# French
## Dictionary

**French ▸ English  English ▸ French**

# French
## Dictionary

**French ▸ English  English ▸ French**

**DICTIONNAIRES LE ROBERT**

### Collins Gem
*An Imprint of HarperCollinsPublishers*

*first published in this edition 1979*
*sixth edition 2001*

© William Collins Sons & Co. Ltd. 1979, 1988
© HarperCollins Publishers 1993, 1997, 2000, 2001

**latest reprint 2001**

ISBN 0-00-711003-0

The Collins Gem website address is
**www.collins-gem.com**

---

*contributors*
Jean-François Allain, Sabine Citron
Catherine Love, Joyce Littlejohn
Val McNulty, John Podbielski

*based on the first edition by*
**Pierre-Henri Cousin**
Renée Birks, Elisabeth Campbell, Hélène Lewis
Claude Nimmo, Philippe Patry
Lorna Sinclair

---

DICTIONNAIRES LE ROBERT
27, rue de la Glacière
75013 PARIS

ISBN 2-85036-624-2

*Dépôt légal avril 2001*
*Achevé d'imprimer avril 2001*

*A catalogue record for this book is available from the British Library*

*Typeset by Morton Word Processing Ltd, Scarborough*

*Printed and bound in Great Britain by Omnia Books Ltd, Glasgow, G64*

# TABLE DES MATIÈRES

# CONTENTS

**Les marques déposées**

**Note on trademarks**

# INTRODUCTION

Nous sommes très heureux que vous ayez décidé d'acheter le dictionnaire anglais Gem de Collins et espérons que vous aimerez l'utiliser et que vous en tirerez profit au lycée, à la maison, en vacances ou au travail.

Cette introduction a pour but de vous donner quelques conseils sur la meilleure façon d'utiliser au mieux votre dictionnaire, en vous référant non seulement à son importante nomenclature mais aussi aux informations contenues dans chaque entrée. Ceci vous aidera à lire et à comprendre, mais aussi à communiquer et à vous exprimer en anglais contemporain.

Le dictionnaire anglais Gem de Collins commence par la liste des abréviations utilisées dans le texte et par la transcription des sons par des symboles phonétiques. À la fin vous trouverez des tables de verbes français ainsi que la liste des verbes irréguliers en anglais, suivis d'une section finale sur les nombres et sur les expressions de temps.

## COMMENT UTILISER VOTRE DICTIONNAIRE GEM COLLINS

Ce dictionnaire offre une masse d'informations et use de divers formes et tailles de caractères, symboles, abréviations, parenthèses et crochets. Les conventions et symboles utilisés sont expliqués dans les sections qui suivent.

### Entrées

Les mots que vous cherchez dans le dictionnaire (les 'entrées') sont classés par ordre alphabétique. Ils sont imprimés en **caractères gras** pour pouvoir être repérés rapidement. Les deux entrées figurant en haut de page indiquent le premier et le dernier mot qui apparaissent sur la page en question.

Des informations sur l'usage ou sur la forme de certaines entrées sont données entre parenthèses, après la transcription phonétique. Ces indications apparaissent sous forme abrégée et en italiques (ex *(fam)*, *(COMM)*).

Dans les cas appropriés, les mots apparentés aux entrées sont regroupés sous la même entrée (**ronger, rongeur; accept,** acceptance) et apparaissent en caractères gras, légèrement plus petits que ceux de l'entrée.

Les expressions courantes dans lesquelles apparaît l'entrée sont indiquées par des caractères romains gras différents (ex **avoir du retard**).

## Transcription phonétique

La transcription phonétique de chaque entrée (indiquant sa prononciation) est indiquée entre crochets immédiatement après l'entrée (ex **fumer** [fyme]; **knead** [ni:d]). Une liste de ces symboles figure à la page xiv.

## Traductions

Les traductions des entrées apparaissent en caractères ordinaires et, lorsque plusieurs sens ou usages coexistent, ces traductions sont séparées par un point-virgule. Vous trouverez souvent entre parenthèses d'autres mots en italiques qui précèdent les traductions. Ces mots fournissent souvent certains des contextes dans lesquels l'entrée est susceptible d'être utilisée (ex **rough** (*voice*) ou (*weather*)) ou offrent des synonymes (ex **rough** (*violent*)).

## 'Mots-clés'

Une importance particulière est accordée à certains mots français et anglais qui sont considérés comme des "mots-clés" dans chacune des langues. Cela peut être dû à leur utilisation très fréquente ou au fait qu'ils ont divers types d'usages (ex **vouloir, plus; get, that**). Une combinaison de losanges et de chiffres vous aident à distinguer différentes catégories grammaticales et différents sens. D'autres renseignements utiles apparaissent en italiques et entre parenthèses dans la langue de l'utilisateur.

## Données grammaticales

Les catégories grammaticales sont données sous forme abrégée et en italiques après la transcription phonétique des entrées (ex *vt, adv, conj*).

Les genres des noms français sont indiqués de la manière suivante: *nm* pour un nom masculin et *nf* pour un nom féminin. Le féminin et le pluriel irréguliers de certains noms sont également indiqués (**directeur, trice; cheval, aux**).

Le masculin et le féminin des adjectif sont indiqués lorsque ces deux formes sont différentes (ex **noir, e**). Lorsque l'adjectif a un féminin ou un pluriel irrégulier, ces formes sont clairement indiquées (ex **net, nette**). Les pluriels irréguliers des noms, et les formes irréguliers des verbes anglais sont indiqués entre parenthèses, avant la catégorie grammaticale (ex **man** ... (*pl* **men**) *n*; **give** (*pt* **gave**, *pp* **given**) *vt*).

# INTRODUCTION

We are delighted you have decided to buy the Collins Gem French Dictionary and hope you will enjoy and benefit from using it at school, at home, on holiday or at work.

This introduction gives you a few tips on how to get the most out of your dictionary — not simply from its comprehensive wordlist but also from the information provided in each entry. This will help you to read and understand modern French, as well as communicate and express yourself in the language.

The Collins Gem French Dictionary begins by listing the abbreviations used in the text and illustrating the sounds shown by the phonetic symbols. You will find French verb tables and English irregular verbs at the back, followed by a final section on numbers and time expressions.

## USING YOUR COLLINS GEM DICTIONARY

A wealth of information is presented in the dictionary, using various typefaces, sizes of type, symbols, abbreviations and brackets. The conventions and symbols used are explained in the following sections.

### Headwords

The words you look up in a dictionary — "headwords" — are listed alphabetically. They are printed in **bold type** for rapid identification. The two headwords appearing at the top of each page indicate the first and last word dealt with on the page in question.

Information about the usage or form of certain headwords is given in brackets after the phonetic spelling. This usually appears in abbreviated form and in italics (e.g. (*fam*), (*COMM*)).

Where appropriate, words related to headwords are grouped in the same entry (**ronger, rongeur; accept, acceptance**) in a slightly smaller bold type than the headword.

Common expressions in which the headword appears are shown in a different bold roman type (e.g. **avoir du retard**).

## Phonetic spellings

The phonetic spelling of each headword (indicating its pronunciation) is given in square brackets immediately after the headword (e.g. **fumer** [fyme]; **knead** [ni:d]). A list of these symbols is given on page xiv.

## Translations

Headword translations are given in ordinary type and, where more than one meaning or usage exists, these are separated by a semi-colon. You will often find other words in italics in brackets before the translations. These offer suggested contexts in which the headword might appear (e.g. **rough** (*voice*) or (*weather*)) or provide synonyms (e.g. **rough** (*violent*)).

## "Key" words

Special status is given to certain French and English words which are considered as "key" words in each language. They may, for example, occur very frequently or have several types of usage (e.g. **vouloir, plus; get, that**). A combination of lozenges and numbers helps you to distinguish different parts of speech and different meanings. Further helpful information is provided in brackets and in italics in the relevant language for the user.

## Grammatical information

Parts of speech are given in abbreviated form in italics after the phonetic spellings of headwords (e.g. *vt, adv, conj*).

Genders of French nouns are indicated as follows: *nm* for a masculine and *nf* for a feminine noun. Feminine and irregular plural forms of nouns are also shown (**directeur, trice; cheval, aux**).

Adjectives are given in both masculine and feminine forms where these forms are different (e.g. **noir, e**). Clear information is provided where adjectives have an irregular feminine or plural form (e.g. **net, nette**).

# ABRÉVIATIONS

# ABBREVIATIONS

| | | |
|---|---|---|
| abréviation | **ab(b)r** | abbreviation |
| adjectif, locution adjective | **adj** | adjective, adjectival phrase |
| adverbe, locution adverbiale | **adv** | adverb, adverbial phrase |
| administration | **ADMIN** | administration |
| agriculture | **AGR** | agriculture |
| anatomie | **ANAT** | anatomy |
| architecture | **ARCHIT** | architecture |
| article défini | **art déf** | definite article |
| article indéfini | **art indéf** | indefinite article |
| l'automobile | **AUT(O)** | the motor car and motoring |
| aviation, voyages aériens | **AVIAT** | flying, air travel |
| biologie | **BIO(L)** | biology |
| botanique | **BOT** | botany |
| anglais de Grande-Bretagne | **BRIT** | British English |
| chimie | **CHEM** | chemistry |
| commerce, finance, banque | **COMM** | commerce, finance, banking |
| comparatif | **compar** | comparative |
| informatique | **COMPUT** | computing |
| conjonction | **conj** | conjunction |
| construction | **CONSTR** | building |
| nom utilisé comme adjectif | **cpd** | compound element |
| cuisine, art culinaire | **CULIN** | cookery |
| article défini | **def art** | definite article |
| déterminant: article; adjectif démonstratif ou indéfini etc | **dét** | determiner: article, demonstrative etc |
| diminutif | **dimin** | diminutive |
| économie | **ECON** | economics |
| électricité, électronique | **ELEC** | electricity, electronics |
| exclamation, interjection | **excl** | exclamation, interjection |
| féminin | **f** | feminine |
| langue familière (! emploi vulgaire) | **fam (!)** | colloquial usage (! particularly offensive) |
| emploi figuré | **fig** | figurative use |
| (verbe anglais) dont la particule est inséparable du verbe | **fus** | (phrasal verb) where the particle cannot be separated from main verb |
| généralement | **gén, gen** | generally |
| géographie, géologie | **GEO** | geography, geology |
| géométrie | **GEOM** | geometry |
| impersonnel | **impers** | impersonal |
| article indéfini | **indef art** | indefinite article |
| langue familière (! emploi vulgaire) | **inf(!)** | colloquial usage (! particularly offensive) |
| infinitif | **infin** | infinitive |
| informatique | **INFORM** | computing |
| invariable | **inv** | invariable |
| irrégulier | **irrég, irreg** | irregular |

# ABRÉVIATIONS

# ABBREVIATIONS

| | | |
|---|---|---|
| domaine juridique | JUR | law |
| grammaire, linguistique | LING | grammar, linguistics |
| masculin | m | masculine |
| mathématiques, algèbre | MATH | mathematics, calculus |
| médecine | MÉD MED | medical term, medicine |
| masculin ou féminin, suivant le sexe | m/f | masculine or feminine depending on sex |
| domaine militaire, armée | MIL | military matters |
| musique | MUS | music |
| nom | n | noun |
| navigation, nautisme | NAVIG, NAUT | sailing, navigation |
| adjectif ou nom numérique | num | numeral adjective or noun |
| | o.s. | oneself |
| péjoratif | péj, pej | derogatory, pejorative |
| photographie | PHOT(O) | photography |
| physiologie | PHYSIOL | physiology |
| pluriel | pl | plural |
| politique | POL | politics |
| participe passé | pp | past participle |
| préposition | prép, prep | preposition |
| pronom | pron | pronoun |
| psychologie, psychiatrie | PSYCH | psychology, psychiatry |
| temps du passé | pt | past tense |
| quelque chose | qch | |
| quelqu'un | qn | |
| religions, domaine ecclésiastique | REL | religions, church service |
| | sb | somebody |
| enseignement, système scolaire et universitaire | SCOL | schooling, schools and universities |
| singulier | sg | singular |
| | sth | something |
| subjonctif | sub | subjunctive |
| sujet (grammatical) | su(b)j | (grammatical) subject |
| superlatif | superl | superlative |
| techniques, technologie | TECH | technical term, technology |
| télécommunications | TEL | telecommunications |
| télévision | TV | television |
| typographie | TYP(O) | typography, printing |
| anglais des USA | US | American English |
| verbe (auxiliaire) | vb (aux) | (auxiliary) verb |
| verbe intransitif | vi | intransitive verb |
| verbe transitif | vt | transitive verb |
| zoologie | ZOOL | zoology |
| marque déposée | ® | registered trademark |
| indique une équivalence culturelle | ≈ | introduces a cultural equivalent |

# TRANSCRIPTION PHONÉTIQUE

## CONSONNES

NB. **p, b, t, d, k, g** sont suivis d'une aspiration en anglais.

## CONSONANTS

NB. **p, b, t, d, k, g** are not aspirated in French.

| | | |
|---|---|---|
| *poupée* | p | *puppy* |
| *bombe* | b | *baby* |
| *tente thermal* | t | *tent* |
| *dinde* | d | *daddy* |
| *coq qui képi* | k | *cork kiss chord* |
| *gag bague* | g | *gag guess* |
| *sale ce nation* | s | *so rice kiss* |
| *zéro rose* | z | *cousin buzz* |
| *tache chat* | ʃ | *sheep sugar* |
| *gilet juge* | ʒ | *pleasure beige* |
| | tʃ | *church* |
| | dʒ | *judge general* |
| *fer phare* | f | *farm raffle* |
| *valve* | v | *very rev* |
| | θ | *thin maths* |
| | ð | *that other* |
| *lent salle* | l | *little ball* |
| *rare rentrer* | R | |
| | r | *rat rare* |
| *maman femme* | m | *mummy comb* |
| *non nonne* | n | *no ran* |
| *agneau vigne* | ɲ | |
| | ŋ | *singing bank* |
| *hop!* | h | *hat reheat* |
| *yeux paille pied* | j | *yet* |
| *nouer oui* | w | *wall bewail* |
| *huile lui* | ɥ | |
| | x | *loch* |

## DIVERS

pour l'anglais: le r final se prononce en liaison devant une voyelle

pour l'anglais: précède la syllabe accentuée

## MISCELLANEOUS

r    in French wordlist: no liaison

'    in French transcription: no liaison

# PHONETIC TRANSCRIPTION

## VOYELLES

NB. La mise en équivalence de certains sons n'indique qu'une ressemblance approximative.

## VOWELS

NB. The pairing of some vowel sounds only indicates approximate equivalence.

| VOYELLES | | VOWELS |
|---|---|---|
| *ici vie lyre* | i i: | heel bead |
| | ɪ | hit pity |
| *jouer été* | e | |
| *lait jouet merci* | ɛ | set tent |
| pl*at* amour | a æ | bat apple |
| *bas pâte* | ɑ ɑ: | after car calm |
| | ʌ | fun cousin |
| *le premier* | ə | over above |
| *beurre peur* | œ | |
| *peu deux* | ø ə: | urn fern work |
| *or homme* | ɔ | wash pot |
| *mot eau gauche* | o ɔ: | born cork |
| *genou roue* | u | full soot |
| | u: | boon lewd |
| *rue urne* | y | |

## DIPHTONGUES

## DIPHTHONGS

| | | |
|---|---|---|
| | ɪə | beer tier |
| | ɛə | tear fair there |
| | eɪ | date plaice day |
| | aɪ | life buy cry |
| | au | owl foul now |
| | əu | low no |
| | ɔɪ | boil boy oily |
| | uə | poor tour |

## NASALES

## NASAL VOWELS

| | |
|---|---|
| *matin plein* | ɛ̃ |
| *brun* | œ̃ |
| *sang an dans* | ɑ̃ |
| *non pont* | ɔ̃ |

xv

# FRANÇAIS – ANGLAIS
# FRENCH – ENGLISH

## A, a

**a** [a] *vb voir* **avoir**

---
**MOT-CLÉ**
---

**à** [a] (*à + le* = **au**, *à + les* = **aux**) *prép* **1** (*endroit, situation*) at, in; **être à Paris/au Portugal** to be in Paris/Portugal; **être à la maison/à l'école** to be at home/at school; **à la campagne** in the country; **c'est à 10 km/à 20 minutes (d'ici)** it's 10 km/20 minutes away

**2** (*direction*) to); **aller à Paris/au Portugal** to go to Paris/Portugal; **aller à la maison/à l'école** to go home/to school; **à la campagne** to the country

**3** (*temps*): **à 3 heures/minuit** at 3 o'clock/midnight; **au printemps/mois de juin** in the spring/the month of June

**4** (*attribution, appartenance*) to); **le livre est à Paul/à lui/à nous** this book is Paul's/his/ours; **donner qch à qn** to give sth to sb

**5** (*moyen*): **se chauffer au gaz** to have gas heating; **à bicyclette** on a *ou* by bicycle; **à la main/machine** by hand/machine

**6** (*provenance*) from; **boire à la bouteille** to drink from the bottle

**7** (*caractérisation, manière*): **l'homme aux yeux bleus** the man with the blue eyes; **à la russe** the Russian way

**8** (*but, destination*): **tasse à café** coffee cup; **maison à vendre** house for sale

**9** (*rapport, évaluation, distribution*): **100 km/unités à l'heure** 100 km/units per *ou* an hour; **payé à l'heure** paid by the hour; **cinq à six** five to six

**abaisser** [abese] *vt* to lower, bring down; (*manette*) to pull down; **s'~** vi to go down; (*fig*) to demean o.s.

**abandon** [abɑ̃dɔ̃] *nm* abandoning; giving up; withdrawal; **être à l'~** to be in a state of neglect

**abandonner** [abɑ̃dɔne] *vt* (*personne*) to abandon; (*projet, activité*) to abandon, give up; (SPORT) to retire *ou* withdraw from; (*céder*) to surrender; **s'~ à** (*paresse, plaisirs*) to give o.s. up to

**abasourdir** [abazurdir] *vt* to stun, stagger

**abat-jour** [abaʒur] *nm inv* lampshade

**abats** [aba] *nmpl* (*de bœuf, porc*) offal *sg*; (*de volaille*) giblets

**abattement** [abatmɑ̃] *nm*: **~ fiscal** ≃ tax allowance

**abattoir** [abatwar] *nm* slaughterhouse

**abattre** [abatr] *vt* (*arbre*) to cut down, fell; (*mur, maison*) to pull down; (*avion, personne*) to shoot down; (*animal*) to shoot, kill; (*fig*) to wear out, tire out; to demoralize; **s'~** vi to crash down; **ne pas se laisser ~** to keep one's spirits up, not to let things get one down; **s'~ sur** to beat down on; (*fig*) to rain down on

**abbaye** [abei] *nf* abbey

**abbé** [abe] *nm* priest; (*d'une abbaye*) abbot

**abcès** [apsɛ] *nm* abscess

**abdiquer** [abdike] *vi* to abdicate

**abdominaux** [abdɔmino] *nmpl*: **faire des ~** to do exercises for one's abdominals, do one's abdominals

**abeille** [abɛj] *nf* bee

**aberrant, e** [aberɑ̃, ɑ̃t] *adj* absurd

**aberration** [aberasjɔ̃] *nf* aberration

**abêtir** [abetir] *vt* to make morons of (*ou* a moron of)

**abîme** [abim] nm abyss, gulf

**abîmer** [abime] vt to spoil, damage; **s'~** vi to get spoilt ou damaged

**ablation** [ablasjɔ̃] nf removal

**aboiement** [abwamɑ̃] nm bark, barking

**abois** [abwa] nmpl: **aux ~** at bay

**abolir** [abɔliʀ] vt to abolish

**abominable** [abɔminabl] adj abominable

**abondance** [abɔ̃dɑ̃s] nf abundance

**abondant, e** [abɔ̃dɑ̃, ɑ̃t] adj plentiful, abundant, copious; **abonder** vi to abound, be plentiful; **abonder dans le sens de qn** to concur with sb

**abonné, e** [abɔne] nm/f subscriber; season ticket holder

**abonnement** [abɔnmɑ̃] nm subscription; (transports, concerts) season ticket

**abonner** [abɔne] vt: **s'~ à** to subscribe, to take out a subscription to

**abord** [abɔʀ] nm: **au premier ~** at first sight, initially; **~s** nmpl (environs) surroundings; **d'~** first

**abordable** [abɔʀdabl] adj (prix) reasonable; (personne) approachable

**aborder** [abɔʀde] vi to land ♦ vt (sujet, difficulté) to tackle; (personne) to approach; (rivage etc) to reach

**aboutir** [abutiʀ] vi (négociations etc) to succeed; **~ à** to end up at; **n'~ à rien** to come to nothing

**aboyer** [abwaje] vi to bark

**abréger** [abʀeʒe] vt to shorten

**abreuver** [abʀœve]: **s'~** vi to drink; **abreuvoir** nm watering place

**abréviation** [abʀevjasjɔ̃] nf abbreviation

**abri** [abʀi] nm shelter; **être à l'~** to be under cover; **se mettre à l'~** to shelter

**abricot** [abʀiko] nm apricot

**abriter** [abʀite] vt to shelter; **s'~** vi to shelter, take cover

**abrupt, e** [abʀypt] adj sheer, steep; (ton) abrupt

**abruti, e** [abʀyti] adj stunned, dazed ♦

nm/f (fam) idiot, moron; **~ de travail** overworked

**absence** [apsɑ̃s] nf absence; (MÉD) blackout; **avoir des ~s** to have mental blanks

**absent, e** [apsɑ̃, ɑ̃t] adj absent ♦ nm/f absentee; **absenter**: **s'absenter** vi to take time off work; (sortir) to leave, go out

**absolu, e** [apsɔly] adj absolute; **absolument** adv absolutely

**absorbant, e** [apsɔʀbɑ̃, ɑ̃t] adj absorbent

**absorber** [apsɔʀbe] vt to absorb; (gén MÉD: manger, boire) to take

**abstenir** [apstəniʀ] vb: **s'~ de qch/de faire** to refrain from sth/from doing

**abstraction** [apstʀaksjɔ̃] nf abstraction

**abstrait, e** [apstʀɛ, ɛt] adj abstract

**absurde** [apsyʀd] adj absurd

**abus** [aby] nm abuse; **~ de confiance** breach of trust; **abuser** vi to go too far, overstep the mark; **abuser de** (duper) to take advantage of; **abusif, -ive** adj exorbitant; (punition) excessive

**acabit** [akabi] nm: **de cet ~** of that type

**académie** [akademi] nf academy; (SCOL: circonscription) ≃ regional education authority

---

**Académie française**

*The Académie française was founded by Cardinal Richelieu in 1635 during the reign of Louis XIII. It consists of forty elected scholars and writers who are known as "les Quarante" or "les Immortels". One of the Académie's functions is to regulate the development of the French language and its recommendations are frequently the subject of lively public debate. It has produced several editions of its famous dictionary and awards various literary prizes.*

---

**acajou** [akaʒu] nm mahogany

**acariâtre** [akarjɑtr] *adj* cantankerous

**accablant, e** [akɑblɑ̃, ɑ̃t] *adj* (*chaleur*) oppressive; (*témoignage, preuve*) overwhelming

**accablement** [akɑbləmɑ̃] *nm* despondency

**accabler** [akɑble] *vt* to overwhelm, overcome; **~ qn d'injures** to heap *ou* shower abuse on sb

**accalmie** [akalmi] *nf* lull

**accaparer** [akapare] *vt* to monopolize; (*suj: travail etc*) to take up (all) the time *ou* attention of

**accéder** [aksede]: **~ à** *vt* (*lieu*) to reach; (*accorder: requête*) to grant, accede to

**accélérateur** [akseleratœr] *nm* accelerator

**accélération** [akselerasjɔ̃] *nf* acceleration

**accélérer** [akselere] *vt* to speed up ♦ *vi* to accelerate

**accent** [aksɑ̃] *nm* accent; (*PHONÉTIQUE, fig*) stress; **mettre l'~ sur** (*fig*) to stress; **~ aigu/grave/circonflexe** acute/grave/circumflex accent; **accentuer** [aksɑ̃tɥe] *vt* (*LING*) to accent; (*fig*) to accentuate, emphasize; **s'accentuer** *vi* to become more marked *ou* pronounced

**acceptation** [aksɛptasjɔ̃] *nf* acceptance

**accepter** [aksɛpte] *vt* to accept; **~ de faire** to agree to do

**accès** [aksɛ] *nm* (à un lieu) access; (*MÉD: de toux*) fit; (: *de fièvre*) bout; **d'~ facile** easily accessible; **facile d'~** easy to get to; **~ de colère** fit of anger; **accessible** [aksesibl] *adj* accessible; (*livre, sujet*) **accessible à** within the reach of sb

**accessoire** [akseswar] *adj* secondary; incidental ♦ *nm* accessory; (*THÉÂTRE*) prop

**accident** [aksidɑ̃] *nm* accident; **par ~** by chance; **~ de la route** road accident; **~ du travail** industrial injury *ou* accident; **accidenté, e** *adj* damaged; injured; (*relief, terrain*) uneven; hilly; **accidentel, le** *adj* accidental

**acclamations** [aklamasjɔ̃] *nfpl* cheers

**acclamer** [aklame] *vt* to cheer, acclaim

**acclimater** [aklimate]: **s'~** *vi* (*personne*) to adapt (o.s.)

**accolade** [akɔlad] *nf* (*amicale*) embrace; (*signe*) brace

**accommodant, e** [akɔmɔdɑ̃, ɑ̃t] *adj* accommodating, easy-going

**accommoder** [akɔmɔde] *vt* (*CULIN*) to prepare; **s'~ de** *vt* to put up with; (*se contenter de*) to make do with

**accompagnateur, -trice** [akɔ̃paɲatœr, tris] *nm/f* (*MUS*) accompanist; (*de voyage: guide*) guide; (*de voyage organisé*) courier

**accompagner** [akɔ̃paɲe] *vt* to accompany, be *ou* go *ou* come with; (*MUS*) to accompany

**accompli, e** [akɔ̃pli] *adj* accomplished

**accomplir** [akɔ̃plir] *vt* (*tâche, projet*) to carry out; (*souhait*) to fulfil; **s'~** *vi* to be fulfilled

**accord** [akɔr] *nm* agreement; (*entre des styles, tons etc*) harmony; (*MUS*) chord; **d'~!** OK!; **se mettre d'~** to come to an agreement; **être d'~ (pour faire qch)** to agree (to do sth)

**accordéon** [akɔrdeɔ̃] *nm* (*MUS*) accordion

**accorder** [akɔrde] *vt* (*faveur, délai*) to grant; (*harmoniser*) to match; (*MUS*) to tune; **s'~** *vi* to get on together; to agree

**accoster** [akɔste] *vt* (*NAVIG*) to draw alongside ♦ *vi* to berth

**accotement** [akɔtmɑ̃] *nm* verge (*BRIT*), shoulder

**accouchement** [akuʃmɑ̃] *nm* delivery, (child)birth; labour

**accoucher** [akuʃe] *vi* to give birth, have a baby; **~ d'un garçon** to give birth to a boy; **accoucheur** *nm*: **(médecin) accoucheur** obstetrician

**accouder** [akude]: **s'~** *vi* to rest one's elbows on/against; **accoudoir** *nm* armrest

**accoupler** [akuple] *vt* to couple; (*pour*

*la reproduction)* to mate; **s'~** *vt* to mate

**accourir** [akuʀiʀ] *vi* to rush *ou* run up

**accoutrement** [akutʀəmã] *(péj) nm* *(tenue)* outfit

**accoutumance** [akutymãs] *nf (gén)* adaptation; *(MÉD)* addiction

**accoutumé, e** [akutyme] *adj (habituel)* customary, usual

**accoutumer** [akutyme] *vt:* **s'~ à** to get accustomed *ou* used to

**accréditer** [akʀedite] *vt (nouvelle)* to substantiate

**accroc** [akʀo] *nm (déchirure)* tear; *(fig)* hitch, snag

**accrochage** [akʀɔʃaʒ] *nm (AUTO)* collision; *(dispute)* clash, brush

**accrocher** [akʀɔʃe] *vt (fig)* to catch, attract; **s'~** *(se disputer)* to have a clash *ou* brush; **~ qch à** *(suspendre)* to hang sth (up) on; *(attacher: remorque)* to hitch sth (up) to; **~ qch (à)** *(déchirer)* to catch sth on(to); **~ un passant** *(heurter)* to knock down a pedestrian; **s'~ à** *(rester pris à)* to catch on; *(agripper, fig)* to hang on *ou* cling to

**accroissement** [akʀwasmã] *nm* increase

**accroître** [akʀwatʀ] *s'~* *vi* to increase

**accroupir** [akʀupiʀ] *s'~* *vi* to squat, crouch (down)

**accru, e** [akʀy] *pp de* **accroître**

**accueil** [akœj] *nm* welcome; **comité d'~** reception committee; **accueillir** *vt* to welcome; *(aller chercher)* to meet, collect

**acculer** [akyle] *vt:* **~ qn à** *ou* **contre** to drive sb back against

**accumuler** [akymyle] *vt* to accumulate, amass; **s'~** *vi* to accumulate; to pile up

**accusation** [akyzasjɔ̃] *nf (gén)* accusation; *(JUR)* charge; *(partie):* **l'~** the prosecution

**accusé, e** [akyze] *nm/f* accused; defendant; **~ de réception** acknowledgement of receipt

**accuser** [akyze] *vt* to accuse; *(fig)* to

emphasize, bring out; to show; **~ qn de** to accuse sb of; *(JUR)* to charge sb with; **~ réception de** to acknowledge receipt of

**acerbe** [asɛʀb] *adj* caustic, acid

**acéré, e** [asere] *adj* sharp

**acharné, e** [aʃaʀne] *adj (efforts)* relentless; *(lutte, adversaire)* fierce, bitter

**acharner** [aʃaʀne] *vt:* **s'~ contre** to set o.s. against; *(suj: malchance)* to dog; **s'~ à faire** to try doggedly to do; *(persister)* to persist in doing

**achat** [aʃa] *nm* purchase; **faire des ~** to do some shopping; **faire l'~ de qch** to purchase sth

**acheminer** [aʃ(ə)mine] *vt (courrier)* to forward, dispatch; **s'~ vers** to head for

**acheter** [aʃ(ə)te] *vt* to buy, purchase; *(soudoyer)* to buy; **~ qch à** *(marchand)* to buy *ou* purchase sth from; *(ami etc: offrir)* to buy sth for; **acheteur, -euse** *nm/f* buyer; shopper; *(COMM)* buyer

**achever** [aʃ(ə)ve] *vt* to complete, finish; *(blessé)* to finish off; **s'~** *vi* to end

**acide** [asid] *adj* sour, sharp; *(CHIMIE)* acid(ic) ♦ *nm (CHIMIE)* acid; **acidulé, e** *adj* slightly acid

**acier** [asje] *nm* steel; **aciérie** *nf* steelworks *sg*

**acné** [akne] *nf* acne

**acolyte** [akɔlit] *(péj) nm* associate

**acompte** [akɔ̃t] *nm* deposit

**à-côté** [akote] *nm* side-issue; *(argent)* extra

**à-coup** [aku] *nm:* **par ~~s** by fits and starts

**acoustique** [akustik] *nf (d'une salle)* acoustics *pl*

**acquéreur** [akeʀœʀ] *nm* buyer, purchaser

**acquérir** [akeʀiʀ] *vt* to acquire

**acquis, e** [aki, iz] *pp de* **acquérir** ♦ *nm* *(accumulated)* experience; **son aide nous est ~e** we can count on her help

**acquit** [aki] *vb voir* **acquérir** ♦ *nm (quittance)* receipt; **par ~ de conscience** to set one's mind at rest

**acquitter** [akite] vt (JUR) to acquit; (facture) to pay, settle; **s'~ de** vt (devoir) to discharge; (promesse) to fulfil

**âcre** [akʀ] adj acrid, pungent

**acrobate** [akʀɔbat] nm/f acrobat; **acrobatie** nf acrobatics sg

**acte** [akt] nm act, action; (THÉÂTRE) act; **prendre ~ de** to note, take note of; **faire ~ de candidature** to apply; **faire ~ de présence** to put in an appearance; **~ de naissance** birth certificate

**acteur** [aktœʀ] nm actor

**actif, -ive** [aktif, iv] adj active ♦ nm (COMM) assets pl; (fig): **avoir à son ~** to have to one's credit; **population active** working population

**action** [aksjɔ̃] nf (gén) action; (COMM) share; **une bonne ~** a good deed; **actionnaire** nm/f shareholder; **actionner** vt (mécanisme) to activate; (machine) to operate

**activer** [aktive] vt to speed up; **s'~** vi to bustle about; to hurry up

**activité** [aktivite] nf activity; **en ~** (volcan) active; (fonctionnaire) in active life

**actrice** [aktʀis] nf actress

**actualiser** [aktyalize] vt to bring up to date

**actualité** [aktyalite] nf (d'un problème) topicality; (événements): **l'~** current events; **les ~s** nfpl (CINÉMA, TV) the news; **d'~** topical

**actuel, le** [aktyɛl] adj (présent) present; (d'actualité) topical; **à l'heure ~le** at the present time; **actuellement** adv at present, at the present time

**acuité** [akyite] nf acuteness

**acuponcteur** [akypɔ̃ktœʀ] nm acupuncturist

**acuponcture** [akypɔ̃ktyʀ] nf acupuncture

**adaptateur** [adaptatœʀ] nm (ÉLEC) adapter

**adapter** [adapte] vt to adapt; **s'~ (à)** (suj: personne) to adapt (to); **~ qch à** (approprier) to adapt sth to (fit); **~ qch sur/dans/à** (fixer) to fit sth on/into/to

**additif** [aditif] nm additive

**addition** [adisjɔ̃] nf addition; (au café) bill; **additionner** vt to add (up)

**adepte** [adɛpt] nm/f follower

**adéquat, e** [adekwa(t), at] adj appropriate, suitable

**adhérent, e** [adeʀɑ̃, ɑ̃t] nm/f member

**adhérer** [adeʀe]: **~ à** vt (coller) to adhere ou stick to; (se rallier à) to join; **adhésif, -ive** adj adhesive, sticky; **ruban adhésif** sticky ou adhesive tape; **adhésion** nf joining; (fait d'être membre) membership; (accord) support

**adieu, x** [adjø] excl goodbye ♦ nm farewell

**adjectif** [adʒɛktif] nm adjective

**adjoindre** [adʒwɛ̃dʀ] vt: **~ qch à** to attach sth to; (ajouter) to add sth to; **s'~** vt (collaborateur etc) to take on, appoint; **adjoint, e** nm/f assistant; **adjoint au maire** deputy mayor; **directeur adjoint** assistant manager

**adjudant** [adʒydɑ̃] nm (MIL) warrant officer

**adjuger** [adʒyʒe] vt (prix, récompense) to award; (lors d'une vente) to auction (off); **s'~** vt to take for o.s.

**adjurer** [adʒyʀe] vt: **~ qn de faire** to implore ou beg sb to do

**admettre** [admɛtʀ] vt (laisser entrer) to admit; (candidat: SCOL) to pass; (tolérer) to allow, accept; (reconnaître) to admit, acknowledge

**administrateur, -trice** [administʀatœʀ, tʀis] nm/f (COMM) director; (ADMIN) administrator

**administration** [administʀasjɔ̃] nf administration; **l'A~** ≈ the Civil Service

**administrer** [administʀe] vt (firme) to manage, run; (biens, remède, sacrement etc) to administer

**admirable** [admiʀabl] adj admirable, wonderful

**admirateur, -trice** [admiʀatœʀ, tʀis] nm/f admirer

**admiration** [admiʀasjɔ̃] nf admiration

**admirer** [admiʀe] vt to admire

**admis, e** [admi, iz] *pp de* **admettre**

**admissible** [admisibl] *adj* (*candidat*) eligible; (*comportement*) admissible, acceptable

**admission** [admisjɔ̃] *nf* admission; acknowledgement; **demande d'~** application for membership

**ADN** *sigle m* (= *acide désoxyribonucléique*) DNA

**adolescence** [adɔlesɑ̃s] *nf* adolescence

**adolescent, e** [adɔlesɑ̃, ɑ̃t] *nm/f* adolescent, teenager

**adonner** [adɔne]: **s'~ à** *vt* (*sport*) to devote o.s. to; (*boisson*) to give o.s. over to

**adopter** [adɔpte] *vt* to adopt; **adoptif, -ive** *adj* (*parents*) adoptive; (*fils, patrie*) adopted

**adorable** [adɔRabl] *adj* delightful, adorable

**adorer** [adɔRe] *vt* to adore; (*REL*) to worship

**adosser** [adose] *vt*: **~ qch à** *ou* **contre** to stand with sth against; **s'~ à** *ou* **contre** to lean with one's back against

**adoucir** [adusiʀ] *vt* (*goût, température*) to make milder; (*avec du sucre*) to sweeten; (*peau, voix*) to soften; (*caractère*) to mellow

**adresse** [adʀɛs] *nf* (*domicile*) address; (*dextérité*) skill, dexterity

**adresser** [adʀese] *vt* (*lettre: expédier*) to send; (: *écrire l'adresse sur*) to address; (*injure, compliments*) to address; **s'~ à** (*parler à*) to speak to; to address; (*s'informer auprès de*) to go and see; (: *bureau*) to enquire at; (*suj: livre, conseil*) to be aimed at; **~ la parole à** to speak to, address

**adroit, e** [adʀwa, wat] *adj* skilful, skilled

**adulte** [adylt] *nm/f* adult, grown-up ♦ *adj* (*chien, arbre*) fully-grown, mature; (*attitude*) adult, grown-up

**adultère** [adylteʀ] *nm* (*acte*) adultery

**advenir** [advəniʀ] *vi* to happen

**adverbe** [adveʀb] *nm* adverb

**adversaire** [adveʀseʀ] *nm/f* (*SPORT, gén*) opponent, adversary

**adverse** [adveʀs] *adj* opposing

**aération** [aeʀasjɔ̃] *nf* airing; (*circulation de l'air*) ventilation

**aérer** [aeʀe] *vt* to air; (*fig*) to lighten; **s'~** *vi* to get some (fresh) air

**aérien, ne** [aeʀjɛ̃, jɛn] *adj* (*AVIAT*) air *cpd*, aerial; (*câble, métro*) overhead; (*fig*) light; **compagnie ~ne** airline

**aéro...** [aeʀo] *préfixe*: **aérobic** *nm* aerobics *sg*; **aérogare** *nf* airport (buildings) (*en ville*) air terminal; **aéroglisseur** *nm* hovercraft; **Aéronavale** *nf* ≈ Fleet Air Arm (*BRIT*), ≈ Naval Air Force (*US*); **aérophagie** *nf* (*MÉD*) wind, aerophagia (*MÉD*); **aéroport** *nm* airport; **aéroporté, e** *adj* airborne, airlifted; **aérosol** *nm* aerosol

**affable** [afabl] *adj* affable

**affaiblir** [afeblir]: **s'~** *vi* to weaken

**affaire** [afeʀ] *nf* (*problème, question*) matter; (*criminelle, judiciaire*) case (*scandaleuse etc*) affair; (*entreprise*) business; (*marché, transaction*) deal; business *no pl*; (*occasion intéressante*) bargain; **~s** *nfpl* (*intérêts publics et privés*) affairs; (*activité commerciale*) business *sg*; (*effets personnels*) things, belongings; **ce sont mes ~s** (*cela me concerne*) that's my business; **ça fera l'~** that will do (nicely); **se tirer d'~** to sort it *ou* things out for o.s.; **avoir ~** (*être en contact*) to be dealing with; **les A~s étrangères** Foreign Affairs; **affairer: s'affairer** *vi* to busy o.s., bustle about

**affaisser** [afese]: **s'~** *vi* (*terrain, immeuble*) to subside, sink; (*personne*) to collapse

**affaler** [afale] *vb*: **s'~ (dans/sur)** to collapse *ou* slump (into/onto)

**affamé, e** [afame] *adj* starving

**affectation** [afɛktasjɔ̃] *nf* (*nomination*) appointment; (*manque de naturel*) affectation

**affecter** [afɛkte] *vt* to affect; **~ qch à** to allocate *ou* allot sth to; **~ qn à** to appoint sb to; (*diplomate*) to post sb to

**affectif, -ive** [afɛktif, iv] *adj* emotional

**affection** [afɛksjɔ̃] *nf* affection; (*mal*) ailment; **affectionner** *vt* to be fond of;

**affectueux, -euse** [afɛktɥø, øz] *adj* affectionate

**affermir** [afɛRmiR] *vt* to consolidate, strengthen; (*muscles*) to tone up

**affichage** [afiʃaʒ] *nm* billposting; (*électronique*) display

**affiche** [afiʃ] *nf* poster; (*officielle*) notice; (*THÉÂTRE*) bill

**afficher** [afiʃe] *vt* (*affiche*) to put up; (*réunion*) to put up a notice about; (*électroniquement*) to display; (*fig*) to exhibit, display; **"défense d'~"** "stick no bills"

**affilée** [afile]: **d'~** *adv* at a stretch

**affiler** [afile] *vt* to sharpen

**affilier** [afilje]: **s'~ à** (*club, société*) to join

**affiner** [afine] *vt* to refine

**affirmatif, -ive** [afiRmatif, iv] *adj* affirmative

**affirmation** [afiRmasjɔ̃] *nf* assertion

**affirmer** [afiRme] *vt* to assert

**affligé, e** [afliʒe] *adj* distressed, grieved; **~ de** (*maladie, tare*) afflicted with

**affliger** [afliʒe] *vt* (*peiner*) to distress, grieve

**affluence** [aflyɑ̃s] *nf* crowds *pl*; **heures d'~** rush hours; **jours d'~** busiest days

**affluent** [aflyɑ̃] *nm* tributary

**affluer** [aflye] *vi* (*secours, biens*) to flood in, pour in; (*sang*) to rush, flow

**affolant, e** [afɔlɑ̃, ɑ̃t] *adj* frightening

**affolement** [afɔlmɑ̃] *nm* panic

**affoler** [afɔle] *vt* to throw into a panic; **s'~** *vi* to panic

**affranchir** [afRɑ̃ʃiR] *vt* to put a stamp *ou* stamps on; (*à la machine*) to frank (*BRIT*), meter (*US*); (*fig*) to free, liberate; **affranchissement** *nm* postage

**affréter** [afRete] *vt* to charter

**affreux, -euse** [afRø, øz] *adj* dreadful, awful

**affront** [afRɔ̃] *nm* affront; **affronte-**

**-ment** *nm* clash, confrontation

**affronter** [afRɔ̃te] *vt* to confront, face

**affubler** [afyble] (*péj*) *vt*: **~ qn de** to rig *ou* deck sb out in

**affût** [afy] *nm*: **à l'~ (de)** (*gibier*) lying in wait (for); (*fig*) on the look-out (for)

**affûter** [afyte] *vt* to sharpen, grind

**afin** [afɛ̃]: **~ que** *conj* so that, in order that; **~ de faire** in order to, so as to do

**africain, e** [afRikɛ̃, ɛn] *adj, nm/f* African

**Afrique** [afRik] *nf*: **l'~** Africa; **l'~ du Sud** South Africa

**agacer** [agase] *vt* to irritate

**âge** [ɑʒ] *nm* age; **quel ~ as-tu?** how old are you?; **prendre de l'~** to be getting on (in years); **âgé, e** *adj* old, elderly; **âgé de 10 ans** 10 years old

**agence** [aʒɑ̃s] *nf* agency, office; (*succursale*) branch; **~ de voyages** travel agency; **~ immobilière** estate (*BRIT*) *ou* real estate (*US*) agent's (office)

**agencer** [aʒɑ̃se] *vt* to put together; (*local*) to arrange, lay out

**agenda** [aʒɛ̃da] *nm* diary

**agenouiller** [aʒ(ə)nuje]: **s'~** *vi* to kneel (down)

**agent** [aʒɑ̃] *nm* (*aussi*: **~ de police**) policeman; (*ADMIN*) official, officer; **~ d'assurances** insurance broker

**agglomération** [aglɔmeRasjɔ̃] *nf* town; built-up area; **l'~ parisienne** the urban area of Paris

**aggloméré** [aglɔmeRe] *nm* (*bois*) chipboard

**aggraver** [agRave]: **s'~** *vi* to worsen

**agile** [aʒil] *adj* agile, nimble

**agir** [aʒiR] *vi* to act; **il s'agit de** (*ça traite de*) it is about; (*il est important de*) it's a matter *ou* question of

**agitation** [aʒitasjɔ̃] *nf* (*hustle and*) bustle; (*trouble*) agitation, excitement; (*politique*) unrest, agitation

**agité, e** [aʒite] *adj* fidgety, restless; (*troublé*) agitated, perturbed; (*mer*) rough

**agiter** [aʒite] *vt* (*bouteille, chiffon*) to

shake; (bras, mains) to wave; (préoccuper, exciter) to perturb; **s'~** vi (enfant, élève) to fidget

**agneau, x** [aɲo] nm lamb

**agonie** [agɔni] nf mortal agony, death pangs pl; (fig) death throes pl

**agrafe** [agraf] nf (de vêtement) hook, fastener; (de bureau) staple; **agrafer** vt to fasten; to staple; **agrafeuse** nf stapler

**agrandir** [agʀɑ̃diʀ] vt to enlarge; **s'~** vi (ville, famille) to grow, expand; (trou, écart) to get bigger; **agrandissement** nm (PHOTO) enlargement

**agréable** [agreabl] adj pleasant, nice

**agréé, e** [agree] adj: **concessionnaire ~** registered dealer

**agréer** [agree] vt (requête) to accept; **~ à** to please, suit; **veuillez ~ ...** (formule épistolaire) yours faithfully

**agrégation** [agregasjɔ̃] nf highest teaching diploma in France; **agrégé, e** nm/f holder of the agrégation

**agrément** [agremɑ̃] nm (accord) consent, approval; **agrémenter** vt to embellish, adorn

**agresser** [agrese] vt to attack; **agresseur** nm aggressor, attacker; (POL, MIL) aggressor; **agressif, -ive** adj aggressive

**agricole** [agrikɔl] adj agricultural; **agriculteur** nm farmer; **agriculture** nf agriculture, farming

**agripper** [agripe] vt to grab, clutch; **s'~** to cling (on) to, clutch, grip

**agroalimentaire** [agroalimɑ̃teʀ] nm farm-produce industry

**agrumes** [agrym] nmpl citrus fruit(s)

**aguerrir** [agerir] vt to harden

**aguets** [age] nmpl: **être aux ~** to be on the look out

**aguicher** [agiʃe] vt to entice

**ahuri, e** [ayri] adj (stupéfait) flabbergasted

**ai** [e, ɛ] vb voir **avoir**

**aide** [ed] nm/f assistant, carer ♦ nf assistance, help; (secours financier) aid; **à l'~**

**de** (avec) with the help ou aid of; **appeler (qn) à l'~** to call for help (from sb); **~ familiale** home help, mother's help; **~ judiciaire** ♦ nf legal aid; **~ sociale** nf (assistance) state aid; **aide-mémoire** nm inv memoranda pages p. (key facts) handbook; **aide-soignant, e** nm/f auxiliary nurse

**aider** [ede] vt to help; **s'~ de** (se servir de) to use, make use of

**aie** etc [ɛ] vb voir **avoir**

**aïe** [aj] excl ouch!

**aïeul, e** [ajœl] nm/f grandparent, grandfather(-mother)

**aïeux** [ajø] nmpl grandparents; (ancêtres) forebears, forefathers

**aigle** [ɛgl] nm eagle

**aigre** [ɛgʀ] adj sour, sharp; (fig) biting, cutting; **aigre-doux, -ce** adj (sauce) sweet and sour; **aigreur** nf sourness, sharpness; **aigreurs d'estomac** heartburn sg; **aigrir** vt (personne) to embitter; (caractère) to sour

**aigu, ë** [egy] adj (objet, douleur) sharp; (son, voix) high-pitched, shrill; (note, high(-pitched)

**aiguille** [eguij] nf needle; (de montre) hand; **~ à tricoter** knitting needle

**aiguiller** [eguije] vt (orienter) to direct; **aiguilleur du ciel** nm air-traffic controller

**aiguillon** [eguijɔ̃] nm (d'abeille) sting; **aiguillonner** vt to spur ou goad on

**aiguiser** [egize] vt to sharpen; (fig) to stimulate; (: sens) to excite

**ail** [aj, o] nm garlic

**aile** [ɛl] nf wing; **aileron** nm (de requin) fin; **ailier** nm winger

**aille** etc [aj] vb voir **aller**

**ailleurs** [ajœʀ] adv elsewhere, somewhere else; **partout/nulle part ~** everywhere/nowhere else; **d'~** (du reste) moreover, besides; **par ~** (d'autre part) moreover, furthermore

**aimable** [ɛmabl] adj kind, nice

**aimant** [ɛmɑ̃] nm magnet

**aimer** [eme] vt to love; (d'amitié, affection, par goût) to like; (souhait): **j'~ais ...** I would like ...; **bien ~ qn/qch** to like sb/sth; **j'~ais mieux faire** I'd much rather do

**aine** [ɛn] nf groin

**aîné, e** [ene] adj elder, older; (le plus âgé) eldest, oldest ♦ nm/f oldest child ou one, oldest boy ou son/girl ou daughter

**ainsi** [ɛ̃si] adv (de cette façon) like this, in this way, thus; (ce faisant) thus ♦ conj thus, so; **~ que** (comme) (just) as; (et aussi) as well as; **pour ~ dire** so to speak; **et ~ de suite** and so on

**aïoli** [ajɔli] nm garlic mayonnaise

**air** [ɛʀ] nm air; (mélodie) tune; (expression) look, air; **prendre l'~** to get some (fresh) air; **avoir l'~** (sembler) to look, appear; **avoir l'~ de** to look like; **avoir l'~ de faire** to look as though one is doing, appear to be doing; **en l'~** (promesses) empty

**aisance** [ɛzɑ̃s] nf ease; (richesse) affluence

**aise** [ɛz] nf comfort; **être à l'~** ou **à son ~** to be comfortable; (pas embarrassé) to be at ease; (financièrement) to be comfortably off; **se mettre à l'~** to make o.s. comfortable; **être mal à l'~** to be uncomfortable; (gêné) to be ill at ease; **en faire à son ~** to do as one likes; **aisé, e** adj easy; (assez riche) well-to-do, well-off

**aisselle** [ɛsɛl] nf armpit

**ait** [ɛ] vb voir **avoir**

**ajonc** [aʒɔ̃] nm gorse no pl

**ajourner** [aʒuʀne] vt (réunion) to adjourn; (décision) to defer, postpone

**ajouter** [aʒute] vt to add

**ajusté, e** [aʒyste] adj: **bien ~** (robe etc) close-fitting

**ajuster** [aʒyste] vt (régler) to adjust; (vêtement) to alter; (coup de fusil) to aim; (cible) to aim at; (TECH, gén: adapter): **~ qch à** to fit sth to

**alarme** [alaʀm] nf alarm; **donner l'~** to give ou raise the alarm; **alarmer** vt

to alarm; **s'alarmer** vi to become alarmed; **alarmiste** adj, nm/f alarmist

**album** [albɔm] nm album

**albumine** [albymin] nf albumin; **avoir de l'~** to suffer from albuminuria

**alcool** [alkɔl] nm: **l'~** alcohol; **un ~** a spirit, a brandy; **bière sans ~** non-alcoholic ou alcohol-free beer; **~ à brûler** methylated spirits (BRIT), wood alcohol (US); **~ à 90°** surgical spirit; **alcoolique** adj, nm/f alcoholic; **alcoolisé, e** adj alcoholic; **une boisson non alcoolisée** a soft drink; **alcoolisme** nm alcoholism; **alcootest** ® nm Breathalyser ®; (test) breath-test

**aléas** [alea] nmpl hazards; **aléatoire** adj uncertain; (INFORM) random

**alentour** [alɑ̃tuʀ] adv around, round about; **~s** nmpl (environs) surroundings; **aux ~s de** (lieu) in the vicinity ou neighbourhood of, round about; (temps) round about

**alerte** [alɛʀt] adj agile, nimble; brisk, lively ♦ nf alert; warning; **~ à la bombe** bomb scare; **alerter** vt to alert

**algèbre** [alʒɛbʀ] nf algebra

**Alger** [alʒe] n Algiers

**Algérie** [alʒeʀi] nf: **l'~** Algeria; **algérien, ne** adj Algerian ♦ nm/f: **Algérien, ne** Algerian

**algue** [alg] nf seaweed no pl; (BOT) alga

**alibi** [alibi] nm alibi

**aliéné, e** [aljene] nm/f insane person, lunatic (péj)

**aligner** [aliɲe] vt to align, line up; (idées, chiffres) to string together; (adapter): **~ qch sur** to bring sth into alignment with; **s'~** (soldats etc) to line up; **s'~ sur** (POL) to align o.s. on

**aliment** [alimɑ̃] nm food; **alimentaire** adj: **denrées alimentaires** foodstuffs; **alimentation** nf (commerce) food trade; (magasin) grocery store; (régime) diet; (en eau etc, de moteur) supplying; (INFORM) feed; **alimenter** vt to feed; (TECH): **alimenter (en)** to supply (with);

**alinéa** [alinea] *nm* paragraph

**aliter** [alite]: **s'~** *vi* to take to one's bed

**allaiter** [alete] *vt* to (breast-)feed, nurse; (*suj: animal*) to suckle

**allant** [alɑ̃] *nm* drive, go

**alléchant, e** [aleʃɑ̃, ɑ̃t] *adj* (*odeur*) mouth-watering; (*offre*) enticing

**allécher** [aleʃe] *vt* to make sb's mouth water; to tempt *ou* entice sb

**allée** [ale] *nf* (*de jardin*) path; (*en ville*) avenue, drive; **~s et venues** comings and goings

**allégé, e** [aleʒe] *adj* (*yaourt etc*) low-fat

**alléger** [aleʒe] *vt* (*voiture*) to make lighter; (*chargement*) to lighten; (*souffrance*) to alleviate, soothe

**allègre** [a(l)lɛgʀ] *adj* lively, cheerful

**alléguer** [a(l)lege] *vt* to put forward (as proof *ou* an excuse)

**Allemagne** [alman] *nf*: **l'~** Germany; **allemand, e** *adj* German ♦ *nm/f*: **Allemand, e** German ♦ *nm* (*LING*) German

**aller** [ale] *nm* (*trajet*) outward journey; (*billet: aussi:* **~ simple**) single (*BRIT*) ou one-way (*US*) ticket ♦ *vi* (*gén*) to go; **~ à** (*convenir*) to suit; (*suj: forme, pointure etc*) to fit; **~ (bien) avec** (*couleurs, style etc*) to go (well) with; **je vais y ~/me fâcher** I'm going to go/to get angry; **~ voir** to go and see, go to see; **allez!** come on!; **allons!** come now!; **comment allez-vous?** how are you?; **comment ça va?** how are you?; (*affaires etc*) how are things?; **il va bien/mal** he's well/not well, he's fine/ill; **ça va bien/mal** (*affaires etc*) it's going well/not going well; **~ mieux** to be better; **s'en ~** (*partir*) to be off, go, leave; (*disparaître*) to go away; **~ retour** return journey (*BRIT*), round trip; (*billet*) return (ticket) (*BRIT*), round trip ticket (*US*)

**allergique** [alɛʀʒik] *adj*: **~ à** allergic to

**alliage** [aljaʒ] *nm* alloy

to feed (with); (*fig*) to sustain, keep going

**alliance** [aljɑ̃s] *nf* (*MIL, POL*) alliance; (*bague*) wedding ring

**allier** [alje] *vt* (*POL, gén*) to ally; (*fig*) to combine; **s'~** to become allies; to combine

**allô** [alo] *excl* hullo, hallo

**allocation** [alɔkasjɔ̃] *nf* allowance; **~ (de) chômage** unemployment benefit; **~s familiales** ≃ child benefit

**allocution** [a(l)lɔkysjɔ̃] *nf* short speech

**allonger** [alɔ̃ʒe] *vt* to lengthen, make longer; (*étendre: bras, jambe*) to stretch (out); **s'~** *vi* to get longer; (*se coucher*) to lie down, stretch out; **~ le pas** to hasten one's step(s)

**allouer** [alwe] *vt* to allocate, allot

**allumage** [alymaʒ] *nm* (*AUTO*) ignition

**allume-cigare** [alymsigaʀ] *nm inv* cigar lighter

**allumer** [alyme] *vt* (*lampe, phare, radio*) to put *ou* switch on; (*pièce*) to put *ou* switch the light(s) on in; (*feu*) to light; **s'~** *vi* (*lumière, lampe*) to come *ou* go on

**allumette** [alymɛt] *nf* match

**allure** [alyʀ] *nf* (*vitesse*) speed, pace; (*démarche*) walk; (*aspect, air*) look; **avoir de l'~** to have style; **à toute ~** at top speed

**allusion** [a(l)lyzjɔ̃] *nf* allusion; (*sous-entendu*) hint; **faire ~ à** to allude *ou* refer to; to hint at

---

**MOT-CLÉ**

---

**alors** [alɔʀ] *adv* **1** (*à ce moment-là*) then, at that time; **il habitait alors à Paris** he lived in Paris at that time

**2** (*par conséquent*) then; **tu as fini? alors je m'en vais** have you finished? I'm going then; **et alors?** so what?

**alors que** *conj* **1** (*au moment où*) when, as; **il est arrivé alors que je partais** he arrived as I was leaving

**2** (*pendant que*) while, when; **alors qu'il était à Paris, il a visité** ... while *ou* when he was in Paris, he visited ...

**3** (*tandis que*) whereas, while; **alors**

que son frère travaillait dur, lui se reposait while his brother was working hard, HE would rest

**alouette** [alwɛt] nf (sky)lark

**alourdir** [aluʀdiʀ] vt to weigh down, make heavy

**aloyau** [alwajo] nm sirloin

**Alpes** [alp] nfpl: **les ~** the Alps

**alphabet** [alfabɛ] nm alphabet; (livre) ABC (book); **alphabétique** adj alphabetical; **alphabétiser** vt to teach to read and write; (pays) to eliminate illiteracy in

**alpinisme** [alpinism] nm mountaineering, climbing; **alpiniste** nm/f mountaineer, climber

**Alsace** [alzas] nf Alsace; **alsacien, ne** adj Alsatian ♦ nm/f: **Alsacien, ne** Alsatian

**altérer** [alteʀe] vt (vérité) to distort; **s'~** vi to deteriorate

**alternateur** [alternatœʀ] nm alternator

**alternatif, -ive** [alternatif, iv] adj alternating; **alternative** nf (choix) alternative; **alternativement** adv alternately; **alterner** vi to alternate

**Altesse** [altɛs] nf Highness

**altitude** [altityd] nf altitude, height

**alto** [alto] nm (instrument) viola

**aluminium** [alyminjɔm] nm aluminium (BRIT), aluminum (US)

**amabilité** [amabilite] nf kindness

**amadouer** [amadwe] vt to mollify, soothe

**amaigrir** [amegʀiʀ] vt to make thin(ner); **amaigrissant, e** adj (régime) slimming

**amalgame** [amalgam] (péj) nm (strange) mixture

**amande** [amɑ̃d] nf (de l'amandier) almond; **amandier** nm (tree) almond (tree)

**amant** [amɑ̃] nm lover

**amarrer** [amaʀe] vt (NAVIG) to moor; (gén) to make fast

**amas** [ama] nm heap, pile; **amasser** vt

to amass; **s'amasser** vi (foule) to gather

**amateur** [amatœʀ] nm amateur; **en ~** (péj) amateurishly; **~ de musique/ sport** etc music/sport etc lover

**amazone** [amazon] nf: **en ~** side-saddle

**ambassade** [ɑ̃basad] nf embassy; **l'~ de France** the French Embassy; **ambassadeur, -drice** nm/f ambassador (-dress)

**ambiance** [ɑ̃bjɑ̃s] nf atmosphere

**ambiant, e** [ɑ̃bjɑ̃, jɑ̃t] adj (air, milieu) surrounding; (température) ambient

**ambigu, ë** [ɑ̃bigy] adj ambiguous

**ambitieux, -euse** [ɑ̃bisjø, jøz] adj ambitious

**ambition** [ɑ̃bisjɔ̃] nf ambition

**ambulance** [ɑ̃bylɑ̃s] nf ambulance; **ambulancier, -ière** nm/f ambulance man(-woman) (BRIT), paramedic (US)

**ambulant, e** [ɑ̃bylɑ̃, ɑ̃t] adj travelling, itinerant

**âme** [am] nf soul

**amélioration** [ameljɔʀasjɔ̃] nf improvement

**améliorer** [ameljɔʀe] vt to improve; **s'~** vi to improve, get better

**aménager** [amenaʒe] vt (agencer, transformer) to fit out; to lay out; (: quartier, territoire) to develop; (installer) to fix up, put in; **ferme aménagée** converted farmhouse

**amende** [amɑ̃d] nf fine; **faire ~ honorable** to make amends

**amener** [am(ə)ne] vt to bring; (causer) to bring about; **s'~** vi to show up (fam), turn up

**amenuiser** [amənɥize]: **s'~** vi (chances) to grow slimmer, lessen

**amer, amère** [amɛʀ] adj bitter

**américain, e** [ameʀikɛ̃, ɛn] adj American ♦ nm/f: **A~, e** American

**Amérique** [ameʀik] nf: **l'~** America; **l'~ centrale/latine** Central/Latin America; **l'~ du Nord/du Sud** North/South America

**amertume** [amɛrtym] nf bitterness

**ameublement** [amœbləmã] nm furnishing; *(meubles)* furniture

**ameuter** [amøte] vt *(peuple)* to rouse

**ami, e** [ami] nm/f friend; *(amant/maîtresse)* boyfriend/girlfriend ♦ adj: **pays/groupe ~** friendly country/group

**amiable** [amjabl]: **à l'~** adv *(JUR)* out of court; *(gén)* amicably

**amiante** [amjãt] nm asbestos

**amical, e, -aux** [amikal, o] adj friendly; **amicalement** adv in a friendly way; *(formule épistolaire)* regards

**amidon** [amidɔ̃] nm starch

**amincir** [amɛ̃sir] vt: **~ qn** to make sb thinner ou slimmer; *(suj: vêtement)* to make sb look slimmer

**amincissant, e** [amɛ̃sisɑ̃, ɑ̃t] adj: **régime ~** (slimming) diet; **crème ~e** slimming cream

**amiral, -aux** [amiral, o] nm admiral

**amitié** [amitje] nf friendship; **prendre en ~** to befriend; **~s, Christèle** best wishes, Christèle; **présenter ses ~s à qn** to send sb one's best wishes

**ammoniaque** [amɔnjak] nf ammonia (water)

**amnistie** [amnisti] nf amnesty

**amoindrir** [amwɛ̃drir] vt to reduce

**amollir** [amɔlir] vt to soften

**amonceler** [amɔ̃s(ə)le] vt to pile ou heap up; **s'~** vi to pile ou heap up; *(fig)* to accumulate

**amont** [amɔ̃]: **en ~** adv upstream

**amorce** [amɔrs] nf *(sur un hameçon)* bait; *(explosif)* cap; primer; priming; *(fig: début)* beginning(s), start; **amorcer** vt to start

**amorphe** [amɔrf] adj passive, lifeless

**amortir** [amɔrtir] vt *(atténuer: choc)* to absorb, cushion; *(bruit, douleur)* to deaden; *(COMM: dette)* to pay off; **~ un achat** to make a purchase pay for itself; **amortisseur** nm shock absorber

**amour** [amur] nm love; **faire l'~ to**

make love; **amouracher: s'amouracher de** *(péj)* vt to become infatuated with; **amoureux, -euse** adj *(regard, tempérament)* amorous; love cpd; *(personne)*: **amoureux (de qn)** in love (with sb) ♦ nmpl courting couple(s); **amour-propre** nm self-esteem, pride

**amovible** [amɔvibl] adj removable, detachable

**ampère** [ɑ̃pɛr] nm amp(ere)

**amphithéâtre** [ɑ̃fiteatr] nm amphitheatre; *(d'université)* lecture hall ou theatre

**ample** [ɑ̃pl] adj *(vêtement)* roomy, ample; *(gestes, mouvement)* broad; *(ressources)* ample; **amplement** adv: **c'est amplement suffisant** that's more than enough; **ampleur** nf *(de dégâts, problème)* extent

**amplificateur** [ɑ̃plifikatœr] nm amplifier

**amplifier** [ɑ̃plifje] vt *(fig)* to expand, increase

**ampoule** [ɑ̃pul] nf *(électrique)* bulb; *(de médicament)* phial; *(aux mains, pieds)* blister; **ampoulé, e** *(péj)* adj pompous, bombastic

**amputer** [ɑ̃pyte] vt *(MÉD)* to amputate; *(fig)* to cut ou reduce drastically

**amusant, e** [amyzɑ̃, ɑ̃t] adj *(divertissant, spirituel)* entertaining, amusing; *(comique)* funny, amusing

**amuse-gueule** [amyzgœl] nm inv appetizer, snack

**amusement** [amyzmɑ̃] nm *(divertissement)* amusement; *(jeu etc)* pastime, diversion

**amuser** [amyze] vt *(divertir)* to entertain, amuse; *(égayer, faire rire)* to amuse; **s'~** *(à jouer)* to play; *(se divertir)* to enjoy o.s., have fun; *(fig)* to mess about

**amygdale** [amidal] nf tonsil

**an** [ɑ̃] nm year; **avoir quinze ~s** to be fifteen (years old); **le jour de l'~, le premier de l'~, le nouvel ~** New

Year's Day

**analogique** [analɔʒik] *adj* (*INFORM, montre*) analog

**analogue** [analɔg] *adj:* **~ (à)** analogous (to), similar (to)

**analphabète** [analfabɛt] *nm/f* illiterate

**analyse** [analiz] *nf* analysis; (*MÉD*) test; **analyser** *vt* to analyse; to test

**ananas** [anana(s)] *nm* pineapple

**anarchie** [anaʀʃi] *nf* anarchy

**anatomie** [anatɔmi] *nf* anatomy

**ancêtre** [ɑ̃sɛtʀ] *nm/f* ancestor

**anchois** [ɑ̃ʃwa] *nm* anchovy

**ancien, ne** [ɑ̃sjɛ̃, jɛn] *adj* old; (*de jadis, de l'antiquité*) ancient; (*précédent, ex-*) former, old; (*par l'expérience*) senior ♦ *nm/f* (*dans une tribu*) elder; **~ combattant** ♦ *nm* war veteran; **anciennement** *adv* formerly; **ancienneté** [ɑ̃sjɛnte] *nf* (*ADMIN*) (length of) service; (*privilèges obtenus*) seniority

**ancre** [ɑ̃kʀ] *nf* anchor; **jeter/lever l'~** to cast/weigh anchor; **ancrer** *vt* (*CONSTR: câble etc*) to anchor; (*fig*) to fix firmly

**Andorre** [ɑ̃dɔʀ] *nf* Andorra

**andouille** [ɑ̃duj] *nf* (*CULIN*) sausage made of chitterlings; (*fam*) clot, nit

**âne** [ɑn] *nm* donkey, ass; (*péj*) dunce

**anéantir** [aneɑ̃tiʀ] *vt* to annihilate, wipe out; (*fig*) to obliterate, destroy

**anémie** [anemi] *nf* anaemia; **anémique** *adj* anaemic

**ânerie** [ɑnʀi] *nf* stupidity; (*parole etc*) stupid *ou* idiotic comment *etc*

**anesthésie** [anɛstezi] *nf* anaesthesia; **faire une ~ locale/générale à qn** to give sb a local/general anaesthetic

**ange** [ɑ̃ʒ] *nm* angel; **être aux ~s** to be over the moon

**angélus** [ɑ̃ʒelys] *nm* angelus; (*cloches*) evening bells *pl*

**angine** [ɑ̃ʒin] *nf* throat infection; **~ de poitrine** angina

**anglais, e** [ɑ̃glɛ, ɛz] *adj* English ♦ *nm/f:* **A~, e** Englishman(-woman) ♦ *nm* (*LING*) English; **les A~** the English; **filer à l'~e**

to take French leave

**angle** [ɑ̃gl] *nm* angle; (*coin*) corner; **~ droit** right angle

**Angleterre** [ɑ̃glətɛʀ] *nf:* **l'~** England

**anglo...** [ɑ̃glɔ] *préfixe* Anglo-, anglo(-); **anglophone** *adj* English-speaking

**angoisse** [ɑ̃gwas] *nf* anguish, distress; **angoissé, e** *adj* (*personne*) distressed; **angoisser** *vt* to harrow, cause anguish to ♦ *vi* to worry, fret

**anguille** [ɑ̃gij] *nf* eel

**anicroche** [anikʀɔʃ] *nf* hitch, snag

**animal, e, -aux** [animal, o] *adj, nm* animal

**animateur, -trice** [animatœʀ, tʀis] *nm/f* (*de télévision*) host; (*de groupe*) leader, organizer

**animation** [animasjɔ̃] *nf* (*voir animé*) busyness; liveliness; (*CINÉMA: technique*) animation; **~s culturelles** cultural activities

**animé, e** [anime] *adj* (*lieu*) busy, lively; (*conversation, réunion*) lively, animated

**animer** [anime] *vt* (*ville, soirée*) to liven up; (*mener*) to lead; **s'~** *vi* to liven up

**anis** [ani(s)] *nm* (*CULIN*) aniseed; (*BOT*) anise

**ankylose** [ɑ̃kiloze]: **s'~** *vi* to get stiff

**anneau, x** [ano] *nm* (*de rideau, bague*) ring; (*de chaîne*) link

**année** [ane] *nf* year

**annexe** [anɛks] *adj* (*problème*) related; (*document*) appended; (*salle*) adjoining ♦ *nf* (*bâtiment*) annex(e); (*jointe à une lettre*) enclosure

**anniversaire** [anivɛʀsɛʀ] *nm* birthday; (*d'un événement, bâtiment*) anniversary

**annonce** [anɔ̃s] *nf* announcement; (*signe, indice*) sign; (*aussi:* **~ publicitaire**) advertisement; **les petites ~s** the classified advertisements; **les petites annonces**, the small ads

**annoncer** [anɔ̃se] *vt* to announce; (*être le signe de*) to herald; **s'~ bien/difficile** to look promising/difficult; **annonceur, -euse** *nm/f* (*publicitaire*) advertiser; (*TV, RADIO: speaker*) announcer

**annuaire** [anɥɛʀ] *nm* yearbook, annual; ~ **téléphonique** (telephone) directory, phone book

**annuel, le** [anɥɛl] *adj* annual, yearly

**annuité** [anɥite] *nf* annual instalment

**annulation** [anylasjɔ̃] *nf* cancellation

**annuler** [anyle] *vt* (*rendez-vous, voyage*) to cancel, call off; (*jugement*) to quash (BRIT), repeal (US); (MATH, PHYSIQUE) to cancel out

**anodin, e** [anɔdɛ̃, in] *adj* (*blessure*) harmless; (*détail*) insignificant, trivial

**anonymat** [anɔnima] *nm* anonymity

**anonyme** [anɔnim] *adj* anonymous; (*fig*) impersonal

**ANPE** *sigle f* (= *Agence nationale pour l'emploi*) national employment agency

**anorak** [anɔʀak] *nm* anorak

**anorexie** [anɔʀɛksi] *nf* anorexia

**anormal, e, -aux** [anɔʀmal, o] *adj* abnormal

**anse** [ɑ̃s] *nf* (*de panier, tasse*) handle

**antan** [ɑ̃tɑ̃]: **d'~** *adj* of long ago

**antarctique** [ɑ̃taʀktik] *adj* Antarctic ♦ *nm*: **l'A~** the Antarctic

**antécédents** [ɑ̃tesedɑ̃] *nmpl* (MÉD etc) past history *sg*

**antenne** [ɑ̃tɛn] *nf* (*de radio*) aerial; (*d'insecte*) antenna, feeler; (*poste avancé*) outpost; (*petite succursale*) sub-branch; **passer à l'~** to go on the air

**antérieur, e** [ɑ̃teʀjœʀ] *adj* (*d'avant*) previous, earlier; (*de devant*) front

**anti...** [ɑ̃ti] *préfixe* anti...; **antialcoolique** *adj* anti-alcohol; **antiatomique** *adj*: **abri antiatomique** fallout shelter; **antibiotique** *nm* antibiotic; **antibrouillard** *adj*: **phare antibrouillard** fog lamp (BRIT) ou light (US)

**anticipation** [ɑ̃tisipasjɔ̃] *nf*: **livre/film d'~** science fiction book/film

**anticipé, e** [ɑ̃tisipe] *adj*: **avec mes remerciements ~s** thanking you in advance *ou* anticipation

**anticiper** [ɑ̃tisipe] *vt* (*événement, coup*) to anticipate, foresee

**anti...**: **anticonceptionnel, le** *adj* contraceptive; **anticorps** *nm* antibody; **antidote** *nm* antidote; **antigel** *nm* antifreeze; **antihistaminique** *nm* antihistamine

**antillais, e** [ɑ̃tijɛ, ɛz] *adj* West Indian, Caribbean ♦ *nm/f*: **A~, e** West Indian, Caribbean

**Antilles** [ɑ̃tij] *nfpl*: **les ~** the West Indies

**antilope** [ɑ̃tilɔp] *nf* antelope

**anti...**: **antimite(s)** *adj, nm*: (*produit*) **antimite(s)** mothproofer; moth repellent; **antipathique** *adj* unpleasant, disagreeable; **antipelliculaire** *adj* anti-dandruff

**antipodes** [ɑ̃tipɔd] *nmpl* (*fig*): **être aux ~ de** to be the opposite extreme of

**antiquaire** [ɑ̃tikɛʀ] *nm/f* antique dealer

**antique** [ɑ̃tik] *adj* antique; (*très vieux*) ancient, antiquated; **antiquité** [ɑ̃tikite] *nf* (*objet*) antique; **l'Antiquité** Antiquity; **magasin d'antiquités** antique shop

**anti...**: **antirabique** *adj* rabies *cpd*; **antirouille** *adj inv* anti-rust *cpd*; **antisémite** *adj* anti-Semitic; **antiseptique** *adj, nm* antiseptic; **antivol** *adj, nm*: (*dispositif*) **antivol** anti-theft device

**antre** [ɑ̃tʀ] *nm* den, lair

**anxiété** [ɑ̃ksjete] *nf* anxiety

**anxieux, -euse** [ɑ̃ksjø, jøz] *adj* anxious, worried

**AOC** *sigle f* (= *appellation d'origine contrôlée*) label guaranteeing the quality of wine

---

**AOC**

AOC is the highest French wine classification. It indicates that the wine meets strict requirements concerning the vineyard of origin, the type of vine grown, the method of production, and the volume of alcohol present.

---

**août** [u(t)] *nm* August

**apaiser** [apeze] *vt* (*colère, douleur*) to soothe; (*personne*) to calm (down), pacify; **s'~** *vi* (*tempête, bruit*) to die down, subside; (*personne*) to calm down

**apanage** [apanaʒ] *nm*: **être l'~ de** to be the privilege *ou* prerogative of

**aparté** [aparte] *nm* (*entretien*) private conversation; **en ~** in an aside

**apathique** [apatik] *adj* apathetic

**apatride** [apatrid] *nm/f* stateless person

**apercevoir** [apɛrsəvwar] *vt* to see; **s'~ de** *vt* to notice; **s'~ que** to notice that

**aperçu** [apɛrsy] *nm* (*vue d'ensemble*) general survey

**apéritif** [aperitif] *nm* (*boisson*) aperitif; (*réunion*) drinks pl

**à-peu-près** [apøprɛ] (*péj*) *nm inv* vague approximation

**apeuré, e** [apœre] *adj* frightened, scared

**aphte** [aft] *nm* mouth ulcer

**apiculture** [apikyltyr] *nf* beekeeping, apiculture

**apitoyer** [apitwaje] *vt* to move to pity; **s'~ (sur)** to feel pity (for)

**aplanir** [aplanir] *vt* to level; (*fig*) to smooth away, iron out

**aplatir** [aplatir] *vt* to flatten; **s'~** *vi* to become flatter; (*écrasé*) to be flattened; **s'~ devant qn** (*fig*): to humiliate o.s.; to crawl to sb

**aplomb** [aplɔ̃] *nm* (*équilibre*) balance, equilibrium; (*fig*) self-assurance; nerve; **d'~** steady

**apogée** [apɔʒe] *nm* (*fig*) peak, apogee

**apologie** [apɔlɔʒi] *nf* vindication, praise

**a posteriori** [aposterjɔri] *adv* after the event

**apostrophe** [apɔstrɔf] *nf* (*signe*) apostrophe

**apostropher** [apɔstrɔfe] *vt* (*interpeller*) to shout at, address sharply

**apothéose** [apoteoz] *nf* pinnacle of achievement; (*mus*) grand finale

**apôtre** [apotr] *nm* apostle

**apparaître** [aparɛtr] *vi* to appear

**apparat** [apara] *nm*: **tenue d'~** ceremonial dress

**appareil** [aparɛj] *nm* (*outil, machine*) piece of apparatus, device; (*électrique, ménager*) appliance; (*avion*) (aero)plane, aircraft *inv*; (*téléphonique*) phone; (*dentier*) brace (*BRIT*), braces (*US*); **"qui est à l'~?"** "who's speaking?"; **dans le plus simple ~** in one's birthday suit; **appareiller** *vi* (*NAVIG*) to cast off, get under way ♦ *vt* (*assortir*) to match up; **appareil(-photo)** *nm* camera

**apparemment** [aparamɑ̃] *adv* apparently

**apparence** [aparɑ̃s] *nf* appearance; **en ~** apparently

**apparent, e** [aparɑ̃, ɑ̃t] *adj* visible; (*évident*) obvious; (*superficiel*) apparent

**apparenté, e** [aparɑ̃te] *adj*: **~ à** related to; (*fig*) similar to

**apparition** [aparisjɔ̃] *nf* appearance; (*surnaturelle*) apparition

**appartement** [apartəmɑ̃] *nm* flat (*BRIT*), apartment (*US*)

**appartenir** [apartənir]: **~ à** *vt* to belong to; **il lui appartient de** it is his duty to

**apparu, e** [apary] *pp de* **apparaître**

**appât** [apa] *nm* (*PÊCHE*) bait; (*fig*) lure, bait; **appâter** *vt* to lure

**appauvrir** [apovrir] *vt* to impoverish

**appel** [apɛl] *nm* call; (*nominal*) roll call; (: *SCOL*) register; (*MIL: recrutement*) call-up; **faire ~ à** (*invoquer*) to appeal to; (*avoir recours à*) to call on; (*nécessiter*) to call for, require; **faire ~** (*JUR*) to appeal; **faire l'~** to call the roll; to call the register; **sans ~** (*fig*) final, irrevocable; **~ d'offres** (*COMM*) invitation to tender; **faire un ~ de phares** to flash one's headlights; **~** (*téléphonique*) (tele)phone call

**appelé** [ap(ə)le] *nm* (*MIL*) conscript

**appeler** [ap(ə)le] *vt* to call; (*faire venir: médecin etc*) to call, send for; **s'~** *vi*: **elle s'appelle Gabrielle** her name is Gabrielle, she's called Gabrielle;

comment ça s'appelle? what is it called?; **être appelé à** (fig) to be destined to

**appendice** [apɛ̃dis] nm appendix; **appendicite** nf appendicitis

**appentis** [apɑ̃ti] nm lean-to

**appesantir** [apəzɑ̃tiʀ]: **s'~** vi to grow heavier; **s'~ sur** (fig) to dwell on

**appétissant, e** [apetisɑ̃, ɑ̃t] adj appetizing, mouth-watering

**appétit** [apeti] nm appetite; **bon ~!** enjoy your meal!

**applaudir** [aplodiʀ] vt to applaud ♦ vi to applaud, clap; **applaudissements** nmpl applause sg, clapping sg

**application** [aplikasjɔ̃] nf application

**applique** [aplik] nf wall lamp

**appliquer** [aplike] vt to apply; (loi) to enforce; **s'~** vi (élève etc) to apply o.s.; **s'~ à** to apply to

**appoint** [apwɛ̃] nm (extra) contribution ou help; **chauffage d'~** extra heating

**appointements** [apwɛ̃təmɑ̃] nmpl salary sg

**apport** [apɔʀ] nm (approvisionnement) supply; (contribution) contribution

**apporter** [apɔʀte] vt to bring

**apposer** [apoze] vt (signature) to affix

**appréciable** [apʀesjabl] adj appreciable

**apprécier** [apʀesje] vt to appreciate; (évaluer) to estimate, assess

**appréhender** [apʀeɑ̃de] vt (craindre) to dread; (arrêter) to apprehend; **appréhension** [apʀeɑ̃sjɔ̃] nf apprehension, anxiety

**apprendre** [apʀɑ̃dʀ] vt to learn; (événement, résultats) to learn of, hear of; **~ qch à qn** (informer) to tell sb (of) sth; (enseigner) to teach sb sth; **~ à faire qch** to learn to do sth; **~ à qn à faire qch** to teach sb to do sth; **apprenti, e** nm/f apprentice; **apprentissage** nm learning; (COMM, SCOL: période) apprenticeship

**apprêté, e** [apʀete] adj (fig) affected

**apprêter** [apʀete] vt: **s'~ à faire qch** to get ready to do sth

**appris, e** [apʀi, iz] pp de **apprendre**

**apprivoiser** [apʀivwaze] vt to tame

**approbation** [apʀɔbasjɔ̃] nf approval

**approchant, e** [apʀɔʃɑ̃, ɑ̃t] adj similar; **quelque chose d'~** something like that

**approche** [apʀɔʃ] nf approach

**approcher** [apʀɔʃe] vi to approach, come near ♦ vt to approach; (rapprocher): **~ qch (de qch)** to bring ou put sth near (to sth); **s'~ de** to approach, go ou come near to; **~ de** (lieu, but) to draw near to; (quantité, moment) to approach

**approfondir** [apʀɔfɔ̃diʀ] vt to deepen; (question) to go further into

**approprié, e** [apʀɔpʀije] adj: **~ (à)** appropriate (to), suited to

**approprier** [apʀɔpʀije]: **s'~** vt to appropriate, take over

**approuver** [apʀuve] vt to agree with; (trouver louable) to approve of

**approvisionner** [apʀɔvizjɔne] vt to supply; (compte bancaire) to pay funds into; **s'~ en** to stock up with

**approximatif, -ive** [apʀɔksimatif, iv] adj approximate, rough; (termes) vague

**appt** abr = **appartement**

**appui** [apɥi] nm support; **prendre ~ sur** to lean on; (objet) to rest on; **l'~ de la fenêtre** the windowsill, the window ledge; **appui(e)-tête** nm inv headrest

**appuyer** [apɥije] vt (poser): **~ qch sur/contre** to lean ou rest sth on/ against; (soutenir: personne, demande) to support, back (up) ♦ vi: **~** (bouton, frein) to press, push; (mot, détail) to stress, emphasize; **s'~ sur** to lean on; (fig: compter sur) to rely on

**âpre** [ɑpʀ] adj acrid, pungent; **~ au gain** grasping

**après** [apʀɛ] prép after ♦ adv afterwards; **2 heures ~** 2 hours later; **~ qu'il est** ou **soit parti** after he left; **~ avoir fait** after having done; **d'~** (selon) according to; **~ coup** after the event, afterwards; **~ tout** (au fond) after all; **et (puis) ~?** so what?; **après-demain** adv the day after tomorrow; **après-guerre** nm post-war years pl; **après-midi** nm ou nf inv afternoon; **après-rasage** nm inv aftershave; **après-shampooing** nm inv conditioner; **après-ski** nm inv snow boot

**à-propos** [aprɔpo] nm (d'une remarque) aptness; **faire preuve d'~~** to show presence of mind

**apte** [apt] adj capable; (MIL) fit

**aquarelle** [akwarɛl] nf watercolour

**aquarium** [akwarjɔm] nm aquarium

**arabe** [arab] adj Arabic; (désert, cheval) Arabian; (nation, peuple) Arab ♦ nm/f: **A~** Arab ♦ nm (LING) Arabic

**Arabie** [arabi] nf: **l'~ (Saoudite)** Saudi Arabia

**arachide** [araʃid] nf (plante) groundnut (plant); (graine) peanut, groundnut

**araignée** [arɛɲe] nf spider

**arbitraire** [arbitrɛr] adj arbitrary

**arbitre** [arbitr] nm (SPORT) referee; (: TENNIS, CRICKET) umpire; (fig) arbiter, judge; (JUR) arbitrator; **arbitrer** vt to referee; to umpire; to arbitrate

**arborer** [arbɔre] vt to bear, display

**arbre** [arbr] nm tree; (TECH) shaft; **~ généalogique** family tree

**arbuste** [arbyst] nm small shrub

**arc** [ark] nm (arme) bow; (GÉOM) arc; (ARCHIT) arch; **en ~ de cercle** semi-circular

**arcade** [arkad] nf arch(way); **~s** (série) arcade sg, arches

**arc-boutant** [arkbutã] nm flying buttress

**arceau, x** [arso] nm (métallique etc) hoop

**arc-en-ciel** [arkãsjɛl] nm rainbow

**arche** [arʃ] nf arch; **~ de Noé** Noah's Ark

**archéologie** [arkeɔlɔʒi] nf arch(a)eology; **archéologue** nm/f arch(a)eologist

**archet** [arʃɛ] nm bow

**archevêque** [arʃəvɛk] nm archbishop

**archi...** [arʃi] (fam) préfixe tremendously; **archicomble** (fam) adj chock-a-block; **archiconnu, e** (fam) adj enormously well-known

**archipel** [arʃipɛl] nm archipelago

**architecte** [arʃitɛkt] nm architect

**architecture** [arʃitɛktyr] nf architecture

**archives** [arʃiv] nfpl (collection) archives

**arctique** [arktik] adj Arctic ♦ nm: **l'A~** the Arctic

**ardemment** [ardamã] adv ardently, fervently

**ardent, e** [ardã, ãt] adj (soleil) blazing; (amour) ardent, passionate; (prière) fervent

**ardeur** [ardœr] nf ardour (BRIT), ardor (US); (du soleil) heat

**ardoise** [ardwaz] nf slate

**ardu, e** [ardy] adj (travail) arduous; (problème) difficult

**arène** [arɛn] nf arena; **~s** nfpl (amphithéâtre) bull-ring sg

**arête** [arɛt] nf (de poisson) bone; (d'une montagne) ridge

**argent** [arʒã] nm (métal) silver; (monnaie) money; **~ de poche** pocket money; **~ liquide** ready money, (ready) cash; **argenté, e** adj (couleur) silver, silvery; **en métal argenté** silver-plated; **argenterie** nf silverware

**argentin, e** [arʒãtɛ̃, in] adj Argentinian, Argentine

**Argentine** [arʒãtin] nf: **l'~** Argentina, the Argentine

**argile** [arʒil] nf clay

**argot** [argo] nm slang; **argotique** adj slang cpd; (très familier) slangy

**argument** [argymã] nm argument

**argumentaire** [argymãtɛr] nm sales leaflet

**argumenter** [argymãte] vi to argue

**argus** [argys] nm guide to second-hand car etc prices

**aride** [aRid] adj arid

**aristocratie** [aRistɔkRasi] nf aristocracy; **aristocratique** adj aristocratic

**arithmétique** [aRitmetik] adj arithmetic(al) ♦ nf arithmetic

**armateur** [aRmatœR] nm shipowner

**armature** [aRmatyR] nf framework; (de tente etc) frame; **soutien-gorge à/ sans ~** underwired/unwired bra

**arme** [aRm] nf weapon; **~s** nfpl (~ment) weapons, arms; (blason) (coat of) arms; **~ à feu** firearm

**armée** [aRme] nf army; **~ de l'air** Air Force; **~ de terre** Army

**armement** [aRməmã] nm (matériel) arms pl, weapons pl

**armer** [aRme] vt to arm; (arme à feu) to cock; (appareil-photo) to wind on; **~ qch de** to reinforce sth with; **s'~ de** to arm o.s. with

**armistice** [aRmistis] nm armistice; **l'A~** ≈ Remembrance (BRIT) ou Veterans (US) Day

**armoire** [aRmwaR] nf (tall) cupboard; (penderie) wardrobe (BRIT), closet (US)

**armoiries** [aRmwaRi] nfpl coat sg of arms

**armure** [aRmyR] nf armour no pl, suit of armour; **armurier** nm gunsmith

**arnaque** [aRnak] (fam) nf swindling; **c'est de l'~** it's a rip-off; **arnaquer** (fam) vt to swindle

**aromates** [aRɔmat] nmpl seasoning sg, herbs (and spices)

**aromathérapie** [aRɔmateRapi] nf aromatherapy

**aromatisé, e** [aRɔmatize] adj flavoured

**arôme** [aRom] nm aroma

**arpenter** [aRpãte] vt (salle, couloir) to pace up and down

**arpenteur** [aRpãtœR] nm surveyor

**arqué, e** [aRke] adj arched; (jambes) bandy

**arrache-pied** [aRaʃpje]: **d'~~** adv relentlessly

**arracher** [aRaʃe] vt to pull out; (page etc) to tear off, tear out; (légumes, herbe) to pull up; (bras etc) to tear off; **s'~** vt (article recherché) to fight over; **~ qch à qn** to snatch sth from sb; (fig) to wring sth out of sb

**arraisonner** [aRezɔne] vt (bateau) to board and search

**arrangeant, e** [aRãʒã, ãt] adj accommodating, obliging

**arrangement** [aRãʒmã] nm agreement, arrangement

**arranger** [aRãʒe] vt (gén) to arrange; (réparer) to fix, put right; (régler: différend) to settle, sort out; (convenir à) to suit, be convenient for; **s'~** vi (se mettre d'accord) to come to an agreement; **je vais m'~** I'll manage; **ça va s'~** it'll sort itself out

**arrestation** [aRestasjɔ̃] nf arrest

**arrêt** [aRe] nm stopping; (de bus etc) stop; (JUR) judgment, decision; **à l'~** stationary; **tomber en ~ devant** to stop short in front of; **sans ~** (sans interruption) non-stop; (très fréquemment) continually; **~ de travail** stoppage (of work); **~ maladie** sick leave

**arrêté** [aRete] nm order, decree

**arrêter** [aRete] vt to stop; (chauffage etc) to turn off, switch off; (fixer: date etc) to appoint, decide on; (criminel, suspect) to arrest; **s'~** vi to stop; **~ de faire** to stop doing

**arrhes** [aR] nfpl deposit sg

**arrière** [aRjɛR] nm back; (SPORT) fullback ♦ adj inv: **siège/roue ~** back ou rear seat/wheel; **à l'~** behind, at the back; **en ~** behind; (regarder) back, behind; (tomber, aller) backwards; **arriéré, e** adj (péj) backward ♦ nm (d'argent) arrears pl; **arrière-goût** nm aftertaste; **arrière-grand-mère** nf great-grandmother; **arrière-grand-père** nm great-grandfather; **arrière-pays** nm inv hinterland; **arrière-pensée** nf ulterior motive; mental reservation; **arrière-plan** nm background; **arrière-saison** nf late autumn; **arrière-train** nm hindquarters pl

**arrimer** [aʀime] vt to secure; (cargaison) to stow

**arrivage** [aʀivaʒ] nm consignment

**arrivée** [aʀive] nf arrival; (ligne d'~) finish

**arriver** [aʀive] vi to arrive; (survenir) to happen, occur; **il arrive à Paris à 8h** he gets to ou arrives Paris at 8; **~ à** (atteindre) to reach; **~ à faire qch** to succeed in doing sth; **en ~ à** (finir par) to come to; **il arrive que** it happens that; **il lui arrive de faire** he sometimes does; **arriviste** nm/f go-getter

**arrobase** [aʀɔbaz] nf(INFORM) @, 'at' sign

**arrogance** [aʀɔgɑ̃s] nf arrogance

**arrogant, e** [aʀɔgɑ̃, ɑ̃t] adj arrogant

**arrondir** [aʀɔ̃diʀ] vt (forme, objet) to round; (somme) to round off

**arrondissement** [aʀɔ̃dismɑ̃] nm (ADMIN) ≈ district

**arroser** [aʀoze] vt to water; (victoire) to celebrate (over a drink); (CULIN) to baste; **arrosoir** nm watering can

**arsenal, -aux** [aʀsənal, o] nm (NAVIG) naval dockyard; (MIL) arsenal; (fig) gear

**art** [aʀ] nm art

**artère** [aʀtɛʀ] nf (ANAT) artery; (rue) main road

**arthrite** [aʀtʀit] nf arthritis

**artichaut** [aʀtiʃo] nm artichoke

**article** [aʀtikl] nm article; (COMM) item, article; **à l'~ de la mort** at the point of death; **~s de luxe** luxury goods

**articulation** [aʀtikylasjɔ̃] nf articulation; (ANAT) joint

**articuler** [aʀtikyle] vt to articulate

**artifice** [aʀtifis] nm device, trick

**artificiel, le** [aʀtifisjɛl] adj artificial

**artisan** [aʀtizɑ̃] nm artisan, (self-employed) craftsman; **artisanal, e, -aux** adj of ou made by craftsmen; (péj) cottage industry cpd; **de fabrication artisanale** home-made; **artisanat** nm arts and crafts pl

**artiste** [aʀtist] nm/f artist; (de variétés) entertainer; (musicien etc) performer; **artistique** adj artistic

**as¹** [a] vb voir **avoir**

**as²** [as] nm ace

**ascendance** [asɑ̃dɑ̃s] nf (origine) ancestry

**ascendant, e** [asɑ̃dɑ̃, ɑ̃t] adj upward ♦ nm influence

**ascenseur** [asɑ̃sœʀ] nm lift (BRIT), elevator (US)

**ascension** [asɑ̃sjɔ̃] nf ascent; (de montagne) climb; **l'A~** (REL) the Ascension

### Ascension

La fête de l'Ascension is a French public holiday, usually in May. As it falls on a Thursday, many people take Friday off work and enjoy a long weekend; see also faire le **pont**.

**aseptisé, e** (péj) sanitized

**aseptiser** [asɛptize] vt (ustensile) to sterilize; (plaie) to disinfect

**asiatique** [azjatik] adj Asiatic, Asian ♦ nm/f: **A~** Asian

**Asie** [azi] nf: **l'~** Asia

**asile** [azil] nm (refuge) refuge, sanctuary; (POL): **droit d'~** (political) asylum; **~ (de vieillards)** old people's home

**aspect** [aspɛ] nm appearance, look; (fig) aspect, side; **à l'~ de** at the sight of

**asperge** [aspɛʀʒ] nf asparagus no pl

**asperger** [aspɛʀʒe] vt to spray, sprinkle

**aspérité** [aspeʀite] nf bump, protruding bit (of rock etc)

**asphalte** [asfalt] nm asphalt

**asphyxier** [asfiksje] vt to suffocate, asphyxiate; (fig) to stifle

**aspirateur** [aspiʀatœʀ] nm vacuum cleaner; **passer l'~** to vacuum

**aspirer** [aspiʀe] vt (air) to inhale; (liquide) to suck (up); (suj: appareil) to suck up; **~ à** to aspire to

**aspirine** [aspiʀin] nf aspirin

**assagir** [asaʒiʀ]: **s'~** vi to quieten down, settle down

**assaillir** [asajiʀ] vt to assail, attack

**assainir** [aseniʀ] vt (logements) to

**up;** *(eau, air)* to purify
**assaisonnement** [asɛzɔnmã] *nm* seasoning
**assaisonner** [asɛzɔne] *vt* to season
**assassin** [asasɛ̃] *nm* murderer; assassin;
**assassiner** *vt* to murder; *(esp POL)* to assassinate
**assaut** [aso] *nm* assault, attack; **prendre d'~** to storm, assault; **donner l'~** to attack
**assécher** [asefe] *vt* to drain
**assemblage** [asãblaʒ] *nm (action)* assembling; *(de couleurs, choses)* collection
**assemblée** [asãble] *nf (réunion)* meeting; *(assistance)* gathering; *(POL)* assembly
**assembler** [asãble] *vt (joindre, monter)* to assemble, put together; *(amasser)* to gather (together), collect (together);
**s'~** *vi* to gather
**assener, asséner** [asene] *vt:* **~ un coup à qn** to deal sb a blow
**assentiment** [asãtimã] *nm* assent, consent
**asseoir** [aswar] *vt (malade, bébé)* to sit up; *(personne debout)* to sit down;
*(autorité, réputation)* to establish; **s'~** *vi* to sit (o.s.) down
**assermenté, e** [asɛrmãte] *adj* sworn, on oath
**asservir** [asɛrvir] *vt* to subjugate, enslave
**assez** [ase] *adv (suffisamment)* enough, sufficiently; *(passablement)* rather, quite, fairly; **~ de pain/livres** enough *ou* sufficient bread/books; **vous en avez ~?** have you got enough?; **j'en ai ~!** I've had enough!
**assidu, e** [asidy] *adj (appliqué)* assiduous, painstaking; *(ponctuel)* regular
**assied** *etc* **vb voir asseoir**
**assiéger** [asjeʒe] *vt* to besiege
**assiérai** *etc* **vb voir asseoir**
**assiette** [asjɛt] *nf* plate; *(contenu)* plate(ful); **il n'est pas dans son ~** he's not feeling quite himself; **~ à des-**

**sert** dessert plate; **~ anglaise** assorted cold meats; **~ creuse** (soup) dish, soup plate; **~ plate** (dinner) plate
**assigner** [asiɲe] *vt:* **~ qch à** *(poste, part, travail)* to assign sth to
**assimiler** [asimile] *vt* to assimilate, absorb; *(comparer):* **~ qch/qn à** to liken *ou* compare sth/sb to
**assis, e** [asi, iz] *pp de* **asseoir** ♦ *adj* sitting (down), seated; **assise** *nf (fig)* basis, foundation; **assises** *nfpl (JUR)* assizes
**assistance** [asistãs] *nf (public)* audience; *(aide)* assistance; **enfant de l'A~ publique** child in care
**assistant, e** [asistã, ãt] *nm/f* assistant; *(d'université)* probationary lecturer; **~(e) social(e)** social worker
**assisté, e** [asiste] *adj (AUTO)* power assisted; **~ par ordinateur** computer-assisted
**assister** [asiste] *vt (aider)* to assist; **~ à** *(scène, événement)* to witness; *(conférence, séminaire)* to attend, be at; *(spectacle, match)* to be at, see
**association** [asɔsjasjɔ̃] *nf* association
**associé, e** [asɔsje] *nm/f* associate; *(COMM)* partner
**associer** [asɔsje] *vt* to associate; **s'~** *vi* to join together; **s'~ à qn pour faire** to join forces with sb to do; **s'~ à** *(couleurs, qualités)* to be combined with; *(opinions, joie de qn)* to share in; **~ qn à** *(profits)* to give sb a share of; *(affaire)* to make sb a partner in; *(joie, triomphe)* to include sb in; **~ qch à** *(allier à)* to combine sth with
**assoiffé, e** [aswafe] *adj* thirsty
**assombrir** [asɔ̃brir] *vt* to darken; *(fig)* to fill with gloom
**assommer** [asɔme] *vt (étourdir, abrutir)* to knock out, stun
**Assomption** [asɔ̃psjɔ̃] *nf:* **l'~** the Assumption

La fête de l'Assomption *on August*

*15 is a French national holiday. Tra-
ditionally, large numbers of holiday-
makers set out on this date, frequently
causing chaos on the roads; see also*
faire le **pont**.

**assorti, e** [asɔʀti] *adj* matched, matching; (*varié*) assorted; ~ **à** matching;
**assortiment** *nm* assortment, selection
**assortir** [asɔʀtiʀ] *vt* to match; ~ **qch à**
to match sth with; ~ **qch de** to accompany sth with

**assoupi, e** [asupi] *adj* dozing, sleeping
**assoupir** [asupiʀ]: **s'~** *vi* to doze off
**assouplir** [asupliʀ] *vt* to make supple;
(*fig*) to relax; **assouplissant** *nm* (fabric) softener
**assourdir** [asuʀdiʀ] *vt* (*bruit*) to dead-
en, muffle; (*suj: bruit*) to deafen
**assouvir** [asuviʀ] *vt* to satisfy, appease
**assujettir** [asyʒetiʀ] *vt* to subject
**assumer** [asyme] *vt* (*fonction, emploi*)
to assume, take on
**assurance** [asyʀɑ̃s] *nf* (*certitude*) assurance; (*confiance en soi*) (self-)
confidence; (*contrat*) insurance (policy); (*secteur commercial*) insurance; ~
**maladie** health insurance; ~ **tous risques** (*AUTO*) comprehensive insurance;
**~s sociales** ≃ National Insurance
(*BRIT*), ≃ Social Security (*US*);
**assurance-vie** *nf* life assurance *ou* insurance
**assuré, e** [asyʀe] *adj* (*certain: réussite,
échec*) certain, sure; (*air*) assured; (*pas*)
steady ♦ *nm/f* insured (person); **assu-
rément** *adv* assuredly, most certainly
**assurer** [asyʀe] *vt* (*FIN*) to insure; (*victoire etc*) to ensure; (*frontières, pouvoir*)
to make secure; (*service*) to provide,
operate; **s'~** (*COMM*) to insure
o.s. (against); **s'~ de/que** (*vérifier*) to
make sure of/that; **s'~ (de)** (*aide de qn*)
to secure; ~ **à qn que** to assure sb
that; ~ **qn de** to assure sb of; **assureur** *nm* insurer
**asthmatique** [asmatik] *adj*, *nm/f* asth-

matic
**asthme** [asm] *nm* asthma
**asticot** [astiko] *nm* maggot
**astiquer** [astike] *vt* to polish, shine
**astre** [astʀ] *nm* star
**astreignant, e** [astʀɛɲɑ̃, ɑ̃t] *adj* demanding
**astreindre** [astʀɛ̃dʀ] *vt*: ~ **qn à faire**
to compel *ou* force sb to do; **s'~** *vi*: **s'~
à faire** to force o.s. to do
**astrologie** [astʀɔlɔʒi] *nf* astrology
**astronaute** [astʀonot] *nm/f* astronaut
**astronomie** [astʀɔnɔmi] *nf* astronomy
**astuce** [astys] *nf* shrewdness, astute-
ness; (*truc*) trick, clever way; **astu-
cieux, -euse** *adj* clever
**atelier** [atalje] *nm* workshop; (*de
peintre*) studio
**athée** [ate] *adj* atheistic ♦ *nm/f* atheist
**Athènes** [atɛn] *n* Athens
**athlète** [atlet] *nm/f* (*SPORT*) athlete;
**athlétisme** *nm* athletics *sg*
**atlantique** [atlɑ̃tik] *adj* Atlantic ♦ *nm*:
**l'(océan) A~** the Atlantic (Ocean)
**atlas** [atlas] *nm* atlas
**atmosphère** [atmɔsfɛʀ] *nf* atmosphere
**atome** [atom] *nm* atom; **atomique** *adj*
atomic, nuclear
**atomiseur** [atɔmizœʀ] *nm* atomizer
**atout** [atu] *nm* trump; (*fig*) asset
**âtre** [ɑtʀ] *nm* hearth
**atroce** [atʀɔs] *adj* atrocious
**attabler** [atable]: **s'~** *vi* to sit down at
(the) table
**attachant, e** [ataʃɑ̃, ɑ̃t] *adj* engaging,
lovable, likeable
**attache** [ataʃ] *nf* clip, fastener; (*fig*) tie
**attacher** [ataʃe] *vt* to tie up; (*étiquette*)
to attach, tie on; (*ceinture*) to fasten
♦ *vi* (*poêle, riz*) to stick; **s'~ à** (*par affection*) to become attached to; **s'~ à fai-
re** to endeavour to do; ~ **qch à** to tie
*ou* attach sth to
**attaque** [atak] *nf* attack; (*cérébrale*)
stroke; (*d'épilepsie*) fit; ~ **à main armée**
armed attack
**attaquer** [atake] *vt* to attack; (*en jus-*

*tice)* to bring an action against, sue ♦ *vi* to attack; **s'~ à** ♦ ♦ *vt (personne)* to attack; *(problème)* to tackle

**attardé, e** [atarde] *adj (enfant)* backward; *(passants)* late

**attarder** [atarde]: **s'~** *vi* to linger

**atteindre** [atɛ̃dʀ] *vt* to reach; *(blesser)* to hit; *(émouvoir)* to affect; **atteint, e** *adj (MÉD):* **être atteint de** to be suffering from; **atteinte** *nf:* **hors d'atteinte** out of reach; **porter atteinte à** to strike a blow at

**atteler** [at(ə)le] *vt (cheval, bœufs)* to hitch up; **s'~ à** *(travail)* to buckle down to

**attelle** [atɛl] *nf* splint

**attenant, e** [at(ə)nɑ̃, ɑ̃t] *adj:* **~ (à)** adjoining

**attendant** [atɑ̃dɑ̃] *adv:* **en ~** meanwhile, in the meantime

**attendre** [atɑ̃dʀ] *vt (gén)* to wait for; *(être destiné ou réservé à)* to await, be in store for ♦ *vi* to wait; **s'~ à (ce que)** to expect (that); **~ un enfant** to be expecting a baby; **~ de faire/d'être** to wait until one does/is; **attendez qu'il vienne** wait until he comes; **~ qch de** to expect sth of

**attendrir** [atɑ̃dʀiʀ] *vt* to move (to pity); *(viande)* to tenderize; **attendrissant, e** *adj* moving, touching

**attendu, e** [atɑ̃dy] *adj (visiteur)* expected; *(événement)* long-awaited; **~ que** considering that, since

**attentat** [atɑ̃ta] *nm* assassination attempt; **~ à la bombe** bomb attack; **~ à la pudeur** indecent assault *no pl*

**attente** [atɑ̃t] *nf* wait; *(espérance)* expectation

**attenter** [atɑ̃te]: **~ à** *vt (liberté)* to violate; **~ à la vie de qn** to make an attempt on sb's life

**attentif, -ive** [atɑ̃tif, iv] *adj (auditeur)* attentive; *(examen)* careful; **~ à** careful to

**attention** [atɑ̃sjɔ̃] *nf* attention; *(prévenance)* attention, thoughtfulness *no pl;*

à l'~ **de** for the attention of; **faire ~ (à)** to be careful (of); **faire ~ (à ce) que** to be *ou* make sure that; **~!** careful!, watch out!; **attentionné, e** *adj* thoughtful, considerate

**atténuer** [atenɥe] *vt (douleur)* to alleviate, ease; *(couleurs)* to soften

**atterrer** [ateʀe] *vt* to dismay, appal

**atterrir** [ateʀiʀ] *vi* to land; **atterrissage** *nm* landing

**attestation** [atɛstasjɔ̃] *nf* certificate

**attester** [atɛste] *vt* to testify to

**attirail** [atiʀaj] *(fam) nm* gear; *(péj)* paraphernalia

**attirant, e** [atiʀɑ̃, ɑ̃t] *adj* attractive, appealing

**attirer** [atiʀe] *vt* to attract; *(appâter)* to lure, entice; **~ qn dans un coin** to draw sb into a corner; **~ l'attention de qn** to attract sb's attention; **~ l'attention de qn sur** to draw sb's attention to; **~ des ennuis** to bring trouble upon o.s., get into trouble

**attiser** [atize] *vt (feu)* to poke (up)

**attitré, e** [atitʀe] *adj (habituel)* regular, usual; *(agréé)* accredited

**attitude** [atityd] *nf* attitude; *(position du corps)* bearing

**attouchements** [atuʃmɑ̃] *nmpl (sexuels)* fondling *sg*

**attraction** [atʀaksjɔ̃] *nf (gén)* attraction; *(de cabaret, cirque)* number

**attrait** [atʀɛ] *nm* appeal, attraction

**attrape-nigaud** [atʀapnigo] *(fam) nm* con

**attraper** [atʀape] *vt (gén)* to catch; *(habitude, amende)* to get, pick up; *(fam: duper)* to con; **se faire ~** *(fam)* to be told off

**attrayant, e** [atʀɛjɑ̃, ɑ̃t] *adj* attractive

**attribuer** [atʀibɥe] *vt (prix)* to award; *(rôle, tâche)* to allocate, assign; *(imputer):* **~ qch à** to attribute sth to; **s'~** *vt (s'approprier)* to claim for o.s.; **attribut** *nm* attribute

**attrister** [atʀiste] *vt* to sadden

**attroupement** [atʀupmɑ̃] *nm* crowd

**attrouper** [atrupe]: **s'~** vi to gather

**au** [o] prép +dét = **à** +**le**

**aubaine** [obɛn] nf godsend

**aube** [ob] nf dawn, daybreak; **à l'~** at dawn ou daybreak

**aubépine** [obepin] nf hawthorn

**auberge** [obɛʀʒ] nf inn; **~ de jeunesse** youth hostel

**aubergine** [obɛʀʒin] nf aubergine

**aubergiste** [obɛʀʒist] nm/f inn-keeper, hotel-keeper

**aucun, e** [okœ̃, yn] dét no, tournure négative +any; (positif) any, tournure négative +any; any(one); **sans ~ doute** without any doubt; **plus qu'~ autre** more than any other; **~ des deux** neither of the two; **~ d'entre eux** none of them, any of them; **aucunement** adv in no way, not in the least

**audace** [odas] nf daring, boldness; (péj) audacity; **audacieux, -euse** adj daring, bold

**au-delà** [od(ə)la] adv beyond ♦ nm: **l'~~** the hereafter; **~~ de** beyond

**au-dessous** [odsu] adv underneath; below; **~~ de** under(neath), below; (limite, somme etc) below, under; (dignité, condition) below

**au-dessus** [odsy] adv above; **~~ de** prép: above

**au-devant** [od(ə)vɑ̃]: **~~ de** prép: **aller ~~ de** (personne, danger) to go (out) and meet; (souhaits de qn) to anticipate

**audience** [odjɑ̃s] nf audience; (JUR: séance) hearing

**audimat** ® [odimat] nm (taux d'écoute) ratings pl

**audio-visuel, le** [odjovizɥɛl] adj audio-visual

**auditeur, -trice** [oditœʀ, tʀis] nm/f listener

**audition** [odisjɔ̃] nf (ouïe, écoute) hearing; (JUR: de témoins) examination; (MUS, THÉÂTRE: épreuve) audition

**auditoire** [oditwaʀ] nm audience

**auge** [oʒ] nf trough

**augmentation** [ɔgmɑ̃tasjɔ̃] nf in-

crease; **~ (de salaire)** rise (in salary) (BRIT), (pay) raise (US)

**augmenter** [ɔgmɑ̃te] vt (gén) to increase; (salaire, prix) to increase, raise, put up; (employé) to increase the salary of ♦ vi to increase

**augure** [ogyʀ] nm: **de bon/mauvais ~** of good/ill omen; **augurer** vt: **augurer bien de** to augur well for

**aujourd'hui** [oʒuʀdɥi] adv today

**aumône** [omon] nf inv alms sg; **aumônier** nm chaplain

**auparavant** [oparavɑ̃] adv before(hand)

**auprès** [opʀɛ]: **~ de** prép next to, close to; (recourir, s'adresser) to; (en comparaison de) compared with

**auquel** [okɛl] prép +pron = **à +lequel**

**aurai** etc [ɔʀe] vb voir **avoir**

**auréole** [ɔʀeɔl] nf halo; (tache) ring

**aurons** etc [ɔʀ5] vb voir **avoir**

**aurore** [ɔʀɔʀ] nf dawn, daybreak

**ausculter** [skylte] vt to sound (the chest of)

**aussi** [osi] adv (également) also, too; (de comparaison) ♦ conj therefore, consequently; **~ fort que** as strong as; **moi ~** me too

**aussitôt** [osito] adv straight away, immediately; **~ que** as soon as

**austère** [ostɛʀ] adj austere

**austral, e** [ɔstʀal] adj southern

**Australie** [ɔstʀali] nf: **l'~** Australia; **australien, ne** adj Australian ♦ nm/f: **Australien, ne** Australian

**autant** [otɑ̃] adv so much; (comparatif: **~ (que)** as much (as); (nombre) as many (as); **~ (de)** so much (ou many); as much (ou many); **~ partir** we (ou you etc) may as well leave; **~ dire que** ... one might as well say that ...; **pour ~** for all that; **d'~ plus/mieux (que)** all the more/the better (since)

**autel** [otɛl] nm altar

**auteur** [otœʀ] nm author

**authenticité** [otɑ̃tisite] nf authenticity

**authentique** [otɑ̃tik] adj authentic,

genuine

**auto** [oto] *nf* car

**auto...: autobiographie** *nf* autobiography; **autobronzant** *nm* self-tanning cream (or lotion etc); **autobus** *nm* bus; **autocar** *nm* coach

**autochtone** [ɔtɔktɔn] *nm/f* native

**auto...: autocollant, e** *adj* self-adhesive; (*enveloppe*) self-seal ♦ *nm* sticker; **auto-couchettes** *car* sleeper train; **auto-couchettes** *adj*: **train auto-couchettes** car sleeper train; **autocuiseur** *nm* pressure cooker; **autodéfense** *nf* self-defence; **autodidacte** *nm/f* self-taught person; **auto-école** *nf* driving school; **autographe** *nm* autograph

**automate** [ɔtɔmat] *nm* (*machine*) (automatic) machine

**automatique** [ɔtɔmatik] *adj* automatic ♦ *nm*: **l'~** direct dialling; **automatiquement** *adv* automatically; **automatiser** *vt* to automate

**automne** [ɔtɔn] *nm* autumn (BRIT), fall (US)

**automobile** [ɔtɔmɔbil] *adj* motor *cpd* ♦ *nf* (motor) car; **automobiliste** *nm/f* motorist

**autonome** [ɔtɔnɔm] *adj* autonomous; **autonomie** *nf* autonomy

**autopsie** [ɔtɔpsi] *nf* post-mortem (examination), autopsy

**autoradio** [ɔtɔradjo] *nm* car radio

**autorisation** [ɔtɔrizasjɔ̃] *nf* permission, authorization; (*papiers*) permit

**autorisé, e** [ɔtɔrize] *adj* (opinion, sources) authoritative

**autoriser** [ɔtɔrize] *vt* to give permission for, authorize; (*fig*) to allow (of)

**autoritaire** [ɔtɔritɛr] *adj* authoritarian

**autorité** [ɔtɔrite] *nf* authority; **faire ~** to be authoritative

**autoroute** [ɔtorut] *nf* motorway (BRIT), highway (US)

**auto-stop** [otostɔp] *nm*: **faire de l'~~** to hitch-hike; **prendre qn en ~~** to give sb a lift; **auto-stoppeur, -euse** *nm/f* hitch-hiker

**autour** [otur] *adv* around; **~ de** around; **tout ~** all around

**autre** [otr] *adj* **1** (*différent*) other, different; **je préférerais un autre verre** I'd prefer another *ou* a different glass

**2** (*supplémentaire*) other; **je voudrais un autre verre d'eau** I'd like another glass of water

**3**: **autre chose** something else; **autre part** somewhere else; **d'autre part** on the other hand

♦ *pron*: **un autre** another (one); **nous/vous autres** us/you; **d'autres** others; **l'autre** the other (one); **les autres** the others; (*autrui*) others; **l'un et l'autre** both of them; **se détester l'un l'autre/les uns les autres** to hate each other *ou* one another; **d'une semaine à l'autre** from one week to the next; (*incessamment*) any week now; **entre autres** among other things

**autrefois** [otrəfwa] *adv* in the past

**autrement** [otrəmɑ̃] *adv* differently; (*d'une manière différente*) in another way; (*sinon*) otherwise; **~ dit** in other words

**Autriche** [otriʃ] *nf*: **l'~** Austria; **autrichien, ne** *adj* Austrian ♦ *nm/f*: **Autrichien, ne** Austrian

**autruche** [otryʃ] *nf* ostrich

**autrui** [otrɥi] *pron* others

**auvent** [ovɑ̃] *nm* canopy

**aux** [o] *prép +dét* = **à +les**

**auxiliaire** [ɔksiljɛr] *adj, nm/f* auxiliary

**auxquelles** [okɛl] *prép +pron* = **à +lesquelles**

**auxquels** [okɛl] *prép +pron* = **à +lesquels**

**avachi, e** [avaʃi] *adj* limp, flabby

**aval** [aval] *nm*: **en ~** downstream, downriver

**avalanche** [avalɑ̃ʃ] *nf* avalanche

**avaler** [avale] *vt* to swallow

**avance** [avɑ̃s] *nf* (de troupes etc) advance; progress; (d'argent) advance; (sur un concurrent) lead; **~s** *nfpl* (amoureuses) advances; **(être) en ~** (to be) early; (sur un programme) (to be) ahead of schedule; **à l'~, d'~** in advance

**avancé, e** [avɑ̃se] *adj* advanced; (travail) well on, well under way

**avancement** [avɑ̃smɑ̃] *nm* (professionnel) promotion

**avancer** [avɑ̃se] *vi* to move forward, advance; (projet, travail) to make progress; (montre, réveil) to be fast; to gain ♦ *vt* to move forward, advance; (argent) to advance; (montre, pendule) to put forward; **s'~** *vi* to move forward, advance; (fig) to commit o.s.

**avant** [avɑ̃] *prép, adv* before ♦ *adj inv*: **siège/roue ~** front seat/wheel ♦ *nm* (d'un véhicule, bâtiment) front; (SPORT: joueur) forward; **qu'il (ne) fasse/de faire** before he does/doing; **~ tout** (surtout) above all; **à l'~** (dans un véhicule) in (the) front; **en ~** forward(s); **en ~ de** in front of

**avantage** [avɑ̃taʒ] *nm* advantage; **~s sociaux** fringe benefits; **avantager** *vt* (favoriser) to favour; (embellir) to flatter; **avantageux, -euse** *adj* (prix) attractive

**avant...: avant-bras** *nm inv* forearm; **avantcoureur** *adj inv*: **signe avantcoureur** advance indication *ou* sign; **avant-dernier, -ière** *adj*, *nm/f* next to last, last but one; **avant-goût** *nm* foretaste; **avant-guerre** *nm* pre-war years; **avant-hier** *adv* the day before yesterday; **avant-première** *nf* (de film) preview; **avant-projet** *nm* (preliminary) draft; **avant-propos** *nm* foreword; **avant-veille** *nf*: **l'avant-veille** two days before

**avare** [avaʀ] *adj* miserly, avaricious ♦ *nm/f* miser; **~ de** (compliments etc) sparing of

**avarié, e** [avaʀje] *adj* (aliment) rotting

**avaries** [avaʀi] *nfpl* (NAVIG) damage *sg*

**avec** [avɛk] *prép* with; (à l'égard de) to(wards); with; **et ~ ça?** (dans magasin) anything else?

**avenant, e** [avnɑ̃, ɑ̃t] *adj* pleasant; **à l'~** in keeping

**avènement** [avɛnmɑ̃] *nm* (d'un changement) advent, coming

**avenir** [avniʀ] *nm* future; **à l'~** in future; **politicien d'~** politician with prospects *ou* a future

**aventure** [avɑ̃tyʀ] *nf* adventure; (amoureuse) affair; **aventurer: s'aventurer** *vi* to venture; **aventureux, -euse** *adj* adventurous, venturesome; (projet) risky, chancy

**avenue** [avny] *nf* avenue

**avérer** [aveʀe]: **s'~** *vb +attrib* to prove (to be)

**averse** [avɛʀs] *nf* shower

**averti, e** [avɛʀti] *adj* (well-)informed

**avertir** [avɛʀtiʀ] *vt*: **~ qn (de qch/que)** to warn sb (of sth/that); (renseigner) to inform sb (of sth/that); **avertissement** *nm* warning; **avertisseur** *nm* horn, siren

**aveu, x** [avø] *nm* confession

**aveugle** [avœgl] *adj* blind ♦ *nm/f* blind man/woman; **aveuglément** *adv* blindly; **aveugler** *vt* to blind

**aviateur, -trice** [avjatœʀ, tʀis] *nm/f* aviator, pilot

**aviation** [avjasjɔ̃] *nf* aviation; (sport) flying; (MIL) air force

**avide** [avid] *adj* eager; (péj) greedy, grasping

**avilir** [aviliʀ] *vt* to debase

**avion** [avjɔ̃] *nm* (aero)plane (BRIT), (air)plane (US); **aller (quelque part) en ~** to go (somewhere) by plane, fly (somewhere); **par ~** by airmail; **~ à réaction** jet (plane)

**aviron** [aviʀɔ̃] *nm* oar; (sport): **l'~** rowing

**avis** [avi] *nm* opinion; (notification) notice; **à mon ~** in my opinion; **changer d'~** to change one's mind; **jusqu'à nouvel ~** until further notice

**avisé, e** [avize] *adj* sensible, wise; **bien/mal ~ de** well-/ill-advised to

**aviser** [avize] *vt* (*informer*): **~ qn de/que** to advise *ou* inform sb of/that ♦ *vi* to think about things, assess the situation; **nous ~ons sur place** we'll work something out once we're there; **s'~ de qch/que** to become suddenly aware of sth/that; **s'~ de faire** to take it into one's head to do

**avocat, e** [avɔka, at] *nm/f* (*JUR*) barrister (*BRIT*), lawyer ♦ *nm* (*CULIN*) avocado (pear); **~ de la défense** counsel for the defence; **~ général** assistant public prosecutor

**avoine** [avwan] *nf* oats *pl*

---

**MOT-CLÉ**

**avoir** [avwaʀ] *nm* assets *pl*, resources *pl*; (*COMM*) credit

♦ *vt* 1 (*posséder*) to have; **elle a 2 enfants/une belle maison** she has (got) 2 children/a lovely house; **il a les yeux bleus** he has (got) blue eyes

2 (*âge, dimensions*) to be; **il a 3 ans** he is 3 (years old); **le mur a 3 mètres de haut** the wall is 3 metres high; *voir aussi* **faim**; **peur** *etc*

3 (*vb: duper*) to do, have; **on vous a eu!** you've been done *ou* had!

4: **en avoir contre qn** to have a grudge against sb; **en avoir assez** to be fed up; **j'en ai pour une demi-heure** it'll take me half an hour

♦ *vb aux* 1 to have; **avoir mangé/dormi** to have eaten/slept

2 (*avoir +à +infinitif*): **avoir à faire qch** to have to do sth; **vous n'avez qu'à lui demander** you only have to ask him

♦ *vb impers* 1: **il y a** (+ *singulier*) there is; (+ *pluriel*) there are; **qu'y-a-t-il?, qu'est-ce qu'il y a?** what's the matter?, what is it?; **il doit y avoir une explication** there must be an explanation; **il n'y a qu'à ...** we (*ou* you *etc*) will just have to ...

---

2 (*temporel*): **il y a 10 ans** 10 years ago; **il y a 10 ans/longtemps que je le sais** I've known it for 10 years/a long time; **il y a 10 ans qu'il est arrivé** it's 10 years since he arrived

**avoisiner** [avwazine] *vt* to be near *ou* close to; (*fig*) to border *ou* verge on

**avortement** [avɔʀtəmã] *nm* abortion

**avorter** [avɔʀte] *vi* (*MÉD*) to have an abortion; (*fig*) to fail

**avoué, e** [avwe] *adj* avowed ♦ *nm* (*JUR*) ≈ solicitor

**avouer** [avwe] *vt* (*crime, défaut*) to confess (to); **~ avoir fait/que** to admit *ou* confess to having done/that

**avril** [avʀil] *nm* April

---

**poisson d'avril**

The traditional prank on April 1 in France is to stick a cut-out paper fish, known as a *poisson d'avril*, to someone's back without being caught.

---

**axe** [aks] *nm* axis; (*de roue etc*) axle; (*fig*) main line; **axer** *vt*: **axer qch sur** to centre sth on

**ayons** *etc* [ɛjɔ̃] *vb voir* **avoir**

**azote** [azɔt] *nm* nitrogen

# B, b

**baba** [baba] *nm*: **~ au rhum** rum baba

**babines** [babin] *nfpl* chops

**babiole** [babjɔl] *nf* (*bibelot*) trinket; (*vétille*) trifle

**bâbord** [babɔʀ] *nm*: **à ~** to port, on the port side

**baby-foot** [babifut] *nm* table football

**baby-sitting** [babisitiŋ] *nm*: **faire du ~ ~** to baby-sit

**bac** [bak] *abr m* = **baccalauréat** ♦ *nm* (*récipient*) tub

**baccalauréat** [bakalɔʀea] *nm* high school diploma

# bâche    27    balcon

**baccalauréat**

*In France the* **baccalauréat** *or* **bac** *is the school-leaving certificate taken at a lycée at the age of seventeen or eighteen, enabling entry to university. Different subject combinations are available from the broad subject range studied.*

**bâche** [baʃ] *nf* tarpaulin

**bachelier, -ière** [baʃəlje, jɛʀ] *nm/f* holder of the *baccalauréat*

**bâcler** [bakle] *vt* to botch (up)

**badaud, e** [bado, od] *nm/f* idle onlooker, stroller

**badigeonner** [badiʒɔne] *vt* (*barbouiller*) to daub

**badiner** [badine] *vi*: **~ avec qch** to treat sth lightly

**baffe** [baf] (*fam*) *nf* slap, clout

**baffle** [bafl] *nm* speaker

**bafouer** [bafwe] *vt* to deride, ridicule

**bafouiller** [bafuje] *vi, vt* to stammer

**bâfrer** [bafʀe] (*fam*) *vi* to guzzle

**bagages** [bagaʒ] *nmpl* luggage *sg*; **~ à main** hand-luggage

**bagarre** [bagaʀ] *nf* fight, brawl; **bagarrer: se bagarrer** [bagaʀe] *vi* to have a fight *ou* scuffle, fight

**bagatelle** [bagatɛl] *nf* trifle

**bagne** [baɲ] *nm* penal colony

**bagnole** [baɲɔl] *nf* car

**bagout** [bagu] *nm*: **avoir du ~** to have the gift of the gab

**bague** [bag] *nf* ring; **~ de fiançailles** engagement ring

**baguette** [bagɛt] *nf* stick; (*cuisine chinoise*) chopstick; (*de chef d'orchestre*) baton; (*pain*) stick of (French) bread; **~ magique** magic wand

**baie** [bɛ] *nf* (GÉO) bay; (*fruit*) berry; (*vitrée*) picture window

**baignade** [bɛɲad] *nf* bathing; **"~ interdite"** "no bathing"

**baigner** [beɲe] *vt* (*bébé*) to bath; **se ~** *vi* to have a swim, go swimming *ou* bathing; **baignoire** *nf* bath(tub)

**bail** [baj, bo] (*pl* **baux**) *nm* lease

**bâillement** [bɑjmɑ̃] *nm* yawn

**bâiller** [bɑje] *vi* to yawn; (*être ouvert*) to gape; **bâillonner** *vt* to gag

**bain** [bɛ̃] *nm* bath; **prendre un ~** to have a bath; **se mettre dans le ~** (*fig*) to get into it *ou* things; **~ de soleil**: **prendre un ~ de soleil** to sunbathe; **~s de mer** sea bathing *sg*; **bain-marie** *nm*: **faire chauffer au bain-marie** (*boîte etc*) to immerse in boiling water

**baiser** [beze] *nm* kiss ♦ *vt* (*main, front*) to kiss; (*fam!*) to screw (!)

**baisse** [bɛs] *nf* fall, drop; **être en ~** to be falling, be declining

**baisser** [bese] *vt* to lower; (*radio, chauffage*) to turn down ♦ *vi* to fall, drop, go down; (*vue, santé*) to fail, dwindle; **se ~** *vi* to bend down

**bal** [bal] *nm* dance; (*grande soirée*) ball; **~ costumé** fancy-dress ball

**balade** [balad] (*fam*) *nf* (*à pied*) walk, stroll; (*en voiture*) drive; **balader** (*fam*): **se balader** *vi* to go for a walk *ou* stroll; to go for a drive; **baladeur** *nm* personal stereo, Walkman ®

**balafre** [balafʀ] *nf* (*cicatrice*) scar

**balai** [bale] *nm* broom, brush; **balai-brosse** *nm* (long-handled) scrubbing brush

**balance** [balɑ̃s] *nf* scales *pl*; (*signe*): **la B~** Libra

**balancer** [balɑ̃se] *vt* to swing; (*fam: lancer*) to fling, chuck; (: *jeter*) to chuck out; **se ~** *vi* to swing, rock; **se ~ de** (*fam*) not to care about; **balançoire** *nf* swing; (*sur pivot*) seesaw

**balayer** [baleje] *vt* (*feuilles etc*) to sweep up, brush up; (*pièce*) to sweep; (*objections*) to sweep aside; (*suj: radar*) to scan; **balayeur, -euse** *nm/f* roadsweeper

**balbutier** [balbysje] *vi, vt* to stammer

**balcon** [balkɔ̃] *nm* balcony; (THÉÂTRE) dress circle

**baleine** [balɛn] nf whale

**balise** [baliz] nf (NAVIG) beacon; (marker) buoy; (AVIAT) runway light, beacon; (AUTO, SKI) sign, marker; **baliser** vt to mark out (with lights etc)

**balivernes** [balivɛrn] nfpl nonsense sg

**ballant, e** [balɑ̃, ɑ̃t] adj dangling

**balle** [bal] nf (de fusil) bullet; (de sport) ball; (fam: franc) franc

**ballerine** [bal(ə)rin] nf (danseuse) ballet dancer; (chaussure) ballet shoe

**ballet** [balɛ] nm ballet

**ballon** [balɔ̃] nm (de sport) ball; (jouet, AVIAT) balloon; ~ **de football** football

**ballot** [balo] nm bundle; (péj) nitwit

**ballottage** [balɔtaʒ] nm (POL) second ballot

**ballotter** [balɔte] vt: **être ballotté** to be thrown about

**balnéaire** [balneɛr] adj seaside cpd; **station ~** seaside resort

**balourd, e** [balur, urd] adj clumsy

**balustrade** [balystrad] nf railings pl, handrail

**bambin** [bɑ̃bɛ̃] nm little child

**bambou** [bɑ̃bu] nm bamboo

**ban** [bɑ̃] nm: **mettre au ~ de** to outlaw from; **~s** nmpl (de mariage) banns

**banal, e** [banal] adj banal, commonplace; (péj) trite; **banalité** nf banality

**banane** [banan] nf banana; (sac) waist-bag, bum-bag

**banc** [bɑ̃] nm seat, bench; (de poissons) shoal; **~ d'essai** (fig) testing ground

**bancaire** [bɑ̃kɛr] adj banking; (chèque, carte) bank cpd

**bancal, e** [bɑ̃kal] adj wobbly

**bandage** [bɑ̃daʒ] nm bandage

**bande** [bɑ̃d] nf (de tissu etc) strip; (MÉD) bandage; (motif) stripe; (magnétique etc) tape; (groupe) band; (: péj) bunch; **faire ~ à part** to keep to o.s.; **~ dessinée** comic strip; **~ sonore** sound track

| **bande dessinée** |

*The **bande dessinée** or **BD** enjoys a huge following in France amongst*

adults as well as children. An international show takes place at Angoulême in January every year. Astérix, Tintin, Lucky Luke and Gaston Lagaffe are among the most famous cartoon characters.

**bandeau, x** [bɑ̃do] nm headband; (sur les yeux) blindfold

**bander** [bɑ̃de] vt (blessure) to bandage; **~ les yeux à qn** to blindfold sb

**banderole** [bɑ̃drɔl] nf banner, streamer

**bandit** [bɑ̃di] nm bandit; **banditisme** nm violent crime, armed robberies pl

**bandoulière** [bɑ̃duljɛr] nf: **en ~** (slung ou worn) across the shoulder

**banlieue** [bɑ̃ljø] nf suburbs pl; **lignes/quartiers de ~** suburban lines/areas; **trains de ~** commuter trains

**banlieusard, e** [bɑ̃ljøzar] nm/f (suburban) commuter

**bannière** [banjɛr] nf banner

**bannir** [banir] vt to banish

**banque** [bɑ̃k] nf bank; (activités) banking; **~ d'affaires** merchant bank; **banqueroute** nf bankruptcy

**banquet** [bɑ̃kɛ] nm dinner; (d'apparat) banquet

**banquette** [bɑ̃kɛt] nf seat

**banquier** [bɑ̃kje] nm banker

**banquise** [bɑ̃kiz] nf ice field

**baptême** [batɛm] nm christening; baptism; **~ de l'air** first flight

**baptiser** [batize] vt to baptize, christen

**baquet** [bakɛ] nm tub, bucket

**bar** [bar] nm bar

**baraque** [barak] nf shed; (fam) house; **baraqué, e** (fam) adj well-built, hefty; **baraquements** nmpl (provisoires) huts

**baratin** [baratɛ̃] (fam) nm smooth talk, patter; **baratiner** vt to chat up

**barbare** [barbar] adj barbaric; **barbarie** nf barbarity

**barbe** [barb] nf beard; **la ~!** (fam)

damn it!; **quelle ~!** (fam) what a drag ou bore!; **à la ~ de qn** under sb's nose; **~ à papa** candy-floss (BRIT), cotton candy (US)

**barbelé** [barbale] adj, nm: **(fil de fer) ~** barbed wire no pl

**barber** [barbe] (fam) vt to bore stiff

**barbiturique** [barbityrik] nm barbiturate

**barboter** [barbɔte] vi (enfant) to paddle

**barbouiller** [barbuje] vt to daub; **avoir l'estomac barbouillé** to feel queasy

**barbu, e** [barby] adj bearded

**barda** [barda] (fam) nm kit, gear

**barder** [barde] (fam) vi: **ça va ~** sparks will fly, things are going to get hot

**barème** [barɛm] nm (SCOL) scale; (table de référence) table

**baril** [baril(l)] nm barrel; (poudre) keg

**bariolé, e** [barjɔle] adj gaudily-coloured

**baromètre** [barɔmɛtr] nm barometer

**baron, ne** [barɔ̃] nm/f baron(ess)

**baroque** [barɔk] adj (ART) baroque; (fig) weird

**barque** [bark] nf small boat

**barquette** [barkɛt] nf (pour repas) tray; (pour fruits) punnet

**barrage** [baraʒ] nm dam; (sur route) roadblock, barricade

**barre** [bar] nf bar; (NAVIG) helm; (écrite) line, stroke

**barreau, x** [baro] nm bar; (JUR): **le ~** the Bar

**barrer** [bare] vt (route etc) to block; (mot) to cross out; (chèque) to cross (BRIT); (NAVIG) to steer; **se ~** (fam) vi to clear off

**barrette** [barɛt] nf (pour cheveux) (hair) slide ou clip (US)

**barricader** [barikade]: **se ~** vi to barricade o.s.

**barrière** [barjɛr] nf fence; (obstacle) barrier; (porte) gate

**barrique** [barik] nf barrel, cask

**bar-tabac** [bartaba] nm bar (which sells tobacco and stamps)

**bas, basse** [ba, bas] adj low ♦ nm bottom, lower part; (vêtement) stocking ♦ adv low; (parler) softly; **au ~ mot** at the lowest estimate; **en ~** down below; (d'une liste, d'un mur etc) at/to the bottom; (dans une maison) downstairs; **en ~ de** at the bottom of; **un enfant en ~ âge** a young child; **à ~ ...!** down with ...!; **~ morceaux** nmpl (viande) cheap cuts

**basané, e** [bazane] adj tanned

**bas-côté** [bakote] nm (de route) verge (BRIT), shoulder (US)

**bascule** [baskyl] nf: **(jeu de) ~** seesaw; **(balance à) ~** scales pl; **fauteuil à ~** rocking chair

**basculer** [baskyle] vi to fall over, topple (over); (benne) to tip up ♦ vt (contenu) to tip out; (benne) to tip up

**base** [baz] nf base; (POL) rank and file; (fondement, principe) basis ♦ adj: **de ~** basic; **à ~ de café etc** coffee etc -based; **~ de données** database; **baser** vt to base; **se baser sur** (preuves) to base one's argument on

**bas-fond** [bafɔ̃] nm (NAVIG) shallow; **~s** nmpl (fig) dregs

**basilic** [bazilik] nm (CULIN) basil

**basket** [baskɛt] nm trainer (BRIT), sneaker (US); (aussi: **~-ball**) basketball

**basque** [bask] adj, nm/f Basque

**basse** [bas] adj voir bas ♦ nf (MUS) bass; **basse-cour** nf farmyard

**bassin** [basɛ̃] nm (pièce d'eau) pond, pool; (de fontaine, GÉO) basin; (ANAT) pelvis; (portuaire) dock

**bassine** [basin] nf (ustensile) basin; (contenu) bowl(ful)

**basson** [basɔ̃] nm bassoon

**bas-ventre** [bavɑ̃tr] nm (lower part of the) stomach

**bat** [ba] vb voir battre

**bataille** [bataj] nf (MIL) battle; (rixe) fight; **batailler** vi to fight

**bâtard, e** [bɑtaʀ, aʀd] *nm/f* illegitimate child, bastard *(pej)*

**bateau, x** [bato] *nm* boat; ship; **bateau-mouche** *nm* passenger pleasure boat *(on the Seine)*

**bâti, e** [bɑti] *adj:* **bien ~** well-built

**batifoler** [batifɔle] *vi* to frolic about

**bâtiment** [bɑtimɑ̃] *nm* building; *(NAVIG)* ship, vessel; *(industrie)* building trade

**bâtir** [bɑtiʀ] *vt* to build

**bâtisse** [bɑtis] *nf* building

**bâton** [bɑtɔ̃] *nm* stick; **à ~s rompus** informally

**bats** [ba] *vb voir* **battre**

**battage** [bataʒ] *nm (publicité)* (hard) plugging

**battant** [batɑ̃, ɑ̃t] *nm:* **porte à double ~** double door

**battement** [batmɑ̃] *nm (de cœur)* beat; *(intervalle)* interval; **10 minutes de ~** 10 minutes to spare

**batterie** [batʀi] *nf (MIL, ÉLEC)* battery; *(MUS)* drums *pl*, drum kit; **~ de cuisine** pots and pans *pl*, kitchen utensils *pl*

**batteur** [batœʀ] *nm (MUS)* drummer; *(appareil)* whisk

**battre** [batʀ] *vt* to beat; *(blé)* to thresh; *(passer au peigne fin)* to scour; *(cartes)* to shuffle ♦ *vi (cœur)* to beat; *(volets etc)* to bang, rattle; **se ~** *vi* to fight; **~ la mesure** to beat time; **~ son plein** to be at its height, be going full swing; **~ des mains** to clap one's hands

**battue** [baty] *nf (chasse)* beat; *(policière etc)* search, hunt

**baume** [bom] *nm* balm

**baux** [bo] *nmpl de* **bail**

**bavard, e** [bavaʀ, aʀd] *adj* (very) talkative; gossipy; **bavarder** *vi* to chatter; *(commérer)* to gossip; *(divulguer un secret)* to blab

**bave** [bav] *nf* dribble; *(de chien etc)* slobber; *(d'escargot)* slime; **baver** *vi* to dribble; *(chien)* to slobber; **en baver** *(fam)* to have a hard time of it; **baveux, -euse** *adj (omelette)* runny; **ba-**

**voir** *nm* bib

**bavure** [bavyʀ] *nf* smudge; *(fig)* hitch; *(policière etc)* blunder

**bayer** [baje] *vi:* **~ aux corneilles** to stand gaping

**bazar** [bazaʀ] *nm* general store; *(fam)* jumble; **bazarder** *(fam)* to chuck out

**BCBG** *sigle adj* (= *bon chic bon genre*) preppy, smart and trendy

**BCE** *sigle f* (= *Banque centrale européenne*) ECB

**BD** *sigle f* = **bande dessinée**

**bd** *abr* = **boulevard**

**béant, e** [beɑ̃, ɑ̃t] *adj* gaping

**béat, e** [bea, at] *adj:* **~ d'admiration** struck dumb with admiration; **béatitude** *nf* bliss

**beau** **(bel), belle** [bo, bɛl] *(mpl* **beaux)** *adj* beautiful, lovely; *(homme)* handsome; *(femme)* beautiful ♦ *adv:* **il fait beau** the weather's fine; **un ~jour** one (fine) day; **de plus belle** more than ever, even more; **on a ~essayer** however hard we try; **bel et bien** well and truly

┌─────────────┐
│ MOT-CLÉ │
└─────────────┘

**beaucoup** [boku] *adv* **1** a lot; **il boit beaucoup** he drinks a lot; **il ne boit pas beaucoup** he doesn't drink much *ou* a lot

**2** *(suivi de plus, trop etc)* much, a lot, far; **il est beaucoup plus grand** he is much *ou* far taller

**3:** **beaucoup de** *(nombre)* many, a lot of; *(quantité)* a lot of; **beaucoup d'étudiants/de touristes** a lot of *ou* many students/tourists; **beaucoup de courage** a lot of courage; **il n'a pas beaucoup d'argent** he hasn't got much *ou* a lot of money

**4:** **de beaucoup** by far

**beau...: beau-fils** *nm* son-in-law; *(re-mariage)* stepson; **beau-frère** *nm* brother-in-law; **beau-père** *nm* fatherin-law; (remariage) stepfather

**beauté** [bote] nf beauty; **de toute ~** beautiful; **finir qch en ~** to complete sth brilliantly

**beaux-arts** [bozar] nmpl fine arts

**beaux-parents** [boparã] nmpl wife's/ husband's family, in-laws

**bébé** [bebe] nm baby

**bec** [bɛk] nm beak, bill; (de théière) spout; (de casserole) lip; (fam) mouth; **~ de gaz** (street) gaslamp

**bécane** [bekan] (fam) nf bike

**bec-de-lièvre** [bɛkdəljɛvʀ] nm harelip

**bêche** [bɛʃ] nf spade; **bêcher** vt to dig

**bécoter** [bekɔte]: **se ~** vi to smooch

**becqueter** [bɛkte] (fam) vt to eat

**bedaine** [bədɛn] nf paunch

**bedonnant, e** [bədɔnã, ãt] adj pot-bellied

**bée** [be] adj: **bouche ~** gaping

**beffroi** [befʀwa] nm belfry

**bégayer** [begeje] vt, vi to stammer

**bègue** [bɛg] nm/f: **être ~** to have a stammer

**beige** [bɛʒ] adj beige

**beignet** [bɛɲɛ] nm fritter

**bel** [bɛl] adj voir **beau**

**bêler** [bele] vi to bleat

**belette** [bəlɛt] nf weasel

**belge** [bɛlʒ] adj Belgian ♦ nm/f: **B~** Belgian

**Belgique** [bɛlʒik] nf: **la ~** Belgium

**bélier** [belje] nm ram; (signe): **le B~** Aries

**belle** [bɛl] adj voir **beau** ♦ nf (SPORT) decider; **belle-fille** nf daughter-in-law; (remariage) stepdaughter; **belle-mère** nf mother-in-law; stepmother; **belle-sœur** nf sister-in-law

**belliqueux, -euse** [belikø, øz] adj aggressive, warlike

**belvédère** [belvedɛʀ] nm panoramic viewpoint (or small building there)

**bémol** [bemɔl] nm (MUS) flat

**bénédiction** [benediksjɔ̃] nf blessing

**bénéfice** [benefis] nm (COMM) profit; (avantage) benefit; **bénéficier: bénéfi-**

cier de vt to enjoy; (situation) to benefit from ou from; **bénéfique** adj beneficial

**bénévole** [benevɔl] adj voluntary, unpaid

**bénin, -igne** [benɛ̃, iɲ] adj minor, mild; (tumeur) benign

**bénir** [beniʀ] vt to bless; **bénit, e** adj consecrated; **eau bénite** holy water

**benjamin, e** [bɛ̃ʒamɛ̃, in] nm/f youngest child

**benne** [bɛn] nf skip; (de téléphérique) (cable) car; **~ basculante** tipper (BRIT), dump truck (US)

**BEP** sigle m (= brevet d'études professionnelles) technical school certificate

**béquille** [bekij] nf crutch; (de bicyclette) stand

**berceau, x** [bɛʀso] nm cradle, crib

**bercer** [bɛʀse] vt to rock, cradle; (suj: musique etc) to lull; **~ qn de** (promesses etc) to delude sb with; **berceuse** nf lullaby

**béret (basque)** [beʀɛ (bask(ə))] nm beret

**berge** [bɛʀʒ] nf bank

**berger, -ère** [bɛʀʒe, ɛʀ] nm/f shepherd(-ess); **~ allemand** alsatian (BRIT), German shepherd

**berlingot** [bɛʀlɛ̃go] nm (bonbon) boiled sweet, humbug (BRIT)

**berlue** [bɛʀly] nf: **j'ai la ~** I must be seeing things

**berner** [bɛʀne] vt to fool

**besogne** [bəzɔɲ] nf work no pl, job

**besoin** [bəzwɛ̃] nm need; **avoir ~ de qch/faire qch** to need sth/to do sth; **au ~** if need be; **le ~** (pauvreté) need, want; **être dans le ~** to be in need ou want; **faire ses ~s** to relieve o.s.

**bestiaux** [bestjo] nmpl cattle

**bestiole** [bestjɔl] nf (tiny) creature

**bétail** [betaj] nm livestock, cattle pl

**bête** [bɛt] nf animal; (bestiole) insect, creature ♦ adj stupid, silly; **il cherche la petite ~** he's being pernickety ou overfussy; **~ noire** pet hate

**bêtement** [bɛtmɑ̃] *adv* stupidly

**bêtise** [betiz] *nf* stupidity; (*action*) stupid thing (*to say ou do*)

**béton** [betɔ̃] *nm* concrete; **{en} ~** (*alibi, argument*) cast iron; **~ armé** reinforced concrete; **bétonnière** *nf* cement mixer

**betterave** [bɛtʀav] *nf* beetroot (BRIT), beet (US); **~ sucrière** sugar beet

**beugler** [bøgle] *vi* to low; (*radio etc*) to blare ♦ *vt* (*chanson*) to bawl out

**Beur** [bœʀ] *nm/f* person of North African origin living in France

**beurre** [bœʀ] *nm* butter; **beurrer** *vt* to butter; **beurrier** *nm* butter dish

**beuverie** [bøvʀi] *nf* drinking session

**bévue** [bevy] *nf* blunder

**Beyrouth** [beʀut] *n* Beirut

**bi...** [bi] *préfixe* bi..., two-

**biais** [bjɛ] *nm* (*moyen*) device, expedient; (*aspect*) angle; **en ~, de ~** (*obliquement*) at an angle; **par le ~ de** by means of; **biaiser** *vi* (*fig*) to sidestep the issue

**bibelot** [biblo] *nm* trinket, curio

**biberon** [bibʀɔ̃] *nm* (*feeding*) bottle; **nourrir au ~** to bottle-feed

**bible** [bibl] *nf* bible

**biblio...** [biblijo] *préfixe*: **bibliobus** *nm* mobile library van; **bibliographie** *nf* bibliography; **bibliothécaire** *nm/f* librarian; **bibliothèque** *nf* library; (*meuble*) bookcase

**bic** ® [bik] *nm* Biro ®

**bicarbonate** [bikaʀbɔnat] *nm*: **~ (de soude)** bicarbonate of soda

**biceps** [bisɛps] *nm* biceps

**biche** [biʃ] *nf* doe

**bichonner** [biʃɔne] *vt* to pamper

**bicolore** [bikɔlɔʀ] *adj* two-coloured

**bicoque** [bikɔk] (*péj*) *nf* shack

**bicyclette** [bisiklɛt] *nf* bicycle

**bide** [bid] (*fam*) *nm* (*ventre*) belly; (*THÉÂTRE*) flop

**bidet** [bidɛ] *nm* bidet

**bidon** [bidɔ̃] *nm* can ♦ *adj inv* (*fam*) phoney

**bidonville** [bidɔ̃vil] *nm* shanty town

**bidule** [bidyl] (*fam*) *nm* thingumajig

MOT-CLÉ

**bien** [bjɛ̃] *nm* 1 (*avantage, profit*): **faire du bien à qn** to do sb good; **dire du bien de** to speak well of; **c'est pour son bien** it's for his own good

2 (*possession, patrimoine*) possession, property; **son bien le plus précieux** his most treasured possession; **avoir du bien** to have property; **biens** (**de consommation** *etc*) (consumer *etc*) goods

3 (*moral*): **le bien** good; **distinguer le bien du mal** to tell good from evil

♦ *adv* 1 (*de façon satisfaisante*) well; **elle travaille/mange bien** she works/eats well; **croyant bien faire, je/il ...** thinking I/he was doing the right thing, I/he ...; **c'est bien fait!** it serves him (*ou* her *etc*) right!

2 (*valeur intensive*) quite; **bien jeune** quite young; **bien assez** quite enough; **bien mieux** (very) much better; **j'espère bien y aller** I do hope to go; **je veux bien le faire** (*concession*) I'm quite willing to do it; **il faut bien le faire** it has to be done

3: **du temps/des gens** quite a time/a number of people

♦ *adj inv* 1 (*en bonne forme, à l'aise*): **je me sens bien** I feel fine; **je ne me sens pas bien** I don't feel well; **on est bien dans ce fauteuil** this chair is very comfortable

2 (*joli, beau*) good-looking; **tu es bien dans cette robe** you look good in that dress

3 (*satisfaisant*) good; **elle est bien, cette maison/secrétaire** it's a good house/she's a good secretary

4 (*moralement*) right; (*: personne*) good, nice; (*respectable*) respectable; **ce n'est pas bien de ...** it's not right to ...; **elle est bien, cette femme** she's a nice woman, she's a good sort; **des gens biens** respectable people

**5** (en bons termes): **être bien avec qn** to be on good terms with sb ♦ préfixe: **bien-aimé** adj, nm/f beloved; **bien-être** nm well-being; **bienfaisance** nf charity; **bienfaisant, e** adj (chose) beneficial; **bienfait** nm act of generosity, benefaction; (de la science etc) benefit; **bienfaiteur, -trice** nm/f benefactor/benefactress; **bienfondé** nm soundness; **bien-fonds** nm property; **bienheureux, -euse** adj happy; (REL) blessed, blest; **bien que** conj (al)though; **bien sûr** adv certainly

**bienséant, e** [bjɛ̃seã, ãt] adj seemly
**bientôt** [bjɛ̃to] adv soon; **à** ~ see you soon
**bienveillant, e** [bjɛ̃vɛjã, ãt] adj kindly
**bienvenu, e** [bjɛ̃vny] adj welcome; **bienvenue** nf: **souhaiter la bienvenue à** to welcome; **bienvenue à** welcome to
**bière** [bjɛʀ] nf (boisson) beer; (cercueil) bier; ~ (à la) **pression** draught beer; ~ **blonde** lager; ~ **brune** brown ale
**biffer** [bife] vt to cross out
**bifteck** [biftɛk] nm steak
**bifurquer** [bifyʀke] vi (route) to fork; (véhicule) to turn off
**bigarré, e** [bigaʀe] adj multicoloured; (disparate) motley
**bigorneau, x** [bigɔʀno] nm winkle
**bigot, e** [bigo, ɔt] (péj) adj bigoted
**bigoudi** [bigudi] nm curler
**bijou, x** [biʒu] nm jewel; **bijouterie** nf jeweller's (shop); **bijoutier, -ière** nm/f jeweller
**bikini** [bikini] nm bikini
**bilan** [bilã] nm (fig) outcome; (: de victimes) toll; (COMM) balance sheet(s); **un** ~ **de santé** a (medical) checkup; **faire le** ~ **de** to assess, review; **déposer son** ~ to file a bankruptcy statement
**bile** [bil] nf bile; **se faire de la** ~ (fam) to worry o.s. sick

**bilieux, -euse** [biljø, øz] adj bilious; (fig: colérique) testy
**bilingue** [bilɛ̃g] adj bilingual
**billard** [bijaʀ] nm (jeu) billiards sg; (table) billiard table; ~ **américain** pool
**bille** [bij] nf (gén) ball; (du jeu de ~s) marble
**billet** [bijɛ] nm (aussi: ~ **de banque**) (bank)note; (de cinéma, de bus etc) ticket; (courte lettre) note; ~ **Bige** cheap rail ticket for under-26s; **billetterie** nf ticket office; (distributeur) ticket machine; (BANQUE) cash dispenser
**billion** [biljɔ̃] nm billion (BRIT), trillion (US)
**billot** [bijo] nm block
**bimensuel, le** [bimãsɥɛl] adj bimonthly
**binette** [binɛt] nf hoe
**bio...** [bjo] préfixe bio...; **biochimie** nf biochemistry; **biodiversité** nf biodiversity; **bioéthique** nf bioethics sg; **biographie** nf biography; **biologie** nf biology; **biologique** adj biological; (produits, aliments) organic; **biologiste** nm/f biologist
**Birmanie** [biʀmani] nf Burma
**bis** [bis] adv: **12** ~ 12a ou A ♦ excl, nm encore
**bisannuel, le** [bizanɥɛl] adj biennial
**biscornu, e** [biskɔʀny] adj twisted
**biscotte** [biskɔt] nf toasted bread (sold in packets)
**biscuit** [biskɥi] nm biscuit; ~ **de savoie** sponge cake
**bise** [biz] nf (fam: baiser) kiss; (vent) North wind; **grosses** ~s (de) (sur lettre) love and kisses (from)
**bisou** [bizu] (fam) nm kiss
**bissextile** [bisɛkstil] adj: **année** ~ leap year
**bistouri** [bisturi] nm lancet
**bistro(t)** [bistro] nm bistro, café
**bitume** [bitym] nm asphalt
**bizarre** [bizaʀ] adj strange, odd
**blafard, e** [blafaʀ, aʀd] adj wan
**blague** [blag] nf (propos) joke; (farce)

trick; **sans ~!** no kidding!; **blaguer** vi
to joke

**blaireau, x** [blεʀo] nm (ZOOL) badger; (brosse) shaving brush

**blairer** [blεʀe] (fam) vt: **je ne peux pas le ~** I can't bear ou stand him

**blâme** [blɑm] nm blame; (sanction) reprimand; **blâmer** vt to blame

**blanc, blanche** [blɑ̃, blɑ̃ʃ] adj white; (non imprimé) ♦ nm/f white, white man(-woman) ♦ nm (couleur) white; (espace non écrit) blank; (aussi: ~ d'œuf) (egg-)white; (aussi: ~ de poulet) breast, white meat; (aussi: vin ~) white wine; **~ cassé** off-white; **chèque en ~** blank cheque; **à ~** (chauffer) white-hot; (tirer, charger) with blanks; **blanche** nf (MUS) minim (BRIT), half-note (US); **blancheur** nf whiteness

**blanchir** [blɑ̃ʃiʀ] vt (gén) to whiten; (linge) to launder; (CULIN) to blanch; (fig: disculper) to clear ♦ vi to grow white; (cheveux) to go white; **blanchisserie** nf laundry

**blason** [blazɔ̃] nm coat of arms

**blasphème** [blasfεm] nm blasphemy

**blazer** [blazεʀ] nm blazer

**blé** [ble] nm wheat; **~ noir** buckwheat

**bled** [blεd] (péj) nm hole

**blême** [blεm] adj pale

**blessant, e** [blεsɑ̃, ɑ̃t] adj offensant) hurtful

**blessé, e** [blese] adj injured ♦ nm/f injured person, casualty

**blesser** [blese] vt to injure; (délibérément) to wound; (offenser) to hurt; **se ~** to injure o.s.; **se au pied** to injure one's foot; **blessure** nf (accidentelle) injury; (intentionnelle) wound

**bleu, e** [blø] adj blue; (bifteck) very rare ♦ nm (couleur) blue; (contusion) bruise; (vêtement: aussi: ~s) overalls pl; **~ marine** navy blue; **bleuet** nm cornflower; **bleuté, e** adj blue-shaded

**blinder** [blεde] vt to armour; (fig) to harden

**bloc** [blɔk] nm (de pierre etc) block; (de papier à lettres) pad; (ensemble) group, block; **serré à ~** tightened right down; **en ~** as a whole; **~ opérateur** operating ou theatre block; **~ sanitaire** toilet block; **blocage** nm (des prix) freezing; (PSYCH) hang-up; **bloc-notes** nm note pad

**blocus** [blɔkys] nm blockade

**blond, e** [blɔ̃, blɔ̃d] adj fair, blond; (sable, blés) golden; **~ cendré** ash blond; **blonde** nf (femme) blonde; (bière) lager; (cigarette) Virginia cigarette

**bloquer** [blɔke] vt (passage) to block; (pièce mobile) to jam; (crédits, compte) to freeze; **se ~** to jam; (PSYCH) to have a mental block

**blottir** [blɔtiʀ]: **se ~** vi to huddle up

**blouse** [bluz] nf overall

**blouson** [bluzɔ̃] nm blouson jacket; **~ noir** (fig) ≈ rocker

**blue-jean** [bludʒin] nm (pair of) jeans

**bluff** [blœf] nm bluff; **bluffer** vi to bluff

**bobard** [bɔbaʀ] (fam) nm tall story

**bobine** [bɔbin] nf reel; (ÉLEC) coil

**bocal, -aux** [bɔkal, o] nm jar

**bock** [bɔk] nm glass of beer

**body** [bɔdi] nm body(suit); (SPORT) leotard

**bœuf** [bœf] nm ox; (CULIN) beef

**bof!** [bɔf] (fam) excl don't care!; (pas terrible) nothing special

**bogue** [bɔg] nm: **le ~ de l'an 2000** the millennium bug

**bohème** [bɔεm] adj happy-go-lucky, unconventional; **bohémien, ne** nm/f gipsy

**boire** [bwaʀ] vt to drink; (s'imprégner de) to soak up; **~ un coup** (fam) to have a drink

**bois** [bwa] nm wood; **de ~, en ~** wooden; **boisé, e** adj woody, wooded

**boisson** [bwasɔ̃] nf drink

**boîte** [bwat] nf box; (fam: entreprise) firm; **aliments en ~** canned ou tinned (BRIT) foods; **~ aux lettres** letter box;

**d'allumettes** box of matches; (*vide*) matchbox; **~ (de conserve)** can *ou* tin (BRIT) (of food); **~ de nuit** night club; **~ de vitesses** gear box; **~ postale** PO Box; **~ vocale** (TEL) voice mail

**boiter** [bwate] *vi* to limp; (*fig: raisonnement*) to be shaky

**boîtier** [bwatje] *nm voir* **boire**

**boive** *etc* [bwav] *vb voir* **boire**

**bol** [bɔl] *nm* bowl; **un ~ d'air** a breath of fresh air; **j'en ai ras le ~** (*fam*) I'm fed up with this; **avoir du ~** (*fam*) to be lucky

**bolide** [bɔlid] *nm* racing car; **comme un ~** at top speed, like a rocket

**bombardement** [bɔ̃bardəmɑ̃] *nm* bombing

**bombarder** [bɔ̃barde] *vt* to bomb; **~ qn de** (*cailloux, lettres*) to bombard sb with

**bombe** [bɔ̃b] *nf* bomb; (*atomiseur*) (aerosol) spray; **bombé, e** *adj* (*forme*) rounded; **bomber** *vt*: **bomber le torse** to swell out one's chest

---
MOT-CLÉ
---

**bon, bonne** [bɔ̃, bɔn] *adj* 1 (*agréable, satisfaisant*) good; **un bon repas/restaurant** a good meal/restaurant; **être bon en maths** to be good at maths

2 (*charitable*): **être bon (envers)** to be good (to)

3 (*correct*) right; **le bon numéro/moment** the right number/moment

4 (*souhaits*): **bon anniversaire** happy birthday; **bon voyage** have a good trip; **bonne chance** good luck; **bonne année** happy New Year; **bonne nuit** good night

5 (*approprié, apte*): **bon à/pour** fit to *ou* for

6: **bon enfant** *adj inv* accommodating, easy-going; **bonne femme** (*péj*) woman; **de bonne heure** early; **bon marché** *adj inv* cheap ♦ *adv* cheap; **bon mot** witticism; **bon sens** common

sense; **bon vivant** jovial chap; **bonnes œuvres** charitable works, charities

♦ *nm* 1 (*billet*) voucher; (*aussi: bon cadeau*) gift voucher; **bon d'essence** petrol coupon; **bon du Trésor** Treasury bond

2: **avoir du bon** to have its good points; **pour de bon** for good

♦ *adv*: **il fait bon** it's *ou* the weather is fine; **sentir bon** to smell good; **tenir bon** to stand firm

♦ *excl* good!; **ah bon?** really?; *voir aussi* **bonne**

---

**bonbon** [bɔ̃bɔ̃] *nm* (boiled) sweet

**bonbonne** [bɔ̃bɔn] *nf* demijohn

**bond** [bɔ̃] *nm* leap; **faire un ~** to leap in the air

**bondé, e** [bɔ̃de] *adj* packed (full)

**bondir** [bɔ̃diʀ] *vi* to leap

**bonheur** [bɔnœʀ] *nm* happiness; **porter ~ (à qn)** to bring (sb) luck; **au petit ~** haphazardly; **par ~** fortunately

**bonhomie** [bɔnɔmi] *nf* goodnaturedness

**bonhomme** [bɔnɔm] (*pl* **bonshommes**) *nm* fellow; **~ de neige** snowman

**bonifier** [bɔnifje] *vt* to improve

**boniment** [bɔnimɑ̃] *nm* patter *no pl*

**bonjour** [bɔ̃ʒuʀ] *excl, nm* hello; (*selon l'heure*) good morning/afternoon; **c'est simple comme ~!** it's easy as pie!

**bonne** [bɔn] *adj voir* **bon** ♦ *nf* (*domestique*) maid; **bonnement** *adv*: **tout bonnement** quite simply

**bonnet** [bɔnɛ] *nm* hat; (*de soutiengorge*) cup; **~ de bain** bathing cap

**bonshommes** [bɔ̃zɔm] *nmpl de* **bonhomme**

**bonsoir** [bɔ̃swaʀ] *excl* good evening

**bonté** [bɔ̃te] *nf* kindness *no pl*

**bonus** [bɔnys] *nm* no-claims bonus

**bord** [bɔʀ] *nm* (*de table, verre, falaise*) edge; (*de rivière, lac*) bank; (*de route*) side; (**monter**) **à ~** (to go) on board;

jeter par-dessus ~ to throw overboard; **le commandant de/les hommes du ~** the ship's master/crew; **au ~ de la mer** at the seaside; **être au ~ des larmes** to be on the verge of tears

**bordeaux** [bɔrdo] nm Bordeaux (wine) ♦ adj inv maroon

**bordel** [bɔrdɛl] nm brothel; (fam!) bloody mess (f)

**bordelais, e** [bɔrdəlɛ, ɛz] adj of ou from Bordeaux

**border** [bɔrde] vt (être le long de) to line; (qn dans son lit) to tuck up; (garnir): **~ qch de** to edge sth with

**bordereau, x** [bɔrdəro] nm (formulaire) slip

**bordure** [bɔrdyr] nf border; **en ~ de** on the edge of

**borgne** [bɔrɲ] adj one-eyed

**borne** [bɔrn] nf boundary stone; (aussi: **~ kilométrique**) kilometre-marker; ~ milestone; **~s** nfpl (fig) limits; **dépasser les ~s** to go too far

**borné, e** [bɔrne] adj (personne) narrow-minded

**borner** [bɔrne] vt: **se ~ à faire** (se contenter de) to content o.s. with doing; (se limiter à) to limit o.s. to doing

**bosquet** [bɔskɛ] nm grove

**bosse** [bɔs] nf (de terrain etc) bump; (enflure) lump; (du bossu, du chameau) hump; **avoir la ~ des maths** etc (fam) to have a gift for maths etc; **il a roulé sa ~** (fam) he's been around

**bosser** [bɔse] (fam) vi (travailler) to work; (travailler dur) to slave (away)

**bossu, e** [bɔsy] nm/f hunchback

**botanique** [bɔtanik] nf botany ♦ adj botanic(al)

**botte** [bɔt] nf (soulier) (high) boot; (gerbe): **~ de paille** bundle of straw; **~ de radis** bunch of radishes; **~s de caoutchouc** wellington boots; **botter** vt: **ça me botte** (fam) I fancy that

**bottin** [bɔtɛ̃] nm directory

**bottine** [bɔtin] nf ankle boot

**bouc** [buk] nm goat; (barbe) goatee; **~ émissaire** scapegoat

**boucan** [bukã] (fam) nm din, racket

**bouche** [buʃ] nf mouth; **rester ~ bée** to stand open-mouthed; **le ~ à ~** the kiss of life; **~ d'égout** manhole; **~ d'incendie** fire hydrant; **~ de métro** metro entrance

**bouché, e** [buʃe] adj (temps, ciel) overcast; **c'est ~** there's no future in it

**bouchée** [buʃe] nf mouthful; **~s à la reine** chicken vol-au-vents

**boucher, -ère** [buʃe, ɛr] nm/f butcher ♦ vt (trou) to fill up; (obstruer) to block up; **se ~** vi (tuyau etc) to block up, get blocked up; **j'ai le nez bouché** my nose is blocked; **se ~ le nez** to hold one's nose; **boucherie** nf butcher's (shop); (fig) slaughter

**bouche-trou** [buʃtru] nm (fig) stop gap

**bouchon** [buʃɔ̃] nm stopper; (de tube) top; (en liège) cork; (fig: embouteillage) holdup; (PÊCHE) float

**boucle** [bukl] nf (forme, figure) loop; (objet) buckle; **~ (de cheveux)** curl; **~ d'oreille** earring

**bouclé, e** [bukle] adj (cheveux) curly

**boucler** [bukle] vt (fermer: ceinture etc) to fasten; (terminer) to finish off; (enfermer) to shut away; (quartier) to seal off ♦ vi to curl

**bouclier** [buklije] nm shield

**bouddhiste** [budist] nm/f Buddhist

**bouder** [bude] vi to sulk ♦ vt to stay away from

**boudin** [budɛ̃] nm: **~ (noir)** black pudding; **~ blanc** white pudding

**boue** [bu] nf mud

**bouée** [bwe] nf buoy; **~ de sauvetage** lifebuoy

**boueux, -euse** [bwø, øz] adj muddy

**bouffe** [buf] (fam) nf grub (fam), food

**bouffée** [buf] nf (de cigarette) puff; **une ~ d'air pur** a breath of fresh air

**bouffer** [bufe] (fam) vi to eat

**bouffi, e** [bufi] adj swollen

**bougeoir** [buʒwaʀ] *nm* candlestick

**bougeotte** [buʒɔt] *nf*: **avoir la ~** (*fam*) to have the fidgets

**bouger** [buʒe] *vi* to move; (*dent etc*) to be loose; (*s'activer*) to get moving ♦ *vt* to move; **les prix/les couleurs n'ont pas bougé** prices/colours haven't changed

**bougie** [buʒi] *nf* candle; (*AUTO*) spark(ing) plug

**bougon, ne** [bugɔ̃, ɔn] *adj* grumpy

**bougonner** [bugɔne] *vi, vt* to grumble

**bouillabaisse** [bujabɛs] *nf* type of fish soup

**bouillant, e** [bujɑ̃, ɑ̃t] *adj* (*qui bout*) boiling; (*très chaud*) boiling (hot)

**bouillie** [buji] *nf* (*de bébé*) cereal; **en ~** (*fig*) crushed

**bouillir** [bujiʀ] *vi, vt* to boil; **~ d'impatience** to seethe with impatience

**bouilloire** [bujwaʀ] *nf* kettle

**bouillon** [bujɔ̃] *nm* (*CULIN*) stock *no pl*; **bouillonner** *vi* to bubble; (*fig: idées*) to bubble up

**bouillotte** [bujɔt] *nf* hot-water bottle

**boulanger, -ère** [bulɑ̃ʒe, ɛʀ] *nm/f* baker; **boulangerie** *nf* bakery; **boulangerie-pâtisserie** *nf* baker's and confectioner's (shop)

**boule** [bul] *nf* (*gén*) ball; **~s** *nfpl* (*jeu*) bowls; **se mettre en ~** (*fig: fam*) to fly off the handle, to blow one's top; **jouer aux ~s** to play bowls; **~ de neige** snowball

**bouleau, x** [bulo] *nm* (silver) birch

**bouledogue** [buldɔg] *nm* bulldog

**boulet** [bulɛ] *nm* (*aussi:* **~ de canon**) cannonball

**boulette** [bulɛt] *nf* (*de viande*) meatball

**boulevard** [bulvaʀ] *nm* boulevard

**bouleversant, e** [bulvɛʀsɑ̃, ɑ̃t] *adj* (*scène, récit*) deeply moving

**bouleversement** [bulvɛʀsəmɑ̃] *nm* upheaval

**bouleverser** [bulvɛʀse] *vt* (*émouvoir*) to overwhelm; (*causer du chagrin*) to distress; (*pays, vie*) to disrupt; (*papiers,*

*objets*) to turn upside down

**boulon** [bulɔ̃] *nm* bolt

**boulot, te** [bulo, ɔt] *adj* plump, tubby ♦ *nm* (*fam: travail*) work

**boum** [bum] *nm* bang ♦ *nf* (*fam*) party

**bouquet** [bukɛ] *nm* (*de fleurs*) bunch (of flowers), bouquet; (*de persil etc*) bunch; **c'est le ~!** (*fam*) that takes the biscuit!

**bouquin** [bukɛ̃] *nm* book; **bouquiner** (*fam*) *vi* to read; **bouquiniste** *nm/f* bookseller

**bourbeux, -euse** [buʀbø, øz] *adj* muddy

**bourbier** [buʀbje] *nm* (quag)mire

**bourde** [buʀd] *nf* (*erreur*) howler; (*gaffe*) blunder

**bourdon** [buʀdɔ̃] *nm* bumblebee; **bourdonner** *vi* to buzz

**bourg** [buʀ] *nm* small market town

**bourgeois, e** [buʀʒwa, waz] *adj* (*péj*) middle class; **bourgeoisie** *nf* ≈ (upper) middle classes *pl*

**bourgeon** [buʀʒɔ̃] *nm* bud

**Bourgogne** [buʀgɔɲ] *nf*: **la ~** Burgundy ♦ *nm*: **b~** burgundy (wine)

**bourguignon, ne** [buʀgiɲɔ̃, ɔn] *adj* of ou from Burgundy, Burgundian

**bourlinguer** [buʀlɛ̃ge] (*fam*) *vi* to knock about a lot, get around a lot

**bourrade** [buʀad] *nf* shove, thump

**bourrage** [buʀaʒ] *nm*: **~ de crâne** brainwashing; (*SCOL*) cramming

**bourrasque** [buʀask] *nf* squall

**bourratif, -ive** [buʀatif, iv] (*fam*) *adj* filling, stodgy (*péj*)

**bourré, e** [buʀe] *adj* (*fam: ivre*) plastered, tanked up (*BRIT*); (*rempli*): **~ de** crammed full of

**bourreau, x** [buʀo] *nm* executioner; (*fig*) torturer; **~ de travail** workaholic

**bourrelet** [buʀlɛ] *nm* fold ou roll (of flesh)

**bourrer** [buʀe] *vt* (*pipe*) to fill; (*poêle*) to pack; (*valise*) to cram (full)

**bourrique** [buʀik] *nf* (*âne*) ass

**bourru, e** [buʀy] *adj* surly, gruff

**bourse** [buʀs] nf (subvention) grant; (porte-monnaie) purse; **la B~** the Stock Exchange

**boursier, -ière** [buʀsje, jɛʀ] nm/f (étudiant) grant holder

**boursoufler** [buʀsufle]: **se ~** vi to swell (up)

**bous** [bu] vb voir **bouillir**

**bousculade** [buskylad] nf (hâte) rush; (cohue) crush; **bousculer** vt (heurter) to knock into; (fig) to push, rush

**bouse** [buz] nf dung no pl

**bousiller** [buzije] (fam) vt (appareil) to wreck

**boussole** [busɔl] nf compass

**bout** [bu] vb voir **bouillir** ♦ nm bit; (d'un bâton etc) tip; (d'une ficelle, table, rue, période) end; **au ~ de** at the end of, after; **pousser qn à ~** to push sb to the limit; **venir à ~ de** to manage to finish

**boutade** [butad] nf quip, sally

**boute-en-train** [butɑ̃tʀɛ̃] nm inv (fig) live wire

**bouteille** [butɛj] nf bottle; (de gaz butane) cylinder

**boutique** [butik] nf shop

**bouton** [butɔ̃] nm button; (sur la peau) spot; (BOT) bud; **~ d'or** buttercup; **boutonner** vt to button up; **boutonnière** nf buttonhole; **bouton-pression** nm press stud

**bouture** [butyʀ] nf cutting

**bovins** [bɔvɛ̃] nmpl cattle pl

**bowling** [buliŋ] nm (tenpin) bowling; (salle) bowling alley

**box** [bɔks] nm (d'écurie) loose-box; (JUR): **~ des accusés** dock

**boxe** [bɔks] nf boxing; **boxeur** nm boxer

**boyaux** [bwajo] nmpl (viscères) entrails, guts

**BP** abr = **boîte postale**

**bracelet** [bʀaslɛ] nm bracelet

**braconnier** [bʀakɔnje] nm poacher

**brader** [bʀade] vt to sell off; **braderie** nf cut-price shop/stall

**braguette** [bʀagɛt] nf fly ou flies (BRIT), zipper (US)

**brailler** [bʀaje] vi to bawl, yell

**braire** [bʀɛʀ] vi to bray

**braise** [bʀɛz] nf embers pl

**brancard** [bʀɑ̃kaʀ] nm (civière) stretcher; **brancardier** nm stretcher-bearer

**branchages** [bʀɑ̃ʃaʒ] nmpl boughs

**branche** [bʀɑ̃ʃ] nf branch

**branché, e** [bʀɑ̃ʃe] (fam) adj trendy

**brancher** [bʀɑ̃ʃe] vt to connect (up), (en mettant la prise) to plug in

**brandir** [bʀɑ̃diʀ] vt to brandish

**branle** [bʀɑ̃l] nm: **mettre en ~** to set in motion; **branle-bas** nm inv commotion

**braquer** [bʀake] vi (AUTO) to turn (the wheel) ♦ vt (revolver etc): **~ qch sur** to aim sth at, point sth at; (mettre en colère): **~ qn** to put sb's back up

**bras** [bʀa] nm arm; **~ dessus, ~ dessous** arm in arm; **se retrouver avec qch sur les ~** (fam) to be landed with sth; **~ droit** (fig) right hand man; **~ de fer** arm wrestling

**brasier** [bʀazje] nm blaze, inferno

**bras-le-corps** [bʀalkɔʀ] adv: **à ~** (a)round the waist

**brassard** [bʀasaʀ] nm armband

**brasse** [bʀas] nf (nage) breast-stroke

**brassée** [bʀase] nf armful

**brasser** [bʀase] vt to mix; **l'argent, les affaires** to handle a lot of money, business

**brasserie** [bʀasʀi] nf (restaurant) café-restaurant; (usine) brewery

**brave** [bʀav] adj (courageux) brave; (bon, gentil) good, kind

**braver** [bʀave] vt to defy

**bravo** [bʀavo] excl bravo ♦ nm cheer

**bravoure** [bʀavuʀ] nf bravery

**break** [bʀɛk] nm (AUTO) estate car

**brebis** [bʀabi] nf ewe; **~ galeuse** black sheep

**brèche** [bʀɛʃ] nf breach, gap; **être toujours sur la ~** (fig) to be always on the go

**redouille** [bʀeduj] adj empty-handed

**redouiller** [bʀeduje] vi, vt to mumble, stammer

**bref, brève** [bʀef, ɛv] adj short, brief ♦ adv in short; **d'un ton ~** sharply, curtly; **en ~** in short, in brief

**Brésil** [bʀezil] nm Brazil; **brésilien, -ne** adj Brazilian ♦ nm/f: **B~, ne** Brazilian

**Bretagne** [bʀətaɲ] nf Brittany

**bretelle** [bʀətɛl] nf (de vêtement, de sac) strap; (d'autoroute) slip road (BRIT), entrance/exit ramp (US); **~s** nfpl (pour pantalon) braces (BRIT), suspenders (US)

**breton, -ne** [bʀətɔ̃, ɔn] adj Breton ♦ nm/f: **B~, ne** Breton

**breuvage** [bʀœvaʒ] nm beverage, drink

**brève** [bʀɛv] adj voir **bref**

**brevet** [bʀəvɛ] nm diploma, certificate; **~ (d'invention)** patent; **breveté, e** adj patented

**bribes** [bʀib] nfpl (de conversation) snatches; **par ~** piecemeal

**bricolage** [bʀikɔlaʒ] nm: **le ~** do-it-yourself

**bricole** [bʀikɔl] nf (babiole) trifle

**bricoler** [bʀikɔle] vi (petits travaux) to potter about ♦ vt (réparer) to fix up; **bricoleur, -euse** nm/f handyman(-woman), DIY enthusiast

**bride** [bʀid] nf bridle; **tenir qn en ~** to keep a tight rein on sb

**bridé, e** [bʀide] adj: **yeux ~s** slit eyes

**bridge** [bʀidʒ] nm (CARTES) bridge

**brièvement** [bʀijɛvmɑ̃] adv briefly

**brigade** [bʀigad] nf (POLICE) squad; (MIL) brigade; **brigadier** nm sergeant

**brigandage** [bʀigɑ̃daʒ] nm robbery

**briguer** [bʀige] vt to aspire to

**brillamment** [bʀijamɑ̃] adv brilliantly

**brillant, e** [bʀijɑ̃, ɑ̃t] adj (remarquable) bright; (luisant) shiny, shining

**briller** [bʀije] vi to shine

**brimer** [bʀime] vt to bully

**brin** [bʀɛ̃] nm (de laine, ficelle etc) strand; (fig): **un ~ de** a bit of; **~ d'herbe** blade of grass; **~ de muguet** sprig of lily of the valley

**brindille** [bʀɛ̃dij] nf twig

**brio** [bʀijo] nm: **avec ~** with panache

**brioche** [bʀijɔʃ] nf brioche (bun); (fam: ventre) paunch

**brique** [bʀik] nf brick; (de lait) carton

**briquer** [bʀike] vt to polish up

**briquet** [bʀikɛ] nm (cigarette) lighter

**brise** [bʀiz] nf breeze

**briser** [bʀize] vt to break; **se ~** vi to break

**britannique** [bʀitanik] adj British ♦ nm/f: **B~** British person, Briton; **les B~s** the British

**brocante** [bʀɔkɑ̃t] nf junk, second-hand goods pl; **brocanteur, -euse** nm/f junkshop owner; junk dealer

**broche** [bʀɔʃ] nf brooch; (CULIN) spit; (MÉD) pin; **à la ~** spit-roasted

**broché, e** [bʀɔʃe] adj (livre) paper-backed

**brochet** [bʀɔʃɛ] nm pike inv

**brochette** [bʀɔʃɛt] nf (ustensile) skewer; (plat) kebab

**brochure** [bʀɔʃyʀ] nf pamphlet, brochure, booklet

**broder** [bʀɔde] vt to embroider ♦ vi to embroider the facts; **broderie** nf embroidery

**broncher** [bʀɔ̃ʃe] vi: **sans ~** without flinching, without turning a hair

**bronches** [bʀɔ̃ʃ] nfpl bronchial tubes; **bronchite** nf bronchitis

**bronze** [bʀɔ̃z] nm bronze

**bronzer** [bʀɔ̃ze] vi to get a tan; **se ~** to sunbathe

**brosse** [bʀɔs] nf brush; **coiffé en ~** with a crewcut; **~ à cheveux** hairbrush; **~ à dents** toothbrush; **~ à habits** clothesbrush; **brosser** vt (nettoyer) to brush; (fig: tableau etc) to paint; **se brosser les dents** to brush one's teeth

**brouette** [bʀuɛt] nf wheelbarrow

**brouhaha** [bʀuaa] nm hubbub

**brouillard** [bʀujaʀ] nm fog

**brouille** [bʀuj] nf quarrel

**brouiller** [bʀuje] vt (œufs, message) to scramble; (idées) to mix up; (rendre trouble) to cloud; (désunir: amis) to set at odds; **se ~** vi (vue) to cloud over; (gens) to fall out

**brouillon, ne** [bʀujɔ̃, ɔn] adj (sans soin) untidy; (qui manque d'organisation) disorganized ♦ nm draft; (papier) ~ rough paper

**broussailles** [bʀusaj] nfpl undergrowth sg; **broussailleux, -euse** adj bushy

**brousse** [bʀus] nf: **la ~** the bush

**brouter** [bʀute] vi to graze

**broutille** [bʀutij] nf trifle

**broyer** [bʀwaje] vt to crush; **~ du noir** to be down in the dumps

**bru** [bʀy] nf daughter-in-law

**brugnon** [bʀyɲɔ̃] nm (BOT) nectarine

**bruiner** [bʀɥine] vb impers: **il bruine** it's drizzling, there's a drizzle

**bruire** [bʀɥiʀ] vi (feuilles) to rustle

**bruit** [bʀɥi] nm: **un ~** a noise, a sound; (fig: rumeur) a rumour; **le ~** noise; **sans ~** without a sound, noiselessly; **~ de fond** background noise; **bruitage** nm sound effects pl

**brûlant, e** [bʀylɑ̃, ɑ̃t] adj burning; (liquide) boiling (hot)

**brûlé, e** [bʀyle] adj (fig: démasqué) blown ♦ nm: **odeur de ~** smell of burning

**brûle-pourpoint** [bʀylpuʀpwɛ̃]: **à ~~** adv point-blank

**brûler** [bʀyle] vt to burn; (suj: eau bouillante) to scald; (: consommer: électricité, essence) to use; (feu rouge, signal) to go through ♦ vi to burn; (jeu: tu brûles) you're getting hot; **se ~** vi to burn o.s.; (s'ébouillanter) to scald o.s.

**brûlure** [bʀylyʀ] nf (lésion) burn; **~s d'estomac** heartburn sg

**brume** [bʀym] nf mist; **brumisateur** nm atomizer

**brun, e** [bʀœ̃, bʀyn] adj (gén, bière) brown; (cheveux, tabac) dark; **elle est ~e** she's got dark hair

**brunch** [bʀœntʃ] nm brunch

**brunir** [bʀyniʀ] vi to get a tan

**brushing** [bʀœʃiŋ] nm blow-dry

**brusque** [bʀysk] adj abrupt; **brusquer** vt to rush

**brut, e** [bʀyt] adj (minerai, soie) raw; (diamant) rough; (COMM) gross; (pétrole) **~** crude (oil)

**brutal, e, -aux** [bʀytal, o] adj brutal; **brutaliser** vt to handle roughly, manhandle

**Bruxelles** [bʀysɛl] n Brussels

**bruyamment** [bʀɥijamɑ̃] adv noisily

**bruyant, e** [bʀɥijɑ̃, ɑ̃t] adj noisy

**bruyère** [bʀɥijɛʀ] nf heather

**BTS** sigle m (= brevet de technicien supérieur) vocational training certificate taken at the end of a higher education course

**bu, e** [by] pp de **boire**

**buccal, e, -aux** [bykal, o] adj: **par voie ~e** orally

**bûche** [byʃ] nf log; **prendre une ~** (fig) to come a cropper; **~ de Noël** Yule log

**bûcher** [byʃe] nm (funéraire) pyre; (supplice) stake ♦ vi (fam) to swot (BRIT), slave (away) ♦ vt (fam) to swot up (BRIT), slave away at; **bûcheron** nm woodcutter; **bûcheur, -euse** (fam) adj hard-working

**budget** [bydʒɛ] nm budget

**buée** [bɥe] nf (sur une vitre) mist

**buffet** [byfɛ] nm (meuble) sideboard; (de réception) buffet; **~ (de gare)** (station) buffet, snack bar

**buffle** [byfl] nm buffalo

**buis** [bɥi] nm box tree; (bois) box(wood)

**buisson** [bɥisɔ̃] nm bush

**buissonnière** [bɥisɔnjɛʀ] adj: **faire l'école ~** to skip school

**bulbe** [bylb] nm (BOT, ANAT) bulb

**Bulgarie** [bylgaʀi] nf Bulgaria

**bulle** [byl] nf bubble

**bulletin** [byltɛ̃] nm (communiqué, jour-

*nal*) bulletin; (*SCOL*) report; **~ d'informations** news bulletin; **~ de salaire** pay-slip; **~ (de vote)** ballot paper; **~ météorologique** weather report

**bureau, x** [byʀo] *nm* (*meuble*) desk; (*pièce*) office; **~ de change** (foreign) exchange office *ou* bureau; **~ de poste** post office; **~ de tabac** tobacconist's (shop); **~ de vote** polling station; **bureaucratie** [byʀokʀasi] *nf* bureaucracy

**burin** [byʀɛ̃] *nm* cold chisel; (*ART*) burin

**burlesque** [byʀlɛsk] *adj* ridiculous; (*LITTÉRATURE*) burlesque

**bus¹** [by] *vb voir* **boire**

**bus²** [bys] *nm* bus

**busqué, e** [byske] *adj* (*nez*) hook(ed)

**buste** [byst] *nm* (*torse*) chest; (*seins*) bust

**but¹** [by] *vb voir* **boire**

**but²** [by(t)] *nm* (*cible*) target; (*fig*) goal, aim; (*FOOTBALL etc*) goal; **de ~ en blanc** point-blank; **avoir pour ~ de faire** to aim to do; **dans le ~ de** with the intention of

**butane** [bytan] *nm* (*camping*) butane; (*usage domestique*) Calor gas ®

**buté, e** [byte] *adj* stubborn, obstinate

**buter** [byte] *vi:* **~ contre** (*cogner*) to bump into; (*trébucher*) to stumble against; **se ~** *vi* to get obstinate, dig in one's heels; **~ contre une difficulté** (*fig*) to hit a snag

**butin** [bytɛ̃] *nm* booty, spoils *pl*; (*d'un vol*) loot

**butiner** [bytine] *vi* (*abeilles*) to gather nectar

**butte** [byt] *nf* mound, hillock; **être en ~ à** to be exposed to

**buvais** *etc* [byvɛ] *vb voir* **boire**

**buvard** [byvaʀ] *nm* blotter

**buvette** [byvɛt] *nf* bar

**buveur, -euse** [byvœʀ, øz] *nm/f* drinker

## C, c

**c'** [s] *dét voir* **ce**

**CA** *sigle m* = **chiffre d'affaires**

**ça** [sa] *pron* (*pour désigner*) this; (: *plus loin*) that; (*comme sujet indéfini*) it; **comment ~ va?** how are you?; **~ va?** (*d'accord?*) OK?, all right?; **où ~?** where's that?; **pourquoi ~?** why's that?; **qui ~?** who's that?; **~ alors!** really!; **~ fait 10 ans (que)** it's 10 years (since); **c'est ~** that's right; **~ y est** that's it

**çà** [sa] *adv:* **~ et là** here and there

**cabane** [kaban] *nf* hut, cabin

**cabaret** [kabaʀɛ] *nm* night club

**cabas** [kaba] *nm* shopping bag

**cabillaud** [kabijo] *nm* cod *inv*

**cabine** [kabin] *nf* (*de bateau*) cabin; (*de piscine etc*) cubicle; (*de camion, train*) cab; (*d'avion*) cockpit; **~ d'essayage** fitting room; **~ (téléphonique)** call *ou* (tele)phone box

**cabinet** [kabinɛ] *nm* (*petite pièce*) closet; (*de médecin*) surgery (*BRIT*), office (*US*); (*de notaire etc*) office; (: *clientèle*) practice; (*POL*) Cabinet; **~s** *nmpl* (*w.-c.*) toilet *sg*; **~ d'affaires** business consultancy; **~ de toilette** toilet

**câble** [kɑbl] *nm* cable

**cabosser** [kabose] *vt* to dent

**cabrer** [kabʀe]: **se ~** *vi* (*cheval*) to rear up

**cabriole** [kabʀijɔl] *nf:* **faire des ~s** to caper about

**cacahuète** [kakaɥɛt] *nf* peanut

**cacao** [kakao] *nm* cocoa

**cache** [kaʃ] *nm* mask, card (for masking)

**cache-cache** [kaʃkaʃ] *nm:* **jouer à ~~** to play hide-and-seek

**cachemire** [kaʃmiʀ] *nm* cashmere

**cache-nez** [kaʃne] *nm inv* scarf, muffler

**cacher** [kaʃe] *vt* to hide, conceal; **se ~** *vi* (*volontairement*) to hide; (*être caché*)

**cachet** [kaʃɛ] *nm (comprimé)* tablet; *(de la poste)* postmark; *(rétribution)* fee; *(fig)* style, character; **cacheter** *vt* to seal

**cachette** [kaʃɛt] *nf* hiding place; **en ~** on the sly, secretly

**cachot** [kaʃo] *nm* dungeon

**cachotterie** [kaʃɔtʀi] *nf*: **faire des ~s** to be secretive

**cactus** [kaktys] *nm* cactus

**cadavre** [kadavʀ] *nm* corpse, (dead) body

**Caddie** ®, **caddy** [kadi] *nm (supermarket)* trolley

**cadeau, x** [kado] *nm* present, gift; **faire un ~ à qn** to give sb a present ou gift; **faire ~ de qch à qn** to make a present of sth to sb, give sb sth as a present

**cadenas** [kadna] *nm* padlock

**cadence** [kadɑ̃s] *nf (tempo)* rhythm; *(de travail etc)* rate; **en ~** rhythmically

**cadet, te** [kade, ɛt] *adj* younger; *(le plus jeune)* youngest ♦ *nm/f* youngest child ou one

**cadran** [kadʀɑ̃] *nm* dial; **~ solaire** sundial

**cadre** [kadʀ] *nm* frame; *(environnement)* surroundings *pl* ♦ *(ADMIN)* managerial employee, executive; **dans le ~ de** *(fig)* within the framework ou context of

**cadrer** [kadʀe] *vi*: **~ avec** tally ou correspond with ♦ *vt* to centre

**cafard** [kafaʀ] *nm* cockroach; **avoir le ~** *(fam)* to be down in the dumps

**café** [kafe] *nm* coffee; *(bistro)* café ♦ *adj inv* coffee(-coloured); **~ au lait** white coffee; **~ noir** black coffee; **~ tabac** *cd* baccoonist's ou newsagent's serving coffee and spirits; **cafetière** *nf (pot)* coffee-pot

**cafouiller** [kafuje] *(fam)* vi to get into a shambles

**cage** [kaʒ] *nf* cage; **~ d'escalier** (stair)well; **~ thoracique** rib cage

**cageot** [kaʒo] *nm* crate

**cagibi** [kaʒibi] *(fam)* nm *(débarras)* boxroom

**cagnotte** [kaɲɔt] *nf* kitty

**cagoule** [kagul] *nf (passe-montagne)* balaclava

**cahier** [kaje] *nm* notebook; **~ de brouillons** roughbook, jotter; **~ d'exercices** exercise book

**cahot** [kao] *nm* jolt, bump

**caïd** [kaid] *nm* big chief, boss

**caille** [kaj] *nf* quail

**cailler** [kaje] *vi (lait)* to curdle; **ça caille** *(fam)* it's freezing; **caillot** [kajo] *nm (blood)* clot

**caillou, x** [kaju] *nm (little) stone*; **caillouteux, -euse** *adj (route)* stony

**Caire** [kɛʀ] *nm*: **le ~** Cairo

**caisse** [kɛs] *nf* box; *(tiroir où l'on met la recette)* till; *(où l'on paye)* cash desk *(BRIT)*, check-out; *(de banque)* cashier's desk; **~ d'épargne** savings bank; **~ de retraite** pension fund; **~ enregistreuse** cash register; **caissier, -ière** *nm/f* cashier

**cajoler** [kaʒɔle] *vt (câliner)* to cuddle; *(amadouer)* to wheedle, coax

**cake** [kɛk] *nm* fruit cake

**calandre** [kalɑ̃dʀ] *nf* radiator grill

**calanque** [kalɑ̃k] *nf* rocky inlet

**calcaire** [kalkɛʀ] *nm* limestone ♦ *adj (eau)* hard; *(GÉO)* limestone *cpd*

**calciné, e** [kalsine] *adj* burnt to ashes

**calcul** [kalkyl] *nm* calculation; **le ~** *(SCOL)* arithmetic; **~ (biliaire)** *(gall)*stone; **calculatrice** *nf* calculator; **calculer** *vt* to calculate, work out; **calculette** *nf* pocket calculator

**cale** [kal] *nf (de bateau)* hold; *(en bois)* wedge; **~ sèche** dry dock

**calé, e** [kale] *(fam) adj* clever, bright

**caleçon** [kalsɔ̃] *nm (d'homme)* boxer shorts; *(de femme)* leggings

**calembour** [kalɑ̃buʀ] *nm* pun

**calendrier** [kalɑ̃dʀije] *nm* calendar; *(fig)* timetable

**calepin** [kalpɛ̃] *nm* notebook

**caler** [kale] vt to wedge ♦ vi (moteur, véhicule) to stall

**calfeutrer** [kalføtʀe] vt to (make) draughtproof; **se ~** vi to make o.s. snug and comfortable

**calibre** [kalibʀ] nm calibre

**califourchon** [kalifuʀʃɔ̃]: **à ~** adv astride

**câlin, e** [kalɛ̃, in] adj cuddly, cuddlesome; (regard, voix) tender; **câliner** vt to cuddle

**calmant** [kalmɑ̃] nm tranquillizer, sedative; (pour la douleur) painkiller

**calme** [kalm] adj calm, quiet ♦ nm calm(ness), quietness; **calmer** vt to calm (down); (douleur, inquiétude) to ease, soothe; **se calmer** vi to calm down

**calomnie** [kalɔmni] nf slander; (écrite) libel; **calomnier** vt to slander; to libel

**calorie** [kalɔʀi] nf calorie

**calotte** [kalɔt] nf (coiffure) skullcap; (fam: gifle) slap; **~ glaciaire** (GÉO) icecap

**calquer** [kalke] vt to trace; (fig) to copy exactly

**calvaire** [kalvɛʀ] nm (croix) wayside cross, calvary; (souffrances) suffering

**calvitie** [kalvisi] nf baldness

**camarade** [kamaʀad] nm/f friend, pal; (POL) comrade; **camaraderie** nf friendship

**cambouis** [kɑ̃bwi] nm dirty oil ou grease

**cambrer** [kɑ̃bʀe] **se ~** vi to arch one's back

**cambriolage** [kɑ̃bʀijɔlaʒ] nm burglary; **cambrioler** vt to burgle (BRIT), burglarize (US); **cambrioleur, -euse** nm/f burglar

**camelote** [kamlɔt] (fam) nf rubbish, trash, junk

**caméra** [kameʀa] nf (CINÉMA, TV) camera; (d'amateur) cine-camera

**caméscope** ® [kameskɔp] nm camcorder ®

**camion** [kamjɔ̃] nm lorry (BRIT), truck; ~ de dépannage breakdown (BRIT) ou tow (US) truck; **camion-citerne** nm tanker; **camionnette** nf (small) van; **camionneur** nm (chauffeur) lorry (BRIT) ou truck driver; (entrepreneur) haulage contractor (BRIT), trucker (US)

**camisole** [kamizɔl] nf: **~ (de force)** straitjacket

**camomille** [kamɔmij] nf camomile; (boisson) camomile tea

**camoufler** [kamufle] vt to camouflage; (fig) to conceal, cover up

**camp** [kɑ̃] nm camp; (fig) side; ~ de vacances children's holiday camp (BRIT), summer camp (US)

**campagnard, e** [kɑ̃paɲaʀ, aʀd] adj country cpd

**campagne** [kɑ̃paɲ] nf country, countryside; (MIL, POL, COMM) campaign; à la ~ in the country

**camper** [kɑ̃pe] vi to camp ♦ vt to sketch; **se ~ devant** to plant o.s. in front of; **campeur, -euse** nm/f camper

**camping** [kɑ̃piŋ] nm camping; (terrain del) ~ campsite, camping site; **faire du ~** to go camping; **camping-car** nm camper, motorhome (US); **camping-gaz** ® nm inv camp(ing) stove

**Canada** [kanada] nm: le ~ Canada; **canadien, ne** adj Canadian ♦ nm/f: **Canadien, ne** Canadian; **canadienne** nf (veste) fur-lined jacket

**canaille** [kanaj] (péj) nf scoundrel

**canal, -aux** [kanal, o] nm canal; (naturel) channel; **canalisation** nf (tuyau) pipe; **canaliser** vt to canalize; (fig) to channel

**canapé** [kanape] nm settee, sofa

**canard** [kanaʀ] nm duck; (fam: journal) rag

**canari** [kanaʀi] nm canary

**cancans** [kɑ̃kɑ̃] nmpl (malicious) gossip sg

**cancer** [kɑ̃sɛʀ] nm cancer; (signe): le C~ Cancer; ~ de la peau skin cancer

**cancre** [kɑ̃kʀ] nm dunce

**candeur** [kɑ̃dœʀ] nf ingenuousness,

guilelessness

**candidat, e** [kɑ̃dida, at] nm/f candidate; (à un poste) applicant, candidate; **candidature** nf (POL) candidature; (à poste) application; **poser sa candidature à un poste** to apply for a job

**candide** [kɑ̃did] adj ingenuous, guileless

**cane** [kan] nf (female) duck

**caneton** [kantɔ̃] nm duckling

**canette** [kanɛt] nf (de bière) (flip-top) bottle

**canevas** [kanva] nm (COUTURE) canvas

**caniche** [kaniʃ] nm poodle

**canicule** [kanikyl] nf scorching heat

**canif** [kanif] nm penknife, pocket knife

**canine** [kanin] nf canine (tooth)

**caniveau, x** [kanivo] nm gutter

**canne** [kan] nf (walking) stick; ~ à **pêche** fishing rod; ~ à **sucre** sugar cane

**cannelle** [kanɛl] nf cinnamon

**canoë** [kanɔe] nm canoe; (sport) canoeing

**canon** [kanɔ̃] nm (arme) gun; (HISTOIRE) cannon; (d'une arme: tube) barrel; (fig: norme) model; (MUS) canon

**canot** [kano] nm ding(h)y; ~ **de sauvetage** lifeboat; ~ **pneumatique** inflatable ding(h)y; **canotier** nm boater

**cantatrice** [kɑ̃tatris] nf (opera) singer

**cantine** [kɑ̃tin] nf canteen

**cantique** [kɑ̃tik] nm hymn

**canton** [kɑ̃tɔ̃] nm district consisting of several communes; (en Suisse) canton

**cantonade** [kɑ̃tɔnad]: **à la ~** adv to everyone in general

**cantonner** [kɑ̃tɔne]: **se ~ à** vt to confine o.s. to

**cantonnier** [kɑ̃tɔnje] nm roadmender

**canular** [kanylar] nm hoax

**caoutchouc** [kautʃu] nm rubber

**cap** [kap] nm (GÉO) cape; (promontoire) headland; (fig: tournant) watershed; (NAVIG): **changer de ~** to change course; **mettre le ~ sur** to head ou steer for

**CAP** sigle m (= Certificat d'aptitude professionnelle) vocational training certificate taken at secondary school

**capable** [kapabl] adj able, capable; ~ **de qch/faire** capable of sth/doing

**capacité** [kapasite] nf (compétence) ability; (JUR, contenance) capacity

**cape** [kap] nf cape, cloak; **rire sous ~** to laugh up one's sleeve

**CAPES** [kapɛs] sigle m (= Certificat d'aptitude pédagogique à l'enseignement secondaire) teaching diploma

**capillaire** [kapilɛr] adj (soins, lotion) hair cpd; (vaisseau etc) capillary

**capitaine** [kapitɛn] nm captain

**capital, e, -aux** [kapital, o] adj (œuvre) major; (question, rôle) fundamental ♦ nm capital; (fig) stock; **d'une importance ~e** of capital importance; **voir aussi capitaux**; ~ **(social)** authorized capital; **capitale** nf (ville) capital; (lettre) capital (letter); **capitalisme** nm capitalism; **capitaliste** adj, nm/f capitalist; **capitaux** nmpl (fonds) capital sg

**capitonné, e** [kapitɔne] adj padded

**caporal, -aux** [kapɔral, o] nm lance corporal

**capot** [kapo] nm (AUTO) bonnet (BRIT), hood (US)

**capote** [kapɔt] nf (de voiture) hood (BRIT), top (US); (fam) condom

**capoter** [kapɔte] vi (négociations) to founder

**câpre** [kapr] nf caper

**caprice** [kapris] nm whim, caprice; **faire des ~s** to make a fuss; **capricieux, -euse** adj (fantasque) capricious, whimsical; (enfant) awkward

**Capricorne** [kaprikɔrn] nm: **le ~** Capricorn

**capsule** [kapsyl] nf (de bouteille) cap; (BOT etc, spatiale) capsule

**capter** [kapte] vt (ondes radio) to pick up; (fig) to win, capture

**captivant, e** [kaptivɑ̃, ɑ̃t] adj captivating

**captivité** [kaptivite] nf captivity

**capturer** [kaptyʀe] vt to capture

**capuche** [kapyʃ] nf hood

**capuchon** [kapyʃɔ̃] nm hood; (de stylo) cap, top

**capucine** [kapysin] nf (BOT) nasturtium

**caquet** [kake] nm: **rabattre le ~ à qn** (fam) to bring sb down a peg or two

**caqueter** [kakte] vi to cackle

**car** [kaʀ] nm coach ♦ conj because, for

**carabine** [kaʀabin] nf rifle

**caractère** [kaʀaktɛʀ] nm (gén) character; **avoir bon/mauvais ~** to be good-/ill-natured; **en ~s gras** in bold type; **en petits ~s** in small print; **~s d'imprimerie** (block) capitals; **caractériel, le** adj (traits) (of) character; (enfant) emotionally disturbed

**caractérisé, e** [kaʀakteʀize] adj sheer, downright

**caractériser** [kaʀakteʀize] vt to be characteristic of

**caractéristique** [kaʀakteʀistik], adj, nf characteristic

**carafe** [kaʀaf] nf (pour eau, vin ordinaire) carafe

**caraïbe** [kaʀaib] adj Caribbean ♦ n: **les C~s** the Caribbean (Islands)

**carambolage** [kaʀãbɔlaʒ] nm multiple crash, pileup

**caramel** [kaʀamɛl] nm (bonbon) caramel, toffee; (substance) caramel

**carapace** [kaʀapas] nf shell

**caravane** [kaʀavan] nf caravan; **caravaning** nm caravanning

**carbone** [kaʀbɔn] nm carbon; (double copy); **carbonique** adj: **gaz carbonique** carbon dioxide; **neige carbonique** dry ice; **carbonisé, e** adj charred

**carburant** [kaʀbyʀã] nm (motor) fuel

**carburateur** [kaʀbyʀatœʀ] nm carburettor

**carcan** [kaʀkã] nm (fig) yoke, shackles pl

**carcasse** [kaʀkas] nf carcass; (de véhicule etc) shell

**cardiaque** [kaʀdjak] adj cardiac, heart

cpd ♦ nm/f heart patient; **être ~** to have heart trouble

**cardigan** [kaʀdigã] nm cardigan

**cardiologue** [kaʀdjɔlɔg] nm/f cardiologist, heart specialist

**carême** [kaʀɛm] nm: **le C~** Lent

**carence** [kaʀãs] nf (manque) deficiency

**caresse** [kaʀɛs] nf caress

**caresser** [kaʀese] vt to caress; (animal) to stroke

**cargaison** [kaʀgɛzɔ̃] nf cargo, freight

**cargo** [kaʀgo] nm cargo boat, freighter

**caricature** [kaʀikatyʀ] nf caricature

**carie** [kaʀi] nf: **la ~ (dentaire)** tooth decay; **une ~** a bad tooth

**carillon** [kaʀijɔ̃] nm (air, de pendule) chimes pl

**caritatif, -ive** [kaʀitatif, iv] adj: **organisation caritative** charity

**carnassier, -ière** [kaʀnasje, jɛʀ] adj carnivorous

**carnaval** [kaʀnaval] nm carnival

**carnet** [kaʀnɛ] nm (calepin) notebook; (de tickets, timbres etc) book; **~ de chèques** cheque book; **~ de notes** school report

**carotte** [kaʀɔt] nf carrot

**carpette** [kaʀpɛt] nf rug

**carré, e** [kaʀe] adj square; (fig: franc) straightforward ♦ nm (MATH) square; **mètre/kilomètre ~** square metre/kilometre

**carreau, x** [kaʀo] nm (par terre) (floor) tile; (au mur) (wall) tile; (de fenêtre) (window) pane; (motif) check, square; (CARTES: couleur) diamonds pl; **tissu à ~x** checked fabric

**carrefour** [kaʀfuʀ] nm crossroads sg

**carrelage** [kaʀlaʒ] nm (sol) (tiled) floor

**carrelet** [kaʀlɛ] nm (poisson) plaice

**carrément** [kaʀemã] adv (franchement) straight out, bluntly; (sans hésiter) straight; (intensif) completely; **c'est ~ impossible** it's completely impossible

**carrière** [kaʀjɛʀ] nf (métier) career; (de roches) quarry; **militaire de ~** professional soldier

**carrossable** [kaʀɔsabl] *adj* suitable for (motor) vehicles

**carrosse** [kaʀɔs] *nm* (horse-drawn) coach

**carrosserie** [kaʀɔsʀi] *nf* body, coachwork *no pl*

**carrure** [kaʀyʀ] *nf* build; (*fig*) stature, calibre

**cartable** [kaʀtabl] *nm* satchel, (school)bag

**carte** [kaʀt] *nf* (*de géographie*) map; (*marine, du ciel*) chart; (*d'abonnement, à jouer*) card; (*au restaurant*) menu; (*aussi:* **~ de visite**) (visiting) card; **à la ~** (*au restaurant*) à la carte; **donner ~ blanche à qn** to give sb a free rein; **~ bancaire** cash card; **~ de crédit** credit card; **~ de fidélité** loyalty card; **~ d'identité** identity card; **~ de séjour** residence permit; **~ grise** (AUTO) ≈ (car) registration book, logbook; **~ postale** postcard; **~ routière** road map; **~ téléphonique** phonecard

**carter** [kaʀtɛʀ] *nm* sump

**carton** [kaʀtɔ̃] *nm* (*matériau*) cardboard; (*boîte*) cardboard box; **faire un ~** (*fam*) to score a hit; **~ (à dessin)** portfolio; **carton-pâte** *nm* pasteboard

**cartouche** [kaʀtuʃ] *nf* cartridge; (*de cigarettes*) carton

**cas** [kɑ] *nm* case; **ne faire aucun ~ de** to take no notice of; **en aucun ~** on no account; **au ~ où** in case; **en ~ de** in case of, in the event of; **en ~ de besoin** if need be; **en tout ~** in any case, at any rate

**casanier, -ière** [kazanje, jɛʀ] *adj* stay-at-home

**cascade** [kaskad] *nf* waterfall, cascade; (*fig*) ruisseau, torrent; **cascadeur, -euse** *nm/f* stuntman(-girl)

**case** [kɑz] *nf* (*hutte*) hut; (*compartiment*) compartment; (*sur un formulaire, de mots croisés etc*) box

**caser** [kɑze] *vt* (*fam*) *vt* (*placer*) to put (away); (*loger*) to put up; **se ~** *vi* (*se marier*) to settle down; (*trouver un em-*

*ploi*) to find a (steady) job

**caserne** [kazɛʀn] *nf* barracks *pl*

**cash** [kaʃ] *adv*: **payer ~** to pay cash down

**casier** [kazje] *nm* (*pour courrier*) pigeonhole; (*compartiment*) compartment; (*à clef*) locker; **~ judiciaire** police record

**casino** [kazino] *nm* casino

**casque** [kask] *nm* helmet; (*chez le coiffeur*) (hair-)drier; (*pour audition*) (head-)phones *pl*, headset

**casquette** [kaskɛt] *nf* cap

**cassant, e** [kasɑ̃, ɑ̃t] *adj* brittle; (*fig: ton*) curt, abrupt

**cassation** [kasasjɔ̃] *nf*: **cour de ~** final court of appeal

**casse** [kas] (*fam*) *nf* (*pour voitures*): **mettre à la ~** to scrap; (*dégâts*): **il y a eu de la ~** there were a lot of breakages; **casse-cou** *adj inv* daredevil, reckless; **casse-croûte** *nm inv* snack; **casse-noix** *nm inv* nutcrackers *pl*; **casse-pieds** (*fam*) *adj inv*: **il est casse-pieds** he's a pain in the neck

**casser** [kase] *vt* to break; (*JUR*) to quash; **se ~** *vi* to break; **~ les pieds à qn** (*fam: irriter*) to get on sb's nerves; **se ~ la tête** (*fam*) to go to a lot of trouble

**casserole** [kasʀɔl] *nf* saucepan

**casse-tête** [kastɛt] *nm inv* (*difficultés*) headache (*fig*)

**cassette** [kasɛt] *nf* (*bande magnétique*) cassette; (*coffret*) casket

**casseur** [kasœʀ] *nm* hooligan

**cassis** [kasis] *nm* blackcurrant

**cassoulet** [kasulɛ] *nm* bean and sausage hot-pot

**cassure** [kasyʀ] *nf* break, crack

**castor** [kastɔʀ] *nm* beaver

**castrer** [kastʀe] *vt* (*mâle*) to castrate; (: *cheval*) to geld; (*femelle*) to spay

**catalogue** [katalɔg] *nm* catalogue

**cataloguer** [katalɔge] *vt* to catalogue, to list; (*péj*) to put a label on

**catalyseur** [katalizœʀ] *nm* catalyst; **ca-talytique** *adj*: **pot catalytique** cataly-

# catastrophe

# célibat

tic convertor

**catastrophe** [katastʀɔf] nf catastrophe, disaster; **catastrophé, e** (fam) adj stunned

**catch** [katʃ] nm (all-in) wrestling

**catéchisme** [kateʃism] nm catechism

**catégorie** [kategɔʀi] nf category; **catégorique** adj categorical

**cathédrale** [katedʀal] nf cathedral

**catholique** [katɔlik] adj, nm/f (Roman) Catholic; **pas très ~** a bit shady ou fishy

**catimini** [katimini]: **en ~** adv on the sly

**cauchemar** [koʃmaʀ] nm nightmare

**cause** [koz] nf cause; (JUR) lawsuit; case; **à ~ de** because of, owing to; **pour ~ de** on account of; **(et) pour ~** and for a (very) good reason; **être en ~** (intérêts) to be at stake; **remettre en ~** to challenge; **causer** vt to cause ♦ vi to chat, talk; **causerie** (conférence) nf talk; **causette** nf: **faire la causette** to have a chat

**caution** [kosjɔ̃] nf guarantee, security; (JUR) bail (bond); (fig) backing, support; **libéré sous ~** released on bail; **cautionner** vt (répondre de) to guarantee; (soutenir) to support

**cavalcade** [kavalkad] nf (fig) stampede

**cavalier, -ière** [kavalje, jɛʀ] adj (désinvolte) offhand ♦ nm/f rider; (au bal) partner ♦ nm (ÉCHECS) knight

**cave** [kav] nf cellar

**caveau, x** [kavo] nm vault

**caverne** [kavɛʀn] nf cave

**CCP** sigle m = **compte chèques postaux**

**CD** sigle m (= compact disc) CD

**CD-ROM** [sedeʀɔm] sigle m CD-ROM

**CE** n abr m (= Communauté Européenne) EC

---

MOT-CLÉ

---

**ce, cette** [sə, sɛt] (devant nm **cet** + voyelle ou h aspiré; pl **ces**) dét (proximité) this; these pl; (non-proximité) that; those pl;

---

cette maison(-ci/là) this/that house; cette nuit (qui vient) tonight; (passée) last night

♦ pron 1: **c'est** it's ou it is; **c'est un peintre** he's ou he is a painter; **ce sont des peintres** they're ou they are painters; **c'est le facteur** (à la porte) it's the postman; **qui est-ce?** who is it?; (en désignant) who is he/she?; **qu'est-ce?** what is it?

**2: ce qui, ce que** what; (chose qui): **il est bête, ce qui me chagrine** he's stupid, which saddens me; **tout ce qui bouge** everything that ou which moves; **tout ce que je sais** all I know; **ce dont j'ai parlé** I talked about; **ce que c'est grand!** it's so big!; voir aussi **-ci**; **est-ce que**; **n'est-ce pas**; **c'est-à-dire**

---

**ceci** [səsi] pron this

**cécité** [sesite] nf blindness

**céder** [sede] vt (donner) to give up ♦ vi (chaise, barrage) to give way; (personne) to give in; **~ à** to yield to, give in to

**CEDEX** [sedɛks] sigle m (= courrier d'entreprise à distribution exceptionnelle) postal service for bulk users

**cédille** [sedij] nf cedilla

**cèdre** [sɛdʀ] nm cedar

**CEI** sigle m (= Communauté des États Indépendants) CIS

**ceinture** [sɛ̃tyʀ] nf belt; (taille) waist; **~ de sécurité** safety ou seat belt

**cela** [s(ə)la] pron that; (comme sujet indéfini): **quand/où ~?** when/where (was that)?

**célèbre** [selɛbʀ] adj famous; **célébrer** vt to celebrate

**céleri** [sɛlʀi] nm: **~(-rave)** celeriac; **~ (en branche)** celery

**célibat** [seliba] nm (homme) bachelorhood; (femme) spinsterhood; (prêtre) celibacy; **célibataire** adj single, unmarried ♦ nm bachelor ♦ nf unmarried woman

**celle(s)** [sɛl] *pron voir* **celui**

**cellier** [selje] *nm* storeroom (for wine)

**cellule** [selyl] *nf* (*gén*) cell

**cellulite** [selylit] *nf* excess fat, cellulite

*MOT-CLÉ*

**celui, celle** [səlɥi, sɛl] (*mpl* **ceux**, *fpl* **celles**) *pron* 1: **celui-ci/là, celle-ci/là** this one/that one; **ceux-ci, celles-ci** these (ones); **ceux-là, celles-là** those (ones); **celui de mon frère** my brother's; **celui du salon/du dessous** the one in (*ou* from) the lounge/below 2: **celui qui bouge** the one which *ou* that moves; (*personne*) the one who moves; **celui que je vois** the one (which *ou* that) I see; **celui dont je parle** the one I'm talking about

3 (*valeur indéfinie*): **celui qui veut** whoever wants

**cendre** [sɑ̃dʀ] *nf* ash; **~s** *nfpl* (*d'un défunt*) ashes; **sous la ~** (*CULIN*) in (the) embers; **cendrier** *nm* ashtray

**cène** [sɛn] *nf*: **la ~** (Holy) Communion

**censé, e** [sɑ̃se] *adj*: **être ~ faire** to be supposed to do

**censeur** [sɑ̃sœʀ] *nm* (*SCOL*) deputy-head (*BRIT*), vice-principal (*US*)

**censure** [sɑ̃syʀ] *nf* censorship; **censurer** *vt* (*CINÉMA, PRESSE*) to censor; (*POL*) to censure

**cent** [sɑ̃] *num* a hundred, one hundred ♦ *nm* (*US, Canada etc*) cent; (*partie de l'euro*) cent; **centaine** *nf*: **une centaine (de)** a hundred or so; **des centaines (de)** hundreds (of); **centenaire** *adj* hundred-year-old ♦ *nm* (*anniversaire*) centenary; **centième** *num* hundredth; **centigrade** *nm* centigrade; **centilitre** *nm* centilitre; **centime** *nm* centime; **centimètre** *nm* centimetre; (*ruban*) tape measure, measuring tape

**central, e, -aux** [sɑ̃tʀal, o] *adj* central ♦ *nm*: **~ (téléphonique)** (telephone)

exchange; **centrale** *nf* power station

**centre** [sɑ̃tʀ] *nm* centre; **~ commercial** shopping centre; **~ d'appels** call centre; **~ de loisirs** leisure centre; **centre-ville** *nm* town centre, downtown (area) (*US*)

**centuple** [sɑ̃typl] *nm*: **le ~ de qch** a hundred times sth; **au ~** a hundred-fold

**cep** [sɛp] *nm* (vine) stock

**cèpe** [sɛp] *nm* (edible) boletus

**cependant** [s(ə)pɑ̃dɑ̃] *adv* however

**céramique** [seʀamik] *nf* ceramics *sg*

**cercle** [sɛʀkl] *nm* circle

**cercueil** [sɛʀkœj] *nm* coffin

**céréale** [seʀeal] *nf* cereal; **~s** *nfpl* breakfast cereal

**cérémonie** [seʀemɔni] *nf* ceremony

**cerf** [sɛʀ] *nm* stag

**cerfeuil** [sɛʀfœj] *nm* chervil

**cerf-volant** [sɛʀvɔlɑ̃] *nm* kite

**cerise** [s(ə)ʀiz] *nf* cherry; **cerisier** *nm* cherry (tree)

**cerne** [sɛʀn] *nm*: **avoir des ~s** to have shadows *ou* dark rings under one's eyes

**cerner** [sɛʀne] *vt* (*MIL etc*) to surround; (*fig: problème*) to delimit, define

**certain, e** [sɛʀtɛ̃, ɛn] *adj* certain ♦ *dét* certain; **d'un ~ âge** past one's prime, not so young; **un ~ temps** (quite) some time; **~s** ♦ *pron* some; **certainement** *adv* (*probablement*) most probably *ou* likely; (*bien sûr*) certainly, of course

**certes** [sɛʀt] *adv* (*sans doute*) admittedly; (*bien sûr*) of course

**certificat** [sɛʀtifika] *nm* certificate

**certifier** [sɛʀtifje] *vt*: **~ qch à qn** to assure sb of sth; **copie certifiée conforme** certified copy of the original

**certitude** [sɛʀtityd] *nf* certainty

**cerveau, x** [sɛʀvo] *nm* brain

**cervelas** [sɛʀvəla] *nm* saveloy

**cervelle** [sɛʀvɛl] *nf* (*ANAT*) brain; (*CULIN*) brains

**ces** [se] *dét voir* **ce**

**CES** *sigle m* (= *Collège d'enseignement*

*secondaire)* ≃ *(junior)* secondary school *(BRIT)*

**cesse** [sɛs]: **sans ~** *adv (tout le temps)* continually, constantly; *(sans interruption)* continuously; **il n'a eu de ~ que** he did not rest until; **cesser** *vt* to stop ♦ *vi* to stop, cease; **cesser de faire** to stop doing; **cessez-le-feu** *nm inv* ceasefire

**c'est-à-dire** [sɛtadir] *adv* that is (to say)

**cet, cette** [sɛt] *dét voir* **ce**

**ceux** [sø] *pron voir* **celui**

**CFC** *abr (= chlorofluorocarbon)* CFC

**CFDT** *sigle f (= Confédération française démocratique du travail)* French trade union

**CGT** *sigle f (= Confédération générale du travail)* French trade union

**chacun, e** [ʃakœ̃, yn] *pron* each; *(indéfini)* everyone, everybody

**chagrin** [ʃagrɛ̃] *nm* grief, sorrow; **avoir du ~** to be grieved; **chagriner** *vt* to grieve

**chahut** [ʃay] *nm* uproar; **chahuter** *vt* to rag, bait ♦ *vi* to make an uproar

**chaîne** [ʃɛn] *nf* chain; *(RADIO, TV: stations)* channel; **~s** *nfpl (AUTO)* (snow) chains; **travail à la ~** production line work; **~ (de montage)** production *ou* assembly line; **~ de montagnes** mountain range; **~ (hi-fi)** hi-fi system; **~ laser** CD player; **~ (stéréo)** stereo (system); **chaînette** *nf* (small) chain

**chair** [ʃɛr] *nf* flesh; **avoir la ~ de poule** to have goosepimples *ou* gooseflesh; **bien en ~** plump, well-padded; **en ~ et en os** in the flesh; **~ à saucisse** sausage meat

**chaire** [ʃɛr] *nf (d'église)* pulpit; *(d'université)* chair

**chaise** [ʃɛz] *nf* chair; **~ longue** deck-chair

**châle** [ʃal] *nm* shawl

**chaleur** [ʃalœr] *nf* heat; *(fig: accueil)* warmth; **chaleureux, -euse** *adj* warm

**chaloupe** [ʃalup] *nf* launch; *(de sauve-*

*tage)* lifeboat

**chalumeau, x** [ʃalymo] *nm* blowlamp, blowtorch

**chalutier** [ʃalytje] *nm* trawler

**chamailler** [ʃamaje]: **se ~** *vi* to squabble, bicker

**chambouler** [ʃɑ̃bule] *(fam) vt* to disrupt, turn upside down

**chambre** [ʃɑ̃br] *nf* bedroom; *(POL, COMM)* chamber; **faire ~ à part** to sleep in separate rooms; **~ à air** *(de pneu)* (inner) tube; **~ à coucher** bedroom; **~ à un lit/deux lits** *(à l'hôtel)* single-/twin-bedded room; **~ d'amis** spare *ou* guest room; **~ noire** *(PHOTO)* dark room; **chambrer** *vt (vin)* to bring to room temperature

**chameau, x** [ʃamo] *nm* camel

**chamois** [ʃamwa] *nm* chamois

**champ** [ʃɑ̃] *nm* field; **~ de bataille** battlefield; **~ de courses** racecourse; **~ de tir** rifle range

**champagne** [ʃɑ̃paɲ] *nm* champagne

**champêtre** [ʃɑ̃pɛtr] *adj* country *cpd*, rural

**champignon** [ʃɑ̃piɲɔ̃] *nm* mushroom; *(terme générique)* fungus; **~ de Paris** button mushroom

**champion, ne** [ʃɑ̃pjɔ̃, jɔn] *adj, nm/f* champion; **championnat** *nm* championship

**chance** [ʃɑ̃s] *nf*: **la ~** luck; **~s** *nfpl (probabilités)* chances; **avoir de la ~** to be lucky; **il a des ~ de réussir** he's got a good chance of passing

**chanceler** [ʃɑ̃s(ə)le] *vi* to totter

**chancelier** [ʃɑ̃səlje] *nm (allemand)* chancellor

**chanceux, -euse** [ʃɑ̃sø, øz] *adj* lucky

**chandail** [ʃɑ̃daj] *nm* (thick) sweater

**Chandeleur** [ʃɑ̃dlœr] *nf*: **la ~** Candlemas

**chandelier** [ʃɑ̃dəlje] *nm* candlestick

**chandelle** [ʃɑ̃dɛl] *nf* (tallow) candle; **dîner aux ~s** candlelight dinner

**change** [ʃɑ̃ʒ] *nm (devises)* exchange

**changement** [ʃɑ̃ʒmɑ̃] *nm* change; **~**

**de vitesses** gears pl

**changer** [ʃɑ̃ʒe] vt (modifier) to change, alter; (remplacer, COMM) to change ♦ vi to change, alter; **se ~** vi to change (o.s.); **~ de** (remplacer: adresse, nom, voiture etc) to change one's; (échanger: place, train etc) to change; **~ d'avis** to change one's mind; **~ de vitesse** to change gear

**chanson** [ʃɑ̃sɔ̃] nf song

**chant** [ʃɑ̃] nm song; (art vocal) singing; (d'église) hymn

**chantage** [ʃɑ̃taʒ] nm blackmail; **faire du ~** to use blackmail

**chanter** [ʃɑ̃te] vt, vi to sing; **si cela lui chante** (fam) if he feels like it; **chanteur, -euse** nm/f singer

**chantier** [ʃɑ̃tje] nm (building) site; (sur une route) roadworks pl; **mettre en ~** to put in hand; **~ naval** shipyard

**chantilly** [ʃɑ̃tiji] nf voir **crème**

**chantonner** [ʃɑ̃tɔne] vi, vt to sing to oneself, hum

**chanvre** [ʃɑ̃vʀ] nm hemp

**chaparder** [ʃapaʀde] (fam) vt to pinch

**chapeau, x** [ʃapo] nm hat; **~!** well done!

**chapelet** [ʃaplɛ] nm (REL) rosary

**chapelle** [ʃapɛl] nf chapel

**chapelure** [ʃaplyʀ] nf (dried) bread-crumbs pl

**chapiteau, x** [ʃapito] nm (de cirque) marquee, big top

**chapitre** [ʃapitʀ] nm chapter

**chaque** [ʃak] dét each, every; (indéfini) every

**char** [ʃaʀ] nm (MIL): **~ (d'assaut)** tank; **~ à voile** sand yacht

**charabia** [ʃaʀabja] (péj) nm gibberish

**charade** [ʃaʀad] nf riddle; (mimée) charade

**charbon** [ʃaʀbɔ̃] nm coal; **~ de bois** charcoal

**charcuterie** [ʃaʀkytʀi] nf (magasin) pork butcher's shop and delicatessen; (produits) cooked pork meats pl; **charcutier, -ière** nm/f pork butcher

**chardon** [ʃaʀdɔ̃] nm thistle

**charge** [ʃaʀʒ] nf (fardeau) load, burden; (explosif, ÉLEC, MIL, JUR) charge; (rôle, mission) responsibility; **~s** nfpl (du loyer) service charges; **à la ~ de** (dépendant de) dependent upon; (aux frais de) chargeable to; **prendre en ~** to take charge of; (suj: véhicule) to take on; (dépenses) to take care of; **~s sociales** social security contributions

**chargé, e** [ʃaʀʒe] adj (emploi du temps, journée) full, heavy

**chargement** [ʃaʀʒəmɑ̃] nm (objets) load

**charger** [ʃaʀʒe] vt (voiture, fusil, caméra) to load; (batterie) to charge ♦ vi (MIL etc) to charge; **se ~ de** vi to see to; **~ qn de (faire) qch** to put sb in charge of (doing) sth

**chariot** [ʃaʀjo] nm trolley; (charrette) waggon

**charité** [ʃaʀite] nf charity

**charmant, e** [ʃaʀmɑ̃, ɑ̃t] adj charming

**charme** [ʃaʀm] nm charm; **charmer** vt to charm

**charnel, le** [ʃaʀnɛl] adj carnal

**charnière** [ʃaʀnjɛʀ] nf hinge; (fig) turning-point

**charnu, e** [ʃaʀny] adj fleshy

**charpente** [ʃaʀpɑ̃t] nf frame(work); **charpentier** nm carpenter

**charpie** [ʃaʀpi] nf: **en ~** (fig) in shreds ou ribbons

**charrette** [ʃaʀɛt] nf cart

**charrier** [ʃaʀje] vt (entraîner: fleuve) to carry (along); (transporter) to cart, carry

**charrue** [ʃaʀy] nf plough (BRIT), plow (US)

**charter** [ʃaʀtɛʀ] nm (vol) charter flight

**chasse** [ʃas] nf hunting; (au fusil) shooting; (poursuite) chase; (aussi: **~ d'eau**) flush; **~ gardée** private hunting grounds pl; **prendre en ~** to give chase to; **tirer la ~ (d'eau)** to flush the toilet, pull the chain; **~ à courre** hunting; **chasse-neige** nm inv snowplough (BRIT), snowplow (US); **chasser** vt to hunt; (*expulser*) to chase away *ou* out, drive away *ou* out; **chasseur, -euse** *nm/f* hunter ♦ *nm* (*avion*) fighter

**châssis** [ʃɑsi] *nm* (AUTO) chassis; (*cadre*) frame

**chat** [ʃa] *nm* cat

**châtaigne** [ʃatɛɲ] *nf* chestnut; **châtaignier** *nm* chestnut (tree)

**châtain** [ʃatɛ̃] *adj inv* (*cheveux*) chestnut (brown); (*personne*) chestnut-haired

**château, x** [ʃɑto] *nm* (*forteresse*) castle; (*résidence royale*) palace; (*manoir*) mansion; ~ **d'eau** water tower; ~ **fort** stronghold, fortified castle

**châtier** [ʃɑtje] *vt* to punish; **châtiment** *nm* punishment

**chaton** [ʃatɔ̃] *nm* (ZOOL) kitten

**chatouiller** [ʃatuje] *vt* to tickle; **chatouilleux, -euse** *adj* ticklish; (*fig*) touchy, over-sensitive

**chatoyer** [ʃatwaje] *vi* to shimmer

**châtrer** [ʃɑtre] *vt* (*mâle*) to castrate; (: *cheval*) to geld; (*femelle*) to spay

**chatte** [ʃat] *nf* (she-)cat

**chaud, e** [ʃo, ʃod] *adj* (*gén*) warm; (*très* ~) hot; **il fait** ~ it's warm; it's hot; **avoir** ~ to be warm; to be hot; **ça me tient** ~ it keeps me warm; **rester au** ~ to stay in the warm

**chaudière** [ʃodjɛr] *nf* boiler

**chaudron** [ʃodrɔ̃] *nm* cauldron

**chauffage** [ʃofaʒ] *nm* heating; ~ **central** central heating

**chauffard** [ʃofar] *nm* (*péj*) reckless driver

**chauffe-eau** [ʃofo] *nm inv* water-heater

**chauffer** [ʃofe] *vt* to heat ♦ *vi* to heat up, warm up; (*trop*: *moteur*) to overheat; **se** ~ *vi* (*au soleil*) to warm o.s up

**chauffeur** [ʃofœr] *nm* driver; (*privé*) chauffeur

**chaume** [ʃom] *nm* (*du toit*) thatch; **chaumière** *nf* (thatched) cottage

**chaussée** [ʃose] *nf* road(way)

**chausse-pied** [ʃospje] *nm* shoe-horn

**chausser** [ʃose] *vt* (*bottes, skis*) to put on; (*enfant*) to put shoes on; ~ **du 38/**

**42** to take size 38/42

**chaussette** [ʃosɛt] *nf* sock

**chausson** [ʃosɔ̃] *nm* slipper; (*de bébé*) bootee; ~ **(aux pommes)** (apple) turnover

**chaussure** [ʃosyr] *nf* shoe; ~**s à talon** high-heeled shoes; ~**s de marche** walking shoes/boots; ~**s de ski** ski boots

**chauve** [ʃov] *adj* bald; **chauve-souris** *nf* bat

**chauvin, e** [ʃovɛ̃, in] *adj* chauvinistic

**chaux** [ʃo] *nf* lime; **blanchi à la** ~ whitewashed

**chavirer** [ʃavire] *vi* to capsize

**chef** [ʃɛf] *nm* head, leader; (*de cuisine*) chef; ~ **d'accusation** charge; ~ **d'entreprise** company head; ~ **d'état** head of state; ~ **de famille** head of the family; ~ **de gare** station master; ~ **d'orchestre** conductor; ~ **de service** department head; **chef-d'œuvre** *nm* masterpiece; **chef-lieu** *nm* county town

**chemin** [ʃ(ə)mɛ̃] *nm* path; (*itinéraire, direction, trajet*) way; **en** ~ on the way; ~ **de fer** railway (BRIT), railroad (US); **par** ~ **de fer** by rail

**cheminée** [ʃ(ə)mine] *nf* chimney; (*à l'intérieur*) chimney piece, fireplace; (*de bateau*) funnel

**cheminement** [ʃ(ə)minmɑ̃] *nm* progress

**cheminot** [ʃ(ə)mino] *nm* railwayman

**chemise** [ʃ(ə)miz] *nf* shirt; (*dossier*) folder; ~ **de nuit** nightdress

**chemisier** [ʃ(ə)mizje, jɛr] *nm* blouse

**chenal, -aux** [ʃ(ə)nal, o] *nm* channel

**chêne** [ʃɛn] *nm* oak (tree); (*bois*) oak

**chenil** [ʃ(ə)nil] *nm* kennels *pl*

**chenille** [ʃ(ə)nij] *nf* (ZOOL) caterpillar

**chèque** [ʃɛk] *nm* cheque (BRIT), check (US); ~ **sans provision** bad cheque; ~ **de voyage** traveller's cheque; **chéquier** [ʃekje] *nm* cheque book

**cher, -ère** [ʃɛr] *adj* (*aimé*) dear; (*coûteux*) expensive, dear ♦ *adv*: **ça**

coûte ~ it's expensive

**chercher** [ʃɛrʃe] vt to look for; (gloire etc) to seek; **aller** ~ to go for, go and fetch; ~ **à faire** to try to do; **chercheur, -euse** nm/f researcher, research worker

**chère** [ʃɛr] adj voir **cher**

**chéri, e** [ʃeri] adj beloved, dear; **(mon)** ~ **darling**

**chérir** [ʃerir] vt to cherish

**cherté** [ʃɛrte] nf: **la** ~ **de la vie** the high cost of living

**chétif, -ive** [ʃetif, iv] adj (enfant) puny

**cheval, -aux** [ʃ(ə)val, o] nm horse; (AUTO): ~ **(vapeur)** horsepower no pl; **faire du** ~ to ride; **à** ~ on horseback; **à** ~ **sur** astride; (fig) overlapping; ~ **de course** racehorse

**chevalet** [ʃ(ə)valɛ] nm easel

**chevalier** [ʃ(ə)valje] nm knight

**chevalière** [ʃ(ə)valjɛr] nf signet ring

**chevalin, e** [ʃ(ə)valɛ̃, in] adj: **boucherie** ~ horse-meat butcher's

**chevaucher** [ʃ(ə)voʃe] vi (aussi: **se** ~) to overlap (each other) ♦ vt to be astride, straddle

**chevaux** [ʃəvo] nmpl de **cheval**

**chevelu, e** [ʃɛv(ə)ly] (péj) adj long-haired

**chevelure** [ʃɛv(ə)lyr] nf hair no pl

**chevet** [ʃ(ə)vɛ] nm: **au** ~ **de qn** at sb's bedside; **lampe de** ~ bedside lamp

**cheveu, x** [ʃ(ə)vø] nm hair; ~**x** nmpl (chevelure) hair; **avoir les** ~**x courts** to have short hair

**cheville** [ʃ(ə)vij] nf (ANAT) ankle; (de bois) peg; (pour une vis) plug

**chèvre** [ʃɛvr] nf (she-)goat

**chevreau, x** [ʃəvro] nm kid

**chèvrefeuille** [ʃɛvrəfœj] nm honeysuckle

**chevreuil** [ʃəvrœj] nm roe deer inv; (CULIN) venison

**chevronné, e** [ʃəvrɔne] adj seasoned

--- MOT-CLÉ ---

**chez** [ʃe] prép 1 (à la demeure de) at;

(: direction) to; **chez qn** at/to sb's house ou place; **chez moi** at home; (direction) home

2 (+profession) at; (: direction) to; **chez le boulanger/dentiste** at ou to the baker's/dentist's

3 (dans le caractère, l'œuvre de) in; **chez les renards/Racine** in foxes/Racine

**chez-soi** [ʃeswa] nm inv home

**chic** [ʃik] adj inv chic, smart; (fam: généreux) nice, decent ♦ nm stylishness; ~! (fam) great!; **avoir le** ~ **de** to have the knack of

**chicane** [ʃikan] nf (querelle) squabble; **chicaner** vi (ergoter): **chicaner sur** to quibble about

**chiche** [ʃiʃ] adj niggardly, mean ♦ excl (à un défi) you're on!

**chichis** [ʃiʃi] (fam) nmpl fuss sg

**chicorée** [ʃikɔre] nf (café) chicory; (salade) endive

**chien** [ʃjɛ̃] nm dog; ~ **de garde** guard dog; **chien-loup** nm wolfhound

**chiendent** [ʃjɛ̃dɑ̃] nm couch grass

**chienne** [ʃjɛn] nf dog, bitch

**chier** [ʃje] (fam!) vi to crap (!)

**chiffon** [ʃifɔ̃] nm (piece) of rag; **chiffonner** vt to crumple; (fam: tracasser) to concern

**chiffre** [ʃifr] nm (représentant un nombre) figure, numeral; (montant, total) total, sum; **en** ~**s ronds** in round figures; ~ **d'affaires** turnover; **chiffrer** vt (dépense) to put a figure to, assess; (message) to (en)code, cipher; **se chiffrer à** to add up to, amount to

**chignon** [ʃiɲɔ̃] nm chignon, bun

**Chili** [ʃili] nm: **le** ~ Chile; **chilien, ne** adj Chilean ♦ nm/f: **Chilien, ne**

**chimie** [ʃimi] nf chemistry; **chimique** adj chemical; **produits chimiques** chemicals

**chimpanzé** [ʃɛ̃pɑ̃ze] nm chimpanzee

**Chine** [ʃin] nf: **la** ~ China; **chinois, e** adj Chinese ♦ nm/f: **Chinois, e** Chinese

♦ *nm* (*LING*) Chinese

**chiot** [ʃjo] *nm* pup(py)

**chiper** [ʃipe] (*fam*) *vt* to pinch

**chipoter** [ʃipɔte] (*fam*) *vi* (*ergoter*) to quibble

**chips** [ʃips] *nfpl* crisps (*BRIT*), (potato) chips (*US*)

**chiquenaude** [ʃiknod] *nf* flick, flip

**chirurgical, e, -aux** [ʃiryʀʒikal, o] *adj* surgical

**chirurgie** [ʃiryʀʒi] *nf* surgery; ~ **esthétique** plastic surgery; **chirurgien, ne** *nm/f* surgeon

**chlore** [klɔʀ] *nm* chlorine

**choc** [ʃɔk] *nm* (*heurt*) impact, shock; (*collision*) crash; (*moral*) shock; (*affrontement*) clash

**chocolat** [ʃɔkɔla] *nm* chocolate; ~ **au lait** milk chocolate; ~ (**chaud**) hot chocolate

**chœur** [kœʀ] *nm* (*chorale*) choir; (*OPÉRA, THÉÂTRE*) chorus; **en** ~ in chorus

**choisir** [ʃwaziʀ] *vt* to choose, select

**choix** [ʃwa] *nm* choice, selection; **avoir le** ~ to have the choice; **premier** ~ (*COMM*) class one; **de** ~ choice, selected; **au** ~ as you wish

**chômage** [ʃomaʒ] *nm* unemployment; **mettre au** ~ to make redundant, put out of work; **être au** ~ to be unemployed *ou* out of work; **chômeur, -euse** *nm/f* unemployed person

**chope** [ʃɔp] *nf* tankard

**choper** [ʃɔpe] (*fam*) *vt* (*objet, maladie*) to catch

**choquer** [ʃɔke] *vt* (*offenser*) to shock; (*deuil*) to shake

**chorale** [kɔʀal] *nf* choir

**choriste** [kɔʀist] *nm/f* choir member; (*OPÉRA*) chorus member

**chose** [ʃoz] *nf* thing; **c'est peu de** ~ it's nothing (really)

**chou, x** [ʃu] *nm* cabbage; **mon petit** ~ (my) sweetheart; ~ **à la crème** choux bun; **~x de Bruxelles** Brussels sprouts; **choucroute** *nf*

sauerkraut

**chouette** [ʃwɛt] *nf* owl ♦ *adj* (*fam*) great, smashing

**chou-fleur** [ʃuflœʀ] *nm* cauliflower

**choyer** [ʃwaje] *vt* (*dorloter*) to cherish; (*: excessivement*) to pamper

**chrétien, ne** [kʀetjɛ̃, jɛn] *adj, nm/f* Christian

**Christ** [kʀist] *nm*: **le** ~ Christ; **christianisme** *nm* Christianity

**chrome** [kʀom] *nm* chromium; **chromé, e** *adj* chromium-plated

**chronique** [kʀɔnik] *adj* chronic ♦ *nf* (*de journal*) column, page; (*historique*) chronicle; (*RADIO, TV*): **la** ~ **sportive** the sports review

**chronologique** [kʀɔnɔlɔʒik] *adj* chronological

**chronomètre** [kʀɔnɔmɛtʀ] *nm* stopwatch; **chronométrer** *vt* to time

**chrysanthème** [kʀizɑ̃tɛm] *nm* chrysanthemum

**chuchotement** [ʃyʃɔtmɑ̃] *nm* whisper

**chuchoter** [ʃyʃɔte] *vt, vi* to whisper

**chut** [ʃyt] *excl* sh!

**chute** [ʃyt] *nf* fall; (*déchet*) scrap; **faire une** ~ (**de 10 m**) to fall (10 m); (**d'eau**) waterfall; **la** ~ **des cheveux** hair loss; ~ **libre** free fall; ~**s de pluie/neige** rain/snowfalls

**Chypre** [ʃipʀ] *nm/f* Cyprus

**-ci** [si] *adv voir* **par** ♦ *dét*: **ce garçon-~/-là** this/that boy; **ces femmes-~/-là** these/those women

**cible** [sibl] *nf* target

**ciboulette** [sibulɛt] *nf* (small) chive

**cicatrice** [sikatʀis] *nf* scar; **cicatriser** *vt* to heal

**ci-contre** [sikɔ̃tʀ] *adv* opposite

**ci-dessous** [sidəsu] *adv* below

**ci-dessus** [sidəsy] *adv* above

**cidre** [sidʀ] *nm* cider

**Cie** *abr* (= *compagnie*): Co.

**ciel** [sjɛl] *nm* sky; (*REL*) heaven; **cieux** *nmpl* (*REL*) heaven; **à** ~ **ouvert** open-air; (*mine*) open-cast

**cierge** [sjɛʀʒ] *nm* candle

**cieux** [sjø] nmpl de **ciel**

**cigale** [sigal] nf cicada

**cigare** [sigaʀ] nm cigar

**cigarette** [sigaʀɛt] nf cigarette

**ci-gît** [siʒi] adv «b here lies

**cigogne** [sigɔɲ] nf stork

**ci-inclus, e** [siɛ̃kly, yz] adj, adv enclosed

**ci-joint, e** [siʒwɛ̃, ɛt] adj, adv enclosed

**cil** [sil] nm (eye)lash

**cime** [sim] nf top; (montagne) peak

**ciment** [simɑ̃] nm cement

**cimetière** [simtjɛʀ] nm cemetery; (d'église) churchyard

**cinéaste** [sineast] nm/f film-maker

**cinéma** [sinema] nm cinema; **cinématographique** adj film cpd, cinema cpd

**cinglant, e** [sɛ̃glɑ̃, ɑ̃t] adj (remarque) biting

**cinglé, e** [sɛ̃gle] (fam) adj crazy

**cinq** [sɛ̃k] num five; **cinquantaine** nf: **une cinquantaine (de)** about fifty; **avoir la cinquantaine** (âge) to be around fifty; **cinquante** num fifty; **cinquantenaire** adj, nm/f fifty-year-old; **cinquième** num fifth

**cintre** [sɛ̃tʀ] nm coat-hanger

**cintré, e** [sɛ̃tʀe] adj (chemise) fitted

**cirage** [siʀaʒ] nm (shoe) polish

**circonflexe** [siʀkɔ̃flɛks] adj: **accent ~** circumflex accent

**circonscription** [siʀkɔ̃skʀipsjɔ̃] nf district; **~ électorale** (d'un député) constituency

**circonscrire** [siʀkɔ̃skʀiʀ] vt (sujet) to define, delimit; (incendie) to contain

**circonstance** [siʀkɔ̃stɑ̃s] nf circumstance; (occasion) occasion; **~s atténuantes** mitigating circumstances

**circuit** [siʀkɥi] nm (ÉLEC, TECH) circuit; (trajet) tour, (round) trip

**circulaire** [siʀkylɛʀ] adj, nf circular

**circulation** [siʀkylasjɔ̃] nf circulation; (AUTO): **la ~** (the) traffic

**circuler** [siʀkyle] vi (sang, devises) to circulate; (véhicules) to drive (along); (passants) to walk along; (train, bus) to

run; **faire ~** (nouvelle) to spread (about), circulate; (badauds) to move on

**cire** [siʀ] nf wax; **ciré** nm oilskin; **cirer** vt to wax, polish

**cirque** [siʀk] nm circus; (fig) chaos, bedlam; **quel ~!** what a carry-on!

**cisaille(s)** [sizaj] nf(pl) (gardening) shears pl

**ciseau, x** [sizo] nm: **~ (à bois)** chisel; **~x** nmpl (paire de ~x) (pair of) scissors

**ciseler** [siz(ə)le] vt to chisel, carve

**citadin, e** [sitadɛ̃, in] nm/f city dweller

**citation** [sitasjɔ̃] nf (d'auteur) quotation; (JUR) summons sg

**cité** [site] nf town; (plus grande) city; **~ universitaire** students' residences sg

**citer** [site] vt (un auteur) to quote (from); (nommer) to name; (JUR) to summon

**citerne** [sitɛʀn] nf tank

**citoyen, ne** [sitwajɛ̃, jɛn] nm/f citizen

**citron** [sitʀɔ̃] nm lemon; **~ vert** lime; **citronnade** nf still lemonade

**citrouille** [sitʀuj] nf pumpkin

**civet** [sivɛ] nm: **~ de lapin** rabbit stew

**civière** [sivjɛʀ] nf stretcher

**civil, e** [sivil] adj (mariage, poli) civil; (non militaire) civilian; **en ~** in civilian clothes; **dans la ~** in civilian life

**civilisation** [sivilizasjɔ̃] nf civilization

**clair, e** [klɛʀ] adj light; (pièce) light, bright; (eau, son, fig) clear ♦ adv: **voir ~** to see clearly; **tirer qch au ~** to clarify sth, clear up sth; **mettre au ~** (notes etc) to tidy up; **~ de lune** ♦ nm moonlight; **clairement** adv clearly

**clairière** [klɛʀjɛʀ] nf clearing

**clairon** [klɛʀɔ̃] nm bugle; **claironner** vt (fig) to trumpet, shout from the rooftops

**clairsemé, e** [klɛʀsəme] adj sparse

**clairvoyant, e** [klɛʀvwajɑ̃, ɑ̃t] adj perceptive, clear-sighted

**clandestin, e** [klɑ̃dɛstɛ̃, in] adj clandestine, secret; (mouvement) underground; (travailleur) illegal; **passager ~**

stowaway

**clapier** [klapje] *nm* (rabbit) hutch

**clapoter** [klapɔte] *vi* to lap

**claque** [klak] *nf* (*gifle*) slap; **claquer** *vi* (*porte*) to bang, slam; (*fam: mourir*) to snuff it ♦ *vt* (*porte*) to slam, bang; (*doigts*) to snap; (*fam: dépenser*) to blow; **il claquait des dents** his teeth were chattering; **être claqué** (*fam*) to be dead tired; **se claquer un muscle** to pull *ou* strain a muscle; **claquettes** *nfpl* tap-dancing *sg*; (*chaussures*) flip-flops

**clarinette** [klarinɛt] *nf* clarinet

**clarté** [klarte] *nf* (*luminosité*) brightness; (*d'un son, de l'eau*) clearness; (*d'une explication*) clarity

**classe** [klɑs] *nf* class; (SCOL: *local*) class(room); (: *leçon, élèves*) class; **aller en ~** to go to school; **classement** *nm* (*rang*: SCOL) place; (: SPORT) placing; (*liste*: SCOL) class list (in order of merit); (: SPORT) placings *pl*

**classer** [klɑse] *vt* (*idées, livres*) to classify; (*papiers*) to file; (*candidat, concurrent*) to grade; (JUR: *affaire*) to close; **se ~ premier/dernier** to come first/last; (SPORT) to finish first/last; **classeur** *nm* (*cahier*) file

**classique** [klasik] *adj* classical; (*sobre*: *coupe etc*) classic(al); (*habituel*) standard, classic

**clause** [kloz] *nf* clause

**clavecin** [klav(ə)sɛ̃] *nm* harpsichord

**clavicule** [klavikyl] *nf* collarbone

**clavier** [klavje] *nm* keyboard

**clé** [kle] *nf* key; (MUS) clef; (*de mécanicien*) spanner (BRIT), wrench (US); **prix ~s en main** (*d'une voiture*) on-the-road price; **~ anglaise** (monkey) wrench; **~ de contact** ignition key

**clef** [kle] *nf* = **clé**

**clément, e** [klemɑ̃, ɑ̃t] *adj* (*temps*) mild; (*indulgent*) lenient

**clerc** [klɛr] *nm*: **~ de notaire** solicitor's clerk

**clergé** [klɛrʒe] *nm* clergy

**cliché** [kliʃe] *nm* (*fig*) cliché; (*négatif*) negative; (*photo*) print

**client, e** [klijɑ̃, klijɑ̃t] *nm/f* (*acheteur*) customer, client; (*d'hôtel*) guest, patron; (*du docteur*) patient; (*de l'avocat*) client; **clientèle** *nf* (*du magasin*) customers *pl*, clientèle; (*du docteur, de l'avocat*) practice

**cligner** [kliɲe] *vi*: **~ des yeux** to blink (one's eyes); **~ de l'œil** to wink; **clignotant** *nm* (AUTO) indicator; **clignoter** *vi* (*étoiles etc*) to twinkle; (*lumière*) to flicker

**climat** [klima] *nm* climate

**climatisation** [klimatizasjɔ̃] *nf* air conditioning; **climatisé, e** *adj* air-conditioned

**clin d'œil** [klɛ̃dœj] *nm* wink; **en un ~** in a flash

**clinique** [klinik] *nf* private hospital

**clinquant, e** [klɛ̃kɑ̃, ɑ̃t] *adj* flashy

**clip** [klip] *nm* (*boucle d'oreille*) clip-on; (*vidéo*) ~ (pop) video

**cliqueter** [klik(ə)te] *vi* (*ferraille*) to jangle; (*clés*) to jingle

**clochard, e** [klɔʃar, ard] *nm/f* tramp

**cloche** [klɔʃ] *nf* (*d'église*) bell; (*fam*) clot; **cloche-pied**: **à cloche-pied** *adv* on one leg, hopping (along); **clocher** *nm* church tower; (*en pointe*) steeple ♦ *vi* (*fam*) to be *ou* go wrong; **de clocher** (*péj*) parochial

**cloison** [klwazɔ̃] *nf* partition (wall)

**cloître** [klwatr] *nm* cloister; **cloîtrer** *vt*: **se cloîtrer** to shut o.s. up *ou* away

**cloque** [klɔk] *nf* blister

**clore** [klɔr] *vt* to close; **clos, e** *adj voir* **maison**; **huis**

**clôture** [klotyr] *nf* closure; (*barrière*) enclosure; **clôturer** *vt* (*terrain*) to enclose; (*débats*) to close

**clou** [klu] *nm* nail; **~s** *nmpl* (*passage ~té*) pedestrian crossing; **pneus à ~s** studded tyres; **le ~ du spectacle** the highlight of the show; **~ de girofle** clove; **clouer** *vt* to nail down *ou* up; **clouer le bec à qn** (*fam*) to shut sb up

**clown** [klun] nm clown

**club** [klœb] nm club

**CMU** nf (= couverture maladie universelle) system of free health care for those on low incomes

**CNRS** sigle m (= Centre nationale de la recherche scientifique) ≃ SERC (BRIT), ≃ NSF (US)

**coaguler** [kɔagyle] vt, vi (aussi: **se ~**: sang) to coagulate

**coasser** [kɔase] vi to croak

**cobaye** [kɔbaj] nm guinea-pig

**coca** [kɔka] nm Coke ®

**cocaïne** [kɔkain] nf cocaine

**cocasse** [kɔkas] adj comical, funny

**coccinelle** [kɔksinɛl] nf ladybird (BRIT), ladybug (US)

**cocher** [kɔʃe] vt to tick off

**cochère** [kɔʃɛr] adj f: **porte ~** carriage entrance

**cochon, ne** [kɔʃɔ̃, ɔn] nm pig ♦ adj (fam) dirty, smutty; **~ d'Inde** guinea pig; **cochonnerie** [kɔʃɔnri] nf (saleté) filth; (marchandise) rubbish, trash

**cocktail** [kɔktɛl] nm cocktail; (réception) cocktail party

**coco** [kɔko] nm voir noix

**cocorico** [kɔkɔriko] excl, nm cock-a-doodle-do

**cocotier** [kɔkɔtje] nm coconut palm

**cocotte** [kɔkɔt] nf (en fonte) casserole; **~ (minute)** pressure cooker; **ma ~** (fam) sweetie (pie)

**cocu** [kɔky] (fam) nm cuckold

**code** [kɔd] nm code ♦ adj: **phares ~s** dipped lights; **se mettre en ~(s)** to dip one's (head)lights; **~ à barres** bar code; **~ civil** Common Law; **~ de la route** highway code; **~ pénal** penal code; **~ postal** (numéro) post (BRIT) ou zip (US) code

**cœur** [kœr] nm heart; (CARTES: couleur) hearts pl; (: carte) heart; **avoir bon ~** to be kind-hearted; **avoir mal au ~** to feel sick; **par ~** by heart; **de bon ~** willingly; **cela lui tient à ~** that's (very) close to his heart

**coffre** [kɔfr] nm (meuble) chest; (d'auto) boot (BRIT), trunk (US); **coffre(-fort)** nm safe; **coffret** nm casket

**cognac** [kɔɲak] nm brandy, cognac

**cogner** [kɔɲe] vi to knock; **se ~ la tête** to bang one's head

**cohérent, e** [kɔerɑ̃, ɑ̃t] adj coherent, consistent

**cohorte** [kɔɔrt] nf troop

**cohue** [kɔy] nf crowd

**coi, coite** [kwa, kwat] adj: **rester ~** to remain silent

**coiffe** [kwaf] nf headdress

**coiffé, e** [kwafe] adj: **bien/mal ~** with tidy/untidy hair

**coiffer** [kwafe] vt (fig: surmonter) to cover, top; **se ~** vi to do one's hair; **~ qn** to do sb's hair; **coiffeur, -euse** nm/f hairdresser; **coiffeuse** nf (table) dressing table; **coiffure** nf (cheveux) hairstyle, hairdo; (art): **la coiffure** hair-dressing

**coin** [kwɛ̃] nm corner; (pour ~cer) wedge; **l'épicerie du ~** the local grocer; **dans le ~** (aux alentours) in the area, around about; (habiter) locally; **je ne suis pas du ~** I'm not from here; **au ~ du feu** by the fireside; **regard ~** sideways glance

**coincé, e** [kwɛ̃se] adj stuck, jammed; (fig: inhibé) inhibited, hung up

**coincer** [kwɛ̃se] vt to jam; (fam: attraper) to pinch

**coïncidence** [kɔɛ̃sidɑ̃s] nf coincidence

**coïncider** [kɔɛ̃side] vi to coincide

**coing** [kwɛ̃] nm quince

**col** [kɔl] nm (de chemise) collar; (encolure, cou) neck; (de montagne) pass; **~ de l'utérus** cervix; **~ roulé** polo-neck

**colère** [kɔlɛr] nf anger; **une ~** a fit of anger; **(se mettre) en ~** (to get) angry; **coléreux, -euse** adj, **colérique** adj quick-tempered, irascible

**colifichet** [kɔlifiʃɛ] nm trinket

**colimaçon** [kɔlimasɔ̃] nm: **escalier en**

~ spiral staircase

**colin** [kɔlɛ̃] nm hake

**colique** [kɔlik] nf diarrhoea

**colis** [kɔli] nm parcel

**collaborateur, -trice** [kɔ(l)labɔʀatœʀ, tʀis] nm/f (aussi POL) collaborator; (d'une revue) contributor

**collaborer** [kɔ(l)labɔʀe] vi to collaborate; ~ à to collaborate on; (revue) to contribute to

**collant, e** [kɔlɑ̃, ɑ̃t] adj sticky; (robe etc) clinging, skintight; (péj) clinging ♦ nm (bas) tights pl; (de danseur) leotard

**collation** [kɔlasjɔ̃] nf light meal.

**colle** [kɔl] nf glue; (à papiers peints) (wallpaper) paste; (fam: devinette) teaser, riddle; (SCOL: fam) detention

**collecte** [kɔlɛkt] nf collection; **collectif, -ive** adj collective; (visite, billet) group cpd

**collection** [kɔlɛksjɔ̃] nf collection; (ÉDITION) series; **collectionner** vt to collect; **collectionneur, -euse** nf collector

**collectivité** [kɔlɛktivite] nf group; ~s locales (ADMIN) local authorities

**collège** [kɔlɛʒ] nm (école) (secondary) school; (assemblée) body; **collégien** nm schoolboy; **collégienne** nf schoolgirl

---

**collège**

The *collège* is a state secondary school for children aged between eleven and fifteen. Pupils follow a nationally prescribed curriculum consisting of a common core and various options. Before leaving the *collège*, pupils are assessed by examination and course work for their *brevet des collèges*.

---

**collègue** [kɔ(l)lɛg] nm/f colleague

**coller** [kɔle] vt (papier, timbre) to stick (à to); (affiche) to stick up; (enveloppe) to stick down; (morceaux) to stick ou glue

together; (fam: mettre, fourrer) to stick, shove; (SCOL: interro) to keep in ♦ vi (être collant) to be sticky; (adhérer) to stick; ~ à to stick to; **être collé à un examen** (fam) to fail an exam

**collet** [kɔlɛ] nm (piège) snare, noose; (cou): **prendre qn au** ~ to grab sb by the throat

**collier** [kɔlje] nm (bijou) necklace; (de chien, TECH) collar

**collimateur** [kɔlimatœʀ] nm: **avoir qn/qch dans le** ~ (fig) to have sb/sth in one's sights

**colline** [kɔlin] nf hill

**collision** [kɔlizjɔ̃] nf collision, crash; **entrer en** ~ **(avec)** to collide (with)

**colloque** [kɔ(l)lɔk] nm symposium

**collyre** [kɔliʀ] nm eye drops

**colmater** [kɔlmate] vt (fuite) to seal off; (brèche) to plug, fill in

**colombe** [kɔlɔ̃b] nf dove

**Colombie** [kɔlɔ̃bi] nf: **la** ~ Colombia

**colon** [kɔlɔ̃] nm settler

**colonel** [kɔlɔnɛl] nm colonel

**colonie** [kɔlɔni] nf colony; ~ **(de vacances)** holiday camp (for children)

**colonne** [kɔlɔn] nf column; **se mettre en** ~ **par deux** to get into twos; ~ **(vertébrale)** spine, spinal column

**colorant** [kɔlɔʀɑ̃, ɑ̃t] nm colouring

**colorer** [kɔlɔʀe] vt to colour

**colorier** [kɔlɔʀje] vt to colour (in)

**coloris** [kɔlɔʀi] nm colour, shade

**colporter** [kɔlpɔʀte] vt to hawk, peddle

**colza** [kɔlza] nm rape(seed)

**coma** [kɔma] nm coma; **être dans le** ~ to be in a coma

**combat** [kɔ̃ba] nm fight, fighting no pl; ~ **de boxe** boxing match; **combattant** nm: **ancien combattant** war veteran; **combattre** vt to fight; (épidémie, ignorance) to combat, fight against

**combien** [kɔ̃bjɛ̃] adv (quantité) how much; (nombre) how many; ~ **de** (quantité) how much; (nombre) how many; ~ **de temps** how long; ~ **ça coûte/pèse?** how much does it cost/

weigh?; **on est le ~ aujourd'hui?** (fam) what's the date today?

**combinaison** [kɔ̃binɛʒɔ̃] nf combination; (astuce) scheme; (de femme) slip; (de plongée) wetsuit; (bleu de travail) boiler suit (BRIT), coveralls pl (US)

**combine** [kɔ̃bin] nf trick; (péj) scheme, fiddle (BRIT)

**combiné** [kɔ̃bine] nm (aussi: ~ télé-phonique) receiver

**combiner** [kɔ̃bine] vt (grouper) to combine; (plan, horaire) to work out, devise

**comble** [kɔ̃bl] adj (salle) packed (full) ♦ nm (du bonheur, plaisir) height; ~ nmpl (CONSTR) attic sg, loft sg; **c'est le ~!** that beats everything!

**combler** [kɔ̃ble] vt (trou) to fill in; (besoin, lacune) to fill; (déficit) to make good; (satisfaire) to fulfil

**combustible** [kɔ̃bystibl] nm fuel

**comédie** [kɔmedi] nf comedy; (fig) playacting no pl; **faire la ~** (fam) to make a fuss; **~ musicale** musical; **co-médien, ne** nm/f actor(-tress)

___Comédie française___

___Founded in 1680 by Louis XIV, the Comédie française is the French national theatre. Subsidized by the state, the company performs mainly in the Palais Royal in Paris and stages mainly classical French plays.___

**comestible** [kɔmɛstibl] adj edible

**comique** [kɔmik] adj (drôle) comical; (THÉÂTRE) comic ♦ nm (artiste) comic, comedian

**comité** [kɔmite] nm committee; ~ **d'entreprise** works council

**commandant** [kɔmɑ̃dɑ̃] nm (gén) commander, commandant; (NAVIG, AVIAT) captain

**commande** [kɔmɑ̃d] nf (COMM) order; ~**s** nfpl (AVIAT etc) controls; **sur ~** to order; **commandement** nm command; (REL) commandment; **commander** vt (COMM) to order; (diriger, ordonner) to

command; **commander à qn de faire** to command ou order sb to do

**commando** [kɔmɑ̃do] nm commando (squad)

___MOT-CLÉ___

**comme** [kɔm] prép **1** (comparaison) like; **tout comme son père** just like his father; **fort comme un bœuf** as strong as an ox; **joli comme tout** ever so pretty

**2** (manière) like; **faites-le comme ça** do it like this, do it this way; **comme ci, comme ça** so-so, middling

**3** (en tant que) as a; **donner comme prix** to give as a prize; **travailler comme secrétaire** to work as a secretary

♦ conj **1** (ainsi que) as; **elle écrit comme elle parle** she writes as she talks; **comme si** as if

**2** (au moment où, alors que) as; **il est parti comme j'arrivais** he left as I arrived

**3** (parce que, puisque) as; **comme il était en retard, il ...** as he was late, he ...

♦ adv: **comme il est fort/c'est bon!** he's so strong/it's so good!

**commémorer** [kɔmemɔʀe] vt to commemorate

**commencement** [kɔmɑ̃smɑ̃] nm beginning, start

**commencer** [kɔmɑ̃se] vt, vi to begin, start; ~ **à** ou **de faire** to begin ou start doing

**comment** [kɔmɑ̃] adv how; ~? (que dites-vous?) pardon?

**commentaire** [kɔmɑ̃tɛʀ] nm (remarque) comment, remark; (exposé) commentary

**commenter** [kɔmɑ̃te] vt (jugement, événement) to comment (up)on; (RADIO, TV: match, manifestation) to cover

**commérages** [kɔmeʀaʒ] nmpl gossip sg

**commerçant, e** [kɔmɛrsã, ãt] nm/f shopkeeper, trader

**commerce** [kɔmɛrs] nm (activité) trade, commerce; (boutique) business; **~ électronique** e-commerce; **commercial, e, -aux** adj commercial, trading; (péj) commercial; **les commerciaux** the sales people; **commercialiser** vt to market

**commère** [kɔmɛr] nf gossip

**commettre** [kɔmɛtr] vt to commit

**commis** [kɔmi] nm (de magasin) (shop) assistant; (de banque) clerk

**commissaire** [kɔmisɛr] nm (de police) ≈ (police) superintendent; **commissaire-priseur** nm auctioneer; **commissariat** nm police station

**commission** [kɔmisjɔ̃] nf (comité, pourcentage) commission; (message) message; (course) errand; **~s** nfpl (achats) shopping sg

**commode** [kɔmɔd] adj (pratique) convenient, handy; (facile) easy; (personne): **pas ~** awkward (to deal with) ♦ nf chest of drawers; **commodité** nf convenience

**commotion** [kɔmosjɔ̃] nf: **~ (cérébrale)** concussion; **commotionné, e** adj shocked, shaken

**commun, e** [kɔmœ̃, yn] adj common; (pièce) communal, shared; (effort) joint; **ça sort du ~** it's out of the ordinary; **le ~ des mortels** the common run of people; **en ~** (faire) jointly; **mettre en ~** to pool, share; voir aussi **communs**

**communauté** [kɔmynote] nf community

**commune** [kɔmyn] nf (ADMIN) commune, ≈ district; (: urbaine) ≈ borough

**communicatif, -ive** [kɔmynikatif, iv] adj (rire) infectious; (personne) communicative

**communication** [kɔmynikasjɔ̃] nf communication; **~ (téléphonique)** (telephone) call

**communier** [kɔmynje] vi (REL) to receive communion

**communion** [kɔmynjɔ̃] nf communion

**communiquer** [kɔmynike] vt (nouvelle, dossier) to pass on, convey; (peur etc) to communicate ♦ vi to communicate; **se ~ à** (se propager) to spread to

**communisme** [kɔmynism] nm communism; **communiste** adj, nm/f communist

**communs** [kɔmœ̃] nmpl (bâtiments) outbuildings

**commutateur** [kɔmytatœr] nm (ÉLEC) (change-over) switch, commutator

**compact, e** [kɔpakt] adj (dense) dense; (appareil) compact

**compagne** [kɔpaɲ] nf companion

**compagnie** [kɔpaɲi] nf (firme, MIL) company; **tenir ~ à qn** to keep sb company; **fausser ~ à qn** to give sb the slip, slip ou sneak away from sb; **~ aérienne** airline (company)

**compagnon** [kɔpaɲɔ̃] nm companion

**comparable** [kɔparabl] adj: **~ (à)** comparable (to)

**comparaison** [kɔparɛzɔ̃] nf comparison

**comparaître** [kɔparɛtr] vi: **~ (devant)** to appear (before)

**comparer** [kɔpare] vt to compare; **~ qch/qn à ou et** (pour choisir) to compare sth/sb with ou and; (pour établir une similitude) to compare sth/sb to

**compartiment** [kɔpartimã] nm compartment

**comparution** [kɔparysjɔ̃] nf (JUR) appearance

**compas** [kɔpɑ] nm (GÉOM) (pair of) compasses pl; (NAVIG) compass

**compatible** [kɔpatibl] adj compatible

**compatir** [kɔpatir] vi to sympathize

**compatriote** [kɔpatriɔt] nm/f compatriot

**compensation** [kɔpãsasjɔ̃] nf compensation

**compenser** [kɔpãse] vt to compensate for, make up for

**compère** [kɔpɛr] nm accomplice

**compétence** [kɔpetãs] nf competence

**compétent, e** [kɔ̃petɑ̃, ɑ̃t] *adj (apte)* competent, capable

**compétition** [kɔ̃petisjɔ̃] *nf (gén)* competition; *(SPORT: épreuve)* event; **la ~ automobile** motor racing

**complainte** [kɔ̃plɛ̃t] *nf* lament

**complaire** [kɔ̃plɛr]: **se ~** *vi:* **se ~ dans** to take pleasure in

**complaisance** [kɔ̃plɛzɑ̃s] *nf* kindness; **pavillon de ~** flag of convenience

**complaisant, e** [kɔ̃plɛzɑ̃, ɑ̃t] *adj (aimable)* kind, obliging

**complément** [kɔ̃plemɑ̃] *nm* complement; *(reste)* remainder; **~ d'information** *(ADMIN)* supplementary *ou* further information; **complémentaire** *adj* complementary; *(additionnel)* supplementary

**complet, -ète** [kɔ̃plɛ, ɛt] *adj* complete; *(plein: hôtel etc)* full ♦ *nm (aussi: ~ veston)* suit; **pain ~** wholemeal bread; **complètement** *adv* completely; **compléter** *vt (porter à la quantité voulue)* to complete; *(augmenter: connaissances, études)* to complement, supplement; *(: garde-robe)* to add to; **se compléter** *(caractères)* to complement one another

**complexe** [kɔ̃plɛks] *adj, nm* complex; **complexé, e** *adj* mixed-up, hung-up

**complication** [kɔ̃plikasjɔ̃] *nf* complexity, intricacy; *(difficulté, ennui)* complication

**complice** [kɔ̃plis] *nm* accomplice; **complicité** *nf* complicity

**compliment** [kɔ̃plimɑ̃] *nm (louange)* compliment; **~s** *nmpl (félicitations)* congratulations

**compliqué, e** [kɔ̃plike] *adj* complicated, complex; *(personne)* complicated

**compliquer** [kɔ̃plike] *vt* to complicate; **se ~** to become complicated

**complot** [kɔ̃plo] *nm* plot

**comportement** [kɔ̃pɔrtəmɑ̃] *nm* behaviour

**comporter** [kɔ̃pɔrte] *vt (consister en)* to consist of, comprise; *(inclure)* to

have; **se ~** *vi* to behave

**composant** [kɔ̃pozɑ̃] *nm*, **composante** *nf* component

**composé** [kɔ̃poze] *nm* compound

**composer** [kɔ̃poze] *vt (musique, texte)* to compose; *(mélange, équipe)* to make up; *(numéro)* to dial; *(constituer)* to make up, form ♦ *vi (transiger)* to come to terms; **se ~ de** to be composed of, be made up of; **compositeur, -trice** *nm/f (MUS)* composer; **composition** *nf* composition; *(SCOL)* test

**composter** [kɔ̃pɔste] *vt (billet)* to punch

**compote** [kɔ̃pɔt] *nf* stewed fruit *no pl*; **~ de pommes** stewed apples

**compréhensible** [kɔ̃preɑ̃sibl] *adj* comprehensible; *(attitude)* understandable

**compréhensif, -ive** [kɔ̃preɑ̃sif, iv] *adj* understanding

**comprendre** [kɔ̃prɑ̃dr] *vt* to understand; *(se composer de)* to comprise, consist of

**compresse** [kɔ̃prɛs] *nf* compress

**compression** [kɔ̃presjɔ̃] *nf* compression; *(de personnes)* reduction

**comprimé** [kɔ̃prime] *nm* tablet

**comprimer** [kɔ̃prime] *vt* to compress; *(fig: crédit etc)* to reduce, cut down

**compris, e** [kɔ̃pri, iz] *pp de* **comprendre** ♦ *adj (inclus)* included; **~ entre** *(situé)* contained between; **l'électricité ~e/non ~e,** **y/non ~ l'électricité** including/excluding electricity; **100 F tout ~** 100 F all inclusive *ou* all-in

**compromettre** [kɔ̃prɔmɛtr] *vt* to compromise; **compromis** *nm* compromise

**comptabilité** [kɔ̃tabilite] *nf (activité)* accounting, accountancy; *(comptes)* accounts *pl*, books *pl*; *(service)* accounts office

**comptable** [kɔ̃tabl] *nm/f* accountant

**comptant** [kɔ̃tɑ̃] *adv:* **payer ~** to pay cash; **acheter ~** to buy for cash

**compte** [kɔ̃t] *nm (total, mon-*

*tant)* count, (right) number; *(bancaire, facture)* account; **~s** nmpl *(FINANCE)* accounts, books; *(fig)* explanation *sg;* **en fin de ~** all things considered; **s'en tirer à bon ~** to get off lightly; **pour le ~ de** on behalf of; **pour son propre ~** for one's own benefit; **tenir ~ de** to take account of sth; **travailler à son ~** to work for oneself; **rendre ~ (à qn) de qch** to give (sb) an account of sth; *voir aussi* **rendre**; **à rebours** countdown; **~ chèques postaux** Post Office account; **~ courant** current account; **~ rendu** account, report; *(de film, livre)* review; **compte-gouttes** nm inv dropper

**compter** [kɔ̃te] vt to count; *(facturer)* to charge for; *(avoir à son actif, comporter)* to have; *(prévoir)* to allow, reckon; *(penser, espérer)*: **~ réussir** to expect to succeed ♦ vi to count; *(être économe)* to economize; *(figurer)*: **~ parmi** to be ou rank among; **~ sur** to count (up)on; **~ avec qch/qn** to reckon with ou take account of sth/sb; **sans ~ que** besides which

**compteur** [kɔ̃tœʀ] nm meter; **~ de vitesse** speedometer

**comptine** [kɔ̃tin] nf nursery rhyme

**comptoir** [kɔ̃twaʀ] nm *(de magasin)* counter; *(bar)* bar

**compulser** [kɔ̃pylse] vt to consult

**comte, comtesse** [kɔ̃t] nm count; **comtesse** nf countess

**con, ne** [kɔ̃, kɔn] *(fam!)* adj damned ou bloody *(BRIT)* stupid (!)

**concéder** [kɔ̃sede] vt to grant; *(défaite, point)* to concede

**concentré** [kɔ̃sɑ̃tʀe] adj *(lait)* condensed ♦ nm: **~ de tomates** tomato purée

**concentrer** [kɔ̃sɑ̃tʀe] vt to concentrate; **se ~** vi to concentrate

**concept** [kɔ̃sɛpt] nm concept

**conception** [kɔ̃sɛpsjɔ̃] nf conception; *(d'une machine etc)* design; *(d'un problème, de la vie)* approach

**concerner** [kɔ̃sɛʀne] vt to concern; **en ce qui me concerne** as far as I am concerned

**concert** [kɔ̃sɛʀ] nm concert; **de ~** *(décider)* unanimously; **concerter: se concerter** vi to put their *etc* heads together

**concession** [kɔ̃sesjɔ̃] nf concession; **concessionnaire** nm/f agent, dealer

**concevoir** [kɔ̃s(ə)vwaʀ] vt *(idée, projet)* to conceive (of); *(comprendre)* to understand; *(enfant)* to conceive; **bien/mal conçu** well-/badly-designed

**concierge** [kɔ̃sjɛʀʒ] nm/f caretaker

**conciliabules** [kɔ̃siljabyl] nmpl (private) discussions, confabulations

**concilier** [kɔ̃silje] vt to reconcile; **se ~** vt to win over

**concis, e** [kɔ̃si, iz] adj concise

**concitoyen, ne** [kɔ̃sitwajɛ̃, jɛn] nm/f fellow citizen

**concluant, e** [kɔ̃klyɑ̃, ɑ̃t] adj conclusive

**conclure** [kɔ̃klyʀ] vt to conclude; **conclusion** nf conclusion

**conçois** *etc* [kɔ̃swa] vb voir **concevoir**

**concombre** [kɔ̃kɔ̃bʀ] nm cucumber

**concorder** [kɔ̃kɔʀde] vi to tally, agree

**concourir** [kɔ̃kuʀiʀ] vi *(SPORT)* to compete; **~ à** *(effet etc)* to work towards

**concours** [kɔ̃kuʀ] nm competition; *(SCOL)* competitive examination; *(assistance)* aid, help; **~ de circonstances** combination of circumstances; **~ hippique** horse show

**concret, -ète** [kɔ̃kʀɛ, ɛt] adj concrete

**concrétiser** [kɔ̃kʀetize] **se ~** vi to materialize

**conçu, e** [kɔ̃sy] pp de **concevoir**

**concubinage** [kɔ̃kybinaʒ] nm *(JUR)* cohabitation

**concurrence** [kɔ̃kyʀɑ̃s] nf competition; **faire ~ à** to be in competition with; **jusqu'à ~ de** up to

**concurrent, e** [kɔ̃kyʀɑ̃, ɑ̃t] nm/f *(SPORT, ÉCON etc)* competitor; *(SCOL)* candidate

**condamner** [kɔ̃dɑne] vt *(blâmer)* to

condemn; (JUR) to sentence; (porte, ouverture) to fill in, block up; **~ qn à 2 ans de prison** to sentence sb to 2 years' imprisonment

**condensation** [kɔ̃dɑ̃sasjɔ̃] nf condensation

**condenser** [kɔ̃dɑse] vt to condense; **se ~ vi** to condense

**condisciple** [kɔ̃disipl] nm/f fellow student

**condition** [kɔ̃disjɔ̃] nf condition; **~s** nfpl (tarif, prix) terms; (circonstances) conditions; **à ~ de** ou **que** provided that; **conditionnel, le** nm conditional (tense)

**conditionnement** [kɔ̃disjɔnmã] nm (emballage) packaging

**conditionner** [kɔ̃disjɔne] vt (déterminer) to determine; (COMM: produit) to package; **air conditionné** air conditioning

**condoléances** [kɔ̃dɔleɑs] nfpl condolences

**conducteur, -trice** [kɔ̃dyktœR, tRis] nm/f driver ♦ nm (ÉLEC etc) conductor

**conduire** [kɔ̃dɥiR] vt to drive; (délégation, troupeau) to lead; **se ~** vi to behave; **~ à** to lead to; **~ qn quelque part** to take sb somewhere; to drive sb somewhere

**conduite** [kɔ̃dɥit] nf (comportement) behaviour; (d'eau, de gaz) pipe; **sous la ~ de** led by; **~ à gauche** left-hand drive

**cône** [kon] nm cone

**confection** [kɔ̃feksjɔ̃] nf (fabrication) making; (COUTURE): **la ~** the clothing industry

**confectionner** [kɔ̃feksjɔne] vt to make

**conférence** [kɔ̃feRɑs] nf conference; (exposé) lecture; **~ de presse** press conference; **conférencier, -ière** nm/f speaker, lecturer

**confesser** [kɔ̃fese] vt to confess; **se ~** vi (REL) to go to confession; **confession** nf confession; (culte: catholique etc) denomination

**confiance** [kɔ̃fjɑ̃s] nf (en l'honnêteté de qn) confidence, trust; (en la valeur de qch) faith; **avoir ~ en** to have confidence ou faith in, trust; **faire ~ à qn** to trust sb; **mettre qn en ~** to win sb's trust; **~ en soi** self-confidence

**confiant, e** [kɔ̃fjɑ, jɑt] adj confident; trusting

**confidence** [kɔ̃fidɑs] nf confidence; **confidentiel, le** adj confidential

**confier** [kɔ̃fje] vt: **~ à qn** (objet, travail) to entrust to sb; (secret, pensée) to confide to sb; **se ~ à qn** to confide in sb

**confins** [kɔ̃fɛ] nmpl: **aux ~ de** on the borders of

**confirmation** [kɔ̃fiRmasjɔ̃] nf confirmation

**confirmer** [kɔ̃fiRme] vt to confirm

**confiserie** [kɔ̃fizRi] nf (magasin) confectioner's ou sweet shop; **~s** nfpl (bonbons) confectionery sg

**confisquer** [kɔ̃fiske] vt to confiscate

**confit, e** [kɔ̃fi, it] adj: **fruits ~s** crystallized fruits ♦ nm: **~ d'oie** conserve of goose

**confiture** [kɔ̃fityR] nf jam; **~ d'oranges** (orange) marmalade

**conflit** [kɔ̃fli] nm conflict

**confondre** [kɔ̃fɔdR] vt (jumeaux, faits) to confuse, mix up; (témoin, accusé) to confound; **~** vi (témoin) to merge; **se ~ en excuses** to apologize profusely; **confondu, e** adj (stupéfait) speechless, overcome

**conforme** [kɔ̃fɔRm] adj: **~ à** (loi, règle) in accordance with; **conformément** adv: **conformément à** in accordance with; **conformer** vt: **se conformer à** to conform to

**confort** [kɔ̃fɔR] nm comfort; **tout ~** (COMM) with all modern conveniences; **confortable** adj comfortable

**confrère** [kɔ̃fRɛR] nm colleague

**confronter** [kɔ̃fRɔte] vt to confront

**confus, e** [kɔ̃fy, yz] adj (vague) confused; (embarrassé) embarrassed; **confusion** nf (voir confus) confusion;

embarrassment; (*voir* **confondre**) confusion, mixing up

**congé** [kɔ̃ʒe] *nm* (*vacances*) holiday; **en ~** on holiday; **semaine de ~** week off; **prendre ~ de qn** to take one's leave of sb; **donner son ~ à** to give in one's notice to; **~ maladie** sick leave; **~ de maternité** maternity leave; **~s payés** paid holiday

**congédier** [kɔ̃ʒedje] *vt* to dismiss

**congélateur** [kɔ̃ʒelatœʀ] *nm* freezer

**congeler** [kɔ̃ʒ(ə)le] *vt* to freeze; **les produits congelés** frozen foods

**congestion** [kɔ̃ʒɛstjɔ̃] *nf* congestion; **~ cérébrale** stroke; **congestionner** (*rue*) to congest; (*visage*) to flush

**congrès** [kɔ̃gʀɛ] *nm* congress

**conifère** [kɔnifɛʀ] *nm* conifer

**conjecture** [kɔ̃ʒɛktyʀ] *nf* conjecture

**conjoint, e** [kɔ̃ʒwɛ̃, wɛ̃t] *adj* joint ♦ *nm/f* spouse

**conjonction** [kɔ̃ʒɔ̃ksjɔ̃] *nf* (LING) conjunction

**conjonctivite** [kɔ̃ʒɔ̃ktivit] *nf* conjunctivitis

**conjoncture** [kɔ̃ʒɔ̃ktyʀ] *nf* circumstances *pl*; **la ~ actuelle** the present (economic) situation

**conjugaison** [kɔ̃ʒyɡɛzɔ̃] *nf* (LING) conjugation

**conjuguer** [kɔ̃ʒyɡe] *vt* (LING) to conjugate; (*efforts etc*) to combine

**conjuration** [kɔ̃ʒyʀasjɔ̃] *nf* conspiracy

**conjurer** [kɔ̃ʒyʀe] *vt* (*sort, maladie*) to avert; (*implorer*) to beseech

**connaissance** [kɔnɛsɑ̃s] *nf* (*savoir*) knowledge *no pl*; (*personne connue*) acquaintance; **être sans ~** to be unconscious; **perdre/reprendre ~** to lose/regain consciousness; **à ma/sa ~** to (the best of) my/his knowledge; **faire la ~ de qn** to meet sb

**connaisseur** [kɔnɛsœʀ, øz] *nm* connoisseur

**connaître** [kɔnɛtʀ] *vt* to know; (*éprouver*) to experience; (*avoir: succès*) to have, enjoy; **~ de nom/vue** to know

by name/sight; **ils se sont connus à Genève** they (first) met in Geneva; **s'y ~ en qch** to know a lot about sth

**connecter** [kɔnekte] *vt* to connect

**connerie** [kɔnʀi] (*fam!*) *nf* stupid thing to do/say)

**connu, e** [kɔny] *adj* (*célèbre*) well-known

**conquérir** [kɔ̃keʀiʀ] *vt* to conquer; **conquête** *nf* conquest

**consacrer** [kɔ̃sakʀe] *vt* (*employer*) to devote, dedicate; (REL) to consecrate

**conscience** [kɔ̃sjɑ̃s] *nf* conscience; **avoir/prendre ~ de** to be/become aware of; **perdre ~** to lose consciousness; **avoir bonne/mauvaise ~** to have a clear/guilty conscience; **consciencieux, -euse** *adj* conscientious; **conscient, e** *adj* conscious

**conscrit** [kɔ̃skʀi] *nm* conscript

**consécutif, -ive** [kɔ̃sekytif, iv] *adj* consecutive; **~ à** following upon

**conseil** [kɔ̃sɛj] *nm* (*avis*) piece of advice; (*assemblée*) council; **des ~s** advice; **prendre ~ (auprès de qn)** to take advice (from sb); **~ d'administration** board (of directors); **le ~ des ministres** ≈ the Cabinet; **~ municipal** town council

**conseiller, -ère** [kɔ̃seje, ɛʀ] *nm/f* adviser ♦ *vt* (*personne*) to advise; (*méthode, action*) to recommend, advise; **~ à qn de** to advise sb to; **~ municipal** town councillor

**consentement** [kɔ̃sɑ̃tmɑ̃] *nm* consent

**consentir** [kɔ̃sɑ̃tiʀ] *vt* to agree, consent

**conséquence** [kɔ̃sekɑ̃s] *nf* consequence; **en ~** (*donc*) consequently; (*de façon appropriée*) accordingly; **conséquent, e** *adj* logical, rational; (*fam: important*) substantial; **par conséquent** consequently

**conservateur, -trice** [kɔ̃sɛʀvatœʀ, tʀis] *nm/f* (POL) conservative; (*de musée*) curator ♦ *nm* (*pour aliments*) preservative

**conservatoire** [kɔ̃sɛrvatwar] *nm* academy

**conserve** [kɔ̃sɛrv] *nf* (*gén pl*) canned *ou* tinned (*BRIT*) food; **en ~** canned, tinned (*BRIT*)

**conserver** [kɔ̃sɛrve] *vt* (*faculté*) to retain, keep; (*amis, livres*) to keep; (*préserver, aussi CULIN*) to preserve

**considérable** [kɔ̃siderabl] *adj* considerable, significant, extensive

**considération** [kɔ̃siderasjɔ̃] *nf* consideration; (*estime*) esteem

**considérer** [kɔ̃sidere] *vt* to consider; **~ qch comme** to regard sth as

**consigne** [kɔ̃siɲ] *nf* (*de gare*) left luggage (office) (*BRIT*), checkroom (*US*); (*ordre, instruction*) instructions *pl*; (*automatique*) left-luggage locker; **consigner** *vt* (*note, pensée*) to record; (*punir: élève*) to put in detention; (*COMM*) to put a deposit on

**consistant, e** [kɔ̃sistɑ̃, ɑ̃t] *adj* (*mélange*) thick; (*repas*) solid

**consister** [kɔ̃siste] *vi*: **~ en/à faire** to consist of/in doing

**consœur** [kɔ̃sœr] *nf* (lady) colleague

**console** [kɔ̃sɔl] *nf*: **~ de jeux** games console

**consoler** [kɔ̃sɔle] *vt* to console

**consolider** [kɔ̃sɔlide] *vt* to strengthen; (*fig*) to consolidate

**consommateur, -trice** [kɔ̃sɔmatœr, tris] *nm/f* (*ÉCON*) consumer; (*dans un café*) customer

**consommation** [kɔ̃sɔmasjɔ̃] *nf* (*boisson*) drink; (*ÉCON*) consumption

**consommer** [kɔ̃sɔme] *vt* (*suj: personne*) to eat *ou* drink, consume; (*: voiture, machine*) to use, consume; (*mariage*) to consummate ♦ *vi* (*dans un café*) to (have a) drink

**consonne** [kɔ̃sɔn] *nf* consonant

**conspirer** [kɔ̃spire] *vi* to conspire

**constamment** [kɔ̃stamɑ̃] *adv* constantly

**constant, e** [kɔ̃stɑ̃, ɑ̃t] *adj* constant; (*personne*) steadfast

**constat** [kɔ̃sta] *nm* (*de police, d'accident*) report; **~ à l'amiable** jointly-agreed statement for insurance purposes; **~ d'échec** acknowledgement of failure

**constatation** [kɔ̃statasjɔ̃] *nf* (*observation*) (observed) fact, observation

**constater** [kɔ̃state] *vt* (*remarquer*) to note; (*ADMIN, JUR: attester*) to certify

**consterner** [kɔ̃stɛrne] *vt* to dismay

**constipé, e** [kɔ̃stipe] *adj* constipated

**constitué, e** [kɔ̃stitye] *adj*: **~ de** made up of, composed of

**constituer** [kɔ̃stitye] *vt* (*équipe*) to set up; (*dossier, collection*) to put together; (*suj: éléments: composer*) to make up, constitute; (*représenter, être*) to constitute; **se ~ prisonnier** to give o.s. up; **constitution** [kɔ̃stitysjɔ̃] *nf* (*composition*) composition; (*santé, POL*) constitution

**constructeur** [kɔ̃stryktœr] *nm* manufacturer, builder

**constructif, -ive** [kɔ̃stryktif, iv] *adj* constructive

**construction** [kɔ̃stryksjɔ̃] *nf* construction, building

**construire** [kɔ̃stryir] *vt* to build, construct

**consul** [kɔ̃syl] *nm* consul; **consulat** *nm* consulate

**consultant, e** [kɔ̃syltɑ̃, ɑ̃t] *adj, nm* consultant

**consultation** [kɔ̃syltasjɔ̃] *nf* consultation; **~s** *nfpl* (*POL*) talks; **heures de ~** (*MÉD*) surgery (*BRIT*) *ou* office (*US*) hours

**consulter** [kɔ̃sylte] *vt* to consult ♦ *vi* (*médecin*) to hold surgery (*BRIT*), be in (the office) (*US*); **se ~** *vi* to confer

**consumer** [kɔ̃syme] *vt* to consume; **se ~** *vi* to burn

**contact** [kɔ̃takt] *nm* contact; **au ~ de** (*air, peau*) on contact with; (*gens*) through contact with; **mettre/couper le ~** (*AUTO*) to switch on/off the ignition; **entrer en** *ou* **prendre ~ avec** to get in touch *ou* contact with; **contacter** *vt* to contact, get in touch with

**contagieux, -euse** [kɔ̃taʒjø, jøz] *adj* infectious; (*par le contact*) contagious

**contaminer** [kɔ̃tamine] *vt* to contaminate

**conte** [kɔ̃t] *nm* tale; ~ **de fées** fairy tale

**contempler** [kɔ̃tɑ̃ple] *vt* to contemplate, gaze at

**contemporain, e** [kɔ̃tɑ̃pɔʀɛ̃, ɛn] *adj, nm/f* contemporary

**contenance** [kɔ̃t(ə)nɑ̃s] *nf* (*d'un récipient*) capacity; (*attitude*) bearing, attitude; **perdre** ~ to lose one's composure

**conteneur** [kɔ̃t(ə)nœʀ] *nm* container

**contenir** [kɔ̃t(ə)niʀ] *vt* to contain; (*avoir une capacité de*) to hold; **se** ~ *vi* to contain o.s.

**content, e** [kɔ̃tɑ̃, ɑ̃t] *adj* pleased, glad; ~ **de** pleased with; **contenter** *vt* to satisfy, please; **se contenter de** to content o.s. with

**contentieux** [kɔ̃tɑ̃sjø] *nm* (COMM) litigation; (*service*) litigation department

**contenu** [kɔ̃t(ə)ny] *nm* (*d'un récipient*) contents *pl*; (*d'un texte*) content

**conter** [kɔ̃te] *vt* to recount, relate

**contestable** [kɔ̃tɛstabl] *adj* questionable

**contestation** [kɔ̃tɛstasjɔ̃] *nf* (POL) protest

**conteste** [kɔ̃tɛst]: **sans** ~ *adv* unquestionably, indisputably; **contester** *vt* to question ♦ *vi* (POL, *gén*) to rebel (against established authority)

**contexte** [kɔ̃tɛkst] *nm* context

**contigu, ë** [kɔ̃tigy] *adj*: ~ **(à)** adjacent (to)

**continent** [kɔ̃tinɑ̃] *nm* continent

**continu, e** [kɔ̃tiny] *adj* continuous; **faire la journée ~e** to work without taking a full lunch break; (*courant*) ~ direct current, DC

**continuel, le** [kɔ̃tinɥɛl] *adj* (*qui se répète*) constant, continual; (*continu*) continuous

**continuer** [kɔ̃tinɥe] *vt* (*travail, voyage etc*) to continue (with), carry on with;

go on (with); (*prolonger: alignement, rue*) to continue ♦ *vi* (*vie, bruit*) to continue, go on; ~ **à** *ou* **de faire** to go on *ou* continue doing

**contorsionner** [kɔ̃tɔʀsjɔne]: **se** ~ *vi* to contort o.s., writhe about

**contour** [kɔ̃tuʀ] *nm* outline, contour; **contourner** *vt* to go round; (*difficulté*) to get round

**contraceptif, -ive** [kɔ̃tʀasɛptif, iv] *adj, nm* contraceptive; **contraception** *nf* contraception

**contracté, e** [kɔ̃tʀakte] *adj* tense

**contracter** [kɔ̃tʀakte] *vt* (*muscle etc*) to tense, contract; (*maladie, dette*) to contract; (*assurance*) to take out; **se** ~ *vi* (*muscles*) to contract

**contractuel, le** [kɔ̃tʀaktɥɛl] *nm/f* (*agent*) traffic warden

**contradiction** [kɔ̃tʀadiksjɔ̃] *nf* contradiction; **contradictoire** *adj* contradictory, conflicting

**contraignant, e** [kɔ̃tʀɛɲɑ̃, ɑ̃t] *adj* restricting

**contraindre** [kɔ̃tʀɛ̃dʀ] *vt*: ~ **qn à faire** to compel sb to do; **contrainte** *nf* constraint

**contraire** [kɔ̃tʀɛʀ] *adj, nm* opposite; ~ **à** contrary to; **au** ~ on the contrary

**contrarier** [kɔ̃tʀaʀje] *vt* (*personne: irriter*) to annoy; (*fig: projets*) to thwart, frustrate; **contrariété** *nf* annoyance

**contraste** [kɔ̃tʀast] *nm* contrast

**contrat** [kɔ̃tʀa] *nm* contract; ~ **de travail** employment contract

**contravention** [kɔ̃tʀavɑ̃sjɔ̃] *nf* parking ticket

**contre** [kɔ̃tʀ] *prép* against; (*en échange*) (in exchange) for; **par** ~ on the other hand

**contrebande** [kɔ̃tʀəbɑ̃d] *nf* (*trafic*) contraband, smuggling; (*marchandise*) smuggled goods *pl*; **faire la** ~ **de** to smuggle; **contrebandier, -ière** *nm/f* smuggler

**contrebas** [kɔ̃tʀəbɑ]: **en** ~ *adv* (down) below

**contrebasse** [kɔ̃trəbas] nf (double) bass

**contre...: contrecarrer** vt to thwart; **contrecœur: à contrecœur** adv (be)grudgingly, reluctantly; **contrecoup** nm repercussions pl; **contredire** vt (personne) to contradict; (faits) to refute

**contrée** [kɔ̃tre] nf (région) region; (pays) land

**contrefaçon** [kɔ̃trəfasɔ̃] nf forgery

**contrefaire** [kɔ̃trəfɛr] vt (document, signature) to forge, counterfeit

**contre...: contre-indication** (pl **contre-indications**) nf (MÉD) contra-indication; **"contre-indication en cas d'eczéma"** "should not be used by people with eczema"; **contre-indiqué, e** adj (MÉD) contraindicated; (déconseillé) unadvisable, ill-advised; **contre-jour: à contre-jour** adv against the sunlight

**contremaître** [kɔ̃trəmɛtr] nm foreman

**contrepartie** [kɔ̃trəparti] nf: **en ~** in return

**contre-pied** [kɔ̃trəpje] nm: **prendre le ~~ de** (opinion) to take the opposing view of; (action) to take the opposite course to

**contre-plaqué** [kɔ̃trəplake] nm plywood

**contrepoids** [kɔ̃trəpwa] nm counterweight, counterbalance

**contrepoison** [kɔ̃trəpwazɔ̃] nm antidote

**contrer** [kɔ̃tre] vt to counter

**contresens** [kɔ̃trəsɑ̃s] nm (erreur) misinterpretation; (de traduction) mistranslation; **à ~** the wrong way

**contretemps** [kɔ̃trətɑ̃] nm hitch; **à ~** (fig) at an inopportune moment

**contrevenir** [kɔ̃trəv(ə)nir]: **~ à** vt to contravene

**contribuable** [kɔ̃tribɥabl] nm/f taxpayer

**contribuer** [kɔ̃tribɥe]: **~ à** vt to contri-

bute towards; **contribution** nf contribution; **contributions directes/indirectes** direct/indirect taxation; **mettre à contribution** to call upon

**contrôle** [kɔ̃trol] nm checking no pl, check; (des prix) monitoring, control; (test) test, examination; (de véhicule) to lose control of; **~ continu** (SCOL) continuous assessment; **~ d'identité** identity check

**contrôler** [kɔ̃trole] vt (vérifier) to check; (surveiller: opérations) to supervise; (: prix) to monitor, control; (maîtriser: prix, COMM: firme) to control; **~ vi** to control o.s.; **contrôleur, -euse** nm/f (de train) (ticket) inspector; (de bus) (bus) conductor(-tress)

**contrordre** [kɔ̃trɔrdr] nm: **sauf ~** unless otherwise directed

**controversé, e** [kɔ̃trɔvɛrse] adj (personnage, question) controversial

**contusion** [kɔ̃tyzjɔ̃] nf bruise, contusion

**convaincre** [kɔ̃vɛ̃kr] vt: **~ qn (de qch)** to convince sb (of sth); **~ qn (de faire)** to persuade sb (to do)

**convalescence** [kɔ̃valesɑ̃s] nf convalescence

**convenable** [kɔ̃vnabl] adj suitable; (assez bon, respectable) decent

**convenance** [kɔ̃vnɑ̃s] nf: **à ma/votre ~** to my/your liking; **~s** nfpl (normes sociales) proprieties

**convenir** [kɔ̃vnir] vi to be suitable; **~ à** to suit; **~ de** (bien-fondé de qch) to admit (to), acknowledge; (date, somme etc) to agree upon; **~ que** (admettre) to admit that; **~ de faire** to agree to do

**convention** [kɔ̃vɑ̃sjɔ̃] nf convention; **~s** nfpl (convenances) convention sg; **~ collective** (ÉCON) collective agreement; **conventionnel, e** adj (ADMIN) applying charges laid down by the state

**convenu, e** [kɔ̃vny] pp de **convenir** ♦ adj agreed

**conversation** [kɔ̃vɛrsasjɔ̃] nf conversation

**convertir** [kɔ̃vɛʀtiʀ] vt: ~ qn (à) to convert sb (to); se ~ (à) to be converted (to); ~ qch en to convert sth into

**conviction** [kɔ̃viksjɔ̃] nf conviction

**convienne** etc [kɔ̃vjɛn] vb voir **convenir**

**convier** [kɔ̃vje] vt: ~ qn à (dîner etc) to (cordially) invite sb to

**convive** [kɔ̃viv] nm/f guest (at table)

**convivial, e, -aux** [kɔ̃vivjal, jo] adj (INFORM) user-friendly

**convocation** [kɔ̃vɔkasjɔ̃] nf (document) notification to attend; (: JUR) summons sg

**convoi** [kɔ̃vwa] nm convoy; (train) train

**convoiter** [kɔ̃vwate] vt to covet

**convoquer** [kɔ̃vɔke] vt (assemblée) to convene; (subordonné) to summon; (candidat) to ask to attend

**convoyeur** [kɔ̃vwajœʀ] nm: ~ de fonds security guard

**coopération** [kɔɔpeʀasjɔ̃] nf cooperation; (ADMIN): la C~ ≈ Voluntary Service Overseas (BRIT), ≈ Peace Corps (US)

**coopérer** [kɔɔpeʀe] vi: ~ (à) to cooperate (in)

**coordonnées** [kɔɔʀdɔne] nfpl: donnez-moi vos ~ (fam) can I have your details please?

**coordonner** [kɔɔʀdɔne] vt to coordinate

**copain** [kɔpɛ̃] (fam) nm mate, pal; (petit ami) boyfriend

**copeau, x** [kɔpo] nm shaving

**copie** [kɔpi] nf copy; (SCOL) script, paper; **copier** vt, vi to copy; **copier sur** to copy from; **copieur** nm (photo)copier

**copieux, -euse** [kɔpjø, jøz] adj copious

**copine** [kɔpin] (fam) nf mate, pal; (petite amie) girlfriend

**copropriété** [kɔpʀɔpʀijete] nf coownership, joint ownership

**coq** [kɔk] nm cock, rooster; **coq-à-**

l'âne nm inv abrupt change of subject

**coque** [kɔk] nf (de noix, mollusque) shell; (de bateau) hull; à la ~ (CULIN) (soft-)boiled

**coquelicot** [kɔkliko] nm poppy

**coqueluche** [kɔklyʃ] nf whooping-cough

**coquet, te** [kɔkɛ, ɛt] adj appearance-conscious; (logement) smart, charming

**coquetier** [kɔk(ə)tje] nm egg-cup

**coquillage** [kɔkijaʒ] nm (mollusque) shellfish inv; (coquille) shell

**coquille** [kɔkij] nf shell; (TYPO) misprint; ~ St Jacques scallop

**coquin, e** [kɔkɛ̃, in] adj mischievous, roguish; (polisson) naughty

**cor** [kɔʀ] nm (MUS) horn; (MÉD): ~ (au pied) corn

**corail, -aux** [kɔʀaj, o] nm coral no pl

**Coran** [kɔʀɑ̃] nm: le ~ the Koran

**corbeau, x** [kɔʀbo] nm crow

**corbeille** [kɔʀbɛj] nf basket; ~ à papier waste paper basket ou bin

**corbillard** [kɔʀbijaʀ] nm hearse

**corde** [kɔʀd] nf rope; (de violon, raquette) string; usé jusqu'à la ~ threadbare; ~ à linge washing ou clothes line; ~ à sauter skipping rope; ~s vocales vocal cords

**cordée** [kɔʀde] nf (d'alpinistes) rope, roped party

**cordialement** [kɔʀdjalmɑ̃] adv (formule épistolaire) (kind) regards

**cordon** [kɔʀdɔ̃] nm cord, string; ~ ombilical umbilical cord; ~ sanitaire/de police sanitary/police cordon

**cordonnerie** [kɔʀdɔnʀi] nf shoe repairer's (shop); **cordonnier** nm shoe repairer

**Corée** [kɔʀe] nf: la ~ du Sud/du Nord South/North Korea

**coriace** [kɔʀjas] adj tough

**corne** [kɔʀn] nf horn; (de cerf) antler

**cornée** [kɔʀne] nf cornea

**corneille** [kɔʀnɛj] nf crow

**cornemuse** [kɔʀnəmyz] nf bagpipes pl

**cornet** [kɔʀnɛ] nm (paper) cone; (de

*glace)* cornet, cone

**corniche** [kɔʀniʃ] *nf (route)* coast road

**cornichon** [kɔʀniʃɔ̃] *nm* gherkin

**Cornouailles** [kɔʀnwaj] *nf* Cornwall

**corporation** [kɔʀpɔʀasjɔ̃] *nf* corporate body

**corporel, le** [kɔʀpɔʀel] *adj* bodily; *(punition)* corporal

**corps** [kɔʀ] *nm* body; **à ~** headlong; **prendre ~** to take shape; **~ à ~** *adv* hand-to-hand ♦ *nm* clinch; **le ~ électoral** the electorate; **le ~ enseignant** the teaching profession

**corpulent, e** [kɔʀpylɑ̃, ɑ̃t] *adj* stout

**correct, e** [kɔʀekt] *adj* correct; *(fam: acceptable)* salaire, hôtel) reasonable, decent; **correcteur, -trice** *nm/f (SCOL)* examiner; **correction** [kɔʀeksjɔ̃] *nf (voir correct)* correctness; *(voir corriger)* correction; *(coups)* thrashing; **correctionnel, le** *adj (JUR)*: **tribunal correctionnel** ≈ criminal court

**correspondance** [kɔʀespɔ̃dɑ̃s] *nf* correspondence; *(de train, d'avion)* connection; **cours par ~** correspondence course; **vente par ~** mail-order business

**correspondant, e** [kɔʀespɔ̃dɑ̃, ɑ̃t] *nm/f* correspondent; *(TÉL)* person phoning *(ou being phoned)*

**correspondre** [kɔʀespɔ̃dʀ] *vi* to correspond, tally; **~ à** to correspond to; **~ avec qn** to correspond with sb

**corrida** [kɔʀida] *nf* bullfight

**corridor** [kɔʀidɔʀ] *nm* corridor

**corrigé** [kɔʀiʒe] *nm (SCOL: d'exercice)* correct version

**corriger** [kɔʀiʒe] *vt (devoir)* to correct; *(punir)* to thrash; **~ qn de** *(défaut)* to cure sb of

**corroborer** [kɔʀɔbɔʀe] *vt* to corroborate

**corrompre** [kɔʀɔ̃pʀ] *vt* to corrupt; *(acheter: témoin etc)* to bribe

**corruption** [kɔʀypsjɔ̃] *nf* corruption; *(de témoins)* bribery

**corsage** [kɔʀsaʒ] *nm* bodice; *(chemisier)* blouse

**corsaire** [kɔʀsɛʀ] *nm* pirate

**corse** [kɔʀs] *adj, nm/f* Corsican ♦ *nf*: **la C~** Corsica

**corsé, e** [kɔʀse] *adj (café)* full-flavoured; *(sauce)* spicy; *(problème)* tough

**corset** [kɔʀsɛ] *nm* corset

**cortège** [kɔʀtɛʒ] *nm* procession

**cortisone** [kɔʀtizɔn] *nf* cortisone

**corvée** [kɔʀve] *nf* chore, drudgery *no pl*

**cosmétique** [kɔsmetik] *nm* beauty care product

**cosmopolite** [kɔsmɔpɔlit] *adj* cosmopolitan

**cossu, e** [kɔsy] *adj (maison)* opulent(-looking)

**costaud, e** [kɔsto, od] *(fam) adj* strong, sturdy

**costume** [kɔstym] *nm (d'homme)* suit; *(de théâtre)* costume; **costumé, e** *adj* dressed up; **bal costumé** fancy dress ball

**cote** [kɔt] *nf (en Bourse)* quotation; **~ d'alerte** danger *ou* flood level

**côte** [kot] *nf (rivage)* coast(line); *(pente)* hill; *(ANAT)* rib; *(d'un tricot, tissu)* rib, ribbing *no pl*; **~ à ~** side by side; **la C~ d'Azur** the (French) Riviera

**coté, e** [kɔte] *adj*: **être bien ~** to be highly rated

**côté** [kote] *nm (gén)* side; *(direction)* way, direction; **de chaque ~ (de)** on each side (of); **de tous ~s** from all directions; **de quel ~ il est parti?** which way did he go?; **de ce/de l'autre ~** this/the other way; **du ~ de** *(provenance)* from; *(direction)* towards; **de ~** *(regarder)* sideways; *(mettre)* aside; **mettre de l'argent de ~** to save some money; **à ~** *(right)* nearby; *(voisins)* next door; **à ~ de** beside, next to; *(en comparaison)* compared to; **être aux ~s de** to be by the side of

**coteau, x** [kɔto] *nm* hill

**côtelette** [kotlɛt] *nf* chop

**côtier, -ière** [kotje, jɛʀ] *adj* coastal

**cotisation** [kɔtizasjɔ̃] nf subscription, dues pl; (pour une pension) contributions pl

**cotiser** [kɔtize] vi: ~ (à) to pay contributions (to); **se** ~ vi to club together

**coton** [kɔtɔ̃] nm cotton; ~ **hydrophile** cotton wool (BRIT), absorbent cotton (US); **Coton-Tige** ® nm cotton bud

**côtoyer** [kotwaje] vt (fréquenter) to rub shoulders with

**cou** [ku] nm neck

**couchant** [kuʃɑ̃] adj: **soleil** ~ setting sun

**couche** [kuʃ] nf layer; (de peinture, vernis) coat; (de bébé) nappy (BRIT), diaper (US); ~ **d'ozone** ozone layer; ~**s sociales** social levels or strata

**couché, e** [kuʃe] adj lying down; (au lit) in bed

**coucher** [kuʃe] nm (du soleil) setting ♦ vt (personne) to put to bed; (: loger) to put up; (objet) to lay on its side ♦ vi to sleep; **se** ~ vi (pour dormir) to go to bed; (pour se reposer) to lie down; (soleil) to set; ~ **de soleil** sunset

**couchette** [kuʃɛt] nf couchette; (pour voyageur, sur bateau) berth

**coucou** [kuku] nm cuckoo

**coude** [kud] nm (ANAT) elbow; (de tuyau, de la route) bend; ~ **à** ~ shoulder to shoulder, side by side

**coudre** [kudʀ] vt (bouton) to sew on ♦ vi to sew

**couenne** [kwan] nf (de lard) rind

**couette** [kwɛt] nf duvet, quilt; ~**s** nfpl (cheveux) bunches

**couffin** [kufɛ̃] nm Moses basket

**couler** [kule] vi to flow, run; (fuir: stylo, récipient) to leak; (nez) to run; (sombrer: bateau) to sink ♦ vt (cloche, sculpture) to cast; (bateau) to sink; (faire échouer: personne) to bring down

**couleur** [kulœʀ] nf colour (BRIT), color (US); (CARTES) suit; **film/télévision en** ~**s** colo(u)r film/television

**couleuvre** [kulœvʀ] nf grass snake

**coulisse** [kulis] nf: ~**s** nfpl (THÉÂTRE) wings; (fig): **dans les** ~**s** behind the scenes; **coulisser** vi to slide, run

**couloir** [kulwaʀ] nm corridor, passage; (de bus) gangway; ~ **aérien/de navigation** air/shipping lane

**coup** [ku] nm (heurt, choc) knock; (affectif) blow, shock; (agressif) blow; (avec arme à feu) shot; (de l'horloge) stroke; (tennis, golf) stroke; (boxe) blow; (fam: fois) time; ~ **de coude** nudge (with the elbow); ~ **de tonnerre** clap of thunder; ~ **de sonnette** ring of the bell; **donner un** ~ **de balai** to give the floor a sweep; **boire un** ~ (fam) to have a drink; **être dans le** ~ (fam) to be in on it; **du** ~ ... as a result; **d'un seul** ~ (subitement) suddenly; (à la fois) at one go; **du premier** ~ first time; **du même** ~ at the same time; **à tous les** ~**s** (fam) every time; **tenir le** ~ to hold out; **après** ~ afterwards; **à** ~ **sûr** definitely, without fail; **sur** ~ in quick succession; **sur le** ~ outright; **sous le** ~ **de** (surprise etc) under the influence of; **en** ~ **de vent** in a tearing hurry; ~ **de chance** stroke of luck; ~ **de couteau** stab (of a knife); ~ **d'État** coup; ~ **de feu** shot; ~ **de fil** (fam) phone call; ~ **de frein** (sharp) braking no pl; ~ **de main: donner un** ~ **de main à qn** to give sb a (helping) hand; ~ **d'œil** glance; ~ **de pied** kick; ~ **de poing** punch; ~ **de soleil** sunburn no pl; ~ **de téléphone** phone call; ~ **de tête** (fig) (sudden) impulse

**coupable** [kupabl] adj guilty ♦ nm/f (gén) culprit; (JUR) guilty party

**coupe** [kup] nf (verre) goblet; (à fruits) dish; (SPORT) cup; (de cheveux, de vêtement) cut; (graphique, plan) (cross) section

**coupe-papier** [kuppapje] nm inv paper knife

**couper** [kupe] vt to cut; (retrancher) to cut (out); (route, courant) to cut off; (appétit) to take away; (vin à table) to dilute ♦ vi to cut; (prendre un raccourci) to take a short-cut; **se ~** vi (se blesser) to cut o.s.; **~ la parole à qn** to cut sb short

**couple** [kupl] nm couple

**couplet** [kuple] nm verse

**coupole** [kupɔl] nf dome

**coupon** [kupɔ̃] nm (ticket) coupon; (reste de tissu) remnant; **coupon-réponse** nm reply coupon

**coupure** [kupyr] nf cut; (billet de banque) note; (de journal) cutting; **~ de courant** power cut

**cour** [kur] nf (de ferme, jardin) (court)yard; (d'immeuble) back yard; (JUR, royale) court; **faire la ~ à qn** to court sb; **~ d'assises** court of assizes; **~ de récréation** playground; **~ martiale** court-martial

**courage** [kuraʒ] nm courage, bravery; **courageux, -euse** adj brave, courageous

**couramment** [kuramɑ̃] adv commonly; (parler) fluently

**courant, e** [kurɑ̃, ɑ̃t] adj (fréquent) common; (COMM, gén: normal) standard; (en cours) current ♦ nm current; (fig) movement; (: d'opinion) trend; **être au ~ (de)** (fait, nouvelle) to know (about); **mettre qn au ~ (de)** to tell sb (about); (nouveau travail etc) to teach sb the basics (of); **se tenir au ~ (de)** (techniques etc) to keep o.s. up-to-date (on); **dans le ~ (de)** (pendant) in the course of; **le 10 ~** (COMM) the 10th inst.; **~ d'air** draught; **~ électrique** (electric) current, power

**courbature** [kurbatyr] nf ache

**courbe** [kurb] adj curved ♦ nf curve; **courber** vt to bend; **se courber** vi (personne) to bend (down), stoop

**coureur, -euse** [kurœr, øz] nm/f (SPORT) runner (ou driver); (péj) womanizer; manhunter; **~ automobile** racing driver

**courge** [kurʒ] nf (CULIN) marrow; **courgette** nf courgette (BRIT), zucchini (US)

**courir** [kurir] vi to run ♦ vt (SPORT: épreuve) to compete in; (risque) to run; (danger) to run; **~ les magasins** to go round the shops; **le bruit court que** the rumour is going round that

**couronne** [kurɔn] nf crown; (de fleurs) wreath, circlet

**courons** etc [kurɔ̃] vb voir **courir**

**courrier** [kurje] nm mail, post; (lettres à écrire) letters pl; **~ électronique** E-mail

**courroie** [kurwa] nf strap; (TECH) belt

**courrons** etc [kurɔ̃] vb voir **courir**

**cours** [kur] nm (leçon) class; (: particulier) lesson; (série de leçons, cheminement) course; (écoulement) flow; (COMM: de devises) rate; (: de denrées) price; **donner libre ~ à** to give free expression to; **avoir ~** (SCOL) to have a class ou lecture; **en ~** (année) current; (travaux) in progress; **en ~ de route** on the way; **au ~ de** in the course of, during; **~ d'eau** waterway; **~ du soir** night school; **~ intensif** crash course

**course** [kurs] nf running; (SPORT: épreuve) race; (d'un taxi) journey, trip; (commission) errand; **~s** nfpl (achats) shopping sg; **faire des ~s** to do some shopping

**court, e** [kur, kurt(ə)] adj short ♦ adv short ♦ nm: **~ (de tennis)** (tennis) court; **à ~ de** short of; **prendre qn de ~** to catch sb unawares; **court-circuit** nm short-circuit

**courtier, -ère** [kurtje, jɛr] nm/f broker

**courtiser** [kurtize] vt to court, woo

**courtois, e** [kurtwa, waz] adj courteous; **courtoisie** nf courtesy

**couru, e** [kury] pp de **courir**

**cousais** etc [kuze] vb voir **coudre**

**couscous** [kuskus] nm couscous

**cousin, e** [kuzɛ̃, in] nm/f cousin

**coussin** [kusɛ̃] nm cushion

**cousu, e** [kuzy] pp de **coudre**

**coût** [ku] nm cost; **le ~ de la vie** the cost of living; **coûtant** adj m: **au prix coûtant** at cost price

**couteau, x** [kuto] nm knife

**coûter** [kute] vt, vi to cost; **combien ça coûte?** how much is it?, what does it cost?; **coûte que coûte** at all costs; **coûteux, -euse** adj costly, expensive

**coutume** [kutym] nf custom

**couture** [kutyʀ] nf sewing; (profession) dressmaking; (points) seam; **couturier** nm fashion designer; **couturière** nf dressmaker

**couvée** [kuve] nf brood, clutch

**couvent** [kuvɑ̃] nm (de sœurs) convent; (de frères) monastery

**couver** [kuve] vt to hatch; (maladie) to be coming down with ♦ vi (feu) to smoulder; (révolte) to be brewing

**couvercle** [kuvɛʀkl] nm lid; (de bombe aérosol etc, qui se visse) cap, top

**couvert, e** [kuvɛʀ, ɛʀt] pp de **couvrir** ♦ adj (ciel) overcast ♦ nm place setting; (place à table) place; **~s** nmpl (ustensiles) cutlery sg; **~ de** covered with ou in; **mettre le ~** to lay the table

**couverture** [kuvɛʀtyʀ] nf blanket; (de livre, assurance, fig) cover; (presse) coverage; **~ chauffante** electric blanket

**couveuse** [kuvøz] nf (de maternité) incubator

**couvre-feu** [kuvʀəfø] nm curfew

**couvre-lit** [kuvʀəli] nm bedspread

**couvreur** [kuvʀœʀ] nm roofer

**couvrir** [kuvʀiʀ] vt to cover; **se ~** (s'habiller) to cover up; (se coiffer) to put on one's hat; (ciel) to cloud over

**cow-boy** [kɔbɔj] nm cowboy

**crabe** [kʀab] nm crab

**cracher** [kʀaʃe] vi, vt to spit

**crachin** [kʀaʃɛ̃] nm drizzle

**crack** [kʀak] nm (fam: as) ace

**craie** [kʀɛ] nf chalk

**craindre** [kʀɛ̃dʀ] vt to fear, be afraid of; (être sensible à: chaleur, froid) to be easily damaged by

**crainte** [kʀɛ̃t] nf fear; **de ~ de/que** for fear of/that; **craintif, -ive** adj timid

**cramoisi, e** [kʀamwazi] adj crimson

**crampe** [kʀɑ̃p] nf cramp

**crampon** [kʀɑ̃pɔ̃] nm (de chaussure de football) stud; (de chaussure de course) spike; (d'alpinisme) crampon; **cramponner** vi: **se cramponner (à)** to hang ou cling on (to)

**cran** [kʀɑ̃] nm (entaille) notch; (de courroie) hole; (fam: courage) guts pl; **~ d'arrêt** safety catch

**crâne** [kʀɑn] nm skull

**crâner** [kʀɑne] (fam) vi to show off

**crapaud** [kʀapo] nm toad

**crapule** [kʀapyl] nf villain

**craquement** [kʀakmɑ̃] nm crack, snap; (du plancher) creak, creaking no pl

**craquer** [kʀake] vi (bois, plancher) to creak; (fil, branche) to snap; (couture) to come apart; (fig: accusé) to break down; (: fam) to crack up ♦ vt (allumette) to strike; **j'ai craqué** (fam) I couldn't resist it

**crasse** [kʀas] nf grime, filth; **crasseux, -euse** adj grimy, filthy

**cravache** [kʀavaʃ] nf (riding) crop

**cravate** [kʀavat] nf tie

**crawl** [kʀol] nm crawl; **dos ~é** backstroke

**crayon** [kʀɛjɔ̃] nm pencil; **~ à bille** ball-point pen; **~ de couleur** crayon, colouring pencil; **crayon-feutre** (pl **crayons-feutres**) nm felt(-tip) pen

**créancier, -ière** [kʀeɑ̃sje, jɛʀ] nm/f creditor

**création** [kʀeasjɔ̃] nf creation

**créature** [kʀeatyʀ] nf creature

**crèche** [kʀɛʃ] nf (de Noël) crib; (garderie) crèche, day nursery

**crédit** [kʀedi] nm (gén) credit; **~s** nmpl (fonds) funds; **payer/acheter à ~** to pay/buy on credit ou on easy terms; **faire ~ à qn** to give sb credit; **créditer** vt: **créditer un compte (de)** to credit an account (with)

**crédule** [kʀedyl] adj credulous, gullible

**créer** [kʀee] vt to create

**crémaillère** [kʀemajɛʀ] nf: **pendre la ~** to have a house-warming party

**crématoire** [kʀematwaʀ] adj: **four ~**

crematorium

**crème** [kʀɛm] *nf* cream; *(entremets)* cream dessert ♦ *adj inv* cream(-coloured); **un (café) ~** ≃ a white coffee; **~ anglaise** (egg) custard; **~ chantilly** whipped cream; **~ fouettée** = **crème chantilly**; **crémerie** *nf* dairy; **crémeux, -euse** *adj* creamy

**créneau, x** [kʀeno] *nm (de fortification)* crenel(le); *(dans marché)* gap, niche; *(AUTO)*: **faire un ~** to reverse into a parking space *(between two cars alongside the kerb)*

**crêpe** [kʀɛp] *nf (galette)* pancake ♦ *nm (tissu)* crêpe; **crêpé, e** *adj (cheveux)* backcombed; **crêperie** *nf* pancake shop *ou* restaurant

**crépiter** [kʀepite] *vi (friture)* to sputter, splutter; *(feu)* to crackle

**crépu, e** [kʀepy] *adj* frizzy, fuzzy

**crépuscule** [kʀepyskyl] *nm* twilight, dusk

**cresson** [kʀesɔ̃] *nm* watercress

**crête** [kʀɛt] *nf (de coq)* comb; *(de vague, montagne)* crest

**creuser** [kʀøze] *vt (trou, tunnel)* to dig; *(sol)* to dig a hole in; *(fig)* to go (deeply) into; **ça creuse** that gives you a real appetite; **se ~ la cervelle** *(fam)* to rack one's brains

**creux, -euse** [kʀø, kʀøz] *adj* hollow ♦ *nm* hollow; **heures creuses** slack periods; *(électricité, téléphone)* off-peak periods; **avoir un ~** *(fam)* to be hungry

**crevaison** [kʀavɛzɔ̃] *nf* puncture

**crevasse** [kʀavas] *nf (dans le sol, la peau)* crack; *(de glacier)* crevasse

**crevé, e** [kʀave] *(fam) adj (fatigué)* all in, exhausted

**crever** [kʀave] *vt (ballon)* to burst ♦ *vi (pneu)* to burst; *(automobiliste)* to have a puncture (BRIT) *ou* a flat (tire) (US); *(fam)* to die

**crevette** [kʀavɛt] *nf*: **~ (rose)** prawn; **~ grise** shrimp

**cri** [kʀi] *nm* cry, shout; *(d'animal: spécifique)* cry, call; **c'est le dernier ~** *(fig)* it's the latest fashion

**criant, e** [kʀijɑ̃, kʀijɑ̃t] *adj (injustice)* glaring

**criard, e** [kʀijaʀ, kʀijaʀd] *adj (couleur)* garish, loud; *(voix)* yelling

**crible** [kʀibl] *nm* riddle; **passer qch au ~** *(fig)* to go over sth with a fine-tooth comb; **criblé, e** *adj*: **criblé de** riddled with; *(de dettes)* crippled with

**cric** [kʀik] *nm (AUTO)* jack

**crier** [kʀije] *vi (pour appeler)* to shout, cry (out); *(de douleur etc)* to scream, yell ♦ *vt (injure)* to shout (out), yell (out)

**crime** [kʀim] *nm* crime; *(meurtre)* murder; **criminel, le** *nm/f* criminal; *(assassin)* murderer

**crin** [kʀɛ̃] *nm (de cheval)* hair *no pl*

**crinière** [kʀinjɛʀ] *nf* mane

**crique** [kʀik] *nf* creek, inlet

**criquet** [kʀike] *nm* grasshopper

**crise** [kʀiz] *nf* crisis; *(MÉD)* attack; *(: d'épilepsie)* fit; **piquer une ~ de nerfs** to go hysterical; **~ cardiaque** heart attack; **~ de foie** bilious attack

**crisper** [kʀispe] *vt (poings)* to clench; **se ~** *vi (visage)* to tense; *(personne)* to get tense

**crisser** [kʀise] *vi (neige)* to crunch; *(pneu)* to screech

**cristal, -aux** [kʀistal, o] *nm* crystal; **cristallin, e** *adj* crystal-clear

**critère** [kʀitɛʀ] *nm* criterion

**critiquable** [kʀitikabl] *adj* open to criticism

**critique** [kʀitik] *adj* critical ♦ *nm/f (de théâtre, musique)* critic ♦ *nf* criticism; *(THÉÂTRE etc: article)* review

**critiquer** [kʀitike] *vt (dénigrer)* to criticize; *(évaluer)* to assess, examine (critically)

**croasser** [kʀɔase] *vi* to caw

**Croatie** [kʀɔasi] *nf* Croatia

**croc** [kʀo] *nm (dent)* fang; *(de boucher)* hook; **croc-en-jambe** *nm*: **faire un croc-en-jambe à qn** to trip sb up

**croche** [kʀɔʃ] *nf (MUS)* quaver (BRIT),

**eighth note** (US); **croche-pied** nm = croc-en-jambe

**crochet** [kʀɔʃɛ] nm hook; (détour) detour; (TRICOT: aiguille) crochet hook; (: technique) crochet; **vivre aux ~s de qn** to live ou sponge off sb

**crochu, e** [kʀɔʃy] adj (nez) hooked; (doigts) claw-like

**crocodile** [kʀɔkɔdil] nm crocodile

**croire** [kʀwaʀ] vt to believe; **se ~ fort** to think one is strong; **~ que** to think ou think that; **~ à, ~ en** to believe in

**crois** [kʀwa] vb voir **croître**

**croisade** [kʀwazad] nf crusade

**croisé, e** [kʀwaze] adj (veste) double-breasted

**croisement** [kʀwazmɑ̃] nm (carrefour) crossroads sg; (BIO) crossing; (: résultat) crossbreed

**croiser** [kʀwaze] vt (personne, route) to pass; (route) to cross, cut across; (BIO) to cross; **se ~** vi (personnes, véhicules) to pass each other; (routes, lettres) to cross; (regards) to meet; **~ les jambes/bras** to cross one's legs/ fold one's arms

**croisière** [kʀwazjɛʀ] nf cruise

**croissance** [kʀwasɑ̃s] nf growth

**croissant** [kʀwasɑ̃] nm (à manger) croissant; (motif) crescent

**croître** [kʀwatʀ] vi to grow

**croix** [kʀwa] nf cross; **~ gammée** swastika; **la C~ Rouge** the Red Cross

**croque-monsieur** [kʀɔkməsjø] nm inv toasted ham and cheese sandwich

**croquer** [kʀɔke] vt (manger) to crunch; (: fruit) to munch; (dessiner) to sketch; **chocolat à ~** plain dessert chocolate

**croquis** [kʀɔki] nm sketch

**cross** [kʀɔs] nm: **faire du ~ (à pied)** to do cross-country running

**crosse** [kʀɔs] nf (de fusil) butt; (de revolver) grip

**crotte** [kʀɔt] nf droppings pl; **crotté, e** adj muddy, mucky; **crottin** nm (dung, manure; (fromage) (small round) cheese (made of goat's milk)

**crouler** [kʀule] vi (s'effondrer) to collapse; (être délabré) to be crumbling

**croupe** [kʀup] nf rump; **en ~** pillion

**croupir** [kʀupiʀ] vi to stagnate

**croustillant, e** [kʀustijɑ̃, ɑ̃t] adj crisp

**croûte** [kʀut] nf crust; (du fromage) rind; (MÉD) scab; **en ~** (CULIN) in pastry

**croûton** [kʀutɔ̃] nm (CULIN) crouton; (bout du pain) crust, heel

**croyable** [kʀwajabl] adj credible

**croyant, e** [kʀwajɑ̃, ɑ̃t] nm/f believer

**CRS** sigle fpl (= Compagnies républicaines de sécurité) state security police force ♦ sigle m member of the CRS

**cru, e** [kʀy] pp de **croire** ♦ adj (non cuit) raw; (lumière, couleur) harsh; (paroles) crude ♦ nm (vignoble) vineyard; (vin) wine; **un grand ~** a great vintage; **jambon ~** Parma ham

**crû** [kʀy] pp de **croître**

**cruauté** [kʀyote] nf cruelty

**cruche** [kʀyʃ] nf pitcher, jug

**crucifix** [kʀysifi] nm crucifix; **crucifixion** nf crucifixion

**crudités** [kʀydite] nfpl (CULIN) salads

**crue** [kʀy] nf (inondation) flood

**cruel, le** [kʀyɛl] adj cruel

**crus** etc [kʀy] vb voir **croire; croître**

**crûs** etc [kʀy] vb voir **croître**

**crustacés** [kʀystase] nmpl shellfish

**Cuba** [kyba] nf Cuba; **cubain, e** adj Cuban ♦ nm/f: **Cubain, e** Cuban

**cube** [kyb] nm cube; (jouet) building brick; **mètre ~** cubic metre; **2 au ~** 2 cubed

**cueillette** [kœjɛt] nf picking; (quantité) crop, harvest

**cueillir** [kœjiʀ] vt (fruits, fleurs) to pick, gather; (fig) to catch

**cuiller, cuillère** [kɥijɛʀ] nf spoon; **~ à café** coffee spoon; **~ à soupe** soup-spoon; teaspoonful; (CULIN) tablespoonful; **cuillerée** nf spoonful

**cuir** [kɥiʀ] nm leather; **~ chevelu** scalp

**cuire** [kɥiʀ] vt (aliments) to cook; (au four) to bake ♦ vi to cook; **bien cuit** (viande) well done; **trop cuit** overdone

**cuisant, e** [kɥizɑ̃, ɑ̃t] *adj (douleur)* stinging; *(fig: souvenir, échec)* bitter

**cuisine** [kɥizin] *nf (pièce)* kitchen; *(art culinaire)* cookery, cooking; *(nourriture)* cooking, food; **faire la ~** to cook; **cuisiné, e** *adj:* **plat cuisiné** ready-made meal *ou* dish; **cuisiner** *vt* to cook; *(fam)* to grill ♦ *vi* to cook; **cuisinier, -ière** *nf* cook; **cuisinière** *nf (poêle)* cooker

**cuisse** [kɥis] *nf* thigh; *(CULIN)* leg

**cuisson** [kɥisɔ̃] *nf* cooking

**cuit, e** [kɥi, kɥit] *pp de* **cuire**

**cuivre** [kɥivʀ] *nm* copper; **les ~s** *(MUS)* the brass

**cul** [ky] *(fam!) nm* arse (!)

**culbute** [kylbyt] *nf* somersault; *(accidentelle)* tumble, fall

**culminant, e** *adj:* **point ~** highest point

**culminer** [kylmine] *vi* to reach its highest point

**culot** [kylo] *(fam) nm (effronterie)* cheek

**culotte** [kylɔt] *nf (de femme)* knickers *pl (BRIT)*, panties *pl*

**culpabilité** [kylpabilite] *nf* guilt

**culte** [kylt] *nm (religion)* religion; *(hommage, vénération)* worship; *(protestant)* service

**cultivateur, -trice** [kyltivatœʀ, tʀis] *nm/f* farmer

**cultivé, e** [kyltive] *adj (personne)* cultured, cultivated

**cultiver** [kyltive] *vt* to cultivate; *(légumes)* to grow, cultivate

**culture** [kyltyʀ] *nf* cultivation; *(connaissances etc)* culture; **les ~s** intensive farming; **~ physique** physical training; **culturel, le** *adj* cultural; **culturisme** *nm* body-building

**cumin** [kymɛ̃] *nm* cumin

**cumuler** [kymyle] *vt (emplois)* to hold concurrently; *(salaires)* to draw concurrently

**cupide** [kypid] *adj* greedy, grasping

**cure** [kyʀ] *nf (MÉD)* course of treatment

**curé** [kyʀe] *nm* parish priest

**cure-dent** [kyʀdɑ̃] *nm* toothpick

**cure-pipe** [kyʀpip] *nm* pipe cleaner

**curer** [kyʀe] *vt* to clean out

**curieusement** [kyʀjøzmɑ̃] *adv* curiously

**curieux, -euse** [kyʀjø, jøz] *adj (indiscret)* curious, inquisitive; *(étrange)* strange, curious ♦ *nmpl (badauds)* onlookers; **curiosité** *nf* curiosity; *(site)* unusual feature

**curriculum vitae** [kyʀikylɔmvite] *nm inv* curriculum vitae

**curseur** [kyʀsœʀ] *nm (INFORM)* cursor

**cutané, e** [kytane] *adj* skin

**cuti-réaction** [kytiʀeaksjɔ̃] *nf (MÉD)* skin-test

**cuve** [kyv] *nf* vat; *(à mazout etc)* tank

**cuvée** [kyve] *nf* vintage

**cuvette** [kyvet] *nf (récipient)* bowl, basin; *(GÉO)* basin

**CV** *sigle m (AUTO)* = **cheval vapeur**; *(COMM)* = **curriculum vitae**

**cyanure** [sjanyʀ] *nm* cyanide

**cybercafé** [siberkafe] *nm* cybercafé

**cyclable** [siklabl] *adj:* **piste ~** cycle track

**cycle** [sikl] *nm* cycle; **cyclisme** *nm* cycling; **cycliste** *nmf* cyclist ♦ *adj* cycle *cpd;* **coureur cycliste** racing cyclist

**cyclomoteur** [siklɔmɔtœʀ] *nm* moped

**cyclone** [siklon] *nm* hurricane

**cygne** [siɲ] *nm* swan

**cylindre** [silɛ̃dʀ] *nm* cylinder; **cylindrée** *nf (AUTO) (cubic)* capacity

**cymbale** [sɛ̃bal] *nf* cymbal

**cynique** [sinik] *adj* cynical

**cystite** [sistit] *nf* cystitis

# D, d

**d'** [d] *prép voir de*

**dactylo** [daktilo] *nf (aussi: ~graphe)* typist; *(aussi: ~graphie)* typing; **dactylographier** *vt* to type (out)

**dada** [dada] *nm* hobby-horse

**daigner** [deɲe] *vt* to deign

# daim
# débandade

**daim** [dɛ̃] *nm* (fallow) deer *inv*; *(cuir suédé)* suede

**dalle** [dal] *nf* paving stone, slab

**daltonien, ne** [daltɔnjɛ̃, jɛn] *adj* colour-blind

**dam** [dã] *nm*: **au grand ~ de** much to the detriment *(ou* annoyance) **of**

**dame** [dam] *nf* lady; *(CARTES, ÉCHECS)* queen; **~s** *nfpl (jeu)* draughts *sg* (BRIT), checkers *sg* (US)

**damner** [dane] *vt* to damn

**dancing** [dãsiŋ] *nm* dance hall

**Danemark** [danmark] *nm* Denmark

**danger** [dãʒe] *nm* danger; **dangereux, -euse** *adj* dangerous

**danois, e** [danwa, waz] *adj* Danish ♦ *nm/f*: **D~, e** Dane ♦ *nm* (LING) Danish

---

## MOT-CLÉ

**dans** [dã] *prép* **1** *(position)* in; *(à l'intérieur de)* inside; **c'est dans le tiroir/le salon** it's in the drawer/lounge; **dans la boîte** in *ou* inside the box; **marcher dans la ville** to walk about the town

**2** *(direction)* into; **elle a couru dans le salon** she ran into the lounge

**3** *(provenance)* out of, from; **je l'ai pris dans le tiroir/salon** I took it out of *ou* from the drawer/lounge; **boire dans un verre** to drink out *ou* from a glass

**4** *(temps)* in; **dans 2 mois** in 2 months, in 2 months' time

**5** *(approximation)* about; **dans les 20 F** about 20F

---

**danse** [dãs] *nf*: **la ~** dancing; **une ~ a** dance; **la ~ classique** ballet; **danser** *vi, vt* to dance; **danseur, -euse** *nm/f* ballet dancer; *(au bal etc)* dancer; (: cavalier) partner

**dard** [dar] *nm (d'animal)* sting

**date** [dat] *nf* date; **de longue ~** long-standing; **~ de naissance** date of birth; **~ de péremption** expiry date; **~ limite** deadline; **dater** *vt, vi* to date;

**dater de** to date from; **à dater de** (as) from

**datte** [dat] *nf* date

**dauphin** [dofɛ̃] *nm* (ZOOL) dolphin

**davantage** [davãtaʒ] *adv* more; *(plus longtemps)* longer; **~ de** more

---

## MOT-CLÉ

**de, d'** [də] *(de + le = du, de + les = des) prép* **1** *(appartenance)* of; **le toit de la maison** the roof of the house; **la voiture d'Ann/de mes parents** Ann's/my parents' car

**2** *(provenance)* from; **il vient de Londres** he comes from London; **elle est sortie du cinéma** she came out of the cinema

**3** *(caractérisation, mesure)*: **un mur de brique/bureau d'acajou** a brick wall/mahogany desk; **un billet de 50 F** a 50F note; **une pièce de 2 m de large** *ou* **large de 2 m** a room 2m wide, a 2m-wide room; **un bébé de 10 mois** a 10-month-old baby; **12 mois de crédit/travail** 12 months' credit/work; **augmenter de 10 F** to increase by 10F; **de 14 à 18** from 14 to 18

♦ *dét* **1** *(phrases affirmatives)* some *(souvent omis)*; **du vin, de l'eau, des pommes** (some) wine, (some) water, (some) apples; **des enfants sont venus** some children came; **pendant des mois** for months

**2** *(phrases interrogatives et négatives)* any; **a-t-il du vin?** has he got any wine?; **il n'a pas de pommes/d'enfants** he hasn't (got) any apples/children, he has no apples/children

---

**dé** [de] *nm (à jouer)* die *ou* dice; *(aussi:* **~ à coudre)** thimble

**dealer** [dilœr] *nm (fam)* (drug) pusher

**déambuler** [deãbyle] *vi* to stroll about

**débâcle** [debakl] *nf* rout

**déballer** [debale] *vt* to unpack

**débandade** [debãdad] *nf (dispersion)* scattering

**débarbouiller** [debarbuje] vt to wash; **se ~** to wash (one's face)

**débarcadère** [debarkadɛʀ] nm wharf

**débardeur** [debardœʀ] nm (maillot) tank top

**débarquer** [debarke] vt to unload, land ♦ vi to disembark; (fig: fam) to turn up

**débarras** [debara] nm (pièce) lumber room; (placard) junk cupboard; **bon ~!** good riddance!; **débarrasser** vt to clear; **se débarrasser de** vt to get rid of; **débarrasser qn de** (vêtements, paquets) to relieve sb of

**débat** [deba] nm discussion, debate; **débattre** vt to discuss, debate; **se débattre** vi to struggle

**débaucher** [deboʃe] vt (licencier) to lay off, dismiss; (entraîner) to lead astray, debauch

**débile** [debil] (fam) adj (idiot) dim-witted

**débit** [debi] nm (d'un liquide, fleuve) flow; (d'un magasin) turnover (of goods); (élocution) delivery; (bancaire) debit; **~ de boissons** drinking establishment; **~ de tabac** tobacconist's; **débiter** vt (compte) to debit; (couper: bois, viande) to cut up; (péj: dire) to churn out; **débiteur, -trice** nm/f debtor ♦ adj in debit; (compte) debit cpd

**déblayer** [debleje] vt to clear

**débloquer** [deblɔke] vt (prix, crédits) to free

**déboires** [debwaʀ] nmpl setbacks

**déboiser** [debwaze] vt to deforest

**déboîter** [debwate] vt (AUTO) to pull out; **se ~ le genou** etc to dislocate one's knee etc

**débonnaire** [debɔnɛʀ] adj easy-going, good-natured

**débordé, e** [debɔʀde] adj: **être ~ (de)** (travail, demandes) to be snowed under (with)

**déborder** [debɔʀde] vi to overflow; (lait etc) to boil over; **~ qch** (dépasser) to extend beyond sth

**débouché** [debuʃe] nm (pour vendre) outlet; (perspective d'emploi) opening

**déboucher** [debuʃe] vt (évier, tuyau etc) to unblock; (bouteille) to uncork ♦ vi: **~ de** to emerge from; **~ sur** (études) to lead on to

**débourser** [deburse] vt to pay out

**déboussolé, e** [debusɔle] (fam) adj disorientated

**debout** [d(ə)bu] adv: **être ~** (personne) to be standing, stand; (: levé, éveillé) to be up; **se mettre ~** to stand up; **se tenir ~** to stand; **~!** stand up!; (du lit) get up!; **cette histoire ne tient pas ~** this story doesn't hold water

**déboutonner** [debutɔne] vt to undo, unbutton

**débraillé, e** [debraje] adj slovenly, untidy

**débrancher** [debrɑ̃ʃe] vt to disconnect; (appareil électrique) to unplug

**débrayage** [debrɛjaʒ] nm (AUTO) clutch; **débrayer** vi (AUTO) to declutch; (cesser le travail) to stop work

**débris** [debri] nmpl fragments; **des ~ de verre** bits of glass

**débrouillard, e** [debrujar, ard] (fam) adj smart, resourceful

**débrouiller** [debruje] vt to disentangle, untangle; **se ~** vi to manage; **débrouillez-vous** you'll have to sort things out yourself

**début** [deby] nm beginning, start; **~s** nmpl (de carrière) début sg; **~ juin** in early June; **débutant, e** nm/f beginner, novice; **débuter** vi to begin, start; (faire ses débuts) to start out

**deçà** [dasa]: **en ~ de** prép this side of

**décadence** [dekadɑ̃s] nf decline

**décaféiné, e** [dekafeine] adj decaffeinated

**décalage** [dekalaʒ] nm gap; **~ horaire** time difference

**décaler** [dekale] vt to shift

**décalquer** [dekalke] vt to trace

**décamper** [dekɑ̃pe] (fam) vi to clear out ou off

**décaper** [dekape] vt (surface peinte) to strip

**décapiter** [dekapite] vt to behead; (par accident) to decapitate

**décapotable** [dekapɔtabl] adj convertible

**décapsuleur** [dekapsylœr] nm bottle-opener

**décarcasser** [dekarkase]: **se ~** (fam) vi to flog o.s. to death

**décédé, e** [desede] adj deceased

**décéder** [desede] vi to die

**déceler** [des(ə)le] vt (trouver) to discover, detect

**décembre** [desãbr] nm December

**décemment** [desamã] adv decently

**décennie** [deseni] nf decade

**décent, e** [desã, ãt] adj decent

**déception** [desɛpsjɔ̃] nf disappointment

**décerner** [desɛrne] vt to award

**décès** [desɛ] nm death

**décevant, e** [des(ə)vã, ãt] adj disappointing

**décevoir** [des(ə)vwar] vt to disappoint

**déchaîner** [defene] vt (violence) to unleash; (enthousiasme) to arouse; **se ~** (tempête) to rage; (personne) to fly into a rage

**déchanter** [defãte] vi to become disillusioned

**décharge** [defarʒ] nf (dépôt d'ordures) rubbish tip ou dump; (électrique) electrical discharge; **décharger** vt (marchandise, véhicule) to unload; (tirer) to discharge; **se décharger** vi (batterie) to go flat; **décharger qn de** (responsabilité) to release sb from

**décharné, e** [defarne] adj emaciated

**déchausser** [defose] vt (skis) to take off; **se ~** vi to take off one's shoes; (dent) to come ou work loose

**déchéance** [defeãs] nf (physique) degeneration; (morale) decay

**déchet** [defɛ] nm (reste) scrap; **~s** nmpl (ordures) refuse sg, rubbish sg; **~s nucléaires** nuclear waste

**déchiffrer** [defifre] vt to decipher

**déchiqueter** [defik(ə)te] vt to tear ou pull to pieces

**déchirant, e** [defirã, ãt] adj heart-rending

**déchirement** [defirmã] nm (chagrin) wrench, heartbreak; (gén pl: conflit) rift, split

**déchirer** [defire] vt to tear; (en morceaux) to tear up; (arracher) to tear out; (fig: conflit) to tear (apart); **se ~** vt to tear, rip; **se ~ un muscle** to tear a muscle

**déchirure** [defiryr] nf (accroc) tear, rip; **~ musculaire** torn muscle

**déchoir** [defwar] vi (personne) to lower o.s., demean o.s.

**déchu, e** [defy] adj (roi) deposed

**décidé, e** [deside] adj (personne, air) determined; **c'est ~** it's decided; **décidément** adv really

**décider** [deside] vt: **~ qch** to decide on sth; **se ~ (à faire)** to decide (to do), make up one's mind (to do); **se ~ pour** to decide on ou in favour of; **~ de faire/que** to decide to do/that; **~ qn (à faire qch)** to persuade sb (to do sth)

**décimal, e, -aux** [desimal, o] adj decimal; **décimale** nf decimal

**décimètre** [desimɛtr] nm decimetre

**décisif, -ive** [desizif, iv] adj decisive

**décision** [desizjɔ̃] nf decision

**déclaration** [deklarasjɔ̃] nf declaration; (discours: POL etc) statement; **~ (d'impôts)** tax return

**déclarer** [deklare] vt to declare; (décès, naissance) to register; **se ~** vi (feu) to break out

**déclencher** [deklãʃe] vt (mécanisme etc) to release; (sonnerie) to set off; (attaque, grève) to launch; (provoquer) to trigger off; **se ~** vi (mécanisme) to release ou go off; (sonnerie) to go off

**déclic** [deklik] nm (bruit) click

**décliner** [dekline] vi to decline ♦ vt (invitation) to decline; (nom, adresse) to state

**décocher** |dekɔʃe| vt (coup de poing) to throw; (flèche, regard) to shoot

**décoiffer** |dekwafe| vt: ~ **qn** to mess up sb's hair; **je suis toute décoiffée** my hair is in a real mess

**déçois** etc |deswa| vb voir **décevoir**

**décollage** |dekɔlaʒ| nm (AVIAT) takeoff

**décoller** |dekɔle| vt to unstick ♦ vi (avion) to take off; **se ~** vi to come unstuck

**décolleté, e** |dekɔlte| adj low-cut ♦ nm low neck(line); (plongeant) cleavage

**décolorer** |dekɔlɔre| **se ~** vi to fade; **se faire ~ les cheveux** to have one's hair bleached

**décombres** |dekɔ̃bʀ| nmpl rubble sg, debris sg

**décommander** |dekɔmɑ̃de| vt to cancel; **se ~** vi to cry off

**décomposé, e** |dekɔ̃poze| adj (pourri) decomposed; (visage) haggard, distorted

**décompte** |dekɔ̃t| nm deduction; (facture) detailed account

**déconcerter** |dekɔ̃sɛʀte| vt to disconcert, confound

**déconfit, e** |dekɔ̃fi, it| adj crestfallen

**décongeler** |dekɔ̃ʒ(ə)le| vt to thaw

**déconner** |dekɔne| (fam) vi to talk rubbish

**déconseiller** |dekɔ̃seje| vt: ~ **qch** (à **qn**) to advise (sb) against sth; **c'est déconseillé** it's not recommended

**décontracté, e** |dekɔ̃tʀakte| adj relaxed, laid-back (fam)

**décontracter** |dekɔ̃tʀakte| **se ~** vi to relax

**déconvenue** |dekɔ̃v(ə)ny| nf disappointment

**décor** |dekɔʀ| nm décor; (paysage) scenery; **~s** nmpl (THÉÂTRE) scenery sg, décor sg; (CINÉMA) set sg; **décorateur** nm (interior) decorator; **décoration** nf decoration; **décorer** vt to decorate

**décortiquer** |dekɔʀtike| vt to shell; (fig: texte) to dissect

**découcher** |dekuʃe| vi to spend the night away from home

**découdre** |dekudʀ| **se ~** vi to come unstitched

**découler** |dekule| vi: ~ **de** to ensue ou follow from

**découper** |dekupe| vt (papier, tissu etc) to cut up; (viande) to carve; (article) to cut out; **se ~ sur** to stand out against

**décourager** |dekuʀaʒe| vt to discourage; **se ~** vi to lose heart, become discouraged

**décousu, e** |dekuzy| adj unstitched; (fig) disjointed, disconnected

**découvert, e** |dekuvɛʀ, ɛʀt| adj (tête) bare, uncovered; (lieu) open, exposed ♦ nm (bancaire) overdraft; **découverte** nf discovery; **faire la découverte de** to discover

**découvrir** |dekuvʀiʀ| vt to discover; (enlever ce qui couvre) to uncover; (dévoiler) to reveal; **se ~** (chapeau) to take off one's hat; (vêtement) to take something off; (ciel) to clear

**décret** |dekʀɛ| nm decree; **décréter** vt to decree

**décrié, e** |dekʀije| adj disparaged

**décrire** |dekʀiʀ| vt to describe

**décrocher** |dekʀɔʃe| vt (détacher) to take down; (téléphone) to take off the hook; (: pour répondre) to lift the receiver; (fam: contrat etc) to get, land ♦ vi (fam: abandonner) to drop out; (: cesser d'écouter) to switch off

**décroître** |dekʀwatʀ| vi to decrease, decline

**décrypter** |dekʀipte| vt to decipher

**déçu, e** |desy| pp de **décevoir**

**décupler** |dekyple| vt, vi to increase tenfold

**dédaigner** |dedeɲe| vt to despise, scorn; (négliger) to disregard, spurn; **dédaigneux, -euse** adj scornful, disdainful; **dédain** nm scorn, disdain

**dédale** |dedal| nm maze

**dedans** |dədɑ̃| adv inside; (pas en plein air) indoors, inside ♦ nm inside; **au ~** inside

**dédicacer** [dedikase] vt: ~ (à qn) to sign (for sb), autograph (for sb)

**dédier** [dedje] vt to dedicate

**dédire** [dedir]: **se** ~ vi to go back on one's word, retract

**dédommagement** [dedɔmaʒmɑ̃] nm compensation

**dédommager** [dedɔmaʒe] vt: ~ qn (de) to compensate sb (for)

**dédouaner** [dedwane] vt to clear through customs

**dédoubler** [deduble] vt (classe, effectifs) to split (into two)

**déduire** [deduir] vt: ~ qch (de) (ôter) to deduct sth (from); (conclure) to deduce ou infer sth (from)

**déesse** [dees] nf goddess

**défaillance** [defajɑ̃s] nf (syncope) blackout; (fatigue) (sudden) weakness no pl; (technique) fault, failure; ~ **cardiaque** heart failure

**défaillir** [defajir] vi to feel faint; (mémoire etc) to fail

**défaire** [defɛr] vt to undo; (installation) to take down, dismantle; **se** ~ vi to come undone; **se** ~ **de** to get rid of

**défait, e** [defɛ, ɛt] adj (visage) haggard, ravaged; **défaite** nf defeat

**défalquer** [defalke] vt to deduct

**défaut** [defo] nm (moral) fault, failing, defect; (tissus) fault, flaw; (manque, carence): ~ **de** shortage of; (COMPUT) bug; **prendre qn en** ~ to catch sb out; **faire** ~ (manquer) to be lacking; **à** ~ **de** for lack ou want of

**défaveur** [defavœr] nf disfavour; **défavorable** [defavɔrabl] adj unfavourable (BRIT), unfavorable (US)

**défavoriser** [defavɔrize] vt to put at a disadvantage

**défection** [defɛksjɔ̃] nf defection, failure to give support

**défectueux, -euse** [defɛktɥø, øz] adj faulty, defective

**défendre** [defɑ̃dr] vt to defend; (interdire) to forbid; **se** ~ vi to defend o.s.; ~ **à qn qch/de faire** to forbid sb sth/to do; **il se défend** (fam: se débrouille) he

can hold his own; **se** ~ **de/contre** (se protéger) to protect o.s. from/against; **se** ~ **de** (se garder de) to refrain from

**défense** [defɑ̃s] nf defence; (d'éléphant etc) tusk; "~ **de fumer**" "no smoking"

**déférer** [defere] vt (JUR) to refer; ~ **à** (requête, décision) to defer to

**déferler** [defɛrle] vi (vagues) to break; (fig: foule) to surge

**défi** [defi] nm challenge; **lancer un** ~ **à qn** to challenge sb; **sur un ton de** ~ defiantly

**déficit** [defisit] nm (COMM) deficit; **déficitaire** adj in deficit

**défier** [defje] vt (provoquer) to challenge; (mort, autorité) to defy

**défigurer** [defigyre] vt to disfigure

**défilé** [defile] nm (GÉO) (narrow) gorge ou pass; (soldats) parade; (manifestants) procession, march; ~ **de mode** fashion parade

**défiler** [defile] vi (troupes) to march past; (sportifs) to parade; (manifestants) to march; (visiteurs) to pour, stream; **se** ~ vi: **il s'est défilé** (fam) he wriggled out of it

**définir** [definir] vt to define

**définitif, -ive** [definitif, iv] adj (final) final, definitive; (pour longtemps) permanent, definitive; (refus) definite; **définitive** nf: **en définitive** eventually; (somme toute) in fact; **définitivement** adv (partir, s'installer) for good

**défoncer** [defɔ̃se] vt (porte) to smash in ou down; **se** ~ (fam) vi (travailler) to work like a dog; (drogué) to get high

**déformer** [defɔrme] vt to put out of shape; (pensée, fait) to distort; **se** ~ vi to lose its shape

**défouler** [defule]: **se** ~ vi to unwind, let off steam

**défraîchir** [defreʃir]: **se** ~ vi to fade

**défricher** [defriʃe] vt to clear (for cultivation)

**défunt, e** [defœ̃, œ̃t] nm/f deceased

**dégagé, e** [degaʒe] adj (route, ciel) clear; **sur un ton** ~ casually

**dégagement** [degaʒmɑ̃] nm: **voie de ~** slip road

**dégager** [degaʒe] vt (exhaler) to give off; (délivrer) to free, extricate; (désencombrer) to clear; (isoler: idée, aspect) to bring out; **se ~** vi (passage, ciel) to clear

**dégarnir** [degarnir] vt (vider) to empty, clear; **se ~** vi (tempes, crâne) to go bald

**dégâts** [dega] nmpl damage sg

**dégel** [deʒel] nm thaw; **dégeler** vt to thaw (out)

**dégénérer** [deʒenere] vi to degenerate

**dégingandé, e** [deʒɛ̃gɑ̃de] adj gangling

**dégivrer** [deʒivre] vt (frigo) to defrost; (vitres) to de-ice

**dégonflé, e** [degɔ̃fle] adj (pneu) flat

**dégonfler** [degɔ̃fle] vt (pneu, ballon) to let down, deflate; **se ~** vi (fam) to chicken out

**dégouliner** [deguline] vi to trickle, drip

**dégourdi, e** [degurdi] adj smart, resourceful

**dégourdir** [degurdir] vt: **se ~ les jambes** to stretch one's legs (fig)

**dégoût** [degu] nm disgust, distaste; **dégoûtant, e** adj disgusting; **dégoûté, e** adj disgusted; **dégoûté de** sick of; **dégoûter** vt to disgust; **dégoûter qn de qch** to put sb off sth

**dégrader** [degrade] vt (MIL: officier) to degrade; (abîmer) to damage, deface; **se ~** vi (relations, situation) to deteriorate

**dégrafer** [degrafe] vt to unclip, unhook

**degré** [dəgre] nm degree

**dégressif, -ive** [degresif, iv] adj on a decreasing scale

**dégringoler** [degrɛ̃gɔle] vi to tumble (down)

**dégrossir** [degrosir] vt (fig: projet) to work out roughly

**déguenillé, e** [deg(ə)nije] adj ragged, tattered

**déguerpir** [degerpir] vi to clear off

**dégueulasse** [degœlas] (fam) adj disgusting

**dégueuler** [degœle] (fam) vi to throw up

**déguisement** [degizmɑ̃] nm (pour s'amuser) fancy dress

**déguiser** [degize]: **se ~** vi (se costumer) to dress up; (pour tromper) to disguise o.s.

**dégustation** [degystasjɔ̃] nf (de fromages etc) sampling; **~ de vins** wine-tasting session

**déguster** [degyste] vt (vins) to taste; (fromages etc) to sample; (savourer) to enjoy, savour

**dehors** [dəɔr] adv outside; (en plein air) outdoors ♦ nm outside ♦ nmpl (apparences) appearances; **mettre** ou **jeter ~** (expulser) to throw out; **au ~** outside; **au ~ de** outside; **en ~** (hormis) apart from

**déjà** [deʒa] adv already; (auparavant) before, already

**déjeuner** [deʒœne] vi to (have) lunch; (le matin) to have breakfast ♦ nm lunch

**déjouer** [deʒwe] vt (complot) to foil

**delà** [dala] adv: **en ~ (de), au ~(de)** beyond

**délabrer** [delabre]: **se ~** vi to fall into decay, become dilapidated

**délacer** [delase] vt (chaussures) to undo

**délai** [dele] nm (attente) waiting period; (sursis) extension of (time); (temps accordé) time limit; **sans ~** without delay; **dans les ~s** within the time limit

**délaisser** [delese] vt to abandon, desert

**délasser** [delase] vt to relax; **se ~** vi to relax

**délavé, e** [delave] adj faded

**délayer** [deleje] vt (CULIN) to mix (with water etc); (peinture) to thin down

**delco** [delko] nm (AUTO) distributor

**délecter** [delekte]: **se ~** vi to revel ou delight in

# délégué 81 démettre

**délégué, e** [delege] *nm/f* representative

**déléguer** [delege] *vt* to delegate

**délibéré, e** [delibeʀe] *adj (conscient)* deliberate

**délibérer** [delibeʀe] *vi* to deliberate

**délicat, e** [delika, at] *adj* delicate; *(plein de tact)* tactful; *(attention)* thoughtful; **délicatement** *adv* delicately; *(avec douceur)* gently

**délice** [delis] *nm* delight

**délicieux, -euse** [delisjø, jøz] *adj (au goût)* delicious; *(sensation)* delightful

**délimiter** [delimite] *vt (terrain)* to delimit, demarcate

**délinquance** [delɛ̃kɑ̃s] *nf* criminality; **délinquant, e** *adj, nm/f* delinquent

**délirant, e** [deliʀɑ̃, ɑ̃t] *(fam) adj* wild

**délirer** [deliʀe] *vi* to be delirious; **tu délires!** *(fam)* you're crazy!

**délit** [deli] *nm (criminal)* offence

**délivrer** [delivʀe] *vt (prisonnier)* to (set) free, release; *(passeport)* to issue

**déloger** [delɔʒe] *vt (objet coincé)* to dislodge

**déloyal, e, -aux** [delwajal, o] *adj (ami)* disloyal; *(procédé)* unfair

**deltaplane** [deltaplan] *nm* hang-glider

**déluge** [delyʒ] *nm (pluie)* downpour; *(biblique)* Flood

**déluré, e** [delyʀe] *(péj) adj* forward, pert

**demain** [d(a)mɛ̃] *adv* tomorrow

**demande** [d(a)mɑ̃d] *nf (requête)* request; *(revendication)* demand; *(d'emploi)* application; *(ÉCON)* **la ~ demand;** **"~s d'emploi"** *(annonces)* "situations wanted"; **~ en mariage** proposal (of marriage)

**demandé, e** [d(a)mɑ̃de] *adj (article etc)*: **très ~** (very) much in demand

**demander** [d(a)mɑ̃de] *vt* to ask for; *(chemin, heure etc)* to ask; *(nécessiter)* to require, demand; **se ~ si/pourquoi etc** to wonder whether/why etc; **~ qch à qn** to ask sb for sth; **~ à qn de faire** to ask sb to do; **demandeur, -euse**

*nm/f*: **demandeur d'emploi** job-seeker

**démangeaison** [demɑ̃ʒɛzɔ̃] *nf* itching; **avoir des ~s** to be itching

**démanger** [demɑ̃ʒe] *vi* to itch

**démanteler** [demɑ̃t(a)le] *vt* to break up

**démaquillant** [demakijɑ̃] *nm* make-up remover

**démaquiller** [demakije] *vt*: **se ~** to remove one's make-up

**démarche** [demaʀʃ] *nf (allure)* gait, walk; *(intervention)* step; *(fig: intellectuelle)* thought processes *pl*; **faire les ~s nécessaires (pour obtenir qch)** to take the necessary steps (to obtain sth)

**démarcheur, -euse** [demaʀʃœʀ, øz] *nm/f (COMM)* door-to-door salesman(-woman)

**démarque** [demaʀk] *nf (article)* markdown

**démarrage** [demaʀaʒ] *nm* start

**démarrer** [demaʀe] *vi (conducteur)* to start (up); *(véhicule)* to move off; *(travaux)* to get moving; **démarreur** *nm (AUTO)* starter

**démêlant** [demelɑ̃] *nm* conditioner

**démêler** [demele] *vt* to untangle; **démêlés** *nmpl* problems

**déménagement** [demenaʒmɑ̃] *nm* move; **camion de ~** removal van

**déménager** [demenaʒe] *vt (meubles)* to (re)move ♦ *vi* to move (house); **déménageur** *nm* removal man

**démener** [dem(ə)ne]: **se ~** *vi (se dépenser)* to exert o.s.; *(pour obtenir qch)* to go to great lengths

**dément, e** [demɑ̃, ɑ̃t] *adj (fou)* mad, crazy; *(fam)* brilliant, fantastic

**démentiel, le** [demɑ̃sjɛl] *adj* insane

**démentir** [demɑ̃tiʀ] *vt* to refute; **~ que** to deny that

**démerder** [demɛʀde] *(fam)*: **se ~** *vi* to sort things out for o.s.

**démesuré, e** [dem(ə)zyʀe] *adj* immoderate

**démettre** [demetʀ] *vt*: **~ qn de** *(fonction, poste)* to dismiss sb from; **se ~**

l'épaule *etc* to dislocate one's shoulder *etc*

**demeurant** [d(ə)mœrɑ̃] : **au ~** *adv* for all that

**demeure** [d(ə)mœr] *nf* residence; **demeurer** *vi* (*habiter*) to live; (*rester*) to remain

**demi, e** [dəmi] *adj* half ♦ *nm* (*bière*) ≈ half-pint (0,25 *litres*) ♦ *préfixe*: **~...** half-, semi..., demi-; **trois heures/bouteilles et ~es** three and a half hours/bottles, three hours/bottles and a half; **il est 2 heures et ~e/midi et ~** it's half past 2/half past 12; **à ~** ~ half-; **à la ~ (heure)** on the half-hour; **demi-cercle** *nm* semicircle; **en demi-cercle** ♦ *adj* semicircular ♦ *adv* in a half circle; **demi-douzaine** *nf* half-dozen, half a dozen; **demi-finale** *nf* semifinal; **demi-frère** *nm* half-brother; **demi-heure** *nf* half-hour, half an hour; **demi-journée** *nf* half-day, half a day; **demi-litre** *nm* half-litre, half a litre; **demi-livre** *nf* half-pound, half a pound; **demi-mot**: **à demi-mot** *adv*. **à demi-mot** without having to spell things out; **demi-pension** *nf* (à l'hôtel) half-board; **demi-pensionnaire** *nm/f*: **être demi-pensionnaire** to take school lunches; **demi-place** *nf* half-fare

**démis, e** [demi, iz] *adj* (*épaule etc*) dislocated

**demi-sel** [dəmisɛl] *adj inv* (*beurre, fromage*) slightly salted

**demi-sœur** [dəmisœr] *nf* half-sister

**démission** [demisjɔ̃] *nf* resignation; **donner sa ~** to give *ou* hand in one's notice; **démissionner** *vi* to resign

**demi-tarif** [dəmitarif] *nm* half-price; **voyager à ~~** to travel half-fare

**demi-tour** [dəmitur] *nm* about-turn; **faire ~~** to turn (and go) back

**démocratie** [demɔkrasi] *nf* democracy; **démocratique** *adj* democratic

**démodé, e** [demɔde] *adj* old-fashioned

**demoiselle** [d(ə)mwazɛl] *nf* (*jeune fille*) young lady; (*célibataire*) single lady,

maiden lady; **~ d'honneur** bridesmaid

**démolir** [demɔlir] *vt* to demolish

**démon** [demɔ̃] *nm* (*enfant turbulent*) devil, demon; **le D~** the Devil

**démonstration** [demɔ̃strasjɔ̃] *nf* demonstration

**démonté, e** [demɔ̃te] *adj* (*mer*) raging, wild

**démonter** [demɔ̃te] *vt* (*machine etc*) to take down, dismantle

**démontrer** [demɔ̃tre] *vt* to demonstrate

**démordre** [demɔrdr] *vi*: **ne pas ~ de** to refuse to give up, stick to

**démouler** [demule] *vt* to turn out

**démuni, e** [demyni] *adj* (*sans argent*) impoverished; **~ de** without

**démunir** [demynir] *vt*: **~ qn de** to deprive sb of; **se ~ de** to part with, give up

**dénaturer** [denatyre] *vt* (*goût*) to alter; (*pensée, fait*) to distort

**dénicher** [denife] *vt* (*fam*) (*objet*) to unearth; (*restaurant etc*) to discover

**dénier** [denje] *vt* to deny

**dénigrer** [denigre] *vt* to denigrate, run down

**dénivellation** [denivelasjɔ̃] *nf* (*pente*) slope

**dénombrer** [denɔ̃bre] *vt* to count

**dénomination** [denɔminasjɔ̃] *nf* designation, appellation

**dénommé, e** [denɔme] *adj*: **un ~ Dupont** a certain Mr Dupont

**dénoncer** [denɔ̃se] *vt* to denounce

**dénouement** [denumɑ̃] *nm* outcome

**dénouer** [denwe] *vt* to unknot, undo; **se ~** (*nœud*) to come undone

**dénoyauter** [denwajote] *vt* to stone

**denrée** [dɑ̃re] *nf*: **~s (alimentaires)** foodstuffs

**dense** [dɑ̃s] *adj* dense; **densité** *nf* density

**dent** [dɑ̃] *nf* tooth; **~ de lait/sagesse** milk/wisdom tooth; **dentaire** *adj* dental

**dentelé, e** [dɑ̃t(ə)le] *adj* jagged, indented

**dentelle** [dɑ̃tɛl] nf lace no pl

**dentier** [dɑ̃tje] nm denture

**dentifrice** [dɑ̃tifʀis] nm toothpaste

**dentiste** [dɑ̃tist] nm/f dentist

**dentition** [dɑ̃tisjɔ̃] nf teeth

**dénuder** [denyde] vt to bare

**dénué, e** [denye] adj: **~ de** devoid of; **dénuement** nm destitution

**déodorant** [deɔdɔʀɑ̃] nm deodorant

**déontologie** [deɔ̃tɔlɔʒi] nf code of practice

**dépannage** [depanaʒ] nm: **service de ~** (AUTO) breakdown service

**dépanner** [depane] vt (voiture, télévision) to fix, repair; (fig) to bail out, help out; **dépanneuse** nf breakdown lorry (BRIT), tow truck (US)

**dépareillé, e** [depaʀeje] adj (collection, service) incomplete; (objet) odd

**départ** [depaʀ] nm departure; (SPORT) start; **au ~** at the start; **la veille du son ~** the day before he leaves/left

**départager** [depaʀtaʒe] vt to decide between

**département** [depaʀtəmɑ̃] nm department

---

**département**

France is divided into 96 administrative units called **départements**. These local government divisions are headed by a state-appointed **préfet**, and administered by an elected **Conseil général**. Départements are usually named after prominent geographical features such as rivers or mountain ranges; see also **DOM-TOM**.

---

**dépassé, e** [depase] adj superseded, outmoded; **il est complètement ~** he's completely out of his depth, he can't cope

**dépasser** [depase] vt (véhicule, concurrent) to overtake; (endroit) to pass, go past; (somme, limite) to exceed; (fig: en beauté etc) to surpass, outshine ♦ vi (ju-

pon etc) to show

**dépaysé, e** [depeize] adj disoriented

**dépaysement** [depeizmɑ̃] nm (changement) change of scenery

**dépecer** [depase] vt to joint, cut up

**dépêche** [depɛʃ] nf dispatch

**dépêcher** [depeʃe]: **se ~** vi to hurry

**dépeindre** [depɛ̃dʀ] vt to depict

**dépendance** [depɑ̃dɑ̃s] nf dependence; (bâtiment) outbuilding

**dépendre** [depɑ̃dʀ]: **~ de** vt to depend on; (financièrement etc) to be dependent on

**dépens** [depɑ̃] nmpl: **aux ~ de** at the expense of

**dépense** [depɑ̃s] nf spending no pl, expense, expenditure no pl; (énergie) to expend, use up; **se dépenser** vi to exert o.s.; **dépensier, -ière** adj: **il est dépensier** he's a spendthrift

**dépérir** [depeʀiʀ] vi (personne) to waste away; (plante) to wither

**dépêtrer** [depetʀe] vt: **se ~ de** to extricate o.s. from

**dépeupler** [depœple]: **se ~** vi to become depopulated

**dépilatoire** [depilatwaʀ] adj depilatory, hair-removing

**dépister** [depiste] vt to detect; (voleur) to track down

**dépit** [depi] nm vexation, frustration; **en ~ de** in spite of; **en ~ du bon sens** contrary to all good sense; **dépité, e** adj vexed, frustrated

**déplacé, e** [deplase] adj (propos) out of place, uncalled-for

**déplacement** [deplasmɑ̃] nm (voyage) trip, travelling no pl

**déplacer** [deplase] vt (table, voiture) to move, shift; **se ~** vi to move; (voyager) to travel; **se ~ une vertèbre** to slip a disc

**déplaire** [deplɛʀ] vt: **ça me déplaît** I don't like this, I dislike this; **se ~** vi to be unhappy; **déplaisant, e** adj disagreeable

**dépliant** [deplijɑ̃] nm leaflet

**déplier** [deplije] vt to unfold

**déplorer** [deplɔʀe] vt to deplore

**déployer** [deplwaje] vt (carte) to open out; (ailes) to spread; (troupes) to deploy

**déporter** [depɔʀte] vt (exiler) to deport; (dévier) to carry off course

**déposer** [depoze] vt (gén: mettre, poser) to lay ou put down; (à la banque, à la consigne) to deposit; (passager) to drop (off), set down; (roi) to depose; (plainte) to lodge; (marque) to register; **se ~** vi to settle; **dépositaire** nm/f (COMM) agent; **déposition** nf statement

**dépôt** [depo] nm (à la banque, sédiment) deposit; (entrepôt) warehouse, store

**dépotoir** [depotwaʀ] nm dumping ground, rubbish dump

**dépouiller** [depuje] vt (documents) to go through, peruse; **~ qn/qch de** to strip sb/sth of; **~ le scrutin** to count the votes

**dépourvu, e** [depuʀvy] adj: **~ de** lacking in, without; **prendre qn au ~** to catch sb unprepared

**déprécier** [depʀesje]: **se ~** vi to depreciate

**dépression** [depʀesjɔ̃] nf depression; **~ (nerveuse)** (nervous) breakdown

**déprimant, e** [depʀimɑ̃, ɑ̃t] adj depressing

**déprimer** [depʀime] vi to be/get depressed

---

_MOT-CLÉ_

**depuis** [dəpɥi] prép 1 (point de départ dans le temps) since; **il habite Paris depuis 1983/l'an dernier** he has been living in Paris since 1983/last year; **depuis quand le connaissez-vous?** how long have you known him?

2 (temps écoulé) for; **il habite Paris depuis 5 ans** he has been living in Paris for 5 years; **je le connais depuis**

3 ans I've known him for 3 years

3 (lieu) since; **il a plu depuis Metz** it's been raining since Metz; **elle a téléphoné depuis Valence** she rang from Valence

4 (quantité, rang) from; **depuis les plus petits jusqu'aux plus grands** from the youngest to the oldest

♦ adv (temps) since (then); **je ne lui ai pas parlé depuis !** I haven't spoken to him since (then)

**depuis que** conj since; **depuis qu'il m'a dit ça** (ever) since he said that to me

**député, e** [depyte] nm/f (POL) ≈ Member of Parliament (BRIT), ≈ Member of Congress (US)

**députer** [depyte] vt to delegate

**déraciner** [deʀasine] vt to uproot

**dérailler** [deʀaje] vi (train) to be derailed; **faire ~** to derail

**déraisonner** [deʀɛzɔne] vi to talk nonsense, rave

**dérangement** [deʀɑ̃ʒmɑ̃] nm (gêne) trouble; (gastrique etc) disorder; **en ~** (téléphone, machine) out of order

**déranger** [deʀɑ̃ʒe] vt (personne) to trouble, bother; (projets) to disrupt, upset; (objets, vêtements) to disarrange; **se ~** vi: **surtout ne vous dérangez pas pour moi** please don't put yourself out on my account; **est-ce que cela vous dérange si ...?** do you mind if ...?

**déraper** [deʀape] vi (voiture) to skid; (personne, semelles) to slip

**dérégler** [deʀegle] vt (mécanisme) to put out of order; (estomac) to upset

**dérider** [deʀide]: **se ~** vi to brighten up

**dérision** [deʀizjɔ̃] nf: **tourner en ~** to deride; **dérisoire** adj derisory

**dérive** [deʀiv] nf: **aller à la ~** (NAVIG, fig) to drift

**dérivé, e** [deʀive] nm (TECH) byproduct

**dériver** [deʀive] vt (MATH) to derive;

(*cours d'eau etc*) to divert ♦ *vi* (*bateau*) to drift; ~ **de** to derive from

**dermatologue** [dɛʀmatɔlɔg] *nm/f* dermatologist

**dernier, -ière** [dɛʀnje, jɛʀ] *adj* last; (*le plus récent*) latest, last; **lundi/le mois** ~ last Monday/month; **c'est le ~ cri** it's the very latest thing; **en** ~ last; **ce** ~ the latter; **dernièrement** *adv* recently

**dérobé, e** [deʀɔbe] *adj*: **à la ~e** surreptitiously

**dérober** [deʀɔbe] *vt* to steal; **se** ~ *vi* (*s'esquiver*) to slip away; **se** ~ **à** (*justice, regards*) to hide from; (*obligation*) to shirk

**dérogation** [deʀɔgasjɔ̃] *nf* (special) dispensation

**déroger** [deʀɔʒe]: ~ **à** *vt* to go against, depart from

**dérouiller** [deʀuje] *vt*: **se** ~ **les jambes** to stretch one's legs (*fig*)

**déroulement** [deʀulmɑ̃] *nm* (*d'une opération etc*) progress

**dérouler** [deʀule] *vt* (*ficelle*) to unwind; **se** ~ *vi* (*avoir lieu*) to take place; (*se passer*) to go (off); **tout s'est déroulé comme prévu** everything went as planned

**dérouter** [deʀute] *vt* (*avion, train*) to reroute, divert; (*étonner*) to disconcert, throw (out)

**derrière** [dɛʀjɛʀ] *adv*, *prép* behind ♦ *nm* (*d'une maison*) back; (*postérieur*) behind, bottom; **les pattes de** ~ the back or hind legs; **par** ~ from behind; (*fig*) behind one's back

**des** [de] *dét voir* **de** ♦ *prép* +*dét* = **de** +**les**

**dès** [dɛ] *prép* from; ~ **que** as soon as; ~ **son retour** as soon as he was (*ou* is) back

**désabusé, e** [dezabyze] *adj* disillusioned

**désaccord** [dezakɔʀ] *nm* disagreement; **désaccordé, e** *adj* (*MUS*) out of tune

**désaffecté, e** [dezafɛkte] *adj* disused

**désagréable** [dezagʀeabl] *adj* unpleas-

ant

**désagréger** [dezagʀeʒe]: **se** ~ *vi* to disintegrate, break up

**désagrément** [dezagʀemɑ̃] *nm* annoyance, trouble *no pl*

**désaltérer** [dezaltere] *vt*: **se** ~ to quench one's thirst

**désapprobateur, -trice** [dezapʀɔbatœʀ, tʀis] *adj* disapproving

**désapprouver** [dezapʀuve] *vt* to disapprove of

**désarmant, e** [dezaʀmɑ̃, ɑ̃t] *adj* disarming

**désarroi** [dezaʀwa] *nm* disarray

**désastre** [dezastʀ] *nm* disaster; **désastreux, -euse** *adj* disastrous

**désavantage** [dezavɑ̃taʒ] *nm* disadvantage; **désavantager** *vt* to put at a disadvantage

**descendre** [desɑ̃dʀ] *vt* (*escalier, montagne*) to go (*ou* come) down; (*valise, paquet*) to take *ou* get down; (*étagère etc*) to lower; (*fam: abattre*) to shoot down ♦ *vi* to go (*ou* come) down; (*passager: s'arrêter*) to get out, alight; ~ **à pied/en voiture** to walk/drive down; ~ **du train** to get out of *ou* get off the train; ~ **de cheval** to dismount; ~ **à l'hôtel** to stay at a hotel

**descente** [desɑ̃t] *nf* descent, going down; (*chemin*) way down; (*SKI*) downhill (race); ~ **de lit** bedside rug; ~ **(de police)** (police) raid

**description** [dɛskʀipsjɔ̃] *nf* description

**désemparé, e** [dezɑ̃paʀe] *adj* bewildered, distraught

**désemplir** [dezɑ̃pliʀ] *vi*: **ne pas** ~ to be always full

**déséquilibre** [dezekilibʀ] *nm* (*position*): **en** ~ unsteady; (*fig: des forces, du budget*) imbalance; **déséquilibré, e** *nm/f* (*PSYCH*) unbalanced person; **déséquilibrer** *vt* to throw off balance

**désert, e** [dezɛʀ, ɛʀt] *adj* deserted ♦ *nm* desert; **déserter** *vi*, *vt* to desert; **désertique** *adj* desert *cpd*

**désespéré, e** [dezɛspeʀe] *adj* desperate

**désespérer** [dezespeʀe] *vi*: ~ **(de)** to despair (of); **désespoir** *nm* despair; **en désespoir de cause** in desperation

**déshabiller** [dezabije] *vt* to undress; **se ~ vi** to undress (o.s.)

**déshériter** [dezeʀite] *vt* to disinherit; **déshérités** *nmpl*: **les déshérités** the underprivileged

**déshonneur** [dezɔnœʀ] *nm* dishonour

**déshydraté, e** [dezidʀate] *adj* dehydrated

**desiderata** [deziderata] *nmpl* requirements

**désigner** [deziɲe] *vt (montrer)* to point out, indicate; *(dénommer)* to denote; *(candidat etc)* to name

**désinfectant, e** [dezɛ̃fɛktɑ̃, ɑ̃t] *adj, nm* disinfectant

**désinfecter** [dezɛ̃fɛkte] *vt* to disinfect

**désintégrer** [dezɛ̃tegʀe]: **se ~ vi** to disintegrate

**désintéressé, e** [dezɛ̃teʀese] *adj* disinterested, unselfish

**désintéresser** [dezɛ̃teʀese] *vt*: **se ~ (de)** to lose interest (in)

**désintoxication** [dezɛ̃tɔksikasjɔ̃] *nf*: **faire une cure de ~** to undergo treatment for alcoholism *(ou* drug addiction)

**désinvolture** [dezɛ̃vɔlt] *adj* casual, offhand; **désinvolture** *nf* casualness

**désir** [deziʀ] *nm* wish; *(sensuel)* desire; **désirer** *vt* to want, wish for; *(sexuellement)* to desire; **je désire ...** *(formule de politesse)* I would like ...

**désister** [deziste]: **se ~ vi** to stand down, withdraw

**désobéir** [dezɔbeiʀ] *vi*: ~ **(à qn/qch)** to disobey (sb/sth); **désobéissant, e** *adj* disobedient

**désobligeant, e** [dezɔbliʒɑ̃, ɑ̃t] *adj* disagreeable

**désodorisant** [dezɔdɔʀizɑ̃] *nm* air freshener, deodorizer

**désœuvré, e** [dezœvʀe] *adj* idle

**désolé, e** [dezɔle] *adj (paysage)* desolate; **je suis ~** I'm sorry

**désoler** [dezɔle] *vt* to distress, grieve

**désopilant, e** [dezɔpilɑ̃, ɑ̃t] *adj* hilarious

**désordonné, e** [dezɔʀdɔne] *adj* untidy

**désordre** [dezɔʀdʀ] *nm* disorder(liness), untidiness; *(anarchie)* disorder; **en ~** in a mess, untidy

**désorienté, e** [dezɔʀjɑ̃te] *adj* disorientated

**désormais** [dezɔʀmɛ] *adv* from now on

**désossé, e** [dezɔse] *adj (viande)* boned

**desquels** [dekɛl] *prép +pron =* **de +lesquelles**

**desquels** [dekɛl] *prép +pron =* **de +lesquels**

**desséché, e** [desefe] *adj* dried up

**dessécher** [desefe]: **se ~ vi** to dry out

**dessein** [desɛ̃] *nm*: **à ~** intentionally, deliberately

**desserrer** [deseʀe] *vt* to loosen; *(frein)* to release

**dessert** [desɛʀ] *nm* dessert, pudding

**desserte** [desɛʀt] *nf (table)* side table; *(transport)*: **la ~ du village est assurée par autocar** there is a coach service to the village

**desservir** [desɛʀviʀ] *vt (ville, quartier)* to serve; *(débarrasser)*: ~ **(la table)** to clear the table

**dessin** [desɛ̃] *nm (œuvre, art)* drawing; *(motif)* pattern, design; ~ **animé** cartoon (film); ~ **humoristique** cartoon; **dessinateur, -trice** *nm/f* drawer; *(de bandes dessinées)* cartoonist; *(industriel)* draughtsman(-woman), draftsman(-woman) *(us)*; **dessiner** *vt* to draw; *(concevoir)* to design

**dessous** [d(ə)su] *adv* underneath, beneath ♦ *nm* underside ♦ *nmpl (sousvêtements)* underwear *sg*; **en ~, par ~** underneath; **au-~** *(de)* below; *(peu digne de)* beneath; **avoir le ~** to get the worst of it; **les voisins du ~** the downstairs neighbours; **dessous-de-plat** *nm inv* tablemat

**dessus** [d(ə)sy] *adv* on top; *(collé, écrit)*

**destin** on it ♦ *nm* top; **en ~** above; **par ~** *adv* over it ♦ *prép* over; **au-~ (de)** above; **avoir le ~** to get the upper hand; **dessus-de-lit** *nm inv* bedspread

**destin** [destɛ̃] *nm* fate; (*avenir*) destiny

**destinataire** [destinatɛR] *nm/f* (POSTES) addressee; (*d'un colis*) consignee

**destination** [destinasjɔ̃] *nf* (*lieu*) destination; (*usage*) purpose; **à ~ de** bound for, travelling to

**destinée** [destine] *nf* fate; (*existence, avenir*) destiny

**destiner** [destine] *vt*: **~ qch à qn** (*envisager de donner*) to intend sb to have sth; (*adresser*) to intend sth for sb; **être destiné à** (*usage*) to be meant for

**désuet, -ète** [dezɥɛ, ɛt] *adj* outdated, outmoded

**détachant** [detaʃɑ̃] *nm* stain remover

**détachement** [detaʃmɑ̃] *nm* detachment

**détacher** [detaʃe] *vt* (*enlever*) to detach, remove; (*délier*) to untie; (ADMIN): **~ qn (auprès de** *ou* **à)** to post sb (to); **se ~** *vi* (*se séparer*) to come off; (: *page*) to come out; (*se défaire*) to come undone; **se ~ sur** to stand out against; **se ~ de** (*se désintéresser*) to grow away from

**détail** [detaj] *nm* detail; (COMM): **le ~** retail; **en ~** in detail; **au ~** (COMM) retail; **détaillant** *nm* retailer; **détaillé, e** *adj* (*plan, explications*) detailed; (*facture*) itemized; **détailler** *vt* (*expliquer*) to explain in detail

**détaler** [detale] (*fam*) *vi* (*personne*) to take off

**détartrant** [detartrɑ̃] *nm* scale remover

**détaxé, e** [detakse] *adj*: **produits ~s** tax-free goods

**détecter** [detɛkte] *vt* to detect

**détective** [detɛktiv] *nm*: **~ (privé)** private detective

**déteindre** [detɛ̃dR] *vi* (*au lavage*) to run, lose its colour

**détendre** [detɑ̃dR] *vt* (*corps, esprit*) to

relax; **se ~** *vi* (*ressort*) to lose its tension; (*personne*) to relax

**détenir** [det(ə)niR] *vt* (*record, pouvoir, secret*) to hold; (*prisonnier*) to detain, hold

**détente** [detɑ̃t] *nf* relaxation

**détention** [detɑ̃sjɔ̃] *nf* (*d'armes*) possession; (*captivité*) detention; **~ préventive** custody

**détenu, e** [det(ə)ny] *nm/f* prisoner

**détergent** [detɛRʒɑ̃] *nm* detergent

**détériorer** [deterjɔre] *vt* to damage; **se ~** *vi* to deteriorate

**déterminé, e** [detɛRmine] *adj* (*résolu*) determined; (*précis*) specific, definite

**déterminer** [detɛRmine] *vt* (*fixer*) to determine; **se ~ à faire qch** to make up one's mind to do sth

**déterrer** [detere] *vt* to dig up

**détestable** [detestabl] *adj* foul, detestable

**détester** [detɛste] *vt* to hate, detest

**détonner** [detɔne] *vi* (*fig*) to clash

**détour** [detuR] *nm* detour; (*tournant*) bend, curve; **ça vaut le ~** it's worth the trip; **sans ~** (*fig*) plainly

**détourné, e** [deturne] *adj* (*moyen*) roundabout

**détournement** [deturnəmɑ̃] *nm*: **~ d'avion** hijacking

**détourner** [deturne] *vt* to divert; (*par la force*) to hijack; (*yeux, tête*) to turn away; (*de l'argent*) to embezzle; **se ~** *vi* to turn away

**détracteur, -trice** [detraktœr, tris] *nm/f* disparager, critic

**détraquer** [detrake] *vt* to put out of order; (*estomac*) to upset; **se ~** *vi* (*machine*) to go wrong

**détrempé, e** [detrɑ̃pe] *adj* (*sol*) sodden, waterlogged

**détresse** [detrɛs] *nf* distress

**détriment** [detrimɑ̃] *nm*: **au ~ de** to the detriment of

**détritus** [detrity(s)] *nmpl* rubbish *sg*, refuse *sg*

**détroit** [detrwa] *nm* strait

**détromper** [detʀɔ̃pe] vt to disabuse

**détruire** [detʀɥiʀ] vt to destroy

**dette** [dɛt] nf debt

**DEUG** sigle m (= diplôme d'études universitaires générales) diploma taken after 2 years at university

**deuil** [dœj] nm (perte) bereavement; (période) mourning; **être en ~** to be in mourning

**deux** [dø] num two; **tous les ~** both; **ses ~ mains** his both, his two hands; **~ fois** twice; **deuxième** num second; **deuxièmement** adv secondly; **deux-pièces** nm inv (tailleur) two-piece suit; (de bain) two-piece (swimsuit); (appartement) two-roomed flat (BRIT) ou apartment (US); **deux-points** nm inv colon sg; **deux-roues** nm inv two-wheeled vehicle

**devais** etc [dəvɛ] vb voir **devoir**

**dévaler** [devale] vt to hurtle down

**dévaliser** [devalize] vt to rob, burgle

**dévaloriser** [devalɔʀize] vt to depreciate; **se ~** vi to depreciate

**dévaluation** [devalɥasjɔ̃] nf devaluation

**devancer** [d(ə)vɑ̃se] vt (coureur, rival) to get ahead of; (arriver) to arrive before; (prévenir: questions, désirs) to anticipate

**devant** [d(ə)vɑ̃] adv in front; (à distance: en avant) ahead ♦ prép in front of; (en avant) ahead of; (avec mouvement: passer) past; (en présence de) before, in front of; (étant donné) in view of ♦ nm front; **prendre les ~s** to make the first move; **les pattes de ~** the front legs, the forelegs; **par ~** (boutonner) at the front; (entrer) the front way; **aller au~ de qn** to go out to meet sb; **aller au~ de** (désirs de qn) to anticipate

**devanture** [d(ə)vɑ̃tyʀ] nf (étalage) display; (vitrine) (shop) window

**déveine** [devɛn] (fam) nf rotten luck no pl

**développement** [dev(ə)lɔpmɑ̃] nm development; **pays en voie de ~** developing countries

**développer** [dev(ə)lɔpe] vt to develop; **se ~** vi to develop

**devenir** [dəv(ə)niʀ] vb +attrib to become; **que sont-ils devenus?** what has become of them?

**dévergondé, e** [devɛʀgɔ̃de] adj wild, shameless

**déverser** [devɛʀse] vt (liquide) to pour (out); (ordures) to tip (out); **se ~ dans** (fleuve) to flow into

**dévêtir** [devetiʀ]: **se ~** vi to undress

**devez** etc [dəve] vb voir **devoir**

**déviation** [devjasjɔ̃] nf (AUTO) diversion (BRIT), detour (US)

**devienne** etc [dəvjɛn] vb voir **devenir**

**dévier** [devje] vt (fleuve, circulation) to divert; (coup) to deflect ♦ vi to veer (off course)

**devin** [dəvɛ̃] nm soothsayer, seer

**deviner** [d(ə)vine] vt to guess; (apercevoir) to distinguish; **devinette** nf riddle

**devins** etc [dəvɛ̃] vb voir **devenir**

**devis** [d(ə)vi] nm estimate, quotation

**dévisager** [deviʒaʒe] vt to stare at

**devise** [dəviz] nf (formule) motto, watchword; **~s** nfpl (argent) currency sg

**deviser** [d(ə)vize] vi to converse

**dévisser** [devise] vt to unscrew, undo

**dévoiler** [devwale] vt to unveil

**devoir** [d(ə)vwaʀ] nm duty; (SCOL) homework no pl; (: en classe) exercise ♦ vt (argent, respect): **~ qch (à qn)** to owe (sb) sth; (+infin: obligation): **il doit le faire** he has to do it, he must do it; (: intention): **le nouveau centre commercial doit ouvrir en mai** the new shopping centre is due to open in May; (: probabilité): **il doit être tard** it must be late

**dévolu, e** [devɔly] adj: **jeter son ~ sur** to fix one's choice on

**dévorer** [devɔʀe] vt to devour

**dévot, e** [devo, ɔt] adj devout, pious; **dévotion** nf devoutness

**dévoué, e** [devwe] *adj* devoted

**dévouement** [devumɑ̃] *nm* devotion

**dévouer** [devwe]: **se ~** *vi* (*se sacrifier*): **se ~ (pour)** to sacrifice o.s. (for); (*se consacrer*): **se ~ à** to devote *ou* dedicate o.s.

**dévoyé, e** [devwaje] *adj* delinquent

**devrai** *etc* [dəvre] *vb voir* **devoir**

**diabète** [djabɛt] *nm* diabetes *sg*; **diabétique** *nm/f* diabetic

**diable** [djɑbl] *nm* devil

**diabolo** [djabɔlo] *nm* (*boisson*) lemonade with fruit cordial

**diagnostic** [djagnɔstik] *nm* diagnosis *sg*; **diagnostiquer** *vt* to diagnose

**diagonal, e, -aux** [djagɔnal, o] *adj* diagonal; **diagonale** *nf* diagonal; **en diagonale** diagonally

**diagramme** [djagram] *nm* chart, graph

**dialecte** [djalɛkt] *nm* dialect

**dialogue** [djalɔg] *nm* dialogue

**diamant** [djamɑ̃] *nm* diamond

**diamètre** [djamɛtr] *nm* diameter

**diapason** [djapazɔ̃] *nm* tuning fork

**diaphragme** [djafragm] *nm* diaphragm

**diapo** [djapo] (*fam*) *nf* slide

**diapositive** [djapozitiv] *nf* transparency, slide

**diarrhée** [djare] *nf* diarrhoea

**dictateur** [diktatœr] *nm* dictator; **dictature** *nf* dictatorship

**dictée** [dikte] *nf* dictation

**dicter** [dikte] *vt* to dictate

**dictionnaire** [diksjɔnɛr] *nm* dictionary

**dicton** [diktɔ̃] *nm* saying, dictum

**dièse** [djɛz] *nm* sharp

**diesel** [djezɛl] *nm* diesel ♦ *adj inv* diesel

**diète** [djɛt] *nf* (*jeûne*) starvation diet; (*régime*) diet; **diététique** *adj*: **magasin diététique** health food shop

**dieu, x** [djø] *nm* god; **D~** God; **mon D~!** good heavens!

**diffamation** [difamasjɔ̃] *nf* slander; (*écrite*) libel

**différé** [difere] *nm* (*TV*): **en ~** (pre-)

recorded

**différemment** [diferamɑ̃] *adv* differently

**différence** [diferɑ̃s] *nf* difference; **à la ~ de** unlike; **différencier** *vt* to differentiate; **différend** *nm* difference (of opinion), disagreement

**différent, e** [diferɑ̃, ɑ̃t] *adj* (*dissemblable*) different; **~ de** different from; (*divers*) different, various

**différer** [difere] *vt* to postpone, put off ♦ *vi*: **~ (de)** to differ (from)

**difficile** [difisil] *adj* difficult; (*exigeant*) hard to please; **difficilement** *adv* with difficulty

**difficulté** [difikylte] *nf* difficulty; **en ~** (*bateau, alpiniste*) in difficulties

**difforme** [difɔrm] *adj* deformed, misshapen

**diffuser** [difyze] *vt* (*chaleur*) to diffuse; (*émission, musique*) to broadcast; (*nouvelle*) to circulate; (*COMM*) to distribute

**digérer** [diʒere] *vt* to digest; (*fam: accepter*) to stomach, put up with; **digestif** *nm* (*after-dinner*) liqueur; **digestion** *nf* digestion

**digne** [diɲ] *adj* dignified; **~ de** worthy of; **~ de foi** trustworthy; **dignité** *nf* dignity

**digue** [dig] *nf* dike, dyke

**dilapider** [dilapide] *vt* to squander

**dilemme** [dilɛm] *nm* dilemma

**dilettante** [diletɑ̃t] *nm/f*: **faire qch en ~** to dabble in sth

**diligence** [diliʒɑ̃s] *nf* stagecoach

**diluer** [dilɥe] *vt* to dilute

**diluvien, ne** [dilyvjɛ̃, jɛn] *adj*: **pluie ~ne** torrential rain

**dimanche** [dimɑ̃ʃ] *nm* Sunday

**dimension** [dimɑ̃sjɔ̃] *nf* (*grandeur*) size; (~s) dimensions

**diminué, e** [diminɥe] *adj*: **il est très ~ depuis son accident** he's not at all the man he was since his accident

**diminuer** [diminɥe] *vt* to reduce, decrease; (*ardeur etc*) to lessen; (*dénigrer*) to belittle ♦ *vi* to decrease, diminish;

**diminutif** nm (surnom) pet name; **diminution** nf decreasing, diminishing

**dinde** [dɛ̃d] nf turkey

**dindon** [dɛ̃dɔ̃] nm turkey

**dîner** [dine] nm dinner ♦ vi to have dinner

**dingue** [dɛ̃g] (fam) adj crazy

**dinosaure** [dinɔzɔr] nm dinosaur

**diplomate** [diplɔmat] nm (secret, mensonge, bande) diplomat; (fig) diplomatist; **diplomatie** nf diplomacy

**diplôme** [diplom] nm diploma; **avoir des ~s** to have qualifications; **diplômé, e** adj qualified

**dire** [dir] nm: **au ~ de** according to ♦ vt to say; (secret, mensonge, heure) to tell; **~ qch à qn** to tell sb sth; **~ à qn qu'il fasse** ou **de faire** to tell sb to do; **on dit que** they say that; **ceci dit** that being said; **si cela lui dit** (plaire) if he fancies it; **que dites-vous de** (penser) what do you think of; **on dirait que** it looks (ou sounds etc) as if; **dis/dites (donc)!** I say!

**direct, e** [dirɛkt] adj direct ♦ nm (TV): **en ~** live; **directement** adv directly

**directeur, -trice** [dirɛktœr, tris] nm/f (d'entreprise) director; (de - service manager(-eress)); (d'école) head(teacher) (BRIT), principal (US)

**direction** [dirɛksjɔ̃] nf (sens) direction; (d'entreprise) management; (AUTO) steering; "**toutes ~s**" "all routes"

**dirent** [dir] vb voir **dire**

**dirigeant, e** [diriʒɑ̃, ɑ̃t] adj (classe) ruling ♦ nm/f (d'un parti etc) leader

**diriger** [diriʒe] vt (entreprise) to manage, run; (véhicule) to steer; (orchestre) to conduct; (recherches, travaux) to supervise; **se ~** vi (s'orienter) to find one's way; **se ~ vers** ou **sur** to make ou head for

**dis** etc [di] vb voir **dire**

**discernement** [disɛrnəmɑ̃] nm (bon sens) discernment, judgement

**discerner** [disɛrne] vt to discern, make out

**discipline** [disiplin] nf discipline; **discipliner** vt to discipline

**discontinu, e** [diskɔ̃tiny] adj intermittent

**discontinuer** [diskɔ̃tinɥe] vi: **sans ~** without stopping, without a break

**discordant, e** [diskɔrdɑ̃, ɑ̃t] adj discordant

**discothèque** [diskɔtɛk] nf (boîte de nuit) disco(thèque)

**discours** [diskur] nm speech

**discret, -ète** [diskrɛ, ɛt] adj discreet; (parfum, maquillage) unobtrusive; **discrétion** nf discretion; **à discrétion** as much as one wants

**discrimination** [diskriminasjɔ̃] nf discrimination; **sans ~** indiscriminately

**disculper** [diskylpe] vt to exonerate

**discussion** [diskysjɔ̃] nf discussion

**discutable** [diskytabl] adj debatable

**discuté, e** [diskyte] adj controversial

**discuter** [diskyte] vt (débattre) to discuss; (contester) to question, dispute ♦ vi to talk; (protester) to argue; **~ de** to discuss

**dise** etc [diz] vb voir **dire**

**diseuse** [dizøz] nf: **~ de bonne aventure** fortuneteller

**disgracieux, -euse** [disgrasjø, jøz] adj ungainly, awkward

**disjoindre** [diswɛ̃dr] vt to take apart; **se ~** vi to come apart

**disjoncteur** [diswɔ̃ktœr] nm (ÉLEC) circuit breaker

**disloquer** [dislɔke]: **se ~** vi (parti, empire) to break up

**disons** [dizɔ̃] vb voir **dire**

**disparaître** [disparɛtr] vi to disappear; (se perdre: traditions etc) to die out; **faire ~** (tache) to remove; (douleur) to get rid of

**disparition** [disparisjɔ̃] nf disappearance; **espèce en voie de ~** endangered species

**disparu, e** [dispary] nm/f missing person ♦ adj: **être porté ~** to be reported missing

**dispensaire** [dispɑ̃sɛʀ] nm community clinic

**dispenser** [dispɑ̃se] vt: ~ qn de to exempt sb from; **se ~ de** vt (corvée) to get out of

**disperser** [dispɛʀse] vt to scatter; **se ~** vi to break up

**disponibilité** [disponibilite] nf availability; **disponible** adj available

**dispos** [dispo] adj m: **(frais et) ~** fresh (as a daisy)

**disposé, e** [dispoze] adj: **bien/mal ~** (humeur) in a good/bad mood; **~ à** (prêt à) willing ou prepared to

**disposer** [dispoze] vt to arrange ♦ vi: **vous pouvez ~** you may leave; **~ de** to have (at one's disposal); **se ~ à faire** to prepare to do, be about to do

**dispositif** [dispozitif] nm device; (fig) system, plan of action

**disposition** [dispozisjɔ̃] nf (arrangement) arrangement, layout; (humeur) mood; **prendre ses ~s** to make arrangements; **avoir des ~s pour la musique** etc to have a special aptitude for music etc; **à la ~ de qn** at sb's disposal; **je suis à votre ~** I am at your service

**disproportionné, e** [dispʀopɔʀsjɔne] adj disproportionate, out of all proportion

**dispute** [dispyt] nf quarrel, argument; **disputer** vt (match) to play; (combat) to fight; **se disputer** vi to quarrel

**disquaire** [diskɛʀ] nm/f record dealer

**disqualifier** [diskalifje] vt to disqualify

**disque** [disk] nm (MUS) record; (forme, pièce) disc; (SPORT) discus; ~ **compact** compact disc; ~ **dur** hard disk; **disquette** nf floppy disk, diskette

**disséminer** [disemine] vt to scatter

**disséquer** [diseke] vt to dissect

**dissertation** [disɛʀtasjɔ̃] nf (SCOL) essay

**dissimuler** [disimyle] vt to conceal

**dissipé, e** [disipe] adj (élève) undisciplined, unruly

**dissiper** [disipe] vt to dissipate; (fortune) to squander; **se ~** vi (brouillard) to clear, disperse

**dissolvant** [disolvɑ̃] nm nail polish remover

**dissonant, e** [disonɑ̃, ɑ̃t] adj discordant

**dissoudre** [disudʀ] vt to dissolve; **se ~** vi to dissolve

**dissuader** [disɥade] vt: ~ **qn de faire** to dissuade sb from doing; **dissuasion** nf: **force de dissuasion** deterrent power

**distance** [distɑ̃s] nf distance; (fig: écart) gap; **à ~** at ou from a distance; **distancer** vt to outdistance

**distant, e** [distɑ̃, ɑ̃t] adj (réservé) distant; ~ **de** (lieu) far away from

**distendre**: **se ~** vi to distend

**distillerie** [distilʀi] nf distillery

**distinct, e** [distɛ̃(kt), ɛ̃kt] adj distinct; **distinctement** adv distinctly, clearly; **distinctif, -ive** adj distinctive

**distingué, e** [distɛ̃ge] adj distinguished

**distinguer** [distɛ̃ge] vt to distinguish

**distraction** [distʀaksjɔ̃] nf (inattention) absent-mindedness; (passe-temps) distraction, entertainment

**distraire** [distʀɛʀ] vt (divertir) to entertain, divert; (déranger) to distract; **se ~** vi to amuse ou enjoy o.s.; **distrait, e** adj absent-minded

**distrayant, e** [distʀɛjɑ̃, ɑ̃t] adj entertaining

**distribuer** [distʀibɥe] vt to distribute, hand out; (CARTES) to deal (out); (courrier) to deliver; **distributeur** nm (COMM) distributor; (automatique) (vending) machine; (: de billets) (cash) dispenser; **distribution** nf distribution; (postale) delivery; (choix d'acteurs) casting, cast

**dit, e** [di, dit] pp de **dire** ♦ adj (fixé): **le jour ~** the arranged day; (surnommé): **X, ~ Pierrot** X, known as Pierrot

**dites** [dit] vb voir **dire**

**divaguer** [divage] vi to ramble; (fam) to rave

**divan** [divã] nm divan

**diverger** [divɛʀʒe] vi to diverge

**divers, e** [divɛʀ, ɛʀs] adj (varié) diverse, varied; (différent) different, various; **~es personnes** various ou several people

**diversifier** [divɛʀsifje] vt to vary

**diversité** [divɛʀsite] nf (variété) diversity

**divertir** [divɛʀtiʀ]: **se ~** vi to amuse ou enjoy o.s.; **divertissement** nm distraction, entertainment

**divin, e** [divɛ̃, in] adj divine

**diviser** [divize] vt to divide; **division** nf division

**divorce** [divɔʀs] nm divorce; **divorcé, e** nm/f divorcee; **divorcer** vi to get a divorce, get divorced

**divulguer** [divylge] vt to disclose

**dix** [dis] num ten; **dixième** num tenth

**dizaine** [dizɛn] nf: **une ~ (de)** about ten, ten or so

**do** [do] nm (note) C; (en chantant la gamme) do(h)

**docile** [dɔsil] adj docile

**dock** [dɔk] nm dock; **docker** nm docker

**docteur** [dɔktœʀ] nm doctor; **doctorat** nm doctorate; **doctoresse** nf lady doctor

**doctrine** [dɔktʀin] nf doctrine

**document** [dɔkymã] nm document; **documentaire** adj, nm documentary; **documentaliste** nm/f (SCOL) librarian; **documentation** nf documentation, literature; **documenter** vt: **se documenter (sur)** to gather information (on)

**dodo** [dodo] nm (langage enfantin): **aller faire ~** to go to bye-byes

**dodu, e** [dody] adj plump

**dogue** [dɔg] nm mastiff

**doigt** [dwa] nm finger; **à deux ~s de** within an inch of; **~ de pied** toe; **doigté** nm (MUS) fingering; (fig: habileté) diplomacy, tact

**doit** etc [dwa] vb voir **devoir**

**doléances** [dɔleãs] nfpl grievances

**dollar** [dɔlaʀ] nm dollar

**domaine** [dɔmɛn] nm estate, property; (fig) domain, field

**domestique** [dɔmɛstik] adj domestic ♦ nm/f servant, domestic; **domestiquer** vt to domesticate

**domicile** [dɔmisil] nm home, place of residence; **à ~** at home; **livrer à ~** to deliver; **domicilié, e** adj: **"domicilié à ..."** "address ..."

**dominant, e** [dɔminã, ãt] adj (opinion) predominant

**dominer** [dɔmine] vt to dominate; (sujet) to master; (surpasser) to outclass, surpass; (surplomber) to tower above, dominate ♦ vi to be in the dominant position; **se ~** vi to control o.s.

**domino** [dɔmino] nm domino

**dommage** [dɔmaʒ] nm: **~s (dégâts)** damage no pl; **c'est ~!** what a shame! **c'est ~ que** it's a shame ou pity that; **dommages-intérêts** nmpl damages

**dompter** [d5(p)te] vt to tame; **dompteur, -euse** nm/f trainer

**DOM-TOM** [dɔmtɔm] sigle m (= départements et territoires d'outre-mer) French overseas departments and territories

**don** [d5] nm gift; (charité) donation; **avoir des ~s pour** to have a gift ou talent for; **elle a le ~ de m'énerver** she's got a knack of getting on my nerves

**donc** [d5k] conj therefore, so; (après une digression) so, then

**donjon** [d535] nm keep

**donné, e** [dɔne] adj (convenu: lieu, heure) given; (pas cher: fam): **c'est ~** it's a gift; **étant ~ ... given ...; données** nfpl data

**donner** [dɔne] vt to give; (vieux habits etc) to give away; (spectacle) to put on; **~ qch à qn** to give sb sth, give sth to sb; **~ sur** (suj: fenêtre, chambre) to look (out) onto; **ça donne soif/faim** it makes you (feel) thirsty/hungry; **se ~ à fond** to give one's all; **se ~ du mal** to take (great) trouble; **s'en ~ à cœur**

**joie** (fam) to have a great time

---
MOT-CLÉ
---

**dont** [dɔ̃] pron relatif **1** (appartenance: objets) whose, of which; (appartenance: êtres animés) whose; **la maison dont le toit est rouge** the house whose roof is red, the house whose roof is red; **l'homme dont je connais la sœur** the man whose sister I know
**2** (parmi lesquel(le)s): **2 livres, dont l'un est ...** 2 books, one of which is ...; **il y avait plusieurs personnes, dont Gabrielle** there were several people, among them Gabrielle; **10 blessés, dont 2 grièvement** 10 injured, 2 of them seriously
**3** (complément d'adjectif, de verbe): **le fils dont il est si fier** the son he's so proud of; **ce dont je parle** what I'm talking about

**doré, e** [dɔʀe] adj golden; (avec dorure) gilt, gilded
**dorénavant** [dɔʀenavɑ̃] adv henceforth
**dorer** [dɔʀe] vt to gild; **(faire) ~** (CULIN) to brown
**dorloter** [dɔʀlɔte] vt to pamper
**dormir** [dɔʀmiʀ] vi to sleep; (être endormi) to be asleep
**dortoir** [dɔʀtwaʀ] nm dormitory
**dorure** [dɔʀyʀ] nf gilding
**dos** [do] nm back; (de livre) spine; **"voir au ~"** "see over"; **de ~** from the back
**dosage** [dozaʒ] nm mixture
**dose** [doz] nf dose; **doser** vt to measure out; **il faut savoir doser ses efforts** you have to be able to pace yourself
**dossard** [dosaʀ] nm number (worn by competitor)
**dossier** [dosje] nm (documents) file; (de chaise) back; (PRESSE) feature; **un ~ scolaire** a school report
**dot** [dɔt] nf dowry
**doter** [dɔte] vt: **~ de** to equip with

**douane** [dwan] nf customs pl; **douanier, -ière** adj customs cpd ♦ nm customs officer
**double** [dubl] adj, adv double ♦ nm (2 fois plus): **le ~ (de)** twice as much (ou many) (as); (autre exemplaire) duplicate, copy; (sosie) double; (TENNIS) doubles sg; **en ~ (exemplaire)** in duplicate; **faire ~ emploi** to be redundant
**double-cliquer** [dublklike] vi (INFORM) to double-click
**doubler** [duble] vt (multiplier par 2) to double; (vêtement) to line; (dépasser) to overtake, pass; (film) to dub; (acteur) to stand in for ♦ vi to double
**doublure** [dublyʀ] nf lining; (CINÉMA) stand-in
**douce** [dus] adj voir **doux; douceâtre** adj sickly sweet; **doucement** adv gently; (lentement) slowly; **doucereux, -euse** (péj) adj sugary; **douceur** nf softness; (de quelqu'un) gentleness; (de climat) mildness
**douche** [duʃ] nf shower; **doucher: se doucher** vi to have ou take a shower
**doudoune** [dudun] nf padded jacket
**doué, e** [dwe] adj gifted, talented; **être ~ pour** to have a gift for
**douille** [duj] nf (ÉLEC) socket
**douillet, te** [dujɛ, ɛt] adj cosy; (péj: à la douleur) soft
**douleur** [dulœʀ] nf pain; (chagrin) grief, distress; **douloureux, -euse** adj painful
**doute** [dut] nm doubt; **sans ~** no doubt; (probablement) probably; **sans aucun ~** without a doubt; **douter** vt to doubt; **douter de** (sincérité de qn) to have (one's) doubts about; (réussite) to be doubtful of; **se douter de qch/que** to suspect sth/that; **je m'en doutais** I suspected as much; **douteux, -euse** adj (incertain) doubtful; (péj) dubious-looking
**Douvres** [duvʀ] nf Dover
**doux, douce** [du, dus] adj soft; (sucré) sweet; (peu fort: moutarde, clément: cli-

*mat*) mild; (*pas brusque*) gentle

**douzaine** [duzɛn] *nf* (12) dozen; (*environ 12*): **une ~ (de)** a dozen or so

**douze** [duz] *num* twelve; **douzième** *num* twelfth

**doyen, ne** [dwajɛ̃, jɛn] *nm/f* (*en âge*) most senior member; (*de faculté*) dean

**dragée** [dʀaʒe] *nf* sugared almond

**dragon** [dʀagɔ̃] *nm* dragon

**draguer** [dʀage] *vt* (*rivière*) to dredge; (*fam*) to try to pick up

**dramatique** [dʀamatik] *adj* dramatic; (*tragique*) tragic ♦ *nf* (*TV*) (television) drama

**dramaturge** [dʀamatyʀʒ] *nm* dramatist, playwright

**drame** [dʀam] *nm* drama

**drap** [dʀa] *nm* (*de lit*) sheet; (*tissu*) woollen fabric

**drapeau, x** [dʀapo] *nm* flag

**drap-housse** [dʀaus] *nm* fitted sheet

**dresser** [dʀese] *vt* (*mettre vertical, monter*) to put up, erect; (*liste*) to draw up; (*animal*) to train; **se ~** *vi* (*obstacle*) to stand; (*personne*) to draw o.s. up; **~ qn contre qn** to set sb against sb; **~ l'oreille** to prick up one's ears

**drogue** [dʀɔg] *nf* drug; **la ~** drugs *pl*; **drogué, e** *nm/f* drug addict; **droguer** *vt* (*victime*) to drug; **se droguer** *vi* (*aux stupéfiants*) to take drugs; (*péj: de médicaments*) to dose o.s. up; **droguerie** *nf* hardware shop; **droguiste** *nm* keeper/ owner of a hardware shop

**droit, e** [dʀwa, dʀwat] *adj* (*non courbe*) straight; (*vertical*) upright, straight; (*fig: loyal*) upright, straight(forward); (*opposé à gauche*) right, right-hand ♦ *adv* straight ♦ *nm* (*prérogative*) right; (*taxe*) duty, tax; (: *d'inscription*) fee; (*JUR*): **le ~** law; **avoir le ~ de** to be allowed to; **avoir ~ à** to be entitled to; **être dans son ~** to be within one's rights; **à ~e** on the right; (*direction*) (to the) right; **~s d'auteur** royalties; **~s de l'homme** human rights; **~ d'inscription** enrolment fee; **droite** *nf* (*POL*): **la droite** the

right (*wing*); **droitier, -ière** *nm/f* right-handed person; **droiture** *nf* uprightness, straightness

**drôle** [dʀol] *adj* funny; **une ~ d'idée** a funny idea; **drôlement** (*fam*) *adv* (*très*) terribly, awfully

**dromadaire** [dʀɔmadɛʀ] *nm* dromedary

**dru, e** [dʀy] *adj* (*cheveux*) thick, bushy; (*pluie*) heavy

**du** [dy] *dét* voir **de ♦** *prép* +*dét* = **de + le**

**dû, due** [dy] *vb* voir **devoir ♦** *adj* (*somme*) owing, owed; (*causé par*): **~ à** due to ♦ *nm* due

**duc** [dyk] *nm* duke; **duchesse** *nf* duchess

**dûment** [dymã] *adv* duly

**dune** [dyn] *nf* dune

**Dunkerque** [dœ̃kɛʀk] *n* Dunkirk

**duo** [dyo] *nm* (*MUS*) duet

**dupe** [dyp] *nf* dupe ♦ *adj*: **(ne pas) être ~ de** (not) to be taken in by

**duplex** [dyplɛks] *nm* (*appartement*) split-level apartment, duplex

**duplicata** [dyplikata] *nm* duplicate

**duquel** [dykɛl] *prép* + *pron* = **de +lequel**

**dur, e** [dyʀ] *adj* (*pierre, siège, travail, problème*) hard; (*voix, climat*) harsh; (*sévère*) hard, harsh; (*cruel*) hard(-hearted); (*porte, col*) stiff; (*viande*) tough ♦ *adv* hard ♦ *nm* (*fam: meneur*) tough nut; **~ d'oreille** hard of hearing

**durant** [dyʀã] *prép* (*au cours de*) during; (*pendant*) for; **des mois ~** for months

**durcir** [dyʀsiʀ] *vt*, *vi* to harden; **se durcir** *vi* to harden

**durée** [dyʀe] *nf* length; (*d'une pile etc*) life; **de courte ~** (*séjour*) short

**durement** [dyʀmã] *adv* harshly

**durer** [dyʀe] *vi* to last

**dureté** [dyʀte] *nf* hardness; harshness; stiffness; toughness

**durit** ® [dyʀit] *nf* (*car radiator*) hose

**dus** *etc* [dy] *vb* voir **devoir**

**duvet** [dyvɛ] *nm* down; (*sac de couchage*) down-filled sleeping bag

**DVD** sigle m (= digital versatile disc) DVD

**dynamique** [dinamik] adj dynamic; **dynamisme** nm dynamism

**dynamite** [dinamit] nf dynamite

**dynamo** [dinamo] nf dynamo

**dyslexie** [disleksi] nf dyslexia, word-blindness

# E, e

**eau, x** [o] nf water; **~x** nfpl (MÉD) waters; **prendre l'~** to leak, let in water; **tomber à l'~** (fig) to fall through; **~ courante** running water; **~ de Javel** bleach; **~ de toilette** toilet water; **~ douce** fresh water; **~ gazeuse** sparkling (mineral) water; **~ minérale** mineral water; **~ plate** still water; **~ potable** drinking water; **eau-de-vie** nf brandy; **eau-forte** nf etching

**ébahi, e** [ebai] adj dumbfounded

**ébattre** [ebatʀ]: **s'~** vi to frolic

**ébaucher** [ebofe] vt to sketch out, outline; **s'~** vi to take shape

**ébène** [eben] nf ebony; **ébéniste** nm cabinetmaker

**éberlué, e** [ebeʀlɥe] adj astounded

**éblouir** [ebluiʀ] vt to dazzle

**éborgner** [ebɔʀɲe] vt to blind in one eye

**éboueur** [ebwœʀ] nm dustman (BRIT), garbageman (US)

**ébouillanter** [ebujɑ̃te] vt to scald; (CU-LIN) to blanch

**éboulement** [ebulmɑ̃] nm rock fall

**ébouler** [ebule]: **s'~** vi to crumble, collapse; **éboulis** nmpl fallen rocks

**ébouriffé, e** [ebuʀife] adj tousled

**ébranler** [ebʀɑ̃le] vt to shake; (affaiblir) to weaken; **s'~** vi (partir) to move off

**ébrécher** [ebʀeʃe] vt to chip

**ébriété** [ebʀijete] nf: **en état d'~** in a state of intoxication

**ébrouer** [ebʀue]: **s'~** vi to shake o.s.

**ébruiter** [ebʀɥite] vt to spread, disclose

**ébullition** [ebylisjɔ̃] nf boiling point

**écaille** [ekaj] nf (de poisson) scale; (matière) tortoiseshell; **écailler** (poisson) to scale; **s'~** vi to flake or peel (off)

**écarlate** [ekaʀlat] adj scarlet

**écarquiller** [ekaʀkije] vt: **~ les yeux** to stare wide-eyed

**écart** [ekaʀ] nm gap; **à l'~** out of the way; **à l'~ de** away from; **faire un ~** (voiture) to swerve; **~ de conduite** misdemeanour

**écarté, e** [ekaʀte] adj (lieu) out-of-the-way, remote; (ouvert): **les jambes ~es** legs apart; **les bras ~s** arms outstretched

**écarter** [ekaʀte] vt (séparer) to move apart, separate; (éloigner) to push back, move away; (ouvrir: bras, jambes) to spread, open; (: rideau) to draw (back); (éliminer: candidat, possibilité) to dismiss; **s'~** vi to part; (s'éloigner) to move away; **s'~ de** to wander from

**écervelé, e** [esɛʀvale] adj scatter-brained, featherbrained

**échafaud** [eʃafo] nm scaffold

**échafaudage** [eʃafodaʒ] nm scaffolding

**échafauder** [eʃafode] vt (plan) to construct

**échalote** [eʃalɔt] nf shallot

**échancrure** [eʃɑ̃kʀyʀ] nf (de robe) scoop neckline

**échange** [eʃɑ̃ʒ] nm exchange; **en ~ de** in exchange ou return for; **échanger** vt: **échanger qch (contre)** to exchange sth (for); **échangeur** nm (AUTO) interchange

**échantillon** [eʃɑ̃tijɔ̃] nm sample

**échappement** [eʃapmɑ̃] nm (AUTO) exhaust

**échapper** [eʃape]: **~ à** vt (gardien) to escape (from); (punition, péril) to escape; **s'~** vi to escape; **~ à qn** (détail, sens) to escape sb; (objet qu'on tient) to slip out of sb's hands; **laisser ~** (cri etc) to let out; **l'~ belle** to have a narrow escape

**écharde** [eʃaʀd] nf splinter (of wood)
**écharpe** [eʃaʀp] nf scarf; **avoir le bras en ~** to have one's arm in a sling
**échasse** [eʃas] nf stilt
**échassier** [eʃasje] nm wader
**échauffer** [eʃofe] vt (moteur) to overheat; vi (SPORT) to warm up; (dans la discussion) to become heated
**échéance** [eʃeɑ̃s] nf (d'un paiement: date) settlement date; (fig) deadline; **brève ~** in the short term; **à longue ~** in the long run
**échéant** [eʃeɑ̃]: **le cas ~** adv if the case arises
**échec** [eʃɛk] nm failure; (ÉCHECS): **~ et mat/au roi** checkmate/check; **~s** nmpl (jeu) chess sg; **tenir en ~** to hold in check
**échelle** [eʃɛl] nf ladder; (fig, d'une carte) scale
**échelon** [eʃ(ə)lɔ̃] nm (d'échelle) rung; (ADMIN) grade; **échelonner** vt to space out
**échevelé, e** [eʃəv(ə)le] adj tousled, dishevelled
**échine** [eʃin] nf backbone, spine
**échiquier** [eʃikje] nm chessboard
**écho** [eko] nm echo; **échographie** nf: **passer une échographie** to have a scan
**échoir** [eʃwaʀ] vi (dette) to fall due; (délais) to expire; **~ à** to fall to
**échouer** [eʃwe] vi to fail; **s'~** vi to run aground
**échu, e** [eʃy] pp de **échoir**
**éclabousser** [eklabuse] vt to splash
**éclair** [eklɛʀ] nm (d'orage) flash of lightning, lightning no pl; (gâteau) éclair
**éclairage** [eklɛʀaʒ] nm lighting
**éclaircie** [eklɛʀsi] nf bright interval
**éclaircir** [eklɛʀsiʀ] vt to lighten; (fig: mystère) to clear up; (: point) to clarify; **s'~** vi (ciel) to clear; **s'~ la voix** to clear one's throat; **éclaircissement** nm (sur un point) clarification
**éclairer** [eklɛʀe] vt (lieu) to light (up);

(personne: avec une lampe etc) to light the way for; (fig: problème) to shed light on ♦ vi: **~ mal/bien** to give poor/good light; **s'~ à la bougie** to use candlelight
**éclaireur, -euse** [eklɛʀœʀ, øz] nm, f (scout) (boy scout/girl guide ♦ nm (MIL) scout
**éclat** [ekla] nm (de bombe, de verre) fragment; (du soleil, d'une couleur etc) brightness, brilliance; (d'une cérémonie) splendour; (scandale): **faire un ~** to cause a commotion; **~s de voix** shouts; **~ de rire** roar of laughter
**éclatant, e** [eklatɑ̃, ɑ̃t] adj brilliant
**éclater** [eklate] vi (pneu) to burst; (bombe) to explode; (guerre) to break out; (groupe, parti) to break up; **~ en sanglots/de rire** to burst out sobbing/laughing
**éclipser** [eklipse]: **s'~** vi to slip away
**éclore** [eklɔʀ] vi (œuf) to hatch; (fleur) to open (out)
**écluse** [eklyz] nf lock
**écœurant, e** [ekœʀɑ̃, ɑ̃t] adj (gâteau etc) sickly; (fig) sickening
**écœurer** [ekœʀe] vt: **~ qn** (nourriture) to make sb feel sick; (conduite, personne) to disgust sb
**école** [ekɔl] nf school; **aller à l'~** to go to school; **~ maternelle/primaire** nursery/primary school; **~ publique** state school; **écolier, -ière** nm, f schoolboy(-girl)

**école maternelle**

*Nursery school (l'école maternelle) is publicly funded in France and, though not compulsory, is attended by most children between the ages of two and six. Statutory education begins with primary school (l'école primaire) from the age of six to ten or eleven.*

**écologie** [ekɔlɔʒi] nf ecology; **écologique** adj environment-friendly; **écolo-**

**giste** nm/f ecologist

**éconduire** [ekɔ̃dɥir] vt to dismiss

**économe** [ekɔnɔm] adj thrifty ♦ nm/f (de lycée etc) bursar (BRIT), treasurer (US)

**économie** [ekɔnɔmi] nf economy; (gain: d'argent, de temps etc) saving; (science) economics sg; **~s** nfpl (pécule) savings; **économique** adj (avantageux) economical; (ÉCON) economic; **économiser** vt, vi to save

**écoper** [ekɔpe] vi to bale out; **~ de 3 ans de prison** (fig: fam) to get sentenced to 3 years

**écorce** [ekɔrs] nf bark; (de fruit) peel

**écorcher** [ekɔrʃe] vt: **s'~ le genou/la main** to graze one's knee/one's hand; **écorchure** nf graze

**écossais, e** [ekɔsɛ, ɛz] adj Scottish ♦ nm/f: **É~, e** Scot

**Écosse** [ekɔs] nf: **l'~** Scotland

**écosser** [ekɔse] vt to shell

**écoulement** [ekulmɑ̃] nm (d'eau) flow

**écouler** [ekule] vt (marchandise) to sell; **s'~** vi (eau) to flow (out); (jours, temps) to pass (by)

**écourter** [ekurte] vt to curtail, cut short

**écoute** [ekut] nf (RADIO, TV): **temps/ heure d'~** listening (ou viewing) time/ hour; **rester à l'~ (de)** to stay tuned in (to); **~s téléphoniques** phone tapping sg

**écouter** [ekute] vt to listen to; **écouteur** [ekutœr] nm (TÉL) receiver; (RADIO) headphones pl, headset

**écoutille** [ekutij] nf hatch

**écran** [ekrɑ̃] nm screen; **petit ~** television; **~ total** sunblock

**écrasant, e** [ekrazɑ̃, ɑ̃t] adj overwhelming

**écraser** [ekraze] vt to crush; (piéton) to run over; **s'~** vi to crash; **s'~ contre** to crash into

**écrémé, e** [ekreme] adj (lait) skimmed

**écrevisse** [ekrəvis] nf crayfish inv

**écrier** [ekrie]: **s'~** vi to exclaim

**écrin** [ekrɛ̃] nm case, box

**écrire** [ekrir] vt to write; **s'~** to write to each other; **ça s'écrit comment?** how is it spelt? **écrit** nm (examen) written paper; **par écrit** in writing

**écriteau, x** [ekrito] nm notice, sign

**écriture** [ekrityr] nf writing; **l'É~, les É~s** the Scriptures

**écrivain** [ekrivɛ̃] nm writer

**écrou** [ekru] nm nut

**écrouer** [ekrue] vt to imprison

**écrouler** [ekrule]: **s'~** vi to collapse

**écru, e** [ekry] adj (couleur) off-white, écru

**ECU** [eky] sigle m ECU

**écueil** [ekœj] nm reef; (fig) pitfall

**éculé, e** [ekyle] adj (chaussure) downat-heel; (fig: péj) hackneyed

**écume** [ekym] nf foam; **écumer** vt (CULIN) to skim; **écumoire** nf skimmer

**écureuil** [ekyrœj] nm squirrel

**écurie** [ekyri] nf stable

**écusson** [ekysɔ̃] nm badge

**écuyer, -ère** [ekɥije, jɛr] nm/f rider

**eczéma** [ɛgzema] nm eczema

**édenté, e** [edɑ̃te] adj toothless

**EDF** sigle f (= Électricité de France) national electricity company

**édifice** [edifis] nm edifice, building

**édifier** [edifje] vt to build, erect; (fig) to edify

**Édimbourg** [edɛ̃bur] n Edinburgh

**éditer** [edite] vt (publier) to publish; (annoter) to edit; **éditeur, -trice** nm/f editor; publisher; **édition** nf edition; (industrie du livre) publishing

**édredon** [edrədɔ̃] nm eiderdown

**éducateur, -trice** [edykatœr, tris] nm/f teacher; (in special school) instructor

**éducatif, -ive** [edykatif, iv] adj educational

**éducation** [edykasjɔ̃] nf education; (familiale) upbringing; (manières) (good) manners pl; **~ physique** physical education

**édulcorant** [edylkɔrɑ̃] nm sweetener

**éduquer** [edyke] vt to educate; (élever)

to bring up

**effacé, e** [efase] *adj* unassuming

**effacer** [efase] *vt* to erase, rub out; **s'~** *vi* (*inscription etc*) to wear off; (*pour laisser passer*) to step aside

**effarant, e** [efaʀɑ̃, ɑ̃t] *adj* alarming

**effarer** [efaʀe] *vt* to alarm

**effaroucher** [efaʀuʃe] *vt* to frighten *ou* scare away

**effectif, -ive** [efektif, iv] *adj* real ♦ *nm* (SCOL) (pupil) numbers *pl*; (*entreprise*) staff, workforce; **effectivement** *adv* (*réellement*) actually, really; (*en effet*) indeed

**effectuer** [efektɥe] *vt* (*opération*) to carry out; (*trajet*) to make

**efféminé, e** [efemine] *adj* effeminate

**effervescent, e** [efɛʀvesɑ̃, ɑ̃t] *adj* effervescent

**effet** [efɛ] *nm* (*résultat*) effect; (*impression*) impression; **~s** *nmpl* (*vêtements etc*) things; **faire** ~ (*médicament*) to take effect; **faire bon/mauvais** ~ **sur qn** to make a good/bad impression on sb; **en** ~ indeed; **~ de serre** greenhouse effect

**efficace** [efikas] *adj* (*personne*) efficient; (*action, médicament*) effective; **efficacité** *nf* efficiency; effectiveness

**effilocher** [efiloʃe]: **s'~** *vi* to fray

**efflanqué, e** [eflɑ̃ke] *adj* emaciated

**effleurer** [eflœʀe] *vt* to brush (against); (*sujet*) to touch upon; (*suj: idée, pensée*): **ça ne m'a pas effleuré** it didn't cross my mind

**effluves** [eflyv] *nmpl* exhalation(s)

**effondrer** [efɔ̃dʀe]: **s'~** *vi* to collapse

**efforcer** [efɔʀse]: **s'~ de** *vt* : **s'~ de faire** to try hard to do

**effort** [efɔʀ] *nm* effort

**effraction** [efʀaksjɔ̃] *nf*: **s'introduire par** ~ **dans** to break into

**effrayant, e** [efʀejɑ̃, ɑ̃t] *adj* frightening

**effrayer** [efʀeje] *vt* to frighten, scare

**effréné, e** [efʀene] *adj* wild

**effriter** [efʀite]: **s'~** *vi* to crumble

**effroi** [efʀwa] *nm* terror, dread *no pl*

**effronté, e** [efʀɔ̃te] *adj* cheeky

**effroyable** [efʀwajabl] *adj* horrifying, appalling

**effusion** [efyzjɔ̃] *nf* effusion; **sans ~ de sang** without bloodshed

**égal, e, -aux** [egal, o] *adj* equal; (*constant: vitesse*) steady ♦ *nm/f* equal; **être ~** (à *prix, nombre*) to be equal to; **ça lui est ~** it's all the same to him, he doesn't mind; **sans ~** matchless, unequalled; **d'~ à ~** as equals; **également** *adv* equally; (*aussi*) too, as well; **égaler** *vt* to equal; **égaliser** *vt* (*sol, salaires*) to level (out); (*chances*) to equalize ♦ *vi* (SPORT) to equalize; **égalité** *nf* equality; **être à égalité** to be level

**égard** [egaʀ] *nm*: **~s** consideration *sg*; **à cet ~** in this respect; **par ~ pour** out of consideration for; **à l'~ de** towards

**égarement** [egaʀmɑ̃] *nm* distraction

**égarer** [egaʀe] *vt* to mislay; **s'~** *vi* to get lost, lose one's way; (*objet*) to go astray

**égayer** [egeje] *vt* to cheer up; (*pièce*) to brighten up

**églantine** [eglɑ̃tin] *nf* wild *ou* dog rose

**églefin** [egləfɛ̃] *nm* haddock

**église** [egliz] *nf* church; **aller à l'~** to go to church

**égoïsme** [egɔism] *nm* selfishness; **égoïste** *adj* selfish

**égorger** [egɔʀʒe] *vt* to cut the throat of

**égosiller** [egozije]: **s'~** *vi* to shout o.s. hoarse

**égout** [egu] *nm* sewer

**égoutter** [egute] *vt* to drip; **s'~** *vi* to drip; **égouttoir** *nm* draining board; (*mobile*) draining rack

**égratigner** [egʀatiɲe] *vt* to scratch; **égratignure** *nf* scratch

**Égypte** [eʒipt] *nf*: **l'~** Egypt; **égyptien, ne** *adj* Egyptian ♦ *nm/f*: **É~, ne** Egyptian

**eh** [e] *excl* hey!; **~ bien** well

**éhonté, e** [eɔ̃te] *adj* shameless, brazen

# éjecter 99 Élysée

**éjecter** [eʒɛkte] *vt* (TECH) to eject; (*fam*) to kick *ou* chuck out

**élaborer** [elabɔʀe] *vt* to elaborate; (*projet, stratégie*) to work out; (*rapport*) to draft

**élan** [elɑ̃] *nm* (ZOOL) elk, moose; (SPORT) run up; (*fig: de tendresse etc*) surge; **prendre de l'~** to gather speed

**élancé, e** [elɑ̃se] *adj* slender

**élancement** [elɑ̃smɑ̃] *nm* shooting pain

**élancer** [elɑ̃se]: **s'~** *vi* to dash, hurl o.s.

**élargir** [elaʀʒiʀ] *vt* to widen; **s'~** *vi* to widen; (*vêtement*) to stretch

**élastique** [elastik] *adj* elastic ♦ *nm* (*de bureau*) rubber band; (*pour la couture*) elastic *no pl*

**électeur, -trice** [elɛktœʀ, tʀis] *nm/f* elector, voter

**élection** [elɛksjɔ̃] *nf* election

**électorat** [elɛktɔʀa] *nm* electorate

**électricien, ne** [elɛktʀisjɛ̃, jɛn] *nm/f* electrician

**électricité** [elɛktʀisite] *nf* electricity; **allumer/éteindre l'~** to put on/off the light

**électrique** [elɛktʀik] *adj* electric(al)

**électrocuter** [elɛktʀɔkyte] *vt* to electrocute

**électroménager** [elɛktʀomenaʒe] *adj*, *nm*: **appareils ~s**, **l'~** domestic (electrical) appliances

**électronique** [elɛktʀɔnik] *adj* electronic ♦ *nf* electronics *sg*

**électrophone** [elɛktʀɔfɔn] *nm* record player

**élégance** [elegɑ̃s] *nf* elegance

**élégant, e** [elegɑ̃, ɑ̃t] *adj* elegant

**élément** [elemɑ̃] *nm* element; (*pièce*) component, part; **~s de cuisine** kitchen units; **élémentaire** *adj* elementary

**éléphant** [elefɑ̃] *nm* elephant

**élevage** [el(ə)vaʒ] *nm* breeding; (*de bovins*) cattle rearing; **truite d'~** farmed trout

**élévation** [elevasjɔ̃] *nf* (*hausse*) rise

**élevé, e** [el(ə)ve] *adj* high; **bien/mal ~** well-/ill-mannered

**élève** [elɛv] *nm/f* pupil

**élever** [el(ə)ve] *vt* (*enfant*) to bring up, raise; (*animaux*) to breed; (*hausser: taux, niveau*) to raise; (*édifier: monument*) to put up, erect; **s'~** (*avion*) to go up; (*niveau, température*) to rise; **s'~ à** (*suj: frais, dégâts*) to amount to, add up to; **s'~ contre qch** to rise up against sth; **~ la voix** to raise one's voice; **éleveur, -euse** *nm/f* breeder

**élimé, e** [elime] *adj* threadbare

**éliminatoire** [eliminatwaʀ] *nf* (SPORT) heat

**éliminer** [elimine] *vt* to eliminate

**élire** [eliʀ] *vt* to elect

**elle** [ɛl] *pron* (*sujet*) she; (: *chose*) it; (*complément*) her; it; **~s** (*sujet*) they; (*complément*) them; **~-même** herself; itself; **~s-mêmes** themselves; *voir aussi* **il**

**élocution** [elɔkysjɔ̃] *nf* delivery; **défaut d'~** speech impediment

**éloge** [elɔʒ] *nm* (*gén no pl*) praise; **faire l'~ de** to praise; **élogieux, -euse** *adj* laudatory, full of praise

**éloigné, e** [elwaɲe] *adj* distant, far-off; (*parent*) distant; **éloignement** *nm* (*distance, aussi fig*) distance

**éloigner** [elwaɲe] *vt* (*échéance*) to put off, postpone; (*soupçons, danger*) to ward off; (*objet*): **~ qch (de)** to move *ou* take sth away (from); (*personne*): **~ qn (de)** to take sb away *ou* remove sb (from); **s'~ (de)** (*personne*) to go away (from); (*véhicule*) to move away (from); (*affectivement*) to become estranged (from); **ne vous éloignez pas!** don't go far away!

**élu, e** [ely] *pp de* **élire** ♦ *nm/f* (POL) elected representative

**éluder** [elyde] *vt* to evade

**Élysée** [elize] *nm*: **(le palais de) l'~** the Élysée Palace (*the French president's residence*)

**émacié, e** [emasje] adj emaciated

**émail, -aux** [emaj, o] nm enamel

**émaillé, e** [emaje] adj (fig): ~ **de** dotted with

**émanciper** [emãsipe]: **s'~** vi (fig) to become emancipated ou liberated

**émaner** [emane]: ~ **de** vt to come from

**emballage** [ãbalaʒ] nm (papier) wrapping; (boîte) packaging

**emballer** [ãbale] vt to wrap (up); (dans un carton) to pack (up); (fig: fam) to thrill (to bits); **s'~** vi (moteur) to race; (cheval) to bolt; (fig: personne) to get carried away

**embarcadère** [ãbarkadεr] nm wharf, pier

**embarcation** [ãbarkasjɔ̃] nf (small) boat, (small) craft inv

**embardée** [ãbarde] nf: **faire une ~** to swerve

**embarquement** [ãbarkəmã] nm (de passagers) boarding; (de marchandises) loading

**embarquer** [ãbarke] vt (personne) to embark; (marchandise) to load; (fam) to cart off ♦ vi (passager) to board; **s'~** vi to board; **s'~ dans** (affaire, aventure) to embark upon

**embarras** [ãbara] nm (gêne) embarrassment; **mettre qn dans l'~** to put sb in an awkward position; **vous n'avez que l'~ du choix** the only problem is choosing

**embarrassant, e** [ãbarasã, ãt] adj embarrassing

**embarrasser** [ãbarase] vt (encombrer) to clutter (up); (gêner) to hinder, hamper; ~ **qn** to put sb in an awkward position; **s'~ de** to burden o.s. with

**embauche** [ãboʃ] nf hiring; **embaucher** vt to take on, hire

**embaumer** [ãbome] vt: ~ **la lavande** etc to be fragrant with (the scent of) lavender etc

**embellie** [ãbeli] nf brighter period

**embellir** [ãbelir] vt to make more at-

tractive; (une histoire) to embellish ♦ vi to grow lovelier ou more attractive

**embêtements** [ãbetmã] nmpl trouble sg

**embêter** [ãbete] vt (to bother); **s'~** vi (s'ennuyer) to be bored

**emblée** [ãble]: **d'~** adv straightaway

**embobiner** [ãbɔbine] vt (fam) to get round

**emboîter** [ãbwate] vt to fit together; **s'~ (dans)** to fit (into); ~ **le pas à qn** to follow in sb's footsteps

**embonpoint** [ãbɔ̃pwε̃] nm stoutness

**embouchure** [ãbuʃyr] nf (GÉO) mouth

**embourber** [ãburbe]: **s'~** vi to get stuck in the mud

**embourgeoiser** [ãburʒwaze]: **s'~** vi to become middle-class

**embouteillage** [ãbutejaʒ] nm traffic jam

**emboutir** [ãbutir] vt (heurter) to crash into, ram

**embranchement** [ãbrãʃmã] nm (routier) junction

**embraser** [ãbraze]: **s'~** vi to flare up

**embrassades** [ãbrasad] nfpl hugging and kissing

**embrasser** [ãbrase] vt to kiss; (sujet, période) to embrace, encompass; **s'~** to kiss (each other)

**embrasure** [ãbrazyr] nf: **dans l'~ de la porte** in the door(way)

**embrayage** [ãbrεjaʒ] nm clutch

**embrayer** [ãbrεje] vi (AUTO) to let in the clutch

**embrocher** [ãbrɔʃe] vt to put on a spit

**embrouiller** [ãbruje] vt to muddle up; (fils) to tangle (up); **s'~** vi (personne) to get in a muddle

**embruns** [ãbrε̃] nmpl sea spray sg

**embryon** [ãbrijɔ̃] nm embryo

**embûches** [ãbyʃ] nfpl pitfalls, traps

**embué, e** [ãbye] adj misted up

**embuscade** [ãbyskad] nf ambush

**éméché, e** [emeʃe] adj tipsy, merry

**émeraude** [em(ə)rod] nf emerald

**émerger** [emεrʒe] vt to emerge; (faire

saillie, *aussi fig*) to stand out

**émeri** [em(ə)ʀi] *nm*: **toile** *ou* **papier ~** emery paper

**émerveillement** [emɛʀvɛjmɑ̃] *nm* wonder

**émerveiller** [emɛʀveje] *vt* to fill with wonder; **s'~ de** to marvel at

**émettre** [emɛtʀ] *vt* (*son, lumière*) to give out, emit; (*message etc: RADIO*) to transmit; (*billet, timbre, emprunt*) to issue; (*hypothèse, avis*) to voice, put forward ♦ *vi* to broadcast

**émeus** *etc* [emø] *vb voir* **émouvoir**

**émeute** [emøt] *nf* riot

**émietter** [emjete] *vt* to crumble

**émigrer** [emigʀe] *vi* to emigrate

**émincer** [emɛ̃se] *vt* to cut into thin slices

**éminent, e** [eminɑ̃, ɑ̃t] *adj* distinguished

**émission** [emisjɔ̃] *nf* (*RADIO, TV*) programme, broadcast; (*d'un message*) transmission; (*de timbre*) issue

**emmagasiner** [ɑ̃magazine] *vt* (*amasser*) to store up

**emmanchure** [ɑ̃mɑ̃ʃyʀ] *nf* armhole

**emmêler** [ɑ̃mele] *vt* to tangle (up); (*fig*) to muddle up; **s'~** *vi* to get in a tangle

**emménager** [ɑ̃menaʒe] *vi* to move in; **~ dans** to move into

**emmener** [ɑ̃m(ə)ne] *vt* to take (with one); (*comme otage, capture*) to take away; **~ qn au cinéma** to take sb to the cinema

**emmerder** [ɑ̃mɛʀde] (*fam!*) *vt* to bug, bother; **s'~** *vi* to be bored stiff

**emmitoufler** [ɑ̃mitufle] *vt*: **s'~** *vi* to wrap up (warmly)

**émoi** [emwa] *nm* commotion

**émotif, -ive** [emɔtif, iv] *adj* emotional

**émotion** [emɔsjɔ̃] *nf* emotion

**émousser** [emuse] *vt* to blunt; (*fig*) to dull

**émouvoir** [emuvwaʀ] *vt* to move; **s'~** *vi* to be moved; (*s'indigner*) to be roused

**empailler** [ɑ̃paje] *vt* to stuff

**empaqueter** [ɑ̃pakte] *vt* to parcel up

**emparer** [ɑ̃paʀe]: **s'~ de** *vt* (*objet*) to seize, grab; (*comme otage, MIL*) to seize; (*suj: peur etc*) to take hold of

**empâter** [ɑ̃pate]: **s'~** *vi* to thicken out

**empêchement** [ɑ̃pɛʃmɑ̃] *nm* (unexpected) obstacle, hitch

**empêcher** [ɑ̃peʃe] *vt* to prevent; **~ qn de faire** to prevent *ou* stop sb (from) doing; **il n'empêche que** nevertheless; **il n'a pas pu s'~ de rire** he couldn't help laughing

**empereur** [ɑ̃pʀœʀ] *nm* emperor

**empester** [ɑ̃pɛste] *vi* to stink, reek

**empêtrer** [ɑ̃petʀe] *vt*: **s'~ dans** (*fils etc*) to get tangled up in

**emphase** [ɑ̃faz] *nf* pomposity, bombast

**empiéter** [ɑ̃pjete] *vi*: **~ sur** to encroach upon

**empiffrer** [ɑ̃pifʀe]: **s'~** (*fam*) *vi* to stuff o.s.

**empiler** [ɑ̃pile] *vt* to pile (up)

**empire** [ɑ̃piʀ] *nm* empire; (*fig*) influence

**empirer** [ɑ̃piʀe] *vi* to worsen, deteriorate

**emplacement** [ɑ̃plasmɑ̃] *nm* site

**emplettes** [ɑ̃plɛt] *nfpl* shopping *sg*

**emplir** [ɑ̃pliʀ] *vt* to fill; **s'~ (de)** to fill (with)

**emploi** [ɑ̃plwa] *nm* use; (*COMM, ÉCON*) employment; (*poste*) job, situation; **mode d'~** directions for use; **~ du temps** timetable, schedule

**employé, e** [ɑ̃plwaje] *nm/f* employee; **~ de bureau** office employee *ou* clerk

**employer** [ɑ̃plwaje] *vt* to use; (*ouvrier, main-d'œuvre*) to employ; **s'~ à faire** to apply *ou* devote o.s. to doing; **employeur, -euse** *nm/f* employer

**empocher** [ɑ̃pɔʃe] *vt* to pocket

**empoigner** [ɑ̃pwaɲe] *vt* to grab

**empoisonner** [ɑ̃pwazɔne] *vt* to poison; (*empester: air, pièce*) to stink out; (*fam*): **~ qn** to drive sb mad

**emporté, e** [ɑ̃pɔʀte] adj quick-tempered

**emporter** [ɑ̃pɔʀte] vt to take (with one); (en dérobant ou enlevant, emmener: blessés, voyageurs) to take away; (entraîner) to carry away; **s'~** vi (de colère) to lose one's temper; **l'~ (sur)** to get the upper hand (of); **plats à ~** take-away meals

**empreint, e** [ɑ̃pʀɛ̃, ɛ̃t] adj: **~ de** (regret, jalousie) marked with; **empreinte** nf: **empreinte (de pas)** footprint; **empreinte (digitale)** fingerprint

**empressé, e** [ɑ̃pʀese] adj attentive

**empressement** [ɑ̃pʀesmɑ̃] nm (hâte) eagerness

**empresser** [ɑ̃pʀese] **s'~** vi: **s'~ auprès de qn** to surround sb with attention; **s'~ de faire** (se hâter) to hasten to do

**emprise** [ɑ̃pʀiz] nf hold, ascendancy

**emprisonnement** [ɑ̃pʀizɔnmɑ̃] nm imprisonment

**emprisonner** [ɑ̃pʀizɔne] vt to imprison

**emprunt** [ɑ̃pʀœ̃] nm loan

**emprunté, e** [ɑ̃pʀœ̃te] adj (fig) ill-at-ease, awkward

**emprunter** [ɑ̃pʀœ̃te] vt to borrow; (itinéraire) to take, follow

**ému, e** [emy] pp de **émouvoir** ♦ adj (gratitude) touched; (compassion) moved

---

MOT-CLÉ

---

**en** [ɑ̃] prép 1 (endroit, pays) in; (direction) to; **habiter en France/ville** to live in France/town; **aller en France/ville** to go to France/town

2 (moment, temps) in; **en été/juin** in summer/June

3 (moyen) by; **en avion/taxi** by plane/taxi

4 (composition) made of; **c'est en verre** it's (made of) glass; **un collier en argent** a silver necklace

5 (description, état): **une femme (ha-**

**billée) en rouge** a woman (dressed) in red; **peindre qch en rouge** to paint sth red; **en T/étoile** T/star-shaped; **en chemise/chaussettes** in one's shirt-sleeves/socks; **en soldat** as a soldier; **cassé en plusieurs morceaux** broken into several pieces; **en réparation** being repaired, under repair; **en vacances** on holiday; **en deuil** in mourning; **le même en plus grand** the same but ou only bigger

6 (avec gérondif) while, on, by; **en dormant** while sleeping, as one sleeps; **en sortant** on going out, as he etc went out; **sortir en courant** to run out

♦ pron 1 (indéfini): **j'en ai/veux** I have/want some; **en as-tu?** have you got any?; **je n'en veux pas** I don't want any; **j'en ai 2** I've got 2; **combien y en a-t-il?** how many (of them) are there?; **j'en ai assez** I've got enough (of it ou them); **(j'en ai marre)** I've had enough

2 (provenance) from there; **j'en viens** I've come from there

3 (cause): **il en est malade/perd le sommeil** he is ill/can't sleep because of it

4 (complément de nom, d'adjectif, de verbe): **j'en connais les dangers** I know its ou the dangers; **j'en suis fier/ai besoin** I am proud of/need it

---

**ENA** sigle f (= École Nationale d'Administration) one of the Grandes Écoles

**encadrement** [ɑ̃kɑdʀəmɑ̃] nm (cadres) managerial staff

**encadrer** [ɑ̃kɑdʀe] vt (tableau, image) to frame; (fig: entourer) to surround; (personnel, soldats etc) to train

**encaissé, e** [ɑ̃kese] adj (vallée) steep-sided; (rivière) with steep banks

**encaisser** [ɑ̃kese] vt (chèque) to cash; (argent) to collect; (fam: coup, défaite) to take

**encart** [ɑ̃kaʀ] nm insert

**en-cas** [ɑ̃kɑ] nm snack

**encastré, e** |ɑ̃kastʀe| *adj:* **four ~** built-in oven

**enceinte** |ɑ̃sɛ̃t| *adj f:* **~ (de 6 mois)** (6 months) pregnant ♦ *nf* (*mur*) wall; (*espace*) enclosure; (*aussi:* **~ acoustique**) (loud)speaker

**encens** |ɑ̃sɑ̃| *nm* incense

**encercler** |ɑ̃sɛʀkle| *vt* to surround

**enchaîner** |ɑ̃ʃene| *vt* to chain up; (*mouvements, séquences*) to link (together) ♦ *vi* to carry on

**enchanté, e** |ɑ̃ʃɑ̃te| *adj* (*ravi*) delighted; (*magique*) enchanted; **~ (de faire votre connaissance)** pleased to meet you

**enchantement** |ɑ̃ʃɑ̃tmɑ̃| *nm* delight; (*magie*) enchantment

**enchère** |ɑ̃ʃɛʀ| *nf* bid; **mettre/vendre aux ~s** to put up for (sale by)/sell by auction

**enchevêtrer** |ɑ̃ʃ(ə)vetʀe|: **s'~** *vi* to get in a tangle

**enclencher** |ɑ̃klɑ̃ʃe| *vt* (*mécanisme*) to engage; **s'~** *vi* to engage

**enclin, e** |ɑ̃klɛ̃, in| *adj:* **~ à** inclined *ou* prone to

**enclos** |ɑ̃klo| *nm* enclosure

**enclume** |ɑ̃klym| *nf* anvil

**encoche** |ɑ̃kɔʃ| *nf* notch

**encoignure** |ɑ̃kɔɲyʀ| *nf* corner

**encolure** |ɑ̃kɔlyʀ| *nf* (*cou*) neck

**encombrant, e** |ɑ̃kɔ̃bʀɑ̃, ɑ̃t| *adj* cumbersome, bulky

**encombre** |ɑ̃kɔ̃bʀ| : **sans ~** *adv* without mishap *ou* trouble; **encombrement** *nm:* **être pris dans un encombrement** to be stuck in a traffic jam

**encombrer** |ɑ̃kɔ̃bʀe| *vt* to clutter (up); (*gêner*) to hamper; **s'~ de** (*bagages etc*) to load *ou* burden o.s. with

**encontre** |ɑ̃kɔ̃tʀ| : **à l'~ de** *prép* against, counter to

MOT-CLÉ

**encore** |ɑ̃kɔʀ| *adv* **1** (*continuation*) still; **il y travaille encore** he's still working on it; **pas encore** not yet

**2** (*de nouveau*) again; **j'irai encore demain** I'll go again tomorrow; **encore une fois** (once) again; **encore deux jours** two more days

**3** (*intensif*) even, still; **encore plus fort/mieux** even louder/better, louder/better still

**4** (*restriction*) even so *ou* then, only; **encore pourrais-je le faire si** ... even so, I might be able to do it if ...; **si encore** if only

**encore que** *conj* although

**encouragement** |ɑ̃kuʀaʒmɑ̃| *nm* encouragement

**encourager** |ɑ̃kuʀaʒe| *vt* to encourage

**encourir** |ɑ̃kuʀiʀ| *vt* to incur

**encrasser** |ɑ̃kʀase| *vt* to make filthy

**encre** |ɑ̃kʀ| *nf* ink; **encrier** *nm* inkwell

**encroûter** |ɑ̃kʀute| : **s'~** (*fam*) *vi* (*fig*) to get into a rut, get set in one's ways

**encyclopédie** |ɑ̃siklɔpedi| *nf* encyclopaedia

**endetter** |ɑ̃dete| : **s'~** *vi* to get into debt

**endiablé, e** |ɑ̃djable| *adj* (*danse*) furious

**endimanché, e** |ɑ̃dimɑ̃ʃe| *adj* in one's Sunday best

**endive** |ɑ̃div| *nf* chicory *no pl*

**endoctriner** |ɑ̃dɔktʀine| *vt* to indoctrinate

**endommager** |ɑ̃dɔmaʒe| *vt* to damage

**endormi, e** |ɑ̃dɔʀmi| *adj* asleep

**endormir** |ɑ̃dɔʀmiʀ| *vt* to put to sleep; (*suj: chaleur etc*) to send to sleep; (*MÉD: dent, nerf*) to anaesthetize; (*fig: soupçons*) to allay; **s'~** *vi* to fall asleep, go to sleep

**endosser** |ɑ̃dose| *vt* (*responsabilité*) to take, shoulder; (*chèque*) to endorse; (*uniforme, tenue*) to put on, don

**endroit** |ɑ̃dʀwa| *nm* place; (*opposé à l'envers*) right side; **à l'~** (*vêtement*) the right way out; (*objet posé*) the right way round

**enduire** [ɑ̃dɥiʀ] vt to coat
**enduit** [ɑ̃dɥi] nm coating
**endurance** [ɑ̃dyʀɑ̃s] nf endurance
**endurant, e** [ɑ̃dyʀɑ̃, ɑ̃t] adj tough, hardy
**endurcir** [ɑ̃dyʀsiʀ]: **s'~** vi (physiquement) to become tougher; (moralement) to become hardened
**endurer** [ɑ̃dyʀe] vt to endure, bear
**énergétique** [enɛʀʒetik] adj (aliment) energy-giving
**énergie** [enɛʀʒi] nf (PHYSIQUE) energy; (TECH) power; (morale) vigour, spirit; **énergique** adj energetic, vigorous; (mesures) drastic, stringent
**énervant, e** [enɛʀvɑ̃, ɑ̃t] adj irritating, annoying
**énerver** [enɛʀve] vt to irritate, annoy; **s'~** vi to get excited, get worked up
**enfance** [ɑ̃fɑ̃s] nf childhood
**enfant** [ɑ̃fɑ̃] nm/f child; **~ de chœur ♦** nm (REL) altar boy; **enfantillage** (péj) nm childish behaviour no pl; **enfantin, e** adj (puéril) childlike; (langage, jeu etc) children's cpd
**enfer** [ɑ̃fɛʀ] nm hell
**enfermer** [ɑ̃fɛʀme] vt to shut up; (à clef, interner) to lock up
**enfiévré, e** [ɑ̃fjevʀe] adj feverish
**enfiler** [ɑ̃file] vt (vêtement) to slip on, slip into; (perles) to string; (aiguille) to thread
**enfin** [ɑ̃fɛ̃] adv at last; (en énumérant) lastly; (toutefois) still; (pour conclure) in a word; (somme toute) after all
**enflammer** [ɑ̃flame]: **s'~** vi to catch fire; (MÉD) to become inflamed
**enflé, e** [ɑ̃fle] adj swollen
**enfler** [ɑ̃fle] vi to swell (up)
**enfoncer** [ɑ̃fɔ̃se] vt (clou) to drive in; (faire pénétrer): **~ qch dans** to push (ou drive) sth into; (forcer: porte) to break open; **s'~** vi to sink; **s'~ dans** to sink into; (forêt, ville) to disappear into
**enfouir** [ɑ̃fwiʀ] vt (dans le sol) to bury; (dans un tiroir etc) to tuck away
**enfourcher** [ɑ̃fuʀʃe] vt to mount

**enfreindre** [ɑ̃fʀɛ̃dʀ] vt to infringe, break
**enfuir** [ɑ̃fɥiʀ]: **s'~** vi to run away ou off
**enfumer** [ɑ̃fyme] vt (pièce) to fill with smoke
**engageant, e** [ɑ̃gaʒɑ̃, ɑ̃t] adj attractive, appealing
**engagement** [ɑ̃gaʒmɑ̃] nm commitment
**engager** [ɑ̃gaʒe] vt (embaucher) to take on; (: artiste) to engage; (commencer) to start; (lier) to bind, commit; (impliquer) to involve; (investir) to invest, lay out; (inciter) to urge; (introduire: clé) to insert; (MIL) to enlist; (débuter: conversation etc) to start (up); **s'~** vi to undertake to do; **s'~ dans** (rue, passage) to turn into; (fig: affaire, discussion) to enter into, embark on
**engelures** [ɑ̃ʒlyʀ] nfpl chilblains
**engendrer** [ɑ̃ʒɑ̃dʀe] vt to breed, create
**engin** [ɑ̃ʒɛ̃] nm machine; (outil) instrument; (AUT) vehicle; (AVIAT) aircraft inv
**englober** [ɑ̃glɔbe] vt to include
**engloutir** [ɑ̃glutiʀ] vt to swallow up
**engoncé, e** [ɑ̃gɔ̃se] adj: **~ dans** cramped in
**engorger** [ɑ̃gɔʀʒe] vt to obstruct, block
**engouement** [ɑ̃gumɑ̃] nm (sudden) passion
**engouffrer** [ɑ̃gufʀe] vt to swallow up, devour; **s'~ dans** to rush into
**engourdir** [ɑ̃guʀdiʀ] vt to numb; (fig) to dull, blunt; **s'~** vi to go numb
**engrais** [ɑ̃gʀɛ] nm manure; **~ (chimique)** (chemical) fertilizer
**engraisser** [ɑ̃gʀese] vt to fatten (up)
**engrenage** [ɑ̃gʀənaʒ] nm gears pl, gearing; (fig) chain
**engueuler** [ɑ̃gœle] (fam) vt to bawl at
**enhardir** [ɑ̃aʀdiʀ]: **s'~** vi to grow bolder
**énigme** [enigm] nf riddle
**enivrer** [ɑ̃nivʀe] vt to get drunk
**enjambée** [ɑ̃ʒɑ̃be] nf stride

**enjamber** [ɑ̃ʒɑ̃be] vt to stride over

**enjeu, x** [ɑ̃ʒø] nm stakes pl

**enjôler** [ɑ̃ʒole] vt to coax, wheedle

**enjoliver** [ɑ̃ʒolive] vt to embellish; **enjoliveur** nm (AUTO) hub cap

**enjoué, e** [ɑ̃ʒwe] adj playful

**enlacer** [ɑ̃lase] vt (étreindre) to embrace, hug

**enlaidir** [ɑ̃ledir] vt to make ugly ♦ vi to become ugly

**enlèvement** [ɑ̃lɛvmɑ̃] nm (rapt) abduction, kidnapping

**enlever** [ɑ̃l(ə)ve] vt (ôter: gén) to remove; (: vêtement, lunettes) to take off; (emporter: ordures etc) to take away; (kidnapper) to abduct, kidnap; (obtenir: prix, contrat) to win; (prendre): ~ qch à qn to take sth (away) from sb

**enliser** [ɑ̃lize]: **s'~** vi to sink, get stuck

**enneigé, e** [ɑ̃neʒe] adj (route, maison) snowed-up; (paysage) snowy

**ennemi, e** [ɛnmi] adj hostile; (MIL) enemy cpd ♦ nm/f enemy

**ennui** [ɑ̃nɥi] nm (lassitude) boredom; (difficulté) trouble no pl; **avoir des ~s** to have problems; **ennuyer** vt to bother; (lasser) to bore; **s'ennuyer** vi to be bored; **ennuyeux, -euse** adj boring, tedious; (embêtant) annoying

**énoncé** [enɔ̃se] nm (de problème) terms pl

**énoncer** [enɔ̃se] vt (faits) to set out, state

**enorgueillir** [ɑ̃nɔrɡœjir]: **s'~ de** vt to pride o.s. on

**énorme** [enɔrm] adj enormous, huge; **énormément** adv enormously ♦ **énormément de neige/gens** an enormous amount of snow/number of people; **énormité** nf (propos) outrageous remark

**enquérir** [ɑ̃kerir]: **s'~ de** vt to inquire about

**enquête** [ɑ̃kɛt] nf (de journaliste, de police) investigation; (judiciaire, administrative) inquiry; (sondage d'opinion) survey; **enquêter** vi to investigate

**enquiers** etc [ɑ̃kje] vb voir **enquérir**

**enquiquiner** [ɑ̃kikine] (fam) vt to annoy, irritate, bother

**enraciné, e** [ɑ̃rasine] adj deep-rooted

**enragé, e** [ɑ̃raʒe] adj (MÉD) rabid, with rabies; (fig) fanatical

**enrageant, e** [ɑ̃raʒɑ̃, ɑ̃t] adj infuriating

**enrager** [ɑ̃raʒe] vi to be in a rage

**enrayer** [ɑ̃reje] vt to check, stop

**enregistrement** [ɑ̃r(ə)ʒistrəmɑ̃] nm recording; **~ des bagages** (à l'aéroport) baggage check-in

**enregistrer** [ɑ̃r(ə)ʒistre] vt (MUS etc) to record; (fig: mémoriser) to make a mental note of; (bagages: à l'aéroport) to check in

**enrhumer** [ɑ̃ryme] vt: **s'~, être enrhumé** to catch a cold

**enrichir** [ɑ̃riʃir] vt to make rich(er); (fig) to enrich; **s'~** vi to get rich(er)

**enrober** [ɑ̃robe] vt: **~ qch de** to coat sth with

**enrôler** [ɑ̃role] vt to enlist; **s'~ (dans)** to enlist (in)

**enrouer** [ɑ̃rwe]: **s'~** vi to go hoarse

**enrouler** [ɑ̃rule] vt (fil, corde) to wind (up)

**ensanglanté, e** [ɑ̃sɑ̃glɑ̃te] adj covered with blood

**enseignant, e** [ɑ̃sɛɲɑ̃, ɑ̃t] nm/f teacher

**enseigne** [ɑ̃sɛɲ] nf sign; **~ lumineuse** neon sign

**enseignement** [ɑ̃sɛɲ(ə)mɑ̃] nm teaching; (ADMIN) education

**enseigner** [ɑ̃sɛɲe] vt, vi to teach; **~ qch à qn** to teach sb sth

**ensemble** [ɑ̃sɑ̃bl] adv together ♦ nm (groupement) set; (vêtements) outfit; (totalité): **l'~ du** ou **de la** whole ou entire; (unité, harmonie) unity; **impression/idée d'~** overall ou general impression/idea; **dans l'~** (en gros) on the whole

**ensemencer** [ɑ̃s(ə)mɑ̃se] vt to sow

**ensevelir** [ɑ̃sɛv(ə)lir] vt to bury

**ensoleillé, e** [ɑ̃sɔleje] adj sunny

**ensommeillé, e** [ɑ̃sɔmeje] *adj* drowsy

**ensorceler** [ɑ̃sɔʀsale] *vt* to enchant, bewitch

**ensuite** [ɑ̃sɥit] *adv* then, next; (*plus tard*) afterwards, later

**ensuivre** [ɑ̃sɥivʀ]: **s'~** *vi* to follow, ensue; **et tout ce qui s'ensuit** and all that goes with it

**entaille** [ɑ̃taj] *nf* cut; (*sur un objet*) notch

**entamer** [ɑ̃tame] *vt* (*pain, bouteille*) to start; (*hostilités, pourparlers*) to open

**entasser** [ɑ̃tase] *vt* (*empiler*) to pile up, heap up; **s'~** *vi* (*s'amonceler*) to pile up; **s'~ dans** (*personnes*) to cram into

**entendre** [ɑ̃tɑ̃dʀ] *vt* to hear; (*comprendre*) to understand; (*vouloir dire*) to mean; **s'~** *vi* (*sympathiser*) to get on; (*se mettre d'accord*) to agree; **j'ai entendu dire que** I've heard (it said) that

**entendu, e** [ɑ̃tɑ̃dy] *adj* (*réglé*) agreed; (*au courant: air*) knowing; **(c'est) ~** all right, agreed; **bien ~** of course

**entente** [ɑ̃tɑ̃t] *nf* understanding; (*accord, traité*) agreement; **à double ~** (*sens*) with a double meaning

**entériner** [ɑ̃teʀine] *vt* to ratify, confirm

**enterrement** [ɑ̃tɛʀmɑ̃] *nm* (*cérémonie*) funeral, burial

**enterrer** [ɑ̃teʀe] *vt* to bury

**entêtant, e** [ɑ̃tetɑ̃, ɑ̃t] *adj* heady

**entêté, e** [ɑ̃tete] *adj* stubborn

**en-tête** [ɑ̃tɛt] *nm* heading; **papier à ~** headed notepaper

**entêter** [ɑ̃tete]: **s'~** *vi*: **~ (à faire)** to persist in (doing)

**enthousiasme** [ɑ̃tuzjasm] *nm* enthusiasm; **enthousiasmer** *vt* to fill with enthusiasm; **s'enthousiasmer (pour qch)** to get enthusiastic (about sth); **enthousiaste** *adj* enthusiastic

**enticher** [ɑ̃tiʃe]: **s'~ de** to become infatuated with

**entier, -ère** [ɑ̃tje, jɛʀ] *adj* whole; (*total: satisfaction etc*) complete; (*fig: caractère*) unbending ♦ *nm* (*MATH*) whole; **en ~** totally; **lait ~** full-cream milk; **en-**

**tièrement** *adv* entirely, wholly

**entonner** [ɑ̃tɔne] *vt* (*chanson*) to strike up

**entonnoir** [ɑ̃tɔnwaʀ] *nm* funnel

**entorse** [ɑ̃tɔʀs] *nf* (*MÉD*) sprain; (*fig*): **~ au règlement** infringement of the rule

**entortiller** [ɑ̃tɔʀtije] *vt* (*enrouler*) to twist, wind; (*fam: cajoler*) to get round

**entourage** [ɑ̃tuʀaʒ] *nm* circle; (*famille*) circle of family/friends; (*ce qui enclôt*) surround

**entourer** [ɑ̃tuʀe] *vt* to surround; (*apporter son soutien à*) to rally round; **~ de** to surround with

**entracte** [ɑ̃tʀakt] *nm* interval

**entraide** [ɑ̃tʀɛd] *nf* mutual aid; **s'~r** *vi* to help each other

**entrain** [ɑ̃tʀɛ̃] *nm* spirit; **avec/sans ~** spiritedly/half-heartedly

**entraînement** [ɑ̃tʀɛnmɑ̃] *nm* training

**entraîner** [ɑ̃tʀene] *vt* (*charrier*) to carry *ou* drag along; (*TECH*) to drive; (*emmener: personne*) to take (off); (*influencer*) to lead; (*SPORT*) to train; (*impliquer*) to entail; **s'~** *vi* (*SPORT*) to train; **s'~ à qch/à faire** to train o.s. for sth/to do; **~ qn à faire** (*inciter*) to lead sb to do; **entraîneur, -euse** *nm/f* (*SPORT*) coach, trainer ♦ *nm* (*HIPPISME*) trainer

**entraver** [ɑ̃tʀave] *vt* (*action, progrès*) to hinder

**entre** [ɑ̃tʀ] *prép* between; (*parmi*) among(st); **l'un d'~ eux/nous** one of them/us; **~ eux** among(st) themselves; **entrebâillé, e** [ɑ̃tʀəbɑje] *adj* half-open, ajar; **entrechoquer: s'entrechoquer** *vi* to knock *ou* bang together; **entrecôte** *nf* entrecôte *ou* rib steak; **entrecouper** *vt*: **entrecouper qch de** to intersperse sth with; **entrecroiser: s'entrecroiser** *vi* to intertwine

**entrée** [ɑ̃tʀe] *nf* entrance; (*accès: au cinéma etc*) admission; (*billet*) (admission) ticket; (*CULIN*) first course

**entre...: entrefaites: sur ces entrefaites** *adv* at this juncture; **entrefilet** *nm* paragraph (*short article*); **entrejam-**

**bes** nm crotch; **entrelacer** vt to intertwine; **entremêler**: s'**entremêler** vi to become entangled; **entremets** nm (cream) dessert; **entremise** nf intervention; **par l'entremise de** through

**entreposer** [ɑ̃trəpoze] vt to store, put into storage

**entrepôt** [ɑ̃trəpo] nm warehouse

**entreprenant, e** [ɑ̃trəprənɑ̃, ɑ̃t] adj (actif) enterprising; (trop galant) forward

**entreprendre** [ɑ̃trəprɑ̃dr] vt (se lancer dans) to undertake; (commencer à) to begin ou start (upon)

**entrepreneur** [ɑ̃trəprənœr, øz] nm: **~ en bâtiment**) building contractor

**entreprise** [ɑ̃trəpriz] nf (société) firm, concern; (action) undertaking, venture

**entrer** [ɑ̃tre] vi to go (ou come) in, enter ♦ vt (INFORM) to enter; input; **faire ~ qch dans** to get sth into; **~ dans** (gén) to enter; (pièce) to go (ou come) into, enter; (club) to join; (heurter) to run into; **~ à l'hôpital** to go into hospital; **faire ~** (visiteur) to show in

**entresol** [ɑ̃trəsɔl] nm mezzanine

**entre-temps** [ɑ̃trətɑ̃] adv meanwhile

**entretenir** [ɑ̃trət(ə)nir] vt to maintain; (famille, maîtresse) to support, keep; **~ qn (de)** to speak to sb (about)

**entretien** [ɑ̃trətjɛ̃] nm maintenance; (discussion) discussion, talk; (pour un emploi) interview

**entrevoir** [ɑ̃trəvwar] vt (à peine) to make out; (brièvement) to catch a glimpse of

**entrevue** [ɑ̃trəvy] nf (audience) interview

**entrouvert, e** [ɑ̃truver, ɛrt] adj halfopen

**énumérer** [enymere] vt to list

**envahir** [ɑ̃vair] vt to invade; (suj: inquiétude, peur) to come over; **envahissant, e** (péj) adj (personne) intrusive

**enveloppe** [ɑ̃v(ə)lɔp] nf (de lettre) envelope; (crédits) budget; **envelopper** vt to wrap; (fig) to envelop, shroud

**envenimer** [ɑ̃v(ə)nime] vt to aggravate

**envergure** [ɑ̃vɛrgyr] nf (fig) scope; (personne) calibre

**enverrai** etc [ɑ̃vere] vb voir **envoyer**

**envers** [ɑ̃ver] prép towards, to, ♦ nm other side; (d'une étoffe) wrong side; **à l'~** (verticalement) upside down; (pull) back to front; (chaussettes) inside out

**envie** [ɑ̃vi] nf (sentiment) envy; (souhait) desire, wish; **avoir ~ de (faire)** to feel like (doing); (plus fort) to want (to do); **avoir ~ que** to wish that; **cette glace me fait ~** I fancy some of that ice cream; **envier** vt to envy; **envieux, -euse** adj envious

**environ** [ɑ̃virɔ̃] adv: **~ 3 h/2 km** (around) about 3 o'clock/2 km; voir aussi **environs**

**environnant, e** [ɑ̃virɔnɑ̃, ɑ̃t] adj surrounding

**environnement** [ɑ̃virɔnmɑ̃] nm environment

**environs** [ɑ̃virɔ̃] nmpl surroundings; **aux ~ de** (round) about

**envisager** [ɑ̃vizaʒe] vt to contemplate, envisage; **~ de faire** to consider doing

**envoi** [ɑ̃vwa] nm (paquet) parcel, consignment; **coup d'~** (SPORT) kick-off

**envoler** [ɑ̃vɔle]: s'**~** vi (oiseau) to fly away ou off; (avion) to take off; (papier, feuille) to blow away; (fig) to vanish (into thin air)

**envoûter** [ɑ̃vute] vt to bewitch

**envoyé, e** [ɑ̃vwaje] nm/f (POL) envoy; (PRESSE) correspondent

**envoyer** [ɑ̃vwaje] vt to send; (lancer) to hurl, throw; **~ chercher** to send for; **~ promener qn** (fam) to send sb packing

**ÉOLE** [eɔl] sigle m (= est-ouest-liaison-express) Paris high-speed, east-west subway service

**épagneul, e** [epaɲœl] nm/f spaniel

**épais, se** [epe, ɛs] adj thick; **épaisseur** nf thickness

**épancher** [epɑ̃ʃe]: s'**~** vi to open one's heart

**épanouir** [epanwir]: s'**~** vi (fleur) to

bloom, open out; (visage) to light up; (personne) to blossom

**épargne** [eparɲ] nf saving

**épargner** [eparɲe] vt to save; (ne pas tuer ou endommager) to spare ♦ vi to save; ~ **qch à qn** to spare sb sth

**éparpiller** [eparpije] vt to scatter; **s'~** vi to scatter; (fig) to dissipate one's efforts

**épars, e** [epar, aʀs] adj scattered

**épatant, e** [epatã, ãt] (fam) adj super

**épater** [epate] (fam) vt (étonner) to amaze; (impressionner) to impress

**épaule** [epol] nf shoulder

**épauler** [epole] vt (aider) to back up, support; (arme) to raise (to one's shoulder) ♦ vi to (take) aim

**épaulette** [epolet] nf (MIL) epaulette; (rembourrage) shoulder pad

**épave** [epav] nf wreck

**épée** [epe] nf sword

**épeler** [ep(ə)le] vt to spell

**éperdu, e** [eperdy] adj distraught, overcome; (amour) passionate

**éperon** [eprɔ̃] nm spur

**épervier** [epervje] nm sparrowhawk

**épi** [epi] nm (de blé, d'orge) ear; (de maïs) cob

**épice** [epis] nf spice

**épicé, e** [epise] adj spicy

**épicer** [epise] vt to spice

**épicerie** [episri] nf grocer's shop; (denrées) groceries pl; ~ **fine** delicatessen; **épicier, -ière** nm/f grocer

**épidémie** [epidemi] nf epidemic

**épiderme** [epiderm] nm skin

**épier** [epje] vt to spy on, watch closely

**épilepsie** [epilepsi] nf epilepsy

**épiler** [epile] vt (jambes) to remove the hair from; (sourcils) to pluck

**épilogue** [epilɔg] nm (fig) conclusion, dénouement; **épiloguer** vi: **épiloguer sur** to hold forth on

**épinards** [epinar] nmpl spinach sg

**épine** [epin] nf thorn, prickle; (d'oursin etc) spine; ~ **dorsale** backbone; **épineux, -euse** adj thorny

**épingle** [epɛ̃gl] nf pin; ~ **à cheveux** hairpin; ~ **de nourrice** ou **de sûreté** safety pin; **épingler** vt (badge, décoration): **épingler qch sur** to pin sth on(to); (fam) to catch, nick

**épique** [epik] adj epic

**épisode** [epizɔd] nm episode; **film/ roman à ~s** serial; **épisodique** adj occasional

**éploré, e** [eplɔre] adj tearful

**épluche-légumes** [eplyʃlegym] nm inv (potato) peeler

**éplucher** [eplyʃe] vt (fruit, légumes) to peel; (fig) to go over with a fine-tooth comb; **épluchures** nfpl peelings

**éponge** [epɔ̃ʒ] nf sponge; **éponger** vt (liquide) to mop up; (surface) to sponge; (fig: déficit) to soak up

**épopée** [epɔpe] nf epic

**époque** [epɔk] nf (de l'histoire) age, era; (de l'année, la vie) time; **d'~** (meuble) period cpd

**époumoner** [epumɔne]: **s'~** vi to shout o.s. hoarse

**épouse** [epuz] nf wife; **épouser** vt to marry

**épousseter** [epuste] vt to dust

**époustouflant, e** [epustuflã, ãt] (fam) adj staggering, mind-boggling

**épouvantable** [epuvãtabl] adj appalling, dreadful

**épouvantail** [epuvãtaj] nm scarecrow

**épouvante** [epuvãt] nf terror; **film d'~** horror film; **épouvanter** vt to terrify

**époux** [epu] nm husband ♦ nmpl (married) couple

**éprendre** [eprãdr]: **s'~ de** vt to fall in love with

**épreuve** [eprœv] nf (d'examen) test; (malheur, difficulté) trial, ordeal; (PHOTO) print; (TYPO) proof; (SPORT) event; **à toute** ~ unfailing; **mettre à l'~** to put to the test

**épris, e** [epri, iz] pp de **éprendre**

**éprouvant, e** [epruvã, ãt] adj trying, testing

**éprouver** [epruve] vt (tester) to test;

(*marquer, faire souffrir*) to afflict, distress; (*ressentir*) to experience

**éprouvette** [epʀuvɛt] *nf* test tube

**épuisé, e** [epɥize] *adj* exhausted; (*livre*) out of print; **épuisement** *nm* exhaustion

**épuiser** [epɥize] *vt* (*fatiguer*) to exhaust, wear *ou* tire out; (*stock, sujet*) to exhaust; **s'~** *vi* to wear *ou* tire o.s. out, exhaust o.s.

**épuisette** [epɥizɛt] *nf* shrimping net

**épurer** [epyʀe] *vt* (*liquide*) to purify; (*parti etc*) to purge

**équateur** [ekwatœʀ] *nm* equator; **(la république de) l'É~** Ecuador

**équation** [ekwasjɔ̃] *nf* equation

**équerre** [ekɛʀ] *nf* (*à dessin*) (set) square

**équilibre** [ekilibʀ] *nm* balance; **garder/perdre l'~** to keep/lose one's balance; **être en ~** to be balanced; **équilibré, e** *adj* well-balanced; **équilibrer** *vt* to balance; **s'équilibrer** *vi* (*poids*) to balance; (*fig: défauts etc*) to balance each other out

**équipage** [ekipaʒ] *nm* crew

**équipe** [ekip] *nf* team

**équipé, e** [ekipe] *adj:* **bien/mal ~** well-/poorly-equipped; **équipée** *nf* escapade

**équipement** [ekipmɑ̃] *nm* equipment; **~s** *nmpl* (*installations*) amenities, facilities

**équiper** [ekipe] *vt* to equip; **~ qn/qch de** to equip sb/sth with

**équipier, -ière** [ekipje, jɛʀ] *nm/f* team member

**équitable** [ekitabl] *adj* fair

**équitation** [ekitasjɔ̃] *nf* (horse-)riding; **faire de l'~** to go riding

**équivalent, e** [ekivalɑ̃, ɑ̃t] *adj, nm* equivalent

**équivaloir** [ekivalwaʀ]: **~ à** *vt* to be equivalent to

**équivoque** [ekivɔk] *adj* equivocal, ambiguous; (*louche*) dubious ♦ *nf* (*incertitude*) doubt

**érable** [eʀabl] *nm* maple

**érafler** [eʀafle] *vt* to scratch; **éraflure** *nf* scratch

**éraillé, e** [eʀaje] *adj* (*voix*) rasping

**ère** [ɛʀ] *nf* era; **en l'an 1050 de notre ~** in the year 1050 A.D.

**érection** [eʀɛksjɔ̃] *nf* erection

**éreinter** [eʀɛ̃te] *vt* to exhaust, wear out; (*critiquer*) to pull to pieces

**ériger** [eʀiʒe] *vt* (*monument*) to erect

**ermite** [ɛʀmit] *nm* hermit

**éroder** [eʀɔde] *vt* to erode

**érotique** [eʀɔtik] *adj* erotic

**errer** [eʀe] *vi* to wander

**erreur** [eʀœʀ] *nf* mistake, error; **faire ~** to be mistaken; **par ~** by mistake; **~ judiciaire** miscarriage of justice

**érudit, e** [eʀydi, it] *adj* erudite, learned

**éruption** [eʀypsjɔ̃] *nf* eruption; (MÉD) rash

**ès** [ɛs] *prép:* **licencié ~ lettres/sciences** ≃ Bachelor of Arts/Science

**escabeau, x** [ɛskabo] *nm* (*tabouret*) stool; (*échelle*) stepladder

**escadron** [ɛskadʀɔ̃] *nm* squadron

**escalade** [ɛskalad] *nf* climbing *no pl;* (POL etc) escalation; **escalader** *vt* to climb

**escale** [ɛskal] *nf* (NAVIG: *durée*) call; (*endroit*) port of call; (AVIAT) stop(over); **faire ~ à** (NAVIG) to put in at; (AVIAT) to stop over at; **vol sans ~** nonstop flight

**escalier** [ɛskalje] *nm* stairs *pl;* **dans l'~** on the stairs; **~ roulant** escalator

**escamoter** [ɛskamɔte] *vt* (*esquiver*) to get round, evade; (*faire disparaître*) to conjure away

**escapade** [ɛskapad] *nf:* **faire une ~** to go on a jaunt; (*s'enfuir*) to run away *ou* off

**escargot** [ɛskaʀgo] *nm* snail

**escarpé, e** [ɛskaʀpe] *adj* steep

**escarpin** [ɛskaʀpɛ̃] *nm* low-fronted shoe, court shoe (BRIT)

**escient** [esjɑ̃] *nm:* **à bon ~** advisedly

**esclaffer** [ɛsklafe]: **s'~** *vi* to guffaw

**esclandre** [ɛsklɑ̃dr] nm scene, fracas

**esclavage** [ɛsklavaʒ] nm slavery

**esclave** [ɛsklav] nm/f slave

**escompte** [ɛskɔ̃t] nm discount; **escompter** vt (fig) to expect

**escorte** [ɛskɔrt] nf escort; **escorter** vt to escort

**escrime** [ɛskrim] nf fencing

**escrimer** [ɛskrime]: **s'~** vi: **s'~ à faire** to wear o.s. out doing

**escroc** [ɛskro] nm swindler, conman; **escroquer** [ɛskrɔke] vt: **escroquer qch (à qn)** to swindle sth (out of sb); **escroquerie** nf swindle

**espace** [ɛspas] nm space

**espacer** [ɛspase] vt to space out; **s'~** vi (visites etc) to become less frequent

**espadon** [ɛspadɔ̃] nm swordfish inv

**espadrille** [ɛspadrij] nf rope-soled sandal

**Espagne** [ɛspaɲ] nf: **l'~** Spain; **espagnol, e** adj Spanish ♦ nm/f: **E~, e** Spaniard ♦ nm (LING) Spanish

**escouade** [ɛskwad] nf squad

**espèce** [ɛspɛs] nf (BIO, BOT, ZOOL) species inv; (gén: sorte) sort, kind, type; (péj): **~ de maladroit!** you clumsy oaf!; **~s** nfpl (COMM) cash sg; **en ~** in cash

**espérance** [ɛsperɑ̃s] nf hope; **~ de vie** life expectancy

**espérer** [ɛspere] vt to hope for; **j'espère (bien)** I hope so; **~ que/faire** to hope that/to do

**espiègle** [ɛspjɛgl] adj mischievous

**espion, ne** [ɛspjɔ̃, jɔn] nm/f spy; **espionnage** nm espionage, spying; **espionner** vt to spy (up)on

**esplanade** [ɛsplanad] nf esplanade

**espoir** [ɛspwar] nm hope

**esprit** [ɛspri] nm (intellect) mind; (humour) wit; (mentalité, d'une loi etc, fantôme etc) spirit; **faire de l'~** to try to be witty; **reprendre ses ~s** to come to; **perdre l'~** to lose one's mind

**esquimau, de, x** [ɛskimo, od] adj Eskimo ♦ nm/f: **E~, de** Eskimo ♦ nm: **E~ ®** ice lolly (BRIT), popsicle (US)

**esquinter** [ɛskɛ̃te] (fam) vt to mess up

**esquisse** [ɛskis] nf sketch; **esquisser** vt to sketch; **esquisser un sourire** to give a vague smile

**esquiver** [ɛskive] vt to dodge; **s'~** vi to slip away

**essai** [ɛse] nm (tentative) attempt, try; (de produit) testing; (RUGBY) try; (LITTÉRATURE) essay; **~s** nmpl (AUTO) trials; **~ gratuit** (COMM) free trial; **à l'~** on a trial basis

**essaim** [ɛsɛ̃] nm swarm

**essayer** [ɛseje] vt to try; (vêtement, chaussures) to try (on); (méthode, voiture) to try (out) ♦ vi to try; **~ de faire** to try out/attempt to do

**essence** [ɛsɑ̃s] nf (de voiture) petrol (BRIT), gas(oline) (US); (extrait de plante) essence; (espèce: d'arbre) species inv

**essentiel, le** [ɛsɑ̃sjɛl] adj essential; **c'est l'~** (ce qui importe) that's the main thing; **l'~ de** the main part of

**essieu, x** [ɛsjø] nm axle

**essor** [ɛsɔr] nm (de l'économie etc) rapid expansion

**essorer** [ɛsɔre] vt (en tordant) to wring (out); (par la force centrifuge) to spin-dry; **essoreuse** nf spin-dryer

**essouffler** [ɛsufle]: **s'~** vi to get out of breath

**essuie-glace** [ɛsɥiglas] nm inv windscreen (BRIT) ou windshield (US) wiper

**essuyer** [ɛsɥije] vt to wipe; (fig: échec) to suffer; **s'~** (après le bain) to dry o.s.; **~ la vaisselle** to dry up

**est** [ɛ] vb voir **être**

**est²** [ɛst] nm east ♦ adj inv east; (région) east(ern); **à l'~** in the east; (direction) to the east, east(wards); **à l'~ de** (to the) east of

**estampe** [ɛstɑ̃p] nf print, engraving

**est-ce que** [ɛskə] adv: **~ c'est cher/c'était bon?** is it expensive/was it good?; **quand est-ce qu'il part?** when does he leave?, when is he leaving?; voir aussi **que**

**esthéticienne** [ɛstetisjɛn] nf beautician

**esthétique** [estetik] *adj* attractive

**estimation** [estimasjɔ̃] *nf* valuation; (*chiffre*) estimate

**estime** [estim] *nf* esteem, regard; **estimer** *vt* (*respecter*) to esteem; (*expertiser: bijou etc*) to value; (*évaluer: coût etc*) to assess, estimate; (*penser*): **estimer que/être** to consider that/o.s. to be

**estival, e, -aux** [estival, o] *adj* summer *cpd*

**estivant, e** [estivɑ̃, ɑ̃t] *nm/f* (summer) holiday-maker

**estomac** [estɔma] *nm* stomach

**estomaqué, e** [estɔmake] (*fam*) *adj* flabbergasted

**estomper** [estɔ̃pe] *vt* (*papiers d'identité, facture*) to make out; (*liste, programme*) to draw up; (*entreprise*) to set up; (*réputation, usage, fait, culpabilité*) to establish; **s'~** *vi* to be established; **s'~** (**à son compte**) to set up in business; **s'~ à/près de** to settle in/near

**étable** [etabl] *nf* cowshed

**établi** [etabli] *nm* (work)bench

**établir** [etablir] *vt* (*papiers d'identité, facture*) to make out; (*liste, programme*) to draw up; (*entreprise*) to set up; (*réputation, usage, fait, culpabilité*) to establish; **s'~** *vi* to be established; **s'~** (**à son compte**) to set up in business; **s'~ à/près de** to settle in/near

**établissement** [etablismɑ̃] *nm* (*entreprise, institution*) establishment; **~ scolaire** school, educational establishment

**étage** [etaʒ] *nm* (*d'immeuble*) storey, floor; **à l'~** upstairs; **au 2ème ~** on the 2nd (BRIT) or 3rd (US) floor

**étagère** [etaʒɛr] *nf* (*rayon*) shelf; (*meuble*) shelves *pl*

**étai** [ete] *nm* stay, prop

**étain** [etɛ̃] *nm* pewter *no pl*

**étais** *etc* [ete] *vb voir* **être**

**étal** [etal] *nm* stall

**étalage** [etalaʒ] *nm* display; (*devanture*) display window; **faire ~ de** to show

off, parade

**étaler** [etale] *vt* (*carte, nappe*) to spread (out); (*peinture*) to spread; (*échelonner: paiements, vacances*) to spread, stagger; (*marchandises*) to display; (*connaissances*) to parade; **s'~** *vi* (*liquide*) to spread out; (*fam*) to fall flat on one's face; **s'~ sur** (*suj: paiements etc*) to be spread out over

**étalon** [etalɔ̃] *nm* (*cheval*) stallion

**étanche** [etɑ̃ʃ] *adj* (*récipient*) watertight; (*montre, vêtement*) waterproof; **étancher** *vt*: **étancher sa soif** to quench one's thirst

**étang** [etɑ̃] *nm* pond

**étant** [etɑ̃] *vb voir* **être**; **donné**

**étape** [etap] *nf* stage; (*lieu d'arrivée*) stopping place; (: CYCLISME) staging point

**état** [eta] *nm* (POL, *condition*) state; **en mauvais ~** in poor condition; **en ~ (de marche)** in (working) order; **remettre en ~** to repair; **hors d'~** out of order; **être en ~/hors d'~ de faire** to be in a/in no fit state to do; **être dans tous ses ~s** to be in a state; **faire ~ de** (*alléguer*) to put forward; **l'É~** the State; **~ civil** civil status; **~ des lieux** inventory of fixtures; **étatiser** *vt* to bring under state control; **état-major** *nm* (MIL) staff; **États-Unis** *nmpl*: **les États-Unis** the United States

**étau, x** [eto] *nm* vice (BRIT), vise (US)

**étayer** [eteje] *vt* to prop up ou shore up

**etc.** [ɛtsetera] *adv* etc

**et c(a)etera** [ɛtsetera] *adv* et cetera, and so on

**été** [ete] *pp de* **être ♦** *nm* summer

**éteindre** [etɛ̃dr] *vt* (*lampe, lumière, radio*) to turn ou switch off; (*cigarette, feu*) to put out, extinguish; **s'~** *vi* (*feu, lumière*) to go out; (*mourir*) to pass away; **éteint, e** *adj* (*fig*) lacklustre, dull; (*volcan*) extinct

**étendard** [etɑ̃dar] *nm* standard

**étendre** [etɑ̃dr] *vt* (*pâte, liquide*) to spread; (*carte etc*) to spread out; (*linge*) to hang up; (*bras, jambes*) to stretch out; (*fig: agrandir*) to extend; **s'~** *vi* (*augmenter, se propager*) to spread; (*terrain, forêt etc*) to stretch; (*s'allonger*) to stretch out; (*se coucher*) to lie down; (*fig: expliquer*) to elaborate

**étendu, e** [etɑ̃dy] *adj* extensive; **étendue** *nf* (*d'eau, de sable*) stretch, expanse; (*importance*) extent, scope

**éternel, le** [etɛrnɛl] *adj* eternal

**éterniser** [etɛrnize]: **s'~** *vi* to last for ages; (*visiteur*) to stay for ages

**éternité** [etɛrnite] *nf* eternity; **ça a duré une ~** it lasted for ages

**éternuement** [etɛrnymɑ̃] *nm* sneeze

**éternuer** [etɛrnɥe] *vi* to sneeze

**êtes** [ɛt(z)] *vb voir* **être**

**éthique** [etik] *adj* ethical

**ethnie** [etni] *nf* ethnic group

**éthylisme** [etilism] *nm* alcoholism

**étiez** [etje] *vb voir* **être**

**étinceler** [etɛ̃s(ə)le] *vi* to sparkle

**étincelle** [etɛ̃sɛl] *nf* spark

**étiqueter** [etik(ə)te] *vt* to label

**étiquette** [etikɛt] *nf* label; (*protocole*): **l'~** etiquette

**étirer** [etire]: **s'~** *vi* (*personne*) to stretch; (*convoi, route*) **s'~ sur** to stretch out over

**étoffe** [etɔf] *nf* material, fabric

**étoffer** [etɔfe] *vt* to fill out

**étoile** [etwal] *nf* star; **à la belle ~** in the open; **~ de mer** starfish; **~ filante** shooting star; **étoilé, e** *adj* starry

**étonnant, e** [etɔnɑ̃, ɑ̃t] *adj* amazing

**étonnement** [etɔnmɑ̃] *nm* surprise, amazement

**étonner** [etɔne] *vt* to surprise, amaze; **s'~ que/de** to be amazed that/at; **cela m'~ait (que)** (*j'en doute*) I'd be surprised (if)

**étouffant, e** [etufɑ̃, ɑ̃t] *adj* stifling

**étouffée** [etufe]: **à l'~** *adv* (*CULIN: légumes*) steamed; (: *viande*) braised

**étouffer** [etufe] *vt* to suffocate; (*bruit*) to muffle; (*scandale*) to hush up ♦ *vt* to suffocate; **s'~** *vi* (*en mangeant etc*) to

choke; **on étouffe** it's stifling

**étourderie** [eturdəri] *nf* (*caractère*) absent-mindedness *no pl;* (*faute*) thoughtless blunder

**étourdi, e** [eturdi] *adj* (*distrait*) scatter-brained, heedless

**étourdir** [eturdir] *vt* (*assommer*) to stun, daze; (*griser*) to make dizzy *ou* giddy; **étourdissement** *nm* dizzy spell

**étourneau, x** [eturno] *nm* starling

**étrange** [etrɑ̃ʒ] *adj* strange

**étranger, -ère** [etrɑ̃ʒe, ɛr] *adj* foreign; (*pas de la famille, non familier*) strange ♦ *nm/f* foreigner; stranger ♦ *nm:* **à l'~** abroad

**étrangler** [etrɑ̃gle] *vt* to strangle; **s'~** *vi* (*en mangeant etc*) to choke

---

**MOT-CLÉ**

**être** [ɛtr] *nm* being; **être humain** human being

♦ *vb +attrib* 1 (*état, description*) to be; **il est instituteur** he is *ou* he's a teacher; **vous êtes grand/intelligent/fatigué** you are *ou* you're tall/clever/tired

2 (*+à: appartenir*): **le livre est à Paul** the book is Paul's *ou* belongs to Paul; **c'est à moi/eux** it is *ou* it's mine/theirs

3 (*+de: provenance*): **il est de Paris** he is from Paris; (: *appartenance*): **il est des nôtres** he is one of us

4 (*date*): **nous sommes le 10 janvier** it's the 10th of January (today)

♦ *vi* to be; **je ne serai pas ici demain** I won't be here tomorrow

♦ *vb aux* 1 to have; to be; **être arrivé/allé** to have arrived/gone; **il est parti** he has left, he has gone

2 (*forme passive*) to be; **être fait par** to be made by; **il a été promu** he has been promoted

3 (*+à: obligation*): **c'est à réparer** it needs repairing; **c'est à essayer** it should be tried

♦ *vb impers* 1: **il est +adjectif** it is +*adjectif*; **il est impossible de le faire** it's impossible to do it

**2** (heure, date): **il est 10 heures, c'est 10 heures** it is ou it's 10 o'clock

**3** (emphatique): **c'est moi** it's me; **c'est à lui de le faire** it's up to him to do it

**étreindre** [etʀɛ̃dʀ] vt to clutch, grip; (amoureusement, amicalement) to embrace; **s'~** vi to embrace

**étrenner** [etʀene] vt to use (ou wear) for the first time; **étrennes** nfpl Christmas box ou present

**étrier** [etʀije] nm stirrup

**étriqué, e** [etʀike] adj skimpy

**étroit, e** [etʀwa, wat] adj narrow; (vêtement) tight; (fig: liens, collaboration) close; **à l'~** cramped; **~ d'esprit** narrow-minded

**étude** [etyd] nf studying; (ouvrage, rapport) study; (SCOL: salle de travail) study room; **~s** nfpl (SCOL) studies; **être à l'~** (projet etc) to be under consideration; **faire des ~s (de droit/médecine)** to study (law/medicine)

**étudiant, e** [etydjɑ̃, jɑ̃t] nm/f student

**étudier** [etydje] vt, vi to study

**étui** [etɥi] nm case

**étuve** [etyv] nf steamroom

**étuvée** [etyve]: **à l'~** adv braised

**eu, eue** [y] pp de **avoir**

**euh** [ø] excl er

**euro** [øʀo] nm euro

**Euroland** [øʀɔlɑ̃d] nm Euroland

**Europe** [øʀɔp] nf: **l'~** Europe; **européen, ne** adj European ♦ nm/f: **Européen, ne** European

**eus** etc [y] vb voir **avoir**

**eux** [ø] pron (sujet) they; (objet) them

**évacuer** [evakɥe] vt to evacuate

**évader** [evade]: **s'~** vi to escape

**évaluer** [evalɥe] vt (expertiser) to appraise, evaluate; (juger approximativement) to estimate

**évangile** [evɑ̃ʒil] nm gospel

**évanouir** [evanwiʀ]: **s'~** vi to faint; (disparaître) to vanish, disappear; **éva-**

**nouissement** nm (syncope) fainting fit

**évaporer** [evapɔʀe]: **s'~** vi to evaporate

**évasé, e** [evaze] adj (manches, jupe) flared

**évasif, -ive** [evazif, iv] adj evasive

**évasion** [evazjɔ̃] nf escape

**évêché** [eveʃe] nm bishop's palace

**éveil** [evej] nm awakening; **être en ~** to be alert; **éveillé, e** adj awake; (vif) alert, sharp; **éveiller** vt to (a)waken; (soupçons etc) to arouse; **s'éveiller** vi to (a)waken; (fig) to be aroused

**événement** [evenmɑ̃] nm event

**éventail** [evɑ̃taj] nm fan; (choix) range

**éventaire** [evɑ̃tɛʀ] nm stall, stand

**éventer** [evɑ̃te] vt (secret) to uncover; **s'~** vi (parfum) to go stale

**éventualité** [evɑ̃tɥalite] nf eventuality; possibility; **dans l'~ de** in the event of; **éventuel, le** [evɑ̃tɥɛl] adj possible; **éventuellement** adv possibly

**évêque** [evɛk] nm bishop

**évertuer** [evɛʀtɥe]: **s'~** vi: **s'~ à faire** to try very hard to do

**éviction** [eviksjɔ̃] nf (de locataire) eviction

**évidemment** [evidamɑ̃] adv (bien sûr) of course; (certainement) obviously

**évidence** [evidɑ̃s] nf obviousness; (fait) obvious fact; **de toute ~** quite obviously ou evidently; **être en ~** to be clearly visible; **mettre en ~** (fait) to highlight; **évident, e** adj obvious, evident; **ce n'est pas évident!** (fam) it's not that easy!

**évider** [evide] vt to scoop out

**évier** [evje] nm (kitchen) sink

**évincer** [evɛ̃se] vt to oust

**éviter** [evite] vt to avoid; **~ de faire** to avoid doing; **~ qch à qn** to spare sb sth

**évolué, e** [evɔlɥe] adj advanced

**évoluer** [evɔlɥe] vi (enfant, maladie) to develop; (situation, moralement) to evolve, develop; (aller et venir) to move about; **évolution** nf development, evolution

**évoquer** [evɔke] *vt* to call to mind, evoke; *(mentionner)* to mention

**ex...** [ɛks] *préfixe* ex-

**exact, e** [ɛgza(kt), ɛgzakt] *adj* exact; *(correct)* correct; *(ponctuel)* punctual; **l'heure ~e** the right *ou* exact time; **exactement** *adv* exactly

**ex aequo** [ɛgzeko] *adj* equally placed; **arriver ~** to finish neck and neck

**exagéré, e** [ɛgzaʒere] *adj (prix etc)* excessive

**exagérer** [ɛgzaʒere] *vt* to exaggerate ♦ *vi* to exaggerate; *(abuser)* to go too far

**exalter** [ɛgzalte] *vt (enthousiasmer)* to excite, elate

**examen** [ɛgzamɛ̃] *nm* examination; *(SCOL)* exam, examination; **à l'~** under consideration

**examinateur, -trice** [ɛgzaminatœr, tris] *nm/f* examiner

**examiner** [ɛgzamine] *vt* to examine

**exaspérant, e** [ɛgzasperã, ãt] *adj* exasperating

**exaspérer** [ɛgzaspere] *vt* to exasperate

**exaucer** [ɛgzose] *vt (vœu)* to grant

**excédent** [ɛksedã] *nm* surplus; **en ~** surplus; **~ de bagages** excess luggage

**excéder** [ɛksede] *vt (dépasser)* to exceed; *(agacer)* to exasperate

**excellent, e** [ɛksela, ãt] *adj* excellent

**excentrique** [ɛksãtrik] *adj* eccentric

**excepté, e** [ɛksepte] *adj, prép*: **les élèves ~s, ~ les élèves** except for the pupils

**exception** [ɛksɛpsjɔ̃] *nf* exception; **à l'~ de** except for, with the exception of; **d'~** *(mesure, loi)* special, exceptional; **exceptionnel, le** *adj* exceptional; **exceptionnellement** *adv* exceptionally

**excès** [ɛksɛ] *nm* surplus ♦ *nmpl* excesses; **faire des ~** to overindulge; **~ de vitesse** speeding *no pl*; **excessif, -ive** *adj* excessive

**excitant, e** [ɛksitã, ãt] *adj* exciting ♦ *nm* stimulant; **excitation** *nf (état)* excitement

**exciter** [ɛksite] *vt* to excite; *(suj: café etc)* to stimulate; **s'~** *vi* to get excited

**exclamation** [ɛksklamasjɔ̃] *nf* exclamation

**exclamer** [ɛksklame]: **s'~** *vi* to exclaim

**exclure** [ɛksklyr] *vt (faire sortir)* to expel; *(ne pas compter)* to exclude, leave out; *(rendre impossible)* to exclude, rule out; **il est exclu que** ... it's out of the question that ...; **il n'est pas exclu que** ... it's not impossible that ...; **exclusif, -ive** *adj* exclusive; **exclusion** *nf* exclusion; **à l'exclusion de** with the exclusion *ou* exception of; **exclusivité** *nf (COMM)* exclusive rights *pl*; **film passant en exclusivité** à film showing only at

**excursion** [ɛkskyrsjɔ̃] *nf (en autocar)* excursion, trip; *(à pied)* walk, hike

**excuse** [ɛkskyz] *nf* excuse; **~s** *nfpl (regret)* apology *sg*, apologies; **excuser** *vt* to excuse; **s'excuser (de)** to apologize (for); **"excusez-moi"** "I'm sorry"; *(pour attirer l'attention)* "excuse me"

**exécrable** [ɛgzekrabl] *adj* atrocious

**exécuter** [ɛgzekyte] *vt (tuer)* to execute; *(tâche etc)* to execute, carry out; *(MUS: jouer)* to perform, execute; **s'~** *vi* to comply; **exécutif, -ive** *adj, nm (POL)* executive; **exécution** *nf* execution; **mettre à exécution** to carry out

**exemplaire** [ɛgzãplɛr] *nm* copy

**exemple** [ɛgzãpl] *nm* example; **par ~** for instance, for example; **donner l'~** to set an example

**exempt, e** [ɛgza, ã(p)t] *adj*: **~ de** *(dispensé de)* exempt from; *(sans)* free from

**exercer** [ɛgzɛrse] *vt (pratiquer)* to exercise, practise; *(influence, contrôle)* to exert; *(former)* to exercise, train; **s'~** *vi (sportif, musicien)* to practise

**exercice** [ɛgzɛrsis] *nm* exercise

**exhaustif, -ive** [ɛgzostif, iv] *adj* exhaustive

**exhiber** [ɛgzibe] vt (montrer: papiers, certificat) to present, produce; (péj) to display, flaunt; **s'~** vi to parade; (suj: exhibitionniste) to expose o.s

**exhibitionniste** [ɛgzibisjɔnist] nm/f flasher

**exhorter** [ɛgzɔrte] vt to urge

**exigeant, e** [ɛgziʒɑ̃, ɑ̃t] adj demanding; (péj) hard to please

**exigence** [ɛgziʒɑ̃s] nf demand, requirement

**exiger** [ɛgziʒe] vt to demand, require

**exigu, ë** [ɛgzigy] adj cramped, tiny

**exil** [ɛgzil] nm exile; **lieu d'~** place of exile

**exiler** [ɛgzile] vt to exile; **s'exiler** vi to go into exile

**existence** [ɛgzistɑ̃s] nf existence

**exister** [ɛgziste] vi to exist; **il existe un/des** there is a/are (some)

**exonérer** [ɛgzɔnere] vt: **~ de** to exempt from

**exorbitant, e** [ɛgzɔrbitɑ̃, ɑ̃t] adj exorbitant

**exorbité, e** [ɛgzɔrbite] adj: **yeux ~s** bulging eyes

**exotique** [ɛgzɔtik] adj exotic; **yaourt aux fruits ~s** tropical fruit yoghurt

**expatrier** [ɛkspatrije] vt: **s'~** to leave one's country

**expectative** [ɛkspɛktativ] nf: **être dans l'~** to be still waiting

**expédient** [ɛkspedjɑ̃, jɑ̃t] (péj) nm: **vivre d'~s** to live by one's wits

**expédier** [ɛkspedje] vt (lettre, paquet) to send; (troupes) to dispatch; (fam: travail etc) to dispose of, dispatch; **expéditeur, -trice** nm/f sender; **expédition** nf sending; (scientifique, sportive, MIL) expedition

**expérience** [ɛksperjɑ̃s] nf (de la vie) experience; (scientifique) experiment

**expérimenté, e** [ɛksperimɑ̃te] adj experienced

**expérimenter** [ɛksperimɑ̃te] vt to test out, experiment with

**expert, e** [ɛkspɛr, ɛrt] adj, nm expert; **expert-comptable** nm ≈ chartered accountant (BRIT), ≈ certified public accountant (US)

**expertise** [ɛkspɛrtiz] nf (évaluation) expert evaluation

**expertiser** [ɛkspɛrtize] vt (objet de valeur) to value; (voiture accidentée etc) to assess damage to

**expier** [ɛkspje] vt to expiate, atone for

**expirer** [ɛkspire] vi (prendre fin, mourir) to expire; (respirer) to breathe out

**explicatif, -ive** [ɛksplikatif, iv] adj explanatory

**explication** [ɛksplikasjɔ̃] nf explanation; (discussion) discussion; (dispute) argument; **~ de texte** (SCOL) critical analysis

**explicite** [ɛksplisit] adj explicit

**expliquer** [ɛksplike] vt to explain; **s'~** to explain (o.s.); **s'~ avec qn** (discuter) to explain o.s. to sb; **son erreur s'explique** one can understand his mistake

**exploit** [ɛksplwa] nm exploit, feat; **exploitant, e** nm/f: **exploitant (agricole)** farmer

**exploitation** nf exploitation; (d'une entreprise) running; **~ agricole** farming concern; **exploiter** vt (personne, don) to exploit; (entreprise, ferme) to run, operate; (mine) to exploit, work

**explorer** [ɛksplɔre] vt to explore

**exploser** [ɛksploze] vi to explode, blow up; (engin explosif) to go off; (personne: de colère) to flare up; **explosif, -ive** adj, nm explosive; **explosion** nf explosion

**exportateur, -trice** [ɛkspɔrtatœr, tris] adj export cpd, exporting ♦ nm exporter

**exportation** [ɛkspɔrtasjɔ̃] nf (action) exportation; (produit) export

**exporter** [ɛkspɔrte] vt to export

**exposant** [ɛkspozɑ̃] nm exhibitor

**exposé, e** [ɛkspoze] nm talk ♦ adj: **~ au sud** facing south

**exposer** [ɛkspoze] vt (marchandise) to display; (peinture) to exhibit, show; (parler de) to explain, set out; (mettre en danger, orienter, PHOTO) to expose;

**exposition** *nf* (*manifestation*) exhibition; (*PHOTO*) exposure

**exprès**[1] [εksprε] *adv* (*délibérément*) on purpose; (*spécialement*) specially

**exprès**[2], **-esse** [εksprε] *adj* (*ordre, défense*) express, formal ♦ *adj inv* (*PTT*) express ♦ *adv* express

**express** [εksprε] *adj, nm:* (**café**) ~ espresso (coffee); (**train**) ~ = fast train

**expressément** [εksprεsemã] *adv* (*spécialement*) specifically

**expressif, -ive** [εksprεsif, iv] *adj* expressive

**expression** [εksprεsjɔ̃] *nf* expression

**exprimer** [εksprime] *vt* (*sentiment, idée*) to express; (*jus, liquide*) to press out; **s'~** *vi* (*personne*) to express o.s

**exproprier** [εksprɔprije] *vt* to buy up by compulsory purchase, expropriate

**expulser** [εkspylse] *vt* to expel; (*locataire*) to evict; (*SPORT*) to send off

**exquis, e** [εkski, iz] *adj* exquisite

**extase** [εkstɑz] *nf* ecstasy; **extasier: s'extasier sur** *vt* to go into raptures over

**extension** [εkstɑ̃sjɔ̃] *nf* (*fig*) extension

**exténuer** [εkstenɥe] *vt* to exhaust

**extérieur, e** [εksterjœr] *adj* (*porte, mur etc*) outer, outside; (*au dehors: escalier, w.-c.*) outside; (*commerce*) foreign; (*influences*) external; (*apparent: calme, gaieté etc*) surface *cpd* ♦ *nm* (*d'une maison, d'un récipient etc*) outside, exterior; (*apparence*) exterior; **à l'~** outside; (*à l'étranger*) abroad; **extérieurement** *adv* on the outside; (*en apparence*) on the surface

**exterminer** [εkstεrmine] *vt* to exterminate, wipe out

**externat** [εkstεrna] *nm* day school

**externe** [εkstεrn] *adj* external, outer ♦ *nm/f* (*MÉD*) non-resident medical student (*BRIT*), extern (*US*); (*SCOL*) day pupil

**extincteur** [εkstɛ̃ktœr] *nm* (fire) extinguisher

**extinction** [εkstɛ̃ksjɔ̃] *nf:* ~ **de voix** loss of voice

**extorquer** [εkstɔrke] *vt* to extort

**extra** [εkstra] *adj inv* first-rate; (*fam*) fantastic ♦ *nm inv* extra help

**extrader** [εkstrade] *vt* to extradite

**extraire** [εkstrεr] *vt* to extract; **extrait** *nm* extract

**extraordinaire** [εkstraɔrdinεr] *adj* extraordinary; (*POL: mesures etc*) special

**extravagant, e** [εkstravagã, ãt] *adj* extravagant

**extraverti, e** [εkstravεrti] *adj* extrovert

**extrême** [εkstrεm] *adj, nm:* extreme; **extrêmement** *adv* extremely; **extrême-onction** *nf* last rites *pl*; **Extrême-Orient** *nm* Far East

**extrémité** [εkstremite] *nf* end; (*situation*) straits *pl*, plight; (*geste désespéré*) extreme action; **~s** *nfpl* (*pieds et mains*) extremities

**exubérant, e** [εgzyberã, ãt] *adj* exuberant

**exutoire** [εgzytwar] *nm* outlet, release

# F, f

**F** *abr* = **franc**

**fa** [fa] *nm inv* (*MUS*) F; (*en chantant la gamme*) fa

**fable** [fabl] *nf* fable

**fabricant** [fabrikã, ãt] *nm* manufacturer

**fabrication** [fabrikasjɔ̃] *nf* manufacture

**fabrique** [fabrik] *nf* factory; **fabriquer** *vt* to make; (*industriellement*) to manufacture; (*fig*): **qu'est-ce qu'il fabrique?** (*fam*) what is he doing?

**fabulation** [fabylasjɔ̃] *nf* fantasizing

**fac** [fak] (*fam*) *abr f* (*SCOL*) = **faculté**

**façade** [fasad] *nf* front, façade

**face** [fas] *nf* face; (*fig: aspect*) side ♦ *adj*: **le côté** ~ heads; **en** ~ **de** opposite; (*fig*) in front of; **de** ~ (*voir*) face on; (*photo*) from the front; **à** ~ facing; (*fig*) faced with, in the face of; **faire** ~ **à** to face; **à** ~ *adv* facing each other ♦ *nm inv* encounter

**fâché, e** [faʃe] *adj* angry; (*désolé*) sorry

**fâcher** [faʃe] *vt* to anger; **se ~** to get angry; **se ~ avec** (*se brouiller*) to fall out with

**fâcheux, -euse** [faʃø, øz] *adj* unfortunate, regrettable

**facile** [fasil] *adj* easy; (*caractère*) easy-going; **facilement** *adv* easily

**facilité** *nf* easiness; (*disposition, don*) aptitude; **facilités de paiement** easy terms; **faciliter** *vt* to make easier

**façon** [fasɔ̃] *nf* (*manière*) way; (*d'une robe etc*) making-up, cut; **~s** *nfpl* (*péj*) fuss *sg*; **de ~ à/à ce que** so as to/that; **de toute ~** anyway, in any case; **façonner** [fasɔne] *vt* (*travailler: matière*) to shape, fashion

**facteur, -trice** [faktœʀ] *nm/f* postman(-woman) (BRIT), mailman(-woman) (US) ♦ *nm* (MATH, *fig*: élément) factor

**factice** [faktis] *adj* artificial

**faction** [faksjɔ̃] *nf* faction; **être de ~** to be on guard (duty)

**facture** [faktyʀ] *nf* (*à payer: gén*) bill; invoice; **facturer** *vt* to invoice

**facultatif, -ive** [fakyltatif, iv] *adj* optional

**faculté** [fakylte] *nf* (*intellectuelle, d'université*) faculty; (*pouvoir, possibilité*) power

**fade** [fad] *adj* insipid

**fagot** [fago] *nm* bundle of sticks

**faible** [fɛbl] *adj* weak; (*voix, lumière, vent*) faint; (*rendement, revenu*) low ♦ *nm* (*pour quelqu'un*) weakness, soft spot; **faiblesse** *nf* weakness; **faiblir** *vi* to weaken; (*lumière*) to dim; (*vent*) to drop

**faïence** [fajɑ̃s] *nf* earthenware *no pl*

**faignant, e** [fɛɲɑ̃, ɑ̃t] *nm/f* = **fainéant, e**

**faille** [faj] *vb voir* **falloir** ♦ *nf* (GÉO) fault; (*fig*) flaw, weakness

**faillir** [fajiʀ] *vi*: **j'ai failli tomber** I almost *ou* very nearly fell

**faillite** [fajit] *nf* bankruptcy

**faim** [fɛ̃] *nf* hunger; **avoir ~** to be hungry; **rester sur sa ~** (*aussi fig*) to be left wanting more

**fainéant, e** [feneɑ̃, ɑ̃t] *nm/f* idler, loafer

---

MOT-CLÉ

---

**faire** [fɛʀ] *vt* **1** (*fabriquer, être l'auteur de*) to make; **faire du vin/une offre/un film** to make wine/an offer/a film; **faire du bruit** to make a noise

**2** (*effectuer: travail, opération*) to do; **que faites-vous?** (*quel métier etc*) what do you do?; (*quelle activité: au moment de la question*) what are you doing?; **faire la lessive** to do the washing

**3** (*études*) to do; (*sport, musique*) to play; **faire du droit/du français** to do law/French; **faire du rugby/piano** to play rugby/the piano

**4** (*simuler*): **faire le malade/l'ignorant** to act the invalid/the fool

**5** (*transformer, avoir un effet sur*): **faire de qn un frustré/avocat** to make sb frustrated/a lawyer; **ça ne me fait rien** (*m'est égal*) I don't care *ou* mind; (*me laisse froid*) it has no effect on me; **ça ne fait rien** it doesn't matter; **faire que** (*impliquer*) to mean that

**6** (*calculs, prix, mesures*): **2 et 2 font 4** 2 and 2 are *ou* make 4; **ça fait 10 m/ 15 F** it's 10 m/15F; **je vous le fais 10 F** I'll let you have it for 10F

**7**: **qu'a-t-il fait de sa valise?** what has he done with his case?

**8**: **ne faire que**: **il ne fait que critiquer** (*sans cesse*) all he (ever) does is criticize; (*seulement*) he's only criticizing

**9** (*dire*) to say; **"vraiment?" fit-il** "really?" he said

**10** (*maladie*) to have; **faire du diabète** to have diabetes *sg*

♦ *vi* **1** (*agir, s'y prendre*) to act, do; **il faut faire vite** we (*ou* you *etc*) must act quickly; **comment a-t-il fait pour?** how did he manage to?; **faites**

**comme chez vous** make yourself at home

**2** (*paraître*) to look; **faire vieux/ démodé** to look old/old-fashioned; **ça fait bien** it looks good

♦ *vb substitut* to do; **ne le casse pas comme je l'ai fait** don't break it as I did; **je peux le voir? - faites!** can I see it? - please do!

♦ *vb impers* **1**: **il fait beau** *etc* the weather is fine *etc*; *voir aussi* **jour**; **froid** *etc*

**2** (*temps écoulé, durée*): **ça fait 2 ans qu'il est parti** it's 2 years since he left; **ça fait 2 ans qu'il y est** he's been there for 2 years

♦ *vb semi-aux* **1**: **faire** +*infinitif* (*action directe*) to make; **faire tomber/bouger qch** to make sth fall/move; **faire démarrer un moteur/chauffer de l'eau** to start up an engine/heat some water; **cela fait dormir** it makes you sleep, **faire travailler les enfants** to make the children work *ou* get the children to work

**2** (*indirectement, par un intermédiaire*): **faire réparer qch** to get *ou* have sth repaired; **faire punir les enfants** to have the children punished; **se faire** *vi* **1** (*vin, fromage*) to mature

**2**: **cela se fait beaucoup/ne se fait pas** it's done a lot/not done

**3**: **se faire** +*nom ou pron*: **se faire une jupe** to make *ou* a skirt; **se faire des amis** to make friends; **se faire du souci** to worry; **il ne s'en fait pas** he doesn't worry

**4**: **se faire** +*adj* (*devenir*): **se faire vieux** to be getting old; (*délibérément*): **se faire beau** to do o.s. up

**5**: **se faire à** (*s'habituer*) to get used to; **je n'arrive pas à me faire à la nourriture/au climat** I can't get used to the food/climate

**6**: **se faire** +*infinitif*: **se faire examiner la vue/opérer** to have one's eyes tested/to have an operation; **se faire**

**couper les cheveux** to get one's hair cut; **il va se faire tuer/punir** he's going to get himself killed/get (himself) punished; **il s'est fait aider** he got somebody to help him; **il s'est fait aider par Simon** he got Simon to help him; **se faire faire un vêtement** to get a garment made for o.s.

**7** (*impersonnel*): **comment se fait-il/ faisait-il que?** how is it/was it that?

**faire-part** [fɛʀpaʀ] *nm inv* announcement (*of birth, marriage etc*)

**faisable** [fəzabl] *adj* feasible

**faisan, e** [fəzɑ̃, an] *nm/f* pheasant; **faisandé, e** *adj* high (*bad*)

**faisceau, x** [fɛso] *nm* (*de lumière etc*) beam

**faisons** [fəzɔ̃] *vb voir* **faire**

**fait, e** [fɛ, fɛt] *adj* (*mûr: fromage, melon*) ripe ♦ *nm* (*événement*) event, occurrence; (*réalité, donnée*) fact; **être au ~ (de)** to be informed (of); **au ~** (*à propos*) by the way; **en venir au ~** to get to the point; **du ~ de ceci/qu'il a menti** because of *ou* on account of this/his having lied; **de ce ~** for this reason; **en ~** in fact; **prendre qn sur le ~** to catch sb in the act; **~ divers** news item

**faîte** [fɛt] *nm* top; (*fig*) pinnacle, height

**faites** [fɛt] *vb voir* **faire**

**faitout** [fɛtu] *nm*, **fait-tout** [fɛtu] *nm inv* stewpot

**falaise** [falɛz] *nf* cliff

**falloir** [falwaʀ] *vb impers*: **il faut qu'il parte/a fallu qu'il parte** (*obligation*) he has to *ou* must leave/had to leave; **il a fallu le faire** it had to be done; **il faut faire attention** you have to be careful; **il me faudrait 100 F** I would need 100 F; **il vous faut tourner à gauche après l'église** you have to turn left past the church; **nous avons ce qu'il (nous) faut** we have what we need; **s'en falloir**: **il s'en est fallu de 100 F/5 minutes** we/they *etc* were 100 F short/5 minutes late (*ou* early); **il s'en faut de beaucoup qu'il soit** he is far from being; **il s'en est fallu de peu que cela n'arrive** it very nearly happened

**falsifier** [falsifje] *vt* to falsify, doctor

**famé, e** [fame] *adj*: **mal ~** disreputable, of ill repute

**famélique** [famelik] *adj* half-starved

**fameux, -euse** [famø, øz] *adj* (*illustre*) famous; (*bon: repas, plat etc*) first-rate, first-class; (*valeur intensive*) real, downright

**familial, e, -aux** [familjal, jo] *adj* family *cpd*

**familiarité** [familjarite] *nf* familiarity; **~s** *nfpl* (*privautés*) familiarities

**familier, -ère** [familje, jɛr] *adj* (*connu*) familiar; (*atmosphère*) informal, friendly; (*LING*) informal, colloquial ♦ *nm* regular (visitor)

**famille** [famij] *nf* family; **il a de la ~ à Paris** he has relatives in Paris

**famine** [famin] *nf* famine

**fanatique** [fanatik] *adj* fanatical ♦ *nm/f* fanatic; **fanatisme** *nm* fanaticism

**faner** [fane]: **se ~** *vi* to fade

**fanfare** [fɑ̃far] *nf* (*orchestre*) brass band; (*musique*) fanfare

**fanfaron, ne** [fɑ̃farɔ̃, ɔn] *nm/f* braggart

**fantaisie** [fɑ̃tezi] *nf* (*spontanéité*) fancy, imagination; (*caprice*) whim ♦ *adj*: **bijou ~** costume jewellery; **fantaisiste** (*péj*) *adj* unorthodox, eccentric

**fantasme** [fɑ̃tasm] *nm* fantasy

**fantasque** [fɑ̃task] *adj* whimsical, capricious

**fantastique** [fɑ̃tastik] *adj* fantastic

**fantôme** [fɑ̃tom] *nm* ghost, phantom

**faon** [fɑ̃] *nm* fawn

**farce** [fars] *nf* (*viande*) stuffing; (*blague*) (practical) joke; (*THÉÂTRE*) farce; **farcir** *vt* (*viande*) to stuff

**fardeau, x** [fardo] *nm* burden

**farder** [farde]: **se ~** *vi* to make (o.s.) up

**farfelu, e** [farfəly] *adj* hare-brained

**farine** [farin] *nf* flour; **farineux, -euse** *adj* (*sauce, pomme*) floury

**farouche** [faruʃ] *adj* (*timide*) shy, timid

**fart** [fart] *nm* (ski) wax

**fascicule** [fasikyl] *nm* volume

**fascination** [fasinasjɔ̃] *nf* fascination

**fasciner** [fasine] *vt* to fascinate

**fascisme** [faʃism] *nm* fascism

**fasse** *etc* [fas] *vb voir* **faire**

**faste** [fast] *nm* splendour

**fastidieux, -euse** [fastidjø, jøz] *adj* tedious, tiresome

**fastueux, -euse** [fastɥø, øz] *adj* sumptuous, luxurious

**fatal, e** [fatal] *adj* fatal; (*inévitable*) inevitable; **fatalité** *nf* (*destin*) fate; (*coïncidence*) fateful coincidence

**fatidique** [fatidik] *adj* fateful

**fatigant, e** [fatigɑ̃, ɑ̃t] *adj* tiring; (*agaçant*) tiresome

**fatigue** [fatig] *nf* tiredness, fatigue; **fatigué, e** *adj* tired; **fatiguer** *vt* to tire, make tired; (*fig: agacer*) to annoy ♦ *vi* (*moteur*) to labour, strain; **se fatiguer** to get tired

**fatras** [fatra] *nm* jumble, hotchpotch

**faubourg** [fobur] *nm* suburb

**fauché, e** [foʃe] *adj* (*fam*) broke

**faucher** [foʃe] *vt* (*herbe*) to cut; (*champs, blés*) to reap; (*fig: véhicule*) to mow down; (*fam: voler*) to pinch

**faucille** [fosij] *nf* sickle

**faucon** [fokɔ̃] *nm* falcon, hawk

**faudra** [fodra] *vb voir* **falloir**

**faufiler** [fofile]: **se ~** *vi*: **~ dans** to edge one's way into; **se ~ parmi/entre** to thread one's way among/between

**faune** [fon] *nf* (*ZOOL*) wildlife, fauna

**faussaire** [fosɛr] *nm* forger

**fausse** [fos] *adj voir* **faux**; **faussement** *adv* (*accuser*) wrongly, wrongfully; (*croire*) falsely

**fausser** [fose] *vt* (*objet*) to bend, buckle; (*fig*) to distort; **~ compagnie à qn** to give sb the slip

**faut** [fo] *vb voir* **falloir**

**faute** [fot] *nf* (*erreur*) mistake, error; (*mauvaise action*) misdemeanour; (FOOTBALL *etc*) offence; (TENNIS) fault; **c'est de sa/ma ~** it's his/my fault; **être en ~** to be in the wrong; **~ de** (*temps, argent*) for *ou* through lack of; **sans ~** without fail; **~ de frappe** typing error; **~ de goût** error of taste; **~ professionnelle** professional misconduct *no pl*

**fauteuil** [fotœj] *nm* armchair; **~ roulant** wheelchair

**fauteur** [fotœr] *nm*: **~ de troubles** trouble-maker

**fautif, -ive** [fotif, iv] *adj* (*responsable*) at fault, in the wrong; (*incorrect*) incorrect, inaccurate; **il se sentait ~** he felt guilty

**fauve** [fov] *nm* wildcat ♦ *adj* (*couleur*) fawn

**faux¹** [fo] *nf* scythe

**faux²**, **fausse** [fo, fos] *adj* (*inexact*) wrong; (*voix*) out of tune; (*billet*) fake, forged; (*sournois, postiche*) false ♦ *adv* (MUS) out of tune ♦ *nm* (*copie*) fake, forgery; (*opposé au vrai*): **le ~** falsehood; **faire ~ bond à qn** to stand sb up; **fausse alerte** false alarm; **fausse couche** miscarriage; **~ frais** *nmpl* extras, incidental expenses; **~ pas** tripping *no pl*; (*fig*) faux pas; **~ témoignage** (*délit*) perjury; **faux-filet** *nm* sirloin; **faux-monnayeur** *nm* counterfeiter, forger

**faveur** [favœr] *nf* favour; **traitement de ~** preferential treatment; **en ~ de** in favour of

**favorable** [favorabl] *adj* favourable

**favori, te** [favori, it] *adj, nm/f* favourite

**favoriser** [favorize] *vt* to favour

**fax** [faks] *nm* fax; **faxer** *vt* to fax

**FB** *abr* (= franc belge) BF

**fébrile** [febril] *adj* feverish, febrile

**fécond, e** [fekɔ̃, ɔ̃d] *adj* fertile; **féconder** *vt* to fertilize; **fécondité** *nf* fertility

**fécule** [fekyl] *nf* potato flour; **féculent** *nm* starchy food

**fédéral, e, -aux** [federal, o] *adj* federal

**fée** [fe] *nf* fairy; **féerique** *adj* magical, fairytale *cpd*

**feignant, e** [fɛɲɑ̃, ɑ̃t] *nm/f* = **fainéant, e**

**feindre** [fɛdr] *vt* to feign; **~ de faire** to pretend to do

**feinte** [fɛt] *nf* (SPORT) dummy

**fêler** [fele] *vt* to crack

**félicitations** [felisitasjɔ̃] *nfpl* congratulations

**féliciter** [felisite] *vt*: **~ qn (de)** to congratulate sb (on)

**félin, e** [felɛ, in] *nm* (big) cat

**fêlure** [felyr] *nf* crack

**femelle** [fəmɛl] *adj, nf* female

**féminin, e** [feminɛ, in] *adj* feminine; (*sexe*) female; (*équipe, vêtements etc*) women's ♦ *nm* (LING) feminine; **féministe** *adj* feminist

**femme** [fam] *nf* woman; (*épouse*) wife; **~ au foyer** housewife; **~ de chambre** chambermaid; **~ de ménage** cleaning lady

**fémur** [femyr] *nm* femur, thighbone

**fendre** [fɑ̃dr] *vt* (*couper en deux*) to split; (*fissurer*) to crack; (*traverser: foule, air*) to cleave through; **se ~** *vi* to crack

**fenêtre** [f(ə)nɛtr] *nf* window

**fenouil** [fənuj] *nm* fennel

**fente** [fɑ̃t] *nf* (*fissure*) crack; (*de boîte à lettres etc*) slit

**féodal, e, -aux** [feodal, o] *adj* feudal

**fer** [fɛr] *nm* iron; **~ à cheval** horseshoe; **~ (à repasser)** iron; **~ forgé** wrought iron

**ferai** *etc* [fəre] *vb voir* **faire**

**fer-blanc** [fɛrblɑ̃] *nm* tin(plate)

**férié, e** [ferje] *adj*: **jour ~** public holiday

**ferions** *etc* [fərjɔ̃] *vb voir* **faire**

**ferme** [fɛrm] *adj* firm ♦ *adv* (*travailler etc*) hard ♦ *nf* (*exploitation*) farm; (*maison*) farmhouse

**fermé, e** [fɛrme] *adj* closed, shut; (*gaz, eau etc*) off; (*fig: milieu*) exclusive

**fermenter** [fɛʀmɑ̃te] vi to ferment

**fermer** [fɛʀme] vt to close, shut; (cesser l'exploitation de) to close down, shut down; (eau, électricité, robinet) to put off, turn off; (aéroport, route) to close ♦ vi to close, shut; (magasin: définitivement) to close down, shut down; se ~ vi to close, shut

**fermeté** [fɛʀmate] nf firmness

**fermeture** [fɛʀmatyʀ] nf closing; (dispositif) catch; **heures de ~** closing times; **~ éclair** ® zip (fastener) (BRIT), zipper (US)

**fermier** [fɛʀmje, jɛʀ] nm farmer; **fermière** nf woman farmer; (épouse) farmer's wife

**fermoir** [fɛʀmwaʀ] nm clasp

**féroce** [feʀɔs] adj ferocious, fierce

**ferons** [fəʀɔ̃] vb voir **faire**

**ferraille** [feʀaj] nf scrap iron; **mettre à la ~** to scrap

**ferrer** [feʀe] vt (cheval) to shoe

**ferronnerie** [feʀɔnʀi] nf ironwork

**ferroviaire** [feʀɔvjɛʀ] adj rail(way) cpd (BRIT), rail(road) cpd (US)

**ferry(boat)** [feʀe(bot)] nm ferry

**fertile** [fɛʀtil] adj fertile; **~ en incidents** eventful, packed with incidents

**féru, e** [feʀy] adj: **~ de** with a keen interest in

**fervent, e** [fɛʀvɑ̃, ɑ̃t] adj fervent

**fesse** [fɛs] nf buttock; **fessée** nf spanking

**festin** [fɛstɛ̃] nm feast

**festival** [fɛstival] nm festival

**festivités** [fɛstivite] nfpl festivities

**festoyer** [fɛstwaje] vi to feast

**fêtard** [fɛtaʀ, aʀd] (fam) nm high liver, merry-maker

**fête** [fɛt] nf (religieuse) feast; (publique) holiday; (réception) party; (kermesse) fête, fair; (du nom) feast day, name day; **faire la ~** to live it up; **faire ~ à qn** to give sb a warm welcome; **les ~s** (de fin d'année) the festive season; **la salle des ~s** the village hall; **~ foraine** (fun) fair; **fêter** vt to celebrate; (per-

sonne) to have a celebration for

**feu, x** [fø] nm (gén) fire; (signal lumineux) light; (de cuisinière) ring; **~x** nmpl (AUTO) (traffic) lights; **au ~!** (incendie) fire!; **à ~ doux/vif** over a slow/brisk heat; **à petit ~** (CULIN) over a gentle heat; (fig) slowly; **faire ~** to fire; **prendre ~** to catch fire; **mettre le ~ à** to set fire to; **faire du ~** to make a fire; **avez-vous du ~?** (pour cigarette) have you (got) a light?; **~ arrière** rear light; **~ d'artifice** (spectacle) fireworks pl; **~ de joie** bonfire; **~ rouge/vert/orange** red/green/amber (BRIT) ou yellow (US) light; **~x de brouillard** fog-lamps; **~x de croisement** dipped (BRIT) ou dimmed (US) headlights; **~x de position** sidelights; **~x de route** headlights

**feuillage** [fœjaʒ] nm foliage, leaves pl

**feuille** [fœj] nf (d'arbre) leaf; (de papier) sheet; **~ de maladie** medical expenses claim form; **~ de paie** pay slip

**feuillet** [fœjɛ] nm leaf

**feuilleté, e** [fœjte] adj: **pâte ~** flaky pastry

**feuilleter** [fœjte] vt (livre) to leaf through

**feuilleton** [fœjtɔ̃] nm serial

**feutre** [føtʀ] nm felt; (chapeau) felt hat; (aussi: stylo-~) felt-tip pen; **feutré, e** adj (atmosphère) muffled

**fève** [fɛv] nf broad bean

**février** [fevʀije] nm February

**FF** abr (= franc français) FF

**fiable** [fjabl] adj reliable

**fiançailles** [fjɑ̃saj] nfpl engagement sg

**fiancé, e** [fjɑ̃se] nm/f fiancé(e) ♦ adj: **être ~ (à)** to be engaged (to)

**fiancer** [fjɑ̃se]: **se ~** vi to become engaged

**fibre** [fibʀ] nf fibre; **~ de verre** fibreglass, glass fibre

**ficeler** [fis(ə)le] vt to tie up

**ficelle** [fisɛl] nf string no pl; (morceau) piece ou length of string

**fiche** [fiʃ] nf (pour fichier) (index) card; (formulaire) form; (ÉLEC) plug

**ficher** [fiʃe] vt (dans un fichier) to file; (POLICE) to put on file; (fam: faire) to do; (: donner) to give; (: mettre) to stick ou shove; **se ~ de** (fam: se gausser) to make fun of; **fiche(-moi) le camp** (fam) clear off; **fiche-moi la paix** (fam) leave me alone; **je m'en fiche!** (fam) I don't care!

**fichier** [fiʃje] nm file

**fichu, e** [fiʃy] pp de **ficher** (fam) ♦ adj (fam: fini, inutilisable) bust, done for; (: intensif) wretched, darned ♦ nm (foulard) (head)scarf; **mal ~** (fam) feeling lousy

**fictif, -ive** [fiktif, iv] adj fictitious

**fiction** [fiksjɔ̃] nf fiction; (fait imaginé) invention

**fidèle** [fidɛl] adj faithful ♦ nm/f (REL): les **~s** (à l'église) the congregation sg; **fidélité** nf fidelity

**fier¹** [fje]: **se ~ à** vt to trust

**fier², fière** [fjɛʀ] adj proud; **fierté** nf pride

**fièvre** [fjɛvʀ] nf fever; **avoir de la ~/39 de ~** to have a high temperature/a temperature of 39°C; **fiévreux, -euse** adj feverish

**figé, e** [fiʒe] adj (manières) stiff; (société) rigid; (sourire) set

**figer** [fiʒe]: **se ~** vi (huile) to congeal; (personne) to freeze

**fignoler** [fiɲɔle] (fam) vt to polish up

**figue** [fig] nf fig; **figuier** nm fig tree

**figurant, e** [figyʀɑ̃, ɑ̃t] nm/f (THÉÂTRE) walk-on; (CINÉMA) extra

**figure** [figyʀ] nf (visage) face; (forme, personnage) figure; (illustration) picture, diagram

**figuré, e** [figyʀe] adj (sens) figurative

**figurer** [figyʀe] vi to appear ♦ vt to represent; **se ~ que** to imagine that

**fil** [fil] nm (brin, fig: d'une histoire) thread; (électrique) wire; (d'un couteau) edge; **au ~ des années** with the passing of the years; **au ~ de l'eau** with the stream ou current; **coup de ~** (fam) phone call; **~ à coudre** (sewing)

thread; **~ de fer** wire; **~ de fer barbelé** barbed wire

**filament** [filamɑ̃] nm (ÉLEC) filament

**filandreux, -euse** [filɑ̃dʀø, øz] adj stringy

**filature** [filatyʀ] nf (fabrique) mill; (policière) shadowing no pl, tailing no pl

**file** [fil] nf line; (AUTO) lane; **en ~ indienne** in single file; **à la ~** (d'affilée) in succession; **~ (d'attente)** queue (BRIT), line (US)

**filer** [file] vt (tissu, toile) to spin; (prendre en filature) to shadow, tail; (fam: donner): **~ qch à qn** to slip sb sth ♦ vi (bas) to run; (aller vite) to fly past; (fam: partir) to make ou be off; **~ doux** to toe the line

**filet** [filɛ] nm (gén; CULIN) fillet; (d'eau, de sang) trickle; **~ (à provisions)** string bag

**filiale** [filjal] nf (COMM) subsidiary

**filière** [filjɛʀ] nf (carrière) path; **suivre la ~** (dans sa carrière) to work one's way up (through the hierarchy)

**filiforme** [filifɔʀm] adj spindly

**filigrane** [filigʀan] nm (d'un billet, timbre) watermark

**fille** [fij] nf girl; (opposé à fils) daughter; **vieille ~** old maid; **fillette** nf (little) girl

**filleul, e** [fijœl] nm/f godchild, godson/daughter

**film** [film] nm (pour photo) (roll of) film; (œuvre) film, picture, movie; **~ d'épouvante** horror film; **~ policier** thriller

**filon** [filɔ̃] nm vein, lode; (fig) lucrative line, money spinner

**fils** [fis] nm son; **~ à papa** daddy's boy

**filtre** [filtʀ] nm filter; **filtrer** vt to filter; (fig: candidats, visiteurs) to screen

**fin¹** [fɛ̃] nf end; **~s** nfpl (but) ends; **prendre ~** to come to an end; **mettre ~ à** to put an end to; **à la ~** in the end, eventually; **en ~ de compte** in the end; **sans ~** endless; **~ juin** at the end of June

**fin², e** [fɛ̃, fin] adj (papier, couche, fil)

thin; (*cheveux, visage*) fine; (*taille*) neat, slim; (*esprit, remarque*) subtle ♦ *adv* (*couper*) finely; **~ prêt** quite ready; **~es herbes** mixed herbs

**final, e** [final, o] *adj* final ♦ *nm* (MUS) finale; **finale** *nf* final; **quarts de finale** quarter finals; **finalement** *adv* finally, in the end; (*après tout*) after all

**finance** [finɑ̃s]: **~s** *nfpl* (*situation*) finances; (*activités*) finance *sg*; **moyennant ~** for a fee; **financer** *vt* to finance; **financier, -ière** *adj* financial

**finaud, e** [fino, od] *adj* wily

**finesse** [fines] *nf* thinness; (*raffinement*) fineness; (*subtilité*) subtlety

**fini, e** [fini] *adj* finished; (MATH) finite ♦ *nm* (*d'un objet manufacturé*) finish

**finir** [finiʀ] *vt* to finish ♦ *vi* to finish, end; **~ par faire** to end up *ou* finish up doing; **~ de faire** to finish doing; (*cesser*) to stop doing; **il finit par m'agacer** he's beginning to get on my nerves; **en ~ avec** to be *ou* have done with; **il va mal ~** he will come to a bad end

**finition** [finisjɔ̃] *nf* (*résultat*) finish

**finlandais, e** [fɛ̃lɑ̃dɛ, ɛz] *adj* Finnish ♦ *nm/f*: **F~, e** Finn

**Finlande** [fɛ̃lɑ̃d] *nf*: **la ~** Finland

**fiole** [fjɔl] *nf* phial

**firme** [fiʀm] *nf* firm

**fis** [fi] *vb voir* **faire**

**fisc** [fisk] *nm* tax authorities *pl*; **fiscal, e, -aux** *adj* tax *cpd*, fiscal; **fiscalité** *nf* tax system

**fissure** [fisyʀ] *nf* crack; **fissurer** *vt* to crack; **se fissurer** *vi* to crack

**fiston** [fistɔ̃] (*fam*) *nm* son, lad

**fit** [fi] *vb voir* **faire**

**fixation** [fiksasjɔ̃] *nf* (*attache*) fastening; (PSYCH) fixation

**fixe** [fiks] *adj* fixed; (*emploi*) steady, regular ♦ *nm* (*salaire*) basic salary; **à heure ~** at a set time; **menu à prix ~** set menu

**fixé, e** [fikse] *adj*: **être ~ (sur)** (*savoir à quoi s'en tenir*) to have made up one's mind (about)

**fixer** [fikse] *vt* (*attacher*): **~ qch (à/sur)** to fix *ou* fasten sth (to/onto); (*déterminer*) to fix, set; (*regarder*) to stare at; **se ~** *vi* (*s'établir*) to settle down; **se ~ sur** (*suj: attention*) to focus on

**flacon** [flakɔ̃] *nm* bottle

**flageoler** [flaʒɔle] *vi* (*jambes*) to sag

**flageolet** [flaʒɔlɛ] *nm* (CULIN) dwarf kidney bean

**flagrant, e** [flagʀɑ̃, ɑ̃t] *adj* flagrant, blatant; **en ~ délit** in the act

**flair** [flɛʀ] *nm* sense of smell; (*fig*) intuition; **flairer** *vt* (*humer*) to sniff (at); (*détecter*) to scent

**flamand, e** [flamɑ̃, ɑ̃d] *adj* Flemish ♦ *nm* (LING) Flemish ♦ *nm/f*: **F~, e** Fleming; **les F~s** the Flemish

**flamant** [flamɑ̃] *nm* flamingo

**flambant, e** [flɑ̃bɑ̃, ɑ̃t] *adv*: **~ neuf** brand new

**flambé, e** [flɑ̃be] *adj* (CULIN) flambé

**flambeau, x** [flɑ̃bo] *nm* (flaming) torch

**flambée** [flɑ̃be] *nf* blaze; (*fig: des prix*) explosion

**flamber** [flɑ̃be] *vi* to blaze (up)

**flamboyer** [flɑ̃bwaje] *vi* to blaze (up)

**flamme** [flam] *nf* flame; (*fig*) fire, fervour; **en ~s** on fire, ablaze

**flan** [flɑ̃] *nm* (CULIN) custard tart *ou* pie

**flanc** [flɑ̃] *nm* side; (MIL) flank

**flancher** [flɑ̃ʃe] (*fam*) *vi* to fail, pack up

**flanelle** [flanɛl] *nf* flannel

**flâner** [flɑne] *vi* to stroll; **flânerie** *nf* stroll

**flanquer** [flɑ̃ke] *vt* to flank; (*fam: mettre*) to chuck, shove; (: *jeter*): **~ par terre/à la porte** to fling to the ground/chuck out

**flaque** [flak] *nf* (*d'eau*) puddle; (*d'huile, de sang etc*) pool

**flash** [flaʃ] (*pl* **~es**) *nm* (PHOTO) flash; **~ (d'information)** newsflash

**flasque** [flask] *adj* flabby

**flatter** [flate] *vt* to flatter; **se ~ de qch** to pride o.s. on sth; **flatterie** *nf* flattery *no pl*; **flatteur, -euse** *adj* flattering

**fléau, x** [fleo] nm scourge

**flèche** [flɛʃ] nf arrow; (de clocher) spire; **monter en ~** (fig) to soar, rocket; **partir en ~** to be off like a shot; **fléchette** nf dart

**fléchir** [fleʃiʀ] vt (corps, genou) to bend; (fig) to sway, weaken ♦ vi (fig) to weaken, flag

**flemmard, e** [flemaʀ, aʀd] (fam) nm/f lazybones sg, loafer

**flemme** [flem] nf (fam) laziness; **j'ai la ~ de le faire** I can't be bothered doing it

**flétrir** [fletʀiʀ] **se ~** vi to wither

**fleur** [flœʀ] nf flower; (d'un arbre) blossom; **en ~** (arbre) in blossom; **à ~s** flowery

**fleuri, e** [flœʀi] adj (jardin) in flower ou bloom; (tissu, papier) flowery

**fleurir** [flœʀiʀ] vi (rose) to flower; (arbre) to blossom; (fig) to flourish ♦ vt (tombe) to put flowers on; (chambre) to decorate with flowers

**fleuriste** [flœʀist] nm/f florist

**fleuve** [flœv] nm river

**flexible** [fleksibl] adj flexible

**flic** [flik] nm (fam: péj) nm cop

**flipper** [flipœʀ] nm pinball (machine)

**flirter** [flœʀte] vi to flirt

**flocon** [flɔkɔ̃] nm flake

**flopée** [flɔpe] (fam) nf: **une ~ de** loads of, masses of

**floraison** [flɔʀezɔ̃] nf flowering

**flore** [flɔʀ] nf flora

**florissant, e** [flɔʀisɑ̃, ɑ̃t] adj (économie) flourishing

**flot** [flo] nm flood, stream; **~s** nmpl (de la mer) waves; **être à ~** (NAVIG) to be afloat; **entrer à ~s** to stream ou pour in

**flottant, e** [flɔtɑ̃, ɑ̃t] adj (vêtement) loose

**flotte** [flɔt] nf (NAVIG) fleet; (fam: eau) water; (: pluie) rain

**flottement** [flɔtmɑ̃] nm (fig) wavering, hesitation

**flotter** [flɔte] vi to float; (nuage, odeur) to drift; (drapeau) to fly; (vêtements) to

hang loose; (fam: pleuvoir) to rain; **faire ~ to float**; **flotteur** nm float

**flou, e** [flu] adj fuzzy, blurred; (fig) woolly, vague

**fluctuation** [flyktɥasjɔ̃] nf fluctuation

**fluet, te** [flyɛ, ɛt] adj thin, slight

**fluide** [flɥid] adj fluid; (circulation etc) flowing freely ♦ nm fluid

**fluor** [flyɔʀ] nm: **dentifrice au ~** fluoride toothpaste

**fluorescent, e** [flyɔʀesɑ̃] adj fluorescent

**flûte** [flyt] nf flute; (verre) flute glass; (pain) long loaf; **~!** drat it!; **~ à bec** recorder

**flux** [fly] nm incoming tide; (écoulement) flow; **le ~ et le reflux** the ebb and flow

**FM** sigle f (= fréquence modulée) FM

**foc** [fɔk] nm jib

**foi** [fwa] nf faith; **digne de ~** reliable; **être de bonne/mauvaise ~** to be sincere/insincere; **ma ~ ...** well ...

**foie** [fwa] nm liver; **crise de ~** stomach upset

**foin** [fwɛ̃] nm hay; **faire du ~** (fig: fam) to kick up a row

**foire** [fwaʀ] nf fair; (fête foraine) (fun) fair; **faire la ~** (fig: fam) to whoop it up; **~ (exposition)** trade fair

**fois** [fwa] nf time; **une/deux ~** once/ twice; **2 ~ 2** 2 times 2; **une ~** (passé) once; (futur) sometime; **une ~ pour toutes** once and for all; **une ~ que** once; **des ~** (parfois) sometimes; **à la ~ (ensemble)** at once

**foison** [fwazɔ̃] nf: **à ~** in plenty; **foisonner** vi to abound

**fol** [fɔl] adj voir **fou**

**folie** [fɔli] nf (d'une décision, d'un acte) madness, folly; (état) madness, insanity; **la ~ des grandeurs** delusions of grandeur; **faire des ~s** (en dépenses) to be extravagant

**folklorique** [fɔlklɔʀik] adj folk cpd; (fam) weird

**folle** [fɔl] adj, nf voir **fou**; **follement**

*adv* (*très*) madly, wildly

**foncé, e** [fɔ̃se] *adj* dark

**foncer** [fɔ̃se] *vi* to go darker; (*fam: aller vite*) to tear *ou* belt along; ~ **sur** to charge at

**foncier, -ère** [fɔ̃sje, jɛʀ] *adj* (*honnêteté etc*) basic, fundamental; (*COMM*) real estate *cpd*

**fonction** [fɔ̃ksjɔ̃] *nf* function; (*emploi, poste*) post, position; ~**s** *nfpl* (*professionnelles*) duties; **voiture de** ~ company car; **en** ~ **de** (*par rapport à*) according to; **faire** ~ **de** to serve as; **la publique** the state *ou* civil (*BRIT*) service; **fonctionnaire** *nm/f* state employee, local authority employee; (*dans l'administration*) ≈ civil servant; **fonctionner** *vi* to work, function

**fond** [fɔ̃] *nm* (*d'un récipient, trou*) bottom; (*d'une salle, scène*) back; (*d'un tableau, décor*) background; (*opposé à la forme*) content; (*SPORT*): **le** ~ long distance (running); **au** ~ **de** at the bottom of; **à** ~ (*connaître, soutenir*) thoroughly; (*appuyer, visser*) right down *ou* home; **à** ~ (**de train**) (*fam*) full tilt; **dans le** ~, **au** ~ (*en somme*) basically, really; **de** ~ **en comble** from top to bottom; *voir aussi* **fonds**; ~ **de teint** foundation (cream)

**fondamental, e, -aux** [fɔ̃damɑ̃tal, o] *adj* fundamental

**fondant, e** [fɔ̃dɑ̃, ɑ̃t] *adj* (*neige*) melting; (*poire*) that melts in the mouth

**fondateur, -trice** [fɔ̃datœʀ, tʀis] *nm/f* founder

**fondation** [fɔ̃dasjɔ̃] *nf* founding; (*établissement*) foundation; ~**s** *nfpl* (*d'une maison*) foundations

**fondé, e** [fɔ̃de] *adj* (*accusation etc*) well-founded; **être** ~ **à** to have grounds for *ou* good reason to

**fondement** [fɔ̃dmɑ̃] *nm*: **sans** ~ (*rumeur etc*) groundless, unfounded

**fonder** [fɔ̃de] *vt* to found; (*fig*) to base; **se** ~ **sur** (*suj: personne*) to base o.s. on

**fonderie** [fɔ̃dʀi] *nf* smelting works *sg*

**fondre** [fɔ̃dʀ] *vt* (*aussi:* **faire** ~) to melt; (*dans l'eau*) to dissolve; (*fig: mélanger*) to merge, blend ♦ *vi* (*à la chaleur*) to melt; (*dans l'eau*) to dissolve; (*fig*) to melt away; (*se précipiter*): ~ **sur** to swoop down on; ~ **en larmes** to burst into tears

**fonds** [fɔ̃] *nm* (*COMM*): ~ (**de commerce**) business ♦ *nmpl* (*argent*) funds

**fondu, e** [fɔ̃dy] *adj* (*beurre, neige*) melted; (*métal*) molten; **fondue** *nf* (*CULIN*) fondue

**font** [fɔ̃] *vb voir* **faire**

**fontaine** [fɔ̃tɛn] *nf* fountain; (*source*) spring

**fonte** [fɔ̃t] *nf* melting; (*métal*) cast iron; **la** ~ **des neiges** (the spring) thaw

**foot** [fut] (*fam*) *nm* football

**football** [futbol] *nm* football, soccer; **footballeur** *nm* footballer

**footing** [futiŋ] *nm* jogging; **faire du** ~ to go jogging

**for** [fɔʀ] *nm*: **dans son** ~ **intérieur** in one's heart of hearts

**forain, e** [fɔʀɛ̃, ɛn] *adj* fairground *cpd* ♦ *nm* (*marchand*) stallholder; (*acteur*) fairground entertainer

**forçat** [fɔʀsa] *nm* convict

**force** [fɔʀs] *nf* strength; (*PHYSIQUE, MÉCANIQUE*) force; ~**s** *nfpl* (*physiques*) strength *sg*; (*MIL*) forces; **à** ~ **d'insister** by dint of insisting; **as he** (*ou* **I** *etc*) kept on insisting; **de** ~ forcibly, by force; **les** ~**s de l'ordre** the police

**forcé, e** [fɔʀse] *adj* forced; **c'est** ~ (*fam*) it's inevitable; **forcément** *adv* inevitably; **pas forcément** not necessarily

**forcené, e** [fɔʀsəne] *nm/f* maniac

**forcer** [fɔʀse] *vt* to strain; (*voix*) to strain ♦ *vi* (*SPORT*) to overtax o.s.; ~ **la dose** (*fam*) to overdo it; **se** ~ (**à faire**) to force o.s. (to do)

**forcir** [fɔʀsiʀ] *vi* (*grossir*) to broaden out

**forer** [fɔʀe] *vt* to drill, bore

**forestier, -ère** [fɔʀɛstje, jɛʀ] *adj* forest

*cpd*

**forêt** [fɔʀɛ] nf forest

**forfait** [fɔʀfɛ] nm (COMM) all-in deal ou price; **forfaitaire** adj inclusive

**forge** [fɔʀʒ] nf forge, smithy; **forger** vt to forge; (fig: prétexte) to contrive, make up; **forgeron** nm (black)smith

**formaliser** [fɔʀmalize]: **se ~** vi: **se ~ (de)** to take offence (at)

**formalité** [fɔʀmalite] nf formality; **simple ~** mere formality

**format** [fɔʀma] nm size; **formater** vt (disque) to format

**formation** [fɔʀmasjɔ̃] nf (développement) forming; (apprentissage) training; **~ permanente** continuing education; **~ professionnelle** vocational training

**forme** [fɔʀm] nf (gén) form; (d'un objet) shape, form; **~s** nfpl (bonnes manières) proprieties; (d'une femme) figure sg; **être en ~** (SPORT etc) to be on form; **en bonne et due ~** in due form

**formel, le** [fɔʀmɛl] adj (catégorique) definite, positive; **formellement** adv (absolument) positively; **formellement interdit** strictly forbidden

**former** [fɔʀme] vt to form; (éduquer) to train; **se ~** vi to form

**formidable** [fɔʀmidabl] adj tremendous

**formulaire** [fɔʀmylɛʀ] nm form

**formule** [fɔʀmyl] nf (gén) formula; (expression) phrase; **~ de politesse** polite phrase; (en fin de lettre) letter ending; **formuler** vt (émettre) to formulate

**fort, e** [fɔʀ, fɔʀt] adj strong; (intensité, rendement) high, great; (corpulent) stout; (doué) good, able ♦ adv (serrer, frapper) hard; (parler) loud(ly); (beaucoup) greatly, very much; (très) very ♦ nm (édifice) fort; (point ~) strong point, forte; **~ tête** rebel; **forteresse** nf stronghold

**fortifiant** [fɔʀtifjɑ̃, jɑ̃t] nm tonic

**fortifier** [fɔʀtifje] vt to strengthen

**fortiori** [fɔʀsjɔʀi]: **à ~** adv all the more so

**fortuit, e** [fɔʀtɥi, it] adj fortuitous, chance *cpd*

**fortune** [fɔʀtyn] nf fortune; **faire ~** to make one's fortune; **de ~** makeshift; **fortuné, e** adj wealthy

**fosse** [fos] nf (grand trou) pit; (tombe) grave

**fossé** [fose] nm ditch; (fig) gulf, gap

**fossette** [fosɛt] nf dimple

**fossile** [fosil] nm fossil

**fossoyeur** [foswajœʀ] nm gravedigger

**fou (fol), folle** [fu, fɔl] adj mad; (déréglé etc) wild, erratic; (fam: extrême, très grand) terrific, tremendous ♦ nm/f madman(-woman) ♦ nm (du roi) jester; **être ~ de** to be mad ou crazy about; **avoir le ~rire** to have the giggles

**foudre** [fudʀ] nf: **la ~** lightning

**foudroyant, e** [fudʀwajɑ̃, ɑ̃t] adj (progrès) lightning cpd; (succès) stunning; (maladie, poison) violent

**foudroyer** [fudʀwaje] vt to strike down; **être foudroyé** to be struck by lightning; **~ qn du regard** to glare at sb

**fouet** [fwɛ] nm whip; (CULIN) whisk; **de plein ~** (se heurter) head on; **fouetter** vt to whip; (crème) to whisk

**fougère** [fuʒɛʀ] nf fern

**fougue** [fug] nf ardour, spirit; **fougueux, -euse** adj fiery

**fouille** [fuj] nf search; **~s** nfpl (archéologiques) excavations; **fouiller** vt to search; (creuser) to dig ♦ vi to rummage; **fouillis** nm jumble, muddle

**fouiner** [fwine] (péj) vi: **~ dans** to nose around ou about in

**foulard** [fulaʀ] nm scarf

**foule** [ful] nf crowd; **la ~** crowds pl; **une ~ de** masses of

**foulée** [fule] nf stride

**fouler** [fule] vt to press; (sol) to tread upon; **se ~ la cheville** to sprain one's ankle; **ne pas se ~** not to overexert o.s.; **il ne se foule pas** he doesn't break himself out; **foulure** nf sprain

**four** [fuʀ] nm oven; (de potier) kiln;

(THÉÂTRE/échec) flop

**fourbe** [furb] adj deceitful

**fourbu, e** [furby] adj exhausted

**fourche** [furʃ] nf pitchfork

**fourchette** [furʃεt] nf fork; (STATISTIQUE) bracket, margin

**fourgon** [furgɔ̃] nm van; (RAIL) wag(g)on; **fourgonnette** nf (small) van

**fourmi** [furmi] nf ant; **~s** nfpl (fig) pins and needles; **fourmilière** nf ant-hill; **fourmiller** vi to swarm

**fournaise** [furnεz] nf blaze; (fig) furnace, oven

**fourneau, x** [furno] nm stove

**fournée** [furne] nf batch

**fourni, e** [furni] adj (barbe, cheveux) thick; (magasin): **bien ~ (en)** well stocked (with)

**fournir** [furnir] vt to supply; (preuve, exemple) to provide, supply; (effort) to put in; **fournisseur, -euse** nm/f supplier; (INTERNET): **fournisseur d'accès à Internet** (Internet) service provider, ISP; **fourniture** nf supply(ing); **fournitures scolaires** school stationery

**fourrage** [furaʒ] nm fodder

**fourré, e** [fure] adj (bonbon etc) filled; (manteau etc) fur-lined ♦ nm thicket

**fourrer** [fure] (fam) vt to stick, shove; **se ~ dans/sous** to get into/under; **fourre-tout** nm inv (sac) holdall; (fig) rag-bag

**fourrière** [furjεr] nf pound

**fourrure** [furyr] nf fur; (sur l'animal) coat

**fourvoyer** [furvwaje]: **se ~** vi to go astray, stray

**foutre** [futr] (fam!) vt = **ficher; foutu, e** (fam!) adj = **fichu, e**

**foyer** [fwaje] nm (maison) home; (famille) family; (de cheminée) hearth; (de jeunes etc) (social) club; (résidence) hostel; (salon) foyer; **lunettes à double ~** bi-focal glasses

**fracas** [fraka] nm (d'objet qui tombe) crash; **fracassant, e** adj (succès) thun-

dering; **fracasser** vt to smash

**fraction** [fraksjɔ̃] nf fraction; **fractionner** vt to divide (up), split (up)

**fracture** [fraktyr] nf fracture; **~ du crâne** fractured skull; **fracturer** vt (coffre, serrure) to break open; (os, membre) to fracture

**fragile** [fraʒil] adj fragile, delicate; (fig) frail; **fragilité** nf fragility

**fragment** [fragmã] nm (d'un objet) fragment, piece

**fraîche** [frεʃ] adj voir **frais; fraîcheur** nf coolness; (d'un aliment) freshness; **fraîchir** vi to get cooler; (vent) to freshen

**frais, fraîche** [frε, frεʃ] adj fresh; (froid) cool ♦ adv (récemment) newly, fresh(ly) ♦ nm: **mettre au ~** to put in a cool place ♦ nmpl (gén) expenses; (COMM) costs; **il fait ~** it's cool; **servir ~** serve chilled; **prendre le ~** to take a breath of cool air; **faire des ~** to go to a lot of expense; **~ de scolarité** school fees (BRIT), tuition (US); **~ généraux** overheads

**fraise** [frεz] nf strawberry; **~ des bois** wild strawberry

**framboise** [frãbwaz] nf raspberry

**franc, franche** [frã, frãʃ] adj (personne) frank, straightforward; (visage) open; (net: refus) clear; (: intensif: coupure) clean; (intensif) downright ♦ nm franc

**français, e** [frãsε, εz] adj French ♦ nm/f: **F~, e** Frenchman(-woman) ♦ nm (LING) French; **les F~** the French

**France** [frãs] nf: **la ~** France

**franche** [frãʃ] adj voir **franc; franchement** adv frankly; (nettement) definitely; (tout à fait: mauvais etc) downright

**franchir** [frãʃir] vt (obstacle) to clear, get over; (seuil, ligne, rivière) to cross; (distance) to cover

**franchise** [frãʃiz] nf frankness; (douanière) exemption; (ASSURANCES) excess

**franc-maçon** [frãmasɔ̃] nm freemason

**franco** [frãko] adv (COMM): **~ (de port)**

postage paid

**francophone** [frɑ̃kɔfɔn] *adj* French-speaking

**franc-parler** [frɑ̃parle] *nm inv* outspokenness; **avoir son ~~** to speak one's mind

**frange** [frɑ̃ʒ] *nf* fringe

**frangipane** [frɑ̃ʒipan] *nf* almond paste

**franquette** [frɑ̃kɛt]: **à la bonne ~** *adv* without any fuss

**frappant, e** [frapɑ̃, ɑ̃t] *adj* striking

**frappé, e** [frape] *adj* iced

**frapper** [frape] *vt* (*lieu*) to hit, strike; (*étonner*) to strike; **~ dans ses mains** to clap one's hands; **frappé de stupeur** dumbfounded

**frasques** [frask] *nfpl* escapades

**fraternel, elle** [fratɛrnɛl] *adj* brotherly, fraternal; **fraternité** *nf* brotherhood

**fraude** [frod] *nf* fraud; (*SCOL*) cheating; **passer qch en ~** to smuggle sth in (*ou* out); **~ fiscale** tax evasion; **frauder** *vi, vt* to cheat; **frauduleux, -euse** *adj* fraudulent

**frayer** [freje] *vt* to open up, clear ♦ *vi* to spawn; **se ~ un chemin dans la foule** to force one's way through the crowd

**frayeur** [frejœr] *nf* fright

**fredonner** [frədɔne] *vt* to hum

**freezer** [frizœr] *nm* freezing compartment

**frein** [frɛ̃] *nm* brake; **mettre un ~ à** (*fig*) to curb, check; **~ à main** hand-brake; **freiner** [frene] *vi* to brake ♦ *vt* (*progrès etc*) to check

**frêle** [frɛl] *adj* frail, fragile

**frelon** [frəlɔ̃] *nm* hornet

**frémir** [fremir] *vi* (*de peur, d'horreur*) to shudder; (*de colère*) to shake; (*feuillage*) to quiver

**frêne** [frɛn] *nm* ash

**frénétique** [frenetik] *adj* frenzied, frenetic

**fréquemment** [frekamɑ̃] *adv* frequently

**fréquent, e** [frekɑ̃, ɑ̃t] *adj* frequent

**fréquentation** [frekɑ̃tasjɔ̃] *nf* frequenting; **~s** *nfpl* (*relations*) company *sg*

**fréquenté, e** [frekɑ̃te] *adj*: **très ~** (very) busy; **mal ~** patronized by disreputable elements

**fréquenter** [frekɑ̃te] *vt* (*lieu*) to frequent; (*personne*) to see; **se ~** to see each other

**frère** [frɛr] *nm* brother

**fresque** [frɛsk] *nf* (*ART*) fresco

**fret** [frɛ(t)] *nm* freight

**frétiller** [fretije] *vi* (*poisson*) to wriggle

**fretin** [frətɛ̃] *nm*: **menu ~** small fry

**friable** [frijabl] *adj* crumbly

**friand, e** [frijɑ̃, frijɑ̃d] *adj*: **~ de** very fond of ♦ *nm*: **~ au fromage** cheese puff

**friandise** [frijɑ̃diz] *nf* sweet

**fric** [frik] (*fam*) *nm* cash, bread

**friche** [friʃ]: **en ~** *adj, adv* (*lying*) fallow

**friction** [friksjɔ̃] *nf* (*massage*) rub, rub-down; (*TECH, fig*) friction; **frictionner** *vt* to rub (down)

**frigidaire** ® [friʒidɛr] *nm* refrigerator

**frigide** [friʒid] *adj* frigid

**frigo** [frigo] (*fam*) *nm* fridge

**frigorifié, e** [frigɔrifje] (*fam*) *adj*: **être ~** to be frozen stiff

**frigorifique** [frigɔrifik] *adj* refrigerating

**frileux, -euse** [frilø, øz] *adj* sensitive to (the) cold

**frime** [frim] (*fam*) *nf*: **c'est de la ~** it's a lot of eyewash, it's all put on; **frimer** (*fam*) *vi* to show off

**frimousse** [frimus] *nf* (*sweet*) little face

**fringale** [frɛ̃gal] (*fam*) *nf*: **avoir la ~** to be ravenous

**fringant, e** [frɛ̃gɑ̃, ɑ̃t] *adj* dashing

**fringues** [frɛ̃g] (*fam*) *nfpl* clothes

**fripé, e** [fripe] *adj* crumpled

**fripon, ne** [fripɔ̃, ɔn] *adj* roguish, mischievous ♦ *nm/f* rascal, rogue

**fripouille** [fripuj] *nf* scoundrel

**frire** [frir] *vt, vi*: **faire ~** to fry

**frisé, e** [fʀize] adj (cheveux) curly; (personne) curly-haired

**frisson** [fʀisɔ̃] nm (de froid) shiver; (de peur) shudder; **frissonner** vi (de fièvre, froid) to shiver; (d'horreur) to shudder

**frit, e** [fʀi, fʀit] pp de **frire**; **frite** nf: (pommes) **frites** chips (BRIT), French fries; **friteuse** nf chip pan; **friture** nf (huile) (deep) fat; (plat): **friture (de poissons)** fried fish

**frivole** [fʀivɔl] adj frivolous

**froid, e** [fʀwa, fʀwad] adj, nm cold; **il fait ~** it's cold; **avoir/prendre ~** to be/catch cold; **être en ~ avec** to be on bad terms with; **froidement** adv (accueillir) coldly; (décider) coolly

**froideur** [fʀwadœʀ] nf coldness

**froisser** [fʀwase] vt to crumple (up), crease; (fig) to hurt, offend; **se ~** vi to crumple, crease; (personne) to take offence; **se ~ un muscle** to strain a muscle

**frôler** [fʀole] vt to brush against; (suj: projectile) to skim past; (fig) to come very close to

**fromage** [fʀɔmaʒ] nm cheese; **~ blanc** soft white cheese

**froment** [fʀɔmɑ̃] nm wheat

**froncer** [fʀɔ̃se] vt to gather; **~ les sourcils** to frown

**frondaisons** [fʀɔ̃dɛzɔ̃] nfpl foliage sg

**front** [fʀɔ̃] nm forehead, brow; (MIL) front; **de ~** (se heurter) head-on; (rouler) together (i.e. 2 or 3 abreast); (simultanément) at once; **faire ~ à** to face up to

**frontalier, -ère** [fʀɔ̃talje, jɛʀ] adj border cpd, frontier cpd

**frontière** [fʀɔ̃tjɛʀ] nf frontier, border

**frotter** [fʀote] vi to rub, scrape ♦ vt to rub; (pommes de terre, plancher) to scrub; **~ une allumette** to strike a match

**fructifier** [fʀyktifje] vi to yield a profit

**fructueux, -euse** [fʀyktɥø, øz] adj fruitful

**frugal, e, -aux** [fʀygal, o] adj frugal

**fruit** [fʀɥi] nm fruit gen no pl; **~ de la passion** passion fruit; **~s de mer** seafood(s); **~s secs** dried fruit sg; **fruité, e** adj fruity; **fruitier, -ère** adj: **arbre fruitier** fruit tree

**fruste** [fʀyst] adj unpolished, uncultivated

**frustrer** [fʀystʀe] vt to frustrate

**FS** abr (= franc suisse) SF

**fuel(-oil)** [fjul(ɔjl)] nm fuel oil; (domestique) heating oil

**fugace** [fygas] adj fleeting

**fugitif, -ive** [fyʒitif, iv] adj (fugace) fleeting ♦ nm/f fugitive

**fugue** [fyg] nf: **faire une ~** to run away, abscond

**fuir** [fɥiʀ] vt to flee from; (éviter) to shun ♦ vi to run away; (gaz, robinet) to leak

**fuite** [fɥit] nf flight; (écoulement, divulgation) leak; **être en ~** to be on the run; **mettre en ~** to put to flight

**fulgurant, e** [fylgyʀɑ̃, ɑ̃t] adj lightning cpd, dazzling

**fulminer** [fylmine] vi to thunder forth

**fumé, e** [fyme] adj (CULIN) smoked; (verre) tinted; **fumée** nf smoke

**fumer** [fyme] vi to smoke; (soupe) to steam ♦ vt to smoke

**fûmes** etc [fym] vb voir **être**

**fumet** [fyme] nm aroma

**fumeur, -euse** [fymœʀ, øz] nm/f smoker

**fumeux, -euse** [fymø, øz] adj (péj) woolly, hazy

**fumier** [fymje] nm manure

**fumiste** [fymist] nm/f (péj: paresseux) shirker

**funèbre** [fynɛbʀ] adj funeral cpd; (fig: atmosphère) gloomy

**funérailles** [fyneʀaj] nfpl funeral sg

**funeste** [fynɛst] adj (erreur) disastrous

**fur** [fyʀ]: **au ~ et à mesure** adv as one goes along; **au ~ et à mesure que** as

**furet** [fyʀɛ] nm ferret

**fureter** [fyʀ(ə)te] vi (péj) vi to nose about

**fureur** [fyʀœʀ] nf fury; **être en ~** to

be infuriated; **faire ~** to be all the rage

**furibond, e** [fyribɔ̃, ɔ̃d] *adj* furious

**furie** [fyri] *nf* fury; *(femme)* shrew, vixen; **en ~** *(mer)* raging; **furieux, -euse** *adj* furious

**furoncle** [fyrɔ̃kl] *nm* boil

**furtif, -ive** [fyrtif, iv] *adj* furtive

**fus** [fy] *vb voir* **être**

**fusain** [fyzɛ̃] *nm* (ART) charcoal

**fuseau, x** [fyzo] *nm (pour filer)* spindle; *(pantalon)* (ski) pants; **~ horaire** time zone

**fusée** [fyze] *nf* rocket; **~ éclairante** flare

**fuser** [fyze] *vi (rires etc)* to burst forth

**fusible** [fyzibl] *nm* (ÉLEC: *fil)* fuse wire; *(: fiche)* fuse

**fusil** [fyzi] *nm (de guerre, à canon rayé)* rifle, gun; *(de chasse, à canon lisse)* shotgun, gun; **fusillade** *nf* gunfire *no pl*, shooting *no pl*; **fusiller** *vt* to shoot; **fusil-mitrailleur** *nm* machine gun

**fusionner** [fyzjɔne] *vi* to merge

**fut** [fy] *vb voir* **être**

**fût** [fy] *vb voir* **être ♦** *nm (tonneau)* barrel, cask

**futé, e** [fyte] *adj* crafty; **Bison ~** ® TV and radio traffic monitoring service

**futile** [fytil] *adj* futile; frivolous

**futur, e** [fytyr] *adj*, *nm* future

**fuyant, e** [fɥijɑ̃, ɑ̃t] *vb voir* **fuir ♦** *adj (regard etc)* evasive; *(lignes etc)* receding

**fuyard, e** [fɥijar, ard] *nm/f* runaway

## G, g

**gâcher** [gɑʃe] *vt (gâter)* to spoil; *(gaspiller)* to waste; **gâchis** *nm* waste *no pl*

**gadoue** [gadu] *nf* sludge

**gaffe** [gaf] *nf* blunder; **faire ~** *(fam)* to be careful

**gage** [gaʒ] *nm (dans un jeu)* forfeit; *(fig: de fidélité, d'amour)* token

**gageure** [gaʒyr] *nf*: **c'est une ~** it's attempting the impossible

**gagnant, e** [gaɲɑ̃, ɑ̃t] *nm/f* winner

**gagne-pain** [gaɲpɛ̃] *nm inv* job

**gagner** [gaɲe] *vt* to win; *(somme d'argent, revenu)* to earn; *(aller vers, atteindre)* to reach; *(envahir: sommeil, peur)* to overcome; *(: mal)* to spread to **♦** *vi* to win; *(fig)* to gain; **~ du temps/ de la place** to gain time/save space; **~ sa vie** to earn one's living

**gai, e** [ge] *adj* cheerful; *(un peu ivre)* merry; **gaiement** *adv* cheerfully; **gaieté** *nf* cheerfulness; **de gaieté de cœur** with a light heart

**gaillard, e** [gajar, ard] *nm (strapping)* fellow

**gain** [gɛ̃] *nm (revenu)* earnings *pl*; *(bénéfice: gén pl)* profits *pl*

**gaine** [gɛn] *nf (corset)* girdle; *(fourreau)* sheath

**gala** [gala] *nm* official reception; **de ~** *(soirée etc)* gala

**galant, e** [galɑ̃, ɑ̃t] *adj (courtois)* courteous, gentlemanly; *(entreprenant)* flirtatious, gallant; *(scène, rendez-vous)* romantic

**galère** [galɛr] *nf* galley; **quelle ~!** *(fam)* it's a real grind!; **galérer** *(fam)* *vi* to slog away, work hard; *(rencontrer des difficultés)* to have a hassle

**galerie** [galri] *nf* gallery; *(THÉÂTRE)* circle; *(de voiture)* roof rack; *(fig: spectateurs)* audience; **~ de peinture** *(privée)* art gallery; **~ marchande** shopping arcade

**galet** [gale] *nm* pebble

**galette** [galɛt] *nf* flat cake; **~ des Rois** cake eaten on Twelfth Night

**galipette** [galipɛt] *nf* somersault

**Galles** [gal] *nfpl*: **le pays de ~** Wales; **gallois, e** *adj* Welsh **♦** *nm/f*: **Gallois, e** Welshman(-woman) **♦** *nm (LING)* Welsh

**galon** [galɔ̃] *nm (MIL)* stripe; *(décoratif)* piece of braid

**galop** [galo] *nm* gallop; **galoper** *vi* to gallop

**galopin** [galopɛ̃] *nm* urchin, ragamuffin

**gambader** [gɑ̃bade] *vi (animal, enfant)*

to leap about

**gambas** [gãbas] *nfpl* Mediterranean prawns

**gamin, e** [gamɛ̃, in] *nm/f* kid ♦ *adj* childish

**gamme** [gam] *nf* (MUS) scale; (fig) range

**gammé, e** [game] *adj*: **croix ~e** swastika

**gang** [gãg] *nm* (de criminels) gang

**gant** [gã] *nm* glove; **~ de toilette** face flannel (BRIT), face cloth

**garage** [garaʒ] *nm* garage; **garagiste** *nm/f* (propriétaire) garage owner; (employé) garage mechanic

**garantie** [garãti] *nf* guarantee; **(bon de) ~** guarantee *ou* warranty slip

**garantir** [garãtir] *vt* to guarantee

**garce** [gars] (fam) *nf* bitch

**garçon** [garsõ] *nm* boy; (célibataire): **vieux ~** bachelor; (serveur): **~ de café** waiter; **~ de courses** messenger; **~ d'honneur** best man; **garçonnière** *nf* bachelor flat

**garde** [gard(ə)] *nm* (de prisonnier) guard; (de domaine etc) warden; (soldat, sentinelle) guardsman ♦ *nf* (soldats) guard; **de ~** on duty; **monter la ~** to stand guard; **mettre en ~** to warn; **prendre ~ (à)** to be careful (of); **~ champêtre** ♦ *nm* rural policeman; **~ du corps** ♦ *nm* bodyguard; **~ des enfants** ♦ *nf* (après divorce) custody of the children; **~ à vue** ♦ *nf* (JUR) ≈ police custody; **garde-à-vous** *nm*: **être/se mettre au garde-à-vous** to be at/ stand to attention; **garde-barrière** *nm/f* level-crossing keeper; **garde-boue** *nm inv* mudguard; **garde-chasse** *nm* gamekeeper; **garde-malade** *nf* home nurse; **garde-manger** *nm inv* (armoire) meat safe; (pièce) pantry, larder

**garder** [garde] *vt* (conserver) to keep; (surveiller: enfants) to look after; (: immeuble, lieu, prisonnier) to guard; **se ~** *vi* (aliment: se conserver) to keep; **se ~**

**de faire** to be careful not to do; **~ le lit/la chambre** to stay in bed/indoors; **pêche/chasse gardée** private fishing/hunting (ground)

**garderie** [gardəri] *nf* day nursery, crèche

**garde-robe** [gardərɔb] *nf* wardrobe

**gardien, ne** [gardjɛ̃, jɛn] *nm/f* (garde) guard; (de prison) warder; (de domaine, réserve) warden; (de musée etc) attendant; (de phare, cimetière) keeper; (d'immeuble) caretaker; (fig) guardian; **~ de but** goalkeeper; **~ de la paix** policeman; **~ de nuit** night watchman

**gare** [gar] *nf* station; **~ routière** bus station

**garer** [gare] *vt* to park; **se ~** *vi* to park

**gargariser** [gargarize]: **se ~** *vi* to gargle

**gargote** [gargɔt] *nf* cheap restaurant

**gargouille** [garguj] *nf* gargoyle

**gargouiller** [garguje] *vi* to gurgle

**garnement** [garnəmã] *nm* rascal, scallywag

**garni, e** [garni] *adj* (plat) served with vegetables (and chips or rice etc)

**garnison** [garnizõ] *nf* garrison

**garniture** [garnityr] *nf* (CULIN) vegetables *pl*; **~ de frein** brake lining

**gars** [ga] (fam) *nm* guy

**Gascogne** [gaskɔɲ] *nf* Gascony; **le golfe de ~** the Bay of Biscay

**gas-oil** [gazɔjl] *nm* diesel (oil)

**gaspiller** [gaspije] *vt* to waste

**gastronome** [gastrɔnɔm] *nm/f* gourmet; **gastronomie** *nf* gastronomy; **gastronomique** *adj* gastronomic

**gâteau, x** [gato] *nm* cake; **~ sec** biscuit

**gâter** [gate] *vt* to spoil; **se ~** *vi* (dent, fruit) to go bad; (temps, situation) to change for the worse

**gâterie** [gatri] *nf* little treat

**gâteux, -euse** [gatø, øz] *adj* senile

**gauche** [goʃ] *adj* left, left-hand; (maladroit) awkward, clumsy ♦ *nf* (POL) left (wing); **le bras ~** the left arm; **le côté ~** the left-hand side; **à ~** on the left;

*(direction)* (to the) left; **gaucher, -ère**
*adj* left-handed; **gauchiste** *nm/f* leftist

**gaufre** [gofʀ] *nf* waffle

**gaufrette** [gofʀɛt] *nf* wafer

**gaulois, e** [golwa, waz] *adj* Gallic ♦
*nm/f*: **G~,** = Gaul

**gaver** [gave] *vt* to force-feed; **se ~ de**
to stuff o.s. with

**gaz** [gaz] *nm inv* gas

**gaze** [gaz] *nf* gauze

**gazer** [gaze] *(fam)* *vi*: **ça gaze?** how's
things?

**gazette** [gazɛt] *nf* news sheet

**gazeux, -euse** [gazø, øz] *adj (boisson)*
fizzy; *(eau)* sparkling

**gazoduc** [gazodyk] *nm* gas pipeline

**gazon** [gazɔ̃] *nm (herbe)* grass; *(pelouse)*
lawn

**gazouiller** [gazuje] *vi* to chirp; *(enfant)*
to babble

**geai** [ʒɛ] *nm* jay

**géant, e** [ʒeɑ̃, ɑ̃t] *adj* gigantic; *(COMM)*
giant-size ♦ *nm/f* giant

**geindre** [ʒɛ̃dʀ] *vi* to groan, moan

**gel** [ʒɛl] *nm* frost

**gélatine** [ʒelatin] *nf* gelatine

**gelée** [ʒ(ə)le] *nf* jelly; *(gel)* frost

**geler** [ʒ(ə)le] *vt, vi* to freeze; **il gèle** it's
freezing

**gélule** [ʒelyl] *nf (MÉD)* capsule

**gelures** [ʒəlyʀ] *nfpl* frostbite *sg*

**Gémeaux** [ʒemo] *nmpl*: **les ~** Gemini

**gémir** [ʒemiʀ] *vi* to groan, moan

**gênant, e** [ʒɛnɑ̃, ɑ̃t] *adj (irritant)* annoying; *(embarrassant)* embarrassing

**gencive** [ʒɑ̃siv] *nf* gum

**gendarme** [ʒɑ̃daʀm] *nm* gendarme;
**gendarmerie** *nf* military police force in
countryside and small towns; their police
station or barracks

**gendre** [ʒɑ̃dʀ] *nm* son-in-law

**gêné, e** [ʒene] *adj* embarrassed

**gêner** [ʒene] *vt (incommoder)* to bother;
*(encombrer)* to be in the way; *(embarrasser)* ~ **qn** to make sb feel ill-at-ease

**général, e -aux** [ʒeneʀal, o] *adj, nm*
general; **en ~** usually, in general; **gé-**

**nérale** *nf*: *(répétition)* **générale** final
dress rehearsal; **généralement** *adv*
generally; **généraliser** *vt, vi* to gener-
alize; **se généraliser** *vi* to become
widespread; **généraliste** *nm/f* general
practitioner, G.P.

**génération** [ʒeneʀasjɔ̃] *nf* generation

**généreux, -euse** [ʒeneʀø, øz] *adj*
generous

**générique** [ʒeneʀik] *nm (CINÉMA)* cred-
its *pl*

**générosité** [ʒeneʀozite] *nf* generosity

**genêt** [ʒ(ə)nɛ] *nm* broom *no pl (shrub)*

**génétique** [ʒenetik] *adj* genetic

**Genève** [ʒ(ə)nɛv] *n* Geneva

**génial, e, -aux** [ʒenjal, jo] *adj (of genius; (fam: formidable)* fantastic, brilliant

**génie** [ʒeni] *nm* genius; *(MIL)*: **le ~** the
Engineers *pl*; **~ civil** civil engineering

**genièvre** [ʒənjɛvʀ] *nm* juniper

**génisse** [ʒenis] *nf* heifer

**génital, e, -aux** [ʒenital, o] *adj* gen-
ital; **les parties ~es** the genitals

**génoise** [ʒenwaz] *nf* sponge cake

**genou, x** [ʒ(ə)nu] *nm* knee; **à ~x** on
one's knees; **se mettre à ~x** to kneel
down

**genre** [ʒɑ̃ʀ] *nm* kind, type, sort; *(LING)*
gender; **avoir bon ~** to look a nice
sort; **avoir mauvais ~** to be coarse-
looking; **ce n'est pas son ~** it's not
like him

**gens** [ʒɑ̃] *nmpl (f in some phrases)*
people *pl*

**gentil, le** [ʒɑ̃ti, ij] *adj* kind; *(enfant:
sage)* good; *(endroit etc)* nice; **gentillesse** *nf* kindness; **gentiment** *adv*
kindly

**géographie** [ʒeɔgʀafi] *nf* geography

**geôlier** [ʒolje, jɛʀ] *nm* jailer

**géologie** [ʒeɔlɔʒi] *nf* geology

**géomètre** [ʒeɔmɛtʀ] *nm/f (arpenteur)*
(land) surveyor

**géométrie** [ʒeɔmetʀi] *nf* geometry;
**géométrique** *adj* geometric

**géranium** [ʒeʀanjɔm] *nm* geranium

**gérant, e** [ʒeʀɑ̃, ɑ̃t] *nm/f* manager/-

# gerbe

# gobelet

eress)

**gerbe** [ʒɛʀb] *nf (de fleurs)* spray; *(de blé)* sheaf

**gercé, e** [ʒɛʀse] *adj* chapped

**gerçure** [ʒɛʀsyʀ] *nf* crack

**gérer** [ʒeʀe] *vt* to manage

**germain, e** [ʒɛʀmɛ̃, ɛn] *adj*: **cousin ~** first cousin

**germe** [ʒɛʀm] *nm* germ; **germer** *vi* to sprout; *(semence)* to germinate

**geste** [ʒɛst] *nm* gesture

**gestion** [ʒɛstjɔ̃] *nf* management

**ghetto** [geto] *nm* ghetto

**gibet** [ʒibɛ] *nm* gallows *pl*

**gibier** [ʒibje] *nm (animaux)* game

**giboulée** [ʒibule] *nf* sudden shower

**gicler** [ʒikle] *vi* to spurt, squirt

**gifle** [ʒifl] *nf* slap (in the face); **gifler** *vt* to slap (in the face)

**gigantesque** [ʒigɑ̃tɛsk] *adj* gigantic

**gigogne** [ʒigɔɲ] *adj*: **lits ~s** *(BRIT)* ou trundle beds

**gigot** [ʒigo] *nm* leg (of mutton ou lamb)

**gigoter** [ʒigɔte] *vi* to wriggle (about)

**gilet** [ʒile] *nm* waistcoat; *(pull)* cardigan; **~ de sauvetage** life jacket

**gin** [dʒin] *nm* gin; **~-tonic** gin and tonic

**gingembre** [ʒɛ̃ʒɑ̃bʀ] *nm* ginger

**girafe** [ʒiʀaf] *nf* giraffe

**giratoire** [ʒiʀatwaʀ] *adj*: **sens ~** roundabout

**girofle** [ʒiʀɔfl] *nf*: **clou de ~** clove

**girouette** [ʒiʀwɛt] *nf* weather vane ou cock

**gitan, e** [ʒitɑ̃, an] *nm/f* gipsy

**gîte** [ʒit] *nm (maison)* home; *(abri)* shelter; **~ (rural)** holiday cottage ou apartment

**givre** [ʒivʀ] *nm* (hoar) frost; **givré, e** *adj* covered in frost; *(fam: fou)* nuts; **orange givrée** orange sorbet *(served in peel)*

**glace** [glas] *nf* ice; *(crème glacée)* ice cream; *(miroir)* mirror; *(de voiture)* window

**glacé, e** [glase] *adj (mains, vent, pluie)* freezing; *(lac)* frozen; *(boisson)* iced

**glacer** [glase] *vt* to freeze; *(gâteau)* to ice; *(fig)*: **~ qn** *(intimider)* to chill sb; *(paralyser)* to make sb's blood run cold

**glacial, e** [glasjal, jo] *adj* icy

**glacier** [glasje] *nm (GÉO)* glacier; *(marchand)* ice-cream maker

**glacière** [glasjɛʀ] *nf* icebox

**glaçon** [glasɔ̃] *nm* icicle; *(pour boisson)* ice cube

**glaïeul** [glajœl] *nm* gladiolus

**glaise** [glɛz] *nf* clay

**gland** [glɑ̃] *nm* acorn; *(décoration)* tassel

**glande** [glɑ̃d] *nf* gland

**glander** [glɑ̃de] *(fam) vi* to fart around (!)

**glauque** [glok] *adj* dull blue-green

**glissade** [glisad] *nf (par jeu)* slide; *(chute)* slip; **faire des ~s sur la glace** to slide on the ice

**glissant, e** [glisɑ̃, ɑ̃t] *adj* slippery

**glissement** [glismɑ̃] *nm*: **~ de terrain** landslide

**glisser** [glise] *vi (avancer)* to glide ou slide along; *(coulisser, tomber)* to slide; *(déraper)* to slip; *(être glissant)* to be slippery ♦ *vt* to slip; **se ~ dans** to slip into

**global, e, -aux** [glɔbal, o] *adj* overall

**globe** [glɔb] *nm* globe

**globule** [glɔbyl] *nm (du sang)* corpuscle

**globuleux, -euse** [glɔbylø, øz] *adj*: **yeux ~** protruding eyes

**gloire** [glwaʀ] *nf* glory; **glorieux, -euse** *adj* glorious

**glousser** [gluse] *vi* to cluck; *(rire)* to chuckle; **gloussement** *nm* cluck; chuckle

**glouton, ne** [glutɔ̃, ɔn] *adj* gluttonous

**gluant, e** [glyɑ̃, ɑ̃t] *adj* sticky, gummy

**glucose** [glykoz] *nm* glucose

**glycine** [glisin] *nf* wisteria

**glouton** — *see glouton*

**goal** [gol] *nm* goalkeeper

**GO** *sigle (= grandes ondes)* LW

**gobelet** [gɔblɛ] *nm (en étain, verre, ar-

**gent)** tumbler; *(d'enfant, de pique-nique)* beaker; *(à dés)* cup

**gober** [gɔbe] *vt* to swallow (whole)

**godasse** [gɔdas] *(fam) nf* shoe

**godet** [gɔde] *nm* pot

**goéland** [gɔelɑ̃] *nm* (sea)gull

**goélette** [gɔelɛt] *nf* schooner

**gogo** [gɔgo]: **à ~** *adv* galore

**goguenard, e** [gɔgnaR, aRd] *adj* mocking

**goinfre** [gwɛ̃fR] *nm* glutton

**golf** [gɔlf] *nm* golf; *(terrain)* golf course

**golfe** [gɔlf] *nm* gulf; *(petit)* bay

**gomme** [gɔm] *nf (à effacer)* rubber *(BRIT)*, eraser; **gommer** *vt* to rub out *(BRIT)*, erase

**gond** [gɔ̃] *nm* hinge; **sortir de ses ~s** *(fig)* to fly off the handle

**gondoler** [gɔ̃dɔle]: **se ~** *vi (planche)* to warp; *(métal)* to buckle

**gonflé, e** [gɔ̃fle] *adj* swollen; **il est ~** *(fam: courageux)* he's got some nerve; *(: impertinent)* he's got a nerve

**gonfler** [gɔ̃fle] *vt (pneu, ballon: en soufflant)* to blow up; *(: avec une pompe)* to pump up; *(nombre, importance)* to inflate ♦ *vi* to swell (up); *(CULIN: pâte)* to rise; **gonfleur** *nm* pump

**gonzesse** [gɔ̃zɛs] *(fam) nf* chick, bird *(BRIT)*

**goret** [gɔRɛ] *nm* piglet

**gorge** [gɔRʒ] *nf (ANAT)* throat; *(vallée)* gorge

**gorgé, e** [gɔRʒe] *adj*: **~ de** filled with; *(eau)* saturated with; **gorgée** *nf (petite)* sip; *(grande)* gulp

**gorille** [gɔRij] *nm* gorilla; *(fam)* bodyguard

**gosier** [gozje] *nm* throat

**gosse** [gɔs] *(fam) nm/f* kid

**goudron** [gudRɔ̃] *nm* tar; **goudronner** *vt* to tar(mac) *(BRIT)*, asphalt *(US)*

**gouffre** [gufR] *nm* abyss, gulf

**goujat** [guʒa] *nm* boor

**goulot** [gulo] *nm* neck; **boire au ~** to drink from the bottle

**goulu, e** [guly] *adj* greedy

**gourd, e** [guR, guRd] *adj* numb (with cold)

**gourde** [guRd] *nf (récipient)* flask; *(fam)* (clumsy) clot *ou* oaf ♦ *adj* oafish

**gourdin** [guRdɛ̃] *nm* club, bludgeon

**gourer** [guRe] *(fam)*: **se ~** *vi* to boob

**gourmand, e** [guRmɑ̃, ɑ̃d] *adj* greedy; **gourmandise** [guRmɑ̃diz] *nf* greed; *(bonbon)* sweet

**gourmet** [guRmɛ] *nm* gourmet

**gourmette** [guRmɛt] *nf* chain bracelet

**gousse** [gus] *nf*: **~ d'ail** clove of garlic

**goût** [gu] *nm* taste; **avoir bon ~** to taste good; **de bon ~** tasteful; **de mauvais ~** tasteless; **prendre ~ à** to develop a taste *ou* a liking for

**goûter** [gute] *vt (essayer)* to taste; *(apprécier)* to enjoy ♦ *vi* to have (afternoon) tea ♦ *nm* (afternoon) tea

**goutte** [gut] *nf* drop; *(MÉD)* gout; *(alcool)* brandy; **tomber ~ à ~** to drip; **goutte-à-goutte** *nm (MÉD)* drip

**gouttelette** [gut(ə)lɛt] *nf* droplet

**gouttière** [gutjɛR] *nf* gutter

**gouvernail** [guveRnaj] *nm* rudder; *(barre)* helm, tiller

**gouvernante** [guveRnɑ̃t] *nf* governess

**gouvernement** [guveRnəmɑ̃] *nm* government

**gouverner** [guveRne] *vt* to govern

**grabuge** [gRabyʒ] *(fam) nm* mayhem

**grâce** [gRɑs] *nf (charme)* grace; *(faveur)* favour; *(JUR)* pardon; **~s** *nfpl (REL)* grace *sg*; **faire ~ à qn de qch** to spare sb sth; **rendre ~(s) à** to give thanks to; **demander ~** to beg for mercy; **~ à** thanks to; **gracier** *vt* to pardon; **gracieux, -euse** *adj* graceful

**grade** [gRad] *nm* rank; **monter en ~** to be promoted

**gradin** [gRadɛ̃] *nm* tier; step; **~s** *nmpl (de stade)* terracing *sg*

**gradué, e** [gRadye] *adj*: **verre ~** measuring jug

**graduel, le** [gRadyɛl] *adj* gradual

**graduer** [gRadye] *vt (effort etc)* to increase gradually; *(règle, verre)* to graduate

**graffiti** [grafiti] *nmpl* graffiti

**grain** [grɛ̃] *nm* (*gén*) grain; (*NAVIG*) squall; **~ de beauté** beauty spot; **~ de café** coffee bean; **~ de poivre** peppercorn; **~ de poussière** speck of dust; **♦ de raisin** grape

**graine** [grɛn] *nf* seed

**graissage** [gresaʒ] *nm* lubrication, greasing

**graisse** [gres] *nf* fat; (*lubrifiant*) grease; **graisser** *vt* to lubricate, grease; (*tacher*) to make greasy; **graisseux, -euse** *adj* greasy

**grammaire** [gra(m)mɛr] *nf* grammar; **grammatical, e, -aux** *adj* grammatical

**gramme** [gram] *nm* gramme

**grand, e** [grɑ̃, grɑ̃d] *adj* (*haut*) tall; (*gros, vaste, large*) big, large; (*long*) long; (*plus âgé*) big; (*adulte*) grown-up; (*sens abstraits*) great **♦** *adv*: **~ ouvert** wide open; **au ~ air** in the open (air); **les ~s blessés** the severely injured; **~ ensemble** housing scheme; **~e magasin** department store; **~e personne** grown-up; **~e surface** hypermarket; **~es écoles** prestige schools of university level; **~es lignes** (*RAIL*) main lines; **~es vacances** summer holidays; **grand-chose** [grɑ̃ʃoz] *nm/f inv*: **pas grand-chose** not much; **Grande-Bretagne** nf (Great) Britain; **grandeur** nf (*dimension*) size; **grandeur nature** life-size; **grandiose** *adj* imposing; **grandir** *vi* to grow **♦** *vt*: **grandir qn** (*suj: vêtement, chaussure*) to make sb look taller; **grand-mère** nf grandmother; **grand-messe** nf high mass; **grand-peine**: **à grand-peine** *adv* with difficulty; **grand-père** nm grandfather; **grand-route** nf main road; **grands-parents** *nmpl* grandparents

**grange** [grɑ̃ʒ] *nf* barn

**granit(e)** [granit] *nm* granite

**graphique** [grafik] *adj* graphic **♦** *nm* graph

**grappe** [grap] *nf* cluster; **~ de raisin** bunch of grapes

**gras, se** [grɑ, grɑs] *adj* (*viande, soupe*) fatty; (*personne*) fat; (*surface, main*) greasy; (*plaisanterie*) coarse; (*TYPO*) bold **♦** *nm* (*CULIN*) fat; **faire la ~se matinée** to have a lie-in (*BRIT*), sleep late (*US*); **grassement** *adv*: **grassement payé** handsomely paid; **grassouillet, te** *adj* podgy, plump

**gratifiant, e** [gratifjɑ̃, jɑ̃t] *adj* gratifying, rewarding

**gratin** [gratɛ̃] *nm* (*plat*) cheese-topped dish; (*croûte*) cheese topping; **gratiné, e** *adj* (*CULIN*) au gratin

**gratis** [gratis] *adv* free

**gratitude** [gratityd] *nf* gratitude

**gratte-ciel** [gratsjɛl] *nm inv* skyscraper

**gratte-papier** [gratpapje] (*péj*) *nm* penpusher

**gratter** [grate] *vt* (*avec un outil*) to scrape; (*enlever: avec un outil*) to scrape off; (: *avec un ongle*) to scratch; (*enlever: avec un ongle*) to scratch off **♦** *vi* (*irriter*) to be scratchy; (*démanger*) to itch; **se ~** to scratch (o.s.)

**gratuit, e** [gratɥi, ɥit] *adj* (*entrée, billet*) free; (*fig*) gratuitous

**gravats** [grava] *nmpl* rubble *sg*

**grave** [grav] *adj* (*maladie, accident*) serious, bad; (*sujet, problème*) serious, grave; (*air*) grave, solemn; (*voix, son*) deep, low-pitched; **gravement** *adv* seriously; (*parler, regarder*) gravely

**graver** [grave] *vt* to engrave

**gravier** [gravje] *nm* gravel *no pl*; **gravillons** *nmpl* loose chippings *ou* gravel

**gravir** [gravir] *vt* to climb (up)

**gravité** [gravite] *nf* (*de maladie, d'accident*) seriousness; (*de sujet, problème*) gravity

**graviter** [gravite] *vi* to revolve

**gravure** [gravyr] *nf* engraving; (*reproduction*) print

**gré** [gre] *nm*: **de bon ~** willingly; **contre le ~ de qn** against sb's will; **de**

son (plein) ~ of one's own free will; **bon ~ mal ~** like it or not; **de ~ ou de force** whether one likes it or not; **savoir ~ à qn de qch** to be grateful to sb for sth

**grec, grecque** [grɛk] adj Greek; (classique: vase etc) Grecian ♦ nm/f: **G~, Grecque** Greek ♦ nm (LING) Greek

**Grèce** [grɛs] nf: **la ~** Greece

**greffe** [grɛf] nf (BOT, MÉD: de tissu) graft; (MÉD: d'organe) transplant; **greffer** vt (BOT, MÉD: tissu) to graft; (MÉD: organe) to transplant

**greffier, jɛr** [grɛfje, jɛr] nm clerk of the court

**grêle** [grɛl] adj (very) thin ♦ nf hail; **grêler** vb impers: **il grêle** it's hailing; **grêlon** nm hailstone

**grelot** [grəlo] nm little bell

**grelotter** [grələte] vi to shiver

**grenade** [grənad] nf (explosive) grenade; (BOT) pomegranate; **grenadine** nf grenadine

**grenat** [grəna] adj inv dark red

**grenier** [grənje] nm attic; (de ferme) loft

**grenouille** [grənuj] nf frog

**grès** [grɛ] nm sandstone; (poterie) stoneware

**grésiller** [grezije] vi to sizzle; (RADIO) to crackle

**grève** [grɛv] nf (d'ouvriers) strike; (plage) shore; **se mettre en/faire ~** to go on/be on strike; **~ de la faim** hunger strike; **~ du zèle** work-to-rule (BRIT), slowdown (US); **~ sauvage** wildcat strike

**gréviste** [grevist] nm/f striker

**gribouiller** [gribuje] vt to scribble, scrawl

**grièvement** [grijɛvmɑ̃] adv seriously

**griffe** [grif] nf claw; (de couturier) label; **griffer** vt to scratch

**griffonner** [grifɔne] vt to scribble

**grignoter** [griɲɔte] vt (personne) to nibble at; (souris) to gnaw at ♦ vi to nibble

**gril** [gril] nm steak ou grill pan; **faire cuire au ~** to grill; **grillade** nf (viande etc) grill

**grillage** [grijaʒ] nm (treillis) wire netting; (clôture) wire fencing

**grille** [grij] nf (clôture) wire fence; (portail) (metal) gate; (d'égout) (metal) grate; (fig) grid

**grille-pain** [grijpɛ̃] nm inv toaster

**griller** [grije] vt (pain) to toast; (viande) to grill; (fig: ampoule etc) to blow; **faire ~** to toast; to grill; (châtaignes) to roast; **~ un feu rouge** to jump the lights

**grillon** [grijɔ̃] nm cricket

**grimace** [grimas] nf grimace; (pour faire rire): **faire des ~s** to pull ou make faces

**grimper** [grɛ̃pe] vi, vt to climb

**grincer** [grɛ̃se] vi (objet métallique) to grate; (plancher, porte) to creak; **~ des dents** to grind one's teeth

**grincheux, -euse** [grɛ̃ʃø, øz] adj grumpy

**grippe** [grip] nf flu, influenza; **grippé, e** adj: **être grippé** to have flu

**gris, e** [gri, griz] adj grey; (ivre) tipsy

**grisaille** [grizaj] nf greyness, dullness

**griser** [grize] vt to intoxicate

**grisonner** [grizɔne] vi to be going grey

**grisou** [grizu] nm firedamp

**grive** [griv] nf thrush

**grivois, e** [grivwa, waz] adj saucy

**Groenland** [grɔenlɑ̃d] nm Greenland

**grogner** [grɔɲe] vi to growl; (fig) to grumble; **grognon, ne** adj grumpy

**groin** [grwɛ̃] nm snout

**grommeler** [grɔm(ə)le] vi to mutter to o.s.

**gronder** [grɔ̃de] vi to rumble; (fig: révolte) to be brewing ♦ vt to scold; **faire ~** to get a telling-off

**groom** [grum] nm bellboy

**gros, se** [gro, gros] adj big, large; (obèse) fat; (travaux, dégâts) extensive; (épais) thick; (rhume, averse) heavy

♦ *adv*: **risquer/gagner** ~ to risk/win a lot ♦ *nm/f* fat man/woman ♦ *nm* (COMM): **le** ~ the wholesale business; **prix de** ~ wholesale price; **par** ~ *temps/grosse mer* in rough weather/ heavy seas; **en** ~ roughly; (COMM) wholesale; ~ **lot** jackpot; ~ **mot** coarse word; ~ **plan** (PHOTO) close-up; ~ **sel** cooking salt; ~ **titre** headline; **~se caisse** big drum

**groseille** [gʀozɛj] *nf*: ~ **(rouge/ blanche)** red/white currant; ~ **à maquereau** gooseberry

**grosse** [gʀos] *adj voir* **gros; grossesse** *nf* pregnancy; **grosseur** *nf* size; (*tumeur*) lump

**grossier, -ière** [gʀosje, jɛʀ] *adj* coarse; (*insolent*) rude; (*dessin*) rough; (*travail*) roughly done; (*imitation, instrument*) crude; (*évident: erreur*) gross; **grossièrement** *adv* (*sommairement*) roughly; (*vulgairement*) coarsely; **grossièretés** *nfpl*: **dire des grossièretés** to use coarse language

**grossir** [gʀosiʀ] *vi* (*personne*) to put on weight ♦ *vt* (*exagérer*) to exaggerate; (*au microscope*) to magnify; (*suj: vêtement*): ~ **qn** to make sb look fatter

**grossiste** [gʀosist] *nm/f* wholesaler

**grosso modo** [gʀosomɔdo] *adv* roughly

**grotesque** [gʀotɛsk] *adj* (*extravagant*) grotesque; (*ridicule*) ludicrous

**grotte** [gʀot] *nf* cave

**grouiller** [gʀuje] *vi*: ~ **de** to be swarming with; **se** ~ (*fam*) ♦ *vi* to get a move on; **grouillant, e** *adj* swarming

**groupe** [gʀup] *nm* group; **le** ~ **des 7** Group of 7; ~ **sanguin** blood group; **groupement** *nm* (*action*) grouping; (*groupe*) group; **grouper** *vt* to group; **se grouper** *vi* to gather

**grue** [gʀy] *nf* crane

**grumeaux** [gʀymo] *nmpl* lumps

**guenilles** [gənij] *nfpl* rags

**guenon** [gənɔ̃] *nf* female monkey

**guépard** [gepaʀ] *nm* cheetah

**guêpe** [gɛp] *nf* wasp

**guêpier** [gepje] *nm* (*fig*) trap

**guère** [gɛʀ] *adv* (*avec adjectif, adverbe*): **ne ...** ~ hardly; (*avec verbe*): **ne ...** ~ (*pas beaucoup*) *tournure négative +much*; (*pas souvent*) hardly ever; (*pas longtemps*) *tournure négative +(very) long*; **il n'y a** ~ **que/de** there's hardly anybody (*ou* anything) but/hardly any; **ce n'est** ~ **difficile** it's hardly difficult; **nous n'avons** ~ **de temps** we have hardly any time

**guéridon** [geʀidɔ̃] *nm* pedestal table

**guérilla** [geʀija] *nf* guerrilla warfare

**guérillero** [geʀijeʀo] *nm* guerrilla

**guérir** [geʀiʀ] *vt* (*personne, maladie*) to cure; (*membre, plaie*) to heal ♦ *vi* (*malade, maladie*) to be cured; (*blessure*) to heal; **guérison** *nf* (*de maladie*) curing; (*de membre, plaie*) healing; (*de malade*) recovery; **guérisseur, -euse** *nm/f* healer

**guerre** [gɛʀ] *nf* war; ~ **civile** civil war; **en** ~ at war; **faire la** ~ **à** to wage war against; **guerrier, -ière** *adj* warlike ♦ *nm/f* warrior

**guet** [gɛ] *nm*: **faire le** ~ to be on the watch *ou* look-out; **guet-apens** [gɛtapɑ̃] *nm* ambush; **guetter** *vt* (*épier*) to watch (intently); (*attendre*) to watch (out) for; (*hostilement*) to be lying in wait for

**gueule** [gœl] *nf* (*d'animal*) mouth; (*fam: figure*) face; (: *bouche*) mouth; **ta** ~! (*fam*) shut up!; ~ **de bois** (*fam*) hangover; **gueuler** (*fam*) *vi* to bawl

**gueuleton** (*fam*) *nm* blow-out

**gui** [gi] *nm* mistletoe

**guichet** [giʃɛ] *nm* (*de bureau, banque*) counter; **les** ~**s** (*à la gare, au théâtre*) the ticket office *sg*; ~ **automatique** cash dispenser (BRIT), automatic telling machine (US)

**guide** [gid] *nm* guide ♦ *nf* (*éclaireuse*) girl guide; **guider** *vt* to guide

**guidon** [gidɔ̃] *nm* handlebars *pl*

**guignol** [giɲɔl] *nm* ≈ Punch and Judy

show; (fig) clown

**guillemets** [gijmɛ] nmpl: **entre ~** in inverted commas

**guillotiner** [gijɔtine] vt to guillotine

**guindé, e** [gɛ̃de] adj (personne, air) stiff, starchy; (style) stilted

**guirlande** [giʀlɑ̃d] nf (fleurs) garland; **~ de Noël** tinsel garland; **~ lumineuse** string of fairy lights; **~ de papier** paper chain

**guise** [giz] nf: **à votre ~** as you wish ou please; **en ~ de** by way of

**guitare** [gitaʀ] nf guitar

**gym** [ʒim] nf (exercices) gym; **gymnase** nm gym(nasium); **gymnaste** nm/f gymnast; **gymnastique** nf gymnastics sg; (au réveil etc) keep-fit exercises pl

**gynécologie** [ʒinekɔlɔʒi] nf gynaecology; **gynécologique** adj gynaecological; **gynécologue** nm/f gynaecologist

## H, h

**habile** [abil] adj skilful; (malin) clever; **habileté** [abilte] nf skill, skilfulness; cleverness

**habillé, e** [abije] adj dressed; (chic) dressy

**habillement** [abijmɑ̃] nm clothes pl

**habiller** [abije] vt to dress; (fournir en vêtements) to clothe; **s'~** vi to dress (o.s.); (se déguiser, mettre des vêtements chic) to dress up

**habit** [abi] nm outfit; **~s** nmpl (vêtements) clothes; **~ (de soirée)** evening dress; (pour homme) tails pl

**habitant, e** [abitɑ̃, ɑ̃t] nm/f inhabitant; (d'une maison) occupant; **loger chez l'~** to stay with the locals

**habitation** [abitasjɔ̃] nf house; **~s à loyer modéré** (block of) council flats

**habiter** [abite] vt to live in ♦ vi: **~ à/dans** to live in

**habitude** [abityd] nf habit; **avoir l'~ de faire** to be in the habit of doing; (expérience) to be used to doing; **d'~** usually; **comme d'~** as usual

**habitué, e** [abitye] nm/f (de maison) regular visitor; (de café) regular (customer)

**habituel, le** [abitɥɛl] adj usual

**habituer** [abitɥe] vt: **~ qn à** to get sb used to; **s'~ à** to get used to

**hache** ['aʃ] nf axe

**hacher** ['aʃe] vt (viande) to mince; (persil) to chop; **'hachis** nm mince no pl; **hachis Parmentier** ≈ shepherd's pie

**hachisch** ['aʃiʃ] nm hashish

**hachoir** ['aʃwaʀ] nm (couteau) chopper; (appareil) (meat) mincer; (planche) chopping board

**hagard, e** ['agaʀ, aʀd] adj wild, distraught

**haie** ['ɛ] nf hedge; (SPORT) hurdle

**haillons** ['ajɔ̃] nmpl rags

**haine** ['ɛn] nf hatred

**haïr** ['aiʀ] vt to detest, hate

**hâlé, e** ['ɑle] adj (sun)tanned, sunburnt

**haleine** [alɛn] nf breath; **hors d'~** out of breath; **tenir en ~** (attention) to hold spellbound; (incertitude) to keep in suspense; **de longue ~** long-term

**haleter** ['alte] vi to pant

**hall** ['ol] nm hall

**halle** ['al] nf (covered) market; **~s** nfpl (d'une grande ville) central food market sg

**hallucinant, e** [alysinɑ̃, ɑ̃t] adj staggering

**hallucination** [alysinasjɔ̃] nf hallucination

**halte** ['alt] nf stop, break; (endroit) stopping place ♦ excl stop!; **faire ~** to stop

**haltère** [altɛʀ] nm dumbbell, barbell; **~s** nmpl: (poids et) **~s** (activité) weightlifting sg; **haltérophilie** nf weightlifting

**hamac** ['amak] nm hammock

**hamburger** ['ɑ̃buʀgœʀ] nm hamburger

**hameau** ['amo] nm hamlet

**hameçon** [amsɔ̃] nm (fish) hook

**hanche** ['ɑ̃ʃ] nf hip

**'hand-ball** ['ɑdbal] nm handball

**handicapé, e** ['ɑdikape] nm/f physically (ou mentally) handicapped person; **~ moteur** spastic

**hangar** ['ɑ̃gar] nm shed; (AVIAT) hangar

**hanneton** ['antɔ̃] nm cockchafer

**hanter** ['ɑte] vt to haunt

**hantise** ['ɑtiz] nf obsessive fear

**happer** ['ape] vt to snatch; (suj: train etc) to hit

**haras** ['aRɑ] nm stud farm

**harassant, e** ['aRasɑ̃, ɑ̃t] adj exhausting

**harcèlement** ['aRsɛlmɑ̃] nm harassment; **~ sexuel** sexual harassment

**harceler** ['aRsəle] vt to harass; **~ qn de questions** to plague sb with questions

**hardi, e** ['aRdi] adj bold, daring

**hareng** ['aRɑ̃] nm herring

**hargne** ['aRɲ] nf aggressiveness; **'hargneux, -euse** adj aggressive

**haricot** ['aRiko] nm bean; **~ blanc** haricot bean; **~ vert** green bean; **~ rouge** kidney bean

**harmonica** [aRmɔnika] nm mouth organ

**harmonie** [aRmɔni] nf harmony; **harmonieux, -euse** adj harmonious; (couleurs, couple) well-matched

**harnacher** ['aRnaʃe] vt to harness

**harnais** ['aRnɛ] nm harness

**harpe** ['aRp] nf harp

**harponner** ['aRpɔne] vt to harpoon; (fam) to collar

**hasard** ['azaR] nm: **le ~** chance, fate; **un ~** a coincidence; **au ~** (aller) aimlessly; (choisir) at random; **par ~** by chance; **à tout ~** (en cas de besoin) just in case; (en espérant trouver ce qu'on cherche) on the off chance (BRIT); **'hasarder** vt (mot) to venture; **se hasarder à faire** to risk doing

**hâte** ['ɑt] nf haste; **à la ~** hurriedly, hastily; **en ~** posthaste, with all possible speed; **avoir ~ de** to be eager ou anxious to; **'hâter** vt to hasten; **se hâter** vi to hurry; **'hâtif, -ive** adj (tra-

vail) hurried; (décision, jugement) hasty

**'hausse** ['os] nf rise, increase; **être en ~** to be going up; **'hausser** vt to raise; **hausser les épaules** to shrug (one's shoulders)

**haut, e** ['o, 'ot] adj high; (grand) tall ♦ adv high ♦ nm top (part); **de 3 m de ~** 3 m high, 3 m in height; **des ~s et des bas** ups and downs; **en ~ lieu** in high places; **à ~e voix, (tout)** aloud, out loud; **du ~ de** from the top of; **de ~ en bas** from top to bottom; **plus ~** higher up, further up; (dans un texte) above; (parler) louder; **en ~** (être/aller) at/to the top; (dans une maison) upstairs; **en ~ de** at the top of

**hautain, e** ['otɛ̃, ɛn] adj haughty

**hautbois** ['obwa] nm oboe

**haut-de-forme** ['odfɔRm] nm top hat

**hauteur** ['otœR] nf height; **à la ~ de** (accident) near; (fig: tâche, situation) equal to; **à la ~** (fig) up to it

**haut...**: **'haut-fourneau** nm blast ou smelting furnace; **'haut-le-cœur** nm inv retch, heave; **'haut-parleur** nm (loud)speaker

**havre** ['ɑvR] nm haven

**Haye** ['ɛ] n: **la ~** the Hague

**hayon** ['ɛjɔ̃] nm hatchback

**hebdo** [ebdo] (fam) nm weekly

**hebdomadaire** [ebdɔmadɛR] adj, nm weekly

**hébergement** [ebɛRʒəmɑ̃] nm accommodation

**héberger** [ebɛRʒe] vt (touristes) to accommodate, lodge; (amis) to put up; (réfugiés) to take in

**hébété, e** [ebete] adj dazed

**hébreu, x** [ebrø] adj m Hebrew

**hécatombe** [ekatɔ̃b] nf slaughter

**hectare** [ɛktaR] nm hectare

**hein** ['ɛ̃] excl eh?

**hélas** [elas] excl alas! ♦ adv unfortunately

**héler** ['ele] vt to hail

**hélice** [elis] nf propeller

**hélicoptère** [elikɔptɛR] nm helicopter

**helvétique** [ɛlvetik] *adj* Swiss

**hématome** [ematom] *nm* nasty bruise

**hémicycle** [emisikl] *nm* (POL): l'~ ≃ the benches (of the Commons) (BRIT), ≃ the floor (of the House of Representatives) (US)

**hémisphère** [emisfɛr] *nm*: l'~ nord/ sud the northern/southern hemisphere

**hémorragie** [emɔraʒi] *nf* bleeding no pl, haemorrhage

**hémorroïdes** [emɔrɔid] *nfpl* piles, haemorrhoids

**'hennir** ['enir] *vi* to neigh, whinny; **'hennissement** *nm* neigh, whinny

**hépatite** [epatit] *nf* hepatitis

**herbe** [ɛrb] *nf* grass; (CULIN, MÉD) herb; **~s de Provence** mixed herbs; **en ~** unripe; (fig) budding; **herbicide** *nm* weed-killer; **herboriste** *nm/f* herbalist

**'here** [ɛr] *nm*: **pauvre ~** poor wretch

**héréditaire** [erediter] *adj* hereditary

**'hérisser** ['erise] *vt*: **~ qn** (fig) to ruffle sb; **se ~** *vi* to bristle, bristle up; **'hérisson** *nm* hedgehog

**héritage** [eritaʒ] *nm* inheritance; (coutumes, système) heritage, legacy

**hériter** [erite] *vi*: **~ de qch (de qn)** to inherit sth (from sb); **héritier, -ière** [eritje, jɛr] *nm/f* heir(-ess)

**hermétique** [ermetik] *adj* airtight; watertight; (fig: obscur) abstruse; (: impénétrable) impenetrable

**hermine** [ermin] *nf* ermine

**hernie** ['erni] *nf* hernia

**héroïne** [erɔin] *nf* heroine; (drogue) heroin

**héroïque** [erɔik] *adj* heroic

**héron** ['erɔ] *nm* heron

**héros** ['ero] *nm* hero

**hésitant, e** [ezitɑ, ɑt] *adj* hesitant

**hésitation** [ezitasjɔ] *nf* hesitation

**hésiter** [ezite] *vi*: **~ (à faire)** to hesitate (to do)

**hétéroclite** [eterɔklit] *adj* heterogeneous; (objets) sundry

**hétérogène** [eterɔʒɛn] *adj* heterogeneous

**hétérosexuel, le** [eterɔsɛkɥɛl] *adj* heterosexual

**'hêtre** ['ɛtr] *nm* beech

**heure** ['ɶr] *nf* hour; (SCOL) period; (moment) time; **c'est l'~** it's time; **quelle est-il?** what time is it?; **2 ~s (du matin)** 2 o'clock (in the morning); **être à l'~** to be on time; (montre) to be right; **mettre à l'~** to set right; **à une ~ avancée (de la nuit)** at a late hour of the night; **à toute ~** at any time; **24 ~s sur 24** round the clock, 24 hours a day; **à l'~ qu'il est** at this time (of day); by now; **sur l'~** at once; **~ de pointe** rush hour; (téléphone) peak period; **~ d'affluence** rush hour; **~s creuses** slack periods; (pour électricité, téléphone etc) off-peak periods; **~s supplémentaires** overtime *sg*

**heureusement** [ɶrøzmɑ] *adv* (par bonheur) fortunately, luckily

**heureux, -euse** [ɶrø, øz] *adj* happy; (chanceux) lucky, fortunate

**'heurter** ['ɶrte] *vt* (mur) to strike, hit; (personne) to collide with; **se ~ à** *vt* (fig) to come up against

**'heurts** ['ɶr] *nmpl* (fig) clashes

**hexagone** [ɛgzagɔn] *nm* hexagon; (la France) France (because of its shape)

**hiberner** [ibɛrne] *vi* to hibernate

**hibou, x** ['ibu] *nm* owl

**hideux, -euse** ['idø, øz] *adj* hideous

**hier** [jɛr] *adv* yesterday; **~ soir** last night, yesterday evening; **toute la journée d'~** all day yesterday; **toute la matinée d'~** all yesterday morning

**hiérarchie** ['jerarʃi] *nf* hierarchy

**hi-fi** ['ifi] *adj inv* hi-fi ♦ *nf* hi-fi

**hilare** [ilar] *adj* mirthful

**hindou, e** [ɛdu] *adj* Hindu ♦ *nm/f*: **H~, e** Hindu

**hippique** [ipik] *adj* equestrian, horse *cpd*; **un club ~** a riding centre; **un concours ~** a horse show; **hippisme** *nm* (horse)riding

**hippodrome** [ipɔdrom] *nm* racecourse

**hippopotame** [ipɔpotam] *nm* hippopotamus

**hirondelle** [iʀɔ̃dɛl] *nf* swallow

**hirsute** [iʀsyt] *adj* (*personne*) shaggy-haired; (*barbe*) shaggy; (*tête*) tousled

**hisser** ['ise] *vt* to hoist, haul up; **se ~** *vi* to heave o.s. up

**histoire** [istwaʀ] *nf* (*science, événements*) history; (*anecdote, récit, événements*) history; (*anecdote, récit, mensonge*) story; (*affaire*) business *no pl*; **~s** *nfpl* (*chichis*) fuss *no pl*; (*ennuis*) trouble *sg*; **historique** *adj* historical; (*important*) historic

**hit-parade** ['itpaʀad] *nm*: **le ~** the charts

**hiver** [ivɛʀ] *nm* winter; **hivernal, e, -aux** *adj* winter *cpd*; (*glacial*) wintry; **hiverner** *vi* to winter

**HLM** *nm ou f* (= *habitation à loyer modéré*) council flat; **des HLM** council housing

**hobby** ['ɔbi] *nm* hobby

**hocher** ['ɔʃe] *vt*: **~ la tête** to nod; (*signe négatif ou dubitatif*) to shake one's head

**hochet** ['ɔʃɛ] *nm* rattle

**hockey** ['ɔkɛ] *nm*: **~ (sur glace/gazon)** (ice/field) hockey

**hold-up** ['ɔldœp] *nm inv* hold-up

**hollandais, e** ['ɔlɑ̃dɛ, ɛz] *adj* Dutch ♦ *nm* (*LING*) Dutch ♦ *nm/f*: **H~, e** Dutchman(-woman); **les H~** the Dutch

**Hollande** ['ɔlɑ̃d] *nf*: **la ~** Holland

**homard** ['ɔmaʀ] *nm* lobster

**homéopathique** [ɔmeɔpatik] *adj* homœopathic

**homicide** [ɔmisid] *nm* murder; **~ involontaire** manslaughter

**hommage** [ɔmaʒ] *nm* tribute; **~s** *nmpl*: **présenter ses ~s** to pay one's respects; **rendre ~ à** to pay tribute ou homage to

**homme** [ɔm] *nm* man; **~ d'affaires** businessman; **~ d'État** statesman; **~ de main** hired man; **~ de paille** stooge; **~ politique** politician; **homme-grenouille** *nm* frogman

**homo...: homogène** *adj* homogeneous; **homologue** *nm/f* counterpart; **homologué, e** *adj* (*SPORT*) ratified; (*tarif*) authorized; **homonyme** *nm* homonym; (*d'une personne*) namesake; **homosexuel, le** *adj* homosexual

**'Hongrie** ['ɔ̃gʀi] *nf*: **la ~** Hungary; **'hongrois, e** *adj* Hungarian ♦ *nm/f*: **Hongrois, e** Hungarian ♦ *nm* (*LING*) Hungarian

**honnête** [ɔnɛt] *adj* (*intègre*) honest; (*juste, satisfaisant*) fair; **honnêtement** *adv* honestly; **honnêteté** *nf* honesty

**honneur** [ɔnœʀ] *nm* honour; (*mérite*) credit; **en l'~ de** in honour of; (*événement*) on the occasion of; **faire ~ à** (*engagements*) to honour; (*famille*) to be a credit to; (*fig: repas etc*) to do justice to

**honorable** [ɔnɔʀabl] *adj* worthy, honourable; (*suffisant*) decent

**honoraire** [ɔnɔʀɛʀ] *adj* honorary; **professeur ~** professor emeritus; **honoraires** *nmpl* fees *pl*

**honorer** [ɔnɔʀe] *vt* to honour; (*estimer*) to hold in high regard; (*faire honneur à*) to do credit to; **honorifique** [ɔnɔʀifik] *adj* honorary

**honte** ['ɔ̃t] *nf* shame; **avoir ~ de** to be ashamed of; **faire ~ à qn** to make sb (feel) ashamed; **honteux, -euse** *adj* ashamed; (*conduite, acte*) shameful, disgraceful

**hôpital, -aux** [ɔpital, o] *nm* hospital

**hoquet** ['ɔkɛ] *nm*: **avoir le ~** to have (the) hiccoughs; **'hoqueter** *vi* to hiccough

**horaire** [ɔʀɛʀ] *adj* hourly ♦ *nm* timetable, schedule; **~s** *nmpl* (*d'employé*) hours; **~ souple** flexitime

**horizon** [ɔʀizɔ̃] *nm* horizon

**horizontal, e, -aux** [ɔʀizɔ̃tal, o] *adj* horizontal

**horloge** [ɔʀlɔʒ] *nf* clock; **l'~ parlante** the speaking clock; **horloger, -ère**

*nm/f* watchmaker; clockmaker

**'hormis** ['ɔrmi] *prép* save

**horoscope** [ɔrɔskɔp] *nm* horoscope

**horreur** [ɔrœr] *nf* horror; **quelle ~!** how awful!; **avoir ~ de** to loathe *ou* detest; **horrible** *adj* horrible; **horrifier** *vt* to horrify

**horripiler** [ɔripile] *vt* to exasperate

**hors** ['ɔr] *prép*: **~ de** out of; **~ pair** outstanding; **~ de propos** inopportune; **être ~ de soi** to be beside o.s.; **~ d'usage** out of service; **'hors-bord** *nm inv* speedboat (*with outboard motor*); **'hors-d'œuvre** *nm inv* hors d'œuvre; **'hors-jeu** *nm inv* offside; **'hors-la-loi** *nm inv* outlaw; **'hors-taxe** *adj* (*boutique, articles*) duty-free

**hortensia** [ɔrtɑ̃sja] *nm* hydrangea

**hospice** [ɔspis] *nm* (*de vieillards*) home

**hospitalier, -ière** [ɔspitalje, jɛr] *adj* (*accueillant*) hospitable; (*MÉD: service, centre*) hospital *cpd*

**hospitaliser** [ɔspitalize] *vt* to take/send to hospital, hospitalize

**hospitalité** [ɔspitalite] *nf* hospitality

**hostie** [ɔsti] *nf* host (REL)

**hostile** [ɔstil] *adj* hostile; **hostilité** *nf* hostility

**hosto** [ɔsto] (*fam*) *nm* hospital

**hôte** [ot] *nm* (*maître de maison*) host; (*invité*) guest

**hôtel** [otɛl] *nm* hotel; **aller à l'~** to stay in a hotel; **~ de ville** town hall; **~ (particulier)** (*private*) mansion; **hôtelier, -ière** *adj* hotel *cpd* ♦ *nm/f* hotelier; **hôtellerie** *nf* hotel business

**hôtesse** [otɛs] *nf* hostess; **~ de l'air** air stewardess; **~ (d'accueil)** receptionist

**'hotte** ['ɔt] *nf* (*panier*) basket (*carried on the back*); **~ aspirante** cooker hood

**houblon** [ublɔ̃] *nm* (BOT) hop; (*pour la bière*) hops *pl*

**houille** ['uj] *nf* coal; **~ blanche** hydroelectric power

**houle** ['ul] *nf* swell; **'houleux, -euse** *adj* stormy

**houligan** ['uligɑ̃] *nm* hooligan

**'hourra** ['ura] *excl* hurrah!

**'houspiller** ['uspije] *vt* to scold

**'housse** ['us] *nf* cover

**'houx** ['u] *nm* holly

**hublot** [yblo] *nm* porthole

**'huche** ['yʃ] *nf*: **~ à pain** bread bin

**'huer** ['ɥe] *vt* to boo

**huile** [ɥil] *nf* oil; **~ solaire** suntan oil; **huiler** *vt* to oil; **huileux, -euse** *adj* oily

**huis** [ɥi] *nm*: **à ~ clos** in camera

**huissier** [ɥisje] *nm* usher; (*JUR*) ≈ bailiff

**'huit** ['ɥi(t)] *num* eight; **samedi en ~** a week on Saturday; **dans ~ jours** in a week; **huitaine** *nf*: **une huitaine (de jours)** a week or so; **huitième** *num* eighth

**huître** [ɥitr] *nf* oyster

**humain, e** [ymɛ̃, ɛn] *adj* human; (*compatissant*) humane ♦ *nm* human (being); **humanitaire** *adj* humanitarian; **humanité** *nf* humanity

**humble** [œ̃bl] *adj* humble

**humecter** [ymɛkte] *vt* to dampen

**humer** ['yme] *vt* (*plat*) to smell; (*parfum*) to inhale

**humeur** [ymœr] *nf* mood; **de bonne/ mauvaise ~** in a good/bad mood

**humide** [ymid] *adj* damp; (*main, yeux*) moist; (*climat, chaleur*) humid; (*saison, route*) wet

**humilier** [ymilje] *vt* to humiliate

**humilité** [ymilite] *nf* humility, humbleness

**humoristique** [ymɔristik] *adj* humorous

**humour** [ymur] *nm* humour; **avoir de l'~** to have a sense of humour; **~ noir** black humour

**'hurlement** ['yrləmɑ̃] *nm* howling *no pl*, howl, yelling *no pl*, yell

**'hurler** ['yrle] *vi* to howl, yell

**hurluberlu** [yrlybɛrly] (*péj*) *nm* crank

**'hutte** ['yt] *nf* hut

**hybride** [ibrid] *adj, nm* hybrid

**hydratant, e** [idʀatɑ̃, ɑ̃t] *adj* (*crème*) moisturizing

**hydraulique** [idʀolik] *adj* hydraulic

**hydravion** [idʀavjɔ̃] *nm* seaplane

**hydrogène** [idʀɔʒɛn] *nm* hydrogen

**hydroglisseur** [idʀogliscœʀ] *nm* hydroplane

**hyène** [jɛn] *nf* hyena

**hygiénique** [iʒenik] *adj* hygienic

**hymne** [imn] *nm* hymn; **~ national** national anthem

**hypermarché** [ipɛʀmaʀʃe] *nm* hypermarket

**hypermétrope** [ipɛʀmetʀɔp] *adj* long-sighted

**hypertension** [ipɛʀtɑ̃sjɔ̃] *nf* high blood pressure

**hypertexte** [ipɛʀtɛkst] *nm* (INFORM) hypertext

**hypnose** [ipnoz] *nf* hypnosis; **hypnotiser** *vt* to hypnotize; **hypnotiseur** *nm* hypnotist

**hypocrisie** [ipɔkʀizi] *nf* hypocrisy; **hypocrite** *adj* hypocritical

**hypothèque** [ipɔtɛk] *nf* mortgage

**hypothèse** [ipɔtɛz] *nf* hypothesis

**hystérique** [isteʀik] *adj* hysterical

# I, i

**iceberg** [ajsbɛʀg] *nm* iceberg

**ici** [isi] *adv* here; **jusqu'~** as far as this; (*temps*) so far; **d'~ demain** by tomorrow; **d'~ là** by then, in the meantime; **d'~ peu** before long

**icône** [ikon] *nf* icon

**idéal, e, -aux** [ideal, o] *adj* ideal ♦ *nm* ideal; **idéaliste** *adj* idealistic ♦ *nm/f* idealist

**idée** [ide] *nf* idea; **avoir dans l'~ que** to have an idea that; **~ fixe** obsession; **~ reçue** generally accepted idea

**identifier** [idɑ̃tifje] *vt* to identify; **s'~ à** (*héros etc*) to identify with

**identique** [idɑ̃tik] *adj*: **~ (à)** identical (to)

**identité** [idɑ̃tite] *nf* identity

**idiot, e** [idjo, idjɔt] *adj* idiotic ♦ *nm/f* idiot; **idiotie** *nf* idiotic thing

**idole** [idɔl] *nf* idol

**if** [if] *nm* yew

**igloo** [iglu] *nm* igloo

**ignare** [iɲaʀ] *adj* ignorant

**ignifugé, e** [iɲifyʒe] *adj* fireproof

**ignoble** [iɲɔbl] *adj* vile

**ignorant, e** [iɲɔʀɑ̃, ɑ̃t] *adj* ignorant

**ignorer** [iɲɔʀe] *vt* not to know; (*personne*) to ignore

**il** [il] *pron* he; (*animal, chose, en tournure impersonnelle*) it; **~s** they; *voir* **avoir**

**île** [il] *nf* island; **l'~ Maurice** Mauritius; **les ~s anglo-normandes** the Channel Islands; **les ~s Britanniques** the British Isles

**illégal, e, -aux** [i(l)legal, o] *adj* illegal

**illégitime** [i(l)leʒitim] *adj* illegitimate

**illettré, e** [i(l)letʀe] *adj, nm/f* illiterate

**illimité, e** [i(l)limite] *adj* unlimited

**illisible** [i(l)lizibl] *adj* illegible; (*roman*) unreadable

**illogique** [i(l)lɔʒik] *adj* illogical

**illumination** [i(l)lyminasjɔ̃] *nf* illumination; (*idée*) flash of inspiration

**illuminer** [i(l)lymine] *vt* to light up; (*monument, rue: pour une fête*) to illuminate; (: *au moyen de projecteurs*) to floodlight

**illusion** [i(l)lyzjɔ̃] *nf* illusion; **se faire des ~s** to delude o.s.; **faire ~** to delude ou fool people; **illusionniste** *nm/f* conjuror

**illustration** [i(l)lystʀasjɔ̃] *nf* illustration

**illustre** [i(l)lystʀ] *adj* illustrious

**illustré, e** [i(l)lystʀe] *adj* illustrated ♦ *nm* comic

**illustrer** [i(l)lystʀe] *vt* to illustrate; **s'~** to become famous, win fame

**îlot** [ilo] *nm* small island, islet

**ils** [il] *pron voir* **il**

**image** [imaʒ] *nf* (*gén*) picture; (*métaphore*) image; **~ de marque** brand image; (*fig*) public image; **imagé, e** *adj* (*texte*) full of imagery; (*langage*) colourful

**imaginaire** [imaʒinɛʀ] adj imaginary

**imagination** [imaʒinasjɔ̃] nf imagination; **avoir de l'~** to be imaginative

**imaginer** [imaʒine] vt to imagine; (inventer: expédient) to devise, think up; **s'~** vt (se figurer: scène etc) to imagine, picture; **s'~ que** to imagine that

**imbattable** [ɛ̃batabl] adj unbeatable

**imbécile** [ɛ̃besil] adj idiotic ♦ nm/f idiot;

**imbécillité** [ɛ̃besilite] nf idiocy; (action) idiotic thing; (film, livre, propos) rubbish

**imbiber** [ɛ̃bibe] vt to soak; **s'~ de** to become saturated with

**imbu, e** [ɛ̃by] adj: **~ de** full of

**imbuvable** [ɛ̃byvabl] adj undrinkable; (personne: fam) unbearable

**imitateur, -trice** [imitatœʀ, tʀis] nm/f (gén) imitator; (MUSIC-HALL) impersonator

**imitation** [imitasjɔ̃] nf imitation; (de personnalité) impersonation

**imiter** [imite] vt to imitate; (contrefaire) to forge; (ressembler à) to look like

**immaculé, e** [imakyle] adj (linge, surface, réputation) spotless; (blancheur) immaculate

**immangeable** [ɛ̃mɑ̃ʒabl] adj inedible

**immatriculation** [imatʀikylasjɔ̃] nf registration

**immatriculer** [imatʀikyle] vt to register; **faire/se faire ~** to register

**immédiat, e** [imedja, jat] adj immediate ♦ nm: **dans l'~** for the time being; **immédiatement** adv immediately

**immense** [i(m)mɑ̃s] adj immense

**immerger** [imɛʀʒe] vt to immerse, submerge

**immeuble** [imœbl] nm building; (à usage d'habitation) block of flats

**immigration** [imigʀasjɔ̃] nf immigration

**immigré, e** [imigʀe] nm/f immigrant

**imminent, e** [iminɑ̃, ɑ̃t] adj imminent

**immiscer** [imise]: **s'~** vi: **s'~ dans** to interfere in ou with

**immobile** [i(m)mɔbil] adj still, motion-less

**immobilier, -ière** [imɔbilje, jɛʀ] adj property cpd ♦ nm: **l'~** the property business

**immobiliser** [imɔbilize] vt (gén) to immobilize; (circulation, véhicule, affaires) to bring to a standstill; **s'~** (personne) to stand still; (machine, véhicule) to come to a halt

**immonde** [i(m)mɔ̃d] adj foul

**immoral, e, -aux** [i(m)mɔʀal, o] adj immoral

**immortel, le** [imɔʀtɛl] adj immortal

**immuable** [imɥabl] adj unchanging

**immunisé, e** [im(m)ynize] adj: **~ contre** immune to

**immunité** [imynite] nf immunity

**impact** [ɛ̃pakt] nm impact

**impair, e** [ɛ̃pɛʀ] adj odd ♦ nm faux pas, blunder

**impardonnable** [ɛ̃paʀdɔnabl] adj unpardonable, unforgiving

**imparfait, e** [ɛ̃paʀfɛ, ɛt] adj imperfect

**impartial, e, -aux** [ɛ̃paʀsjal, jo] adj impartial, unbiased

**impasse** [ɛ̃pas] nf dead end, cul-de-sac; (fig) deadlock

**impassible** [ɛ̃pasibl] adj impassive

**impatience** [ɛ̃pasjɑ̃s] nf impatience

**impatient, e** [ɛ̃pasjɑ̃, jɑ̃t] adj impatient; **impatienter: s'impatienter** vi to get impatient

**impeccable** [ɛ̃pekabl] adj (parfait) perfect; (propre) impeccable; (fam) smashing

**impensable** [ɛ̃pɑ̃sabl] adj (événement hypothétique) unthinkable; (événement qui a eu lieu) unbelievable

**imper** [ɛ̃pɛʀ] (fam) nm raincoat

**impératif, -ive** [ɛ̃peʀatif, iv] adj imperative ♦ nm (LING) imperative; **impératifs** nmpl (exigences: d'une fonction, d'une charge) requirements; (: de la mode) demands

**impératrice** [ɛ̃peʀatʀis] nf empress

**imperceptible** [ɛ̃pɛʀsɛptibl] adj imperceptible

**impérial, e, -aux** [ɛ̃peʀjal, jo] *adj* impérial; **impériale** *nf* top deck

**impérieux, -euse** [ɛ̃peʀjø, jøz] *adj* (*caractère, ton*) imperious; (*obligation, besoin*) pressing, urgent

**impérissable** [ɛ̃peʀisabl] *adj* undying

**imperméable** [ɛ̃peʀmeabl] *adj* waterproof; (*fig*): ~ **à** impervious to ♦ *nm* raincoat

**impertinent, e** [ɛ̃peʀtinɑ̃, ɑ̃t] *adj* impertinent

**imperturbable** [ɛ̃peʀtyʀbabl] *adj* (*personne, caractère*) unperturbable; (*sangfroid, gaieté, sérieux*) unshakeable

**impétueux, -euse** [ɛ̃petɥø, øz] *adj* impetuous

**impitoyable** [ɛ̃pitwajabl] *adj* pitiless, merciless

**implanter** [ɛ̃plɑ̃te]: **s'~** *vi* to be set up

**impliquer** [ɛ̃plike] *vt* to imply; **~ qn (dans)** to implicate sb (in)

**impoli, e** [ɛ̃pɔli] *adj* impolite, rude

**impopulaire** [ɛ̃pɔpylɛʀ] *adj* unpopular

**importance** [ɛ̃pɔʀtɑ̃s] *nf* importance; **sans ~** unimportant

**important, e** [ɛ̃pɔʀtɑ̃, ɑ̃t] *adj* important; (*en quantité: somme, retard*) considerable, sizeable; (: *dégâts*) extensive; (*péj: airs, ton*) self-important ♦ *nm*: **l'~** the important thing

**importateur, -trice** [ɛ̃pɔʀtatœʀ, tʀis] *nm/f* importer

**importation** [ɛ̃pɔʀtasjɔ̃] *nf* importation; (*produit*) import

**importer** [ɛ̃pɔʀte] *vt* (*COMM*) to import; (*maladies, plantes*) to introduce ♦ *vi* (*être important*) to matter; **il importe qu'il fasse** it is important that he should do; **peu m'importe** (*je n'ai pas de préférence*) I don't mind; (*je m'en moque*) I don't care; **peu importe (que)** it doesn't matter (if); *voir aussi* **n'importe**

**importun, e** [ɛ̃pɔʀtœ̃, yn] *adj* irksome, importunate; (*arrivée, visite*) inopportune, ill-timed ♦ *nm* intruder; **importuner** *vt* to bother

**imposable** [ɛ̃pozabl] *adj* taxable

**imposant, e** [ɛ̃pozɑ̃, ɑ̃t] *adj* imposing

**imposer** [ɛ̃poze] *vt* (*taxer*) to tax; **s'~** (*être nécessaire*) to be imperative; **~ qch à qn** to impose sth on sb; **en ~ à** to impress; **s'~ comme** to emerge as; **s'~ par** to win recognition through

**impossibilité** [ɛ̃posibilite] *nf* impossibility; **être dans l'~ de faire qch** to be unable to do sth

**impossible** [ɛ̃posibl] *adj* impossible; **il m'est ~ de le faire** it is impossible for me to do it, I can't possibly do it; **faire l'~** to do one's utmost

**imposteur** [ɛ̃pɔstœʀ] *nm* impostor

**impôt** [ɛ̃po] *nm* tax; **~s** *nmpl* (*contributions*) (income) tax *sg*; **payer 1000 F d'~s** to pay 1,000F in tax; **~ foncier** land tax; **~ sur le chiffre d'affaires** corporation (BRIT) *ou* corporate (US) tax; **~ sur le revenu** income tax

**impotent, e** [ɛ̃pɔtɑ̃, ɑ̃t] *adj* disabled

**impraticable** [ɛ̃pʀatikabl] *adj* (*projet*) impracticable, unworkable; (*piste*) impassable

**imprécis, e** [ɛ̃pʀesi, iz] *adj* imprecise

**imprégner** [ɛ̃pʀeɲe] *vt* (*tissu*) to impregnate; (*lieu, air*) to fill; **s'~ de** (*fig*) to absorb

**imprenable** [ɛ̃pʀənabl] *adj* (*forteresse*) impregnable; **vue ~** unimpeded outlook

**imprésario** [ɛ̃pʀesaʀjo] *nm* manager

**impression** [ɛ̃pʀesjɔ̃] *nf* impression; (*d'un ouvrage, tissu*) printing; **faire bonne ~** to make a good impression; **impressionnant, e** *adj* (*imposant*) impressive; (*bouleversant*) upsetting; **impressionner** *vt* (*frapper*) to impress; (*bouleverser*) to upset

**imprévisible** [ɛ̃pʀevizibl] *adj* unforeseeable

**imprévoyant, e** [ɛ̃pʀevwajɑ̃, ɑ̃t] *adj* lacking in foresight; (*en matière d'argent*) improvident

**imprévu, e** [ɛ̃pʀevy] *adj* unforeseen, unexpected ♦ *nm* (*incident*) unexpected

incident; **des vacances pleines d'~**
holidays full of surprises; **en cas d'~** if
anything unexpected happens; **sauf ~**
unless anything unexpected crops up
**imprimante** [ɛ̃pʀimɑ̃t] *nf* printer
**imprimé** [ɛ̃pʀime] *nm* (*formulaire*)
printed form; (*POSTES*) printed matter *no*
*pl*; (*tissu*) printed fabric; **~ à fleur** floral
print
**imprimer** [ɛ̃pʀime] *vt* to print; (*publier*)
to publish; **imprimerie** *nf* printing;
(*établissement*) printing works *sg*; **imprimeur** *nm* printer
**impromptu, e** [ɛ̃pʀɔ̃pty] *adj* (*repas,
discours*) impromptu; (*départ*) sudden;
(*visite*) surprise
**impropre** [ɛ̃pʀɔpʀ] *adj* inappropriate; **~**
**à** unfit for
**improviser** [ɛ̃pʀɔvize] *vt, vi* to improvise
**improviste** [ɛ̃pʀɔvist]: **à l'~** *adv* unex-
pectedly, without warning
**imprudence** [ɛ̃pʀydɑ̃s] *nf* (*d'une personne, d'une action*) carelessness *no pl*;
(*d'une remarque*) imprudence *no pl*;
**commettre une ~** to do something
foolish
**imprudent, e** [ɛ̃pʀydɑ̃, ɑ̃t] *adj* (*conducteur, geste, action*) careless; (*remarque*) unwise, imprudent; (*projet*) fool-
hardy
**impudent, e** [ɛ̃pydɑ̃, ɑ̃t] *adj* impudent
**impudique** [ɛ̃pydik] *adj* shameless
**impuissant, e** [ɛ̃pɥisɑ̃, ɑ̃t] *adj* help-
less; (*sans effet*) ineffectual; (*sexuellement*) impotent
**impulsif, -ive** [ɛ̃pylsif, iv] *adj* impulsive
**impulsion** [ɛ̃pylsjɔ̃] *nf* (*ÉLEC, instinct*)
impulse; (*élan, influence*) impetus
**impunément** [ɛ̃pynemɑ̃] *adv* with im-
punity
**inabordable** [inabɔʀdabl] *adj* (*cher*)
prohibitive
**inacceptable** [inaksɛptabl] *adj* unacceptable
**inaccessible** [inaksesibl] *adj* inacces-

sible
**inachevé, e** [inaʃ(ə)ve] *adj* unfinished
**inactif, -ive** [inaktif, iv] *adj* inactive;
(*remède*) ineffective; (*BOURSE: marché*)
slack ♦ *nm:* **les ~s** the non-working
population
**inadapté, e** [inadapte] *adj* (*gén*): **~** not adapted to, unsuited to; (*PSYCH*)
maladjusted
**inadéquat, e** [inadekwa(t), kwat] *adj*
inadequate
**inadmissible** [inadmisibl] *adj* inadmissible
**inadvertance** [inadvɛʀtɑ̃s]: **par ~** *adv*
inadvertently
**inaltérable** [inalteʀabl] *adj* (*matière*)
stable; (*fig*) unfailing; **~ à** unaffected
by
**inanimé, e** [inanime] *adj* (*matière*) inanimate; (*évanoui*) unconscious; (*sans
vie*) lifeless
**inanition** [inanisjɔ̃] *nf*: **tomber d'~** to
faint with hunger (and exhaustion)
**inaperçu, e** [inapɛʀsy] *adj*: **passer ~**
to go unnoticed
**inapte** [inapt] *adj*: **~ à** incapable of;
(*MIL*) unfit for
**inattaquable** [inatakabl] *adj* (*texte,
preuve*) irrefutable
**inattendu, e** [inatɑ̃dy] *adj* unexpected
**inattentif, -ive** [inatɑ̃tif, iv] *adj* inat-
tentive; **~ à** (*dangers, détails*) heedless
of; **inattention** *nf*: **faute d'inattention** careless mistake
**inauguration** [inogyʀasjɔ̃] *nf* inauguration
**inaugurer** [inogyʀe] *vt* (*monument*) to
unveil; (*exposition, usine*) to open; (*fig*)
to inaugurate
**inavouable** [inavwabl] *adj* shameful;
(*bénéfices*) undisclosable
**incalculable** [ɛ̃kalkylabl] *adj* incalculable
**incandescence** [ɛ̃kɑ̃desɑ̃s] *nf*: **porter
à ~** to heat white-hot
**incapable** [ɛ̃kapabl] *adj* incapable; **~
de faire** incapable of doing; (*empêché*)

unable to do

**incapacité** [ɛ̃kapasite] *nf* (*incompétence*) incapability; (*impossibilité*) incapacity; **dans l'~ de faire** unable to do

**incarcérer** [ɛ̃karsere] *vt* to incarcerate, imprison

**incarné, e** [ɛ̃karne] *adj* (*ongle*) ingrown

**incarner** [ɛ̃karne] *vt* to embody, personify; (*THÉÂTRE*) to play

**incassable** [ɛ̃kasabl] *adj* unbreakable

**incendiaire** [ɛ̃sɑ̃djɛr] *adj* incendiary; (*fig: discours*) inflammatory

**incendie** [ɛ̃sɑ̃di] *nm* fire; **~ criminel** arson *no pl*; **~ de forêt** forest fire; **incendier** *vt* (*mettre le feu à*) to set fire to, set alight; (*brûler complètement*) to burn down; **se faire incendier** (*fam*) to get a rocket

**incertain, e** [ɛ̃sɛrtɛ̃, ɛn] *adj* uncertain; (*temps*) unsettled; (*imprécis: contours*) indistinct, blurred; **incertitude** *nf* uncertainty

**incessamment** [ɛ̃sesamɑ̃] *adv* very shortly

**incident** [ɛ̃sidɑ̃, ɑ̃t] *nm* incident; **~ de parcours** minor hitch *ou* setback; **~ technique** technical difficulties *pl*

**incinérer** [ɛ̃sinere] *vt* (*ordures*) to incinerate; (*mort*) to cremate

**incisive** [ɛ̃siziv] *nf* incisor

**inciter** [ɛ̃site] *vt*: **~ qn à (faire) qch** to encourage sb to do sth; (*à la révolte etc*) to incite sb to do sth

**inclinable** [ɛ̃klinabl] *adj*: **siège à dossier ~** reclining seat

**inclinaison** [ɛ̃klinɛzɔ̃] *nf* (*déclivité: d'une route etc*) incline; (: *d'un toit*) slope; (*état penché*) tilt

**inclination** [ɛ̃klinasjɔ̃] *nf* (*penchant*) inclination; **~ de (la) tête** nod (of the head); **~ de buste** bow

**incliner** [ɛ̃kline] *vt* (*pencher*) to tilt ♦ *vi*: **~ à qch/à faire** to incline towards sth/doing; **s'~** (*devant*) to bow down; (*céder*) to give in *ou* yield (to); **~ la tête** to give a slight bow

**inclure** [ɛ̃klyr] *vt* to include; (*joindre à un envoi*) to enclose; **jusqu'au 10 mars inclus** until 10th March inclusive

**incognito** [ɛ̃kɔɲito] *adv* incognito ♦ *nm*: **garder l'~** to remain incognito

**incohérent, e** [ɛ̃kɔerɑ̃, ɑ̃t] *adj* (*comportement*) inconsistent; (*geste, langage, texte*) incoherent

**incollable** [ɛ̃kɔlabl] *adj* (*riz*) non-stick; **il est ~** (*fam*) he's got all the answers

**incolore** [ɛ̃kɔlɔr] *adj* colourless

**incommoder** [ɛ̃kɔmɔde] *vt* (*chaleur, odeur*): **~ qn** to bother sb

**incomparable** [ɛ̃kɔ̃parabl] *adj* incomparable

**incompatible** [ɛ̃kɔ̃patibl] *adj* incompatible

**incompétent, e** [ɛ̃kɔ̃petɑ̃, ɑ̃t] *adj* incompetent

**incomplet, -ète** [ɛ̃kɔ̃plɛ, ɛt] *adj* incomplete

**incompréhensible** [ɛ̃kɔ̃preɑ̃sibl] *adj* incomprehensible

**incompris, e** [ɛ̃kɔ̃pri, iz] *adj* misunderstood

**inconcevable** [ɛ̃kɔ̃s(ə)vabl] *adj* inconceivable

**inconciliable** [ɛ̃kɔ̃siljabl] *adj* irreconcilable

**inconditionnel, le** [ɛ̃kɔ̃disjɔnɛl] *adj* unconditional; (*partisan*) unquestioning ♦ *nm/f* (*d'un homme politique*) ardent supporter; (*d'un écrivain, d'un chanteur*) ardent admirer; (*d'une activité*) fanatic

**inconfort** [ɛ̃kɔ̃fɔr] *nm* discomfort; **inconfortable** *adj* uncomfortable

**incongru, e** [ɛ̃kɔ̃gry] *adj* unseemly

**inconnu, e** [ɛ̃kɔny] *adj* unknown ♦ *nm/f* stranger ♦ *nm*: **l'~** the unknown; **inconnue** *nf* unknown factor

**inconsciemment** [ɛ̃kɔ̃sjamɑ̃] *adv* unconsciously

**inconscient, e** [ɛ̃kɔ̃sjɑ̃, jɑ̃t] *adj* unconscious; (*irréfléchi*) thoughtless, reckless; (*sentiment*) subconscious ♦ *nm*: **l'~** the unconscious; **~ de** unaware of

**inconsidéré, e** [ɛ̃kɔ̃sidere] *adj* ill-considered

**inconsistant, e** [ɛ̃kɔ̃sistɑ̃, ɑ̃t] *adj* (fig) flimsy, weak

**inconsolable** [ɛ̃kɔ̃sɔlabl] *adj* inconsolable

**incontestable** [ɛ̃kɔ̃testabl] *adj* indisputable

**incontinent, e** [ɛ̃kɔ̃tinɑ̃, ɑ̃t] *adj* incontinent

**incontournable** [ɛ̃kɔ̃turnabl] *adj* unavoidable

**incontrôlable** [ɛ̃kɔ̃trolabl] *adj* unverifiable; (*irrépressible*) uncontrollable

**inconvenant, e** [ɛ̃kɔ̃v(ə)nɑ̃, ɑ̃t] *adj* unseemly, improper

**inconvénient** [ɛ̃kɔ̃venjɑ̃] *nm* disadvantage, drawback; **si vous n'y voyez pas d'~** if you have no objections

**incorporer** [ɛ̃kɔrpɔre] *vt*: **~ (à)** to mix in (with); **~ (dans)** (*paragraphe etc*) to incorporate (in); (MIL: *appeler*) to recruit (into); **il a très bien su s'~ à notre groupe** he was very easily incorporated into our group

**incorrect, e** [ɛ̃kɔrekt] *adj* (*impropre, inconvenant*) improper; (*défectueux*) faulty; (*inexact*) incorrect; (*impoli*) impolite; (*déloyal*) underhand

**incorrigible** [ɛ̃kɔriʒibl] *adj* incorrigible

**incrédule** [ɛ̃kredyl] *adj* incredulous; (REL) unbelieving

**increvable** [ɛ̃krəvabl] (*fam*) *adj* tireless

**incriminer** [ɛ̃krimine] *vt* (*personne*) to incriminate; (*action, conduite*) to bring under attack; (*bonne foi, honnêteté*) to call into question

**incroyable** [ɛ̃krwajabl] *adj* incredible

**incruster** [ɛ̃kryste] *vt* (ART) to inlay; **s'~** *vi* (*invité*) to take root

**inculpé, e** [ɛ̃kylpe] *nm/f* accused

**inculper** [ɛ̃kylpe] *vt*: **~ (de)** to charge (with)

**inculquer** [ɛ̃kylke] *vt*: **~ qch à** to inculcate sth in *ou* instil into

**inculte** [ɛ̃kylt] *adj* uncultivated; (*esprit, peuple*) uncultured

**Inde** [ɛ̃d] *nf*: **l'~** India

**indécent, e** [ɛ̃desɑ̃, ɑ̃t] *adj* indecent

**indéchiffrable** [ɛ̃deʃifrabl] *adj* indecipherable

**indécis, e** [ɛ̃desi, iz] *adj* (*par nature*) indecisive; (*temporairement*) undecided

**indéfendable** [ɛ̃defɑ̃dabl] *adj* indefensible

**indéfini, e** [ɛ̃defini] *adj* (*imprécis, incertain*) undefined; (*illimité*, LING) indefinite; **indéfiniment** *adv* indefinitely; **indéfinissable** *adj* indefinable

**indélébile** [ɛ̃delebil] *adj* indelible

**indélicat, e** [ɛ̃delika, at] *adj* tactless

**indemne** [ɛ̃demn] *adj* unharmed; **indemniser** *vt*: **indemniser qn (de)** to compensate sb (for)

**indemnité** [ɛ̃demnite] *nf* (*dédommagement*) compensation *no pl*; (*allocation*) allowance; **indemnité de licenciement** redundancy payment

**indépendamment** [ɛ̃depɑ̃damɑ̃] *adv* independently; **~ de** (*abstraction faite de*) irrespective of; (*en plus de*) over and above

**indépendance** [ɛ̃depɑ̃dɑ̃s] *nf* independence

**indépendant, e** [ɛ̃depɑ̃dɑ̃, ɑ̃t] *adj* independent; **~ de** independent of

**indescriptible** [ɛ̃dɛskriptibl] *adj* indescribable

**indésirable** [ɛ̃dezirabl] *adj* undesirable

**indestructible** [ɛ̃dɛstryktibl] *adj* indestructible

**indétermination** [ɛ̃detɛrminasjɔ̃] *nf* (*irrésolution: chronique*) indecision; (: *temporaire*) indecisiveness

**indéterminé, e** [ɛ̃detɛrmine] *adj* (*date, cause, nature*) unspecified; (*forme, longueur, quantité*) indeterminate

**index** [ɛ̃dɛks] *nm* (*doigt*) index finger; (*d'un livre etc*) index; **mettre à l'~** to blacklist; **indexé, e** *adj* (ÉCON): **indexé (sur)** index-linked (to)

**indic** [ɛ̃dik] (*fam*) *nm* (POLICE) grass

**indicateur** [ɛ̃dikatœr] *nm* (POLICE) informer; (TECH) gauge, indicator

**indicatif, -ive** [ɛ̃dikatif, iv] *adj*: **à titre**

~ for (your) information ♦ *nm* (*LING*) indicative; (*RADIO*) interval tune ou signature tune; (*TÉL*) dialling code

**indication** [ɛ̃dikasjɔ̃] *nf* indication; (*renseignement*) information *no pl*; ~s *nfpl* (*directives*) instructions

**indice** [ɛ̃dis] *nm* (*marque, signe*) indication, sign; (*POLICE: lors d'une enquête*) clue; (*JUR: présomption*) piece of evidence; (*SCIENCE, ÉCON, TECH*) index

**indicible** [ɛ̃disibl] *adj* inexpressible

**indien, ne** [ɛ̃djɛ̃, jɛn] *adj* Indian ♦ *nm/f*: **I~, ne** Indian

**indifféremment** [ɛ̃diferamɑ̃] *adv* (*sans distinction*) equally (well)

**indifférence** [ɛ̃diferɑ̃s] *nf* indifference

**indifférent, e** [ɛ̃diferɑ̃, ɑ̃t] *adj* (*peu intéressé*) indifferent; **ça m'est** ~ it doesn't matter to me; **elle m'est** ~**e** I am indifferent to her

**indigence** [ɛ̃diʒɑ̃s] *nf* poverty

**indigène** [ɛ̃diʒɛn] *adj* native, indigenous; (*des gens du pays*) local ♦ *nm/f* native

**indigeste** [ɛ̃diʒɛst] *adj* indigestible

**indigestion** [ɛ̃diʒɛstjɔ̃] *nf* indigestion *no pl*

**indigne** [ɛ̃diɲ] *adj* unworthy

**indigner** [ɛ̃diɲe] *vt*: **s'~ (de** ou **contre)** to get indignant (at)

**indiqué, e** [ɛ̃dike] *adj* (*date, lieu*) agreed; (*traitement*) appropriate; (*conseillé*) advisable

**indiquer** [ɛ̃dike] *vt* (*suj: pendule, aiguille*) to show; (: *étiquette, panneau*) to show, indicate; (*renseigner sur*) to point out, tell; (*déterminer: date, lieu*) to give, state; (*signaler, dénoter*) to indicate, point to; ~ **qch/qn à qn** (*montrer du doigt*) to point sth/sb out to sb; (*faire connaître: médecin, restaurant*) to tell sb of sth/sb

**indirect, e** [ɛ̃dirɛkt] *adj* indirect

**indiscipliné, e** [ɛ̃disipline] *adj* undisciplined

**indiscret, -ète** [ɛ̃diskrɛ, ɛt] *adj* indiscreet

**indiscutable** [ɛ̃diskytabl] *adj* indisputable

**indispensable** [ɛ̃dispɑ̃sabl] *adj* indispensable, essential

**indisposé, e** [ɛ̃dispoze] *adj* indisposed

**indisposer** [ɛ̃dispoze] *vt* (*incommoder*) to upset; (*déplaire à*) to antagonize; (*énerver*) to irritate

**indistinct, e** [ɛ̃distɛ̃(kt), ɛ̃kt] *adj* indistinct; **indistinctement** *adv* (*voir, prononcer*) indistinctly; (*sans distinction*) indiscriminately

**individu** [ɛ̃dividy] *nm* individual; **individuel, le** *adj* (*gén*) individual; (*responsabilité, propriété, liberté*) personal; **chambre individuelle** single room; **maison individuelle** detached house

**indolore** [ɛ̃dɔlɔr] *adj* painless

**indomptable** [ɛ̃dɔ̃(p)tabl] *adj* untameable; (*fig*) invincible

**Indonésie** [ɛ̃dɔnezi] *nf* Indonesia

**indu, e** [ɛ̃dy] *adj*: **à une heure ~e** at some ungodly hour

**induire** [ɛ̃dɥir] *vt*: ~ **qn en erreur** to lead sb astray, mislead sb

**indulgent, e** [ɛ̃dylʒɑ̃, ɑ̃t] *adj* (*parent, regard*) indulgent; (*juge, examinateur*) lenient

**industrialisé, e** [ɛ̃dystrijalize] *adj* industrialized

**industrie** [ɛ̃dystri] *nf* industry; **industriel, le** *adj* industrial ♦ *nm* industrialist

**inébranlable** [inebrɑ̃labl] *adj* (*masse, colonne*) solid; (*personne, certitude, foi*) unshakeable

**inédit, e** [inedi, it] *adj* (*correspondance, livre*) hitherto unpublished; (*spectacle, moyen*) novel, original; (*film*) unreleased

**ineffaçable** [inefasabl] *adj* indelible

**inefficace** [inefikas] *adj* (*remède, moyen*) ineffective; (*machine, employé*) inefficient

**inégal, e, -aux** [inegal, o] *adj* unequal; (*irrégulier*) uneven; **inégalable** *adj* matchless; **inégalé, e** *adj* (*record*) unequalled; (*beauté*) unrivalled; **inégalité** *nf* inequality

**inépuisable** [inepɥizabl] *adj* inexhaustible

**inerte** [inɛʀt] *adj* (*immobile*) lifeless; (*sans réaction*) passive

**inespéré, e** [inɛspeʀe] *adj* unexpected, unhoped-for

**inestimable** [inɛstimabl] *adj* priceless; (*fig: bienfait*) invaluable

**inévitable** [inevitabl] *adj* unavoidable; (*fatal, habituel*) inevitable

**inexact, e** [inɛgza(kt), akt] *adj* inaccurate

**inexcusable** [inɛkskyzabl] *adj* unforgivable

**inexplicable** [inɛksplikabl] *adj* inexplicable

**in extremis** [inɛkstʀemis] *adv* at the last minute ♦ *adj* last-minute

**infaillible** [ɛ̃fajibl] *adj* infallible

**infâme** [ɛ̃fam] *adj* vile

**infarctus** [ɛ̃faʀktys] *nm*: ~ (du myocarde) coronary (thrombosis)

**infatigable** [ɛ̃fatigabl] *adj* tireless

**infect, e** [ɛ̃fɛkt] *adj* revolting; (*personne*) obnoxious; (*temps*) foul

**infecter** [ɛ̃fɛkte] *vt* (*atmosphère, eau*) to contaminate; (*MÉD*) to infect; **s'~** to become infected *ou* septic; **infection** *nf* infection; (*puanteur*) stench

**inférieur, e** [ɛ̃feʀjœʀ] *adj* lower; (*en qualité, intelligence*) inferior; **~ à** (*somme, quantité*) less *ou* smaller than; (*moins bon que*) inferior to

**infernal, e, -aux** [ɛ̃fɛʀnal, o] *adj* (*insupportable: chaleur, rythme*) infernal; (*: enfant*) horrid; (*satanique, effrayant*) diabolical

**infidèle** [ɛ̃fidɛl] *adj* unfaithful

**infiltrer** [ɛ̃filtʀe] *vb*: **s'~ dans** to get into; (*liquide*) to seep through; (*fig: groupe, ennemi*) to infiltrate

**infime** [ɛ̃fim] *adj* minute, tiny

**infini, e** [ɛ̃fini] *adj* infinite ♦ *nm* infinity; **à l'~** endlessly; **infiniment** *adv* infinitely; **infinité** *nf*: **une infinité de** an infinite number of

**infinitif** [ɛ̃finitif, iv] *nm* infinitive

**infirme** [ɛ̃fiʀm] *adj* disabled ♦ *nm/f* disabled person

**infirmerie** [ɛ̃fiʀməʀi] *nf* medical room

**infirmier, -ière** [ɛ̃fiʀmje] *nm/f* nurse; **infirmière chef** sister

**infirmité** [ɛ̃fiʀmite] *nf* disability

**inflammable** [ɛ̃flamabl] *adj* (in)flammable

**inflation** [ɛ̃flasjɔ̃] *nf* inflation

**infliger** [ɛ̃fliʒe] *vt*: **~ qch (à qn)** to inflict sth (on sb); (*amende, sanction*) to impose sth (on sb)

**influençable** [ɛ̃flyɑ̃sabl] *adj* easily influenced

**influence** [ɛ̃flyɑ̃s] *nf* influence; **influencer** *vt* to influence; **influent, e** *adj* influential

**informateur, -trice** [ɛ̃fɔʀmatœʀ, tʀis] *nm/f* (*POLICE*) informer

**informaticien, ne** [ɛ̃fɔʀmatisjɛ̃, jɛn] *nm/f* computer scientist

**information** [ɛ̃fɔʀmasjɔ̃] *nf* (*renseignement*) piece of information; (*PRESSE, TV: nouvelle*) item of news; (*diffusion de renseignements , INFORM*) information; (*JUR*) inquiry, investigation; **~s** *nfpl* (*TV*) news *sg*

**informatique** [ɛ̃fɔʀmatik] *nf* (*technique*) data processing; (*science*) computer science ♦ *adj* computer *cpd*; **informatiser** *vt* to computerize

**informe** [ɛ̃fɔʀm] *adj* shapeless

**informer** [ɛ̃fɔʀme] *vt*: **~ qn (de)** to inform sb (of); **s'~ (de)** to inquire *ou* find out (about/whether *ou* if)

**infos** [ɛ̃fo] *nfpl*: **les ~** the news *sg*

**infraction** [ɛ̃fʀaksjɔ̃] *nf* offence; **~ à** violation *ou* breach of; **être en ~** to be in breach of the law

**infranchissable** [ɛ̃fʀɑ̃ʃisabl] *adj* impassable; (*fig*) insuperable

**infrarouge** [ɛ̃fʀaʀuʒ] *adj* infrared

**infrastructure** [ɛ̃fʀastʀyktyʀ] *nf* (*AVIAT, MIL*) ground installations *pl*; (*ÉCON: touristique etc*) infrastructure

**infuser** [ɛ̃fyze] *vt, vi* (*thé*) to brew; (*tisane*) to infuse; **infusion** *nf* (*tisane*) herb tea

**ingénier** [ɛ̃ʒenje]: **s'~** vi: **s'~ à faire to** strive to do

**ingénierie** [ɛ̃ʒeniʀi] nf engineering; **~ génétique** genetic engineering

**ingénieur** [ɛ̃ʒenjœʀ] nm engineer; **ingénieur du son** sound engineer

**ingénieux, -euse** [ɛ̃ʒenjø, jøz] adj ingenious, clever

**ingénu, e** [ɛ̃ʒeny] adj ingenuous, artless

**ingérer** [ɛ̃ʒeʀe] vb: **s'~ dans** to interfere in

**ingrat, e** [ɛ̃gʀa, at] adj (personne) ungrateful; (travail, sujet) thankless; (visage) unprepossessing

**ingrédient** [ɛ̃gʀedjɑ̃] nm ingredient

**ingurgiter** [ɛ̃gyʀʒite] vt to swallow

**inhabitable** [inabitabl] adj uninhabitable

**inhabité, e** [inabite] adj uninhabited

**inhabituel, le** [inabituɛl] adj unusual

**inhibition** [inibisjɔ̃] nf inhibition

**inhumain, e** [inymɛ̃, ɛn] adj inhuman

**inhumation** [inymasjɔ̃] nf burial

**inhumer** [inyme] vt to inter, bury

**inimaginable** [inimaʒinabl] adj unimaginable

**ininterrompu, e** [inɛ̃teʀɔ̃py] adj (file, série) unbroken; (flot, vacarme) uninterrupted, non-stop; (effort) unremitting, continuous; (suite, ligne) unbroken

**initial, e, -aux** [inisjal, jo] adj initial; **initiale** nf initial; **initialiser** vt to initialize

**initiation** [inisjasjɔ̃] nf: **~ à** introduction to

**initiative** [inisjativ] nf initiative

**initier** [inisje] vt: **~ qn à** to initiate sb into; (faire découvrir: art, jeu) to introduce sb to

**injecté, e** [ɛ̃ʒɛkte] adj: **yeux ~s de sang** bloodshot eyes

**injecter** [ɛ̃ʒɛkte] vt to inject; **injection** nf injection; **à injection** (AUTO) fuel injection cpd

**injure** [ɛ̃ʒyʀ] nf insult, abuse no pl; **inju-**

**rier** vt to insult, abuse; **injurieux, -euse** adj abusive, insulting

**injuste** [ɛ̃ʒyst] adj unjust, unfair; **injustice** nf injustice

**inlassable** [ɛ̃lasabl] adj tireless

**inné, e** [i(n)ne] adj innate, inborn

**innocent, e** [inɔsɑ̃, ɑ̃t] adj innocent; **innocenter** vt to clear, prove innocent

**innombrable** [i(n)nɔ̃bʀabl] adj innumerable

**innommable** [i(n)nɔmabl] adj unspeakable

**innover** [inɔve] vi to break new ground

**inoccupé, e** [inɔkype] adj unoccupied

**inodore** [inɔdɔʀ] adj (gaz) odourless; (fleur) scentless

**inoffensif, -ive** [inɔfɑ̃sif, iv] adj harmless, innocuous

**inondation** [inɔ̃dasjɔ̃] nf flood

**inonder** [inɔ̃de] vt to flood; **~ de** to flood with

**inopiné, e** [inɔpine] adj unexpected; (mort) sudden

**inopportun, e** [inɔpɔʀtœ̃, yn] adj illtimed, untimely

**inoubliable** [inubliabl] adj unforgettable

**inouï, e** [inwi] adj unheard-of, extraordinary

**inox** [inɔks] nm stainless steel

**inqualifiable** [ɛ̃kalifjabl] adj unspeakable

**inquiet, -ète** [ɛ̃kjɛ, ɛkjɛt] adj anxious; **inquiétant, e** adj worrying, disturbing; **inquiéter** vt to worry; **s'inquiéter** to worry; **s'inquiéter de** to worry about; (s'enquérir de) to inquire about; **inquiétude** nf anxiety

**insaisissable** [ɛ̃sezisabl] adj (fugitif, ennemi) elusive; (différence, nuance) imperceptible

**insalubre** [ɛ̃salybʀ] adj insalubrious

**insatisfaisant, e** [ɛ̃satisfazɑ̃, ɑ̃t] adj unsatisfactory

**insatisfait, e** [ɛ̃satisfɛ, ɛt] adj (non comblé) unsatisfied; (mécontent) dissatisfied

**inscription** [ɛ̃skripsjɔ̃] *nf* inscription; (*immatriculation*) enrolment

**inscrire** [ɛ̃skrir] *vt* (*marquer: sur son calepin etc*) to note *ou* write down; (: *sur un mur, une affiche etc*) to write; (: *dans la pierre, le métal*) to inscribe; (*mettre: sur une liste, un budget etc*) to put down; **s'~** (*pour une excursion etc*) to put one's name down; **s'~ (à)** (*club, parti*) to join; (*université*) to register *ou* enrol (*examen, concours*) to register (for); **~ qn à** (*club, parti*) to enrol sb at

**insecte** [ɛ̃sɛkt] *nm* insect; **insecticide** *nm* insecticide

**insensé, e** [ɛ̃sɑ̃se] *adj* mad

**insensibiliser** [ɛ̃sɑ̃sibilize] *vt* to anaesthetize

**insensible** [ɛ̃sɑ̃sibl] *adj* (*nerf, membre*) numb; (*dur, indifférent*) insensitive

**inséparable** [ɛ̃separabl] *adj* inseparable ♦ *nm*: **~s** (*oiseaux*) lovebirds

**insigne** [ɛ̃siɲ] *nm* (*d'un parti, club*) badge; (*d'une fonction*) insignia ♦ *adj* distinguished

**insignifiant, e** [ɛ̃siɲifjɑ̃, jɑ̃t] *adj* insignificant, trivial

**insinuer** [ɛ̃sinɥe] *vt* to insinuate; **s'~ dans** (*fig*) to worm one's way into

**insipide** [ɛ̃sipid] *adj* insipid

**insister** [ɛ̃siste] *vi* to insist; (*continuer à sonner*) to keep on trying; **~ sur** (*détail, sujet*) to lay stress on

**insolation** [ɛ̃sɔlasjɔ̃] *nf* (*MÉD*) sunstroke *no pl*

**insolent, e** [ɛ̃sɔlɑ̃, ɑ̃t] *adj* insolent

**insolite** [ɛ̃sɔlit] *adj* strange, unusual

**insomnie** [ɛ̃sɔmni] *nf* insomnia *no pl*

**insonoriser** [ɛ̃sɔnɔrize] *vt* to soundproof

**insouciant, e** [ɛ̃susjɑ̃, jɑ̃t] *adj* carefree; **~ du danger** heedless of *ou* careless of danger

**insoumis, e** [ɛ̃sumi, iz] *adj* (*caractère, enfant*) rebellious, refractory; (*contrée, tribu*) unsubdued

**insoupçonnable** [ɛ̃supsɔnabl] *adj* un-

suspected; (*personne*) above suspicion

**insoupçonné, e** [ɛ̃supsɔne] *adj* unsuspected

**insoutenable** [ɛ̃sut(ə)nabl] *adj* (*argument*) untenable; (*chaleur*) unbearable

**inspecter** [ɛ̃spɛkte] *vt* to inspect; **inspecteur, -trice** *nm/f* inspector; **inspecteur d'Académie** (regional) director of education; **inspecteur des finances** ≈ tax inspector (*BRIT*), ≈ Internal Revenue Service agent (*US*); **inspection** *nf* inspection

**inspirer** [ɛ̃spire] *vt* (*gén*) to inspire ♦ *vi* (*aspirer*) to breathe in; **s'~ de** (*suj: artiste*) to draw one's inspiration from

**instable** [ɛ̃stabl] *adj* unstable; (*meuble, équilibre*) unsteady; (*temps*) unsettled

**installation** [ɛ̃stalasjɔ̃] *nf* installation; **~s** *nfpl* facilities

**installer** [ɛ̃stale] *vt* (*loger, placer*) to put; (*meuble, gaz, électricité*) to put in; (*rideau, étagère, tente*) to put up; (*appartement*) to fit out; **s'~** (*s'établir: artisan, dentiste etc*) to set o.s. up; (*se loger*) to settle; (*emménager*) to settle in; (*sur un siège, à un emplacement*) to settle (down); (*fig: maladie, grève*) to take a firm hold

**instance** [ɛ̃stɑ̃s] *nf* (*ADMIN: autorité*) authority; **affaire en ~** matter pending; **être en ~ de divorce** to be awaiting a divorce

**instant** [ɛ̃stɑ̃] *nm* moment, instant; **dans un ~** in a moment; **à l'~** this instant; **pour l'~** for the moment, for the time being

**instantané, e** [ɛ̃stɑ̃tane] *adj* (*lait, café*) instant; (*explosion, mort*) instantaneous ♦ *nm* snapshot

**instar** [ɛ̃star] : **à l'~ de** *prép* following the example of, like

**instaurer** [ɛ̃store] *vt* to institute; (*couvre-feu*) to impose

**instinct** [ɛ̃stɛ̃] *nm* instinct; **instinctivement** *adv* instinctively

**instit** [ɛ̃stit] (*fam*) *nm/f* (primary school) teacher

**instituer** [ɛ̃stitɥe] vt to establish

**institut** [ɛ̃stity] nm institute; **~ de beauté** beauty salon; **Institut universitaire de technologie** ≈ polytechnic

**instituteur, -trice** [ɛ̃stitytœʀ, tʀis] nm/f (primary school) teacher

**institution** [ɛ̃stitysjɔ̃] nf institution; (collège) private school

**instructif, -ive** [ɛ̃stʀyktif, iv] adj instructive

**instruction** [ɛ̃stʀyksjɔ̃] nf (enseignement, savoir) education; (JUR) (preliminary) investigation and enquiry; **~s** nfpl (ordres, mode d'emploi) instructions; **~ civique** civics sg

**instruire** [ɛ̃stʀɥiʀ] vt (élèves) to teach; (recrues) to train; (JUR: affaire) to conduct the investigation for; **s'~** to educate o.s.; **instruit, e** adj educated

**instrument** [ɛ̃stʀymã] nm instrument; **~ à cordes/vent** stringed/wind instrument; **~ de mesure** measuring instrument; **~ de musique** musical instrument; **~ de travail** (working) tool

**insu** [ɛ̃sy] nm: **à l'~ de** without sb knowing (it)

**insubmersible** [ɛ̃sybmɛʀsibl] adj unsinkable

**insuffisant, e** [ɛ̃syfizã, ãt] adj (en quantité) insufficient; (en qualité) inadequate; (sur une copie) poor

**insulaire** [ɛ̃sylɛʀ] adj island cpd; (attitude) insular

**insuline** [ɛ̃sylin] nf insulin

**insulte** [ɛ̃sylt] nf insult; **insulter** vt to insult

**insupportable** [ɛ̃sypɔʀtabl] adj unbearable

**insurger** [ɛ̃syʀʒe] vb: **s'~ (contre)** to rise up ou rebel (against)

**insurmontable** [ɛ̃syʀmɔ̃tabl] adj (difficulté) insuperable; (aversion) unconquerable

**insurrection** [ɛ̃syʀɛksjɔ̃] nf insurrection

**intact, e** [ɛ̃takt] adj intact

**intangible** [ɛ̃tãʒibl] adj intangible; (principe) inviolable

**intarissable** [ɛ̃taʀisabl] adj inexhaustible

**intégral, e, -aux** [ɛ̃tegʀal, o] adj complete; **texte ~** unabridged version; **bronzage ~** all-over suntan; **intégralement** adv in full; **intégralité** nf whole; **dans son intégralité** in full; **intégrant, e** adj: **faire partie intégrante de** to be an integral part of

**intègre** [ɛ̃tɛgʀ] adj upright

**intégrer** [ɛ̃tegʀe] vt: **bien s'~** to integrate well

**intégrisme** [ɛ̃tegʀism] nm fundamentalism

**intellectuel, le** [ɛ̃telɛktɥel] adj intellectual ♦ nm/f intellectual; (péj) highbrow

**intelligence** [ɛ̃teliʒãs] nf intelligence; (compréhension): **l'~ de** the understanding of; (complicité): **regard d'~** glance of complicity; (accord): **vivre en bonne ~ avec qn** to be on good terms with sb

**intelligent, e** [ɛ̃teliʒã, ãt] adj intelligent

**intelligible** [ɛ̃teliʒibl] adj intelligible

**intempéries** [ɛ̃tãpeʀi] nfpl bad weather sg

**intempestif, -ive** [ɛ̃tãpestif, iv] adj untimely

**intenable** [ɛ̃t(ə)nabl] adj (chaleur) unbearable

**intendant, e** [ɛ̃tãdã] nm/f (MIL) quartermaster; (SCOL) bursar

**intense** [ɛ̃tãs] adj intense; **intensif, -ive** adj intensive; **un cours intensif** a crash course

**intenter** [ɛ̃tãte] vt: **~ un procès contre** ou **à** to start proceedings against

**intention** [ɛ̃tãsjɔ̃] nf intention; (JUR) intent; **avoir l'~ de faire** to intend to do; **à l'~ de** for; (renseignement) for the benefit of; (film, ouvrage) aimed at; **à cette ~** with this aim in view; **intentionné, e** adj: **bien intentionné** well-meaning ou -intentioned; **mal inten-**

tionné ill-intentioned

**interactif, -ive** [ɛ̃teraktif, iv] adj (COM-PUT) interactive

**intercalaire** [ɛ̃terkalɛr] nm divider

**intercaler** [ɛ̃terkale] vt to insert

**intercepter** [ɛ̃tersɛpte] vt to intercept; (lumière, chaleur) to cut off

**interchangeable** [ɛ̃terʃɑ̃ʒabl] adj interchangeable

**interclasse** [ɛ̃terklas] nm (SCOL) break (between classes)

**interdiction** [ɛ̃terdiksjɔ̃] nf ban; **~ de stationner** no parking; **~ de fumer** no smoking

**interdire** [ɛ̃terdir] vt to forbid; (ADMIN) to ban, prohibit; (: journal, livre) to ban; **~ à qn de faire** to forbid sb to do; (suj: empêchement) to prevent sb from doing

**interdit, e** [ɛ̃terdi, it] adj (stupéfait) taken aback

**intéressant, e** [ɛ̃teresɑ̃, ɑ̃t] adj interesting; (avantageux) attractive

**intéressé, e** [ɛ̃terese] adj (parties) involved, concerned; (amitié, motifs) self-interested

**intéresser** [ɛ̃terese] vt (captiver) to interest; (toucher) to be of interest to; (ADMIN: concerner) to affect, concern; **s'~ à** to be interested in

**intérêt** [ɛ̃terɛ] nm interest; (égoïsme) self-interest; **tu as ~ à accepter** it is in your interest to accept; **tu as ~ à te dépêcher** you'd better hurry

**intérieur, e** [ɛ̃terjœr] adj (mur, escalier, poche) inside; (commerce, politique) domestic; (cour, calme, vie) inner; (navigation) inland ♦ nm (d'une maison, d'un récipient etc) inside; (d'un pays, aussi décor, mobilier) interior; **à l'~ (de)** inside; **intérieurement** adv inwardly

**intérim** [ɛ̃terim] nm interim period; **faire de l'~** to temp; **assurer l'~ (de)** to deputize (for); **par ~** interim

**intérimaire** [ɛ̃terimɛr] adj (directeur, ministre) acting; (secrétaire, personnel) temporary ♦ nm/f (secrétaire) temporary

secretary, temp (BRIT)

**interlocuteur, -trice** [ɛ̃terlɔkytœr, tris] nm/f speaker; **son ~** the person he was speaking to

**interloquer** [ɛ̃terlɔke] vt to take aback

**intermède** [ɛ̃termɛd] nm interlude

**intermédiaire** [ɛ̃termedjɛr] adj intermediate; (solution) temporary ♦ nm/f intermediary; (COMM) middleman; **sans ~** directly; **par l'~ de** through

**interminable** [ɛ̃terminabl] adj endless

**intermittence** [ɛ̃termitɑ̃s] nf: **par ~** sporadically, intermittently

**internat** [ɛ̃terna] nm boarding school

**international, e, -aux** [ɛ̃ternasjɔnal, o] adj, nm/f international

**interne** [ɛ̃tern] adj internal ♦ nm/f (SCOL) boarder; (MÉD) houseman

**interner** [ɛ̃terne] vt (POL) to intern; (MÉD) to confine to a mental institution

**Internet** [ɛ̃ternɛt] nm: **l'~** the Internet

**interpeller** [ɛ̃terpale] vt (appeler) to call out to; (apostropher) to shout at; (POLICE, POL) to question; (concerner) to concern

**interphone** [ɛ̃terfɔn] nm intercom; (d'immeuble) entry phone

**interposer** [ɛ̃terpoze] vt: **s'~** to intervene; **par personnes interposées** through a third party

**interprétation** [ɛ̃terpretasjɔ̃] nf interpretation

**interprète** [ɛ̃terprɛt] nm/f interpreter; (porte-parole) spokesperson

**interpréter** [ɛ̃terprete] vt to interpret; (jouer) to play; (chanter) to sing

**interrogatif, -ive** [ɛ̃terɔgatif, iv] adj (LING) interrogative

**interrogation** [ɛ̃terɔgasjɔ̃] nf question; (action) questioning; (SCOL) (written ou oral) test

**interrogatoire** [ɛ̃terɔgatwar] nm (PO-LICE) questioning no pl; (JUR, aussi fig) cross-examination

**interroger** [ɛ̃terɔʒe] vt to question; (IN-

*FORM)* to consult; *(SCOL)* to test

**interrompre** [ɛ̃teʀɔ̃pʀ] *vt* (gén) to interrupt; *(négociations)* to break off; *(match)* to stop; **s'~** to break off; **interrupteur** nm switch; **interruption** nf interruption; *(pause)* break; **sans interruption** without stopping

**intersection** [ɛ̃tɛʀsɛksjɔ̃] nf intersection

**interstice** [ɛ̃tɛʀstis] nm crack; *(de volet)* slit

**interurbain, e** [ɛ̃teʀyʀbɛ̃, ɛn] adj *(TÉL)* long-distance

**intervalle** [ɛ̃tɛʀval] nm *(espace)* space; *(de temps)* interval; **à deux jours d'~** two days apart

**intervenir** [ɛ̃tɛʀvəniʀ] vi *(gén)* to intervene; **~ auprès de qn** to intervene with sb

**intervention** [ɛ̃tɛʀvɑ̃sjɔ̃] nf intervention; *(discours)* speech; **intervention chirurgicale** (surgical) operation

**intervertir** [ɛ̃tɛʀvɛʀtiʀ] vt to invert (the order of), reverse

**interview** [ɛ̃tɛʀvju] nf interview

**intestin** [ɛ̃tɛstɛ̃, in] nm intestine

**intime** [ɛ̃tim] adj intimate; *(vie)* private; *(conviction)* inmost; *(dîner, cérémonie)* quiet ♦ nm/f close friend; **un journal ~** a diary

**intimider** [ɛ̃timide] vt to intimidate

**intimité** [ɛ̃timite] nf: **dans l'~** in private; *(sans formalités)* with only a few friends, quietly

**intitulé, e** [ɛ̃tityle] adj entitled

**intolérable** [ɛ̃tɔleʀabl] adj intolerable

**intox** [ɛ̃tɔks] *(fam)* nf brainwashing

**intoxication** [ɛ̃tɔksikasjɔ̃] nf: **~ alimentaire** food poisoning

**intoxiquer** [ɛ̃tɔksike] vt to poison; *(fig)* to brainwash

**intraduisible** [ɛ̃tʀaduizibl] adj untranslatable; *(fig)* inexpressible

**intraitable** [ɛ̃tʀɛtabl] adj inflexible, uncompromising

**intranet** [ɛ̃tʀanɛt] nm intranet

**intransigeant, e** [ɛ̃tʀɑ̃ziʒɑ̃, ɑ̃t] adj in-

transigent

**intransitif, -ive** [ɛ̃tʀɑ̃zitif, iv] adj *(LING)* intransitive

**intrépide** [ɛ̃tʀepid] adj dauntless

**intrigue** [ɛ̃tʀig] nf *(scénario)* plot; **intriguer** v/t to puzzle, intrigue

**intrinsèque** [ɛ̃tʀɛ̃sɛk] adj intrinsic

**introduction** [ɛ̃tʀɔdyksjɔ̃] nf introduction

**introduire** [ɛ̃tʀɔduiʀ] vt to introduce; *(visiteur)* to show in; *(aiguille, clef)*: **~ qch dans** to insert ou introduce sth into; **s'~ (dans)** to get in(to); *(dans un groupe)* to get o.s. accepted (into)

**introuvable** [ɛ̃tʀuvabl] adj which cannot be found; *(COMM)* unobtainable

**introverti, e** [ɛ̃tʀɔvɛʀti] nm/f introvert

**intrus, e** [ɛ̃tʀy, yz] nm/f intruder

**intrusion** [ɛ̃tʀyzjɔ̃] nf intrusion

**intuition** [ɛ̃tɥisjɔ̃] nf intuition

**inusable** [inyzabl] adj hard-wearing

**inusité, e** [inyzite] adj rarely used

**inutile** [inytil] adj useless; *(superflu)* unnecessary; **inutilement** adv unnecessarily; **inutilisable** adj unusable

**invalide** [ɛ̃valid] adj disabled ♦ nm: **~ de guerre** disabled ex-serviceman

**invariable** [ɛ̃vaʀjabl] adj invariable

**invasion** [ɛ̃vazjɔ̃] nf invasion

**invectiver** [ɛ̃vɛktive] vt to hurl abuse at

**invendable** [ɛ̃vɑ̃dabl] adj unsaleable; *(COMM)* unmarketable; **invendus** nmpl unsold goods

**inventaire** [ɛ̃vɑ̃tɛʀ] nm inventory; *(COMM: liste)* stocklist; *(: opération)* stocktaking no pl

**inventer** [ɛ̃vɑ̃te] vt to invent; *(subterfuge)* to devise, invent; *(histoire, excuse)* to make up, invent; **inventeur** nm inventor; **inventif, -ive** adj inventive; **invention** nf invention

**inverse** [ɛ̃vɛʀs] adj opposite ♦ nm opposite; **dans l'ordre ~** in the reverse order; **en sens ~** in *(ou* from) the opposite direction; **dans le sens ~ des aiguilles d'une montre** anticlockwise;

tu t'es trompé, c'est l'~ you've got it wrong, it's the other way round; **inversement** adv conversely; **inverser** vt to invert, reverse; (ÉLEC) to reverse

**investigation** [ɛ̃vɛstigasjɔ̃] nf investigation

**investir** [ɛ̃vɛstiʀ] vt to invest; **investissement** nm investment; **investiture** nf nomination

**invétéré, e** [ɛ̃vetere] adj inveterate

**invisible** [ɛ̃vizibl] adj invisible

**invitation** [ɛ̃vitasjɔ̃] nf invitation

**invité, e** [ɛ̃vite] nm/f guest

**inviter** [ɛ̃vite] vt to invite

**invivable** [ɛ̃vivabl] adj unbearable

**involontaire** [ɛ̃vɔlɔ̃tɛʀ] adj (mouvement) involuntary; (insulte) unintentional; (complice) unwitting

**invoquer** [ɛ̃vɔke] vt (Dieu, muse) to call upon, invoke; (prétexte) to put forward (as an excuse); (loi, texte) to refer to

**invraisemblable** [ɛ̃vʀɛsɑ̃blabl] adj (fait, nouvelle) unlikely, improbable; (insolence, habit) incredible

**iode** [jɔd] nm iodine

**irai** etc [iʀe] vb voir **aller**

**Irak** [iʀak] nm Iraq; **irakien, ne** adj Iraqi ♦ nm/f: **Irakien, ne** Iraqi

**Iran** [iʀɑ̃] nm Iran; **iranien, ne** adj Iranian ♦ nm/f: **Iranien, ne** Iranian

**irascible** [iʀasibl] adj short-tempered

**irions** etc [iʀjɔ̃] vb voir **aller**

**iris** [iʀis] nm iris

**irlandais, e** [iʀlɑ̃dɛ, ɛz] adj Irish ♦ nm/f: **Irlandais, e** Irishman(-woman); **les Irlandais** the Irish

**Irlande** [iʀlɑ̃d] nf Ireland; **du Nord** Northern Ireland; **la République d'~** the Irish Republic

**ironie** [iʀɔni] nf irony; **ironique** adj ironical; **ironiser** vi to be ironical

**irons** etc [iʀɔ̃] vb voir **aller**

**irradier** [iʀadje] vt to irradiate

**irraisonné, e** [iʀɛzɔne] adj irrational

**irrationnel, le** [iʀasjɔnɛl] adj irrational

**irréalisable** [iʀealizabl] adj unrealisable; (projet) impracticable

**irrécupérable** [iʀekyperabl] adj beyond repair; (personne) beyond redemption

**irréductible** [iʀedyktibl] adj (volonté) indomitable; (ennemi) implacable

**irréel, le** [iʀeɛl] adj unreal

**irréfléchi, e** [iʀefleʃi] adj thoughtless

**irrégularité** [iʀegylaʀite] nf irregularity; (de travail, d'effort, de qualité) unevenness no pl

**irrégulier, -ière** [iʀegylje, jɛʀ] adj irregular; (travail, effort, qualité) uneven; (élève, athlète) erratic

**irrémédiable** [iʀemedjabl] adj irreparable

**irremplaçable** [iʀɑ̃plasabl] adj irreplaceable

**irréparable** [iʀepaʀabl] adj (objet) beyond repair; (dommage etc) irreparable

**irréprochable** [iʀepʀɔʃabl] adj irreproachable, beyond reproach; (tenue) impeccable

**irrésistible** [iʀezistibl] adj irresistible; (besoin, désir, preuve, logique) compelling; (amusant) hilarious

**irrésolu, e** [iʀezɔly] adj (personne) irresolute; (problème) unresolved

**irrespectueux, -euse** [iʀɛspɛktyø, øz] adj disrespectful

**irrespirable** [iʀɛspiʀabl] adj unbreathable; (fig) oppressive

**irresponsable** [iʀɛspɔ̃sabl] adj irresponsible

**irriguer** [iʀige] vt to irrigate

**irritable** [iʀitabl] adj irritable

**irriter** [iʀite] vt to irritate

**irruption** [iʀypsjɔ̃] nf: **faire ~ (chez qn)** to burst in (on sb)

**Islam** [islam] nm Islam; **islamique** adj Islamic; **islamiste** adj (militant) Islamic; (mouvement) Islamic fundamentalist ♦ nm/f Islamic fundamentalist

**Islande** [islɑ̃d] nf Iceland

**isolant, e** [izɔlɑ̃, ɑ̃t] adj insulating; (insonorisant) soundproofing

**isolation** [izɔlasjɔ̃] nf insulation

**isolé, e** [izɔle] adj isolated; (contre le

*froid)* insulated

**isoler** [izɔle] *vt* to isolate; *(prisonnier)* to put in solitary confinement; *(ville)* to cut off, isolate; *(contre le froid)* to insulate; **s'~** *vi* to isolate o.s.; **isoloir** [izɔlwaʀ] *nm* polling booth

**Israël** [israɛl] *nm* Israel; **israélien, ne** *adj* Israeli ♦ *nm/f:* **Israélien, ne** Israeli; **israélite** *adj* Jewish ♦ *nm/f:* **Israélite** Jew (Jewess)

**issu, e** [isy] *adj:* **~ de** *(né de)* descended from; *(résultant de)* stemming from; **issue** *nf (ouverture, sortie)* exit; *(solution)* way out, solution; *(dénouement)* outcome; **à l'issue de** at the conclusion *ou* close of; **voie sans issue** dead end; **issue de secours** emergency exit

**Italie** [itali] *nf* Italy; **italien, ne** *adj* Italian ♦ *nm/f:* **Italien, ne** Italian ♦ *nm (LING)* Italian

**italique** [italik] *nm:* **en ~** in italics

**itinéraire** [itineʀɛʀ] *nm* itinerary, route; **~ bis** diversion

**IUT** *sigle m* = **Institut universitaire de technologie**

**IVG** *sigle f* (= *interruption volontaire de grossesse)* abortion

**ivoire** [ivwaʀ] *nm* ivory

**ivre** [ivʀ] *adj* drunk; **~ de** *(colère, bonheur)* wild with; **ivresse** *nf* drunkenness; **ivrogne** *nm/f* drunkard

# J, j

**j'** [ʒ] *pron voir* **je**

**jacasser** [ʒakase] *vi* to chatter

**jacinthe** [ʒasɛ̃t] *nf* hyacinth

**jadis** [ʒadis] *adv* long ago

**jaillir** [ʒajiʀ] *vi (liquide)* to spurt out; *(cris, responses)* to burst forth

**jais** [ʒɛ] *nm* jet; **(d'un noir) de ~** jet-black

**jalousie** [ʒaluzi] *nf* jealousy; *(store)* slatted blind

**jaloux, -ouse** [ʒalu, uz] *adj* jealous

**jamais** [ʒamɛ] *adv* never; *(sans négation)* ever; **ne ... ~** never; **à ~** for ever

**jambe** [ʒɑ̃b] *nf* leg

**jambon** [ʒɑ̃bɔ̃] *nm* ham; **~ blanc** boiled *ou* cooked ham; **jambonneau, x** *nm* knuckle of ham

**jante** [ʒɑ̃t] *nf* (wheel) rim

**janvier** [ʒɑ̃vje] *nm* January

**Japon** [ʒapɔ̃] *nm* Japan; **japonais, e** *adj* Japanese ♦ *nm/f:* **Japonais, e** Japanese ♦ *nm (LING)* Japanese

**japper** [ʒape] *vi* to yap, yelp

**jaquette** [ʒakɛt] *nf (de cérémonie)* morning coat

**jardin** [ʒaʀdɛ̃] *nm* garden; **~ d'enfants** nursery school; **jardinage** *nm* gardening; **jardiner** *vi* to do some gardening; **jardinier, -ière** *nm/f* gardener; **jardinière** *nf* planter; *(de fenêtre)* window box; **jardinière de légumes** mixed vegetables

**jargon** [ʒaʀgɔ̃] *nm (baragouin)* gibberish; *(langue professionnelle)* jargon

**jarret** [ʒaʀɛ] *nm* back of knee; *(CULIN)* knuckle, shin

**jarretelle** [ʒaʀtɛl] *nf* suspender *(BRIT)*, garter *(US)*

**jarretière** [ʒaʀtjɛʀ] *nf* garter

**jaser** [ʒaze] *vi (médire)* to gossip

**jatte** [ʒat] *nf* basin, bowl

**jauge** [ʒoʒ] *nf (instrument)* gauge; **~ d'essence** petrol gauge; **~ d'huile** (oil) dipstick

**jaune** [ʒon] *adj, nm* yellow ♦ *adv (fam):* **rire ~** to laugh on the other side of one's face; **~ d'œuf** (egg) yolk; **jaunir** *vi, vt* to turn yellow; **jaunisse** *nf* jaundice

**Javel** [ʒavɛl] *nf voir* **eau**

**javelot** [ʒavlo] *nm* javelin

**J.-C.** *abr* = **Jésus-Christ**

**je, j'** [ʒə] *pron* I

**jean** [dʒin] *nm* jeans *pl*

**Jésus-Christ** [ʒezykri(st)] *n* Jesus Christ; **600 avant/après ~~** *ou* **J.-C.** 600 B.C./A.D.

**jet**[1] *nm (lancer: action)* throwing *no*

**pl;** (: *résultat*) throw; (*jaillissement: d'eaux*) jet; (: *de sang*) spurt; **~ d'eau** spray

**jet²** [dʒɛt] nm (*avion*) jet

**jetable** [ʒ(ə)tabl] adj disposable

**jetée** [ʒəte] nf jetty; (*grande*) pier

**jeter** [ʒ(ə)te] vt (*gén*) to throw; (*se défaire de*) to throw away ou out; **se ~ dans** to flow into; **~ qch à qn** to throw sth to sb; (*de façon aggresive*) to throw sth at sb; **~ un coup d'œil (à)** to take a look (at); **~ un sort à qn** to cast a spell on sb; **se ~ sur qn** to rush at sb

**jeton** [ʒ(ə)tɔ̃] nm (*au jeu*) counter

**jette** *etc* [ʒɛt] vb voir **jeter**

**jeu, x** [ʒø] nm (*divertissement*, TECH: *d'une pièce*) play; (TENNIS: *partie*, FOOTBALL etc: *façon de jouer*) game; (THÉÂTRE etc) acting; (*série d'objets, jouet*) set; (CARTES) hand; (*au casino*): **le ~** gambling; **être en ~** to be at stake; **entrer/mettre en ~** to come/bring into play; **~ de cartes** pack of cards; **~ d'échecs** chess set; **~ de hasard** game of chance; **~ de mots** pun; **~ de société** parlour game; **~ télévisé** television quiz; **~ vidéo** video game

**jeudi** [ʒødi] nm Thursday

**jeun** [ʒœ̃]: **à ~** adv on an empty stomach; **être à ~** to have eaten nothing; **rester à ~** not to eat anything

**jeune** [ʒœn] adj young; **les ~s** young people; **~ fille** girl; **~ homme** young man; **~s mariés** newly-weds

**jeûne** [ʒøn] nm fast

**jeunesse** [ʒœnɛs] nf youth; (*aspect*) youthfulness

**joaillerie** [ʒɔajri] nf jewellery; (*magasin*) jeweller's; **joaillier, -ière** nm/f jeweller

**jogging** [dʒɔgiŋ] nm jogging; (*survêtement*) tracksuit; **faire du ~** to go jogging

**joie** [ʒwa] nf joy

**joindre** [ʒwɛ̃dr] vt to join; (à *une lettre*) **~ qch à** to enclose sth with;

(*contacter*) to contact, get in touch with; **se ~ à** to join; **~ les mains** to put one's hands together

**joint, e** [ʒwɛ̃, ɛt] adj: **pièce ~e** enclosure ♦ nm (*ligne*) join; **~ de culasse** cylinder head gasket; **~ de robinet** washer

**joker** [(d)ʒɔkɛr] nm (INFORM): (*caractère ~*) wildcard

**joli, e** [ʒɔli] adj pretty, attractive; **c'est du ~!** (*ironique*) that's very nice!; **c'est joli, mais ...** that's all very well but ...

**jonc** [ʒɔ̃] nm (bul)rush

**jonction** [ʒɔ̃ksjɔ̃] nf junction

**jongleur, -euse** [ʒɔ̃glœr, øz] nm/f juggler

**jonquille** [ʒɔ̃kij] nf daffodil

**Jordanie** [ʒɔrdani] nf: **la ~** Jordan

**joue** [ʒu] nf cheek

**jouer** [ʒwe] vt to play; (*somme d'argent, réputation*) to stake, wager; (*simuler: sentiment*) to affect, feign ♦ vi to play; (THÉÂTRE, CINÉMA) to act; (*au casino*) to gamble; (*bois, porte: se voiler*) to warp; (*clef, pièce: avoir du jeu*) to be loose; **~ sur** (*miser*) to gamble on; **~ de** (MUS) to play; **~ à** (*jeu, sport, roulette*) to play; **~ un tour à qn** to play a trick on sb; **~ serré** to play a close game; **~ la comédie** to put on an act; **bien joué!** well done!; **on joue Hamlet au théâtre X** Hamlet is on at the X theatre

**jouet** [ʒwɛ] nm toy; **être le ~ de** (*illusion etc*) to be the victim of

**joueur, -euse** [ʒwœr, øz] nm/f player; **être beau ~** to be a good loser

**joufflu, e** [ʒufly] adj chubby-cheeked

**joug** [ʒu] nm yoke

**jouir** [ʒwir] vi (*sexe: fam*) to come ♦ vi: **~ de** to enjoy; **jouissance** nf pleasure; (JUR) use

**joujou** [ʒuʒu] (fam) nm toy

**jour** [ʒur] nm day; (*opposé à la nuit*) day, daytime; (*clarté*) daylight; (*fig: aspect*) light; (*ouverture*) gap; **au ~ le ~**

from day to day; **de nos ~s** these days; **du ~ au lendemain** overnight; **il fait ~** it's daylight; **au grand ~** (fig) in the open; **mettre au ~** to disclose; **mettre à ~** to update; **donner le ~ à** to give birth to; **voir le ~** to be born; **~ férié** public holiday; **~ de fête** holiday; **~ ouvrable** working day

**journal, -aux** [ʒuʀnal, o] nm (news)paper; (spécialisé) journal; (intime) diary; **~ de bord** log; **~ télévisé** television news sg

**journalier, -ière** [ʒuʀnalje, jɛʀ] adj daily; (banal) everyday

**journalisme** [ʒuʀnalism] nm journalism; **journaliste** nm/f journalist

**journée** [ʒuʀne] nf day; **faire la ~ continue** to work over lunch

**journellement** [ʒuʀnɛlmɑ̃] adv daily

**joyau, x** [ʒwajo] nm gem, jewel

**joyeux, -euse** [ʒwajø, øz] adj joyful, merry; **~ Noël!** merry Christmas!; **~ anniversaire!** happy birthday!

**jubiler** [ʒybile] vi to be jubilant, exult

**jucher** [ʒyʃe] vt, vi to perch

**judas** [ʒyda] nm (trou) spy-hole

**judiciaire** [ʒydisjɛʀ] adj judicial

**judicieux, -euse** [ʒydisjø, jøz] adj judicious

**judo** [ʒydo] nm judo

**juge** [ʒyʒ] nm judge; **~ d'instruction** examining (BRIT) ou committing (US) magistrate; **~ de paix** justice of the peace; **~ de touche** linesman

**jugé** [ʒyʒe] : **au ~** adv by guesswork

**jugement** [ʒyʒmɑ̃] nm judgment; (JUR: au pénal) sentence; (: au civil) decision

**jugeote** [ʒyʒɔt] (fam) nf commonsense

**juger** [ʒyʒe] vt to judge; (estimer) to consider; **~ qn/qch satisfaisant** to consider sb/sth (to be) satisfactory; **~ bon de faire** to see fit to do; **~ de** to appreciate

**juif, -ive** [ʒɥif, ʒɥiv] adj Jewish ♦ nm/f: **J~, ive** Jew (Jewess)

**juillet** [ʒɥijɛ] nm July

**juin** [ʒɥɛ̃] nm June

**jumeau, -elle, x** [ʒymo, ɛl] adj, nm/f twin

**jumeler** [ʒym(ə)le] vt to twin

**jumelle** [ʒymɛl] adj, nf voir **jumeau**; **~s** nfpl (appareil) binoculars

**jument** [ʒymɑ̃] nf mare

**jungle** [ʒœ̃gl] nf jungle

**jupe** [ʒyp] nf skirt

**jupon** [ʒypõ] nm waist slip

**juré, e** [ʒyʀe] nm/f juror

**jurer** [ʒyʀe] vt (obéissance etc) to swear, vow ♦ vi (dire des jurons) to swear, curse; (dissoner) : **~ (avec)** to clash (with); **~ de faire/que** to swear to do/that; **~ de qch** (s'en porter garant) to swear to sth

**juridique** [ʒyʀidik] adj legal

**juron** [ʒyʀõ] nm curse, swearword

**jury** [ʒyʀi] nm jury; (ART, SCOL) panel of judges; (SCOL) board of examiners

**jus** [ʒy] nm juice; (de viande) gravy, (meat) juice; **~ de fruit** fruit juice

**jusque** [ʒyskə]: **jusqu'à** prép (endroit) as far as, (up) to; (moment) until, till; (limite) up to; **~ sur/dans** up to; (y compris) even on/in; **jusqu'à ce que** until; **jusqu'à présent** so far; **jusqu'où?** how far?

**justaucorps** [ʒystokɔʀ] nm leotard

**juste** [ʒyst] adj (équitable) just, fair; (légitime) just; (exact) right; (pertinent) apt; (étroit) tight; (insuffisant) on the short side ♦ adv rightly, correctly; (chanter) in tune; (exactement, seulement) just; **~ assez/au-dessus** just enough/above; **au ~** exactly; **le ~ milieu** the happy medium; **c'était ~** it was a close thing; **justement** *adv* justly; (*précisément*) just, precisely; **justesse** *nf* (*précision*) accuracy; (*d'une remarque*) aptness; (*d'une opinion*) soundness; **de justesse** only just

**justice** [ʒystis] *nf* (*équité*) fairness, justice; (ADMIN) law; **rendre ~ à qn** to do sb justice; **justicier, -ière** *nm/f* righter of wrongs

**justificatif, -ive** [ʒystifikatif, iv] *adj* (*document*) supporting; **pièce justificative** written proof

**justifier** [ʒystifje] *vt* to justify; **~ de** to prove

**juteux, -euse** [ʒytø, øz] *adj* juicy

**juvénile** [ʒyvenil] *adj* youthful

# K, k

**K** [ka] *nm* (INFORM) K

**kaki** [kaki] *adj inv* khaki

**kangourou** [kãguʀu] *nm* kangaroo

**karaté** [kaʀate] *nm* karate

**karting** [kaʀtiŋ] *nm* go-carting, karting

**kascher** [kaʃeʀ] *adj* kosher

**kayak** [kajak] *nm* canoe, kayak; **faire du ~** to go canoeing

**kermesse** [kɛʀmɛs] *nf* fair; (*fête de charité*) bazaar, (charity) fête

**kidnapper** [kidnape] *vt* to kidnap

**kilo** [kilo] *nm* = **kilogramme**

**kilo...: kilogramme** *nm* kilogramme; **kilométrage** *nm* number of kilometres travelled; ≃ mileage; **kilomètre** *nm* kilometre; **kilométrique** *adj* (*distance*) in kilometres

**kinésithérapeute** [kineziteʀapøt] *nm/f* physiotherapist

**kiosque** [kjɔsk] *nm* kiosk, stall; **~ à musique** bandstand

**kir** [kiʀ] *nm* kir (*white wine with black-currant liqueur*)

**kit** [kit] *nm*: **en ~** in kit form

**kiwi** [kiwi] *nm* kiwi

**klaxon** [klaksɔn] *nm* horn; **klaxonner** *vi, vt* to hoot (BRIT), honk (US)

**km** *abr* = **kilomètre**

**km/h** *abr* (= kilomètres/heure) ≃ mph

**K.-O.** (*fam*) *adj inv* shattered, knackered

**Kosovo** [kɔsɔvo] *nm* Kosovo

**k-way** ® [kawe] *nm* (lightweight nylon) cagoule

**kyste** [kist] *nm* cyst

# L, l

**l'** [l] *art* déf *voir* **le**

**la** [la] *art* déf *voir* **le ♦** *nm* (MUS) A; (*en chantant la gamme*) la

**là** [la] *adv* there; (*ici*) here; (*dans le temps*) then; **elle n'est pas ~** she isn't here; **c'est ~ que** this is where; **~ où** where; **de ~** (*fig*) hence; **par ~** (*fig*) by that; *voir aussi* **-ci**; **ce**; **celui**; **là-bas** *adv* there

**label** [label] *nm* stamp, seal

**labeur** [labœʀ] *nm* toil *no pl*, toiling *no pl*

**labo** [labo] (*fam*) *nm* (= *laboratoire*) lab

**laboratoire** [labɔʀatwaʀ] *nm* laboratory; **~ de langues** language laboratory

**laborieux, -euse** [labɔʀjø, jøz] *adj* (*tâche*) laborious

**labour** [labuʀ] *nm* ploughing *no pl*; **~s** *nmpl* (*champs*) ploughed fields; **cheval de ~** plough- *ou* cart-horse; **labourer** *vt* to plough

**labyrinthe** [labiʀɛ̃t] *nm* labyrinth, maze

**lac** [lak] *nm* lake

**lacer** [lase] *vt* to lace *ou* do up

**lacérer** [laseʀe] *vt* to tear to shreds

**lacet** [lasɛ] *nm* (*de chaussure*) lace; (*de route*) sharp bend; (*piège*) snare

**lâche** [lɑʃ] *adj* (*poltron*) cowardly; (*desserré*) loose, slack ♦ *nm/f* coward

**lâcher** [lɑʃe] *vt* to let go of; (*ce qui tombe, abandonner*) to drop; (*oiseau, animal: libérer*) to release, set free; (*fig: mot, remarque*) to let slip, come out with ♦ vi (freins) to fail; ~ **les amarres** (NAVIG) to cast off (the moorings); ~ **prise** to let go

**lâcheté** [lɑʃte] nf cowardice

**lacrymogène** [lakʀimɔʒɛn] adj: **gaz** ~ teargas

**lacté, e** [lakte] adj (produit, régime) milk cpd

**lacune** [lakyn] nf gap

**là-dedans** [ladədɑ̃] adv inside (there), in it; (fig) in that

**là-dessous** [ladsu] adv underneath, under there; (fig) behind that

**là-dessus** [ladsy] adv on there; (fig: sur ces mots) at that point; (: à ce sujet) about that

**ladite** [ladit] dét voir **ledit**

**lagune** [lagyn] nf lagoon

**là-haut** [lao] adv up there

**laïc** [laik] adj, nm/f = **laïque**

**laid, e** [lɛ, lɛd] adj ugly; **laideur** nf ugliness no pl

**lainage** [lɛnaʒ] nm (vêtement) woollen garment; (étoffe) woollen material

**laine** [lɛn] nf wool

**laïque** [laik] adj lay, civil; (SCOL) state cpd ♦ nm/f layman(-woman)

**laisse** [lɛs] nf (de chien) lead, leash; **tenir en** ~ to keep on a lead ou leash

**laisser** [lese] vt to leave ♦ vb aux: ~ **qn faire** to let sb do; **se** ~ **aller** to let o.s. go; **laisse-toi faire** let me (ou him etc) do it; **laisser-aller** nm carelessness, slovenliness; **laissez-passer** nm inv pass

**lait** [lɛ] nm milk; **frère/sœur de** ~ foster brother/sister; ~ **condensé/ concentré** evaporated/condensed milk; **laita- ge** nm dairy product; **laiterie** nf dairy; **laitier, -ière** adj dairy cpd ♦ nm/f milkman (dairywoman)

**laiton** [lɛtɔ̃] nm brass

**laitue** [lety] nf lettuce

**laïus** [lajys] (péj) nm spiel

**lambeau, x** [lɑ̃bo] nm scrap; **en ~x** in tatters, tattered

**lambris** [lɑ̃bʀi] nm panelling no pl

**lame** [lam] nf blade; (vague) wave; (~lle) strip; ~ **de fond** ground swell no pl; ~ **de rasoir** razor blade; **lamelle** nf thin strip ou blade

**lamentable** [lamɑ̃tabl] adj appalling

**lamenter** [lamɑ̃te] vt: **se** ~ **(sur)** to moan (over)

**lampadaire** [lɑ̃padɛʀ] nm (de salon) standard lamp; (dans la rue) street lamp

**lampe** [lɑ̃p] nf lamp; (TECH) valve; ~ **à souder** blowlamp; ~ **de chevet** bedside lamp; ~ **de poche** torch (BRIT), flashlight (US)

**lampion** [lɑ̃pjɔ̃] nm Chinese lantern

**lance** [lɑ̃s] nf spear; ~ **d'incendie** fire hose

**lancée** [lɑ̃se] nf: **être/continuer sur sa** ~ to be under way/keep going

**lancement** [lɑ̃smɑ̃] nm launching

**lance-pierres** [lɑ̃spjɛʀ] nm inv catapult

**lancer** [lɑ̃se] nm (SPORT) throwing no pl, throw ♦ vt to throw; (émettre, projeter) to throw out, send out; (produit, fusée, bateau, artiste) to launch; (injure) to hurl, fling; **se** ~ (prendre de l'élan) to build up speed; (se précipiter): **se** ~ **sur** ou **contre** to rush at; **se** ~ **dans** (discussion) to launch into; (aventure) to embark on; ~ **qch à qn** to throw sth to sb; (de façon agressive) to throw sth at sb; ~ **du poids** putting the shot

**lancinant, e** [lɑ̃sinɑ̃, ɑ̃t] adj (douleur) shooting

**landau** [lɑ̃do] nm pram (BRIT), baby carriage (US)

**lande** [lɑ̃d] nf moor

**langage** [lɑ̃gaʒ] nm language

**langouste** [lɑ̃gust] nf crayfish inv; **langoustine** nf Dublin Bay prawn

**langue** [lɑ̃g] nf (ANAT, CULIN) tongue; (LING) language; **tirer la** ~ **(à)** to stick out one's tongue (at); **de** ~ **française** French-speaking; ~ **maternelle** native language, mother tongue; ~ **vivante/ étrangère** modern/foreign language

**langueur** [lɑ̃gœʀ] nf languidness

**languir** [lɑ̃giʀ] vi to languish; (conversation) to flag; **faire ~ qn** to keep sb waiting

**lanière** [lanjɛʀ] nf (de fouet) lash; (de sac, bretelle) strap

**lanterne** [lɑ̃tɛʀn] nf (portable) lantern; (électrique) light, lamp; (de voiture) (side)light

**laper** [lape] vt to lap up

**lapidaire** [lapidɛʀ] adj (fig) terse

**lapin** [lapɛ̃] nm rabbit; (peau) rabbitskin; (fourrure) coney; **poser un ~ à qn** (fam) to stand sb up

**Laponie** [laponi] nf Lapland

**laps** [laps] nm: **~ de temps** space of time, lapse of time

**laque** [lak] nf (vernis) lacquer; (pour cheveux) hair spray

**laquelle** [lakɛl] pron voir **lequel**

**larcin** [laʀsɛ̃] nm theft

**lard** [laʀ] nm (bacon) (streaky) bacon; (graisse) fat

**lardon** [laʀdɔ̃] nm: **~s** chopped bacon

**large** [laʀʒ] adj wide, broad; (fig) generous ♦ adv: **calculer/voir ~** to allow extra/think big ♦ nm (largeur): **5 m de ~ 5 m** wide ou in width; (mer): **le ~** the open sea; **au ~ de** off; **~ d'esprit** broad-minded; **largement** adv widely; (de loin) greatly; (au moins) easily; (généreusement) generously; **c'est largement suffisant** that's ample; **largesse** nf generosity; **largesses** nfpl (dons) liberalities; **largeur** nf (qu'on mesure) width; (impression visuelle) wideness, width; (d'esprit) broadness

**larguer** [laʀge] vt to drop; **~ les amarres** to cast off (the moorings)

**larme** [laʀm] nf tear; (fam: goutte): **une ~** a drop; **en ~s** in tears; **larmoyer** vi (yeux) to water; (se plaindre) to whimper

**larvé, e** [laʀve] adj (fig) latent

**laryngite** [laʀɛ̃ʒit] nf laryngitis

**las, lasse** [lɑ, lɑs] adj weary

**laser** [lazɛʀ] nm: (rayon) **~** laser

(beam); **chaîne ~** compact disc (player); **disque ~** compact disc

**lasse** [lɑs] adj voir **las**

**lasser** [lase] vt to weary, tire; **se ~ de** vt to grow weary ou tired of

**latéral, e, -aux** [lateʀal, o] adj side cpd, lateral

**latin, e** [latɛ̃, in] adj Latin ♦ nm/f: **L~, e** Latin ♦ nm (LING) Latin

**latitude** [latityd] nf latitude

**latte** [lat] nf lath, slat; (de plancher) board

**lauréat, e** [lɔʀea, at] nm/f winner

**laurier** [lɔʀje] nm (BOT) laurel; (CULIN) bay leaves pl

**lavable** [lavabl] adj washable

**lavabo** [lavabo] nm washbasin; **~s** nmpl (toilettes) toilet sg

**lavage** [lavaʒ] nm washing no pl, wash; **~ de cerveau** brainwashing no pl

**lavande** [lavɑ̃d] nf lavender

**lave** [lav] nf lava no pl

**lave-linge** [lavlɛ̃ʒ] nm inv washing machine

**laver** [lave] vt to wash; (tache) to wash off; **se ~** vi to have a wash; wash; **se ~ les mains/dents** to wash one's hands/clean one's teeth; **~ qn de** (accusation) to clear sb of; **laverie** nf: **laverie (automatique)** launderette; **lavette** nf dish cloth; (fam) drip; **laveur, -euse** nm/f cleaner; **lave-vaisselle** nm inv dishwasher; **lavoir** nm wash house; (évier) sink

**laxatif, -ive** [laksatif, iv] adj, nm laxative

**layette** [lɛjɛt] nf baby clothes

---

**MOT-CLÉ**

**le** [lə], **la, l'** (pl **les**) art déf **1** the; **le livre/la pomme/l'arbre** the book/the apple/the tree; **les étudiants** the students

**2** (noms abstraits): **le courage/l'amour/la jeunesse** courage/love/youth

**3** (indiquant la possession): **se casser**

jambe *etc* to break one's leg *etc*; **levez la main** put your hand up; **avoir les yeux gris/le nez rouge** to have grey eyes/a red nose

**4** (*temps*): **le matin/soir** in the morning/evening; mornings/evenings; **le jeudi** *etc* (on) Thursdays *etc*; (*ce jeudi-là etc*) (on) the Thursday

**5** (*distribution, évaluation*) a, an; **10 F le mètre/kilo** 10F a *ou* per metre/kilo; **le tiers/quart de** a third/quarter of

♦ *pron* **1** (*personne: mâle*) him; (*personne: femelle*) her; (: *pluriel*) them; **je le/la/les vois** I can see him/her/them; **2** (*animal, chose: singulier*) it; (: *pluriel*) them; **je le vois** I can see it; **je les vois** I can see them

**3** (*remplaçant une phrase*): **je ne le savais pas** I didn't know (about it); **il était riche et ne l'est plus** he was once rich but no longer

**lécher** [leʃe] *vt* to lick; (*laper: lait, eau*) to lick *ou* lap up; **lèche-vitrines** *nm*: **faire du lèche-vitrines** to go window-shopping

**leçon** [l(ə)sɔ̃] *nf* lesson; **faire la** ~ (*fig*) to give a lecture to; **~s de conduite** driving lessons

**lecteur, -trice** [lɛktœr, tris] *nm/f* reader; (*d'université*) foreign language assistant ♦ *nm* (*TECH*): ~ **de cassettes/CD** cassette/CD player; ~ **de disquette** disk drive

**lecture** [lɛktyr] *nf* reading

**ledit** [lədi], **ladite** (*mpl* **lesdits**, *fpl* **lesdites**) *dét* the aforesaid

**légal, e, -aux** [legal, o] *adj* legal; **légaliser** *vt* to legalize; **légalité** *nf* law

**légendaire** [leʒɑ̃dɛr] *adj* legendary

**légende** [leʒɑ̃d] *nf* (*mythe*) legend; (*de carte, plan*) key; (*de dessin*) caption

**léger, -ère** [leʒe, ɛr] *adj* light; (*bruit, retard*) slight; (*personne: superficiel*) thoughtless; (: *volage*) free and easy; **à la légère** (*parler, agir*) rashly, thoughtlessly; **légèrement** *adv* (*s'habiller, bou-*

*ger*) lightly; (*un peu*) slightly; **manger légèrement** to eat a light meal; **légèreté** *nf* lightness; (*d'une remarque*) flippancy

**législatif, -ive** [leʒislatif, iv] *adj* legislative; **législatives** *nfpl* general election *sg*

**légitime** [leʒitim] *adj* (*JUR*) lawful, legitimate; (*fig*) rightful, legitimate; **en état de ~ défense** in self-defence

**legs** [lɛg] *nm* legacy

**léguer** [lege] *vt*: ~ **qch à qn** (*JUR*) to bequeath sth to sb

**légume** [legym] *nm* vegetable

**lendemain** [lɑ̃dmɛ̃] *nm*: **le ~** the next *ou* following day; **le ~ matin/soir** the next *ou* following morning/evening; **le ~** the day after

**lent, e** [lɑ̃, lɑ̃t] *adj* slow; **lentement** *adv* slowly; **lenteur** *nf* slowness *no pl*

**lentille** [lɑ̃tij] *nf* (*OPTIQUE*) lens *sg*; (*CULIN*) lentil

**léopard** [leɔpar] *nm* leopard

**lèpre** [lɛpr] *nf* leprosy

---

**MOT-CLÉ**

**lequel, laquelle** [ləkɛl, lakɛl] (*mpl* **lesquels**, *fpl* **lesquelles**) (*à + lequel* = **auquel**, *de + lequel* = **duquel** *etc*) *pron* **1** (*interrogatif*) which, which one

**2** (*relatif: personne: sujet*) who; (: *objet, après préposition*) whom; (: *chose*) which

♦ *adj*: **auquel cas** in which case

---

**les** [le] *dét voir* **le**

**lesbienne** [lɛsbjɛn] *nf* lesbian

**lesdites** [ledit], **lesdits** [ledi] *dét pl*

**léser** *voir* **ledit**

**léser** [leze] *vt* to wrong

**lésiner** [lezine] *vi*: **ne pas ~ sur les moyens** (*pour mariage etc*) to push the boat out

**lésion** [lezjɔ̃] *nf* lesion, damage *no pl*

**lesquelles, lesquels** [lekɛl] *pron* *voir* **lequel**

**lessive** [lesiv] *nf* (*poudre*) washing powder; (*linge*) washing *no pl*, wash; **lessiver** *vt* to wash; (*fam: fatiguer*) to tire out, exhaust

**lest** [lɛst] *nm* ballast

**leste** [lɛst] *adj* sprightly, nimble

**lettre** [lɛtr] *nf* letter; **~s** *nfpl* (*littérature*) literature *sg*; (*SCOL*) arts (subjects); **à la ~** literally; **en toutes ~s** in full

**leucémie** [løsemi] *nf* leukaemia

MOT-CLÉ

**leur** [lœr] *adj possessif* their; **leur maison** their house; **leurs amis** their friends
♦ *pron* **1** (*objet indirect*) (to) them; **je leur ai dit la vérité** I told them the truth; **je le leur ai donné** I gave it to them, I gave them it
**2** (*possessif*): **le(la) leur, les leurs** theirs

**leurre** [lœr] *nm* (*fig: illusion*) delusion; (*: duperie*) deception; **leurrer** *vt* to delude, deceive

**leurs** [lœr] *adj voir* **leur**

**levain** [ləvɛ̃] *nm* leaven

**levé, e** [ləve] *adj*: **être ~** to be up; **levée** *nf* (*POSTES*) collection

**lever** [l(ə)ve] *vt* (*vitre, bras etc*) to raise; (*soulever de terre, supprimer: interdiction, siège*) to lift; (*impôts, armée*) to levy ♦ *vi* to rise ♦ *nm*: **au ~** on getting up; **se ~** *vi* to get up; (*soleil*) to rise; (*jour*) to break; (*brouillard*) to lift; **~ de soleil** sunrise; **~ du jour** daybreak

**levier** [ləvje] *nm* lever

**lèvre** [lɛvr] *nf* lip

**lévrier** [levrije] *nm* greyhound

**levure** [l(ə)vyr] *nf* yeast; **~ chimique** baking powder

**lexique** [lɛksik] *nm* vocabulary; (*glossaire*) lexicon

**lézard** [lezar] *nm* lizard

**lézarde** [lezard] *nf* crack

**liaison** [ljɛzɔ̃] *nf* (*rapport*) connection; (*transport*) link; (*amoureuse*) affair; (*PHONÉTIQUE*) liaison; **entrer/être en ~ avec** to get/be in contact with

**liane** [ljan] *nf* creeper

**liant, e** [ljɑ̃, ljɑ̃t] *adj* sociable

**liasse** [ljas] *nf* wad, bundle

**Liban** [libɑ̃] *nm*: **le ~** (the) Lebanon; **libanais, e** *adj* Lebanese ♦ *nm/f*: **Libanais, e** Lebanese

**libeller** [libele] *vt* (*chèque, mandat*): (**au nom de**) to make out (to); (*lettre*) to word

**libellule** [libelyl] *nf* dragonfly

**libéral, e, -aux** [liberal, o] *adj, nm/f* liberal; **profession ~e** (liberal) profession

**libérer** [libere] *vt* (*délivrer*) to free, liberate; (*relâcher: prisonnier*) to discharge, release; (*: d'inhibitions*) to liberate; (*gaz*) to release; **se ~** *vi* (*de rendez-vous*) to get out of previous engagements

**liberté** [liberte] *nf* freedom; (*loisir*) free time; **~s** *nfpl* (*privautés*) liberties; **mettre/être en ~** to set/be free; **en ~ provisoire/surveillée/conditionnelle** on bail/probation/parole

**libraire** [librɛr] *nm/f* bookseller

**librairie** [librɛri] *nf* bookshop

**libre** [libr] *adj* free; (*route, voie*) clear; (*place, salle*) free; (*ligne*) not engaged; (*SCOL*) non-state; **~ de qch/de faire** free from sth/to do; **~ arbitre** free will; **libre-échange** *nm* free trade; **libre-service** *nm* self-service store

**Libye** [libi] *nf*: **la ~** Libya

**licence** [lisɑ̃s] *nf* (*permis*) permit; (*diplôme*) degree; (*liberté*) licence; **licencié, e** *nm/f* (*SCOL*): **licencié ès lettres/en droit** ≃ Bachelor of Arts/Law

**licenciement** [lisɑ̃simɑ̃] nm redundancy

**licencier** [lisɑ̃sje] vt (débaucher) to make redundant, lay off; (renvoyer) to dismiss

**licite** [lisit] adj lawful

**lie** [li] nf dregs pl, sediment

**lié, e** [lje] adj: **très ~ avec** very friendly with ou close to

**liège** [ljɛʒ] nm cork

**lien** [ljɛ̃] nm (corde, fig: affectif) bond; (rapport) link, connection; **~ de parenté** family tie

**lier** [lje] vt (attacher) to tie up; (joindre) to link up; (fig: unir, engager) to bind; **se ~ avec** to make friends with; **~ qch à** to tie ou link sth to; **~ conversation avec** to strike up a conversation with

**lierre** [ljɛr] nm ivy

**liesse** [ljɛs] nf: **être en ~** to be celebrating ou jubilant

**lieu, x** [ljø] nm place; **~x** nmpl (locaux) premises; (endroit: d'un accident etc) scene sg; **en ~ sûr** in a safe place; **en premier ~** in the first place; **en dernier ~** lastly; **avoir ~** to take place; **tenir ~ de** to serve as; **donner ~ à** to give rise to; **au ~ de** instead of; **lieudit** (pl lieux-dits) nm locality

**lieutenant** [ljøt(ə)nɑ̃] nm lieutenant

**lièvre** [ljɛvr] nm hare

**ligament** [ligamɑ̃] nm ligament

**ligne** [liɲ] nf (gén) line; (TRANSPORTS; liaison) service; (: trajet) route; (silhouette) figure; **entrer en ~ de compte** to come into it

**lignée** [liɲe] nf line, lineage

**ligoter** [ligɔte] vt to tie up

**ligue** [lig] nf league; **liguer** vt: **se liguer contre** (fig) to combine against

**lilas** [lila] nm lilac

**limace** [limas] nf slug

**limande** [limɑ̃d] nf dab

**lime** [lim] nf file; **~ à ongles** nail file; **limer** vt to file

**limier** [limje] nm bloodhound; (détec-

tive) sleuth

**limitation** [limitasjɔ̃] nf: **~ de vitesse** speed limit

**limite** [limit] nf (de terrain) boundary; (partie ou point extrême) limit; **vitesse/charge ~** maximum speed/load; **cas ~** borderline case; **date ~** deadline; **limiter** vt (restreindre) to limit, restrict; (délimiter) to border; **limitrophe** adj border cpd

**limoger** [limɔʒe] vt to dismiss

**limon** [limɔ̃] nm silt

**limonade** [limɔnad] nf lemonade

**linceul** [lɛ̃sœl] nm shroud

**linge** [lɛ̃ʒ] nm (serviettes etc) linen; (lessive) washing; (aussi: **~ de corps**) underwear; **lingerie** nf lingerie, underwear

**lingot** [lɛ̃go] nm ingot

**linguistique** [lɛ̃gɥistik] adj linguistic ♦ nf linguistics sg

**lion, ne** [ljɔ̃, ljɔn] nm/f lion (lioness); (signe): **le L~** Leo; **lionceau, x** nm lion cub

**liqueur** [likœr] nf liqueur

**liquidation** [likidasjɔ̃] nf (vente) sale

**liquide** [likid] adj liquid ♦ nm liquid; (COMM): **en ~** in ready money ou cash; **liquider** vt to liquidate; (COMM: articles) to clear, sell off; **liquidités** nfpl (COMM) liquid assets

**lire** [lir] nf (monnaie) lira ♦ vt, vi to read

**lis** [lis] nm = **lys**

**lisible** [lizibl] adj legible

**lisière** [lizjɛr] nf (de forêt) edge

**lisons** [lizɔ̃] vb voir **lire**

**lisse** [lis] adj smooth

**liste** [list] nf list; **faire la ~ de** to list; **~ électorale** electoral roll; **listing** nm (INFORM) printout

**lit** [li] nm bed; **petit ~**, **lit à une place** single bed; **grand ~**, **lit à deux places** double bed; **faire son ~** to make one's bed; **aller/se mettre au ~** to go to/get into bed; **~ de camp** campbed; **~ d'enfant** cot (BRIT), crib (US)

**literie** [litʀi] nf bedding, bedclothes pl

**litière** [litjɛʀ] nf litter

**litige** [litiʒ] nm dispute

**litre** [litʀ] nm litre

**littéraire** [liteʀɛʀ] adj literary ♦ nm/f arts student; **elle est très ~** (she's very literary)

**littéral, e, -aux** [liteʀal, o] adj literal

**littérature** [liteʀatyʀ] nf literature

**littoral, -aux** [litɔʀal, o] nm coast

**liturgie** [lityʀʒi] nf liturgy

**livide** [livid] adj livid, pallid

**livraison** [livʀɛzɔ̃] nf delivery

**livre** [livʀ] nm book ♦ nf (poids, monnaie) pound; **~ de bord** logbook; **~ de poche** paperback

**livré, e** [livʀe] adj: **~ à soi-même** left to o.s. ou one's own devices; **livrée** f livery

**livrer** [livʀe] vt (COMM) to deliver; (otage, coupable) to hand over; (secret, information) to give away; **se ~ à** (se confier) to confide in; (se rendre, s'abandonner) to give o.s. up to; (faire: pratiques, actes) to indulge in; (enquête) to carry out

**livret** [livʀɛ] nm booklet; (d'opéra) libretto; **~ de caisse d'épargne** (savings) bank-book; **~ de famille** (official) family record book; **~ scolaire** (school) report book

**livreur, -euse** [livʀœʀ, øz] nm/f delivery boy ou man/girl ou woman

**local, e, -aux** [lɔkal] adj local ♦ nm (salle) premises pl; voir aussi **locaux**; **localiser** vt (repérer) to locate, place; (limiter) to confine; **localité** nf locality

**locataire** [lɔkatɛʀ] nm/f tenant; (de chambre) lodger

**location** [lɔkasjɔ̃] nf (par le locataire, le loueur) renting; (par le propriétaire) renting out, letting; (THÉÂTRE) booking office; **"~ de voitures"** "car rental"; **habiter en ~** to live in rented accommodation; **prendre une ~** (pour les vacances) to rent a house etc (for the holidays)

**locaux** [lɔko] nmpl premises

**locomotive** [lɔkɔmɔtiv] nf locomotive, engine

**locution** [lɔkysjɔ̃] nf phrase

**loge** [lɔʒ] nf (THÉÂTRE: d'artiste) dressing room; (de spectateurs) box; (de concierge, franc-maçon) lodge

**logement** [lɔʒmɑ̃] nm accommodation no pl (BRIT), accommodations pl (US); (appartement) flat (BRIT), apartment (US); (hébergement) housing no pl

**loger** [lɔʒe] vt to accommodate ♦ vi to live; **se ~ dans** (suj: balle, flèche) to lodge itself in; **trouver à se ~** to find accommodation; **logeur, -euse** nm/f landlord(-lady)

**logiciel** [lɔʒisjɛl] nm software

**logique** [lɔʒik] adj logical ♦ nf logic

**logis** [lɔʒi] nm abode, dwelling

**logo** [lɔgo] nm logo

**loi** [lwa] nf law; **faire la ~** to lay down the law

**loin** [lwɛ̃] adv far; (dans le temps: futur) a long way off; (: passé) a long time ago; **plus ~** further; **~ de** far from; **au ~** far off; **de ~** from a distance; (fig: de beaucoup) by far

**lointain, e** [lwɛ̃tɛ̃, ɛn] adj faraway, distant; (dans le futur, passé) distant; (cause, parent) remote, distant ♦ nm: **dans le ~** in the distance

**loir** [lwaʀ] nm dormouse

**loisir** [lwaziʀ] nm: **heures de ~** spare time; **~s** nmpl (temps libre) leisure sg; (activités) leisure activities; **avoir le ~ de faire** to have the time ou opportunity to do; **à ~** at leisure

**londonien, ne** [lɔ̃dɔnjɛ̃, jɛn] adj London cpd, of London ♦ nm/f: **L~, ne** Londoner

**Londres** [lɔ̃dʀ] n London

**long, longue** [lɔ̃, lɔ̃g] adj long ♦ adv: **en savoir ~** to know a great deal ♦ nm: **de 3 m de ~** 3 m long, 3 m in length; **ne pas faire ~ feu** not to last long; **(tout) le ~ de** (all) along; **tout au ~ de** (année, vie) throughout; **de ~**

**en large** (*marcher*) to and fro, up and down; *voir aussi* **longue**

**longer** [lɔ̃ʒe] vt to go (*ou* walk *ou* drive) along(side); (*suj: mur, route*) to border

**longiligne** [lɔ̃ʒiliɲ] *adj* long-limbed

**longitude** [lɔ̃ʒityd] *nf* longitude

**longtemps** [lɔ̃tɑ̃] *adv* (for) a long time, (for) long; **avant** ~ before long; **pour** *ou* **pendant** ~ for a long time; **mettre** ~ **à faire** to take a long time to do

**longue** [lɔ̃g] *adj voir* **long** ♦ *nf*: **à la** ~ in the end; **longuement** *adv* (*longtemps*) for a long time; (*en détail*) at length

**longueur** [lɔ̃gœʀ] *nf* length; ~**s** *nfpl* (*fig: d'un film etc*) tedious parts; **en** ~ lengthwise; **tirer en** ~ to drag on; **à** ~ **de journée** all day long; ~ **d'onde** wavelength

**longue-vue** [lɔ̃gvy] *nf* telescope

**look** [luk] (*fam*) *nm* look, image

**lopin** [lɔpɛ̃] *nm*: ~ **de terre** patch of land

**loque** [lɔk] *nf* (*personne*) wreck; ~**s** *nfpl* (*habits*) rags

**loquet** [lɔkɛ] *nm* latch

**lorgner** [lɔʀɲe] vt to eye; (*fig*) to have one's eye on

**lors** [lɔʀ] : ~ **de** *prép* at the time of; during

**lorsque** [lɔʀsk] *conj* when, as

**losange** [lɔzɑ̃ʒ] *nm* diamond

**lot** [lo] *nm* (*part*) share; (*de ~erie*) prize; (*fig: destin*) fate, lot; (*COMM, INFORM*) batch; **le gros** ~ the jackpot

**loterie** [lɔtʀi] *nf* lottery

**loti, e** [lɔti] *adj*: **bien/mal** ~ well-/badly off

**lotion** [losjɔ̃] *nf* lotion

**lotissement** [lɔtismɑ̃] *nm* housing development; (*parcelle*) plot, lot

**loto** [lɔto] *nm* lotto

---
**Loto**

Le Loto is a state-run national lottery with large cash prizes. Participants select 7 numbers out of 49. The
---

more correct numbers, the greater the prize. The draw is televised twice weekly.

---

**lotte** [lɔt] *nf* monkfish

**louable** [lwabl] *adj* commendable

**louanges** [lwɑ̃ʒ] *nfpl* praise *sg*

**loubard** [lubaʀ] (*fam*) *nm* lout

**louche** [luʃ] *adj* shady, fishy, dubious ♦ *nf* ladle; **loucher** vi to squint

**louer** [lwe] vt (*maison: suj: propriétaire*) to let, to rent (out); (: *locataire*) to rent; (*voiture etc: entreprise*) to hire out (*BRIT*), rent (out); (: *locataire*) to hire, rent; (*réserver*) to book; (*faire l'éloge de*) to praise; **"à** ~**"** "to let" (*BRIT*), "for rent" (*US*)

**loup** [lu] *nm* wolf

**loupe** [lup] *nf* magnifying glass

**louper** [lupe] (*fam*) vt (*manquer*) to miss; (*examen*) to flunk

**lourd, e** [luʀ, luʀd] *adj, adv* heavy; ~ **de** (*conséquences, menaces*) charged with; **il fait** ~ the weather is close, it's sultry; **lourdaud, e** (*péj*) *adj* clumsy; **lourdement** *adv* heavily; **lourdeur** *nf* weight; **lourdeurs d'estomac** indigestion

**loutre** [lutʀ] *nf* otter

**louveteau, x** [luv(ə)to] *nm* wolf-cub; (*scout*) cub (scout)

**louvoyer** [luvwaje] vi (*fig*) to hedge, evade the issue

**loyal, e, -aux** [lwajal, o] *adj* (*fidèle*) loyal, faithful; (*fair-play*) fair; **loyauté** *nf* loyalty, faithfulness; fairness

**loyer** [lwaje] *nm* rent

**lu, e** [ly] *pp de* **lire**

**lubie** [lybi] *nf* whim, craze

**lubrifiant** [lybʀifjɑ̃, jɑ̃t] *nm* lubricant

**lubrifier** [lybʀifje] vt to lubricate

**lubrique** [lybʀik] *adj* lecherous

**lucarne** [lykaʀn] *nf* skylight

**lucide** [lysid] *adj* lucid; (*accidenté*) conscious

**lucratif, -ive** [lykʀatif, iv] *adj* lucrative, profitable; **à but non** ~ non profit-making

**lueur** [lɥœʀ] nf (pâle) (faint) light; (chatoyante) glimmer no pl; (fig) glimmer; gleam

**luge** [lyʒ] nf sledge (BRIT), sled (US)

**lugubre** [lygybʀ] adj gloomy, dismal

MOT-CLÉ

**lui** [lɥi] pron 1 (objet indirect: mâle) (to) him; (: femelle) (to) her; (: chose, animal) (to) it; **je lui ai parlé** I have spoken to him (ou to her); **il lui a offert un cadeau** he gave him (ou her) a present

2 (après préposition, comparatif: personne) him; (: chose, animal) it; **elle est contente de lui** she is pleased with him; **je le connais mieux que lui** I know him better than he does; I know her better than him

3 (sujet, forme emphatique) he; **lui, il est à Paris** HE is in Paris

4: **lui-même** himself; itself

**luire** [lɥiʀ] vi to shine; (en rougeoyant) to glow

**lumière** [lymjɛʀ] nf light; **mettre en ~** (fig) to highlight; **~ du jour** daylight

**luminaire** [lyminɛʀ] nm lamp, light

**lumineux, -euse** [lyminø, øz] adj luminous; (éclairé) illuminated; (ciel, couleur) bright; (rayon) of light, light cpd; (fig: regard) radiant

**lunatique** [lynatik] adj whimsical, temperamental

**lundi** [lœdi] nm Monday; **~ de Pâques** Easter Monday

**lune** [lyn] nf moon; **~ de miel** honeymoon

**lunette** [lynɛt] nf: **~s** nfpl glasses, spectacles; (protectrices) goggles; **~ arrière** (AUTO) rear window; **~s de soleil** sunglasses

**lus** etc [ly] vb voir **lire**

**lustre** [lystʀ] nm (de plafond) chandelier; (fig: éclat) lustre; **lustrer** vt to shine

**lut** [ly] vb voir **lire**

**luth** [lyt] nm lute

**lutin** [lytɛ̃] nm imp, goblin

**lutte** [lyt] nf (conflit) struggle; (sport) wrestling; **lutter** vi to fight, struggle

**luxe** [lyks] nm luxury; **de ~** luxury cpd

**Luxembourg** [lyksɑ̃buʀ] nm: **le ~** Luxembourg

**luxer** [lykse] vt: **se ~ l'épaule** to dislocate one's shoulder

**luxueux, -euse** [lyksɥø, øz] adj luxurious

**luxure** [lyksyʀ] nf lust

**luxuriant, e** [lyksyʀjɑ̃, ɑ̃t] adj luxuriant

**lycée** [lise] nm secondary school; **lycéen, ne** nm/f secondary school pupil

**lyophilisé, e** [ljɔfilize] adj (café) freeze-dried

**lyrique** [liʀik] adj lyrical; (OPÉRA) lyric; **artiste ~** opera singer

**lys** [lis] nm lily

# M, m

**M** abr = **Monsieur**

**m'** [m] pron voir **me**

**ma** [ma] adj voir **mon**

**macaron** [makaʀɔ̃] nm (gâteau) macaroon; (insigne) (round) badge

**macaronis** [makaʀɔni] nmpl macaroni sg

**macédoine** [masedwan] nf: **~ de fruits** fruit salad; **~ de légumes** mixed vegetables

**macérer** [maseʀe] vi, vt to macerate; (dans du vinaigre) to pickle

**mâcher** [mɑʃe] vt to chew; **ne pas ~ ses mots** not to mince one's words

**machin** [maʃɛ̃] (fam) nm thing(umajig)

**machinal, e, -aux** [maʃinal, o] adj mechanical, automatic; **machinalement** adv mechanically, automatically

**machination** [maʃinasjɔ̃] nf frame-up

**machine** [maʃin] nf machine; (locomotive) engine; **~ à écrire** typewriter; **~ à laver/coudre** washing/sewing machine; ~ **à sous** fruit machine

**macho** [matʃo] (*fam*) *nm* male chauvinist

**mâchoire** [mɑʃwaʀ] *nf* jaw

**mâchonner** [mɑʃɔne] *vt* to chew (at)

**maçon** [masɔ̃] *nm* builder; (*poseur de briques*) bricklayer; **maçonnerie** *nf* (*murs*) brickwork; (*pierres*) masonry, stonework

**maculer** [makyle] *vt* to stain

**Madame** [madam] (*pl* **Mesdames**) *nf*: ~ **X** Mrs X; **occupez-vous de ~/ Monsieur/Mademoiselle** please serve this lady/gentleman/(young) lady; **bonjour ~/Monsieur/Mademoiselle** good morning; (*ton déférent*) good morning Madam/Sir/Madam; (*le nom est connu*) good morning Mrs/Mr/Miss X; **~/ Monsieur/Mademoiselle** (*pour appeler*) Madam/Sir/Miss!; **~/Monsieur/ Mademoiselle** (*sur lettre*) Dear Madam/Sir/Madam; **chère ~/cher Monsieur/chère Mademoiselle** Dear Mrs/Mr/Miss X; **Mesdames** Ladies

**madeleine** [madlɛn] *nf* madeleine; small sponge cake

**Mademoiselle** [madmwazɛl] (*pl* **Mesdemoiselles**) *nf* Miss; *voir aussi* **Madame**

**madère** [madɛʀ] *nm* Madeira (wine)

**magasin** [magazɛ̃] *nm* (*boutique*) shop; (*entrepôt*) warehouse; **en ~** (*COMM*) in stock

**magazine** [magazin] *nm* magazine

**Maghreb** [magʀɛb] *nm*: **le ~** North Africa; **maghrébin, e** *adj* North African ♦ *nm/f*: **M~** Maghrébin, e North African

**magicien, ne** [maʒisjɛ̃, jɛn] *nm/f* magician

**magie** [maʒi] *nf* magic; **magique** *adj* magic; (*enchanteur*) magical

**magistral, e, -aux** [maʒistral, o] *adj* (*œuvre, adresse*) masterly; (*ton*) authoritative; **cours ~** lecture

**magistrat** [maʒistra] *nm* magistrate

**magnat** [magna] *nm* tycoon

**magnétique** [manetik] *adj* magnetic

**magnétiser** [manetize] *vt* to magnetize; (*fig*) to mesmerize, hypnotize

**magnétophone** [manetɔfɔn] *nm* tape recorder; ~ **à cassettes** cassette recorder

**magnétoscope** [manetɔskɔp] *nm* video-tape recorder

**magnifique** [manifik] *adj* magnificent

**magot** [mago] (*fam*) *nm* (*argent*) pile (of money); (*économies*) nest egg

**magouille** [maguj] (*fam*) *nf* scheming; **magouiller** (*fam*) *vi* to scheme

**magret** [magʀɛ] *nm*: ~ **de canard** duck steaklet

**mai** [mɛ] *nm* May

---

**mai**

Le premier mai *is a public holiday in France marking union demonstrations in the United States in 1886 to secure the eight-hour working day. It is traditional to exchange and wear sprigs of lily of the valley. The 8 mai is a public holiday in France commemorating the surrender of the German army to Eisenhower on May 7, 1945. There are parades of ex-servicemen in most towns. The social upheavals of May and June 1968, marked by student demonstrations, strikes and rioting, are generally referred to as* "les événements de mai 68". *De Gaulle's government survived, but reforms in education and a move towards decentralization ensued.*

---

**maigre** [mɛgʀ] *adj* (*very*) thin, skinny; (*viande*) lean; (*fromage*) low-fat; (*végétation*) thin, sparse; (*fig*) poor, meagre, skimpy; **jours ~s** days of abstinence, fish days; **maigreur** *nf* thinness; **maigrir** *vi* to get thinner, lose weight; **maigrir de 2 kilos** to lose 2 kilos

**maille** [maj] *nf* stitch; **avoir ~ à partir avec qn** to have a brush with sb; ~ **à l'endroit/à l'envers** plain/purl stitch

**maillet** [majɛ] *nm* mallet

**maillon** [majɔ̃] *nm* link

**maillot** [majo] *nm* (*aussi:* ~ **de corps**) vest; (*de sportif*) jersey; ~ **de bain** swimsuit; (*d'homme*) bathing trunks *pl*

**main** [mɛ̃] *nf* hand; **à la** ~ in one's hand; **se donner la** ~ to hold hands; **donner** *ou* **tendre la** ~ **à qn** to hold out one's hand to sb; **serrer la** ~ **à qn** to shake hands with sb; **sous la** ~ *to ou* at hand; **à remettre en** ~s **propres** to be delivered personally; **mettre la dernière** ~ **à** to put the finishing touches to; **se faire/perdre la** ~ to get one's hand in/lose one's touch; **avoir qch bien en** ~ to have (got) the hang of sth; **main-d'œuvre** *nf* manpower, labour; **main-forte** *nf*: **prêter main-forte à qn** to come to sb's assistance; **mainmise** *nf* (*fig*): **mainmise sur** complete hold on

**maint, e** [mɛ̃, mɛ̃t] *adj* many a; ~s many; **à** ~**es reprises** time and (time) again

**maintenant** [mɛ̃t(ə)nɑ̃] *adv* now; (*actuellement*) nowadays

**maintenir** [mɛ̃t(ə)niʀ] *vt* (*retenir, soutenir*) to support; (*contenir: foule etc*) to hold back; (*conserver, affirmer*) to maintain; **se** ~ *vi* (*prix*) to keep steady; (*amélioration*) to persist

**maintien** [mɛ̃tjɛ̃] *nm* (*sauvegarde*) maintenance; (*attitude*) bearing

**maire** [mɛʀ] *nm* mayor; **mairie** *nf* (*bâtiment*) town hall; (*administration*) town council

**mais** [mɛ] *conj* but; ~ **non!** of course not!; ~ **enfin** but after all; (*indignation*) look here!

**maïs** [mais] *nm* maize (BRIT), corn (US)

**maison** [mɛzɔ̃] *nf* house; (*chez-soi*) home; (COMM) firm; **~ adj** (CULIN) home-made; (*fig*) in-house, own; **à la** ~ at home; (*direction*) home; ~ **close** *ou* **de passe** brothel; ~ **de repos** convalescent home; ~ **de santé** mental home; ~ **des jeunes** ≈ youth club; ~

**mère** parent company; **maisonnée** *nf* household, family; **maisonnette** *nf* small house, cottage

---

**maisons des jeunes et de la culture**

Maisons des jeunes et de la culture are centres for young people which organize a wide range of sporting and cultural activities, and are also engaged in welfare work. The centres are, in part, publicly financed.

---

**maître, -esse** [mɛtʀ, mɛtʀɛs] *nm/f* master (mistress); (SCOL) teacher, schoolmaster(-mistress) ♦ *nm* (*peintre etc*) master; (*titre*): **M~** Maître, term of address gen for a barrister ♦ *adj* (*principal, essentiel*) main; **être ~ de** (*soi, situation*) to be in control of; **une maîtresse femme** a managing woman; ~ **chanteur** blackmailer; **~ d'école** schoolmaster; ~ **d'hôtel** (*domestique*) butler; (*d'hôtel*) head waiter; ~ **nageur** lifeguard; **maîtresse** *nf* (*amante*) mistress; **maîtresse d'école** teacher, (school)mistress; **maîtresse de maison** hostess; (*ménagère*) housewife

**maîtrise** [mɛtʀiz] *nf* (*aussi:* ~ **de soi**) self-control, self-possession; (*habileté*) skill, mastery; (*suprématie*) mastery, command; (*diplôme*) ≈ master's degree; **maîtriser** *vt* (*cheval, incendie*) to (bring under) control; (*sujet*) to master; (*émotion*) to control, master; **se maîtriser** to control o.s.

**maïzena** ® [maizena] *nf* cornflour

**majestueux, -euse** [maʒɛstɥø, øz] *adj* majestic

**majeur, e** [maʒœʀ] *adj* (*important*) major; (JUR) of age ♦ *nm* (*doigt*) middle finger; **en ~e partie** for the most part; **la ~e partie de** most of

**majoration** [maʒɔʀasjɔ̃] *nf* rise, increase

**majorer** [maʒɔʀe] *vt* to increase

**majoritaire** [maʒɔʀitɛʀ] *adj* majority

*cpd*

**majorité** [maʒɔʀite] *nf* (*gén*) majority; (*parti*) party in power; **en ~** mainly

**majuscule** [maʒyskyl] *adj, nf:* (**lettre**) **~** capital (letter)

**mal** [mal, mo] (*pl* **maux**) *nm* (*opposé au bien*) evil; (*tort, dommage*) harm; (*douleur physique*) pain, ache; (~*adie*) illness, sickness *no pl* ♦ *adv* badly ♦ *adj* bad, wrong; **être ~ à l'aise** to be uncomfortable; **être ~ avec qn** to be on bad terms with sb; **il a ~ compris** he misunderstood; **dire/penser du ~ de** to speak/think ill of; **ne voir aucun ~ à** to see no harm in, see nothing wrong in; **faire ~ à qn** to hurt sb; **se faire ~** to hurt o.s.; **se donner du ~ pour faire qch** to go to a lot of trouble to do sth; **ça fait ~** it hurts; **j'ai au dos** my back hurts; **avoir ~ à la tête/à la gorge/aux dents** to have a headache/a sore throat/toothache; **avoir le ~ du pays** to be homesick; *voir aussi* **cœur; maux; ~ de mer** seasickness; **~ en point** in a bad state

**malade** [malad] *adj* ill, sick; (*poitrine, jambe*) bad; (*plante*) diseased ♦ *nm/f* invalid, sick person; (*à l'hôpital etc*) patient; **tomber ~** to fall ill; **être ~ du cœur** to have heart trouble ou a bad heart; **~ mental** mentally sick ou ill person; **maladie** [maladi] *nf* (*spécifique*) disease, illness; (*mauvaise santé*) illness, sickness; **maladif, -ive** *adj* sickly; (*curiosité, besoin*) pathological

**maladresse** [maladrɛs] *nf* clumsiness *no pl*; (*gaffe*) blunder

**maladroit, e** [maladrwa, wat] *adj* clumsy

**malaise** [malɛz] *nm* (*MÉD*) feeling of faintness; (*fig*) uneasiness, malaise; **avoir un ~** to feel faint

**malaisé, e** [maleze] *adj* difficult

**malaria** [malaʀja] *nf* malaria

**malaxer** [malakse] *vt* (*pétrir*) to knead; (*mélanger*) to mix

**malchance** [malʃɑ̃s] *nf* misfortune, ill

luck *no pl*; **par ~** unfortunately; **malchanceux, -euse** *adj* unlucky

**mâle** [mɑl] *adj* (*aussi ÉLEC, TECH*) male; (*viril: voix, traits*) manly ♦ *nm* male

**malédiction** [malediksjɔ̃] *nf* curse

**mal...: malencontreux, -euse** *adj* unfortunate, untoward; **mal-en-point** *adj inv* in a sorry state; **malentendant, e** *nm/f:* **les malentendants** the hard of hearing; **malentendu** *nm* misunderstanding; **malfaçon** *nf* fault; **malfaisant, e** *adj* evil, harmful; **malfaiteur** *nm* lawbreaker, criminal; (*voleur*) burglar, thief; **malfamé, e** *adj* disreputable

**malgache** [malgaʃ] *adj* Madagascan, Malagasy ♦ *nm/f:* **M~** Madagascan, Malagasy ♦ *nm* (*LING*) Malagasy

**malgré** [malgre] *prép* in spite of, despite; **~ tout** all the same

**malhabile** [malabil] *adj* clumsy, awkward

**malheur** [malœʀ] *nm* (*situation*) adversity, misfortune; (*événement*) misfortune; (*: très grave*) disaster, tragedy; **faire un ~** to be a smash hit; **malheureusement** *adv* unfortunately; **malheureux, -euse** *adj* (*triste*) unhappy, miserable; (*infortuné, regrettable*) unfortunate; (*malchanceux*) unlucky; (*insignifiant*) wretched ♦ *nm/f* poor soul; **les malheureux** the destitute

**malhonnête** [malɔnɛt] *adj* dishonest; **malhonnêteté** *nf* dishonesty

**malice** [malis] *nf* mischievousness; (*méchanceté*) spite; **par ~** out of malice ou spite; **sans ~** guileless; **malicieux, -euse** *adj* mischievous

**malin, -igne** [malɛ̃, maliɲ] *adj* (*futé: f gén: ~e*) smart, shrewd; (*MÉD*) malignant

**malingre** [malɛ̃gʀ] *adj* puny

**malle** [mal] *nf* trunk; **mallette** *nf* (*small*) suitcase; (*porte-documents*) attaché case

**malmener** [malməne] *vt* to manhandle; (*fig*) to give a rough handling to

**malodorant, e** [malɔdɔrɑ̃, ɑ̃t] adj foul- ou ill-smelling

**malotru** [malɔtry] nm lout, boor

**malpoli, e** [malpɔli] adj impolite

**malpropre** [malprɔpr] adj dirty

**malsain, e** [malsɛ̃, ɛn] adj unhealthy

**malt** [malt] nm malt

**Malte** [malt] nf Malta

**maltraiter** [maltrete] vt to manhandle, ill-treat

**malveillance** [malvejɑ̃s] nf (animosité) ill will; (intention de nuire) malevolence

**malversation** [malvɛrsasjɔ̃] nf embezzlement

**maman** [mamɑ̃] nf mum(my), mother

**mamelle** [mamɛl] nf teat

**mamelon** [mam(ə)lɔ̃] nm (ANAT) nipple

**mamie** [mami] (fam) nf granny

**mammifère** [mamifɛr] nm mammal

**mammouth** [mamut] nm mammoth

**manche** [mɑ̃ʃ] nf (de vêtement) sleeve; (d'un jeu, tournoi) round; (GÉO): **la M~** the Channel ♦ nm (d'outil, casserole) handle; (de pelle, pioche etc) shaft; **à ~s courtes/longues** short-/long-sleeved

**manchette** [mɑ̃ʃɛt] nf (de chemise) cuff; (coup) forearm blow; (titre) headline

**manchot** [mɑ̃ʃo, ɔt] nm one-armed man; armless man; (ZOOL) penguin

**mandarine** [mɑ̃darin] nf mandarin (orange), tangerine

**mandat** [mɑ̃da] nm (postal) postal ou money order; (d'un député etc) mandate; (procuration) power of attorney, proxy; (POLICE) warrant; **~ d'arrêt** warrant for arrest; **mandataire** nm/f (représentant) representative; (JUR) proxy

**manège** [manɛʒ] nm riding school; (à la foire) roundabout, merry-go-round; (fig) game, ploy

**manette** [manɛt] nf lever, tap; **~ de jeu** joystick

**mangeable** [mɑ̃ʒabl] adj edible, eatable

**mangeoire** [mɑ̃ʒwar] nf trough, manger

**manger** [mɑ̃ʒe] vt to eat; (ronger: suj: rouille etc) to eat into ou away ♦ vi to eat; **donner à ~ à** (enfant) to feed; **mangeur, -euse** nm/f eater; **gros mangeur** big eater

**mangue** [mɑ̃g] nf mango

**maniable** [manjabl] adj (outil) handy; (voiture, voilier) easy to handle

**maniaque** [manjak] adj finicky, fussy ♦ nm/f (méticuleux) fusspot; (fou) maniac

**manie** [mani] nf (tic) odd habit; (obsession) mania; **avoir la ~ de** to be obsessive about

**manier** [manje] vt to handle

**manière** [manjɛr] nf (façon) way, manner; **~s** nfpl (attitude) manners; (chichis) fuss sg; **de ~ à** so as to; **de cette ~** in this way ou manner; **d'une certaine ~** in a way; **de toute ~** in any case

**maniéré, e** [manjere] adj affected

**manif** [manif] (fam) nf demo

**manifestant, e** [manifestɑ̃, ɑ̃t] nm/f demonstrator

**manifestation** [manifestasjɔ̃] nf (de joie, mécontentement) expression, demonstration; (symptôme) outward sign; (culturelle etc) event; (POL) demonstration

**manifeste** [manifest] adj obvious, evident ♦ nm manifesto; **manifester** vt (volonté, intentions) to show, indicate; (joie, peur) to express, show ♦ vi to demonstrate; **se manifester** vi (émotion) to show ou express itself; (difficultés) to arise; (symptômes) to appear

**manigance** [manigɑ̃s] nf scheme; **manigancer** vt to plot

**manipulation** [manipylasjɔ̃] nf handling; (POL, génétique) manipulation

**manipuler** [manipyle] vt to handle; (fig) to manipulate

**manivelle** [manivel] nf crank

**mannequin** [mankɛ̃] nm (COUTURE) dummy; (MODE) model

**manœuvre** [manœvr] nf (gén) manœuvre (BRIT), maneuver (US) ♦ nm labourer; **manœuvrer** vt to manœuvre

(BRIT), maneuver (US); (levier, machine) to operate ♦ vi to manoeuvre

**manoir** [manwar] nm manor ou country house

**manque** [mɑ̃k] nm (insuffisance): ~ **de** lack of; (vide) emptiness, gap; (MÉD) withdrawal; **être en état de** ~ to suffer withdrawal symptoms

**manqué, e** [mɑ̃ke] adj failed; **garçon** ~ tomboy

**manquer** [mɑ̃ke] vi (faire défaut) to be lacking; (être absent) to be missing; (échouer) to fail ♦ vt to miss ♦ vb impers: **il (nous) manque encore 100 F** we are still 100 F short; **il manque des pages (au livre)** there are some pages missing (from the book); **il/cela me manque** I miss him/this; ~ **à** (règles etc) to be in breach of, fail to observe; ~ **de** to lack; **je ne ~ai pas de le lui dire** I'll be sure to tell him; **il a manqué (de) se tuer** he very nearly got killed

**mansarde** [mɑ̃sard] nf attic; **mansardé, e** adj: **chambre mansardée** attic room

**manteau, x** [mɑ̃to] nm coat

**manucure** [manykyr] nf manicurist

**manuel, le** [manɥɛl] adj manual ♦ nm (ouvrage) manual, handbook

**manufacture** [manyfaktyr] nf factory; **manufacturé, e** adj manufactured

**manuscrit, e** [manyskri, it] adj handwritten ♦ nm manuscript

**manutention** [manytɑ̃sjɔ̃] nf (COMM) handling

**mappemonde** [mapmɔ̃d] nf (plane) map of the world; (sphère) globe

**maquereau, x** [makro] nm (ZOOL) mackerel inv; (fam) pimp

**maquette** [makɛt] nf (à échelle réduite) (scale) model; (d'une page illustrée) paste-up

**maquillage** [makijaʒ] nm making up; (crème etc) make-up

**maquiller** [makije] vt (personne, visage) to make up; (truquer: passeport, statisti-

que) to take; (: voiture volée) to do over (respray etc); **se** ~ vi to make up (one's face)

**maquis** [maki] nm (GÉO) scrub; (MIL) maquis, underground fighting no pl

**maraîcher, -ère** [marɛʃe, ɛr] adj: **cultures maraîchères** market gardening sg ♦ nm/f market gardener

**marais** [marɛ] nm marsh, swamp

**marasme** [marasm] nm stagnation, slump

**marathon** [maratɔ̃] nm marathon

**maraudeur, øz** [marodœr, øz] nm prowler

**marbre** [marbr] nm marble

**marc** [mar] nm (de raisin, pommes) marc; ~ **de café** coffee grounds pl ou dregs pl

**marchand, e** [marʃɑ̃, ɑ̃d] nm/f shopkeeper, tradesman(-woman); (au marché) stallholder; (de vins, charbon) merchant ♦ adj: **prix/valeur ~(e)** market price/value; **~(e) de fruits** fruiterer (BRIT), fruit seller (US); **~(e) de journaux** newsagent; **~(e) de légumes** greengrocer (BRIT), produce dealer (US); **~(e) de poissons** fishmonger; **marchander** vi to bargain, haggle; **marchandise** nf goods pl, merchandise no pl

**marche** [marʃ] nf (d'escalier) step; (activité) walking; (promenade, trajet, allure) walk; (démarche) walk, gait; (MIL etc) march; (fonctionnement) running; (des événements) course; **dans le sens de la** ~ (RAIL) facing the engine; **en** ~ (monter etc) while the vehicle is moving ou in motion; **mettre en** ~ to start; **se mettre en** ~ (personne) to get moving; (machine) to start; **être en état de** ~ to be in working order; ~ **à suivre** (correct) procedure; **arrière** reverse (gear); **faire** ~ **arrière** to reverse; (fig) to backtrack, back-pedal

**marché** [marʃe] nm market; (transaction) bargain, deal; **faire du** ~ **noir** to buy and sell on the black market; ~ **aux puces** flea market; **M~ commun**

Common Market

**marchepied** [maʁʃəpje] nm (RAIL) step

**marcher** [maʁʃe] vi to walk; (MIL) to march; (aller: voiture, train, affaires) to go; (prospérer) to go well; (fonctionner) to work, run; (fam: consentir) to go along, agree; (: croire naïvement) to be taken in; **faire ~ qn** (taquiner) to pull sb's leg; (tromper) to lead sb up the garden path; **marcheur, -euse** nm/f walker

**mardi** [maʁdi] nm Tuesday; **M~ gras** Shrove Tuesday

**mare** [maʁ] nf pond; (flaque) pool

**marécage** [maʁekaʒ] nm marsh, swamp; **marécageux, -euse** adj marshy

**maréchal, -aux** [maʁeʃal, o] nm marshal; **maréchal-ferrant** [maʁeʃalferɑ̃, maʁeʃo-] (pl **maréchaux-ferrants**) nm blacksmith, farrier

**marée** [maʁe] nf tide; (poissons) fresh (sea) fish; **~ haute/basse** high/low tide; **~ montante/descendante** rising/ebb tide; **~ noire** oil slick

**marelle** [maʁɛl] nf hopscotch

**margarine** [maʁɡaʁin] nf margarine

**marge** [maʁʒ] nf margin; **en ~ de** (fig) on the fringe of; **~ bénéficiaire** profit margin

**marginal, e, -aux** [maʁʒinal, o] nm/f (original) eccentric; (déshérité) dropout

**marguerite** [maʁɡəʁit] nf marguerite, (oxeye) daisy; (d'imprimante) daisy-wheel

**mari** [maʁi] nm husband

**mariage** [maʁjaʒ] nm marriage; (noce) wedding; **~ civil/religieux** registry office (BRIT) ou civil/church wedding

**marié, e** [maʁje] adj married ♦ nm (bride)groom; **les ~s** the bride and groom; **les (jeunes) ~s** the newlyweds; **mariée** nf bride

**marier** [maʁje] vt to marry; (fig) to blend; **se ~** vt to get married; **se ~ (avec)** to marry

**marin, e** [maʁɛ̃, in] adj sea cpd, marine

♦ nm sailor

**marine** [maʁin] adj voir **marin** ♦ adj inv navy (blue) ♦ nm (MIL) marine ♦ nf navy; **~ de guerre** navy; **~ marchande** merchant navy

**mariner** [maʁine] vt: **faire ~** to marinade

**marionnette** [maʁjɔnɛt] nf puppet

**maritalement** [maʁitalmɑ̃] adv: **vivre ~** to live as husband and wife

**maritime** [maʁitim] adj sea cpd, maritime

**mark** [maʁk] nm mark

**marmelade** [maʁməlad] nf stewed fruit, compote; **~ d'oranges** marmalade

**marmite** [maʁmit] nf (cooking-)pot

**marmonner** [maʁmɔne] vt, vi to mumble, mutter

**marmot** [maʁmo] (fam) nm kid

**marmotter** [maʁmɔte] vt to mumble

**Maroc** [maʁɔk] nm: **le ~** Morocco; **marocain, e** [maʁɔkɛ̃, ɛn] adj Moroccan ♦ nm/f: **Marocain, e** Moroccan

**maroquinerie** [maʁɔkinʁi] nf (articles) fine leather goods pl; (boutique) shop selling fine leather goods

**marquant, e** [maʁkɑ̃, ɑ̃t] adj outstanding

**marque** [maʁk] nf mark; (COMM: de nourriture) brand; (: de voiture, produits manufacturés) make; (de disques) label; **de ~** (produits) high-class; (visiteur etc) distinguished, well-known; **une grande ~ de vin** a well-known brand of wine; **~ de fabrique** trademark; **~ déposée** registered trademark

**marquer** [maʁke] vt to mark; (inscrire) to write down; (bétail) to brand; (SPORT: but etc) to score; (: joueur) to mark; (accentuer: taille etc) to emphasize; (manifester: refus, intérêt) to show ♦ vi (événement) to stand out, be outstanding; (SPORT) to score

**marqueterie** [maʁkɛtʁi] nf inlaid work, marquetry

**marquis** [maʁki] nm marquis, marquess; **marquise** nf marchioness; (auvent) glass canopy ou awning

**marraine** [maʀɛn] nf godmother

**marrant, e** [maʀɑ̃, ɑ̃t] (fam) adj funny

**marre** [maʀ] (fam) adv: **en avoir ~ de** to be fed up with

**marrer** [maʀe]: **se ~** (fam) vi to have a (good) laugh

**marron** [maʀɔ̃] nm (fruit) chestnut ♦ adj inv brown; **~s glacés** candied chestnuts; **marronnier** nm chestnut (tree)

**mars** [maʀs] nm March

**Marseille** [maʀsɛj] n Marseilles

**marsouin** [maʀswɛ̃] nm porpoise

**marteau, x** [maʀto] nm hammer; **être ~** (fam) to be nuts; **marteau-piqueur** nm pneumatic drill

**marteler** [maʀtəle] vt to hammer

**martien, ne** [maʀsjɛ̃, jɛn] adj Martian, of ou from Mars

**martyr, e** [maʀtiʀ] nm/f martyr; **martyre** nm martyrdom; (fig: sens affaibli) agony, torture; **martyriser** vt (REL) to martyr; (fig) to bully; (enfant) to batter, beat

**marxiste** [maʀksist] adj, nm/f Marxist

**mascara** [maskaʀa] nm mascara

**masculin, e** [maskylɛ̃, in] adj masculine; (sexe, population) male; (équipe, vêtements) men's; (viril) manly ♦ nm masculine; **masculinité** nf masculinity

**masochiste** [mazɔʃist] adj masochistic

**masque** [mask] nm mask; **masquer** vt (cacher: paysage, porte) to hide, conceal; (dissimuler: vérité, projet) to mask, obscure

**massacre** [masakʀ] nm massacre, slaughter; **massacrer** vt to massacre, slaughter; (fam: texte etc) to murder

**massage** [masaʒ] nm massage

**masse** [mas] nf mass; (ÉLEC) earth; (maillet) sledgehammer; (péj): **la ~** the masses pl; **une ~ de** (fam) masses ou loads of; **en ~** ♦ adv (acheter) in bulk; (en foule) en masse ♦ adj (exécutions, production) mass cpd

**masser** [mase] vt (assembler: gens) to gather; (pétrir) to massage; **se ~** vi (foule) to gather; **masseur, -euse** nm/f masseur(-euse)

**massif, -ive** [masif, iv] adj (porte) solid, massive; (visage) heavy, large; (bois, or) solid; (dose) massive; (déportations etc) mass cpd ♦ nm (montagneux) massif; (de fleurs) clump, bank

**massue** [masy] nf club, bludgeon

**mastic** [mastik] nm (pour vitres) putty; (pour fentes) filler

**mastiquer** [mastike] vt (aliment) to chew, masticate

**mat, e** [mat] adj (couleur, métal) mat(t); (bruit, son) dull ♦ adj inv (ÉCHECS): **être ~** to be checkmate

**mât** [mɑ] nm (NAVIG) mast; (poteau) pole, post

**match** [matʃ] nm match; **faire ~ nul** to draw; **~ aller** first leg; **~ retour** second leg, return match

**matelas** [mat(ə)la] nm mattress; **~ pneumatique** air bed ou mattress; **matelassé, e** adj (vêtement) padded; (tissu) quilted

**matelot** [mat(ə)lo] nm sailor, seaman

**mater** [mate] vt (personne) to bring to heel, subdue; (révolte) to put down

**matérialiser** [mateʀjalize]: **se ~** vi to materialize

**matérialiste** [mateʀjalist] adj materialistic

**matériaux** [mateʀjo] nmpl material(s)

**matériel, le** [materjel] adj material ♦ nm equipment no pl; (de camping etc) gear no pl; (INFORM) hardware

**maternel, le** [maternel] adj (amour, geste) motherly, maternal; (grand-père, oncle) maternal; **maternelle** nf (aussi: **école maternelle**) (state) nursery school

**maternité** [maternite] nf (établissement) maternity hospital; (état de mère) motherhood, maternity; (grossesse) pregnancy; **congé de ~** maternity leave

**mathématique** [matematik] adj mathematical; **mathématiques** nfpl (science) mathematics sg

**maths** [mat] (fam) nfpl maths

**matière** [matjɛr] nf matter; (COMM, TECH) material, matter no pl; (fig: d'un livre etc) subject matter, material; (SCOL) subject; **en ~ de** as regards; **~s grasses** fat content sg; **~s premières** raw materials

---

hôtel Matignon

L'hôtel Matignon is the Paris office and residence of the French Prime Minister. By extension, the term "Matignon" is often used to refer to the Prime Minister or his staff.

---

**matin** [matɛ̃] nm, adv morning; **du ~ au soir** from morning till night; **de bon ou grand ~** early in the morning; **matinal, e, -aux** adj (toilette, gymnastique) morning (cpd); **être matinal** (personne) to be up early; to be an early riser; **matinée** nf morning; (spectacle) matinée

**matou** [matu] nm tom(cat)

**matraque** [matrak] nf (de policier) truncheon (BRIT), billy (US)

**matricule** [matrikyl] nm (MIL) regimental number; (ADMIN) reference number

**matrimonial, e, -aux** [matrimɔnjal, jo] adj marital, marriage cpd

**maudire** [modir] vt to curse; **maudit, e** (fam) adj (satané) blasted, confounded

**maugréer** [mogree] vi to grumble

**maussade** [mosad] adj sullen; (temps) gloomy

**mauvais, e** [mɔvɛ, ɛz] adj bad; (faux): **le ~ numéro/moment** the wrong number/moment; (méchant, malveillant) malicious, spiteful; **il fait ~** the weather is bad; **la mer est ~e** the sea is rough; **~ plaisant** hoaxer; **~e herbe** weed; **~e langue** gossip, scandalmonger (BRIT); **~e passe** bad patch

**mauve** [mov] adj mauve

**maux** [mo] nmpl de mal; **~ de ventre** stomachache sg

**maximum** [maksimɔm] adj, nm maximum; **au ~** (le plus possible) as much as one can; (tout au plus) at the (very) most ou maximum; **faire le ~** to do one's level best

**mayonnaise** [majɔnɛz] nf mayonnaise

**mazout** [mazut] nm (fuel) oil

**Me** abr = **Maître**

**me, m'** [m(ə)] pron (direct: téléphoner, attendre etc) me; (indirect: parler, donner etc) (to) me; (réfléchi) myself

**mec** [mɛk] (fam) nm bloke, guy

**mécanicien, ne** [mekanisjɛ̃, jɛn] nm/f mechanic; (RAIL) (train ou engine) driver

**mécanique** [mekanik] adj mechanical ♦ nf (science) mechanics sg; (mécanisme) mechanism; **ennui ~** engine trouble no pl

**mécanisme** [mekanism] nm mechanism

**méchamment** [meʃamɑ̃] adv nastily, maliciously, spitefully

**méchanceté** [meʃɑ̃ste] nf nastiness, maliciousness; **dire des ~s à qn** to say spiteful things to sb

**méchant, e** [meʃɑ̃, ɑ̃t] adj nasty, malicious, spiteful; (enfant: pas sage) naughty; (animal) vicious

**mèche** [mɛʃ] nf (de cheveux) lock; (de lampe, bougie) wick; (d'un explosif) fuse;

de ~ avec in league with
**méchoui** [meʃwi] nm barbecue of a
whole roast sheep
**méconnaissable** [mekɔnɛsabl] adj un-
recognizable
**méconnaître** [mekɔnɛtʀ] vt (ignorer)
to be unaware of; (mésestimer) to misjudge
**mécontent, e** [mekɔ̃tɑ̃, ɑ̃t] adj: ~ (de)
discontented ou dissatisfied ou dis-
pleased (with); (contrarié) annoyed (at);
**mécontentement** nm dissatisfaction,
discontent, displeasure; (irritation) annoyance
**médaille** [medaj] nf medal
**médaillon** [medajɔ̃] nm (bijou) locket
**médecin** [med(ə)sɛ̃] nm doctor; ~ légiste forensic surgeon
**médecine** [med(ə)sin] nf medicine
**média** [medja] nmpl: les ~ the media;
**médiatique** adj media cpd; **médiatisé, e** adj reported in the media; **ce
procès a été très médiatisé** (péj) this
trial was turned into a media event
**médical, e, -aux** [medikal, o] adj
medical; **passer une visite ~e** to have
a medical
**médicament** [medikamɑ̃] nm medicine, drug
**médiéval, e, -aux** [medjeval, o] adj
medieval
**médiocre** [medjɔkʀ] adj mediocre,
poor
**médire** [mediʀ] vi: ~ de to speak ill of;
**médisance** nf scandalmongering (BRIT)
**méditer** [medite] vi to meditate
**Méditerranée** [mediteʀane] nf: la
(mer) ~ the Mediterranean (Sea); **méditerranéen, ne** adj Mediterranean ♦
nm/f: **Méditerranéen, ne** native ou inhabitant of a Mediterranean country
**méduse** [medyz] nf jellyfish
**meeting** [mitiŋ] nm (POL, SPORT) rally
**méfait** [mefɛ] nm (faute) misdemeanour, wrongdoing; **~s** nmpl (ravages)
ravages, damage sg
**méfiance** [mefjɑ̃s] nf mistrust, distrust

**méfiant, e** [mefjɑ̃, jɑ̃t] adj mistrustful,
distrustful
**méfier** [mefje]: **se** ~ vi to be wary; to
be careful; **se** ~ **de** to mistrust, distrust,
be wary of
**mégarde** [megaʀd] nf: **par** ~ (accidentellement) accidentally; (par erreur) by
mistake
**mégère** [meʒɛʀ] nf shrew
**mégot** [mego] (fam) nm cigarette end
**meilleur, e** [mejœʀ] adj, adv better ♦
nm: **le** ~ the best; **le** ~ **des deux** the
better of the two; ~ **marché** (inv)
cheaper; **meilleure** nf: **la meilleure**
the best (one)
**mélancolie** [melɑ̃kɔli] nf melancholy,
gloom; **mélancolique** adj melan-
cholic, melancholy
**mélange** [melɑ̃ʒ] nm mixture; **mélanger** vt to mix; (vins, couleurs) to blend;
(mettre en désordre) to mix up, muddle
(up)
**mélasse** [melas] nf treacle, molasses sg
**mêlée** [mele] nf mêlée, scramble; (RUG-
BY) scrum(mage)
**mêler** [mele] vt (unir) to mix; (embrouiller) to muddle (up), mix up; **se** ~ vi to
mix, mingle; **se** ~ **à** (personne: se
joindre) to join; (: s'associer à) to mix
with; **se** ~ **de** (suj: personne) to meddle
with, interfere in; **mêle-toi de ce qui
te regarde!** mind your own business!
**mélodie** [melɔdi] nf melody; **mélo-
dieux, -euse** adj melodious
**melon** [m(ə)lɔ̃] nm (BOT) (honeydew)
melon; (aussi: **chapeau** ~) bowler (hat)
**membre** [mɑ̃bʀ] nm (ANAT) limb; (personne, pays, élément) member ♦ adj
member cpd
**mémé** [meme] (fam) nf granny

MOT-CLÉ

**même** [mɛm] adj 1 (avant le nom):
same; **en même temps** at the same
time
2 (après le nom: renforcement): **il est la
loyauté même** he is loyalty itself; **ce**

sont ses paroles/celles-là mêmes they are his very words/the very ones ♦ *pron*: le(la) **même** the same one ♦ *adv* **1** (*renforcement*): **il n'a même pas pleuré** he didn't even cry; **même lui l'a dit** even HE said it; **ici même** at this very place **2**: **à même**: **à même la bouteille** straight from the bottle; **à même la peau** next to the skin; **être à même de faire** to be in a position to do, be able to do **3**: **de même**: **faire de même** to do likewise; **lui de même** so does (*ou* did *ou* is) he; **de même que** just as; **il en va de même pour** the same goes for

**mémo** [memo] (*fam*) *nm* memo

**mémoire** [memwar] *nf* memory ♦ *nm* (*SCOL*) dissertation, paper; **~s** *nmpl* (*souvenirs*) memoirs; **à la ~ de** to the memory of; **de ~** from memory; **~ morte/vive** (*INFORM*) ROM/RAM

**mémorable** [memɔrabl] *adj* memorable, unforgettable

**menace** [mənas] *nf* threat; **menacer** *vt* to threaten

**ménage** [menaʒ] *nm* (*travail*) housework; (*couple*) (married) couple; (*famille*, *ADMIN*) household; **faire le ~** to do the housework; **ménagement** *nm* care and attention; **ménager, -ère** *adj* household *cpd*, domestic ♦ *vt* (*traiter*: *personne*) to handle with tact; (*utiliser*) to use sparingly; (*prendre soin de*) to take (great) care of, look after; (*organiser*) to arrange; **ménager qch à qn** (*réserver*) to have sth in store for sb; **ménagère** *nf* housewife

**mendiant, e** [mãdjã, jãt] *nm/f* beggar

**mendier** [mãdje] *vi* to beg ♦ *vt* to beg (for)

**mener** [m(ə)ne] *vt* to lead; (*enquête*) to conduct; (*affaires*) to manage ♦ *vi*: **~ à/dans** (*emmener*) to take to/into; **~ qch à bien** to see sth through (to a successful conclusion), complete sth

successfully

**meneur, -euse** [mənœr, øz] *nm/f* leader; (*péj*) agitator

**méningite** [menɛʒit] *nf* meningitis no pl

**ménopause** [menopoz] *nf* menopause

**menottes** [mənɔt] *nfpl* handcuffs

**mensonge** [mãsɔʒ] *nm* lie; (*action*) lying no pl; **mensonger, -ère** *adj* false

**mensualité** [mãsyalite] *nf* (*traite*) monthly payment

**mensuel, le** [mãsyɛl] *adj* monthly

**mensurations** [mãsyrasjɔ̃] *nfpl* measurements

**mental, e, -aux** [mãtal, o] *adj* mental; **mentalité** *nf* mentality

**menteur, -euse** [mãtœr, øz] *nm/f* liar

**menthe** [mãt] *nf* mint

**mention** [mãsjɔ̃] *nf* (*annotation*) note, comment; (*SCOL*) grade; **~ bien** *etc* ≈ grade B *etc* (*ou* upper 2nd class *etc*) pass (*BRIT*), ≈ pass with (high) honors (*US*); (*ADMIN*): **"rayer les ~s inutiles"** "delete as appropriate"; **mentionner** *vt* to mention

**mentir** [mãtir] *vi* to lie

**menton** [mãtɔ̃] *nm* chin

**menu, e** [məny] *adj* (*personne*) slim, slight; (*frais*, *difficulté*) minor ♦ *adv* (*couper*, *hacher*) very fine ♦ *nm* menu; **~ touristique/gastronomique** economy/gourmet's menu

**menuiserie** [mənɥizri] *nf* (*métier*) joinery, carpentry; (*passe-temps*) woodwork; **menuisier** *nm* joiner, carpenter

**méprendre** [meprãdr]: **se ~** *vi*: **se ~ sur** to be mistaken (about)

**mépris** [mepri] *nm* (*dédain*) contempt, scorn; **au ~ de** regardless of, in defiance of; **méprisable** *adj* contemptible, despicable; **méprisant, e** *adj* scornful; **méprise** *nf* mistake, error; **mépriser** *vt* to scorn, despise; (*gloire*, *danger*) to scorn, spurn

**mer** [mɛr] *nf* sea; (*marée*) tide; **en ~** at sea; **en haute** *ou* **pleine ~** off shore, on the open sea; **la ~ du Nord/Rouge**

the North/Red Sea

**mercenaire** [mɛʀsənɛʀ] *nm* mercenary, hired soldier

**mercerie** [mɛʀsəʀi] *nf* (*boutique*) haberdasher's shop (*BRIT*), notions store (*US*)

**merci** [mɛʀsi] *excl* thank you ♦ *nf*: **à la ~ de** qn/qch at sb's mercy/the mercy of sth; **~ beaucoup** thank you very much; **~ de** thank you for; **sans ~** merciless(ly)

**mercredi** [mɛʀkʀədi] *nm* Wednesday

**mercure** [mɛʀkyʀ] *nm* mercury

**merde** [mɛʀd] (*fam!*) *nf* ♦ shit (*!*) ♦ *excl* (bloody) hell (*!*)

**mère** [mɛʀ] *nf* mother; **~ célibataire** unmarried mother

**merguez** [mɛʀgɛz] *nf* merguez sausage (*type of spicy sausage from N Africa*)

**méridional, e, -aux** [meʀidjɔnal, o] *adj* southern ♦ *nm/f* Southerner

**meringue** [məʀɛ̃g] *nf* meringue

**mérite** [meʀit] *nm* merit; **avoir du ~ (à faire** qch) to deserve credit (for doing sth); **mériter** *vt* to deserve

**merlan** [mɛʀlɑ̃] *nm* whiting

**merle** [mɛʀl] *nm* blackbird

**merveille** [mɛʀvɛj] *nf* marvel, wonder; **faire ~** to work wonders; **à ~** perfectly, wonderfully; **merveilleux, -euse** *adj* marvellous, wonderful

**mes** [me] *adj voir* **mon**

**mésange** [mezɑ̃ʒ] *nf* tit(mouse)

**mésaventure** [mezavɑ̃tyʀ] *nf* misadventure, misfortune

**Mesdames** [medam] *nfpl de* **Madame**

**Mesdemoiselles** [medmwazɛl] *nfpl de* **Mademoiselle**

**mesquin, e** [mɛskɛ̃, in] *adj* mean, petty; **mesquinerie** *nf* meanness; (*procédé*) mean trick

**message** [mesaʒ] *nm* message; **messager, -ère** *nm/f* messenger; **messagerie** *nf* (*INTERNET*) **messagerie électronique** bulletin board

**messe** [mɛs] *nf* mass

**Messieurs** [mesjø] *nmpl de* **Monsieur**

**mesure** [m(ə)zyʀ] *nf* (*évaluation, dimension*) measurement; (*récipient*) measure; (*MUS: cadence*) time, tempo; (: *division*) bar; (*retenue*) moderation; (*disposition*) measure, step; **sur ~** (*costume*) made-to-measure; **dans la ~ où** insofar as, inasmuch as; **à ~ que** as; **être en ~ de** to be in a position to; **dans une certaine ~** to a certain extent

**mesurer** [məzyʀe] *vt* to measure; (*juger*) to weigh up, assess; (*modérer: ses paroles etc*) to moderate; **se ~ avec** to have a confrontation with; **il mesure 1 m 80** he's 1 m 80 tall

**met** [me] *vb voir* **mettre**

**métal, -aux** [metal, o] *nm* metal; **métallique** *adj* metallic

**météo** [meteo] *nf* (*bulletin*) weather report

**météorologie** [meteɔʀɔlɔʒi] *nf* meteorology

**méthode** [metɔd] *nf* method; (*livre, ouvrage*) manual, tutor

**méticuleux, -euse** [metikylø, øz] *adj* meticulous

**métier** [metje] *nm* (*profession: gén*) job; (: *manuel*) trade; (*artisanal*) craft; (*technique, expérience*) (acquired) skill ou technique; (*aussi:* **~ à tisser**) (weaving) loom; **avoir du ~** to have practical experience

**métis, se** [metis] *adj, nm/f* half-caste, half-breed

**métrage** [metʀaʒ] *nm*: **long/moyen/court ~** full-length/medium-length/short film

**mètre** [mɛtʀ] *nm* metre; (*règle*) ruler; (*ruban*) tape measure; **métrique** *adj* metric

**métro** [metʀo] *nm* underground (*BRIT*), subway

**métropole** [metʀɔpɔl] *nf* (*capitale*) metropolis; (*pays*) home country

**mets** [me] *nm* dish

**metteur** [metœʀ] *nm*: **~ en scène** (*THÉÂTRE*) producer; (*CINÉMA*) director

MOT-CLÉ

**mettre** [mɛtʀ] vt 1 (placer) to put; **mettre en bouteille/en sac** to bottle/put in bags ou sacks; **mettre en charge (pour)** to charge (with), indict (for)

2 (vêtements: revêtir) to put on; (: porter) to wear; **mets ton gilet** put your cardigan on; **je ne mets plus mon manteau** I no longer wear my coat

3 (faire fonctionner: chauffage, électricité) to put on; (: reveil, minuteur) to set; (installer: gaz, eau) to put in, lay on; **mettre en marche** to start up

4 (consacrer) **mettre du temps à faire qch** to take time to do sth ou over sth

5 (noter, écrire) to say, put (down); **qu'est-ce qu'il a mis sur la carte?** what did he say ou write on the card?; **mettez au pluriel** put ... into the plural

6 (supposer) **mettons que ...** let's suppose ou say that ...

7: **se mettre du sien** to pull one's weight

**se mettre** vi 1 (se placer) **vous pouvez vous mettre là** you can sit (ou stand) there; **où ça se met?** where does it go?; **se mettre au lit** to get into bed; **se mettre au piano** to sit down at the piano; **se mettre de l'encre sur les doigts** to get ink on one's fingers

2 (s'habiller) **se mettre en maillot de bain** to get into ou put on a swimsuit; **n'avoir rien à se mettre** to have nothing to wear

3: **se mettre à** to begin, start; **se mettre à faire** to begin ou start doing ou to do; **se mettre au piano** to start learning the piano; **se mettre au travail/à l'étude** to get down to work/one's studies

**meuble** [mœbl] nm piece of furniture; **des ~s** furniture; **meublé** nm furnished

flatlet (BRIT) ou room; **meubler** vt to furnish

**meugler** [møgle] vi to low, moo

**meule** [møl] nf (de foin, blé) stack; (de fromage) round; (à broyer) millstone

**meunier, ière** [mønje, jɛʀ] nm miller; **meunière** nf miller's wife

**meure** etc [mœʀ] vb voir **mourir**

**meurtre** [mœʀtʀ] nm murder; **meurtrier, ière** adj (arme etc) deadly; (fureur, instincts) murderous ♦ nm/f murderer(-ess)

**meurtrir** [mœʀtʀiʀ] vt to bruise; (fig) to wound; **meurtrissure** nf bruise

**meus** etc [mœ] vb voir **mouvoir**

**meute** [møt] nf pack

**mexicain, e** [mɛksikɛ̃, ɛn] adj Mexican ♦ nm/f: **M~, e** Mexican

**Mexico** [mɛksiko] n Mexico City

**Mexique** [mɛksik] nm: **le ~** Mexico

**Mgr** abr = **Monseigneur**

**mi** [mi] nm (MUS) E; (en chantant la gamme) mi ♦ préfixe: ~... half(-); mid-; **à la ~-janvier** in mid-January; **à ~-hauteur** halfway up; **mi-bas** nm inv knee sock

**miauler** [mjole] vi to miaow

**miche** [miʃ] nf round ou cob loaf

**mi-chemin** [miʃmɛ̃]: **à ~~** adv halfway, midway

**mi-clos, e** [miklo, kloz] adj half-closed

**micro** [mikʀo] nm mike, microphone; (INFORM) micro

**microbe** [mikʀɔb] nm germ, microbe

**micro...**: **micro-onde** nf: **four à micro-ondes** microwave oven; **micro-ordinateur** nm microcomputer; **microscope** nm microscope; **microscopique** adj microscopic

**midi** [midi] nm midday, noon; (moment du déjeuner) lunchtime; (sud) south; **à ~** at 12 (o'clock) ou midday ou noon; **le M~** the South of France, the Midi

**mie** [mi] nf crumb (of the loaf)

**miel** [mjɛl] nm honey; **mielleux, -euse** adj (personne) unctuous, syrupy

**mien, ne** [mjɛ̃, mjɛn] pron: **le(la)**

~(ne), les ~(ne)s mine; les ~s my family

**miette** [mjɛt] *nf* (*de pain, gâteau*)
crumb; (*fig: de la conversation etc*)
scrap; **en ~s** in pieces *ou* bits

---

MOT-CLÉ

---

**mieux** [mjø] *adv* **1** (*d'une meilleure
façon*): **mieux (que)** better (than); **elle
travaille/mange mieux** she works/
eats better; **elle va mieux** she is better
**2** (*de la meilleure façon*) best; **ce que je
sais le mieux** what I know best; **les livres les mieux faits** the best made
books
**3: de mieux en mieux** better and better
♦ *adj* **1** (*plus à l'aise, en meilleure forme*)
better; **se sentir mieux** to feel better
**2** (*plus satisfaisant*) better; **c'est mieux
ainsi** like this; **c'est le mieux des deux**
it's the better of the two; **le(la) mieux**,
**les mieux** the best; **demandez-lui, c'est
le mieux** ask him, it's the best thing
**3** (*plus joli*) better-looking
**4: au mieux** at best; **au mieux avec**
on the best of terms with; **pour le
mieux** for the best
♦ *nm* **1** (*progrès*) improvement
**2: de mon/ton mieux** as best I/you
can (*ou* could); **faire de son mieux** to
do one's best

**mièvre** [mjɛvʀ] *adj* mawkish (*BRIT*),
sickly sentimental

**mignon, ne** [miɲɔ̃, ɔn] *adj* sweet, cute

**migraine** [migʀɛn] *nf* headache; (*MÉD*)
migraine

**mijoter** [miʒɔte] *vt* to simmer; (*préparer
avec soin*) to cook lovingly; (*fam: tra-
mer*) to plot, cook up ♦ *vi* to simmer

**mil** [mil] *num* = **mille**

**milieu, x** [miljø] *nm* (*centre*) middle;
(*BIO, GÉO*) environment; (*entourage social*) milieu; (*provenance*) background;
(*pègre*): **le ~** the underworld; **au ~ de**

in the middle of; **au beau** *ou* **en plein
~ (de)** right in the middle (of); **un juste ~** a happy medium

**militaire** [militɛʀ] *adj* military, army
*cpd* ♦ *nm* serviceman

**militant, e** [militɑ̃, ɑ̃t] *adj*, *nm/f* militant

**militer** [milite] *vi* to be a militant

**mille** [mil] *num* a *ou* one thousand
♦ *nm* (*mesure*): **~ (marin)** nautical mile;
**mettre dans le ~** (*fig*) to be bang on
target; **millefeuille** *nm* cream *ou* vanilla slice; **millénaire** *nm* millennium
♦ *adj* thousand-year-old; (*fig*) ancient;
**mille-pattes** *nm inv* centipede

**millésimé, e** [milezime] *adj* vintage
*cpd*

**millet** [mijɛ] *nm* millet

**milliard** [miljaʀ] *nm* milliard, thousand
million (*BRIT*), billion (*US*); **milliardaire**
*nm/f* multimillionaire (*BRIT*), billionaire
(*US*)

**millier** [milje] *nm* thousand; **un ~ (de)**
a thousand or so, about a thousand;
**par ~s** in (their) thousands, by the
thousand

**milligramme** [miligʀam] *nm* milligramme

**millimètre** [milimɛtʀ] *nm* millimetre

**million** [miljɔ̃] *nm* million; **deux ~s de**
two million; **millionnaire** *nm/f* million-
aire

**mime** [mim] *nm/f* (*acteur*) mime(r)
♦ *nm* (*art*) mime, miming; **mimer** *vt* to
mime; (*singer*) to mimic, take off

**mimique** [mimik] *nf* (*grimace*) (funny)
face; (*signes*) gesticulations *pl*, sign language *no pl*

**minable** [minabl] *adj* (*décrépit*)
shabby(-looking); (*médiocre*) pathetic

**mince** [mɛ̃s] *adj* thin; (*personne, taille*)
slim, slender; (*fig: profit, connaissances*)
slight, small, weak ♦ *excl*: **~ alors!** drat
it!, darn it! (*US*); **minceur** *nf* thinness;
(*d'une personne*) slimness, slenderness;
**mincir** *vi* to get slimmer

**mine** [min] *nf* (*physionomie*) expression,

look; (*allure*) exterior, appearance; (*de crayon*) lead; (*gisement, explosif, fig: source*) mine; **avoir bonne ~** (*personne*) to look well; (*ironique*) to look an utter idiot; **avoir mauvaise ~** to look unwell or poorly; **faire ~ de faire** to make a pretence of doing; **~ de rien** although you wouldn't think so

**miner** [mine] *vt* (*saper*) to undermine, erode; (MIL) to mine

**minerai** [minʀɛ] *nm* ore

**minéral, e, -aux** [mineʀal, o] *adj, nm* mineral

**minéralogique** [mineʀalɔʒik] *adj:* **numéro ~** registration number

**minet, te** [minɛ, ɛt] *nm/f* (*chat*) pussycat; (*péj*) young trendy

**mineur, e** [minœʀ] *adj* minor ♦ *nm/f* (JUR) minor, person under age ♦ *nm* (*travailleur*) miner

**miniature** [minjatyʀ] *adj, nf* miniature

**minibus** [minibys] *nm* minibus

**mini-cassette** [minikasɛt] *nf* cassette (recorder)

**minier, -ière** [minje, jɛʀ] *adj* mining

**mini-jupe** [miniʒyp] *nf* mini-skirt

**minime** [minim] *adj* minor, minimal

**minimiser** [minimize] *vt* to minimize; (*fig*) to play down

**minimum** [minimɔm] *adj, nm* minimum; **au ~** (*au moins*) at the very least

**ministère** [ministɛʀ] *nm* (*aussi* REL) ministry; (*cabinet*) government

**ministre** [ministʀ] *nm* (*aussi* REL) minister

**Minitel** ® [minitɛl] *nm* videotext terminal and service

---

**Minitel**

**Minitel** *is a personal computer terminal supplied free of change by France-Télécom to telephone subscribers. It serves as a computerized telephone directory as well as giving access to various services, including information on train timetables, the*

stock market and situations vacant. Services are accessed by phoning the relevant number and charged to the subscriber's phone bill.

---

**minoritaire** [minɔʀitɛʀ] *adj* minority

**minorité** [minɔʀite] *nf* minority; **être en ~** to be in the *ou* a minority

**minuit** [minɥi] *nm* midnight

**minuscule** [minyskyl] *adj* minute, tiny ♦ *nf*: (**lettre**) ~ small letter

**minute** [minyt] *nf* minute; **à la ~** (*just*) this instant; (*faire*) there and then; **minuter** *vt* to time; **minuterie** *nf* time switch

**minutieux, -euse** [minysjø, jøz] *adj* (*personne*) meticulous; (*travail*) minutely detailed

**mirabelle** [miʀabɛl] *nf* (*cherry*) plum

**miracle** [miʀakl] *nm* miracle

**mirage** [miʀaʒ] *nm* mirage

**mire** [miʀ] *nf*: **point de ~** (*fig*) focal point

**miroir** [miʀwaʀ] *nm* mirror

**miroiter** [miʀwate] *vi* to sparkle, shimmer; **faire ~ qch à qn** to paint sth in glowing colours for sb, dangle sth in front of sb's eyes

**mis, e** [mi, miz] *pp de* **mettre** ♦ *adj*: **bien ~** well-dressed

**mise** [miz] *nf* (*argent: au jeu*) stake; (*tenue*) clothing, attire; **être de ~** to be acceptable *ou* in season; **~ au point** (*fig*) clarification; **~ de fonds** capital outlay; **~ en examen** charging, indictment; **~ en plis** set; **~ en scène** production

**miser** [mize] *vt* (*enjeu*) to stake, bet; **~ sur** (*cheval, numéro*) to bet on; (*fig*) to bank *ou* count on

**misérable** [mizeʀabl] *adj* (*lamentable, malheureux*) pitiful, wretched; (*pauvre*) poverty-stricken; (*insignifiant, mesquin*) miserable ♦ *nm/f* wretch

**misère** [mizeʀ] *nf* (*extreme*) poverty, destitution; **~s** *nfpl* (*malheurs*) woes, miseries; (*ennuis*) little troubles; **salaire**

de ~ starvation wage

**missile** [misil] *nm* missile

**mission** [misjɔ̃] *nf* mission; **partir en ~** (ADMIN, POL) to go on an assignment; **missionnaire** *nm/f* missionary

**mit** [mi] *vb voir* **mettre**

**mité, e** [mite] *adj* moth-eaten

**mi-temps** [mitɑ̃] *nf inv* (SPORT: *période*) half; (: *pause*) half-time; **à ~~** part-time

**miteux, -euse** [mitø, øz] *adj* (*lieu*) seedy

**mitigé, e** [mitiʒe] *adj*: **sentiments ~s** mixed feelings

**mitonner** [mitɔne] *vt* to cook with loving care; (*fig*) to cook up quietly

**mitoyen, ne** [mitwajɛ̃, jɛn] *adj* (*mur*) common, party *cpd*

**mitrailler** [mitraje] *vt* to machine-gun; (*fig*) to pelt, bombard; (: *photographier*) to take shot after shot of; **mitraillette** *nf* submachine gun; **mitrailleuse** *nf* machine gun

**mi-voix** [mivwa]: **à ~~** *adv* in a low or hushed voice

**mixage** [miksaʒ] *nm* (CINÉMA) (sound) mixing

**mixer** [miksœr] *nm* (food) mixer

**mixte** [mikst] *adj* (*gén*) mixed; (SCOL) mixed, coeducational

**mixture** [mikstyr] *nf* mixture; (*fig*) concoction

**Mlle** (*pl* **Mlles**) *abr* = **Mademoiselle**

**MM** *abr* = **Messieurs**

**Mme** (*pl* **Mmes**) *abr* = **Madame**

**mobile** [mɔbil] *adj* mobile; (*pièce de machine*) moving ♦ *nm* (*motif*) motive; (*œuvre d'art*) mobile

**mobilier, -ière** [mɔbilje, jɛʀ] *nf* furniture

**mobiliser** [mɔbilize] *vt* to mobilize

**mocassin** [mɔkasɛ̃] *nm* moccasin

**moche** [mɔʃ] (*fam*) *adj* (*laid*) ugly; (*mauvais*) rotten

**modalité** [mɔdalite] *nf* form, mode; **~s de paiement** methods of payment

**mode** [mɔd] *nf* fashion ♦ *nm* (*manière*)

form, mode; **à la ~** fashionable, in fashion; **~ d'emploi** directions *pl* (for use)

**modèle** [mɔdɛl] *adj*, *nm* model; (*qui pose: de peintre*) sitter; **~ déposé** registered design; **~ réduit** small-scale model; **modeler** *vt* to model

**modem** [mɔdɛm] *nm* modem

**modéré, e** [mɔdere] *adj*, *nm/f* moderate

**modérer** [mɔdere] *vt* to moderate; **se ~** *vi* to restrain o.s.

**moderne** [mɔdern] *adj* modern ♦ *nm* (*style*) modern style; (*meubles*) modern furniture; **moderniser** *vt* to modernize

**modeste** [mɔdɛst] *adj* modest; **modestie** *nf* modesty

**modifier** [mɔdifje] *vt* to modify, alter; **se ~** *vi* to alter

**modique** [mɔdik] *adj* modest

**modiste** [mɔdist] *nf* milliner

**module** [mɔdyl] *nm* module

**moelle** [mwal] *nf* marrow; **~ épinière** spinal cord

**moelleux, -euse** [mwalø, øz] *adj* soft; (*gâteau*) light and moist

**mœurs** [mœr] *nfpl* (*conduite*) morals; (*manières*) manners; (*pratiques sociales, mode de vie*) habits

**mohair** [mɔɛr] *nm* mohair

**moi** [mwa] *pron* me; (*emphatique*): **~, je ...** for my part, I ..., I myself ...; **à ~** mine; **moi-même** *pron* myself; (*emphatique*) I myself

**moindre** [mwɛ̃dr] *adj* lesser; lower; **le(la) ~s** the least, the slightest; **merci – c'est la ~ des choses!** thank you – it's a pleasure!

**moine** [mwan] *nm* monk, friar

**moineau, x** [mwano] *nm* sparrow

---
MOT-CLÉ
---

**moins** [mwɛ̃] *adv* 1 (*comparatif*): **moins (que)** less (than); **moins grand que** less tall than, not as tall as; **moins je travaille, mieux je me porte** the less I work, the better I feel

**2** (superlatif): **le moins** (the) least; **c'est ce que j'aime le moins** it's what I like the least; **le(la) moins douée** the least gifted; **au moins, du moins** at least; **pour le moins** at the very least

**3: moins de** (quantité) less (than); (nombre) fewer (than); **moins de sable/d'eau** less sand/water; **moins de livres/gens** fewer books/people; **moins de 2 ans** less than 2 years; **moins de midi** not yet midday

**4: de moins, en moins: 100 F/3 jours de moins** 100F/3 days less; **3 livres en moins** 3 books fewer; **3 books too few; de l'argent en moins** less money; **le soleil en moins** but for the sun, minus the sun; **de moins en moins** less and less

**5: à moins de, à moins que** unless; **à moins de faire** unless we do (ou he does etc); **à moins que tu ne fasses** unless you do; **à moins d'un accident** barring any accident

♦ prép: **4 moins 2** 4 minus 2; **il est moins 5** it's 5 to; **il fait moins 5** it's 5 (degrees) below (freezing), it's minus 5

**mois** [mwa] nm month

**moisi** [mwazi] nm mould, mildew; **odeur de ~** musty smell; **moisir** vi to go mouldy; **moisissure** nf mould no pl

**moisson** [mwasɔ̃] nf harvest; **moissonner** vt to harvest, reap; **moissonneuse** nf (machine) harvester

**moite** [mwat] adj sweaty, sticky

**moitié** [mwatje] nf half; **la ~** half; **la ~ de** half (of); **la ~ du temps** half the time; **à la ~** halfway through; **à ~** (avant le verbe) half; (avant l'adjectif) half-; **à ~ prix** (at) half-price; **~ moitié** half-and-half

**moka** [mɔka] nm coffee gateau

**mol** [mɔl] adj voir **mou**

**molaire** [mɔlɛr] nf molar

**molester** [mɔlɛste] vt to manhandle, maul (about)

**molle** [mɔl] adj voir **mou**; **mollement** adv (péj: travailler) sluggishly; (protester) feebly

**mollet** [mɔlɛ] nm calf ♦ adj m: **œuf ~** soft-boiled egg

**molletonné, e** [mɔltɔne] adj fleece-lined

**mollir** [mɔlir] vi (fléchir) to relent; (substance) to go soft

**mollusque** [mɔlysk] nm mollusc

**môme** [mom] (fam) nm/f (enfant) brat

**moment** [mɔmɑ̃] nm moment; **ce n'est pas le ~** this is not the (right) time; **pour un bon ~** for a good while; **pour le ~** for the moment, for the time being; **au ~ de** at the time of; **au ~ où** just as; **à tout ~** (peut arriver etc) at any time ou moment; (constamment) constantly, continually; **en ce ~** at the moment; at present; **sur le ~** at the time; **par ~s** now and then, at times; **du ~ où** ou que seeing that, since; **momentané, e** adj temporary, momentary; **momentanément** adv (court instant) for a short while

**momie** [mɔmi] nf mummy

**mon, ma** [mɔ̃, ma] (pl **mes**) adj my

**Monaco** [mɔnako] nm Monaco

**monarchie** [mɔnarʃi] nf monarchy

**monastère** [mɔnastɛr] nm monastery

**monceau, x** [mɔ̃so] nm heap

**mondain, e** [mɔ̃dɛ̃, ɛn] adj (vie) society cpd

**monde** [mɔ̃d] nm world; (haute société): **le ~** (high) society; **il y a du ~** (beaucoup de gens) there are a lot of people; (quelques personnes) there are some people; **beaucoup/peu de ~** many/few people; **mettre au ~** to bring into the world; **pas le moins du ~** not in the least; **se faire un ~ de qch** to make a great deal of fuss about sth; **mondial, e, -aux** adj (population) world cpd; (influence) world-wide; **mondialement** adv throughout the world

**monégasque** [mɔnegask] adj Monégasque, of *ou* from Monaco

**monétaire** [mɔnetɛr] *adj* monetary

**moniteur, -trice** [mɔnitœr, tris] *nm/f* (SPORT) instructor(-tress); (*de colonie de vacances*) supervisor ♦ *nm* (*écran*) monitor

**monnaie** [mɔnɛ] *nf* (ÉCON, gén: *moyen d'échange*) currency; (*petites pièces*): **avoir de la ~** to have (some) change; **une pièce de ~** a coin; **faire de la ~** to get (some) change; **avoir/faire la de 20 F** to have change of/get change for 20 F; **rendre à qn la ~** (**sur 20 F**) to give sb the change (out of *ou* from 20 F); **monnayer** *vt* to convert into cash; (*talent*) to capitalize on

**monologue** [mɔnɔlɔg] *nm* monologue, soliloquy; **monologuer** *vi* to soliloquize

**monopole** [mɔnɔpɔl] *nm* monopoly

**monotone** [mɔnɔtɔn] *adj* monotonous

**Monsieur** [məsjø] (*pl* **Messieurs**) *titre* Mr ♦ *nm* (*homme quelconque*): **un/le m~** a/the gentleman; **~ ...** (*en tête de lettre*) Dear Sir, ...; *voir aussi* **Madame**

**monstre** [mɔ̃str] *nm* monster ♦ *adj* (fam: *colossal*) monstrous; **un travail ~** a fantastic amount of work; **monstrueux, -euse** *adj* monstrous

**mont** [mɔ̃] *nm*: **par ~s et par vaux** up hill and down dale; **le M~ Blanc** Mont Blanc

**montage** [mɔ̃taʒ] *nm* (*assemblage*: *d'appareil*) assembly; (PHOTO) photomontage; (CINÉMA) editing

**montagnard, e** [mɔ̃taɲar, ard] *adj* mountain *cpd* ♦ *nm/f* mountain-dweller

**montagne** [mɔ̃taɲ] *nf* (*cime*) mountain; (*région*): **la ~** the mountains *pl*; **~s russes** big dipper *sg*, switchback *sg*; **montagneux, -euse** *adj* mountainous; (*basse montagne*) hilly

**montant, e** [mɔ̃tɑ̃, ɑ̃t] *adj* rising; **pull à col ~** high-necked jumper ♦ *nm* (*somme, total*) (sum) total, (total) amount; (*de fenêtre*) upright; (*de lit*) post

**monte-charge** [mɔ̃tʃarʒ] *nm inv* goods lift, hoist

**montée** [mɔ̃te] *nf* (*des prix, hostilités*) rise; (*escalade*) climb; (*côte*) hill; **au lieu de la ~** halfway up

**monter** [mɔ̃te] *vt* (*escalier, côte*) to go (*ou* come) up; (*valise, paquet*) to take (*ou* bring) up; (*étagère*) to raise; (*tente, échafaudage*) to put up; (*machine*) to assemble; (CINÉMA) to edit; (*société etc*) to set up ♦ *vi* to go (*ou* come) up; (*prix, niveau, température*) to go up, rise; (*passager*) to get up; **se ~ à** (*frais etc*) to add up to, come to; **~ à pied** to walk up, go up on foot; **~ dans le train/l'avion** to get into the train/plane, board the train/plane; **~ sur** to climb up onto; **~ à cheval** (*faire du cheval*) to ride, go riding

**montre** [mɔ̃tr] *nf* watch; **contre la ~** (SPORT) against the clock; **montre-bracelet** *nf* wristwatch

**montrer** [mɔ̃tre] *vt* to show; **~ qch à qn** to show sb sth

**monture** [mɔ̃tyr] *nf* (*cheval*) mount; (*de lunettes*) frame; (*d'une bague*) setting

**monument** [mɔnymɑ̃] *nm* monument; **~ aux morts** war memorial

**moquer** [mɔke]: **se ~ de** *vt* to make fun of, laugh at; (fam: *se désintéresser de*) not to care about; (*tromper*): **se ~ de qn** to take sb for a ride; **moquerie** *nf* mockery

**moquette** [mɔkɛt] *nf* fitted carpet

**moqueur, -euse** [mɔkœr, øz] *adj* mocking

**moral, e, -aux** [mɔral, o] *adj* moral ♦ *nm*: **avoir le ~** (fam) to be in good spirits; **avoir le ~ à zéro** (fam) to be really down; **morale** *nf* (*mœurs*) morals *pl*; (*valeurs*) moral standards *pl*, morality; (*d'une fable etc*) moral; **faire la morale à** to lecture, preach at; **moralité** *nf* morality; (*de fable*) moral

**morceau, x** [mɔrso] *nm* piece,

(*d'une œuvre*) passage, extract; (MUS) piece; (CULIN: *de viande*) cut; (*de sucre*) lump; **mettre en ~x** to pull to pieces *ou* bits; **manger un ~** to have a bite (to eat)

**morceler** [mɔʀsəle] *vt* to break up, divide up

**mordant, e** [mɔʀdɑ̃, ɑ̃t] *adj* (*ton, remarque*) scathing, cutting; (*ironie, froid*) biting ♦ *nm* (*style*) bite, punch

**mordiller** [mɔʀdije] *vt* to nibble at, chew at

**mordre** [mɔʀdʀ] *vt* to bite ♦ *vi* (*poisson*) to bite; ~ **sur** (*fig*) to go over into, overlap into; ~ **à l'hameçon** to bite, rise to the bait

**mordu, e** [mɔʀdy] (*fam*) *nm/f* enthusiast; **un ~ de jazz** a jazz fanatic

**morfondre** [mɔʀfɔ̃dʀ]: **se ~** *vi* to mope

**morgue** [mɔʀg] *nf* (*arrogance*) haughtiness; (*lieu: de la police*) morgue; (: *à l'hôpital*) mortuary

**morne** [mɔʀn] *adj* dismal, dreary

**morose** [mɔʀoz] *adj* sullen, morose

**mors** [mɔʀ] *nm* bit

**morse** [mɔʀs] *nm* (ZOOL) walrus; (TÉL) Morse (code)

**morsure** [mɔʀsyʀ] *nf* bite

**mort¹** [mɔʀ] *nf* death

**mort², e** [mɔʀ, mɔʀt] *pp de* **mourir** ♦ *adj* dead ♦ *nm/f* (*défunt*) dead man/woman; (*victime*): **il y a eu plusieurs ~s** several people were killed, there were several killed; ~ **de peur/fatigue** frightened to death/dead tired

**mortalité** [mɔʀtalite] *nf* mortality, death rate

**mortel, le** [mɔʀtɛl] *adj* (*poison etc*) deadly, lethal; (*accident, blessure*) fatal; (*silence, ennemi*) deadly; (*péché*) mortal; (*fam: ennuyeux*) deadly boring

**mortier** [mɔʀtje] *nm* (*gén*) mortar

**mort-né, e** [mɔʀne] *adj* (*enfant*) stillborn

**mortuaire** [mɔʀtɥɛʀ] *adj*: **avis ~** death announcement

**morue** [mɔʀy] *nf* (ZOOL) cod *inv*

**mosaïque** [mɔzaik] *nf* mosaic

**Moscou** [mɔsku] *n* Moscow

**mosquée** [mɔske] *nf* mosque

**mot** [mo] *nm* word; (*message*) line, note; ~ **à ~** word for word; ~ **d'ordre** watchword; ~ **de passe** password; ~**s croisés** crossword (puzzle) *sg*

**motard** [mɔtaʀ] *nm* biker; (*policier*) motorcycle cop

**motel** [mɔtɛl] *nm* motel

**moteur, -trice** [mɔtœʀ, tʀis] *adj* (ANAT, PHYSIOL) motor; (TECH) driving; (AUTO): **à 4 roues motrices** 4-wheel drive ♦ *nm* engine, motor; **à ~** power-driven, motor *cpd*

**motif** [mɔtif] *nm* (*cause*) motive; (*décoratif*) design, pattern, motif; **sans ~** groundless

**motivation** [mɔtivasjɔ̃] *nf* motivation

**motiver** [mɔtive] *vt* to motivate; (*justifier*) to justify, account for

**moto** [mɔto] *nf* (*motor*)bike; **motocycliste** *nm/f* motorcyclist

**motorisé, e** [mɔtɔʀize] *adj* (*personne*) having transport *ou* a car

**motrice** [mɔtʀis] *adj voir* **moteur**

**motte** [mɔt] *nf*: ~ **de terre** lump of earth, clod (of earth); ~ **de beurre** lump of butter

**mou (mol), molle** [mu, mɔl] *adj* soft; (*personne*) lethargic; (*protestations*) weak ♦ *nm*: **avoir du mou** to be slack

**moucharder** [muʃaʀde] (*fam*) *vt* (SCOL) to sneak on; (POLICE) to grass on

**mouche** [muʃ] *nf* fly

**moucher** [muʃe]: **se ~** *vi* to blow one's nose

**moucheron** [muʃʀɔ̃] *nm* midge

**mouchoir** [muʃwaʀ] *nm* handkerchief, hanky; ~ **en papier** tissue, paper hanky

**moudre** [mudʀ] *vt* to grind

**moue** [mu] *nf* pout; **faire la ~** to pout; (*fig*) to pull a face

**mouette** [mwɛt] *nf* (sea)gull

**moufle** [mufl] *nf* (*gant*) mitt(en)

**mouillé, e** [muje] *adj* wet

mouiller 187 mule

**mouiller** [muje] vt (humecter) to wet, moisten; (tremper): ~ **qn/qch** to make sb/sth wet ◆ vi (NAVIG) to lie ou be at anchor; **se** ~ (fam: prendre des risques) to commit o.s.

**moulant, e** [mulã, ãt] adj figure-hugging

**moule** [mul] nm mussel ◆ nf (CULIN) mould; ~ **à gâteaux** ◆ nm cake tin (BRIT) ou pan (US)

**moulent** [mul] voir moudre; mouler

**mouler** [mule] vt (suj: vêtement) to hug, fit closely round

**moulin** [mulẽ] nm mill; ~ **à café/à poivre** coffee/pepper mill; ~ **à légumes** (vegetable) shredder; ~ **à paroles** (fig) chatterbox; ~ **à vent** windmill

**moulinet** [muline] nm (de canne à pêche) reel; (mouvement): **faire des ~s avec qch** to whirl sth around

**moulinette** ® [mulinɛt] nf (vegetable) shredder

**moulu, e** [muly] pp de moudre

**mourant, e** [murã, ãt] adj dying

**mourir** [murir] vi to die; (civilisation) to die out; ~ **de froid/faim** to die of exposure/hunger; ~ **de faim/d'ennui** (fig) to be starving/be bored to death; ~ **d'envie de faire** to be dying to do

**mousse** [mus] nf (BOT) moss; (de savon) lather; (écume: sur eau, bière) froth, foam; (CULIN) mousse ◆ nm (NAVIG) ship's boy; ~ **à raser** shaving foam

**mousseline** [muslin] nf muslin; **pommes** ~ mashed potatoes

**mousser** [muse] vi (bière, détergent) to foam; (savon) to lather; **mousseux, -euse** adj frothy ◆ nm: **(vin) mousseux** sparkling wine

**mousson** [musõ] nf monsoon

**moustache** [mustaʃ] nf moustache; ~**s** nfpl (du chat) whiskers pl; **moustachu, e** adj with a moustache

**moustiquaire** [mustikɛR] nf mosquito net

**moustique** [mustik] nm mosquito

**moutarde** [mutaRd] nf mustard

**mouton** [mutõ] nm sheep inv; (peau) sheepskin; (CULIN) mutton

**mouvement** [muvmã] nm movement; (fig: impulsion) gesture; **avoir un bon** ~ to make a nice gesture; **en** ~ in motion; on the move; **mouvementé, e** adj (vie, poursuite) eventful; (réunion) turbulent

**mouvoir** [muvwar]: **se** ~ vi to move

**moyen, ne** [mwajẽ, ɛn] adj average; (tailles, prix) medium; (de grandeur moyenne) medium-sized ◆ nm (façon) means sg, way; ~**s** nmpl (capacités) means; **très** ~ (résultats) pretty poor; **je n'en ai pas les** ~**s** I can't afford it; **au** ~ **de** by means of; **par tous les** ~**s** by every possible means, every possible way; **par ses propres** ~**s** all by oneself; ~ **âge** Middle Ages; ~ **de transport** means of transport

**moyennant** [mwajenã] prép (somme) for; (service, conditions) in return for; (travail, effort) with

**moyenne** [mwajen] nf average; (MATH) mean; (SCOL) pass mark; **en** ~ on (an) average; ~ **d'âge** average age

**Moyen-Orient** [mwajẽnɔrjã] nm: **le ~~** the Middle East

**moyeu, x** [mwajø] nm hub

**MST** sigle f (= maladie sexuellement transmissible) STD

**MTC** sigle m (= mécanisme du taux de change) ERM

**mû, mue** [my] pp de mouvoir

**muer** [mɥe] vi (oiseau, mammifère) to moult; (serpent) to slough; (jeune garçon): **il mue** his voice is breaking; **se** ~ **en** to transform into

**muet, te** [mɥe, mɥet] adj dumb; (fig): ~ **d'admiration** etc speechless with admiration etc; (CINÉMA) silent ◆ nm/f mute

**mufle** [myfl] nm muzzle; (fam: goujat) boor

**mugir** [myʒir] vi (taureau) to bellow; (vache) to low; (fig) to howl

**muguet** [mygɛ] nm lily of the valley

**mule** [myl] nf (ZOOL) (she-)mule

**mulet** [mylɛ] nm (ZOOL) (he-)mule

**multinationale** [myltinasjɔnal] nf multinational

**multiple** [myltipl] adj multiple, numerous; (varié) many, manifold; **multiplication** nf multiplication; **multiplier** vt to multiply; **se multiplier** vi to multiply

**municipal, e, -aux** [mynisipal, o] adj (élections, stade) municipal; (conseil) town cpd; **piscine/bibliothèque ~e** public swimming pool/library; **municipalité** nf (ville) municipality; (conseil) town council

**munir** [mynir] vt: ~ qch de to equip sth with; **se ~ de** to arm o.s. with

**munitions** [mynisjɔ̃] nfpl ammunition sg

**mur** [myr] nm wall; ~ **du son** sound barrier

**mûr, e** [myr] adj ripe; (personne) mature

**muraille** [myrɑj] nf (high) wall

**mural, e, -aux** [myral, o] adj wall cpd; (art) mural

**mûre** [myr] nf blackberry

**muret** [myrɛ] nm low wall

**mûrir** [myrir] vi (fruit, blé) to ripen; (abcès) to come to a head; (fig: idée, personne) to mature ♦ vt (projet) to nurture; (personne) to (make) mature

**murmure** [myrmyr] nm murmur; **murmurer** vi to murmur

**muscade** [myskad] nf (aussi: **noix (de) ~**) nutmeg

**muscat** [myska] nm (raisins) muscat grape; (vin) muscatel (wine)

**muscle** [myskl] nm muscle; **musclé, e** adj muscular; (fig) strong-arm

**museau, x** [myzo] nm muzzle; (CULIN) brawn

**musée** [myze] nm museum; (de peinture) art gallery

**museler** [myz(ə)le] vt to muzzle; **muselière** nf muzzle

**musette** [myzɛt] nf (sac) lunchbag

**musical, e, -aux** [myzikal, o] adj musical

**music-hall** [myzikol] nm (salle) variety theatre; (genre) variety

**musicien, ne** [myzisjɛ̃, jɛn] adj musical ♦ nm/f musician

**musique** [myzik] nf music; ~ **d'ambiance** background music

**musulman, e** [myzylmɑ̃, an] adj, nm/f Moslem, Muslim

**mutation** [mytasjɔ̃] nf (ADMIN) transfer

**muter** [myte] vt to transfer, move

**mutilé, e** [mytile] nm/f disabled person (through loss of limbs)

**mutiler** [mytile] vt to mutilate, maim

**mutin, e** [mytɛ̃, in] adj (air, ton) mischievous, impish ♦ nm/f (MIL, NAVIG) mutineer; **mutinerie** nf mutiny

**mutisme** [mytism] nm silence

**mutuel, le** [mytɥɛl] adj mutual; **mutuelle** nf voluntary insurance premiums for back-up health cover

**myope** [mjɔp] adj short-sighted

**myosotis** [mjɔzɔtis] nm forget-me-not

**myrtille** [mirtij] nf bilberry

**mystère** [mistɛr] nm mystery; **mystérieux, -euse** adj mysterious

**mystifier** [mistifje] vt to fool

**mythe** [mit] nm myth

**mythologie** [mitɔlɔʒi] nf mythology

# N, n

**n'** [n] adv voir **ne**

**nacre** [nakr] nf mother of pearl

**nage** [naʒ] nf swimming; (manière) style of swimming, stroke; **traverser/s'éloigner à la ~** to swim across/away; **en ~** bathed in sweat; **nageoire** nf fin; **nager** vi to swim; **nageur, -euse** nm/f swimmer

**naguère** [nagɛr] adv formerly

**naïf, -ïve** [naif, naiv] adj naïve

**nain, e** [nɛ̃, nɛn] nm/f dwarf

**naissance** [nesɑ̃s] nf birth; **donner ~ à** to give birth to; (fig) to give rise to

**naître** [nɛtr] vi to be born; (fig): ~ **de** to arise from, be born out of; **il est né**

en 1960 he was born in 1960; **faire ~** (fig) to give rise to, arouse

**naïve** [naiv] *adj voir* **naïf**

**naïveté** [naivte] *nf* naïveté

**nana** [nana] (fam) *nf* (fille) chick, bird (BRIT)

**nantir** [nɑ̃tiʀ] *vt*: **~ qn de** to provide sb with; **les nantis** (péj) the well-to-do

**nappe** [nap] *nf* tablecloth; (de pétrole, gaz) layer; **~ phréatique** ground water; **napperon** *nm* table-mat

**naquit** etc [naki] *vb voir* **naître**

**narcodollars** [narkodɔlaʀ] *nmpl* drug money pl

**narguer** [naʀge] *vt* to taunt

**narine** [naʀin] *nf* nostril

**narquois, e** [naʀkwa, waz] *adj* mocking

**natal, e** [natal] *adj* native; **natalité** *nf* birth rate

**natation** [natasjɔ̃] *nf* swimming

**natif, -ive** [natif, iv] *adj* native

**nation** [nasjɔ̃] *nf* nation; **national, e, -aux** [nasjɔnal, o] *adj* national; **nationale** *nf*: (route) **nationale** ≈ A road (BRIT), ≈ state highway (US); **nationaliser** *vt* to nationalize; **nationalisme** *nm* nationalism; **nationalité** *nf* nationality

**natte** [nat] *nf* (cheveux) plait; (tapis) mat

**naturaliser** [natyʀalize] *vt* to naturalize

**nature** [natyʀ] *nf* nature ♦ *adj, adv* (CULIN) plain, without seasoning or sweetening; (café, thé) black, without sugar; (yaourt) natural; **payer en ~** to pay in kind; **~ morte** still-life; **naturel, le** [natyʀɛl] *adj* (gén, aussi enfant) natural; (absence d'affectation) naturalness; (caractère) disposition, nature; **naturellement** *adv* naturally; (bien sûr) of course

**naufrage** [nofʀaʒ] *nm* (ship)wreck; **faire ~** to be shipwrecked

**nauséabond, e** [nozeabɔ̃, ɔ̃d] *adj* foul

**nausée** [noze] *nf* nausea

**nautique** [notik] *adj* nautical, water *cpd*; **sports ~s** water sports

**naval, e** [naval] *adj* naval; (industrie) shipbuilding

**navet** [navɛ] *nm* turnip; (péj: film) rubbishy film

**navette** [navɛt] *nf* shuttle; **faire la ~ (entre)** to go to and fro ou shuttle (between)

**navigateur** [navigatœʀ, tʀis] *nm* (NAVIG) seafarer; (INFORM) browser

**navigation** [navigasjɔ̃] *nf* navigation, sailing

**naviguer** [navige] *vi* to navigate, sail

**navire** [naviʀ] *nm* ship

**navrer** [navʀe] *vt* to upset, distress; **je suis navré** I'm so sorry

**ne, n'** [n(ə)] *adv voir* **pas; plus; jamais** etc; (sans valeur négative: non traduit): **c'est plus loin que je ~ le croyais** it's further than I thought

**né, e** [ne] *pp* (voir **naître**): **~ en 1960** born in 1960; **~e Scott** née Scott

**néanmoins** [neɑ̃mwɛ̃] *adv* nevertheless

**néant** [neɑ̃] *nm* nothingness; **réduire à ~** to bring to nought; (espoir) to dash

**nécessaire** [neseseʀ] *adj* necessary ♦ *nm* necessary; (sac) kit; **je vais faire le ~** I'll see to it; **~ de couture** sewing kit; **nécessité** *nf* necessity; **nécessiter** *vt* to require

**nécrologique** [nekʀɔlɔʒik] *adj*: **rubrique ~** obituary column

**nectar** [nɛktaʀ] *nm* nectar

**néerlandais, e** [neeʀlɑ̃dɛ, ɛz] *adj* Dutch

**nef** [nɛf] *nf* (d'église) nave

**néfaste** [nefast] *adj* (nuisible) harmful; (funeste) ill-fated

**négatif, -ive** [negatif, iv] *adj* negative ♦ *nm* (PHOTO) negative

**négligé, e** [negliʒe] *adj* (en désordre) slovenly ♦ *nm* (tenue) negligee

**négligeable** [negliʒabl] *adj* negligible

**négligent, e** [negliʒɑ̃, ɑ̃t] *adj* careless, negligent

**négliger** [negliʒe] *vt* (tenue) to be careless about; (avis, précautions) to disregard; (épouse, jardin) to neglect; **~ de**

**faire à** to fail to do, not bother to do
**négoce** [negɔs] nm trade
**négociant, e** [negɔsjɑ̃, ɑ̃t] nm merchant
**négociation** [negɔsjasjɔ̃] nf negotiation; **négocier** vi, vt to negotiate
**nègre** [nɛgʀ] (péj) nm (écrivain) ghost (writer)
**neige** [nɛʒ] nf snow; **neiger** vi to snow
**nénuphar** [nenyfaʀ] nm water-lily
**néon** [neɔ̃] nm neon
**néo-zélandais, e** [neozelɑ̃dɛ, ɛz] adj New Zealand cpd ♦ nm/f: **N~-Z~, e** New Zealander
**nerf** [nɛʀ] nm nerve; **être sur les ~s** to be all keyed up; **allons, du ~!** come on, buck up!; **nerveux, -euse** adj nervous; (irritable) touchy, nervy; (voiture) nippy, responsive; **nervosité** nf excitability, tenseness; (irritabilité passagère) irritability, nervousness
**nervure** [nɛʀvyʀ] nf vein
**n'est-ce pas** [nɛspa] adv isn't it?, won't you? etc, selon le verbe qui précède
**Net** [nɛt] nm (Internet): **le ~** the Net
**net, nette** [nɛt] adj (sans équivoque, distinct) clear; (évident: amélioration, différence) marked, distinct; (propre) neat, clean; (COMM: prix, salaire) net ♦ adv (refuser) flatly ♦ nm: **mettre au ~** to copy out; **s'arrêter ~** to stop dead; **netteté** nf clearness
**nettoyage** [netwajaʒ] nm cleaning; **~ à sec** dry cleaning
**nettoyer** [netwaje] vt to clean
**neuf¹** [nœf] num nine
**neuf², neuve** [nœf, nœv] adj new ♦ nm: **remettre à ~** to do up (as good as new), refurbish; **quoi de ~?** what's new?
**neutre** [nøtʀ] adj neutral; (LING) neuter
**neuve** [nœv] adj voir **neuf²**
**neuvième** [nœvjɛm] num ninth
**neveu, x** [n(ə)vø] nm nephew
**névrose, e** [nevʀoze] adj, nm/f neurotic

**nez** [ne] nm nose; **~ à ~ avec** face to face with; **avoir du ~** to have flair
**ni** [ni] conj: **~ ... ~** neither ... nor; **je n'aime ~ les lentilles ~ les épinards** I like neither lentils nor spinach; **il n'a dit ~ oui ~ non** he didn't say either yes or no; **elles ne sont venues ~ l'une ~ l'autre** neither of them came
**niais, e** [njɛ, njɛz] adj silly, thick
**niche** [niʃ] nf (du chien) kennel; (de mur) recess, niche; **nicher** vi to nest
**nid** [ni] nm nest; **~ de poule** pothole
**nièce** [njɛs] nf niece
**nier** [nje] vt to deny
**nigaud, e** [nigo, od] nm/f booby, fool
**Nil** [nil] nm: **le ~** the Nile
**n'importe** [nɛ̃pɔʀt] adv: **~ qui/quoi/où** anybody/anything/anywhere; **~ quand** any time; **~ quel/quelle** any; **~ lequel/laquelle** any (one); **~ comment** (sans soin) carelessly
**niveau, x** [nivo] nm level; (des élèves, études) standard; **~ de vie** standard of living
**niveler** [niv(ə)le] vt to level
**NN** abr (= nouvelle norme) revised standard of hotel classification
**noble** [nɔbl] adj noble; **noblesse** nf nobility; (d'une action etc) nobleness
**noce** [nɔs] nf wedding; (gens) wedding party (ou guests pl); **faire la ~** (fam) to go on a binge
**nocif, -ive** [nɔsif, iv] adj harmful
**nocturne** [nɔktyʀn] adj nocturnal ♦ nf late-night opening
**Noël** [nɔɛl] nm Christmas
**nœud** [nø] nm knot; (ruban) bow; **~ papillon** bow tie
**noir, e** [nwaʀ] adj black; (obscur, sombre) dark ♦ nm/f black man/woman ♦ nm: **dans le ~** in the dark; **travail au ~** moonlighting; **travailler au ~** to work on the side; **noircir** vt, vi to blacken; **noire** nf (MUS) crotchet (BRIT), quarter note (US)
**noisette** [nwazɛt] nf hazelnut
**noix** [nwa] nf walnut; (CULIN): **une ~ de**

beurre a knob of butter; ~ **de cajou**
cashew nut; ~ **de coco** coconut; **à la** ~
*(fam)* worthless

**nom** [nɔ̃] *nm* name; *(LING)* noun; ~ **de
famille** surname; ~ **de jeune fille**
maiden name; ~ **déposé** trade name;
~ **propre** proper noun

**nomade** [nɔmad] *nm/f* nomad

**nombre** [nɔ̃br] *nm* number; **venir en**
~ to come in large numbers; **depuis** ~
**d'années** for many years; **au** ~ **de
mes amis** among my friends; **nombreux, -euse** *adj* many, numerous;
*(avec nom sg: foule)* large; **peu
nombreux** few

**nombril** [nɔ̃bri(l)] *nm* navel

**nommer** [nɔme] *vt* to name; *(élire)* to
appoint, nominate; **se** ~: **il se nomme
Pascal** his name's Pascal, he's called
Pascal

**non** [nɔ̃] *adv (réponse)* no; *(avec loin,
sans, seulement)* not; ~ **(pas) que** not
that; **moi** ~ **plus** neither do I, I don't
either; **c'est bon** ~? *(exprimant le
doute)* it's good, isn't it?

**non-alcoolisé, e** [nɔ̃alkɔlize] *adj* non-
alcoholic

**nonante** [nɔnɑ̃t] *(BELGIQUE, SUISSE) num*
ninety

**non-fumeur** [nɔ̃fymœr, øz] *nm* non-
smoker

**non-sens** [nɔ̃sɑ̃s] *nm* absurdity

**nonchalant, e** [nɔ̃ʃalɑ̃, ɑ̃t] *adj* nonchalant

**nord** [nɔr] *nm* North ♦ *adj* northern;
north; **au** ~ *(situation)* in the north;
*(direction)* to the north; **au** ~ **de** ~ *(à
the north of)* of; **nord-est** *nm* North-East;
**nord-ouest** *nm* North-West

**normal, e, -aux** [nɔrmal, o] *adj* normal; **c'est tout à fait** ~ it's perfectly
natural; **vous trouvez ça** ~? does it
seem right to you?; **normale** *nf*: **la
normale** the norm, the average; **normalement** *adv (en général)* normally

**normand, e** [nɔrmɑ̃, ɑ̃d] *adj* of Normandy

**Normandie** [nɔrmɑ̃di] *nf* Normandy

**norme** [nɔrm] *nf* norm; *(TECH)* standard

**Norvège** [nɔrvɛʒ] *nf* Norway; **norvégien, ne** *adj* Norwegian ♦ *nm/f*: **Norvégien, ne** Norwegian ♦ *nm (LING)*
Norwegian

**nos** [no] *adj voir* **notre**

**nostalgie** [nɔstalʒi] *nf* nostalgia; **nos-
talgique** *adj* nostalgic

**notable** [nɔtabl] *adj (fait)* notable,
noteworthy; *(marqué)* noticeable,
marked ♦ *nm* prominent citizen

**notaire** [nɔtɛr] *nm* solicitor

**notamment** [nɔtamɑ̃] *adv* in particular, among others

**note** [nɔt] *nf (écrite, MUS)* note; *(SCOL)*
mark *(BRIT)*, grade; *(facture)* bill; ~ **de
service** memorandum

**noté, e** [nɔte] *adj*: **être bien/mal** ~
*(employé etc)* to have a good/bad
record

**noter** [nɔte] *vt (écrire)* to write down;
*(remarquer)* to note, notice; *(devoir)* to
mark, grade

**notice** [nɔtis] *nf* summary, short article;
*(brochure)* leaflet, instruction book

**notifier** [nɔtifje] *vt*: ~ **qch à qn** to notify sb of sth, notify sth to sb

**notion** [nɔsjɔ̃] *nf* notion, idea

**notoire** [nɔtwar] *adj* widely known; *(en
mal)* notorious

**notre** [nɔtr] *(pl* **nos)** *adj* our

**nôtre** [nɔtr] *pron*: **la** ~, **la** ~, **les** ~**s**
ours ♦ *adj*: **les** ~**s** ours; *(alliés etc)*
our own people; **soyez des** ~**s** join us

**nouer** [nwe] *vt* to tie, knot; *(fig: alliance
etc)* to strike up

**noueux, -euse** [nwø, øz] *adj* gnarled

**nouilles** [nuj] *nfpl* noodles

**nourrice** [nuris] *nf (gardienne)* child-
minder

**nourrir** [nurir] *vt* to feed; *(fig: espoir)*
to harbour, nurse; **se** ~ to eat; **se** ~
**de** to feed (o.s.) on; **nourrissant, e**
*adj* nourishing, nutritious; **nourrisson**
*nm* (unweaned) infant; **nourriture** *nf*
food

**nous** [nu] *pron* (*sujet*) we; (*objet*) us; **nous-mêmes** *pron* ourselves

**nouveau** (**nouvel**), **-elle, x** [nuvo, nuvɛl] *adj* new ♦ *nm:* **y a-t-il du ~?** is there anything new on this? ♦ *nm/f* new pupil (*ou* employee); **de ~, à ~** again; **~ venu, nouvelle venue** newcomer; **~x mariés** newly-weds; **nouveau-né, e** *nm* newborn baby; **nouveauté** *nf* novelty; (*objet*) new thing *ou* article

**nouvel** [nuvɛl] *adj voir* **nouveau**; **N~ An** New Year

**nouvelle** [nuvɛl] *adj voir* **nouveau** ♦ *nf* (*piece*) of news *sg*; (*LITTÉRATURE*) short story; **les ~s** the news; **je suis sans ~ de lui** I haven't heard from him; **Nouvelle-Calédonie** *nf* New Caledonia; **nouvellement** *adv* recently, newly; **Nouvelle-Zélande** *nf* New Zealand

**novembre** [nɔvɑ̃br] *nm* November

**novice** [nɔvis] *adj* inexperienced

**noyade** [nwajad] *nf* drowning *no pl*

**noyau, x** [nwajo] *nm* (*de fruit*) stone; (*BIO, PHYSIQUE*) nucleus; (*fig: centre*) core; **noyauter** *vt* (*POL*) to infiltrate

**noyer** [nwaje] *nm* walnut (tree); (*bois*) walnut ♦ *vt* to drown; (*moteur*) to flood; **se ~** *vi* to be drowned, drown; (*suicide*) to drown o.s.

**nu, e** [ny] *adj* naked; (*membres*) naked, bare; (*pieds, mains, chambre, fil électrique*) bare ♦ *nm* (*ART*) nude; **tout ~** stark naked; **se mettre ~** to strip; **mettre à ~** to bare

**nuage** [nɥaʒ] *nm* cloud; **nuageux, -euse** *adj* cloudy

**nuance** [nɥɑ̃s] *nf* (*de couleur, sens*) shade; **il y a une ~ (entre)** there's a slight difference (between); **nuancer** *vt* (*opinion*) to bring some reservations *ou* qualifications to

**nucléaire** [nykleɛr] *adj* nuclear ♦ *nm:* **le ~** nuclear energy

**nudiste** [nydist] *nm/f* nudist

**nuée** [nɥe] *nf:* **une ~ de** a cloud *ou* host *ou* swarm of

**nues** [ny] *nfpl:* **tomber des ~** to be taken aback; **porter qn aux ~** to praise sb to the skies

**nuire** [nɥir] *vi* to be harmful; **~ à** to harm, do damage to; **nuisible** *adj* harmful; **animal nuisible** pest

**nuit** [nɥi] *nf* night; **il fait ~** it's dark; **cette ~** (*hier*) last night; (*aujourd'hui*) tonight; **~ blanche** sleepless night

**nul, nulle** [nyl] *adj* (*aucun*) no; (*minime*) nil, non-existent; (*non valable*) null; (*péj*) useless, hopeless ♦ *pron* none, no one; **match ou résultat ~** draw; **~ le part** nowhere; **nullement** *adv* by no means; **nullité** *nf* (*personne*) nonentity

**numérique** [nymerik] *adj* numerical; (*affichage*) digital

**numéro** [nymero] *nm* number; (*spectacle*) act, turn; (*PRESSE*) issue; number; **~ de téléphone** (*phone*) number; **~ vert** freefone ® number (*BRIT*); toll-free number (*US*); **numéroter** *vt* to number

**nu-pieds** [nypje] *adj inv, adv* barefoot

**nuque** [nyk] *nf* nape of the neck

**nu-tête** [nytɛt] *adj inv, adv* bareheaded

**nutritif, -ive** [nytritif, iv] *adj* (*besoins, valeur*) nutritional; (*nourrissant*) nutritious

**nylon** [nilɔ̃] *nm* nylon

# O, o

**oasis** [ɔazis] *nf* oasis

**obéir** [ɔbeir] *vi* to obey; **~ à** to obey; **obéissance** *nf* obedience; **obéissant, e** *adj* obedient

**obèse** [ɔbɛz] *adj* obese; **obésité** *nf* obesity

**objecter** [ɔbʒɛkte] *vt* (*prétexter*) to plead, put forward as an excuse; **~ (à qn) que** to object (to sb) that; **objecteur** *nm:* **objecteur de conscience** conscientious objector

**objectif, -ive** [ɔbʒɛktif, iv] *adj* objective ♦ *nm* objective; (*PHOTO*) lens *sg*, objective; **objectivité** nf objectivity

**objection** [ɔbʒɛksjɔ̃] nf objection

**objet** [ɔbʒɛ] nm object; (d'une discussion, recherche) subject; **être ~ l'~ de** (discussion) to be the subject of; (soins) to be given ou shown; **sans ~** purposeless; groundless; **~ d'art** objet d'art; **~s trouvés** lost property sg (BRIT), lost-and-found sg (US); **~s de valeur** valuables

**obligation** [ɔbligasjɔ̃] nf obligation; (COMM) bond, debenture; **obligatoire** adj compulsory, obligatory; **obligatoirement** adv necessarily; (fam: sans aucun doute) inevitably

**obligé, e** [ɔbliʒe] adj (redevable): **être très ~ à qn** to be most obliged to sb

**obligeance** [ɔbliʒɑ̃s] nf: **avoir l'~ de ...** to be kind ou good enough to ...; **obligeant, e** adj (personne) obliging, kind

**obliger** [ɔbliʒe] vt (contraindre): **~ qn à faire** to force ou oblige sb to do; **je suis bien obligé** I have to

**oblique** [ɔblik] adj oblique; **en ~** diagonally; **obliquer** vi: **obliquer vers** to turn off towards

**oblitérer** [ɔblitere] vt (timbre-poste) to cancel

**obnubiler** [ɔbnybile] vt to obsess

**obscène** [ɔpsɛn] adj obscene

**obscur, e** [ɔpskyr] adj dark; (méconnu) obscure; **obscurcir** vt to darken; (fig) to obscure; **s'obscurcir** vi to grow dark; **obscurité** nf darkness; **dans l'obscurité** in the dark, in darkness

**obsédé, e** [ɔpsede] nm/f: **un ~ (sexuel)** a sex maniac

**obséder** [ɔpsede] vt to obsess, haunt

**obsèques** [ɔpsɛk] nfpl funeral sg

**observateur, -trice** [ɔpsɛrvatœr, tris] adj observant, perceptive ♦ nm/f observer

**observation** [ɔpsɛrvasjɔ̃] nf observation; (d'un règlement etc) observance; (reproche) reproof; **être en ~** (MÉD) to be under observation

**observatoire** [ɔpsɛrvatwar] nm observatory

**observer** [ɔpsɛrve] vt (regarder) to observe, watch; (scientifiquement; aussi règlement etc) to observe; (surveiller) to watch; (remarquer) to observe, notice; **faire ~ qch à qn** (dire) to point out sth to sb

**obsession** [ɔpsesjɔ̃] nf obsession

**obstacle** [ɔpstakl] nm obstacle; (ÉQUITATION) jump, hurdle; **faire ~ à** (projet) to hinder, put obstacles in the path of

**obstiné, e** [ɔpstine] adj obstinate

**obstiner** [ɔpstine]: **s'~** vi to insist, dig one's heels in; **s'~ à faire** to persist (obstinately) in doing

**obstruer** [ɔpstrye] vt to block, obstruct

**obtenir** [ɔptənir] vt to obtain, get; (résultat) to achieve, obtain; **~ de pouvoir faire** to obtain permission to do

**obturateur** [ɔptyratœr, tris] nm (PHOTO) shutter

**obus** [ɔby] nm shell

**occasion** [ɔkazjɔ̃] nf (aubaine, possibilité) opportunity; (circonstance) occasion; (COMM: article non neuf) secondhand buy; (: acquisition avantageuse) bargain; **à plusieurs ~s** on several occasions; **à l'~** sometimes, on occasions; **d'~** secondhand; **occasionnel, le** adj (non régulier) occasional; **occasionnellement** adv occasionally, from time to time

**occasionner** [ɔkazjɔne] vt to cause

**occident** [ɔksidɑ̃] nm: **l'O~** the West; **~ occidental, e, -aux** adj western; (POL) Western ♦ nm/f Westerner

**occupation** [ɔkypasjɔ̃] nf occupation

**occupé, e** [ɔkype] adj (personne) busy; (place, sièges) taken; (toilettes) engaged; (ligne) engaged (BRIT), busy (US); (MIL, POL) occupied

**occuper** [ɔkype] vt to occupy; (poste) to hold; **s'~ de** (être responsable de) to be in charge of; (se charger de: affaire) to take charge of, deal with; (: clients) *etc*) to attend to; **s'~ (à qch)** to occupy o.s. with sth; to keep o.s. busy (with sth)

**occurrence** [ɔkyʀɑ̃s] *nf*: **en l'~** in this case

**océan** [ɔseɑ̃] *nm* ocean

**octante** [ɔktɑ̃t] *adj (regional)* eighty

**octet** [ɔktɛ] *nm* byte

**octobre** [ɔktɔbʀ] *nm* October

**octroyer** [ɔktʀwaje]: **s'~** *vt (vacances etc)* to treat o.s. to

**oculiste** [ɔkylist] *nm/f* eye specialist

**odeur** [ɔdœʀ] *nf* smell

**odieux, -euse** [ɔdjø, jøz] *adj* hateful

**odorant, e** [ɔdɔʀɑ̃, ɑ̃t] *adj* sweet-smelling, fragrant

**odorat** [ɔdɔʀa] *nm* (sense of) smell

**œil** [œj] *(pl* **yeux**) *nm* eye; **à l'œil** *(fam)* for free; **à l'œil nu** with the naked eye; **tenir qn à l'œil** to keep an eye on; **avoir l'œil à** to keep an eye on; **fermer les yeux (sur)** *(fig)* to turn a blind eye (to); **voir qch d'un bon/mauvais œil** to look on sth favourably/unfavourably

**œillères** [œjɛʀ] *nfpl* blinkers *(BRIT)*, blinders *(US)*

**œillet** [œjɛ] *nm (BOT)* carnation

**œuf** [œf, *pl* ø] *nm* egg; **œuf à la coque/au plat/dur** boiled/fried/hard-boiled egg; **œuf de Pâques** Easter egg; **œufs brouillés** scrambled eggs

**œuvre** [œvʀ] *nf (tâche)* task, undertaking; *(livre, tableau etc)* work; *(ensemble de la production artistique)* works *pl* ♦ *nm (CONSTR)*: **le gros œuvre** the shell; **œuvre (de bienfaisance)** charity; **mettre en œuvre** *(moyens)* to make use of; **œuvre d'art** work of art

**offense** [ɔfɑ̃s] *nf* insult; **offenser** *vt* to offend, hurt

**offert, e** [ɔfɛʀ, ɛʀt] *pp de* **offrir**

**office** [ɔfis] *nm (agence)* bureau, agency; *(REL)* service ♦ *nm ou nf (pièce)* pantry; **faire ~ de** to act as; **d'~** automatically; **~ du tourisme** tourist bureau

**officiel, le** [ɔfisjɛl] *adj, nm/f* official

**officier** [ɔfisje] *nm* officer

**officieux, -euse** [ɔfisjø, jøz] *adj* unofficial

**offrande** [ɔfʀɑ̃d] *nf* offering

**offre** [ɔfʀ] *nf* offer; *(aux enchères)* bid; *(ADMIN: soumission)* tender; *(ÉCON)*: **l'~ et la demande** supply and demand; **"~s d'emploi"** "situations vacant"; **~ d'emploi** job advertised

**offrir** [ɔfʀiʀ] *vt*: **~ (à qn)** to offer (to sb); *(faire cadeau de)* to give (to sb); **s'~** *vt (vacances, voiture)* to treat o.s. to; **~ (à qn) de faire qch** to offer to do sth (for sb); **~ à boire à qn** *(chez soi)* to offer sb a drink

**offusquer** [ɔfyske] *vt* to offend

**OGM** *sigle m* (= *organisme génétiquement modifié*) GMO

**oie** [wa] *nf (ZOOL)* goose

**oignon** [ɔɲɔ̃] *nm* onion; *(de tulipe etc)* bulb

**oiseau, x** [wazo] *nm* bird; **~ de proie** bird of prey

**oisif, -ive** [wazif, iv] *adj* idle

**oléoduc** [ɔleɔdyk] *nm* (oil) pipeline

**olive** [ɔliv] *nf (BOT)* olive; **olivier** *nm* olive (tree)

**OLP** *sigle f* (= *Organisation de libération de la Palestine*) PLO

**olympique** [ɔlɛ̃pik] *adj* Olympic

**ombragé, e** [ɔ̃bʀaʒe] *adj* shaded, shady; **ombrageux, -euse** *adj (personne)* touchy, easily offended

**ombre** [ɔ̃bʀ] *nf (espace non ensoleillé)* shade; *(~ portée, tache)* shadow; **à l'~** in the shade; **dans l'~** *(fig)* in the dark; **~ à paupières** eyeshadow; **ombrelle** *nf* parasol, sunshade

**omelette** [ɔmlɛt] *nf* omelette; **~ norvégienne** baked Alaska

**omettre** [ɔmɛtʀ] *vt* to omit, leave out

**omnibus** [ɔmnibys] *nm* slow ou stopping train

**omoplate** [ɔmɔplat] *nf* shoulder blade

---

**MOT-CLÉ**

**on** [ɔ̃] *pron* **1** *(indéterminé)* you, one; **on peut le faire ainsi** you ou one can do

it like this, it can be done like this
**2** (*quelqu'un*): **on les a attaqués** they were attacked; **on vous demande au téléphone** there's a phone call for you, you're wanted on the phone
**3** (*nous*) we; **on va y aller demain** we're going tomorrow
**4** (*les gens*) they; **autrefois, on croyait** ... they used to believe ...
**5: on ne peut plus**
♦ *adv*: **on ne peut plus stupide** as stupid as can be

**oncle** [ɔ̃kl] *nm* uncle

**onctueux, -euse** [ɔ̃ktɥø, øz] *adj* creamy, smooth

**onde** [ɔ̃d] *nf* wave; **sur les ~s** on the radio; **sur ~s courtes** on short wave *sg*; **moyennes/longues ~s** medium/long wave *sg*

**ondée** [ɔ̃de] *nf* shower

**on-dit** [ɔ̃di] *nm inv* rumour

**onduler** [ɔ̃dyle] *vi* to undulate; (*cheveux*) to wave

**onéreux, -euse** [ɔnerø, øz] *adj* costly

**ongle** [ɔ̃gl] *nm* nail

**ont** [ɔ̃] *vb voir* **avoir**

**ONU** *sigle f* (= *Organisation des Nations Unies*) UN

**onze** [ɔ̃z] *num* eleven; **onzième** *num* eleventh

**OPA** *sigle f* = **offre publique d'achat**

**opaque** [ɔpak] *adj* opaque

**opéra** [ɔpera] *nm* opera; (*édifice*) opera house

**opérateur, -trice** [ɔperatœr, tris] *nm/f* operator; **~ (de prise de vues)** cameraman

**opération** [ɔperasjɔ̃] *nf* operation; (*COMM*) dealing

**opératoire** [ɔperatwar] *adj* (*choc etc*) post-operative

**opérer** [ɔpere] *vt* (*personne*) to operate on; (*faire, exécuter*) to carry out, make ♦ *vi* (*remède: faire effet*) to act, work; (*MÉD*) to operate; **s'~** *vi* (*avoir lieu*) to occur, take place; **se faire ~** to have

an operation

**opérette** [ɔperɛt] *nf* operetta, light opera

**ophtalmologiste** [ɔftalmɔlɔʒist] *nm/f* ophthalmologist, optician

**opiner** [ɔpine] *vi*: **~ de la tête** to nod assent

**opinion** [ɔpinjɔ̃] *nf* opinion; **l'~ (publique)** public opinion

**opportun, e** [ɔpɔrtœ̃, yn] *adj* timely, opportune; **opportuniste** *nm/f* opportunist

**opposant, e** [ɔpozɑ̃, ɑ̃t] *nm/f* opponent

**opposé, e** [ɔpoze] *adj* (*direction*) opposite; (*faction*) opposing; (*opinions, intérêts*) conflicting; (*contre*): **~ à** opposed to, against ♦ *nm*: **l'~** the other *ou* place opposite (*ou* direction); (*contraire*) the opposite; **à l'~** (*fig*) on the other hand; **à l'~ de** (*fig*) contrary to, unlike

**opposer** [ɔpoze] *vt* (*personnes, équipes*) to oppose; (*couleurs*) to contrast; **s'~** *vi* (*équipes*) to confront each other; (*opinions*) to conflict; (*couleurs, styles*) to contrast; **s'~ à** (*interdire*) to oppose; **~ qch à** (*comme obstacle, défense*) to set sth against; (*comme objection*) to put sth forward against

**opposition** [ɔpozisjɔ̃] *nf* opposition; **par ~ à** as opposed to, **entrer en ~ avec** to come into conflict with; **faire ~ à un chèque** to stop a cheque

**oppressant, e** [ɔpresɑ̃, ɑ̃t] *adj* oppressive

**oppresser** [ɔprese] *vt* to oppress; **oppression** *nf* oppression

**opprimer** [ɔprime] *vt* to oppress

**opter** [ɔpte] *vi*: **~ pour** to opt for

**opticien, ne** [ɔptisjɛ̃, jɛn] *nm/f* optician

**optimisme** [ɔptimism] *nm* optimism; **optimiste** *nm/f* optimist ♦ *adj* optimistic

**option** [ɔpsjɔ̃] *nf* option; **matière à ~** (*SCOL*) optional subject

**optique** [ɔptik] *adj* (*nerf*) optic; (*verres*) optical ♦ *nf* (*fig: manière de voir*) perspective

**opulent, e** [ɔpylɑ̃, ɑ̃t] *adj* wealthy, opulent; (*formes, poitrine*) ample, generous

**or** [ɔʀ] *nm* gold ♦ *conj* now, but; **en ~** (*objet*) gold *cpd*; **une affaire en ~** a real bargain; **il croyait gagner ~ il a perdu** he was sure he would win and yet he lost

**orage** [ɔʀaʒ] *nm* (thunder)storm; **orageux, -euse** *adj* stormy

**oral, e, -aux** [ɔʀal, o] *adj, nm* oral; **par voie ~** (*MÉD*) orally

**orange** [ɔʀɑ̃ʒ] *nf* orange ♦ *adj inv* orange; **orangeade** *nf* orangeade; **orangé, e** *adj* orangey, orange-coloured; **oranger** *nm* orange tree

**orateur** [ɔʀatœʀ, tʀis] *nm* speaker

**orbite** [ɔʀbit] *nf* (*ANAT*) (eye-)socket; (*PHYSIQUE*) orbit

**orchestre** [ɔʀkɛstʀ] *nm* orchestra; (*de jazz*) band; (*places*) stalls *pl* (*BRIT*), orchestra (*US*); **orchestrer** *vt* to orchestrate

**orchidée** [ɔʀkide] *nf* orchid

**ordinaire** [ɔʀdinɛʀ] *adj* ordinary; (*qualité*) standard; (*péj: commun*) common ♦ *nm* ordinary; (*menus*) everyday fare ♦ *nf* (*essence*) ≈ two-star (petrol) (*BRIT*), ≈ regular gas (*US*); **d'~** usually, normally; **comme à l'~** as usual

**ordinateur** [ɔʀdinatœʀ] *nm* computer

**ordonnance** [ɔʀdɔnɑ̃s] *nf* (*MÉD*) prescription; (*MIL*) orderly, batman (*BRIT*)

**ordonné, e** [ɔʀdɔne] *adj* tidy, orderly

**ordonner** [ɔʀdɔne] *vt* (*agencer*) to organize, arrange; (*donner un ordre*): **~ à qn de faire** to order sb to do; (*REL*) to ordain; (*MÉD*) to prescribe

**ordre** [ɔʀdʀ] *nm* order; (*propreté et soin*) orderliness, tidiness; (*nature*): **d'~ pratique** of a practical nature; **~s** *nmpl* (*REL*) holy orders; **mettre en ~** to tidy (up), put in order; **à l'~ de qn** payable to sb; **être aux ~s de qn/sous les ~s de qn** at sb's disposal/under sb's command; **jusqu'à nouvel ~** until

further notice; **de premier ~** first-rate; **~ du jour** (*d'une réunion*) agenda; **à l'~ du jour** (*fig*) topical

**ordure** [ɔʀdyʀ] *nf* filth *no pl*; **~s** *nfpl* (*balayures, déchets*) rubbish *sg*, refuse *sg*; **~s ménagères** household refuse

**oreille** [ɔʀɛj] *nf* ear; **avoir de l'~** to have a good ear (for music)

**oreiller** [ɔʀeje] *nm* pillow

**oreillons** [ɔʀɛjɔ̃] *nmpl* mumps *sg*

**ores** [ɔʀ]: **d'~ et déjà** *adv* already

**orfèvrerie** [ɔʀfɛvʀəʀi] *nf* goldsmith's (*ou* silversmith's) trade; (*ouvrage*) gold (*ou* silver) plate

**organe** [ɔʀgan] *nm* organ; (*porte-parole*) representative, mouthpiece

**organigramme** [ɔʀganigʀam] *nm* (*tableau hiérarchique*) organization chart; (*schéma*) flow chart

**organique** [ɔʀganik] *adj* organic

**organisateur, -trice** [ɔʀganizatœʀ, tʀis] *nm/f* organizer

**organisation** [ɔʀganizasjɔ̃] *nf* organization

**organiser** [ɔʀganize] *vt* to organize; (*mettre sur pied: service etc*) to set up; **s'~** to get organized

**organisme** [ɔʀganism] *nm* (*BIO*) organism; (*corps, ADMIN*) body

**organiste** [ɔʀganist] *nm/f* organist

**orgasme** [ɔʀgasm] *nm* orgasm, climax

**orge** [ɔʀʒ] *nf* barley

**orgue** [ɔʀg] *nm* organ; **~s** *nfpl* (*MUS*) organ *sg*

**orgueil** [ɔʀgœj] *nm* pride; **orgueilleux, -euse** *adj* proud

**Orient** [ɔʀjɑ̃] *nm*: **l'~** the East, the Orient; **oriental, e, -aux** *adj* (*langue, produit*) oriental; (*frontière*) eastern

**orientation** [ɔʀjɑ̃tasjɔ̃] *nf* (*de recherches*) orientation; (*d'une maison etc*) aspect; (*d'un journal*) leanings *pl*; **avoir le sens de l'~** to have a (good) sense of direction; **~ professionnelle** careers advisory service

**orienté, e** [ɔʀjɑ̃te] *adj* (*fig: article, journal*) slanted; **bien/mal ~** (*apparte-*

ment) well/badly positioned; **~ au sud** facing south, with a southern aspect

**orienter** [ɔʀjɑ̃te] vt (tourner: antenne) to direct, turn; (personne, recherches) to direct; (fig: élève) to orientate; **s'~** (se repérer) to find one's bearings; **s'~ vers** (fig) to turn towards

**origan** [ɔʀiɡɑ̃] nm oregano

**originaire** [ɔʀiʒinɛʀ] adj: **être ~ de** to be a native of

**original, e, -aux** [ɔʀiʒinal, o] adj original; (bizarre) eccentric ♦ nm/f eccentric ♦ nm (document etc, ART) original

**origine** [ɔʀiʒin] nf origin; **dès l'~** at ou from the outset; **à l'~** originally; **originel, le** adj original

**orme** [ɔʀm] nm elm

**ornement** [ɔʀnəmɑ̃] nm ornament

**orner** [ɔʀne] vt to decorate, adorn

**ornière** [ɔʀnjɛʀ] nf rut

**orphelin, e** [ɔʀfəlɛ̃, in] adj orphan(ed) ♦ nm/f orphan; **~ de père/mère** fatherless/motherless; **orphelinat** nm orphanage

**orteil** [ɔʀtɛj] nm toe; **gros ~** big toe

**orthographe** [ɔʀtɔɡʀaf] nf spelling

**ortie** [ɔʀti] nf (stinging) nettle

**os** [ɔs] nm bone; **tomber sur un ~** (fam) to hit a snag

**osciller** [ɔsile] vi (au vent etc) to rock; (fig): **~ entre** to waver ou fluctuate between

**osé, e** [ɔze] adj daring, bold

**oseille** [ozɛj] nf sorrel

**oser** [oze] vi, vt to dare; **~ faire** to dare (to) do

**osier** [ozje] nm willow; **d'~, en ~** wicker(work)

**ossature** [ɔsatyʀ] nf (ANAT) frame, skeletal structure; (fig) framework

**osseux, -euse** [ɔsø, øz] adj bony; (tissu, maladie, greffe) bone cpd

**ostensible** [ɔstɑ̃sibl] adj conspicuous

**otage** [ɔtaʒ] nm hostage; **prendre qn comme ~** to take sb hostage

**OTAN** sigle f (= Organisation du traité de l'Atlantique Nord) NATO

**otarie** [ɔtaʀi] nf sea-lion

**ôter** [ote] vt to remove; (soustraire) to take away; **~ qch à qn** to take sth (away) from sb; **~ qch de** to remove sth from

**otite** [ɔtit] nf ear infection

**ou** [u] conj or; **~ ... ~** either ... or; **~ bien** or (else)

---

MOT-CLÉ

---

**où** [u] pron relatif **1** (position, situation) where, that (souvent omis); **la chambre où il était** the room (that) he was in, the room where he was; **la ville où je l'ai rencontré** the town where I met him; **la pièce d'où il est sorti** the room he came out of; **le village d'où je viens** the village I come from; **les villes par où il est passé** the towns he went through

**2** (temps, état) that (souvent omis); **le jour où il est parti** the day (that) he left; **au prix où c'est** at the price it is ♦ adv **1** (interrogation) where; **où est-il/va-t-il?** where is he/is he going?; **par où?** which way?; **d'où vient que ...?** how come ...?

**2** (position) where; **je sais où il est** I know where he is; **où que l'on aille** wherever you go

**ouate** ['wat] nf cotton wool (BRIT), cotton (US)

**oubli** [ubli] nm (acte): **l'~ de** forgetting; (trou de mémoire) lapse of memory; (négligence) omission, oversight; **tomber dans l'~** to sink into oblivion

**oublier** [ublije] vt to forget; (laisser quelque part: chapeau etc) to leave behind; (ne pas voir: erreurs etc) to miss

**oubliettes** [ublijɛt] nfpl dungeon sg

**ouest** [wɛst] nm west ♦ adj inv west; (région) western; **à l'~** in the west; (direction) (to the) west, westwards; **à l'~ de** (to the) west of

**ouf** ['uf] excl phew!

**oui** ['wi] adv yes

**ouï-dire** ['widiʀ]: **par ~-~** *adv* by hear-say

**ouie** [wi] *nf* hearing; **~s** *nfpl* (*de poisson*) gills

**ouille** ['uj] *excl* ouch!

**ouragan** [uʀagã] *nm* hurricane

**ourlet** [uʀlɛ] *nm* hem

**ours** [uʀs] *nm* bear; **~ brun/blanc** brown/polar bear; **~ (en peluche)** teddy (bear)

**oursin** [uʀsɛ̃] *nm* sea urchin

**ourson** [uʀsɔ̃] *nm* (bear-)cub

**ouste** [ust] *excl* hop it!

**outil** [uti] *nm* tool; **outiller** *vt* to equip

**outrage** [utʀaʒ] *nm* insult; **~ à la pudeur** indecent conduct *no pl*; **outrager** *vt* to offend gravely

**outrance** [utʀɑ̃s]: **à ~** *adv* excessively, to excess

**outre** [utʀ] *prép* besides ♦ *adv*: **passer ~ à** to disregard, take no notice of; **en ~** besides, moreover; **~ mesure** to excess; (*manger, boire*) immoderately; **outre-Atlantique** *adv* across the Atlantic; **outre-Manche** *adv* across the Channel; **outre-mer** *adv* overseas; **outrepasser** *vt* to go beyond, exceed

**ouvert, e** [uvɛʀ, ɛʀt] *pp de* **ouvrir** ♦ *adj* open; (*robinet, gaz etc*) on; **ouvertement** *adv* openly; **ouverture** *nf* opening; (*MUS*) overture; **ouverture d'esprit** open-mindedness

**ouvrable** [uvʀabl] *adj*: **jour ~** working day, weekday

**ouvrage** [uvʀaʒ] *nm* (*tâche, de tricot etc*) work *no pl*; (*texte, livre*) work; **ouvragé, e** *adj* finely embroidered (*ou* worked *ou* carved)

**ouvre-boîte(s)** [uvʀəbwat] *nm inv* tin (*BRIT*) *ou* can opener

**ouvre-bouteille(s)** [uvʀəbutɛj] *nm inv* bottle-opener

**ouvreuse** [uvʀøz] *nf* usherette

**ouvrier, -ière** [uvʀije, ijɛʀ] *nm/f* worker ♦ *adj* working-class; (*conflit*) industrial; (*mouvement*) labour *cpd*; **classe ouvrière** working class

**ouvrir** [uvʀiʀ] *vt* (*gén*) to open; (*brèche, passage*, MÉD: *abcès*) to open up; (*commencer l'exploitation de, créer*) to open (up); (*eau, électricité, chauffage, robinet*) to turn on ♦ *vi* to open; to open up; **s'~** *vi* to open; **s'~ à qn** to open one's heart to sb; **~ l'appétit à qn** to whet sb's appetite

**ovaire** [ovɛʀ] *nm* ovary

**ovale** [ɔval] *adj* oval

**ovni** [ɔvni] *sigle m* (= *objet volant non identifié*) UFO

**oxyder** [ɔkside]: **s'~** *vi* to become oxidized

**oxygène** [ɔksiʒɛn] *nm* oxygen

**oxygéné, e** [ɔksiʒene] *adj*: **eau ~e** hydrogen peroxide

**oxygéner** [ɔksiʒene]: **s'~** (*fam*) *vi* to get some fresh air

**ozone** [ozɔn] *nm* ozone; **la couche d'~** the ozone layer

# P, p

**pacifique** [pasifik] *adj* peaceful ♦ *nm*: **le P~, l'océan P~** the Pacific (Ocean)

**pacotille** [pakɔtij] *nf* cheap junk

**pack** [pak] *nm* pack

**pacte** [pakt] *nm* pact, treaty

**pagaie** [pagɛ] *nf* paddle

**pagaille** [pagaj] *nf* mess, shambles *sg*

**pagayer** *vi* to paddle

**page** [paʒ] *nf* page ♦ *nm* page (boy); **à la ~** (*fig*) up-to-date; **~ d'accueil** (INFORM) home page

**paiement** [pemã] *nm* payment

**païen, ne** [pajɛ̃, pajɛn] *adj, nm/f* pagan, heathen

**paillasson** [pajasɔ̃] *nm* doormat

**paille** [pɑj] *nf* straw

**paillettes** [pajet] *nfpl* (*décoratives*) sequins, spangles

**pain** [pɛ̃] *nm* (*substance*) bread; (*unité*) loaf (of bread); (*morceau*) cake; **~ de savon** *etc* bar of soap *etc*; **~ au chocolat** chocolate-filled pastry; **~ aux raisins**

currant bun; **~ bis/complet** brown/
wholemeal (*BRIT*) ou wholewheat (*US*)
bread; **~ d'épice** gingerbread; **~ de
mie** sandwich loaf; **~ grillé** toast

**pair, e** [pɛʀ] *adj (nombre)* even ♦ *nm*
peer; **aller de ~** to go hand in hand
ou together; **jeune fille au ~** au pair;
**paire** *nf* pair

**paisible** [pezibl] *adj* peaceful, quiet

**paître** [pɛtʀ] *vi* to graze

**paix** [pɛ] *nf* peace; **faire/avoir la ~** to
make/have peace; **fiche-lui la ~!** *(fam)*
leave him alone!

**Pakistan** [pakistā] *nm:* **le ~** Pakistan

**palace** [palas] *nm* luxury hotel

**palais** [palɛ] *nm* palace; *(ANAT)* palate

**pâle** [pɑl] *adj* pale; **bleu ~** pale blue

**Palestine** [palɛstin] *nf:* **la ~** Palestine

**palet** [palɛ] *nm* disc; *(HOCKEY)* puck

**paletot** [palto] *nm* (thick) cardigan

**palette** [palɛt] *nf (de peintre)* palette;
*(produits)* range

**pâleur** [palœʀ] *nf* paleness

**palier** [palje] *nm (d'escalier)* landing;
*(fig)* level, plateau; **par ~s** in stages

**pâlir** [paliʀ] *vi* to turn ou go pale; *(couleur)* to fade

**palissade** [palisad] *nf* fence

**pallier** [palje]: **~ à** *vt* to offset, make
up for

**palmarès** [palmaʀɛs] *nm* record (of
achievements); *(SPORT)* list of winners

**palme** [palm] *nf (de plongeur)* flipper;
**palmé, e** *adj (pattes)* webbed

**palmier** [palmje] *nm* palm tree;
*(gâteau)* heart-shaped biscuit made of flaky
pastry

**pâlot, te** [palo, ɔt] *adj* pale, peaky

**palourde** [paluʀd] *nf* clam

**palper** [palpe] *vt* to feel, finger

**palpitant, e** [palpitā, āt] *adj* thrilling

**palpiter** [palpite] *vi (cœur, pouls)* to
beat; *(: plus fort)* to pound, throb

**paludisme** [palydism] *nm* malaria

**pamphlet** [pāflɛ] *nm* lampoon, satirical
tract

**pamplemousse** [pāpləmus] *nm* grapefruit

**pan** [pā] *nm* section, piece ♦ *excl* bang!

**panache** [panaʃ] *nm* plume; *(fig)* spirit,
panache

**panaché, e** [panaʃe] *adj:* **glace ~e**
mixed-flavour ice cream ♦ *nm (bière)*
shandy

**pancarte** [pākaʀt] *nf* sign, notice

**pancréas** [pākʀeas] *nm* pancreas

**pané, e** [pane] *adj* fried in breadcrumbs

**panier** [panje] *nm* basket; **mettre au ~**
to chuck away; **~ à provisions** shopping basket; **panier-repas** *nm* packed
lunch

**panique** [panik] *nf, adj* panic; **paniquer** *vi* to panic

**panne** [pan] *nf* breakdown; **être/
tomber en ~** to have broken down/
break down; **être en ~ d'essence** ou
**sèche** to have run out of petrol *(BRIT)*
ou gas *(US)*; **~ d'électricité** ou **de courant power** ou electrical failure

**panneau, x** [pano] *nm (écriteau)* sign,
notice; **~ d'affichage** notice board; **~
de signalisation** roadsign

**panoplie** [panɔpli] *nf (jouet)* outfit;
*(fig)* array

**panorama** [panɔʀama] *nm* panorama

**panse** [pãs] *nf* paunch

**pansement** [pāsmā] *nm* dressing,
bandage; **~ adhésif** sticking plaster

**panser** [pāse] *vt (plaie)* to dress, bandage; *(bras)* to put a dressing on, bandage; *(cheval)* to groom

**pantalon** [pātalɔ̃] *nm* trousers *pl*, pair
of trousers; **~ de ski** ski pants *pl*

**panthère** [pātɛʀ] *nf* panther

**pantin** [pātɛ̃] *nm* puppet

**pantois** [pātwa] *adj m:* **rester ~** to be
flabbergasted

**pantoufle** [pātufl] *nf* slipper

**paon** [pā] *nm* peacock

**papa** [papa] *nm* dad(dy)

**pape** [pap] *nm* pope

**paperasse** [papʀas] *(péj) nf* bumf *no pl,*
papers *pl;* **paperasserie** *(péj) nf* paper-
work *no pl; (tracasserie)* red tape *no pl*

**papeterie** [papetʀi] *nf* (*magasin*) stationer's (shop)

**papi** *nm* (*fam*) granddad

**papier** [papje] *nm* paper; (*article*) article; **~s** *nmpl* (*aussi:* **~s d'identité**) (identity) papers; **~ à lettres** writing paper, notepaper; **~ carbone** carbon paper; **~ d')aluminium** aluminium (*BRIT*) *ou* aluminum (*US*) foil, tinfoil; **~ de verre** sandpaper; **~ hygiénique** *ou* **de toilette** toilet paper; **~ journal** newspaper; **~ peint** wallpaper

**papillon** [papijɔ̃] *nm* butterfly; (*fam: contravention*) (parking) ticket; **~ de nuit** moth

**papillote** [papijɔt] *nf:* **en ~** cooked in tinfoil

**papoter** [papote] *vi* to chatter

**paquebot** [pak(ə)bo] *nm* liner

**pâquerette** [pakʀɛt] *nf* daisy

**Pâques** [pak] *nm, nfpl* Easter

**paquet** [pakɛ] *nm* packet; (*colis*) parcel; (*fig: tas*): **~ de** pile *ou* heap of; **paquet-cadeau** *nm:* **faites-moi un ~** gift-wrap it for me

**par** [paʀ] *prép* by; **finir** *etc* **~** to end *etc* with; **~ amour** out of love; **passer ~ Lyon/la côte** to go via *ou* through Lyons/along by the coast; **~ la fenêtre** (*jeter, regarder*) out of the window; **3 ~ jour/personne** 3 a *ou* per day/head; **2 ~ 2** in twos; **~ ici** this way; (*dans le coin*) round here; **~-ci, ~-là** here and there; **~ temps de pluie** in wet weather

**parabolique** [paʀabɔlik] *adj:* **antenne ~** parabolic *ou* dish aerial

**parachever** [paʀaʃ(ə)ve] *vt* to perfect

**parachute** [paʀaʃyt] *nm* parachute; **parachutiste** *nm/f* parachutist; (*MIL*) paratrooper

**parade** [paʀad] *nf* (*spectacle, défilé*) parade; (*ESCRIME, BOXE*) parry

**paradis** [paʀadi] *nm* heaven, paradise

**paradoxe** [paʀadɔks] *nm* paradox

**paraffine** [paʀafin] *nf* paraffin

**parages** [paʀaʒ] *nmpl:* **dans les ~ (de)** in the area *ou* vicinity (of)

**paragraphe** [paʀagʀaf] *nm* paragraph

**paraître** [paʀɛtʀ] *vb* +attrib to seem, look, appear ♦ *vi* to appear; (*être visible*) to show; (*PRESSE, ÉDITION*) to be published, come out, appear ♦ *vb impers:* **il paraît que** it seems *ou* appears that; **they say that; chercher à ~** to show off

**parallèle** [paʀalɛl] *adj* parallel; (*non officiel*) unofficial ♦ *nm* (*comparaison*): **faire un ~ entre** to draw a parallel between ♦ *nf* parallel (line)

**paralyser** [paʀalize] *vt* to paralyse

**paramédical, e, -aux** [paʀamedikal, o] *adj:* **personnel ~** paramedics *ou* paramedical workers *pl*

**paraphrase** [paʀafʀɑz] *nf* paraphrase

**parapluie** [paʀaplɥi] *nm* umbrella

**parasite** [paʀazit] *nm* parasite; **~s** *nmpl* (*TÉL*) interference *sg*

**parasol** [paʀasɔl] *nm* parasol, sunshade

**paratonnerre** [paʀatɔnɛʀ] *nm* lightning conductor

**paravent** [paʀavɑ̃] *nm* folding screen

**parc** [paʀk] *nm* (*public*) park, gardens *pl*; (*de château etc*) grounds *pl*; (*d'enfant*) playpen; (*ensemble d'unités*) stock; (*de voitures etc*) fleet; **~ d'attractions** theme park; **~ de stationnement** car park

**parcelle** [paʀsɛl] *nf* fragment, scrap; (*de terrain*) plot, parcel

**parce que** [paʀsk(ə)] *conj* because

**parchemin** [paʀʃəmɛ̃] *nm* parchment

**parcmètre** [paʀkmɛtʀ] *nm* parking meter

**parcourir** [paʀkuʀiʀ] *vt* (*trajet, distance*) to cover; (*article, livre*) to skim *ou* glance through; (*lieu*) to go all over, travel up and down; (*suj: frisson*) to run through

**parcours** [paʀkuʀ] *nm* (*trajet*) journey; (*itinéraire*) route

**par-derrière** [paʀdɛʀjɛʀ] *adv* round the back; **dire du mal de qn ~~** to speak ill of sb behind his back

**par-dessous** [pard(ə)su] *prép, adv* under(neath)

**pardessus** [pardəsy] *nm* overcoat

**par-dessus** [pard(ə)sy] *prép* over (the top of) ♦ *adv* over (the top); **~~ le marché** on top of all that; **~~ tout** above all; **en avoir ~~ la tête** to have had enough

**par-devant** [pard(ə)vã] *adv* (*passer*) round the front

**pardon** [pardɔ̃] *nm* forgiveness *no pl* ♦ *excl* sorry!; (*pour interpeller etc*) excuse me!; **demander ~ à qn** (**de**) to apologize to sb (for); **je vous demande ~** I'm sorry; (*pour interpeller*) excuse me; **pardonner** *vt* to forgive; **pardonner qch à qn** to forgive sb for sth

**pare...: pare-balles** *adj inv* bulletproof; **pare-brise** *nm inv* windscreen (*BRIT*), windshield (*US*); **pare-chocs** *nm inv* bumper

**paré, e** [pare] *adj* ready, all set

**pareil, le** [parɛj] *adj* (*identique*) the same, alike; (*similaire*) such; (*tel*): **un courage/livre ~** such courage/a book, courage/a book like this; **de ~s livres** such books; **ne pas avoir son(sa) ~(le)** to be second to none; **~ à** the same as; (*similaire*) similar to; **sans ~** unparalleled, unequalled

**parent, e** [parã, ãt] *nm/f*: **un(e) ~(e)** a relative *ou* relation; **~s** *nmpl* (*père et mère*) parents; **parenté** *nf* (*lien*) relationship

**parenthèse** [parãtɛz] *nf* (*ponctuation*) bracket, parenthesis; (*digression*) parenthesis, digression; **entre ~s** in brackets; (*fig*) incidentally

**parer** [pare] *vt* to adorn; (*éviter*) to ward off; **~ au plus pressé** to attend to the most urgent things first

**paresse** [parɛs] *nf* laziness; **paresseux, -euse** *adj* lazy

**parfaire** [parfɛr] *vt* to perfect

**parfait, e** [parfɛ, ɛt] *adj* perfect ♦ *nm* (*LING*) perfect (tense); **parfaitement** *adv* perfectly ♦ *excl* (most) certainly

**parfois** [parfwa] *adv* sometimes

**parfum** [parfœ̃] *nm* (*produit*) perfume, scent; (*odeur: de fleur*) scent, fragrance; (*goût*) flavour; (*de fleur, fruit*) fragrant; (*femme*) perfumed; **parfumé, e** *adj* (*fleur, fruit*) fragrant; (*femme*) perfumed; **parfumé au café** coffee-flavoured; **parfumer** *vt* (*suj: odeur, bouquet*) to perfume; (*crème, gâteau*) to flavour; **parfumerie** *nf* (*produits*) perfumes *pl*; (*boutique*) perfume shop

**pari** [pari] *nm* bet; **parier** *vt* to bet

**Paris** [pari] *n* Paris; **parisien, ne** *adj* Parisian; (*GÉO, ADMIN*) Paris *cpd* ♦ *nm/f*: **Parisien, ne** Parisian

**parjure** [parʒyr] *nm* perjury

**parking** [parkiŋ] *nm* (*lieu*) car park

**parlant, e** [parlã, ãt] *adj* (*regard*) eloquent; (*CINÉMA*) talking; **les chiffres sont ~s** the figures speak for themselves

**parlement** [parləmã] *nm* parliament; **parlementaire** *adj* parliamentary ♦ *nm/f* member of parliament; **parlementer** *vi* to negotiate, parley

**parler** [parle] *vi* to speak, talk; (*avouer*) to talk; (**à qn**) **de** to talk *ou* speak (to sb) about; **le/en français** to speak French/in French; **~ affaires** to talk business; **sans ~ de** (*fig*) not to mention, to say nothing of; **tu parles!** (*fam: bien sûr*) you bet!

**parloir** [parlwar] *nm* (*de prison, d'hôpital*) visiting room

**parmi** [parmi] *prép* among(st)

**paroi** [parwa] *nf* wall; (*cloison*) partition; **~ rocheuse** rock face

**paroisse** [parwas] *nf* parish

**parole** [parɔl] *nf* (*faculté*): **la ~** speech; (*mot, promesse*) word; **~s** *nfpl* (*MUS*) words, lyrics; **tenir ~** to keep one's word; **prendre la ~** to speak; **demander la ~** to ask for permission to speak; **je te crois sur ~** I'll take your word for it

**parquer** [parke] *vt* (*voiture, matériel*) to park; (*bestiaux*) to pen (in *ou* up)

**parquet** [parke] *nm* (*parquet*) floor;

*(JUR):* **le ~** the Public Prosecutor's department

**parrain** [paʀɛ̃] *nm* godfather; **parrainer** *vt (suj: entreprise)* to sponsor

**pars** [paʀ] *vb voir* **partir**

**parsemer** [paʀsəme]* *vt (suj: feuilles, papiers)* to be scattered over; **~ qch de** to scatter sth with

**part** [paʀ] *nf (qui revient à qn)* share; *(fraction, -ie)* part; **prendre ~ à** *(débat etc)* to take part in; *(soucis, douleur de qn)* to share in; **faire ~ de qch à qn** to announce sth to sb, inform sb of sth; **pour ma ~** as for me, as far as I'm concerned; **à ~ entière** full; **de la ~ de** *(au nom de)* on behalf of; *(donné par)* from; **de toute(s) ~(s)** from all sides or quarters; **de ~ et d'autre** on both sides, on either side; **d'une ~ ... d'autre ~** on the one hand ... on the other hand; **d'autre ~** *(de plus)* moreover; **à ~** *(séparément)* separately; *(de côté)* aside ♦ *prép* apart from, except for; **faire la ~ des choses** to make allowances

**partage** [paʀtaʒ] *nm (fractionnement)* dividing up; *(répartition)* sharing out; *no pl*, share-out

**partager** [paʀtaʒe] *vt* to share; *(distribuer, répartir)* to share (out); *(morceler, diviser)* to divide (up); **se ~** *(héritage etc)* to share between themselves (*ou* ourselves)

**partance** [paʀtɑ̃s]: **en ~** *adv:* **en ~ pour** (bound) for

**partenaire** [paʀtənɛʀ] *nm/f* partner

**parterre** [paʀtɛʀ] *nm (de fleurs)* (flower) bed; *(THÉÂTRE)* stalls *pl*

**parti** [paʀti] *nm (POL)* party; *(décision)* course of action; *(personne à marier)* match; **tirer ~ de** to take advantage of, turn to good account; **prendre ~ (pour/contre)** to take sides *ou* a stand (for/against); **~ pris** bias

**partial, e, -aux** [paʀsjal, jo] *adj* biased, partial

**participant, e** [paʀtisipɑ̃, ɑ̃t] *nm/f* participant; *(à un concours)* entrant

**participation** [paʀtisipasjɔ̃] *nf* participation; *(financière)* contribution

**participer** [paʀtisipe]: **~ à** *vt (course, réunion)* to take part in; *(frais etc)* to contribute to; *(chagrin, succès de qn)* to share (in)

**particularité** [paʀtikylaʀite] *nf* (distinctive) characteristic

**particulier, -ière** [paʀtikylje, jɛʀ] *adj (spécifique)* particular; *(spécial)* special, particular; *(personnel, privé)* private; *(étrange)* peculiar, odd ♦ *nm (individu: ADMIN)* private individual; **~ à** peculiar to; **en ~** *(surtout)* in particular, particularly; *(en privé)* in private; **particulièrement** *adv* particularly

**partie** [paʀti] *nf (gén)* part; *(JUR etc: protagonistes)* party; *(de cartes, tennis etc)* game; **une ~ de pêche** a fishing party *ou* trip; **en ~** partly, in part; **faire ~ de** *(suj: chose)* to be part of; **prendre qn à ~** to take sb to task; **en grande ~** largely, in the main; **~ civile** *(JUR)* party claiming damages in a criminal case

**partiel, le** [paʀsjɛl] *adj* partial ♦ *nm (SCOL)* class exam

**partir** [paʀtiʀ] *vi (gén)* to go; *(quitter)* to go, leave; *(tache)* to go, come out; *(de: lieu: quitter)* to leave; *(: commencer à)* to start from; **à ~ de** from

**partisan, e** [paʀtizɑ̃, an] *nm/f* partisan ♦ *adj:* **être ~ de qch/de faire** to be in favour of sth/doing

**partition** [paʀtisjɔ̃] *nf (MUS)* score

**partout** [paʀtu] *adv* everywhere; **~ où il allait** everywhere *ou* wherever he went

**paru** [paʀy] *pp de* **paraître**

**parure** [paʀyʀ] *nf (bijoux etc)* finery *no pl*; jewellery *no pl*; *(assortiment)* set

**parution** [paʀysjɔ̃] *nf* publication

**parvenir** [paʀvəniʀ]: **~ à** *vt (atteindre)* to reach; *(réussir):* **~ à faire** to manage to do, succeed in doing; **~ à ses fins** to achieve one's ends

**pas¹** [pɑ] *nm (enjambée, DANSE)* step;

# pas

(allure, mesure) pace; (bruit) (foot)step; (trace) footprint; **~ à ~** step by step; **au ~** at walking pace; **faire les cent ~** to pace up and down; **faire les premiers ~** to make the first move; **sur le ~ de la porte** on the doorstep

---
**MOT-CLÉ**
---

**pas²** [pɑ] adv **1** (en corrélation avec: ne, non etc) not; **il ne pleure pas** he does not ou doesn't cry; he's not ou isn't crying; **il n'a pas pleuré/ne pleurera pas** he did not ou didn't/will not ou won't cry; **ils n'ont pas de voiture/d'enfants** they haven't got a car/any children, they have no car/children; **il m'a dit de ne pas le faire** he told me not to do it; **non pas que ...** not that ...

**2** (employé seule ou etc): **pas moi** not me; not I, I don't (ou can't etc); **une pomme pas mûre** an apple which isn't ripe; **pas plus tard qu'hier** only yesterday; **pas du tout** not at all

**3**: **pas mal** not bad; not badly; **pas mal** quite a lot of

---

**passage** [pɑsaʒ] nm (fait de passer) voir **passer**; (lieu, prix de la traversée, extrait) passage; (chemin) way; **de ~** (touristes) passing through; **~ à niveau** level crossing; **~ clouté** pedestrian crossing; **"~ interdit"** "no entry"; **~ souterrain** subway (BRIT), underpass

**passager, -ère** [pɑsaʒe, ɛʀ] adj passing ♦ nm/f passenger; **~ clandestin** stowaway

**passant, e** [pɑsɑ̃, ɑ̃t] adj (rue, endroit) busy ♦ nm/f passer-by; **en ~** in passing

**passe¹** [pɑs] nf (SPORT, NAVIG) pass; **être en ou de faire** to be on the way to doing; **être dans une mauvaise ~** to be going through a rough patch

**passe²** [pɑs] nm (~-partout) master ou skeleton key

**passé, e** [pɑse] adj (révolu) past; (dernier: semaine etc) last; (couleur) faded ♦

---

prép after ♦ nm past; (LING) past (tense); **~ de mode** out of fashion; **~ composé** perfect (tense); **~ simple** past historic

**passe-partout** [pɑspaʀtu] nm inv master ou skeleton key ♦ adj inv all-purpose

**passeport** [pɑspɔʀ] nm passport

**passer** [pɑse] vi (aller) to go; (voiture, piétons: défiler) to pass (by), go by; (facteur, laitier etc) to come, call; (pour rendre visite) to call ou drop in; (film, émission) to be on; (temps, jours) to pass, go by; (couleur) to fade; (mode) to die out; (douleur) to pass, go away; (SCOL) to go up (to the next class) ♦ vt (frontière, rivière etc) to cross; (douane) to go through; (examen) to sit, take; (visite médicale etc) to have; (journée, temps) to spend; (enfiler: vêtement) to slip on; (film, pièce) to show, put on; (disque) to play, put on; (marché, accord) to agree on; **se ~** vi (avoir lieu: scène, action) to take place; (se dérouler: entretien etc) to go; (s'écouler: semaine etc) to pass, go by; (arriver): **que s'est-il passé?** what happened?; **~ qch à qn** (sel etc) to pass sth to sb; (prêter) to lend sth to sb; (transmettre: message) to pass sth on to sb; (tolérer) to let sb get away with sth; **~ par** to go through; **~ avant qch/qn** (fig) to come before sth/sb; **~ un coup de fil à qn** (fam) to give sb a ring; **laisser ~** (air, lumière, personne) to let through; (occasion) to let slip, miss; (erreur) to overlook; **~ la seconde** (AUTO) to change into second; **~ le balai/l'aspirateur** to sweep up/hoover; **je vous passe M. X** (je vous mets en communication avec X) I'm putting you through to Mr X; (je lui passe l'appareil) here's Mr X, I'll hand you over to Mr X; **se ~ de** to go ou do without

**passerelle** [pɑsʀɛl] nf footbridge; (de navire, avion) gangway

**passe-temps** [pɑstɑ̃] nm inv pastime

**passible** [pɑsibl] adj: **~ de** liable to

**passif, -ive** [pɑsif, iv] adj passive

**passion** [pasjɔ̃] *nf* passion; **passionnant, e** *adj* fascinating; **passionné, e** *adj* (*personne*) passionate; (*récit*) impassioned; **être passionné de** to have a passion for; **passionner** *vt* (*personne*) to fascinate, grip; **se passionner pour** (*sport*) to have a passion for

**passoire** [paswaʀ] *nf* sieve; (*à légumes*) colander; (*à thé*) strainer

**pastèque** [pastɛk] *nf* watermelon

**pasteur** [pastœʀ] *nm* (*protestant*) minister, pastor

**pasteurisé, e** [pastœʀize] *adj* pasteurized

**pastille** [pastij] *nf* (*à sucer*) lozenge, pastille

**patate** [patat] *nf* (*fam: pomme de terre*) spud; ~ **douce** sweet potato

**patauger** [patoʒe] *vi* to splash about

**pâte** [pat] *nf* (*à tarte*) pastry; (*à pain*) dough; (*à frire*) batter; ~**s** *nfpl* (*macaroni etc*) pasta *sg*; ~ **à modeler** modelling clay, Plasticine Ⓡ (*BRIT*); ~ **brisée** shortcrust pastry; ~ **d'amandes** almond paste; ~ **de fruits** crystallized fruit *no pl*; ~ **feuilletée** puff ou flaky pastry

**pâté** [pate] *nm* (*charcuterie*) pâté; (*tache*) ink blot; (*de sable*) sandpie; ~ **de maisons** block (of houses); ~ **en croûte** ≈ pork pie

**pâtée** [pate] *nf* mash, feed

**patente** [patɑ̃t] *nf* (*COMM*) trading licence

**paternel, le** [patɛʀnɛl] *adj* (*amour, soins*) fatherly; (*ligne, autorité*) paternal

**pâteux, -euse** [patø, øz] *adj* pasty; (*langue*) coated

**pathétique** [patetik] *adj* moving

**patience** [pasjɑ̃s] *nf* patience

**patient, e** [pasjɑ̃, jɑ̃t] *adj*, *nm/f* patient; **patienter** *vi* to wait

**patin** [patɛ̃] *nm* skate; (*sport*) skating; ~**s (à glace)** (ice) skates; ~**s à roulettes** roller skates

**patinage** [patinaʒ] *nm* skating

**patiner** [patine] *vi* to skate; (*roue, voi-*

*ture*) to spin; **se** ~ *vi* (*meuble, cuir*) to acquire a sheen; **patineur, -euse** *nm/f* skater; **patinoire** *nf* skating rink, (*ice*) rink

**pâtir** [patiʀ]: ~ **de** *vt* to suffer because of

**pâtisserie** [patisʀi] *nf* (*boutique*) cake shop; (*gâteau*) cake, pastry; (*à la maison*) pastry- ou cake-making, baking; **pâtissier, -ière** *nm/f* pastrycook

**patois** [patwa, waz] *nm* dialect, patois

**patraque** [patʀak] (*fam*) *adj* peaky, off-colour

**patrie** [patʀi] *nf* homeland

**patrimoine** [patʀimwan] *nm* (*culture*) heritage

**patriotique** [patʀijɔtik] *adj* patriotic

**patron, ne** [patʀɔ̃, ɔn] *nm/f* boss; (*REL*) patron saint ♦ *nm* (*COUTURE*) pattern; **patronat** *nm* employers *pl*; **patronner** *vt* to sponsor, support

**patrouille** [patʀuj] *nf* patrol

**patte** [pat] *nf* (*jambe*) leg; (*pied: de chien, chat*) paw; (: *d'oiseau*) foot

**pâturage** [patyʀaʒ] *nm* pasture

**paume** [pom] *nf* palm

**paumé, e** [pome] (*fam*) *nm/f* drop-out

**paumer** [pome] (*fam*) *vt* to lose

**paupière** [popjɛʀ] *nf* eyelid

**pause** [poz] *nf* (*arrêt*) break; (*en parlant, MUS*) pause

**pauvre** [povʀ] *adj* poor; **pauvreté** (*état*) poverty

**pavaner** [pavane]: **se** ~ *vi* to strut about

**pavé, e** [pave] *adj* (*cour*) paved; (*chaussée*) cobbled ♦ *nm* (*bloc*) paving stone, cobblestone

**pavillon** [pavijɔ̃] *nm* (*de banlieue*) small (detached) house; pavilion; (*drapeau*) flag

**pavoiser** [pavwaze] *vi* (*fig*) to rejoice, exult

**pavot** [pavo] *nm* poppy

**payant, e** [pɛjɑ̃, ɑ̃t] *adj* (*spectateurs etc*) paying; (*fig: entreprise*) profitable; (*effort*) which pays off; **c'est** ~ you have to pay, there is a charge

**paye** [pɛj] nf pay, wages pl

**payer** [peje] vt (créancier, employé, loyer) to pay; (achat, réparations, fig: faute) to pay for ♦ vi to pay; (métier) to be well-paid; (tactique etc) to pay off; **il me l'a fait ~ 10 F** he charged me 10 F for it; **~ qch à qn** to buy sth for sb, buy sth sb; **se ~ la tête de qn** (fam) to take the mickey out of sb

**pays** [pei] nm country; (région) region; **du ~** local

**paysage** [peizaʒ] nm landscape

**paysan, ne** [peizɑ̃, an] nm/f farmer; (péj) peasant ♦ adj (agricole) farming; (rural) country

**Pays-Bas** [peiba] nmpl: **les ~~** the Netherlands

**PC** nm (INFORM) PC ♦ sigle m = **parti communiste**

**P.D.G.** sigle m = **président directeur général**

**péage** [peaʒ] nm toll; (endroit) tollgate

**peau, x** [po] nf skin; **gants de ~** leather gloves; **être bien/mal dans sa ~** to be quite at ease/ill-at-ease; **~ de chamois** (chiffon) chamois leather, shammy; **Peau-Rouge** nm/f Red Indian, redskin

**pêche** [pɛʃ] nf (sport, activité) fishing; (poissons pêchés) catch; (fruit) peach; **~ à la ligne** (en rivière) angling

**péché** [peʃe] nm sin

**pécher** [peʃe] vi (REL) to sin

**pêcher** [peʃe] nm peach tree ♦ vi to go fishing ♦ vt (attraper) to catch; (être pêcheur de) to fish for

**pécheur, -eresse** [peʃœr, peʃrɛs] nm/f sinner

**pêcheur** [pɛʃœr] nm fisherman; (à la ligne) angler

**pécule** [pekyl] nm savings pl, nest egg

**pédagogie** [pedagɔʒi] nf educational methods pl, pedagogy; **pédagogique** adj educational

**pédale** [pedal] nf pedal

**pédalo** [pedalo] nm pedal-boat

**pédant, e** [pedɑ̃, ɑ̃t] adj pedantic

**pédestre** [pedɛstr] adj: **randonnée ~** ramble; **sentier ~** pedestrian footpath

**pédiatre** [pedjatr] nm/f paediatrician, child specialist

**pédicure** [pedikyr] nm/f chiropodist

**pègre** [pɛgr] nf underworld

**peignais** etc [peɲɛ] vb voir **peindre**

**peigne** [peɲ] nm comb; **peigner** vt to comb (the hair of); **se peigner** vi to comb one's hair

**peignoir** [peɲwar] nm dressing gown; **peignoir de bain** bathrobe

**peindre** [pɛ̃dr] vt to paint; (fig) to portray, depict

**peine** [pɛn] nf (affliction) sorrow, sadness no pl; (mal, effort) trouble no pl, effort; (difficulté) difficulty; (JUR) sentence; **avoir de la ~** to be sad; **faire de la ~ à qn** to distress or upset sb; **prendre la ~ de faire** to go to the trouble of doing; **se donner de la ~** to make an effort; **ce n'est pas la ~ de faire** there's no point in doing, it's not worth doing; **à ~** scarcely, hardly, barely; **à ~ ... que** hardly ... than; **~ capitale** ou **de mort** capital punishment, death sentence; **peiner** vi (personne) to work hard; (moteur, voiture) to labour ♦ vt to grieve, sadden

**peintre** [pɛ̃tr] nm painter; **~ en bâtiment** house painter

**peinture** [pɛ̃tyr] nf painting; (matière) paint; (surfaces peintes: aussi: ~s) paintwork; **"~ fraîche"** "wet paint"

**péjoratif, -ive** [peʒɔratif, iv] adj pejorative, derogatory

**pelage** [pəlaʒ] nm coat, fur

**pêle-mêle** [pɛlmɛl] adv higgledy-piggledy

**peler** [pəle] vt, vi to peel

**pèlerin** [pɛlrɛ̃] nm pilgrim

**pèlerinage** [pɛlrinaʒ] nm pilgrimage

**pelle** [pɛl] nf shovel; (d'enfant, de terrassier) spade

**pellicule** [pelikyl] nf film; **~s** nfpl (MÉD)

dandruff sg

**pelote** [p(ə)lɔt] nf (de fil, laine) ball

**peloton** [p(ə)lɔtɔ̃] nm group, squad, (CYCLISME) pack; ~ **d'exécution** firing squad

**pelotonner** [p(ə)lɔtɔne]: **se ~** vi to curl (o.s.) up

**pelouse** [p(ə)luz] nf lawn

**peluche** [p(ə)lyʃ] nf (animal en) ~ fluffy animal, soft toy; **chien/lapin en ~** fluffy dog/rabbit

**pelure** [p(ə)lyʀ] nf peeling, peel no pl

**pénal, e, -aux** [penal, o] adj penal; **pénalité** nf penalty

**penaud, e** [pəno, od] adj sheepish, contrite

**penchant** [pɑ̃ʃɑ̃] nm (tendance) tendency, propensity; (faible) liking, fondness

**pencher** [pɑ̃ʃe] vi to tilt, lean over ♦ vt to tilt; **se ~** vi to lean over; (se baisser) to bend down; **se ~ sur** (fig: problème) to look into; **~ pour** to be inclined to favour

**pendaison** [pɑ̃dɛzɔ̃] nf hanging

**pendant** [pɑ̃dɑ̃] prép (au cours de) during; (indique la durée) for; ~ **que** while

**pendentif** [pɑ̃dɑ̃tif] nm pendant

**penderie** [pɑ̃dʀi] nf wardrobe

**pendre** [pɑ̃dʀ] vi, vt to hang; **se ~** (se suicider) to hang o.s.; ~ **la crémaillère** to have a house-warming party

**pendule** [pɑ̃dyl] nf clock ♦ nm pendulum

**pénétrer** [penetʀe] vi, vt to penetrate; ~ **dans** to enter

**pénible** [penibl] adj (travail) hard; (sujet) painful; (personne) tiresome; **péniblement** adv with difficulty

**péniche** [peniʃ] nf barge

**pénicilline** [penisilin] nf penicillin

**péninsule** [penɛ̃syl] nf peninsula

**pénis** [penis] nm penis

**pénitence** [penitɑ̃s] nf (peine) penance; (repentir) penitence; **pénitencier** nm penitentiary

**pénombre** [penɔ̃bʀ] nf (faible clarté)

half-light; (obscurité) darkness

**pensée** [pɑ̃se] nf thought; (démarche, doctrine) thinking no pl; (fleur) pansy; **en ~** in one's mind

**penser** [pɑ̃se] vi, vt to think; ~ **à** (ami, vacances) to think of ou about; (réfléchir à: problème, offre) to think about ou over; (prévoir) to think of; **faire ~ à** to remind one of; ~ **faire qch** to be thinking of doing sth, intend to do sth; **pensif, -ive** adj pensive, thoughtful

**pension** [pɑ̃sjɔ̃] nf (allocation) pension; (prix du logement) board and lodgings, bed and board; (école) boarding school; ~ **alimentaire** (de divorcée) maintenance allowance, alimony; ~ **complète** full board; ~ **(de famille)** boarding house, guesthouse; **pensionnaire** nm/f (SCOL) boarder; **pensionnat** nm boarding school

**pente** [pɑ̃t] nf slope; **en ~** sloping

**Pentecôte** [pɑ̃tkot] nf: **la ~** Whitsun (BRIT), Pentecost

**pénurie** [penyʀi] nf shortage

**pépé** [pepe] (fam) nm grandad

**pépin** [pepɛ̃] nm (BOT: graine) pip; (ennui) snag, hitch

**pépinière** [pepinjɛʀ] nf nursery

**perçant, e** [pɛʀsɑ̃, ɑ̃t] adj (cri) piercing, shrill; (regard) piercing

**percée** [pɛʀse] nf (trouée) opening; (MIL, technologique) breakthrough

**perce-neige** [pɛʀsənɛʒ] nf inv snowdrop

**percepteur** [pɛʀsɛptœʀ, tʀis] nm tax collector

**perception** [pɛʀsɛpsjɔ̃] nf perception; (bureau) tax office

**percer** [pɛʀse] vt to pierce; (ouverture etc) to make; (mystère, énigme) to penetrate ♦ vi to break through; **perceuse** nf drill

**percevoir** [pɛʀsəvwaʀ] vt (distinguer) to perceive, detect; (taxe, impôt) to collect; (revenu, indemnité) to receive

**perche** [pɛʀʃ] nf (bâton) pole

**percher** [pɛʀʃe] vt, vi to perch; **se ~** vi

to perch; **perchoir** nm perch

**perçois** etc [pɛʀswa] vb voir **percevoir**

**percolateur** [pɛʀkɔlatœʀ] nm percolator

**perçu, e** [pɛʀsy] pp de **percevoir**

**percussion** [pɛʀkysjɔ̃] nf percussion

**percuter** [pɛʀkyte] vt to strike; (suj: véhicule) to crash into

**perdant, e** [pɛʀdɑ̃, ɑ̃t] nm/f loser

**perdre** [pɛʀdʀ] vt to lose; (gaspiller: temps, argent) to waste; (personne: moralement etc) to ruin ♦ vi to lose; (sur une vente etc) to lose; **se ~** (s'égarer) to get lost, lose one's way; (denrées) to go to waste

**perdrix** [pɛʀdʀi] nf partridge

**perdu, e** [pɛʀdy] pp de **perdre** ♦ adj (isolé) out-of-the-way; (COMM: emballage) non-returnable; (malade): **il est ~** there's no hope left for him; **à vos moments ~s** in your spare time

**père** [pɛʀ] nm father; **~ de famille** father; **le ~ Noël** Father Christmas

**perfection** [pɛʀfɛksjɔ̃] nf perfection; **à la ~** to perfection; **perfectionné, e** adj sophisticated; **perfectionner** vt to improve, perfect

**perforatrice** [pɛʀfɔʀatʀis] nf (de bureau) punch

**perforer** [pɛʀfɔʀe] vt (poinçonner) to punch

**performant, e** [pɛʀfɔʀmɑ̃, ɑ̃t] adj: **très ~** high-performance cpd

**perfusion** [pɛʀfyzjɔ̃] nf: **faire une ~ à qn** to put sb on a drip

**péricliter** [peʀiklite] vi to collapse

**péril** [peʀil] nm peril

**périmé, e** [peʀime] adj (ADMIN) out-of-date, expired

**périmètre** [peʀimɛtʀ] nm perimeter

**période** [peʀjɔd] nf period; **périodique** adj periodic ♦ nm periodical

**péripéties** [peʀipesi] nfpl events, episodes

**périphérique** [peʀifeʀik] adj (quartiers) outlying ♦ nm (AUTO) ring road

**périple** [peʀipl] nm journey

**périr** [peʀiʀ] vi to die, perish

**périssable** [peʀisabl] adj perishable

**perle** [pɛʀl] nf pearl; (de plastique, métal, sueur) bead

**permanence** [pɛʀmanɑ̃s] nf permanence; (local) (duty) office; **assurer une ~** (service public, bureaux) to operate ou maintain a basic service; **être de ~** to be on call ou duty; **en ~** continuously

**permanent, e** [pɛʀmanɑ̃, ɑ̃t] adj permanent; (spectacle) continuous; **permanente** nf perm

**perméable** [pɛʀmeabl] adj (terrain) permeable; **~ à** (fig) receptive ou open to

**permettre** [pɛʀmɛtʀ] vt to allow, permit; **~ à qn de faire/qch** to allow sb to do/sth; **se ~ de faire** to take the liberty of doing

**permis** [pɛʀmi, iz] nm permit, licence; **~ de chasse** hunting permit; **~ (de conduire)** (driving) licence (BRIT), (driver's) license (US); **~ de construire** planning permission (BRIT), building permit (US); **~ de séjour** residence permit; **~ de travail** work permit

**permission** [pɛʀmisjɔ̃] nf permission; (MIL) leave; **avoir la ~ de faire** to have permission to do; **en ~** on leave

**permuter** [pɛʀmyte] vt to change around, permutate ♦ vi to change, swap

**Pérou** [peʀu] nm Peru

**perpétuel, le** [pɛʀpetɥɛl] adj perpetual; **perpétuité** nf: **à perpétuité** for life; **être condamné à perpétuité** to receive a life sentence

**perplexe** [pɛʀplɛks] adj perplexed, puzzled

**perquisitionner** [pɛʀkizisjɔne] vi to carry out a search

**perron** [pɛʀɔ̃] nm steps pl (leading to entrance)

**perroquet** [pɛʀɔkɛ] nm parrot

**perruche** [pɛʀyʃ] nf budgerigar (BRIT), budgie (BRIT), parakeet (US)

**perruque** [peʀyk] *nf* wig

**persan, e** [pεʀsɑ̃, an] *adj* Persian

**persécuter** [pεʀsekyte] *vt* to persecute

**persévérer** [pεʀsevere] *vi* to persevere

**persiennes** [pεʀsjεn] *nfpl* shutters

**persil** [pεʀsi] *nm* parsley

**Persique** [pεʀsik] *adj*: **le golfe ~** the (Persian) Gulf

**persistant, e** [pεʀsistɑ̃, ɑ̃t] *adj* persistent

**persister** [pεʀsiste] *vi* to persist; **~ à faire qch** to persist in doing sth

**personnage** [pεʀsɔnaʒ] *nm* (*individu*) character, individual; (*célébrité*) important person; (*de roman, film*) character; (*PEINTURE*) figure

**personnalité** [pεʀsɔnalite] *nf* personality; (*personnage*) prominent figure

**personne** [pεʀsɔn] *nf* person ♦ *pron* nobody, no one; (*avec négation en anglais*) anybody, anyone; **~s** *nfpl* (*gens*) people *pl*; **il y a ~** there isn't anybody there; there is n't anybody there; **~ âgée** elderly person; **personnel, le** *adj* personal; (*égoïste*) selfish ♦ *nm* staff, personnel; **personnellement** *adv* personally

**perspective** [pεʀspεktiv] *nf* (*ART*) perspective; (*vue*) view; (*point de vue*) viewpoint, angle; (*chose envisagée*) prospect; **en ~** in prospect

**perspicace** [pεʀspikas] *adj* clearsighted, gifted with (*ou* showing) insight; **perspicacité** *nf* clearsightedness

**persuader** [pεʀsɥade] *vt*: **~ qn (de faire)** to persuade sb (to do); **persuasif, -ive** *adj* persuasive

**perte** [pεʀt] *nf* loss; (*de temps*) waste; (*fig: morale*) ruin; **à ~ de vue** as far as the eye can (*ou* could) see; **~s blanches** (vaginal) discharge *sg*

**pertinemment** [pεʀtinamɑ̃] *adv* (*savoir*) full well

**pertinent, e** [pεʀtinɑ̃, ɑ̃t] *adj* apt, relevant

**perturbation** [pεʀtyʀbasjɔ̃] *nf*: **~ (at-** mosphérique) atmospheric disturbance

**perturber** [pεʀtyʀbe] *vt* to disrupt; (*PSYCH*) to perturb, disturb

**pervers, e** [pεʀvεʀ, εʀs] *adj* perverted

**pervertir** [pεʀvεʀtiʀ] *vt* to pervert

**pesant, e** [pəzɑ̃, ɑ̃t] *adj* heavy; (*fig: présence*) burdensome

**pèse-personne** [pεzpεʀsɔn] *nm* (bathroom) scales *pl*

**peser** [pəze] *vt* to weigh ♦ *vi* to weigh; (*fig: avoir de l'importance*) to carry weight; **~ lourd** to be heavy

**pessimisme** [pesimism] *nm* pessimism

**pessimiste** [pesimist] *adj* pessimistic ♦ *nm/f* pessimist

**peste** [pεst] *nf* plague

**pester** [pεste] *vi*: **~ contre** to curse

**pétale** [petal] *nm* petal

**pétanque** [petɑ̃k] *nf* type of bowls

Pétanque, which originated in the south of France, is a version of the game of *boules* played on a variety of hard surfaces. Standing with their feet together, players throw steel bowls towards a wooden jack.

**pétarader** [petaʀade] *vi* to backfire

**pétard** [petaʀ] *nm* banger (*BRIT*), firecracker

**péter** [pete] *vi* (*fam: casser*) to bust; (*fam!*) to fart (*!*)

**pétillant, e** [petijɑ̃, ɑ̃t] *adj* (*eau etc*) sparkling

**pétiller** [petije] *vi* (*feu*) to crackle; (*champagne*) to bubble; (*yeux*) to sparkle

**petit, e** [p(ə)ti, it] *adj* small; (*avec nuance affective: voyage*) short, little; (*bruit etc*) faint, slight; **~s** *nmpl* (*d'un animal*) young *pl*; **les tout~s** the little ones, the tiny tots; **~ à ~** bit by bit, gradually; **~(e) ami(e)** boyfriend/girlfriend; **~ déjeuner** breakfast; **~ pain** (bread) roll; **les ~es annonces** the small ads; **~s pois** garden peas; **petite-fille** *nf* granddaughter; **petit-fils** *nm* grandson

**pétition** [petisj5] *nf* petition

**petits-enfants** [pətizɑ̃fɑ̃] *nmpl* grandchildren

**petit-suisse** [pətisɥis] (*pl* **~s ~s**) *nm* small individual pot of cream cheese

**pétrin** [petrɛ̃] *nm* (*fig*): **dans le ~** (*fam*) in a jam *ou* fix

**pétrir** [petRiR] *vt* to knead

**pétrole** [petRɔl] *nm* oil; (*pour lampe, réchaud etc*) paraffin (oil); **pétrolier, -ière** *nm* oil tanker

---
MOT-CLÉ
---

**peu** [pø] *adv* 1 (*modifiant verbe, adjectif, adverbe*) 1 **il boit peu** he doesn't drink (very) much; **il est peu bavard** he's not very talkative; **peu avant/après** shortly before/afterwards

2 (*modifiant nom*): **peu de: peu de gens/d'arbres** few *ou* not (very) many people/trees; **il a peu d'espoir** he hasn't (got) much hope, he has little hope; **pour peu de temps** for (only) a short while

3: **peu à peu** little by little; **à peu près** just about, more *ou* less; **à peu près 10 kg/10 F** approximately 10 kg/10F

♦ *nm* 1: **le peu de gens qui** the few people who; **le peu de sable qui** what little sand, the little sand

2: **un peu** a little; **un petit peu** a little bit; **un peu d'espoir** a little hope

♦ *pron*: **peu le savent** few know (it); **avant** *ou* **sous peu** shortly, before long; **de peu** (only) just

---

**peuple** [pœpl] *nm* people; **peupler** *vt* (*pays, région*) to populate; (*étang*) to stock; (*suj: hommes, poissons*) to inhabit

**peuplier** [pøplije] *nm* poplar (tree)

**peur** [pœR] *nf* fear; **avoir ~ (de/faire/que)** to be frightened *ou* afraid (of/of doing/that); **faire ~ à** to frighten; **de ~ de/que** for fear of/that; **peu-**

**reux, -euse** *adj* fearful, timorous

**peut** [pø] *vb voir* **pouvoir**

**peut-être** [pøtɛtR] *adv* perhaps, maybe; **~~ que** perhaps, maybe; **~~ bien qu'il fera/est** he may well do/be

**peux** *etc* [pø] *vb voir* **pouvoir**

**phare** [faR] *nm* (*en mer*) lighthouse; (*de véhicule*) headlight; **~s de recul** reversing lights

**pharmacie** [faRmasi] *nf* (*magasin*) chemist's (BRIT), pharmacy; (*de salle de bain*) medicine cabinet; **pharmacien, ne** *nm* pharmacist, chemist (BRIT)

**phénomène** [fenɔmɛn] *nm* phenomenon

**philatélie** [filateli] *nf* philately, stamp collecting

**philosophe** [filɔzɔf] *nm/f* philosopher ♦ *adj* philosophical

**philosophie** [filɔzɔfi] *nf* philosophy

**phobie** [fɔbi] *nf* phobia

**phonétique** [fɔnetik] *nf* phonetics *sg*

**phoque** [fɔk] *nm* seal

**phosphorescent, e** [fɔsfɔResɑ̃, ɑ̃t] *adj* luminous

**photo** [fɔto] *nf* photo(graph); **prendre en ~** to take a photo of; **faire de la ~** to take photos; **~ d'identité** passport photograph; **photocopie** *nf* photocopy; **photocopier** *vt* to photocopy; **photocopieuse** *nf* photocopier; **photographe** *nm/f* photographer; **photographie** *nf* (*technique*) photography; (*cliché*) photograph; **photographier** *vt* to photograph

**phrase** [fRaz] *nf* sentence

**physicien, ne** [fizisjɛ̃, jɛn] *nm/f* physicist

**physionomie** [fizjɔnɔmi] *nf* face

**physique** [fizik] *adj* physical ♦ *nm* physique ♦ *nf* physics *sg*; **au ~** physically; **physiquement** *adv* physically

**piailler** [pjaje] *vi* to squawk

**pianiste** [pjanist] *nm/f* pianist

**piano** [pjano] *nm* piano; **pianoter** *vi* to tinkle away (at the piano)

**pic** [pik] *nm* (*instrument*) pick(axe);

# pichet

(montagne) peak; (ZOOL) woodpecker; **à ~** vertically; (fig: tomber, arriver) just at the right time

**pichet** [piʃɛ] nm jug

**picorer** [pikɔʀe] vt to peck

**picoter** [pikɔte] vt (suj: oiseau) to peck ♦ vi (irriter) to smart, prickle

**pie** [pi] nf magpie

**pièce** [pjɛs] nf (d'un logement) room; (THÉÂTRE) play; (de machine) part; (de monnaie) coin; (document) document; (fragment, de collection) piece; **dix francs ~** ten francs each; **vendre à la ~** to sell separately; **travailler à la ~** to do piecework; **un maillot une ~** a one-piece swimsuit; **un deux-~s cuisine** a two-room(ed) flat (BRIT) ou apartment (US) with kitchen; **à conviction** exhibit; **~ d'identité: avez-vous une ~ d'identité?** have you got any (means of) identification?; **~ montée** tiered cake; **~s détachées** spares, (spare) parts; **~s justificatives** supporting documents

**pied** [pje] nm foot; (de table) leg; (de lampe) base; **à ~** on foot; **au ~ de la lettre** literally; **avoir ~** to be able to touch the bottom, not to be out of one's depth; **avoir le ~ marin** to be a good sailor; **sur ~** (debout, rétabli) up and about; **mettre sur ~** (entreprise) to set up; **c'est le ~** (fam) it's brilliant; **mettre les ~s dans le plat** (fam) to put one's foot in it; **il se débrouille comme un ~** (fam) he's completely useless; **pied-noir** nm Algerian-born Frenchman

**piège** [pjɛʒ] nm trap; **prendre au ~** to trap; **piéger** vt (avec une bombe) to booby-trap; **lettre/voiture piégée** letter/car-bomb

**pierre** [pjɛʀ] nf stone; **~ précieuse** precious stone, gem; **~ tombale** tombstone; **pierreries** nfpl gems, precious stones

**piétiner** [pjetine] vi (trépigner) to stamp (one's foot); (fig) to be at a standstill ♦ vt to trample on

**piéton, ne** [pjetɔ̃, ɔn] nm/f pedestrian; **piétonnier, ière** adj: **rue ou zone piétonnière** pedestrian precinct

**pieu, x** [pjø] nm post; (pointu) stake

**pieuvre** [pjœvʀ] nf octopus

**pieux, -euse** [pjø, pjøz] adj pious

**piffer** [pife] (fam) vt: **je ne peux pas le ~** I can't stand him

**pigeon** [piʒɔ̃] nm pigeon

**piger** [piʒe] (fam) vi, vt to understand

**pigiste** [piʒist] nm/f freelance(r)

**pignon** [piɲɔ̃] nm (de mur) gable

**pile** [pil] nf (tas) pile; (ÉLEC) battery ♦ adv (fam: s'arrêter etc) dead; **à deux heures ~** at two on the dot; **jouer à ~ ou face** to toss up (for it); **~ ou face?** heads or tails?

**piler** [pile] vt to crush, pound

**pilier** [pilje] nm pillar

**piller** [pije] vt to pillage, plunder, loot

**pilote** [pilɔt] nm pilot; (de voiture) driver ♦ adj pilot cpd; **~ de course** racing driver; **~ de ligne/d'essai/de chasse** airline/test/fighter pilot; **piloter** vt (avion) to pilot, fly; (voiture) to drive

**pilule** [pilyl] nf pill; **prendre la ~** to be on the pill

**piment** [pimɑ̃] nm (aussi: ~ rouge) chilli; (fig) spice, piquancy; **~ doux** pepper, capsicum; **pimenté, e** adj (plat) hot, spicy

**pimpant, e** [pɛ̃pɑ̃, ɑ̃t] adj spruce

**pin** [pɛ̃] nm pine

**pinard** [pinaʀ] (fam) nm (cheap) wine, plonk (BRIT)

**pince** [pɛ̃s] nf (outil) pliers pl; (de homard, crabe) pincer, claw; (COUTURE: pli) dart; **~ à épiler** tweezers pl; **~ à linge** clothes peg (BRIT) ou pin (US)

**pincé, e** [pɛ̃se] adj (air) stiff

**pinceau, x** [pɛ̃so] nm (paint)brush

**pincée** [pɛ̃se] nf: **une ~ de** a pinch of

**pincer** [pɛ̃se] vt to pinch; (fam) to nab

**pinède** [pinɛd] nf pinewood, pine forest

**pingouin** [pɛ̃gwɛ̃] nm penguin

**ping-pong** ® [piŋpɔ̃g] *nm* table tennis

**pingre** [pɛ̃gʀ] *adj* niggardly

**pinson** [pɛ̃sɔ̃] *nm* chaffinch

**pintade** [pɛ̃tad] *nf* guinea-fowl

**pioche** [pjɔʃ] *nf* pickaxe; **piocher** *vt* to dig up (with a pickaxe); **piocher dans** (*le tas, ses économies*) to dig into

**pion** [pjɔ̃] *nm* (ÉCHECS) pawn; (DAMES) piece; (SCOL) supervisor

**pionnier** [pjɔnje] *nm* pioneer

**pipe** [pip] *nf* pipe; **fumer la ~** to smoke a pipe

**pipeau, x** [pipo] *nm* (reed-)pipe

**piquant, e** [pikɑ̃, ɑ̃t] *adj* (*barbe, rosier etc*) prickly; (*saveur, sauce*) hot, pungent; (*détail*) titillating; (*froid*) biting ♦ *nm* (*épine*) thorn, prickle; (*fig*) spiciness, spice

**pique** [pik] *nf* pike; (*fig*) cutting remark ♦ *nm* (CARTES) spades *pl*

**pique-nique** [piknik] *nm* picnic; **pique-niquer** *vi* to have a picnic

**piquer** [pike] *vt* (*suj: guêpe, fumée, orties*) to sting; (*suj: moustique*) to bite; (: *barbe*) to prick; (: *froid*) to bite; (MÉD) to give a jab to; (: *chien, chat*) to put to sleep; (*intérêt*) to arouse; (*fam: voler*) to pinch ♦ *vi* (*avion*) to go into a dive; **se ~** (*avec une aiguille*) to prick o.s.; (*dans les orties*) to get stung; (*suj: toxicomane*) to shoot up; **une colère** to fly into a rage

**piquet** [pike] *nm* (*pieu*) post, stake; (*de tente*) peg; **~ de grève** (strike-)picket

**piqûre** [pikyʀ] *nf* (*d'épingle*) prick; (*d'ortie*) sting; (*de moustique*) bite; (MÉD) injection, shot (US); **faire une ~ à qn** to give sb an injection

**pirate** [piʀat] *nm, adj* pirate; **~ de l'air** hijacker

**pire** [piʀ] *adj* worse; (*superlatif*): **le(la) ~ ... the worst** ♦ *nm*: **le ~ (de)** the worst (of); **au ~** at the (very) worst

**pis** [pi] *nm* (*de vache*) udder; (*pire*): **le ~** the worst ♦ *adj, adv* worse; **de mal en ~** from bad to worse

**piscine** [pisin] *nf* (swimming) pool; **~ couverte** indoor (swimming) pool

**pissenlit** [pisɑ̃li] *nm* dandelion

**pistache** [pistaʃ] *nf* pistachio (nut)

**piste** [pist] *nf* (*d'un animal, sentier*) track, trail; (*indice*) lead; (*de stade*) track; (*de cirque*) ring; (*de danse*) floor; (*de patinage*) rink; (*de ski*) run; (AVIAT) runway; **~ cyclable** cycle track

**pistolet** [pistɔlɛ] *nm* (*arme*) pistol, gun; (*à peinture*) spray gun; **pistolet-mitrailleur** *nm* submachine gun

**piston** [pistɔ̃] *nm* (TECH) piston; **avoir du ~** (*fam*) to have friends in the right places; **pistonner** *vt* (*candidat*) to pull strings for

**piteux, -euse** [pitø, øz] *adj* pitiful, sorry (*avant le nom*)

**pitié** [pitje] *nf* pity; **il me fait ~** I feel sorry for him; **avoir ~ de** (*compassion*) to pity, feel sorry for; (*merci*) to have pity ou mercy on

**pitoyable** [pitwajabl] *adj* pitiful

**pitre** [pitʀ] *nm* clown; **pitrerie** *nf* tomfoolery *no pl*

**pittoresque** [pitɔʀɛsk] *adj* picturesque

**pivot** [pivo] *nm* pivot; **pivoter** *vi* to revolve; (*fauteuil*) to swivel

**P.J.** *sigle f* (= *police judiciaire*) ≈ CID (BRIT), ≈ FBI (US)

**placard** [plakaʀ] *nm* (*armoire*) cupboard; (*affiche*) poster, notice

**place** [plas] *nf* (*emplacement, classement*) place; (*de ville, village*) square; (*espace libre*) room, space; (*de parking*) space; (*siège: de train, cinéma, voiture*) seat; (*emploi*) job; **en ~** (*mettre*) in its place; **sur ~** on the spot; **faire ~ à** to give way to; **ça prend de la ~** it takes up a lot of room *ou* space; **à la ~ de** in place of, instead of; **à ta ~ ...** if I were you ...; **se mettre à la ~ de qn** to put o.s. in sb's place *ou* in sb's shoes

**placé, e** [plase] *adj*: **être bien/mal ~** (*spectateur*) to have a good/a poor seat; (*concurrent*) to be in a good/bad position; **il est bien ~ pour le savoir**

he is in a position to know
**placement** [plasmɑ̃] *nm* (FINANCE) investment; **bureau de ~** employment agency
**placer** [plase] *vt* to place; (*convive, spectateur*) to seat; (*argent*) to place, invest; **il n'a pas pu ~ un mot** he couldn't get a word in; **se ~ au premier rang** to go and stand (*ou* sit) in the first row
**plafond** [plafɔ̃] *nm* ceiling
**plage** [plaʒ] *nf* beach
**plagiat** [plaʒja] *nm* plagiarism
**plaid** [plɛd] *nm* (tartan) car rug
**plaider** [plede] *vi* (*avocat*) to plead ♦ *vt* to plead; **~ pour** (*fig*) to speak for; **plaidoyer** [pledwaje] *nm* (JUR) speech for the defence; (*fig*) plea
**plaie** [plɛ] *nf* wound
**plaignant, e** [plɛɲɑ̃, ɑ̃t] *nm/f* plaintiff
**plaindre** [plɛ̃dʀ] *vt* to pity, feel sorry for; **se ~** (*gémir*) to moan; (*protester*): **se ~ (à qn) (de)** to complain (to sb) (about); (*souffrir*): **se ~ de** to complain of
**plaine** [plɛn] *nf* plain
**plain-pied** [plɛ̃pje] *adv*: **de ~~ (avec)** on the same level (as)
**plainte** [plɛ̃t] *nf* (*gémissement*) moan, groan; (*doléance*) complaint; **porter ~** to lodge a complaint
**plaire** [plɛʀ] *vi* to be a success, be successful; **ça plaît beaucoup aux jeunes** it's very popular with young people; **~ à: cela me plaît** I like it; **se ~ quelque part** to like being somewhere *ou* to like being somewhere; **j'irai si ça me plaît** I'll go if I feel like it; **s'il vous plaît** please
**plaisance** [plɛzɑ̃s] *nf* (*aussi*: **navigation de ~**) (pleasure) sailing, yachting
**plaisant, e** [plɛzɑ̃, ɑ̃t] *adj* pleasant; (*histoire, anecdote*) amusing
**plaisanter** [plɛzɑ̃te] *vi* to joke; **plaisanterie** *nf* joke
**plaise** *etc* [plɛz] *vb voir* **plaire**
**plaisir** [plɛziʀ] *nm* pleasure; **faire ~ à qn** (*délibérément*) to be nice to sb, please sb; **ça me fait ~** I like (*ou* doing)

it; **j'espère que ça te fera ~** I hope you'll like it; **pour le ~** for pleasure
**plaît** [plɛ] *vb voir* **plaire**
**plan, e** [plɑ̃, an] *adj* flat ♦ *nm* plan; (*fig*) level, plane; (CINÉMA) shot; **au premier/second ~** in the foreground/middle distance; **à l'arrière ~** in the background; **rester en ~** (*fam*) to be left stranded; **laisser en ~** (*fam: travail*) to drop, abandon; **~ d'eau** lake
**planche** [plɑ̃ʃ] *nf* (*pièce de bois*) plank, (wooden) board; (*illustration*) plate; **~ à repasser** ironing board; **~ à roulettes** skateboard; **~ à voile** (*sport*) windsurfing
**plancher** [plɑ̃ʃe] *nm* floor; floorboards *pl* ♦ *vi* (*fam*) to work hard
**planer** [plane] *vi* to glide; (*fam: rêveur*) to have one's head in the clouds; **~ sur** (*fig: danger*) to hang over
**planète** [planɛt] *nf* planet
**planeur** [planœʀ] *nm* glider
**planification** [planifikasjɔ̃] *nf* (economic) planning
**planifier** [planifje] *vt* to plan
**planning** [planiŋ] *nm* programme, schedule
**planque** [plɑ̃k] *(fam) nf* (*emploi peu fatigant*) cushy (BRIT) *ou* easy number; (*cachette*) hiding place
**plant** [plɑ̃] *nm* seedling, young plant
**plante** [plɑ̃t] *nf* plant; **~ d'appartement** house *ou* pot plant; **~ des pieds** sole (of the foot)
**planter** [plɑ̃te] *vt* (*plante*) to plant; (*enfoncer*) to hammer *ou* drive in; (*tente*) to put up, pitch; (*fam: personne*) to dump; **se ~** (*fam: se tromper*) to get it wrong
**plantureux, -euse** [plɑ̃tyʀø, øz] *adj* copious, lavish; (*femme*) buxom
**plaque** [plak] *nf* plate; (*de verglas, d'eczéma*) patch; (*avec inscription*) plaque; **~ chauffante** hotplate; **~ de chocolat** bar of chocolate; **~ (minéralogique ou d'immatriculation)** number

**plaqué** (BRIT) ou **license** (US) **plate**; ~ **tournante** (fig) centre

**plaqué, e** [plake] adj: ~ **or/argent** gold-/silver-plated

**plaquer** [plake] vt (aplatir): ~ **qch sur** ou **contre** to make sth stick ou cling to; (RUGBY) to bring down; (fam: laisser tomber) to drop

**plaquette** [plaket] nf (de chocolat) bar; (beurre) pack(et); ~ **de frein** brake pad

**plastique** [plastik] adj, nm plastic; **plastiquer** vt to blow up (with a plastic bomb)

**plat, e** [pla, -at] adj flat; (cheveux) straight; (style) flat, dull ♦ nm (récipient, CULIN) dish; (d'un repas) course; **à ~ ventre** face down; **à ~** (pneu, batterie) flat; (fam: personne) dead beat; ~ **cuisiné** pre-cooked meal; ~ **de résistance** main course; ~ **du jour** dish of the day

**platane** [platan] nm plane tree

**plateau, x** [plato] nm (support) tray; (GÉO) plateau; (CINÉMA) set; ~ **de fromages** cheeseboard

**plate-bande** [platbɑ̃d] nf flower bed

**plate-forme** [platfɔrm] nf platform; ~-~ **de forage/pétrolière** drilling/oil rig

**platine** [platin] nm platinum ♦ nf (d'un tourne-disque) turntable

**plâtre** [platr] nm (matériau) plaster; (statue) plaster statue; (MÉD) (plaster) cast; **avoir un bras dans le ~** to have an arm in plaster

**plein, e** [plɛ̃, plɛn] adj full ♦ nm: **faire le ~** (d'essence) to fill up (with petrol); **à ~es mains** (ramasser) in handfuls; **à ~ temps** full-time; **en ~ air** in the open air; **en ~ soleil** in direct sunlight; **en ~e nuit/rue** in the middle of the night/street; **en ~ jour** in broad daylight

**pleurer** [plœre] vi to cry; (yeux) to water ♦ vt to mourn (for); ~ **sur** to lament (over), to bemoan

**pleurnicher** [plœrnife] vi to snivel, whine

**pleurs** [plœr] nmpl: **en ~** in tears

**pleut** [plø] vb voir **pleuvoir**

**pleuvoir** [pløvwar] vb impers to rain ♦ vi (coups) to rain; (critiques, invitations) to shower down; **il pleut** it's raining

**pli** [pli] nm fold; (de jupe) pleat; (de pantalon) crease; **prendre le ~ de faire** to get into the habit of doing; **un mauvais ~** a bad habit

**pliant, e** [plijɑ̃, plijɑ̃t] adj folding

**plier** [plije] vt to fold; (pour ranger) to fold up; (genou, bras) to bend ♦ vi to bend; (fig) to yield; **se ~** to fold; **se ~ à** to submit to

**plinthe** [plɛ̃t] nf skirting board

**plisser** [plise] vt (jupe) to put pleats in; (yeux) to screw up; (front) to crease

**plomb** [plɔ̃] nm (métal) lead; (d'une cartouche) (lead) shot; (PÊCHE) sinker; (ÉLEC) fuse; **sans ~** (essence etc) unleaded

**plombage** [plɔ̃baʒ] nm (de dent) filling

**plomberie** [plɔ̃bri] nf plumbing

**plombier** [plɔ̃bje] nm plumber

**plonge** [plɔ̃ʒ] nf washing-up

**plongeant, e** [plɔ̃ʒɑ̃, ɑ̃t] adj (vue) from above; (décolleté) plunging

**plongée** [plɔ̃ʒe] nf (SPORT) diving no pl; (sans scaphandre) skin diving; ~ **sous-marine** diving

**plongeoir** [plɔ̃ʒwar] nm diving board

**plongeon** [plɔ̃ʒɔ̃] nm dive

**plonger** [plɔ̃ʒe] vi to dive ♦ vt: ~ **qch dans** to plunge sth into; **se ~ dans** (études, lecture) to bury ou immerse o.s. in; **plongeur** nm diver

**ployer** [plwaje] vt, vi to bend

**plu** [ply] pp de **plaire**, **pleuvoir**

**pluie** [plɥi] nf rain

**plume** [plym] nf feather; (pour écrire) (pen) nib; (fig) pen

**plupart** [plypar]: **la ~** pron the majority, most (of them); **la ~ des** the majority, the most (of); **la ~ du temps/d'entre nous** most of the time/of us; **pour la ~** for the most part, mostly

**pluriel** [plyrjɛl] nm plural

**plus¹** [ply] *vb voir* **plaire**

---
MOT-CLÉ
---

**plus²** [ply] *adv* **1** (*forme négative*): **ne ... plus** no more, no longer; **je n'ai plus d'argent** I've got no more money *ou* no money left; **il ne travaille plus** he's no longer working, he doesn't work any more

**2** (*comparatif*) more, ...+er; (*superlatif*): **le plus** the most, the ...+est; **plus grand/intelligent (que)** bigger/more intelligent (than); **le plus grand/intelligent** the biggest/most intelligent; **tout au plus** at the very most

**3** (*davantage*) more; **il travaille plus (que)** he works more (than); **plus il travaille, plus il est heureux** the more he works, the happier he is; **plus de pain** more bread; **plus de 10 personnes** more than 10 people, over 10 people; **3 heures de plus que** 3 hours more than; **de plus** what's more, moreover; **3 kilos en plus** 3 kilos more; **en plus de** in addition to; **de plus en plus** more and more; **plus ou moins** more or less; **ni plus ni moins** no more, no less

♦ *prép*: **4 plus 2** 4 plus 2

**plusieurs** [plyzjœr] *dét, pron* several; **ils sont ~** there are several of them

**plus-value** [plyvaly] *nf* (*bénéfice*) surplus

**plut** [ply] *vb voir* **plaire**

**plutôt** [plyto] *adv* rather; **je préfère ~ celui-ci** I'd rather have this one; **~ que (de) faire** rather than *ou* instead of doing

**pluvieux, -euse** [plyvjø, jøz] *adj* rainy, wet

**PME** *sigle f* (= petite(s) et moyenne(s) entreprise(s)) small business(es)

**PMU** *sigle m* (= Pari mutuel urbain) system of betting on horses; (*café*) betting agency

**PNB** *sigle m* (= produit national brut)

GNP

**pneu** [pnø] *nm* tyre (BRIT), tire (US)

**pneumonie** [pnømɔni] *nf* pneumonia

**poche** [pɔʃ] *nf* pocket; (*sous les yeux*) bag, pouch; **argent de ~** pocket money

**pocher** [pɔʃe] *vt* (CULIN) to poach

**pochette** [pɔʃɛt] *nf* (*d'aiguilles etc*) case; (*mouchoir*) breast pocket handkerchief; (*sac à main*) clutch bag; **~ de disque** record sleeve

**poêle** [pwal] *nm* stove ♦ *nf*: **~ (à frire)** frying pan

**poème** [pɔɛm] *nm* poem

**poésie** [pɔezi] *nf* (*poème*) poem; (*art*): **la ~** poetry

**poète** [pɔɛt] *nm* poet

**poids** [pwa] *nm* weight; (SPORT) shot; **vendre au ~** to sell by weight; **prendre du ~** to put on weight; **~ lourd** (*camion*) lorry (BRIT), truck (US)

**poignant, e** [pwaɲɑ̃, ɑ̃t] *adj* poignant

**poignard** [pwaɲar] *nm* dagger; **poignarder** *vt* to stab, knife

**poigne** [pwaɲ] *nf* grip; **avoir de la ~** (*fig*) to rule with a firm hand

**poignée** [pwaɲe] *nf* (*de sel etc, fig*) handful; (*de couvercle, porte*) handle; **~ de main** handshake

**poignet** [pwaɲɛ] *nm* (ANAT) wrist; (*de chemise*) cuff

**poil** [pwal] *nm* (ANAT) hair; (*de pinceau, brosse*) bristle; (*de tapis*) strand; (*pelage*) coat; **à ~** (*fam*) starkers; **au ~** (*fam*) hunky-dory; **poilu, e** *adj* hairy

**poinçon** [pwɛ̃sɔ̃] *nm* (*marque*) hallmark; **poinçonner** [pwɛ̃sɔne] *vt* (*bijou*) to hallmark; (*billet*) to punch

**poing** [pwɛ̃] *nm* fist; **coup de ~** punch

**point** [pwɛ̃] *nm* point; (*endroit*) spot; (*marque, signe*) dot; (: *de ponctuation*) full stop, period (US); (COUTURE, TRICOT) stitch ♦ *adv* = **pas²**; **faire le ~** (*fig*) to take stock (of the situation); **sur le ~ de faire** (just) about to do; **à tel ~ que** so much so that; **mettre au ~** (*procédé*) to develop; (*affaire*) to settle; **à ~**

(CULIN: viande) medium; **à ~ (nommé)** just at the right time; **deux ~s** colon; **~ (de côté)** stitch (pain); **~ d'exclamation/d'interrogation** exclamation/question mark; **~ de repère** landmark; (dans le temps) point of reference; **~ de suture** (MÉD) stitch; **~ de vente** retail outlet; **~ de vue** viewpoint; (fig: opinion) point of view; **d'honneur: mettre un ~ d'honneur à faire qch** to make it a point of honour to do sth; **~ faible/fort** weak/strong point; **~ noir** blackhead; **~s de suspension** suspension points

**pointe** [pwɛ̃t] nf (clou) tack; (fig): **une ~** a hint of; **être à la ~ de** (fig) to be in the forefront; **sur la ~ des pieds** on tiptoe; **en ~** pointed, tapered; **de ~** (technique etc) leading; **heures de ~** peak hours

**pointer** [pwɛ̃te] vt (diriger: canon, doigt); **~ sur qch** to point at sth ♦ vi (employé) to clock in

**pointillé** [pwɛ̃tije] nm (trait) dotted line

**pointilleux, -euse** [pwɛ̃tijø, øz] adj particular, pernickety

**pointu, e** [pwɛ̃ty] adj pointed; (voix) shrill; (analyse) precise

**pointure** [pwɛ̃tyr] nf size

**point-virgule** [pwɛ̃virgyl] nm semi-colon

**poire** [pwar] nf pear; (péj: fam) mug

**poireau, x** [pwaro] nm leek

**poireauter** [pwarote] vi (fam) to be left kicking one's heels

**poirier** [pwarje] nm pear tree

**pois** [pwa] nm (BOT) pea; (sur une étoffe) dot, spot; **~ chiche** chickpea; **à ~** (cravate etc) spotted, polka-dot cpd

**poison** [pwazɔ̃] nm poison

**poisse** [pwas] nf (fam) rotten luck

**poisseux, -euse** [pwasø, øz] adj sticky

**poisson** [pwasɔ̃] nm fish ⊕ gén inv; **les P~s** (signe) Pisces; **d'avril!** April fool!; **~ rouge** goldfish; **poissonnerie** nf fish-shop; **poissonnier, -ière** nm/f

fishmonger (BRIT), fish merchant (US)

**poitrine** [pwatrin] nf chest; (seins) bust, bosom; (CULIN) breast

**poivre** [pwavr] nm pepper

**poivron** [pwavrɔ̃] nm pepper, capsicum

**polaire** [pɔlɛr] adj polar

**polar** [pɔlar] nm (fam) detective novel

**pôle** [pol] nm (GÉO, ÉLEC) pole

**poli, e** [pɔli] adj polite; (lisse) smooth

**police** [pɔlis] nf police; **~ d'assurance** insurance policy; **~ judiciaire** ≈ Criminal Investigation Department (BRIT), ≈ Federal Bureau of Investigation (US); **~ secours** ≈ emergency services pl (BRIT), ≈ paramedics pl (US); **policier, -ière** adj police cpd ♦ nm policeman; (aussi: **roman policier**) detective novel

**polio** [pɔljo] nf polio

**polir** [pɔlir] vt to polish

**polisson, ne** [pɔlisɔ̃, ɔn] nm/f (enfant) (little) rascal

**politesse** [pɔlitɛs] nf politeness

**politicien, ne** [pɔlitisjɛ̃, jɛn] nm/f politician

**politique** [pɔlitik] adj political ♦ nf politics sg; (mesures, méthode) policies pl

**pollen** [pɔlɛn] nm pollen

**polluant, e** [pɔlɥɑ̃, ɑ̃t] adj polluting; **produit ~** pollutant

**polluer** [pɔlɥe] vt to pollute; **pollution** nf pollution

**polo** [pɔlo] nm (chemise) polo shirt

**Pologne** [pɔlɔɲ] nf: **la ~** Poland; **polonais, e** adj Polish ♦ nm/f: **Polonais, e** Pole ♦ nm (LING) Polish

**poltron, ne** [pɔltrɔ̃, ɔn] adj cowardly

**polycopier** [pɔlikɔpje] vt to duplicate

**Polynésie** [pɔlinezi] nf: **la ~** Polynesia

**polyvalent, e** [pɔlivalɑ̃, ɑ̃t] adj (rôle) varied; (salle) multi-purpose

**pommade** [pɔmad] nf ointment, cream

**pomme** [pɔm] nf apple; **tomber dans les ~s** (fam) to pass out; **~ d'Adam** Adam's apple; **~ de pin** pine ou fir cone; **~ de terre** potato

**pommeau, x** [pɔmo] nm (boule) knob; (de selle) pommel

**pommette** [pɔmɛt] nf cheekbone

**pommier** [pɔmje] nm apple tree

**pompe** [pɔ̃p] nf pump; (faste) pomp (and ceremony); **~ à essence** petrol pump; **~s funèbres** funeral parlour sg, undertaker's sg; **pomper** vt to pump; (aspirer) to pump up; (absorber) to soak up

**pompeux, -euse** [pɔ̃pø, øz] adj pompous

**pompier** [pɔ̃pje] nm fireman

**pompiste** [pɔ̃pist] nm/f petrol (BRIT) ou gas (US) pump attendant

**poncer** [pɔ̃se] vt to sand (down)

**ponctuation** [pɔ̃ktɥasjɔ̃] nf punctuation

**ponctuel, le** [pɔ̃ktɥɛl] adj punctual

**pondéré, e** [pɔ̃dere] adj level-headed, composed

**pondre** [pɔ̃dʀ] vt to lay

**poney** [pɔne] nm pony

**pont** [pɔ̃] nm bridge; (NAVIG) deck; **faire le ~** to take the extra day off; **~ suspendu** suspension bridge; **pont-levis** nm drawbridge

---

faire le pont

---

*The expression "faire le pont" refers to the practice of taking a Monday or Friday off to make a long weekend if a public holiday falls on a Tuesday or Thursday. The French often do this at l'Ascension, l'Assomption and le 14 juillet.*

---

**pop** [pɔp] adj inv pop

**populace** [pɔpylas] (péj) nf rabble

**populaire** [pɔpylɛʀ] adj popular; (manifestation) mass cpd; (milieux, quartier) working-class; (expression) vernacular

**popularité** [pɔpylaʀite] nf popularity

**population** [pɔpylasjɔ̃] nf population; **~ active** working population

**populeux, -euse** [pɔpylø, øz] adj densely populated

**porc** [pɔʀ] nm pig; (CULIN) pork

**porcelaine** [pɔʀsəlɛn] nf porcelain, china; piece of china(ware)

**porc-épic** [pɔʀkepik] nm porcupine

**porche** [pɔʀʃ] nm porch

**porcherie** [pɔʀʃəʀi] nf pigsty

**pore** [pɔʀ] nm pore

**porno** [pɔʀno] adj porno ♦ nm porn

**port** [pɔʀ] nm harbour, port; (ville) port; (de l'uniforme etc) wearing; (pour lettre) postage; (pour colis, aussi: posture) carriage; **~ de pêche/de plaisance** fishing/sailing harbour

**portable** [pɔʀtabl] nm (COMPUT) laptop (computer)

**portail** [pɔʀtaj] nm gate

**portant, e** [pɔʀtɑ̃, ɑ̃t] adj: **bien/mal ~** in good/poor health

**portatif, -ive** [pɔʀtatif, iv] adj portable

**porte** [pɔʀt] nf door; (de ville, jardin) gate; **mettre à la ~** to throw out; **~ à ~** nm door-to-door selling; **~ d'entrée** front door; **porte-avions** nm inv aircraft carrier; **porte-bagages** nm inv luggage rack; **porte-bonheur** nm inv lucky charm; **porte-clefs** nm inv key ring; **porte-documents** nm inv attaché ou document case

**porté, e** [pɔʀte] adj: **être ~ à faire** to be inclined to do; **être ~ sur qch** to be keen on sth; **portée** nf (d'une arme) range; (fig: effet) impact, import; (: capacité) scope; (d'une chatte etc) litter; (MUS) stave, staff; **à/hors de portée (de)** within/out of reach (of); **à la portée de (la) main** within (arm's) reach; **à la portée de qn** (fig) at sb's level; **within sb's capabilities**

**porte...: porte-fenêtre** nf French window; **portefeuille** nm wallet; **portemanteau, x** nm (cintre) coat hanger; (au mur) coat rack; **porte-monnaie** nm inv purse; **porte-parole** nm inv spokesman

**porter** [pɔʀte] vt to carry; (sur soi: vêtement, barbe, bague) to wear; (fig: responsabilité etc) to bear, carry; (ins-

*cription, nom, fruits)* to bear; *(coup)* to deal; *(attention)* to turn; *(apporter):* ~ **qch à qn** to take sth to sb ♦ *vi (voix)* to carry; *(coup, argument)* to hit home; ~ *vi (se sentir):* **se ~ bien/mal** to be well/unwell; ~ **sur** *(recherches)* to be concerned with; **se faire ~ malade** to report sick

**porteur** [pɔʀtœʀ, øz] *nm (de bagages)* porter; *(de chèque)* bearer

**porte-voix** [pɔʀtavwa] *nm inv* megaphone

**portier** [pɔʀtje] *nm* doorman

**portière** [pɔʀtjɛʀ] *nf* door

**portillon** [pɔʀtijɔ̃] *nm* gate

**portion** [pɔʀsjɔ̃] *nf (part)* portion, share; *(partie)* portion, section

**porto** [pɔʀto] *nm* port (wine)

**portrait** [pɔʀtʀɛ] *nm (peinture)* portrait; *(photo)* photograph; **portrait-robot** *nm* Identikit ® *ou* photo-fit ® picture

**portuaire** [pɔʀtɥɛʀ] *adj* port *cpd*, harbour *cpd*

**portugais, e** [pɔʀtyɡɛ, ɛz] *adj* Portuguese ♦ *nm/f:* **P~, e** Portuguese ♦ *nm* (LING) Portuguese

**Portugal** [pɔʀtyɡal] *nm:* **le ~** Portugal

**pose** [poz] *nf (de moquette)* laying; *(attitude, d'un modèle)* pose; *(PHOTO)* exposure

**posé, e** [poze] *adj* serious

**poser** [poze] *vt* to put; *(installer: moquette, carrelage)* to lay; *(rideaux, papier peint)* to hang; *(question)* to ask; *(principe, conditions)* to lay *ou* set down; *(problème)* to formulate; *(difficulté)* to pose ♦ *vi (modèle)* to pose; ~ *vi (oiseau, avion)* to land; *(question)* to arise: ~ **qch (sur)** *(déposer)* to put sth down (on); ~ **qch sur/quelque part** *(placer)* to put sth on/somewhere; ~ **sa candidature à un poste** to apply for a post

**positif, -ive** [pozitif, iv] *adj* positive

**position** [pozisjɔ̃] *nf* position; **prendre ~** *(fig)* to take a stand

**posologie** [pozɔlɔʒi] *nf* dosage

**posséder** [pɔsede] *vt* to own, possess; *(qualité, talent)* to have, possess; *(sexuellement)* to possess; **possession** *nf* ownership *no pl*, possession

**possibilité** [pɔsibilite] *nf* possibility; **~s** *nfpl (potentiel)* potential *sg*

**possible** [pɔsibl] *adj* possible; *(projet, entreprise)* feasible ♦ *nm:* **faire son ~** to do all one can, do one's utmost; **le plus/moins de livres ~** as many/few books as possible; **le plus vite ~** as quickly as possible; **dès que ~** as soon as possible

**postal, e, -aux** [pɔstal, o] *adj* postal

**poste** [pɔst] *nf (service)* post service; *(administration, bureau)* post office ♦ *nm (fonction, MIL)* post; *(TÉL)* extension; *(de radio etc)* set; **mettre à la ~** to post; ~ **(de police)** *nm* police station; ~ **de secours** *nm* first-aid post; ~ **restante** *nf* poste restante (BRIT), general delivery (US)

**poster¹** [pɔste] *vt* to post

**poster²** [pɔstɛʀ] *nm* poster

**postérieur, e** [pɔsteʀjœʀ] *adj (date)* later; *(partie)* back ♦ *nm (fam)* behind

**posthume** [pɔstym] *adj* posthumous

**postulant, e** [pɔstylɑ̃, ɑ̃t] *nm/f* applicant

**postuler** [pɔstyle] *vi:* ~ **à** *ou* **pour un emploi** to apply for a job

**posture** [pɔstyʀ] *nf* position

**pot** [po] *nm (en verre)* jar; *(en terre)* pot; *(en plastique, carton)* carton; *(en métal)* tin; *(fam: chance)* luck; **avoir du ~** *(fam)* to be lucky; **boire** *ou* **prendre un ~** *(fam)* to have a drink; **petit ~** *(pour bébé)* (jar of) baby food; ~ **catalytique** catalytic converter; ~ **d'échappement** exhaust pipe; ~ **de fleurs** plant pot, flowerpot; *(plante)* pot plant

**potable** [pɔtabl] *adj:* **eau (non) ~** (non-)drinking water

**potage** [pɔtaʒ] *nm* soup; **potager, -ère** *adj:* **(jardin) potager** kitchen *ou* vegetable garden

**pot-au-feu** [pɔtofø] *nm inv* (beef) stew

**pot-de-vin** [podvɛ̃] nm bribe

**pote** [pɔt] (fam) nm pal

**poteau, x** [pɔto] nm post; **~ indicateur** signpost

**potelé, e** [pɔt(ə)le] adj plump, chubby

**potence** [pɔtɑ̃s] nf gallows sg

**potentiel, le** [pɔtɑ̃sjɛl] adj, nm potential

**poterie** [pɔtʀi] nf pottery; (objet) piece of pottery

**potier** [pɔtje, jɛʀ] nm potter

**potins** [pɔtɛ̃] (fam) nmpl gossip sg

**potiron** [pɔtiʀɔ̃] nm pumpkin

**pou, x** [pu] nm louse

**poubelle** [pubɛl] nf (dust)bin

**pouce** [pus] nm thumb

**poudre** [pudʀ] nf powder; (fard) (face) powder; (explosif) gunpowder; **en ~**: **café en ~** instant coffee; **lait en ~** dried ou powdered milk; **poudreuse** nf powder snow; **poudrier** nm (powder) compact

**pouffer** [pufe] vi: **~ (de rire)** to burst out laughing

**poulailler** [pulaje] nm henhouse

**poulain** [pulɛ̃] nm foal; (fig) protégé

**poule** [pul] nf hen; (CULIN) (boiling) fowl

**poulet** [pulɛ] nm chicken; (fam) cop

**poulie** [puli] nf pulley

**pouls** [pu] nm pulse; **prendre le ~ de qn** to feel sb's pulse

**poumon** [pumɔ̃] nm lung

**poupe** [pup] nf stern; **en ~** astern

**poupée** [pupe] nf doll

**pouponnière** [pupɔnjɛʀ] nf crèche, day nursery

**pour** [puʀ] prép for ♦ nm: **le ~ et le contre** the pros and cons; **~ faire** (so as) to do, in order to; **~ avoir fait** for having done; **~ que** so that, in order that; **~ 100 francs d'essence** 100 francs' worth of petrol; **~ cent** per cent; **~ ce qui est de** as for

**pourboire** [puʀbwaʀ] nm tip

**pourcentage** [puʀsɑ̃taʒ] nm percentage

**pourchasser** [puʀʃase] vt to pursue

**pourparlers** [puʀpaʀle] nmpl talks, negotiations

**pourpre** [puʀpʀ] adj crimson

**pourquoi** [puʀkwa] adv, conj why ♦ nm inv: **le ~ (de)** the reason (for)

**pourrai** etc [puʀe] vb voir **pouvoir**

**pourri, e** [puʀi] adj rotten

**pourrir** [puʀiʀ] vi to rot; (fruit) to go rotten ou bad ♦ vt to rot; (fig) to spoil thoroughly; **pourriture** nf rot

**pourrons** etc [puʀɔ̃] vb voir **pouvoir**

**poursuite** [puʀsɥit] nf pursuit, chase; **~s** nfpl (JUR) legal proceedings

**poursuivre** [puʀsɥivʀ] vt to pursue, chase (after); (obséder) to haunt; (JUR) to bring proceedings against, prosecute; (: au civil) to sue; (but) to strive towards; (continuer: études etc) to carry on with, continue; **se ~** vi to go on, continue

**pourtant** [puʀtɑ̃] adv yet; **c'est ~ facile** (and) yet it's easy

**pourtour** [puʀtuʀ] nm perimeter

**pourvoir** [puʀvwaʀ] vt: **~ qch/qn de** to equip sth/sb with ♦ vi: **~ à** to provide for; **pourvoyeur** nm supplier; **pourvu, e** adj: **pourvu de** equipped with; **pourvu que** (+ sub: condition) so long as; (espérons que) let's hope (that)

**pousse** [pus] nf growth; (bourgeon) shoot

**poussé, e** [puse] adj (enquête) exhaustive; (études) advanced; **poussée** nf thrust; (d'acné) eruption; (fig: prix) upsurge

**pousser** [puse] vt to push; (émettre: cri, soupir) to give; (stimuler: élève) to urge on; (poursuivre: études, discussion) to carry on (further) ♦ vi (croître) to grow; **se ~** vi to move over; **~ qn à** (inciter) to urge ou press sb to; (acculer) to drive sb to; **faire ~** (plante) to grow

**poussette** [pusɛt] nf push chair (BRIT), stroller (US)

**poussière** [pusjɛʀ] nf dust; **poussié-**

reux, -euse *adj* dusty

**poussin** [pusɛ̃] *nm* chick

**poutre** [putʀ] *nf* beam

MOT-CLÉ

**pouvoir** [puvwaʀ] *nm* power; (POL: dirigeants): **le pouvoir** those in power; **les pouvoirs publics** the authorities; **pouvoir d'achat** purchasing power

♦ *vb semi-aux* **1** (être en état de) can, be able to; **je ne peux pas le réparer** I can't *ou* I am not able to repair it; **déçu de ne pas pouvoir le faire** disappointed not to be able to do it

**2** (avoir la permission) may, can, be allowed to; **vous pouvez aller au cinéma** you can *ou* may go to the pictures

**3** (probabilité, hypothèse) may, might, could; **il a pu avoir un accident** he may *ou* might *ou* could have had an accident; **il aurait pu le dire!** he might *ou* could have said (so)!

♦ *vb impers* may, might, could; **il peut arriver que** it may *ou* might *ou* could happen that

♦ *vb* can, be able to; **j'ai fait tout ce que j'ai pu** I did all I could; **je n'en peux plus** (épuisé) I'm exhausted; (à bout) I can't take any more; **se pouvoir** *vi*: **il se peut que** it may *ou* might be that; **cela se pourrait** that's quite possible

**prairie** [pʀeʀi] *nf* meadow

**praline** [pʀalin] *nf* sugared almond

**praticable** [pʀatikabl] *adj* passable, practicable

**pratiquant, e** [pʀatikɑ̃, ɑ̃t] *nm/f* (regular) churchgoer

**pratique** [pʀatik] *nf* practice ♦ *adj* practical; **pratiquement** *adv* (pour ainsi dire) practically, virtually; **pratiquer** *vt* to practise; (l'équitation, la pêche) to go in for; (le golf, football) to play; (intervention, opération) to carry out

**pré** [pʀe] *nm* meadow

**préalable** [pʀealabl] *adj* preliminary;

au ~ beforehand

**préambule** [pʀeɑ̃byl] *nm* preamble; (fig) prelude; **sans** ~ straight away

**préau** [pʀeo] *nm* (SCOL) covered playground

**préavis** [pʀeavi] *nm* notice

**précaution** [pʀekosjɔ̃] *nf* precaution; **avec** ~ cautiously; **par** ~ as a precaution

**précédemment** [pʀesedamɑ̃] *adv* before, previously

**précédent, e** [pʀesedɑ̃, ɑ̃t] *adj* previous ♦ *nm* precedent

**précéder** [pʀesede] *vt* to precede

**précepteur, -trice** [pʀesɛptœʀ, tʀis] *nm/f* (private) tutor

**prêcher** [pʀeʃe] *vt* to preach

**précieux, -euse** [pʀesjø, jøz] *adj* precious; (aide, conseil) invaluable

**précipice** [pʀesipis] *nm* drop, chasm

**précipitamment** [pʀesipitamɑ̃] *adv* hurriedly, hastily

**précipitation** [pʀesipitasjɔ̃] *nf* (hâte) haste; **~s** *nfpl* (pluie) rain *sg*

**précipité, e** [pʀesipite] *adj* hurried, hasty

**précipiter** [pʀesipite] *vt* (hâter: départ) to hasten; (faire tomber): **~ qn/qch du haut de** to throw *ou* hurl sb/sth off *ou* from; **se** ~ *vi* to speed up; **se** ~ **sur/vers** to rush at/towards

**précis, e** [pʀesi, iz] *adj* precise; (mesures) accurate, precise; **à 4 heures ~es** at 4 o'clock sharp; **précisément** *adv* precisely; **préciser** *vt* (expliquer) to be more specific about, clarify; (spécifier) to state, specify; **se préciser** *vi* to become clear(er); **précision** *nf* precision; (détail) point *ou* detail; **demander des précisions** to ask for further explanation

**précoce** [pʀekɔs] *adj* early; (enfant) precocious

**préconçu, e** [pʀekɔ̃sy] *adj* preconceived

**préconiser** [pʀekɔnize] *vt* to advocate

**prédécesseur** [pʀedesesœʀ] *nm* predecessor

**prédilection** [predileksjɔ̃] *nf*: **avoir une ~ pour** to be partial to

**prédire** [predir] *vt* to predict

**prédominer** [predɔmine] *vi* to predominate

**préface** [prefas] *nf* preface

**préfecture** [prefektyr] *nf* prefecture; **~ de police** police headquarters *pl*

**préférable** [preferabl] *adj* preferable

**préféré, e** [prefere] *adj, nm/f* favourite

**préférence** [preferɑ̃s] *nf* preference; **de ~** preferably

**préférer** [prefere] *vt*: **~ qn/qch (à)** to prefer sb/sth (to), like sb/sth better (than); **~ faire** to prefer to do; **je ~ais du thé** I would rather have tea, I'd prefer tea

**préfet** [prefe] *nm* prefect

**préhistorique** [preistɔrik] *adj* prehistoric

**préjudice** [preʒydis] *nm* (*matériel, moral*) harm *no pl*; **porter ~ à** to harm, be detrimental to; **au ~ de** at the expense of

**préjugé** [preʒyʒe] *nm* prejudice; **avoir un ~ contre** to be prejudiced ou biased against

**préjuger** [preʒyʒe]: **~ de** *vt* to prejudge

**prélasser** [prelase]: **se ~** *vi* to lounge

**prélèvement** [prelɛvmɑ̃] *nm* (*montant*) deduction; **faire un ~ de sang** to take a blood sample

**prélever** [prel(ə)ve] *vt* (*échantillon*) to take; **~ (sur)** (*montant*) to deduct (from); (*argent: sur son compte*) to withdraw (from)

**prématuré, e** [prematyre] *adj* premature ♦ *nm* premature baby

**premier, -ière** [prəmje, jɛr] *adj* first; (*rang*) front; (*fig: objectif*) basic; **le ~ venu** the first person to come along; **de ~ ordre** first-rate; **P~ Ministre** Prime Minister; **première** *nf* (*SCOL*) lower sixth form; (*THÉÂTRE*) first night; (*AUTO*) first (gear); (*AVIAT, RAIL etc*) first

class; (*CINÉMA*) première; (*exploit*) first; **premièrement** *adv* firstly

**prémonition** [premɔnisjɔ̃] *nf* premonition

**prémunir** [premynir]: **se ~** *vi*: **se ~ contre** to guard against

**prenant, e** [prənɑ̃, ɑ̃t] *adj* absorbing, engrossing

**prénatal, e** [prenatal] *adj* (*MÉD*) antenatal

**prendre** [prɑ̃dr] *vt* to take; (*repas*) to have; (*se procurer*) to get; (*malfaiteur, poisson*) to catch; (*passager*) to pick up; (*personnel*) to take on; (*traiter: personne*) to handle; (*voix, ton*) to put on; (*ôter*): **~ qch à** to take sth from; (*coincer*): **se ~ les doigts dans** to get one's fingers caught in ♦ *vi* (*liquide, ciment*) to set; (*greffe, vaccin*) to take; (*feu: foyer*) to go; (*: allumette*) to light; **~ à gauche** to turn (to the) left; **~ froid** to catch cold; **se ~ pour** to think one is; **s'en ~ à** to attack; **se ~ d'amitié pour** to befriend; **s'y ~** (*procéder*) to set about it

**preneur** [prənœr, øz] *nm*: **être/trouver ~** to be willing to buy/find a buyer

**preniez** [prənje] *vb voir* prendre

**prenne** *etc* [prɛn] *vb voir* prendre

**prénom** [prenɔ̃] *nm* first ou Christian name

**préoccupation** [preɔkypasjɔ̃] *nf* (*souci*) concern; (*idée fixe*) preoccupation

**préoccuper** [preɔkype] *vt* (*inquiéter*) to worry; (*absorber*) to preoccupy; **se ~ de** to be concerned with

**préparatifs** [preparatif] *nmpl* preparations

**préparation** [preparasjɔ̃] *nf* preparation

**préparer** [prepare] *vt* to prepare; (*café, thé*) to make; (*examen*) to prepare for; (*voyage, entreprise*) to plan; **se ~** *vi* (*orage, tragédie*) to brew, be in the air; **~ qch à qn** (*surprise etc*) to have sth in store for sb; **se ~ (à qch/à faire)** to prepare (o.s.) ou get ready (for sth/to do)

**prépondérant, e** [prepɔ̃derɑ̃, ɑ̃t] *adj* major, dominating

**préposé, e** [prepoze] *nm/f* employee; *(facteur)* postman

**préposition** [prepozisjɔ̃] *nf* preposition

**près** [prɛ] *adv* near, close; ~ **de** near (to), close to; *(environ)* nearly, almost; **de** ~ closely; **à 5 kg** ~ to within about 5 kg; **à cela** ~ **que** apart from the fact that; **il n'est pas à 10 minutes** ~ he can spare 10 minutes

**présage** [prezaʒ] *nm* omen; **présager** *vt* to foresee

**presbyte** [prɛsbit] *adj* long-sighted

**presbytère** [prɛsbitɛr] *nm* presbytery

**prescription** [prɛskripsjɔ̃] *nf* prescription

**prescrire** [prɛskrir] *vt* to prescribe

**présence** [prezɑ̃s] *nf* presence; *(au bureau, à l'école)* attendance

**présent, e** [prezɑ̃, ɑ̃t] *adj, nm* present; **à** ~ **(que)** now (that)

**présentation** [prezɑ̃tasjɔ̃] *nf* presentation; *(de nouveau venu)* introduction; *(allure)* appearance; **faire les** ~**s** to do the introductions

**présenter** [prezɑ̃te] *vt* to present; *(excuses, condoléances)* to offer; *(invité, conférencier)*: ~ **qn (à)** to introduce sb (to) ♦ *vi*: ~ **bien** to have a pleasing appearance; **se** ~ *vi (occasion)* to arise; **se** ~ **à** *(examen)* to sit; *(élection)* to stand at, run for

**préservatif** [prezɛrvatif, iv] *nm* sheath, condom

**préserver** [prezɛrve] *vt*: ~ **de** *(protéger)* to protect from

**président** [prezidɑ̃] *nm* (POL) president; *(d'une assemblée, COMM)* chairman; ~ **directeur général** chairman and managing director; **présidentielles** *nfpl* presidential elections

**présider** [prezide] *vt* to preside over; *(dîner)* to be the guest of honour at

**présomptueux, -euse** [prezɔ̃ptɥø,

øz] *adj* presumptuous

**presque** [prɛsk] *adv* almost, nearly; ~ **personne** hardly anyone; ~ **rien** hardly anything; ~ **pas** hardly (at all); ~ **pas (de)** hardly any

**presqu'île** [prɛskil] *nf* peninsula

**pressant, e** [prɛsɑ̃, ɑ̃t] *adj* urgent

**presse** [prɛs] *nf* press; *(affluence)*: **heures de** ~ busy times

**pressé, e** [prese] *adj* in a hurry; *(travail)* urgent; **orange** ~**e** freshly-squeezed orange juice

**pressentiment** [presɑ̃timɑ̃] *nm* foreboding, premonition

**pressentir** [presɑ̃tir] *vt* to sense

**presse-papiers** [prɛspapje] *nm inv* paperweight

**presser** [prese] *vt (fruit, éponge)* to squeeze; *(bouton)* to press; *(allure)* to speed up; *(inciter)*: ~ **qn de faire** to urge ou press sb to do ♦ *vi* to be urgent; **se** ~ *vi (se hâter)* to hurry (up); **se** ~ **contre qn** to squeeze up against sb; **rien ne presse** there's no hurry

**pressing** [presiŋ] *nm (magasin)* dry-cleaner's

**pression** [presjɔ̃] *nf* pressure; *(bouton)* press stud; *(fam: bière)* draught beer; **faire** ~ **sur** to put pressure on; ~ **artérielle** blood pressure

**prestance** [prɛstɑ̃s] *nf* presence, imposing bearing

**prestataire** [prɛstatɛr] *nm/f* supplier

**prestation** [prɛstasjɔ̃] *nf (allocation)* benefit; *(d'une entreprise)* service provided; *(d'un artiste)* performance

**prestidigitateur, -trice** [prɛstidiʒitatœr, tris] *nm/f* conjurer

**prestige** [prɛstiʒ] *nm* prestige; **prestigieux, -euse** *adj* prestigious

**présumer** [prezyme] *vt*: ~ **que** to presume ou assume that

**prêt, e** [prɛ, prɛt] *adj* ready ♦ *nm (somme)* loan; **prêt-à-porter** *nm* ready-to-wear ou off-the-peg (BRIT) clothes *pl*

**prétendre** [pretɑ̃dr] *vt (affirmer)*: ~

que to claim that; *(avoir l'intention de):* ~ **faire qch** to mean ou intend to do sth; **prétendu, e** adj *(supposé)* so-called

**prétentieux, -euse** [pretɑ̃sjø, jøz] adj pretentious

**prétention** [pretɑ̃sjɔ̃] nf claim; *(vanité)* pretentiousness; ~**s** nfpl *(salaire)* expected salary

**prêter** [prete] vt *(livres, argent):* ~ **qch (à)** to lend sth (to); *(supposer):* ~ **à** *(caractère, propos)* to attribute to sb; **se** ~ **à** to lend o.s. *(ou itself)* to; *(manigances etc)* to going along with; ~ **à** *(critique, commentaires etc)* to be open to, give rise to; ~ **attention à** to pay attention to; ~ **serment** to take the oath

**prétexte** [pretekst] nm pretext, excuse; **sous aucun** ~ on no account; **prétexter** to give as a pretext ou an excuse

**prêtre** [prɛtr] nm priest

**preuve** [prœv] nf proof; *(indice)* proof, evidence no pl; **faire** ~ **de** to show; **faire ses** ~**s** to prove o.s. *(ou itself)*

**prévaloir** [prevalwar] vi to prevail

**prévenant, e** [prev(ə)nɑ̃, ɑ̃t] adj thoughtful, kind

**prévenir** [prev(ə)nir] vt *(éviter: catastrophe etc)* to avoid, prevent; *(anticiper: désirs, besoins)* to anticipate; ~ **qn (de)** *(avertir)* to warn sb (about); *(informer)* to tell ou inform sb (about)

**préventif, -ive** [prevɑ̃tif, iv] adj preventive

**prévention** [prevɑ̃sjɔ̃] nf prevention; ~ **routière** road safety

**prévenu, e** [prev(ə)ny] nm/f *(JUR)* defendant, accused

**prévision** [previzjɔ̃] nf: ~**s** predictions; *(ÉCON)* forecast sg; **en** ~ **de** in anticipation of; ~**s météorologiques** weather forecast sg

**prévoir** [prevwar] vt *(anticiper)* to foresee; *(s'attendre à)* to expect, reckon on; *(organiser: voyage etc)* to plan; *(envisager)* to allow; **comme prévu** as

planned; **prévoyant, e** adj gifted with *(ou showing)* foresight; **prévu, e**, pp de **prévoir**

**prier** [prije] vi to pray ♦ vt *(Dieu)* to pray to; *(implorer)* to beg; *(demander):* ~ **qn de faire** to ask sb to do; **se faire** ~ to need coaxing ou persuading; **je vous en prie** *(allez-y)* please do; *(de rien)* don't mention it; **prière** nf prayer; **"prière de ..."** "please ..."

**primaire** [primɛr] adj primary ♦ nm *(SCOL)* primary education

**prime** [prim] nf *(bonus)* bonus; *(subvention)* premium; *(COMM: cadeau)* free gift; *(ASSURANCES, BOURSE)* premium ♦ adj: **de** ~ **abord** at first glance; **primer** vt *(récompenser)* to award a prize to ♦ vi to dominate; to be most important

**primeurs** [primœr] nfpl early fruits and vegetables

**primevère** [primvɛr] nf primrose

**primitif, -ive** [primitif, iv] adj primitive; *(originel)* original

**primordial, e, -iaux** [primɔrdjal, jo] adj essential

**prince** [prɛ̃s] nm prince; **princesse** nf princess

**principal, e, -aux** [prɛ̃sipal, o] adj principal, main ♦ nm *(SCOL)* principal, head(master); *(essentiel)* main thing

**principe** [prɛ̃sip] nm principle; **par** ~ on principle; **en** ~ *(habituellement)* as a rule; *(théoriquement)* in principle

**printemps** [prɛ̃tɑ̃] nm spring

**priorité** [prijɔrite] nf priority; *(AUTO)* right of way; ~ **à droite** right of way to vehicles coming from the right

**pris, e** [pri, priz] pp de **prendre** ♦ adj *(place)* taken; *(mains)* full; *(personne)* busy; **avoir le nez/la gorge** ~**(e)** to have a stuffy nose/a hoarse throat; **être** ~ **de panique** to be panic-stricken

**prise** [priz] nf *(d'une ville)* capture; *(PÊCHE, CHASSE)* catch; *(point d'appui ou pour empoigner)* hold; *(ÉLEC: fiche)* plug; *(: femelle)* socket; **être aux** ~**s avec** to be grappling with; ~ **de conscience**

# priser 223 profond

**priser** [prize] *vt* (*estimer*) to prize, value

**prison** [prizɔ̃] *nf* prison; **aller/être en ~** to go to/be in prison *ou* jail; **prisonnier, -ière** *nm/f* prisoner ♦ *adj* captive

**prit** [pri] *vb voir* **prendre**

**privé, e** [prive] *adj* private ♦ *nm* (COMM) private sector; **en ~** in private

**priver** [prive] *vt*: **~ qn de** to deprive sb of; **se ~ de** to go *ou* do without

**privilège** [privilɛʒ] *nm* privilege

**prix** [pri] *nm* price; (*récompense, SCOL*) prize; **hors de ~** exorbitantly priced; **à aucun ~** not at any price; **à tout ~** at all costs; **~ d'achat/de vente/de revient** purchasing/selling/cost price

**probable** [prɔbabl] *adj* likely, probable; **probablement** *adv* probably

**probant, e** [prɔbɑ̃, ɑ̃t] *adj* convincing

**problème** [prɔblɛm] *nm* problem

**procédé** [prɔsede] *nm* (*méthode*) process; (*comportement*) behaviour *no pl*

**procéder** [prɔsede] *vi* to proceed; (*moralement*) to behave; **~ à** to carry out

**procès** [prɔsɛ] *nm* trial; (*poursuites*) proceedings *pl*; **être en ~ avec** to be involved in a lawsuit with

**processus** [prɔsesys] *nm* process

**procès-verbal, -aux** [prɔsɛverbal, o] *nm* (*de réunion*) minutes *pl*; (*aussi*: **P.V.**) parking ticket

**prochain, e** [prɔʃɛ̃, ɛn] *adj* next; (*proche: départ, arrivée*) impending ♦ *nm* fellow man; **la ~e fois/semaine** ~e next time/week; **prochainement** *adv* soon, shortly

**proche** [prɔʃ] *adj* nearby; (*dans le temps*) imminent; (*parent, ami*) close; **~s** *nmpl* (*parents*) close relatives; **être ~ (de)** to be near, be close (to); **le P~-Orient** the Middle East

**proclamer** [prɔklame] *vt* to proclaim

**procuration** [prɔkyrasjɔ̃] *nf* proxy

**procurer** [prɔkyre] *vt*: **~ qch à qn** (*fournir*) to obtain sth for sb; (*causer: plaisir etc*) to bring sb sth; **se ~** *vt* to get; **procureur** *nm* public prosecutor

**prodige** [prɔdiʒ] *nm* marvel, wonder; (*personne*) prodigy; **prodiguer** *vt* (*soins, attentions*): **prodiguer qch à qn** to give sb sth

**producteur, -trice** [prɔdyktœr, tris] *nm/f* producer

**productif, -ive** [prɔdyktif, iv] *adj* productive

**production** [prɔdyksjɔ̃] *nf* production; (*rendement*) output

**productivité** [prɔdyktivite] *nf* productivity

**produire** [prɔdɥir] *vt* to produce; **se ~** *vi* (*événement*) to happen, occur; (*acteur*) to perform, appear

**produit** [prɔdɥi] *nm* product; **~ chimique** chemical; **~ d'entretien** cleaning product; **~ national brut** gross national product; **~s alimentaires** foodstuffs

**prof** [prɔf] (*fam*) *nm* teacher

**profane** [prɔfan] *adj* (REL) secular ♦ *nm/f* layman(-woman)

**proférer** [prɔfere] *vt* to utter

**professeur** [prɔfesœr] *nm* teacher; (*de faculté*) (university) lecturer; (: *titulaire d'une chaire*) professor

**profession** [prɔfesjɔ̃] *nf* occupation; **~ libérale** (liberal) profession; **sans ~** unemployed; **professionnel, le** *adj*, *nm/f* professional

**profil** [prɔfil] *nm* profile; **de ~** in profile

**profit** [prɔfi] *nm* (*avantage*) benefit, advantage; (COMM, FINANCE) profit; **au ~ de** in aid of; **tirer ~ de** to profit from; **profitable** *adj* (*utile*) beneficial; (*lucratif*) profitable; **profiter** *vi*: **profiter de** (*situation, occasion*) to take advantage of; (*vacances, jeunesse etc*) to make the most of

**profond, e** [prɔfɔ̃, ɔ̃d] *adj* deep; (*senti-*

ment, *intérêt*) profound; **profondément** *adv* deeply; **il dort profondément** he is sound asleep; **profondeur** *nf* depth

**progéniture** [prɔʒenityr] *nf* offspring *inv*

**programme** [prɔgram] *nm* programme; (*SCOL*) syllabus, curriculum; (*INFORM*) program; **programmer** *vt* (*émission*) to schedule; (*INFORM*) to program; **programmeur, -euse** *nm/f* programmer

**progrès** [prɔgrɛ] *nm* progress *no pl*; **faire des ~** to make progress; **progresser** *vi* to progress; **progressif, -ive** *adj* progressive

**prohiber** [prɔibe] *vt* to prohibit, ban

**proie** [prwa] *nf* prey *no pl*

**projecteur** [prɔʒɛktœr] *nm* (*pour film*) projector; (*de théâtre, cirque*) spotlight

**projectile** [prɔʒɛktil] *nm* missile

**projection** [prɔʒɛksjɔ̃] *nf* projection; (*séance*) showing

**projet** [prɔʒɛ] *nm* plan; (*ébauche*) draft; **~ de loi** bill; **projeter** *vt* (*envisager*) to plan; (*film, photos*) to project; (*ombre, lueur*) to throw, cast; (*jeter*) to throw up (*ou* off *ou* out)

**prolétaire** [prɔleter] *adj, nmf* proletarian

**prolongement** [prɔlɔ̃ʒmɑ̃] *nm* extension; **dans le ~ de** running on from

**prolonger** [prɔlɔ̃ʒe] *vt* (*débat, séjour*) to prolong; (*délai, billet, rue*) to extend; **se ~** *vi* to go on

**promenade** [prɔm(ə)nad] *nf* walk (*ou* drive *ou* ride); **faire une ~** to go for a walk; **une ~ en voiture/à vélo** a drive/(bicycle) ride

**promener** [prɔm(ə)ne] *vt* (*chien*) to take out for a walk; (*doigts, regard*): **~ qch sur** to run sth over; **se ~** *vi* to go for (*ou* be out for) a walk

**promesse** [prɔmɛs] *nf* promise

**promettre** [prɔmɛtr] *vt* to promise ♦ *vi* to be *ou* look promising; **~ à qn de faire** to promise sb that one will do

**promiscuité** [prɔmiskɥite] *nf* (*chambre*) lack of privacy

**promontoire** [prɔmɔ̃twar] *nm* headland

**promoteur, -trice** [prɔmɔtœr, tris] *nm/f*: **~ (immobilier)** property developer (*BRIT*), real estate promoter (*US*)

**promotion** [prɔmosjɔ̃] *nf* promotion; **en ~** on special offer

**promouvoir** [prɔmuvwar] *vt* to promote

**prompt, e** [prɔ̃(pt), prɔ̃(p)t] *adj* swift, rapid

**prôner** [prone] *vt* (*préconiser*) to advocate

**pronom** [prɔnɔ̃] *nm* pronoun

**prononcer** [prɔnɔ̃se] *vt* to pronounce; (*dire*) to utter; (*discours*) to deliver; **se ~** *vi* to be pronounced; **se ~ (sur)** (*se décider*) to reach a decision (*ou* on about), give a verdict (*on*); **prononciation** *nf* pronunciation

**pronostic** [prɔnɔstik] *nm* (*MÉD*) prognosis; (*fig: aussi:* **~s**) forecast

**propagande** [prɔpagɑ̃d] *nf* propaganda

**propager** [prɔpaʒe] *vt* to spread; **se ~** *vi* to spread

**prophète** [prɔfɛt] *nm* prophet

**prophétie** [prɔfesi] *nf* prophecy

**propice** [prɔpis] *adj* favourable

**proportion** [prɔpɔrsjɔ̃] *nf* proportion; **toute(s) ~(s) gardée(s)** making due allowance(s)

**propos** [prɔpo] *nm* (*intention*) intention, aim; (*sujet*): **à quel ~** what about? ♦ *nmpl* (*paroles*) talk *no pl*, remarks; **à ~ de** about, regarding; **à tout ~** for the slightest thing *ou* reason; **à ~** by the way; (*opportunément*) at the right moment

**proposer** [prɔpoze] *vt* to propose; **~ qch (à qn)** (*suggérer*) to suggest sth (to sb), propose sth (to sb); (*offrir*) to offer (sb) sth; **se ~** to offer one's services; **se ~ de faire** to intend *ou* propose to do; **proposition** (*suggestion*) *nf* proposal, suggestion; (*LING*) clause

**propre** [prɔpr] *adj* clean; (*net*) neat,
tidy; (*possessif*) own; (*sens*) literal; (*particulier*): **à** peculiar to; (*approprié*):
**à** suitable for ♦ *nm*: **recopier au ~** to
make a fair copy of; **proprement** *adv*
(*avec propreté*) cleanly; **le village proprement dit** the village itself; **à proprement parler** strictly speaking; **propreté** *nf* cleanliness

**propriétaire** [prɔprijetɛr] *nm/f* owner;
(*pour le locataire*) landlord(-lady)

**propriété** [prɔprijete] *nf* property;
(*droit*) ownership

**propulser** [prɔpylse] *vt* to propel

**proroger** [prɔrɔʒe] *vt* (*prolonger*) to
extend

**proscrire** [prɔskrir] *vt* (*interdire*) to
ban, prohibit

**prose** [proz] *nf* (*style*) prose

**prospecter** [prɔspɛkte] *vt* to prospect;
(*COMM*) to canvass

**prospectus** [prɔspɛktys] *nm* leaflet

**prospère** [prɔspɛr] *adj* prosperous;
**prospérer** *vi* to prosper

**prosterner** [prɔstɛrne]: **se ~** *vi* to
bow low, prostrate o.s.

**prostituée** [prɔstitɥe] *nf* prostitute

**prostitution** [prɔstitysjɔ̃] *nf* prostitution

**protecteur, -trice** [prɔtɛktœr, tris]
*adj* protective; (*air, ton: péj*) patronizing
♦ *nm/f* protector

**protection** [prɔtɛksjɔ̃] *nf* protection;
(*d'un personnage influent: aide*) patronage

**protéger** [prɔteʒe] *vt* to protect; **se ~
de** *ou* **contre** to protect o.s. from

**protéine** [prɔtein] *nf* protein

**protestant, e** [prɔtɛstɑ̃, ɑ̃t] *adj, nm/f*
Protestant

**protestation** [prɔtɛstasjɔ̃] *nf* (*plainte*)
protest

**protester** [prɔtɛste] *vi*: **~ (contre)** to
protest (against *ou* about); **~ de** (*son innocence*) to protest

**prothèse** [prɔtɛz] *nf*: **~ dentaire** denture

**protocole** [prɔtɔkɔl] *nm* (*fig*) etiquette

**proue** [pru] *nf* bow(s *pl*), prow

**prouesse** [prues] *nf* feat

**prouver** [pruve] *vt* to prove

**provenance** [prɔv(ə)nɑ̃s] *nf* origin;
**avion en ~ de** plane (arriving) from

**provenir** [prɔv(ə)nir]: **~ de** *vt* to come
from

**proverbe** [prɔvɛrb] *nm* proverb

**province** [prɔvɛ̃s] *nf* province

**proviseur** [prɔvizœr] *nm* ≈
head(teacher) (*BRIT*), ≈ principal (*US*)

**provision** [prɔvizjɔ̃] *nf* (*réserve*) stock,
supply; **~s** *nfpl* (*vivres*) provisions, food
*no pl*

**provisoire** [prɔvizwar] *adj* temporary;
**provisoirement** *adv* temporarily

**provocant, e** [prɔvɔkɑ̃, ɑ̃t] *adj* provocative

**provoquer** [prɔvɔke] *vt* (*défier*) to provoke; (*causer*) to cause, bring about;
(*inciter*): **~ qn à** to incite sb to

**proxénète** [prɔksenɛt] *nm* procurer

**proximité** [prɔksimite] *nf* nearness,
closeness; (*dans le temps*) imminence,
closeness; **à ~** near *ou* close by; **à ~ de**
near (to), close to

**prudemment** [prydamɑ̃] *adv* carefully; wisely, sensibly

**prudence** [prydɑ̃s] *nf* carefulness;
**avec ~** carefully; **par ~** as a precaution

**prudent, e** [prydɑ̃, ɑ̃t] *adj* (*pas téméraire*) careful; (: *en général*) safety-conscious; (*sage, conseillé*) wise, sensible; **c'est plus ~** it's wiser

**prune** [pryn] *nf* plum

**pruneau, x** [pryno] *nm* prune

**prunelle** [prynɛl] *nf* (*BOT*) sloe; **il y
tient comme à la ~ de ses yeux** he
treasures *ou* cherishes it

**prunier** [prynje] *nm* plum tree

**PS** *sigle m* = **parti socialiste**

**psaume** [psom] *nm* psalm

**pseudonyme** [psødɔnim] *nm* (*gén*)
fictitious name; (*d'écrivain*) pseudonym,

pen name

**psychanalyse** [psikanaliz] *nf* psycho-analysis

**psychiatre** [psikjatʀ] *nm/f* psychiatrist; **psychiatrique** *adj* psychiatric

**psychique** [psiʃik] *adj* psychological

**psychologie** [psikɔlɔʒi] *nf* psychology; **psychologique** *adj* psychological; **psychologue** *nm/f* psychologist

**P.T.T.** *sigle fpl* = **Postes, Télécommunications et Télédiffusion**

**pu** [py] *pp de* **pouvoir**

**puanteur** [pɥɑ̃tœʀ] *nf* stink, stench

**pub** [pyb] *nf* (*fam: annonce*) ad, advert; (*pratique*) advertising

**public, -ique** [pyblik] *adj* public; (*école, instruction*) state *cpd* ♦ *nm* public; (*assistance*) audience; **en ~** in public

**publicitaire** [pyblisitɛʀ] *adj* advertising *cpd*; (*film*) publicity *cpd*

**publicité** [pyblisite] *nf* (*méthode, profession*) advertising; (*annonce*) advertisement; (*révélations*) publicity

**publier** [pyblije] *vt* to publish

**publique** [pyblik] *adj voir* **public**

**puce** [pys] *nf* flea; (*INFORM*) chip; **carte à ~** smart card; **~s** *nfpl* (*marché*) flea market *sg*

**pudeur** [pydœʀ] *nf* modesty; **pudique** *adj* (*chaste*) modest; (*discret*) discreet

**puer** [pɥe] (*péj*) *vi* to stink

**puériculture** [pɥeʀikyltʀis] *nf* p(a)ediatric nurse

**puéril, e** [pɥeʀil] *adj* childish

**puis** [pɥi] *vb voir* **pouvoir** ♦ *adv* then

**puiser** [pɥize] *vt*: **~ (dans)** to draw (from)

**puisque** [pɥisk] *conj* since

**puissance** [pɥisɑ̃s] *nf* power; **en ~** *adj* potential

**puissant, e** [pɥisɑ̃, ɑ̃t] *adj* powerful

**puisse** *etc* [pɥis] *vb voir* **pouvoir**

**puits** [pɥi] *nm* well

**pull(-over)** [pyl(ɔvɛʀ)] *nm* sweater

**pulluler** [pylyle] *vi* to swarm

**pulpe** [pylp] *nf* pulp

**pulvérisateur** [pylveʀizatœʀ] *nm*

spray

**pulvériser** [pylveʀize] *vt* to pulverize; (*liquide*) to spray

**punaise** [pynɛz] *nf* (*ZOOL*) bug; (*clou*) drawing pin (*BRIT*), thumbtack (*US*)

**punch¹** [pɔ̃ʃ] *nm* (*boisson*) punch

**punch²** [pœnʃ] *nm* (*BOXE, fig*) punch

**punir** [pyniʀ] *vt* to punish; **punition** *nf* punishment

**pupille** [pypij] *nf* (*ANAT*) pupil ♦ *nm/f* (*enfant*) ward

**pupitre** [pypitʀ] *nm* (*SCOL*) desk

**pur, e** [pyʀ] *adj* pure; (*vin*) undiluted; (*whisky*) neat; **en ~e perte** to no avail; **c'est de la folie ~e** it's sheer madness; **purement** *adv* purely

**purée** [pyʀe] *nf*: **~ (de pommes de terre)** mashed potatoes *pl*; **~ de marrons** chestnut purée

**purgatoire** [pyʀgatwaʀ] *nm* purgatory

**purger** [pyʀʒe] *vt* (*MÉD, POL*) to purge; (*JUR: peine*) to serve

**purin** [pyʀɛ̃] *nm* liquid manure

**pur-sang** [pyʀsɑ̃] *nm inv* thoroughbred

**pus** [py] *nm* pus

**putain** [pytɛ̃] (*fam!*) *nf* whore (!)

**puzzle** [pœzl] *nm* jigsaw (puzzle)

**P.-V.** *sigle m* = **procès-verbal**

**pyjama** [piʒama] *nm* pyjamas *pl* (*BRIT*), pajamas *pl* (*US*)

**pyramide** [piʀamid] *nf* pyramid

**Pyrénées** [piʀene] *nfpl*: **les ~** the Pyrenees

## Q, q

**QI** *sigle m* (= *quotient intellectuel*) IQ

**quadragénaire** [k(w)adʀaʒenɛʀ] *nm/f* man/woman in his/her forties

**quadriller** [kadʀije] *vt* (*POLICE*) to keep under tight control

**quadruple** [k(w)adʀypl] *nm*: **le ~ de** four times as much as; **quadruplés, -ées** *nm/fpl* quadruplets, quads

**quai** [ke] *nm* (*de port*) quay; (*de gare*) platform; **être à ~** (*navire*) to be alongside

**qualification** [kalifikasjɔ̃] nf (aptitude) qualification

**qualifié, e** [kalifje] adj qualified; (main d'œuvre) skilled

**qualifier** [kalifje] vt to qualify; **se ~** vi to qualify; **~ qch/qn de** to describe sth/sb as

**qualité** [kalite] nf quality

**quand** [kɑ̃] conj, adv when; **~ je serai riche** when I'm rich; **~ même** all the same; **~ même, il exagère!** really, he overdoes it!; **~ bien même** even though

**quant** [kɑ̃]: **~ à** prép (pour ce qui est de) as for, as to; (au sujet de) regarding; **quant-à-soi** nm: **rester sur son quant-à-soi** to remain aloof

**quantité** [kɑ̃tite] nf quantity, amount; (grand nombre): **une ou des ~(s) de** a great deal of

**quarantaine** [karɑ̃tɛn] nf (MÉD) quarantine; **avoir la ~** (âge) to be around forty; **une ~ (de)** forty or so, about forty

**quarante** [karɑ̃t] num forty

**quart** [kar] nm (fraction) quarter; (surveillance) watch; **un ~ de vin** a quarter litre of wine; **le ~ de** a quarter of; **~ d'heure** quarter of an hour; **~s de finale** quarter finals

**quartier** [kartje] nm (de ville) district, area; (de bœuf) quarter; (de fruit) piece; **cinéma de ~** local cinema; **avoir ~ libre** (fig) to be free; **~ général** headquarters pl

**quartz** [kwarts] nm quartz

**quasi** [kazi] adv almost, nearly; **quasiment** adv almost, nearly; **quasiment jamais** hardly ever

**quatorze** [katɔrz] num fourteen

**quatre** [katr] num four; **à ~ pattes** on all fours; **se mettre en ~ pour qn** to go out of one's way for sb; **~ à ~** (monter, descendre) four at a time; **quatre-quarts** nm inv pound cake; **quatre-vingt-dix** num ninety;

**quatre-vingts** num eighty; **quatre-vingt-un** num eighty-one; **quatrième** num fourth ♦ nf (SCOL) third form ou year

**quatuor** [kwatɥɔr] nm quartet(te)

─────────────
**MOT-CLÉ**
─────────────

**que** [kə] conj 1 (introduisant complétive) that; **il sait que tu es là** he knows (that) you're here; **je veux que tu acceptes** I want you to accept; **il a dit que oui** he said he would (ou it was) yes

2 (reprise d'autres conjonctions): **quand il rentrera et qu'il aura mangé** when he gets back and (when) he has eaten; **si vous y allez ou que vous ...** if you go there or if you ...

3 (en tête de phrase: hypothèse, souhait etc): **qu'il le veuille ou non** whether he likes it or not; **qu'il fasse ce qu'il voudra!** let him do as he pleases!

4 (après comparatif) than, as; voir aussi **plus; aussi; autant** etc

5 (seulement): **ne ... que** only; **il ne boit que de l'eau** he only drinks water

♦ adv (exclamation): **qu'il ou qu'est-ce qu'il est bête/court vite!** he's so silly/he runs so fast!; **que de livres!** what a lot of books!

♦ pron 1 (relatif: personne) whom; (: chose) that, which; **l'homme que je vois** the man (whom) I see; **le livre que tu vois** the book (that ou which) you see; **un jour que j'étais ...** a day when I was ...

2 (interrogatif) what; **que fais-tu?, qu'est-ce que tu fais?** what are you doing?; **qu'est-ce que c'est?** what is it?, what's that?; **que faire?** what can one do?

**Québec** [kebɛk] n: **le ~** Québec; **québecois; a** adj Québec ♦ nm/f: **Québecois, e** Quebecker ♦ nm (LING) Quebec French

---
**MOT-CLÉ**
---

**quel, quelle** [kɛl] *adj* **1** (*interrogatif: personne*) who; (: *chose*) what; which; **quei est cet homme?** who is this man?; **quel est ce livre?** what is this book?; **quel livre/homme?** what book/man?; (*parmi un certain choix*) which book/man?; **quels acteurs préférez-vous?** which actors do you prefer?; **dans quels pays êtes-vous allé?** which *ou* what countries did you go to?

**2** (*exclamatif*): **quelle surprise!** what a surprise!

**3**: **quel que soit le coupable** whoever is guilty; **quel que soit votre avis** whatever your opinion

---

**quelconque** [kɛlkɔ̃k] *adj* (*indéfini*): **un ami/prétexte ~** some friend/pretext or other; (*médiocre: repas*) indifferent, poor; (*laid: personne*) plain-looking

---
**MOT-CLÉ**
---

**quelque** [kɛlk] *adj* **1** some; a few; (*tournure interrogative*) any; **quelque espoir** some hope; **il a quelques amis** he has a few *ou* some friends; **a-t-il quelques amis?** has he any friends?; **les quelques livres qui** the few books which; **20 kg et quelque(s)** a bit over 20 kg

**2**: **quelque ... que**: **quelque livre qu'il choisisse** whatever (*ou* whichever) book he chooses

**3**: **quelque chose** something; (*tournure interrogative*) anything; **quelque chose d'autre** something else; anything else; **quelque part** somewhere; anywhere; **en quelque sorte** as it were

♦ *adv* **1** (*environ*): **quelque 100 mètres** some 100 metres

**2**: **quelque peu** rather, somewhat

**quelquefois** [kɛlkəfwa] *adv* sometimes
**quelques-uns, -unes** [kɛlkəzœ̃, yn]

*pron* a few, some

**quelqu'un** [kɛlkœ̃] *pron* someone, somebody; (*+tournure interrogative*) anyone, anybody; **~ d'autre** someone *ou* somebody else; (*+ tournure interrogative*) anybody else

**quémander** [kemɑ̃de] *vt* to beg for
**qu'en dira-t-on** [kɑ̃diratɔ̃] *nm inv*: **le ~ ~-~** gossip, what people say
**querelle** [kaʀɛl] *nf* quarrel; **quereller: se quereller** *vi* to quarrel
**qu'est-ce que** [kɛskə] *voir* **que**
**qu'est-ce qui** [kɛski] *voir* **qui**
**question** [kɛstjɔ̃] *nf* question; (*fig*) matter, issue; **il a été ~ de** we (*ou* they) spoke about; **de quoi est-il ~?** what is it about?; **il n'en est pas ~** there's no question of it; **hors de ~** out of the question; **remettre en ~** to question; **questionnaire** *nm* questionnaire; **questionner** *vt* to question
**quête** [kɛt] *nf* collection; (*recherche*) quest, search; **faire la ~** (*à l'église*) to take the collection; (*artiste*) to pass the hat round
**quetsche** [kwɛtʃ] *nf* kind of dark-red plum
**queue** [kø] *nf* tail; (*fig: du classement*) bottom; (: *de poêle*) handle; (: *de fruit, feuille*) stalk; (: *de train, colonne, file*) rear; **faire la ~** to queue (up) (BRIT), line up (US); **~ de cheval** ponytail; **~ de poisson** (AUT): **faire une ~ de poisson à qn** to cut in front of sb
**qui** [ki] *pron* (*personne*) who; (*+prép*) whom; (*chose, animal*) which, that; **qu'est-ce ~ est sur la table?** what is on the table?; **~ est-ce ~?** who?; **~ est-ce que?** who?; **à ~ est ce sac?** whose bag is this?; **à ~ parlais-tu?** who were you talking to?, to whom were you talking?; **amenez ~ vous voulez** bring who you like; **~ que ce soit** whoever it may be
**quiconque** [kikɔ̃k] *pron* (*celui qui*) whoever, anyone who; (*n'importe qui*) anyone, anybody

**quiétude** [kjetyd] nf: **en toute ~** in complete peace

**quille** [kij] nf: **(jeu de) ~s** skittles sg (BRIT), bowling (US)

**quincaillerie** [kɛ̃kajʀi] nf (ustensiles) hardware; (magasin) hardware shop; **quincaillier, -ière** nm/f hardware dealer

**quinquagénaire** [kɛ̃kaʒenɛʀ] nm/f man/woman in his/her fifties

**quintal, -aux** [kɛ̃tal, o] nm quintal (100 kg)

**quinte** [kɛ̃t] nf (de toux) coughing fit

**quintuple** [kɛ̃typl] nm: **le ~ de** five times as much as; **quintuplés, -ées** nm/fpl quintuplets, quins

**quinzaine** [kɛ̃zɛn] nf: **une ~ (de)** about fifteen, fifteen or so; **une ~ (de jours)** a fortnight, two weeks

**quinze** [kɛ̃z] num fifteen; **dans ~ jours** in a fortnight('s time), in two weeks('(time)

**quiproquo** [kipʀɔko] nm misunderstanding

**quittance** [kitɑ̃s] nf (reçu) receipt

**quitte** [kit] adj: **être ~ envers qn** to no longer be in sb's debt; (fig) to be quits with sb; **~ à faire** even if it means doing

**quitter** [kite] vt to leave; (vêtement) to take off; **se ~** vi (couples, interlocuteurs) to part; **ne quittez pas** (au téléphone) hold the line

**qui-vive** [kiviv] nm: **être sur le ~~** to be on the alert

**quoi** [kwa] pron (interrogatif) what; **~ de neuf?** what's the news?; **as-tu de quoi écrire** have you anything to write with?; **~ qu'il arrive** whatever happens; **~ qu'il en soit** be that as it may; **~ que ce soit** anything at all; **il n'y a pas de ~** "(please) don't mention it"; **il n'y a pas de ~ rire** there's nothing to laugh about; **à ~ bon?** what's the use?; **en ~ puis-je vous aider?** how can I help you?

**quoique** [kwak] conj (al)though

**quote-part** [kɔtpaʀ] nf share

**quotidien, ne** [kɔtidjɛ̃, jɛn] adj daily; (banal) everyday ♦ nm (journal) daily (paper); **quotidiennement** adv daily

# R, r

**r.** abr = route; rue

**rab** [ʀab] (fam) nm (nourriture) extra; **est-ce qu'il y a du ~?** is there any extra (left)?

**rabâcher** [ʀabaʃe] vt to keep on repeating

**rabais** [ʀabɛ] nm reduction, discount; **rabaisser** vt (dénigrer) to belittle; (ra-battre: prix) to reduce

**rabat-joie** [ʀabaʒwa] nm inv killjoy

**rabattre** [ʀabatʀ] vt (couvercle, siège) to pull down; (déduire) to reduce; **se ~** vi (se refermer: couvercle) to fall shut; (vé-hicule, coureur) to cut in; **se ~ sur** to fall back on

**rabbin** [ʀabɛ̃] nm rabbi

**râblé, e** [ʀɑble] adj stocky

**rabot** [ʀabo] nm plane

**rabougri, e** [ʀabugʀi] adj stunted

**rabrouer** [ʀabʀue] vt to snub

**racaille** [ʀakaj] (péj) nf rabble, riffraff

**raccommoder** [ʀakɔmɔde] vt to mend, repair; **se ~** vi (fam) to make it up

**raccompagner** [ʀakɔ̃paɲe] vt to take ou see back

**raccord** [ʀakɔʀ] nm link; (retouche) touch up; **raccorder** vt to join (up), link up; (suj: pont etc) to connect, link

**raccourci** [ʀakuʀsi] nm short cut

**raccourcir** [ʀakuʀsiʀ] vt to shorten ♦ vi (jours) to grow shorter, draw in

**raccrocher** [ʀakʀɔʃe] vt (tableau) to hang back up; (récepteur) to put down ♦ vi (au tél) to hang up, ring off; **se ~** vi à vt to cling to, hang on to

**race** [ʀas] nf race; (d'animaux, fig) breed; **de ~** purebred, pedigree

**rachat** [Raʃa] nm buying; (du même objet) buying back

**racheter** [Raʃ(ə)te] vt (article perdu) to buy another; (après avoir vendu) to buy back; (d'occasion) to buy; (COMM: part, firme) to buy up; (davantage): **~ du lait/3 œufs** to buy more milk/another 3 eggs ou 3 more eggs; **se ~** vi (fig) to make amends

**racial, e, -aux** [Rasjal, jo] adj racial

**racine** [Rasin] nf root; **~ carrée/cubique** square/cube root

**raciste** [Rasist] adj, nm/f raci(al)ist

**racket** [Raket] nm racketeering no pl

**raclée** [Rɑkle] (fam) nf hiding, thrashing

**racler** [Rɑkle] vt (gratter) to scrape; **se ~ la gorge** to clear one's throat

**racoler** [Rɑkɔle] vt (suj: prostituée) to solicit; (: parti, marchand) to tout for

**racontars** [Rɑkɔ̃taR] nmpl story, lie

**raconter** [Rɑkɔ̃te] vt: **~ (à qn)** (décrire) to relate (to sb), tell (sb) about; (dire de mauvaise foi) to tell (sb); **~ une histoire** to tell a story

**racornir** [RɑkɔRniR] adj hard(ened)

**radar** [RadaR] nm radar

**rade** [Rad] nf (natural) harbour; **rester en ~** (fig) to be left stranded

**radeau, x** [Rado] nm raft

**radiateur** [RadjatœR] nm radiator, heater; (AUTO) radiator; **~ électrique/à gaz** electric/gas heater ou fire

**radiation** [Radjasjɔ̃] nf (PHYSIQUE) radiation

**radical, e, -aux** [Radikal, o] adj radical

**radier** [Radje] vt to strike off

**radieux, -euse** [Radjø, jøz] adj radiant

**radin, e** [Radɛ̃, in] (fam) adj stingy

**radio** [Radjo] nf radio; (MÉD) X-ray ♦ nm radio operator; **à la ~** on the radio; **radioactif, -ive** adj radioactive; **radio-cassette** nf cassette radio, radio cassette player; **radiodiffuser** vt to broadcast; **radiographie** nf radiography; (photo) X-ray photograph; **radiophonique** adj radio cpd; **radio-réveil** (pl

**radios-réveils**) nm radio alarm clock

**radis** [Radi] nm radish

**radoter** [Radɔte] vi to ramble on

**radoucir** [RadusiR]: **se ~** vi (temps) to become milder; (: se calmer) to calm down

**rafale** [Rafal] nf (vent) gust of wind); (tir) burst of gunfire

**raffermir** [RafɛRmiR] vt to firm up; **se ~** vi (fig: autorité, prix) to strengthen

**raffiner** [Rafine] vt to refine; **raffinerie** nf refinery

**raffoler** [Rafɔle]: **~ de** vt to be very keen on

**rafistoler** [Rafistɔle] (fam) vt to patch up

**rafle** [Rafl] nf (de police) raid; **rafler** (fam) vt to swipe, nick

**rafraîchir** [RafReʃiR] vt (atmosphère, température) to cool (down); (aussi: **mettre à ~**) to chill; (fig: rénover) to brighten up; **se ~** vi (temps) to grow cooler; (en se lavant) to freshen up; (en buvant) to refresh o.s.; **rafraîchissant, e** adj refreshing; **rafraîchissement** nm (boisson) cool drink; **rafraîchissements** nmpl (boissons, fruits etc) refreshments

**rage** [Raʒ] nf (MÉD): **la ~** rabies; (fureur) rage, fury; **faire ~** to rage; **~ de dents** (raging) toothache

**ragot** [Rago] nm (fam) malicious gossip no pl

**ragoût** [Ragu] nm stew

**raide** [Rɛd] adj stiff; (câble) taut, tight; (escarpé) steep; (droit: cheveux) straight; (fam: sans argent) flat broke; (osé) daring, bold ♦ adv (en pente) steeply; **~ mort** stone dead; **raidir** vt (muscles) to stiffen; **se raidir** vi (tissu) to stiffen; (personne) to tense up; (: se préparer moralement) to brace o.s.; (fig: position) to harden; **raideur** nf (rigidité) stiffness; **avec raideur** (répondre) stiffly, abruptly

**raie** [Rɛ] nf (ZOOL) skate, ray; (rayure) stripe; (des cheveux) parting

**raifort** [RefɔR] nm horseradish

**rail** [Raj] nm rail; (*chemins de fer*) railways pl; **par ~** by rail

**railler** [Raje] vt to scoff at, jeer at

**rainure** [RenyR] nf groove

**raisin** [Rezɛ̃] nm (aussi: **~s**) grapes pl; **~s secs** raisins

**raison** [Rezɔ̃] nf reason; **avoir ~** to be right; **donner ~ à qn** to agree with sb; (*événement*) to prove sb right; **perdre la ~** to become insane; **~ de plus** all the more reason; **à plus forte ~** all the more so; **en ~ de** because of; **à ~ de** at the rate of; **sans ~** for no real reason; **raisonnable** adj reasonable, sensible

**raisonnement** [Rezɔnmɑ̃] nm (*façon de réfléchir*) reasoning; (*argumentation*) argument

**raisonner** [Rezɔne] vi (*penser*) to reason; (*argumenter, discuter*) to argue ♦ vt (*personne*) to reason with

**rajeunir** [RaʒœniR] vt (suj: *coiffure, robe*): **~ qn** to make sb look younger; (*fig: personnel*) to inject new blood into ♦ vi to become (ou look) younger

**rajouter** [Raʒute] vt to add

**rajuster** [RaʒystE] vt (*vêtement*) to straighten, tidy; (*salaires*) to adjust

**ralenti** [Rɑ̃lɑ̃ti] nm: **au ~** (*fig*) at a slower pace; **tourner au ~** (AUTO) to tick over (AUTO), idle

**ralentir** [Rɑ̃lɑ̃tiR] vt to slow down

**râler** [Rɑle] vi to groan; (*fam*) to grouse, moan (and groan)

**rallier** [Ralje] vt (*rejoindre*) to rejoin; (*gagner à sa cause*) to win over; **se ~ à** (*avis*) to come over ou round to

**rallonge** [Ralɔ̃ʒ] nf (*de table*) (extra) leaf

**rallonger** [Ralɔ̃ʒe] vt to lengthen

**rallye** [Rali] nm rally; (POL) march

**ramassage** [Ramasaʒ] nm: **~ scolaire** school bus service

**ramassé, e** [Ramase] adj (*trapu*) squat

**ramasser** [Ramase] vt (*objet tombé ou par terre, fam*) to pick up; (*recueillir: copies, ordures*) to collect; (*récolter*) to

gather; **se ~** vi (*sur soi-même*) to huddle up; **ramassis** (*péj*) nm (*de voyous*) bunch; (*d'objets*) jumble

**rambarde** [Rɑ̃baRd] nf guardrail

**rame** [Ram] nf (*aviron*) oar; (*de métro*) train; (*de papier*) ream

**rameau, x** [Ramo] nm (small) branch; **les R~x** (REL) Palm Sunday sg

**ramener** [Ram(ə)ne] vt to bring back; (*reconduire*) to take back; **~ qch à** (*réduire à*) to reduce sth to

**ramer** [Rame] vi to row

**ramollir** [RamɔliR] vt to soften; **se ~** vi to go soft

**ramoner** [Ramone] vt to sweep

**rampe** [Rɑ̃p] nf (*d'escalier*) banister(s) pl; (*dans un garage*) ramp; (THÉÂTRE): **la ~** the footlights pl; **~ de lancement** launching pad

**ramper** [Rɑ̃pe] vi to crawl

**rancard** [Rɑ̃kaR] (fam) nm (*rendez-vous*) date

**rancart** [Rɑ̃kaR] nm: **mettre au ~** (fam) to scrap

**rance** [Rɑ̃s] adj rancid

**rancœur** [Rɑ̃kœR] nf rancour

**rançon** [Rɑ̃sɔ̃] nf ransom

**rancune** [Rɑ̃kyn] nf grudge, rancour; **garder à ~ à qn (de qch)** to bear sb a grudge (for sth); **sans ~!** no hard feelings!; **rancunier, -ière** adj vindictive, spiteful

**randonnée** [Rɑ̃dɔne] nf ride; (*pédestre*) walk, ramble; (: *en montagne*) hike, hiking no pl

**rang** [Rɑ̃] nm (*rangée*) row; (*grade, classement*) rank; **~s** nmpl (MIL) ranks; **se mettre en ~s** to get into ou form rows; **au premier ~** in the first row; (*fig*) ranking first

**rangé, e** [Rɑ̃ʒe] adj (*vie*) well-ordered; (*personne*) steady

**rangée** [Rɑ̃ʒe] nf row

**ranger** [Rɑ̃ʒe] vt (*mettre de l'ordre dans*) to tidy up; (*classer, grouper*) to order, arrange; (*mettre à sa place*) to put away; (*fig: classer*): **~ qn/qch parmi** to rank sb/sth among); **se ~** vi (véhicule, conducteur) to pull over ou in; (piéton) to step aside; (s'assagir) to settle down; **se ~ à** (avis) to come round to

**ranimer** [Ranime] vt (personne) to bring round; (débat, souvenir) to revive; (feu) to rekindle

**rap** [Rap] nm rap (music)

**rapace** [Rapas] nm bird of prey

**râpe** [Rɑp] nf (CULIN) grater; **râper** vt (CULIN) to grate

**rapetisser** [Rap(ə)tise] vt to shorten

**rapide** [Rapid] adj fast; (prompt: coup d'œil, mouvement) quick ♦ nm express (train); (de cours d'eau) rapid; **rapidement** adv fast; quickly

**rapiécer** [Rapjese] vt to patch

**rappel** [Rapel] nm (THÉÂTRE) curtain call; (MÉD: vaccination) booster; (deuxième avis) reminder; **rappeler** vt to call back; (ambassadeur, MIL) to recall; (faire se souvenir): **rappeler qch à qn** to remind sb of sth; **se rappeler** vt (se souvenir de) to remember, recall

**rapport** [Rapɔʀ] nm (lien, analogie) connection; (compte rendu) report; (profit) yield, return; **~s** nmpl (entre personnes, pays) relations; **avoir ~ à** to have something to do with; **être/se mettre en ~ avec qn** to be/get in touch with sb; **par ~ à** in relation to; **~s (sexuels)** (sexual) intercourse sg

**rapporter** [Rapɔʀte] vt (rendre, ramener) to bring back; (bénéfice) to yield, bring in; (mentionner, répéter) to report ♦ vi (investissement) to give a good return ou (: activité) to be very profitable; **se ~ à** (correspondre à) to relate to; **rapporteur, -euse** nm/f (péj) telltale ♦ nm (GÉOM) protractor

**rapprochement** [RapRɔʃmɑ̃] nm (de nations) reconciliation; (rapport) parallel

**rapprocher** [RapRɔʃe] vt (deux objets) to bring closer together; (fig: ennemis, partis etc) to bring together; (comparer) to establish a parallel between; (chaise d'une table): **~ qch (de)** to bring sth

closer (to); **se ~** vi to draw closer ou nearer; **se ~ de** to come closer to; (présenter une analogie avec) to be close to

**rapt** [Rapt] nm abduction

**raquette** [Raket] nf (de tennis) racket; (de ping-pong) bat

**rare** [RɑR] adj rare; **se faire ~** to become scarce; **rarement** adv rarely, seldom

**ras, e** [Rɑ, Rɑz] adj (poil, herbe) short; (tête) close-cropped ♦ adv short; **en ~ campagne** in open country; **à ~ bords** to the brim; **en avoir ~ le bol** (fam) to be fed up; **~ du cou** (pull, robe) crew-neck

**rasade** [Razad] nf glassful

**raser** [Raze] vt (barbe, cheveux) to shave off; (menton, personne) to shave; (fam: ennuyer) to bore; (démolir) to raze (to the ground); (frôler) to graze, skim; **se ~** to shave; (fam) to be bored ou (tears); **rasoir** nm razor

**rassasier** [Rasazje] vt: **être rassasié** to have eaten one's fill

**rassemblement** [Rasɑ̃bləmɑ̃] nm (groupe) gathering; (POL) union

**rassembler** [Rasɑ̃ble] vt (réunir) to assemble, gather; (documents, notes) to gather together, collect; **se ~** vi to gather

**rassis, e** [Rasi, iz] adj (pain) stale

**rassurer** [RasyRe] vt to reassure; **se ~** vi to reassure o.s.; **rassure-toi** don't worry

**rat** [Ra] nm rat

**raté, e** [Rate] adj (tentative) unsuccessful, failed ♦ nm/f (fam: personne) failure

**râteau, x** [Rɑto] nm rake

**rater** [Rate] vi (affaire, projet etc) to go wrong, fail ♦ vt (fam: cible, train, occasion) to miss; (plat) to spoil; (fam: examen) to fail

**ration** [Rasjɔ̃] nf ration

**ratisser** [Ratise] vt (allée) to rake; (feuilles) to rake up; (suj: armée, police) to comb

**RATP** sigle f (= Régie autonome des transports parisiens) Paris transport authority

**rattacher** [Rataʃe] vt (animal, cheveux) to tie up again; (fig: relier): ~ qch à to link sth with

**rattrapage** [Ratrapaʒ] nm: cours de ~ remedial class

**rattraper** [Ratrape] vt (fugitif) to recapture; (empêcher de tomber) to catch (hold of); (atteindre, rejoindre) to catch up with; (réparer: erreur) to make up for; se ~ to make up for it; se ~ (à) (se raccrocher) to stop o.s. falling (by catching hold of)

**rature** [Ratyr] nf deletion, erasure

**rauque** [Rok] adj (voix) hoarse

**ravages** [Ravaʒ] nmpl: faire des ~ to wreak havoc

**ravaler** [Ravale] vt (mur, façade) to restore; (déprécier) to lower

**ravi, e** [Ravi] adj: être ~ de/que to be delighted with/that

**ravigoter** [Ravigɔte] (fam) vt to buck up

**ravin** [Ravɛ̃] nm gully, ravine

**ravir** [Ravir] vt (enchanter) to delight; à ~ adv beautifully

**raviser** [Ravize]: se ~ vi to change one's mind

**ravissant, e** [Ravisɑ̃, ɑ̃t] adj delightful

**ravisseur, -euse** [Ravisœr, øz] nm/f abductor, kidnapper

**ravitaillement** [Ravitajmɑ̃] nm (réserves) supplies pl

**ravitailler** [Ravitaje] vt (en vivres, ammunitions) to provide with fresh supplies; (avion) to refuel; se ~ vi to get fresh supplies; (avion) to refuel

**raviver** [Ravive] vt (feu, douleur) to revive; (couleurs) to brighten up

**rayé, e** [Reje] adj (à rayures) striped

**rayer** [Reje] vt (érafler) to scratch; (barrer) to cross out; (d'une liste) to cross off

**rayon** [Rejɔ̃] nm (de soleil etc) ray; (GÉOM) radius; (de roue) spoke; (étagère)

shelf; (de grand magasin) department; dans un ~ de within a radius of; ~ de soleil sunbeam; ~s X X-rays

**rayonnement** [Rejɔnmɑ̃] nm (fig: d'une culture) influence

**rayonner** [Rejɔne] vi (fig) to shine forth; (personne: de joie, de beauté) to be radiant; (touriste) to go touring (from one base)

**rayure** [Rejyr] nf (motif) stripe; (éraflure) scratch; à ~s striped

**raz-de-marée** [Rɑdmare] nm inv tidal wave

**ré** [Re] nm (MUS) D; (en chantant la gamme) re

**réacteur** [Reaktœr] nm (d'avion) jet engine; (nucléaire) reactor

**réaction** [Reaksjɔ̃] nf reaction

**réadapter** [Readapte]: se ~ (à) vi to readjust (to)

**réagir** [Reaʒir] vi to react

**réalisateur, -trice** [Realizatœr, tris] nm/f (TV, CINÉMA) director

**réalisation** [Realizasjɔ̃] nf realization; (cinéma) production; en cours de ~ under way

**réaliser** [Realize] vt (projet, opération) to carry out, realize; (rêve, souhait) to realize, fulfil; (exploit) to achieve; (film) to produce; (se rendre compte de) to realize; se ~ vi to be realized

**réaliste** [Realist] adj realistic

**réalité** [Realite] nf reality; en ~ in (actual) fact; dans la ~ in reality

**réanimation** [Reanimasjɔ̃] nf resuscitation; service de ~ intensive care unit

**rébarbatif, -ive** [Rebarbatif, iv] adj forbidding

**rebattu, e** [R(ə)baty] adj hackneyed

**rebelle** [Rəbɛl] nm/f rebel ♦ adj (troupes) rebel; (enfant) rebellious; (mèche etc) unruly

**rebeller** [R(ə)bele]: se ~ vi to rebel

**rebondi, e** [R(ə)bɔ̃di] adj (joues) chubby

**rebondir** [R(ə)bɔ̃dir] vi (ballon: au sol) to bounce; (: contre un mur) to rebound; (fig) to get moving again; **re-bondissement** nm new development

**rebord** [R(ə)bɔR] nm edge; **le ~ de la fenêtre** the windowsill

**rebours** [R(ə)buR]: **à ~** adv the wrong way

**rebrousser** [R(ə)bRuse] vt: **~ chemin** to turn back

**rebut** [Rəby] nm: **mettre au ~** to scrap; **rebutant, e** adj off-putting; **rebuter** vt to put off

**récalcitrant, e** [RekalsitRã, ãt] adj refractory

**recaler** [R(ə)kale] vt (SCOL) to fail; **se faire ~** to fail

**récapituler** [Rekapityle] vt to recapitulate, sum up

**receler** [R(ə)səle] vt (produit d'un vol) to receive; (fig) to conceal; **receleur, -euse** nm/f receiver

**récemment** [Resamã] adv recently

**recensement** [R(ə)sãsmã] nm (population) census

**recenser** [R(ə)sãse] vt (population) to take a census of; (inventorier) to list

**récent, e** [Resã, ãt] adj recent

**récépissé** [Resepise] nm receipt

**récepteur** [ReseptœR, tRis] nm receiver

**réception** [Resepsjɔ̃] nf receiving no pl; (accueil) reception, welcome; (bureau) reception desk; (réunion mondaine) reception, party; **réceptionniste** nm/f receptionist

**recette** [R(ə)sɛt] nf recipe; (COMM) takings pl; **~s** nfpl (COMM: rentrées) receipts

**receveur, -euse** [R(ə)savœR, øz] nm/f (des contributions) tax collector; (des postes) postmaster(-mistress)

**recevoir** [R(ə)savwaR] vt to receive; (client, patient) to see; **être reçu (à un examen)** to pass

**rechange** [R(ə)ʃãʒ]: **de ~** adj (pièces, roue) spare; (fig: solution) alternative; **des vêtements de ~** a change of clothes

**réchapper** [Reʃape]: **~ de** ou **à** vt (accident, maladie) to come through

**recharge** [R(ə)ʃaRʒ] nf refill; **rechargeable** adj (stylo etc) refillable; **recharger** vt (stylo) to refill; (batterie) to recharge

**réchaud** [Reʃo] nm (portable) stove

**réchauffer** [Reʃofe] vt (plat) to reheat; (mains, personne) to warm; **se ~** vi (température) to get warmer; (personne) to warm o.s.

**rêche** [Rɛʃ] adj rough

**recherche** [R(ə)ʃɛRʃ] nf (action) search; (raffinement) studied elegance; (scientifique etc): **la ~** research; **~s** nfpl (de la police) investigations; (scientifiques) research sg; **la ~ de** the search for; **être à la ~ de qch** to be looking for sth

**recherché, e** [R(ə)ʃɛRʃe] adj (rare, demandé) much sought-after; (raffiné: style) mannered; (: tenue) elegant

**rechercher** [R(ə)ʃɛRʃe] vt (objet égaré, personne) to look for; (causes, nouveau procédé) to try to find; (bonheur, compliments) to seek

**rechigner** [R(ə)ʃiɲe] vi: **~ à faire qch** to balk ou jib at doing sth

**rechute** [R(ə)ʃyt] nf (MÉD) relapse

**récidiver** [Residive] vi to commit a subsequent offence; (fig) to do it again

**récif** [Resif] nm reef

**récipient** [Resipjã] nm container

**réciproque** [Resiprɔk] adj reciprocal

**récit** [Resi] nm story; **récital** nm recital; **réciter** vt to recite

**réclamation** [Reklamasjɔ̃] nf complaint; **~s** nfpl (bureau) complaints department sg

**réclame** [Reklam] nf ad, advert(isement); **en ~** on special offer; **réclamer** vt to ask for; (revendiquer) to claim, demand ♦ vi to complain

**réclusion** [Reklyzjɔ̃] nf imprisonment

**recoin** [Rəkwɛ̃] nm nook, corner

**reçois** etc [Rəswa] vb voir **recevoir**

**récolte** [Rekɔlt] nf harvesting, gathering; (produits) harvest, crop; **récolter** vt to harvest, gather (in); (fig) to collect

**recommandé** [R(ə)kɔmãde] nm

*(POSTES)*: **en** ~ by registered mail

**recommander** [R(ə)kɔmɑ̃de] vt to recommend; *(POSTES)* to register

**recommencer** [R(ə)kɔmɑ̃se] vt *(reprendre: lutte, séance)* to resume, start again; *(refaire: travail, explications)* to start afresh, start (over) again ♦ vi to start again; *(récidiver)* to do it again

**récompense** [Rekɔ̃pɑ̃s] nf reward; *(prix)* award; **récompenser** vt: **récompenser qn (de** ou **pour)** to reward sb (for)

**réconcilier** [Rekɔ̃silje] vt to reconcile; **se ~ (avec)** to be reconciled (with)

**reconduire** [R(ə)kɔ̃dɥiR] vt *(raccompagner)* to take ou see back; *(renouveler)* to renew

**réconfort** [Rekɔ̃fɔR] nm comfort; **réconforter** vt *(consoler)* to comfort

**reconnaissance** [R(ə)kɔnɛsɑ̃s] nf *(gratitude)* gratitude, gratefulness; *(action de reconnaître)* recognition; *(MIL)* reconnaissance, recce; **reconnaissant, e** adj grateful

**reconnaître** [R(ə)kɔnɛtR] vt to recognize; *(MIL: lieu)* to reconnoitre; *(JUR: enfant, torts)* to acknowledge; ~ **que** to admit ou acknowledge that; **reconnu, e** adj *(indiscuté, connu)* recognized

**reconstituant, e** [R(ə)kɔ̃stitɥɑ̃, ɑ̃t] adj *(aliment, régime)* strength-building

**reconstituer** [R(ə)kɔ̃stitɥe] vt *(événement, accident)* to reconstruct; *(fresque, vase brisé)* to piece together, reconstitute

**reconstruction** [R(ə)kɔ̃stRyksjɔ̃] nf rebuilding

**reconstruire** [R(ə)kɔ̃stRɥiR] vt to rebuild

**reconvertir** [R(ə)kɔ̃vɛRtiR]: **se ~ dans** vt *(un métier, une branche)* to go into

**record** [R(ə)kɔR] nm, adj record

**recoupement** [R(ə)kupmɑ̃] nm: **par ~** by cross-checking

**recouper** [R(ə)kupe] vt *(témoignages)* to tie ou match up

**recourbe** [R(ə)kuRbe]: **se ~** vi to curve (up), bend (up)

**recourir** [R(ə)kuRiR]: ~ **à** vt *(ami, agence)* to turn ou appeal to; *(force, ruse, emprunt)* to resort to

**recours** [R(ə)kuR] nm: **avoir ~ à = recourir à; en dernier ~** as a last resort

**recouvrer** [R(ə)kuvRe] vt *(vue, santé etc)* to recover, regain

**recouvrir** [R(ə)kuvRiR] vt *(couvrir à nouveau)* to re-cover; *(couvrir entièrement, aussi fig)* to cover

**récréation** [RekReasjɔ̃] nf *(SCOL)* break

**récrier** [RekRije]: **se ~** vi to exclaim

**récriminations** [RekRiminasjɔ̃] nfpl remonstrations, complaints

**recroqueviller** [R(ə)kRɔk(ə)vije]: **se ~** vi *(personne)* to huddle up

**recrudescence** [R(ə)kRydesɑ̃s] nf fresh outbreak

**recrue** [RəkRy] nf recruit

**recruter** [R(ə)kRyte] vt to recruit

**rectangle** [Rɛktɑ̃gl] nm rectangle; **rectangulaire** adj rectangular

**rectificatif** [Rɛktifikatif, iv] nm correction

**rectifier** [Rɛktifje] vt *(calcul, adresse, paroles)* to correct; *(erreur)* to rectify

**rectiligne** [Rɛktilin] adj straight

**recto** [Rɛkto] nm front (of a page); ~ **verso** on both sides (of the page)

**reçu, e** [R(ə)sy] pp de **recevoir** ♦ adj *(candidat)* successful; *(admis, consacré)* accepted ♦ nm *(COMM)* receipt

**recueil** [Rəkœj] nm collection; **recueillir** vt to collect; *(voix, suffrages)* to win; *(accueillir: réfugiés, chat)* to take in; **se recueillir** vi to gather one's thoughts, meditate

**recul** [R(ə)kyl] nm *(éloignement)* distance; *(déclin)* decline; **être en ~** to be on the decline; **avec du ~** with hindsight; **avoir un mouvement de ~** to recoil; **prendre du ~** to stand back; **reculé, e** adj remote; **reculer** vi to move back, back away; *(AUTO)* to reverse, back (up); *(fig)* to (be on the) decline ♦ vt to move back; *(véhicule)* to reverse, back (up); (date, décision) to postpone; **reculons: à reculons** adv backwards

**récupérer** [rekypere] vt to recover, get back; (heures de travail) to make up; (déchets) to salvage ♦ vi to recover

**récurer** [rekyre] vt to scour

**récuser** [rekyze] vt to challenge; **se ~** vi to decline to give an opinion

**reçut** [rəsy] vb voir **recevoir**

**recycler** [r(ə)sikle] vt (TECH) to recycle; **se ~** vi to retrain

**rédacteur, -trice** [redaktœr, tris] nm/f (journaliste) writer; subeditor; (d'ouvrage de référence) editor, compiler; **~ en chef** chief editor

**rédaction** [redaksjɔ̃] nf writing; (rédacteurs) editorial staff; (SCOL: devoir) essay, composition

**redemander** [rədmɑ̃de] vt (une nouvelle fois) to ask again for; (davantage) to ask for more

**redescendre** [r(ə)desɑ̃dr] vi to go back down ♦ vt (pente etc) to go down

**redevance** [r(ə)dəvɑ̃s] nf (TÉL) rental charge; (TV) licence fee

**rédiger** [redize] vt to write; (contrat) to draw up

**redire** [r(ə)dir] vt to repeat; **trouver à ~ à** to find fault with

**redonner** [r(ə)dɔne] vt (rendre) to give back; (resservir: nourriture) to give more

**redoubler** [r(ə)duble] vi (tempête, violence) to intensify; (SCOL) to repeat a year; **~ de patience/prudence** to be doubly patient/careful

**redoutable** [r(ə)dutabl] adj formidable, fearsome

**redouter** [r(ə)dute] vt to dread

**redressement** [r(ə)drɛsmɑ̃] nm (économique) recovery

**redresser** [r(ə)drɛse] vt (relever) to set upright; (pièce tordue) to straighten out; (situation, économie) to put right; **se ~** vi (personne) to sit ou stand up (straight); (économie) to recover

**réduction** [redyksjɔ̃] nf reduction

**réduire** [redɥir] vt to reduce; (prix, dépenses) to cut, reduce; **se ~ à** (revenir à) to boil down to; **réduit** nm (pièce) tiny room

**rééducation** [reedykasjɔ̃] nf (d'un membre) re-education; (de délinquants, d'un blessé) rehabilitation

**réel, le** [reɛl] adj real; **réellement** adv really

**réexpédier** [reɛkspedje] vt (à l'envoyeur) to return, send back; (au destinataire) to send on, forward

**refaire** [r(ə)fɛr] vt to do again; (faire de nouveau: sport) to take up again; (réparer, restaurer) to do up

**réfection** [refɛksjɔ̃] nf repair

**réfectoire** [refɛktwar] nm refectory

**référence** [referɑ̃s] nf reference; **~s** nfpl (recommandations) reference sg

**référer** [refere]: **se ~ à** vt to refer to

**refermer** [r(ə)fɛrme] vt to close ou shut again; **se ~** vi (porte) to close ou shut (again)

**refiler** [r(ə)file] vt (fam) to palm off

**réfléchi, e** [refleʃi] adj (caractère) thoughtful; (action) well-thought-out; (LING) reflexive; **c'est tout ~** my mind's made up

**réfléchir** [refleʃir] vt to reflect ♦ vi to think; **~ à** to think about

**reflet** [r(ə)flɛ] nm reflection; (sur l'eau etc) sheen no pl, glint; **refléter** vt to reflect; **se refléter** vi to be reflected

**réflexe** [reflɛks] nm, adj reflex

**réflexion** [reflɛksjɔ̃] nf (de la lumière etc) reflection; (fait de penser) thought; (remarque) remark; **~ faite, à la ~** on reflection

**refluer** [r(ə)flye] vi to flow back; (foule) to surge back

**reflux** [r(ə)fly] nm (de la mer) ebb

**réforme** [refɔrm] nf reform; (REL): **la R~** the Reformation; **réformer** vt to reform; (MIL) to declare unfit for service

**refouler** [r(ə)fule] vt (envahisseurs) to drive back; (larmes) to force back; (désir, colère) to repress

**refrain** [R(ə)fRɛ̃] nm refrain, chorus

**refréner** [RəfRene] vt, **réfréner** [RefRene] vt to curb, check

**réfrigérateur** [RefRiʒeRatœR] nm refrigerator, fridge

**refroidir** [R(ə)fRwadiR] vt to cool; (fig: personne) to put off ♦ vi to cool (down); **se ~** vi (temps) to get cool ou colder; (fig: ardeur) to cool (off); **refroidissement** nm (grippe etc) chill

**refuge** [R(ə)fyʒ] nm refuge; **réfugié, e,** adj, nm/f refugee; **réfugier: se réfugier** vi to take refuge

**refus** [R(ə)fy] nm refusal; **ce n'est pas de ~** I won't say no, it's welcome; **refuser** vt to refuse; (SCOL: candidat) to fail; (personne) to turn away; **refuser qch à qn** to refuse sb sth; **se refuser à faire** to refuse to do

**réfuter** [Refyte] vt to refute

**regagner** [R(ə)ɡaɲe] vt (faveur) to win back; (lieu) to get back to

**regain** [Rəɡɛ̃] nm (renouveau): **un ~ de** renewed +nom

**régal** [Reɡal] nm treat; **régaler: se régaler** vi to have a delicious meal; (fig) to enjoy o.s.

**regard** [R(ə)ɡaR] nm (coup d'œil) look, glance; (expression) look (in one's eye); **au ~ de** (loi, morale) from the point of view of; **en ~ de** in comparison with

**regardant, e** [R(ə)ɡaRdɑ̃, ɑ̃t] adj (économe) tight-fisted; **peu ~ (sur)** very free (about)

**regarder** [R(ə)ɡaRde] vt to look at; (film, télévision, match) to watch; (concerner) to concern ♦ vi to look; **ne pas ~ à la dépense** to spare no expense; **~ qn/qch comme** to regard sb/sth as

**régie** [Reʒi] nf (COMM, INDUSTRIE) state-owned company; (THÉÂTRE, CINÉMA) production; (RADIO, TV) control room

**regimber** [R(ə)ʒɛ̃be] vi to balk, jib

**régime** [Reʒim] nm (POL) régime; (MÉD) diet; (ADMIN: carcéral, fiscal etc) system; (de bananes, dattes) bunch; **se mettre au/suivre un ~** to go on/be on a diet

**régiment** [Reʒimɑ̃] nm regiment

**région** [Reʒjɔ̃] nf region; **régional, e, -aux** adj regional

**régir** [ReʒiR] vt to govern

**régisseur** [ReʒisœR] nm (d'un domaine) steward; (CINÉMA, TV) assistant director; (THÉÂTRE) stage manager

**registre** [RəʒistR] nm register

**réglage** [Reɡlaʒ] nm adjustment

**règle** [Reɡl] nf (instrument) ruler; (loi) rule; **~s** nfpl (menstruation) period sg; **en ~** (papiers d'identité) in order; **en ~ générale** as a (general) rule; **réglé, e** [Reɡle] adj (vie) well-ordered; (arrangé) settled

**règlement** [RɛɡlЭmɑ̃] nm (paiement) settlement; (arrêté) regulation; (règles, statuts) regulations pl, rules pl; **~ de compte(s)** settling of old scores; **réglementaire** adj conforming to the regulations; (tenue) regulation cpd; **réglementation** nf (règles) regulations; **réglementer** vt to regulate

**régler** [Reɡle] vt (conflit, facture) to settle; (personne) to settle up with; (mécanisme, machine) to regulate, adjust; (thermostat etc) to set, adjust

**réglisse** [Reɡlis] nf liquorice

**règne** [Rɛɲ] nm (d'un roi etc, fig) reign; **régner** vi (roi) to rule, reign; (fig) to reign

**regorger** [R(ə)ɡɔRʒe] vi: **~ de** to overflow with, be bursting with

**regret** [R(ə)ɡRɛ] nm regret; **à ~** with regret; **sans ~** with no regrets; **regrettable** adj regrettable; **regretter** vt to regret; (personne) to miss; **je regrette mais ...** I'm sorry but ...

**regrouper** [R(ə)ɡRupe] vt (grouper) to group together; (contenir) to include, comprise; **se ~** vi to gather (together)

**régulier, -ière** [Reɡylje, jɛR] adj (gén) regular; (vitesse, qualité) steady; (égal: couche, ligne) even; (TRANSPORTS: ligne, service) scheduled, regular; (légal) lawful, in order; (honnête) straight, on the level; **régulièrement** adv regularly; (uniformément) evenly

**rehausser** [Rəose] vt (relever) to heighten, raise; (fig: souligner) to set off, enhance

**rein** [Rɛ̃] nm kidney; ~s nmpl (dos) back sg

**reine** [Rɛn] nf queen

**reine-claude** [Rɛnklod] nf greengage

**réinsertion** [Rɛ̃sɛRsjɔ̃] nf (de délinquant) reintegration, rehabilitation

**réintégrer** [Rɛ̃tegRe] vt (lieu) to return to; (fonctionnaire) to reinstate

**rejaillir** [R(ə)ʒajiR] vi to splash up; ~ **sur** (fig: scandale) to rebound on; (: gloire) to be reflected on

**rejet** [Rəʒɛ] nm rejection; **rejeter** vt (relancer) to throw back; (écarter) to reject; (déverser) to throw out, discharge; (vomir) to bring or throw up; **rejeter la responsabilité de qch sur qn** to lay the responsibility for sth at sb's door

**rejoindre** [R(ə)ʒwɛ̃dR] vt (famille, régiment) to rejoin, return to; (lieu) to get (back) to; (suj: route etc) to meet, join; (rattraper) to catch up (with); **se ~** vi to meet; **je te rejoins à la gare** I'll see ou meet you at the station

**réjouir** [ReʒwiR] vt to delight; **se ~ (de)** vi to be delighted (about); **réjouissances** [Reʒwisɑ̃s] nfpl (fête) festivities

**relâche** [Rəlɑʃ] nm ou nf: **sans ~** without respite ou a break; **relâché, e** adj loose, lax; **relâcher** vt (libérer) to release; (desserrer) to loosen; **se relâcher** vi (discipline) to become slack ou lax; (élève etc) to slacken off

**relais** [R(ə)lɛ] nm (SPORT: course de) ~ relay (race); **prendre le ~ (de)** to take over (from); ~ **routier** ≈ transport café (BRIT), ≈ truck stop (US)

**relancer** [R(ə)lɑ̃se] vt (balle) to throw back; (moteur) to restart; (fig) to boost, revive; (harceler): ~ **qn** to pester sb

**relatif, -ive** [R(ə)latif, iv] adj relative

**relation** [R(ə)lasjɔ̃] nf (rapport) relation(ship); (connaissance) acquaintance; ~s nfpl (rapports) relations; (connaissances) connections; **être/entrer en**

~**(s) avec** to be/get in contact with

**relaxe** [Rəlaks] (fam) adj (tenue) informal; (personne) relaxed; **relaxer: se relaxer** vi to relax

**relayer** [R(ə)leje] vt (collaborateur, coureur etc) to relieve; **se ~** vi (dans une activité) to take it in turns

**reléguer** [R(ə)lege] vt to relegate

**relent(s)** [Rəlɑ̃] nm(pl) (foul) smell

**relevé, e** [Rəl(ə)ve] adj (manches) rolled-up; (sauce) highly-seasoned ♦ nm (de compteur) reading; (bancaire) statement

**relève** [Rəlɛv] nf (personne) relief; **prendre la ~** to take over

**relever** [Rəl(ə)ve] vt (meuble) to stand up again; (personne tombée) to help up; (vitre, niveau de vie) to raise; (col) to turn up; (style) to elevate; (plat, sauce) to season; (sentinelle, équipe) to relieve; (fautes) to pick out; (défi) to accept, take up; (noter: adresse etc) to take down, note; (: plan) to sketch; (compteur) to read; (ramasser: cahiers) to collect, take in; **se ~** vi (se remettre debout) to get up; ~ **de** (maladie) to be recovering from; (être du ressort de) to be a matter for; (fig) to pertain to; ~ **qn de** (fonctions) to relieve sb of

**relief** [Rəljɛf] nm relief; **mettre en ~** (fig) to bring out, highlight

**relier** [Rəlje] vt to link up with; (livre) to bind; ~ **qch à** to link sth to

**religieuse** [R(ə)liʒjøz] nf nun; (gâteau) cream bun

**religieux, -euse** [R(ə)liʒjø, jøz] adj religious ♦ nm monk

**religion** [R(ə)liʒjɔ̃] nf religion

**relire** [R(ə)liR] vt (à nouveau) to reread; (vérifier) to read over

**reliure** [RəljyR] nf binding

**reluire** [R(ə)lɥiR] vi to gleam

**remanier** [R(ə)manje] vt to reshape, recast; (POL) to reshuffle

**remarquable** [R(ə)maRkabl] adj remarkable

**remarque** [R(ə)maRk] nf remark;

(écrite) note

**remarquer** [R(ə)marke] vt (voir) to notice; **se ~** vi to be noticeable; **faire ~ (à qn) que** to point out (to sb) that; **faire ~ qch (à qn)** to point sth out (to sb); **remarquez, ...** mind you ...; **se faire ~** to draw attention to o.s.

**rembourrer** [Rābure] vt to stuff

**remboursement** [Rābursəmā] nm (de dette, d'emprunt) repayment; (de frais) refund; **rembourser** vt to pay back, repay; (frais, billet etc) to refund; **se faire rembourser** to get a refund

**remède** [R(ə)mɛd] nm (médicament) medicine; (traitement, fig) remedy, cure

**remémorer** [R(ə)memɔre] vt: **se ~** to recall, recollect

**remerciements** [Rəmɛrsimā] nmpl thanks

**remercier** [R(ə)mɛrsje] vt to thank; (congédier) to dismiss; **~ qn de/d'avoir fait** to thank sb for/for having done

**remettre** [R(ə)mɛtR] vt (replacer) to put back; (vêtement) to put back on; (ajouter) to add; (ajourner): **~ qch (à)** to postpone sth (until); **se ~** vi: **se ~ de** to recover (from); **~ qch à qn** (donner: lettre, clé etc) to hand over sth to sb; (: prix, décoration) to present sb with sth; **se ~ à faire qch** to start doing sth again

**remise** [R(ə)miz] nf (rabais) discount; (local) shed; **~ de peine** reduction of sentence; **~ en jeu** (FOOTBALL) throw-in

**remontant** [R(ə)mɔtā, āt] nm tonic, pick-me-up

**remonte-pente** [R(ə)mɔtpāt] nm ski-lift

**remonter** [R(ə)mɔte] vi to go back up; (prix, température) to go up again **♦** vt (pente) to go up; (fleuve) to sail (ou swim etc) up; (manches, pantalon) to roll up; (col) to turn up; (niveau, limite) to raise; (fig: personne) to buck up; (qch de démonté) to put back together, reassemble; (montre) to wind up; **♦ le moral à qn** to raise sb's spirits; **~ à** (dater de) to date ou go back to

**remontrance** [R(ə)mɔtrās] nf reproof, reprimand

**remontrer** [R(ə)mɔtre] vt (fig): **en ~ à** to prove one's superiority over

**remords** [R(ə)mɔR] nm remorse no pl; **avoir des ~** to feel remorse

**remorque** [R(ə)mɔrk] nf trailer; **remorquer** vt to tow; **remorqueur** nm tug(boat)

**remous** [Rəmu] nm (d'un navire) (back)wash no pl; (de rivière) swirl, eddy **♦** nmpl (fig) stir sg

**remparts** [Rāpar] nmpl walls, ramparts

**remplaçant, e** [Rāplasā, āt] nm/f replacement, stand-in; (SCOL) supply teacher

**remplacement** [Rāplasmā] nm replacement; **faire des ~s** (professeur) to do supply teaching; (secrétaire) to temp

**remplacer** [Rāplase] vt to replace; **~ qch/qn par** to replace sth/sb with

**rempli, e** [Rāpli] adj (emploi du temps) full, busy; **~ de** full of, filled with

**remplir** [RāpliR] vt to fill (up); (questionnaire) to fill out ou up; (obligations, fonction, condition) to fulfil; **se ~** vi to fill up

**remporter** [Rāpɔrte] vt (marchandise) to take away; (fig) to win, achieve

**remuant, e** [Rəmɥā, āt] adj restless

**remue-ménage** [R(ə)mymenaʒ] nm inv commotion

**remuer** [Rəmɥe] vt to move; (café, sauce) to stir **♦** vi to move; **se ~** vi to move; (fam: s'activer) to get a move on

**rémunérer** [Remynere] vt to remunerate

**renard** [R(ə)nar] nm fox

**renchérir** [RāʃeriR] vi (fig): **~ (sur)** (en paroles) to add something (to)

**rencontre** [RākɔtR] nf meeting; (imprévue) encounter; **aller à la ~ de qn** to go and meet sb; **rencontrer** vt to meet; (mot, expression) to come across; (difficultés) to meet with; **se rencontrer** vi to meet

**rendement** [Rɑ̃dmɑ̃] nm (d'un travailleur, d'une machine) output; (d'un champ) yield

**rendez-vous** [Rɑ̃devu] nm appointment; (d'amoureux) date; (lieu) meeting place; **donner ~ à qn** to arrange to meet sb; **avoir/prendre ~~ (avec)** to have/make an appointment (with)

**rendre** [Rɑ̃dR] vt (restituer) to give back, return; (invitation) to return, repay; (vomir) to bring up; (exprimer, traduire) to render; (faire devenir): ~ **qn célèbre/qch possible** to make sb famous/sth possible; **se ~** vi (capituler) to surrender, give o.s. up; (aller): **se ~ quelque part** to go somewhere; ~ **la monnaie à qn** to give sb his change; **se ~ compte de qch** to realize sth

**rênes** [Rɛn] nfpl reins

**renfermé, e** [Rɑ̃fɛRme] adj (fig) withdrawn ♦ nm: **sentir le ~** to smell stuffy

**renfermer** [Rɑ̃fɛRme] vt to contain

**renflouer** [Rɑ̃flue] vt to refloat; (fig) to set back on its (ou his/her) feet

**renfoncement** [Rɑ̃fɔ̃smɑ̃] nm recess

**renforcer** [Rɑ̃fɔRse] vt to reinforce; **renfort: renforts** nmpl reinforcements; **à grand renfort de** with a great deal of

**renfrogné, e** [Rɑ̃fRɔɲe] adj sullen

**rengaine** [Rɑ̃gɛn] (péj) nf old tune

**renier** [Rənje] vt (personne) to disown, repudiate; (foi) to renounce

**renifler** [R(ə)nifle] vi, vt to sniff

**renne** [Rɛn] nm reindeer inv

**renom** [Rənɔ̃] nm reputation; (célébrité) renown; **renommé, e** adj celebrated, renowned; **renommée** nf fame

**renoncer** [R(ə)nɔ̃se]: ~ **à** vt to give up; ~ **à faire** to give up the idea of doing

**renouer** [Rənwe] vt: ~ **avec** (habitude) to take up again

**renouvelable** [R(ə)nuv(ə)labl] adj (énergie etc) renewable

**renouveler** [R(ə)nuv(ə)le] vt to renew; (exploit, méfait) to repeat; **se ~** vi (incident) to recur, happen again; **renouvellement** nm (remplacement) renewal

**rénover** [Renɔve] vt (immeuble) to renovate, do up; (quartier) to redevelop

**renseignement** [Rɑ̃sɛɲmɑ̃] nm information, no pl, piece of information; (bureau des) ~s information office

**renseigner** [Rɑ̃seɲe] vt: ~ **qn (sur)** to give information to sb (about); **se ~** vi to ask for information, make inquiries

**rentabilité** [Rɑ̃tabilite] nf profitability

**rentable** [Rɑ̃tabl] adj profitable

**rente** [Rɑ̃t] nf private income; (pension) pension

**rentrée** [Rɑ̃tRe] nf: ~ **(d'argent)** cash no pl coming in; **la ~ (des classes)** the start of the new school year

---

La **rentrée (des classes)** in September marks an important point in the French year. Children and teachers return to school, and political and social life begins again after the long summer break.

---

**rentrer** [Rɑ̃tRe] vi (revenir chez soi) to go (ou come) back home; (entrer de nouveau) to go (ou come) back in; (entrer) to go (ou come) in; (air, clou: pénétrer) to go in; (revenu) to come in ♦ vt to bring in; (: véhicule) to put away; (chemise dans pantalon etc) to tuck in; (griffes) to draw in; ~ **le ventre** to pull in one's stomach; ~ **dans** (heurter) to crash into; ~ **dans l'ordre** to be back to normal; ~ **dans ses frais** to recover one's expenses

**renverse** [Rɑ̃vɛRs]: **à la ~** adv backwards

**renverser** [Rɑ̃vɛRse] vt (faire tomber: chaise, verre) to knock over, overturn; (liquide, contenu) to spill, upset; (piéton) to knock down; (retourner) to turn upside down; (: ordre des mots etc) to reverse; (fig: gouvernement etc) to overthrow; (stupéfier) to bowl over; **se ~** vi (verre, vase) to fall over; (contenu) to spill

**renvoi** [ʀɑ̃vwa] nm (d'employé) dismissal; (d'élève) expulsion; (référence) cross-reference; (éructation) belch; **renvoyer** vt to send back; (congédier) to dismiss; (élève: définitivement) to expel; (lumière) to reflect; (ajourner): **renvoyer qch (à)** to put sth off ou postpone sth (until)

**repaire** [ʀ(ə)pɛʀ] nm den

**répandre** [ʀepɑ̃dʀ] vt (renverser) to spill; (étaler, diffuser) to spread; (odeur) to give off; **se ~** vi to spill; (se propager) to spread; **répandu, e** adj (opinion, usage) widespread

**réparation** [ʀepaʀasjɔ̃] nf repair

**réparer** [ʀepaʀe] vt to repair; (fig: offense) to make up for, atone for; (: oubli, erreur) to put right

**repartie** [ʀəpaʀti] nf retort; **avoir de la ~** to be quick at repartee

**repartir** [ʀ(ə)paʀtiʀ] vi to leave again; (voyageur) to set off again; (fig) to get going again; **~ à zéro** to start from scratch (again)

**répartir** [ʀepaʀtiʀ] vt (pour attribuer) to share out; (pour disposer, disposer) to divide up; (poids) to distribute; **se ~** vt (travail, rôles) to share out between themselves; **répartition** nf (des richesses etc) distribution

**repas** [ʀ(ə)pɑ] nm meal

**repassage** [ʀ(ə)pɑsaʒ] nm ironing

**repasser** [ʀ(ə)pɑse] vi to come (ou go) back ♦ vt (vêtement, tissu) to iron; (examen) to retake, resit; (film) to show again; (leçon) to go over (again)

**repêcher** [ʀ(ə)peʃe] vt to fish out; (candidat) to pass (by inflating marks)

**repentir** [ʀapɑ̃tiʀ] nm repentance; **se ~** vi to repent; **~ d'avoir fait qch** (regretter) to regret having done sth

**répercussions** [ʀepɛʀkysjɔ̃] nfpl (fig) repercussions

**répercuter** [ʀepɛʀkyte] : **se ~** vi (bruit) to reverberate; (fig): **se ~ sur** to have repercussions on

**repère** [ʀ(ə)pɛʀ] nm mark; (monument,

événement) landmark

**repérer** [ʀ(ə)peʀe] vt (fam: erreur, personne) to spot; (: endroit) to locate; **se ~** vi to find one's way about

**répertoire** [ʀepɛʀtwaʀ] nm (liste) (alphabetical) list; (carnet) index notebook; (INFORM) folder, directory; (d'un artiste) repertoire

**répéter** [ʀepete] vt to repeat; (préparer: leçon) to learn, go over; (THÉÂTRE) to rehearse; **~** vi (redire) to repeat o.s.; (se reproduire) to be repeated, recur

**répétition** [ʀepetisjɔ̃] nf repetition; (THÉÂTRE) rehearsal

**répit** [ʀepi] nm respite

**replier** [ʀ(ə)plije] vt (rabattre) to fold down ou over; **se ~** vi (troupes, armée) to withdraw, fall back; (sur soi-même) to withdraw into o.s.

**réplique** [ʀeplik] nf (repartie, fig) reply; (THÉÂTRE) line; (copie) replica; **répliquer** vi to reply; (riposter) to retaliate

**répondeur** [ʀepɔ̃dœʀ, øz] nm: **~ automatique** (TÉL) answering machine

**répondre** [ʀepɔ̃dʀ] vi to answer, reply; (freins) to respond; **~ à** to reply to, answer; (affection, salut) to return; (provocation) to respond to; (correspondre à: besoin) to answer; (: conditions) to meet; (: description) to match; (avec impertinence): **~ à qn** to answer sb back; **~ de** to answer for

**réponse** [ʀepɔ̃s] nf answer, reply; **en ~ à** in reply to

**reportage** [ʀ(ə)pɔʀtaʒ] nm report; **~ en direct** (live) commentary

**reporter¹** [ʀapɔʀtɛʀ] nm reporter

**reporter²** [ʀapɔʀte] vt (ajourner): **~ qch (à)** to postpone sth (until); (transférer): **~ qch sur** to transfer sth to; **se ~ à** (époque) to think back to; (document) to refer to

**repos** [ʀ(ə)po] nm rest; (tranquillité) peace and quiet; (MIL): **~!** stand at ease!; **ce n'est pas de tout ~!** it's no picnic!

**reposant, e** [ʀ(ə)pozɑ̃, ɑ̃t] adj restful

**reposer** [R(ə)poze] vt (verre, livre) to put down; (délasser) to rest ♦ vi: laisser ~ (pâte) to leave to stand; se ~ vi to rest; se ~ sur qn to rely on sb; ~ sur (fig) to rest on

**repoussant, e** [R(ə)pusɑ̃, ɑ̃t] adj repulsive

**repousser** [R(ə)puse] vi to grow again ♦ vt to repel, repulse; (offre) to turn down, reject; (personne) to push back; (différer) to put back

**reprendre** [R(ə)pRɑ̃dR] vt (objet prêté, donné) to take back; (prisonnier, ville) to recapture; (firme, entreprise) to take over; (le travail) to resume; (emprunter: argument, idée) to take up, use; (refaire: article etc) to go over again; (vêtement) to alter; (réprimander) to tell off; (corriger) to correct; (chercher): je viendrai te ~ à 4 h I'll come and fetch you at 4; (se resservir de): ~ du pain/un œuf to take (ou eat) more bread/another egg ♦ vi (classes, pluie) to start (up) again; (activités, travaux, combats) to resume, start (up) again; (affaires) to pick up; (dire): reprit-il he went on; se ~ vi (se ressaisir) to recover; ~ des forces to recover one's strength; ~ courage to take new heart; ~ la route to set off again; ~ haleine ou son souffle to get one's breath back

**représailles** [R(ə)pRezaj] nfpl reprisals

**représentant, e** [R(ə)pRezɑ̃tɑ̃, ɑ̃t] nm/f representative

**représentation** [R(ə)pRezɑ̃tasjɔ̃] nf (symbole, image) representation; (spectacle) performance

**représenter** [R(ə)pRezɑ̃te] vt to represent; (donner: pièce, opéra) to perform; se ~ vt (se figurer) to imagine

**répression** [RepResjɔ̃] nf repression

**réprimer** [RepRime] vt (émotions) to suppress; (peuple etc) to repress

**repris** [R(ə)pRi, iz] nm: ~ de justice ex-prisoner, ex-convict

**reprise** [R(ə)pRiz] nf (recommencement) resumption; (économique) recovery; (TV) repeat; (COMM) trade-in, part exchange; (raccommodage) mend; à plusieurs ~s on several occasions

**repriser** [R(ə)pRize] vt (chaussette, lainage) to darn; (tissu) to mend

**reproche** [R(ə)pRɔʃ] nm (remontrance) reproach; faire des ~s à qn to reproach sb; sans ~(s) beyond reproach;

**reprocher** vt: reprocher qch à qn to reproach ou blame sb for sth; reprocher qch à (critiquer) to have sth against

**reproduction** [R(ə)pRɔdyksjɔ̃] nf reproduction

**reproduire** [R(ə)pRɔdɥiR] vt to reproduce; se ~ vi (BIO) to reproduce; (recommencer) to recur, re-occur

**reprouver** [RepRuve] vt to reprove

**reptile** [Reptil] nm reptile

**repu, e** [Rəpy] adj satisfied, sated

**république** [Repyblik] nf republic

**répugnant, e** [Repyɲɑ̃, ɑ̃t] adj disgusting

**répugner** [Repyɲe]: ~ à vt: ~ à qn to repel ou disgust sb; ~ à faire to be loath ou reluctant to do

**réputation** [Repytasjɔ̃] nf reputation; **réputé, e** adj renowned

**requérir** [RəkeRiR] vt (nécessiter) to require, call for

**requête** [Rəkɛt] nf request

**requin** [Rəkɛ̃] nm shark

**requis, e** [Rəki, iz] adj required

**RER** sigle m (= réseau express régional) Greater Paris high-speed train service

**rescapé, e** [Reskape] nm/f survivor

**rescousse** [Reskus] nf: aller à la ~ de qn to go to sb's aid ou rescue

**réseau, x** [Rezo] nm network

**réservation** [RezeRvasjɔ̃] nf booking, reservation

**réserve** [RezeRv] nf (retenue) reserve; (entrepôt) storeroom; (restriction, d'Indiens) reservation; (de pêche, chasse) preserve; de ~ (provisions etc) in reserve

**réservé, e** [RezeRve] adj reserved;

chasse/pêche ~e private hunting/ fishing

**réserver** [Rezerve] vt to reserve; (chambre, billet etc) to book, reserve; (fig: destiner) to have in store; (garder): ~ qch pour/à to keep ou save sth for

**réservoir** [Rezervwar] nm tank

**résidence** [Rezidās] nf residence; ~ secondaire second home; **résidentiel, le** adj residential; **résider** vi: **résider à/dans/en** to reside in; **résider dans** (fig) to lie in

**résidu** [Rezidy] nm residue no pl

**résigner** [Rezine]: se ~ vi: se ~ (à qch/à faire) to resign o.s. (to sth/to doing)

**résilier** [Rezilje] vt to terminate

**résistance** [Rezistās] nf resistance; (de réchaud, bouilloire: fil) element

**résistant, e** [Rezistā, āt] adj (personne) robust, tough; (matériau) strong, hard-wearing

**résister** [Reziste] vi to resist; ~ à (assaut, tentation) to resist; (supporter: gel etc) to withstand; (désobéir à) to stand up to, oppose

**résolu, e** [Rezɔly] pp de **résoudre** ♦ adj: **être ~ à qch/faire** to be set upon sth/doing

**résolution** [Rezɔlysjɔ̃] nf (fermeté, décision) resolution; (d'un problème) solution

**résolve** etc [Rezɔlv] vb voir **résoudre**

**résonner** [Rezɔne] vi (cloche, pas) to reverberate, resound; (salle) to be resonant

**résorber** [Rezɔrbe]: se ~ vi (fig: chômage) to be reduced; (: déficit) to be absorbed

**résoudre** [Rezudr] vt to solve; se ~ à faire to bring o.s. to do

**respect** [Respɛ] nm respect; **tenir en ~** to keep at bay; **respecter** vt to respect; **respectueux, -euse** adj respectful

**respiration** [Respirasjɔ̃] nf breathing no pl

**respirer** [Respire] vi to breathe; (se détendre) to get one's breath; (: se rassurer) to breathe again ♦ vt to breathe (in), inhale; (manifester: santé, calme etc) to exude

**resplendir** [Resplādir] vi to shine; (fig): ~ (de) to be radiant (with)

**responsabilité** [Respɔ̃sabilite] nf responsibility; (légale) liability

**responsable** [Respɔ̃sabl] adj responsible ♦ nm/f (coupable) person responsible; (personne compétente) person in charge; (de parti, syndicat) official; ~ de responsible for

**resquiller** [Reskije] (fam) vi to get in without paying; (ne pas faire la queue) to jump the queue

**ressaisir** [R(ə)sezir]: se ~ vi to regain one's self-control

**ressasser** [R(ə)sase] vt to keep going over

**ressemblance** [R(ə)sāblās] nf resemblance, similarity, likeness

**ressemblant, e** [R(ə)sāblā, āt] adj (portrait) lifelike, true to life

**ressembler** [R(ə)sāble]: ~ à vt to be like, resemble; (visuellement) to look like; se ~ vi to be (ou look) alike

**ressemeler** [R(ə)səm(ə)le] vt to (re)sole

**ressentiment** [R(ə)sātimā] nm resentment

**ressentir** [R(ə)sātir] vt to feel

**resserrer** [R(ə)sere] vt (nœud, boulon) to tighten (up); (fig: liens) to strengthen

**resservir** [R(ə)servir] vt to do ou serve again; se ~ vi to help o.s. again

**ressort** [Rəsɔr] nm (pièce) spring; (énergie) spirit; (recours): **en dernier ~** as a last resort; (compétence): **être du ~ de** to fall within the competence of

**ressortir** [Rəsɔrtir] vi to go (ou come) out (again); (contraster) to stand out; ~ **de** to emerge from; **faire ~** (fig: souligner) to bring out

**ressortissant, e** [R(ə)sɔrtisā, āt] nm/f

national

**ressources** [R(ə)suRs] nfpl (moyens) ressources

**ressusciter** [Resysite] vt (fig) to revive, bring back ♦ vi to rise (from the dead)

**restant, e** [Rɛstɑ̃, ɑ̃t] adj remaining ♦ nm: **le ~ (de)** the remainder (of); **un ~ de** (de trop) some left-over

**restaurant** [RɛstɔRɑ̃] nm restaurant

**restauration** [RɛstɔRasjɔ̃] nf restoration; (hôtellerie) catering; **~ rapide** fast food

**restaurer** [RɛstɔRe] vt to restore; **se ~** vi to have something to eat

**reste** [Rɛst] nm (restant): **le ~ (de)** the rest (of); (de trop): **un ~ (de)** some left-over; (nourriture) left-overs; (d'une cité etc, dépouille mortelle) remains; **du ~, au ~** besides, moreover

**rester** [Rɛste] vi to stay, remain; (subsister) to remain, be left; (durer) to last, live on ♦ vb impers: **il reste du pain/2 œufs** there's some bread/there are 2 eggs left (over); **restons-en là** let's leave it at that; **il me reste assez de temps** I have enough time left; **il ne me reste plus qu'à ...** I've just got to ...

**restituer** [Rɛstitɥe] vt (objet, somme): **~ qch (à qn)** to return sth (to sb)

**restreindre** [RɛstRɛ̃dR] vt to restrict, limit

**restriction** [Rɛstriksjɔ̃] nf restriction

**résultat** [Rezylta] nm result; (d'examen, d'élection) results pl

**résulter** [Rezylte]: **~ de** vt to result from, be the result of

**résumé** [Rezyme] nm summary, résumé

**résumer** [Rezyme] vt (texte) to summarize; (récapituler) to sum up

**résurrection** [RezyRɛksjɔ̃] nf resurrection

**rétablir** [RetabliR] vt to restore, reestablish; **se ~** vi (guérir) to recover; (silence, calme) to return, be restored; **rétablissement** nm restoring; (guéri-

son) recovery

**retaper** [R(ə)tape] (fam) vt (maison, voiture etc) to do up; (revigorer) to buck up

**retard** [R(ə)taR] nm (d'une personne attendue) lateness no pl; (sur l'horaire, un programme) delay; (fig: scolaire, mental etc) backwardness; **en ~ (de 2 heures)** (2 hours) late; **avoir du ~** to be late; (sur un programme) to be behind (schedule); **prendre du ~** (train, avion) to be delayed; **sans ~** without delay

**retardataire** [R(ə)taRdatɛR] nmf latecomer

**retardement** [R(ə)taRdəmɑ̃]: **à ~** delayed action cpd; **bombe à ~** time bomb

**retarder** [R(ə)taRde] vt to delay; (montre) to put back ♦ vi (montre) to be slow; (sur un horaire) to delay sb (an hour); **~ qch (de 2 jours)** (départ, date) to put sth back (2 days)

**retenir** [Rət(ə)niR] vt (garder, retarder) to keep, detain; (maintenir: objet qui glisse, fig: colère, larmes) to hold back; (se rappeler) to retain; (réserver) to reserve; (accepter: proposition etc) to accept; (fig: empêcher d'agir): **~ qn (de faire)** to hold sb back (from doing); (prélever): **~ qch (sur)** to deduct sth (from); **se ~** vi (se raccrocher): **se ~ à** to hold onto; (se contenir): **se ~ de faire** to restrain o.s. from doing; **~ son souffle** to hold one's breath

**retentir** [R(ə)tɑ̃tiR] vi to ring out; (salle): **~ de** to ring ou resound with; **retentissant, e** adj resounding; **retentissement** nm repercussion

**retenu, e** [Rət(ə)ny] adj (place) reserved; (personne: empêché) held up; **retenue** nf (prélèvement) deduction; (scol) detention; (modération) (self-) restraint

**réticence** [Retisɑ̃s] nf hesitation, reluctance no pl; **réticent, e** adj hesitant, reluctant

**rétine** [Retin] nf retina

**retiré, e** [R(ə)tiRe] adj (vie) secluded; (lieu) remote

**retirer** [R(ə)tiRe] vt (vêtement, lunettes) to take off, remove; (argent, plainte) to withdraw; (reprendre: bagages, billets) to collect, pick up; (extraire): **~ qch de** to take sth out of, remove sth from

**retombées** [Rətɔ̃be] nfpl (radioactives) fallout sg; (fig: répercussions) effects

**retomber** [R(ə)tɔ̃be] vi (à nouveau) to fall again; (atterrir: après un saut etc) to land; (échoir): **~ sur qn** to fall on sb

**rétorquer** [RetɔRke] vt: **~ (à qn) que** to retort (to sb) that

**retouche** [R(ə)tuʃ] nf (sur vêtement) alteration; **retoucher** vt (photographie) to touch up; (texte, vêtement) to alter

**retour** [R(ə)tuR] nm return; **au ~** (en route) on the way back; **à mon ~** when I get/got back; **être de ~ (de)** to be back (from); **par ~ du courrier** by return of post

**retourner** [R(ə)tuRne] vt (dans l'autre sens: matelas, crêpe etc) to turn (over); (: sac, vêtement) to turn inside out; (fam: bouleverser) to shake; (renvoyer, restituer): **~ qch à qn** to return sth to sb ♦ vi (aller, revenir): **~ quelque part/ à** to go back o return somewhere/to; **se ~** vi (tourner la tête) to turn round; **~ à** (état, activité) to return to, go back to; **se ~ contre** (fig) to turn against

**retrait** [R(ə)tRɛ] nm (d'argent) withdrawal; **en ~** set back; **~ du permis (de conduire)** disqualification from driving (BRIT), revocation of driver's license (US)

**retraite** [R(ə)tRɛt] nf (d'un employé) retirement; (revenu) pension; (d'une armée, REL) retreat; **prendre sa ~** to retire; **~ anticipée** early retirement; **retraité, e** adj retired ♦ nm/f pensioner

**retrancher** [R(ə)tRɑ̃ʃe] vt (nombre, somme): **~ qch de** to take away o deduct sth from; **se ~ derrière/dans** to take refuge behind/in

**retransmettre** [R(ə)tRɑ̃smɛtR] vt (RADIO) to broadcast; (TV) to show

**rétrécir** [RetResiR] vt (vêtement) to take in ♦ vi to shrink

**rétribution** [RetRibysjɔ̃] nf payment

**rétro** [RetRo] adj inv: **la mode ~** the nostalgia vogue

**rétrograde** [RetRogRad] adj reactionary, backward-looking

**rétroprojecteur** [RetRopRɔʒɛktœR] nm overhead projector

**rétrospective** [RetRospɛktiv] nf retrospective exhibition/season; **rétrospectivement** adv in retrospect

**retrousser** [R(ə)tRuse] vt to roll up

**retrouvailles** [R(ə)tRuvaj] nfpl reunion sg

**retrouver** [R(ə)tRuve] vt (fugitif, objet perdu) to find; (calme, santé) to regain; (revoir) to see again; (rejoindre) to meet (again), join; **se ~** vi to meet; (s'orienter) to find one's way; **se ~ quelque part** to find o.s. somewhere; **s'y ~** (y voir clair) to make sense of it; (rentrer dans ses frais) to break even

**rétroviseur** [RetRovizœR] nm (rearview) mirror

**réunion** [Reynjɔ̃] nf (séance) meeting

**réunir** [ReyniR] vt (rassembler) to gather together; (inviter: amis, famille) to have round, have in; (cumuler: qualités etc) to combine; (rapprocher: ennemis) to bring together (again), reunite; (rattacher: parties) to join (together); **se ~** vi (se rencontrer) to meet

**réussi, e** [Reysi] adj successful

**réussir** [ReysiR] vi to succeed, be successful; (à un examen) to pass ♦ vt to make a success of; **~ à faire** to succeed in doing; **~ à qn** (être bénéfique à) to agree with sb; **réussite** nf success; (CARTES) patience

**revaloir** [R(ə)valwaR] vt: **je vous revaudrai cela** I'll repay you some day; (en mal) I'll pay you back for this

**revanche** [R(ə)vɑ̃ʃ] nf revenge; (sport) revenge match; **en ~** on the other hand

**rêve** [REV] nm dream; **de ~** dream cpd; **faire un ~** to have a dream

**revêche** [Rəvεʃ] adj surly, sour-tempered

**réveil** [Revεj] nm waking up no pl; (fig) awakening; (pendule) alarm (clock); **au ~** on waking (up); **réveille-matin** nm inv alarm clock; **réveiller** (personne) to wake up; (fig) to awaken, revive; **se réveiller** vi to wake up

**réveillon** [Revεjɔ̃] nm Christmas Eve; (de la Saint-Sylvestre) New Year's Eve; **réveillonner** vi (d'Occasion) to celebrate Christmas Eve (ou New Year's Eve)

**révélateur, -trice** [Revelatœr, tRis] adj: **~ (de qch)** revealing (sth)

**révéler** [Revele] vt to reveal; **se ~** vi to be revealed, reveal itself ♦ vb +attrib: **se ~ difficile/aisé** to prove difficult/easy

**revenant, e** [R(ə)vənɑ̃, ɑ̃t] nm/f ghost

**revendeur, -euse** [R(ə)vɑ̃dœr, øz] nm/f (détaillant) retailer; (de drogue) (drug-)dealer

**revendication** [R(ə)vɑ̃dikasjɔ̃] nf claim, demand

**revendiquer** [R(ə)vɑ̃dike] vt to claim, demand; (responsabilité) to claim

**revendre** [R(ə)vɑ̃dR] vt (d'Occasion) to resell; (détailler) to sell; **à ~** (en abondance) to spare

**revenir** [Rəv(ə)niR] vi to come back; (coûter): **~ cher/à 100 F** (à qn) to cost (sb) a lot/100 F; **~ à** (reprendre: études, projet) to return to, go back to; (équivaloir à) to amount to; **~ à qn** (part, honneur) to go to sb, be sb's; (souvenir, nom) to come back to sb; **~ sur** (question, sujet) to go back over; (engagement) to go back on; **~ à soi** to come round; **n'en pas ~: je n'en reviens pas** I can't get over it; **~ sur ses pas** to retrace one's steps; **cela revient à dire que/au même** it amounts to saying that/the same thing; **faire ~** (CULIN) to brown

**revenu** [Rəv(ə)ny] nm income; **~s** nmpl income sg

**rêver** [Reve] vi, vt to dream; **~ de/à** to dream of

**réverbère** [ReveRbεR] nm street lamp ou light; **réverbérer** vt to reflect

**révérence** [ReveRɑ̃s] nf (salut) bow; (: de femme) curtsey

**rêverie** [RevRi] nf daydreaming no pl, daydream

**revers** [R(ə)vεR] nm (de feuille, main) back; (d'étoffe) wrong side; (de pièce, médaille) back, reverse; (TENNIS, PING-PONG) backhand; (de veste) lapel; (fig: échec) setback

**revêtement** [R(ə)vεtmɑ̃] nm (des sols) flooring; (de chaussée) surface

**revêtir** [R(ə)vetiR] vt (habit) to don, put on; (prendre: importance, apparence) to take on; **~ qch de** to cover sth with

**rêveur, -euse** [RevœR, øz] adj dreamy ♦ nm/f dreamer

**revient** [Rəvjε̃] vb voir **revenir**

**revigorer** [R(ə)vigɔRe] vt (air frais) to invigorate, brace up; (repas, boisson) to revive, buck up

**revirement** [R(ə)viRmɑ̃] nm change of mind; (d'une situation) reversal

**réviser** [Revize] vt to revise; (machine) to overhaul, service

**révision** [Revizjɔ̃] nf revision; (de voiture) servicing no pl

**revivre** [R(ə)vivR] vi (reprendre des forces) to come alive again ♦ vt (épreuve, moment) to relive

**revoir** [RəvwaR] vt to see again; (réviser) to revise ♦ nm: **au ~** goodbye

**révoltant, e** [Revɔltɑ̃, ɑ̃t] adj revolting

**révolte** [Revɔlt] nf rebellion, revolt

**révolter** [Revɔlte] vt to revolt; **se ~ (contre)** to rebel (against); **ça me révolte (de voir que ...)** I'm revolted ou appalled (to see that ...)

**révolu, e** [Revɔly] adj past; (ADMIN): **âgé de 18 ans ~** over 18 years of age

**révolution** [Revɔlysjɔ̃] nf revolution; **révolutionnaire** adj, nm/f revolutionary

**revolver** [ʀevɔlvɛʀ] nm gun; (à barillet) revolver

**révoquer** [ʀevɔke] vt (fonctionnaire) to dismiss; (arrêt, contrat) to revoke

**revue** [ʀ(ə)vy] nf (périodique) review, magazine; (de music-hall) variety show; **passer en ~** (mentalement) to go through

**rez-de-chaussée** [ʀed(ə)ʃose] nm inv ground floor

**RF** sigle f = **République française**

**Rhin** [ʀɛ̃] nm Rhine

**rhinocéros** [ʀinɔseʀɔs] nm rhinoceros

**Rhône** [ʀon] nm Rhone

**rhubarbe** [ʀybaʀb] nf rhubarb

**rhum** [ʀɔm] nm rum

**rhumatisme** [ʀymatism] nm rheumatism no pl

**rhume** [ʀym] nm cold; **~ de cerveau** head cold; **le ~ des foins** hay fever

**ri** [ʀi] pp de **rire**

**riant, e** [ʀ(i)jɑ̃, ʀ(i)jɑ̃t] adj smiling, cheerful

**ricaner** [ʀikane] vi (avec méchanceté) to snigger; (bêtement) to giggle

**riche** [ʀiʃ] adj rich; (personne, pays) rich, wealthy; **~ en** rich in; **richesse** nf wealth; (fig: de sol, musée etc) richness; **richesses** nfpl (ressources, argent) wealth sg; (fig: trésors) treasures

**ricochet** [ʀikɔʃɛ] nm: **faire des ~s** to skip stones; **par ~** (fig) as an indirect result

**rictus** [ʀiktys] nm grin

**ride** [ʀid] nf wrinkle

**rideau, x** [ʀido] nm curtain; **~ de fer** (boutique) metal shutter(s)

**rider** [ʀide] vt to wrinkle; **se ~** vi to become wrinkled

**ridicule** [ʀidikyl] adj ridiculous ♦ nm: **le ~** ridicule; **ridiculiser: se ridiculiser** vi to make a fool of o.s.

MOT-CLÉ

**rien** [ʀjɛ̃] pron 1: **(ne) ... rien** nothing; tournure négative + anything; **qu'est-ce**

que vous avez? – **rien** what have you got? – nothing; **il n'a rien dit/fait** he said/did nothing; he hasn't said/done anything; **il n'a rien** (n'est pas blessé) he's all right; **de rien!** not at all!

2 (quelque chose): **a-t-il jamais rien fait pour nous?** has he ever done anything for us?

3: **rien de: rien d'intéressant** nothing interesting; **rien d'autre** nothing else; **rien du tout** nothing at all

4: **rien que** just, only; nothing but; **rien que pour lui faire plaisir** only ou just to please him; **rien que la vérité** nothing but the truth; **rien que cela** that alone

♦ nm: **un petit rien** (cadeau) a little something; **des riens** trivia pl; **un rien de** a hint of; **en un rien de temps** in no time at all

**rieur, -euse** [ʀ(i)jœʀ, ʀ(i)jøz] adj cheerful

**rigide** [ʀiʒid] adj stiff; (fig) rigid; strict

**rigole** [ʀigɔl] nf (conduit) channel

**rigoler** [ʀigɔle] vi (fam: rire) to laugh; (s'amuser) to have (some) fun; (plaisanter) to be joking ou kidding; **rigolo, -ote** (fam) adj funny ♦ nm/f comic; (péj) fraud, phoney

**rigoureusement** [ʀiguʀøzmɑ̃] adv (vrai) absolutely; (interdit) strictly

**rigoureux, -euse** [ʀiguʀø, øz] adj rigorous; (hiver) hard, harsh

**rigueur** [ʀigœʀ] nf rigour; **être de ~** to be the rule; **à la ~** at a pinch; **tenir ~ à qn de qch** to hold sth against sb

**rillettes** [ʀijɛt] nfpl potted meat (made from pork or goose)

**rime** [ʀim] nf rhyme

**rinçage** [ʀɛ̃saʒ] nm rinsing (out); (opération) rinse

**rincer** [ʀɛ̃se] vt to rinse; (récipient) to rinse out

**ring** [ʀiŋ] nm (boxing) ring

**ringard, e** [ʀɛ̃gaʀ, aʀd] (fam) adj old-fashioned

**rions** [ʀi͡ɔ̃] vb voir **rire**

**riposter** [ʀipɔste] vi to retaliate ♦ vt: ~ **que** to retort that

**rire** [ʀiʀ] vi to laugh; (se divertir) to have fun ♦ nm laugh; **le ~** laughter; **~ de** to laugh at; **pour ~** (pas sérieusement) for a joke ou a laugh

**risée** [ʀize] nf: **être la ~** de to be the laughing stock of

**risible** [ʀizibl] adj laughable

**risque** [ʀisk] nm risk; **le ~** danger; **à ses ~s et périls** at his own risk; **risqué, e** adj risky; (plaisanterie) risqué, daring; **risquer** [ʀiske] vt to risk; (allusion, question) to venture, hazard; **ça ne risque rien** it's quite safe; **risquer de: il risque de se tuer** he could get himself killed; **ce qui risque de se produire** what might ou could well happen; **il ne risque pas de recommencer** there's no chance of him doing that again; **se risquer à faire** (tenter) to venture ou dare to do

**rissoler** [ʀisɔle] vi, vt: **(faire) ~** to brown

**ristourne** [ʀistuʀn] nf discount

**rite** [ʀit] nm rite; (fig) ritual

**rivage** [ʀivaʒ] nm shore

**rival, e, -aux** [ʀival, -o] adj, nm/f rival; **rivaliser** vi: **rivaliser avec** (personne) to rival, vie with; **rivalité** nf rivalry

**rive** [ʀiv] nf shore; (de fleuve) bank; **riverain, e** nm/f riverside ou (au lakeside) resident; (d'une route) local resident

**rivet** [ʀivɛ] nm rivet

**rivière** [ʀivjɛʀ] nf river

**rixe** [ʀiks] nf brawl, scuffle

**riz** [ʀi] nm rice; **rizière** nf paddy-field, ricefield

**RMI** sigle m (= revenu minimum d'insertion) = income support (BRIT), welfare (US)

**RN** sigle f = **route nationale**

**robe** [ʀɔb] nf dress; (de juge) robe; (pelage) coat; **~ de chambre** dressing gown; **~ de soirée/de mariée** evening/wedding dress

**robinet** [ʀɔbinɛ] nm tap

**robot** [ʀɔbo] nm robot

**robuste** [ʀɔbyst] adj robust, sturdy; **robustesse** nf robustness, sturdiness

**roc** [ʀɔk] nm rock

**rocade** [ʀɔkad] nf bypass

**rocaille** [ʀɔkaj] nf loose stones pl; (jardin) rockery, rock garden

**roche** [ʀɔʃ] nf rock

**rocher** [ʀɔʃe] nm rock

**rocheux, -euse** [ʀɔʃø, øz] adj rocky

**rodage** [ʀɔdaʒ] nm: **en ~** running in

**roder** [ʀɔde] vt (AUTO) to run in

**rôder** [ʀode] vi to roam about; (de façon suspecte) to lurk (about ou around); **rôdeur, -euse** nm/f prowler

**rogne** [ʀɔɲ] (fam) nf: **être en ~** to be in a temper

**rogner** [ʀɔɲe] vt to clip; **~ sur** (fig) to cut down ou back on

**rognons** [ʀɔɲɔ̃] nmpl (CULIN) kidneys

**roi** [ʀwa] nm king; **la fête des R~s, les R~s** Twelfth Night

| fête des Rois |
| --- |

La **fête des Rois** is celebrated on January 6. Figurines representing the magi are traditionally added to the Christmas crib and people eat la **galette des Rois**, a plain, flat cake in which a porcelain charm (la **fève**) is hidden. Whoever finds the charm is king or queen for the day and chooses a partner.

**rôle** [ʀol] nm role, part

**romain, e** [ʀɔmɛ̃, ɛn] adj Roman ♦ nm/f: **R~, e** Roman

**roman, e** [ʀɔmã, an] adj (ARCHIT) Romanesque ♦ nm novel; **~ d'espionnage** spy novel ou story; **~ policier** detective story

**romance** [ʀɔmãs] nf ballad

**romancer** [ʀɔmãse] vt (agrémenter) to romanticize; **romancier, -ière** nm/f novelist; **romanesque** adj (amours, aventures) storybook cpd; (sentimental;

*personne)* romantic

**roman-feuilleton** [ʀɔmɑ̃fœjtɔ̃] nm serialized novel

**romanichel, le** [ʀɔmaniʃɛl] (*péj*) nm/f gipsy

**romantique** [ʀɔmɑ̃tik] adj romantic

**romarin** [ʀɔmaʀɛ̃] nm rosemary

**rompre** [ʀɔ̃pʀ] vt to break; (*entretien, fiançailles*) to break off ♦ vi (*fiancés*) to break it off; **se ~** vi to break; **rompu, e** adj (*fourbu*) exhausted

**ronces** [ʀɔ̃s] nfpl brambles

**ronchonner** [ʀɔ̃ʃɔne] (*fam*) vi to grouse, grouch

**rond, e** [ʀɔ̃, ʀɔ̃d] adj round; (*joues, mollets*) well-rounded; (*fam: ivre*) tight ♦ nm (*cercle*) ring; (*fam: sou*): **je n'ai plus un ~** I haven't a penny left; **en ~** (*s'asseoir, danser*) in a ring; **ronde** nf (*gén: de surveillance*) rounds pl, patrol; (*danse*) round (dance); (*MUS*) semibreve (*BRIT*), whole note (*US*); **à la ronde** (*alentour*): **à 10 km à la ronde** for 10 km round; **rondelet, te** adj plump

**rondelle** [ʀɔ̃dɛl] nf (*tranche*) slice, round; (*TECH*) washer

**rondement** [ʀɔ̃dmɑ̃] adv (*efficacement*) briskly

**rondin** [ʀɔ̃dɛ̃] nm log

**rond-point** [ʀɔ̃pwɛ̃] nm roundabout

**ronflant, e** [ʀɔ̃flɑ̃, ɑ̃t] (*péj*) adj high-flown, grand

**ronflement** [ʀɔ̃fləmɑ̃] nm snore, snoring

**ronfler** [ʀɔ̃fle] vi to snore; (*moteur, poêle*) to hum

**ronger** [ʀɔ̃ʒe] vt to gnaw (at); (*suj: vers, rouille*) to eat into; **se ~ les ongles** to bite one's nails; **se ~ les sangs** to worry o.s. sick; **rongeur** nm rodent

**ronronner** [ʀɔ̃ʀɔne] vi to purr

**rosace** [ʀozas] nf (*vitrail*) rose window

**rosbif** [ʀɔsbif] nm: **du ~** roasting beef; (*cuit*) roast beef

**rose** [ʀoz] nf rose ♦ adj pink

**rosé, e** [ʀoze] adj pinkish; (*vin*) ~ rosé

**roseau, x** [ʀozo] nm reed

**rosée** [ʀoze] nf dew

**rosette** [ʀozɛt] nf (*nœud*) bow

**rosier** [ʀozje] nm rosebush, rose tree

**rosse** [ʀɔs] nf (*fam*) adj nasty, vicious

**rossignol** [ʀɔsiɲɔl] nm (*ZOOL*) nightingale

**rot** [ʀo] nm belch; (*de bébé*) burp

**rotatif, -ive** [ʀɔtatif, iv] adj rotary

**rotation** [ʀɔtasjɔ̃] nf rotation

**roter** [ʀɔte] (*fam*) vi to burp, belch

**rôti** [ʀoti] nm: **du ~** roasting meat; (*cuit*) roast meat; **~ de bœuf/porc** joint of beef/pork

**rotin** [ʀɔtɛ̃] nm rattan (cane); **fauteuil en ~** cane (arm)chair

**rôtir** [ʀotiʀ] vi, vt (*aussi:* **faire ~**) to roast; **rôtisserie** nf (*restaurant*) steakhouse; (*traiteur*) roast meat shop; **rôtissoire** nf (roasting) spit

**rotule** [ʀɔtyl] nf kneecap

**roturier, -ière** [ʀɔtyʀje, jɛʀ] nm/f commoner

**rouage** [ʀwaʒ] nm cog(wheel), gearwheel; **les ~s de l'État** the wheels of State

**roucouler** [ʀukule] vi to coo

**roue** [ʀu] nf wheel; **~ de secours** spare wheel

**roué, e** [ʀwe] adj wily

**rouer** [ʀwe] vt: **~ qn de coups** to give sb a thrashing

**rouge** [ʀuʒ] adj, nm/f red ♦ nm red; (*vin*) ~ red wine; (*sur la liste*) ~ exdirectory (*BRIT*), unlisted (*US*); **passer au ~** (*signal*) to go red; (*automobiliste*) to go through a red light; **~ (à lèvres)** lipstick; **rouge-gorge** nm robin (redbreast)

**rougeole** [ʀuʒɔl] nf measles sg

**rougeoyer** [ʀuʒwaje] vi to glow red

**rouget** [ʀuʒɛ] nm mullet

**rougeur** [ʀuʒœʀ] nf redness; (*MÉD: tache*) red blotch

**rougir** [ʀuʒiʀ] vi to turn red; (*de honte, timidité*) to blush, flush; (*de plaisir, colère*) to flush

**rouille** [ʀuj] nf rust; **rouillé, e** adj

rusty; **rouiller** *vt* to rust ♦ *vi* to rust, go rusty; **se rouiller** *vi* to rust

**roulant, e** [Rulɑ̃, ɑ̃t] *adj* (*meuble*) on wheels; (*tapis etc*) moving; **escalier ~** escalator

**rouleau, x** [Rulo] *nm* roll; (*à mise en plis, à peinture, vague*) roller; **~ à pâtisserie** rolling pin

**roulement** [Rulmɑ̃] *nm* (*rotation*) rotation; (*bruit*) rumbling *no pl*, rumble; **travailler par ~** to work on a rota (BRIT) *ou* rotation (US) basis; **~ (à billes)** ball bearings *pl*; **~ de tambour** drum roll

**rouler** [Rule] *vt* to roll; (*papier, tapis*) to roll up; (CULIN: *pâte*) to roll out; (*fam: duper*) to do ♦ *vi* (*bille, boule*) to roll; (*voiture, train*) to go, run; (*automobiliste*) to drive; (*bateau*) to roll; **se ~ dans** (*boue*) to roll in; (*couverture*) to roll o.s. (up) in

**roulette** [Rulɛt] *nf* (*de table, fauteuil*) castor; (*de dentiste*) drill; (*jeu*) roulette; **à ~s** on castors; **ça a marché comme sur des ~s** (*fam*) it went off very smoothly

**roulis** [Ruli] *nm* roll(ing)

**roulotte** [Rulɔt] *nf* caravan

**roumain, e** [Rumɛ̃, ɛn] *adj* Rumanian ♦ *nm/f*: **R~, e** Rumanian

**Roumanie** [Rumani] *nf* Rumania

**rouquin, e** [Rukɛ̃, in] (*péj*) *nm/f* redhead

**rouspéter** [Ruspete] (*fam*) *vi* to moan

**rousse** [Rus] *adj voir* **roux**

**roussir** [Rusir] *vt* to scorch ♦ *vi* (CULIN): **faire ~** to brown

**route** [Rut] *nf* road; (*fig: chemin*) way; (*itinéraire, parcours*) route; (*fig: voie*) road, path; **il y a 3h de ~** it's a 3-hour ride *ou* journey; **en ~** on the way; **mettre en ~** to start up; **se mettre en ~** to set off; **~ nationale** ≈ A road (BRIT), ≈ state highway (US); **routier, -ière** *adj road cpd* ♦ *nm* (*camionneur*) (long-distance) lorry (BRIT) *ou* truck (US) driver; (*restaurant*) ≈ transport café

(BRIT), ≈ truck stop (US)

**routine** [Rutin] *nf* routine; **routinier, -ière** (*péj*) *adj* (*activité*) humdrum; (*personne*) addicted to routine

**rouvrir** [Ruvrir] *vt, vi* to reopen, open again; **se ~** *vi* to reopen, open again

**roux, rousse** [Ru, Rus] *adj* red; (*personne*) red-haired ♦ *nm/f* redhead

**royal, e, -aux** [Rwajal, o] *adj* royal; (*cadeau etc*) fit for a king

**royaume** [Rwajom] *nm* kingdom; (*fig*) realm; **le R~-Uni** the United Kingdom

**royauté** [Rwajote] *nf* (*régime*) monarchy

**RPR** *sigle m*: **Rassemblement pour la République** French right-wing political party

**ruban** [Rybɑ̃] *nm* ribbon; **~ adhésif** adhesive tape

**rubéole** [Rybeɔl] *nf* German measles *sg*, rubella

**rubis** [Rybi] *nm* ruby

**rubrique** [Rybrik] *nf* (*titre, catégorie*) heading; (PRESSE: *article*) column

**ruche** [Ryʃ] *nf* hive

**rude** [Ryd] *adj* (*au toucher*) rough; (*métier, tâche*) hard, tough; (*climat*) severe, harsh; (*bourru*) harsh, rough; (*fruste: manières*) rugged, tough; (*fam: fameux*) jolly good; **rudement** (*fam*) *adv* (*très*) terribly

**rudimentaire** [Rydimɑ̃tɛr] *adj* rudimentary, basic

**rudiments** [Rydimɑ̃] *nmpl*: **avoir des ~ d'anglais** to have a smattering of English

**rudoyer** [Rydwaje] *vt* to treat harshly

**rue** [Ry] *nf* street

**ruée** [Rɥe] *nf* rush

**ruelle** [Rɥɛl] *nf* alley(-way)

**ruer** [Rɥe] *vi* (*cheval*) to kick out; **se ~ vi: se ~ sur** to pounce on; **se ~ vers/dans/hors de** to rush *ou* dash towards/into/out of

**rugby** [Rygbi] *nm* rugby (football)

**rugir** [Ryʒir] *vi* to roar

**rugueux, -euse** [Rygø, øz] *adj* rough

**ruine** [ʀɥin] nf ruin; **ruiner** vt to ruin; **ruineux, -euse** adj ruinous

**ruisseau, X** [ʀɥiso] nm stream, brook

**ruisseler** [ʀɥis(ə)le] vi to stream

**rumeur** [ʀymœʀ] nf (nouvelle) rumour; (bruit confus) rumbling

**ruminer** [ʀymine] vt (herbe) to ruminate; (fig) to ruminate on ou over, chew over

**rupture** [ʀyptyʀ] nf (séparation, désunion) break-up, split; (de négociations etc) breakdown; (de contrat) breach; (dans continuité) break

**rural, e, -aux** [ʀyʀal, o] adj rural, country cpd

**ruse** [ʀyz] nf: **la ~** cunning, craftiness; (pour tromper) trickery; **une ~** a trick, a ruse; **rusé, e** adj cunning, crafty

**russe** [ʀys] adj Russian ♦ nm/f: **R~** Russian ♦ nm (LING) Russian

**Russie** [ʀysi] nf: **la ~** Russia

**rustine** ® [ʀystin] nf rubber repair patch (for bicycle tyre)

**rustique** [ʀystik] adj rustic

**rustre** [ʀystʀ] nm boor

**rutilant, e** [ʀytilɑ̃, ɑ̃t] adj gleaming

**rythme** [ʀitm] nm rhythm; (vitesse) rate; (: de la vie) pace, tempo; **rythmé, e** adj rhythmic(al)

## S, s

**s'** [s] pron voir **se**

**sa** [sa] adj voir **son**

**SA** sigle (= société anonyme) ≃ Ltd (BRIT), ≃ Inc. (US)

**sable** [sabl] nm sand; **~s mouvants** quicksand(s)

**sablé** [sable] nm shortbread biscuit

**sabler** [sable] vt (contre le verglas) to grit; **~ le champagne** to drink champagne

**sablier** [sablije] nm hourglass; (de cuisine) egg timer

**sablonneux, -euse** [sablɔnø, øz] adj sandy

**saborder** [sabɔʀde] vt (navire) to scuttle; (fig: projet) to put paid to, scupper

**sabot** [sabo] nm clog; (de cheval) hoof; **~ de frein** brake shoe

**saboter** [sabɔte] vt to sabotage; (bâcler) to make a mess of, botch

**sac** [sak] nm bag; (à charbon etc) sack; **~ à dos** rucksack; **~ à main** handbag; **~ de couchage** sleeping bag; **~ de voyage** travelling bag; **~ poubelle** bin liner

**saccadé, e** [sakade] adj jerky; (respiration) spasmodic

**saccager** [sakaʒe] vt (piller) to sack; (dévaster) to create havoc in

**saccharine** [sakaʀin] nf saccharin

**sacerdoce** [sasɛʀdɔs] nm priesthood; (fig) calling, vocation

**sache** etc [saʃ] vb voir **savoir**

**sachet** [saʃɛ] nm (small) bag; (de sucre, café) sachet; **du potage en ~** packet soup; **~ de thé** tea bag

**sacoche** [sakɔʃ] nf (gén) bag; (de bicyclette) saddlebag

**sacquer** [sake] (fam) vt (employé) to fire; (détester): **je ne peux pas le ~** I can't stand him

**sacre** [sakʀ] nm (roi) coronation

**sacré, e** [sakʀe] adj sacred; (fam: satané) blasted; (: fameux): **un ~ toupé** a heck of a cheek

**sacrement** [sakʀəmɑ̃] nm sacrament

**sacrifice** [sakʀifis] nm sacrifice; **sacrifier** vt to sacrifice

**sacristie** [sakʀisti] nf (catholique) sacristy; (protestante) vestry

**sadique** [sadik] adj sadistic

**safran** [safʀɑ̃] nm saffron

**sage** [saʒ] adj wise; (enfant) good

**sage-femme** [saʒfam] nf midwife

**sagesse** [saʒɛs] nf wisdom

**Sagittaire** [saʒitɛʀ] nm: **le ~** Sagittarius

**Sahara** [saaʀa] nm: **le ~** the Sahara (desert)

**saignant, e** [sɛɲɑ̃, ɑ̃t] adj (viande) rare

**saignée** [seɲe] nf (fig) heavy losses pl

**saigner** [seɲe] vi to bleed ♦ vt to bleed; (animal) to kill (by bleeding); ~ **du nez** to have a nosebleed

**saillie** [saji] nf (sur un mur etc) projection

**saillir** [sajiʀ] vi to project, stick out; (veine, muscle) to bulge

**sain, e** [sɛ̃, sɛn] adj healthy; ~ **d'esprit** sound in mind, sane; ~ **et sauf** safe and sound, unharmed

**saindoux** [sɛ̃du] nm lard

**saint, e** [sɛ̃, sɛ̃t] adj holy ♦ nm/f saint; **le S~ Esprit** the Holy Spirit ou Ghost; **la S~e Vierge** the Blessed Virgin; **la S~-Sylvestre** New Year's Eve; **sainteté** nf holiness

**sais** etc [sɛ] vb voir **savoir**

**saisi, e** [sezi] adj: ~ **de panique** panic-stricken; **être** ~ (**par le froid**) to be struck by the sudden cold

**saisie** nf seizure; ~**e** (**de données**) (data) capture

**saisir** [seziʀ] vt to take hold of, grab; (fig: occasion) to seize; (comprendre) to grasp; (entendre) to get, catch; (données) to capture; (CULIN) to fry quickly; (JUR: biens, publication) to seize; **se** ~ **de** vt to seize; **saisissant, e** adj startling, striking

**saison** [sɛzɔ̃] nf season; **morte** ~ slack season; **saisonnier, -ière** adj seasonal

**sait** [sɛ] vb voir **savoir**

**salade** [salad] nf (BOT) lettuce etc; (CULIN) (green) salad; (fam: confusion) tangle, muddle; ~ **composée** mixed salad; ~ **de fruits** fruit salad; **saladier** nm (salad) bowl

**salaire** [salɛʀ] nm (annuel, mensuel) salary; (hebdomadaire, journalier) pay, wages pl; ~ **minimum interprofessionnel de croissance** index-linked guaranteed minimum wage

**salarié, e** [salaʀje] nm/f salaried employee; wage-earner

**salaud** [salo] (fam!) nm sod (!), bastard (!)

**sale** [sal] adj dirty, filthy; (fam: mauvais)

nasty

**salé, e** [sale] adj (mer, goût) salty; (CULIN: amandes, beurre etc) salted; (: gâteaux) savoury; (fam: grivois) spicy; (: facture) steep

**saler** [sale] vt to salt

**saleté** [salte] nf (état) dirtiness; (crasse) dirt, filth; (tache etc) dirt no pl; (fam: méchanceté) dirty trick; (: camelote) rubbish no pl; (: obscénité) filthy thing (to say)

**salière** [saljɛʀ] nf saltcellar

**salin, e** [salɛ̃, in] adj saline

**salir** [saliʀ] vt to (make) dirty; (fig: quelqu'un) to soil the reputation of; **se** ~ vi to get dirty; **salissant, e** adj (tissu) which shows the dirt; (travail) dirty, messy

**salle** [sal] nf room; (d'hôpital) ward; (de restaurant) dining room; (d'un cinéma) auditorium; (: public) audience; ~ **à manger** dining room; ~ **d'attente** waiting room; ~ **de bain(s)** bathroom; ~ **de classe** classroom; ~ **de concert** concert hall; ~ **de douches** shower-room; ~ **d'embarquement** (à l'aéroport) departure lounge; ~ **de jeux** (pour enfants) playroom; ~ **d'opération** (d'hôpital) operating theatre; ~ **de séjour** living room; ~ **des ventes** saleroom

**salon** [salɔ̃] nm lounge, sitting room; (mobilier) lounge suite; (exposition) exhibition, show; ~ **de coiffure** hair-dressing salon; ~ **de thé** tearoom

**salope** [salɔp] (fam!) nf bitch (!); **saloperie** (fam!) nf (action) dirty trick; (chose sans valeur) rubbish no pl

**salopette** [salɔpɛt] nf dungarees pl; (d'ouvrier) overall(s)

**salsifis** [salsifi] nm salsify

**salubre** [salybʀ] adj healthy, salubrious

**saluer** [salɥe] vt (pour dire bonjour, fig) to greet; (pour dire au revoir) to take one's leave; (MIL) to salute

**salut** [saly] nm (geste) wave; (parole) greeting; (MIL) salute; (sauvegarde) safety; (REL) salvation ♦ excl (fam: bonjour) hi (there); (: au revoir) see you, bye

**salutations** [salytasjɔ̃] *nfpl* greetings; **Veuillez agréer, Monsieur, mes ~ distinguées** yours faithfully

**samedi** [samdi] *nm* Saturday

**SAMU** [samy] *sigle m* (= *service d'assistance médicale d'urgence*) ≃ ambulance (service) (BRIT), ≃ paramedics *pl* (US)

**sanction** [sɑ̃ksjɔ̃] *nf* sanction; **sanctionner** *vt* (loi, usage) to sanction; (punir) to punish

**sandale** [sɑ̃dal] *nf* sandal; **~s à lanières** strappy sandals

**sandwich** [sɑ̃dwi(t)ʃ] *nm* sandwich

**sang** [sɑ̃] *nm* blood; **en ~** covered in blood; **se faire du mauvais ~** to fret, get in a state; **sang-froid** *nm* calm, sangfroid; **de sang-froid** in cold blood; **sanglant, e** *adj* bloody

**sangle** [sɑ̃gl] *nf* strap

**sanglier** [sɑ̃glije] *nm* (wild) boar

**sanglot** [sɑ̃glo] *nm* sob; **sangloter** *vi* to sob

**sangsue** [sɑ̃sy] *nf* leech

**sanguin, e** [sɑ̃gɛ̃, in] *adj* blood *cpd*; **sanguinaire** *adj* bloodthirsty

**sanitaire** [saniteʀ] *adj* health *cpd*; **~s** *nmpl* (lieu) bathroom *sg*

**sans** [sɑ̃] *prép* without; **un pull ~ manches** a sleeveless jumper; **~ faute** without fail; **~ arrêt** without a break; **~ ça** (fam) otherwise; **~ qu'il s'en aperçoive** without him ou his noticing; **sans-abri** *nmpl* homeless; **sans-emploi** *nmf inv* unemployed person; **les sans-emploi** the unemployed; **sans-gêne** *adj inv* inconsiderate

**santé** [sɑ̃te] *nf* health; **en bonne ~** in good health; **boire à la ~ de qn** to drink (to) sb's health; **à ta/votre ~!** cheers!

**saoudien, ne** [saudjɛ̃, jen] *adj* Saudi Arabian ♦ *nm/f:* **S~, ne** Saudi Arabian

**saoul, e** [su, sul] *adj* = soûl

**saper** [sape] *vt* to undermine, sap

**sapeur-pompier** [sapœʀpɔ̃pje] *nm* fireman

**saphir** [safiʀ] *nm* sapphire

**sapin** [sapɛ̃] *nm* fir (tree); (bois) fir; **~ de Noël** Christmas tree

**sarcastique** [saʀkastik] *adj* sarcastic

**Sardaigne** [saʀdɛɲ] *nf:* **la ~** Sardinia

**sarrasin** [saʀazɛ̃] *nm* buckwheat

**SARL** *sigle f* (= *société à responsabilité limitée*) ≃ plc (BRIT), ≃ Inc. (US)

**sas** [sɑs] *nm* (de sous-marin, d'engin spatial) airlock; (d'écluse) lock

**satané, e** [satane] (fam) *adj* confounded

**satellite** [satelit] *nm* satellite

**satin** [satɛ̃] *nm* satin

**satire** [satiʀ] *nf* satire; **satirique** *adj* satirical

**satisfaction** [satisfaksjɔ̃] *nf* satisfaction

**satisfaire** [satisfɛʀ] *vt* to satisfy; **~ à** (conditions) to meet; **satisfaisant, e** *adj* (acceptable) satisfactory; **satisfait, e** *adj* satisfied; **satisfait de** happy ou satisfied with

**saturer** [satyʀe] *vt* to saturate

**sauce** [sos] *nf* sauce; (avec un rôti) gravy; **saucière** *nf* sauceboat

**saucisse** [sosis] *nf* sausage

**saucisson** [sosisɔ̃] *nm* (slicing) sausage

**sauf, sauve** [sof, sov] *adj* unharmed, unhurt; (fig: honneur) intact, saved ♦ *prép* except; **laisser la vie sauve à qn** to spare sb's life; **~ si** (à moins que) unless; **~ erreur** if I'm not mistaken; **~ avis contraire** unless you hear to the contrary

**sauge** [soʒ] *nf* sage

**saugrenu, e** [sogʀany] *adj* preposterous

**saule** [sol] *nm* willow (tree)

**saumon** [somɔ̃] *nm* salmon *inv*

**saumure** [somyʀ] *nf* brine

**saupoudrer** [sopudʀe] *vt:* **~ qch de** to sprinkle sth with

**saur** [sɔʀ] *adj m:* **hareng ~** smoked ou red herring, kipper

**saurai** etc [sɔʀe] *vb voir* savoir

**saut** [so] nm jump; (discipline sportive) jumping; **faire un ~ chez qn** to pop over to sb's (place); **~ à l'élastique** bungee jumping; **~ à la perche** vaulting; **~ en hauteur/longueur** high/long jump; **~ périlleux** somersault

**saute** [sot] nf: **~ d'humeur** sudden change of mood

**sauter** [sote] vi to jump, leap; (exploser) to blow up, explode; (: fusibles) to blow; (se détacher) to pop out (ou off) ♦ vt to skip, miss (out); **faire ~** to blow up; (CULIN) to sauté; **~ au cou de qn** to fly into sb's arms; **~ sur une occasion** to jump at an opportunity; **~ aux yeux** to be (quite) obvious

**sauterelle** [sotʀɛl] nf grasshopper

**sautiller** [sotije] vi (oiseau) to hop; (enfant) to skip

**sauvage** [sovaʒ] adj (gén) wild; (peuplade) savage; (farouche: personne) unsociable; (barbare) wild, savage; (non officiel) unauthorized, unofficial; **faire du camping ~** to camp in the wild ♦ nm/f savage; (timide) unsociable type

**sauve** [sov] adj f voir **sauf**

**sauvegarde** [sovgaʀd] nf safeguard; (INFORM) backup; **sauvegarder** vt to safeguard; (INFORM: enregistrer) to save; (: copier) to back up

**sauve-qui-peut** [sovkipø] excl run for your life!

**sauver** [sove] vt to save; (porter secours à) to rescue; (récupérer) to salvage, rescue; **se ~** vi (s'enfuir) to run away; (fam: partir) to be off; **sauvetage** nm rescue; **sauveteur** nm rescuer; **sauvette**: **à la sauvette** adv (se marier etc) hastily, hurriedly; **sauveur** nm saviour (BRIT), savior (US)

**savais** etc [save] vb voir **savoir**

**savamment** [savamɑ̃] adv (avec érudition) learnedly; (habilement) skilfully, cleverly

**savant, e** [savɑ̃, ɑ̃t] adj scholarly,

learned ♦ nm scientist

**saveur** [savœʀ] nf flavour; (fig) savour

**savoir** [savwaʀ] vt to know; (être capable de): **il sait nager** he can swim ♦ nm knowledge; **se ~** vi (être connu) to be known; **à ~** that is, namely; **faire ~ qch à qn** to let sb know sth; **pas que je sache** not as far as I know

**savon** [savɔ̃] nm (produit) soap; (morceau) bar of soap; (fam): **passer un ~ à qn** to give sb a good dressing-down; **savonner** vt to soap; **savonnette** ♦ nf bar of soap

**savons** [savɔ̃] vb voir **savoir**

**savourer** [savuʀe] vt to savour; **savoureux, -euse** adj tasty; (fig: anecdote) spicy, juicy

**saxo(phone)** [sakso(fɔn)] nm sax(ophone)

**scabreux, -euse** [skabʀø, øz] adj risky; (indécent) improper, shocking

**scandale** [skɑ̃dal] nm scandal; (tapage): **faire un ~** to make a scene, create a disturbance; **faire ~** to scandalize people; **scandaleux, -euse** adj scandalous, outrageous

**scandinave** [skɑ̃dinav] adj Scandinavian ♦ nm/f: **S~** Scandinavian

**Scandinavie** [skɑ̃dinavi] nf Scandinavia

**scaphandre** [skafɑ̃dʀ] nm (de plongeur) diving suit

**scarabée** [skaʀabe] nm beetle

**scarlatine** [skaʀlatin] nf scarlet fever

**scarole** [skaʀɔl] nf endive

**sceau, x** [so] nm seal

**scélérat** [seleʀa, at] nm/f villain

**sceller** [sele] vt to seal

**scénario** [senaʀjo] nm scenario

**scène** [sɛn] nf (gén) scene; (estrade, fig: théâtre) stage; **entrer en ~** to come on stage; **mettre en ~** (THÉÂTRE) to stage; (CINÉMA) to direct; **~ de ménage** domestic scene

**sceptique** [sɛptik] adj sceptical

**schéma** [ʃema] nm (diagramme) diagram, sketch; **schématique** adj dia-

## sciatique

grammatical(al), schematic; *(fig)* oversimplified

**sciatique** [sjatik] *nf* sciatica

**scie** [si] *nf saw; ~ à métaux* hacksaw

**sciemment** [sjamɑ̃] *adv* knowingly

**science** [sjɑ̃s] *nf* science; *(savoir)* knowledge; **~s naturelles** *(SCOL)* natural science *sg*, biology *sg*; **~s po** political science *ou* studies *pl*; **science-fiction** *nf* science fiction; **scientifique** *adj* scientific ♦ *nm/f* scientist; *(étudiant)* science student

**scier** [sje] *vt* to saw; *(retrancher)* to saw off; **scierie** *nf* sawmill

**scinder** [sɛ̃de] *vt* to split up; **se ~** *vi* to split up

**scintiller** [sɛ̃tije] *vi* to sparkle; *(étoile)* to twinkle

**scission** [sisjɔ̃] *nf* split

**sciure** [sjyʀ] *nf*: **~ (de bois)** sawdust

**sclérose** [skleʀoz] *nf*: **~ en plaques** multiple sclerosis

**scolaire** [skɔleʀ] *adj* school *cpd*; **scolariser** *vt* to provide with schooling/schools; **scolarité** *nf* schooling

**scooter** [skutœʀ] *nm* (motor) scooter

**score** [skɔʀ] *nm* score

**scorpion** [skɔʀpjɔ̃] *nm (signe)*: **le S~** Scorpio

**Scotch ®** [skɔtʃ] *nm* adhesive tape

**scout, e** [skut] *adj, nm* scout

**script** [skʀipt] *nm (écriture)* printing; *(CINÉMA)* (shooting) script

**scrupule** [skʀypyl] *nm* scruple

**scruter** [skʀyte] *vt* to scrutinize; *(l'obscurité)* to peer into

**scrutin** [skʀytɛ̃] *nm (vote)* ballot; *(ensemble des opérations)* poll

**sculpter** [skylte] *vt* to sculpt; *(bois)* to carve; **sculpteur** *nm* sculptor; **sculpture** *nf* sculpture; **sculpture sur bois** wood carving

**SDF** *sigle m (= sans domicile fixe)* homeless person; **les SDF** the homeless

---

MOT-CLÉ

**se** [sə], **s'** *pron* **1** *(emploi réfléchi)* oneself;

(: *masc*) himself; (: *fém*) herself; (: *sujet non humain*) itself; (: *pl*) themselves; **se voir comme l'on est** to see o.s. as one is

**2** *(réciproque)* one another, each other; **ils s'aiment** they love one another *ou* each other

**3** *(passif)*: **cela se répare facilement** it is easily repaired

**4** *(possessif)*: **se casser la jambe/laver les mains** to break one's leg/wash one's hands

---

**séance** [seɑ̃s] *nf (d'assemblée)* meeting, session; *(de tribunal)* sitting, session; *(musicale, CINÉMA, THÉÂTRE)* performance; **~ tenante** forthwith

**seau, x** [so] *nm* bucket, pail

**sec, sèche** [sek, sɛʃ] *adj* dry; *(raisins, figues)* dried; *(cœur: insensible)* hard, cold ♦ *nm*: **tenir au ~** to keep in a dry place ♦ *adv* hard; **je le bois ~** I drink it straight *ou* neat; **à ~** *(puits)* dried up

**sécateur** [sekatœʀ] *nm* secateurs *pl* *(BRIT)*, shears *pl*

**sèche** [sɛʃ] *adj f voir* **sec**; **sèche-cheveux** *nm inv* hair-drier; **sèche-linge** *nm inv* tumble dryer; **sèchement** *adv (répondre)* drily

**sécher** [seʃe] *vt* to dry; *(dessécher: peau, blé)* to dry (out); *(: étang)* to dry up; *(fam: cours)* to skip ♦ *vi* to dry; to dry out; to dry up; *(fam: candidat)* to be stumped; **se ~** *(après le bain)* to dry o.s.; **sécheresse** *nf* dryness; *(absence de pluie)* drought; **séchoir** *nm* drier

**second, e** [s(ə)gɔ̃, ɔ̃d] *adj* second ♦ *nm (assistant)* second in command; *(NAVIG)* first mate; **voyager en ~e** to travel second-class; **secondaire** *adj* secondary; **seconde** *nf* second; **seconder** *vt* to assist

**secouer** [s(ə)kwe] *vt* to shake; *(passagers)* to rock; *(traumatiser)* to shake (up); **se ~** *vi (fam: faire un effort)* to shake o.s. up; (: *se dépêcher*) to get a move on

**secourir** [s(ə)kuʀiʀ] vt (venir en aide à) to assist, aid; **secourisme** nm first aid; **secouriste** nmf first-aid worker

**secours** [s(ə)kuʀ] nm help, aid, assistance ♦ nmpl aid sg; **au ~!** help!; **appeler au ~** to shout ou call for help; **porter ~ à qn** to give sb assistance, help sb; **les premiers ~** first aid sg

**secousse** [s(ə)kus] nf jolt, bump; (électrique) shock; (fig: psychologique) jolt, shock; **~ sismique** earth tremor

**secret, -ète** [sakʀε, εt] adj secret; (fig: renfermé) reserved ♦ nm secret; (discrétion absolue): **le ~** secrecy

**secrétaire** [s(ə)kʀetεʀ] nm/f secretary ♦ nm (meuble) writing desk; **~ de direction** private ou personal secretary; **~ d'État** junior minister; **~ général** (COMM) company secretary; **secrétariat** nm (profession) secretarial work; (bureau) office; (: d'organisation internationale) secretariat

**secteur** [sεktœʀ] nm sector; (zone) area; (ÉLEC): **branché sur ~** plugged into the mains (supply)

**section** [sεksjɔ̃] nf section; (de parcours d'autobus) fare stage; (MIL: unité) platoon; **sectionner** vt to sever

**Sécu** [seky] abr f = sécurité sociale

**séculaire** [sekylεʀ] adj (très vieux) age-old

**sécuriser** [sekyʀize] vt to give a feeling of) security to

**sécurité** [sekyʀite] nf (absence de danger) safety; (absence de troubles) security; **système de ~** security system; **être en ~** to be safe; **la ~ routière** road safety; **la ~ sociale** ≈ (the) Social Security (BRIT), ≈ Welfare (US)

**sédentaire** [sedɑ̃tεʀ] adj sedentary

**séduction** [sedyksjɔ̃] nf seduction; (charme, attrait) appeal, charm

**séduire** [seduiʀ] vt to charm; (femme: abuser de) to seduce; **séduisant, e** adj (femme) seductive; (homme, offre) very attractive

**ségrégation** [segʀegasjɔ̃] nf segregation

**seigle** [sεgl] nm rye

**seigneur** [sεɲœʀ] nm lord

**sein** [sε̃] nm breast; (entrailles) womb; **au ~ de** (équipe, institution) within

**séisme** [seism] nm earthquake

**seize** [sεz] num sixteen; **seizième** num sixteenth

**séjour** [seʒuʀ] nm stay; (pièce) living room; **séjourner** vi to stay

**sel** [sεl] nm salt; (fig: piquant) spice

**sélection** [selεksjɔ̃] nf selection; **sélectionner** vt to select

**self-service** [sεlfsεʀvis] adj, nm self-service

**selle** [sεl] nf saddle; **~s** nfpl (MÉD) stools; **seller** vt to saddle

**sellette** [sεlεt] nf: **être sur la ~** to be in the hot seat

**selon** [s(ə)lɔ̃] prép according to; (en se conformant à) in accordance with; **~ que** according to whether; **~ moi** as I see it

**semaine** [s(ə)mεn] nf week; **en ~** during the week, on weekdays

**semblable** [sɑ̃blabl] adj similar; (de ce genre): **de ~s mésaventures** such mishaps ♦ nm fellow creature ou man; **~ à** similar to, like

**semblant** [sɑ̃blɑ̃] nm: **un ~ de ...** a semblance of ...; **faire ~ (de faire)** to pretend (to do)

**sembler** [sɑ̃ble] vb +attrib to seem ♦ vb impers: **il semble (bien) que/inutile de** it (really) seems ou appears that/ useless to; **il me semble que** it seems to me that; **comme bon lui semble** as he sees fit

**semelle** [s(ə)mεl] nf sole; (intérieure) insole, inner sole

**semence** [s(ə)mɑ̃s] nf (graine) seed

**semer** [s(ə)me] vt to sow; (fig: éparpiller) to scatter; (: confusion) to spread; (fam: poursuivants) to lose, shake off; **semé de** (difficultés) riddled with

**semestre** [s(ə)mεstʀ] nm half-year; (SCOL) semester

**séminaire** [seminɛʀ] nm seminar
**semi-remorque** [səmiʀəmɔʀk] nm articulated lorry (BRIT), semi(trailer) (US)
**semoule** [s(ə)mul] nf semolina
**sempiternel, le** [sɑ̃piteʀnɛl] adj eternal, never-ending
**sénat** [sena] nm senate; **sénateur** [senatœʀ] nm senator
**sens** [sɑ̃s] nm (PHYSIOL, instinct) sense; (signification) meaning, sense; (direction) direction; à mon ~ to my mind; dans le ~ des aiguilles d'une montre clockwise; ~ dessus dessous upside down; ~ interdit one-way street; ~ unique one-way street
**sensation** [sɑ̃sasjɔ̃] nf sensation; à ~ (péj) sensational; faire ~ to cause ou create a sensation; **sensationnel, le** adj (fam) fantastic, terrific
**sensé, e** [sɑ̃se] adj sensible
**sensibiliser** [sɑ̃sibilize] vt: ~ qn à to make sb sensitive to
**sensibilité** [sɑ̃sibilite] nf sensitivity
**sensible** [sɑ̃sibl] adj sensitive; (aux sens) perceptible; (appréciable: différence, progrès) appreciable, noticeable; **sensiblement** adv (à peu près): ils sont sensiblement du même âge they are approximately the same age; **sensiblerie** nf sentimentality
**sensuel, le** [sɑ̃sɥɛl] adj (personne) sensual; (musique) sensuous
**sentence** [sɑ̃tɑ̃s] nf (jugement) sentence
**sentier** [sɑ̃tje] nm path
**sentiment** [sɑ̃timɑ̃] nm feeling; **sentimental, e, -aux** adj sentimental; (vie, aventure) love cpd
**sentinelle** [sɑ̃tinɛl] nf sentry
**sentir** [sɑ̃tiʀ] vt (par l'odorat) to smell; (par le goût) to taste; (au toucher, fig) to feel; (répandre une odeur de) to smell of; (: ressemblance) to smell like ♦ vi to smell; ~ mauvais to smell bad; se ~ bien to feel good; se ~ mal (être indisposé) to feel unwell ou ill; se ~ le courage/la force de faire to feel

brave/strong enough to do; il ne peut pas le ~ (fam) he can't stand him
**séparation** [separasjɔ̃] nf separation; (cloison) division, partition
**séparé, e** [separe] adj (distinct) separate; (époux) separated; **séparément** adv separately
**séparer** [separe] vt to separate; (désunir) to drive apart; (détacher): ~ qch de to pull sth (off) from; se ~ vi (époux, amis) to separate, part; (se diviser: route etc) to divide; se ~ de (époux) to separate ou part from; (employé, objet personnel) to part with
**sept** [sɛt] num seven; **septante** (BELGIQUE, SUISSE) adj inv seventy
**septembre** [sɛptɑ̃bʀ] nm September
**septennat** [septena] nm seven year term of office (of French President)
**septentrional, e, -aux** [sɛptɑ̃tʀijɔnal, o] adj northern
**septicémie** [sɛptisemi] nf blood poisoning, septicaemia
**septième** [sɛtjɛm] num seventh
**septique** [sɛptik] adj: fosse ~ septic tank
**sépulture** [sepyltyʀ] nf (tombeau) burial place, grave
**séquelles** [sekɛl] nfpl after-effects; (fig) aftermath sg
**séquestrer** [sekɛstʀe] vt (personne) to confine illegally; (biens) to impound
**serai** etc [səʀe] vb voir **être**
**serein, e** [səʀɛ, ɛn] adj serene
**serez** [səʀe] vb voir **être**
**sergent** [sɛʀʒɑ̃] nm sergeant
**série** [seʀi] nf series inv; (de clés, casseroles, outils) set; (catégorie: SPORT) rank; en ~ in quick succession; (COMM) mass cpd; hors ~ (COMM) custom-built
**sérieusement** [seʀjøzmɑ̃] adv seriously
**sérieux, -euse** [seʀjø, jøz] adj serious; (élève, employé) reliable, responsible; (client, maison) reliable, dependable ♦ nm seriousness; (d'une entreprise etc) reliability; **garder son ~** to keep a

straight face; **prendre qch/qn au ~** to
take sth/sb seriously

**serin** [s(ə)ʀɛ̃] nm canary

**seringue** [s(ə)ʀɛ̃g] nf syringe

**serions** [sərjɔ̃] vb voir **être**

**serment** [sɛʀmɑ̃] nm (juré): (promesse) pledge, vow

**sermon** [sɛʀmɔ̃] nm sermon

**séronégatif, -ive** [seronegatif, iv] adj
(MÉD) HIV negative

**séropositif, -ive** [seropozitif, iv] adj
(MÉD) HIV positive

**serpent** [sɛʀpɑ̃] nm snake; **serpenter**
vi to wind

**serpillière** [sɛʀpijɛʀ] nf floorcloth

**serre** [sɛʀ] nf (AGR) greenhouse; **~s** nfpl
(griffes) claws, talons

**serré, e** [sɛʀe] adj (habits) tight; (fig:
lutte, match) tight, close-fought; (passagers etc) (tightly) packed; (réseau)
dense; **avoir le cœur ~** to have a
heavy heart

**serrer** [sɛʀe] vt (tenir) to grip ou hold
tight; (comprimer, coincer) to squeeze;
(poings, mâchoires) to clench; (suj:
vêtement) to be too tight for; (ceinture,
nœud, vis) to tighten ♦ vi: **~ à droite**
to keep ou get over to the right; **se ~**
vi (se rapprocher) to squeeze up; **se ~
contre qn** to huddle up to sb; **~ la
main à qn** to shake sb's hand; **~ qn
dans ses bras** to hug sb, clasp sb in
one's arms

**serrure** [sɛʀyʀ] nf lock; **serrurier** nm
locksmith

**sert** etc [sɛʀ] vb voir **servir**

**servante** [sɛʀvɑ̃t] nf (maid)servant

**serveur, -euse** [sɛʀvœʀ, øz] nm/f
waiter (waitress)

**serviable** [sɛʀvjabl] adj obliging, willing to help

**service** [sɛʀvis] nm service; (assortiment
de vaisselle) set, service; (bureau: de la
vente etc) department, section; (travail)
duty; **premier ~** (série de repas) first
sitting; **être de ~** to be on duty; **faire
le ~** to serve; **rendre un ~ à qn** to do

sb a favour; (objet: s'avérer utile) to
come in useful ou handy for sb; **mettre
en ~** to put into service ou operation;
**~ compris/non compris** service
included/not included; **hors ~** out of
order; **~ après-vente** after-sales service; **~ d'ordre** police (ou stewards) in
charge of maintaining order; **~ militaire** military service; **~s secrets** secret
service sg

### service militaire

French men over eighteen are required
to do ten months' **service militaire**
if pronounced fit. The call-up can be
delayed if the conscript is in full-time
higher education. Conscientious objec-
tors are required to do two years' public service. Since 1970, women have
been able to do military service,
though few do.

**serviette** [sɛʀvjɛt] nf (de table) (table)
napkin, serviette; (de toilette) towel;
(porte-documents) briefcase; **~ hygiénique** sanitary towel

**servir** [sɛʀviʀ] vt to serve; (au restaurant) to wait on; (au magasin) to serve,
attend to ♦ vi (TENNIS) to serve; (CARTES)
to deal; **se ~** vi (prendre d'un plat) to
help o.s.; **vous êtes servi?** are you
being served?; **~ à qn** (diplôme, livre) to
be of use to sb; **~ à qch/faire** (outil
etc) to be used for sth/doing; **ça ne
sert à rien** it's no use; **~ (à qn) de** to
serve as (for sb); **se ~ de** (plat) to help
o.s. to; (voiture, outil, relations) to use

**serviteur** [sɛʀvitœʀ] nm servant

**ses** [se] adj voir **son**[1]

**set** [sɛt] nm: **~ (de table)** tablemat,
place mat

**seuil** [sœj] nm doorstep; (fig) threshold

**seul, e** [sœl] adj (sans compagnie)
alone; (unique): **un ~ livre** only one
book, a single book ♦ adv (entirely) on
one's own ♦ nm, nf: **il en reste
un(e) ~(e)** there's only one left; **le ~ li-**

vre the only book; **parler tout ~** to talk to oneself; **faire qch (tout) ~** to do sth (all) on one's own ou (all) by oneself; **à lui (tout) ~** single-handed, on his own; **se sentir ~** to feel lonely; **seulement** adv only; **non seulement ... mais aussi** ou **encore** not only ... but also

**sève** [sɛv] nf sap

**sévère** [sevɛʀ] adj severe

**sévices** [sevis] nmpl (physical) cruelty sg, ill treatment sg

**sévir** [seviʀ] vi (punir) to use harsh measures, crack down; (suj: fléau) to rage, be rampant

**sevrer** [səvʀe] vt (enfant etc) to wean

**sexe** [sɛks] nm sex; (organes génitaux) genitals, sex organs; **sexuel, le** adj sexual

**seyant, e** [sejɑ̃, ɑ̃t] adj becoming

**shampooing** [ʃɑ̃pwɛ̃] nm shampoo

**short** [ʃɔʀt] nm (pair of) shorts pl

---
MOT-CLÉ
---

**si** [si] nm (MUS) B; (en chantant la gamme) ti

♦ adv **1** (oui) yes

**2** (tellement) so; **si gentil/rapidement** so kind/fast; **(tant et)** si bien que so much so that; **si rapide qu'il soit** however fast he may be

♦ conj if; **si tu veux** if you want; **je me demande si** I wonder if ou whether; **si seulement** if only

**Sicile** [sisil] nf: **la ~** Sicily

**SIDA** [sida] sigle m (= syndrome immuno-déficitaire acquis) AIDS sg

**sidéré, e** [sideʀe] adj staggered

**sidérurgie** [sideʀyʀʒi] nf steel industry

**siècle** [sjɛkl] nm century

**siège** [sjɛʒ] nm seat; (d'entreprise) head office; (d'organisation) headquarters pl; (MIL) siege; **~ social** registered office; **siéger** vi to sit

**sien, ne** [sjɛ̃, sjɛn] pron: **le(la) ~(ne), les ~(ne)s** (homme) his; (femme) hers;

(chose, animal) its; **les ~s** (sa famille) one's family; **faire des ~nes** (fam) to be up to one's (usual) tricks

**sieste** [sjɛst] nf (afternoon) snooze ou nap; **faire la ~** to have a snooze ou nap

**sifflement** [siflǝmɑ̃] nm: **un ~** a whistle

**siffler** [sifle] vi (gén) to whistle; (en respirant) to wheeze; (serpent, vapeur) to hiss ♦ vt (chanson) to whistle; (chien etc) to whistle for; (fille) to whistle at; (pièce, orateur) to hiss, boo; (fin du match, départ) to blow one's whistle for; (fam: verre) to guzzle

**sifflet** [siflɛ] nm whistle; **coup de ~** whistle

**siffloter** [siflɔte] vi, vt to whistle

**sigle** [sigl] nm acronym

**signal, -aux** [siɲal, o] nm signal; (indice, écriteau) sign; **donner le ~ de** to give the signal for; **~ d'alarme** alarm signal; **signaux (lumineux)** (AUTO) traffic signals; **signalement** nm description, particulars pl

**signaler** [siɲale] vt to indicate; (personne: faire un signe) to signal; (vol, perte) to report; (faire remarquer): **~ qch à qn/(à qn) que** to point out sth to sb/(to sb) that; **se ~ (par)** to distinguish o.s. (by)

**signature** [siɲatyʀ] nf signature; (action) signing

**signe** [siɲ] nm sign; (TYPO) mark; **faire un ~ de la main** to give a sign with one's hand; **faire ~ à qn** (fig: contacter) to get in touch with sb; **faire ~ à qn d'entrer** to motion (to) sb to come in; **signer** vt to sign; **se signer** vi to cross o.s.

**significatif, -ive** [siɲifikatif, iv] adj significant

**signification** [siɲifikasjɔ̃] nf meaning

**signifier** [siɲifje] vt (vouloir dire) to mean; (faire connaître): **~ qch (à qn)** to make sth known (to sb)

**silence** [silɑ̃s] nm silence; (MUS) rest;

**garder le ~** to keep silent, say nothing; **silencieux, -euse** adj quiet, silent ♦ nm silencer

**silex** [sileks] nm flint

**silhouette** [silwet] nf outline, silhouette; (allure) figure

**silicium** [silisjɔm] nm silicon

**sillage** [sijaʒ] nm wake

**sillon** [sijɔ̃] nm furrow; (de disque) groove; **sillonner** vt to criss-cross

**simagrées** [simaɡre] nfpl fuss sg

**similaire** [similɛr] adj similar; **similicuir** nm imitation leather; **similitude** nf similarity

**simple** [sɛ̃pl] adj simple; (non multiple) single; **~ messieurs** nm (TENNIS) men's singles sg; **~ soldat** private

**simplicité** [sɛ̃plisite] nf simplicity

**simplifier** [sɛ̃plifje] vt to simplify

**simulacre** [simylakr] nm (péj): **un ~ de** a pretence of

**simuler** [simyle] vt to sham, simulate

**simultané, e** [simyltane] adj simultaneous

**sincère** [sɛ̃sɛr] adj sincere; **sincèrement** adv sincerely; (pour parler franchement) honestly, really; **sincérité** nf sincerity

**sine qua non** [sinekwanɔn] adj: **condition ~** indispensable condition

**singe** [sɛ̃ʒ] nm monkey; (de grande taille) ape; **singer** vt to ape, mimic; **singeries** nfpl antics

**singulariser** [sɛ̃ɡylarize]: **se ~** vi to call attention to o.s.

**singularité** [sɛ̃ɡylarite] nf peculiarity

**singulier, -ière** [sɛ̃ɡylje, jɛr] adj remarkable, singular ♦ nm singular

**sinistre** [sinistr] adj sinister ♦ nm (incendie) blaze; (catastrophe) disaster; (ASSURANCES) damage (giving rise to a claim); **sinistré, e** adj disaster-stricken ♦ nm/f disaster victim

**sinon** [sinɔ̃] conj (autrement, sans quoi) otherwise, or else; (sauf) except, other than; (si ce n'est) if not

**sinueux, -euse** [sinɥø, øz] adj winding

**sinus** [sinys] nm (ANAT) sinus; (GÉOM) sine; **sinusite** nf sinusitis

**siphon** [sifɔ̃] nm (tube, d'eau gazeuse) siphon; (d'évier etc) U-bend

**sirène** [sirɛn] nf siren; **~ d'alarme** fire alarm; (en temps de guerre) air-raid siren

**sirop** [siro] nm (à diluer: de fruit etc) syrup; (pharmaceutique) syrup, mixture; **~ pour la toux** cough mixture

**siroter** [sirɔte] vt to sip

**sismique** [sismik] adj seismic

**site** [sit] nm (paysage, environnement) setting; (d'une ville etc: emplacement) site; **~ (pittoresque)** beauty spot; **~s touristiques** places of interest; **~ Web** (INFORM) website

**sitôt** [sito] adv: **~ parti** as soon as he etc had left; **~ que** as soon as; **pas de ~** not for a long time

**situation** [sitɥasjɔ̃] nf situation; (d'un édifice, d'une ville) position, location; **~ de famille** marital status

**situé, e** [sitɥe] adj situated

**situer** [sitɥe] vt to site, situate; (en pensée) to set, place; **se ~** vi to be situated

**six** [sis] num six; **sixième** num sixth ♦ nf (SCOL) first form

**Skaï** ® [skaj] nm Leatherette ®

**ski** [ski] nm (objet) ski; (sport) skiing; **faire du ~** to ski; **~ de fond** cross-country skiing; **~ nautique** waterskiing; **~ de piste** downhill skiing; **~ de randonnée** cross-country skiing; **skier** vi to ski; **skieur, -euse** nm/f skier

**slip** [slip] nm (sous-vêtement) pants pl, briefs pl; (de bain: d'homme) trunks pl; (: du bikini) (bikini) briefs pl

**slogan** [slɔɡã] nm slogan

**SMIC** [smik] sigle m = **salaire minimum interprofessionnel de croissance**

In France, the SMIC is the minimum

*legal hourly rate for workers over eighteen. It is index-linked and is raised each time the cost of living rises by 2%.*

**smicard, e** [smikaʀ, aʀd] (*fam*) *nm/f* minimum wage earner

**smoking** [smɔkiŋ] *nm* dinner *ou* evening suit

**SNCF** *sigle f* (= *Société nationale des chemins de fer français*) French railways

**snob** [snɔb] *adj* snobbish ♦ *nm/f* snob; **snobisme** *nm* snobbery, snobbishness

**sobre** [sɔbʀ] *adj* (*personne*) temperate, abstemious; (*élégance, style*) sober

**sobriquet** [sɔbʀikɛ] *nm* nickname

**social, e, -aux** [sɔsjal, jo] *adj* social

**socialisme** [sɔsjalism] *nm* socialism; **socialiste** *nm/f* socialist

**société** [sɔsjete] *nf* society; (*sportive*) club; (*COMM*) company; **la ~ de consommation** the consumer society; **~ anonyme** ≈ limited (*BRIT*) *ou* incorporated (*US*) company

**sociologie** [sɔsjɔlɔʒi] *nf* sociology

**socle** [sɔkl] *nm* (*de colonne, statue*) plinth, pedestal; (*de lampe*) base

**socquette** [sɔkɛt] *nf* ankle sock

**sœur** [sœʀ] *nf* sister; (*religieuse*) nun, sister

**soi** [swa] *pron* oneself; **en ~** (*intrinsèquement*) in itself; **cela va de ~** that *ou* it goes without saying; **soi-disant** *adj inv* so-called ♦ *adv* supposedly

**soie** [swa] *nf* silk; **soierie** *nf* (*tissu*) silk

**soif** [swaf] *nf* thirst; **avoir ~** to be thirsty; **donner ~ à qn** to make sb thirsty

**soigné, e** [swaɲe] *adj* (*tenue*) well-groomed, neat; (*travail*) careful, meticulous

**soigner** [swaɲe] *vt* (*malade, maladie: suj: docteur*) to treat; (*suj: infirmière, mère*) to nurse, look after; (*travail, détails*) to take care over; (*jardin, invités*) to look after; **soigneux, -euse** *adj* (*propre*) tidy, neat; (*appliqué*) painstaking, careful

**soi-même** [swamɛm] *pron* oneself

**soin** [swɛ̃] *nm* (*application*) care; (*propreté, ordre*) tidiness, neatness; **~s** *nmpl* (*à un malade, blessé*) treatment *sg*, medical attention *sg*; (*hygiène*) care *sg*; **prendre ~ de** to take care of, look after; **prendre ~ de faire** to take care to do; **les premiers ~s** first aid *sg*

**soir** [swaʀ] *nm* evening; **ce ~** this evening, tonight; **demain ~** tomorrow evening, tomorrow night; **soirée** *nf* evening; (*réception*) party

**soit** [swa] *vb voir* **être** ♦ *conj* (*à savoir*) namely; (*ou*): **~ ... ~** either ... or ♦ *adv* so be it, very well; **~ que ... ~ que** *ou* **ou que** whether ... or whether

**soixantaine** [swasɑ̃tɛn] *nf:* **une ~ (de)** sixty *ou* so, about sixty; **avoir la ~** (*âge*) to be around sixty

**soixante** [swasɑ̃t] *num* sixty; **soixante-dix** *num* seventy

**soja** [sɔʒa] *nm* soya; (*graines*) soya beans *pl*; **germes de ~** beansprouts

**sol** [sɔl] *nm* ground; (*de logement*) floor; (*AGR*) soil; (*MUS*) G; (: *en chantant la gamme*) so(h)

**solaire** [sɔlɛʀ] *adj* (*énergie etc*) solar; (*crème etc*) sun *cpd*

**soldat** [sɔlda] *nm* soldier

**solde** [sɔld] *nf* pay ♦ *nm* (*COMM*) balance; **~s** *nm ou f pl* (*articles*) sale goods; (*vente*) sales; **en ~** at sale price; **solder** *vt* (*marchandise*) to sell at sale price, sell off; **se solder par** (*fig*) to end in; **article soldé (à) 10 F** item reduced to 10 F

**sole** [sɔl] *nf* sole *inv* (*fish*)

**soleil** [sɔlɛj] *nm* sun; (*lumière*) sun(light); (*temps ensoleillé*) sun(shine); **il fait du ~** it's sunny; **au ~** in the sun

**solennel, le** [sɔlanɛl] *adj* solemn

**solfège** [sɔlfɛʒ] *nm* musical theory

**solidaire** [sɔlidɛʀ] *adj:* **être ~s** to show solidarity, stand *ou* stick together; **être ~ de** (*collègues*) to stand by; **solidarité** *nf* solidarity; **par solidarité (avec)** in sympathy (with)

**solide** [sɔlid] adj solid; (mur, maison, meuble) solid, sturdy; (connaissances, argument) sound; (personne, estomac) robust, sturdy ♦ nm solid

**soliste** [sɔlist] nm/f soloist

**solitaire** [sɔlitɛr] adj (sans compagnie) solitary, lonely; (lieu) lonely ♦ nm/f (ermite) recluse; (fig: ours) loner

**solitude** [sɔlityd] nf loneliness; (tranquillité) solitude

**solive** [sɔliv] nf joist

**solliciter** [sɔlisite] vt (personne) to appeal to; (emploi, faveur) to seek

**sollicitude** [sɔlisityd] nf concern

**soluble** [sɔlybl] adj soluble

**solution** [sɔlysjɔ̃] nf solution; **~ de facilité** easy way out

**solvable** [sɔlvabl] adj solvent

**sombre** [sɔ̃br] adj dark; (fig) gloomy; **sombrer** vi (bateau) to sink; **sombrer dans** (misère, désespoir) to sink into

**sommaire** [sɔmɛr] adj (simple) basic; (expéditif) summary ♦ nm summary

**sommation** [sɔmasjɔ̃] nf (JUR) summons sg; (avant de faire feu) warning

**somme** [sɔm] nf (MATH) sum; (quantité) amount; (argent) sum, amount ♦ nm: **faire un ~** to have a (short) nap; **en ~** all in all; **~ toute** all in all

**sommeil** [sɔmɛj] nm sleep; **avoir ~** to be sleepy; **sommeiller** vi to doze

**sommer** [sɔme] vt: **~ qn de faire** to command ou order sb to do

**sommes** [sɔm] vb voir **être**

**sommet** [sɔmɛ] nm top; (d'une montagne) summit, top; (fig: de la perfection, gloire) height

**sommier** [sɔmje] nm (bed) base

**somnambule** [sɔmnɑ̃byl] nm/f sleepwalker

**somnifère** [sɔmnifɛr] nm sleeping drug no pl (ou pill)

**somnoler** [sɔmnɔle] vi to doze

**somptueux, -euse** [sɔ̃ptɥø, øz] adj sumptuous

**son1, sa** [sɔ̃, sa] (pl **ses**) adj (antécédent humain: mâle) his; (: femelle) her; (: va-

leur indéfinie) one's, his/her; (antécédent non humain) its

**son2** [sɔ̃] nm sound; (de blé) bran

**sondage** [sɔ̃daʒ] nm: **~ (d'opinion)** (opinion) poll

**sonde** [sɔ̃d] nf (NAVIG) lead ou sounding line; (MÉD) probe; (TECH: de forage) borer, driller

**sonder** [sɔ̃de] vt (NAVIG) to sound; (TECH) to bore, drill; (fig: personne) to sound out; **~ le terrain** (fig) to test the ground

**songe** [sɔ̃ʒ] nm dream; **songer** vi: **songer à** (penser à) to think over; (envisager) to consider, think of; **songer que** to think that; **songeur, -euse** adj pensive

**sonnant, e** [sɔnɑ̃, ɑ̃t] adj: **à 8 heures ~es** on the stroke of 8

**sonné, e** [sɔne] adj (fam) cracked; **il est midi ~** it's gone twelve

**sonner** [sɔne] vi to ring ♦ vt (cloche) to ring; (glas, tocsin) to sound; (portier, infirmière) to ring for; **~ faux** (instrument) to sound out of tune; (rire) to ring false

**sonnerie** [sɔnri] nf (son) ringing; (sonnette) bell; **~ d'alarme** alarm bell

**sonnette** [sɔnɛt] nf bell; **~ d'alarme** alarm bell

**sono** [sɔno] abr f = **sonorisation**

**sonore** [sɔnɔr] adj (voix) sonorous, ringing; (salle) resonant; (film, signal) sound cpd; **sonorisation** nf (équipement: de salle de conférences) public address system, P.A. system; (: de discothèque) sound system; **sonorité** nf (de piano, violon) tone; (d'une salle) acoustics pl

**sont** [sɔ̃] vb voir **être**

**sophistiqué, e** [sɔfistike] adj sophisticated

**sorbet** [sɔrbɛ] nm water ice, sorbet

**sorcellerie** [sɔrsɛlri] nf witchcraft no pl

**sorcier** [sɔrsje] nm sorcerer; **sorcière** nf witch ou sorceress

**sordide** [sɔrdid] adj (lieu) squalid; (action) sordid

**sornettes** [sɔʀnɛt] *nfpl* twaddle *sg*

**sort** [sɔʀ] *nm* (*destinée*) fate; (*condition*) lot; (*magique*) curse, spell; **tirer au ~** to draw lots

**sorte** [sɔʀt] *nf* sort, kind; **de la ~** in that way; **de (telle) ~ que** ou **en quelque ~** in a way; **faire en ~ que** to see to it that

**sortie** [sɔʀti] *nf* (*issue*) way out, exit; (*remarque drôle*) sally; (*promenade*) outing; (*le soir: au restaurant etc*) night out; (*COMM: d'un disque*) release; (*: d'un livre*) publication; (*: d'un modèle*) launching; **~s** *nfpl* (*COMM: somme*) items of expenditure, outgoings; **~ de bain** (*vêtement*) bathrobe; **~ de secours** emergency exit

**sortilège** [sɔʀtilɛʒ] *nm* (magic) spell

**sortir** [sɔʀtiʀ] *vi* (*gén*) to come out; (*partir, se promener, aller au spectacle*) to go out; (*numéro gagnant*) to come up ♦ *vt* to take out; (*produit, modèle*) to bring out; (*fam: dire*) to come out with; **~ avec qn** to be going out with sb; **s'en ~** (*malade*) to pull through; (*d'une difficulté etc*) to get through; **~ de** (*endroit*) to come out of, leave; (*provenir de*) to come from; (*compétence*) to be outside

**sosie** [sɔzi] *nm* double

**sot, sotte** [so, sɔt] *adj* silly, foolish ♦ *nm/f* fool; **sottise** *nf* (*caractère*) silliness, foolishness; (*action*) silly ou foolish thing

**sou** [su] *nm*: **près de ses ~s** tightfisted; **sans le ~** penniless

**soubresaut** [subʀəso] *nm* start; (*cahot*) jolt

**souche** [suʃ] *nf* (*d'arbre*) stump; (*de carnet*) counterfoil (*BRIT*), stub

**souci** [susi] *nm* (*inquiétude*) concern; (*préoccupation*) concern; (*BOT*) marigold; **se faire du ~** to worry; **soucier**: **se soucier de** *vt* to care about; **soucieux, -euse** *adj* concerned, worried

**soucoupe** [sukup] *nf* saucer; **~ volante** flying saucer

**soudain, e** [sudɛ̃, ɛn] *adj* (*douleur,*

*mort*) sudden ♦ *adv* suddenly, all of a sudden

**soude** [sud] *nf* soda

**souder** [sude] *vt* (*avec fil à* ~) to solder; (*par soudure autogène*) to weld; (*fig*) to bind together

**soudoyer** [sudwaje] (*péj*) *vt* to bribe

**soudure** [sudyʀ] *nf* soldering; welding; (*joint*) soldered joint; weld

**souffert, e** [sufɛʀ, ɛʀt] *pp de* **souffrir**

**souffle** [sufl] *nm* (*en expirant*) breath; (*en soufflant*) puff, blow; (*respiration*) breathing; (*d'explosion, de ventilateur*) blast; (*du vent*) blowing; **être à bout de ~** to be out of breath; **un ~ d'air** a breath of air

**soufflé, e** [sufle] *adj* (*fam: stupéfié*) staggered ♦ *nm* (*CULIN*) soufflé

**souffler** [sufle] *vi* (*gén*) to blow; (*haleter*) to puff (and blow) ♦ *vt* (*feu, bougie*) to blow out; (*chasser: poussière etc*) to blow away; (*TECH: verre*) to blow; (*dire*): **~ qch à qn** to whisper sth to sb; **soufflet** [suflɛ] *nm* (*instrument*) bellows *pl*; (*gifle*) slap (in the face); **souffleur** *nm* (*THÉÂTRE*) prompter

**souffrance** [sufʀɑ̃s] *nf* suffering; **en ~** (*affaire*) pending

**souffrant, e** [sufʀɑ̃, ɑ̃t] *adj* unwell

**souffre-douleur** [sufʀədulœʀ] *nm inv* butt, underdog

**souffrir** [sufʀiʀ] *vi* to suffer, be in pain ♦ *vt* to suffer, endure; (*supporter*) to bear, stand; **~ de** (*maladie, froid*) to suffer from; **elle ne peut pas le ~** she can't stand ou bear him

**soufre** [sufʀ] *nm* sulphur

**souhait** [swɛ] *nm* wish; **tous nos ~s de** good wishes ou best wishes for; **à vos ~s!** bless you!; **souhaitable** *adj* desirable

**souhaiter** [swete] *vt* to wish; **~ la bonne année à qn** to wish sb a happy New Year; **~ que** to hope that

**souiller** [suje] *vt* to dirty, soil; (*fig: réputation etc*) to sully, tarnish

**soûl, e** [su, sul] *adj* drunk ♦ *tout*

**son ~** to one's heart's content

**soulagement** [sulaʒmã] *nm* relief

**soulager** [sulaʒe] *vt* to relieve

**soûler** [sule] *vt*: **~ qn** to get sb drunk; (*suj: boisson*) to make sb drunk; (*fig*) to make sb's head spin *ou* reel; **se ~** *vi* to get drunk

**soulever** [sul(ə)ve] *vt* to lift; (*poussière*) to send up; (*enthousiasme*) to arouse; (*question, débat*) to raise; **se ~** *vi* (*peuple*) to rise up; (*personne couchée*) to lift o.s. up

**soulier** [sulje] *nm* shoe

**souligner** [suliɲe] *vt* to underline; (*fig*) to emphasize, stress

**soumettre** [sumɛtʀ] *vt* (*pays*) to subject, subjugate; (*rebelle*) to put down, subdue; **se ~ (à)** (to submit (to)); **~ qch à qn** (*projet etc*) to submit sth to sb

**soumis, e** [sumi, iz] *adj* submissive; **soumission** *nf* submission

**soupape** [supap] *nf* valve

**soupçon** [supsõ] *nm* suspicion; (*petite quantité*) **un ~ de** a hint *ou* touch of; **soupçonner** *vt* to suspect; **soupçonneux, -euse** *adj* suspicious

**soupe** [sup] *nf* soup

**souper** [supe] *vi* to have supper ♦ *nm* supper

**soupeser** [supəze] *vt* to weigh in one's hand(s); (*fig*) to weigh up

**soupière** [supjɛʀ] *nf* (*soup*) tureen

**soupir** [supiʀ] *nm* sigh; **pousser un ~ de soulagement** to heave a sigh of relief

**soupirail, -aux** [supiʀaj, o] *nm* (small) basement window

**soupirer** [supiʀe] *vi* to sigh

**souple** [supl] *adj* supple; (*fig: règlement, caractère*) flexible; (: *démarche, taille*) lithe, supple; **souplesse** *nf* suppleness; (*de caractère*) flexibility

**source** [suʀs] *nf* (*point d'eau*) spring; (*d'un cours d'eau, fig*) source; **de bonne ~** on good authority

**sourcil** [suʀsi] *nm* (eye)brow; **sourciller** *vi*: **sans sourciller** without turning

a hair *ou* batting an eyelid

**sourd, e** [suʀ, suʀd] *adj* deaf; (*bruit*) muffled; (*douleur*) dull ♦ *nm/f* deaf person; **faire la ~e oreille** to turn a deaf ear; **sourdine** *nf* (MUS) mute; **en sourdine** softly, quietly; **sourd-muet, sourde-muette** *adj* deaf-and-dumb ♦ *nm/f* deaf-mute

**souriant, e** [suʀjã, jãt] *adj* cheerful

**souricière** [suʀisjɛʀ] *nf* mousetrap; (*fig*) trap

**sourire** [suʀiʀ] *nm* smile ♦ *vi* to smile; **~ à qn** to smile at sb; (*fig: plaire à*) to appeal to sb; (*suj: chance*) to smile on sb; **garder le ~** to keep smiling

**souris** [suʀi] *nf* mouse

**sournois, e** [suʀnwa, waz] *adj* deceitful, underhand

**sous** [su] *prép* under; **~ la pluie** in the rain; **~ terre** underground; **~ peu** shortly, before long; **sous-bois** *nm inv* undergrowth

**souscrire** [suskʀiʀ]: **~ à** *vt* to subscribe to

**sous...:** **sous-directeur, -trice** *nm/f* assistant manager(-manageress); **sous-entendre** *vt* to imply, infer; **sous-entendu, e** *adj* implied ♦ *nm* innuendo, insinuation; **sous-estimer** *vt* to underestimate; **sous-jacent, e** *adj* underlying; **sous-louer** *vt* to sublet; **sous-marin, e** *adj* (*flore, faune*) submarine; (*pêche*) underwater ♦ *nm* submarine; **sous-officier** *nm* = non-commissioned officer (N.C.O.); **sous-produit** *nm* by-product; **sous-pull** *nm* thin poloneck jersey; **soussigné, e** *adj*: **je soussigné I** the undersigned; **sous-sol** *nm* basement; **sous-titre** *nm* subtitle

**soustraction** [sustʀaksjɔ̃] *nf* subtraction

**soustraire** [sustʀɛʀ] *vt* to subtract, take away; (*dérober*): **~ qch à qn** to remove sth from sb; **se ~ à** (*autorité etc*) to elude, escape from

**sous...:** **sous-traitant** *nm* subcontractor; **sous-traiter** vt to sub-contract; **sous-vêtements** nmpl underwear sg

**soutane** [sutan] nf cassock, soutane

**soute** [sut] nf hold

**soutenir** [sut(ə)niʀ] vt to support; (assaut, choc) to stand up to, withstand; (intérêt, effort) to keep up; (assurer): ~ **que** to maintain that; **soutenu, e** (efforts) sustained, unflagging; (style) elevated

**souterrain, e** [suteʀɛ̃, ɛn] adj underground ♦ nm underground passage

**soutien** [sutjɛ̃] nm support; **soutien-gorge** nm bra

**soutirer** [sutiʀe] vt: ~ **qch à qn** to squeeze ou get sth out of sb

**souvenir** [suv(ə)niʀ] nm (réminiscence) memory; (objet) souvenir ♦ vb: **se ~ de** ♦ vt to remember; **se ~ que** to remember that; **en ~ de** in memory ou remembrance of

**souvent** [suvɑ̃] adv often; **peu ~** seldom, infrequently

**souverain, e** [suv(ə)ʀɛ̃, ɛn] nm/f sovereign, monarch

**soyeux, -euse** [swajø, øz] adj silky

**soyons** etc [swajɔ̃] vb voir **être**

**spacieux, -euse** [spasjø, jøz] adj spacious, roomy

**spaghettis** [spageti] nmpl spaghetti sg

**sparadrap** [spaʀadʀa] nm sticking plaster (BRIT), Bandaid ® (US)

**spatial, e, -aux** [spasjal, jo] adj (AVIAT) space cpd

**speaker, ine** [spikœʀ, kʀin] nm/f announcer

**spécial, e, -aux** [spesjal, jo] adj special; (bizarre) peculiar; **spécialement** adv especially, particularly; (tout exprès) specially; **spécialiser**: **se spécialiser** vi to specialize; **spécialiste** nm/f specialist; **spécialité** nf speciality; (branche) special field

**spécifier** [spesifje] vt to specify, state

**spécimen** [spesimɛn] nm specimen

**spectacle** [spɛktakl] nm (scène) sight;

(représentation) show; (industrie) show business; **spectaculaire** adj spectacular

**spectateur, -trice** [spɛktatœʀ, tʀis] nm/f (CINÉMA etc) member of the audience; (SPORT) spectator; (d'un événement) onlooker, witness

**spéculer** [spekyle] vi to speculate

**spéléologie** [speleɔlɔʒi] nf potholing

**sperme** [spɛʀm] nm semen, sperm

**sphère** [sfɛʀ] nf sphere

**spirale** [spiʀal] nf spiral

**spirituel, le** [spiʀitɥɛl] adj spiritual; (fin, piquant) witty

**splendide** [splɑ̃did] adj splendid

**sponsoriser** [spɔ̃sɔʀize] vt to sponsor

**spontané, e** [spɔ̃tane] adj spontaneous; **spontanéité** nf spontaneity

**sport** [spɔʀ] nm sport ♦ adj inv (vêtement) casual; **faire du ~** to do sport; **~s d'hiver** winter sports; **sportif, -ive** adj (journal, association, épreuve) sports cpd; (allure, démarche) athletic; (attitude, esprit) sporting

**spot** [spɔt] nm (lampe) spot(light); (annonce): ~ **(publicitaire)** commercial (break)

**square** [skwaʀ] nm public garden(s)

**squelette** [skəlɛt] nm skeleton; **squelettique** adj scrawny

**stabiliser** [stabilize] vt to stabilize

**stable** [stabl] adj stable, steady

**stade** [stad] nm (SPORT) stadium; (phase, niveau) stage

**stage** [staʒ] nm (cours) training course; ~ **de formation (professionnelle)** vocational (training) course; ~ **de perfectionnement** advanced training course; **stagiaire** nm/f, adj trainee

**stagner** [stagne] vi to stagnate

**stalle** [stal] nf stall, box

**stand** [stɑ̃d] nm (d'exposition) stand; (de foire) stall; ~ **de tir** (à la foire, SPORT) shooting range

**standard** [stɑ̃daʀ] adj inv standard ♦ nm switchboard; **standardiste** nm/f switchboard operator

**standing** [stãdiŋ] *nm* standing; **de grand ~** luxury

**starter** [staʀtɛʀ] *nm* (AUTO) choke

**station** [stasjɔ̃] *nf* station; (*de bus*) stop; (*de villégiature*) resort; **~ balnéaire** seaside resort; **~ de ski** ski resort; **~ de taxis** taxi rank (BRIT) *ou* stand (US); **stationnement** *nm* parking; **stationner** *vi* to park; **station-service** *nf* service station

**statistique** [statistik] *nf* (*science*) statistics *sg*; (*rapport, étude*) statistic ♦ *adj* statistical

**statue** [staty] *nf* statue

**statu quo** [statykwo] *nm* status quo

**statut** [staty] *nm* status; **~s** *nmpl* (JUR, ADMIN) statutes; **statutaire** *adj* statutory

**Sté** *abr* = **société**

**steak** [stɛk] *nm* steak; **~ haché** hamburger

**sténo(dactylo)** [steno(daktilo)] *nf* shorthand typist (BRIT), stenographer (US)

**sténo(graphie)** [steno(grafi)] *nf* shorthand

**stéréo** [steʀeo] *adj* stereo

**stérile** [steʀil] *adj* sterile

**stérilet** [steʀilɛ] *nm* coil, loop

**stériliser** [steʀilize] *vt* to sterilize

**stigmates** [stigmat] *nmpl* scars, marks

**stimulant, e** [stimylã, ãt] *adj* (*fig*) stimulus, incentive; (*physique*) stimulant

**stimuler** [stimyle] *vt* to stimulate

**stipuler** [stipyle] *vt* to stipulate

**stock** [stɔk] *nm* stock; **stocker** *vt* to stock

**stop** [stɔp] *nm* (AUTO: *écriteau*) stop sign; (: *feu arrière*) brake-light; **faire du ~** (*fam*) to hitch(hike); **stopper** *vt, vi* to stop, halt

**store** [stɔʀ] *nm* blind; (*de magasin*) shade, awning

**strabisme** [stʀabism] *nm* squinting

**strapontin** [stʀapɔ̃tɛ̃] *nm* jump ou foldaway seat

**stratégie** [stʀateʒi] *nf* strategy; **straté-**

**gique** *adj* strategic

**stress** [stʀɛs] *nm* stress; **stressant, e** *adj* stressful; **stresser** *vt*: **stresser qn** to make sb (feel) tense

**strict, e** [stʀikt] *adj* strict; (*tenue, décor*) severe, plain; **le ~ nécessaire/minimum** the bare essentials/minimum

**strident, e** [stʀidã, ãt] *adj* shrill, strident

**strophe** [stʀɔf] *nf* verse, stanza

**structure** [stʀyktyʀ] *nf* structure

**studieux, -euse** [stydjø, jøz] *adj* studious

**studio** [stydjo] *nm* (*logement*) (one-roomed) flatlet (BRIT) ou apartment (US); (*d'artiste, TV etc*) studio

**stupéfait, e** [stypefɛ, ɛt] *adj* astonished

**stupéfiant, e** [stypefjã, jãt] *adj* (*étonnant*) stunning, astounding ♦ *nm* (MÉD) drug, narcotic

**stupéfier** [stypefje] *vt* (*étonner*) to stun, astonish

**stupeur** [stypœʀ] *nf* astonishment

**stupide** [stypid] *adj* stupid; **stupidité** *nf* stupidity; (*parole, acte*) stupid thing (to do ou say)

**style** [stil] *nm* style

**stylé, e** [stile] *adj* well-trained

**styliste** [stilist] *nm/f* designer

**stylo** [stilo] *nm*: **~ (à encre)** (fountain) pen; **~ (à) bille** ball-point pen; **~-feutre** felt-tip pen

**su, e** [sy] *pp de* **savoir** ♦ *nm*: **au ~ de** with the knowledge of

**suave** [sɥav] *adj* sweet

**subalterne** [sybaltɛʀn] *adj* (*employé, officier*) junior; (*rôle*) subordinate, subsidiary ♦ *nm/f* subordinate

**subconscient** [sypkɔ̃sjã] *nm* subconscious

**subir** [sybiʀ] *vt* (*affront, dégâts*) to suffer; (*opération, châtiment*) to undergo

**subit, e** [sybi, it] *adj* sudden; **subitement** *adv* suddenly, all of a sudden

**subjectif, -ive** [sybʒɛktif, iv] *adj* subjective

**subjonctif** [sybʒɔ̃ktif] *nm* subjunctive

**subjuguer** [sybʒyge] *vt* to captivate

**submerger** [sybmɛrʒe] *vt* to submerge; (*fig*) to overwhelm

**subordonné, e** [sybɔrdɔne] *adj, nm/f* subordinate

**subrepticement** [sybrɛptismɑ̃] *adv* surreptitiously

**subside** [sybzid] *nm* grant

**subsidiaire** [sybzidjɛr] *adj*: **question ~** deciding question

**subsister** [sybziste] *vi* (*rester*) to remain, subsist; (*survivre*) to live on

**substance** [sypstɑ̃s] *nf* substance

**substituer** [sypstitɥe] *vt*: **~ qn/qch à** to substitute sb/sth for; **se ~ à qn** (*évincer*) to substitute o.s. for sb

**substitut** [sypstity] *nm* (*succédané*) substitute

**subterfuge** [sybtɛrfyʒ] *nm* subterfuge

**subtil, e** [sybtil] *adj* subtle

**subtiliser** [sybtilize] *vt*: **~ qch (à qn)** to spirit sth away (from sb)

**subvenir** [sybvənir]: **~ à** *vt* to meet

**subvention** [sybvɑ̃sjɔ̃] *nf* subsidy, grant; **subventionner** *vt* to subsidize

**suc** [syk] *nm* (*BOT*) sap; (*de viande, fruit*) juice

**succédané** [syksedane] *nm* substitute

**succéder** [syksede]: **~ à** *vt* to succeed; **se ~** *vi* (*accidents, années*) to follow one another

**succès** [syksɛ] *nm* success; **avoir du ~** to be a success, be successful; **à ~** successful; **~ de librairie** bestseller; **~ (féminins)** conquests

**successif, -ive** [syksesif, iv] *adj* successive

**successeur** [syksesœr] *nm* successor

**succession** [syksɛsjɔ̃] *nf* (*série, POL*) succession; (*JUR: patrimoine*) estate, inheritance

**succomber** [sykɔ̃be] *vi* to die, succumb; (*fig*): **~ à** to succumb to

**succulent, e** [sykylɑ̃, ɑ̃t] *adj* (*repas, mets*) delicious

**succursale** [sykyrsal] *nf* branch

**sucer** [syse] *vt* to suck; **sucette** *nf* (*bonbon*) lollipop; (*de bébé*) dummy (*BRIT*), pacifier (*US*)

**sucre** [sykr] *nm* (*substance*) sugar; (*morceau*) lump of sugar, sugar lump ou cube; **~ d'orge** barley sugar; **~ en morceaux/en poudre** lump/caster sugar; **~ glace/roux** icing/brown sugar; **sucré, e** *adj* (*produit alimentaire*) sweetened; (*au goût*) sweet; **sucrer** (*thé, café*) to sweeten, put sugar in; **sucreries** *nfpl* (*bonbons*) sweets, sweet things; **sucrier** *nm* (*récipient*) sugar bowl

**sud** [syd] *nm*: **le ~** the south ♦ *adj inv* south; (*côte*) south, southern; **au ~** (*situation*) in the south; (*direction*) to the south; **au ~ de** (*position*) south of; **sud-africain, e** *adj* South African ♦ *nm/f*: **Sud-Africain, e** South African; **sud-américain, e** *adj* South American ♦ *nm/f*: **Sud-Américain, e** South American ♦ *nm* south-east; **sud-ouest** *nm, adj inv* south-west

**Suède** [sɥɛd] *nf*: **la ~** Sweden; **suédois, e** *adj* Swedish ♦ *nm/f*: **Suédois, e** Swede ♦ *nm* (*LING*) Swedish

**suer** [sɥe] *vi* to sweat; (*suinter*) to ooze; **sueur** *nf* sweat; **en sueur** sweating, in a sweat; **donner des sueurs froids à qn** to put sb in(to) a cold sweat

**suffire** [sɥfir] *vi* (*être assez*): **~ (à qn/ pour qch/pour faire)** to be enough ou sufficient (for sb/for sth/to do); **il suffit d'une négligence ...** it only takes one act of carelessness ...; **il suffit qu'on oublie pour que ...** one only needs to forget for ...; **ça suffit!** that's enough!

**suffisamment** [syfizamɑ̃] *adv* sufficiently, enough; **~ de** sufficient, enough

**suffisant, e** [syfizɑ̃, ɑ̃t] *adj* sufficient; (*résultats*) satisfactory; (*vaniteux*) self-important, bumptious

**suffixe** [syfiks] *nm* suffix

**suffoquer** [syfɔke] *vt* to choke, suffocate; (*stupéfier*) to stagger, astound ♦ *vi* to choke, suffocate

**suffrage** [syfʀaʒ] *nm* (POL: *voix*) vote

**suggérer** [sygʒeʀe] *vt* to suggest; **suggestion** *nf* suggestion

**suicide** [sɥisid] *nm* suicide; **suicider**: **se suicider** *vi* to commit suicide

**suie** [sɥi] *nf* soot

**suinter** [sɥɛ̃te] *vi* to ooze

**suis** [sɥi] *vb voir* **être**; **suivre**

**suisse** [sɥis] *adj* Swiss ♦ *nm*: **S~** Swiss *pl inv* ♦ *nf*: **la S~** Switzerland; **la S~ romande/allemande** French-speaking/German-speaking Switzerland; **Suissesse** *nf* Swiss (woman *ou* girl)

**suite** [sɥit] *nf* (*continuation: d'énumération etc*) rest, remainder; (: *de feuilleton*) continuation; (: *film etc sur le même thème*) sequel; (*série*) series, series, succession; (*conséquence*) result; (*ordre, liaison logique*) coherence; (*appartement , MUS*) suite; (*escorte*) retinue, suite; **~s** *nfpl* (*d'une maladie etc*) effects; **prendre la ~ de** (*directeur etc*) to succeed, take over from; **donner ~ à** (*requête, projet*) to follow up; **faire ~ à** (*suite: faisant*) **~ à votre lettre du ...** further to your letter of the ...; **de ~** (*d'affilée*) in succession; (*immédiatement*) at once; **par la ~** afterwards (*d'affilée*); **à la ~** one after the other; **à la ~ de** (*derrière*) behind; (*en conséquence de*) following

**suivant, e** [sɥivã, ãt] *adj* next, following ♦ *prép* (*selon*) according to; **au ~!** next!

**suivi, e** [sɥivi] *adj* (*effort, qualité*) consistent; (*cohérent*) coherent; **très/peu ~** (*cours*) well-/poorly-attended

**suivre** [sɥivʀ] *vt* (*gén*) to follow; (SCOL: *cours*) to attend; (*comprendre*) to keep up with; (COMM: *article*) to continue to stock ♦ *vi* to follow; (*élève: assimiler*) to keep up; **se ~** *vi* (*accidents etc*) to follow one after the other; **faire ~** (*lettre*) to forward; **"à ~"** "to be continued"

**sujet, te** [syʒɛ, ɛt] *adj*: **être ~ à** (*vertige etc*) to be liable *ou* subject to ♦

*nm/f* (*d'un souverain*) subject ♦ *nm* subject; **au ~ de** about; **~ de conversation** topic *ou* subject of conversation; **~ d'examen** (SCOL) examination question

**summum** [sɔ(m)mɔm] *nm*: **le ~ de** the height of

**super** [sypɛʀ] (*fam*) *adj inv* terrific, great, fantastic, super

**superbe** [sypɛʀb] *adj* magnificent, superb

**super(carburant)** [sypɛʀ(kaʀbyʀɑ̃)] *nm* ≈ 4-star petrol (BRIT), ≈ high-octane gasoline (US)

**supercherie** [sypɛʀʃəʀi] *nf* trick

**supérette** [sypeʀɛt] *nf* (COMM) mini-market, superette (US)

**superficie** [sypɛʀfisi] *nf* (*surface*) area

**superficiel, le** [sypɛʀfisjɛl] *adj* superficial

**superflu, e** [sypɛʀfly] *adj* superfluous

**supérieur, e** [sypeʀjœʀ] *adj* (*lèvre, étages, classes*) upper; (*plus élevé: température, niveau, enseignement*): **~ (à)** higher (than); (*meilleur: qualité, produit*): **~ (à)** superior (to); (*excellent, hautain*) superior ♦ *nm, nf* superior; **supériorité** *nf* superiority

**superlatif** [sypɛʀlatif] *nm* superlative

**supermarché** [sypɛʀmaʀʃe] *nm* supermarket

**superposer** [sypɛʀpoze] *vt* (*faire chevaucher*) to superimpose; **lits superposés** bunk beds

**superproduction** [sypɛʀpʀɔdyksjɔ̃] *nf* (*film*) spectacular

**superpuissance** [sypɛʀpɥisɑ̃s] *nf* super-power

**superstitieux, -euse** [sypɛʀstisjø, jøz] *adj* superstitious

**superviser** [sypɛʀvize] *vt* to supervise

**supplanter** [syplɑ̃te] *vt* to supplant

**suppléance** [sypleɑ̃s] *nf*: **faire des ~s** (*professeur*) to do supply teaching; **suppléant, e** *adj* (*professeur*) supply *cpd*; (*juge, fonctionnaire*) deputy *cpd* ♦ *nm/f* (*professeur*) supply teacher

**suppléer** [syplee] vt (ajouter: mot manquant etc) to supply, provide; (compenser: lacune) to fill in; ~ **à** to make up for

**supplément** [syplemã] nm supplement; (de frites etc) extra portion; **un ~ de travail** extra ou additional work; **payer un ~** to pay an additional charge; **le vin est en ~** wine is extra; **supplémentaire** adj additional, further; (train, bus) relief cpd, extra

**supplications** [syplikasjɔ̃] nfpl pleas, entreaties

**supplice** [syplis] nm torture no pl

**supplier** [syplije] vt to implore, beseech

**support** [sypɔʀ] nm support; (publicitaire) medium; (audio-visuel) aid

**supportable** [sypɔʀtabl] adj (douleur) bearable

**supporter¹** [sypɔʀtɛʀ] nm supporter, fan

**supporter²** [sypɔʀte] vt (conséquences, épreuve) to bear, endure; (défauts, personne) to put up with; (suj: chose: chaleur etc) to withstand; (: personne: chaleur, vin) to be able to take

**supposer** [sypoze] vt to suppose; (impliquer) to presuppose; **à ~ que** supposing (that)

**suppositoire** [sypozitwaʀ] nm suppository

**suppression** [sypʀesjɔ̃] nf (voir supprimer) cancellation; removal; deletion

**supprimer** [sypʀime] vt (congés, service d'autobus etc) to cancel; (emplois, privilèges, témoin gênant) to do away with; (cloison, cause, anxiété) to remove; (clause, mot) to delete

**suprême** [sypʀɛm] adj supreme

MOT-CLÉ

**sur** [syʀ] prép **1** (position) on; (pardessus) over; (au-dessus) above; **pose-le sur la table** put it on the table; **je n'ai pas d'argent sur moi** I haven't any money on me

**2** (direction) towards; **en allant sur Paris** going towards Paris; **sur votre droite** on ou to your right

**3** (à propos de) on, about; **un livre/une conférence sur Balzac** a book/lecture on ou about Balzac

**4** (proportion, mesures) out of, by; **un sur 10** one in 10; (SCOL) one out of 10; **4 m sur 2** 4 m by 2

**sur ce** adv hereupon

**sûr, e** [syʀ] adj sure, certain; (digne de confiance) reliable; (sans danger) safe; (diagnostic, goût) reliable; **le plus ~ est de** the safest thing is to; **~ de soi** self-confident; **~ et certain** absolutely certain

**surcharge** [syʀʃaʀʒ] nf (de passagers, marchandises) excess load; **surcharger** vt to overload

**surchoix** [syʀʃwa] adj inv top-quality

**surclasser** [syʀklase] vt to outclass

**surcroît** [syʀkʀwa] nm: **un ~ de** additional +nom; **par ou de ~** moreover; **en ~ in addition**

**surdité** [syʀdite] nf deafness

**surélever** [syʀel(ə)ve] vt to raise, heighten

**sûrement** [syʀmã] adv (certainement) certainly; (sans risques) safely

**surenchère** [syʀãʃɛʀ] nf (aux enchères) higher bid; **surenchérir** vi to bid higher; (fig) to try and outdo each other

**surent** [syʀ] vb voir **savoir**

**surestimer** [syʀɛstime] vt to overestimate

**sûreté** [syʀte] nf (sécurité) safety; (exactitude: de renseignements) reliability; (d'un geste) steadiness; **mettre en ~** to put in a safe place; **pour plus de ~** as an extra precaution, to be on the safe side

**surf** [sœʀf] nm surfing

**surface** [syʀfas] nf surface; (superficie) surface area; **une grande ~** a supermarket; **faire ~** to surface; **en ~** near the surface; (fig) superficially

**surfait, e** [syʀfɛ, ɛt] *adj* overrated

**surgelé, e** [syʀʒəle] *adj* (deep-)frozen ♦ *nm:* **les ~s** (deep-)frozen food

**surgir** [syʀʒiʀ] *vi* to appear suddenly; (*fig: problème, conflit*) to arise

**sur...:** **surhumain**, e *adj* superhuman; **sur-le-champ** *adv* immediately; **surlendemain** *nm:* **le surlendemain (soir)** two days later (in the evening); **le surlendemain de** two days after; **surmenage** *nm* overwork(ing); **surmener: se surmener** *vi* to overwork

**surmonter** [syʀmɔ̃te] *vt* (*vaincre*) to overcome; (*être au-dessus de*) to top

**surnaturel, le** [syʀnatyʀɛl] *adj, nm* supernatural

**surnom** [syʀnɔ̃] *nm* nickname

**surnombre** [syʀnɔ̃bʀ] *nm:* **être en ~** to be too many (*ou* one too many)

**surpeuplé, e** [syʀpœple] *adj* over-populated

**sur-place** [syʀplas] *nm:* **faire du ~~** to mark time

**surplomber** [syʀplɔ̃be] *vt, vi* to overhang

**surplus** [syʀply] *nm* (COMM) surplus; (*reste*): **~ de bois** wood left over

**surprenant, e** [syʀpʀənɑ̃, ɑ̃t] *adj* amazing

**surprendre** [syʀpʀɑ̃dʀ] *vt* (*étonner*) to surprise; (*tomber sur: intrus etc*) to catch; (*entendre*) to overhear

**surpris, e** [syʀpʀi, iz] *adj* surprised (*at/that*); **surprise** *nf* surprise; **faire une surprise à qn** to give sb a surprise; **surprise-partie** *nf* party

**surréservation** [syʀʀezɛʀvasjɔ̃] *nf* double booking, overbooking

**sursaut** [syʀso] *nm* start, jump; **~ de** (*énergie, indignation*) sudden burst of; **en ~** with a start; **sursauter** *vi* to (give a) start, jump

**sursis** [syʀsi] *nm* (JUR: *gén*) suspended sentence; (*fig*) reprieve

**surtaxe** [syʀtaks] *nf* surcharge

**surtout** [syʀtu] *adv* (*avant tout, d'abord*) above all; (*spécialement, parti-*

culièrement) especially; **~, ne dites rien!** whatever you do, don't say anything!; **~ pas!** certainly not ou definitely not!; **~ que ...** especially as ...

**surveillance** [syʀvejɑ̃s] *nf* watch; (PO-LICE, MIL) surveillance; **sous ~ médicale** under medical supervision

**surveillant, e** [syʀvejɑ̃, ɑ̃t] *nm/f* (*de prison*) warder; (SCOL) monitor

**surveiller** [syʀveje] *vt* (*enfant, élèves, bagages*) to watch, keep an eye on; (*prisonnier, suspect*) to keep (a) watch on; (*territoire, bâtiment*) to (keep) watch over; (*travaux, cuisson*) to supervise; (SCOL: *examen*) to invigilate; **~ son langage/sa ligne** to watch one's language/figure

**survenir** [syʀvəniʀ] *vi* (*incident, retards*) to occur, arise; (*événement*) to take place

**survêt(ement)** [syʀvɛt(mɑ̃)] *nm* tracksuit

**survie** [syʀvi] *nf* survival; **survivant, e** *nm/f* survivor; **survivre** *vi* to survive; **survivre à** (*accident etc*) to survive

**survoler** [syʀvɔle] *vt* to fly over; (*fig: livre*) to skim through

**survolté, e** [syʀvɔlte] *adj* (*fig*) worked up

**sus** [sy(s)] : **en ~ de** *prép* in addition to, over and above; **en ~** in addition

**susceptible** [syseptibl] *adj* touchy, sensitive; **~ de faire** (*hypothèse*) liable to do

**susciter** [sysite] *vt* (*admiration*) to arouse; (*ennuis*): **~ (à qn)** to create (for sb)

**suspect, e** [syspɛ(kt), ɛkt] *adj* suspicious; (*témoignage, opinions*) suspect ♦ *nm/f* suspect; **suspecter** *vt* to suspect; (*honnêteté de qn*) to question, have one's suspicions about

**suspendre** [syspɑ̃dʀ] *vt* (*accrocher: vêtement*): **~ qch (à)** to hang sth up (on); (*interrompre, démettre*) to suspend; **se ~ à** to hang from

**suspendu, e** [syspɑ̃dy] *adj* (*accroché*):

~ hanging on (*ou* from); (*perché*): ~ **au-dessus de** suspended over

**suspens** [syspɑ̃]: **en ~** *adv* (*affaire*) in abeyance; **tenir en ~** to keep in suspense

**suspense** [syspens, syspɑ̃s] *nm* suspense

**suspension** [syspɑ̃sjɔ̃] *nf* suspension; (*lustre*) light fitting *ou* fitment

**sut** [sy] *vb voir* **savoir**

**suture** [sytyʀ] *nf* (MÉD): **point de ~** stitch

**svelte** [svɛlt] *adj* slender, svelte

**SVP** *abr* (= *s'il vous plaît*) please

**sweat-shirt** [switʃœʀt] (*pl* ~-~**s**) *nm* sweatshirt

**syllabe** [si(l)lab] *nf* syllable

**symbole** [sɛ̃bɔl] *nm* symbol; **symbolique** *adj* symbolic(al); (*geste, offrande*) token *cpd*; **symboliser** *vt* to symbolize

**symétrique** [simetʀik] *adj* symmetrical

**sympa** [sɛ̃pa] (*fam*) *adj inv* nice; **sois ~, prête-le moi** be a pal and lend it to me

**sympathie** [sɛ̃pati] *nf* (*inclination*) liking; (*affinité*) friendship; (*condoléances*) sympathy; **j'ai beaucoup de ~ pour lui** I like him a lot; **sympathique** *adj* nice, friendly

**sympathisant, e** [sɛ̃patizɑ̃, ɑ̃t] *nm/f* sympathizer

**sympathiser** [sɛ̃patize] *vi* (*voisins etc*: *s'entendre*) to get on (BRIT) *ou* along (US) (well)

**symphonie** [sɛ̃fɔni] *nf* symphony

**symptôme** [sɛ̃ptom] *nm* symptom

**synagogue** [sinagɔg] *nf* synagogue

**syncope** [sɛ̃kɔp] *nf* (MÉD) blackout; **tomber en ~** to faint, pass out

**syndic** [sɛ̃dik] *nm* (*d'immeuble*) managing agent

**syndical, e, -aux** [sɛ̃dikal, o] *adj* (trade) union *cpd*; **syndicaliste** *nm/f* trade unionist

**syndicat** [sɛ̃dika] *nm* (*d'ouvriers, employés*) (trade) union; **~ d'initiative** tourist office; **syndiqué, e** *adj* belong-

ing to a (trade) union; **syndiquer: se syndiquer** *vi* to form a trade union; (*adhérer*) to join a trade union

**synonyme** [sinɔnim] *adj* synonymous ♦ *nm* synonym; **~ de** synonymous with

**syntaxe** [sɛ̃taks] *nf* syntax

**synthèse** [sɛ̃tɛz] *nf* synthesis

**synthétique** [sɛ̃tetik] *adj* synthetic

**Syrie** [siʀi] *nf*: **la ~** Syria

**systématique** [sistematik] *adj* systematic

**système** [sistɛm] *nm* system; **~ D** (*fam*) resourcefulness

# T, t

**t'** [t] *pron voir* **te**

**ta** [ta] *adj voir* **ton**[1]

**tabac** [taba] *nm* tobacco; (*magasin*) tobacconist's (shop); **~ blond/brun** light/dark tobacco

**tabagisme** [tabaʒism] *nm*: **~ passif** passive smoking

**tabasser** [tabase] (*fam*) *vt* to beat up

**table** [tabl] *nf* table; **à ~!** dinner *etc* is ready!; **se mettre à ~** to sit down to eat; **mettre la ~** to lay the table; **faire ~ rase de** to make a clean sweep of; **~ à repasser** ironing board; **~ de cuisson** (à *l'électricité*) hotplate; (*au gaz*) gas ring; **~ de nuit** *ou* **de chevet** bedside table; **~ des matières** table of contents *pl*; **~ d'orientation** viewpoint indicator; **~ roulante** trolley

**tableau, x** [tablo] *nm* (*peinture*) painting; (*reproduction, fig*) picture; (*panneau*) board; (*schéma*) table, chart; **~ d'affichage** notice board; **~ de bord** (AVIAT) instrument panel; **~ noir** blackboard

**tabler** [table] *vi*: **~ sur** to bank on

**tablette** [tablɛt] *nf* (*planche*) shelf; **~ de chocolat** bar of chocolate

**tableur** [tablœʀ] *nm* spreadsheet

**tablier** [tablije] *nm* apron

**tabou** [tabu] *nm* taboo

**tabouret** [taburɛ] nm stool

**tac** [tak] nm: **il m'a répondu du ~ au ~** he answered me right back

**tache** [taʃ] nf (saleté) stain, mark; (ART, de couleur, lumière) spot; **~ de rousseur** freckle

**tâche** [taʃ] nf task

**tacher** [taʃe] vt to stain, mark

**tâcher** [taʃe] vi: **~ de faire** to try ou endeavour to do

**tacheté, e** [taʃte] adj spotted

**tacot** [tako] (péj) nm banger (BRIT), (old) heap

**tact** [takt] nm tact; **avoir du ~** to be tactful

**tactique** [taktik] adj tactical ♦ nf (technique) tactics sg; (plan) tactic

**taie** [tɛ] nf **(d'oreiller)** pillowslip, pillowcase

**taille** [taj] nf cutting; (d'arbre etc) pruning; (milieu du corps) waist; (hauteur) height; (grandeur) size; **de ~ à faire** capable of doing; **de ~** sizeable; **taille-crayon(s)** nm pencil sharpener

**tailler** [taje] vt (pierre, diamant) to cut; (arbre, plante) to prune; (vêtement) to cut out; (crayon) to sharpen

**tailleur** [tajœʀ] nm (couturier) tailor; (vêtement) suit; **en ~** (assis) cross-legged

**taillis** [taji] nm copse

**taire** [tɛʀ] vi: **faire ~ qn** to make sb be quiet; **se ~** vi to be silent ou quiet

**talc** [talk] nm talc, talcum powder

**talent** [talɑ̃] nm talent

**talkie-walkie** [tokiwoki] nm walkie-talkie

**taloche** [talɔʃ] (fam) nf clout, cuff

**talon** [talɔ̃] nm heel; (de chèque, billet) stub, counterfoil (BRIT); **~s plats/ aiguilles** flat/stiletto heels

**talonner** [talɔne] vt (suivre) to follow hot on the heels of; (harceler) to hound

**talus** [taly] nm embankment

**tambour** [tɑ̃buʀ] nm (MUS, aussi) drum; (musicien) drummer; (porte) revolving door(s pl); **tambourin** nm tambourine

**tambouriner** vi to drum; **tambouriner à/sur** to drum on

**tamis** [tami] nm sieve

**Tamise** [tamiz] nf: **la ~** the Thames

**tamisé, e** [tamize] adj (fig) subdued, soft

**tampon** [tɑ̃pɔ̃] nm (de coton, d'ouate) wad, pad; (amortisseur) buffer; (bouchon) plug, stopper; (cachet, timbre) stamp; (mémoire) ~ (INFORM) buffer; **(hygiénique) tampon; tamponner** vt (timbres) to stamp; (heurter) to crash ou ram into; **tamponneuse** adj f: **autos tamponneuses** dodgems

**tandem** [tɑ̃dɛm] nm tandem

**tandis** [tɑ̃di]: **~ que** conj while

**tanguer** [tɑ̃ge] vi to pitch (and toss)

**tanière** [tanjɛʀ] nf lair, den

**tanné, e** [tane] adj weather-beaten

**tanner** [tane] vt to tan; (fam: harceler) to badger

**tant** [tɑ̃] adv so much; **~ de** (sable, eau) so much; (gens, livres) so many; **~ que** as long as; (autant que) as much as; **~ mieux** that's great; (avec une certaine réserve) so much the better; **~ pis** too bad; (conciliant) never mind

**tante** [tɑ̃t] nf aunt

**tantôt** [tɑ̃to] adv (parfois): **~ ... ~** now ... now; (cet après-midi) this afternoon

**taon** [tɑ̃] nm horsefly

**tapage** [tapaʒ] nm uproar, din

**tapageur, -euse** [tapaʒœʀ, øz] adj noisy; (voyant) loud, flashy

**tape** [tap] nf slap

**tape-à-l'œil** [tapalœj] adj inv flashy, showy

**taper** [tape] vt (porte) to bang, slam; (enfant) to slap; (dactylographier) to type; (fam: emprunter): **~ qn de 10 F** to touch sb for 10 F ♦ vi (soleil) to beat down; **se ~** vt (repas) to put away; (corvée) to get landed with; **~ sur qn** to thump sb; (fig) to run sb down; **~ sur un clou** to hit a nail; **~ sur la table** to bang on the table; **~ à** (porte etc) to knock on; **~ dans** (se ser-

*vir*) to dig into; **~ des mains/pieds** to clap one's hands/stamp one's feet; **(à la machine)** to type; **se ~ un travail** *(fam)* to land o.s. a job

**tapi, e** [tapi] *adj (blotti)* crouching; *(caché)* hidden away

**tapis** [tapi] *nm* carpet; *(petit)* rug; **mettre sur le ~** *(fig)* to bring up for discussion; **~ de bain** bath mat; **~ de sol** *(de tente)* groundsheet; **~ de souris** *(INFORM)* mouse mat; **~ roulant** *(pour piétons)* moving walkway; *(pour bagages)* carousel

**tapisser** [tapise] *vt (avec du papier peint)* to paper; *(recouvrir)* : **~ qch (de)** to cover sth (with); **tapisserie** *nf (tenture, broderie)* tapestry; *(papier peint)* wallpaper; **tapissier-décorateur** *nm* interior decorator

**tapoter** [tapɔte] *vt (joue, main)* to pat; *(objet)* to tap

**taquin, e** [takɛ̃, in] *adj* teasing; **taquiner** *vt* to tease

**tarabiscoté, e** [taʀabiskɔte] *adj* overornate, fussy

**tard** [taʀ] *adv* late; **plus ~** later (on); **au plus ~** at the latest; **sur le ~** late in life

**tarder** [taʀde] *vi (chose)* to be a long time coming; *(personne)* : **~ à faire** to delay doing; **il me tarde d'être** I am longing to be; **sans (plus)** ~ without (further) delay

**tardif, -ive** [taʀdif, iv] *adj* late

**taré, e** [taʀe] *nm/f* cretin

**tarif** [taʀif] *nm* : **~s des consommations** price list; **~s postaux/douaniers** postal/customs rates; **~ des taxis** taxi fares; **~ plein/réduit** *(train)* full/reduced fare; *(téléphone)* peak/off-peak rate

**tarir** [taʀiʀ] *vi* to dry up, run dry

**tarte** [taʀt] *nf* tart; **~ aux fraises** strawberry tart; **~ Tatin** ≃ apple upside-down tart

**tartine** [taʀtin] *nf* slice of bread; **~ de miel** slice of bread and honey; **tarti-**

**ner** *vt* to spread; **fromage à tartiner** cheese spread

**tartre** [taʀtʀ] *nm (des dents)* tartar; *(de bouilloire)* fur, scale

**tas** [ta] *nm* heap, pile; *(fig)* : **un ~ de** heaps of, lots of; **en ~** in a heap *ou* pile; **formé sur le ~** trained on the job

**tasse** [tas] *nf* cup; **~ à café** coffee cup

**tassé, e** [tase] *adj* : **bien ~** *(café etc)* strong

**tasser** [tase] *vt (terre, neige)* to pack down; *(entasser)* : **~ qch dans** to cram sth into; **se ~** *vi (se serrer)* to squeeze up; *(s'affaisser)* to settle; *(fig)* to settle down

**tata** [tata] *nf* auntie

**tâter** [tate] *vt* to feel; *(fig)* to try out; **se ~** *(hésiter)* to be in two minds; **~ de** *(prison etc)* to have a taste of

**tatillon, ne** [tatijɔ̃, ɔn] *adj* pernickety

**tâtonnement** [tɑtɔnmɑ̃] *nm* : **par ~s** by trial and error

**tâtonner** [tɑtɔne] *vi* to grope one's way along

**tâtons** [tɑtɔ̃] : **à ~** *adv* : **chercher/avancer à ~** to grope around for/grope one's way forward

**tatouage** [tatwaʒ] *nm* tattoo

**tatouer** [tatwe] *vt* to tattoo

**taudis** [todi] *nm* hovel, slum

**taule** [tol] *(fam)* *nf* nick *(fam)*, prison

**taupe** [top] *nf* mole

**taureau, x** [tɔʀo] *nm* bull; *(signe)* : **le T~** Taurus

**tauromachie** [tɔʀɔmaʃi] *nf* bullfighting

**taux** [to] *nm* rate; *(d'alcool)* level; **~ de change** exchange rate; **~ d'intérêt** interest rate

**taxe** [taks] *nf* tax; *(douanière)* duty; **toutes ~s comprises** inclusive of tax; **la boutique hors ~s** the duty free shop; **~ à la valeur ajoutée** value added tax

**taxer** [takse] *vt (personne)* to tax; *(produit)* to put a tax on, tax

**taxi** [taksi] *nm* taxi; *(chauffeur: fam)* taxi

driver

**Tchécoslovaquie** [tʃekɔslɔvaki] *nf* Czechoslovakia; **tchèque** *adj* Czech ♦ *nm/f*: **Tchèque** Czech ♦ *nm* (*LING*) Czech; **la République tchèque** the Czech Republic

**te, t'** [tə] *pron* you; (*réfléchi*) yourself

**technicien, ne** [teknisjɛ̃, jɛn] *nm/f* technician

**technico-commercial, e, -aux** [teknikokɔmersjal, jo] *adj*: **agent ~** sales technician

**technique** [teknik] *adj* technical ♦ *nf* technique; **techniquement** *adv* technically

**technologie** [teknɔlɔʒi] *nf* technology; **technologique** *adj* technological

**teck** [tek] *nm* teak

**tee-shirt** [tiʃœrt] *nm* T-shirt, tee-shirt

**teignais** *etc* [tɛɲɛ] *vb voir* **teindre**

**teindre** [tɛ̃dr] *vt* to dye; **se ~ les cheveux** to dye one's hair; **teint, e** *adj* dyed ♦ *nm* (*du visage*) complexion; (*momentané*) colour ♦ *nf* shade; **grand teint** colourfast

**teinté, e** [tɛ̃te] *adj*: **~ de** (*fig*) tinged with

**teinter** [tɛ̃te] *vt* (*verre, papier*) to tint; (*bois*) to stain

**teinture** [tɛ̃tyr] *nf* dye; **~ d'iode** tincture of iodine; **teinturerie** *nf* dry cleaner's; **teinturier** *nm* dry cleaner

**tel, telle** [tel] *adj* (*pareil*) such; (*comme*): **~ un/des** ... like a/like ...; (*indéfini*) such-and-such a; (*intensif*): **un ~/de tels** ... such (a)/such ...; **rien de ~** nothing like it; **~ que** like, such as; **~ quel** as it is ou stands (*ou* was etc); **venez ~ jour** come on such-and-such a day

**télé** [tele] (*fam*) *nf* TV

**télé...**: **télécabine** *nf* (*benne*) cable car; **télécarte** *nf* phonecard; **télécommande** *nf* remote control; **télécopie** *nf* fax; **envoyer qch par télécopie** to fax sth; **télécopieur** *nm* fax machine; **télédistribution** *nf* cable TV; **téléférique** *nm* = **téléphérique**;

**télégramme** *nm* telegram; **télégraphier** *vt* to telegraph, cable; **téléguider** *vt* to radio-control; **télématique** *nf* telematics *sg*; **téléobjectif** *nm* telephoto lens *sg*; **télépathie** *nf* telepathy; **téléphérique** *nm* cable car

**téléphone** [telefɔn] *nm* telephone; **avoir le ~** to be on the (tele)phone; **au ~** on the phone; **~ mobile** mobile phone; **~ rouge** hot line; **~ sans fil** cordless (tele)phone; **~ de voiture** car phone; **téléphoner** *vi* to make a phone call; **téléphoner à** to phone, call up; **téléphonique** *adj* (tele)phone *cpd*

**télescope** [teleskɔp] *nm* telescope

**télescoper** [teleskɔpe] *vt* to smash up; **se ~** (*véhicules*) to concertina

**télé...**: **téléscripteur** *nm* teleprinter; **télésiège** *nm* chairlift; **téléski** *nm* ski-tow; **téléspectateur, -trice** *nm/f* (television) viewer; **télévente** *nf* telesales; **téléviseur** *nm* television set; **télévision** *nf* television; **à la télévision** on television; **télévision numérique** digital TV

**télex** [teleks] *nm* telex

**telle** [tel] *adj voir* **tel**; **tellement** *adv* (*tant*) so much; (*si*) so; **tellement de** (*sable, eau*) so much; (*gens, livres*) so many; **il s'est endormi tellement il était fatigué** he was so tired (that) he fell asleep; **pas tellement** not (all) that much; **pas tellement** not (all) that much; not (all) that +*adjectif*

**téméraire** [temerer] *adj* reckless, rash; **témérité** *nf* recklessness, rashness

**témoignage** [temwaɲaʒ] *nm* (*JUR*: *déclaration*) testimony *no pl*, evidence *no pl*; (*rapport, récit*) account; (*fig*: *d'affection etc*: *cadeau*) token, mark; (: *geste*) expression

**témoigner** [temwaɲe] *vt* (*intérêt, gratitude*) to show ♦ *vi* (*JUR*) to testify, give evidence; **~ de** to bear witness to, testify to

**témoin** [temwɛ̃] *nm* witness ♦ *adj*: **appartement ~** show flat (*BRIT*); **être ~**

de to witness; **~ oculaire** eyewitness

**tempe** [tɑ̃p] nf temple

**tempérament** [tɑ̃peʀamɑ̃] nm temperament, disposition; **à ~** (vente) on deferred (payment) terms; (achat) by instalments, hire purchase cpd

**température** [tɑ̃peʀatyʀ] nf temperature; **avoir ou faire de la ~** to be running ou have a temperature

**tempéré, e** [tɑ̃peʀe] adj temperate

**tempête** [tɑ̃pɛt] nf storm; **~ de sable/neige** sand/snowstorm

**temple** [tɑ̃pl] nm temple; (protestant) church

**temporaire** [tɑ̃pɔʀɛʀ] adj temporary

**temps** [tɑ̃] nm (atmosphérique) weather; (durée) time; (époque) time, times pl; (LING) tense; (MUS) beat; (TECH) stroke; **un ~ de chien** (fam) rotten weather; **quel ~ fait-il?** what's the weather like?; **il fait beau/mauvais ~** the weather is fine/bad; **avoir le ~/tout son ~** to have time/plenty of time; **en ~ de paix/guerre** in peacetime/wartime; **en ~ utile ou voulu** in due time ou course; **ces derniers ~** lately; **dans quelque ~** in a (little) while; **de ~ en ~, de ~ à autre** from time to time; **à ~** (partir, arriver) in time; **à ~ complet, à plein ~** fulltime; **à ~ partiel** part-time; **dans le ~** at one time; **~ d'arrêt** pause, halt; **~ mort** (COMM) slack period

**tenable** [t(ə)nabl] adj bearable

**tenace** [tənas] adj persistent

**tenailler** [tənaje] vt (fig) to torment

**tenailles** [tənaj] nfpl pincers

**tenais** etc [t(ə)nɛ] vb voir tenir

**tenancier, -ière** [tənɑ̃sje] nm/f manager/manageress

**tenant, e** [tənɑ̃, ɑ̃t] nm/f (SPORT): **du titre** title-holder

**tendance** [tɑ̃dɑ̃s] nf tendency; (opinions) leanings pl, sympathies pl; (évolution) trend; **avoir ~ à** to have a tendency to, tend to

**tendeur** [tɑ̃dœʀ] nm (attache) elastic strap

**tendre** [tɑ̃dʀ] adj tender; (bois, roche, couleur) soft ♦ vt (élastique, peau) to stretch; to tighten; (muscle) to tense; (fig: piège) to set, lay; (donner): **~ qch à qn** to hold sth out to sb; (offrir) to offer sth to sb; **se ~** vi (corde) to tighten; (relations) to become strained; **~ à qch/à faire** to tend towards sth/to do; **~ l'oreille** to prick up one's ears; **~ la main/le bras** to hold out one's hand/stretch out one's arm; **tendrement** adv tenderly; **tendresse** nf tenderness

**tendu, e** [tɑ̃dy] pp de tendre ♦ adj (corde) tight; (muscles) tensed; (relations) strained

**ténèbres** [tenɛbʀ] nfpl darkness sg

**teneur** [tənœʀ] nf content; (d'une lettre) terms pl, content

**tenir** [t(ə)niʀ] vt to hold; (magasin, hôtel) to run; (promesse) to keep ♦ vi to hold; (neige, gel) to last; **se ~** vi (avoir lieu) to be held, take place; (être: personne) to stand; **~ à** (personne, objet) to be attached to; (réputation) to care about; **~ à faire** to want ou be determined to do; **~ de** (ressembler à) to take after; **ça ne tient qu'à lui** it is entirely up to him; **~ qn pour** to regard sb as; **~ qch de qn** (histoire) to have heard ou learnt sth from sb; (qualité, défaut) to have inherited ou got sth from sb; **~ dans** to fit into; **~ compte de qch** to take sth into account; **~ les comptes** to keep the books; **~ bon** to stand fast; **~ le coup** to hold out; **~ au chaud** to keep hot; **tiens/tenez, voilà le stylo** there's the pen!; **tiens, voilà Alain!** look, here's Alain!; **tiens?** (surprise) really?; **se ~ droit** to stand (ou sit) up straight; **bien se ~** to behave well; **se ~ à qch** to hold on to sth; **s'en ~ à qch** to confine o.s. to sth

**tennis** [tenis] nm tennis; (court) tennis court ♦ nm ou f pl (aussi: **chaussures de ~**) tennis ou gym shoes; **~ de table** table tennis; **tennisman** nm tennis player

**tension** [tɑ̃sjɔ̃] *nf* tension; (MÉD) blood pressure; **avoir de la ~** to have high blood pressure

**tentation** [tɑ̃tasjɔ̃] *nf* temptation

**tentative** [tɑ̃tativ] *nf* attempt

**tente** [tɑ̃t] *nf* tent

**tenter** [tɑ̃te] *vt* (éprouver, attirer) to tempt; (essayer): **~ qch/de faire** to attempt ou try sth/to do; **~ sa chance** to try one's luck

**tenture** [tɑ̃tyʀ] *nf* hanging

**tenu, e** [t(ə)ny] *pp de* **tenir ♦** *adj* (maison, comptes): **bien ~** well-kept; (obligé): **~ de faire** obliged to do **♦** *nf* (vêtements) clothes *pl*; (comportement) (good) manners *pl*, good behaviour; (d'une maison) upkeep; **en petite ~** scantily dressed ou clad; **~e de route** (AUTO) road-holding; **~e de soirée** evening dress

**ter** [tɛʀ] *adj*: **16** ~ **16b** ou **B**

**térébenthine** [teʀebɑ̃tin] *nf*: (essence de) ~ (oil of) turpentine

**Tergal** ® [tɛʀgal] *nm* Terylene ®

**terme** [tɛʀm] *nm* term; (fin) end; **à court/long ~ ♦** *adj* short-/long-term **♦** *adv* in the short/long term; **avant ~** (MÉD) prematurely; **mettre un ~ à** to put an end ou a stop to; **en bons ~s** on good terms

**terminaison** [tɛʀminɛzɔ̃] *nf* (LING) ending

**terminal, o** [tɛʀminal, o] *nm* terminal; **terminale** *nf* (SCOL) ≈ sixth form ou year (BRIT), ≈ twelfth grade (US)

**terminer** [tɛʀmine] *vt* to finish; **se ~** *vi* to end

**terne** [tɛʀn] *adj* dull

**ternir** [tɛʀniʀ] *vt* to dull; (fig) to sully, tarnish; **se ~** *vi* to become dull

**terrain** [tɛʀɛ̃] *nm* (sol, fig) ground; (COMM: étendue de terre) land *no pl*; (parcelle) plot of land); (à bâtir) site; **sur le ~** (fig) on the field; **~ d'aviation** airfield; **~ de camping** campsite; **~ de football/rugby** football/rugby

pitch (BRIT) ou field (US); **~ de golf** golf course; **~ de jeu** games field; (pour les petits) playground; **~ de sport** sports ground; **~ vague** waste ground *no pl*

**terrasse** [tɛʀas] *nf* terrace; **à la ~** (café) outside; **terrasser** *vt* (adversaire) to floor; (suj: maladie etc) to strike down

**terre** [tɛʀ] *nf* (gén, aussi ÉLEC) earth; (substance) soil, earth; (opposé à mer) land *no pl*; (contrée) land; **~s** *nfpl* (terrains) lands, land *sg*; **en ~** (pipe, poterie) clay *cpd*; **à ~** ou **par ~** (mettre, être, s'asseoir) on the ground (ou floor); (jeter, tomber) to the ground, down; **~ à ~** *adj* inv down-to-earth; **~ cuite** terracotta; **la ~ ferme** dry land; **~ glaise** clay

**terreau** [tɛʀo] *nm* compost

**terre-plein** [tɛʀplɛ̃] *nm* platform; (sur chaussée) central reservation

**terrer** [tɛʀe]: **se ~** *vi* to hide away

**terrestre** [tɛʀɛstʀ] *adj* (surface) earth's, of the earth; (BOT, ZOOL, MIL) land *cpd*; (REL) earthly

**terreur** [tɛʀœʀ] *nf* terror *no pl*

**terrible** [tɛʀibl] *adj* terrible, dreadful; (fam) terrific; **pas ~** nothing special

**terrien, ne** [tɛʀjɛ̃, jɛn] *adj*: **propriétaire ~** landowner **♦** *nm/f* (non martien etc) earthling

**terrier** [tɛʀje] *nm* burrow, hole; (chien) terrier

**terrifier** [tɛʀifje] *vt* to terrify

**terrine** [tɛʀin] *nf* (récipient) terrine; (CULIN) pâté

**territoire** [tɛʀitwaʀ] *nm* territory

**terroir** [tɛʀwaʀ] *nm*: **accent du ~** country accent

**terroriser** [tɛʀɔʀize] *vt* to terrorize

**terrorisme** [tɛʀɔʀism] *nm* terrorism; **terroriste** *nm/f* terrorist

**tertiaire** [tɛʀsjɛʀ] *adj* tertiary **♦** *nm* (ÉCON) service industries *pl*

**tertre** [tɛʀtʀ] *nm* hillock, mound

**tes** [te] *adj voir* **ton**[1]

**tesson** [tesɔ̃] *nm*: **~ de bouteille** piece

of broken bottle

**test** [tɛst] nm test

**testament** [tɛstamɑ̃] nm (JUR) will; (REL) Testament; (fig) legacy

**tester** [tɛste] vt to test

**testicule** [tɛstikyl] nm testicle

**tétanos** [tetanos] nm tetanus

**têtard** [tɛtaʀ] nm tadpole

**tête** [tɛt] nf head; (cheveux) hair no pl; (visage) face; **de ~** adj (wagon etc) front cpd ♦ adv (calculer) mentally; **tenir ~ à qn** to stand up to sb; **la ~ en bas** with one's head down; **la ~ la première** (tomber) headfirst; **faire une ~** (FOOTBALL) to head the ball; **faire la ~** (fig) to sulk; **en ~** at the front; (SPORT) in the lead; **à la ~ de** at the head of; **à ~ reposée** in a more leisurely moment; **n'en faire qu'à sa ~** to do as one pleases; **en avoir par-dessus la ~** to be fed up; **en ~ à ~** in private, alone together; **de la ~ aux pieds** from head to toe; **~ de lecture** (playback) head; **~ de liste** (POL) chief candidate; **~ de série** (TENNIS) seeded player, seed; **tête-à-queue** nm inv: **faire un tête-à-queue** to spin round

**téter** [tete] vt: **~ (sa mère)** to suck at one's mother's breast, feed

**tétine** [tetin] nf teat; (sucette) dummy (BRIT), pacifier (US)

**têtu, e** [tety] adj stubborn, pigheaded

**texte** [tɛkst] nm text; (morceau choisi) passage

**textile** [tɛkstil] adj textile cpd ♦ nm textile; **le ~** the textile industry

**texto** [tɛksto] (fam) adj word for word

**texture** [tɛkstyʀ] nf texture

**thaïlandais, e** [tajlɑ̃dɛ, ɛz] adj Thai ♦ nm/f: **T~, e** Thai

**Thaïlande** [tajlɑ̃d] nf Thailand

**TGV** sigle m (= train à grande vitesse) high-speed train

**thé** [te] nm tea; **~ au citron** lemon tea; **~ au lait** tea with milk; **prendre le ~** to have tea; **faire le ~** to make the tea

**théâtral, e, -aux** [teatʀal, o] adj theatrical

**théâtre** [teatʀ] nm theatre; (péj: simulation) playacting; (fig: lieu): **le ~ de** the scene of; **faire du ~** to act

**théière** [tejɛʀ] nf teapot

**thème** [tɛm] nm theme; (SCOL: traduction) prose (composition)

**théologie** [teɔlɔʒi] nf theology

**théorie** [teɔʀi] nf theory; **théorique** adj theoretical

**thérapie** [teʀapi] nf therapy

**thermal, e, -aux** [tɛʀmal, o] adj: **station ~e** spa; **cure ~e** water cure

**thermes** [tɛʀm] nmpl thermal baths

**thermomètre** [tɛʀmɔmɛtʀ] nm thermometer

**thermos** ® [tɛʀmos] nm ou nf: **(bouteille) ~** vacuum ou Thermos ® flask

**thermostat** [tɛʀmɔsta] nm thermostat

**thèse** [tɛz] nf thesis

**thon** [tɔ̃] nm tuna (fish)

**thym** [tɛ̃] nm thyme

**tibia** [tibja] nm shinbone, tibia; (partie antérieure de la jambe) shin

**tic** [tik] nm tic, (nervous) twitch; (de langage etc) mannerism

**ticket** [tikɛ] nm ticket; **~ de caisse** receipt; **~ de quai** platform ticket

**tic-tac** [tiktak] nm ticking; **faire ~~** to tick

**tiède** [tjɛd] adj lukewarm; (vent, air) mild, warm; **tiédir** vi to cool; (se réchauffer) to grow warmer

**tien, ne** [tjɛ̃, tjɛn] pron: **le(la) ~(ne), les ~(ne)s** yours; **à la ~ne!** cheers!

**tiens** [tjɛ̃] vb, excl voir **tenir**

**tierce** [tjɛʀs] adj voir **tiers**

**tiercé** [tjɛʀse] nm system of forecast betting giving first 3 horses

**tiers, tierce** [tjɛʀ, tjɛʀs] adj third ♦ nm (JUR) third party; (fraction) third; **le ~ monde** the Third World

**tifs** [tif] (fam) nmpl hair

**tige** [tiʒ] nf stem; (baguette) rod

**tignasse** [tiɲas] (péj) nf mop of hair

**tigre** [tigʀ] nm tiger; **tigresse** nf tigress; **tigré, e** adj (rayé) striped; (tacheté) spotted; (chat) tabby

**tilleul** [tijœl] nm lime (tree), linden (tree); (boisson) lime(-blossom) tea

**timbale** [tɛ̃bal] nf (metal) tumbler; **~s** nfpl (MUS) timpani, kettledrums

**timbre** [tɛ̃bʀ] nm (tampon) stamp; (aussi: **~poste**) (postage) stamp; (MUS: de voix, instrument) stamp

**timbré, e** [tɛ̃bʀe] (fam) adj cracked

**timide** [timid] adj shy; (timoré) timid; **timidement** adv shyly; timidly; **timidité** nf shyness; timidity

**tins** etc [tɛ̃] vb voir **tenir**

**tintamarre** [tɛ̃tamaʀ] nm din, uproar

**tinter** [tɛ̃te] vi to ring, chime; (argent, clefs) to jingle

**tique** [tik] nf (parasite) tick

**tir** [tiʀ] nm (sport) shooting; (fait ou manière de ~er) fire no pl; (rafale) fire; (stand) shooting gallery; **~ à l'arc** archery; **~ au pigeon** clay pigeon shooting

**tirage** [tiʀaʒ] nm (action) printing; (PHOTO) print; (de journal) circulation; (de livre: nombre d'exemplaires) (print) run; (: édition) edition; (de loterie) draw; **par ~ au sort** by drawing lots

**tirailler** [tiʀaje] vt: **être tiraillé entre** to be torn between

**tire** [tiʀ] nf: **vol à la ~** pickpocketing

**tiré, e** [tiʀe] adj (traits) drawn; **~ par les cheveux** far-fetched

**tire-au-flanc** [tiʀoflɑ̃] (péj) nm inv skiver

**tire-bouchon** [tiʀbuʃɔ̃] nm corkscrew

**tirelire** [tiʀliʀ] nf moneybox

**tirer** [tiʀe] vt (gén) to pull; (extraire): **~ qch de** to take ou pull sth out of; (trait, rideau, carte, conclusion, chèque) to draw; (langue) to stick out; (en faisant feu: balle, coup) to fire; (: animal) to shoot; (journal, livre, photo) to shoot; (FOOTBALL: corner etc) to take ♦ vi (faire feu) to fire; (faire du tir, FOOTBALL) to shoot; **se ~** vi (fam) to push off; **s'en ~** (éviter le pire) to get off; (survivre) to

pull through; (se débrouiller) to manage; **~ sur** (corde) to pull on ou at; (faire feu sur) to shoot ou fire at; (pipe) to draw on; (approcher de: couleur) to verge ou border on; **~ qn de** (embarras etc) to help ou get sb out of; **~ à l'arc/ la carabine** to shoot with a bow and arrow/with a rifle; **~ à sa fin** to be drawing to a close; **~ qch au clair** to clear sth up; **~ au sort** to draw lots; **~ parti de** to take advantage of; **~ profit de** to profit from

**tiret** [tiʀɛ] nm dash

**tireur** [tiʀœʀ] nm gunman; **~ d'élite** marksman

**tiroir** [tiʀwaʀ] nm drawer; **tiroir-caisse** nm till

**tisane** [tizan] nf herb tea

**tisonnier** [tizɔnje] nm poker

**tisser** [tise] vt to weave; **tisserand** nm weaver

**tissu** [tisy] nm fabric, material, cloth no pl; (ANAT, BIO) tissue; **tissu-éponge** nm (terry) towelling no pl

**titre** [titʀ] nm (gén) title; (de journal) headline; (diplôme) qualification; (COMM) security; **en ~** (champion) official; **à juste ~** rightly; **à quel ~?** on what grounds?; **à aucun ~** on no account; **au même ~ (que)** in the same way (as); **à ~ d'information** (for your) information; **à ~ gracieux** free of charge; **à ~ d'essai** on a trial basis; **à ~ privé** in a private capacity; **~ de propriété** title deed; **~ de transport** ticket

**tituber** [titybe] vi to stagger (along)

**titulaire** [titylɛʀ] adj (ADMIN) with tenure ♦ nm/f (de permis) holder

**toast** [tost] nm slice ou piece of toast; (de bienvenue) (welcoming) toast; **porter un ~ à qn** to propose ou drink a toast to sb

**toboggan** [tɔbɔgɑ̃] nm slide; (AUTO) flyover

**toc** [tɔk] excl: **~, toc** knock knock ♦ nm: **en ~** fake

**tocsin** [tɔksɛ̃] nm alarm (bell)

**toge** [tɔʒ] nf toga; (de juge) gown

**tohu-bohu** [tɔyby] nm hubbub

**toi** [twa] pron you

**toile** [twal] nf (tableau) canvas; **de ou en ~** (pantalon) cotton; (sac) canvas; **~ cirée** oilcloth; **~ d'araignée** cobweb; **~ de fond** (fig) backdrop

**toilette** [twalɛt] nf (habits) outfit; **~s** nfpl (w.-c.) toilet sg; **faire sa ~** to have a wash, get washed; **articles de ~** toiletries

**toi-même** [twamɛm] pron yourself

**toiser** [twaze] vt to eye up and down

**toison** [twazɔ̃] nf (de mouton) fleece

**toit** [twa] nm roof; **~ ouvrant** sunroof

**toiture** [twatyʀ] nf roof

**tôle** [tol] nf (plaque) steel ou iron sheet; **~ ondulée** corrugated iron

**tolérable** [tɔleʀabl] adj tolerable

**tolérant, e** [tɔleʀɑ̃, ɑ̃t] adj tolerant

**tolérer** [tɔleʀe] vt to tolerate; (ADMIN: hors taxe etc) to allow

**tollé** [tɔ(l)le] nm outcry

**tomate** [tɔmat] nf tomato; **~s farcies** stuffed tomatoes

**tombe** [tɔ̃b] nf (sépulture) grave; (avec monument) tomb

**tombeau, x** [tɔ̃bo] nm tomb

**tombée** [tɔ̃be] nf: **à la ~ de la nuit** at nightfall

**tomber** [tɔ̃be] vi to fall; (fièvre, vent) to drop; **laisser ~** (objet) to drop; (personne) to let down; (activité) to give up; **laisse ~!** forget it!; **faire ~** to knock over; **~ sur** (rencontrer) to bump into; **~ de fatigue/sommeil** to drop from exhaustion/be falling asleep on one's feet; **ça tombe bien** that's come at the right time; **il est bien tombé** he's been lucky; **~ en panne** to break down

**tombola** [tɔ̃bɔla] nf raffle

**tome** [tom] nm volume

**ton¹, ta** [tɔ̃, ta] (pl **tes**) adj your

**ton²** [tɔ̃] nm (gén) tone; (couleur) shade, tone; **de bon ~** in good taste

**tonalité** [tɔnalite] nf (au téléphone) dialling tone

**tondeuse** [tɔ̃døz] nf (à gazon) (lawn)mower; (du coiffeur) clippers pl; (pour les moutons) shears pl

**tondre** [tɔ̃dʀ] vt (pelouse, herbe) to mow; (haie) to cut, clip; (mouton, toison) to shear; (cheveux) to crop

**tongs** [tɔ̃g] nfpl flip-flops

**tonifier** [tɔnifje] vt (peau, organisme) to tone up

**tonique** [tɔnik] adj fortifying ♦ nm tonic

**tonne** [tɔn] nf metric ton, tonne

**tonneau, x** [tɔno] nm (à vin, cidre) barrel; **faire des ~x** (voiture, avion) to roll over

**tonnelle** [tɔnɛl] nf bower, arbour

**tonner** [tɔne] vi to thunder; **il tonne** it is thundering, there's some thunder

**tonnerre** [tɔnɛʀ] nm thunder

**tonton** [tɔ̃tɔ̃] nm uncle

**tonus** [tɔnys] nm energy

**top** [tɔp] nm: **au 3ème ~** at the 3rd stroke

**topinambour** [tɔpinɑ̃buʀ] nm Jerusalem artichoke

**topo** [tɔpo] (fam) nm rundown; **c'est le même ~** it's the same old story

**toque** [tɔk] nf (de fourrure) fur hat; **~ de cuisinier** chef's hat; **~ de jockey/juge** jockey's/judge's cap

**toqué, e** [tɔke] (fam) adj cracked

**torche** [tɔʀʃ] nf torch

**torchon** [tɔʀʃɔ̃] nm cloth; (à vaisselle) tea towel ou cloth

**tordre** [tɔʀdʀ] vt (chiffon) to wring; (barre, fig: visage) to twist; **se ~** : **se ~ le poignet/la cheville** to twist one's wrist/ankle; **se ~ de douleur/rire** to be doubled up with pain/laughter; **tordu, e** adj bent; (fig) crazy

**tornade** [tɔʀnad] nf tornado

**torpille** [tɔʀpij] nf torpedo

**torréfier** [tɔʀefje] vt to roast

**torrent** [tɔʀɑ̃] nm mountain stream

**torsade** [tɔʀsad] nf: **un pull à ~s** a

cable sweater

**torse** [tɔʀs] nm chest; (ANAT, SCULPTURE) torso; ~ **nu** stripped to the waist

**tort** [tɔʀ] nm (défaut) fault; ~**s** nmpl (JUR) fault sg; **avoir** ~ to be wrong; **être dans son** ~ to be in the wrong; **donner** ~ **à qn** to lay the blame on sb; **causer du** ~ **à** to harm; ~ **wrongly**; **à** ~ **et à travers** wildly

**torticolis** [tɔʀtikɔli] nm stiff neck

**tortiller** [tɔʀtije] vt to twist; (moustache) to twirl; **se** ~ vi to wriggle; (en dansant) to wiggle

**tortionnaire** [tɔʀsjɔnɛʀ] nm torturer

**tortue** [tɔʀty] nf tortoise; (d'eau douce) terrapin; (d'eau de mer) turtle

**tortueux, euse** [tɔʀtɥø, øz] adj (rue) twisting; (fig) tortuous

**torture** [tɔʀtyʀ] nf torture; **torturer** vt to torture; (fig) to torment

**tôt** [to] adv early; ~ **ou tard** sooner or later; **si** ~ so early; (déjà) so soon; **plus** ~ earlier; **au plus** ~ at the earliest; **il eut** ~ **fait de faire** he soon did

**total, e, -aux** [tɔtal, o] adj, nm total; **au** ~ in total; (fig) on the whole; **faire le** ~ to work out the total; **totalement** adv totally; **totaliser** vt to total; **totalitaire** adj totalitarian; **totalité** nf: **la totalité de** (all of); the whole +sg; **en totalité** entirely

**toubib** [tubib] (fam) nm doctor

**touchant, e** [tuʃɑ̃, ɑ̃t] adj touching

**touche** [tuʃ] nf (de piano, de machine à écrire) key; (de téléphone) button; (PEIN-TURE etc) stroke, touch; (fig: de nostalgie) touch; (FOOTBALL: aussi: **remise en** ~) throw-in; (aussi: **ligne de** ~) touch-line

**toucher** [tuʃe] nm touch ♦ vt to touch; (palper) to feel; (atteindre: d'un coup de feu etc) to hit; (concerner) to concern, affect; (contacter) to reach, contact; (recevoir: récompense) to receive, get; (: salaire) to draw, get; (: chèque) to cash; **se** ~ (être en contact) to touch; **au** ~

to the touch; ~ **à** to touch; (concerner) to have to do with, concern; **je vais lui en** ~ **un mot** I'll have a word with him about it; ~ **à sa fin** to be drawing to a close

**touffe** [tuf] nf tuft

**touffu, e** [tufy] adj thick, dense

**toujours** [tuʒuʀ] adv always; (encore) still; (constamment) forever; ~ **plus** more and more; **pour** ~ forever; ~ **est-il que** the fact remains that; **essaie** ~ (you can) try anyway

**toupet** [tupɛ] (fam) nm cheek

**toupie** [tupi] nf (spinning) top

**tour** [tuʀ] nf tower; (immeuble) high-rise block (BRIT) ou building (US); (ÉCHECS) castle, rook ♦ nm (excursion) trip; (à pied) stroll, walk; (: revolving run, ride; (SPORT: aussi: ~ **de piste**) lap; (d'être servi ou de jouer etc) turn; (de roue etc) revolution; (POL: aussi: ~ **de scrutin**) ballot; (ruse, de prestidigitation) trick; (de potier) wheel; (à bois, métaux) lathe; (circonférence): **de 3 m** ~ = 3 m round, with a circumference ou girth of 3 m; **faire le** ~ **de** to go round; (à pied) to walk round; **c'est au** ~ **de Renée** it's Renée's turn; **à** ~ **de rôle**, ~ **à** ~ in turn; ~ **de chant** nm song recital; ~ **de contrôle** nf control tower; ~ **de garde** nm spell of duty; ~ **d'horizon** nm (fig) general survey; ~ **de taille/tête** nm waist/head measurement; **un 33** ~**s** an LP; **un 45** ~**s** a single

**tourbe** [tuʀb] nf peat

**tourbillon** [tuʀbijɔ̃] nm whirlwind; (d'eau) whirlpool; (fig) whirl, swirl; **tourbillonner** vi to whirl (round)

**tourelle** [tuʀɛl] nf turret

**tourisme** [tuʀism] nm tourism; **agence de** ~ tourist agency; **faire du** ~ to go touring; (en ville) to go sightseeing; **touriste** nm/f tourist; **touristique** adj tourist cpd; (région) touristic

**tourment** [tuʀmɑ̃] nm torment; **tourmenter** vt to torment; **se tourmenter** vi to fret, worry o.s.

**tournage** [turnaʒ] *nm* (CINÉMA) shooting

**tournant** [turnɑ̃] *nm* (*de route*) bend; (*fig*) turning point

**tournebroche** [turnəbrɔʃ] *nm* roasting spit

**tourne-disque** [turnədisk] *nm* record player

**tournée** [turne] *nf* (*du facteur etc*) round; (*d'artiste, politicien*) tour; (*au café*) round (of drinks)

**tournemain** [turnəmɛ̃]: **en un ~** *adv* (as) quick as a flash

**tourner** [turne] *vt* to turn; (*sauce, mélange*) to stir; (CINÉMA: *faire les prises de vues*) to shoot; (: *produire*) to make ♦ *vi* to turn; (*moteur*) to run; (*taximètre*) to tick away; (*lait etc*) to turn (sour); **se ~** *vi* to turn round; **mal ~** to go wrong; **~ autour de** to go round; (*péj*) to hang round; **~ à/en** to turn into; **~ à gauche/droite** to turn left/right; **~ le dos à** to turn one's back on; to have one's back to; **~ de l'œil** to pass out; **se ~ vers** to turn towards; (*fig*) to turn to

**tournesol** [turnəsɔl] *nm* sunflower

**tournevis** [turnəvis] *nm* screwdriver

**tourniquet** [turnikɛ] *nm* (*pour arroser*) sprinkler; (*portillon*) turnstile; (*présentoir*) revolving stand

**tournoi** [turnwa] *nm* tournament

**tournoyer** [turnwaje] *vi* to swirl (round)

**tournure** [turnyr] *nf* (LING) turn of phrase; (*évolution*): **la ~ de qch** the way sth is developing; **~ d'esprit** turn ou cast of mind; **la ~ des événements** the turn of events

**tourte** [turt] *nf* pie

**tourterelle** [turtərɛl] *nf* turtledove

**tous** [tu] *adj*, *pron voir* **tout**

**Toussaint** [tusɛ̃] *nf*: **la ~** All Saints' Day

*lic holiday in France. People traditionally visit the graves of friends and relatives to lay wreaths of heather and chrysanthemums.*

────────────────────

**tousser** [tuse] *vi* to cough

─── MOT-CLÉ ───

**tout, e** [tu, tut] (*mpl* **tous**, *fpl* **toutes**) *adj* **1** (*avec article singulier*) all; **tout le lait** all the milk; **toute la nuit** all night, the whole night; **tout le livre** the whole book; **tout un pain** a whole loaf; **tout le temps** all the time; the whole time; **c'est tout le contraire** it's quite the opposite

**2** (*avec article pluriel*) every, all; **tous les livres** all the books; **toutes les nuits** every night; **toutes les trois/deux semaines** every third/other ou second week, every three/two weeks; **tous les deux** both ou each of us (ou them ou you); **toutes les trois** all three of us (ou them ou you)

**3** (*sans article*): **à tout âge** at any age; **pour toute nourriture, il avait** ... his only food was ...

♦ *pron* everything, all; **il a tout fait** he's done everything; **je les vois tous** I can see them all ou all of them; **nous y sommes tous allés** all of us went, we all went; **en tout** in all; **tout ce qu'il sait** all he knows

♦ *nm* whole; **le tout** all of it (ou them); **le tout est de ...** the main thing is to ...; **pas du tout** not at all

♦ *adv* **1** (*très, complètement*) very; **tout près** very near; **le tout premier** the very first; **tout seul** all alone; **le livre tout entier** the whole book; **tout en haut** right at the top; **tout droit** straight ahead

**2**: **tout en** while; **tout en travaillant** while working, as he *etc* works

**3**: **tout d'abord** first of all; **tout à coup** suddenly; **tout à fait** absolutely;

**tout à l'heure** a short while ago; (*futur*) in a short while, shortly; **à tout à l'heure!** see you later!; **tout de même** all the same; **tout le monde** everybody; **tout de suite** immediately, straight away; **tout terrain** ou **tous terrains** all-terrain

---

**toutefois** [tutfwa] *adv* however

**toutes** [tut] *adj, pron voir* **tout**

**toux** [tu] *nf* cough

**toxicomane** [tɔksikɔman] *nm/f* drug addict

**toxique** [tɔksik] *adj* toxic

**trac** [tʀak] *nm* (*au théâtre, en public*) stage fright; (*aux examens*) nerves *pl*; **avoir le ~** (*au théâtre, en public*) to have stage fright; (*aux examens*) to be feeling nervous

**tracasser** [tʀakase] *vt* to worry, bother; **se ~** to worry

**trace** [tʀas] *nf* (*empreintes*) tracks *pl*; (*marques, aussi fig*) mark; (*quantité infime, indice, vestige*) trace; **~s de pas** footprints

**tracé** [tʀase] *nm* (*parcours*) line; (*plan*) layout

**tracer** [tʀase] *vt* to draw; (*piste*) to open up

**tract** [tʀakt] *nm* tract, pamphlet

**tractations** [tʀaktasjɔ̃] *nfpl* dealings, bargaining *sg*

**tracteur** [tʀaktœʀ] *nm* tractor

**traction** [tʀaksjɔ̃] *nf*: **~ avant/arrière** front-wheel/rear-wheel drive

**tradition** [tʀadisjɔ̃] *nf* tradition; **traditionnel, le** *adj* traditional

**traducteur, -trice** [tʀadyktœʀ, tʀis] *nm/f* translator

**traduction** [tʀadyksjɔ̃] *nf* translation

**traduire** [tʀadɥiʀ] *vt* to translate; (*exprimer*) to convey; **~ qn en justice** to bring sb before the courts

**trafic** [tʀafik] *nm* traffic; **~ d'armes** arms dealing; **trafiquant, e** *nm/f* trafficker; (*d'armes*) dealer; **trafiquer** (*péj*) *vt* (*vin*) to doctor; (*moteur, docu-*

*ment*) to tamper with

**tragédie** [tʀaʒedi] *nf* tragedy; **tragique** *adj* tragic

**trahir** [tʀaiʀ] *vt* to betray; **trahison** *nf* betrayal; (*JUR*) treason

**train** [tʀɛ̃] *nm* (RAIL) train; (*allure*) pace; **être en ~ de faire qch** to be doing sth; **mettre qn en ~** to put sb in good spirits; **se sentir en ~** to feel in good form; **~ d'atterrissage** undercarriage; **~ de vie** style of living; **~ électrique** (*jouet*) (electric) train set; **~ autos-couchettes** car-sleeper train

**traîne** [tʀɛn] *nf* (*de robe*) train; **être à la ~** to lag behind

**traîneau, x** [tʀɛno] *nm* sleigh, sledge

**traînée** [tʀɛne] *nf* trail; (*sur un mur, dans le ciel*) streak; (*péj*) slut

**traîner** [tʀɛne] *vt* (*remorque*) to pull; (*enfant, chien*) to drag ou trail along ♦ *vi* (*robe, manteau*) to trail; (*être en désordre*) to lie around; (*aller lentement*) to dawdle (along); (*vagabonder, agir lentement*) to hang about; (*durer*) to drag on; **se ~** to drag o.s. along; **~ les pieds** to drag one's feet

**train-train** [tʀɛ̃tʀɛ̃] *nm* humdrum routine

**traire** [tʀɛʀ] *vt* to milk

**trait** [tʀɛ] *nm* (*ligne*) line; (*de dessin*) stroke; (*caractéristique*) feature, trait; **~s** *nmpl* (*du visage*) features; **d'un ~** (*boire*) in one gulp; **de ~** (*animal*) draught; **avoir ~ à** to concern; **d'union** hyphen

**traitant, e** [tʀɛtɑ̃, ɑ̃t] *adj* (*shampooing*) medicated; **votre médecin ~** your usual ou family doctor

**traite** [tʀɛt] *nf* (COMM) draft; (AGR) milking; **d'une ~** without stopping; **la ~ des noirs** the slave trade

**traité** [tʀɛte] *nm* treaty

**traitement** [tʀɛtmɑ̃] *nm* treatment; (*salaire*) salary; **~ de données** data processing; **~ de texte** word processing; (*logiciel*) word processing package

**traiter** [tʀɛte] *vt* to treat; (*qualifier*)

qn d'idiot to call sb a fool ♦ *vi* to deal;
~ **de** to deal with

**traiteur** |tʀɛtœʀ| *nm* caterer

**traître, -esse** |tʀɛtʀ, tʀɛtʀɛs| *adj (dangereux)* treacherous ♦ *nm* traitor

**trajectoire** |tʀaʒɛktwaʀ| *nf* path

**trajet** |tʀaʒɛ| *nm (parcours, voyage)* journey; *(itinéraire)* route; *(distance à parcourir)* distance

**trame** |tʀam| *nf (de tissu)* weft; *(fig)* framework; **usé jusqu'à la** ~ threadbare

**tramer** |tʀame| *vt*: **il se trame quelque chose** there's something brewing

**trampoline** |tʀɑ̃pɔlin| *nm* trampoline

**tramway** |tʀamwɛ| *nm* tram(way); *(voiture)* tram(car) *(BRIT)*, streetcar *(US)*

**tranchant, e** |tʀɑ̃ʃɑ̃, ɑ̃t| *adj* sharp; *(fig)* peremptory ♦ *nm (d'un couteau)* cutting edge; *(de la main)* edge; **à double** ~ double-edged

**tranche** |tʀɑ̃ʃ| *nf (morceau)* slice; *(arête)* edge; ~ **d'âge/de salaires** age/wage bracket

**tranché, e** |tʀɑ̃ʃe| *adj (couleurs)* distinct; *(opinions)* clear-cut; **tranchée** *nf* trench

**trancher** |tʀɑ̃ʃe| *vt* to cut, sever ♦ *vi* to take a decision; ~ **avec** to contrast sharply with

**tranquille** |tʀɑ̃kil| *adj* quiet; *(rassuré)* easy in one's mind, with one's mind at rest; **se tenir** ~ *(enfant)* to be quiet; **laisse-moi/laisse-ça** ~ leave me/it alone; **avoir la conscience** ~ to have a clear conscience; **tranquillisant** *nm* tranquillizer; **tranquillité** *nf* peace (and quiet); *(d'esprit)* peace of mind

**transat** |tʀɑ̃zat| *nm* deckchair

**transbordeur** |tʀɑ̃sbɔʀdœʀ| *nm* to tran(s)ship

**transcription** |tʀɑ̃skʀipsjɔ̃| *nf* transcription; *(copie)* transcript

**transférer** |tʀɑ̃sfeʀe| *vt* to transfer; **transfert** *nm* transfer

**transformation** |tʀɑ̃sfɔʀmasjɔ̃| *nf* change; transformation; alteration;

*(RUGBY)* conversion

**transformer** |tʀɑ̃sfɔʀme| *vt* to change; *(radicalement)* to transform; *(vêtement)* to alter; *(matière première, appartement, RUGBY)* to convert; **(se)** ~ **en** to turn into

**transfusion** |tʀɑ̃sfyzjɔ̃| *nf*: ~ **sanguine** blood transfusion

**transgresser** |tʀɑ̃sgʀese| *vt* to contravene

**transi, e** |tʀɑ̃zi| *adj* numb (with cold), chilled to the bone

**transiger** |tʀɑ̃ziʒe| *vi* to compromise

**transit** |tʀɑ̃zit| *nm* transit; **transiter** *vi* to pass in transit

**transitif, -ive** |tʀɑ̃zitif, iv| *adj* transitive

**transition** |tʀɑ̃zisjɔ̃| *nf* transition; **transitoire** *adj* transitional

**translucide** |tʀɑ̃slysid| *adj* translucent

**transmettre** |tʀɑ̃smɛtʀ| *vt (passer)*: ~ **qch à qn** to pass sth on to sb; *(TECH, TÉL, MÉD)* to transmit; *(TV, RADIO: retransmettre)* to broadcast; **transmission** *nf* transmission

**transparent, e** |tʀɑ̃spaʀɑ̃, ɑ̃t| *adj* transparent

**transpercer** |tʀɑ̃spɛʀse| *vt (froid, pluie)* to go through, pierce; *(balle)* to go through

**transpiration** |tʀɑ̃spiʀasjɔ̃| *nf* perspiration

**transpirer** |tʀɑ̃spiʀe| *vi* to perspire

**transplanter** |tʀɑ̃splɑ̃te| *vt (MÉD, BOT)* to transplant; **transplantation** *nf* *(MÉD)* transplant

**transport** |tʀɑ̃spɔʀ| *nm* transport; ~**s en commun** public transport *sg*; **transporter** *vt* to carry, move; *(COMM)* to transport, convey; **transporteur** *nm* haulage contractor *(BRIT)*, trucker *(US)*

**transvaser** |tʀɑ̃svaze| *vt* to decant

**transversal, e, -aux** |tʀɑ̃svɛʀsal, o| *adj (rue)* which runs across; **coupe ~e** cross section

**trapèze** |tʀapɛz| *nm (au cirque)* trapeze

**trappe** |tʀap| *nf* trap door

**trapu, e** [trapy] *adj* squat, stocky

**traquenard** [traknar] *nm* trap

**traquer** [trake] *vt* to track down; *(harceler)* to hound

**traumatiser** [tromatize] *vt* to traumatize

**travail, -aux** [travaj] *nm (gén)* work; *(tâche, métier)* work *no pl;* job; *(ÉCON, MÉD)* labour; **être sans ~** *(employé)* to be unemployed; *voir aussi* **travaux;** **~ (au) noir** moonlighting

**travailler** [travaje] *vi* to work; *(bois)* to warp ♦ *vt (bois, métal)* to work on; *(objet d'art, discipline)* to work on; **cela le fait travailler** it is on his mind; **travailleur, -euse** *adj* hard-working ♦ *nm/f* worker; **travailliste** *adj* ≈ Labour *cpd*

**travaux** [travo] *nmpl (de réparation, agricoles etc)* work *sg;* *(sur route)* roadworks *pl;* *(de construction)* building *(work);* **travaux des champs** farmwork *sg;* **travaux dirigés** *(SCOL)* tutorial; **travaux forcés** hard labour *sg;* **travaux manuels** *(SCOL)* handicrafts; **travaux ménagers** housework *sg;* **travaux pratiques** *(SCOL)* practical work *(en laboratoire)* lab work

**travers** [traver] *nm* fault, failing; **en ~ (de)** across; **au ~ (de)/à ~** through; **de ~** *(nez, bouche)* crooked; *(chapeau)* askew; **comprendre de ~** to misunderstand; **regarder de ~** *(fig)* to look askance at

**traverse** [travers] *nf (de voie ferrée)* sleeper; **chemin de ~** shortcut

**traversée** [traverse] *nf* crossing

**traverser** [traverse] *vt (gén)* to cross; *(ville, tunnel, aussi: percer, fig)* to go through; *(suj: ligne, trait)* to run across

**traversin** [travers] *nm* bolster

**travesti** [travesti] *nm* transvestite

**trébucher** [trebyʃe] *vi:* **~ (sur)** to stumble (over), trip (against)

**trèfle** [trefl] *nm (BOT)* clover; *(CARTES: couleur)* clubs *pl;* *(: carte)* club

**treille** [trej] *nf* vine arbour

**treillis** [treji] *nm (métallique)* wire-

mesh; *(MIL: tenue)* combat uniform; *(pantalon)* combat trousers *pl*

**treize** [trez] *num* thirteen; **treizième** *num* thirteenth

**tréma** [trema] *nm* diaeresis

**tremblement** [trɑ̃bləmɑ̃] *nm:* **~ de terre** earthquake

**trembler** [trɑ̃ble] *vi* to tremble, shake; **~ de (froid, fièvre)** to shiver *ou* tremble with; *(peur)* to shake *ou* tremble with; **~ pour qn** to fear for sb

**trémousser** [tremuse] **se ~** *vi* to jig about, wriggle about

**trempe** [trɑ̃p] *nf (fig):* **de cette/sa ~** of this/his calibre

**trempé, e** [trɑ̃pe] *adj* soaking (wet), drenched; *(TECH)* tempered

**tremper** [trɑ̃pe] *vt* to soak, drench; *(aussi:* **faire ~, mettre à ~)** to soak; *(plonger):* **~ qch dans** to dip sth in(to) ♦ *vi* to soak; *(fig):* **~ dans** to be involved *ou* have a hand in; **se ~** *vi* to have a quick dip; **trempette** *nf:* **faire trempette** to go paddling

**tremplin** [trɑ̃plɛ̃] *nm* springboard; *(SKI)* ski-jump

**trentaine** [trɑ̃ten] *nf:* **une ~ (de)** thirty or so, about thirty; **avoir la ~** *(âge)* to be around thirty

**trente** [trɑ̃t] *num* thirty; **être sur son ~ et un** to be wearing one's Sunday best; **trentième** *num* thirtieth

**trépidant, e** [trepidɑ̃, ɑ̃t] *adj (fig: rythme)* pulsating; *(: vie)* hectic

**trépied** [trepje] *nm* tripod

**trépigner** [trepiɲe] *vi* to stamp (one's feet)

**très** [tre] *adv* very; much +*pp*, highly +*pp*

**trésor** [trezɔr] *nm* treasure; **T~** *(pu-*

blic) public revenue; **trésorerie** nf (gestion) accounts pl; (bureaux) accounts department; **difficultés de trésorerie** cash problems, shortage of cash ou funds; **trésorier, -ière** nm/f treasurer

**tressaillir** [tʀesajiʀ] vi to shiver, shudder

**tressauter** [tʀesote] vi to start, jump

**tresse** [tʀɛs] nf braid, plait; **tresser** vt (cheveux) to braid, plait; (fil, jonc) to plait; (corbeille) to weave; (corde) to twist

**tréteau, x** [tʀeto] nm trestle

**treuil** [tʀœj] nm winch

**trêve** [tʀɛv] nf (MIL, POL) truce; (fig) respite; **~ de ...** enough of this ...

**tri** [tʀi] nm: **faire le ~ (de)** to sort out; **le (bureau de) ~** (POSTES) the sorting office

**triangle** [tʀijɑ̃gl] nm triangle; **triangulaire** adj triangular

**tribord** [tʀibɔʀ] nm: **à ~** to starboard, on the starboard side

**tribu** [tʀiby] nf tribe

**tribunal, -aux** [tʀibynal, o] nm (JUR) court; (MIL) tribunal

**tribune** [tʀibyn] nf (estrade) platform, rostrum; (débat) forum; (d'église, de tribunal) gallery; (de stade) stand

**tribut** [tʀiby] nm tribute

**tributaire** [tʀibytɛʀ] adj: **être ~ de** to be dependent on

**tricher** [tʀiʃe] vi to cheat; **tricheur, -euse** nm/f cheat(er)

**tricolore** [tʀikɔlɔʀ] adj three-coloured; (français) red, white and blue

**tricot** [tʀiko] nm (technique, ouvrage) knitting no pl; (vêtement) jersey, sweater; **~ de corps** vest; **tricoter** vt to knit

**trictrac** [tʀiktʀak] nm backgammon

**tricycle** [tʀisikl] nm tricycle

**triennal, e, -aux** [tʀijenal, o] adj three-year

**trier** [tʀije] vt to sort out; (POSTES, fruits) to sort

**trimestre** [tʀimɛstʀ] nm (SCOL) term;

(COMM) quarter; **trimestriel, le** adj quarterly; (SCOL) end-of-term

**tringle** [tʀɛ̃gl] nf rod

**trinquer** [tʀɛ̃ke] vi to clink glasses

**triomphe** [tʀijɔ̃f] nm triumph; **triompher** vi to triumph, win; **triompher de** to triumph over, overcome

**tripes** [tʀip] nfpl (CULIN) tripe sg

**triple** [tʀipl] adj triple ♦ nm: **le ~ (de)** (comparaison) three times as much (as); **en ~ exemplaire** in triplicate; **tripler** vi, vt to triple, treble

**triplés, -ées** [tʀiple] nm/fpl triplets

**tripoter** [tʀipɔte] vt to fiddle with

**triste** [tʀist] adj sad; (couleur, temps, journée) dreary; (péj): **~ personnage/ affaire** sorry individual/affair; **tristesse** nf sadness

**trivial, e, -aux** [tʀivjal, jo] adj coarse, crude; (commun) mundane

**troc** [tʀɔk] nm barter

**troène** [tʀɔɛn] nm privet

**trognon** [tʀɔɲɔ̃] nm (de fruit) core; (de légume) stalk

**trois** [tʀwa] num three; **troisième** num third; **trois quarts** nmpl: **les trois quarts de** three-quarters of

**trombe** [tʀɔ̃b] nf: **des ~s d'eau** a downpour; **en ~** like a whirlwind

**trombone** [tʀɔ̃bɔn] nm (MUS) trombone; (de bureau) paper clip

**trompe** [tʀɔ̃p] nf (d'éléphant) trunk; (MUS) trumpet, horn

**tromper** [tʀɔ̃pe] vt to deceive; (vigilance, poursuivants) to elude; **se ~** vi to make a mistake, be mistaken; **se ~ de voiture/jour** to take the wrong car/get the day wrong; **se ~ de 3 cm/20 F** to be out by 3 cm/20 F; **tromperie** nf deception, trickery no pl

**trompette** [tʀɔ̃pɛt] nf trumpet; **en ~ (nez)** turned-up

**trompeur, -euse** [tʀɔ̃pœʀ, øz] adj deceptive

**tronc** [tʀɔ̃] nm (BOT, ANAT) trunk; (d'église) collection box

**tronçon** [tʀɔ̃sɔ̃] nm section; **tron-**

**çonner** vt to saw up

**trône** [tʀon] nm throne

**trop** [tʀo] adv (+vb) too much; (+adjectif, adverbe) too; ~ (nombreux) too many; ~ peu (nombreux) too few; ~ (souvent) too often; ~ (longtemps) (for) too long; ~ de (nombre) too many; (quantité) too much; de ~, en ~: des livres en ~ a few books too many; du lait en ~ too much milk; 3 livres/3 F de ~ 3 books too many/3 F too much

**tropical, e, -aux** [tʀɔpikal, o] adj tropical

**tropique** [tʀɔpik] nm tropic

**trop-plein** [tʀoplɛ̃] nm (tuyau) overflow ou outlet (pipe); (liquide) overflow

**troquer** [tʀɔke] vt: ~ qch contre to barter ou trade sth for; (fig) to swap sth for

**trot** [tʀo] nm trot; **trotter** vi to trot

**trotteuse** [tʀɔtøz] nf (sweep) second hand

**trottinette** [tʀɔtinɛt] nf (child's) scooter

**trottoir** [tʀɔtwaʀ] nm pavement; **faire le ~** (péj) to walk the streets; ~ **roulant** moving walkway, travellator

**trou** [tʀu] nm hole; (fig) gap; (COMM) deficit; ~ **d'air** air pocket; ~ **d'ozone** ozone hole; ~ **de la serrure** keyhole; ~ **de mémoire** blank, lapse of memory

**troublant, e** [tʀublɑ̃, ɑ̃t] adj disturbing

**trouble** [tʀubl] adj (liquide) cloudy; (image, photo) blurred; (affaire) shady, murky ♦ adv indistinctly; ~s nmpl (POL) disturbances, troubles, unrest sg; (MÉD) trouble sg, disorders; **trouble-fête** nm spoilsport

**troubler** [tʀuble] vt to disturb; (liquide) to make cloudy; (intriguer) to bother; **se ~** vi (personne) to become flustered ou confused

**trouer** [tʀue] vt to make a hole (ou holes) in

**trouille** [tʀuj] (fam) nf: **avoir la ~** to

be scared to death

**troupe** [tʀup] nf troop; ~ **(de théâtre)** (theatrical) company

**troupeau, x** [tʀupo] nm (de moutons) flock; (de vaches) herd

**trousse** [tʀus] nf case, kit; (d'écolier) pencil case; **aux ~s de** (fig) on the heels ou tail of; ~ **à outils** toolkit; ~ **de toilette** toilet bag

**trousseau, x** [tʀuso] nm (de mariée) trousseau; ~ **de clefs** bunch of keys

**trouvaille** [tʀuvaj] nf find

**trouver** [tʀuve] vt to find; (rendre visite): **aller/venir ~ qn** to go/come and see sb; **se ~** vi (être) to be; **je trouve que** I find ou think that; ~ **à boire/ critiquer** to find something to drink/ criticize; **se ~ bien** to feel well; **se ~ mal** to pass out

**truand** [tʀyɑ̃] nm gangster; **truander** vt: **se faire truander** to be swindled

**truc** [tʀyk] nm (astuce) way, trick; (de cinéma, prestidigitateur) trick, effect; (chose) thing, thingumajig; **avoir le ~** to have the knack

**truelle** [tʀyɛl] nf trowel

**truffe** [tʀyf] nf truffle; (nez) nose

**truffé, e** [tʀyfe] adj: ~ **de** (fig) peppered with; (fautes) riddled with; (pièges) bristling with

**truie** [tʀyi] nf sow

**truite** [tʀyit] nf trout inv

**truquage** [tʀykaʒ] nm special effects

**truquer** [tʀyke] vt (élections, serrure, dés) to fix

**TSVP** sigle (= tournez svp) PTO

**TTC** sigle (= toutes taxes comprises) inclusive of tax

**tu¹** [ty] pron you

**tu², e** [ty] pp de **taire**

**tuba** [tyba] nm (MUS) tuba; (SPORT) snorkel

**tube** [tyb] nm tube; (chanson) hit

**tuberculose** [tybɛʀkyloz] nf tuberculosis

**tuer** [tɥe] vt to kill; **se ~** vi to be killed;

(suicide) to kill o.s.; **tuerie** nf slaughter no pl

**tue-tête** [tytɛt]: **à ~-~** adv at the top of one's voice

**tueur** [tɥœʀ] nm killer; **~ à gages** hired killer

**tuile** [tɥil] nf tile; (fam) spot of bad luck, blow

**tulipe** [tylip] nf tulip

**tuméfié, e** [tymefje] adj puffed-up, swollen

**tumeur** [tymœʀ] nf growth, tumour

**tumulte** [tymylt] nm commotion; **tumultueux, -euse** adj stormy, turbulent

**tunique** [tynik] nf tunic

**Tunisie** [tynizi] nf: **la ~** Tunisia; **tunisien, ne** adj Tunisian ♦ nm/f: **Tunisien, ne** Tunisian

**tunnel** [tynɛl] nm tunnel; **le ~ sous la Manche** the Channel Tunnel

**turbulences** [tyʀbylɑ̃s] nfpl (AVIAT) turbulence sg

**turbulent, e** [tyʀbylɑ̃, ɑ̃t] adj boisterous, unruly

**turc, turque** [tyʀk] adj Turkish ♦ nm/f: **T~, -que** Turk/Turkish woman ♦ nm (LING) Turkish

**turf** [tyʀf] nm racing; **turfiste** nm/f racegoer

**Turquie** [tyʀki] nf: **la ~** Turkey

**turquoise** [tyʀkwaz] nf turquoise ♦ adj inv turquoise

**tus** etc [ty] vb voir **taire**

**tutelle** [tytɛl] nf (JUR) guardianship; (POL) trusteeship; **sous la ~ de** (fig) under the supervision of

**tuteur** [tytœʀ] nm (JUR) guardian; (de plante) stake, support

**tutoyer** [tytwaje] vt: **~ qn** to address sb as "tu"

**tuyau, x** [tɥijo] nm pipe; (flexible) tube; (fam) tip; **~ d'arrosage** hosepipe; **~ d'échappement** exhaust pipe; **tuyauterie** nf piping no pl

**TVA** sigle f (= taxe à la valeur ajoutée) VAT

**tympan** [tɛ̃pɑ̃] nm (ANAT) eardrum

**type** [tip] nm type; (fam) chap, guy ♦ adj typical, classic

**typé, e** [tipe] adj ethnic

**typique** [tipik] adj typical

**tyran** [tiʀɑ̃] nm tyrant; **tyrannique** adj tyrannical

**tzigane** [dzigan] adj gipsy, tzigane

# U, u

**UEM** sigle f (= union économique et monétaire) EMU

**ulcère** [ylsɛʀ] nm ulcer; **ulcérer** vt (fig) to sicken, appal

**ultérieur, e** [ylteʀjœʀ] adj later, subsequent; **remis à une date ~e** postponed to a later date; **ultérieurement** adv later, subsequently

**ultime** [yltim] adj final

**ultra...** [yltʀa] préfixe: **~moderne/ ~rapide** ultra-modern/-fast

MOT-CLÉ

**un, une** [œ̃, yn] art indéf a; (devant voyelle) an; **un garçon/vieillard** a boy/an old man; **une fille** a girl ♦ pron one; **l'un des meilleurs** one of the best; **l'un ..., l'autre** (the) one ..., the other; **les uns ..., les autres** ..., others; **l'un et l'autre** both (of them); **l'un ou l'autre** either (of them); **l'un l'autre, les uns les autres** each other, one another; **pas un seul** not a single one; **un par un** one by one ♦ num one; **une pomme seulement** one apple only

**unanime** [ynanim] adj unanimous; **unanimité** nf: **à l'unanimité** unanimously

**uni, e** [yni] adj (ton, tissu) plain; (surface) smooth, even; (famille) close (-knit); (pays) united

**unifier** [ynifje] vt to unite, unify

**uniforme** [ynifɔʀm] adj uniform; (surface, ton) even ♦ nm uniform; **uniformiser** vt (systèmes) to standardize

**union** [ynjɔ̃] nf (de consommateurs) consumers' association; U~ européenne European Union; U~ soviétique Soviet Union

**unique** [ynik] adj (seul) only; (exceptionnel) unique; (le même): **un prix/ système ~** a single price/system; **fils/ fille ~** only son/daughter, only child; **sens ~** one-way street; **uniquement** adv only, solely; (juste) only, merely

**unir** [yniʀ] vt (nations) to unite; (en mariage) to unite, join together; **s'~** vi to unite; (en mariage) to be joined together

**unitaire** [yniteʀ] adj: **prix ~** unit price

**unité** [ynite] nf unit; (harmonie, cohésion) unity

**univers** [yniveʀ] nm universe; **universel, le** adj universal

**universitaire** [yniveʀsiteʀ] adj university cpd; (diplôme, études) academic, university cpd ♦ nm/f academic

**université** [yniveʀsite] nf university

**urbain, e** [yʀbɛ̃, ɛn] adj urban, city cpd, town cpd; **urbanisme** nm town planning

**urgence** [yʀʒɑ̃s] nf urgency; (MÉD etc) emergency; **d'~** emergency cpd ♦ adv as a matter of urgency; **(service des) ~s** casualty

**urgent, e** [yʀʒɑ̃, ɑ̃t] adj urgent

**urine** [yʀin] nf urine; **urinoir** nm (public) urinal

**urne** [yʀn] nf (électorale) ballot box; (vase) urn

**urticaire** [yʀtikɛʀ] nf nettle rash

**us** [ys] nmpl: **~ et coutumes** (habits and) customs

**USA** sigle mpl: **les USA** the USA

**usage** [yzaʒ] nm (emploi, utilisation) use; (coutume) custom; **à l'~** with use; **à l'~ de** (pour) for (use of); **hors d'~** out of service; **à ~ interne** (MÉD) to be taken; **à ~ externe** (MÉD) for external

use only; **usagé, e** adj (usé) worn; **usager, -ère** nm/f user

**usé, e** [yze] adj worn; (banal: argument etc) hackneyed

**user** [yze] vt (outil) to wear down; (vêtement) to wear out; (matière) to wear away; (consommer: charbon etc) to use; **s'~** vi (tissu, vêtement) to wear out; **~ de** (moyen, procédé) to use, employ; (droit) to exercise

**usine** [yzin] nf factory

**usité, e** [yzite] adj common

**ustensile** [ystɑ̃sil] nm implement; **~ de cuisine** kitchen utensil

**usuel, le** [yzɥɛl] adj everyday, common

**usure** [yzyʀ] nf wear

**utérus** [yteʀys] nm uterus, womb

**utile** [ytil] adj useful

**utilisation** [ytilizasjɔ̃] nf use

**utiliser** [ytilize] vt to use

**utilitaire** [ytilitɛʀ] adj utilitarian

**utilité** [ytilite] nf usefulness no pl; **de peu d'~** of little use ou help

**utopie** [ytɔpi] nf utopia

## V, v

**va** [va] vb voir **aller**

**vacance** [vakɑ̃s] nf (ADMIN) vacancy; **~s** nfpl holiday(s pl), vacation sg; **les grandes ~s** the summer holidays; **prendre des/ses ~s** to take a holiday/one's holiday(s); **aller en ~s** to go on holiday; **vacancier, -ière** nm/f holiday-maker

**vacant, e** [vakɑ̃, ɑ̃t] adj vacant

**vacarme** [vakaʀm] nm (bruit) racket

**vaccin** [vaksɛ̃] nm vaccine; (opération) vaccination; **vaccination** nf vaccination; **vacciner** vt to vaccinate; **être vacciné contre qch** (fam) to be cured of sth

**vache** [vaʃ] nf (ZOOL) cow; (cuir) cowhide ♦ adj (fam) rotten, mean; **vachement** (fam) adv (très) really; (pleuvoir, travailler) a hell of a lot; **vacherie** nf (action) dirty trick; (remarque) nasty remark

**vaciller** [vasije] *vi* to sway, wobble; *(bougie, lumière)* to flicker; *(fig)* to be failing, faltering

**va-et-vient** [vaevjɛ̃] *nm inv (de personnes, véhicules)* comings and goings *pl*, to-ings and fro-ings *pl*

**vagabond, e** [vagabɔ̃, ɔ̃d] *nm (rôdeur)* tramp, vagrant; *(voyageur)* wanderer; **vagabonder** *vi* to roam, wander

**vagin** [vaʒɛ̃] *nm* vagina

**vague** [vag] *nf* wave ♦ *adj* vague; *(regard)* faraway; *(manteau, robe)* loose *(-fitting)*; *(quelconque)*: **un ~ bureau/cousin** some office/cousin or other; **~ de fond** ground swell; **~ de froid** cold spell

**vaillant, e** [vajɑ̃, ɑ̃t] *adj (courageux)* gallant; *(robuste)* hale and hearty

**vaille** [vaj] *vb voir* **valoir**

**vain, e** [vɛ̃, vɛn] *adj* vain; **en ~** in vain

**vaincre** [vɛ̃kʀ] *vt* to defeat; *(fig)* to conquer, overcome; **vaincu, e** *nm/f* defeated party; **vainqueur** *nm* victor; *(SPORT)* winner

**vais** [vɛ] *vb voir* **aller**

**vaisseau, x** [veso] *nm (ANAT)* vessel; *(NAVIG)* ship, vessel; **~ spatial** spaceship

**vaisselier** [vesəlje] *nm* dresser

**vaisselle** [vesɛl] *nf (service)* crockery; *(plats et à laver)* (dirty) dishes *pl*; **faire la ~** to do the washing-up *(BRIT)* ou the dishes

**val** [val, vo] *(pl* **vaux** *ou* **~s)** *nm* valley

**valable** [valabl] *adj* valid; *(acceptable)* decent, worthwhile

**valent** *etc* [val] *vb voir* **valoir**

**valet** [valɛ] *nm* manservant; *(CARTES)* jack

**valeur** [valœʀ] *nf (gén)* value; *(mérite)* worth, merit; *(COMM: titre)* security; **mettre en ~** *(détail)* to highlight; *(objet décoratif)* to show off to advantage; **avoir de la ~** to be valuable; **sans ~** worthless; **prendre de la ~** to go up *ou* gain in value

*(valable)* valid; **valider** *vt* to validate

**valions** [valjɔ̃] *vb voir* **valoir**

**valise** [valiz] *nf* (suit)case; **faire ses ~s** to pack one's bags

**vallée** [vale] *nf* valley

**vallon** [valɔ̃] *nm* small valley; **vallonné, e** *adj* hilly

**valoir** [valwaʀ] *vi (être valable)* to hold, apply ♦ *vt (prix, valeur, effort)* to be worth; *(causer)*: **~ qch à qn** to earn sb sth; **se ~** *vi* to be of equal merit; *(péj)* to be two of a kind; **faire ~** *(droits, prérogatives)* to assert; **faire ~ que** to point out that; **à ~ sur** to be deducted from; **vaille que vaille** somehow or other; **cela ne me dit rien qui vaille** I don't like the look of it at all; **ce climat ne me vaut rien** this climate doesn't suit me; **~ le coup** *ou* **la peine** to be worth the trouble *ou* being worth it; **~ mieux: il vaut mieux se taire** it's better to say nothing; **ça ne vaut rien** it's worthless; **que vaut ce candidat?** how good is this applicant?

**valse** [vals] *nf* waltz

**valu, e** [valy] *pp de* **valoir**

**vandalisme** [vɑ̃dalism] *nm* vandalism

**vanille** [vanij] *nf* vanilla

**vanité** [vanite] *nf* vanity; **vaniteux, -euse** *adj* vain, conceited

**vanne** [van] *nf* gate; *(fig)* joke

**vannerie** [vanʀi] *nf* basketwork

**vantard, e** [vɑ̃taʀ, aʀd] *adj* boastful

**vanter** [vɑ̃te] *vt* to speak highly of, praise; **se ~** *vi* to boast, brag; **se ~ de** to pride o.s. on; *(péj)* to boast of

**vapeur** [vapœʀ] *nf (émanation)* vapour, fumes *pl*; **~s** *nfpl (bouffées)* vapours; **à ~** steam-powered, steam *cpd*; **cuit à la ~** steamed; **vaporeux, -euse** *adj (flou)* hazy, misty; *(léger)* filmy; **vaporisateur** *nm* spray; **vaporiser** *vt (parfum etc)* to spray

**varappe** [vaʀap] *nf* rock climbing

**vareuse** [vaʀøz] *nf (blouson)* pea jacket; *(d'uniforme)* tunic

**variable** [vaʀjabl] *adj* variable; *(temps,*

humeur) changeable; (divers: résultats) varied, various

**varice** [vaʀis] nf varicose vein

**varicelle** [vaʀisɛl] nf chickenpox

**varié, e** [vaʀje] adj varied; (divers) various

**varier** [vaʀje] vi to vary; (temps, humeur) to change ♦ vt to vary; **variété** nf variety; **variétés** nfpl: spectacle/ émission de variétés variety show

**variole** [vaʀjɔl] nf smallpox

**vas** [va] vb voir **aller**

**vase** [vaz] nm vase ♦ nf silt, mud; **vaseux, -euse** adj silty, muddy; (fig: confus) woolly, hazy; (: fatigué) woozy

**vasistas** [vazistɑs] nm fanlight

**vaste** [vast] adj vast, immense

**vaudrai** etc [vodʀe] vb voir **valoir**

**vaurien, ne** [voʀjɛ̃, jɛn] nm/f good-for-nothing

**vaut** [vo] vb voir **valoir**

**vautour** [votuʀ] nm vulture

**vautrer** [votʀe] vb: se ~ dans/sur to wallow in/sprawl on

**vaux** [vo] nmpl de **val** ♦ vb voir **valoir**

**va-vite** [vavit]: à la ~~ adv in a rush ou hurry

**veau, x** [vo] nm (ZOOL) calf; (CULIN) veal; (peau) calfskin

**vécu, e** [veky] pp de **vivre**

**vedette** [vədɛt] nf (artiste etc) star; (canot) motor boat; (police) launch

**végétal, e, -aux** [veʒetal, o] adj vegetable ♦ nm vegetable, plant; **végétalien, ne** nm, adj, nm/f vegan

**végétarien, ne** [veʒetaʀjɛ̃, jɛn] adj, nm/f vegetarian

**végétation** [veʒetasjɔ̃] nf vegetation; **~s** nfpl (MÉD) adenoids

**véhicule** [veikyl] nm vehicle; **~ utilitaire** commercial vehicle

**veille** [vɛj] nf (état) wakefulness; (jour): la ~ (de) the day before; la ~ au soir the previous evening; à la ~ de on the eve of; la ~ de Noël Christmas Eve; la ~ du jour de l'An New Year's Eve

**veillée** [veje] nf (soirée) evening; (réunion) evening gathering; ~ (funèbre) wake

**veiller** [veje] vi to stay up ♦ vt (malade, mort) to watch over, sit up with; ~ à to attend to, see to; ~ à ce que to make sure that; ~ sur to watch over; **veilleur** nm: **veilleur de nuit** night watchman; **veilleuse** nf (lampe) night light; (AUTO) sidelight; (flamme) pilot light

**veinard, e** [vɛnaʀ, aʀd] nm/f lucky devil

**veine** [vɛn] nf (ANAT, du bois etc) vein; (filon) vein, seam; (fam: chance): avoir de la ~ to be lucky

**véliplanchiste** [veliplɑ̃ʃist] nm/f wind-surfer

**vélo** [velo] nm bike, cycle; faire du ~ to go cycling; ~ tout-terrain mountain bike; **vélomoteur** nm moped

**velours** [v(ə)luʀ] nm velvet; ~ côtelé corduroy; **velouté, e** adj velvety ♦ nm: **~ de tomates** cream of tomato soup

**velu, e** [vəly] adj hairy

**venais** etc [vəne] vb voir **venir**

**venaison** [vənɛzɔ̃] nf venison

**vendange** [vɑ̃dɑ̃ʒ] nf (aussi: ~s) grape harvest; **vendanger** vi to harvest the grapes

**vendeur, -euse** [vɑ̃dœʀ, øz] nm/f shop assistant ♦ nm (JUR) vendor, seller; ~ de journaux newspaper seller

**vendre** [vɑ̃dʀ] vt to sell; ~ qch à qn to sell sb sth; "à ~" "for sale"

**vendredi** [vɑ̃dʀədi] nm Friday; V~ saint Good Friday

**vénéneux, -euse** [venenø, øz] *adj* poisonous

**vénérien, ne** [venerjɛ̃, jɛn] *adj* venereal

**vengeance** [vɑ̃ʒɑ̃s] *nf* vengeance *no pl*, revenge *no pl*

**venger** [vɑ̃ʒe] *vt* to avenge; **se ~ vi** to avenge o.s.; **se ~ de qch** to avenge o.s. for sth, take one's revenge for sth; **se ~ de qn** to take revenge on sb; **se ~ sur** to take revenge on

**venimeux, -euse** [vanimø, øz] *adj* poisonous, venomous; *(fig: haineux)* venomous, vicious

**venin** [vanɛ̃] *nm* venom, poison

**venir** [v(ə)niʀ] *vi* to come; **~ de** to come from; **~ de faire: je viens d'y aller/de le voir** I've just been there/seen him; **s'il vient à pleuvoir** if it should rain; **j'en viens à croire que** I have come to believe that; **faire ~** *(docteur, plombier)* to call (out)

**vent** [vɑ̃] *nm* wind; **il y a du ~** it's windy; **c'est du ~** it's all hot air; **au ~** to windward; **sous le ~** to leeward; **avoir le ~ debout/arrière** to head into the wind/have the wind astern; **dans le ~** *(fam)* trendy

**vente** [vɑ̃t] *nf* sale; **~** *(activité)* selling; *(secteur)* sales *pl*; **mettre en ~** *(produit)* to put on sale; *(maison, objet personnel)* to put up for sale; **aux enchères** auction sale; **~ de charité** jumble sale

**venteux, -euse** [vɑ̃tø, øz] *adj* windy

**ventilateur** [vɑ̃tilatœʀ] *nm* fan

**ventiler** [vɑ̃tile] *vt* to ventilate

**ventouse** [vɑ̃tuz] *nf* *(de caoutchouc)* suction pad

**ventre** [vɑ̃tʀ] *nm* *(ANAT)* stomach; *(légèrement péj)* belly; *(utérus)* womb; **avoir mal au ~** to have stomach ache *(BRIT)* ou a stomach ache *(US)*

**ventriloque** [vɑ̃tʀilɔk] *nm/f* ventriloquist

**venu, e** [v(ə)ny] *pp de* **venir** ♦ *adj:* **bien ~** timely; **mal ~** out of place;

**être mal ~ à** *ou* **de faire** to have no grounds for faire, be in no position to do

**ver** [vɛʀ] *nm* worm; *(des fruits etc)* maggot; *(du bois)* woodworm *no pl*; *voir aussi* **vers**; **~ à soie** silkworm; **~ de terre** earthworm; **~ luisant** glowworm; **~ solitaire** tapeworm

**verbaliser** [vɛʀbalize] *vi* *(POLICE)* to book *ou* report an offender

**verbe** [vɛʀb] *nm* verb

**verdâtre** [vɛʀdɑtʀ] *adj* greenish

**verdict** [vɛʀdik(t)] *nm* verdict

**verdir** [vɛʀdiʀ] *vi, vt* to turn green; **verdure** *nf* greenery

**véreux, -euse** [veʀø, øz] *adj* wormeaten; *(malhonnête)* shady, corrupt

**verge** [vɛʀʒ] *nf* *(ANAT)* penis

**verger** [vɛʀʒe] *nm* orchard

**verglacé, e** [vɛʀglase] *adj* icy, icedover

**verglas** [vɛʀgla] *nm* (black) ice

**vergogne** [vɛʀgɔɲ]: **sans ~** *adv* shamelessly

**véridique** [veʀidik] *adj* truthful

**vérification** [veʀifikasjɔ̃] *nf* *(action)* checking *no pl*; *(contrôle)* check

**vérifier** [veʀifje] *vt* to check; *(corroborer)* to confirm, bear out

**véritable** [veʀitabl] *adj* real; *(ami, amour)* true

**vérité** [veʀite] *nf* truth; **en ~** really, actually

**vermeil, le** [vɛʀmɛj] *adj* ruby red

**vermine** [vɛʀmin] *nf* vermin *pl*

**vermoulu, e** [vɛʀmuly] *adj* wormeaten

**verni, e** [vɛʀni] *adj* *(fam)* lucky; **cuir ~** patent leather

**vernir** [vɛʀniʀ] *vt* *(bois, tableau, ongles)* to varnish; *(poterie)* to glaze

**vernis** [vɛʀni] *nm* *(enduit)* varnish; *(pour poterie)* glaze; *(fig)* veneer; **~ à ongles** nail polish *ou* varnish; **vernissage** *nm* *(d'une exposition)* preview

**vérole** [veʀɔl] *nf* *(variole)* smallpox

**verrai** *etc* [veʀe] *vb voir* **voir**

**verre** [vɛʀ] nm glass; (de lunettes) lens sg; **boire** ou **prendre un** ~ to have a drink; ~ **dépoli** frosted glass; **~s de contact** contact lenses; **verrerie** nf (fabrique) glassworks sg; (activité) glassmaking; (objets) glassware; **verrière** nf (paroi vitrée) glass wall; (toit vitré) glass roof

**verrons** etc [vɛʀɔ̃] vb voir **voir**

**verrou** [vɛʀu] nm (targette) bolt; **mettre qn sous les ~s** to put sb behind bars; **verrouillage** nm locking; **verrouillage centralisé** central locking; **verrouiller** vt (porte) to bolt; (ordinateur) to lock

**verrue** [vɛʀy] nf wart

**vers** [vɛʀ] nm line ♦ nmpl (poésie) verse sg ♦ prép (en direction de) toward(s); (près de) around (about); (temporel) about, around

**versant** [vɛʀsɑ̃] nm slopes pl, side

**versatile** [vɛʀsatil] adj fickle, changeable

**verse** [vɛʀs]: **à** ~ adv: **il pleut à** ~ it's pouring (with rain)

**Verseau** [vɛʀso] nm: **le** ~ Aquarius

**versement** [vɛʀsəmɑ̃] nm payment; **en 3 ~s** in 3 instalments

**verser** [vɛʀse] vt (liquide, grains) to pour; (larmes, sang) to shed; (argent) to pay ♦ vi (véhicule) to overturn; (fig): ~ **dans** to lapse into

**verset** [vɛʀsɛ] nm verse

**version** [vɛʀsjɔ̃] nf version; (SCOL) translation (into the mother tongue); **film en** ~ **originale** film in the original language

**verso** [vɛʀso] nm back; **voir au** ~ see over(leaf)

**vert, e** [vɛʀ, vɛʀt] adj green; (vin) young; (vigoureux) sprightly ♦ nm green

**vertèbre** [vɛʀtɛbʀ] nf vertebra

**vertement** [vɛʀtəmɑ̃] adv (réprimander) sharply

**vertical, e, -aux** [vɛʀtikal, o] adj vertical; **verticale** nf vertical; **à la verticale** vertically; **verticalement** adv vertically

**vertige** [vɛʀtiʒ] nm (peur du vide) vertigo; (étourdissement) dizzy spell; (fig) fever; **vertigineux, -euse** adj breathtaking

**vertu** [vɛʀty] nf virtue; **en** ~ **de** in accordance with; **vertueux, -euse** adj virtuous

**verve** [vɛʀv] nf witty eloquence; **être en** ~ to be in brilliant form

**verveine** [vɛʀvɛn] nf (BOT) verbena, vervain; (infusion) verbena tea

**vésicule** [vezikyl] nf vesicle; ~ **biliaire** gall-bladder

**vessie** [vesi] nf bladder

**veste** [vɛst] nf jacket; ~ **droite/croisée** single-/double-breasted jacket

**vestiaire** [vɛstjɛʀ] nm (au théâtre etc) cloakroom; (de stade etc) changing-room (BRIT), locker-room (US)

**vestibule** [vɛstibyl] nm hall

**vestige** [vɛstiʒ] nm relic; (fig) vestige; **~s** nmpl (de ville) remains

**vestimentaire** [vɛstimɑ̃tɛʀ] adj (détail) of dress; (élégance) sartorial; **dépenses ~s** clothing expenditure

**veston** [vɛstɔ̃] nm jacket

**vêtement** [vɛtmɑ̃] nm garment, item of clothing; **~s** nmpl clothes

**vétérinaire** [veteʀinɛʀ] nm/f vet, veterinary surgeon

**vêtir** [vetiʀ] vt to clothe, dress

**veto** [veto] nm veto; **opposer un** ~ to veto

**vêtu, e** [vety] pp de **vêtir**

**vétuste** [vetyst] adj ancient, timeworn

**veuf, veuve** [vœf, vœv] adj widowed ♦ nm widower

**veuille** [vœj] vb voir **vouloir**

**veuillez** [vœje] vb voir **vouloir**

**veule** [vøl] adj spineless

**veuve** [vœv] nf widow

**veux** [vø] vb voir **vouloir**

**vexant, e** [vɛksɑ̃, ɑ̃t] adj (contrariant) annoying; (blessant) hurtful

**vexation** [vɛksasjɔ̃] nf humiliation

**vexer** [vɛkse] vt: ~ **qn** to hurt sb's feelings; **se** ~ vi to be offended

**viable** [vjabl] *adj* viable; (*économie, industrie etc*) sustainable

**viaduc** [vjadyk] *nm* viaduct

**viager, -ère** [vjaʒe, ɛʀ] *adj*: **rente viagère** life annuity

**viande** [vjãd] *nf* meat

**vibrer** [vibʀe] *vi* to vibrate; (*son, voix*) to be vibrant; (*fig*) to be stirred; **faire ~** to (cause to) vibrate; (*fig*) to stir, thrill

**vice** [vis] *nm* vice; (*défaut*) fault ♦ *préfixe*: **~... vice-**; **~ de forme** legal flaw *ou* irregularity

**vichy** [viʃi] *nm* (*toile*) gingham

**vicié, e** [visje] *adj* (*air*) polluted, tainted; (*JUR*) invalidated

**vicieux, -euse** [visjø, jøz] *adj* (*pervers*) lecherous; (*rétif*) unruly ♦ *nm/f* lecher

**vicinal, e, -aux** [visinal, o] *adj*: **chemin ~** by-road, byway

**victime** [viktim] *nf* victim; (*d'accident*) casualty

**victoire** [viktwaʀ] *nf* victory

**victuailles** [viktɥɑj] *nfpl* provisions

**vidange** [vidãʒ] *nf* (*d'un fossé, réservoir*) emptying; (*AUTO*) oil change; (*de lavabo: bonde*) waste outlet; **~s** *nfpl* (*matières*) sewage *sg*; **vidanger** *vt* to empty

**vide** [vid] *adj* empty ♦ *nm* (PHYSIQUE) vacuum; (*espace*) (empty) space, gap; (*futilité, néant*) void; **avoir peur du ~** to be afraid of heights; **emballé sous ~** vacuum packed; **à ~** (*sans occupants*) empty; (*sans charge*) unladen

**vidéo** [video] *nf* video ♦ *adj*: **cassette ~** video cassette; **jeu ~** video game; **vidéoclip** *nm* music video; **vidéoclub** *nm* video shop

**vide-ordures** [vidɔʀdyʀ] *nm inv* (*rubbish*) chute

**vidéothèque** [videotɛk] *nf* video library

**vide-poches** [vidpɔʃ] *nm inv* tidy; (*AUTO*) glove compartment

**vider** [vide] *vt* to empty; (*CULIN: volaille, poisson*) to gut, clean out; **se ~** *vi* to empty; **~ les lieux** to quit *ou* vacate the premises; **videur** *nm* (*de boîte de nuit*) bouncer

**vie** [vi] *nf* life; **être en ~** to be alive; **sans ~** lifeless; **à ~** for life

**vieil** [vjɛj] *adj voir* **vieux**; **vieillard** *nm* old man; **les vieillards** old people, the elderly; **vieille** *adj, nf voir* **vieux**; **vieilleries** *nfpl* old things; **vieillesse** *nf* old age; **vieillir** *vi* (*prendre de l'âge*) to grow old; (*population, vin*) to age; (*doctrine, auteur*) to become dated ♦ *vt* to age; **vieillissement** *nm* growing old; ageing

**Vienne** [vjɛn] *nf* Vienna

**viens** [vjɛ̃] *vb voir* **venir**

**vierge** [vjɛʀʒ] *adj* virgin; (*page*) clean, blank ♦ *nf* virgin; (*signe*): **la V~** Virgo

**Vietnam, Viêt-Nam** [vjɛtnam] *nm* Vietnam; **vietnamien, ne** *adj* Vietnamese ♦ *nm/f*: **Vietnamien, ne** Vietnamese

**vieux (vieil), vieille** [vjø, vjɛj] *adj* old ♦ *nm/f* old man (woman) ♦ *nmpl* old people; **mon ~/ma vieille** (*fam*) old man/girl; **prendre un coup de ~** to put years on; **vieille fille** spinster; **~ garçon** bachelor; **~ jeu** *adj inv* old-fashioned

**vif, vive** [vif, viv] *adj* (*animé*) lively; (*alerte, brusque, aigu*) sharp; (*lumière, couleur*) bright; (*air*) crisp; (*vent, émotion*) keen; (*fort: regret, déception*) great, deep; (*vivant*): **brûlé ~** burnt alive; **de vive voix** personally; **avoir l'esprit ~** to be quick-witted; **piquer qn au ~** to cut sb to the quick; **à ~** (*plaie*) open; **avoir les nerfs à ~** to be on edge

**vigne** [viɲ] *nf* (*plante*) vine; (*plantation*) vineyard; **vigneron** *nm* wine grower

**vignette** [viɲɛt] *nf* (ADMIN) ≃ (road) tax disc (BRIT); ≃ license plate sticker (US); (*de médicament*) price label (*used for reimbursement*)

**vignoble** [viɲɔbl] *nm* (*plantation*) vineyard; (*vignes d'une région*) vineyards *pl*

**vigoureux, -euse** [viguʀø, øz] *adj* vigorous, robust

**vigueur** [vigœʀ] *nf* vigour; **entrer en ~** to come into force; **en ~** current

**vil, e** [vil] *adj* vile, base

**vilain, e** [vilɛ̃, ɛn] *adj* (affaire, blessure) nasty; (pas sage: enfant) naughty

**villa** [vila] *nf* (detached) house; **~ en multipropriété** time-share villa

**village** [vilaʒ] *nm* village; **villageois, e** *adj* village *cpd* ♦ *nm/f* villager

**ville** [vil] *nf* town; (importante) city; (administration): **la ~** = the Corporation; = the (town) council; **~ d'eaux** spa

**villégiature** [vi(l)leʒjatyʀ] *nf* holiday; (lieu de) ~ (holiday) resort

**vin** [vɛ̃] *nm* wine; **avoir le ~ gai** to get happy after a few drinks; **~ d'honneur** reception (with wine and snacks); **~ de pays** local wine; **~ ordinaire** table wine

**vinaigre** [vinɛgʀ] *nm* vinegar; **vinaigrette** *nf* vinaigrette, French dressing

**vindicatif, -ive** [vɛ̃dikatif, iv] *adj* vindictive

**vineux, -euse** [vinø, øz] *adj* win(e)y

**vingt** [vɛ̃] *num* twenty; **vingtaine** *nf*: **une vingtaine (de)** about twenty, twenty or so; **vingtième** *num* twentieth

**vinicole** [vinikɔl] *adj* wine *cpd*, wine-growing

**vins** *etc* [vɛ̃] *vb voir* **venir**

**vinyle** [vinil] *nm* vinyl

**viol** [vjɔl] *nm* (d'une femme) rape; (d'un lieu sacré) violation

**violacé, e** [vjɔlase] *adj* purplish, mauvish

**violemment** [vjɔlamɑ̃] *adv* violently

**violence** [vjɔlɑ̃s] *nf* violence

**violent, e** [vjɔlɑ̃, ɑ̃t] *adj* violent; (remède) drastic

**violer** [vjɔle] *vt* (femme) to rape; (sépulture, loi, traité) to violate

**violet, te** [vjɔlɛ, ɛt] *adj, nm* purple, mauve; **violette** (fleur) violet

**violon** [vjɔlɔ̃] *nm* violin; (fam: prison) lock-up; **~ d'Ingres** hobby; **violoncel-**

le *nm* cello; **violoniste** *nm/f* violinist

**vipère** [vipɛʀ] *nf* viper, adder

**virage** [viʀaʒ] *nm* (d'un véhicule) turn; (d'une route, piste) bend

**virée** [viʀe] *nf* trip; (à pied) walk; (longue) walking tour; (dans les cafés) tour

**virement** [viʀmɑ̃] *nm* (COMM) transfer

**virent** [viʀ] *vb voir* **voir**

**virer** [viʀe] *vt* (COMM): **~ qch (sur)** to transfer sth (into); (fam: expulser): **~ qn** to kick sb out ♦ *vi* (CHIMIE) to change colour; **~ de bord** to tack

**virevolter** [viʀvɔlte] *vi* to twirl around

**virgule** [viʀgyl] *nf* comma; (MATH) point

**viril, e** [viʀil] *adj* (propre à l'homme) masculine; (énergique, courageux) manly, virile

**virtuel, le** [viʀtɥɛl] *adj* potential; (théorique) virtual

**virtuose** [viʀtɥoz] *nm/f* (MUS) virtuoso; (gén) master

**virus** [viʀys] *nm* virus

**vis¹** [vi] *vb voir* **voir; vivre**

**vis²** [vi] *nf* screw

**visa** [viza] *nm* (sceau) stamp; (validation de passeport) visa

**visage** [vizaʒ] *nm* face

**vis-à-vis** [vizavi] *prép*: **~-~-~ de qn** to(wards) sb; **en ~-~-~** facing each other

**viscéral, e, -aux** [viseʀal, o] *adj* (fig) deep-seated, deep-rooted

**visées** [vize] *nfpl* (intentions) designs

**viser** [vize] *vi* to aim ♦ *vt* to aim at; (concerner) to be aimed or directed at; (apposer un visa sur) to stamp, visa; **~ à qch/faire** to aim at sth/at doing ou to do; **viseur** *nm* (d'arme) sights *pl*; (PHOTO) viewfinder

**visibilité** [vizibilite] *nf* visibility

**visible** [vizibl] *adj* visible; (disponible): **est-il ~?** can he see me?, will he see visitors?

**visière** [vizjɛʀ] *nf* (de casquette) peak; (qui s'attache) eyeshade

**vision** [vizjɔ̃] *nf* vision; (sens) (eye)sight,

vision; *(fait de voir)*: **la ~ de** the sight of; **visionneuse** *nf* viewer

**visite** [vizit] *nf* visit; **~ médicale** medical examination; **~ accompagnée** *ou* **guidée** guided tour; **faire une ~ à qn** to call on sb, pay sb a visit; **rendre ~ à qn** to visit sb, pay sb a visit; **être en ~ (chez qn)** to be visiting (sb); **avoir de la ~** to have visitors; **heures de ~** *(hôpital, prison)* visiting hours

**visiter** [vizite] *vt* to visit; **visiteur, -euse** *nm/f* visitor

**vison** [viz5] *nm* mink

**visser** [vise] *vt*: **~ qch** *(fixer, serrer)* to screw sth on

**visuel, le** [vizɥɛl] *adj* visual

**vit** [vi] *vb voir* **voir; vivre**

**vital, e, -aux** [vital, o] *adj* vital

**vitamine** [vitamin] *nf* vitamin

**vite** [vit] *adv* quickly, fast; *(sans délai)* quickly; *(sous peu)* soon; **~!** quick!; **faire ~** to be quick; **le temps passe ~** time flies

**vitesse** [vites] *nf* speed; *(AUTO: dispositif)* gear; **prendre de la ~** to pick up *ou* gather speed; **à toute ~** at full *ou* top speed; **en ~** *(rapidement)* quickly; *(en hâte)* in a hurry

**viticole** [vitikɔl] *adj* wine *cpd*, winegrowing; **viticulteur** *nm* wine grower

**vitrage** [vitraʒ] *nm*: **double ~** double glazing

**vitrail, -aux** [vitraj, o] *nm* stained-glass window

**vitre** [vitr] *nf* (window) pane; *(de portière, voiture)* window; **vitré, e** *adj* glass *cpd*; **vitrer** *vt* to glaze; **vitreux, -euse** *adj* *(terne)* glassy

**vitrine** [vitrin] *nf* (shop) window; *(petite armoire)* display cabinet; **en ~** in the window; **~ publicitaire** display case, showcase

**vivable** [vivabl] *adj* *(personne)* livable-with; *(maison)* fit to live in

**vivace** [vivas] *adj* *(arbre, plante)* hardy; *(fig)* indestructible, inveterate

**vivacité** [vivasite] *nf* liveliness, vivacity

**vivant, e** [vivã, ãt] *adj* *(qui vit)* living, alive; *(animé)* lively; *(preuve, exemple)* living ♦ *nm*: **du ~ de qn** in sb's lifetime; **les ~s** the living

**vive** [viv] *adj voir* **vif** ♦ *vb voir* **vivre** ♦ *excl*: **le roi!** long live the king!; **~ment** *adv* deeply ♦ *excl*: **vivement les vacances!** roll on the holidays!

**vivier** [vivje] *nm* *(étang)* fish tank; *(réservoir)* fishpond

**vivifiant, e** [vivifjã, jãt] *adj* invigorating

**vivions** [vivjɔ̃] *vb voir* **vivre**

**vivoter** [vivɔte] *vi* *(personne)* to scrape a living, get by; *(fig: affaire etc)* to struggle along

**vivre** [vivr] *vi, vt* to live; *(période)* to live through; **~ de** to live on; **il vit encore** he is still alive; **se laisser ~** to take life as it comes; **ne plus ~** *(être anxieux)* to live on one's nerves; **il a vécu** *(eu une vie aventureuse)* he has seen life; **être facile à ~** to be easy to get on with (fig); **faire ~ qn** *(pourvoir à sa substance)* to provide (a living) for sb; **vivres** *nmpl* provisions, food supplies

**vlan** [vlã] *excl* wham!, bang!

**VO** [veo] *nf*: **film en ~** film in the original version; **en ~ sous-titrée** in the original version with subtitles

**vocable** [vɔkabl] *nm* term

**vocabulaire** [vɔkabylɛr] *nm* vocabulary

**vocation** [vɔkasjɔ̃] *nf* vocation, calling

**vociférer** [vɔsifere] *vi, vt* to scream

**vœu, x** [vø] *nm* wish; *(promesse)* vow; **faire ~ de** to take a vow of; **tous nos ~x de bonne année, meilleurs ~x** best wishes for the New Year

**vogue** [vɔg] *nf* fashion, vogue

**voguer** [vɔge] *vi* to sail

**voici** [vwasi] *prép* *(pour introduire, désigner)* here is +*sg*, here are +*pl*; **et ~ que ...** and now (*ou* he) ...; *voir aussi* **voilà**

**voie** [vwa] *nf* way; *(RAIL)* track, line; *(AUTO)* lane; **être en bonne ~** to be going well; **mettre qn sur la ~** to put sb on the right track; **pays en ~ de développement** developing country; **être en ~ d'achèvement/de rénovation** to be nearing completion/in the process of renovation; **par ~ buccale** ou **orale** orally; **à ~ étroite** narrowgauge; (NAVIG) leak; **~ de garage** (RAIL) siding; **~ ferrée** track; railway line; **la ~ publique** the public highway

**voilà** [vwala] *prép* (*en désignant*) there is +*sg*, there are +*pl*; **les ~** ou **voici** here ou there they are; **~** ou **voici here** ou **voici** here's one, there's one; **mon frère et ~ ma sœur** this is my brother and that's my sister; **~** ou **voici deux ans** two years ago; **~** ou **voici deux ans que** it's two years since; **et ~!** there we are!; **~ tout** that's all; **~** ou **voici** (*en offrant etc*) there ou here you are; **tiens! ~ Paul** look! there's Paul

**voile** [vwal] *nm* veil; (*tissu léger*) net ♦ *nf* sail; (*sport*) sailing; **voiler** *vt* to veil; (*fausser: roue*) to buckle; (: *bois*) to warp; **se voiler** *vi* (*lune, regard*) to mist over; (*voix*) to become husky; (*roue, disque*) to buckle; (*planche*) to warp; **voilier** *nm* sailing ship; (*de plaisance*) sailing boat; **voilure** *nf* (*de voilier*) sails *pl*

**voir** [vwar] *vi, vt* to see; **se ~** *vt* (*être visible*) to show; (*se fréquenter*) to see each other; (*se produire*) to happen; **se ~ critiquer/transformer** to be criticized/transformed; **cela se voit** (*c'est visible*) that's obvious, it shows; **faire ~ qch à qn** to show sb sth; **en faire ~ à qn** (*fig*) to give sb a hard time; **ne pas pouvoir ~ qn** not to be able to stand sb; **voyons!** let's see now; (*indignation etc*) come on!; **avoir quelque chose à ~ avec** to have something to do with

**voire** [vwar] *adv* even

**voisin, e** [vwazɛ̃, in] *adj* (*proche*) neighbouring; (*contigu*) next; (*ressemblant*) connected ♦ *nm/f* neighbour;

**voisinage** *nm* (*proximité*) proximity; (*environs*) vicinity; (*quartier, voisins*) neighbourhood

**voiture** [vwatyR] *nf* car; (*wagon*) coach, carriage; **~ de course** racing car; **~ de sport** sports car

**voix** [vwa] *nf* voice; (POL) vote; **à haute ~** aloud; **à ~ basse** in a low voice; **à 2/4 ~** (MUS) in 2/4 parts; **avoir ~ au chapitre** to have a say in the matter

**vol** [vɔl] *nm* (*d'oiseau, d'avion*) flight; (*larcin*) theft; **~ régulier** scheduled flight; **à ~ d'oiseau** as the crow flies; **au ~: attraper qch au ~** to catch sth as it flies past; **en ~** in flight; **~ à main armée** armed robbery; **~ à voile** gliding; **~ libre** hang-gliding

**volage** [vɔlaʒ] *adj* fickle

**volaille** [vɔlaj] *nf* (*oiseaux*) poultry *pl*; (*viande*) poultry *no pl*; (*oiseau*) fowl

**volant, e** [vɔlɑ̃, ɑ̃t] *adj voir* **feuille** *etc* ♦ *nm* (*d'automobile*) (steering) wheel; (*de commande*) wheel; (*objet lancé*) shuttlecock; (*bande de tissu*) flounce

**volcan** [vɔlkɑ̃] *nm* volcano

**volée** [vɔle] *nf* (TENNIS) volley; **à la ~: rattraper à la ~** to catch in mid-air; **à toute ~** (*sonner les cloches*) vigorously; (*lancer un projectile*) with full force; **~ de coups/de flèches** volley of blows/arrows

**voler** [vɔle] *vi* (*avion, oiseau, fig*) to fly; (*voleur*) to steal ♦ *vt* (*objet*) to steal; (*personne*) to rob; **~ qch à qn** to steal sth from sb; **il ne l'a pas volé!** he asked for it!

**volet** [vɔlɛ] *nm* (*de fenêtre*) shutter; (*de feuillet, document*) section

**voleur, -euse** [vɔlœR, øz] *nm/f* thief ♦ *adj* thieving; **"au ~!"** "stop thief!"

**volière** [vɔljɛR] *nf* aviary

**volley** [vɔlɛ] *nm* volleyball

**volontaire** [vɔlɔ̃tɛR] *adj* (*acte, enrôlement, prisonnier*) voluntary; (*oubli*) intentional; (*caractère, personne: décidé*) self-willed ♦ *nm/f* volunteer

**volonté** [vɔlɔ̃te] *nf* (*faculté de vouloir*)

will; (énergie, fermeté) will(power); (souhait, désir) wish; **à ~** as much as one likes; **bonne ~** goodwill, willingness; **mauvaise ~** lack of goodwill, unwillingness

**volontiers** [vɔlɔ̃tje] adv (avec plaisir) willingly, gladly; (habituellement, souvent) readily, willingly; **voulez-vous boire quelque chose? - ~!** would you like something to drink? - yes, please!

**volt** [vɔlt] nm volt

**volte-face** [vɔltəfas] nf inv: **faire ~~** to turn round

**voltige** [vɔltiʒ] nf (ÉQUITATION) trick riding; (au cirque) acrobatics sg; **voltiger** vi to flutter (about)

**volubile** [vɔlybil] adj voluble

**volume** [vɔlym] nm volume; (GÉOM: solide) solid; **volumineux, -euse** adj voluminous, bulky

**volupté** [vɔlypte] nf sensual delight ou pleasure

**vomi** [vɔmi] nm vomit; **vomir** vi to vomit, be sick ♦ vt to vomit, bring up; (fig) to belch out, spew out; (exécrer) to loathe, abhor; **vomissements** nmpl: **être pris de vomissements** to (suddenly) start vomiting

**vont** [vɔ̃] vb voir **aller**

**vorace** [vɔras] adj voracious

**vos** [vo] adj voir **votre**

**vote** [vɔt] nm vote; **~ par correspondance/procuration** postal/proxy vote; **voter** vi to vote ♦ vt (projet de loi) to vote for; (loi, réforme) to pass

**votre** [vɔtr] (pl **vos**) adj your

**vôtre** [votr] pron: **le ~, la ~, les ~s** yours; **les ~s** (fig) your family ou folks; **à la ~** (toast) your (good) health!

**voudrai** etc [vudre] vb voir **vouloir**

**voué, e** [vwe] adj: **~ à** doomed to

**vouer** [vwe] vt: **~ qch à** (Dieu, un saint) to dedicate sth to; **~ sa vie à** (étude, cause etc) to devote one's life to; **~ une amitié éternelle à qn** to vow undying friendship to sb

---

MOT-CLÉ

**vouloir** [vulwar] nm: **le bon vouloir de qn** sb's goodwill; sb's pleasure

♦ vt 1 (exiger, désirer) to want; **vouloir faire/que qn fasse** to want to do/sb to do; **voulez-vous du thé?** would you like ou do you want some tea?; **que me veut-il?** what does he want with me?; **sans le vouloir** (involontairement) without meaning to, unintentionally; **je voudrais ceci/faire** I would ou I'd like this/to do

2 (consentir): **je veux bien** (bonne volonté) I'll be happy to; (concession) fair enough, that's fine; **oui, si on veut** (en quelque sorte) yes, if you like; **veuillez attendre** please wait; **veuillez agréer ...** (formule épistolaire) yours faithfully

**en vouloir à qn** to bear sb a grudge; **s'en vouloir (de)** to be annoyed with o.s. (for); **il en veut à mon argent** he's after my money

4: **vouloir de: l'entreprise ne veut plus de lui** the firm doesn't want him any more; **elle ne veut pas de son aide** she doesn't want his help

5: **vouloir dire** to mean

**voulu, e** [vuly] adj (requis) required, requisite; (délibéré) deliberate, intentional; voir aussi **vouloir**

**vous** [vu] pron (sujet, objet direct) you; (réfléchi: sg) yourself; (: pl) yourselves; (réciproque) each other; **~-même** yourself; **~-mêmes** yourselves

**voûte** [vut] nf vault; **voûter: se voûter** vi (dos, personne) to become stooped

**vouvoyer** [vuvwaje] vt: **~ qn** to address sb as "vous"

**voyage** [vwajaʒ] nm journey, trip; (fait de ~r): **le ~** travel(ling); **partir/être en ~** to go off/be away on a journey ou trip; **faire bon ~** to have a good journey; **~ d'agrément/d'affaires** pleasure/business trip; **~ de noces** honeymoon; **~ organisé** package tour

**voyager** [vwajaʒe] vi to travel; **voyageur, -euse** nm/f traveller; (passager) passenger

**voyant, e** [vwajɑ̃, ɑ̃t] adj (couleur) loud, gaudy ♦ nm (signal) (warning) light; **voyante** nf clairvoyant

**voyelle** [vwajɛl] nf vowel

**voyons** etc [vwajɔ̃] vb voir **voir**

**voyou** [vwaju] nm hooligan

**vrac** [vʀak]: **en ~** adv (au détail) loose; (en gros) in bulk; (en désordre) in a jumble

**vrai, e** [vʀɛ] adj (véridique: récit, faits) true; (non factice, authentique) real; **à ~ dire** to tell the truth; **vraiment** adv really; **vraisemblable** adj likely; (excuse) convincing; **vraisemblablement** adv probably; **vraisemblance** nf likelihood; (romanesque) verisimilitude

**vrille** [vʀij] nf (de plante) tendril; (outil) gimlet; (spirale) spiral; (AVIAT) spin

**vrombir** [vʀɔ̃biʀ] vi to hum

**VRP** sigle m (= voyageur, représentant, placier) sales rep (fam)

**VTT** sigle m (= vélo tout-terrain) mountain bike

**vu, e** [vy] pp de **voir** ♦ adj: **bien/mal ~** (fig: personne) popular/unpopular; (: chose) approved/disapproved of ♦ prép (en raison de) in view of; **~ que** in view of the fact that

**vue** [vy] nf (fait de voir): **la ~ de** the sight of; (sens, faculté) (eye)sight; (panorama, image, photo) view; **~s** nfpl (idées) views; (dessein) designs; **hors de ~** out of sight; **avoir en ~** to have in mind; **tirer à ~** to shoot on sight; **à ~ d'œil** visibly; **de ~** by sight; **perdre de ~** to lose sight of; **en ~** (visible) in sight; (célèbre) in the public eye; **en ~ de faire** with a view to doing

**vulgaire** [vylgɛʀ] adj (grossier) vulgar, coarse; (ordinaire) commonplace; (péj: quelconque): **de ~s touristes** common tourists; (BOT, ZOOL: non latin) common; **vulgariser** vt to popularize

**vulnérable** [vylneʀabl] adj vulnerable

# W, w

**wagon** [vagɔ̃] nm (de voyageurs) carriage; (de marchandises) truck, wagon; **wagon-lit** nm sleeper, sleeping car; **wagon-restaurant** nm restaurant ou dining car

**wallon, ne** [walɔ̃, ɔn] adj Walloon

**waters** [watɛʀ] nmpl toilet sg

**watt** [wat] nm watt

**WC** sigle mpl (= water-closet(s)) toilet

**Web** [wɛb] nm inv: **le ~** the (World Wide) Web

**week-end** [wikɛnd] nm weekend

**western** [wɛstɛʀn] nm western

**whisky** [wiski] (pl whiskies) nm whisky

# X, x

**xénophobe** [gzenɔfɔb] adj xenophobic ♦ nm/f xenophobe

**xérès** [gzeʀɛs] nm sherry

**xylophone** [gzilɔfɔn] nm xylophone

# Y, y

**y** [i] adv (à cet endroit) there; (dessus) on it (ou them); (dedans) in it (ou them) ♦ pron (about ou on ou of) it (d'après le verbe employé); **j'~ pense** I'm thinking about it; **ça ~ est!** that's it!; voir aussi **aller; avoir**

**yacht** [jɔt] nm yacht

**yaourt** [jauʀt] nm yoghurt; **~ nature/aux fruits** plain/fruit yogurt

**yeux** [jø] nmpl de **œil**

**yoga** [jɔga] nm yoga

**yogourt** [jɔguʀt] nm = yaourt

**yougoslave** [jugɔslav] (HISTOIRE) adj Yugoslav(ian) ♦ nm/f: **Y~** Yugoslav

**Yougoslavie** [jugɔslavi] (HISTOIRE) nf Yugoslavia

# Z, z

**zapper** [zape] *vi* to zap

**zapping** [zapiŋ] *nm*: **faire du ~** to flick through the channels

**zèbre** [zɛbʀ(ə)] *nm* (*ZOOL*) zebra; **zébré, e** *adj* striped, streaked

**zèle** [zɛl] *nm* zeal; **faire du ~** (*péj*) to be over-zealous; **zélé, e** *adj* zealous

**zéro** [zeʀo] *nm* zero, nought (*BRIT*); **au-dessous de ~** below zero (Centigrade) *ou* freezing; **partir de ~** to start from scratch; **trois (buts) à ~** 3 (goals to) nil

**zeste** [zɛst] *nm* peel, zest

**zézayer** [zezeje] *vi* to have a lisp

**zigzag** [zigzag] *nm* zigzag; **zigzaguer** *vi* to zigzag

**zinc** [zɛ̃g] *nm* (*CHIMIE*) zinc

**zizanie** [zizani] *nf*: **semer la ~** to stir up ill-feeling

**zizi** [zizi] *nm* (*langage enfantin*) willy

**zodiaque** [zɔdjak] *nm* zodiac

**zona** [zona] *nm* shingles *sg*

**zone** [zon] *nf* zone, area; **~ bleue** ≃ restricted parking area; **~ industrielle** industrial estate

**zoo** [zo(o)] *nm* zoo

**zoologie** [zɔɔlɔʒi] *nf* zoology; **zoologique** *adj* zoological

**zut** [zyt] *excl* dash (it)! (*BRIT*), nuts! (*US*)

# ENGLISH – FRENCH
# ANGLAIS – FRANÇAIS

# A, a

**A** [eɪ] n (MUS) la m

> KEYWORD

**a** [eɪ, ə] (before vowel or silent h: an) indef art **1** un(e); **a book** un livre; **an apple** une pomme; **she's a doctor** elle est médecin

**2** (instead of the number "one") un(e); **a year ago** il y a un an; **a hundred/ thousand etc pounds** cent/mille etc livres

**3** (in expressing ratios, prices etc): **3 a day/week** 3 par jour/semaine; **10 km an hour** 10 km à l'heure; **30p a kilo** 30p le kilo

**A.A.** n abbr = **Alcoholics Anonymous**; (BRIT: Automobile Association) ≈ TCF m

**A.A.A.** (US) n abbr = **American Automobile Association**) ≈ TCF m

**aback** [ə'bæk] adv: **to be taken ~** être stupéfait(e), être décontenancé(e)

**abandon** [ə'bændən] vt abandonner

**abate** [ə'beɪt] vi s'apaiser, se calmer

**abbey** ['æbɪ] n abbaye f

**abbot** ['æbət] n père supérieur

**abbreviation** [əbriːvɪ'eɪʃən] n abréviation f

**abdicate** ['æbdɪkeɪt] vt, vi abdiquer

**abdomen** ['æbdəmen] n abdomen m

**abduct** [æb'dʌkt] vt enlever

**aberration** [æbə'reɪʃən] n anomalie f

**abide** [ə'baɪd] vt: **I can't ~ it/him** je ne peux pas le souffrir or supporter; **~ by** vt fus observer, respecter

**ability** [ə'bɪlɪtɪ] n compétence f; capacité f; (skill) talent m

**abject** ['æbdʒekt] adj (poverty) sordide; (apology) plat(e)

**ablaze** [ə'bleɪz] adj en feu, en flammes

**able** ['eɪbl] adj capable, compétent(e); **to be ~ to do sth** être capable de faire qch, pouvoir faire qch; **~-bodied** adj robuste; **ably** adv avec compétence or talent, habilement

**abnormal** [æb'nɔːməl] adj anormal(e)

**aboard** [ə'bɔːd] adv à bord ♦ prep à bord de

**abode** [ə'bəud] n (LAW): **of no fixed ~** sans domicile fixe

**abolish** [ə'bɔlɪʃ] vt abolir

**aborigine** [æbə'rɪdʒɪnɪ] n aborigène m/f

**abort** [ə'bɔːt] vt faire avorter; **~ion** [ə'bɔːʃən] n avortement m; **to have an ~ion** se faire avorter; **~ive** [ə'bɔːtɪv] adj manqué(e)

> KEYWORD

**about** [ə'baut] adv **1** (approximately) environ, à peu près; **about a hundred/thousand etc** environ cent/ mille etc, une centaine/un millier etc; **it takes about 10 hours** ça prend environ or à peu près 10 heures; **at about 2 o'clock** vers 2 heures; **I've just about finished** j'ai presque fini

**2** (referring to place) çà et là, de côté et d'autre; **to run about** courir çà et là; **to walk about** se promener, aller et venir

**3**: **to be about to do sth** être sur le point de faire qch

♦ prep **1** (relating to) au sujet de, à propos de; **a book about London** un livre sur Londres; **what is it about?** de quoi s'agit-il? **we talked about it** nous en avons parlé; **what or how about doing this?** et si nous faisions ceci?

**2** (referring to place) dans; **to walk**

**about the town** se promener dans la ville

**about-face** [əˈbautˈfeɪs] n demi-tour m

**about-turn** [əˈbautˈtɜːn] n (MIL) demi-tour m; (fig) volte-face f

**above** [əˈbʌv] adv au-dessus ♦ prep au-dessus de; (more) plus de; **mentioned ~** mentionné ci-dessus; **~ all** par-dessus tout, surtout; **~board** adj franc (franche); honnête

**abrasive** [əˈbreɪzɪv] adj abrasif(-ive); (fig) caustique, agressif(-ive)

**abreast** [əˈbrest] adv de front; **to keep ~ of** se tenir au courant de

**abroad** [əˈbrɔːd] adv à l'étranger

**abrupt** [əˈbrʌpt] adj (steep, blunt) abrupt(e); (sudden, gruff) brusque; **~ly** adv (speak, end) brusquement

**abscess** [ˈæbsɪs] n abcès m

**absence** [ˈæbsəns] n absence f

**absent** [ˈæbsənt] adj absent(e); **~ee** [æbsənˈtiː] n absent(e); (habitual) absentéiste m/f; **~-minded** adj distrait(e)

**absolute** [ˈæbsəluːt] adj absolu(e); **~ly** [æbsəˈluːtli] adv absolument

**absolve** [əbˈzɒlv] vt: **to ~ sb (from)** (blame, responsibility, sin) absoudre qn (de)

**absorb** [əbˈzɔːb] vt absorber; **to be ~ed in a book** être plongé(e) dans un livre; **~ent cotton** (US) n coton m hydrophile

**abstain** [əbˈsteɪn] vi: **to ~ (from)** s'abstenir (de)

**abstract** [ˈæbstrækt] adj abstrait(e)

**absurd** [əbˈsɜːd] adj absurde

**abundant** [əˈbʌndənt] adj abondant(e)

**abuse** [n əˈbjuːs, vb əˈbjuːz] n abus m; (insults) insultes fpl, injures fpl ♦ vt (ill-use) abuser de; (insult) insulter; **abusive** [əˈbjuːsɪv] adj grossier(-ère), injurieux(-euse)

**abysmal** [əˈbɪzməl] adj exécrable; (ignorance etc) sans bornes

**abyss** [əˈbɪs] n abîme m, gouffre m

**AC** abbr (= alternating current) courant

alternatif

**academic** [ækəˈdemɪk] adj universitaire; (person: scholarly) intellectuel(le); (pej: issue) oiseux-euse), purement théorique ♦ n universitaire m/f; **~ year** n année f universitaire

**academy** [əˈkædəmɪ] n (learned body) académie f; (school) collège m; **~ of music** conservatoire m

**accelerate** [ækˈseləreɪt] vt, vi accélérer; **accelerator** n accélérateur m

**accent** [ˈæksent] n accent m

**accept** [əkˈsept] vt accepter; **~able** adj acceptable; **~ance** n acceptation f

**access** [ˈækses] n accès m; (LAW: in divorce) droit m de visite; **~ible** [ækˈsesəbl] adj accessible

**accessory** [ækˈsesərɪ] n accessoire m

**accident** [ˈæksɪdənt] n accident m; (chance) hasard m; **by ~** accidentellement; par hasard; **~al** [æksɪˈdentl] adj accidentel(le); **~ally** [æksɪˈdentəlɪ] adv accidentellement; **~ insurance** n assurance f accident; **~-prone** adj sujet(te) aux accidents

**acclaim** [əˈkleɪm] n acclamations fpl ♦ vt acclamer

**accommodate** [əˈkɒmədeɪt] vt loger, recevoir; (oblige, help) obliger; (car etc) contenir; **accommodating** adj obligeant(e), arrangeant(e); **accommodation** [əkɒməˈdeɪʃən] (US **accommodations**) n logement m

**accompany** [əˈkʌmpənɪ] vt accompagner

**accomplice** [əˈkʌmplɪs] n complice m/f

**accomplish** [əˈkʌmplɪʃ] vt accomplir; **~ment** n accomplissement m, réussite f; (skill: gen pl) talent m

**accord** [əˈkɔːd] n accord m ♦ vt accorder; **of his own ~** de son plein gré; **~ance** n: **in ~ance with** conformément à; **~ing: ~ing to** prep selon; **~ingly** adv en conséquence

**accordion** [əˈkɔːdɪən] n accordéon m

**account** [əˈkaunt] n (COMM) compte m; (report) compte rendu; récit m; **~s** npl

(COMM) comptabilité f, comptes; **of no ~** sans importance; **on ~** en acompte; **on no ~** en aucun cas; **on ~ of** à cause de; **to take into ~, take ~ of** tenir compte de; **~ for** fus expliquer, rendre compte de; **~able** adj: **~able (to)** responsable (devant); **~ancy** n comptabilité f; **~ant** n comptable m/f; **~ number** n (at bank etc) numéro m de compte

**accrued interest** [ə'kru:d-] n intérêt m cumulé

**accumulate** [ə'kju:mjuleɪt] vt accumuler, amasser ♦ vi s'accumuler, s'amasser

**accuracy** ['ækjurəsɪ] n exactitude f, précision f

**accurate** ['ækjurɪt] adj exact(e), précis(e); **~ly** adv avec précision

**accusation** [ækju'zeɪʃən] n accusation f

**accuse** [ə'kju:z] vt: **to ~ sb (of sth)** accuser qn (de qch); **the ~d** l'accusé(e)

**accustom** [ə'kʌstəm] vt accoutumer, habituer; **~ed** adj (usual) habituel(le); (in the habit): **~ed to** habitué(e) or accoutumé(e) à

**ace** [eɪs] n as m

**ache** [eɪk] n mal m, douleur f ♦ vi (yearn): **to ~ to do** mourir d'envie de faire qch; **my head ~s** j'ai mal à la tête

**achieve** [ə'tʃi:v] vt (aim) atteindre; (victory, success) remporter, obtenir; **~ment** n exploit m, réussite f

**acid** ['æsɪd] adj acide ♦ n acide m; **~ rain** n pluies fpl acides

**acknowledge** [ək'nɔlɪdʒ] vt (letter: also: **~ receipt of**) accuser réception de; (fact) reconnaître; **~ment** n (of letter) accusé m de réception

**acne** ['æknɪ] n acné m

**acorn** ['eɪkɔ:n] n gland m

**acoustic** [ə'ku:stɪk] adj acoustique; **~s** n, npl acoustique f

**acquaint** [ə'kweɪnt] vt: **to ~ sb with sth** mettre qn au courant de qch; **to be ~ed with** connaître; **~ance** n

connaissance f

**acquire** [ə'kwaɪə*] vt acquérir

**acquit** [ə'kwɪt] vt acquitter; **to ~ o.s. well** bien se comporter, s'en tirer très honorablement

**acre** ['eɪkə*] n acre f (= 4047 m²)

**acrid** ['ækrɪd] adj âcre

**acrobat** ['ækrəbæt] n acrobate m/f

**across** [ə'krɔs] prep (on the other side) de l'autre côté de; (crosswise) en travers de ♦ adv de l'autre côté; en travers; **to run/swim ~** traverser en courant/à la nage; **~ from** en face de

**acrylic** [ə'krɪlɪk] adj acrylique

**act** [ækt] n acte m, action f; (of play) acte; (in music-hall etc) numéro m; (LAW) loi f ♦ vi agir; (THEATRE) jouer; (pretend) jouer la comédie ♦ vt (part) jouer, tenir; **in the ~ of** en train de; **to ~ as** servir de; **~ing** adj suppléant(e), par intérim ♦ n (activity): **to do some ~ing** faire du théâtre (or du cinéma)

**action** ['ækʃən] n action f; (MIL) combat(s) m(pl); **out of ~** hors de combat; (machine) hors d'usage; **to take ~** agir, prendre les mesures; **~ replay** n (TV) ralenti m

**activate** ['æktɪveɪt] vt (mechanism) actionner, faire fonctionner

**active** ['æktɪv] adj actif(-ive); (volcano) en activité; **~ly** adv activement; **activity** [æk'tɪvɪtɪ] n activité f; **activity holiday** n vacances actives

**actor** ['æktə*] n acteur m

**actress** ['æktrɪs] n actrice f

**actual** ['æktjuəl] adj réel(le), véritable; **~ly** adv (really) réellement, véritablement; (in fact) en fait

**acute** [ə'kju:t] adj aigu(ë); (mind, observer) pénétrant(e), perspicace

**ad** [æd] n abbr = **advertisement**

**A.D.** adv abbr (= anno Domini) ap. J.-C.

**adamant** ['ædəmənt] adj inflexible

**adapt** [ə'dæpt] vt adapter ♦ vi: **to ~ (to)** s'adapter (à); **~able** adj (device) adaptable; (person) qui s'adapte facilement; **~er**, **~or** n (ELEC) adaptateur m

**add** [æd] vt ajouter; (figures: also: **~ up**) additionner ♦ vi: **to ~ to** (increase) ajouter à, accroître

**adder** ['ædə<sup>r</sup>] n vipère f

**addict** ['ædɪkt] n intoxiqué(e); (fig) fanatique m/f; **~ed** [ə'dɪktɪd] adj: **to be ~ed to** (drugs, drink etc) être adonné(e) à; (fig: football etc) être un(e) fanatique de; **~ion** [ə'dɪkʃən] (MED) dépendance f; **~ive** adj qui crée une dépendance

**addition** [ə'dɪʃən] n addition f; (thing added) ajout m; **in ~** de plus; de surcroît; **in ~ to** en plus de; **~al** adj supplémentaire

**additive** ['ædɪtɪv] n additif m

**address** [ə'drɛs] n adresse f; (talk) discours m, allocution f ♦ vt adresser; (speak to) s'adresser à; **to ~ (o.s. to) a problem** s'attaquer à un problème

**adept** ['ædɛpt] adj: **~ at** expert(e) à or en

**adequate** ['ædɪkwɪt] adj adéquat(e); suffisant(e)

**adhere** [əd'hɪə<sup>r</sup>] vi: **to ~ to** adhérer à; (fig: rule, decision) se tenir à

**adhesive** [əd'hi:zɪv] n adhésif m; **~ tape** n (BRIT) ruban adhésif; (US: MED) sparadrap m

**ad hoc** [æd'hɔk] adj improvisé(e), ad hoc

**adjacent** [ə'dʒeɪsənt] adj: **~ (to)** adjacent (à)

**adjective** ['ædʒɛktɪv] n adjectif m

**adjoining** [ə'dʒɔɪnɪŋ] adj voisin(e), adjacent(e), attenant(e)

**adjourn** [ə'dʒə:n] vt ajourner ♦ vi suspendre la séance; clore la session

**adjust** [ə'dʒʌst] vt (machine) ajuster, régler; (prices, wages) rajuster ♦ vi: **to ~ (to)** s'adapter (à); **~able** adj réglable; **~ment** n (PSYCH) adaptation f; (to machine) ajustage m, réglage m; (of prices, wages) rajustement m

**ad-lib** [æd'lɪb] vt, vi improviser; **ad lib** adv à volonté, à loisir

**administer** [əd'mɪnɪstə<sup>r</sup>] vt adminis-

trer; (justice) rendre; **administration** [ədmɪnɪs'treɪʃən] n administration f; **administrative** [əd'mɪnɪstrətɪv] adj administratif(-ive)

**admiral** ['ædmərəl] n amiral m; **A~ty** ['ædmərəltɪ] (BRIT) n: **the A~ty** ministère m de la Marine

**admire** [əd'maɪə<sup>r</sup>] vt admirer

**admission** [əd'mɪʃən] n admission f; (to exhibition, night club etc) entrée f; (confession) aveu m; **~ charge** n droits mpl d'admission

**admit** [əd'mɪt] vt laisser entrer; admettre; (agree) reconnaître, admettre; **to ~** vt fus reconnaître; avouer; **~tance** n admission f, (droit m d')entrée f; **~tedly** adv il faut en convenir

**ado** [ə'du:] n: **without (any) more ~** sans plus de cérémonies

**adolescence** [ædəu'lɛsns] n adolescence f; **adolescent** adj, n adolescent(e)

**adopt** [ə'dɔpt] vt adopter; **~ed** adj adoptif(-ive), adopté(e); **~ion** n adoption f

**adore** [ə'dɔ:<sup>r</sup>] vt adorer

**adorn** [ə'dɔ:n] vt orner

**Adriatic (Sea)** [eɪdrɪ'ætɪk-] n Adriatique f

**adrift** [ə'drɪft] adv à la dérive

**adult** ['ædʌlt] n adulte m/f ♦ adj adulte; (literature, education) pour adultes

**adultery** [ə'dʌltərɪ] n adultère m

**advance** [əd'vɑːns] n avance f ♦ adj: **~ booking** réservation f ♦ vt avancer ♦ vi avancer, s'avancer; **~ notice** avertissement m; **to make ~s (to sb)** faire des propositions (à qn); (amorously) faire des avances (à qn); **in ~** à l'avance, d'avance; **~d** adj avancé(e); (SCOL: studies) supérieur(e)

**advantage** [əd'vɑːntɪdʒ] n (also TENNIS) avantage m; **to take ~ of** (person) exploiter

**advent** ['ædvənt] n avènement m, venue f; **A~** Avent m

**adventure** [əd'vɛntʃə<sup>r</sup>] n aventure f

**adverb** ['ædvə:b] n adverbe m

**adverse** ['ædvəːs] *adj* défavorable, contraire

**advert** ['ædvəːt] (BRIT) *n abbr* = **advertisement**

**advertise** ['ædvətaɪz] *vi, vt* faire de la publicité (pour); (*in classified ads etc*) mettre une annonce (pour vendre); **to ~ for** (*staff, accommodation*) faire paraître une annonce pour trouver; **~ment** [ədˈvəːtɪsmənt] *n* (COMM) réclame *f*, publicité *f*; (*in classified ads etc*) annonce *f*; **advertising** *n* publicité *f*

**advice** [ədˈvaɪs] *n* conseils *mpl*; (*notification*) avis *m*; **piece of ~** conseil; **to take legal ~** consulter un avocat

**advisable** [ədˈvaɪzəbl] *adj* conseillé(e), indiqué(e)

**advise** [ədˈvaɪz] *vt* conseiller; **to ~ sb of sth** aviser *or* informer qn de qch; **to ~ against sth/doing sth** déconseiller qch/conseiller de ne pas faire qch; **~r**, **advisor** *n* conseiller(-ère); **advisory** *adj* consultatif(-ive)

**advocate** [*n* ˈædvəkɪt, *vb* ˈædvəkeɪt] *n* (*upholder*) défenseur *m*, avocat(e); (LAW) avocat(e) ♦ *vt* recommander, prôner

**Aegean (Sea)** [iːˈdʒiːən-] *n* (mer *f*) Égée *f*

**aerial** [ˈɛərɪəl] *n* antenne *f* ♦ *adj* aérien(ne)

**aerobics** [ɛəˈrəubɪks] *n* aérobic *f*

**aeroplane** [ˈɛərəpleɪn] (BRIT) *n* avion *m*

**aerosol** [ˈɛərəsɔl] *n* aérosol *m*

**aesthetic** [iːsˈθɛtɪk] *adj* esthétique

**afar** [əˈfɑː] *adv*: **from ~** de loin

**affair** [əˈfɛə] *n* affaire *f*; (*also:* **love ~**) liaison *f*, aventure *f*

**affect** [əˈfɛkt] *vt* affecter; (*disease*) atteindre; **~ed** *adj* affecté(e); **~ion** *n* affection *f*; **~ionate** *adj* affectueux(-euse)

**affinity** [əˈfɪnɪtɪ] *n* (*bond, rapport*): **to have an ~ with/for** avoir une affinité avec/pour

**afflict** [əˈflɪkt] *vt* affliger

**affluence** [ˈæfluəns] *n* abondance *f*, opulence *f*

**affluent** [ˈæfluənt] *adj* (*person, family,* surroundings) aisé(e), riche; **the ~ society** la société d'abondance

**afford** [əˈfɔːd] *vt* se permettre; (*provide*) fournir, procurer

**afloat** [əˈfləut] *adv* à flot; **to stay ~** surnager

**afoot** [əˈfut] *adv*: **there is something ~** il se prépare quelque chose

**afraid** [əˈfreɪd] *adj* effrayé(e); **to be ~ of** *or* **to** avoir peur de; **I am ~ that** je suis désolé(e), mais ...; **I am ~ so/ not** hélas oui/non

**Africa** [ˈæfrɪkə] *n* Afrique *f*; **~n** *adj* africain(e) ♦ *n* Africain(e)

**after** [ˈɑːftə] *prep, adv* après ♦ *conj* après que, après avoir *or* être +*pp*; **what/who are you ~?** que *or* qui cherchez-vous?; **he left/having done** après qu'il fut parti/après avoir fait; **ask ~ him** demandez de ses nouvelles; **to name sb ~ sb** donner à qn le nom de qn; **twenty ~ eight** (US) huit heures vingt; **~ all** après tout; **~ you!** après vous, Monsieur (*or* Madame *etc*); **~effects** *npl* (*of disaster, radiation, drink etc*) répercussions *fpl*; (*of illness*) séquelles *fpl*, suites *fpl*; **~math** *n* conséquences *fpl*, suites *fpl*; **~noon** *n* après-midi *m or f*; **~s** (*inf*) *n* (*dessert*) dessert *m*; **~sales service** *n* (BRIT) *n* (*for car, washing machine etc*) service *m* après-vente; **~shave (lotion)** *n* after-shave *m*; **~sun** *n* après-soleil *m inv*; **~thought** *n*: **I had an ~thought** il m'est venu une idée après coup; **~wards** (US **afterward**) *adv* après

**again** [əˈgɛn] *adv* de nouveau; encore (une fois); **to do sth ~** refaire qch; **not ... ~** ne ... plus; **~ and ~** à plusieurs reprises

**against** [əˈgɛnst] *prep* contre; (*compared to*) par rapport à

**age** [eɪdʒ] *n* âge *m* ♦ *vt, vi* vieillir; **it's been ~s since** ça fait une éternité que ... ne; **he is 20 years of ~** il a 20 ans; **to come of ~** atteindre sa majorité; **~d** [*adj* eɪdʒd, *npl* eɪdʒɪd] *adj*: **~d 10**

âgé(e) de 10 ans ♦ *npl:* **the ~d** les personnes âgées; **~ group** *n* tranche *f* d'âge; **~ limit** *n* limite *f* d'âge

**agency** ['eɪdʒənsɪ] *n* agence *f;* (*government body*) organisme *m,* office *m*

**agenda** [ə'dʒɛndə] *n* ordre *m* du jour

**agent** ['eɪdʒənt] *n* agent *m,* représentant *m;* (*firm*) concessionnaire *m*

**aggravate** ['ægrəveɪt] *vt* aggraver; (*annoy*) exaspérer

**aggressive** [ə'grɛsɪv] *adj* agressif(-ive)

**agitate** ['ædʒɪteɪt] *vt* (*person*) agiter, émouvoir, troubler ♦ *vi:* **to ~ for/against** faire campagne pour/contre

**AGM** *n abbr* = **annual general meeting** AG *f*

**ago** [ə'gəʊ] *adv:* **2 days ~** il y a deux jours; **not long ~** il n'y a pas longtemps; **how long ~?** il y a combien de temps de cela?

**agony** ['ægənɪ] *n* (*pain*) douleur *f* atroce; **to be in ~** souffrir le martyre

**agree** [ə'griː] *vt* (*price*) convenir de ♦ *vi:* **to ~ with** (*person*) être d'accord avec; (*statements etc*) concorder avec; (*LING*) s'accorder avec; **to ~ to do** accepter de *or* consentir à faire; **to ~ to sth** consentir à qch; **to ~ that** (*admit*) convenir *or* reconnaître que; **garlic doesn't ~ with me** je ne supporte pas l'ail; **~able** *adj* agréable; (*willing*) consentant(e), d'accord; **~d** *adj* (*time, place*) convenu(e); **~ment** *n* accord *m;* **in ~ment** d'accord

**agricultural** [ægrɪ'kʌltʃərəl] *adj* agricole

**agriculture** ['ægrɪkʌltʃə] *n* agriculture *f*

**aground** [ə'graʊnd] *adv:* **to run ~** échouer, s'échouer

**ahead** [ə'hɛd] *adv* (*in front: of position, place*) devant; (: *at the head*) en avant; (*look, plan, think*) en avant; **~ of** devant; (*fig: schedule etc*) en avance sur; **~ of time** en avance; **go right** *or* **straight ~** allez tout droit; **go ~!** (*fig: permission*) allez-y!

**aid** [eɪd] *n* aide *f;* (*device*) appareil *m* ♦ *vt* aider; **in ~ of** en faveur de; *see also* **hearing**

**aide** [eɪd] *n* (*person*) aide *m,* assistant(e)

**AIDS** [eɪdz] *n abbr* (= acquired immune deficiency syndrome) SIDA *m;* **AIDS-related** *adj* associé(e) au sida

**aim** [eɪm] *vt:* **to ~ sth (at)** (*gun, camera*) braquer *or* pointer qch (sur); (*missile*) lancer qch (à *or* contre *or* en direction de); (*blow*) allonger qch (à); (*remark*) destiner *or* adresser qch (à) ♦ *vi* (*also: **to take ~**) viser ♦ *n but m;* (*skill*): **his ~** is bad il vise mal; **to ~ at** viser (à); (*fig*) viser (à); **to ~ to do** avoir l'intention de faire; **~less** *adj* sans but

**ain't** [eɪnt] (*inf*) = **am not; aren't; isn't**

**air** [eə] *n* air *m* ♦ *vt* (*room, bed, clothes*) aérer; (*grievances, views, ideas*) exposer, faire connaître ♦ *cpd* (*currents, attack etc*) aérien(ne); **to throw sth into the ~** jeter qch en l'air; **by ~** (*travel*) par avion; **to be on the ~** (*RADIO, TV: programme*) être diffusé(e); (: *station*) diffuser; **~bed** *n* matelas *m* pneumatique; **~-conditioned** *adj* climatisé(e); **~ conditioning** *n* climatisation *f;* **~craft** *n inv* avion *m;* **~craft carrier** *n* porte-avions *m inv;* **~field** *n* terrain *m* d'aviation; **A~ Force** *n* armée *f* de l'air; **~ freshener** *n* désodorisant *m;* **~gun** *n* fusil *m* à air comprimé; **~ hostess** *n* (*BRIT*) hôtesse *f* de l'air; **~ letter** *n* aérogramme *m;* **~lift** *n* pont aérien; **~line** *n* ligne aérienne, compagnie *f* d'aviation; **~liner** *n* avion *m* de ligne; **~mail** *n:* **by ~mail** par avion; **~ mile** *n* air mile *m;* **~plane** *n* (*US*) avion *m;* **~port** *n* aéroport *m;* **~ raid** *n* attaque *or* raid aérien(ne); **~sick** *adj:* **to be ~sick** avoir le mal de l'air; **~tight** *adj* hermétique; **~-traffic controller** *n* aiguilleur *m* du ciel; **~y** *adj* bien aéré(e); (*manners*) dégagé(e)

**aisle** [aɪl] *n* (*of church*) allée centrale; nef latérale; (*of theatre etc*) couloir *m,*

passage *m*, allée; **~ seat** *n* place *f* côté
couloir

**ajar** [əˈdʒɑːʳ] *adj* entrouvert(e)

**akin** [əˈkɪn] *adj*: **~ to** (*similar*) qui tient
de *or* ressemble à

**alarm** [əˈlɑːm] *n* alarme *f* ♦ *vt* alarmer;
**~ call** *n* coup de fil *m* pour réveiller; **~
clock** *n* réveille-matin *m inv*, réveil *m*

**alas** [əˈlæs] *excl* hélas!

**album** [ˈælbəm] *n* album *m*

**alcohol** [ˈælkəhɔl] *n* alcool *m*; **~-free**
*adj* sans alcool; **~ic** [ælkəˈhɔlɪk] *adj* alcoolique ♦ *n* alcoolique *m/f*; **A~ics
Anonymous** Alcooliques anonymes

**ale** [eɪl] *n* bière *f*

**alert** [əˈlɜːt] *adj* alerte, vif (vive); vigi-
lant(e) ♦ *n* alerte *f* ♦ *vt* alerter; **on the ~**
sur le qui-vive; (*MIL*) en état d'alerte

**algebra** [ˈældʒɪbrə] *n* algèbre *m*

**Algeria** [ælˈdʒɪərɪə] *n* Algérie *f*

**alias** [ˈeɪlɪəs] *adv* alias ♦ *n* faux nom,
nom d'emprunt; (*writer*) pseudonyme
*m*

**alibi** [ˈælɪbaɪ] *n* alibi *m*

**alien** [ˈeɪlɪən] *n* étranger(-ère); (*from
outer space*) extraterrestre *mf* ♦ *adj*: **~
(to)** étranger(-ère) à

**alight** [əˈlaɪt] *adj, adv* en feu ♦ *vi* mettre
pied à terre; (*passenger*) descendre

**alike** [əˈlaɪk] *adj* semblable, pareil(le) ♦
*adv* de même; **to look ~** se ressembler

**alimony** [ˈælɪmənɪ] *n* (*payment*) pension *f* alimentaire

**alive** [əˈlaɪv] *adj* vivant(e); (*lively*)
plein(e) de vie

*KEYWORD*

**all** [ɔːl] *adj* (*singular*) tout(e); (*plural*)
tous (toutes); **all day** toute la journée;
**all night** toute la nuit; **all men** tous les
hommes; **all five** tous les cinq; **all the
food** toute la nourriture; **all the books**
tous les livres; **all the time** tout le
temps; **all his life** toute sa vie
♦ *pron* 1 tout; **I ate it all, I ate all of it**
j'ai tout mangé; **all of us went** nous y
sommes tous allés; **all of the boys**

went tous les garçons y sont allés
2 (*in phrases*): **above all** surtout, par-
dessus tout; **after all** après tout; **not at
all** (*in answer to question*) pas du tout;
(*in answer to thanks*) je vous en prie!;
**I'm not at all tired** je ne suis pas du
tout fatigué(e); **anything at all will do**
n'importe quoi fera l'affaire; **all in all**
tout bien considéré, en fin de compte
♦ *adv*: **all alone** tout(e) seul(e); **it's not
as hard as all that** ce n'est pas si difficile que ça; **all the more/the better**
d'autant plus/mieux; **all but** presque,
pratiquement; **the score is 2 all** le
score est de 2 partout

**allege** [əˈledʒ] *vt* alléguer, prétendre;
**~dly** [əˈledʒɪdlɪ] *adv* à ce que l'on pré-
tend, paraît-il

**allegiance** [əˈliːdʒəns] *n* allégeance *f*,
fidélité *f*, obéissance *f*

**allergic** [əˈlɜːdʒɪk] *adj*: **~ to** allergique à

**allergy** [ˈælədʒɪ] *n* allergie *f*

**alleviate** [əˈliːvɪeɪt] *vt* soulager, adoucir

**alley** [ˈælɪ] *n* ruelle *f*

**alliance** [əˈlaɪəns] *n* alliance *f*

**allied** [ˈælaɪd] *adj* allié(e)

**all-in** [ˈɔːlˈɪn] (*BRIT*) *adj* (*also adv*: *charge*)
tout compris

**all-night** [ˈɔːlˈnaɪt] *adj* ouvert(e) *or* qui
dure toute la nuit

**allocate** [ˈæləkeɪt] *vt* (*share out*) répartir, distribuer; **to ~ sth to** (*duties*) assigner *or* attribuer qch à; (*sum, time*) allouer qch à

**allot** [əˈlɔt] *vt*: **to ~ (to)** (*money*) répartir (entre), distribuer (à); (*time*) allouer
(à); **~ment** *n* (*share*) part *f*; (*garden*)
lopin *m* de terre (loué à la municipalité)

**all-out** [ˈɔːlaut] *adj* (*effort etc*) total(e) ♦
*adv*: **all out** à fond

**allow** [əˈlaʊ] *vt* (*practice, behaviour*)
permettre, autoriser; (*sum to spend etc*)
accorder; allouer; (*sum, time estimated*)
compter, prévoir; (*claim, goal*) admettre; (*concede*): **to ~ that** convenir que;
**to ~ sb to do** permettre à qn de faire,

autoriser qn à faire; **he is ~ed to** ... on lui permet de ...; **~ for** vt fus tenir compte de; **~ance** [ə'lauəns] n (money received) allocation f; indemnité f; (TAX) somme f déductible du revenu imposable, abattement m; **to make ~ances for** tenir compte de

**alloy** ['ælɔɪ] n alliage m

**all: ~ right** adv (feel, work) bien; (as answer) d'accord; **~-rounder** n: **to be a good ~-rounder** être doué(e) en tout; **~-time** adj (record) sans précédent, absolu(e)

**ally** [n 'ælaɪ, vb ə'laɪ] n allié m ♦ vt: **to ~ o.s. with** s'allier avec

**almighty** [ɔːl'maɪtɪ] adj tout-puissant; (tremendous) énorme

**almond** ['ɑːmənd] n amande f

**almost** ['ɔːlməʊst] adv presque

**alone** [ə'ləʊn] adj, adv seul(e); **to leave sb ~** laisser qn tranquille; **to leave sth ~** ne pas toucher à qch; **let ~** ... sans parler de ...; encore moins ...

**along** [ə'lɒŋ] prep le long de ♦ adv: **is he coming ~ with us?** vient-il avec nous?; **he was hopping/limping ~** il avançait en sautillant/boitant; **~ with** (together with: person) en compagnie de; (: thing) avec, en plus de; **all ~** (all the time) depuis le début; **~side** prep le long de, à côté de ♦ adv bord à bord

**aloof** [ə'luːf] adj distant(e) ♦ adv: **to stand ~** se tenir à distance or à l'écart

**aloud** [ə'laʊd] adv à haute voix

**alphabet** ['ælfəbet] n alphabet m; **~ical** [ælfə'betɪkl] adj alphabétique

**alpine** ['ælpaɪn] adj alpin(e), alpestre

**Alps** [ælps] npl: **the ~** les Alpes fpl

**already** [ɔːl'redɪ] adv déjà

**alright** [ɔːl'raɪt] (BRIT) adv = **all right**

**Alsatian** [æl'seɪʃən] n (BRIT) (dog) berger allemand

**also** ['ɔːlsəʊ] adv aussi

**altar** ['ɒltə*] n autel m

**alter** ['ɒltə*] vt, vi changer

**alternate** [adj ɒl'tɜːnɪt, vb 'ɒltəneɪt] adj alterné(e), alternant(e), alternatif(-ive) ♦

vi alterner; **on ~ days** un jour sur deux, tous les deux jours; **alternating current** n courant alternatif

**alternative** [ɒl'tɜːnətɪv] adj (solutions) possible, au choix; (plan) autre, de rechange; (lifestyle etc) parallèle ♦ n (choice) alternative f; (other possibility) solution f de remplacement or de rechange, autre possibilité f; **~ medicine** médicines fpl parallèles or douces; **~ly** adv: **~ly one could** on pourrait aussi or une autre or l'autre solution serait de, on pourrait aussi

**alternator** ['ɒltəneɪtə*] n (AUT) alternateur m

**although** [ɔːl'ðəʊ] conj bien que +sub

**altitude** ['æltɪtjuːd] n altitude f

**alto** ['æltəʊ] n (female) contralto m; (male) haute-contre f

**altogether** [ɔːltə'geðə*] adv entièrement, tout à fait; (on the whole) tout compte fait; (in all) en tout

**aluminium** [æljʊ'mɪnɪəm] (BRIT), **aluminum** [ə'luːmɪnəm] (US) n aluminium m

**always** ['ɔːlweɪz] adv toujours

**Alzheimer's (disease)** ['æltshaɪməz-] n maladie f d'Alzheimer

**AM** n abbr (= Assembly Member) député m au Parlement gallois

**am** [æm] vb see **be**

**a.m.** adv abbr (= ante meridiem) du matin

**amalgamate** [ə'mælgəmeɪt] vt, vi fusionner

**amateur** ['æmətə*] n amateur m; **~ish** (pej) adj d'amateur

**amaze** [ə'meɪz] vt stupéfier; **to be ~d (at)** être stupéfait(e) (de); **~ment** n stupéfaction f, stupeur f; **amazing** adj étonnant(e), incroyable

**ambassador** [æm'bæsədə*] n ambassadeur m

**amber** ['æmbə*] n ambre m; **at ~** (BRIT: AUT) à l'orange

**ambiguous** [æm'bɪgjuəs] adj ambigu(ë)

**ambition** [æm'bɪʃən] n ambition f;

**ambitious** *adj* ambitieux(-euse)

**ambulance** [ˈæmbjuləns] *n* ambulance *f*

**ambush** [ˈæmbuʃ] *n* embuscade *f* ♦ *vt* tendre une embuscade à

**amenable** [əˈmiːnəbl] *adj*: **~ to** (*advice etc*) disposé(e) à écouter

**amend** [əˈmɛnd] *vt* (*law*) amender; (*text*) corriger; **to make ~s** réparer ses torts, faire amende honorable

**amenities** [əˈmiːnɪtɪz] *npl* aménagements *mpl*, équipements *mpl*

**America** [əˈmɛrɪkə] *n* Amérique *f*; **~n** *adj* américain(e) ♦ *n* Américain(e)

**amiable** [ˈeɪmɪəbl] *adj* aimable, affable

**amicable** [ˈæmɪkəbl] *adj* amical(e); (*LAW*) à l'amiable

**amid(st)** [əˈmɪd(st)] *prep* parmi, au milieu de

**amiss** [əˈmɪs] *adj*, *adv*: **there's something ~** il y a quelque chose qui ne va pas *or* qui cloche; **to take sth ~** prendre qch mal *or* de travers

**ammonia** [əˈməʊnɪə] *n* (*gas*) ammoniac *m*; (*liquid*) ammoniaque *f*

**ammunition** [æmjuˈnɪʃən] *n* munitions *fpl*

**amok** [əˈmɔk] *adv*: **to run ~** être pris(e) d'un accès de folie furieuse

**among(st)** [əˈmʌŋ(st)] *prep* parmi, entre

**amorous** [ˈæmərəs] *adj* amoureux(-euse)

**amount** [əˈmaʊnt] *n* (*sum*) somme *f*, montant *m*; (*quantity*) quantité *f*, nombre *m* ♦ *vi*: **to** (*total*) s'élever à; (*be same as*) équivaloir à, revenir à

**amp(ere)** [ˈæmp(ɛəʳ)] *n* ampère *m*

**ample** [ˈæmpl] *adj* ample, spacieux(-euse); (*enough*): **this is ~** c'est largement suffisant; **to have ~ time/room** avoir bien assez de temps/place

**amplifier** [ˈæmplɪfaɪəʳ] *n* amplificateur *m*

**amuse** [əˈmjuːz] *vt* amuser, divertir; **~ment** *n* amusement *m*; **~ment arcade** *n* salle *f* de jeu; **~ment park** *n* parc *m* d'attractions

**an** [æn, ən] *indef art see* **a**

**anaemic** [əˈniːmɪk] (*US* **anemic**) *adj* anémique

**anaesthetic** [ænɪsˈθetɪk] (*US* **anesthetic**) *n* anesthésique *m*

**analog(ue)** [ˈænəlɔg] *adj* (*watch, computer*) analogique

**analyse** [ˈænəlaɪz] (*US* **analyze**) *vt* analyser; **analysis** [əˈnæləsɪs] (*pl* **analyses**) *n* analyse *f*; **analyst** [ˈænəlɪst] *n* (*POL etc*) spécialiste *m/f*; (*US*) psychanalyste *m/f*

**analyze** [ˈænəlaɪz] (*US*) *vt* = **analyse**

**anarchist** [ˈænəkɪst] *n* anarchiste *m/f*

**anarchy** [ˈænəkɪ] *n* anarchie *f*

**anatomy** [əˈnætəmɪ] *n* anatomie *f*

**ancestor** [ˈænsɪstəʳ] *n* ancêtre *m*

**anchor** [ˈæŋkəʳ] *n* ancre *f* ♦ *vi* (*also*: **to drop ~**) jeter l'ancre, mouiller ♦ *vt* mettre à l'ancre; (*fig*): **to ~ sth to** fixer qch à

**anchovy** [ˈæntʃəvɪ] *n* anchois *m*

**ancient** [ˈeɪnʃənt] *adj* ancien(ne), antique; (*person*) d'un âge vénérable; (*car*) antédiluvien(ne)

**ancillary** [ænˈsɪlərɪ] *adj* auxiliaire

**and** [ænd] *conj* et; **~ so on** et ainsi de suite; **try ~ come** tâchez de venir; **he talked ~ talked** il n'a pas arrêté de parler; **better ~ better** de mieux en mieux

**anew** [əˈnjuː] *adv* à nouveau

**angel** [ˈeɪndʒəl] *n* ange *m*

**anger** [ˈæŋgəʳ] *n* colère *f*

**angina** [ænˈdʒaɪnə] *n* angine *f* de poitrine

**angle** [ˈæŋgl] *n* angle *m*; **from their ~** de leur point de vue

**angler** [ˈæŋgləʳ] *n* pêcheur(-euse) à la ligne

**Anglican** [ˈæŋglɪkən] *adj*, *n* anglican(e)

**angling** [ˈæŋglɪŋ] *n* pêche *f* à la ligne

**Anglo-** [ˈæŋgləʊ] *prefix* anglo(-)

**angrily** [ˈæŋgrɪlɪ] *adv* avec colère

**angry** [ˈæŋgrɪ] *adj* en colère, furieux(-euse); (*wound*) enflammé(e); **to be ~**

**anguish** with sb/sth être furieux contre qn/ de qch; **to get ~** se fâcher, se mettre en colère

**anguish** ['æŋgwɪʃ] n (mental) angoisse f

**animal** ['ænɪməl] n animal m ♦ adj animal(e)

**animate** [vb 'ænɪmeɪt, adj 'ænɪmɪt] vt animer ♦ adj animé(e), vivant(e); **~d** adj animé(e)

**aniseed** ['ænɪsiːd] n anis m

**ankle** ['æŋkl] n cheville f; **~ sock** n socquette f

**annex** ['æneks] n (BRIT: **~e**) annexe f

**anniversary** [ænɪ'vɜːsərɪ] n anniversaire m

**announce** [ə'naʊns] vt annoncer; **~ment** n (birth, death) faire part de m; (for births etc: in newspaper) avis m de faire-part; (: letter, card) faire-part m; **~r** n (RADIO, TV: between programmes) speaker(ine)

**annoy** [ə'nɔɪ] vt agacer, ennuyer, contrarier; **don't get ~ed!** ne vous fâchez pas!; **~ance** n mécontentement m, contrariété f; **~ing** adj agaçant(e), contrariant(e)

**annual** ['ænjuəl] adj annuel(le) ♦ n (BOT) plante annuelle; (children's book) album m

**annul** [ə'nʌl] vt annuler

**annum** ['ænəm] n see **per**

**anonymous** [ə'nɒnɪməs] adj anonyme

**anorak** ['ænəræk] n anorak m

**anorexia** [ænə'reksɪə] n anorexie f

**another** [ə'nʌðə*] adj, pron ~ **book** (one more) un autre livre, encore un livre, un livre de plus; (a different one) un autre livre ♦ pron (a) autre, encore un(e), un(e) de plus; see also **one**

**answer** ['ɑːnsə*] n réponse f; (to problem) solution f ♦ vi répondre ♦ vt (reply to) répondre à; (problem) résoudre; (prayer) exaucer; **in ~ to your letter** en réponse à votre lettre; **to ~ the phone** répondre (au téléphone); **to ~ the bell** or **the door** aller or venir

ouvrir (la porte); **~ back** vi répondre, répliquer; **~ for** vt fus (person) répondre de, se porter garant de; (crime, one's actions) être responsable de; **~ to** vt fus (description) répondre or correspondre à; **~able** adj: **~able (to sb/for sth)** responsable (devant qn/de qch); **~ing machine** n répondeur m automatique

**ant** [ænt] n fourmi f

**antagonism** [æn'tægənɪzəm] n antagonisme m

**antagonize** [æn'tægənaɪz] vt éveiller l'hostilité de, contrarier

**Antarctic** [ænt'ɑːktɪk] n: **the ~** l'Antarctique m

**antenatal** ['æntɪ'neɪtl] adj prénatal(e); **~ clinic** n service m de consultation prénatale

**anthem** ['ænθəm] n: **national ~** hymne national

**anti** ['æntɪ]: **~-aircraft** adj (missile) antiaérien(ne); **~biotic** ['æntɪbaɪ'ɒtɪk] n antibiotique m; **~body** n anticorps m

**anticipate** [æn'tɪsɪpeɪt] vt s'attendre à, prévoir; (wishes, request) aller au devant de, devancer

**anticipation** [æntɪsɪ'peɪʃən] n attente f; **in ~** par anticipation, à l'avance

**anticlimax** ['æntɪ'klaɪmæks] n déception f, douche froide (fam)

**anticlockwise** ['æntɪ'klɒkwaɪz] adj, adv dans le sens inverse des aiguilles d'une montre

**antics** ['æntɪks] npl singeries fpl

**antidepressant** ['æntɪdɪ'presənt] n antidépresseur m

**antifreeze** ['æntɪfriːz] n antigel m

**antihistamine** ['æntɪ'hɪstəmin] n antihistaminique m

**antiquated** ['æntɪkweɪtɪd] adj vieilli(e), suranné(e), vieillot(te)

**antique** [æn'tiːk] n objet m d'art ancien, meuble ancien or d'époque, antiquité f ♦ adj ancien(ne); **~ dealer** n antiquaire m; **~ shop** n magasin m d'antiquités

**anti** ['æntɪ]: **~-Semitism** ['æntɪ'semɪtɪzəm]

antisémitisme m; **~septic** [æntɪˈsɛptɪk] n antiseptique m; **~social** [ˈæntɪˈsəʊʃəl] adj peu liant(e), sauvage, insociable; (against society) antisocial(e)

**antlers** [ˈæntləz] npl bois mpl, ramure f

**anvil** [ˈænvɪl] n enclume f

**anxiety** [æŋˈzaɪətɪ] n anxiété f; (keenness): **~ to do** grand désir or impatience f de faire

**anxious** [ˈæŋkʃəs] adj anxieux(-euse), angoissé(e); (worrying: time, situation) inquiétant(e); (keen): **~ to do/that** qui tient beaucoup à faire/à ce que; impatient(e) de faire/que

---

KEYWORD

---

**any** [ˈɛnɪ] adj 1 (in questions etc: singular) du, de l', de la, de; (: plural) des; **have you any butter/children/ink?** avez-vous du beurre/des enfants/de l'encre?

2 (with negative) de, d'; **I haven't any money/books** je n'ai pas d'argent/de livres

3 (no matter which) n'importe quel(le); **choose any book you like** vous pouvez choisir n'importe quel livre

4 (in phrases): **in any case** de toute façon; **any day now** d'un jour à l'autre; **at any moment** à tout moment, d'un instant à l'autre; **at any rate** en tout cas

♦ pron 1 (in questions etc) en; **have you got any?** est-ce que vous en avez?; **can any of you sing?** est-ce que parmi vous il y en a qui savent chanter?

2 (with negative): **I haven't any** (of them) je n'en ai pas, je n'en ai aucun

3 (no matter which one(s)) n'importe lequel (or laquelle); **take any of these books (you like)** vous pouvez prendre n'importe lequel de ces livres

♦ adv 1 (in questions etc): **do you want any more soup/sandwiches?** voulez-vous encore de la soupe/des sandwichs?; **are you feeling any better?** est-ce que vous vous sentez mieux?

2 (with negative): **I can't hear him any more** je ne l'entends plus; **don't wait any longer** n'attendez pas plus longtemps

**any: ~body** pron n'importe qui; (in interrogative sentences) quelqu'un; (in negative sentences): **I don't see anybody** je ne vois personne; **~how** adv (at any rate) de toute façon, quand même; (haphazard) n'importe comment; **~one** pron = anybody; **~thing** pron n'importe quoi, quelque chose, ne ... rien; **~way** adv de toute façon; **~where** adv n'importe où, quelque part; **I don't see him ~where** je ne le vois nulle part

**apart** [əˈpɑːt] adv (to one side) à part; de côté; à l'écart; (separately) séparément; **10 miles ~** à 10 miles l'un de l'autre; **to take ~** démonter; **~ from** à part, excepté

**apartheid** [əˈpɑːteɪt] n apartheid m

**apartment** [əˈpɑːtmənt] n (US) appartement m, logement m; (room) chambre f; **~ building** (US) n immeuble m; (divided house) maison divisée en appartements

**ape** [eɪp] n (grand) singe ♦ vt singer

**aperitif** [əˈpɛrɪtɪf] n apéritif m

**aperture** [ˈæpətjuəʳ] n orifice m, ouverture f; (PHOT) ouverture f (du diaphragme)

**APEX** [ˈeɪpɛks] n abbr (AVIAT) (= advance purchase excursion) APEX m

**apologetic** [əpɔləˈdʒɛtɪk] adj (tone, letter) d'excuse; (person): **to be ~** s'excuser

**apologize** [əˈpɔlədʒaɪz] vi: **to ~ (for sth to sb)** s'excuser (de qch auprès de qn), présenter des excuses (à qn pour qch)

**apology** [əˈpɔlədʒɪ] n excuses fpl

**apostle** [əˈpɔsl] n apôtre m

**apostrophe** [əˈpɔstrəfɪ] n apostrophe f

**appalling** [əˈpɔːlɪŋ] adj épouvantable; (stupidity) consternant(e)

**apparatus** [æpə'reɪtəs] n appareil m, dispositif m; (in gymnasium) agrès mpl; (of government) dispositif m

**apparel** [ə'pærəl] (US) n habillement m

**apparent** [ə'pærənt] adj apparent(e); ~ly adv apparemment

**appeal** [ə'piːl] vi (LAW) faire or interjeter appel ♦ n appel m; (request) prière f, appel m; (charm) attrait m, charme m; to ~ for faire un appel pour; to ~ to (beg) faire appel à; (be attractive) plaire à; it doesn't ~ to me cela ne m'attire pas; ~ing adj (attractive) attrayant(e)

**appear** [ə'pɪə'] vi apparaître, se montrer; (LAW) comparaître; (publication) paraître, sortir, être publié(e); (seem) paraître, sembler; it would ~ that il semble que; to ~ in Hamlet jouer dans Hamlet; to ~ on TV passer à la télé; ~ance n apparition f, parution f; (look, aspect) apparence f, aspect m

**appease** [ə'piːz] vt apaiser, calmer

**appendicitis** [əpendɪ'saɪtɪs] n appendicite f

**appendix** [ə'pendɪks] (pl appendices) n appendice m

**appetite** ['æpɪtaɪt] n appétit m; appetizer n amuse-gueule m; (drink) apéritif m

**applaud** [ə'plɔːd] vt, vi applaudir

**applause** [ə'plɔːz] n applaudissements mpl

**apple** ['æpl] n pomme f; ~ tree n pommier m

**appliance** [ə'plaɪəns] n appareil m

**applicable** [ə'plɪkəbl] adj (relevant): to be ~ to valoir pour

**applicant** ['æplɪkənt] n: ~ (for) candidat(e) (à)

**application** [æplɪ'keɪʃən] n application f; (for a job, a grant etc) demande f; candidature f; ~ form n formulaire m de demande

**applied** [ə'plaɪd] adj appliqué(e)

**apply** [ə'plaɪ] vt: to ~ (to) (paint, ointment) appliquer (sur); (law etc) appli-

quer (à) ♦ vi: to ~ to (be suitable for, relevant to) s'appliquer à; (ask) s'adresser à; to ~ (for) (permit, grant) faire une demande (en vue d'obtenir); (job) poser sa candidature (pour), faire une demande d'emploi (concernant); to ~ o.s. s'appliquer à

**appoint** [ə'pɔɪnt] vt nommer, engager; ~ed adj: at the ~ed time à l'heure dite; ~ment n nomination f; (meeting) rendez-vous m; to make an ~ment (with) prendre rendez-vous (avec)

**appraisal** [ə'preɪzl] n évaluation f

**appreciate** [ə'priːʃɪeɪt] vt (like) apprécier; (be grateful for) être reconnaissant(e) de; (understand) comprendre; se rendre compte de ♦ vi (FINANCE) prendre de la valeur

**appreciation** [əpriːʃɪ'eɪʃən] n appréciation f; (gratitude) reconnaissance f; (COMM) hausse f, valorisation f

**appreciative** [ə'priːʃɪətɪv] adj (person) sensible; (comment) élogieux(-euse)

**apprehensive** [æprɪ'hensɪv] adj inquiet(-ète), appréhensif(-ive)

**apprentice** [ə'prentɪs] n apprenti m; ~ship n apprentissage m

**approach** [ə'prəutʃ] vi approcher ♦ vt (come near) approcher de; (ask, apply to) s'adresser à; (situation, problem) aborder ♦ n approche f; (access) accès m; ~able adj accessible

**appropriate** [adj ə'prəuprɪɪt, vb ə'prəuprɪeɪt] adj (moment, remark) opportun(e); (tool etc) approprié(e) ♦ vt (take) s'approprier

**approval** [ə'pruːvəl] n approbation f; on ~ (COMM) à l'examen

**approve** [ə'pruːv] vt approuver; ~ of vt fus approuver

**approximate** [adj ə'prɒksɪmɪt, vb ə'prɒksɪmeɪt] adj approximatif(-ive) ♦ vt se rapprocher de, être proche de; ~ly adv approximativement

**apricot** ['eɪprɪkɒt] n abricot m

**April** ['eɪprəl] n avril m; ~ Fool's Day n le premier avril

**April Fool's Day**

April Fool's Day est le 1er avril, à l'occasion duquel on fait des farces de toutes sortes. Les victimes de ces farces sont les "April fools". Les médias britanniques se prennent aussi au jeu, diffusant de fausses nouvelles, comme la découverte d'îles de la taille de l'Irlande, ou faisant des reportages bidon, montrant par exemple la culture d'arbres à spaghettis en Italie.

**apron** ['eɪprən] n tablier m

**apt** [æpt] adj (suitable) approprié(e); (likely): ~ **to do** susceptible de faire; qui a tendance à faire

**Aquarius** [ə'kwɛərɪəs] n le Verseau

**Arab** ['ærəb] adj arabe ♦ n Arabe m/f; **~ian** [ə'reɪbɪən] adj arabe; **~ic** adj arabe ♦ n arabe m

**arbitrary** ['ɑːbɪtrərɪ] adj arbitraire

**arbitration** [ɑːbɪ'treɪʃən] n arbitrage m

**arcade** [ɑː'keɪd] n arcade f; (passage with shops) passage m, galerie marchande; (with video games) salle f de jeu

**arch** [ɑːtʃ] n arc m; (of foot) cambrure f, voûte f plantaire ♦ vt arquer, cambrer

**archaeologist** [ɑːkɪ'ɔlədʒɪst] n archéologue m/f

**archaeology** [ɑːkɪ'ɔlədʒɪ] n archéologie f

**archbishop** [ɑːtʃ'bɪʃəp] n archevêque m

**archeology** etc (US) [ɑːkɪ'ɔlədʒɪ] = **archaeology** etc

**archery** ['ɑːtʃərɪ] n tir m à l'arc

**architect** ['ɑːkɪtekt] n architecte m; **~ure** n architecture f

**archives** ['ɑːkaɪvz] npl archives fpl

**Arctic** ['ɑːktɪk] adj arctique ♦ n Arctique m

**ardent** ['ɑːdənt] adj fervent(e)

**are** [ɑː] vb see **be**

**area** ['ɛərɪə] n (GEOM) superficie f; (zone) région f; (: smaller) secteur m, partie f;

(in room) coin m; (knowledge, research) domaine m; **~ code** (US) n (TEL) indicatif m téléphonique

**aren't** [ɑːnt] = **are not**

**Argentina** [ɑːdʒən'tiːnə] n Argentine f;

**Argentinian** [ɑːdʒən'tɪnɪən] adj argentin(e) ♦ n Argentin(e)

**arguably** ['ɑːgjuəblɪ] adv: **it is ~ ...** on peut soutenir que c'est ...

**argue** ['ɑːgjuː] vi (quarrel) se disputer; (reason) argumenter; **to ~ that** objecter or alléguer que

**argument** ['ɑːgjumənt] n (reasons) argument m; (quarrel) dispute f; **~ative** [ɑːgju'mentətɪv] adj ergoteur(-euse), raisonneur(-euse)

**Aries** ['ɛərɪz] n le Bélier

**arise** [ə'raɪz] (pt **arose**, pp **arisen**) vi survenir, se présenter

**aristocrat** ['ærɪstəkræt] n aristocrate m/f

**arithmetic** [ə'rɪθmətɪk] n arithmétique f

**ark** [ɑːk] n: **Noah's A~** l'Arche f de Noé

**arm** [ɑːm] n bras m ♦ vt armer; **~s** npl (weapons, HERALDRY) armes fpl; **~ in ~** bras dessus bras dessous

**armaments** ['ɑːməmənts] npl armement m

**armchair** ['ɑːmtʃɛəʳ] n fauteuil m

**armed** [ɑːmd] adj armé(e); **~ robbery** n vol m à main armée

**armour** ['ɑːməʳ] (US **armor**) n armure f; (MIL: tanks) blindés mpl; **~ed car** n véhicule blindé

**armpit** ['ɑːmpɪt] n aisselle f

**armrest** ['ɑːmrest] n accoudoir m

**army** ['ɑːmɪ] n armée f

**A road** (BRIT) n (AUT) route nationale

**aroma** [ə'rəumə] n arôme m; **~therapy** n aromathérapie f

**arose** [ə'rəuz] pt of **arise**

**around** [ə'raund] adv autour; (nearby) dans les parages ♦ prep autour de; (near) près de; (fig: approx) environ; (: date, time) vers

**arouse** [ə'rauz] vt (sleeper) éveiller; (curiosity, passions) éveiller, susciter; (anger) exciter

**arrange** [ə'reɪndʒ] vt arranger; **to ~ to do sth** prévoir de faire qch; **~ment** n arrangement m; **~ments** npl (plans etc) arrangements mpl, dispositions fpl

**array** [ə'reɪ] n: **~ of** déploiement m or étalage m de

**arrears** [ə'rɪəz] npl arriéré m; **to be in ~ with one's rent** devoir un arriéré de loyer

**arrest** [ə'rest] vt arrêter; (sb's attention) retenir, attirer ♦ n arrestation f; **under ~** en état d'arrestation

**arrival** [ə'raɪvl] n arrivée f; **new ~** nouveau venu, nouvelle venue; (baby) nouveau-né(e)

**arrive** [ə'raɪv] vi arriver

**arrogant** [ˈærəgənt] adj arrogant(e)

**arrow** [ˈærəu] n flèche f

**arse** [ɑːs] (BRIT: inf!) n cul m (!)

**arson** [ˈɑːsn] n incendie criminel

**art** [ɑːt] n art m; **A~s** npl (SCOL) les lettres fpl

**artery** [ˈɑːtərɪ] n artère f

**art gallery** n musée m d'art; (small and private) galerie f de peinture

**arthritis** [ɑːˈθraɪtɪs] n arthrite f

**artichoke** [ˈɑːtɪtʃəuk] n (also: **globe ~**) artichaut m; (also: **Jerusalem ~**) topinambour m

**article** [ˈɑːtɪkl] n article m; **~s** npl (BRIT: LAW: training) ≈ stage m; **~ of clothing** vêtement m

**articulate** [adj ɑːˈtɪkjulɪt, vb ɑːˈtɪkjuleɪt] adj (person) qui s'exprime bien; (speech) bien articulé(e), prononcé(e) clairement ♦ vt exprimer; **~d lorry** (BRIT) n (camion m) semi-remorque m

**artificial** [ɑːtɪˈfɪʃl] adj artificiel(le); **~ respiration** n respiration artificielle

**artist** [ˈɑːtɪst] n artiste m/f; **~ic** [ɑːˈtɪstɪk] adj artistique; **~ry** n art m, talent m

**art school** n ≈ école f des beaux-arts

---

**KEYWORD**

**as** [æz, əz] conj **1** (referring to time) comme, alors que; **he came in as I was leaving** il est arrivé comme je partais; **as the years went by** à mesure que les années passaient; **as from tomorrow** à partir de demain

**2** (in comparisons): **as big as** aussi grand que; **twice as big as** deux fois plus grand que; **as much or many as** autant que; **as much money/many books** autant d'argent/de livres que; **as soon as** dès que

**3** (since, because) comme, puisque; **he had to be home by 10 ...** comme il or puisqu'il devait être de retour avant 10 h ...

**4** (referring to manner, way) comme; **do as you wish** faites comme vous voudrez

**5** (concerning): **as for or to that** quant à cela, pour ce qui est de cela

**6**: **as if or though** comme si; **he looked as if he was ill** il avait l'air d'être malade; see also **long; such; well**

♦ prep: **he works as a driver** il travaille comme chauffeur; **as chairman of the company, he ...** en tant que président de la société, il ...; **dressed up as a cowboy** déguisé en cowboy; **he gave me it as a present** il me l'a offert, il m'en a fait cadeau

**a.s.a.p.** abbr (= as soon as possible) dès que possible

**asbestos** [æzˈbestəs] n amiante f

**ascend** [əˈsend] vt gravir; (throne) monter sur

**ascertain** [æsəˈteɪn] vt vérifier

**ash** [æʃ] n (dust) cendre f; (also: **~ tree**) frêne m

**ashamed** [əˈʃeɪmd] adj honteux(-euse), confus(e); **to be ~ of** avoir honte de

**ashore** [əˈʃɔː] adv à terre

**ashtray** [ˈæʃtreɪ] n cendrier m

**Ash Wednesday** n mercredi m des cendres

**Asia** ['eɪʃə] n Asie f; **~n** n Asiatique m/f ♦ adj asiatique

**aside** [ə'saɪd] adv de côté; à l'écart ♦ n aparté m

**ask** [ɑːsk] vt demander; (invite) inviter; **to ~ sb sth/to do sth** demander à qn qch/de faire qch; **to ~ sb about sth** questionner qn sur qch; se renseigner auprès de qn sur qch; **to ~ (sb) a question** poser une question (à qn); **to ~ sb out to dinner** inviter qn au restaurant; **to ~ after** vt fus demander des nouvelles de; **to ~ for** vt fus demander; (trouble) chercher

**asking price** ['ɑːskɪŋ-] n: **the ~** le prix de départ

**asleep** [ə'sliːp] adj endormi(e); **to fall ~** s'endormir

**asparagus** [əs'pærəgəs] n asperges fpl

**aspect** ['æspekt] n aspect m; (direction in which a building etc faces) orientation f, exposition f

**aspire** [əs'paɪə] vi: **to ~ to** aspirer à

**aspirin** ['æsprɪn] n aspirine f

**ass** [æs] n âne m; (inf) imbécile m/f; (US: inf!) cul m (!)

**assailant** [ə'seɪlənt] n agresseur m; assaillant m

**assassinate** [ə'sæsɪneɪt] vt assassiner

**assassination** [əsæsɪ'neɪʃən] n assassinat m

**assault** [ə'sɔːlt] n (MIL) assaut m; (gen: attack) agression f ♦ vt attaquer; (sexually) violenter

**assemble** [ə'sembl] vt assembler ♦ vi s'assembler, se rassembler; **assembly** n assemblée f, réunion f; (institution) assemblée; (construction) assemblage m; **assembly line** n chaîne f de montage

**assent** [ə'sent] n assentiment m, consentement m

**assert** [ə'sɜːt] vt affirmer, déclarer; (one's authority) faire valoir; (one's innocence) protester de

**assess** [ə'ses] vt évaluer; (tax, payment)

établir or fixer le montant de; (property etc: for tax) calculer la valeur imposable de; (person) juger la valeur de; **~ment** n évaluation f, fixation f, calcul m de la valeur imposable, jugement m; **~or** n expert m (impôt et assurance)

**asset** ['æset] n avantage m, atout m; **~s** npl (FINANCE) capital m; avoir(s) m(pl); actif m

**assign** [ə'saɪn] vt (date) fixer; (task) assigner à; (resources) affecter à; **~ment** n tâche f, mission f

**assist** [ə'sɪst] vt aider, assister; **~ance** n aide f, assistance f; **~ant** n assistant(e), adjoint(e); (BRIT: also: **shop ~ant**) vendeur(-euse)

**associate** [n, adj ə'səʊʃɪɪt, vb ə'səʊʃɪeɪt] adj, n associé(e) ♦ vt associer ♦ vi: **to ~ with sb** fréquenter qn; **association** [əsəʊsɪ'eɪʃən] n association f

**assorted** [ə'sɔːtɪd] adj assorti(e)

**assortment** [ə'sɔːtmənt] n assortiment m

**assume** [ə'sjuːm] vt supposer; (responsibilities etc) assumer; (attitude, name) prendre, adopter; **assumption** [ə'sʌmpʃən] n supposition f, hypothèse f; (of power) assomption f, prise f

**assurance** [ə'ʃʊərəns] n assurance f

**assure** [ə'ʃʊə] vt assurer

**asthma** ['æsmə] n asthme m

**astonish** [əs'tɒnɪʃ] vt étonner, stupéfier; **~ment** n étonnement m

**astound** [əs'taʊnd] vt stupéfier, sidérer

**astray** [əs'streɪ] adv: **to go ~** s'égarer; (fig) quitter le droit chemin; **to lead ~** détourner du droit chemin

**astride** [əs'traɪd] prep à cheval sur

**astrology** [əs'trɒlədʒɪ] n astrologie f

**astronaut** ['æstrənɔːt] n astronaute m/f

**astronomy** [əs'trɒnəmɪ] n astronomie f

**asylum** [ə'saɪləm] n asile m

─────────────
| KEYWORD |
─────────────

**at** [æt] prep **1** (referring to position, direction) à; **at the top** au sommet; **at home/school** à la maison or chez soi/à

**ate** l'école; **at the baker's** à la boulangerie, chez le boulanger; **to look at sth** regarder qch

**2** (referring to time): **at 4 o'clock** à 4 heures; **at Christmas** à Noël; **at night** la nuit; **at times** par moments, parfois

**3** (referring to rates, speed etc) à: **at £1 a kilo** une livre le kilo; **two at a time** deux à la fois; **at 50 km/h** à 50 km/h

**4** (referring to manner): **at a stroke** d'un seul coup; **at peace** en paix

**5** (referring to activity): **to be at work** être au travail, travailler; **to play at cowboys** jouer aux cowboys; **to be good at sth** être bon en qch

**6** (referring to cause): **shocked/surprised/annoyed at sth** choqué par/étonné de/agacé par qch; **I went at his suggestion** j'y suis allé sur son conseil

**ate** [eɪt] pt of eat

**atheist** ['eɪθɪɪst] n athée m/f

**Athens** ['æθɪnz] n Athènes

**athlete** ['æθliːt] n athlète m/f; **athletic** [æθ'letɪk] adj athlétique; **athletics** n athlétisme m

**Atlantic** [ət'læntɪk] adj atlantique ♦ n: **the ~ (Ocean)** l'(océan m) Atlantique m

**atlas** ['ætləs] n atlas m

**ATM** n abbr (= automated telling machine) guichet m automatique

**atmosphere** ['ætməsfɪər] n atmosphère f

**atom** ['ætəm] n atome m; **~ic** [ə'tɒmɪk] adj atomique; **~(ic) bomb** n bombe f atomique; **~izer** n atomiseur m

**atone** [ə'təʊn] vi: **to ~ for** expier, racheter

**atrocious** [ə'trəʊʃəs] adj (very bad) atroce, exécrable

**attach** [ə'tætʃ] vt attacher; (document, letter) joindre; **to be ~ed to sb/sth** être attaché à qn/qch

**attaché case** [ə'tæʃeɪ] n mallette f, attaché-case m

**attachment** [ə'tætʃmənt] n (tool) accessoire m; (love): ~ (**to**) affection f (pour), attachement m (à)

**attack** [ə'tæk] vt attaquer; (task etc) s'attaquer à ♦ n attaque f; (also: **heart** ~) crise f cardiaque

**attain** [ə'teɪn] vt (also: **to ~ to**) parvenir à, atteindre; (: knowledge) acquérir

**attempt** [ə'tempt] n tentative f ♦ vt essayer, tenter; **to make an ~ on sb's life** attenter à la vie de qn; ~**ed** adj: ~**ed murder/suicide** tentative de meurtre/suicide

**attend** [ə'tend] vt (course) suivre; (meeting, talk) assister à; (school, church) aller à, fréquenter; (patient) soigner, s'occuper de; ~ **to** vt fus (needs, affairs etc) s'occuper de; (customer, patient) s'occuper de; ~**ance** n (being present) présence f; (people present) assistance f; ~**ant** n employé(e) ♦ adj (dangers) inhérent(e), concomitant(e)

**attention** [ə'tenʃən] n attention f; ~! (MIL) garde-à-vous!; **for the ~ of** (ADMIN) à l'attention de

**attentive** [ə'tentɪv] adj attentif(-ive); (kind) prévenant(e)

**attest** [ə'test] vi: **to ~ to** (demonstrate) démontrer; (confirm) témoigner

**attic** ['ætɪk] n grenier m

**attitude** ['ætɪtjuːd] n attitude f; pose f, maintien m

**attorney** [ə'tɜːnɪ] n (US: lawyer) avoué m; **A~ General** (BRIT) ≈ procureur général; (US) ≈ garde m des Sceaux, ministre m de la Justice

**attract** [ə'trækt] vt attirer; ~**ion** (gen pl: pleasant things) attraction f; attrait m; (PHYSICS) attraction f; (fig: towards sb or sth) attirance f; ~**ive** adj attrayant(e); (person) séduisant(e)

**attribute** [n 'ætrɪbjuːt, vb ə'trɪbjuːt] n attribut m ♦ vt: **to ~ sth to** attribuer qch à

**attrition** [ə'trɪʃən] n: **war of ~** guerre f d'usure

**aubergine** ['əʊbəʒiːn] n aubergine f

**auction** ['ɔːkʃən] n (also: **sale by ~**) vente f aux enchères ♦ vt (also: **sell by ~**) vendre aux enchères; (also: **put up for ~**) mettre aux enchères; **~eer** [ɔːkʃə'nɪəʳ] n commissaire-priseur m

**audience** ['ɔːdɪəns] n (people) assistance f, public m; spectateurs mpl; (interview) audience f

**audiovisual** ['ɔːdɪəʊ'vɪzjuəl] adj audiovisuel(le); **~ aids** npl supports or moyens audiovisuels

**audit** ['ɔːdɪt] vt vérifier

**audition** [ɔː'dɪʃən] n audition f

**auditor** ['ɔːdɪtəʳ] n vérificateur m des comptes

**augur** ['ɔːgəʳ] vi: **it ~s well** c'est bon signe or de bon augure

**August** ['ɔːgəst] n août m

**aunt** [aːnt] n tante f; **~ie, ~y** ['aːntɪ] n dimin of **aunt**

**au pair** ['əu'pɛəʳ] n (also: **~ girl**) jeune fille f au pair

**auspicious** [ɔːs'pɪʃəs] adj de bon augure, propice

**Australia** [ɔs'treɪlɪə] n Australie f; **~n** adj australien(ne) ♦ n Australien(ne)

**Austria** ['ɔstrɪə] n Autriche f; **~n** adj autrichien(ne) ♦ n Autrichien(ne)

**authentic** [ɔː'θɛntɪk] adj authentique

**author** ['ɔːθəʳ] n auteur m

**authoritarian** [ɔːθɔrɪ'tɛərɪən] adj autoritaire

**authoritative** [ɔː'θɔrɪtətɪv] adj (account) digne de foi; (study, treatise) qui fait autorité; (person, manner) autoritaire

**authority** [ɔː'θɔrɪtɪ] n autorité f; (permission) autorisation (formelle); **the authorities** npl (ruling body) les autorités fpl, l'administration f

**authorize** ['ɔːθəraɪz] vt autoriser

**auto** ['ɔːtəu] n (US) auto f, voiture f

**auto: ~biography** [ɔːtəbaɪ'ɔgrəfɪ] n autobiographie f; **~graph** ['ɔːtəgrɑːf] n autographe m ♦ vt signer, dédicacer; **~mated** ['ɔːtəmeɪtɪd] adj automatisé(e), automatique; **~matic** [ɔːtə'mæt-

ik] adj automatique ♦ n (gun) automatique m; (washing machine) machine f à laver automatique; (BRIT: AUT) voiture f à transmission automatique; **~matically** adv automatiquement; **~mation** [ɔːtə'meɪʃən] n automatisation f (électronique); **~mobile** ['ɔːtəməbiːl] (US) n automobile f; **~nomy** [ɔː'tɔnəmɪ] n autonomie f

**autumn** ['ɔːtəm] n automne m; **in ~** en automne

**auxiliary** [ɔːg'zɪlɪərɪ] adj auxiliaire ♦ n auxiliaire m/f

**avail** [ə'veɪl] vt: **to ~ o.s. of** profiter de ♦ n: **to no ~** sans résultat, en vain, en pure perte

**availability** [əveɪlə'bɪlɪtɪ] n disponibilité f

**available** [ə'veɪləbl] adj disponible

**avalanche** ['ævəlɑːnʃ] n avalanche f

**Ave** abbr = **avenue**

**avenge** [ə'vɛndʒ] vt venger

**avenue** ['ævənjuː] n avenue f; (fig) moyen m

**average** ['ævərɪdʒ] n moyenne f; (fig) moyen m ♦ adj moyen(ne) ♦ vt (a certain figure) atteindre or faire etc en moyenne; **on ~** en moyenne; **~ out** vi: **to ~ out at** représenter en moyenne, donner une moyenne de

**averse** [ə'vɜːs] adj: **to be ~ to sth/ doing sth** éprouver une forte répugnance envers qch/à faire qch

**avert** [ə'vɜːt] vt (danger) prévenir, écarter; (one's eyes) détourner

**aviary** ['eɪvɪərɪ] n volière f

**avocado** [ævə'kɑːdəu] n (BRIT: ~ pear) avocat m

**avoid** [ə'vɔɪd] vt éviter

**await** [ə'weɪt] vt attendre

**awake** [ə'weɪk] (pt **awoke**, pp **awoken**) adj éveillé(e) ♦ vt éveiller ♦ vi s'éveiller; **~ to** (dangers, possibilities) conscient(e) de; **to be ~** être réveillé(e); **he was still ~** il ne dormait pas encore; **~ning** n réveil m

**award** [ə'wɔːd] n récompense f, prix m

(LAW: damages) dommages-intérêts mpl
♦ vt (prize) décerner; (LAW: damages)
accorder

**aware** [ə'wɛəʳ] adj: ~ (of) (conscious)
conscient(e) (de); (informed) au courant
(de); **to become ~ of/that** prendre
conscience de/que; se rendre compte
de/que; **~ness** n conscience f, connaissance f

**away** [ə'weɪ] adj, adv (au) loin; ab-
sent(e); **two kilometres ~** à (une distance de) deux kilomètres, à deux kilomètres de distance; **two hours ~ by
car** à deux heures de voiture or de route; **the holiday was two weeks ~** il
restait deux semaines jusqu'aux vacances; **~ from** loin de; **he's ~ for a week**
il est parti (pour) une semaine; **to
pedal/work/laugh ~** être en train de
pédaler/travailler/rire; **~ to fade
(sound)** s'affaiblir; (colour) s'estomper;
**to wither ~** (plant) se dessécher; **~
to take ~** emporter; (subtract) enlever; **~
game** n (SPORT) match m à l'extérieur

**awe** [ɔː] n respect mêlé de crainte; **~-
inspiring** ['ɔːɪnspaɪərɪŋ] adj impres-
sionnant(e)

**awful** ['ɔːfəl] adj affreux(-euse); **an ~
lot (of)** un nombre incroyable (de); **~ly**
adv (very) terriblement, vraiment

**awkward** ['ɔːkwəd] adj (clumsy) gauche, maladroit(e); (inconvenient) peu
pratique; (embarrassing) gênant(e), dé-
licat(e)

**awning** ['ɔːnɪŋ] n (of tent) auvent m;
(of shop) store m; (of hotel etc) marquise f

**awoke** [ə'wəuk] pt of **awake**; **~n**
[ə'wəukən] pp of **awake**

**axe** [æks] (US **ax**) n hache f ♦ vt (project
etc) abandonner; (jobs) supprimer

**axes**[1] ['æksɪz] npl of **axe**

**axes**[2] ['æksiːz] npl of **axis**

**axis** ['æksɪs] (pl **axes**) n axe m

**axle** ['æksl] n (also: **~-tree**: AUT) essieu m

**ay(e)** [aɪ] excl (yes) oui

# B, b

**B** [biː] n (MUS) si m; **~ road** (BRIT) route
départementale

**B.A.** abbr = **Bachelor of Arts**

**babble** ['bæbl] vi bredouiller; (baby,
stream) gazouiller

**baby** ['beɪbɪ] n bébé m; (US: inf: darling): **come on, ~!** viens ma belle/mon
gars!; **~ carriage** (US) n voiture f d'enfant; **~ food** n aliments mpl pour bé-
bé(s); **~-sit** vi garder les enfants; **~-
sitter** n baby-sitter m/f; **~ wipe** n lin-
gette f (pour bébé)

**bachelor** ['bætʃələʳ] n célibataire m; **B~
of Arts/Science** ≈ licencié(e) ès or en
lettres/sciences

**back** [bæk] n (of person, horse, book)
dos m; (of hand) dos, revers m; (of
house) derrière m; (of car, train) arrière
m; (of chair) dossier m; (of page) verso
m; (of room, audience) fond m; (SPORT)
arrière m ♦ vt (candidate: also: **~ up**)
soutenir, appuyer; (horse: at races) parier or miser sur; (car) (faire) reculer ♦ vi
(also: **~ up**) reculer; (also: **~ up**: car etc)
faire marche arrière ♦ adj (in compounds)
de derrière, à l'arrière ♦ adv (not forward) en arrière; (returned): **he's ~** il
est rentré, il est de retour; (restitution):
**throw the ball ~** renvoie la balle;
(again): **he called ~** il a rappelé; **~
seat/wheels** (AUT) sièges mpl/roues fpl
arrières; **~ payments/rent** arriéré m de
paiements/loyer; **he ran ~** il est revenu en courant; **~ down** vi rabattre de
ses prétentions; **~ out** vi (of promise) se
dédire; **~ up** vt (candidate etc) soutenir,
appuyer; (COMPUT) sauvegarder; **~ache**
n mal m de dos; **~bencher** (BRIT) n
membre du parlement sans portefeuille;
**~bone** n colonne vertébrale, épine
dorsale; **~date** vt (letter) antidater;
**~dated pay rise** augmentation f avec
effet rétroactif; **~fire** vi (AUT) pétarader;

*(plans)* mal tourner; **~ground** *n* arrière-plan *m*; *(of events)* situation *f*, conjoncture *f*; *(basic knowledge)* éléments *mpl* de base; *(experience)* formation *f*; **family ~ground** milieu familial; **~hand** *n (TENNIS: also:* **~hand stroke)** revers *m*; **~hander** *(BRIT) n (bribe)* pot-de-vin *m*; **~ing** *n (fig)* soutien *m*, appui *m*; **~lash** *n* contre-coup *m*, répercussion *f*; **~log** *n:* **~log of work** travail *m* en retard; **~ number** *(of magazine etc)* vieux numéro; **~pack** *n* sac *m* à dos; **~packer** *n* randonneur(-euse); **~ pay** *n* rappel *m* de salaire; **~side** *(inf) n* derrière *m*, postérieur *m*; **~stage** *adv ♦ n* derrière la scène, dans la coulisse; **~stroke** *n* dos crawlé; **~up** *adj (train, plane)* supplémentaire, de réserve; *(COMPUT)* de sauvegarde *♦ n (support)* appui *m*, soutien *m*; *(also:* **~up disk/file)** sauvegarde *f*; **~ward** *adj (movement)* en arrière; *(person, country)* arriéré(e); attardé(e); **~wards** *adv (move, go)* en arrière; *(read a list)* à l'envers, à rebours; *(fall)* à la renverse; *(walk)* à reculons; **~water** *n (fig)* trou reculé; bled perdu *(péj)*; **~yard** *n* arrière-cour *f*

**bacon** ['beɪkən] *n* bacon *m*, lard *m*

**bacteria** [bæk'tɪərɪə] *npl* bactéries *fpl*

**bad** [bæd] *adj* mauvais(e); *(child)* vilain(e); *(mistake, accident etc)* grave; *(meat, food)* gâté(e), avarié(e); **his ~ leg** sa jambe malade; **to go ~** *(meat, food)* se gâter

**badge** [bædʒ] *n* insigne *m*; *(of policeman)* plaque *f*

**badger** ['bædʒəʳ] *n* blaireau *m*

**badly** ['bædlɪ] *adv (work, dress etc)* mal; **~ wounded** grièvement blessé; **he needs it ~** il en a absolument besoin; **~ off** *adj, adv* dans la gêne

**badminton** ['bædmɪntən] *n* badminton *m*

**bad-tempered** ['bæd'tɛmpəd] *adj (person: by nature)* ayant mauvais caractère; *(: on one occasion)* de mauvaise

humeur

**baffle** ['bæfl] *vt (puzzle)* déconcerter

**bag** [bæg] *n* sac *m ♦ vt (inf: take)* empocher; s'approprier; **~s of** *(inf: lots of)* des masses de; **~gage** *n* bagages *mpl*; **~gage allowance** *n* franchise *f* de bagages; **~gy** *adj* avachi(e), qui fait des poches; **~pipes** *npl* cornemuse *f*

**bail** [beɪl] *n (payment)* caution *f*; *(release)* mise *f* en liberté sous caution *♦ vt (prisoner: also:* **grant ~ to)** mettre en liberté sous caution; *(boat: also:* **~ out)** écoper; **on ~** *(prisoner)* sous caution; *see also* **bale**; **~ out** *vt (prisoner)* payer la caution de

**bailiff** ['beɪlɪf] *n (BRIT)* ≃ huissier *m*; *(US)* ≃ huissier-audiencier *m*

**bait** [beɪt] *n* appât *m ♦ vt* appâter; *(fig: tease)* tourmenter

**bake** [beɪk] *vt (faire)* cuire au four *♦ vi (bread etc)* cuire *(au four)*; *(make cakes etc)* faire de la pâtisserie; **~d beans** *npl* haricots blancs à la sauce tomate; **~d potato** *n* pomme *f* de terre en robe des champs; **~r** *n* boulanger *m*; **~ry** *n* boulangerie *f*; boulangerie industrielle; **baking** *n* cuisson *f*; **baking powder** *n* levure *f* (chimique)

**balance** ['bæləns] *n* équilibre *m*; *(COMM: sum)* solde *m*; *(remainder)* reste *m*; *(scales)* balance *f ♦ vt* mettre ou faire tenir en équilibre; *(pros and cons)* peser; *(budget)* équilibrer; *(account)* balancer; **~ of trade/payments** balance commerciale des comptes *or* paiements; **~d** *adj (personality, diet)* équilibré(e); *(report)* objectif(-ive); **~ sheet** *n* bilan *m*

**balcony** ['bælkənɪ] *n* balcon *m*; *(in theatre)* deuxième balcon

**bald** [bɔːld] *adj* chauve; *(tyre)* lisse

**bale** [beɪl] *n* balle *f*, ballot *m*; **~ out** *vi (of a plane)* sauter en parachute

**ball** [bɔːl] *n* boule *f*; *(football)* ballon *m*; *(for tennis, golf)* balle *f*; *(of wool)* pelote *f*; *(of string)* bobine *f*; *(dance)* bal *m*; **to**

play ~ (with sb) (fig) coopérer (avec qn)

**ballast** ['bæləst] n lest m

**ball bearings** npl roulement m à billes

**ballerina** [bælə'ri:nə] n ballerine f

**ballet** ['bæleɪ] n ballet m; (art) danse f (classique); ~ **dancer** n danceur(-euse) m/f de ballet; ~ **shoe** n chausson m de danse

**balloon** [bə'lu:n] n ballon m; (in comic strip) bulle f

**ballot** ['bælət] n scrutin m; ~ **paper** n bulletin m de vote

**ballpoint (pen)** ['bɔ:lpɔɪnt(-)] n stylo m à bille

**ballroom** ['bɔ:lrum] n salle f de bal

**ban** [bæn] n interdiction f ♦ vt interdire

**banana** [bə'nɑ:nə] n banane f

**band** [bænd] n bande f; (at a dance) orchestre m; (MIL) musique f, fanfare f; ~ **together** vi se liguer

**bandage** ['bændɪdʒ] n bandage m, pansement m ♦ vt bander

**Band-Aid** ® ['bændeɪd] (US) n pansement adhésif

**bandit** n bandit m

**bandy-legged** ['bændɪ'legɪd] adj aux jambes arquées

**bang** [bæŋ] n détonation f; (of door) claquement m; (blow) coup (violent) ♦ vt frapper (violemment); (door) claquer ♦ vi détoner, claquer ♦ excl pan!; ~**s** (US) npl (fringe) frange f

**banish** ['bænɪʃ] vt bannir

**banister(s)** ['bænɪstə(z)] n(pl) rampe f (d'escalier)

**bank** [bæŋk] n banque f; (of river, lake) bord m, rive f; (of earth) talus m, remblai m ♦ vi (AVIAT) virer sur l'aile; ~ **on** vt fus miser or tabler sur; ~ **account** n compte m en banque; ~ **card** n carte f d'identité bancaire; ~**er** n banquier m; ~**er's card** (BRIT) n = bank card; ~ **holiday** (BRIT) n jour férié (les banques sont fermées); ~**ing** n opérations fpl bancaires; profession f de banquier; ~**note** n billet m de banque; ~ **rate** n

taux m de l'escompte

| bank holiday |
| --- |

Un **bank holiday** en Grande-Bretagne est un lundi férié et donc l'occasion d'un week-end prolongé. La circulation sur les routes et le trafic dans les gares et les aéroports augmentent considérablement à ces périodes. Les principaux **bank holidays**, à part Pâques et Noël, ont lieu au mois de mai et fin août.

**bankrupt** ['bæŋkrʌpt] adj en faillite; to **go ~** faire faillite; ~**cy** n faillite f

**bank statement** n relevé m de compte

**banner** ['bænə'] n bannière f

**bannister(s)** ['bænɪstə(z)] n(pl) = **bannister(s)**

**baptism** ['bæptɪzəm] n baptême m

**bar** [bɑ:'] n (pub) bar m; (counter: in pub) comptoir m, bar; (rod: of metal etc) barre f; (on window etc) barreau m; (of chocolate) tablette f, plaque f; (fig) obstacle m; (prohibition) mesure f d'exclusion; (MUS) mesure f ♦ vt (road) barrer; (window) munir de barreaux; (person) exclure; (activity) interdire; ~ **of soap** savonnette f; the **B~** (LAW) le barreau; **behind ~s** (prisoner) sous les verrous; ~ **none** sans exception

**barbaric** [bɑ:'bærɪk] adj barbare

**barbecue** ['bɑ:bɪkju:] n barbecue m

**barbed wire** ['bɑ:bd-] n fil m de fer barbelé

**barber** ['bɑ:bə'] n coiffeur m (pour hommes)

**bar code** n (on goods) code m à barres

**bare** [bɛə'] adj nu(e) ♦ vt mettre à nu, dénuder; (teeth) montrer; the ~ **necessities** le strict nécessaire; ~**back** adv à cru, sans selle; ~**faced** adj impudent(e), effronté(e); ~**foot** adj, adv nu-pieds, (les) pieds nus; ~**ly** adv à peine

**bargain** ['bɑ:gɪn] n (transaction) marché m; (good buy) affaire f, occasion f

# barge 323 batter

**barge** *vi* (*haggle*) marchander; (*negotiate*): **to ~ (with sb)** négocier (avec qn), traiter (avec qn); **into the ~** par-dessus le marché; **~ for** *vt fus*: **he expected no more than he ~ed for** il ne s'attendait pas à un coup pareil

**barge** [baːdʒ] *n* péniche *f*; **~ in** *vi* (*walk in*) faire irruption; (*interrupt talk*) intervenir mal à propos

**bark** [baːk] *n* (*of tree*) écorce *f*; (*of dog*) aboiement *m* ♦ *vi* aboyer

**barley** ['baːlɪ] *n* orge *f*; **~ sugar** *n* sucre *m* d'orge

**bar**: **~maid** *n* serveuse *f* de bar, barmaid *f*; **~man** (*irreg*) *n* barman *m*; **~ meal** *n* repas *m* de bistrot; **to go for a ~ meal** aller manger au bistrot

**barn** [baːn] *n* grange *f*

**barometer** [bə'rɒmɪtər] *n* baromètre *m*

**baron** ['bærən] *n* baron *m*; **~ess** ['bærənɪs] *n* baronne *f*

**barracks** ['bærəks] *npl* caserne *f*

**barrage** ['bæraːʒ] *n* (*MIL*) tir *m* de barrage; (*dam*) barrage *m*; (*fig*) pluie *f*

**barrel** ['bærəl] *n* tonneau *m*; (*of oil*) baril *m*; (*of gun*) canon *m*

**barren** ['bærən] *adj* stérile

**barricade** [bærɪ'keɪd] *n* barricade *f*

**barrier** ['bærɪər] *n* barrière *f*; (*fig: progress etc*) obstacle *m*

**barring** ['baːrɪŋ] *prep* sauf

**barrister** ['bærɪstər] (*BRIT*) *n* avocat (plaidant)

**barrow** ['bærəʊ] *n* (*wheelbarrow*) charrette *f* à bras

**bartender** ['baːtendər] (*US*) *n* barman *m*

**barter** ['baːtər] *vt*: **to ~ sth for** échanger qch contre

**baseball** ['beɪsbɔːl] *n* base-ball *m*

**basement** ['beɪsmənt] *n* sous-sol *m*

**bases**[1] ['beɪsɪz] *npl of* **base**

**bases**[2] ['beɪsiːz] *npl of* **basis**

**bash** [bæʃ] (*inf*) *vt* frapper, cogner

**bashful** ['bæʃful] *adj* timide; modeste

**basic** ['beɪsɪk] *adj* fondamental(e), de base; (*minimal*) rudimentaire; **~ally** *adv* fondamentalement, à la base; (*in fact*) en fait, au fond; **~s** *npl*: **the ~s** l'essentiel *m*

**basil** ['bæzl] *n* basilic *m*

**basin** ['beɪsn] *n* (*vessel, also GEO*) cuvette *f*, bassin *m*; (*also*: **washbasin**) lavabo *m*

**basis** ['beɪsɪs] (*pl* **bases**) *n* base *f*; **on a trial ~** à titre d'essai; **on a part-time ~** à temps partiel

**bask** [baːsk] *vi*: **to ~ in the sun** se chauffer au soleil

**basket** ['baːskɪt] *n* corbeille *f*; (*with handle*) panier *m*; **~ball** *n* basket-ball *m*

**bass** [beɪs] *n* (*MUS*) basse *f*; **~ drum** *n* grosse caisse *f*

**bassoon** [bə'suːn] *n* (*MUS*) basson *m*

**bastard** ['baːstəd] *n* enfant naturel(le), bâtard(e); (*inf!*) salaud *m* (!)

**bat** [bæt] *n* chauve-souris *f*; (*for baseball etc*) batte *f*; (*BRIT: for table tennis*) raquette *f* ♦ *vt*: **he didn't ~ an eyelid** il n'a pas sourcillé or bronché

**batch** [bætʃ] *n* (*of bread*) fournée *f*; (*of papers*) liasse *f*

**bated** ['beɪtɪd] *adj*: **with ~ breath** en retenant son souffle

**bath** [baːθ] *n* bain *m*; (*~tub*) baignoire *f* ♦ *vt* baigner, donner un bain à; **to have a ~** prendre un bain; *see also* **baths**

**bathe** [beɪð] *vi* se baigner ♦ *vt* (*wound*) laver; **bathing** *n* baignade *f*; **bathing costume**, **bathing suit** (*US*) *n* maillot *m* (de bain)

**bath**: **~robe** *n* peignoir *m* de bain; **~room** *n* salle *f* de bains; **~s** *npl* (*also*: **swimming ~s**) piscine *f*; **~ towel** *n* serviette *f* de bain

**baton** ['bætən] *n* bâton *m*; (*MUS*) baguette *f*; (*club*) matraque *f*

**batter** ['bætər] *vt* battre ♦ *n* pâte *f* à frire; **~ed** ['bætəd] *adj* (*hat, pan*) cabossé(e)

**battery** ['bætərɪ] n batterie f; (of torch) pile f; ~ **farming** n élevage f en batterie

**battle** ['bætl] n bataille f, combat m ♦ vi se battre, lutter; ~**field** n champ m de bataille; ~**ship** n cuirassé m

**Bavaria** [bə'veərɪə] n Bavière f

**bawl** [bɔːl] vi hurler; (child) brailler

**bay** [beɪ] n (of sea) baie f; **to hold sb at** ~ tenir qn à distance ou en échec; ~ **leaf** n laurier m; ~ **window** n baie vitrée

**bazaar** [bə'zɑː'] n bazar m; vente f de charité

**B & B** n abbr = **bed and breakfast**

**BBC** n abbr (= British Broadcasting Corporation) office de la radiodiffusion et télévision britannique

**B.C.** adv abbr (= before Christ) av. J.-C.

---KEYWORD---

**be** [biː] (pt was, were, pp been) aux vb
**1** (with present participle: forming continuous tenses): **what are you doing?** que faites-vous?; **they're coming tomorrow** ils viennent demain; **I've been waiting for you for 2 hours** je t'attends depuis 2 heures
**2** (with pp: forming passives) être; **to be killed** être tué(e); **he was nowhere to be seen** on ne le voyait nulle part
**3** (in tag questions): **it was fun, wasn't it?** c'était drôle, n'est-ce pas?; **she's back, is she?** elle est rentrée, n'est-ce pas ou alors?
**4** (+to +infinitive): **the house is to be sold** la maison doit être vendue; **he's not to open it** il ne doit pas l'ouvrir
♦ vb + complement **1** (gen) être; **I'm English** je suis anglais(e); **I'm tired** je suis fatigué(e); **I'm hot/cold** j'ai chaud/froid; **he's a doctor** il est médecin; **2 and 2 are 4** 2 et 2 font 4
**2** (of health): **how are you?** comment allez-vous?; **he's fine now** il va bien maintenant; **he's very ill** il est

très malade
**3** (of age) avoir; **how old are you?** quel âge avez-vous?; **I'm sixteen (years old)** j'ai seize ans
**4** (cost) coûter; **how much was the meal?** combien a coûté le repas?; **that'll be £5, please** ça fera 5 livres, s'il vous plaît
♦ vi **1** (exist, occur etc) être, exister; **the prettiest girl that ever was** la fille la plus jolie qui ait jamais existé; **be that as it may** quoi qu'il en soit; **so be it** soit
**2** (referring to place) être, se trouver; **I won't be here tomorrow** je ne serai pas là demain; **Edinburgh is in Scotland** Édimbourg est ou se trouve en Écosse
**3** (referring to movement) aller; **where have you been?** où êtes-vous allé(s)?
♦ impers vb **1** (referring to time, distance) être; **it's 5 o'clock** il est 5 heures; **it's the 28th of April** c'est le 28 avril; **it's 10 km to the village** le village est à 10 km
**2** (referring to the weather) faire; **it's too hot/cold** il fait trop chaud/froid; **it's windy** il y a du vent
**3** (emphatic): **it's me/the postman** c'est moi/le facteur

**beach** [biːtʃ] n plage f ♦ vt échouer

**beacon** ['biːkən] n (lighthouse) fanal m; (marker) balise f

**bead** [biːd] n perle f

**beak** [biːk] n bec m

**beaker** ['biːkə'] n gobelet m

**beam** [biːm] n poutre f; (of light) rayon m ♦ vi rayonner

**bean** [biːn] n haricot m; (of coffee) grain m; **runner** ~ haricot m (à rames); **broad** ~ fève f; ~**sprouts** npl germes mpl de soja

**bear** [bɛə'] (pt bore, pp borne) n ours m ♦ vt porter; (endure) supporter ♦ vi: **to** ~ **right/left** obliquer à droite/gauche,

se diriger vers la droite/gauche; **~ out**
vt corroborer, confirmer; **~ up** vi (person) tenir le coup

**beard** [bɪəd] n barbe f; **~ed** adj bar-
bu(e)

**bearer** ['bɛərəʳ] n porteur m; (of passport) titulaire m/f

**bearing** ['bɛərɪŋ] n maintien m, allure f;
(connection) rapport m; **~s** npl (also:
**ball ~s**) roulement m (à billes); **to take
a ~** faire le point

**beast** [biːst] n bête f; (inf: person) brute
f; **~ly** adj infect(e)

**beat** [biːt] (pt **beat**, pp **beaten**) n battement m; (MUS) temps m, mesure f; (of
policeman) ronde f ♦ vt, vi battre; **off
the ~en track** hors des chemins or sen-
tiers battus; **~ it!** (inf) fiche(-moi) le
camp!; **~ off** vt repousser; **~ up** vt (inf:
person) tabasser; (eggs) battre; **~ing** n
raclée f

**beautiful** ['bjuːtɪful] adj beau (belle);
**~ly** adv admirablement

**beauty** ['bjuːtɪ] n beauté f; **~ salon** n
institut de beauté; **~ spot** (BRIT) n
(TOURISM) site naturel (d'une grande
beauté)

**beaver** ['biːvəʳ] n castor m

**because** [bɪˈkɒz] conj parce que; **~ of**
prep à cause de

**beck** [bɛk] n: **to be at sb's ~ and call**
être à l'entière disposition de qn

**beckon** ['bɛkən] vt (also: **~ to**) faire signe (de venir) à

**become** [bɪˈkʌm] (irreg: like **come**) vi
devenir; **to ~ fat/thin** grossir/maigrir;
**to ~ angry** se mettre en colère

**becoming** adj (behaviour) convenable,
bienséant(e); (clothes) seyant(e)

**bed** [bɛd] n lit m; (of flowers) parterre m;
(of coal, clay) couche f; (of sea) fond m;
**to go to ~** aller se coucher; **~ and
breakfast** n (terms) chambre et petit
déjeuner; (place) ≈ chambre f d'hôte;
**~clothes** npl couvertures fpl et draps
mpl; **~ding** n literie f; **~ linen** n draps
mpl de lit (et taies fpl d'oreillers), literie
f

---

Un **bed and breakfast** est une petite
pension dans une maison particulière
ou une ferme où l'on peut louer une
chambre avec petit déjeuner compris
pour un prix modique par rapport à ce
que l'on paierait dans un hôtel. Ces
établissements sont communément
appelés B & B, et sont signalés par
une pancarte dans le jardin ou au-
dessus de la porte.

---

**bed: ~ridden** adj cloué(e) au lit;
**~room** n chambre f (à coucher); **~**
**side** n: **at sb's ~side** au chevet de
qn; **~sit(ter)** (BRIT) chambre meublée, studio m; **~spread** n couvre-lit m,
dessus-de-lit m inv; **~time** n heure f du
coucher

**bee** [biː] n abeille f

**beech** [biːtʃ] n hêtre m

**beef** [biːf] n bœuf m; **roast ~** rosbif m;
**~burger** n hamburger m; **~eater** n
hallebardier m de la Tour de Londres

**bee: ~hive** n ruche f; **~line** n: **to make
a ~line for** se diriger tout droit vers

**been** [biːn] pp of **be**

**beer** [biəʳ] n bière f

**beet** [biːt] n (vegetable) betterave f; (US:
also: **red ~**) betterave (potagère)

**beetle** ['biːtl] n scarabée m

**beetroot** ['biːtruːt] (BRIT) n betterave f

**before** [bɪˈfɔːʳ] prep (in time) avant; (in
space) devant ♦ conj avant que +sub;
avant de ♦ adv avant; devant; **~ going**
avant de partir; **~ she goes** avant
qu'elle ne parte; **the week ~** la semaine précédente or d'avant; **I've seen it
~** je l'ai déjà vu; **~hand** adv au préalable, à l'avance

**beg** [bɛg] vi mendier ♦ vt mendier; (forgiveness, mercy etc) demander; (entreat)
supplier; see also **pardon**

**began** [bɪ'gæn] *pt of* begin

**beggar** ['begə'] *n* mendiant(e)

**begin** [bɪ'gɪn] (*pt* began, *pp* begun) *vt, vi* commencer; **to ~ doing** *or* **to do sth** commencer à *or* de faire qch; **~ner** *n* débutant(e); **~ning** *n* commencement *m*, début *m*

**behalf** [bɪ'hɑːf]: *n*: **on ~ of**, (US) **in ~ of** (*representing*) de la part de; (*for benefit of*) pour le compte de; **on my/his ~** pour moi/lui

**behave** [bɪ'heɪv] *vi* se conduire, se comporter; (*well: also:* **~ o.s.**) se conduire bien *or* comme il faut; **behaviour** (US **behavior**) *n* comportement *m*, conduite *f*

**behead** [bɪ'hed] *vt* décapiter

**behind** [bɪ'haɪnd] *prep* derrière; (*time, progress*) en retard sur; (*work, studies*) en retard dans ♦ *adv* derrière ♦ *n* derrière *m*; **to be ~** (*schedule*) avoir du retard; **~ the scenes** dans les coulisses

**behold** [bɪ'həʊld] (*irreg: like* hold) *vt* apercevoir, voir

**beige** [beɪʒ] *adj* beige

**Beijing** ['beɪ'dʒɪŋ] *n* Bei-jing, Pékin

**being** ['biːɪŋ] *n* être *m*

**Beirut** [beɪ'ruːt] *n* Beyrouth

**Belarus** [belə'ruːs] *n* Bélarus *f*

**belated** [bɪ'leɪtɪd] *adj* tardif(-ive)

**belch** [beltʃ] *vi* avoir un renvoi, roter ♦ *vt* (*also:* **~ out**: *smoke etc*) vomir, cracher

**Belgian** ['beldʒən] *adj* belge, de Belgique ♦ *n* Belge *m/f*

**Belgium** ['beldʒəm] *n* Belgique *f*

**belie** [bɪ'laɪ] *vt* démentir

**belief** [bɪ'liːf] *n* (*opinion*) conviction *f*; (*trust, faith*) foi *f*

**believe** [bɪ'liːv] *vt, vi* croire; **to ~ in** (*God*) croire en; (*method, ghosts*) croire à; **~r** *n* (*in idea, activity*): **~r in** partisan(e) de; (*REL*) croyant(e)

**belittle** [bɪ'lɪtl] *vt* déprécier, rabaisser

**bell** [bel] *n* cloche *f*; (*small*) clochette *f*, grelot *m*; (*on door*) sonnette *f*; (*electric*) sonnerie *f*

**belligerent** [bɪ'lɪdʒərənt] *adj* (*person, attitude*) agressif(-ive)

**bellow** ['beləʊ] *vi* (*bull*) meugler; (*person*) brailler

**belly** ['belɪ] *n* ventre *m*

**belong** [bɪ'lɒŋ] *vi*: **to ~ to** appartenir à; (*club etc*) faire partie de; **this book ~s here** ce livre va ici; **~ings** *npl* affaires *fpl*, possessions *fpl*

**beloved** [bɪ'lʌvd] *adj* (bien-)aimé(e)

**below** [bɪ'ləʊ] *prep* sous, au-dessous de ♦ *adv* en dessous; **see ~** voir plus bas *or* plus loin *or* ci-dessous

**belt** [belt] *n* ceinture *f*; (*of land*) région *f*; (*TECH*) courroie *f* ♦ *vt* (*thrash*) donner une raclée à; **~way** (US) *n* (*AUT*) route *f* de ceinture; (: *motorway*) périphérique *m*

**bemused** [bɪ'mjuːzd] *adj* stupéfié(e)

**bench** [bentʃ] *n* (*gen, also SPORT: POL*) banc *m*; (*in workshop*) établi *m*; **the B~** (*LAW: judge*) le juge; (: *judges collectively*) la magistrature, la Cour

**bend** [bend] (*pt, pp* **bent**) *vt* courber; (*leg, arm*) plier ♦ *vi* se courber ♦ *n* (*BRIT: in road*) virage *m*, tournant *m*; (*in pipe, river*) coude *m*; **~ down** *vi* se baisser; **~ over** *vi* se pencher

**beneath** [bɪ'niːθ] *prep* sous, au-dessous de; (*unworthy of*) indigne de ♦ *adv* dessous, au-dessous, en bas

**benefactor** ['benɪfæktə'] *n* bienfaiteur *m*

**beneficial** [benɪ'fɪʃl] *adj* salutaire; avantageux(-euse); **~ to the health** bon(ne) pour la santé

**benefit** ['benɪfɪt] *n* avantage *m*, profit *m*; (*allowance of money*) allocation *f* ♦ *vt* faire du bien à, profiter à ♦ *vi*: **he'll ~ from it** cela lui fera du bien, il y gagnera *or* s'en trouvera bien

**Benelux** ['benɪlʌks] *n* Bénélux *m*

**benevolent** [bɪ'nevələnt] *adj* bienveillant(e); (*organization*) bénévole

**benign** [bɪ'naɪn] *adj* (*person, smile*) bienveillant(e), affable; (*MED*) bénin(-igne)

**bent** [bɛnt] *pt, pp of* **bend** ♦ *n* inclination *f*, penchant *m*; **to be ~ on** être résolu(e) à

**bequest** [bɪ'kwɛst] *n* legs *m*

**bereaved** [bɪ'riːvd] *n*: **the ~** la famille du disparu

**beret** ['bɛreɪ] *n* béret *m*

**Berlin** [bəː'lɪn] *n* Berlin

**berm** [bəːm] (US) *n* (AUT) accotement *m*

**Bermuda** [bəː'mjuːdə] *n* Bermudes *fpl*

**berry** ['bɛrɪ] *n* baie *f*

**berserk** [bə'səːk] *adj*: **to go ~** (*madman, crowd*) se déchaîner

**berth** [bəːθ] *n* (*bed*) couchette *f*; (*for ship*) poste *m* d'amarrage, mouillage *m* ♦ *vi* (*in harbour*) venir à quai; (*at anchor*) mouiller

**beseech** [bɪ'siːtʃ] (*pt, pp* **besought**) *vt* implorer, supplier

**beset** [bɪ'sɛt] (*pt, pp* **beset**) *vt* assaillir

**beside** [bɪ'saɪd] *prep* à côté de; **to be ~ o.s. (with anger)** être hors de soi; **that's ~ the point** cela n'a rien à voir; **~s** *adv* en outre, de plus; (*in any case*) d'ailleurs ♦ *prep* (*as well as*) en plus de

**besiege** [bɪ'siːdʒ] *vt* (*town*) assiéger; (*fig*) assaillir

**best** [bɛst] *adj* meilleur(e) ♦ *adv* le mieux; **the ~ part of** (*quantity*) le plus clair de, la plus grande partie de; **at ~** au mieux; **to make the ~ of sth** s'accommoder de qch (du mieux que l'on peut); **to do one's ~** faire de son mieux; **to the ~ of my knowledge** pour autant que je sache; **to the ~ of my ability** du mieux que je pourrai; **~ before date** *n* date *f* de limite d'utilisation or de consommation; **~ man** *n* garçon *m* d'honneur

**bestow** [bɪ'stəu] *vt*: **to ~ sth on sb** accorder qch à qn; (*title*) conférer qch à qn

**bet** [bɛt] (*pt, pp* **bet** *or* **betted**) *n* pari *m* ♦ *vt, vi* parier

**betray** [bɪ'treɪ] *vt* trahir

**better** ['bɛtəʳ] *adj* meilleur(e) ♦ *adv* mieux ♦ *vt* améliorer ♦ *n*: **to get the ~**

**of** triompher de, l'emporter sur; **you had ~ do it** vous feriez mieux de le faire; **he thought ~ of it** il s'est ravisé; **to get ~** aller mieux; s'améliorer; **~ off** *adj* plus à l'aise financièrement; (*fig*): **you'd be ~ off this way** vous vous en trouveriez mieux ainsi

**betting** ['bɛtɪŋ] *n* paris *mpl*; **~ shop** (BRIT) *n* bureau *m* de paris

**between** [bɪ'twiːn] *prep* entre ♦ *adv*: **(in)~** au milieu; dans l'intervalle; (*in time*) dans l'intervalle

**beverage** ['bɛvərɪdʒ] *n* boisson *f* (*gén sans alcool*)

**beware** [bɪ'wɛəʳ] *vi*: **to ~ (of)** prendre garde (à); **"~ of the dog"** "(attention) chien méchant"

**bewildered** [bɪ'wɪldəd] *adj* dérouté(e), ahuri(e)

**beyond** [bɪ'jɔnd] *prep* (*in space, time*) au-delà de; (*exceeding*) au-dessus de ♦ *adv* au-delà; **~ doubt** hors de doute; **~ repair** irréparable

**bias** ['baɪəs] *n* (*prejudice*) préjugé *m*, parti pris; **~(s)ed** partial(e), montrant un parti pris

**bib** [bɪb] *n* bavoir *m*, bavette *f*

**Bible** ['baɪbl] *n* Bible *f*

**bicarbonate of soda** [baɪ'kɑːbənɪt-] *n* bicarbonate *m* de soude

**bicker** ['bɪkəʳ] *vi* se chamailler

**bicycle** ['baɪsɪkl] *n* bicyclette *f*

**bid** [bɪd] (*pt* **bid** *or* **bade**, *pp* **bid(den)**) *n* offre *f*; (*at auction*) enchère *f*; (*attempt*) tentative *f* ♦ *vi* faire une enchère *or* offre ♦ *vt* faire une enchère *or* offre de; **to ~ sb good day** souhaiter le bonjour à qn; **~der** *n*: **the highest ~der** le plus offrant; **~ding** *n* enchères *fpl*

**bide** [baɪd] *vt*: **to ~ one's time** attendre son heure

**bifocals** [baɪ'fəuklz] *npl* verres *mpl* à double foyer, lunettes bifocales

**big** [bɪg] *adj* grand(e); gros(se); **~-headed** *adj* prétentieux(-euse)

**bigot** ['bɪgət] *n* fanatique *m/f*, sectaire *m/f*; **~ed** *adj* fanatique, sectaire; **~ry**

fanatisme m, sectarisme m

**big top** n grand chapiteau

**bike** [baɪk] n vélo m, bécane f

**bikini** [bɪˈkiːnɪ] n bikini m

**bilingual** [baɪˈlɪŋgwəl] adj bilingue

**bill** [bɪl] n note f, facture f; (POL) projet m de loi; (US: banknote) billet m (de banque); (of bird) bec m; (THEATRE): **on the ~** à l'affiche; **to fit** or **fill the ~** (fig) faire l'affaire; **~board** n panneau m d'affichage

**billet** [ˈbɪlɪt] n cantonnement m (chez l'habitant)

**billfold** [ˈbɪlfəʊld] n (US) portefeuille m

**billiards** [ˈbɪljədz] n (jeu de) billard m

**billion** [ˈbɪljən] n (BRIT) billion m (million de millions); (US) milliard m

**bimbo** [ˈbɪmbəʊ] (inf) n ravissante idiote f, potiche f

**bin** [bɪn] n boîte f; (also: **dustbin**) poubelle f; (for coal) coffre m

**bind** [baɪnd] (pt, pp **bound**) vt attacher; (book) relier; (oblige) obliger, contraindre ♦ n (inf: nuisance) scie f; **~ing** adj (contract) constituant une obligation

**binge** [bɪndʒ] (inf) n: **to go on a/the ~** aller faire la bringue

**bingo** [ˈbɪŋgəʊ] n jeu de loto pratiqué dans des établissements publics

**binoculars** [bɪˈnɒkjʊləz] npl jumelles fpl

**bio** prefix: **~chemistry** n biochimie f; **~degradable** adj biodégradable; **~graphy** n biographie f; **~logical** adj biologique; **~logy** n biologie f

**birch** [bɜːtʃ] n bouleau m

**bird** [bɜːd] n oiseau m; (BRIT: inf: girl) nana f; **~'s-eye view** n vue f à vol d'oiseau; (fig) vue d'ensemble or générale; **~-watcher** n ornithologue m/f amateur

**Biro** [ˈbaɪərəʊ] ® n stylo m à bille

**birth** [bɜːθ] n naissance f; **to give ~ to** (subj: woman) donner naissance à; (: animal) mettre bas; **~ certificate** n

acte m de naissance; **~ control** n (policy) limitation f des naissances; (method) méthode(s) contraceptive(s); **~day** n anniversaire m ♦ cpd d'anniversaire; **~place** n lieu m de naissance; (fig) berceau m; **~ rate** n (taux m de) natalité f

**biscuit** [ˈbɪskɪt] n (BRIT) biscuit m; (US) petit pain au lait

**bisect** [baɪˈsɛkt] vt couper or diviser en deux

**bishop** [ˈbɪʃəp] n évêque m; (CHESS) fou m

**bit** [bɪt] pt of **bite** ♦ n morceau m; (of tool) mèche f; (of horse) mors m; (COMPUT) élément m binaire; **a ~ of** un peu de; **a ~ mad** un peu fou; **~ by ~** petit à petit

**bitch** [bɪtʃ] n (dog) chienne f; (inf!) salope f (!), garce f

**bite** [baɪt] (pt **bit**, pp **bitten**) vt, vi mordre; (insect) piquer ♦ n (insect ~) piqûre f; (mouthful) bouchée f; **let's have a ~ (to eat)** (inf) mangeons un morceau; **to ~ one's nails** se ronger les ongles

**bitter** [ˈbɪtə*] adj amer(-ère); (weather, wind) glacial(e); (criticism) cinglant(e); (struggle) acharné(e) ♦ n (BRIT: beer) bière f (forte); **~ness** n amertume f; (taste) goût amer

**black** [blæk] adj noir(e) ♦ n (colour) noir m; (person): **B~** noir(e) ♦ vt (BRIT: INDUSTRY) boycotter; **to give sb a ~ eye** pocher l'œil à qn, faire un œil au beurre noir à qn; **~ and blue** couvert(e) de bleus; **to be in the ~** (in credit) être créditeur(-trice); **~berry** n mûre f; **~bird** n merle m; **~board** n tableau m; **~ coffee** n café noir; **~currant** n cassis m; **~en** vt noircir; **~ ice** n verglas m; **~leg** (BRIT) n briseur m de grève, jaune m; **~list** n liste noire f; **~mail** n chantage m ♦ vt faire chanter, soumettre au chantage; **~ market** n marché noir; **~out** n panne f d'électricité; (TV etc) interruption f d'émission; (fainting) syncope f; **~ pudding** n boudin (noir); **B~ Sea** n: **the B~ Sea** la mer Noire; **~**

sheep *n* brebis galeuse; **~smith** *n* forgeron *m*; **~ spot** (AUT) *n* point noir

**bladder** ['blædə*] *n* vessie *f*

**blade** [bleɪd] *n* lame *f*; (of propeller) pale *f*; **~ of grass** brin *m* d'herbe

**blame** [bleɪm] *n* faute *f*, blâme *m* ♦ *vt*: **to ~ sb/sth for sth** attribuer à qn/qch la responsabilité de qch; reprocher qch à qn/qch; **who's to ~?** qui est le fautif *or* coupable *or* responsable?

**bland** [blænd] *adj* (taste, food) doux (douce), fade

**blank** [blæŋk] *adj* blanc (blanche); (look) sans expression, dénué(e) d'expression ♦ *n* espace *m* vide, blanc *m*; (cartridge) cartouche *f* à blanc; **his mind was a ~** il avait la tête vide; **~ cheque** chèque *m* en blanc

**blanket** ['blæŋkɪt] *n* couverture *f*; (of snow, cloud) couche *f*

**blare** [blɛə*] *vi* beugler

**blast** [blɑːst] *n* souffle *m*; (of explosive) explosion *f* ♦ *vt* faire sauter *or* exploser; **~-off** *n* (SPACE) lancement *m*

**blatant** ['bleɪtənt] *adj* flagrant(e), criant(e)

**blaze** [bleɪz] *n* (fire) incendie *m*; (fig) flamboiement *m* ♦ *vi* (fire) flamber; (fig: eyes) flamboyer; (: guns) crépiter ♦ *vt*: **to ~ a trail** (fig) montrer la voie

**blazer** ['bleɪzə*] *n* blazer *m*

**bleach** [bliːtʃ] *n* (also: **household ~**) eau *f* de Javel ♦ *vt* (linen etc) blanchir; **~ed** *adj* (hair) oxygéné(e), décoloré(e)

**bleak** [bliːk] *adj* morne, (countryside) désolé(e)

**bleat** [bliːt] *vi* bêler

**bleed** [bliːd] (*pt, pp* **bled**) *vt, vi* saigner; **my nose is ~ing** je saigne du nez

**bleeper** ['bliːpə*] *n* (device) bip *m*

**blemish** ['blemɪʃ] *n* défaut *m*; (on fruit, reputation) tache *f*

**blend** [blend] *n* mélange *m* ♦ *vt* mélanger ♦ *vi* (colours etc: also: **~ in**) se mélanger, se fondre; **~er** *n* mixeur *m*

**bless** [bles] (*pt, pp* **blessed** *or* **blest**) *vt* bénir; **~ you!** (after sneeze) à vos sou-

haits!; **~ing** *n* bénédiction *f*; (godsend) bienfait *m*

**blew** [bluː] *pt of* **blow**

**blight** [blaɪt] *vt* (hopes etc) anéantir; (life) briser

**blimey** ['blaɪmɪ] (BRIT: inf) excl mince alors!

**blind** [blaɪnd] *adj* aveugle ♦ *n* (for window) store *m* ♦ *vt* aveugler; **~ alley** *n* impasse *f*; **~ corner** (BRIT) *n* virage *m* sans visibilité; **~fold** *n* bandeau *m* ♦ *adj, adv* les yeux bandés ♦ *vt* bander les yeux à; **~ly** *adv* aveuglément; **~ness** *n* cécité *f*; **~ spot** *n* (AUT etc) angle mort; **that is her ~ spot** (fig) elle refuse d'y voir clair sur ce point

**blink** [blɪŋk] *vi* cligner des yeux; (light) clignoter; **~ers** *npl* œillères *fpl*

**bliss** [blɪs] *n* félicité *f*, bonheur *m* sans mélange

**blister** ['blɪstə*] *n* (on skin) ampoule *f*, cloque *f*; (on paintwork, rubber) boursouflure *f* ♦ *vi* (paint) se boursoufler, se cloquer

**blizzard** ['blɪzəd] *n* blizzard *m*, tempête *f* de neige

**bloated** ['bləʊtɪd] *adj* (face) bouffi(e); (stomach, person) gonflé(e)

**blob** [blɒb] *n* (drop) goutte *f*; (stain, spot) tache *f*

**block** [blɒk] *n* bloc *m*; (in pipes) obstruction *f*; (toy) cube *m*; (of buildings) pâté *m* (de maisons) ♦ *vt* bloquer; **to ~ flats** (BRIT) immeuble (locatif); **mental ~** trou *m* de mémoire; **~ade** [blɒ'keɪd] *n* blocus *m*; **~age** *n* obstruction *f*; **~buster** *n* (film, book) grand succès; **~ letters** *npl* majuscules *fpl*

**bloke** [bləʊk] (BRIT: inf) *n* type *m*

**blond(e)** [blɒnd] *adj, n* blond(e)

**blood** [blʌd] *n* sang *m*; **~ donor** *n* donneur(-euse) de sang; **~ group** *n* groupe sanguin; **~hound** *n* limier *m*; **~ poisoning** *n* empoisonnement *m* du sang; **~ pressure** *n* tension *f* (artérielle); **~shed** *n* effusion *f* de sang, carnage *m*; **~ sports** *npl* sports *mpl* sanguinaires; **~shot** *adj*: **~shot eyes** yeux injectés de sang; **~stream** *n* sang *m*, système sanguin; **~ test** *n* prise *f* de sang; **~thirsty** *adj* sanguinaire; **~ vessel** *n* vaisseau sanguin; **~y** *adj* sanglant(e); (*nose*) en sang; (BRIT: infl): **this ~y ...** ce foutu ... (*!*), ce putain de ... (*!*); **~y strong/good** vachement *or* sacrément fort/bon; **~y-minded** (BRIT: inf) *adj* contrariant(e), obstiné(e)

**bloom** [bluːm] *n* fleur *f* ♦ *vi* être en fleur

**blossom** ['blɒsəm] *n* fleur(s) *f(pl)* ♦ *vi* être en fleurs; (*fig*) s'épanouir; **to ~ into** devenir

**blot** [blɒt] *n* tache *f* ♦ *vt* tacher; **~ out** *vt* (*memories*) effacer; (*view*) cacher, masquer

**blotchy** ['blɒtʃɪ] *adj* (*complexion*) couvert(e) de marbrures

**blotting paper** ['blɒtɪŋ-] *n* buvard *m*

**blouse** [blauz] *n* chemisier *m*, corsage *m*

**blow** [bləu] (*pt* **blew**, *pp* **blown**) *n* coup *m* ♦ *vi* souffler ♦ *vt* souffler; (*fuse*) faire sauter; (*instrument*) jouer de; **to ~ one's nose** se moucher; **to ~ a whistle** siffler; **~ away** *vt* chasser, faire s'envoler; **~ down** *vt* faire tomber, renverser; **~ off** *vt* emporter; **~ out** *vi* (*fire, flame*) s'éteindre; **~ over** *vi* s'apaiser; **~ up** *vi* faire sauter; (*tyre*) gonfler; (PHOT) agrandir ♦ *vi* exploser, sauter; **~dry** *n* brushing *m*; **~lamp** (BRIT) *n* chalumeau *m*; **~out** *n* (*of tyre*) éclatement *m*; **~torch** *n* = blowlamp

**blue** [bluː] *adj* bleu(e); (*fig*) triste; **~s** *n* (MUS): **the ~s** le blues; **~ film/joke** film *m*/histoire *f* pornographique; **to come out of the ~** (*fig*) être complètement inattendu; **~bell** *n* jacinthe *f* des bois; **~bottle** *n* mouche *f* à viande; **~print** *n* (*fig*) projet *m*, plan directeur

**bluff** [blʌf] *vi* bluffer ♦ *n* bluff *m*; **to call sb's ~** mettre qn au défi d'exécuter ses menaces

**blunder** ['blʌndə<sup>r</sup>] *n* gaffe *f*, bévue *f* ♦ *vi* faire une gaffe *or* une bévue

**blunt** [blʌnt] *adj* (*person*) brusque, ne mâchant pas ses mots; (*knife*) émoussé(e), peu tranchant(e); (*pencil*) mal taillé

**blur** [bləː<sup>r</sup>] *n* tache *or* masse floue *or* confuse ♦ *vt* brouiller

**blush** [blʌʃ] *vi* rougir ♦ *n* rougeur *f*

**blustery** ['blʌstərɪ] *adj* (*weather*) à bourrasques

**boar** [bɔː<sup>r</sup>] *n* sanglier *m*

**board** [bɔːd] *n* planche *f*; (*on wall*) panneau *m*; (*for chess*) échiquier *m*; (*cardboard*) carton *m*; (*committee*) conseil *m*, comité *m*; (*in firm*) conseil d'administration; (NAUT, AVIAT): **on ~** à bord ♦ *vt* (*ship*) monter à bord de; (*train*) monter dans; **full ~** (BRIT) pension complète; **half ~** demi-pension *f*; **~ and lodging** chambre *f* avec pension; **which goes by the ~** (*fig*) qu'on laisse tomber, qu'on abandonne; **~ up** *vt* (*door, window*) boucher; **~er** *n* (SCOL) interne *m/f*, pensionnaire; **~ game** *n* jeu *m* de société; **~ing card** *n* **= boarding pass**; **~ing house** *n* pension *f*; **~ing pass** *n* (AVIAT, NAUT) carte *f* d'embarquement; **~ing school** *n* internat *m*, pensionnat *m*; **~ room** *n* salle *f* du conseil d'administration

**boast** [bəust] *vi*: **to ~ (about** *or* **of)** se vanter (de)

**boat** [bəut] *n* bateau *m*; (*small*) canot *m*; barque *f*; **~ train** *n* train *m* (qui assure correspondance avec le ferry)

**bob** [bɒb] *vi* (*boat, cork on water: also:* **~ up and down**) danser, se balancer

**bobby** ['bɒbɪ] (BRIT: inf) *n* ≈ agent *m* (de police)

**bobsleigh** ['bɒbsleɪ] *n* bob *m*

**bode** [bəud] *vi*: **to ~ well/ill (for)** être de bon/mauvais augure (pour)

**bodily** ['bɒdɪlɪ] *adj* corporel(le) ♦ *adv* dans ses bras

**body** ['bɒdɪ] *n* corps *m*; (*of car*) carrosserie *f*; (*of plane*) fuselage *m*; (*fig*: society) organe m, organisme m; (: quantity) ensemble m, masse f; (of wine) corps; **~building** n culturisme; **~guard** n garde m du corps; **~work** n carrosserie f

**bog** [bɔg] n tourbière f ♦ vt: **to get ~ged down** (fig) s'enliser

**bog-standard** (inf) adj tout à fait ordinaire

**bogus** ['bəugəs] adj bidon inv; fantôme

**boil** [bɔil] vt (faire) bouillir ♦ vi bouillir ♦ n (MED) furoncle m; **to come to the** (BRIT) **~** or **a** (US) **~** bouillir; **~ down to** vt fus (fig) se réduire or ramener à; **~ over** vi déborder; **~ed egg** n œuf m à la coque; **~ed potatoes** npl pommes fpl à l'anglaise or à l'eau; **~er** n chaudière f; **~er suit** (BRIT) n bleu m or cotte f de travail; **~ing** adj (person): **I'm ~ing** (hot) (inf) je crève de chaud; **~ing point** n point m d'ébullition

**boisterous** ['bɔistərəs] adj bruyant(e), tapageur(-euse)

**bold** [bəuld] adj hardi(e), audacieux(-euse); (pej) effronté(e); (outline, colour) franc (franche), tranché(e), marqué(e); (pattern) grand(e)

**bollard** ['bɔlɑːd] (BRIT) n (AUT) borne lumineuse or de signalisation

**bolt** [bəult] n (lock) verrou m; (with nut) boulon m ♦ adv: **~ upright** droit(e) comme un piquet ♦ vt verrouiller; (TECH: also: **~ on, ~ together**) boulonner; (food) engloutir ♦ vi (horse) s'emballer

**bomb** [bɔm] n bombe f ♦ vt bombarder; **~ing** n (by terrorist) attentat m à la bombe; **~ disposal unit** n section f de déminage; **~er** n (AVIAT) bombardier m; **~shell** n (fig) bombe f

**bond** [bɔnd] n lien m; (binding promise) engagement m, obligation f; (COMM) obligation; **in ~** (of goods) en douane

**bondage** ['bɔndidʒ] n esclavage m

**bone** [bəun] n os m; (of fish) arête f ♦ vt désosser; ôter les arêtes de; **~ dry** adj complètement sec (sèche); **~ idle** adj fainéant(e); **~ marrow** n moelle f osseuse

**bonfire** ['bɔnfaiər] n feu m (de joie);

(for rubbish) feu

**bonnet** ['bɔnit] n bonnet m; (BRIT: of car) capot m

**bonus** ['bəunəs] n prime f, gratification f

**bony** ['bəuni] adj (arm, face, MED: tissue) osseux(-euse); (meat) plein(e) d'os; (fish) plein d'arêtes

**boo** [buː] excl hou!, peuh! ♦ vt huer

**booby trap** ['buːbi-] n engin piégé

**book** [buk] n livre m; (of stamps, tickets) carnet m ♦ vt (ticket) prendre; (seat, room) réserver; (driver) dresser un procès-verbal à; (football player) prendre le nom de; **~s** npl (accounts) comptes mpl, comptabilité f; **~case** n bibliothèque f (meuble); **~ing office** (BRIT) n bureau m de location; **~keeping** n comptabilité f; **~let** n brochure f; **~maker** n bookmaker m; **~seller** n libraire m/f; **~shelf** n (single) étagère f (à livres); **~shop** n librairie f; **~store** n librairie f

**boom** [buːm] n (noise) grondement m; (in prices, population) forte augmentation f ♦ vi gronder; prospérer

**boon** [buːn] n bénédiction f, grand avantage

**boost** [buːst] n stimulant m, remontant m ♦ vt stimuler; **~er** n (MED) rappel m

**boot** [buːt] n botte f; (for hiking) chaussure f (de marche); (for football etc) soulier m; (BRIT: of car) coffre m ♦ vt (COMPUT) amorcer, initialiser; **to ~** (in addition) par-dessus le marché

**booth** [buːð] n (at fair) baraque (foraine); (telephone etc) cabine f; (also: **voting ~**) isoloir m

**booze** [buːz] (inf) n boissons fpl alcooliques, alcool m

**border** ['bɔːdər] n bordure f; bord m; (of a country) frontière f; (also: **~ on**: country) être limitrophe de; **B~s** (BRIT) n: **the B~s** la région frontière entre l'Écosse et l'Angleterre; **~ on** vt fus être voisin(e) de, toucher à; **~line** n (fig) ligne f de démarcation; **~line case**

cas *m* limite

**bore** [bɔːʳ] *pt of* **bear** ♦ *vt* (*hole*) percer; (*oil well, tunnel*) creuser; (*person*) ennuyer, raser ♦ *n* raseur(-euse); (*of gun*) calibre *m*; **to be ~d** s'ennuyer; **~dom** *n* ennui *m*; **boring** *adj* ennuyeux(-euse)

**born** [bɔːn] *adj*: **to be ~** naître; **I was ~ in 1960** je suis né en 1960

**borne** [bɔːn] *pp of* **bear**

**borough** ['bʌrə] *n* municipalité *f*

**borrow** ['bɔrəu] *vt*: **to ~ sth (from sb)** emprunter qch (à qn)

**Bosnia (and) Herzegovina** ['bɔznɪə(ænd)hɜːtsəgəu'viːnə] *n* Bosnie-Herzégovine *f*; **Bosnian** *adj* bosniaque, bosnien(ne) ♦ *n* Bosniaque *m/f*

**bosom** ['buzəm] *n* poitrine *f*; (*fig*) sein *m*

**boss** [bɔs] *n* patron(ne) ♦ *vt* (*also: ~ around/about*) mener à la baguette; **~y** *adj* autoritaire

**bosun** ['bəusn] *n* maître *m* d'équipage

**botany** ['bɔtənɪ] *n* botanique *f*

**botch** [bɔtʃ] *vt* (*also: ~ up*) saboter, bâcler

**both** [bəuθ] *adj* les deux, l'un(e) et l'autre ♦ *pron*: **~ (of them)** les deux, tous (toutes) (les) deux, l'un(e) et l'autre; **they sell ~ the fabric and the finished curtains** ils vendent (et) le tissu et les rideaux (finis), ils vendent à la fois le tissu et les rideaux (finis); **~ of us went, we ~ went** nous sommes allés (tous) les deux

**bother** ['bɔðəʳ] *vt* (*worry*) tracasser; (*disturb*) déranger ♦ *vi* (*also: ~ o.s.*) se tracasser, se faire du souci ♦ *n*: **it is a ~ to have to do** c'est vraiment ennuyeux d'avoir à faire; **it's no ~** aucun problème; **to ~ doing** prendre la peine de faire

**bottle** ['bɔtl] *n* bouteille *f*; (*baby's*): biberon *m* ♦ *vt* mettre en bouteille(s); **~d beer** bière *f* en canette; **~d water** eau minérale; **~ up** *vt* refouler, contenir; **~ bank** *n* conteneur *m* à verre; **~neck** *n* étranglement *m*; **~-opener** *n* ouvre-

bouteille *m*

**bottom** ['bɔtəm] *n* (*of container, sea etc*) fond *m*; (*buttocks*) derrière *m*; (*of page, list*) bas *m* ♦ *adj* du fond; du bas; **the ~ of the class** le dernier de la classe

**bough** [bau] *n* branche *f*, rameau *m*

**bought** [bɔːt] *pt, pp of* **buy**

**boulder** ['bəuldəʳ] *n* gros rocher

**bounce** [bauns] *vi* (*ball*) rebondir; (*cheque*) être refusé(e); (*étant sans provision*) ♦ *vt* faire rebondir ♦ *n* (*rebound*) rebond *m*; **~r** (*inf*) *n* (*at dance, club*) videur *m*

**bound** [baund] *pt, pp of* **bind** ♦ *n* (*gen pl*) limite *f*; (*leap*) bond *m* ♦ *vi* (*leap*) bondir ♦ *vt* (*limit*) borner ♦ *adj*: **to be ~ to do sth** (*obliged*) être obligé(e) or avoir obligation de faire qch; **he's ~ to fail** (*likely*) il est sûr d'échouer, son échec est inévitable or assuré; **~ by** (*law, regulation*) engagé(e) par; **~ for** à destination de; **out of ~s** dont l'accès est interdit

**boundary** ['baundrɪ] *n* frontière *f*

**bout** [baut] *n* période *f*; (*of malaria etc*) accès *m*, crise *f*, attaque *f*; (*BOXING etc*) combat *m*, match *m*

**bow**[1] [bəu] *n* nœud *m*; (*weapon*) arc *m*; (*MUS*) archet *m*

**bow**[2] [bau] *n* (*with body*) révérence *f*, inclination *f* (du buste *or* corps); (*NAUT*: *also*: **~s**) proue *f* ♦ *vi* faire une révérence, s'incliner; (*yield*): **to ~ to** *or* **before** s'incliner devant, se soumettre à

**bowels** [bauəlz] *npl* intestins *mpl*; (*fig*) entrailles *fpl*

**bowl** [bəul] *n* (*for eating*) bol *m*; (*ball*) boule *f* ♦ *vi* (*CRICKET, BASEBALL*) lancer (la balle)

**bow-legged** ['bəu'legɪd] *adj* aux jambes arquées

**bowler** ['bəuləʳ] *n* (*CRICKET, BASEBALL*) lanceur *m* (de la balle); (*BRIT*: *also*: **~ hat**) (chapeau *m*) melon *m*

**bowling** ['bəulɪŋ] *n* (*game*) jeu *m* de boules; jeu *m* de quilles; **~ alley** *n* bowling *m*; **~ green** *n* terrain *m* de boules (*gazonné et carré*)

**bowls** [bəʊlz] *n* (*game*) (jeu *m* de) boules *fpl*

**bow tie** [bəʊ-] *n* nœud *m* papillon

**box** [bɒks] *n* boîte *f*; (*also:* **cardboard ~**) carton *m*; (THEATRE) loge *f* ♦ *vt* mettre en boîte; (SPORT) boxer avec ♦ *vi* boxer, faire de la boxe; **~er** *n* (*person*) boxeur *m*; **~er shorts** *npl* caleçon *msg*; **~ing** *n* (SPORT) boxe *f*; **B~ing Day** *n* le lendemain de Noël; **~ing gloves** *npl* gants *mpl* de boxe; **~ing ring** *n* ring *m*; **~ office** *n* bureau *m* de location; **~room** *n* débarras *m*; chambrette *f*

**boy** [bɔɪ] *n* garçon *m*

**boycott** ['bɔɪkɒt] *n* boycottage *m* ♦ *vt* boycotter

**boyfriend** ['bɔɪfrɛnd] *n* (petit) ami

**boyish** ['bɔɪɪʃ] *adj* (*behaviour*) de garçon; (*girl*) garçonnier(-ière)

**BR** *n abbr* = **British Rail**

**bra** [brɑː] *n* soutien-gorge *m*

**brace** [breɪs] *n* (*on teeth*) appareil *m* (dentaire); (*tool*) vilbrequin *m* ♦ *vt* (*knees, shoulders*) appuyer; **~s** *npl* (BRIT: *for trousers*) bretelles *fpl*; **to ~ o.s.** (*lit*) s'arc-bouter; (*fig*) se préparer mentalement

**bracelet** ['breɪslɪt] *n* bracelet *m*

**bracing** ['breɪsɪŋ] *adj* tonifiant(e), tonique

**bracket** ['brækɪt] *n* (TECH) tasseau *m*, support *m*; (*group*) classe *f*, tranche *f*; (*also:* **brace ~**) accolade *f*; (*also:* **round ~**) parenthèse *f*; (*also:* **square ~**) cro-

chet *m* ♦ *vt* mettre entre parenthèse(s); (*fig: also:* **~ together**) regrouper

**brag** [bræg] *vi* se vanter

**braid** [breɪd] *n* (*trimming*) galon *m*; (*of hair*) tresse *f*

**brain** [breɪn] *n* cerveau *m*; **~s** *npl* (*intellect,* CULIN) cervelle *f*; **he's got ~s** il est intelligent; **~wash** *vt* faire subir un lavage de cerveau à; **~wave** *n* idée *f* géniale; **~y** *adj* intelligent(e), doué(e)

**braise** [breɪz] *vt* braiser

**brake** [breɪk] *n* (*on vehicle, also fig*) frein *m* ♦ *vi* freiner; **~ light** *n* feu *m* de stop

**bran** [bræn] *n* son *m*

**branch** [brɑːntʃ] *n* branche *f*; (COMM) succursale *f* ♦ *vi* bifurquer; **~ out** *vi* (*fig*): **to ~ out into** étendre ses activités à

**brand** [brænd] *n* marque (commerciale) ♦ *vt* (*cattle*) marquer (au fer rouge); **~new** *adj* tout(e) neuf (neuve), flambant neuf (neuve)

**brandy** ['brændɪ] *n* cognac *m*, fine *f*

**brash** [bræʃ] *adj* effronté(e)

**brass** [brɑːs] *n* cuivre *m* (jaune), laiton *m*; **the ~** (MUS) les cuivres; **~ band** *n* fanfare *f*

**brat** [bræt] (*pej*) *n* mioche *m/f*, môme *m/f*

**brave** [breɪv] *adj* courageux(-euse), brave ♦ *n* guerrier indien ♦ *vt* braver, affronter; **~ry** *n* bravoure *f*, courage *m*

**brawl** [brɔːl] *n* rixe *f*, bagarre *f*

**brazen** ['breɪzn] *adj* impudent(e), effronté(e) ♦ *vt*: **to ~ it out** payer d'effronterie, crâner

**brazier** ['breɪzɪə] *n* brasero *m*

**Brazil** [brə'zɪl] *n* Brésil *m*

**breach** [briːtʃ] *vt* ouvrir une brèche dans ♦ *n* (*gap*) brèche *f*; (*breaking*): **~ of contract** rupture *f* de contrat; **~ of the peace** attentat *m* à l'ordre public

**bread** [brɛd] *n* pain *m*; **~ and butter** *n* tartines (beurrées); (*fig*) subsistance *f*; **~bin** (BRIT) *n* boîte *f* à pain; (*bigger*) huche *f* à pain; **~crumbs** *npl* miettes *fpl* de pain; (CULIN) chapelure f, panure f; **~line** n: **to be on the ~line** être sans le sou or dans l'indigence

**breadth** [brɛtθ] n largeur f; (fig) ampleur f

**breadwinner** ['brɛdwɪnə*] n soutien m de famille

**break** [breɪk] (pt **broke**, pp **broken**) vt casser, briser; (promise) rompre; (law) violer ♦ vi (se) casser, se briser; (weather) tourner; (story, news) se répandre; (day) se lever ♦ n (gap) brèche f; (fracture) cassure f; (pause, interval) interruption f, arrêt m; (: short) pause f; (at school) récréation f; (chance) chance f, occasion f favorable; **to ~ one's leg** etc se casser la jambe etc; **to ~ a record** battre un record; **to ~ the news to sb** annoncer la nouvelle à qn; **~ even** rentrer dans ses frais; **~ free** or **loose** se dégager, s'échapper; **~ open** (door etc) forcer, fracturer; **~ down** vt (figures, data) décomposer, analyser ♦ vi s'effondrer; (MED) faire une dépression (nerveuse); (AUT) tomber en panne; **~ in** vt (horse etc) dresser ♦ vi (burglar) entrer par effraction; (interrupt) interrompre; **~ into** vt fus (house) s'introduire or pénétrer par effraction dans; **~ off** vi (speaker) s'interrompre; (branch) se rompre; **~ out** vi éclater, se déclarer; (prisoner) s'évader; **to ~ out in spots** or **a rash** avoir une éruption de boutons; **~ up** vi (ship) se disloquer; (crowd, meeting) se disperser, se séparer; (marriage) se briser; (SCOL) entrer en vacances ♦ vt casser; (fight etc) interrompre, faire cesser; **~age** n casse f; **~down** n (AUT) panne f; (in communications, marriage) rupture f; (MED: also: **nervous ~down**) dépression (nerveuse); (of statistics) ventilation f; **~down van** (BRIT) dépanneuse f; **~er** n brisant m

**breakfast** ['brɛkfəst] n petit déjeuner

**break:** **~-in** n cambriolage m; **~ing and entering** n (LAW) effraction f; **~through** n percée f; **~water** n brise-

lames m inv, digue f

**breast** [brɛst] n (of woman) sein m; (chest, of meat) poitrine f; **~-feed** (irreg: like **feed**) vt, vi allaiter; **~-stroke** n brasse f

**breath** [brɛθ] n haleine f; **out of ~** à bout de souffle, essoufflé(e); **B~alyser ®** ['brɛθəlaɪzə*] n Alcootest ®

**breathe** [briːð] vt, vi respirer; **~ in** vt, vi aspirer, inspirer; **~ out** vt, vi expirer; **~r** n moment m de repos or de répit; **breathing** n respiration f

**breathless** ['brɛθlɪs] adj essoufflé(e), haletant(e)

**breathtaking** ['brɛθteɪkɪŋ] adj stupéfiant(e)

**breed** [briːd] (pt, pp **bred**) vt élever, faire l'élevage de ♦ vi se reproduire ♦ n race f, variété f; **~ing** n (upbringing) éducation f

**breeze** [briːz] n brise f; **breezy** adj frais (fraîche); aéré(e); (manner etc) désinvolte, jovial(e)

**brevity** ['brɛvɪtɪ] n brièveté f

**brew** [bruː] vt (tea) faire infuser; (beer) brasser ♦ vi (fig) se préparer, couver; **~ery** n brasserie f (fabrique)

**bribe** [braɪb] n pot-de-vin m ♦ vt acheter; soudoyer; **~ry** n corruption f

**brick** [brɪk] n brique f; **~layer** n maçon m

**bridal** ['braɪdl] adj nuptial(e)

**bride** [braɪd] n mariée f, épouse f; **~groom** n marié m, époux m; **~smaid** n demoiselle f d'honneur

**bridge** [brɪdʒ] n pont m; (NAUT) passerelle f (de commandement); (of nose) arête f; (CARDS, DENTISTRY) bridge m ♦ vt (fig: gap, gulf) combler

**bridle** ['braɪdl] n bride f; **~ path** n piste or allée cavalière

**brief** [briːf] adj bref (brève) ♦ n (LAW) dossier m, cause f; (gen) tâche f ♦ vt mettre au courant; **~s** npl (undergarment) slip m; **~case** n serviette f, porte-documents m inv; **~ly** adv brièvement

**bright** [braɪt] *adj* brillant(e); *(room, weather)* clair(e); *(clever: person, idea)* intelligent(e); *(cheerful: colour, person)* vif *(vive)*

**brighten** ['braɪtn] *(also: ~ up) vt (room)* éclaircir, égayer; *(event)* égayer ♦ *vi* s'éclaircir; *(person)* retrouver un peu de sa gaieté; *(face)* s'éclairer; *(prospects)* s'améliorer

**brilliance** ['brɪljəns] *n* éclat *m*

**brilliant** ['brɪljənt] *adj* brillant(e); *(sunshine, light)* éclatant(e); *(inf: holiday etc)* super

**brim** [brɪm] *n* bord *m*

**brine** [braɪn] *n (CULIN)* saumure *f*

**bring** [brɪŋ] *(pt, pp brought) vt* apporter; *(person)* amener; **~ about** *vt* provoquer, entraîner; **~ back** *vt* rapporter; *(restore: hanging)* réinstaurer; **~ down** *vt (price)* faire baisser; *(enemy plane)* descendre; *(government)* faire tomber; **~ forward** *vt* avancer; **~ off** *vt (task, plan)* réussir, mener à bien; **~ out** *vt (meaning)* faire ressortir; *(book)* publier; *(object)* sortir; **~ round** *vt (unconscious person)* ranimer; **~ up** *vt (child)* élever; *(carry up)* monter; *(question)* soulever; *(food: vomit)* vomir, rendre

**brink** [brɪŋk] *n* bord *m*

**brisk** [brɪsk] *adj* vif *(vive)*

**bristle** ['brɪsl] *n* poil *m* ♦ *vi* se hérisser

**Britain** ['brɪtən] *n (also: Great ~)* Grande-Bretagne *f*

**British** ['brɪtɪʃ] *adj* britannique ♦ *npl*: **the ~** les Britanniques *mpl*; **~ Isles** *npl*: **the ~ Isles** les îles *fpl* Britanniques; **~ Rail** *n* compagnie ferroviaire britannique

**Briton** ['brɪtən] *n* Britannique *m/f*

**Brittany** ['brɪtənɪ] *n* Bretagne *f*

**brittle** ['brɪtl] *adj* cassant(e), fragile

**broach** [brəʊtʃ] *vt (subject)* aborder

**broad** [brɔːd] *adj* large; *(general: outlines)* grand(e); *(: distinction)* général(e); *(accent)* prononcé(e); **in ~ daylight** en plein jour; **~cast** *(pt, pp broadcast) n* émission *f* ♦ *vt* radiodiffuser; téléviser ♦

*vi* émettre; **~en** *vt* élargir ♦ *vi* s'élargir; **to ~en one's mind** élargir ses horizons; **~ly** *adv* en gros, généralement; **~-minded** *adj* large d'esprit

**broccoli** ['brɒkəlɪ] *n* brocoli *m*

**brochure** ['brəʊʃjʊə] *n* prospectus *m*, dépliant *m*

**broil** [brɔɪl] *vt* griller

**broke** [brəʊk] *pt of* **break** ♦ *adj* fauché(e)

**broken** ['brəʊkn] *pp of* **break** ♦ *adj* cassé(e); *(machine: also: ~ down)* fichu(e); **in ~ English/French** dans un anglais/ français approximatif *or* hésitant; **~ leg** *etc* jambe *etc* cassée; **~-hearted** *adj* (ayant) le cœur brisé

**broker** ['brəʊkə] *n* courtier *m*

**brolly** ['brɒlɪ] *(BRIT: inf) n* pépin *m*, parapluie *m*

**bronchitis** [brɒŋ'kaɪtɪs] *n* bronchite *f*

**bronze** [brɒnz] *n* bronze *m*

**brooch** [brəʊtʃ] *n* broche *f*

**brood** [bruːd] *n* couvée *f* ♦ *vi (person)* méditer (sombrement), ruminer

**broom** [bruːm] *n* balai *m*; *(BOT)* genêt *m*; **~stick** *n* manche *m* à balai

**Bros.** *abbr* = **Brothers**

**broth** [brɒθ] *n* bouillon *m* de viande et de légumes

**brothel** ['brɒθl] *n* maison close, bordel *m*

**brother** ['brʌðə] *n* frère *m*; **~-in-law** *n* beau-frère *m*

**brought** [brɔːt] *pt, pp of* **bring**

**brow** [braʊ] *n* front *m*; *(eyebrow)* sourcil *m*; *(of hill)* sommet *m*

**brown** [braʊn] *adj* brun(e), marron *inv*; *(hair)* châtain *inv*, brun; *(eyes)* marron *inv*; *(tanned)* bronzé(e) ♦ *n (colour)* brun *m* ♦ *vt (CULIN)* faire dorer; **~ bread** *n* pain *m* bis; **B~ie** *n (also: B~ie Guide)* jeannette *f*, éclaireuse *(cadette)*; **~ie** *n (US) (n cake)* gâteau *m* au chocolat et aux noix; **~ paper** *n* papier *m* d'emballage; **~ sugar** *n* cassonade *f*

**browse** [braʊz] *vi (among books)* bouquiner, feuilleter les livres; **to ~**

**through a book** feuilleter un livre
**browser** ['brauzə*] n (COMPUT) navigateur m
**bruise** [bru:z] n bleu m, contusion f ♦ vt
contusionner, meurtrir
**brunette** [bru:'net] n (femme) brune
**brunt** [brʌnt] n: **the ~ of** (attack, criticism etc) le plus gros de
**brush** [brʌʃ] n brosse f; (painting) pinceau m; (shaving) blaireau m; (quarrel)
accrochage m, prise f de bec ♦ vt brosser; (also: ~ against) effleurer, frôler; **~
aside** vt écarter, balayer; **~ up** vt
(knowledge) rafraîchir, réviser; **~wood**
n broussailles fpl, taillis m
**Brussels** ['brʌslz] n Bruxelles; **~
sprout** n chou m de Bruxelles
**brutal** ['bru:tl] adj brutal(e)
**brute** [bru:t] n brute f ♦ adj: **by ~ force**
par la force
**BSc** abbr = Bachelor of Science
**BSE** n abbr (= bovine spongiform encepha-
lopathy) ESB f, BSE f
**bubble** ['bʌbl] n bulle f ♦ vi bouillonner, faire des bulles; (sparkle) pétiller; **~
bath** n bain moussant; **~ gum** n bub-
blegum m
**buck** [bʌk] n mâle m (d'un lapin, daim
etc); (US: inf) dollar m ♦ vi ruer, lancer
une ruade; **to pass the ~ (to sb)** se
décharger de la responsabilité (sur qn);
**~ up** vi (cheer up) reprendre du poil de
la bête, se remonter
**bucket** ['bʌkɪt] n seau m

**buckle** ['bʌkl] n boucle f ♦ vt (belt etc)
boucler, attacher ♦ vi (warp) tordre,
gauchir; (: wheel) se voiler; se déformer
**bud** [bʌd] n bourgeon m; (of flower)

**bouton** m ♦ vi bourgeonner; (flower)
éclore
**Buddhism** ['budɪzəm] n bouddhisme m
**Buddhist** adj bouddhiste ♦ n Bouddhiste m/f
**budding** ['bʌdɪŋ] adj (poet etc) en herbe; (passion etc) naissant(e)
**buddy** ['bʌdɪ] (US) n copain m
**budge** [bʌdʒ] vt faire bouger; (fig: person) faire changer d'avis ♦ vi bouger;
changer d'avis
**budgerigar** ['bʌdʒərɪɡɑ:*] n (BRIT) n perruche f
**budget** ['bʌdʒɪt] n budget m ♦ vi: **to ~
for sth** inscrire qch au budget
**budgie** ['bʌdʒɪ] (BRIT) n = budgerigar
**buff** [bʌf] adj (colour f) chamois m ♦ n
(inf: enthusiast) mordu(e); **he's a ~ ...**
c'est un mordu de ...
**buffalo** ['bʌfələu] (pl ~ or ~es) n buffle
m; (US) bison m
**buffer** ['bʌfə*] n tampon m; (COMPUT)
mémoire f tampon
**buffet¹** ['bʌfeɪ] vt secouer, ébranler
**buffet²** ['bufeɪ] n (food, BRIT: bar) buffet
m; **~ car** n (BRIT) n (RAIL) voiture-buffet f
**bug** [bʌɡ] n (insect) punaise f; (: insect)
insecte m, bestiole f; (fig: germ) virus m,
microbe m; (COMPUT) erreur f; (fig: spy
device) dispositif m d'écoute (électronique) ♦ vt garnir de dispositifs d'écoute;
(inf: annoy) embêter; **~ged** adj sur
écoute
**bugle** ['bju:ɡl] n clairon m
**build** [bɪld] (pt, pp **built**) n (of person)
carrure f, charpente f ♦ vt construire,
bâtir; **~ up** vt accumuler, amasser; accroître; **~er** n entrepreneur m; **~ing** n
(trade) construction f; (house, structure)
bâtiment m, construction; (offices, flats)
immeuble m; **~ing society** (BRIT) n société f de crédit immobilier

tuelles offrent deux services principaux: on peut y avoir un compte
d'épargne duquel on peut retirer son
argent sur demande ou moyennant un
court préavis; et on peut également y
faire des emprunts à long terme, par
exemple pour acheter une maison.

**built** [bɪlt] pt, pp of **build**; **~-in** ['bɪlt'ɪn]
adj (cupboard, oven) encastré(e); (de-
vice) incorporé(e); **~-up area** ['bɪltʌp-] n zone urbanisée

**bulb** [bʌlb] n (BOT) bulbe m, oignon m;
(ELEC) ampoule f

**Bulgaria** [bʌl'gɛərɪə] n Bulgarie f

**bulge** [bʌldʒ] n renflement m, gonfle-
ment m ♦ vi (pocket, file etc) être
plein(e) à craquer; (cheeks) être gon-
flé(e)

**bulk** [bʌlk] n masse f, volume m; (of
person) corpulence f; **in ~** (COMM) en
vrac; **the ~ of** la plus grande or grosse
partie de; **~y** adj volumineux(-euse),
encombrant(e)

**bull** [bul] n taureau m; (male elephant/
whale) mâle m; **~dog** n bouledogue m

**bulldozer** ['buldəuzə'] n bulldozer m

**bullet** [bulɪt] n balle f (de fusil etc)

**bulletin** ['bulɪtɪn] n bulletin m,
communiqué m; (news ~) (bulletin
d'informations fpl; **~ board** n (INTER-
NET) messagerie f électronique

**bulletproof** ['bulɪtpruːf] adj (car) blin-
dé(e); (vest etc) pare-balles inv

**bullfight** ['bulfaɪt] n corrida f, course f
de taureaux; **~er** n torero m; **~ing** n
tauromachie f

**bullion** ['buljən] n or m or argent m en
lingots

**bullock** ['bulək] n bœuf m

**bullring** ['bulrɪŋ] n arènes fpl

**bull's-eye** ['bulzaɪ] n centre m (de la cible)

**bully** ['bulɪ] n brute f, tyran m ♦ vt ty-
ranniser, rudoyer

**bum** [bʌm] n (inf: backside) derrière m;
(esp US: tramp) vagabond(e), traîne-

savates m/f inv

**bumblebee** ['bʌmblbiː] n bourdon m

**bump** [bʌmp] n (in car: minor accident)
accrochage m; (jolt) cahot m; (on road
etc, on head) bosse f ♦ vt heurter, cogner; **~ into** vt fus rentrer dans, tamponner; (meet) tomber sur; **~er** n
pare-chocs m inv ♦ adj: **~er crop/
harvest** récolte/moisson exceptionnelle; **~er cars** (US) npl autos tamponneuses; **~y** adj cahoteux(-euse)

**bun** [bʌn] n petit pain au lait; (of hair)
chignon m

**bunch** [bʌntʃ] n (of flowers) bouquet m;
(of keys) trousseau m; (of bananas) régime m; (of people) groupe m; **~es** npl (in
hair) couettes fpl; **~ of grapes** grappe f
de raisin

**bundle** ['bʌndl] n paquet m ♦ vt (also:
**~ up**) faire un paquet de; (put): **to ~
sth/sb into** fourrer or enfourner qch/
qn dans

**bungalow** ['bʌŋgələu] n bungalow m

**bungle** ['bʌŋgl] vt bâcler, gâcher

**bunion** ['bʌnjən] n oignon m (au pied)

**bunk** [bʌŋk] n couchette f; **~ beds** npl
lits superposés

**bunker** ['bʌŋkə'] n (coal store) soute f à
charbon; (MIL, GOLF) bunker m

**bunting** ['bʌntɪŋ] n pavoisement m,
drapeaux mpl

**buoy** [bɔɪ] n bouée f; **~ up** vt faire flotter; (fig) soutenir, épauler; **~ant** adj (capable de flotter; (carefree) gai(e),
plein(e) d'entrain; (economy) ferme, actif

**burden** ['bɜːdn] n fardeau m ♦ vt (trouble) accabler, surcharger

**bureau** ['bjuərəu] (pl **~x**) n (BRIT: writing
desk) bureau m, secrétaire m; (US: chest
of drawers) commode f; (office) bureau,
m; **~cracy** [bjuə'rɔkrəsɪ] n bureaucratie f

**burglar** ['bɜːglə'] n cambrioleur m; **~
alarm** n sonnerie f d'alarme

**Burgundy** ['bɜːgəndɪ] n Bourgogne f

**burial** ['bɛrɪəl] n enterrement m

**burly** ['bəːlɪ] *adj* de forte carrure, costaud(e)

**Burma** ['bəːmə] *n* Birmanie *f*

**burn** [bəːn] (*pt, pp* **burned** *or* **burnt**) *vt* incendier, détruire par le feu; **~er** *n* brûleur *m*; **~ing** *adj* brûlant(e); (*house*) en flammes; (*ambition*) dévorant(e)

**burrow** ['bʌrəu] *n* terrier *m* ♦ *vt* creuser

**bursary** ['bəːsərɪ] (BRIT) *n* bourse *f* (d'études)

**burst** [bəːst] (*pt,pp* **burst**) *vt* crever; faire éclater; (*subj: river: banks etc*) rompre ♦ *vi* éclater; (*tyre*) crever ♦ *n* (*of gunfire*) rafale *f* (de tir); (*also:* ~ **pipe**) rupture *f*; fuite *f*; **a ~ of enthusiasm/energy** un accès d'enthousiasme/d'énergie; **to ~ into flames** s'enflammer soudainement; **to ~ out laughing** éclater de rire; **to ~ into tears** fondre en larmes; **to be ~ing with** être plein (à craquer) de; (*fig*) être débordant(e) de; **~ into** *vt fus* (*room etc*) faire irruption dans

**bury** ['bɛrɪ] *vt* enterrer

**bus** [bʌs] (*pl* **~es**) *n* autobus *m*

**bush** [buʃ] *n* buisson *m*; (*scrubland*) brousse *f*; **to beat about the ~** tourner autour du pot; **~y** *adj* broussailleux(-euse), touffu(e)

**busily** ['bɪzɪlɪ] *adv* activement

**business** ['bɪznɪs] *n* (*matter, firm*) affaire *f*; (*trading*) affaires *fpl*; (*job, duty*) travail *m*; **to be away on ~** être en déplacement d'affaires; **it's none of my ~** cela ne me regarde pas, ce ne sont pas mes affaires; **he means ~** il ne plaisante pas, il est sérieux; **~like** *adj* (*firm*) sérieux(-euse); (*method*) efficace; **~man** (*irreg*) *n* homme *m* d'affaires; **~ trip** *n* voyage *m* d'affaires; **~woman** (*irreg*) *n* femme *f* d'affaires

**busker** ['bʌskəʳ] (BRIT) *n* musicien ambulant

**bus: ~ shelter** *n* abribus *m*; **~ station** *n* gare routière; **~ stop** *n* arrêt *m* d'autobus

**bust** [bʌst] *n* buste *m*; (*measurement*)

tour *m* de poitrine ♦ *adj* (*inf: broken*) fichu(e), fini(e); **to go ~** faire faillite

**bustle** ['bʌsl] *n* remue-ménage *m*, affairement *m* ♦ *vi* s'affairer, se démener; **bustling** *adj* (*town*) bruyant(e), affairé(e)

**busy** ['bɪzɪ] *adj* occupé(e); (*shop, street*) très fréquenté(e) ♦ *vt*: **to ~ o.s.** s'occuper; **~body** *n* mouche *f* du coche, âme *f* charitable; **~ signal** (US) *n* (TEL) tonalité *f* occupé *inv*

---

KEYWORD

**but** [bʌt] *conj* mais; **I'd love to come, but I'm busy** j'aimerais venir mais je suis occupé

♦ *prep* (*apart from, except*) sauf, excepté; **we've had nothing but trouble** nous n'avons eu que des ennuis; **no-one but him can do it** il n'y a que lui qui puisse le faire; **but for you/your help** sans toi/ton aide; **anything but that** tout sauf or excepté ça, tout mais pas ça

♦ *adv* (*just, only*) ne ...; **she's but a child** elle n'est qu'une enfant; **had I but known** si seulement j'avais su; **all but finished** pratiquement terminé

**butcher** ['butʃəʳ] *n* boucher *m* ♦ *vt* massacrer; (*cattle etc for meat*) tuer; **~'s (shop)** *n* boucherie *f*

**butler** ['bʌtləʳ] *n* maître *m* d'hôtel

**butt** [bʌt] *n* (*large barrel*) gros tonneau; (*of gun*) crosse *f*; (*of cigarette*) mégot *m*; (BRIT: fig: *target*) cible *f* ♦ *vt* donner un coup de tête à; **~ in** *vi* (*interrupt*) s'immiscer dans la conversation

**butter** ['bʌtəʳ] *n* beurre *m* ♦ *vt* beurrer; **~cup** *n* bouton *m* d'or

**butterfly** ['bʌtəflaɪ] *n* papillon *m*; (SWIMMING: *also:* ~ **stroke**) brasse *f* papillon

**buttocks** ['bʌtəks] *npl* fesses *fpl*

**button** ['bʌtn] *n* bouton *m*; (US: *badge*) pin *m* ♦ *vt* (*also:* ~ **up**) boutonner ♦ *vi* se boutonner

**buttress** ['bʌtrɪs] *n* contrefort *m*

**buy** [baɪ] (*pt, pp* **bought**) *vt* acheter ♦ *n* achat *m*; **to ~ sb sth/sth from sb** acheter qch à qn; **to ~ sb a drink** offrir un verre *or* à boire à qn; **~er** *n* acheteur(-euse)

**buzz** [bʌz] *n* bourdonnement *m*; (*inf: phone call*): **to give sb a ~** passer un coup *m* de fil à qn ♦ *vi* bourdonner; **~er** *n* timbre *m* électrique; **~ word** *n* (*inf*) mot *m* à la mode

KEYWORD

**by** [baɪ] *prep* **1** (*referring to cause, agent*) par, de; **killed by lightning** tué par la foudre; **surrounded by a fence** entouré d'une barrière; **a painting by Picasso** un tableau de Picasso

**2** (*referring to method, manner, means*): **by bus/car** en autobus/voiture; **by train** par le *or* en train; **to pay by cheque** payer par chèque; **by saving hard, he ...** à force d'économiser, il ...

**3** (*via, through*) par; **we came by Dover** nous sommes venus par Douvres

**4** (*close to, past*) à côté de; **the house by the school** la maison à côté de l'école; **a holiday by the sea** des vacances au bord de la mer; **she sat by his bed** elle était assise à son chevet; **she went by me** elle est passée à côté de moi; **I go by the post office every day** je passe devant la poste tous les jours

**5** (*with time: not later than*) avant; (: *during*): **by daylight** à la lumière du jour; **by night** la nuit, de nuit; **by 4 o'clock** avant 4 heures; **by this time tomorrow** d'ici demain à la même heure; **by the time I got here it was too late** lorsque je suis arrivé il était déjà trop tard

**6** (*amount*) à; **by the kilo/metre** au kilo/au mètre; **paid by the hour** payé à l'heure

**7** (*MATH, measure*): **to divide/multiply by 3** diviser/multiplier par 3; **a room 3 metres by 4** une pièce de 3 mètres sur 4; **it's broader by a metre** c'est plus large d'un mètre; **one by one** un à un; **little by little** à petit, peu à peu

**8** (*according to*) d'après, selon; **it's 3 o'clock by my watch** il est 3 heures à ma montre; **it's all right by me** je n'ai rien contre

**9:** (**all**) **by oneself** *etc* tout(e) seul(e)

**10: by the way** au fait, à propos

♦ *adv* **1** *see* **go; pass** *etc*

**2: by and by** un peu plus tard, bientôt; **by and large** dans l'ensemble

**bye(-bye)** ['baɪ('baɪ)] *excl* au revoir!, salut!

**bye(e)-law** ['baɪlɔː] *n* arrêté municipal

**by-:** **~-election** (*BRIT*) *n* élection (législative) partielle; **~gone** *adj* passé(e) ♦ *n*: **let ~gones be ~gones** passons l'éponge, oublions le passé; **~pass** *n* (route *f* de) contournement *m*; (*MED*) pontage *m* ♦ *vt* éviter; **~product** *n* sous-produit *m*, dérivé *m*; (*fig*) conséquence *f* secondaire, retombée *f*; **~stander** *n* spectateur(-trice), badaud(e)

**byte** [baɪt] *n* (*COMPUT*) octet *m*

**byword** ['baɪwɜːd] *n*: **to be a ~ for** être synonyme de (*fig*)

# C, c

**C** [siː] *n* (*MUS*) do *m*

**CA** *abbr* **= chartered accountant**

**cab** [kæb] *n* taxi *m*; (*of train, truck*) cabine *f*

**cabaret** ['kæbəreɪ] *n* (*show*) spectacle *m* de cabaret

**cabbage** ['kæbɪdʒ] *n* chou *m*

**cabin** ['kæbɪn] *n* (*house*) cabane *f*, hutte *f*; (*on ship*) cabine *f*; (*on plane*) compartiment *m*; **~ crew** *n* (*AVIAT*) équipage *m*; **~ cruiser** *n* cruiser *m*

**cabinet** ['kæbɪnɪt] *n* (*POL*) cabinet *m*; (*furniture*) petit meuble à tiroirs et rayons; (*also:* **display ~**) vitrine *f*, petite armoire vitrée

**cable** ['keɪbl] *n* câble *m* ♦ *vt* câbler, télégraphier; **~car** *n* téléphérique *m*; **~ television** *n* télévision *f* par câble

**cache** [kæʃ] *n* stock *m*

**cackle** ['kækl] *vi* caqueter

**cactus** ['kæktəs] (*pl* **cacti**) *n* cactus *m*

**cadet** [kə'dɛt] *n* (*MIL*) élève *m* officier

**cadge** [kædʒ] (*inf*) *vt*: **to ~ (from** *or* **off)** se faire donner (par)

**Caesarian** [sɪ'zɛərɪən] *n* (*also:* **~ section**) césarienne *f*

**café** ['kæfeɪ] *n* ≈ café(-restaurant) *m* (*sans alcool*)

**cage** [keɪdʒ] *n* cage *f*

**cagey** ['keɪdʒɪ] (*inf*) *adj* réticent(e); méfiant(e)

**cagoule** [kə'guːl] *n* K-way ® *m*

**Cairo** ['kaɪərəu] *n* le Caire

**cajole** [kə'dʒəul] *vt* couvrir de flatteries *or* de gentillesses

**cake** [keɪk] *n* gâteau *m*; **~d** *adj*: **~d with** raidi(e) par, couvert(e) d'une croûte de

**calculate** ['kælkjuleɪt] *vt* calculer; (*estimate: chances, effect*) évaluer; **calculation** *n* calcul *m*; **calculator** *n* machine *f* à calculer, calculatrice *f*; (*pocket*) calculette *f*

**calendar** ['kæləndə*] *n* calendrier *m*; **~ year** *n* année civile

**calf** [kɑːf] (*pl* **calves**) *n* (*of cow*) veau *m*; (*of other animals*) petit *m*; (*also:* **~skin**) veau *m*, vachette *f*; (*ANAT*) mollet *m*

**calibre** ['kælɪbə*] (*US* **caliber**) *n* calibre *m*

**call** [kɔːl] *vt* appeler; (*meeting*) convoquer ♦ *vi* appeler; (*visit: also:* **~ in**, **~ round**) passer ♦ *n* (*shout*) appel *m*, cri *m*; (*also:* **telephone ~**) coup *m* de téléphone; (*visit*) visite *f*; **she's ~ed Suzanne** elle s'appelle Suzanne; **to be on ~** être de permanence; **~ back** *vi* (*return*) repasser; (*TEL*) rappeler; **~ for** *vt fus* (*demand*) demander; (*fetch*) passer prendre; **~ off** *vt* annuler; **~ on** *vt fus* (*visit*) rendre visite à, passer voir; (*request:* **to ~ on sb to do** inviter qn à faire; **~ out** *vi* pousser un cri *or* des cris; **~ up** *vt* (*MIL*) appeler, mobiliser; (*TEL*) appeler; **~box** *n* (*TEL*) cabine *f* téléphonique; **~ centre** *n* centre *m* d'appels; **~er** *n* (*TEL*) personne *f* qui appelle; (*visitor*) visiteur *m*; **~ girl** *n* call-girl *f*; **~-in** (*US*) *n* (*RADIO, TV: phone-in*) programme *m* à ligne ouverte; **~ing** *n* vocation *f*; (*trade, occupation*) état *m*; **~ing card** (*US*) *n* carte *f* de visite

**callous** ['kæləs] *adj* dur(e), insensible

**calm** [kɑːm] *adj* calme *m* ♦ *n* calme *m* ♦ *vt* calmer, apaiser; **~ down** *vi* se calmer ♦ *vt* calmer, apaiser

**Calor gas** ® ['kælɑ*-] *n* butane *m*, butagaz *m* ®

**calorie** ['kælərɪ] *n* calorie *f*

**calves** [kɑːvz] *npl* of **calf**

**camber** ['kæmbə*] *n* (*of road*) bombement *m*

**Cambodia** [kæm'bəudɪə] *n* Cambodge *m*

**camcorder** ['kæmkɔːdə*] *n* caméscope *m*

**came** [keɪm] *pt* of **come**

**camel** ['kæməl] *n* chameau *m*

**camera** ['kæmərə] *n* (*PHOT*) appareil-photo *m*; (*also:* **cine-~, movie ~**) caméra *f*; **in ~** à huis clos; **~man** (*irreg*) *n* caméraman *m*

**camouflage** ['kæməflɑːʒ] *n* camouflage *m* ♦ *vt* camoufler

**camp** [kæmp] *n* camp *m* ♦ *vi* camper ♦ *adj* (*man*) efféminé(e)

**campaign** [kæm'peɪn] *n* (*MIL, POL etc*) campagne *f* ♦ *vi* faire campagne

**camp: ~bed** (*BRIT*) *n* lit *m* de camp; **~er** *n* campeur(-euse); (*vehicle*) camping-car *m*; **~ing** *n* camping *m*; **to go ~ing** faire du camping; **~ing gas** ® *n* butane *m*; **~site** *n* campement *m*, (terrain *m* de) camping *m*

**campus** ['kæmpəs] *n* campus *m*

**can¹** [kæn] *n* (*of milk, oil, water*) bidon *m*; (*tin*) boîte *f* de conserve ♦ *vt* mettre en conserve

**KEYWORD**

**can²** [kæn] (*negative* **cannot, can't**, *conditional and pt* **could**) *aux vb* 1 (*be able to*) pouvoir; **you can do it if you try** vous pouvez le faire si vous essayez; **I can't hear you** je ne t'entends pas

2 (*know how to*) savoir; **I can swim/play tennis/drive** je sais nager/jouer au tennis/conduire; **can you speak French?** parlez-vous français?

3 (*may*) pouvoir; **can I use your phone?** puis-je me servir de votre téléphone?

4 (*expressing disbelief, puzzlement etc*): **it can't be true!** ce n'est pas possible!; **what CAN he want?** qu'est-ce qu'il peut bien vouloir?

5 (*expressing possibility, suggestion etc*): **he could be in the library** il est peut-être dans la bibliothèque; **she could have been delayed** il se peut qu'elle ait été retardée

**Canada** ['kænədə] *n* Canada *m*; **Canadian** [kə'neɪdɪən] *adj* canadien(ne) ♦ *n* Canadien(ne)

**canal** [kə'næl] *n* canal *m*

**canapé** ['kænəpeɪ] *n* canapé *m*

**canary** [kə'nɛərɪ] *n* canari *m*, serin *m*

**cancel** ['kænsəl] *vt* annuler; (*train*) supprimer; (*party, appointment*) décommander; (*cross out*) barrer, rayer; **~lation** [kænsə'leɪʃən] *n* annulation *f*, suppression *f*

**cancer** ['kænsər] *n* (*MED*) cancer *m*; **C~** (*ASTROLOGY*) le Cancer

**candid** ['kændɪd] *adj* (très) franc (franche), sincère

**candidate** ['kændɪdeɪt] *n* candidat(e)

**candle** ['kændl] *n* bougie *f*; (*of tallow*) chandelle *f*; (*in church*) cierge *m*; **~light** *n*: **by ~light** à la lumière d'une bougie; (*dinner*) aux chandelles; **~stick** *n* (*also*: **~ holder**) bougeoir *m*; (*bigger, ornate*) chandelier *m*

**candour** ['kændər] (*US* **candor**) *n* (grande) franchise *or* sincérité

**candy** ['kændɪ] *n* sucre candi; (*US*) bonbon *m*; **~-floss** (*BRIT*) *n* barbe *f* à papa

**cane** [keɪn] *n* canne *f*; (*for furniture, baskets etc*) rotin *m* ♦ *vt* (*BRIT: SCOL*) administrer des coups de bâton à

**canister** ['kænɪstər] *n* boîte *f*; (*of gas, pressurized substance*) bombe *f*

**cannabis** ['kænəbɪs] *n* (*drug*) cannabis *m*

**canned** [kænd] *adj* (*food*) en boîte, en conserve

**cannon** ['kænən] (*pl* ~ *or* ~**s**) *n* (*gun*) canon *m*

**cannot** ['kænɔt] = **can not**

**canoe** [kə'nu:] *n* pirogue *f*; (*SPORT*) canoë *m*; **~ing** *n*: **to go ~ing** faire du canoë

**canon** ['kænən] *n* (*clergyman*) chanoine *m*; (*standard*) canon *m*

**can-opener** ['kænəupnər] *n* ouvreboîte *m*

**canopy** ['kænəpɪ] *n* baldaquin *m*; dais *m*

**can't** [kænt] = **cannot**

**canteen** [kæn'ti:n] *n* cantine *f*; (*BRIT: of cutlery*) ménagère *f*

**canter** ['kæntər] *vi* (*horse*) aller au petit galop

**canvas** ['kænvəs] *n* toile *f*

**canvass** ['kænvəs] *vi* (*POL*): **to ~ for** faire campagne pour ♦ *vt* (*investigate: opinions etc*) sonder

**canyon** ['kænjən] *n* cañon *m*, gorge *f* (profonde)

**cap** [kæp] *n* casquette *f*; (*of pen*) capuchon *m*; (*of bottle*) capsule *f*; (*contraceptive: also*: **Dutch ~**) diaphragme *m*; (*for toy gun*) amorce *f* ♦ *vt* (*outdo*) surpasser; (*put limit on*) plafonner

**capability** [keɪpə'bɪlɪtɪ] *n* aptitude *f*, capacité *f*

**capable** ['keɪpəbl] *adj* capable

**capacity** [kə'pæsɪtɪ] *n* capacité *f*; (*capability*) aptitude *f*; (*of factory*) rendement *m*

**cape** [keɪp] *n* (*garment*) cape *f*; (*GEO*)

cap m

**caper** ['keɪpər] n (CULIN: gen pl) câpre f; (prank) farce f

**capital** ['kæpɪtl] n (also: ~ city) capitale f; (money) capital m; (also: ~ letter) majuscule f; ~ **gains tax** n (COMM) impôt m sur les plus-values; ~**ism** n capitalisme m; ~**ist** adj capitaliste ♦ n capitaliste m/f; ~**ize** ['kæpɪtəlaɪz] vi: to ~**ize on** tirer parti de; ~ **punishment** n peine capitale

| Capitol |
| --- |

Le Capitol est le siège du Congress, à Washington. Il est situé sur Capitol Hill.

**Capricorn** ['kæprɪkɔːn] n le Capricorne

**capsize** [kæp'saɪz] vt faire chavirer ♦ vi chavirer

**capsule** ['kæpsjuːl] n capsule f

**captain** ['kæptɪn] n capitaine m

**caption** ['kæpʃən] n légende f

**captive** ['kæptɪv] adj, n captif(-ive)

**capture** ['kæptʃər] vt capturer, prendre; (attention) capter; (COMPUT) saisir ♦ n capture f; (data ~) saisie f de données

**car** [kɑː<sup>r</sup>] n voiture f, auto f; (RAIL) wagon m, voiture

**caramel** ['kærəməl] n caramel m

**caravan** ['kærəvæn] n caravane f; ~**ning** n: to go ~**ning** faire du caravaning; ~ **site** (BRIT) n camping m pour caravanes

**carbohydrate** [kɑːbəʊ'haɪdreɪt] n hydrate m de carbone; (food) féculent m

**carbon** ['kɑːbən] n carbone m; ~ **dioxide** n gaz m carbonique; ~ **monoxide** n oxyde m de carbone; ~ **paper** n papier m carbone

**car boot sale** n marché aux puces où les particuliers vendent des objets entreposés dans le coffre de leur voiture

**carburettor** [kɑːbjʊ'retə<sup>r</sup>] (US **carburetor**) n carburateur m

**card** [kɑːd] n carte f; (material) carton m; ~**board** n carton m; ~ **game** n jeu

m de cartes

**cardiac** ['kɑːdɪæk] adj cardiaque

**cardigan** ['kɑːdɪgən] n cardigan m

**cardinal** ['kɑːdɪnl] adj cardinal(e) ♦ n cardinal m

**card index** n fichier m

**cardphone** n téléphone m à carte

**care** [keə<sup>r</sup>] n soin m, attention f; (worry) souci m; (charge) charge f, garde f ♦ vi: to ~ **about** se soucier de, s'intéresser à; (person) être attaché à; ~ **of** chez, aux bons soins de; **in sb's** ~ à la garde de qn, confié(e) à; **to take** ~ (**to do**) faire attention (à faire); **to take** ~ **of** s'occuper de; **I don't** ~ ça m'est bien égal; **I couldn't** ~ **less** je m'en fiche complètement (inf); ~ **for** vt fus s'occuper de; (like) aimer

**career** [kə'rɪə<sup>r</sup>] n carrière f ♦ vi (also: ~ **along**) aller à toute allure; ~ **woman** (irreg) n femme ambitieuse

**care:** ~**free** adj sans souci, insouciant(e); ~**ful** adj (thorough) soigneux(-euse); (cautious) prudent(e); **(be)** ~**ful!** (fais) attention!; ~**fully** adv avec soin, soigneusement, prudemment; ~**less** adj négligent(e); (heedless) insouciant(e); ~**r** n (MED) aide f

**caress** [kə'res] n caresse f ♦ vt caresser

**caretaker** ['keəteɪkə<sup>r</sup>] n gardien(ne), concierge m/f

**car-ferry** ['kɑːferɪ] n (on sea) ferry(-boat) m

**cargo** ['kɑːgəʊ] (pl ~**es**) n cargaison f, chargement m

**car hire** n location f de voitures

**Caribbean** [kærɪ'bɪən] adj: **the** ~ **(Sea)** la mer des Antilles or Caraïbes

**caring** ['keərɪŋ] adj (person) bienveillant(e); (society, organization) humanitaire

**carnation** [kɑː'neɪʃən] n œillet m

**carnival** ['kɑːnɪvl] n (public celebration) carnaval m; (US: funfair) fête foraine

**carol** ['kærəl] n: **(Christmas)** ~ chant m de Noël

**carp** [kɑːp] n (fish) carpe f

**car park** (BRIT) n parking m, parc m de stationnement

**carpenter** ['kɑ:pɪntər] n charpentier m; **carpentry** n menuiserie f

**carpet** ['kɑ:pɪt] n tapis m ♦ vt recouvrir d'un tapis; **~ sweeper** n balai m mécanique

**car phone** (TEL) téléphone m de voiture

**car rental** n location f de voitures

**carriage** ['kærɪdʒ] n voiture f; (of goods) transport m; (: cost) port m; **~way** (BRIT) n (part of road) chaussée f

**carrier** ['kærɪər] n transporteur m, camionneur m; (company) entreprise f de transport; (MED) porteur(-euse); **~ bag** (BRIT) n sac m (en papier or en plastique)

**carrot** ['kærət] n carotte f

**carry** ['kærɪ] vt (subj: person) porter; (vehicle) transporter; (involve: responsibilities etc) comporter, impliquer ♦ vi (sound) porter; **to get carried away** (fig) s'emballer, s'enthousiasmer; **~ out** vi **to ~ on with sth/doing** continuer qch/de faire ♦ vt poursuivre; **~ out** vt (orders) exécuter; (investigation) mener; **~cot** (BRIT) n porte-bébé m; **~on** (inf) n (fuss) histoires fpl

**cart** [kɑ:t] n charrette f ♦ vt (inf) transporter, trimballer (inf)

**carton** ['kɑ:tən] n (box) carton m; (of yogurt) pot m; (of cigarettes) cartouche f

**cartoon** [kɑ:'tu:n] n (PRESS) dessin m (humoristique), caricature f; (BRIT: comic strip) bande dessinée; (CINEMA) dessin animé

**cartridge** ['kɑ:trɪdʒ] n cartouche f

**carve** [kɑ:v] vt (meat) découper; (wood, stone) tailler, sculpter; **~ up** vt découper; (fig: country) morceler; **carving** n sculpture f; **carving knife** n couteau m à découper

**car wash** n station f de lavage (de voitures)

**case** [keɪs] n cas m; (LAW) affaire f, pro-

cès m; (box) caisse f, boîte f, étui m; (BRIT: also: **suitcase**) valise f; **in ~** of en cas de; **in ~ he** ... au cas où il ...; **just in ~** à tout hasard; **in any ~** en tout cas, de toute façon

**cash** [kæʃ] n argent m; (COMM) argent liquide, espèces fpl ♦ vt encaisser; **to pay (in)** ~ payer comptant; **~ on delivery** payable or paiement à la livraison; **~-book** n livre m de caisse; **~ card** n carte f de retrait; **~ desk** (BRIT) n caisse f; **~ dispenser** (BRIT) n distributeur m automatique de billets, billetterie f

**cashew** [kæ'ʃuː] n (also: **~ nut**) noix f de cajou

**cashier** [kæ'ʃɪər] n caissier(-ère)

**cashmere** ['kæʃmɪər] n cachemire m

**cash register** n caisse (enregistreuse)

**casing** ['keɪsɪŋ] n revêtement (protecteur), enveloppe (protectrice)

**casino** [kə'siːnəu] n casino m

**casket** ['kɑːskɪt] n coffret m; (US: coffin) cercueil m

**casserole** ['kæsərəul] n (container) cocotte f; (food) ragoût m (en cocotte)

**cassette** [kæ'set] n cassette f, musicassette f; **~ player** n lecteur m de cassettes; **~ recorder** n magnétophone m à cassettes

**cast** [kɑːst] (pt, pp cast) vt (throw) jeter; (shed) perdre; se dépouiller de; (statue) mouler; (THEATRE): **to ~ sb as Hamlet** attribuer à qn le rôle de Hamlet ♦ n (THEATRE) distribution f; (also: **plaster** ~) plâtre m; **to ~ one's vote** voter; **~ off** vi (NAUT) larguer les amarres; (KNITTING) arrêter les mailles; **~ on** vi (KNITTING) monter les mailles

**castaway** ['kɑːstəweɪ] n naufragé(e)

**caster sugar** ['kɑːstə-] (BRIT) n sucre m semoule

**casting vote** ['kɑːstɪŋ-] n voix prépondérante (pour départager)

**cast iron** n fonte f

**castle** ['kɑːsl] n château (fort); (CHESS) tour f

**castor** ['kɑːstər] n (wheel) roulette f

oil *n* huile *f* de ricin

**castrate** [kæs'treɪt] *vt* châtrer

**casual** ['kæʒjʊl] *adj (by chance)* de hasard, fait(e) au hasard, fortuit(e); *(unconcerned)* désinvolte; *(irregular: work etc)* temporaire; *(unconcerned)* désinvolte; **~ly** *adv* avec désinvolture, négligemment; *(dress)* de façon décontractée

**casualty** ['kæʒjʊltɪ] *n* accidenté(e), blessé(e); *(dead)* victime *f*, mort(e); *(MED: department)* urgences *fpl*

**casual wear** *n* vêtements *mpl* décontractés

**cat** [kæt] *n* chat *m*

**catalogue** (*US* **catalog**) *n* catalogue *m* ♦ *vt* cataloguer

**catalyst** ['kætəlɪst] *n* catalyseur *m*

**catalytic    converter** [kætə'lɪtɪk kən'vɜːtər] *n* pot *m* catalytique

**catapult** ['kætəpʌlt] *(BRIT)* *n (sling)* lance-pierres *m inv*, fronde *f*

**catarrh** [kə'tɑːr] *n* rhume *m* chronique, catarrhe *m*

**catastrophe** [kə'tæstrəfɪ] *n* catastrophe *f*

**catch** [kætʃ] *(pt, pp caught)* *vt* attraper; *(person: by surprise)* prendre, surprendre; *(understand, hear)* saisir ♦ *vi (fire)* prendre; *(become trapped)* se prendre, s'accrocher ♦ *n* prise *f*; *(trick)* attrape *f*; *(of lock)* loquet *m*; **to ~ sb's attention** *or* **eye** attirer l'attention de qn; **to ~ one's breath** retenir son souffle; **to ~ fire** prendre feu; **to ~ sight of** apercevoir; **~ on** *vi* saisir; *(grow popular)* prendre; **~ up** *vi* se rattraper, combler son retard ♦ *vt (also:* **~ up with)** rattraper; **~ing** *adj (MED)* contagieux(-euse); **~ment area** ['kætʃmənt-] *(BRIT)* *n (SCOL)* secteur *m* de recrutement; *(of hospital)* circonscription hospitalière; **~phrase** *n* slogan *m*; expression *f* (à la mode); **~y** *adj (tune)* facile à retenir

**category** ['kætɪgərɪ] *n* catégorie *f*

**cater** ['keɪtər] *vi (provide food)*: **to ~ (for)** préparer des repas (pour), se charger de la restauration (pour); **~ for**

*(BRIT)* *vt fus (needs)* satisfaire, pourvoir à; *(readers, consumers)* s'adresser à, pourvoir aux besoins de; **~er** *n* traiteur *m*; fournisseur *m*; **~ing** *n* restauration *f*; approvisionnement *m*, ravitaillement *m*

**caterpillar** ['kætəpɪlər] *n* chenille *f*

**cathedral** [kə'θiːdrəl] *n* cathédrale *f*

**catholic** ['kæθəlɪk] *adj (tastes)* éclectique, varié(e); **C~** *adj* catholique *m* ♦ *n* catholique *m/f*

**Catseye** ® ['kæts'aɪ] *(BRIT)* *n (AUT)* catadioptre *m*

**cattle** ['kætl] *npl* bétail *m*

**catty** ['kætɪ] *adj* méchant(e)

**caucus** ['kɔːkəs] *n (POL: group)* comité local d'un parti politique; *(US: POL)* comité électoral (pour désigner des candidats)

**caught** [kɔːt] *pt, pp of* **catch**

**cauliflower** ['kɔlɪflaʊər] *n* chou-fleur *m*

**cause** [kɔːz] *n* cause *f* ♦ *vt* causer

**caution** ['kɔːʃən] *n* prudence *f*; *(warning)* avertissement *m* ♦ *vt* avertir, donner un avertissement à; **cautious** *adj* prudent(e)

**cavalry** ['kævəlrɪ] *n* cavalerie *f*

**cave** [keɪv] *n* caverne *f*, grotte *f*; **~ in** *vi (roof etc)* s'effondrer; **~man** ['keɪvmæn] *(irreg)* *n* homme *m* des cavernes

**caviar(e)** ['kævɪɑː] *n* caviar *m*

**CB** *n abbr (= Citizens' Band (Radio))* CB *f*

**CBI** *n abbr (= Confederation of British Industries)* groupement du patronat

**cc** *abbr* **= carbon copy; cubic centimetres**

**CD** *n abbr (= compact disc (player))* CD *m*; **CDI** *n abbr (= Compact Disk Interactive)* CD-I *m*; **CD player** *n* platine *f* laser; **CD-ROM** [siːdiːˈrɔm] *n abbr (= compact disc read-only memory)* CD-Rom *m*

**cease** [siːs] *vt, vi* cesser; **~fire** *n* cessez-le-feu *m*; **~less** *adj* incessant(e), continuel(le)

**cedar** ['siːdər] *n* cèdre *m*

**ceiling** ['siːlɪŋ] *n* plafond *m*

**celebrate** ['selɪbreɪt] *vt, vi* célébrer; **~d** *adj* célèbre; **celebration** [selɪ'breɪʃən] *n* célébration *f*; **celebrity** [sɪ'lebrɪtɪ] *n* célébrité *f*

**celery** ['selərɪ] *n* céleri *m* (à côtes)

**cell** [sel] *n* cellule *f*; (ELEC) élément *m* (de pile)

**cellar** ['selər] *n* cave *f*

**cello** ['tʃeləu] *n* violoncelle *m*

**cellphone** ['selfəun] *n* téléphone *m* cellulaire

**Celt** [kɛlt, sɛlt] *n* Celte *m/f*; **~ic** *adj* celte

**cement** [sə'ment] *n* ciment *m*; **~ mixer** *n* bétonnière *f*

**cemetery** ['semɪtrɪ] *n* cimetière *m*

**censor** ['sensər] *n* censeur *m* ♦ *vt* censurer; **~ship** *n* censure *f*

**censure** ['senʃər] *vt* blâmer, critiquer

**census** ['sensəs] *n* recensement *m*

**cent** [sent] *n* (US, euro etc: coin) cent *m* (= un centième du dollar); see also **per**

**centenary** [sen'ti:nərɪ] *n* centenaire *m*

**center** ['sentər] (US) *n* = **centre**

**centigrade** ['sentɪgreɪd] *adj* centigrade

**centimetre** ['sentɪmi:tər] (US **centimeter**) *n* centimètre *m*

**centipede** ['sentɪpi:d] *n* mille-pattes *m* inv

**central** ['sentrəl] *adj* central(e); **C~ America** *n* Amérique centrale; **~ heating** *n* chauffage central; **~ reservation** (BRIT) *n* (AUT) terre-plein central

**centre** ['sentər] (US **center**) *n* centre *m* ♦ *vt* centrer; **~-forward** *n* (SPORT) avant-centre *m*; **~-half** *n* (SPORT) demi-centre *m*

**century** ['sentjurɪ] *n* siècle *m*; **20th ~** XXe siècle

**ceramic** [sɪ'ræmɪk] *adj* céramique

**cereal** ['si:rɪəl] *n* céréale *f*

**ceremony** ['serɪmənɪ] *n* cérémonie *f*; **to stand on ~** faire des façons

**certain** ['sɜ:tən] *adj* certain(e); **for ~** certainement, sûrement; **~ly** *adv* certainement; **~ty** *n* certitude *f*

**certificate** [sə'tɪfɪkɪt] *n* certificat *m*

**certified** ['sɜ:tɪfaɪd] *adj*: **by ~ mail** (US)

en recommandé, avec avis de réception; **~ public accountant** (US) expert-comptable *m*

**certify** ['sɜ:tɪfaɪ] *vt* certifier; (*award diploma to*) conférer un diplôme *etc* à; (*declare insane*) déclarer malade mental(e)

**cervical** ['sɜ:vɪkl] *adj*: **~ cancer** cancer *m* du col de l'utérus; **~ smear** frottis vaginal

**cervix** ['sɜ:vɪks] *n* col *m* de l'utérus

**cf.** *abbr* (= *compare*) cf., voir

**CFC** *n abbr* (= *chlorofluorocarbon*) CFC *m* (*gen pl*)

**ch.** *abbr* (= *chapter*) chap

**chafe** [tʃeɪf] *vt* irriter, frotter contre

**chain** [tʃeɪn] *n* chaîne *f* ♦ *vt* (*also*: **~ up**) enchaîner, attacher (avec une chaîne); **~ reaction** *n* réaction *f* en chaîne; **~-smoke** *vi* fumer cigarette sur cigarette; **~ store** *n* magasin *m* à succursales multiples

**chair** [tʃeər] *n* chaise *f*; (*armchair*) fauteuil *m*; (*of university*) chaire *f*; (*of meeting, committee*) présidence *f* ♦ *vt* (*meeting*) présider; **~lift** *n* télésiège *m*; **~man** (*irreg*) *n* président *m*

**chalet** ['ʃæleɪ] *n* chalet *m*

**chalk** [tʃɔ:k] *n* craie *f*

**challenge** ['tʃælɪndʒ] *n* défi *m* ♦ *vt* défier; (*statement, right*) mettre en question, contester; **to ~ sb to do** mettre qn au défi de faire; **challenging** *adj* (*tone, look*) de défi, provocateur(-trice); (*task, career*) qui représente un défi *or* une gageure

**chamber** ['tʃeɪmbər] *n* chambre *f*; **~ of commerce** chambre de commerce; **~maid** *n* femme *f* de chambre; **~ music** *n* musique *f* de chambre

**champagne** [ʃæm'peɪn] *n* champagne *m*

**champion** ['tʃæmpɪən] *n* champion(ne); **~ship** *n* championnat *m*

**chance** [tʃɑ:ns] *n* (*opportunity*) occasion *f*, possibilité *f*; (*hope, likelihood*) chance *f*; (*risk*) risque *m* ♦ *vt*: **to ~ it** risquer (le coup), essayer ♦ *adj* fortuit(e), de hasard; **to take a** ~ prendre un risque; **by** ~ par hasard

**chancellor** ['tʃɑːnsələ'] *n* chancelier *m*; **C~ of the Exchequer** (BRIT) *n* chancelier *m* de l'Échiquier; ≃ ministre *m* des Finances

**chandelier** [ʃændə'lɪə'] *n* lustre *m*

**change** [tʃeɪndʒ] *vt* (*alter, replace*, COMM: *money*) changer; (*hands, trains, clothes, one's name*) changer de; (*transform*): **to** ~ **sb into** changer ou transformer qn en ♦ *vi* (*gen*) changer; (*one's clothes*) se changer; (*be transformed*): **to** ~ **into** se changer ou transformer en ♦ *n* changement *m*; (*money*) monnaie *f*; **to** ~ **gear** (AUT) changer de vitesse; **to** ~ **one's mind** changer d'avis; **a** ~ **of clothes** des vêtements de rechange; **for a** ~ pour changer; ~**able** *adj* (*weather*) variable; ~ **machine** *n* distributeur *m* de monnaie; ~**over** *n* (*to new system*) changement *m*, passage *m*, changing *adj* changeant(e); **changing room** (BRIT) *n* (*in shop*) salon *m* d'essayage; (SPORT) vestiaire *m*

**channel** ['tʃænl] *n* (TV) chaîne *f*; (*navigable passage*) chenal *m*; (*irrigation*) canal *m* ♦ *vt* canaliser; **the (English) C~** la Manche; **the C~ Islands** les îles de la Manche, les îles Anglo-Normandes; **the C~ Tunnel** le tunnel sous la Manche; ~**hopping** (TV) *n* zapping *m*

**chant** [tʃɑːnt] *n* chant *m*; (REL) psalmodie *f* ♦ *vt* chanter, scander

**chaos** ['keɪɒs] *n* chaos *m*

**chap** [tʃæp] (BRIT: *inf*) *n* (*man*) type *m*

**chapel** ['tʃæpl] *n* chapelle *f*; (BRIT: *nonconformist* ~) église *f*

**chaplain** ['tʃæplɪn] *n* aumônier *m*

**chapped** [tʃæpt] *adj* (*skin, lips*) gercé(e)

**chapter** ['tʃæptə'] *n* chapitre *m*

**char** [tʃɑː'] *vt* (*burn*) carboniser

**character** ['kærɪktə'] *n* caractère *m*; (*in novel, film*) personnage *m*; (*eccentric*) numéro *m*, phénomène *m*; ~**istic** [kærɪktə'rɪstɪk] *adj* caractéristique ♦ *n*

caractéristique *f*

**charcoal** ['tʃɑːkəʊl] *n* charbon *m* de bois; (*for drawing*) charbon *m*

**charge** [tʃɑːdʒ] *n* (*cost*) prix (demandé); (*accusation*) accusation *f*; (LAW) inculpation *f* ♦ *vt*: **to** ~ **sb (with)** inculper qn (de); (*battery, enemy*) charger; (*customer, sum*) faire payer ♦ *vi* foncer; ~**s** *npl* (*costs*) frais *mpl*; **to reverse the** ~**s** (TEL) téléphoner en P.C.V.; **to take** ~ **of** se charger de; **to be in** ~ **of** être responsable de, s'occuper de; **how much do you** ~**?** combien prenez-vous?; **to** ~ **an expense (up) to sb** mettre une dépense sur le compte de qn; ~ **card** *n* carte *f* de client

**charity** ['tʃærɪtɪ] *n* charité *f*; (*organization*) institution *f* charitable *ou* de bienfaisance, œuvre *f* (de charité)

**charm** [tʃɑːm] *n* charme *m*; (*on bracelet*) breloque *f* ♦ *vt* charmer, enchanter; ~**ing** *adj* charmant(e)

**chart** [tʃɑːt] *n* tableau *m*, diagramme *m*, graphique *m*; (*map*) carte marine *f* ♦ *vt* dresser *ou* établir la carte de; ~**s** *npl* (*hit parade*) hit-parade *f*

**charter** ['tʃɑːtə'] *vt* (*plane*) affréter ♦ *n* (*document*) charte *f*; ~**ed accountant** (BRIT) *n* expert-comptable *m*; ~ **flight** *n* charter *m*

**chase** [tʃeɪs] *vt* poursuivre, pourchasser; (*also:* ~ **away**) chasser ♦ *n* poursuite *f*, chasse *f*

**chasm** ['kæzəm] *n* gouffre *m*, abîme *m*

**chat** [tʃæt] *vi* (*also:* **have a** ~) bavarder, causer ♦ *n* conversation *f*; ~ **show** (BRIT) *n* causerie télévisée

**chatter** ['tʃætə'] *vi* (*person*) bavarder; (*animal*) jacasser ♦ *n* bavardage *m*; jacassement *m*; **my teeth are** ~**ing** je claque des dents; ~**box** (*inf*) *n* moulin *m* à paroles

**chatty** ['tʃætɪ] *adj* (*style*) familier(-ère); (*person*) bavard(e)

**chauffeur** ['ʃəʊfə'] *n* chauffeur *m* (de maître)

**chauvinist** ['ʃəʊvɪnɪst] *n* (*male* ~) phallocrate m; (nationalist) chauvin(e)

**cheap** [tʃiːp] adj bon marché inv, pas cher (chère); (joke) facile, d'un goût douteux; (poor quality) de mauvaise qualité, de qualité médiocre ♦ adv à bon marché, pour pas cher; **~ day return** billet m d'aller et retour réduit (valable pour la journée); **~er** adj moins cher (chère); **~ly** adv à bon marché, à bon compte

**cheat** [tʃiːt] vi tricher ♦ vt tromper, duper; (rob): **to ~ sb out of** sth escroquer qch à qn ♦ n tricheur(-euse); escroc m

**check** [tʃɛk] vt vérifier; (passport, ticket) contrôler; (halt) arrêter; (restrain) maîtriser ♦ n vérification f; contrôle m; (curb) frein m; (us: bill) addition f; (pattern: gen pl) carreaux mpl; (us) = **cheque** ♦ adj (pattern, cloth) à carreaux; **~ in** vi (in hotel) remplir sa fiche (d'hôtel); (at airport) se présenter à l'enregistrement ♦ vt (luggage) (faire) enregistrer; **~ out** vi (in hotel) régler sa note; **~ up** vi: **to ~ up (on** sth) vérifier (qch); **to ~ up on sb** se renseigner sur le compte de qn; **~ered** (us) adj = **chequered**; **~ers** (us) npl jeu m de dames; **~-in (desk)** n enregistrement m; **~ing account** (us) n (current account) compte courant; **~mate** n échec et mat m; **~out** n (in shop) caisse f; **~point** n contrôle m; **~room** (us) n (left-luggage office) consigne f; **~up** n (MED) examen médical, check-up m

**cheek** [tʃiːk] n joue f; (impudence) toupet m, culot m; **~bone** n pommette f; **~y** adj effronté(e), culotté(e)

**cheep** [tʃiːp] vi piauler

**cheer** [tʃɪər] vt acclamer, applaudir; (gladden) réjouir, réconforter ♦ vi applaudir ♦ n (gen pl) acclamations fpl, applaudissements mpl; bravos mpl, hourras mpl; **~s!** à la vôtre!; **~ up** vi se dérider, reprendre courage ♦ vt remonter le moral à qn, dérider; **~ful** adj gai(e), joyeux(-euse)

**cheerio** [tʃɪəriˈəu] excl salut!, au

revoir!

**cheese** [tʃiːz] n fromage m; **~board** n plateau m de fromages

**cheetah** [ˈtʃiːtə] n guépard m

**chef** [ʃɛf] n chef (cuisinier)

**chemical** [ˈkɛmɪkl] adj chimique ♦ n produit m chimique

**chemist** [ˈkɛmɪst] n (BRIT: pharmacist) pharmacien(ne); (scientist) chimiste m/f; **~ry** n chimie f; **~'s (shop)** (BRIT) n pharmacie f

**cheque** [tʃɛk] (BRIT) n chèque m; **~book** n chéquier m, carnet m de chèques; **~ card** n carte f (d'identité) bancaire

**chequered** [ˈtʃɛkəd] (US **checkered**) adj (fig) varié(e)

**cherish** [ˈtʃɛrɪʃ] vt chérir

**cherry** [ˈtʃɛrɪ] n cerise f; (also: ~ tree) cerisier m

**chess** [tʃɛs] n échecs mpl; **~board** n échiquier m

**chest** [tʃɛst] n poitrine f; (box) coffre m, caisse f; **~ of drawers** n commode f

**chestnut** [ˈtʃɛsnʌt] n châtaigne f; (also: ~ tree) châtaignier m

**chew** [tʃuː] vt mâcher; **~ing gum** n chewing-gum m

**chic** [ʃiːk] adj chic inv, élégant(e)

**chick** [tʃɪk] n poussin m; (inf) nana f

**chicken** [ˈtʃɪkɪn] n poulet m; (inf: cow-ard) poule mouillée; **~ out** (inf) vi se dégonfler; **~pox** n varicelle f

**chicory** [ˈtʃɪkərɪ] n (for coffee) chicorée f; (salad) endive f

**chief** [tʃiːf] n chef m ♦ adj principal(e); **~ executive** (us **chief executive officer**) n directeur(-trice) général(e); **~ly** adv principalement, surtout

**chiffon** [ˈʃɪfɔn] n mousseline f de soie

**chilblain** [ˈtʃɪlbleɪn] n engelure f

**child** [tʃaɪld] (pl **~ren**) n enfant m/f; **~birth** n accouchement m; **~hood** n enfance f; **~ish** adj puéril(e), enfantin(e); **~like** adj d'enfant, innocent(e); **~ minder** (BRIT) n garde f d'enfants; **~ren** [ˈtʃɪldrən] npl of **child**

**Chile** ['tʃɪlɪ] n Chili m

**chill** [tʃɪl] n (of water) froid m; (of air) fraîcheur f; (MED) refroidissement m, coup m de froid ♦ vt (person) faire frissonner; (CULIN) mettre au frais, rafraîchir

**chil(l)i** [tʃɪlɪ] n piment m (rouge)

**chilly** ['tʃɪlɪ] adj froid(e), glacé(e); (sensitive to cold) frileux(-euse); **to feel ~** avoir froid

**chime** [tʃaɪm] n carillon m ♦ vi carillonner, sonner

**chimney** ['tʃɪmnɪ] n cheminée f; **~ sweep** n ramoneur m

**chimpanzee** [tʃɪmpæn'ziː] n chimpanzé m

**chin** [tʃɪn] n menton m

**China** ['tʃaɪnə] n Chine f

**china** ['tʃaɪnə] n porcelaine f; (crockery) (vaisselle f en) porcelaine

**Chinese** [tʃaɪ'niːz] adj chinois(e) ♦ n inv (person) Chinois(e); (LING) chinois m

**chink** [tʃɪŋk] n (opening) fente f, fissure f; (noise) tintement m

**chip** [tʃɪp] n (gen pl: CULIN: BRIT) frite f; (: US: potato ~) chip m; (of wood) copeau m; (of glass, stone) éclat m; (also: **microchip**) puce f ♦ vt (cup, plate) ébrécher

| chip shop |

Un **chip shop**, que l'on appelle également un "fish-and-chip shop", est un magasin où l'on vend des plats à emporter. Les chip shops sont d'ailleurs à l'origine des *takeaways*. On y achète en particulier du poisson frit et des frites, mais on y trouve également des plats traditionnels britanniques (steak pies, saucisses, etc). Tous les plats étaient à l'origine emballés dans du papier journal. Dans certains de ces magasins, on peut s'asseoir pour consommer sur place.

**chiropodist** [kɪ'rɔpədɪst] (BRIT) n pédicure m/f

**chirp** [tʃəːp] vi pépier, gazouiller

**chisel** ['tʃɪzl] n ciseau m

**chit** [tʃɪt] n mot m, note f

**chitchat** ['tʃɪttʃæt] n bavardage m

**chivalry** ['ʃɪvəlrɪ] n esprit m chevaleresque, galanterie f

**chives** [tʃaɪvz] npl ciboulette f, civette f

**chock-a-block** ['tʃɔkə'blɔk], **chock-full** ['tʃɔk'ful] adj plein(e) à craquer

**chocolate** ['tʃɔklɪt] n chocolat m

**choice** [tʃɔɪs] n choix m ♦ adj de choix

**choir** ['kwaɪə'] n chœur m, chorale f; **~boy** n jeune choriste m

**choke** [tʃəuk] vi étouffer ♦ vt étrangler; étouffer ♦ n (AUT) starter m; **street ~d with traffic** rue engorgée or emboutteillée

**cholesterol** [kə'lestərɔl] n cholestérol m

**choose** [tʃuːz] (pt **chose**, pp **chosen**) vt choisir; **to ~ to do** décider de faire, juger bon de faire; **choosy** adj: **(to be) choosy** (faire le/la) difficile

**chop** [tʃɔp] vt (wood) couper (à la hache); (CULIN: also: **~ up**) couper (fin), émincer, hacher (en morceaux) ♦ n (CULIN) côtelette f; **~s** npl (jaws) mâchoires fpl

**chopper** ['tʃɔpə'] n (helicopter) hélicoptère m, hélico m

**choppy** ['tʃɔpɪ] adj (sea) un peu agité(e)

**chopsticks** ['tʃɔpstɪks] npl baguettes fpl

**chord** [kɔːd] n (MUS) accord m

**chore** [tʃɔː'] n travail m de routine; **household ~s** travaux mpl du ménage

**chortle** ['tʃɔːtl] vi glousser

**chorus** ['kɔːrəs] n chœur m; (repeated part of song: also fig) refrain m

**chose** [tʃəuz] pt of **choose**; **~n** pp of **choose**

**chowder** ['tʃaudə'] n soupe f de poisson

**Christ** [kraɪst] n Christ m

**christen** ['krɪsn] vt baptiser

**christening** n baptême m

**Christian** ['krɪstɪən] adj, n chrétien(ne); **~ity** [krɪstɪ'ænɪtɪ] n christianisme m

**name** n prénom m

**Christmas** ['krɪsməs] n Noël m or f; **Happy** or **Merry ~!** joyeux Noël!; **~ card** n carte f de Noël; **~ Day** n le jour de Noël; **~ Eve** n la veille de Noël; la nuit de Noël; **~ tree** n arbre m de Noël

**chrome** [krəum] n chrome m

**chromium** ['krəumɪəm] n chrome m

**chronic** ['krɒnɪk] adj chronique

**chronicle** ['krɒnɪkl] n chronique f

**chronological** [krɒnə'lɒdʒɪkl] adj chronologique

**chrysanthemum** [krɪ'sænθəməm] n chrysanthème m

**chubby** ['tʃʌbɪ] adj potelé(e), rondelet(te)

**chuck** [tʃʌk] (inf) vt (throw) lancer, jeter; (BRIT: person) plaquer; (: also: **~ up**: job) lâcher; **~ out** vt flanquer dehors or à la porte; (rubbish) jeter

**chuckle** ['tʃʌkl] vi glousser

**chug** [tʃʌg] vi faire teuf-teuf; (also: **~ along**) avancer en faisant teuf-teuf

**chum** [tʃʌm] n copain (copine)

**chunk** [tʃʌŋk] n gros morceau

**church** [tʃəːtʃ] n église f; **~yard** n cimetière m

**churn** [tʃəːn] n (for butter) baratte f; (also: **milk ~**) (grand) bidon à lait; **~ out** vt débiter

**chute** [ʃuːt] n glissoire f; (also: **rubbish ~**) vide-ordures m inv

**chutney** ['tʃʌtnɪ] n condiment m à base de fruits au vinaigre

**CIA** n abbr (= Central Intelligence Agency) CIA f

**CID** (BRIT) n abbr (= Criminal Investigation Department) P.J. f

**cider** ['saɪdəʳ] n cidre m

**cigar** [sɪ'gɑːʳ] n cigare m

**cigarette** [sɪgə'rɛt] n cigarette f; **~ case** n étui m à cigarettes; **~ end** n mégot m

**Cinderella** [sɪndə'rɛlə] n Cendrillon

**cinders** ['sɪndəz] npl cendres fpl

**cine-camera** ['sɪnɪ'kæmərə] (BRIT) n caméra f

**cinema** ['sɪnəmə] n cinéma m

**cinnamon** ['sɪnəmən] n cannelle f

**circle** ['səːkl] n cercle m; (in cinema, theatre) balcon m ♦ vi décrire des cercles ♦ vt (move round) faire le tour de, tourner autour de; (surround) entourer, encercler

**circuit** ['səːkɪt] n circuit m; **~ous** [səː'kjuːɪtəs] adj indirect(e), qui fait un détour

**circular** ['səːkjuləʳ] adj circulaire ♦ n circulaire f

**circulate** ['səːkjuleɪt] vi circuler ♦ vt faire circuler; **circulation** [səːkju'leɪʃən] n circulation f; (of newspaper) tirage m

**circumflex** ['səːkəmflɛks] n (also: **~ accent**) accent m circonflexe

**circumstances** ['səːkəmstənsɪz] npl circonstances fpl; (financial condition) moyens mpl, situation financière

**circus** ['səːkəs] n cirque m

**CIS** n abbr (= Commonwealth of Independent States) CEI f

**cistern** ['sɪstən] n réservoir m (d'eau); (in toilet) réservoir de la chasse d'eau

**citizen** ['sɪtɪzn] n citoyen(ne); (resident): the **~s** of this town les habitants de cette ville; **~ship** n citoyenneté f

**citrus fruit** ['sɪtrəs-] n agrume m

**city** ['sɪtɪ] n ville f, cité f; the **C~** la Cité de Londres (centre des affaires); **~ technology college** n établissement m d'enseignement technologique

**civic** ['sɪvɪk] adj civique; (authorities) municipal(e); **~ centre** (BRIT) n centre administratif (municipal)

**civil** ['sɪvɪl] adj civil(e); (polite) poli(e), courtois(e); (disobedience, defence) passif(-ive); **~ engineer** n ingénieur m des travaux publics; **~ian** [sɪ'vɪlɪən] adj, n civil(e)

**civilization** [sɪvɪlaɪ'zeɪʃən] n civilisation f

**civilized** ['sɪvɪlaɪzd] adj civilisé(e); (fig) où règnent les bonnes manières

**civil: ~ law** n code civil; (study) droit civil; **~ servant** n fonctionnaire m/f; **C~**

**Service** n fonction publique, administration f; **~ war** n guerre civile

**clad** [klæd] adj: **~ (in)** habillé(e) (de)

**claim** [kleɪm] vt revendiquer; (rights, inheritance) demander, prétendre à; (assert) déclarer, prétendre ♦ vi (for insurance) faire une déclaration de sinistre ♦ n revendication f; demande f; prétention f, déclaration f; (right) droit m, titre m; **~ant** n (ADMIN, LAW) requérant(e)

**clairvoyant** [klɛə'vɔɪənt] n voyant(e), extra-lucide m/f

**clam** [klæm] n palourde f

**clamber** ['klæmbə'] vi grimper, se hisser

**clammy** ['klæmɪ] adj humide (et froid(e)), moite

**clamour** ['klæmə'] (US **clamor**) vi: **to ~ for** réclamer à grands cris

**clamp** [klæmp] n agrafe f, crampon m ♦ vt serrer; (sth to sth) fixer; (wheel) mettre un sabot à; **~ down on** vt fus sévir or prendre des mesures draconiennes contre

**clan** [klæn] n clan m

**clang** [klæŋ] vi émettre un bruit or fracas métallique

**clap** [klæp] vi applaudir; **~ping** n applaudissements mpl

**claret** ['klærət] n (vin m de) bordeaux m (rouge)

**clarinet** [klærɪ'net] n clarinette f

**clarity** ['klærɪtɪ] n clarté f

**clash** [klæʃ] n choc m, (fig) conflit m ♦ vi se heurter; être or entrer en conflit; (colours) jurer; (two events) tomber en même temps

**clasp** [klɑːsp] n (of necklace, bag) fermoir m; (hold, embrace) étreinte f ♦ vt serrer, étreindre

**class** [klɑːs] n classe f ♦ vt classer, classifier

**classic** ['klæsɪk] adj classique ♦ n (author, work) classique m; **~al** classique

**classified** ['klæsɪfaɪd] adj (information) secret(-ète); **~ advertisement** n petite annonce

**classmate** ['klɑːsmeɪt] n camarade m/f de classe

**classroom** ['klɑːsrum] n (salle f de) classe f

**clatter** ['klætə'] n cliquetis m ♦ vi cliqueter

**clause** [klɔːz] n clause f; (LING) proposition f

**claw** [klɔː] n griffe f; (of bird of prey) serre f; (of lobster) pince f

**clay** [kleɪ] n argile f

**clean** [kliːn] adj propre; (clear, smooth) net(te); (record, reputation) sans tache; (joke, story) correct(e) ♦ vt nettoyer; **~ out** vt nettoyer (à fond); **~ up** vt nettoyer; (fig) remettre de l'ordre dans; **~-cut** adj (person) net(te), soigné(e); **~er** n (person) nettoyeur(-euse), femme f de ménage; (product) détachant m; **~er's** n (also: **dry ~er's**) teinturier m; **~ing** n nettoyage m; **~liness** ['klɛnlɪnɪs] n propreté f

**cleanse** [klɛnz] vt nettoyer; (purify) purifier; **~r** n (for face) démaquillant m

**clean-shaven** ['kliːn'ʃeɪvn] adj rasé(e) de près

**cleansing department** ['klɛnzɪŋ-] (BRIT) n service m de voirie

**clear** [klɪə'] adj clair(e); (glass, plastic) transparent(e); (road, way) libre, dégagé(e); (conscience) net(te) ♦ vt (room) débarrasser; (of people) faire évacuer; (cheque) compenser; (LAW: suspect) innocenter; (obstacle) franchir or sauter sans heurter ♦ vi (weather) s'éclaircir; (fog) se dissiper ♦ adv: **~ of** à distance de, à l'écart de; **to ~ the table** desservir, débarrasser la table; **~ up** vt ranger, mettre en ordre; (mystery) éclaircir, résoudre; **~ance** n (removal) déblaiement m; (permission) autorisation f; **~-cut** adj clair(e), nettement défini(e); **~ing** n (in forest) clairière f; **~ing bank** (BRIT) n banque qui appartient à une chambre de compensation; **~ly** adv clairement; (evidently) de toute évidence;

**~way** (BRIT) n route f à stationnement interdit

**clef** [klɛf] n (MUS) clé f

**cleft** [klɛft] n (in rock) crevasse f, fissure f

**clementine** ['klɛməntain] n clémentine f

**clench** [klɛntʃ] vt serrer

**clergy** ['klɜːdʒi] n clergé m; **~man** (irreg) n ecclésiastique m

**clerical** ['klɛrikl] adj de bureau, d'employé de bureau; (REL) clérical(e), du clergé

**clerk** [klɑːk, (US) klɜːrk] n employé(e) de bureau; (US: salesperson) vendeur (-euse)

**clever** ['klɛvə'] adj (mentally) intelligent(e); (deft, crafty) habile, adroit(e); (device, arrangement) ingénieux(-euse), astucieux(-euse)

**click** [klik] vi faire un bruit sec or un déclic

**client** ['klaiənt] n client(e)

**cliff** [klif] n falaise f

**climate** ['klaimit] n climat m

**climax** ['klaimæks] n apogée m, point culminant; (sexual) orgasme m

**climb** [klaim] vi grimper, monter ♦ vt gravir, escalader, monter sur ♦ n montée f, escalade f; **~down** n reculade f, dérobade f; **~er** n (mountaineer) grimpeur(-euse), varappeur(-euse); (plant) plante grimpante; **~ing** n (mountaineering) escalade f, varappe f

**clinch** [klintʃ] vt (deal) conclure, sceller

**cling** [kliŋ] (pt, pp **clung**) vi: **to ~ (to)** se cramponner (à), s'accrocher (à); (of clothes) coller (à)

**clinic** ['klinik] n centre médical; **~al** adj clinique; (attitude) froid(e), détaché(e)

**clink** [kliŋk] vi tinter, cliqueter

**clip** [klip] n (for hair) barrette f; (also: **paper ~**) trombone m ♦ vt (fasten) attacher; (hair, nails) couper; (hedge) tailler; **~pers** npl (for hedge) sécateur m; (also: **nail ~pers**) coupe-ongles m inv; **~ping** n (from newspaper) coupure f de journal

**cloak** [kləuk] n grande cape ♦ vt (fig) masquer, cacher; **~room** n (for coats etc) vestiaire m; (BRIT: WC) toilettes fpl

**clock** [klɔk] n (large) horloge f; (small) pendule f; **~ in** (BRIT) vi pointer (en arrivant); **~ off** (BRIT) vi pointer (en partant); **~ on** (BRIT) vi = **clock in**; **~ out** (BRIT) vi = **clock off**; **~wise** adv dans le sens des aiguilles d'une montre; **~work** n rouages mpl, mécanisme m; (of clock) mouvement m d'horlogerie ♦ adj mécanique

**clog** [klɔg] n sabot m ♦ vt boucher ♦ vi (also: **~ up**) se boucher

**cloister** ['klɔistə'] n cloître m

**close¹** [kləus] adj (near) près, proche; (contact, link) étroit(e); (contest) très serré(e); (watch) étroit(e), strict(e); (examination) attentif(-ive), minutieux (-euse); (weather) lourd(e), étouffant(e) ♦ adv près, à proximité; **~ to** près de, proche de; **~ by** adj proche ♦ adv tout(e) près; **~ at hand** = **close by; a ~ friend** un ami intime; **to have a ~ shave** (fig) l'échapper belle

**close²** [kləuz] vt fermer ♦ vi (shop etc) fermer; (lid, door etc) se fermer; (end) se terminer, se conclure ♦ n (end) conclusion f, fin f; **~ down** vt, vi fermer (définitivement); **~d** adj fermé(e); **~d shop** n organisation f qui n'admet que des travailleurs syndiqués

**close-knit** ['kləus'nit] adj (family, community) très uni(e)

**closely** ['kləusli] adv (examine, watch) de près

**closet** ['klɔzit] n (cupboard) placard m, réduit m

**close-up** ['kləusʌp] n gros plan

**closure** ['kləuʒə'] n fermeture f

**clot** [klɔt] n (gen: blood ~) caillot m; (inf: person) ballot m ♦ vi (blood) se coaguler; **~ted cream** crème fraîche très épaisse

**cloth** [klɔθ] n (material) tissu m, étoffe f; (also: **teacloth**) torchon m; lavette f

**clothe** [kləuð] vt habiller, vêtir; **~s** npl

vêtements *mpl*, habits *mpl*; **~s brush** *n* brosse *f* à habits; **~s line** *n* corde *f* (à linge); **~s peg** (*US* **clothes pin**) *n* pince *f* à linge; **clothing** *n* = **clothes**

**cloud** [klaud] *n* nuage *m*; **~burst** *n* grosse averse; **~y** *adj* nuageux(-euse), couvert(e); (*liquid*) trouble

**clout** [klaut] *vt* flanquer une taloche à

**clove** [kləuv] *n* (*CULIN: spice*) clou *m* de girofle; **~ of garlic** gousse *f* d'ail

**clover** ['kləuvə<sup>r</sup>] *n* trèfle *m*

**clown** [klaun] *n* clown *m* ♦ *vi* (*also: ~ about, ~ around*) faire le clown

**cloying** ['klɔɪɪŋ] *adj* (*taste, smell*) écœurant(e)

**club** [klʌb] *n* (*society, place: also: golf ~*) club *m*; (*weapon*) massue *f*, matraque *f* ♦ *vt* matraquer ♦ *vi:* **to ~ together** s'associer; **~s** *npl* (*CARDS*) trèfle *m*; **~ class** *n* (*AVIAT*) classe *f* club; **~house** *n* club *m*

**cluck** [klʌk] *vi* glousser

**clue** [klu:] *n* indice *m*; (*in crosswords*) définition *f*; **I haven't a ~** je n'en ai pas la moindre idée

**clump** [klʌmp] *n:* **~ of trees** bouquet *m* d'arbres

**clumsy** ['klʌmzɪ] *adj* gauche, maladroit(e)

**clung** [klʌŋ] *pt, pp of* **cling**

**cluster** ['klʌstə<sup>r</sup>] *n* (*of people*) (petit) groupe; (*of flowers*) grappe *f*; (*of stars*) amas *m* ♦ *vi* se rassembler

**clutch** [klʌtʃ] *n* (*grip, grasp*) étreinte *f*, prise *f*; (*AUT*) embrayage *m* ♦ *vt* (*grasp*) agripper; (*hold tightly*) serrer fort; (*grab hold on to*) se cramponner à

**clutter** ['klʌtə<sup>r</sup>] *vt* (*also: ~ up*) encombrer

**CND** *n abbr* (= *Campaign for Nuclear Disarmament*) mouvement pour le désarmement nucléaire

**Co.** *abbr* = **county; company**

**c/o** *abbr* (= *care of*) c/o, aux bons soins de

**coach** [kəutʃ] *n* (*bus*) autocar *m*; (*horse-drawn*) diligence *f*; (*of train*) voiture *f*, wagon *m*; (*SPORT: trainer*) entraîneur(-euse); (*SCOL: tutor*) répétiteur(-trice) ♦ *vt* entraîner; (*student*) faire travailler; **~ trip** *n* excursion *f* en car

**coal** [kəul] *n* charbon *m*; **~ face** *n* front *m* de taille; **~field** *n* bassin houiller

**coalition** [kəuə'lɪʃən] *n* coalition *f*

**coalman** (*irreg*) *n* charbonnier *m*, marchand *m* de charbon

**coalmine** *n* mine *f* de charbon

**coarse** [kɔ:s] *adj* grossier(-ère), rude

**coast** [kəust] *n* côte *f* ♦ *vi* (*car, cycle etc*) descendre en roue libre; **~al** *adj* côtier(-ère); **~guard** *n* garde-côte *m*; (*service*) gendarmerie *f* maritime; **~line** *n* côte *f*, littoral *m*

**coat** [kəut] *n* manteau *m*; (*of animal*) pelage *m*, poil *m*; (*of paint*) couche *f* ♦ *vt* couvrir, enduire; **~ hanger** *n* cintre *m*; **~ing** *n* couche *f*, revêtement *m*; **~ of arms** *n* blason *m*, armoiries *fpl*

**coax** [kəuks] *vt* persuader par des cajoleries

**cobbler** ['kɔblə<sup>r</sup>] *n* cordonnier *m*

**cobbles** ['kɔblz] (*also: ~tones*) *npl* pavés (ronds)

**cobweb** ['kɔbwɛb] *n* toile *f* d'araignée

**cocaine** [kə'keɪn] *n* cocaïne *f*

**cock** [kɔk] *n* (*rooster*) coq *m*; (*male bird*) mâle *m* ♦ *vt* (*gun*) armer; **~erel** *n* jeune coq *m*

**cockle** ['kɔkl] *n* coque *f*

**cockney** ['kɔknɪ] *n* cockney *m*, habitant *des quartiers populaires de l'East End de Londres*; ≈ faubourien(ne)

**cockpit** ['kɔkpɪt] *n* (*in aircraft*) poste *m* de pilotage, cockpit *m*

**cockroach** ['kɔkrəutʃ] *n* cafard *m*

**cocktail** ['kɔkteɪl] *n* cocktail *m*; (*fruit ~ etc*) salade *f*; **~ cabinet** *n* (*meuble-*)bar *m*; **~ party** *n* cocktail *m*

**cocoa** ['kəukəu] *n* cacao *m*

**coconut** ['kəukənʌt] *n* noix *f* de coco

**COD** *abbr* = **cash on delivery**

**cod** [kɔd] *n* morue fraîche, cabillaud *m*

**code** [kəud] *n* code *m*

**cod-liver oil** n huile f de foie de morue

**coercion** [kəu'əːʃən] n contrainte f

**coffee** ['kɒfɪ] n café m; ~ **bar** (BRIT) n café m; ~ **bean** n grain m de café; ~ **break** n pause-café f; **~pot** n cafetière f; ~ **table** n (petite) table basse

**coffin** ['kɒfɪn] n cercueil m

**cog** [kɒg] n dent f (d'engrenage); (wheel) roue dentée

**cogent** ['kəudʒənt] adj puissant(e), convaincant(e)

**coil** [kɔɪl] n rouleau m, bobine f; (contraceptive) stérilet m ♦ vt enrouler

**coin** [kɔɪn] n pièce f de monnaie ♦ vt (word) inventer; ~ **age** n monnaie f, système m monétaire; ~ **box** (BRIT) n cabine f téléphonique

**coincide** [kəuɪn'saɪd] vi coïncider; **~nce** [kəu'ɪnsɪdəns] n coïncidence f

**Coke** [kəuk] ® n coca m

**coke** [kəuk] n coke m

**colander** ['kɒləndər] n passoire f

**cold** [kəuld] adj froid(e) ♦ n froid m; (MED) rhume m; **it's** ~ il fait froid; **to be** or **feel** ~ (person) avoir froid; **to catch** ~ prendre or attraper froid; **to catch a** ~ attraper un rhume; **in** ~ **blood** de sang-froid; **~-shoulder** vt se montrer froid(e) envers, snober; ~ **sore** n bouton m de fièvre

**coleslaw** ['kəulslɔː] n sorte de salade de chou cru

**colic** ['kɒlɪk] n colique(s) f(pl)

**collapse** [kə'læps] vi s'effondrer, s'écrouler ♦ n effondrement m, écroulement m; **collapsible** adj pliant(e); télescopique

**collar** ['kɒlər] n (of coat, shirt) col m; (for animal) collier m; **~bone** n clavicule f

**collateral** [kə'lætərl] n nantissement m

**colleague** ['kɒliːg] n collègue m/f

**collect** [kə'lekt] vt rassembler; ramasser; (as a hobby) collectionner; (BRIT: call and pick up) (passer) prendre; (mail) faire la levée de, ramasser; (money owed) encaisser; (donations, subscriptions) re-

cueillir ♦ vi (people) se rassembler; (things) s'amasser; **to call** ~ (US: TEL) téléphoner en P.C.V.; **~ion** n collection f; (of mail) levée f; (for money) collecte f, quête f; **~or** n collectionneur m

**college** ['kɒlɪdʒ] n collège m

**collide** [kə'laɪd] vi entrer en collision

**colliery** ['kɒlɪərɪ] (BRIT) n mine f de charbon, houillère f

**collision** [kə'lɪʒən] n collision f

**colloquial** [kə'ləukwɪəl] adj familier (-ère)

**colon** ['kəulən] n (sign) deux-points m inv; (MED) côlon m

**colonel** ['kəːnl] n colonel m

**colony** ['kɒlənɪ] n colonie f

**colour** ['kʌlər] (US **color**) n couleur f ♦ vt (paint) peindre; (dye) teindre; (news) fausser, exagérer ♦ vi (blush) rougir; ~s npl (of party, club) couleurs fpl; vt ~ it colorier; ~ **bar** n discrimination raciale (dans un établissement); **~-blind** adj daltonien(ne); **~ed** adj (person) de couleur; (illustration) en couleur; ~ **film** n (for camera) pellicule f (en couleur); **~ful** adj coloré(e), vif(-vive); (personality) pittoresque, haut(e) en couleurs; **~ing** ['kʌlərɪŋ] n colorant m; (complexion) teint m; ~ **scheme** n combinaison f de(s) couleurs; ~ **television** n télévision f (en) couleur

**colt** [kəult] n poulain m

**column** ['kɒləm] n colonne f; **~ist** ['kɒləmnɪst] n chroniqueur(-euse)

**coma** ['kəumə] n coma m

**comb** [kəum] n peigne m ♦ vt (hair) peigner; (area) ratisser, passer au peigne fin

**combat** ['kɒmbæt] n combat m ♦ vt combattre, lutter contre

**combination** [kɒmbɪ'neɪʃən] n combinaison f

**combine** [vb kəm'baɪn, n 'kɒmbaɪn] ♦ vt **to** ~ **sth with sth** combiner qch avec qch; (one quality with another) joindre or allier qch à qch ♦ vi s'associer; (CHEM) se combiner ♦ n (ECON) trust m; (har-

**vester)** n moissonneuse-batteuse(-lieuse) f

**come** [kʌm] (pt **came**, pp **come**) vi venir, arriver; **to ~ to** (decision etc) parvenir or arriver à; **to ~ undone/loose** se défaire/desserrer; **~ about** vi se produire, arriver; **~ across** vt fus rencontrer par hasard, tomber sur; **~ along** vi = come on; **~ away** vi partir, s'en aller, se détacher; **~ back** vi revenir; **~ by** vt fus (acquire) obtenir, se procurer; **~ down** vi descendre; (prices) baisser; (buildings) s'écrouler, être démoli(e); **~ forward** vi s'avancer, se présenter, s'annoncer; **~ from** vt fus être originaire de, venir de; **~ in** vi entrer; **~ in for** vt fus (criticism etc) être l'objet de; **~ into** vt fus (money) hériter de; **~ off** vi (button) se détacher; (stain) s'enlever; (attempt) réussir; **~ on** vi (pupil, work, project) faire des progrès, s'avancer; (lights, electricity) s'allumer; (central heating) se mettre en marche; **~ on!** viens!, allons!, allez!; **~ out** vi sortir; (book) paraître; (strike) cesser le travail, se mettre en grève; **~ round** vi (after faint, operation) revenir à soi, reprendre connaissance; **~ to** vi revenir à soi; **~ up** vi monter; **~ up against** vt fus (resistance, difficulties) rencontrer; **~ up with** vt fus: he came up with an idea il a eu une idée, il a proposé quelque chose; **~ upon** vt fus tomber sur; **~back** n (THEATRE etc) rentrée f

**comedian** [kə'miːdɪən] n (in music hall etc) comique m; (THEATRE) comédien m

**comedy** ['kɒmɪdɪ] n comédie f

**comeuppance** [kʌm'ʌpəns] n: **to get one's ~** recevoir ce qu'on mérite

**comfort** ['kʌmfət] n confort m, bien-être m; (relief) soulagement m, réconfort m ♦ vt consoler, réconforter; **the ~s of home** les commodités fpl de la maison; **~able** adj confortable; (person) à l'aise; (patient) dont l'état est stationnaire; (walk etc) facile; **~ably** adv (sit) confortablement; (live) à l'aise; **~**

**station** (US) n toilettes fpl

**comic** ['kɒmɪk] adj (also: **~al**) comique ♦ n comique m; (BRIT: magazine) illustré m; **~ strip** n bande dessinée

**coming** ['kʌmɪŋ] n arrivée f ♦ adj prochain(e), à venir; **~(s) and going(s)** n(pl) va-et-vient m inv

**comma** ['kɒmə] n virgule f

**command** [kə'mɑːnd] n ordre m, commandement m; (MIL: authority) commandement m; (mastery) maîtrise f ♦ vt (troops) commander; **to ~ sb to do** ordonner à qn de faire; **~er** [kə'mɑːndɪə*] n réquisitionner; **~er** (MIL) commandant m

**commando** [kə'mɑːndəʊ] n commando m; membre m d'un commando

**commemorate** [kə'meməreɪt] vt commémorer

**commence** [kə'mens] vt, vi commencer

**commend** [kə'mend] vt louer; (recommend) recommander

**commensurate** [kə'menʃərɪt] adj: **~ with** or to en proportion de, proportionné(e) à

**comment** ['kɒment] n commentaire m ♦ vi: **to ~ (on)** faire des remarques (sur); **"no ~"** "je n'ai rien à dire"; **~ary** ['kɒməntərɪ] n commentaire m; (SPORT) reportage m (en direct); **~ator** ['kɒmənteɪtə*] n commentateur m; reporter m

**commerce** ['kɒmɜːs] n commerce m

**commercial** [kə'mɜːʃəl] adj commercial(e) ♦ n (TV, RADIO) annonce f publicitaire, spot m publicitaire)

**commiserate** [kə'mɪzəreɪt] vi: **to ~ with sb** témoigner de la sympathie pour qn

**commission** [kə'mɪʃən] n (order for work) commande f; (committee, fee) commission f ♦ vt (work of art) commander, charger un artiste de l'exécution de; **out of ~** (not working) hors service; **~aire** [kəmɪʃə'neə*] (BRIT) n (at shop, cinema etc) portier m (en uniforme); **~er** n (POLICE) préfet m (de police)

**commit** [kə'mɪt] vt (act) commettre; (resources) consacrer; (to sb's care) confier (à); **to ~ o.s. (to do)** s'engager (à faire); **to ~ suicide** se suicider; **~ment** n engagement m; (obligation) responsabilité(s) f(pl)

**committee** [kə'mɪtɪ] n comité m

**commodity** [kə'mɔdɪtɪ] n produit m, marchandise f, article m

**common** ['kɔmən] adj commun(e); (usual) courant(e) ♦ n terrain communal; **the C~s** (BRIT) npl la chambre des Communes; **in ~** en commun; **~er** n roturier(-ière); **~ law** n droit coutumier; **~ly** adv communément, généralement; couramment; **C~ Market** n Marché commun; **~place** adj banal(e), ordinaire; **~ room** n salle commune; **~ sense** n bon sens; **C~wealth** (BRIT) n Commonwealth m

**commotion** [kə'məuʃən] n désordre m, tumulte m

**communal** ['kɔmju:nl] adj (life) communautaire; (for common use) commun(e)

**commune** [n 'kɔmju:n, vb kə'mju:n] n (group) communauté f ♦ vi: **to ~ with** communier avec

**communicate** [kə'mju:nɪkeɪt] vt, vi communiquer; **communication** [kə-mju:nɪ'keɪʃən] n communication f; **communication cord** (BRIT) n sonnette f d'alarme

**communion** [kə'mju:nɪən] n (also: Holy C~) communion f

**communism** ['kɔmjunɪzəm] n communisme m; **communist** adj communiste ♦ n communiste m/f

**community** [kə'mju:nɪtɪ] n communauté f; **~ centre** n centre m de loisirs; **~ chest** (US) n fonds commun

**commutation ticket** [kɔmju'teɪʃən-] (US) n carte f d'abonnement

**commute** [kə'mju:t] vi faire un trajet journalier pour se rendre à son travail ♦

vt (LAW) commuer; **~r** n banlieusard(e) (qui fait un trajet journalier pour se rendre à son travail)

**compact** [adj kəm'pækt, n 'kɔmpækt] adj compact(e) ♦ n (also: powder ~) poudrier m; **~ disc** n disque compact; **~ disc player** n lecteur m de disque compact

**companion** [kəm'pænjən] n compagnon (compagne); **~ship** n camaraderie f

**company** ['kʌmpənɪ] n compagnie f; **to keep sb ~** tenir compagnie à qn; **~ secretary** (BRIT) n (COMM) secrétaire général (d'une société)

**comparative** [kəm'pærətɪv] adj (study) comparatif(-ive); (relative) relatif(-ive); **~ly** adv (relatively) relativement

**compare** [kəm'peə'] vt: **to ~ sth/sb with/to** comparer qch/qn avec or et/à ♦ vi: **to ~ (with)** se comparer (à); être comparable (à); **comparison** [kəm-'pærɪsn] n comparaison f

**compartment** [kəm'pɑ:tmənt] n compartiment m

**compass** ['kʌmpəs] n boussole f; **~es** npl (GEOM: also: **pair of ~es**) compas m

**compassion** [kəm'pæʃən] n compassion f; **~ate** adj compatissant(e)

**compatible** [kəm'pætɪbl] adj compatible

**compel** [kəm'pel] vt contraindre, obliger

**compensate** ['kɔmpənseɪt] vt indemniser, dédommager ♦ vi: **to ~ for** compenser; **compensation** [kɔmpən'seɪʃən] n compensation f; (money) dédommagement m, indemnité f

**compère** ['kɔmpeə'] n (TV) animateur(-trice)

**compete** [kəm'pi:t] vi: **to ~ (with)** rivaliser (avec), faire concurrence (à)

**competent** ['kɔmpɪtənt] adj compétent(e), capable

**competition** [kɔmpɪ'tɪʃən] n (contest) compétition f, concours m; (ECON) concurrence f

**competitive** [kəm'petɪtɪv] adj (ECON) concurrentiel(le); (sport) de compétition; (person) qui a l'esprit de compétition; **competitor** n concurrent n

**complacency** [kəm'pleɪsnsɪ] n suffisance f, vaine complaisance

**complain** [kəm'pleɪn] vi: **to ~ (about)** se plaindre (de); (in shop etc) réclamer (au sujet de); **to ~ of** (pain) se plaindre de; **~t** n plainte f; réclamation f; (MED) affection f

**complement** [n 'kɒmplɪmənt, vb -'kɒmplɪment] n complément m; (especially of ship's crew etc) effectif complet ♦ vt (enhance) compléter; **~ary** [kɒmplɪ'mentərɪ] adj complémentaire

**complete** [kəm'pliːt] adj complet(-ète) ♦ vt achever, parachever; (set, group) compléter; (a form) remplir; **~ly** adv complètement; **completion** [kəm'pliːʃən] n achèvement m; (of contract) exécution f

**complex** ['kɒmpleks] adj complexe ♦ n complexe m

**complexion** [kəm'plekʃən] n (of face) teint m

**compliance** [kəm'plaɪəns] n (submission) docilité f; (agreement): **~ with** le fait de se conformer à; **in ~ with** en accord avec

**complicate** ['kɒmplɪkeɪt] vt compliquer; **~d** adj compliqué(e); **complication** [kɒmplɪ'keɪʃən] n complication f

**compliment** [n 'kɒmplɪmənt, vb -'kɒmplɪment] n compliment m ♦ vt complimenter; **~s** npl (respects) hommages mpl; **to pay sb a ~** faire or adresser un compliment à qn; **~ary** [kɒmplɪ'mentərɪ] adj flatteur(-euse); (free) (offert(e)) à titre gracieux; **~ary ticket** n billet m de faveur

**comply** [kəm'plaɪ] vi: **to ~ with** se soumettre à, se conformer à

**component** [kəm'pəʊnənt] n composant m, élément m

**compose** [kəm'pəʊz] vt composer;

(form): **to be ~d of** se composer de; **to ~ o.s.** se calmer, se maîtriser; (person) prendre une contenance; **~d** adj calme, posé(e); **~r** n (MUS) compositeur m; **composition** [kɒmpə'zɪʃən] n composition f; **composure** [kəm'pəʊʒəʳ] n calme m, maîtrise f de soi

**compound** ['kɒmpaʊnd] n composé m; (enclosure) enclos m; (LING) mot m composé ♦ adj composé(e); **~ fracture** n fracture compliquée; **~ interest** n intérêt m composé

**comprehend** [kɒmprɪ'hend] vt comprendre; **comprehension** n compréhension f

**comprehensive** [kɒmprɪ'hensɪv] adj (très) complet(-ète); **~ policy** n (INSURANCE) assurance f tous risques; **~ (school)** (BRIT) n école secondaire polyvalente; ≃ C.E.S. m

**compress** [vb kəm'pres, n 'kɒmpres] vt comprimer; (text, information) condenser ♦ n (MED) compresse f

**comprise** [kəm'praɪz] vt (also: **be ~d of**) comprendre; (constitute) constituer, représenter

**compromise** ['kɒmprəmaɪz] n compromis m ♦ vt compromettre ♦ vi transiger, accepter un compromis

**compulsion** [kəm'pʌlʃən] n contrainte f, force f

**compulsive** [kəm'pʌlsɪv] adj (PSYCH) compulsif(-ive); (book, film etc) captivant(e)

**compulsory** [kəm'pʌlsərɪ] adj obligatoire

**computer** [kəm'pjuːtəʳ] n ordinateur m; **~ game** n jeu m vidéo; **~-generated** adj de synthèse; **~ize** vt informatiser; **~ programmer** n programmeur(-euse); **~ programming** n programmation f; **~ science** n informatique f; **computing** n = computer science

**comrade** ['kɒmrɪd] n camarade m/f

**con** [kɒn] vt duper; (cheat) escroquer ♦ n escroquerie f

**conceal** [kən'siːl] vt cacher, dissimuler

**conceit** [kən'si:t] n vanité f, suffisance f, prétention f; **~ed** adj vaniteux(-euse), suffisant(e)

**conceive** [kən'si:v] vt, vi concevoir

**concentrate** ['kɔnsəntreit] vi se concentrer ♦ vt concentrer; **concentration** n concentration f; **concentration camp** n camp m de concentration

**concept** ['kɔnsept] n concept m

**concern** [kən'sə:n] n affaire f, (COMM) entreprise f, firme f; (anxiety) inquiétude f, souci m ♦ vt (worry) inquiéter, tourmenter; **to be ~ed (about)** s'inquiéter (de), être inquiet (-ète) (au sujet de); **~ing** prep en ce qui concerne, à propos de

**concert** ['kɔnsət] n concert m; **~ed** [kən'sə:tid] adj concerté(e); **~ hall** n salle f de concert

**concerto** [kən'tʃə:təu] n concerto m

**concession** [kən'sɛʃən] n concession f; **tax ~** dégrèvement fiscal

**conclude** [kən'klu:d] vt conclure; **conclusion** [kən'klu:ʒən] n conclusion f; **conclusive** [kən'klu:siv] adj concluant(e), définitif(-ive)

**concoct** [kən'kɔkt] vt confectionner, composer; (fig) inventer; **~ion** n mélange m

**concourse** ['kɔnkɔːs] n (hall) hall m, salle f des pas perdus

**concrete** ['kɔnkri:t] n béton m ♦ adj concret(-ète); (floor etc) en béton

**concur** [kən'kə:] vi (agree) être d'accord

**concurrently** [kən'kʌrntli] adv simultanément

**concussion** [kən'kʌʃən] n (MED) commotion (cérébrale)

**condemn** [kən'dem] vt condamner

**condensation** [kɔndɛn'seiʃən] n condensation f

**condense** [kən'dens] vi se condenser ♦ vt condenser; **~d milk** n lait concentré (sucré)

**condition** [kən'diʃən] n condition f; (MED) état m ♦ vt déterminer, condition-

ner; **on ~ that** à condition que *+sub*, à condition de; **~al** adj conditionnel(le); **~er** n (for hair) baume après-shampooing m; (for fabrics) assouplissant m

**condolences** [kən'dəulənsiz] npl condoléances fpl

**condom** ['kɔndəm] n préservatif m

**condominium** [kɔndə'miniəm] n (US) (building) immeuble m (en copropriété)

**condone** [kən'dəun] vt fermer les yeux sur, approuver (tacitement)

**conducive** [kən'dju:siv] adj: **~ to** favorable à, qui contribue à

**conduct** [n 'kɔndʌkt, vb kən'dʌkt] n conduite f ♦ vt conduire; (MUS) diriger; **to ~ o.s.** se conduire, se comporter; **~ed tour** n voyage organisé; (of building) visite guidée; **~or** n (of orchestra) chef m d'orchestre; (on bus) receveur m; (US: on train) chef m de train; (ELEC) conducteur m; **~ress** n (on bus) receveuse f

**cone** [kəun] n cône m; (for ice-cream) cornet m; (BOT) pomme f de pin, cône m

**confectioner** [kən'fɛkʃənə*] n confiseur(-euse); **~'s (shop)** n confiserie f; **~y** n confiserie f

**confer** [kən'fə:*] vt: **to ~ sth on** conférer qch à ♦ vi conférer, s'entretenir

**conference** ['kɔnfərəns] n conférence f

**confess** [kən'fes] vt confesser, avouer ♦ vi se confesser; **~ion** n confession f

**confetti** [kən'feti] n confettis mpl

**confide** [kən'faid] vi: **to ~ in** se confier à

**confidence** ['kɔnfidns] n confiance f; (also: self-~) assurance f, confiance en soi; (secret) confidence f; **in ~** (speak, write) en confidence, confidentiellement; **~ trick** n escroquerie f; **confident** adj sûr(e), assuré(e); **confidential** [kɔnfi'dɛnʃəl] adj confidentiel(le)

**confine** [kən'fain] vt limiter, borner; (shut up) confiner, enfermer; **~d** adj (space) restreint(e), réduit(e); **~ment** n emprisonnement m, détention f; **~s**

['kɒnfaɪnz] npl confins mpl, bornes fpl
**confirm** [kən'fə:m] vt confirmer; (appointment) ratifier; **~ation** [kɒnfə'mei-
ʃən] n confirmation f; **~ed** adj invété-
ré(e), incorrigible
**confiscate** ['kɒnfɪskeɪt] vt confisquer
**conflict** [n 'kɒnflɪkt, vb kən'flɪkt] n
conflit m, lutte f ♦ vi être or entrer en
conflit; (opinions) s'opposer, se heurter;
**~ing** [kən'flɪktɪŋ] adj contradictoire
**conform** [kən'fɔ:m] vi: **to ~ (to)** se
conformer (à)
**confound** [kən'faund] vt confondre
**confront** [kən'frʌnt] vt confronter,
mettre en présence; (enemy, danger) affronter, faire face à; **~ation**
[kɒnfrən'teiʃən] n confrontation f
**confuse** [kən'fju:z] vt (person) troubler;
(situation) embrouiller; (one thing with
another) confondre; **~d** adj (person) dé-
routé(e), désorienté(e); **confusing** adj
peu clair(e), déroutant(e); **confusion**
[kən'fju:ʒən] n confusion f
**congeal** [kən'dʒi:l] vi (blood) se coaguler; (oil etc) se figer
**congenial** [kən'dʒi:nɪəl] adj sympathique, agréable
**congested** [kən'dʒestɪd] adj (MED)
congestionné(e); (area) surpeuplé(e);
(road) bloqué(e); **congestion** n
congestion f; (fig) encombrement m
**congratulate** [kən'grætjuleɪt] vt: **to ~
sb on** féliciter qn (de); **congratulations** [kəngrætju'leiʃənz] npl félicitations fpl
**congregate** ['kɒŋgrɪgeɪt] vi se rassembler, se réunir; **congregation**
[kɒŋgrɪ'geiʃən] n assemblée f (des
fidèles)
**congress** ['kɒŋgres] n congrès m;
**~man** (irreg) (US) n membre du
Congrès
**conjunction** [kən'dʒʌŋkʃən] n (LING)
conjonction f
**conjunctivitis** [kəndʒʌŋktɪ'vaɪtɪs] n
conjonctivite f
**conjure** ['kʌndʒər] vi faire des tours de

passe-passe; **~ up** vt (ghost, spirit) faire
apparaître; (memories) évoquer; **~r** n
prestidigitateur m, illusionniste m/f
**con man** (irreg) n escroc m
**connect** [kə'nekt] vt joindre, relier;
(ELEC) connecter; (TEL: caller) mettre en
connection (with avec); (: new subscriber) brancher; (fig) établir un rapport
entre, faire un rapprochement entre ♦
vi (train): **to ~ with** assurer la correspondance avec; **to be ~ed with** (fig)
avoir un rapport avec, avoir des rapports avec, être en relation avec; **~ion**
n relation f, lien m; (ELEC) connexion f;
(train, plane etc) correspondance f; (TEL)
branchement m, communication f
**connive** [kə'naiv] vi: **to ~ at** se faire le
complice de
**conquer** ['kɒŋkər] vt conquérir; (feelings) vaincre, surmonter; **conquest**
['kɒŋkwest] n conquête f
**cons** [kɒnz] npl see **convenience**; **pro**
**conscience** ['kɒnʃəns] n conscience f;
**conscientious** [kɒnʃɪ'enʃəs] adj
consciencieux(-euse)
**conscious** ['kɒnʃəs] adj conscient(e);
**~ness** n conscience f; (MED) connaissance f
**conscript** ['kɒnskrɪpt] n conscrit m
**consent** [kən'sent] n consentement m
♦ vi: **to ~ (to)** consentir (à)
**consequence** ['kɒnsɪkwəns] n conséquence f, suites fpl; (significance) importance f; **consequently** adv par conséquent, donc
**conservation** [kɒnsə'veiʃən] n préser-
vation f, protection f
**conservative** [kən'sə:vətɪv] adj
conservateur(-trice); **at a ~ estimate**
au bas mot; **C~** (BRIT) adj, n (POL)
conservateur(-trice)
**conservatory** [kən'sə:vətrɪ] n (greenhouse) serre f
**conserve** [kən'sə:v] vt conserver, préserver; (supplies, energy) économiser
♦ n confiture f
**consider** [kən'sɪdər] vt (study) considé-

rer, réfléchir à; (take into account) penser à, prendre en considération; (regard, judge) considérer, estimer; **to ~ doing sth** envisager de faire qch; **~able** adj considérable; **~ably** adv nettement; **~ate** adj prévenant(e), plein(e) d'égards; **~ation** [kənsɪdə'reɪʃən] n considération f; **~ing** prep étant donné

**consign** [kən'saɪn] vt expédier; (to sb's care) confier; (fig) livrer; **~ment** n arrivage m, envoi m

**consist** [kən'sɪst] vi: **to ~ of** consister en, se composer de

**consistency** [kən'sɪstənsɪ] n consistance f; (fig) cohérence f

**consistent** [kən'sɪstənt] adj logique, cohérent(e)

**consolation** [kɔnsə'leɪʃən] n consolation f

**console¹** [kən'səul] vt consoler

**console²** ['kɔnsəul] n (COMPUT) console f

**consonant** ['kɔnsənənt] n consonne f

**conspicuous** [kən'spɪkjuəs] adj voyant(e), qui attire l'attention

**conspiracy** [kən'spɪrəsɪ] n conspiration f, complot m

**constable** ['kʌnstəbl] (BRIT) n ≃ agent m de police, gendarme m; **chief ~** ≃ préfet m de police; **constabulary** [kən'stæbjulərɪ] (BRIT) n ≃ police f, gendarmerie f

**constant** ['kɔnstənt] adj constant(e); incessant(e); **~ly** adv constamment, sans cesse

**constipated** ['kɔnstɪpeɪtɪd] adj constipé(e); **constipation** [kɔnstɪ'peɪʃən] n constipation f

**constituency** [kən'stɪtjuənsɪ] n circonscription électorale

**constituent** [kən'stɪtjuənt] n (POL) électeur(-trice); (part) élément constitutif, composant m

**constitution** [kɔnstɪ'tjuːʃən] n constitution f; **~al** adj constitutionnel(le)

**constraint** [kən'streɪnt] n contrainte f

**construct** [kən'strʌkt] vt construire;

**~ion** n construction f; **~ive** adj constructif(-ive); **~ive dismissal** démission forcée

**consul** ['kɔnsl] n consul m; **~ate** ['kɔnsjulɪt] n consulat m

**consult** [kən'sʌlt] vt consulter; **~ant** n (MED) médecin consultant; (other specialist) consultant m, (expert-)conseil m; **~ing room** (BRIT) n cabinet m de consultation

**consume** [kən'sjuːm] vt consommer; **~r** n consommateur(-trice); **~r goods** npl biens mpl de consommation; **~r society** n société f de consommation

**consummate** ['kɔnsʌmeɪt] vt consommer

**consumption** [kən'sʌmpʃən] n consommation f

**cont.** abbr (= continued) suite

**contact** ['kɔntækt] n contact m; (person) connaissance f, relation f ♦ vt contacter, se mettre en contact or en rapport avec; **~ lenses** npl verres mpl de contact, lentilles fpl

**contagious** [kən'teɪdʒəs] adj contagieux(-euse)

**contain** [kən'teɪn] vt contenir; **to ~ o.s.** se contenir, se maîtriser; **~er** n récipient m; (for shipping etc) container m

**contaminate** [kən'tæmɪneɪt] vt contaminer

**cont'd** abbr (= continued) suite

**contemplate** ['kɔntəmpleɪt] vt contempler; (consider) envisager

**contemporary** [kən'təmpərɪ] adj contemporain(e); (design, wallpaper) moderne ♦ n contemporain(e)

**contempt** [kən'tempt] n mépris m, dédain m; **~ of court** (LAW) outrage m à l'autorité de la justice; **~uous** [kən'temptjuəs] adj dédaigneux(-euse), méprisant(e)

**contend** [kən'tend] vt: **to ~ that** soutenir or prétendre que ♦ vi: **to ~** (compete) rivaliser avec; (struggle) lutter avec; **~er** n concurrent(e); (POL) candidat(e)

**content** [adj, vb kən'tent, n 'kɔntent] adj content(e), satisfait(e) ♦ vt contenter, satisfaire ♦ n contenu m; (of fat, moisture) teneur f; ~s npl (of container etc) contenu m; (table of) ~s table f des matières; ~ed adj content(e), satisfait(e)

**contention** [kən'tenʃən] n dispute f, contestation f; (argument) assertion f, affirmation f

**contest** [n 'kɔntest, vb kən'test] n combat m, lutte f; (competition) concours m ♦ vt (decision, statement) contester, discuter; (compete for) disputer; ~ant [kən'testənt] n concurrent(e); (in fight) adversaire m/f

**context** ['kɔntekst] n contexte m

**continent** ['kɔntinənt] n continent m; **the C~** (BRIT) l'Europe continentale; ~al [kɔnti'nentl] adj continental(e); ~al breakfast n petit déjeuner m à la française; ~al quilt (BRIT) n couette f

**contingency** [kən'tindʒənsi] n éventualité f, événement imprévu

**continual** [kən'tinjuəl] adj continuel(le)

**continuation** [kəntinju'eiʃən] n continuation f; (after interruption) reprise f; (of story) suite f

**continue** [kən'tinju:] vi, vt continuer; (after interruption) reprendre, poursuivre; **continuity** [kɔnti'nju:iti] n continuité f; (TV etc) enchaînement m; **continuous** [kən'tinjuəs] adj continu(e); (LING) progressif(-ive)

**contort** [kən'tɔ:t] vt tordre, crisper

**contour** ['kɔntuə'] n contour m, profil m; (on map: also: ~ line) courbe f de niveau

**contraband** ['kɔntrəbænd] n contrebande f

**contraceptive** [kɔntrə'septiv] adj contraceptif(-ive), anticonceptionnel(le) ♦ n contraceptif m

**contract** [n 'kɔntrækt, vb kən'trækt] n contrat m ♦ vi (become smaller) se contracter, se resserrer; (COMM): to ~ to

do sth s'engager (par contrat) à faire qch; ~ion [kən'trækʃən] n contraction f; ~or [kən'træktə'] n entrepreneur m

**contradict** [kɔntrə'dikt] vt contredire

**contraflow** ['kɔntrəfləu] n (AUT): ~ lane voie f à contresens; **there's a ~ system in operation on ...** une voie a été mise en sens inverse sur ...

**contraption** [kən'træpʃən] (pej) n machin m, truc m

**contrary¹** ['kɔntrəri] adj contraire, opposé(e) ♦ n contraire m; **on the ~** au contraire; **unless you hear to the ~** sauf avis contraire

**contrary²** [kən'treəri] adj (perverse) contrariant(e), entêté(e)

**contrast** [n 'kɔntrɑːst, vb kən'trɑːst] n contraste m ♦ vt mettre en contraste, contraster; **in ~ to or with** contrairement à

**contravene** [kɔntrə'vi:n] vt enfreindre, violer, contrevenir à

**contribute** [kən'tribju:t] vi contribuer ♦ vt: to ~ £10/an article to donner 10 livres/un article à; to ~ to contribuer à; (newspaper) collaborer à; **contribution** [kɔntri'bju:ʃən] n contribution f; **contributor** [kən'tribjutə'] n (to newspaper) collaborateur(-trice)

**contrive** [kən'traiv] vi: to ~ to do s'arranger pour faire, trouver le moyen de faire

**control** [kən'trəul] vt maîtriser, commander; (check) contrôler ♦ n contrôle m, autorité f; maîtrise f; ~s npl (of machine etc) commandes fpl; (on radio, TV) boutons mpl de réglage; ~led substance narcotique m; **everything is under ~** tout va bien, j'ai (or il a etc) la situation en main; **to be in ~ of** être maître de, maîtriser; **the car went out of ~** j'ai (or il a etc) perdu le contrôle du véhicule; ~ **panel** n tableau m de commande; ~ **room** n salle f des commandes; ~ **tower** n (AVIAT) tour f de contrôle

**controversial** [kɔntrə'və:ʃl] adj (topic)

discutable, controversé(e); (*person*) qui fait beaucoup parler de lui; **controversy** ['kɒntrəvɜːsɪ] n controverse f, polémique f

**convalesce** [kɒnvə'les] vi relever de maladie, se remettre (d'une maladie)

**convector** [kən'vektə] n (*heater*) radiateur m (à convexion)

**convene** [kən'viːn] vt convoquer, assembler ♦ vi se réunir, s'assembler

**convenience** [kən'viːnɪəns] n commodité f; **at your ~** quand or comme cela vous convient; **all modern ~s**, (BRIT) **all mod cons** avec tout le confort moderne, tout confort

**convenient** [kən'viːnɪənt] adj commode

**convent** ['kɒnvənt] n couvent m; **~ school** n couvent m

**convention** [kən'venʃən] n convention f; **~al** adj conventionnel(le)

**conversant** [kən'vɜːsnt] adj: **to be ~ with** s'y connaître; être au courant de

**conversation** [kɒnvə'seɪʃən] n conversation f

**converse** [n 'kɒnvɜːs, vb kən'vɜːs] n contraire m, inverse m ♦ vi s'entretenir; **~ly** [kən'vɜːslɪ] adv inversement, réciproquement

**convert** [vb kən'vɜːt, n 'kɒnvɜːt] vt (REL, COMM) convertir; (*alter*) transformer; (*house*) aménager ♦ n converti(e); **~ible** [kən'vɜːtəbl] n (voiture f) décapotable f

**convey** [kən'veɪ] vt transporter; (*thanks*) transmettre; (*idea*) communiquer; **~or belt** n convoyeur m, tapis roulant

**convict** [vb kən'vɪkt, n 'kɒnvɪkt] vt déclarer (or reconnaître) coupable ♦ n forçat m, détenu m; **~ion** [kən'vɪkʃən] n (LAW) condamnation f; (*belief*) conviction f

**convince** [kən'vɪns] vt convaincre, persuader; **convincing** adj persuasif(-ive), convaincant(e)

**convoluted** ['kɒnvəlu:tɪd] adj (argu-

ment) compliqué(e)

**convulse** [kən'vʌls] vt: **to be ~d with laughter/pain** se tordre de rire/douleur

**cook** [kuk] vt (faire) cuire ♦ vi cuire; (*person*) faire la cuisine ♦ n cuisinier(-ière); **~book** n livre m de cuisine; **~er** n cuisinière f; **~ery** n cuisine f; **~ery book** (BRIT) n = **cookbook**; **~ie** (US) n biscuit m, petit gâteau sec; **~ing** n cuisine f

**cool** [kuːl] adj frais (fraîche); (*calm*, *unemotional*) calme; (*unfriendly*) froid(e) ♦ vt, vi rafraîchir, refroidir

**coop** [kuːp] n poulailler m; (*for rabbits*) clapier m ♦ vt: **to ~ up** (*fig*) cloîtrer, enfermer

**cooperate** [kəu'ɒpəreɪt] vi coopérer, collaborer; **cooperation** [kəuɒpə'reɪʃən] n coopération f, collaboration f; **cooperative** [kəu'ɒpərətɪv] adj coopératif(-ive) ♦ n coopérative f

**coordinate** [vb kəu'ɔːdɪneɪt, n kəu'ɔːdɪnət] vt coordonner ♦ n (MATH) coordonnée f; **~s** npl (*clothes*) ensemble m, coordonnés mpl

**co-ownership** [kəu'əunəʃɪp] n copropriété f

**cop** [kɒp] (*inf*) n flic m

**cope** [kəup] vi: **to ~ with** faire face à; (*solve*) venir à bout de

**copper** ['kɒpə] n cuivre m; (BRIT: inf: *policeman*) flic m; **~s** npl (*coins*) petite monnaie

**copy** ['kɒpɪ] n copie f; (*of book etc*) exemplaire m ♦ vt copier; **~right** n droit m d'auteur, copyright m

**coral** ['kɒrəl] n corail m

**cord** [kɔːd] n corde f; (*fabric*) velours côtelé; (ELEC) cordon m, fil m

**cordial** ['kɔːdɪəl] adj cordial(e), chaleureux(-euse) ♦ n cordial m

**cordon** ['kɔːdn] n cordon m; **~ off** vt boucler (*par cordon de police*)

**corduroy** ['kɔːdərɔɪ] n velours côtelé

**core** [kɔː] n noyau m; (*of fruit*) trognon m, cœur m; (*of building, problem*) cœur

♦ vt enlever le trognon or le cœur de

**cork** [kɔːk] n liège m; (of bottle) bouchon m; **~screw** n tire-bouchon m

**corn** [kɔːn] n (BRIT: wheat) blé m; (US: maize) maïs m; (on foot) cor m; **~ on the cob** (CULIN) épi m de maïs; **~ed beef** n corned-beef m

**corner** ['kɔːnər] n coin m; (AUT) tournant m, virage m; (FOOTBALL: also: **~ kick**) corner m ♦ vt acculer, mettre au pied du mur; coincer; (COMM: market) accaparer ♦ vi prendre un virage; **~stone** n pierre f angulaire

**cornet** ['kɔːnɪt] n (MUS) cornet m à pistons; (BRIT: of ice-cream) cornet (de glace)

**cornflakes** ['kɔːnfleɪks] npl corn-flakes mpl

**cornflour** ['kɔːnflaʊər] (BRIT), **cornstarch** ['kɔːnstɑːtʃ] (US) n farine f de maïs, maïzena f ®

**Cornwall** ['kɔːnwəl] n Cornouailles f

**corny** ['kɔːnɪ] (inf) adj rebattu(e)

**coronary** ['kɔrənərɪ] n (also: **~ thrombosis**) infarctus m (du myocarde), thrombose f coronarienne

**coronation** [kɔrə'neɪʃən] n couronnement m

**coroner** ['kɔrənər] n officiel chargé de déterminer les causes d'un décès

**corporal** ['kɔːpərəl] n caporal m, brigadier m ♦ adj: **~ punishment** châtiment corporel

**corporate** ['kɔːpərɪt] adj en commun, collectif(-ive); (COMM) de l'entreprise

**corporation** [kɔːpə'reɪʃən] n (of town) municipalité f, conseil municipal; (COMM) société f

**corps** [kɔːr] (pl ~) n corps m

**corpse** [kɔːps] n cadavre m

**correct** [kə'rɛkt] adj (also: accurate) correct(e), exact(e); (proper) correct, convenable ♦ vt corriger; **~ion** n correction f

**correspond** [kɔrɪs'pɔnd] vi correspondre; **~ence** n correspondance f; **~ence course** n cours m par correspondance;

**~ent** n correspondant(e)

**corridor** ['kɔrɪdɔːr] n couloir m, corridor m

**corrode** [kə'rəud] vt corroder, ronger ♦ vi se corroder

**corrugated** ['kɔrəgeɪtɪd] adj plissé(e); ondulé(e); **~ iron** n tôle ondulée

**corrupt** [kə'rʌpt] adj corrompu(e) ♦ vt corrompre; **~ion** n corruption f

**Corsica** ['kɔːsɪkə] n Corse f

**cosmetic** [kɔz'mɛtɪk] n produit m de beauté, cosmétique m

**cost** [kɔst] (pt, pp cost) n coût m ♦ vi coûter ♦ vt établir or calculer le prix de revient de; **~s** npl (COMM) frais mpl; (LAW) dépens mpl; **it ~s £5/too much** cela coûte cinq livres/c'est trop cher; **at all ~s** à coûte que coûte, à tout prix

**co-star** ['kəustɑːr] n partenaire m/f

**cost: ~-effective** adj rentable; **~ly** adj coûteux(-euse); **~-of-living** adj: **~-of-living allowance** indemnité f de vie chère; **~-of-living index** index m du coût de la vie; **~ price** (BRIT) n prix coûtant or de revient

**costume** ['kɔstjuːm] n costume m; (lady's suit) tailleur m; (BRIT: also: **swimming ~**) maillot m (de bain); **~ jewellery** n bijoux mpl fantaisie

**cosy** ['kəuzɪ] (US **cozy**) adj douillet(te); (person) à l'aise, au chaud

**cot** [kɔt] n (BRIT: child's) lit m d'enfant, petit lit; (US: campbed) lit de camp

**cottage** ['kɔtɪdʒ] n petite maison (à la campagne), cottage m; **~ cheese** n fromage blanc (maigre)

**cotton** ['kɔtn] n coton m; (thread) fil m (de coton); **~ on** (inf) vi: **to ~ on to** piger; **~ candy** (US) n barbe f à papa; **~ wool** (BRIT) n ouate f, coton m hydrophile

**couch** [kautʃ] n canapé m; divan m

**couchette** [kuː'ʃɛt] n couchette f

**cough** [kɔf] vi tousser ♦ n toux f; **~ sweet** n pastille f pour or contre la toux

**could** [kud] pt of **can²**; **~n't** = **could not**

**council** ['kaʊnsl] *n* conseil *m*; **city** *or* **town** ~ conseil municipal; ~ **estate** (*BRIT*) *n* (zone *f* de) logements loués *à*/ par la municipalité; ~ **house** (*BRIT*) *n* maison *f* (à loyer modéré) louée par la municipalité; ~**lor** *n* conseiller(-ère)

**counsel** ['kaʊnsl] *n* (*lawyer*) avocat(e); (*advice*) conseil *m*, consultation *f*; ~**lor** *n* conseiller(-ère); (*US: lawyer*) avocat(e)

**count** [kaʊnt] *vt, vi* compter ♦ *n* compte *m*; (*nobleman*) comte *m*; ~ **on** *vt* fus compter sur; ~**down** *n* compte *m* à rebours

**countenance** ['kaʊntɪnəns] *n* expression *f* ♦ *vt* approuver

**counter** ['kaʊntə] *n* comptoir *m*; (*in post office, bank*) guichet *m*; (*in game*) jeton *m* ♦ *vt* aller à l'encontre de, opposer ♦ *adv*: ~ **to** contrairement à; ~**act** *vt* neutraliser, contrebalancer; ~**feit** *n* faux *m*, contrefaçon *f* ♦ *vt* contrefaire ♦ *adj* faux (fausse); ~**foil** *n* talon *m*, souche *f*; ~**part** *n* (*of person etc*) homologue *m/f*

**countess** ['kaʊntɪs] *n* comtesse *f*

**countless** ['kaʊntlɪs] *adj* innombrable

**country** ['kʌntrɪ] *n* pays *m*; (*native land*) patrie *f*; (*as opposed to town*) campagne *f*; (*region*) région *f*, pays; ~ **dancing** (*BRIT*) *n* danse *f* folklorique; ~ **house** *n* manoir *m*, (petit) château; ~**man** (*irreg*) *n* (*compatriot*) compatriote *m*; (*country dweller*) habitant *m* de la campagne, campagnard *m*; ~**side** *n* campagne *f*

**county** ['kaʊntɪ] *n* comté *m*

**coup** [kuː] (*pl* ~**s**) *n* beau coup *m*; (*also:* ~ **d'état**) coup d'État

**couple** ['kʌpl] *n* couple *m*; **a** ~ **of** deux; (*a few*) quelques

**coupon** ['kuːpɒn] *n* coupon *m*, bon-prime *m*, bon-réclame *m*; (*COMM*) coupon

**courage** ['kʌrɪdʒ] *n* courage *m*

**courier** ['kʊrɪə] *n* messager *m*, courrier *m*; (*for tourists*) accompagnateur(-trice), guide *m/f*

**course** [kɔːs] *n* cours *m*; (*of ship*) route *f*; (*for golf*) terrain *m*; (*part of meal*) plat *m*; **first** ~ entrée *f*; **of** ~ bien sûr; ~ **of action** parti *m*, ligne *f* de conduite; ~ **of treatment** (*MED*) traitement *m*

**court** [kɔːt] *n* cour *f*; (*LAW*) cour, tribunal *m*; (*TENNIS*) court *m* ♦ *vt* (*woman*) courtiser, faire la cour à; **to take to** ~ actionner or poursuivre en justice

**courteous** ['kɜːtɪəs] *adj* courtois(e), poli(e); **courtesy** ['kɜːtəsɪ] *n* courtoisie *f*, politesse *f*; **(by) courtesy of** avec l'aimable autorisation de; **courtesy bus** *or* **coach** navette gratuite

**court**: ~**-house** (*US*) *n* palais *m* de justice; ~**ier** *n* courtisan *m*, dame *f* de la cour; ~ **martial** (*pl* **courts martial**) *n* cour martiale, conseil *m* de guerre; ~**room** *n* salle *f* de tribunal; ~**yard** *n* cour *f*

**cousin** ['kʌzn] *n* cousin(e); **first** ~ cousin(e) germain(e)

**cove** [kəʊv] *n* petite baie, anse *f*

**covenant** ['kʌvənənt] *n* engagement *m*

**cover** ['kʌvə] *vt* couvrir ♦ *n* couverture *f*; (*of pan*) couvercle *m*; (*over furniture*) housse *f*; (*shelter*) abri *m*; **to take to** ~ se mettre à l'abri; **under** ~ à l'abri; **under** ~ **of darkness** à la faveur de la nuit; **under separate** ~ (*COMM*) sous pli séparé; **to** ~ **up for sb** couvrir qn; ~**age** *n* (*TV, PRESS*) reportage *m*; ~ **charge** *n* couvert *m* (*supplément à payer*); ~**ing** *n* couche *f*; ~**ing letter** (*US* **cover letter**) *n* lettre explicative; ~ **note** *n* (*INSURANCE*) police *f* provisoire

**covert** ['kʌvət] *adj* (*threat*) voilé(e), caché(e); (*glance*) furtif(-ive)

**cover-up** ['kʌvərʌp] *n* tentative *f* pour étouffer une affaire

**covet** ['kʌvɪt] *vt* convoiter

**cow** [kaʊ] *n* vache *f* ♦ *vt* effrayer, intimider

**coward** ['kaʊəd] *n* lâche *m/f*; ~**ice** *n* lâcheté *f*; ~**ly** *adj* lâche

**cowboy** ['kaʊbɔɪ] *n* cow-boy *m*

**cower** ['kaʊə] *vi* se recroqueviller

**coy** [kɔɪ] adj faussement effarouché(e) or timide

**cozy** ['kəʊzɪ] (US) adj = **cosy**

**CPA** (US) n abbr = **certified public accountant**

**crab** [kræb] n crabe m; ~ **apple** n pomme f sauvage

**crack** [kræk] n (split) fente f, fissure f; (in cup, bone etc) fêlure f; (in wall) lézarde f; (noise) craquement m, coup (sec); (drug) crack m ♦ vt fendre, fissurer; fêler; lézarder; (whip) faire claquer; (nut) casser; (code) déchiffrer; (joke) résoudre ♦ adj (athlete) de première classe, d'élite; ~ **down on** vt fus mettre un frein à; ~ **up** vi être au bout du rouleau, s'effondrer; ~**ed** adj (cup, bone) fêlé(e); (broken) cassé(e); (wall) lézardé(e); (surface) craquelé(e); (inf: mad) cinglé(e); ~**er** n (Christmas cracker) pétard m; (biscuit) biscuit m

**crackle** ['krækl] vi crépiter, grésiller

**cradle** ['kreɪdl] n berceau m

**craft** [krɑːft] n métier (artisanal); (pl inv: boat) embarcation f, barque f; (: plane) appareil m; ~**sman** (irreg) n artisan m, ouvrier (qualifié); ~**smanship** n travail m; ~**y** adj rusé(e), malin(-igne)

**crag** [kræg] n rocher escarpé

**cram** [kræm] vt (fill): to ~ **sth with** bourrer qch de; (put): to ~ **sth into** fourrer qch dans ♦ vi (for exams) bachoter

**cramp** [kræmp] n crampe f ♦ vt gêner, entraver; ~**ed** adj à l'étroit, très serré(e)

**cranberry** ['krænbərɪ] n canneberge f

**crane** [kreɪn] n grue f

**crank** [kræŋk] n manivelle f; (person) excentrique m/f

**cranny** ['krænɪ] n see **nook**

**crash** [kræʃ] n fracas m; (of car) collision f; (of plane) accident m ♦ vt (plane) s'écraser; (two cars) se percuter, s'emboutir; (COMM) s'effondrer; to ~ **into** se jeter or se fracasser contre; ~ **course** n cours intensif; ~ **helmet** n casque (protecteur); ~

**landing** n atterrissage forcé or en catastrophe

**crate** [kreɪt] n cageot m; (for bottles) caisse f

**cravat(e)** [krə'væt] n foulard (noué autour du cou)

**crave** [kreɪv] vt, vi: to ~ (**for**) avoir une envie irrésistible de

**crawl** [krɔːl] vi ramper; (vehicle) avancer au pas ♦ n (SWIMMING) crawl m

**crayfish** ['kreɪfɪʃ] n inv (freshwater) écrevisse f; (saltwater) langoustine f

**crayon** ['kreɪən] n crayon m (de couleur)

**craze** [kreɪz] n engouement m

**crazy** ['kreɪzɪ] adj fou (folle)

**creak** [kriːk] vi grincer; craquer

**cream** [kriːm] n crème f ♦ adj (colour) crème inv; ~ **cake** n (petit) gâteau m à la crème; ~ **cheese** n fromage m à la crème, fromage blanc; ~**y** adj crémeux(-euse)

**crease** [kriːs] n pli m ♦ vt froisser, chiffonner ♦ vi se froisser, se chiffonner

**create** [kriː'eɪt] vt créer; **creation** n création f; **creative** adj (artistic) créatif(-ive); (ingenious) ingénieux (-euse)

**creature** ['kriːtʃə*] n créature f

**crèche** [kreʃ] n garderie f, crèche f

**credence** ['kriːdns] n: to **lend** or **give** ~ to ajouter foi à

**credentials** [krɪ'denʃlz] npl (references) références fpl; (papers of identity) pièce f d'identité

**credit** ['kredɪt] n crédit m; (recognition) honneur m ♦ vt (COMM) créditer; (believe: also: ~ **with**) ajouter foi à, croire; ~**s** npl (CINEMA, TV) générique m; **to be in** ~ (person, bank account) être créditeur(-trice); **to** ~ **sb with** (fig) prêter or attribuer à qn; ~ **card** n carte f de crédit; ~**or** n créancier(-ière)

**creed** [kriːd] n croyance f; credo m

**creek** [kriːk] n crique f, anse f; (US: stream) ruisseau m, petit cours d'eau

**creep** [kriːp] (pt, pp **crept**) vi ramper;

**~er** n plante grimpante; **~y** adj (frightening) qui fait frissonner, qui donne la chair de poule

**cremate** ['kriːmeit] vt incinérer; **crematorium** [kremə'tɔːriəm] (pl crematoria) n four m crématoire

**crêpe** [kreip] n crêpe m; **~ bandage** (BRIT) n bande f Velpeau ®

**crept** [krept] pt, pp of **creep**

**crescent** ['kresnt] n croissant m; (street) rue f (en arc de cercle)

**cress** [kres] n cresson m

**crest** [krest] n crête f; **~fallen** adj déconfit(e), découragé(e)

**Crete** [kriːt] n Crète f

**crevice** ['krevis] n fissure f, lézarde f, fente f

**crew** [kruː] n équipage m; (CINEMA) équipe f; **~cut** n: to have a **~cut** avoir les cheveux en brosse; **~neck** n col m ras du cou

**crib** [krib] n lit m d'enfant; (for baby) berceau m ♦ vt (inf) copier

**crick** [krik] n: **~ in the neck** torticolis m; **~ in the back** tour m de reins

**cricket** ['krikit] n (insect) grillon m, cricri m inv; (game) cricket m

**crime** [kraim] n crime m; **criminal** ['kriminl] adj, n criminel(le)

**crimson** ['krimzn] adj cramoisi(e)

**cringe** [krindʒ] vi avoir un mouvement de recul

**crinkle** ['kriŋkl] vt froisser, chiffonner

**cripple** ['kripl] n boiteux(-euse), infirme m/f ♦ vt estropier

**crisis** ['kraisis] (pl crises) n crise f

**crisp** [krisp] adj croquant(e); (weather) vif (vive); (manner etc) brusque; **~s** (BRIT) npl (pommes) chips fpl

**crisscross** ['kriskrɔs] adj entrecroisé(e)

**criterion** [krai'tiəriən] (pl criteria) n critère m

**critic** ['kritik] n critique m; **~al** adj critique; **~ally** adv (examine) d'un œil critique; (speak etc) sévèrement; **~ally ill** gravement malade; **~ism** ['kritisizəm] n critique f; **~ize** ['kritisaiz] vt critiquer

**croak** [krəuk] vi (frog) coasser; (raven) croasser; (person) parler d'une voix rauque

**Croatia** [krəu'eiʃə] n Croatie f

**crochet** ['krəuʃei] n travail m au crochet

**crockery** ['krɔkəri] n vaisselle f

**crocodile** ['krɔkədail] n crocodile m

**crocus** ['krəukəs] n crocus m

**croft** [krɔft] n petite ferme

**crony** ['krəuni] (inf: pej) n copain (copine)

**crook** [kruk] n escroc m; (of shepherd) houlette f; **~ed** ['krukid] adj courbé(e), tordu(e); (action) malhonnête

**crop** [krɔp] n (produce) culture f; (amount produced) récolte f; (riding ~) cravache f ♦ vt (hair) tondre; **~ up** vi surgir, se présenter, survenir

**cross** [krɔs] n croix f; (BIO etc) croisement m ♦ vt (street etc) traverser; (arms, legs, BIO) croiser; (cheque) barrer ♦ adj en colère, fâché(e); **~ out** vt barrer, biffer; **~ over** vi traverser; **~bar** n barre (transversale); **~country (race)** n cross(-country); **~examine** vt (LAW) faire subir un examen contradictoire à; **~eyed** adj qui louche; **~fire** n feux croisés; **~ing** n (sea passage) traversée f; (also: **pedestrian ~ing**) passage clouté; **~ing guard** (US) n contractuel qui fait traverser la rue aux enfants; **~ purposes** npl: to be at **~ purposes** with sb comprendre qn de travers; **~reference** n renvoi m, référence f; **~roads** n carrefour m; **~ section** n (of object) coupe transversale; (in population) échantillon m, tranche f; **~walk** (US) n passage clouté; **~wind** n vent m de travers; **~word** n mots mpl croisés

**crotch** [krɔtʃ] n (ANAT, of garment) entre-jambes m inv

**crouch** [krautʃ] vi s'accroupir; se tapir

**crow** [krəu] n (bird) corneille f; (of cock) chant m du coq, cocorico m ♦ vi (cock) chanter

**crowbar** ['krəubaː] n levier m

**crowd** [kraud] n foule f ♦ vt remplir ♦ vi affluer, s'attrouper, s'entasser; **to ~ in** entrer en foule; **~ed** adj bondé(e), plein(e)

**crown** [kraun] n couronne f; (of head) sommet m de la tête; (of hill) sommet ♦ vt couronner; **~ jewels** npl joyaux mpl de la Couronne

**crow's-feet** [ˈkrəuzfiːt] npl pattes fpl d'oie

**crucial** [ˈkruːʃl] adj crucial(e), décisif (-ive)

**crucifix** [ˈkruːsɪfɪks] n (REL) crucifix m; **~ion** [kruːsɪˈfɪkʃən] n (REL) crucifixion f

**crude** [kruːd] adj (materials) brut(e); non raffiné(e); (fig: basic) rudimentaire, sommaire; (: vulgar) grossier (-ère); **~ (oil)** n (pétrole) brut m

**cruel** [ˈkruəl] adj cruel(le); **~ty** cruauté f

**cruise** [kruːz] n croisière f ♦ vi (ship) croiser; (car) rouler; **~r** n croiseur m; (motorboat) yacht m de croisière

**crumb** [krʌm] n miette f

**crumble** [ˈkrʌmbl] vt émietter ♦ vi (plaster etc) s'effriter; (land, earth) s'ébouler; (building) s'écrouler, crouler; (fig) s'effondrer; **crumbly** adj friable

**crumpet** [ˈkrʌmpɪt] n petite crêpe (épaisse)

**crumple** [ˈkrʌmpl] vt froisser, friper

**crunch** [krʌntʃ] vt croquer; (underfoot) faire craquer or crisser, écraser ♦ n (fig) instant m or moment m critique, moment m de vérité; **~y** adj croquant(e), croustillant(e)

**crusade** [kruːˈseɪd] n croisade f

**crush** [krʌʃ] n foule f, cohue f; (love): **to have a ~ on sb** avoir le béguin pour qn (inf); (drink): **lemon ~** citron pressé ♦ vt écraser; (crumple) froisser; (fig: hopes) anéantir

**crust** [krʌst] n croûte f

**crutch** [krʌtʃ] n béquille f

**crux** [krʌks] n point crucial

**cry** [kraɪ] vi pleurer; (shout: also: **~ out**) crier ♦ n cri m; **~ off** (inf) vi se dédire; se décommander

**cryptic** [ˈkrɪptɪk] adj énigmatique

**crystal** [ˈkrɪstl] n cristal m; **~-clear** adj clair(e) comme de l'eau de roche

**CSA** n abbr (= Child Support Agency) organisme pour la protection des enfants de parents séparés, qui contrôle le versement des pensions alimentaires

**CTC** n abbr = **city technology college**

**cub** [kʌb] n petit m (d'un animal); (also: **C~ scout**) louveteau m

**Cuba** [ˈkjuːbə] n Cuba m

**cube** [kjuːb] n cube m ♦ vt (MATH) élever au cube; **cubic** adj cubique; **cubic metre** etc mètre m etc cube; **cubic capacity** n cylindrée f

**cubicle** [ˈkjuːbɪkl] n (in hospital) box m; (at pool) cabine f

**cuckoo** [ˈkuːkuː] n coucou m; **~ clock** n (pendule f à) coucou m

**cucumber** [ˈkjuːkʌmbəʳ] n concombre m

**cuddle** [ˈkʌdl] vt câliner, caresser ♦ vi se blottir l'un contre l'autre

**cue** [kjuː] n (snooker ~) queue f de billard; (THEATRE etc) signal m

**cuff** [kʌf] n (BRIT: of shirt, coat etc) poignet m, manchette f; (US: of trousers) revers m; (blow) tape f; **off the ~** à l'improviste; **~ links** npl boutons mpl de manchette

**cul-de-sac** [ˈkʌldəsæk] n cul-de-sac m, impasse f

**cull** [kʌl] vt sélectionner ♦ n (of animals) massacre m

**culminate** [ˈkʌlmɪneɪt] vi: **to ~ in** finir or se terminer par; (end in) mener à; **culmination** [kʌlmɪˈneɪʃən] n point culminant

**culottes** [kjuːˈlɒts] npl jupe-culotte f

**culprit** [ˈkʌlprɪt] n coupable m/f

**cult** [kʌlt] n culte m

**cultivate** [ˈkʌltɪveɪt] vt cultiver; **cultivation** [kʌltɪˈveɪʃən] n culture f

**cultural** [ˈkʌltʃərəl] adj culturel(le)

**culture** [ˈkʌltʃəʳ] n culture f; **~d** adj (person) cultivé(e)

**cumbersome** [ˈkʌmbəsəm] adj encombrant(e), embarrassant(e)

**cunning** [ˈkʌnɪŋ] n ruse f, astuce f
♦ adj rusé(e), malin(-igne); (device, idea) astucieux(-euse)

**cup** [kʌp] n tasse f; (as prize) coupe f; (of bra) bonnet m

**cupboard** [ˈkʌbəd] n armoire f; (built-in) placard m

**cup tie** (BRIT) n match m de coupe

**curate** [ˈkjuərɪt] n vicaire m

**curator** [kjuəˈreɪtə] n conservateur m (d'un musée etc)

**curb** [kə:b] vt refréner, mettre un frein à ♦ n (fig) frein m, restriction f; (US: kerb) bord m du trottoir

**curdle** [ˈkə:dl] vi se cailler

**cure** [kjuə] vt guérir; (CULIN: salt) saler; (: smoke) fumer; (: dry) sécher ♦ n remède m

**curfew** [ˈkə:fju:] n couvre-feu m

**curiosity** [kjuərɪˈɔsɪti] n curiosité f

**curious** [ˈkjuərɪəs] adj curieux(-euse)

**curl** [kə:l] n boucle f (de cheveux) ♦ vt, vi boucler; (tightly) friser; **~ up** vi s'enrouler; se pelotonner; **~er** n bigoudi m, rouleau m; **~y** adj bouclé(e); frisé(e)

**currant** [ˈkʌrnt] n (dried) raisin m de Corinthe, raisin sec; (bush) groseiller m; (fruit) groseille f

**currency** [ˈkʌrnsɪ] n monnaie f; **to gain ~** (fig) s'accréditer

**current** [ˈkʌrnt] n courant m ♦ adj courant(e); **~ account** (BRIT) n compte courant; **~ affairs** npl (questions fpl d')actualité f; **~ly** adv actuellement

**curriculum** [kəˈrɪkjuləm] (pl **~s** or **curricula**) n programme m d'études; **~ vitae** n curriculum vitae m

**curry** [ˈkʌrɪ] n curry m ♦ vt: **to ~ favour with** chercher à s'attirer les bonnes grâces de

**curse** [kə:s] vi jurer, blasphémer ♦ vt maudire ♦ n (spell) malédiction f; (problem, scourge) fléau m; (swearword) juron m

**cursor** [ˈkə:sə] n (COMPUT) curseur m

**cursory** [ˈkə:sərɪ] adj superficiel(le), hâtif(-ive)

**curt** [kə:t] adj brusque, sec (sèche)

**curtail** [kə:ˈteɪl] vt (visit etc) écourter; (expenses, freedom etc) réduire

**curtain** [ˈkə:tn] n rideau m

**curts(e)y** [ˈkə:tsɪ] vi faire une révérence

**curve** [kə:v] n courbe f; (in the road) tournant m, virage m ♦ vi se courber; (road) faire une courbe

**cushion** [ˈkuʃən] n coussin m ♦ vt (fall, shock) amortir

**custard** [ˈkʌstəd] n (for pouring) crème anglaise

**custody** [ˈkʌstədɪ] n (of child) garde f; **to take sb into ~** (suspect) placer en détention préventive

**custom** [ˈkʌstəm] n coutume f, usage m; (COMM) clientèle f; **~ary** adj habituel(le)

**customer** [ˈkʌstəmə] n client(e)

**customized** [ˈkʌstəmaɪzd] adj (car etc) construit(e) sur commande

**custom-made** [ˈkʌstəmˈmeɪd] adj (clothes) fait(e) sur mesure; (other goods) hors série, fait(e) sur commande

**customs** [ˈkʌstəmz] npl douane f; **~ officer** n douanier(-ière)

**cut** [kʌt] (pt, pp **cut**) vt couper; (meat) découper; (reduce) réduire ♦ vi couper ♦ n coupure f; (of clothes) coupe f; (in salary etc) réduction f; (of meat) morceau m; **to ~ one's hand** se couper la main; **to ~ a tooth** percer une dent; **~ down** vt fus (tree etc) couper, abattre; (consumption) réduire; **~ off** vt couper; (fig) isoler; **~ out** vt découper; (stop) arrêter; (remove) ôter; **~ up** vt (paper, meat) découper; **~back** n réduction f

**cute** [kju:t] adj mignon(ne), adorable

**cutlery** [ˈkʌtlərɪ] n couverts mpl

**cutlet** [ˈkʌtlɪt] n côtelette f

**cut: ~out** n (switch) coupe-circuit m inv; (cardboard cutout) découpage m; **~-price** (US **cut-rate**) adj au rabais, à prix réduit; **~-throat** n assassin m ♦ adj acharné(e); **~ting** adj tranchant(e),

**coupant(e)**; (fig) cinglant(e), mordant(e) ♦ n (BRIT: from newspaper) coupure f (de journal); (from plant) bouture f

**CV** n abbr = **curriculum vitae**

**cwt** abbr = **hundredweight(s)**

**cyanide** ['saɪənaɪd] n cyanure m

**cybercafé** ['saɪbəkæfeɪ] n cybercafé m

**cyberspace** ['saɪbəspeɪs] n cyberspace m

**cycle** ['saɪkl] n cycle m; (bicycle) bicyclette f, vélo m ♦ vi faire de la bicyclette; ~ **hire** n location f de vélos; ~ **lane** or **path** n piste f cyclable; **cycling** n cyclisme m; **cyclist** ['saɪklɪst] n cycliste m/f

**cygnet** ['sɪgnɪt] n jeune cygne m

**cylinder** ['sɪlɪndə'] n cylindre m; ~ **head gasket** n joint m de culasse

**cymbals** ['sɪmblz] npl cymbales fpl

**cynic** ['sɪnɪk] n cynique m/f; ~**al** adj cynique; ~**ism** ['sɪnɪsɪzəm] n cynisme m

**Cypriot** ['sɪprɪət] adj cypriote, chypriote ♦ n Cypriote m/f, Chypriote m/f

**Cyprus** ['saɪprəs] n Chypre f

**cyst** [sɪst] n kyste m

**cystitis** [sɪs'taɪtɪs] n cystite f

**czar** [zɑː'] n tsar m

**Czech** [tʃɛk] adj tchèque ♦ n Tchèque m/f; (LING) tchèque m

**Czechoslovak** [tʃɛkə'sləuvæk] adj, n = **Czechoslovakian**

**Czechoslovakia** [tʃɛkəslə'vækɪə] n Tchécoslovaquie f

# D, d

**D** [diː] n (MUS) ré m

**dab** [dæb] vt (eyes, wound) tamponner; (paint, cream) appliquer (par petites touches or rapidement)

**dabble** ['dæbl] vi: **to ~ in** faire or se mêler or s'occuper un peu de

**dad** [dæd] n, **daddy** ['dædɪ] n papa m

**daffodil** ['dæfədɪl] n jonquille f

**daft** [dɑːft] adj idiot(e), stupide

**dagger** ['dægə'] n poignard m

**daily** ['deɪlɪ] adj quotidien(ne), journalier(-ère) ♦ n quotidien m ♦ adv tous les jours

**dainty** ['deɪntɪ] adj délicat(e), mignon(ne)

**dairy** ['dɛərɪ] n (BRIT: shop) crémerie f, laiterie f; (on farm) laiterie; ~ **products** npl produits laitiers; ~ **store** n (US) n crémerie f, laiterie f

**daisy** ['deɪzɪ] n pâquerette f

**dale** [deɪl] n vallon m

**dam** [dæm] n barrage m ♦ vt endiguer

**damage** ['dæmɪdʒ] n dégâts mpl, dommages mpl; (fig) tort m ♦ vt endommager, abîmer; (fig) faire du tort à; ~**s** npl (LAW) dommages-intérêts mpl

**damn** [dæm] vt condamner; (curse) maudire ♦ adj (inf): **I don't give a ~** je m'en fous ♦ adj (inf: also: ~**ed**): **this ... ...** ce sacré or foutu ...; ~ **(it)!** zut!; ~**ing** adj accablant(e)

**damp** [dæmp] adj humide ♦ n humidité f ♦ vt (also: ~**en**: cloth, rag) humecter; (: enthusiasm) refroidir

**damson** ['dæmzən] n prune f de Damas

**dance** [dɑːns] n danse f; (social event) bal m ♦ vi danser; ~ **hall** n salle f de bal, dancing m; ~**r** n danseur(-euse)

**dancing** n danse f

**dandelion** ['dændɪlaɪən] n pissenlit m

**dandruff** ['dændrəf] n pellicules fpl

**Dane** [deɪn] n Danois(e)

**danger** ['deɪndʒə'] n danger m; **there is a ~ of fire** il y a (un) risque d'incendie; **in ~** en danger; **he was in ~ of falling** il risquait de tomber; ~**ous** adj dangereux(-euse)

**dangle** ['dæŋgl] vt balancer ♦ vi pendre

**Danish** ['deɪnɪʃ] adj danois(e) ♦ n (LING) danois m

**dare** [dɛə'] vt: **to ~ sb to do** défier qn de faire ♦ vi: **to ~ (to) do sth** oser faire qch; **I ~ say** (I suppose) il est probable (que); **daring** adj hardi(e), audacieux(-euse); (dress) osé(e) ♦ n audace f, hardiesse f

**dark** [dɑːk] adj (night, room) obscur(e), sombre; (colour, complexion) foncé(e), sombre ♦ n: **in the ~** dans le noir; **in the ~ about** (fig) ignorant tout de; **after ~** après la tombée de la nuit; **~en** vt obscurcir, assombrir ♦ vi s'obscurcir, s'assombrir; **~ glasses** npl lunettes noires; **~ness** n obscurité f; **~room** n chambre noire

**darling** [ˈdɑːlɪŋ] adj chéri(e) ♦ n chéri(e); (favourite): **to be the ~ of** être la coqueluche de

**darn** [dɑːn] vt repriser, raccommoder

**dart** [dɑːt] n fléchette f; (sewing) pince f ♦ vi: **to ~ towards** (also: **make a ~ towards**) se précipiter ou s'élancer vers; **to ~ away/along** partir/passer comme une flèche; **~board** n cible f (de jeu de fléchettes); **~s** n (jeu de) fléchettes fpl

**dash** [dæʃ] n (sign) tiret m; (small quantity) goutte f, larme f ♦ vt (missile) jeter ou lancer violemment; (hopes) anéantir ♦ vi: **to ~ towards** (also: **make a ~ towards**) se précipiter ou se ruer vers; **~ away** vi partir à toute allure, filer; **~ off** vi = dash away

**dashboard** [ˈdæʃbɔːd] n (AUT) tableau m de bord

**dashing** [ˈdæʃɪŋ] adj fringant(e)

**data** [ˈdeɪtə] npl données fpl; **~base** n (COMPUT) base f de données; **~ processing** n traitement m de données

**date** [deɪt] n date f; (with sb) rendez-vous m; (fruit) datte f ♦ vt dater; (person) sortir avec; **~ of birth** date de naissance; **to ~** (until now) à ce jour; **out of ~** (passport) périmé(e); (theory etc) dépassé(e); (clothes etc) démodé(e); **up to ~** moderne; (news) très récent; **~d** [ˈdeɪtɪd] adj démodé(e); **~ rape** n viol m à (à l'issue d'un rendez-vous galant)

**daub** [dɔːb] vt barbouiller

**daughter** [ˈdɔːtə] n fille f; **~-in-law** n belle-fille f, bru f

**daunting** [ˈdɔːntɪŋ] adj décourageant(e)

**dawdle** [ˈdɔːdl] vi traîner, lambiner

**dawn** [dɔːn] n aube f, aurore f ♦ vi (day) se lever, poindre; (fig): **it ~ed on him that ...** il lui vint à l'esprit que ...

**day** [deɪ] n jour m; (as duration) journée f; (period of time, age) époque f, temps m; **the ~ before** la veille, le jour précédent; **the ~ after, the following ~** le lendemain, le jour suivant; **the ~ after tomorrow** après-demain; **the ~ before yesterday** avant-hier; **by ~** de jour; **~break** n point m du jour; **~dream** vi rêver (tout éveillé); **~light** n (lumière f du) jour m; **~return** (BRIT) n billet m d'aller-retour (valable pour la journée); **~time** n jour m, journée f; **~-to-~** adj quotidien(ne); (event) journalier(-ère)

**daze** [deɪz] vt (stun) étourdir ♦ n: **in a ~** étourdi(e), hébété(e)

**dazzle** [ˈdæzl] vt éblouir, aveugler

**DC** abbr (= direct current) courant continu

**D-day** [ˈdiːdeɪ] n le jour J

**dead** [ded] adj mort(e); (numb) engourdi(e), insensible; (battery) à plat; (telephone): **the line is ~** la ligne est coupée ♦ adv absolument, complètement ♦ npl: **the ~** les morts; **he was shot ~** il a été tué d'un coup de revolver; **on time** à l'heure pile; **~ tired** éreinté(e), complètement fourbu(e); **to stop ~** s'arrêter pile ou net; **~en** vt (blow, sound) amortir; (pain) calmer; **~ end** n impasse f; **~ heat** n (SPORT): **to finish in a ~ heat** terminer ex-æquo; **~line** n date f ou heure f limite; **~lock** n impasse f (fig); **~ loss** n: **to be a ~ loss** (inf: person) n'être bon(ne) à rien; **~ly** adj mortel(le); (weapon) meurtrier(-ère); (accuracy) extrême; **~pan** adj impassible; **D~ Sea** n: **the D~ Sea** la mer Morte

**deaf** [def] adj sourd(e); **~en** vt rendre sourd; **~ening** adj assourdissant(e);

**mute** n sourd(e)-muet(te); **~ness** n surdité f

**deal** [di:l] (pt, pp **dealt**) n affaire f, marché m ♦ vt (blow) porter; (cards) donner, distribuer; **a great ~ (of)** beaucoup (de); **~ in** vt fus faire le commerce de; **~ with** vt fus (person, problem) s'occuper de; se charger de; (be about: book etc) traiter de; **~er** n marchand m; **~ings** npl (COMM) transactions fpl; (relations) relations fpl, rapports mpl

**dean** [di:n] n (REL, BRIT: SCOL) doyen m; (US: SCOL) conseiller(-ère) (principal(e)) d'éducation

**dear** [dɪəʳ] adj cher (chère); (expensive) cher, coûteux(-euse) ♦ n: **my ~** mon cher/ma chère; **~ me!** mon Dieu!; **D~ Sir/Madam** (in letter) Monsieur/Madame; **D~ Mr/Mrs X** Cher Monsieur/Chère Madame; **~ly** adv (love) tendrement; (pay) cher

**death** [deθ] n mort f; (fatality) mort m; (ADMIN) décès m; **~ certificate** n acte m de décès; **~ly** adj de mort; **~ penalty** n peine f de mort; **~ rate** n (taux m de) mortalité f; **~ toll** n nombre m de morts

**debase** [dɪ'beɪs] vt (value) déprécier, dévaloriser

**debatable** [dɪ'beɪtəbl] adj discutable

**debate** [dɪ'beɪt] n discussion f, débat m ♦ vt discuter, débattre

**debit** [debɪt] n débit m ♦ vt: **to ~ a sum to sb** or **to sb's account** porter une somme au débit de qn, débiter qn d'une somme; see also **direct**

**debt** [dɛt] n dette f; **to be in ~** avoir des dettes, être endetté(e); **~or** n débiteur(-trice)

**decade** [dɛkeɪd] n décennie f, décade f

**decadence** [dɛkədəns] n décadence f

**decaff** [di:kæf] n (inf) déca m

**decaffeinated** [dɪ'kæfɪneɪtɪd] adj décaféiné(e)

**decanter** [dɪ'kæntəʳ] n carafe f

**decay** [dɪ'keɪ] n (of building) délabrement m; (also: **tooth ~**) carie f (dentai-

re) ♦ vi (rot) se décomposer, pourrir; (: teeth) se carier

**deceased** [dɪ'si:st] n défunt(e)

**deceit** [dɪ'si:t] n tromperie f, supercherie f; **~ful** adj trompeur(-euse); **deceive** [dɪ'si:v] vt tromper

**December** [dɪ'sɛmbəʳ] n décembre m

**decent** [di:sənt] adj décent(e), convenable

**deception** [dɪ'sɛpʃən] n tromperie f

**deceptive** [dɪ'sɛptɪv] adj trompeur (-euse)

**decide** [dɪ'saɪd] vt (person) décider; (question, argument) trancher, régler ♦ vi se décider, décider; **to ~ to do/that** décider de faire/que; **to ~ on** décider, se décider pour; **~d** adj (resolute) résolu(e), décidé(e); (clear, definite) net(te), marqué(e); **~dly** adv résolument; (distinctly) incontestablement, nettement

**deciduous** [dɪ'sɪdjuəs] adj à feuilles caduques

**decimal** [dɛsɪməl] adj décimal(e) ♦ n décimale f; **~ point** n ≈ virgule f

**decipher** [dɪ'saɪfəʳ] vt déchiffrer

**decision** [dɪ'sɪʒən] n décision f

**decisive** [dɪ'saɪsɪv] adj décisif(-ive); (person) décidé(e)

**deck** [dɛk] n (NAUT) pont m; (of bus): **top ~** impériale f; (of cards) jeu m; (record) platine f; **~chair** n chaise longue

**declare** [dɪ'klɛəʳ] vt déclarer

**decline** [dɪ'klaɪn] n (decay) déclin m; (lessening) baisse f ♦ vt refuser, décliner ♦ vi décliner; (business) baisser

**decoder** [dɪ'kəudəʳ] n (TV) décodeur m

**decorate** [dɛkəreɪt] vt (adorn, give a medal to) décorer; (paint and paper) peindre et tapisser; **decoration** [dɛkə'reɪʃən] n (medal etc, adornment) décoration f; **decorator** n peintre-décorateur m

**decoy** [di:kɔɪ] n piège m; (person) compère m

**decrease** [n 'di:kri:s, vb di:'kri:s] n: **~ (in)** diminution f (de) ♦ vt, vi diminuer

**decree** [dɪ'kriː] n (POL, REL) décret m; (LAW) arrêt m, jugement m; ~ **nisi** ['-'naɪsaɪ] n jugement m provisoire de divorce

**dedicate** ['dedɪkeɪt] vt consacrer; (book etc) dédier; ~**d** adj (person) dévoué(e); (COMPUT) spécialisé(e), dédié(e); **dedication** [dedɪ'keɪʃən] n (devotion) dévouement m; (in book) dédicace f

**deduce** [dɪ'djuːs] vt déduire, conclure

**deduct** [dɪ'dʌkt] vt: to ~ **sth** (from) déduire qch (de), retrancher qch (de); ~**ion** [dɪ'dʌkʃən] n (deducting, deducing) déduction f; (from wage etc) prélèvement m, retenue f

**deed** [diːd] n action f, acte m; (LAW) acte notarié, contrat m

**deep** [diːp] adj profond(e); (voice) grave ♦ adv: spectators stood 20 ~ il y avait 20 rangs de spectateurs; **4 metres** ~ de 4 mètres de profondeur; ~ **end** n (of swimming pool) grand bain; ~**en** vt approfondir ♦ vi (fig) s'épaissir; ~**freeze** n congélateur m; ~**fry** vt faire frire (en friteuse); ~**ly** adv profondément; (interested) vivement; ~**sea diver** n sous-marin(e); ~**sea diving** n plongée sous-marine; ~**sea fishing** n grande pêche; ~**seated** adj profond(e), profondément enraciné(e)

**deer** [dɪə²] n inv: (red) ~ cerf m, biche f; (fallow) ~ daim m; (roe) ~ chevreuil m; ~**skin** n daim

**deface** [dɪ'feɪs] vt dégrader; (notice, poster) barbouiller

**default** [dɪ'fɔːlt] n (COMPUT: also: ~ **value**) valeur f par défaut; **by** ~ (LAW) par défaut, par contumace; (SPORT) par forfait

**defeat** [dɪ'fiːt] n défaite f ♦ vt (team, opponents) battre

**defect** [n 'diːfekt, vb dɪ'fekt] n défaut m ♦ vi: to ~ **to the enemy** passer à l'ennemi; ~**ive** [dɪ'fektɪv] adj défectueux (-euse)

**defence** [dɪ'fens] (US **defense**) n défense f; ~**less** adj sans défense

**defend** [dɪ'fend] vt défendre; ~**ant** n (LAW) défendeur(-deresse); (in criminal case) accusé(e), prévenu(e); ~**er** n défenseur m

**defer** [dɪ'fəː²] vt (postpone) différer, ajourner

**defiance** [dɪ'faɪəns] n défi m; **in** ~ **of** au mépris de; **defiant** [dɪ'faɪənt] adj provocant(e), de défi; (person) rebelle, intraitable

**deficiency** [dɪ'fɪʃənsɪ] n insuffisance f, déficience f; **deficient** adj (inadequate) insuffisant(e); **to be deficient in** manquer de

**deficit** ['defɪsɪt] n déficit m

**define** [dɪ'faɪn] vt définir

**definite** ['defɪnɪt] adj (fixed) défini(e), (bien) déterminé(e); (clear, obvious) net(te), manifeste; (certain) sûr(e); **he was** ~ **about it** il a été catégorique; ~**ly** adv sans aucun doute

**definition** [defɪ'nɪʃən] n définition f; (clearness) netteté f

**deflate** [diː'fleɪt] vt dégonfler

**deflect** [dɪ'flekt] vt détourner, faire dévier

**deformed** [dɪ'fɔːmd] adj difforme

**defraud** [dɪ'frɔːd] vt frauder; **to** ~ **sb of sth** escroquer qch à qn

**defrost** [diː'frɒst] vt dégivrer; (food) décongeler; ~**er** n (US) n (demister) dispositif m anti-buée inv

**deft** [deft] adj adroit(e), preste

**defunct** [dɪ'fʌŋkt] adj défunt(e)

**defuse** [diː'fjuːz] vt désamorcer

**defy** [dɪ'faɪ] vt défier; (efforts etc) résister à

**degenerate** [vb dɪ'dʒenəreɪt, adj dɪ'dʒenərɪt] vi dégénérer ♦ adj dégénéré(e)

**degree** [dɪ'griː] n degré m; (SCOL) diplôme m (universitaire); **a (first)** ~ **in maths** une licence en maths; **by** ~**s** (gradually) par degrés; **to some** ~, **to a certain** ~ jusqu'à un certain point, dans une certaine mesure

**dehydrated** [diːhaɪ'dreɪtɪd] adj déshydraté(e); (milk, eggs) en poudre

**de-ice** ['di:'aɪs] vt (windscreen) dégivrer

**deign** [deɪn] vi: to ~ to do daigner faire

**dejected** [dɪ'dʒɛktɪd] adj abattu(e), déprimé(e)

**delay** [dɪ'leɪ] vt retarder ♦ vi s'attarder ♦ n délai m, retard m; to be ~ed être en retard

**delectable** [dɪ'lɛktəbl] adj délicieux(-euse)

**delegate** [n 'dɛlɪgɪt, vb 'dɛlɪgeɪt] n délégué(e) ♦ vt déléguer

**delete** [dɪ'li:t] vt rayer, supprimer

**deliberate** [adj dɪ'lɪbərɪt, vb dɪ'lɪbəreɪt] adj (intentional) délibéré(e); (slow) mesuré(e) ♦ vi délibérer, réfléchir; ~ly [dɪ'lɪbərɪtlɪ] adv (on purpose) exprès, délibérément

**delicacy** ['dɛlɪkəsɪ] n délicatesse f; (food) mets fin ou délicat, friandise f

**delicate** ['dɛlɪkɪt] adj délicat(e)

**delicatessen** [dɛlɪkə'tɛsn] n épicerie fine

**delicious** [dɪ'lɪʃəs] adj délicieux(-euse)

**delight** [dɪ'laɪt] n (grande) joie, grand plaisir ♦ vt enchanter; to take (a) ~ in prendre grand plaisir à; ~ed adj: ~ed (at ou with/to do) ravi(e) (de/de faire); ~ful adj (person) adorable; (meal, evening) merveilleux-eux

**delinquent** [dɪ'lɪŋkwənt] adj, n délinquant(e)

**delirious** [dɪ'lɪrɪəs] adj: to be ~ délirer

**deliver** [dɪ'lɪvə*] vt (mail) distribuer; (goods) livrer; (message) remettre; (speech) prononcer; (MED: baby) mettre au monde; ~y n distribution f; livraison f; (of speaker) élocution f; (MED) accouchement m; to take ~y of prendre livraison de

**delude** [dɪ'lu:d] vt tromper, leurrer; **delusion** n illusion f

**demand** [dɪ'mɑ:nd] vt réclamer, exiger ♦ n exigence f; (claim) revendication f; (ECON) demande f; in ~ demandé(e), recherché(e); on ~ sur demande; ~ing

adj (person) exigeant(e); (work) astreignant(e)

**demean** [dɪ'mi:n] vt: to ~ o.s. s'abaisser

**demeanour** [dɪ'mi:nə*] (US **demeanor**) n comportement m; maintien m

**demented** [dɪ'mɛntɪd] adj dément(e), fou (folle)

**demise** [dɪ'maɪz] n mort f

**demister** [di:'mɪstə*] (BRIT) n (AUT) dispositif m anti-buée inv

**demo** ['dɛməu] (inf) n abbr (= demonstration) manif f

**democracy** [dɪ'mɔkrəsɪ] n démocratie f; **democrat** ['dɛməkræt] n démocrate m/f; **democratic** [dɛmə'krætɪk] adj démocratique

**demolish** [dɪ'mɔlɪʃ] vt démolir

**demonstrate** ['dɛmənstreɪt] vt démontrer, prouver; (show) faire une démonstration de ♦ vi: to ~ (for/against) manifester (en faveur de/contre); **demonstration** [dɛmən'streɪʃən] n démonstration f, manifestation f; **demonstrator** n (POL) manifestant(e)

**demote** [dɪ'məut] vt rétrograder

**demure** [dɪ'mjuə*] adj sage, réservé(e)

**den** [dɛn] n tanière f, antre m

**denial** [dɪ'naɪəl] n démenti m; (refusal) dénégation f

**denim** ['dɛnɪm] n jean m; ~s npl (jeans) (blue-)jean(s) m(pl)

**Denmark** ['dɛnmɑ:k] n Danemark m

**denomination** [dɪnɔmɪ'neɪʃən] n (of money) valeur f; (REL) confession f

**denounce** [dɪ'nauns] vt dénoncer

**dense** [dɛns] adj dense; (stupid) obtus(e), bouché(e); ~ly adv: ~ly populated à forte densité de population; **density** ['dɛnsɪtɪ] n densité f; **double/high-density diskette** n disquette f double densité/haute densité

**dent** [dɛnt] n bosse f ♦ vt (also: make a ~ in) cabosser

**dental** ['dɛntl] adj dentaire; ~ surgeon n (chirurgien(ne)) dentiste

**dentist** ['dɛntɪst] n dentiste m/f

**dentures** ['dentʃəz] npl dentier m sg

**deny** [dɪ'naɪ] vt nier; (refuse) refuser

**deodorant** [diː'əudərənt] n déodorant m, désodorisant m

**depart** [dɪ'pɑːt] vi partir; **to ~ from** (fig: differ from) s'écarter de

**department** [dɪ'pɑːtmənt] n (COMM) rayon m; (SCOL) section f; (POL) ministère m, département m; **~ store** n grand magasin

**departure** [dɪ'pɑːtʃəʳ] n départ m; **a new ~** une nouvelle voie; **~ lounge** n (at airport) salle f d'embarquement

**depend** [dɪ'pend] vi: **to ~ on** dépendre de; (rely on) compter sur; **it ~s** cela dépend; **~ing on the result** selon le résultat; **~able** adj (person) sérieux (-euse), sûr(e); (car, watch) solide, fiable; **~ant** n personne f à charge; **~ent** adj: **to be ~ent (on)** dépendre (de) ♦ n = dependant

**depict** [dɪ'pɪkt] vt (in picture) représenter; (in words) dépeindre, décrire

**depleted** [dɪ'pliːtɪd] adj (considerable-ment) réduit(e) ou diminué(e)

**deport** [dɪ'pɔːt] vt expulser

**deposit** [dɪ'pɔzɪt] n (CHEM, COMM, GEO) dépôt m; (of ore, oil) gisement m; (part payment) arrhes fpl, acompte m; (on bottle etc) consigne f; (for hired goods etc) cautionnement m, garantie f ♦ vt déposer; **~ account** n compte m sur livret

**depot** ['depau] n dépôt m; (US: RAIL) gare f

**depress** [dɪ'pres] vt déprimer; (press down) appuyer sur, abaisser; (prices, wages) faire baisser; **~ed** adj (person) déprimé(e); (area) en déclin, touché(e) par le sous-emploi; **~ing** adj déprimant(e); **~ion** n dépression f; (hollow) creux m

**deprivation** [deprɪ'veɪʃən] n privation f; (loss) perte f

**deprive** [dɪ'praɪv] vt: **to ~ sb of** priver qn de; **~d** adj déshérité(e)

**depth** [depθ] n profondeur f; **in the ~s** of despair au plus profond du désespoir; **to be out of one's ~** avoir perdu pied, nager

**deputize** ['depjutaɪz] vi: **to ~ for** assurer l'intérim de

**deputy** ['depjuti] adj adjoint(e) ♦ n (second in command) adjoint(e); (US: also: ~ sheriff) shérif adjoint; **~ head** directeur adjoint, sous-directeur m

**derail** [dɪ'reɪl] vt: **to be ~ed** dérailler

**deranged** [dɪ'reɪndʒd] adj: **to be (mentally) ~** avoir le cerveau dérangé

**derby** ['dɑːrbɪ] (US) n (bowler hat) (chapeau m) melon m

**derelict** ['derɪlɪkt] adj abandonné(e), à l'abandon

**derisory** [dɪ'raɪsərɪ] adj (sum) dérisoire; (smile, person) moqueur(-euse)

**derive** [dɪ'raɪv] vt: **to ~ sth from** tirer qch de; trouver qch dans ♦ vi: **to ~ from** provenir de, dériver de

**derogatory** [dɪ'rɔgətərɪ] adj désobligeant(e); péjoratif(-ive)

**descend** [dɪ'send] vt, vi descendre; **to ~ from** descendre de, être issu(e) de; **to ~ to (doing) sth** s'abaisser à (faire) qch; **descent** n descente f; (origin) origine f

**describe** [dɪs'kraɪb] vt décrire; **description** [dɪs'krɪpʃən] n description f; (sort) sorte f, espèce f

**desecrate** ['desɪkreɪt] vt profaner

**desert** [n 'dezət, vb dɪ'zɜːt] n désert m ♦ vt déserter, abandonner ♦ vi (MIL) déserter; **~s** npl: **to get one's just ~s** n'avoir que ce qu'on mérite; **~er** [dɪ'zɜːtəʳ] n déserteur m; **~ion** [dɪ'zɜːʃən] n (MIL) désertion f; (LAW: of spouse) abandon m du domicile conjugal; **~ island** n île déserte

**deserve** [dɪ'zɜːv] vt mériter; **deserving** adj (person) méritant(e); (action, cause) méritoire

**design** [dɪ'zaɪn] n (sketch) plan m, dessin m; (layout, shape) conception f, ligne f; (pattern) dessin m, motif(s) m(pl); (COMM, art) design m, stylisme m; (intention) dessein m ♦ vt dessiner; élaborer; ~er n (TECH) concepteur-projeteur m; (ART) dessinateur(-trice), designer m; (fashion) styliste m/f

**desire** [dɪ'zaɪər] n désir m ♦ vt désirer

**desk** [dɛsk] n (in office) bureau m; (for pupil) pupitre m; (BRIT: in shop, restaurant) caisse f; (in hotel, at airport) réception f; **~-top publishing** n publication assistée par ordinateur, PAO f

**desolate** ['dɛsəlɪt] adj désolé(e); (person) affligé(e)

**despair** [dɪs'pɛər] n désespoir m ♦ vi: to ~ of désespérer de

**despatch** [dɪs'pætʃ] n, vt = dispatch

**desperate** ['dɛspərɪt] adj désespéré(e); (criminal) prêt(e) à tout; **to be ~ for sth/to do sth** avoir désespérément besoin de qch/de faire qch; **~ly** adv désespérément; (very) terriblement, extrêmement; **desperation** [dɛspə-'reɪʃən] n désespoir m; **in (sheer) desperation** en désespoir de cause

**despicable** [dɪs'pɪkəbl] adj méprisable

**despise** [dɪs'paɪz] vt mépriser

**despite** [dɪs'paɪt] prep malgré, en dépit de

**despondent** [dɪs'pɒndənt] adj découragé(e), abattu(e)

**dessert** [dɪ'zɜːt] n dessert m; **~spoon** n cuiller f à dessert

**destination** [dɛstɪ'neɪʃən] n destination f

**destined** ['dɛstɪnd] adj: **to be ~ to do/for sth** être destiné(e) à faire/à qch

**destiny** ['dɛstɪnɪ] n destinée f, destin m

**destitute** ['dɛstɪtjuːt] adj indigent(e)

**destroy** [dɪs'trɔɪ] vt détruire; (injured horse) abattre; (dog) faire piquer; **~er** n (NAUT) contre-torpilleur m

**destruction** [dɪs'trʌkʃən] n destruction f

**detach** [dɪ'tætʃ] vt détacher; **~ed** adj (attitude, person) détaché(e); **~ed house** n pavillon m, maison(nette) (individuelle); **~ment** n (MIL) détachement m; (fig) détachement, indifférence

f

**detail** ['diːteɪl] n détail m ♦ vt raconter en détail, énumérer; **in ~** en détail; **~ed** adj détaillé(e)

**detain** [dɪ'teɪn] vt retenir; (in captivity) détenir; (in hospital) hospitaliser

**detect** [dɪ'tɛkt] vt déceler, percevoir; (MED, POLICE) dépister; (MIL RADAR, TECH) détecter; **~ion** n découverte f; détection f; **~ive** n agent m de la sûreté, policier m; **private ~ive** détective privé; **~ive story** n roman policier

**detention** [dɪ'tɛnʃən] n détention f; (SCOL) retenue f, consigne f

**deter** [dɪ'tɜː'] vt dissuader

**detergent** [dɪ'tɜːdʒənt] n détergent m, détersif m

**deteriorate** [dɪ'tɪərɪəreɪt] vi se détériorer, se dégrader

**determine** [dɪ'tɜːmɪn] vt déterminer; **to ~ to do** résoudre de faire, se déterminer à faire; **~d** adj (person) déterminé(e), décidé(e)

**deterrent** [dɪ'tɛrənt] n effet m de dissuasion; force f de dissuasion

**detest** [dɪ'tɛst] vt détester, avoir horreur de

**detonate** ['dɛtəneɪt] vt faire détoner or exploser

**detour** ['diːtuər] n détour m; (US: AUT: diversion) déviation f

**detract** [dɪ'trækt] vt: **to ~ from** (quality, pleasure) diminuer; (reputation) porter atteinte à

**detriment** ['dɛtrɪmənt] n: **to the ~ of** au détriment de, au préjudice de; **~al** [dɛtrɪ'mɛntl] adj: **~al to** préjudiciable à, nuisible à

**devaluation** [dɪvælju'eɪʃən] n dévaluation f

**devastate** ['dɛvəsteɪt] vt dévaster; **~d** adj (fig) anéanti(e); **devastating** adj dévastateur(-trice); (news) accablant(e)

**develop** [dɪ'vɛləp] vt développer; (disease) commencer à souffrir de; (resources) mettre en valeur, exploiter ♦ vi se développer; (situation, disease:

*evolve*) évoluer; (*facts, symptoms: appear*) se manifester; **~ing country** pays *m* en voie de développement; **the machine has ~ed a fault** un problème s'est manifesté dans cette machine; **~er** [dɪ'veləpə*r*] *n* (*also: property ~er*) promoteur *m*; **~ment** [dɪ'veləpmənt] *n* développement *m*; (*of affair, case*) rebondissement *m*, fait(s) nouveau(x)

**device** [dɪ'vaɪs] *n* (*apparatus*) engin *m*, dispositif *m*

**devil** ['devl] *n* diable *m*; démon *m*

**devious** ['di:vɪəs] *adj* (*person*) sournois(e), dissimulé(e)

**devise** [dɪ'vaɪz] *vt* imaginer, concevoir

**devoid** [dɪ'vɔɪd] *adj*: **~ of** dépourvu(e) de, dénué(e) de

**devolution** [di:və'lu:ʃən] *n* (*POL*) décentralisation *f*

**devote** [dɪ'vəut] *vt*: **to ~ sth to** consacrer qch à; **~d** [dɪ'vəutɪd] *adj* dévoué(e); **to be ~d to** (*book etc*) être consacré(e) à; (*person*) être très attaché(e) à; **~e** [devəu'ti:] *n* (*REL*) adepte *m/f*; (*MUS, SPORT*) fervent(e); **devotion** *n* dévouement *m*, attachement *m*; (*REL*) dévotion *f*, piété *f*

**devour** [dɪ'vauə*r*] *vt* dévorer

**devout** [dɪ'vaut] *adj* pieux(-euse), dévot(e)

**dew** [dju:] *n* rosée *f*

**diabetes** [daɪə'bi:ti:z] *n* diabète *m*; **diabetic** [daɪə'betɪk] *adj* diabétique ♦ *n* diabétique *m/f*

**diabolical** [daɪə'bɔlɪkl] (*inf*) *adj* (*weather*) atroce; (*behaviour*) infernal(e)

**diagnosis** [daɪəg'nəusɪs] (*pl* **diagnoses**) *n* diagnostic *m*

**diagonal** [daɪ'ægənl] *adj* diagonal(e) ♦ *n* diagonale *f*

**diagram** ['daɪəgræm] *n* diagramme *m*, schéma *m*

**dial** ['daɪəl] *n* cadran *m* ♦ *vt* (*number*) faire, composer

**dialect** ['daɪəlɛkt] *n* dialecte *m*

**dialling code** (*BRIT*) *n* indicatif *m* (téléphonique)

**dialling tone** (*BRIT*) *n* tonalité *f*

**dialogue** ['daɪəlɔg] *n* dialogue *m*

**dial tone** (*US*) *n* = **dialling tone**

**diameter** [daɪ'æmɪtə*r*] *n* diamètre *m*

**diamond** ['daɪəmənd] *n* diamant *m*; (*shape*) losange *m*; **~s** *npl* (*CARDS*) carreau *m*

**diaper** ['daɪəpə*r*] (*US*) *n* couche *f*

**diaphragm** ['daɪəfræm] *n* diaphragme *m*

**diarrhoea** [daɪə'ri:ə] (*US* **diarrhea**) *n* diarrhée *f*

**diary** ['daɪərɪ] *n* (*daily account*) journal *m*; (*book*) agenda *m*

**dice** [daɪs] *n inv* dé *m* ♦ *vt* (*CULIN*) couper en dés *or* en cubes

**dictate** [dɪk'teɪt] *vt* dicter; **dictation** *n* dictée *f*

**dictator** [dɪk'teɪtə*r*] *n* dictateur *m*; **~ship** *n* dictature *f*

**dictionary** ['dɪkʃənrɪ] *n* dictionnaire *m*

**did** [dɪd] *pt of* **do**; **~n't** = **did not**

**die** [daɪ] *vi* mourir; **to be dying for sth** avoir une envie folle de qch; **to be dying to do sth** mourir d'envie de faire qch; **~ away** *vi* s'éteindre; **~ down** *vi* se calmer, s'apaiser; **~ out** *vi* disparaître

**diesel** ['di:zl] *n* (*vehicle*) diesel *m*; (*also: ~ oil*) carburant *m* diesel, gas-oil *m*; **~ engine** *n* moteur *m* diesel

**diet** ['daɪət] *n* alimentation *f*; (*restricted food*) régime *m* ♦ *vi* (*also: be on a ~*) suivre un régime

**differ** ['dɪfə*r*] *vi* (*be different*): **to ~ (from)** être différent (de); différer (de); (*disagree*): **to ~ (from sb over sth)** ne pas être d'accord (avec qn au sujet de qch); **~ence** *n* différence *f*; (*quarrel*) différend *m*, désaccord *m*; **~ent** différent(e); **~entiate** [dɪfə'renʃɪeɪt] *vi*: **to ~entiate (between)** faire une différence (entre)

**difficult** ['dɪfɪkəlt] *adj* difficile; **~y** *n* difficulté *f*

**diffident** ['dɪfɪdənt] *adj* qui manque de

confiance or d'assurance

**dig** [dɪg] (pt, pp **dug**) vt (hole) creuser; (garden) bêcher ♦ n (prod) coup m de coude; (fig) coup de griffe or de patte; (archeological) fouilles fpl; ~ **in** vi (MIL: also: ~ **o.s. in**) se retrancher; ~ **into** vt fus (savings) puiser dans; **to ~ one's nails into sth** enfoncer ses ongles dans qch; ~ **up** vt déterrer

**digest** [vb daɪˈdʒɛst, n ˈdaɪdʒɛst] vt digérer ♦ n sommaire m, résumé m; **~ion** [dɪˈdʒɛstʃən] n digestion f

**digit** [ˈdɪdʒɪt] n (number) chiffre m; (finger) doigt m; **~al** adj digital(e), à affichage numérique or digital(e), à **~al computer** n calculateur m numérique; **~al TV** n télévision f numérique; **~al watch** n montre f à affichage numérique

**dignified** [ˈdɪgnɪfaɪd] adj digne

**dignity** [ˈdɪgnɪtɪ] n dignité f

**digress** [daɪˈgrɛs] vi: **to ~ from** s'écarter de, s'éloigner de

**digs** [dɪgz] npl (BRIT: inf) piaule f, chambre meublée

**dilapidated** [dɪˈlæpɪdeɪtɪd] adj délabré(e)

**dilemma** [daɪˈlɛmə] n dilemme m

**diligent** [ˈdɪlɪdʒənt] adj appliqué(e), assidu(e)

**dilute** [daɪˈluːt] vt diluer

**dim** [dɪm] adj (light) faible; (memory, outline) vague, indécis(e); (figure) vague, indistinct(e); (room) sombre; (stupid) borné(e), obtus(e) ♦ vt (light) réduire, baisser; (US: AUT) mettre en veilleuse

**dime** [daɪm] (US) n = **10 cents**

**dimension** [daɪˈmɛnʃən] n dimension f

**diminish** [dɪˈmɪnɪʃ] vt, vi diminuer

**diminutive** [dɪˈmɪnjutɪv] adj minuscule, tout(e) petit(e)

**dimmers** [ˈdɪməz] (US) npl (AUT) phares mpl code inv; feux mpl de position

**dimple** [ˈdɪmpl] n fossette f

**din** [dɪn] n vacarme m

**dine** [daɪn] vi dîner; **~r** n (person) dîneur(-euse); (US: restaurant) petit restaurant

**dinghy** [ˈdɪŋgɪ] n youyou m; (also: rubber ~) canot m pneumatique; (also: sailing ~) voilier m, dériveur m

**dingy** [ˈdɪndʒɪ] adj miteux(-euse), minable

**dining car** (BRIT) n wagon-restaurant m

**dining room** n salle f à manger

**dinner** [ˈdɪnəʳ] n dîner m; (lunch) déjeuner m; (public) banquet m; **~ jacket** n smoking m; **~ party** n dîner m; **~ time** n heure f du dîner; (midday) heure f du déjeuner

**dinosaur** [ˈdaɪnəsɔːʳ] n dinosaure m

**dip** [dɪp] n déclivité f; (in sea) baignade f, bain m; (CULIN) ≈ sauce f ♦ vt tremper, plonger; (BRIT: AUT: lights) mettre en code, baisser ♦ vi plonger

**diploma** [dɪˈpləʊmə] n diplôme m

**diplomacy** [dɪˈpləʊməsɪ] n diplomatie f

**diplomat** [ˈdɪpləmæt] n diplomate m; **~ic** [dɪpləˈmætɪk] adj diplomatique

**dipstick** [ˈdɪpstɪk] n (AUT) jauge f de niveau d'huile

**dipswitch** [ˈdɪpswɪtʃ] (BRIT: AUT) interrupteur m de lumière réduite

**dire** [daɪəʳ] adj terrible, extrême, affreux(-euse)

**direct** [daɪˈrɛkt] adj direct(e) ♦ vt diriger, orienter; (letter, remark) adresser; (film, programme) réaliser; (play) mettre en scène; (order): **to ~ sb to do sth** ordonner à qn de faire qch ♦ adv directement; **can you ~ me to ...?** pouvez-vous m'indiquer le chemin de ...?; **~ debit** (BRIT) n prélèvement m automatique

**direction** [dɪˈrɛkʃən] n direction f; **~s** npl (advice) indications fpl; **sense of ~** sens m de l'orientation; **~s for use** mode m d'emploi

**directly** [dɪˈrɛktlɪ] adv (in a straight line) directement, tout droit; (at once) tout de suite, immédiatement

**director** [dɪˈrɛktəʳ] n directeur m; (THEATRE) metteur m en scène; (CINEMA, TV) réalisateur(-trice)

**directory** [dı'rɛktərı] n annuaire m; (COMPUT) répertoire m; **~ enquiries** (US **directory assistance**) n renseignements mpl

**dirt** [də:t] n saleté f; crasse f; (earth) terre f, boue f; **~-cheap** adj très bon marché inv; **~y** adj sale ♦ vt salir; **~y trick** coup tordu

**disability** [dısə'bılıtı] n invalidité f, infirmité f

**disabled** [dıs'eıbld] adj infirme, invalide ♦ npl: **the ~** les handicapés

**disadvantage** [dısəd'vɑ:ntıdʒ] n désavantage m, inconvénient m

**disagree** [dısə'gri:] vi (be different) ne pas concorder; (be against, think otherwise): **to ~ (with)** ne pas être d'accord (avec); **~able** adj désagréable; **~ment** n désaccord m, différend m

**disallow** ['dısə'lau] vt rejeter

**disappear** [dısə'pıəᵣ] vi disparaître; **~ance** n disparition f

**disappoint** [dısə'pɔınt] vt décevoir; **~ed** adj déçu(e); **~ing** adj décevant(e); **~ment** n déception f

**disapproval** [dısə'pru:vəl] n désapprobation f

**disapprove** [dısə'pru:v] vi: **to ~ (of)** désapprouver

**disarmament** [dıs'ɑ:məmənt] n désarmement m

**disarray** [dısə'reı] n: **in ~** (army) en déroute; (organization) en désarroi; (hair, clothes) en désordre

**disaster** [dı'zɑ:stəᵣ] n catastrophe f, désastre m; **disastrous** adj désastreux(-euse)

**disband** [dıs'bænd] vt démobiliser; disperser ♦ vi se séparer; se disperser

**disbelief** ['dısbə'li:f] n incrédulité f

**disc** [dısk] n disque m; (COMPUT) = **disk**

**discard** [dıs'kɑ:d] vt (old things) se débarrasser de; (fig) écarter, renoncer à

**discern** [dı'sə:n] vt discerner, distinguer; **~ing** adj perspicace

**discharge** [vb dıs'tʃɑ:dʒ, n 'dıstʃɑ:dʒ] vt décharger; (duties) s'acquitter de; (patient) renvoyer (chez lui); (employee) congédier, licencier; (soldier) rendre à la vie civile, réformer; (defendant) relaxer, élargir ♦ n décharge f; (dismissal) renvoi m; licenciement m; élargissement m; (MED) écoulement m

**discipline** ['dısıplın] n discipline f

**disc jockey** n disc-jockey m

**disclaim** [dıs'kleım] vt nier

**disclose** [dıs'kləuz] vt révéler, divulguer; **disclosure** n révélation f

**disco** ['dıskəu] n abbr = discothèque

**discomfort** [dıs'kʌmfət] n malaise m, gêne f; (lack of comfort) manque m de confort

**disconcert** [dıskən'sə:t] vt déconcerter

**disconnect** [dıskə'nekt] vt (ELEC, RADIO, pipe) débrancher; (TEL, supply) couper

**discontent** [dıskən'tent] n mécontentement m; **~ed** adj mécontent(e)

**discontinue** [dıskən'tınju:] vt cesser, interrompre; **"~d"** (COMM) "fin de série"

**discord** [dıs'kɔ:d] n discorde f, dissension f; (MUS) dissonance f

**discotheque** [dıs'kəutek] n discothèque f

**discount** [n 'dıskaunt, vb dıs'kaunt] n remise f, rabais m ♦ vt (sum) faire une remise de; (fig) ne pas tenir compte de

**discourage** [dıs'kʌrıdʒ] vt décourager

**discover** [dıs'kʌvəᵣ] vt découvrir; **~y** n découverte f

**discredit** [dıs'kredıt] vt (idea) mettre en doute; (person) discréditer

**discreet** [dıs'kri:t] adj discret(-ète)

**discrepancy** [dıs'krepənsı] n divergence f, contradiction f

**discretion** [dıs'kreʃən] n discrétion f; **use your own ~** à vous de juger

**discriminate** [dıs'krımıneıt] vi: **to ~ between** établir une distinction entre, faire la différence entre; **to ~ against** pratiquer une discrimination contre; **discriminating** adj qui a du discernement; **discrimination** [dıskrımı'neıʃən] n discrimination f; (judgment) discernement m

**discuss** [dɪsˈkʌs] vt discuter de; (debate) discuter; **~ion** n discussion f

**disdain** [dɪsˈdeɪn] n dédain m

**disease** [dɪˈziːz] n maladie f

**disembark** [dɪsɪmˈbɑːk] vi débarquer

**disentangle** [dɪsɪnˈtæŋgl] vt (wool, wire) démêler, débrouiller; (from wreckage) dégager

**disfigure** [dɪsˈfɪɡəʳ] vt défigurer

**disgrace** [dɪsˈɡreɪs] n honte f; (disfavour) disgrâce f ♦ vt déshonorer, couvrir de honte; **~ful** adj scandaleux(-euse), honteux(-euse)

**disgruntled** [dɪsˈɡrʌntld] adj mécontent(e)

**disguise** [dɪsˈɡaɪz] n déguisement m ♦ vt déguiser; **in ~** déguisé(e)

**disgust** [dɪsˈɡʌst] n dégoût m, aversion f ♦ vt dégoûter, écœurer; **~ing** adj dégoûtant(e); révoltant(e)

**dish** [dɪʃ] n plat m; **to do** or **wash the ~es** faire la vaisselle; **~ out** vt servir, distribuer; **~ up** vt servir; **~cloth** n (for washing) lavette f

**dishearten** [dɪsˈhɑːtn] vt décourager

**dishevelled** [dɪˈʃevəld] (US **disheveled**) adj ébouriffé(e); décoiffé(e); débraillé(e)

**dishonest** [dɪsˈɒnɪst] adj malhonnête

**dishonour** [dɪsˈɒnəʳ] (US **dishonor**) n déshonneur m; **~able** adj (behaviour) déshonorant(e); (person) peu honorable

**dishtowel** [ˈdɪʃtaʊəl] (US) n torchon m

**dishwasher** [ˈdɪʃwɒʃəʳ] n lave-vaisselle m

**disillusion** [dɪsɪˈluːʒən] vt désabuser, désillusionner

**disinfect** [dɪsɪnˈfekt] vt désinfecter; **~ant** n désinfectant m

**disintegrate** [dɪsˈɪntɪɡreɪt] vi se désintégrer

**disinterested** [dɪsˈɪntrəstɪd] adj désintéressé(e)

**disjointed** [dɪsˈdʒɔɪntɪd] adj décousu(e), incohérent(e)

**disk** [dɪsk] n (COMPUT) disque m; (: floppy ~) disquette f; **single-/double-sided ~** disquette simple/double face; **~ drive** n lecteur m de disquettes; **~ette** [dɪsˈket] n disquette f, disque m souple

**dislike** [dɪsˈlaɪk] n aversion f, antipathie f ♦ vt ne pas aimer

**dislocate** [ˈdɪsləkeɪt] vt disloquer; déboîter

**dislodge** [dɪsˈlɒdʒ] vt déplacer, faire bouger

**disloyal** [dɪsˈlɔɪəl] adj déloyal(e)

**dismal** [ˈdɪzml] adj lugubre, maussade

**dismantle** [dɪsˈmæntl] vt démonter

**dismay** [dɪsˈmeɪ] n consternation f

**dismiss** [dɪsˈmɪs] vt congédier, renvoyer; (soldiers) faire rompre les rangs à; (idea) écarter; (LAW): **to ~ a case** rendre une fin de non-recevoir; **~al** n renvoi m

**dismount** [dɪsˈmaʊnt] vi mettre pied à terre, descendre

**disobedient** [dɪsəˈbiːdɪənt] adj désobéissant(e)

**disobey** [dɪsəˈbeɪ] vt désobéir à

**disorder** [dɪsˈɔːdəʳ] n désordre m; (rioting) désordres mpl; (MED) troubles mpl; **~ly** adj en désordre; désordonné(e)

**disorientated** [dɪsˈɔːrɪenteɪtɪd] adj désorienté(e)

**disown** [dɪsˈaʊn] vt renier

**disparaging** [dɪsˈpærɪdʒɪŋ] adj désobligeant(e)

**dispassionate** [dɪsˈpæʃənət] adj calme, froid(e); impartial(e), objectif(-ive)

**dispatch** [dɪsˈpætʃ] vt expédier, envoyer ♦ n envoi m, expédition f; (MIL, PRESS) dépêche f

**dispel** [dɪsˈpel] vt dissiper, chasser

**dispense** [dɪsˈpens] vt distribuer, administrer; **~ with** vt fus se passer de; **~r** n (machine) distributeur m; **dispensing chemist** (BRIT) n pharmacie f

**disperse** [dɪsˈpɜːs] vt disperser ♦ vi se disperser

**dispirited** [dɪsˈpɪrɪtɪd] adj découragé(e), déprimé(e)

**displace** [dɪs'pleɪs] vt déplacer

**display** [dɪs'pleɪ] n étalage m; déploiement m; affichage m; (screen) écran m, visuel m; (of feeling) manifestation f ♦ vt montrer; (goods) mettre à l'étalage, exposer; (results, departure times) afficher; (pej) faire étalage de

**displease** [dɪs'pliːz] vt mécontenter, contrarier; **~d** adj: **~d with** mécontent(e) de; **displeasure** [dɪs'plɛʒə*] n mécontentement m

**disposable** [dɪs'pəuzəbl] adj (pack etc) jetable, à jeter; (income) disponible; **nappy** (BRIT) n couche f à jeter, couche-culotte f

**disposal** [dɪs'pəuzl] n (of goods for sale) vente f; (of property) disposition f, cession f; (of rubbish) enlèvement m; destruction f; **at one's ~** à sa disposition

**dispose** [dɪs'pəuz] vt disposer; **~ of** fus (unwanted goods etc) se débarrasser de, se défaire de; (problem) expédier; **~d** adj: **to be ~d to do sth** être disposé(e) à faire qch; **disposition** [dɪspə'zɪʃən] n disposition f; (temperament) naturel m

**disprove** [dɪs'pruːv] vt réfuter

**dispute** [dɪs'pjuːt] n discussion f; (also: **industrial ~**) conflit m ♦ vt contester; (matter) discuter; (victory) disputer

**disqualify** [dɪs'kwɔlɪfaɪ] vt (SPORT) disqualifier; **to ~ sb for sth/from doing** rendre qn inapte à qch/à faire

**disquiet** [dɪs'kwaɪət] n inquiétude f, trouble m

**disregard** [dɪsrɪ'gɑːd] vt ne pas tenir compte de

**disrepair** ['dɪsrɪ'pɛə*] n: **to fall into ~** (building) tomber en ruine

**disreputable** [dɪs'rɛpjutəbl] adj (person) de mauvaise réputation; (behaviour) déshonorant(e)

**disrespectful** [dɪsrɪ'spɛktful] adj irrespectueux(-euse)

**disrupt** [dɪs'rʌpt] vt (plans) déranger; (conversation) interrompre

**dissatisfied** [dɪs'sætɪsfaɪd] adj: **~ (with)** insatisfait(e) (de)

**dissect** [dɪ'sɛkt] vt disséquer

**dissent** [dɪ'sɛnt] n dissentiment m, différence f d'opinion

**dissertation** [dɪsə'teɪʃən] n mémoire m

**disservice** [dɪs'sɜːvɪs] n: **to do sb a ~** rendre un mauvais service à qn

**dissimilar** [dɪ'sɪmɪlə*] adj: **~ (to)** dissemblable (à), différent(e) (de)

**dissipate** ['dɪsɪpeɪt] vt dissiper; (money, efforts) disperser

**dissolute** ['dɪsəluːt] adj débauché(e), dissolu(e)

**dissolve** [dɪ'zɔlv] vt dissoudre ♦ vi se dissoudre, fondre; **to ~ in(to) tears** fondre en larmes

**distance** ['dɪstns] n distance f; **in the ~** au loin

**distant** ['dɪstnt] adj lointain(e), éloigné(e); (manner) distant(e), froid(e)

**distaste** [dɪs'teɪst] n dégoût m; **~ful** adj déplaisant(e), désagréable

**distended** [dɪs'tɛndɪd] adj (stomach) dilaté(e)

**distil** [dɪs'tɪl] (US **distill**) vt distiller; **~lery** n distillerie f

**distinct** [dɪs'tɪŋkt] adj distinct(e); (clear) marqué(e); **as ~ from** par opposition à; **~ion** n distinction f; (in exam) mention f très bien; **~ive** adj distinctif(-ive)

**distinguish** [dɪs'tɪŋgwɪʃ] vt distinguer; **~ed** adj (eminent) distingué(e); **~ing** adj (feature) distinctif(-ive), caractéristique

**distort** [dɪs'tɔːt] vt déformer

**distract** [dɪs'trækt] vt distraire, déranger; **~ed** adj distrait(e); (anxious) éperdu(e), égaré(e); **~ion** n distraction f; égarement m

**distraught** [dɪs'trɔːt] adj éperdu(e)

**distress** [dɪs'trɛs] n détresse f ♦ vt affliger; **~ing** adj douloureux(-euse), pénible

**distribute** [dɪs'trɪbjuːt] vt distribuer; **distribution** [dɪstrɪ'bjuːʃən] n distribution f; **distributor** n distributeur m

**district** ['dɪstrɪkt] n (of country) région f; (of town) quartier m; (ADMIN) district m; ~ **attorney** (US) ≃ procureur m de la République; ~ **nurse** (BRIT) n infirmière visiteuse

**distrust** [dɪs'trʌst] n méfiance f ♦ vt se méfier de

**disturb** [dɪs'tɜ:b] vt troubler; (inconvenience) déranger; **~ance** n dérangement m; (violent event, political etc) troubles mpl; **~ed** adj (worried, upset) agité(e), troublé(e); **to be emotionally ~ed** avoir des problèmes affectifs; **~ing** adj troublant(e), inquiétant(e)

**disuse** [dɪs'ju:s] n: **to fall into** ~ tomber en désuétude; **~d** [dɪs'ju:zd] adj désaffecté(e)

**ditch** [dɪtʃ] n fossé m; (irrigation) rigole f ♦ vt (inf) abandonner; (person) plaquer

**dither** ['dɪðə*] vi hésiter

**ditto** ['dɪtəʊ] adv idem

**dive** [daɪv] n plongeon m; (of submarine) plongée f ♦ vi plonger; **to ~ into** (bag, drawer etc) plonger la main dans; (shop, car etc) se précipiter dans; **~r** n plongeur m

**diversion** [daɪ'vɜ:ʃən] n (BRIT AUT) déviation f; (distraction, MIL) diversion f

**divert** [daɪ'vɜ:t] vt (funds, BRIT: traffic) dévier; (river, attention) détourner

**divide** [dɪ'vaɪd] vt diviser; (separate) séparer ♦ vi se diviser; **~d highway** (US) n route f à quatre voies

**dividend** ['dɪvɪdend] n dividende m

**divine** [dɪ'vaɪn] adj divin(e)

**diving** ['daɪvɪŋ] n plongée (sousmarine); ~ **board** n plongeoir m

**divinity** [dɪ'vɪnɪtɪ] n divinité f; (SCOL) théologie f

**division** [dɪ'vɪʒən] n division f

**divorce** [dɪ'vɔ:s] n divorce m ♦ vt divorcer d'avec; (dissociate) séparer; **~d** adj divorcé(e); **~e** n divorcé(e)

**D.I.Y.** (BRIT) n abbr = do-it-yourself

**dizzy** ['dɪzɪ] adj: **to make sb** ~ donner le vertige à qn; **to feel** ~ avoir la tête

qui tourne

**DJ** n abbr = disc jockey

**DNA fingerprinting** n technique f des empreintes génétiques

┌─────────────────────┐
│ KEYWORD │
└─────────────────────┘

**do** [du:] (pt **did**, pp **done**) n (inf: party etc) soirée f, fête f

♦ vb 1 (in negative constructions) non traduit; **I don't understand** je ne comprends pas

2 (to form questions) non traduit; **didn't you know?** vous ne le saviez pas?; **why didn't you come?** pourquoi n'êtes-vous pas venu?

3 (for emphasis, in polite expressions): **she does seem rather late** je trouve qu'elle est bien en retard; **do sit down/help yourself** asseyez-vous/ servez-vous je vous en prie

4 (used to avoid repeating vb): **she swims better than I do** elle nage mieux que moi; **do you agree? - yes, I do/no, I don't** vous êtes d'accord? - oui/non; **she lives in Glasgow - so do I** elle habite Glasgow - moi aussi; **who broke it? - I did** qui l'a cassé? - c'est moi

5 (in question tags): **he laughed, didn't he?** il a ri, n'est-ce pas?; **I don't know him, do I?** je ne crois pas le connaître

♦ vt (gen: carry out, perform etc) faire; **what are you doing tonight?** qu'est-ce que vous faites ce soir?; **to do the cooking/washing-up** faire la cuisine/la vaisselle; **to do one's teeth/hair/nails** se brosser les dents/se coiffer/se faire les ongles; **the car was doing 100** ≃ la voiture faisait du 160 (à l'heure)

♦ vi 1 (act, behave) faire; **do as I do** faites comme moi

2 (get on, fare) marcher; **the firm is doing well** l'entreprise marche bien; **how do you do?** comment allez-vous?; (on being introduced) enchanté(e)!

**3** (*suit*) aller; **will it do?** est-ce que ça ira?

**4** (*be sufficient*) suffire, aller; **will £10 do?** est-ce que 10 livres suffiront?; **that'll do** ça suffit, ça ira; **that'll do!** (*in annoyance*) ça va ou suffit comme ça!; **to make do** (*with*) se contenter (de)

**do away with** vt fus supprimer

**do up** vt (*laces, dress*) attacher; (*buttons*) boutonner; (*zip*) fermer; (*renovate: room*) refaire; (: *house*) remettre à neuf

**do with** vt fus (*need*): **I could do with a drink/some help** quelque chose à boire/un peu d'aide ne serait pas de refus; (*be connected*): **that has nothing to do with you** cela ne vous concerne pas; **I won't have anything to do with it** je ne veux pas m'en mêler

**do without** vi s'en passer ♦ vt fus se passer de

**dock** [dɔk] n dock m; (LAW) banc m des accusés ♦ vi se mettre à quai; (SPACE) s'arrimer; **~er** n docker m; **~yard** n chantier m de construction navale

**doctor** ['dɔktər] n médecin m, docteur m; (*PhD etc*) docteur m ♦ vt (*drink*) frelater; **D~ of Philosophy** n (*degree*) doctorat m; (*person*) Docteur m en Droit ou Lettres etc, titulaire m/f d'un doctorat

**document** ['dɔkjumənt] n document m; **~ary** [dɔkju'mentərɪ] adj documentaire ♦ n documentaire m

**dodge** [dɔdʒ] n truc m; combine f ♦ vt esquiver, éviter

**dodgems** ['dɔdʒəmz] (BRIT) npl autos tamponneuses

**doe** [dəu] n (*deer*) biche f; (*rabbit*) lapine f

**does** [dʌz] vb see **do**; **~n't** = **does not**

**dog** [dɔg] n chien(ne) ♦ vt suivre de près; poursuivre, harceler; **~ collar** n collier m de chien; (*fig*) faux-col m d'ecclésiastique; **~-eared** adj corné(e);

**~ged** ['dɔgɪd] adj obstiné(e), opiniâtre; **~sbody** n bonne f à tout faire, tâcheron m

**doings** ['duːɪŋz] npl activités fpl

**do-it-yourself** ['duːɪtjɔː'self] n bricolage m

**doldrums** ['dɔldrəmz] npl: **to be in the ~** avoir le cafard; (*business*) être dans le marasme

**dole** [dəul] n (BRIT: *payment*) allocation f de chômage; **on the ~** au chômage; **~ out** vt donner au compte-goutte

**doll** [dɔl] n poupée f

**dollar** ['dɔlər] n dollar m

**dolled up** (*inf*) adj: **(all) ~** sur son trente et un

**dolphin** ['dɔlfɪn] n dauphin m

**dome** [dəum] n dôme m

**domestic** [də'mestɪk] adj (*task, appliances*) ménager(-ère); (*of country: trade, situation etc*) intérieur(e); (*animal*) domestique; **~ated** adj (*animal*) domestiqué(e); (*husband*) pantouflard(e)

**dominate** ['dɔmɪneɪt] vt dominer

**domineering** [dɔmɪ'nɪərɪŋ] adj dominateur(-trice), autoritaire

**dominion** [də'mɪnɪən] n (*territory*) territoire m; **to have ~ over** contrôler

**domino** ['dɔmɪnəu] (*pl* **~es**) n domino m; **~es** n (*game*) dominos mpl

**don** [dɔn] (BRIT) n professeur m d'université

**donate** [də'neɪt] vt faire don de, donner

**done** [dʌn] pp of **do**

**donkey** ['dɔŋkɪ] n âne m

**donor** ['dəunər] n (*of blood etc*) donneur(-euse); (*to charity*) donateur (-trice); **~ card** n carte f de don d'organes

**don't** [dəunt] vb = **do not**

**donut** ['dəunʌt] (US) n = **doughnut**

**doodle** ['duːdl] vi griffonner, gribouiller

**doom** [duːm] n destin m ♦ vt: **to be ~ed (to failure)** être voué(e) à l'échec

**door** [dɔːr] n porte f; (RAIL, *car*) portière f; **~bell** n sonnette f; **~handle** n poi-

# dope                          382                          draft

gnée f de la porte; (car) poignée de portière; **~man** (irreg) n (in hotel) portier m; **~mat** n paillasson m; **~step** n pas m de (la) porte, seuil m; **~way** n (embrasure f de la) porte f

**dope** [dəup] n (inf: drug) drogue f; (: person) andouille f ♦ vt (horse etc) doper

**dormant** ['dɔːmənt] adj assoupi(e), en veilleuse

**dormitory** ['dɔːmɪtrɪ] n dortoir m; (US: building) résidence f universitaire

**dormouse** ['dɔːmaus] (pl dormice) n loir m

**DOS** [dɔs] n abbr (= disk operating system) DOS

**dose** [dəus] n dose f

**dosh** [dɔʃ] (inf) n fric m

**doss house** ['dɔs-] (BRIT) n asile m de nuit

**dot** [dɔt] n point m; (on material) pois m ♦ vt: **~ted with** parsemé(e) de; **on the ~ à** l'heure tapante or pile; **~ted line** n pointillé(s) m(pl)

**double** ['dʌbl] adj double ♦ adv (twice): **to cost ~ (sth)** coûter le double (de qch) or deux fois plus (que qch) ♦ n double m ♦ vt doubler; (fold) plier en deux ♦ vi doubler; **~s** n (TENNIS) double m; **on** or (BRIT) **at the ~** au pas de course; **~ bass** (BRIT) n contrebasse f; **~ bed** n grand lit; **~ bend** (BRIT) n virage m en s; **~breasted** adj croisé(e); **~-click** vi (COMPUT) double-cliquer; **~-cross** vt trahir; **~-decker** n autobus m à impériale; **~ glazing** (BRIT) n double vitrage m; **~ room** n chambre f pour deux personnes; **doubly** adv doublement, deux fois plus

**doubt** [daut] n doute m ♦ vt douter de; **to ~ that** douter que; **~ful** adj douteux(-euse); (person) incertain(e); **~less** adv sans doute, sûrement

**dough** [dəu] n pâte f; **~nut** (US donut) n beignet m

**dove** [dʌv] n colombe f

**Dover** ['dəuvəʳ] n Douvres

**dovetail** ['dʌvteɪl] vi (fig) concorder

**dowdy** ['daudɪ] adj démodé(e); mal fagoté(e) (inf)

**down** [daun] n (soft feathers) duvet m ♦ adv en bas, vers le bas; (on the ground) par terre ♦ prep en bas de; (along) le long de ♦ vt (inf: drink, food) s'envoyer; **~ with X!** à bas X!; **~-and-out** n clochard(e); **~-at-heel** adj éculé(e); (fig) miteux(-euse); **~cast** adj démoralisé(e); **~fall** n chute f; ruine f; **~hearted** adj découragé(e); **~hill** adv: **to go ~hill** descendre; (fig) péricliter; **~ payment** n acompte m; **~pour** n pluie torrentielle, déluge m; **~right** adj (lie etc) effronté(e); (refusal) catégorique; **~size** vt (ECON) réduire ses effectifs

---

### Downing Street

Downing Street est une rue de Westminster (à Londres) où se trouve la résidence officielle du Premier ministre (numéro 10) et celle du ministre des Finances (numéro 11). Le nom "Downing Street" est souvent utilisé pour désigner le gouvernement britannique.

---

**Down's syndrome** [daunz-] n (MED) trisomie f

**down: ~stairs** adv au rez-de-chaussée; à l'étage inférieur; **~stream** adv en aval; **~-to-earth** adj terre à terre inv; **~town** adv en ville; **~ under** adv en Australie/Nouvelle-Zélande; **~ward** adj, adv vers le bas; **~wards** adv vers le bas

**dowry** ['dauri] n dot f

**doz.** abbr = dozen

**doze** [dəuz] vi sommeiller; **~ off** vi s'assoupir

**dozen** ['dʌzn] n douzaine f; **a ~ books** une douzaine de livres; **~s of** des centaines de

**Dr.** abbr = doctor; drive

**drab** [dræb] adj terne, morne

**draft** [drɑːft] n ébauche f; (of letter, essay etc) brouillon m; (COMM) traite f;

**draftsman** (*US: call-up*) conscription *f* ♦ *vt* faire le brouillon or un projet de; (*MIL: send*) détacher; *see also* **draught**

**draftsman** ['drɑːftsmən] (*irreg*) (*US*) *n* = **draughtsman**

**drag** [dræg] *vt* traîner; (*river*) draguer ♦ *vi* traîner ♦ *n* (*inf*) casse-pieds *m/f*; (*women's clothing*): **in ~** (en) travesti; **~ on** *vi* s'éterniser

**dragon** ['drægn] *n* dragon *m*

**dragonfly** ['drægənflaɪ] *n* libellule *f*

**drain** [dreɪn] *n* égout *m*, canalisation *f*; (*on resources*) saignée *f* ♦ *vt* (*land, marshes etc*) drainer, assécher; (*vegetables*) égoutter; (*glass*) vider ♦ *vi* (*water*) s'écouler; **~age** *n* drainage *m*; système *m* d'égouts or de canalisations; **~ing board** (*US* **drain board**) *n* égouttoir *m*; **~pipe** *n* tuyau *m* d'écoulement

**drama** ['drɑːmə] *n* (*art*) théâtre *m*, art *m* dramatique; (*play*) pièce *f* (de théâtre); (*event*) drame *m*; **~tic** [drə'mætɪk] *adj* dramatique; spectaculaire; **~tist** ['dræmətɪst] *n* auteur *m* dramatique; **~tize** ['dræmətaɪz] *vt* (*events*) dramatiser; (*adapt: for TV/cinema*) adapter pour la télévision/pour l'écran

**drank** [dræŋk] *pt of* **drink**

**drape** [dreɪp] *vt* draper; **~s** (*US*) *npl* rideaux *mpl*

**drastic** ['dræstɪk] *adj* sévère; énergique; (*change*) radical(e)

**draught** [drɑːft] (*US* **draft**) *n* courant *m* d'air; (*NAUT*) tirant *m* d'eau; **on ~** (*beer*) à la pression; **~board** (*BRIT*) *n* damier *m*; **~s** (*BRIT*) *n* (jeu *m* de) dames *fpl*

**draughtsman** ['drɑːftsmən] (*irreg*) (*US*) *n* = **draftsman**

**draw** [drɔː] (*pt* **drew**, *pp* **drawn**) *vt* tirer; (*tooth*) arracher, extraire; (*attract*) attirer; (*picture*) dessiner; (*line, circle*) tracer; (*money*) retirer; (*wages*) toucher ♦ *vi* (*SPORT*) faire match nul ♦ *n* match nul; (*lottery*) tirage *m* au sort; loterie *f*; **to ~ near** s'approcher; approcher; **~ out** *vi* (*lengthen*) s'allonger ♦ *vt* (*money*) retirer; **~ up** *vi* (*stop*) s'arrêter ♦ *vt*

(*chair*) approcher; (*document*) établir, dresser; **~back** *n* inconvénient *m*, désavantage *m*; **~bridge** *n* pont-levis *m*

**drawer** [drɔːʳ] *n* tiroir *m*

**drawing** ['drɔːɪŋ] *n* dessin *m*; **~ board** *n* planche *f* à dessin; **~ pin** (*BRIT*) *n* punaise *f*; **~ room** *n* salon *m*

**drawl** [drɔːl] *n* accent traînant

**drawn** [drɔːn] *pp of* **draw**

**dread** [dred] *n* terreur *f*, effroi *m* ♦ *vt* redouter, appréhender; **~ful** *adj* affreux(-euse)

**dream** [driːm] (*pt, pp* **dreamed** or **dreamt**) *n* rêve *m* ♦ *vt, vi* rêver; **~y** *adj* rêveur(-euse); (*music*) langoureux(-euse)

**dreary** ['drɪərɪ] *adj* morne; monotone

**dredge** [dredʒ] *vt* draguer

**dregs** [dregz] *npl* lie *f*

**drench** [drentʃ] *vt* tremper

**dress** [dres] *n* robe *f*; (*no pl: clothing*) habillement *m*, tenue *f* ♦ *vi* s'habiller ♦ *vt* habiller; (*wound*) panser; (*CULIN*) préparer; (*food*) garnir; **to get ~ed** s'habiller; **~ up** *vi* s'habiller; (*in fancy ~*) se déguiser; **~ circle** (*BRIT*) (*THEATRE*) premier balcon; **~er** *n* (*furniture*) vaisselier *m*; (: *US*) coiffeuse *f*, commode *f*; **~ing** *n* (*MED*) pansement *m*; (*CULIN*) sauce *f*, assaisonnement *m*; **~ing gown** (*BRIT*) *n* robe *f* de chambre; **~ing room** *n* (*THEATRE*) loge *f*; (*SPORT*) vestiaire *m*; **~ing table** *n* coiffeuse *f*; **~maker** *n* couturière *f*; **~ rehearsal** *n* (répétition *f*) générale *f*

**drew** [druː] *pt of* **draw**

**dribble** ['drɪbl] *vi* (*baby*) baver ♦ *vt* (*ball*) dribbler

**dried** [draɪd] *adj* (*fruit, beans*) sec (sèche); (*eggs, milk*) en poudre

**drier** ['draɪəʳ] *n* = **dryer**

**drift** [drɪft] *n* (*of current etc*) force *f*; direction *f*, mouvement *m*; (*of snow*) rafale *f*; (: *on ground*) congère *f*; (*general meaning*) sens (général) *m*; (*boat*) aller à la dérive, dériver; (*sand, snow*) s'amonceler, s'entasser; **~wood** *n* bois flotté

**drill** [drɪl] n perceuse f; (~ bit) foret m, mèche f; (of dentist) roulette f, fraise f; (MIL) exercice m ♦ vt percer; (troops) entraîner ♦ vi (for oil) faire un or des forage(s)

**drink** [drɪŋk] (pt **drank**, pp **drunk**) n boisson f; (alcoholic) verre m ♦ vt, vi boire; **to have a ~** boire quelque chose, boire un verre; prendre l'apéritif; a ~ **of water** un verre d'eau; **~er** n buveur(-euse); **~ing water** n eau f potable

**drip** [drɪp] n goutte f; (MED) goutte-à-goutte m, perfusion f ♦ vi tomber goutte à goutte; (tap) goutter; **~-dry** adj (shirt) sans repassage; **~ping** n graisse f (de rôti)

**drive** [draɪv] (pt **drove**, pp **driven**) n promenade f or trajet m en voiture; (also: **~way**) allée f; (energy) dynamisme m, énergie f; (push) effort (concerté), campagne f; (also: **disk ~**) lecteur m de disquettes ♦ vt conduire; (push) chasser, pousser; (TECH: motor, wheel) faire fonctionner; entraîner; (nail, stake etc): **to ~ sth into sth** enfoncer qch dans qch ♦ vi (AUT: at controls) conduire; (: travel) aller en voiture; **left-/right-hand ~** conduite f à gauche/droite; **to ~ sb mad** rendre qn fou (folle); **to ~ sb home/to the airport** reconduire qn chez l'/conduire qn à l'aéroport; **~-by shooting** n (tentative d'assassinat) coups de feu tirés d'un voiture

**drivel** ['drɪvl] (inf) n idioties fpl

**driver** ['draɪvə*] n conducteur(-trice); (of taxi, bus) chauffeur m; **~'s license** (US) n permis m de conduire

**driveway** ['draɪvweɪ] n allée f

**driving** ['draɪvɪŋ] n conduite f; ~ **instructor** n moniteur m d'auto-école; ~ **lesson** n leçon f de conduite; ~ **licence** (BRIT) n permis m de conduire; ~ **school** n auto-école f; ~ **test** n examen m du permis de conduire

**drizzle** ['drɪzl] n bruine f, crachin m

**drool** [druːl] vi baver

**droop** [druːp] vi (shoulders) tomber; (head) pencher; (flower) pencher la tête

**drop** [drɔp] n goutte f; (fall) baisse f; (also: **parachute ~**) saut m ♦ vt laisser tomber; (voice, eyes, price) baisser; (set down from car) déposer ♦ vi tomber; ~s npl (MED) gouttes; ~ **off** vi (sleep) s'assoupir ♦ vt (passenger) déposer; ~ **out** vi (withdraw) se retirer; (student etc) abandonner, décrocher; **~out** n marginal(e); **~per** n compte-gouttes m inv; **~pings** npl crottes fpl

**drought** [draut] n sécheresse f

**drove** [drəuv] pt of **drive**

**drown** [draun] vt noyer ♦ vi se noyer

**drowsy** ['drauzɪ] adj somnolent(e)

**drug** [drʌg] n médicament m; (narcotic) drogue f ♦ vt droguer; **to be on ~s** se droguer; ~ **addict** n toxicomane m/f; **~gist** (US) n pharmacien-droguiste; **~store** (US) n pharmacie-droguerie f, drugstore m

**drum** [drʌm] n tambour m; (for oil, petrol) bidon m; **~s** npl (pop) batterie f; **~mer** n (joueur m de) tambour m

**drunk** [drʌŋk] pp of **drink** ♦ adj ivre, soûl(e) ♦ n (also: **~ard**) ivrogne m/f; **~en** adj (person) ivre, soûl(e); (rage, stupor) ivrogne, d'ivrogne

**dry** [draɪ] adj sec (sèche); (day) sans pluie; (humour) pince-sans-rire ♦ vt (lake, riverbed, wash) à sec ♦ vt sécher; (clothes) faire sécher ♦ vi sécher; ~ **up** vi tarir; **~-cleaner's** n teinturerie f; **~-cleaning** n (spin-dryer) essoreuse f; **~ness** n sécheresse f; **~ rot** n pourriture sèche (du bois)

**DSS** n abbr (= Department of Social Security) ≈ Sécurité sociale

**DTP** n abbr (= desk-top publishing) PAO f

**dual** ['djuəl] adj double; ~ **carriageway** (BRIT) n route f à quatre voies or à chaussées séparées; **~-purpose** adj à double usage

**dubbed** [dʌbd] adj (CINEMA) doublé(e)

**dubious** ['djuːbɪəs] adj hésitant(e), incertain(e); (reputation, company) douteux(-euse)

**duchess** ['dʌtʃɪs] n duchesse f

**duck** [dʌk] n canard m ♦ vi se baisser vivement, baisser subitement la tête; **~ling** ['dʌklɪŋ] n caneton m

**duct** [dʌkt] n conduite f, canalisation f; (ANAT) conduit m

**dud** [dʌd] n (object, tool): **it's a ~** c'est de la camelote, ça ne marche pas ♦ adj: **~ cheque** (BRIT) chèque sans provision

**due** [dju:] adj dû (due); (expected) attendu(e); (fitting) qui convient ♦ n: **to give sb his** (or **her**) **~** être juste envers qn ♦ adv: **~ north** droit vers le nord; **~s** npl (for club, union) cotisation f; **in ~ course** en temps utile or voulu; finalement; **~ to** dû (due) à; causé(e) par; **he's ~ to finish tomorrow** normalement il doit finir demain

**duet** [dju:'et] n duo m

**duffel bag** ['dʌfl-] n sac m marin

**duffel coat** n duffel-coat m

**dug** [dʌg] pt, pp of **dig**

**dull** [dʌl] adj terne, morne; (boring) ennuyeux(-euse); (sound, pain) sourd(e); (weather, day) gris(e), maussade ♦ vt (pain, grief) atténuer; (mind, senses) engourdir

**duly** ['dju:lɪ] adv (on time) en temps voulu; (as expected) comme il se doit

**dumb** [dʌm] adj muet(te); (stupid) bête; **~founded** adj sidéré(e)

**dummy** ['dʌmɪ] n (tailor's model) mannequin m; (mock-up) factice m, maquette f; (BRIT: for baby) tétine f ♦ adj faux (fausse), factice

**dump** [dʌmp] n (also: **rubbish ~**) décharge (publique); (pej) trou m ♦ vt (put down) déposer; déverser; (get rid of) se débarrasser de; (COMPUT: data) vider, transférer

**dumpling** ['dʌmplɪŋ] n boulette f (de pâte)

**dumpy** ['dʌmpɪ] adj boulot(te)

**dunce** [dʌns] n âne m, cancre m

**dune** [dju:n] n dune f

**dung** [dʌŋ] n fumier m

**dungarees** [dʌŋgə'ri:z] npl salopette f; bleu(s) m(pl)

**dungeon** ['dʌndʒən] n cachot m

**duplex** ['dju:pleks] (US) n maison jumelée; (apartment) duplex m

**duplicate** [n 'dju:plɪkət, vb 'dju:plɪkeɪt] n double m ♦ vt faire un double de; (on machine) polycopier; photocopier; **in ~** en deux exemplaires

**durable** ['djuərəbl] adj durable; (clothes, metal) résistant(e), solide

**duration** [djuə'reɪʃən] n durée f

**during** ['djuərɪŋ] prep pendant, au cours de

**dusk** [dʌsk] n crépuscule m

**dust** [dʌst] n poussière f ♦ vt (furniture) épousseter, essuyer; (cake etc): **to ~ with** saupoudrer de; **~bin** (BRIT) n poubelle f; **~er** n chiffon m; **~man** (BRIT) (irreg) n éboueur m, boueux m; **~y** adj poussièreux(-euse)

**Dutch** [dʌtʃ] adj hollandais(e), néerlandais(e) ♦ n (LING) hollandais m ♦ adv (inf): **to go ~** partager les frais; **the ~** npl (people) les Hollandais; **~man** (irreg) n Hollandais m; **~woman** (irreg) n Hollandaise f

**duty** ['dju:tɪ] n devoir m; (tax) droit m, taxe f; **on ~** de service; (at night etc) de garde; **off ~** libre, pas de service or de garde; **~-free** adj exempté(e) de douane, hors taxe inv

**duvet** ['du:veɪ] (BRIT) n couette f

**DVD** [di:vi:di:] n abbr (= digital versatile disc) DVD m

**dwarf** [dwɔ:f] (pl **dwarves**) n nain(e) ♦ vt écraser

**dwell** [dwel] (pt, pp **dwelt**) vi demeurer; **~ on** vt fus s'appesantir sur

**dwindle** ['dwɪndl] vi diminuer

**dye** [daɪ] n teinture f ♦ vt teindre

**dying** ['daɪɪŋ] adj mourant(e), agonisant(e)

**dyke** [daɪk] (BRIT) n digue f

**dynamic** [daɪ'næmɪk] adj dynamique

**dynamite** ['daɪnəmaɪt] n dynamite f
**dynamo** ['daɪnəməu] n dynamo f
**dyslexia** [dɪs'leksɪə] n dyslexie f

# E, e

**E** [iː] n (MUS) mi m

**each** [iːtʃ] adj chaque ♦ pron chacun(e);
~ **other** l'un(e) l'autre; **they hate** ~
**other** ils se détestent (mutuellement);
**you are jealous of** ~ **other** vous êtes
jaloux l'un de l'autre; **they have 2**
**books** — ils ont 2 livres chacun

**eager** ['iːgər] adj (keen) avide; **to be** ~
**to do sth** avoir très envie de faire qch;
**to be** ~ **for** désirer vivement, être avide
de

**eagle** ['iːgl] n aigle m

**ear** [ɪər] n oreille f; (of corn) épi m;
~**ache** n mal m aux oreilles; ~**drum** n
tympan m

**earl** [əːl] (BRIT) n comte m

**earlier** ['əːlɪər] adj (date etc) plus rap-
proché(e); (edition, fashion etc) plus an-
cien(ne), antérieur(e) ♦ adv plus tôt

**early** ['əːlɪ] adv tôt, de bonne heure;
(ahead of time) en avance; (near the beginning) au début ♦ adj qui se manifeste
(or se fait) tôt or de bonne heure;
(work) de jeunesse; (settler, Christian)
premier(-ère); (reply) rapide; (death)
prématuré(e); **to have an** ~ **night** se
coucher tôt or de bonne heure; **in the**
~ **or** ~ **in the spring/19th century** au
début du printemps/19ème siècle; ~
**retirement** n: **to take** ~ **retirement**
prendre sa retraite anticipée

**earmark** ['ɪəmɑːk] vt: **to** ~ **sth for** réserver or destiner qch à

**earn** [əːn] vt gagner; (COMM: yield) rapporter

**earnest** ['əːnɪst] adj sérieux(-euse); **in** ~
♦ adv sérieusement

**earnings** ['əːnɪŋz] npl salaire m; (of
company) bénéfices mpl

**ear:** ~**phones** npl écouteurs mpl; ~**ring**

n boucle f d'oreille; ~**shot** n: **within**
~**shot** à portée de voix

**earth** [əːθ] n (gen, also BRIT: ELEC) terre f
♦ vt relier à la terre; ~**enware** n poterie
f; faïence f; ~**quake** n tremblement m
de terre, séisme m; ~**y** adj (vulgar: humour) truculent(e)

**ease** [iːz] n facilité f, aisance f; (comfort)
bien-être m ♦ vt (soothe) calmer; (loos-
en) relâcher, détendre; **to** ~ **sth in/out**
faire pénétrer/sortir qch délicatement or
avec douceur; faciliter la pénétration/la
sortie de qch; **at** ~! (MIL) repos!; ~ **off**
or **up** vi diminuer; (slow down) ralentir

**easel** ['iːzl] n chevalet m

**east** [iːst] n est m ♦ adj (wind) d'est;
(side) est inv ♦ adv à l'est, vers l'est; **the**
**E~** l'Orient m; les pays mpl de l'Est

**Easter** ['iːstər] n Pâques fpl; ~ **egg** n:
œuf m de Pâques

**east:** ~**erly** ['iːstəlɪ] adj (wind) d'est; (direction) est inv; (point) à l'est; ~**ern**
['iːstən] adj de l'est, oriental(e);
~**ward(s)** ['iːstwəd(z)] adv vers l'est, à
l'est

**easy** ['iːzɪ] adj facile; (manner) aisé(e)
♦ adv: **to take it** or **things** ~ ne pas se
fatiguer; (not worry) ne pas (trop) s'en
faire; ~ **chair** n fauteuil m; ~-**going** adj
accommodant(e), facile à vivre

**eat** [iːt] (pt **ate**, pp **eaten**) vt, vi manger;
~ **away at**, ~ **into** vt fus ronger, attaquer; (savings) entamer

**eaves** [iːvz] npl avant-toit m

**eavesdrop** ['iːvzdrɔp] vi: **to** ~ (**on a**
**conversation**) écouter (une conversation) de façon indiscrète

**ebb** [ɛb] n reflux m ♦ vi refluer; (fig: also:
~ **away**) décliner

**ebony** ['ɛbənɪ] n ébène f

**EC** n abbr (= European Community) C.E.
E. f

**ECB** n abbr (= European Central Bank)
BCE f

**eccentric** [ɪk'sɛntrɪk] adj excentrique
♦ n excentrique m f

**echo** ['ɛkəu] (pl ~**es**) n écho m ♦ vt ré-

**péter** ♦ *vi* résonner, faire écho

**eclipse** [ɪˈklɪps] *n* éclipse *f*

**ecology** [ɪˈkɔlədʒɪ] *n* écologie *f*

**e-commerce** [ˈiːkɔmɜːs] *n* commerce *m* électronique

**economic** [iːkəˈnɔmɪk] *adj* économique; (*business etc*) rentable; **~al** *adj* économique; (*person*) économe

**economics** [iːkəˈnɔmɪks] *n* économie *f* politique ♦ *npl* (*of project, situation*) aspect *m* financier

**economize** [ɪˈkɔnəmaɪz] *vi* économiser, faire des économies

**economy** [ɪˈkɔnəmɪ] *n* économie *f*; **~ class** *n* classe *f* touriste; **~ size** *n* format *m* économique

**ecstasy** [ˈɛkstəsɪ] *n* extase *f* (*drogue aussi*); **ecstatic** [ɛksˈtætɪk] *adj* extatique

**ECU** [ˈeɪkjuː] *n abbr* (= *European Currency Unit*) ECU *m f*

**eczema** [ˈɛksɪmə] *n* eczéma *m*

**edge** [ɛdʒ] *n* bord *m*; (*of knife etc*) tranchant *m*, fil *m* ♦ *vt* border; **on** ~ (*fig*) crispé(e), tendu(e); **to** ~ **away from** s'éloigner furtivement de; **~ways** *adv*: **he couldn't get a word in ~ways** il ne pouvait pas placer un mot

**edgy** [ˈɛdʒɪ] *adj* crispé(e), tendu(e)

**edible** [ˈɛdɪbl] *adj* comestible

**Edinburgh** [ˈɛdɪnbərə] *n* Édimbourg

**edit** [ˈɛdɪt] *vt* (*text, book*) éditer; (*report*) préparer; (*film*) monter; (*broadcast*) réaliser; **~ion** [ɪˈdɪʃən] *n* édition *f*; **~or** *n* (*of column*) rédacteur(-trice); (*of newspaper*) rédacteur(-trice) en chef; (*of book's work*) éditeur(-trice); **~orial** [ɛdɪˈtɔːrɪəl] *adj* de la rédaction, éditorial(e) ♦ *n* éditorial *m*

**educate** [ˈɛdjukeɪt] *vt* (*teach*) instruire; (*instruct*) éduquer; **~d** *adj* (*person*) cultivé(e); **education** [ɛdjuˈkeɪʃən] *n* éducation *f*; (*studies*) études *fpl*; (*teaching*) enseignement *m*, instruction *f*; **educational** *adj* (*experience, toy*) pédagogique; (*institution*) scolaire; (*policy*) d'éducation

**eel** [iːl] *n* anguille *f*

**eerie** [ˈɪərɪ] *adj* inquiétant(e)

**effect** [ɪˈfɛkt] *n* effet *m* ♦ *vt* effectuer; **to take** ~ (*law*) entrer en vigueur, prendre effet; (*drug*) agir, faire son effet; **in** ~ en fait; **~ive** [ɪˈfɛktɪv] *adj* efficace; (*actual*) véritable; **~ively** *adv* efficacement; (*in reality*) effectivement; **~iveness** *n* efficacité *f*

**effeminate** [ɪˈfɛmɪnɪt] *adj* efféminé(e)

**effervescent** [ɛfəˈvɛsnt] *adj* (*drink*) gazeux(-euse)

**efficiency** [ɪˈfɪʃənsɪ] *n* efficacité *f*; (*of machine*) rendement *m*

**efficient** [ɪˈfɪʃənt] *adj* efficace; (*machine*) qui a un bon rendement

**effort** [ˈɛfət] *n* effort *m*; **~less** *adj* (*style*) aisé(e); (*achievement*) facile

**effusive** [ɪˈfjuːsɪv] *adj* chaleureux(-euse)

**e.g.** *adv abbr* (= *exempli gratia*) par exemple, p. ex.

**egg** [ɛg] *n* œuf *m*; **hard-boiled/soft-boiled** ~ œuf dur/à la coque; **to** ~ **on** *vt* pousser; **~cup** *n* coquetier *m*; **~plant** *n* (*esp us*) aubergine *f*; **~shell** *n* coquille *f* d'œuf

**ego** [ˈiːɡəu] *n* (*self-esteem*) amour-propre *m*

**egotism** [ˈɛɡəutɪzəm] *n* égotisme *m*

**egotist** [ˈɛɡəutɪst] *n* égocentrique *m/f*

**Egypt** [ˈiːdʒɪpt] *n* Égypte *f*; **~ian** [ɪˈdʒɪpʃən] *adj* égyptien(ne) ♦ *n* Égyptien(ne)

**eiderdown** [ˈaɪdədaun] *n* édredon *m*

**Eiffel Tower** [ˈaɪfəl-] *n* tour *f* Eiffel

**eight** [eɪt] *num* huit; **~een** [eɪˈtiːn] *num* dix-huit; **~h** [eɪtθ] *num* huitième; **~y** [ˈeɪtɪ] *num* quatre-vingt(s)

**Eire** [ˈɛərə] *n* République *f* d'Irlande

**either** [ˈaɪðə] *adj* l'un ou l'autre; (*both, each*) chaque ♦ *pron*: ~ (*of them*) l'un ou l'autre ♦ *adv* non plus ♦ *conj*: ~ **good or bad** ou bien bon ou bien mauvais, soit bon soit mauvais; **on** ~ **side** de chaque côté; **I don't like** ~ je n'aime ni l'un ni l'autre; **no, I don't** ~ moi non plus

**eject** [ɪˈdʒɛkt] *vt* (*tenant etc*) expulser;

(*object*) éjecter

**elaborate** [*adj* ɪ'læbərɪt, *vb* ɪ'læbəreɪt] *adj* compliqué(e), recherché(e) ♦ *vt* élaborer ♦ *vi*: **to ~ (on)** entrer dans les détails (de)

**elastic** [ɪ'læstɪk] *adj* élastique ♦ *n* élastique *m*; **~ band** *n* élastique *m*

**elated** [ɪ'leɪtɪd] *adj* transporté(e) de joie

**elation** [ɪ'leɪʃən] *n* allégresse *f*

**elbow** ['ɛlbəʊ] *n* coude *m*

**elder** ['ɛldə*r*] *adj* aîné(e) ♦ *n* (*tree*) sureau *m*; **one's ~s** ses aînés; **~ly** *adj* âgé(e) ♦ *npl*: **the ~ly** les personnes âgées

**eldest** ['ɛldɪst] *adj*, *n*: **the ~ (child)** l'aîné(e) (des enfants)

**elect** [ɪ'lɛkt] *vt* élire ♦ *adj*: **the president ~** le président désigné; **to ~ to do** choisir de faire; **~ion** *n* élection *f*; **~ioneering** [ɪlɛkʃə'nɪərɪŋ] *n* propagande électorale, manœuvres électorales; **~or** *n* électeur(-trice); **~orate** *n* électorat *m*

**electric** [ɪ'lɛktrɪk] *adj* électrique; **~al** *adj* électrique; **~ blanket** *n* couverture chauffante; **~ fire** (*BRIT*) *n* radiateur *m* électrique; **~ian** [ɪlɛk'trɪʃən] *n* électricien *m*; **~ity** [ɪlɛk'trɪsɪtɪ] *n* électricité *f*

**electrify** [ɪ'lɛktrɪfaɪ] *vt* (*RAIL, fence*) électrifier; (*audience*) électriser

**electronic** [ɪlɛk'trɒnɪk] *adj* électronique; **~ mail** *n* courrier *m* électronique; **~s** *n* électronique *f*

**elegant** ['ɛlɪgənt] *adj* élégant(e)

**element** ['ɛlɪmənt] *n* (*gen*) élément *m*; (*of heater, kettle etc*) résistance *f*; **~ary** [ɛlɪ'mɛntərɪ] *adj* élémentaire; (*school, education*) primaire

**elephant** ['ɛlɪfənt] *n* éléphant *m*

**elevation** [ɛlɪ'veɪʃən] *n* (*raising, promotion*) avancement *m*, promotion *f*; (*height*) hauteur *f*

**elevator** ['ɛlɪveɪtə*r*] *n* (*in warehouse etc*) élévateur *m*, monte-charge *m inv*; (*US: lift*) ascenseur *m*

**eleven** [ɪ'lɛvn] *num* onze; **~ses** [ɪ'lɛvnzɪz] *npl* ≈ pause-café *f*; **~th** *num*

onzième

**elicit** [ɪ'lɪsɪt] *vt*: **to ~ (from)** obtenir (de), arracher (à)

**eligible** ['ɛlɪdʒəbl] *adj*: **to be ~ for** remplir les conditions requises pour; **an ~ young man/woman** un beau parti

**elm** [ɛlm] *n* orme *m*

**elocution** [ɛlə'kju:ʃən] *n* élocution *f*

**elongated** ['i:lɒŋgeɪtɪd] *adj* allongé(e)

**elope** [ɪ'ləʊp] *vi* (*lovers*) s'enfuir (ensemble)

**eloquent** ['ɛləkwənt] *adj* éloquent(e)

**else** [ɛls] *adv* d'autre; **something ~** quelque chose d'autre, autre chose; **somewhere ~** ailleurs, autre part; **everywhere ~** partout ailleurs; **nobody ~** personne d'autre; **where ~?** à quel autre endroit?; **little ~** pas grand-chose d'autre; **~where** *adv* ailleurs, autre part

**elude** [ɪ'lu:d] *vt* échapper à

**elusive** [ɪ'lu:sɪv] *adj* insaisissable

**emaciated** [ɪ'meɪsɪeɪtɪd] *adj* émacié(e), décharné(e)

**e-mail** ['i:meɪl] *n* courrier *m* électronique ♦ *vt* (*person*) envoyer un message électronique à

**emancipate** [ɪ'mænsɪpeɪt] *vt* émanciper

**embankment** [ɪm'bæŋkmənt] *n* (*of road, railway*) remblai *m*, talus *m*; (*of river*) berge *f*, quai *m*

**embark** [ɪm'bɑːk] *vi* s'embarquer; **to ~ on** (*journey*) entreprendre; (*fig*) se lancer or s'embarquer dans; **~ation** [ɛmbɑː'keɪʃən] *n* embarquement *m*

**embarrass** [ɪm'bærəs] *vt* embarrasser, gêner; **~ed** *adj* gêné(e); **~ing** *adj* gênant(e), embarrassant(e); **~ment** *n* embarras *m*, gêne *f*

**embassy** ['ɛmbəsɪ] *n* ambassade *f*

**embedded** [ɪm'bɛdɪd] *adj* enfoncé(e)

**embellish** [ɪm'bɛlɪʃ] *vt* orner, décorer; (*fig: account*) enjoliver

**embers** ['ɛmbəz] *npl* braise *f*

**embezzle** [ɪm'bɛzl] *vt* détourner; **~ment** *n* détournement *m* de fonds

**embitter** [ɪm'bɪtə*r*] *vt* (*person*) aigrir;

(*relations*) envenimer

**embody** [ɪm'bɔdɪ] vt (*features*) réunir, comprendre; (*ideas*) formuler, exprimer

**embossed** [ɪm'bɔst] adj (*metal*) estampé(e); (*leather*) frappé(e); **~ wallpaper** papier gaufré

**embrace** [ɪm'breɪs] vt embrasser, étreindre; (*include*) embrasser ♦ vi s'étreindre, s'embrasser ♦ n étreinte f

**embroider** [ɪm'brɔɪdə'] vt broder; **~y** n broderie f

**emerald** ['emərəld] n émeraude f

**emerge** [ɪ'mɜːdʒ] vi apparaître; (*from room, car*) surgir; (*from sleep, imprisonment*) sortir

**emergency** [ɪ'mɜːdʒənsɪ] n urgence f; **in an ~** en cas d'urgence; **~ cord** n sonnette f d'alarme; **~ exit** n sortie f de secours; **~ landing** n atterrissage forcé; **~ services** npl: **the ~ services** (*fire, police, ambulance*) les services mpl d'urgence

**emery board** ['emərɪ-] n lime f à ongles (*en carton émerisé*)

**emigrate** ['emɪgreɪt] vi émigrer

**eminent** ['emɪnənt] adj éminent(e)

**emissions** [ɪ'mɪʃənz] npl émissions fpl

**emit** [ɪ'mɪt] vt émettre

**emotion** [ɪ'məuʃən] n émotion f; **~al** adj (*person*) émotif(-ive), très sensible; (*needs, exhaustion*) affectif(-ive); (*scene*) émouvant(e); (*tone, speech*) qui fait appel aux sentiments; **emotive** adj chargé(e) d'émotion; (*subject*) sensible

**emperor** ['empərə'] n empereur m

**emphasis** ['emfəsɪs] (pl **-ases**) n (*stress*) accent m; (*importance*) insistance f

**emphasize** ['emfəsaɪz] vt (*syllable, word, point*) appuyer sur, accentuer; (*feature*) souligner, accentuer

**emphatic** [em'fætɪk] adj (*strong*) énergique, vigoureux(-euse); (*unambiguous, clear*) catégorique

**empire** ['empaɪə'] n empire m

**employ** [ɪm'plɔɪ] vt employer; **~ee** n employé(e); **~er** n employeur(-euse);

**~ment** n emploi m; **~ment agency** n agence f or bureau m de placement

**empower** [ɪm'pauə'] vt: **to ~ sb to do** autoriser or habiliter qn à faire

**empress** ['empris] n impératrice f

**emptiness** ['emptinis] n (*of area, region*) aspect m désertique m; (*of life*) vide m, vacuité f

**empty** ['emptɪ] adj vide; (*street, promise*) en l'air, vain(e) ♦ vt vider ♦ vi se vider; (*liquid*) s'écouler; **~-handed** adj les mains vides

**EMU** n abbr (= *economic and monetary union*) UME f

**emulate** ['emjuleɪt] vt rivaliser avec, imiter

**emulsion** [ɪ'mʌlʃən] n émulsion f; (*also: ~ paint*) peinture mate

**enable** [ɪ'neɪbl] vt: **to ~ sb to do** permettre à qn de faire

**enamel** [ɪ'næml] n émail m; (*also: ~ paint*) peinture laquée

**enchant** [ɪn'tʃɑːnt] vt enchanter; **~ing** adj ravissant(e), enchanteur(-teresse)

**encl.** abbr = **enclosed**

**enclose** [ɪn'kləuz] vt (*land*) clôturer; (*space, object*) entourer; (*letter etc*): **to ~ (with)** joindre (à); **please find ~d** veuillez trouver ci-joint; **enclosure** n enceinte f

**encompass** [ɪn'kʌmpəs] vt (*include*) contenir, inclure

**encore** [ɔŋ'kɔː'] excl bis ♦ n bis m

**encounter** [ɪn'kauntə'] n rencontre f ♦ vt rencontrer

**encourage** [ɪn'kʌrɪdʒ] vt encourager; **~ment** n encouragement m

**encroach** [ɪn'krəutʃ] vi: **to ~ (up)on** empiéter sur

**encyclop(a)edia** [ensaɪkləu'piːdɪə] n encyclopédie f

**end** [end] n (*gen, also: aim*) fin f; (*of table, street, rope etc*) bout m, extrémité f ♦ vt terminer; (*also: bring to an ~, put an ~ to*) mettre fin à ♦ vi se terminer, finir; **in the ~** finalement; **on ~** (*object*) debout, dressé(e); **to stand on ~**

*(hair)* se dresser sur la tête; **for hours on ~** pendant des heures et des heures; **~ up** vi: **to ~ up in** *(condition)* finir *or* se terminer par; *(place)* finir *or* aboutir à **p**

**endanger** [ɪnˈdeɪndʒəʳ] vt mettre en danger; **an ~ed species** une espèce en voie de disparition

**endearing** [ɪnˈdɪərɪŋ] adj attachant(e)

**endeavour** [ɪnˈdevəʳ] *(US* **endeavor)** n tentative f, effort m ♦ vi: **to ~ to do** tenter *or* s'efforcer de faire

**ending** [ˈendɪŋ] n dénouement m, fin f; *(LING)* terminaison f

**endive** [ˈendaɪv] n chicorée f; *(smooth)* endive f

**endless** [ˈendlɪs] adj sans fin, interminable

**endorse** [ɪnˈdɔːs] vt *(cheque)* endosser; *(approve)* appuyer, approuver, sanctionner; **~ment** n *(approval)* appui m, aval m; *(BRIT: on driving licence)* contravention portée au permis de conduire

**endure** [ɪnˈdjuəʳ] vt supporter, endurer ♦ vi durer

**enemy** [ˈenəmɪ] adj, n ennemi(e)

**energetic** [enəˈdʒetɪk] adj énergique; *(activity)* qui fait se dépenser (physiquement)

**energy** [ˈenədʒɪ] n énergie f

**enforce** [ɪnˈfɔːs] vt *(law)* appliquer, faire respecter

**engage** [ɪnˈgeɪdʒ] vt engager; *(attention etc)* retenir ♦ vi *(TECH)* s'enclencher, s'engrener; **to ~ in** se lancer dans; **~d** adj *(BRIT: busy, in use)* occupé(e); *(betrothed)* fiancé(e); **to get ~d** se fiancer; **~d tone** n *(TEL)* tonalité f occupé *inv or* pas libre; **~ment** n obligation f, engagement m; rendez-vous m inv; *(to marry)* fiançailles fpl; **~ment ring** n bague f de fiançailles; **engaging** adj engageant(e), attirant(e)

**engine** [ˈendʒɪn] n *(AUT)* moteur m; *(RAIL)* locomotive f; **~ driver** n mécanicien m

**engineer** [endʒɪˈnɪəʳ] n ingénieur m;

*(BRIT: repairer)* dépanneur m; *(NAVY, US RAIL)* mécanicien m; **~ing** n engineering m, ingénierie f; *(of bridges, ships)* génie m; *(of machine)* mécanique f

**England** [ˈɪŋglənd] n Angleterre f; **English** adj anglais(e) ♦ n *(LING)* anglais m; **the English** npl *(people)* les Anglais; **the English Channel** la Manche; **Englishman** *(irreg)* n Anglais; **Englishwoman** *(irreg)* n Anglaise f

**engraving** [ɪnˈgreɪvɪŋ] n gravure f

**engrossed** [ɪnˈgrəust] adj: **~ in** absorbé(e) par, plongé(e) dans

**engulf** [ɪnˈgʌlf] vt engloutir

**enhance** [ɪnˈhɑːns] vt rehausser, mettre en valeur

**enjoy** [ɪnˈdʒɔɪ] vt aimer, prendre plaisir à; *(have: health, fortune)* connaître; *(: success)* connaître; **to ~ o.s.** s'amuser; **~able** adj agréable; **~ment** n plaisir m

**enlarge** [ɪnˈlɑːdʒ] vt accroître; *(PHOT)* agrandir ♦ vi: **to ~ on** *(subject)* s'étendre sur; **~ment** [ɪnˈlɑːdʒmənt] n *(PHOT)* agrandissement m

**enlighten** [ɪnˈlaɪtn] vt éclairer; **~ed** adj éclairé(e); **~ment** n: **the E~ment** *(HISTORY)* ≈ le Siècle des lumières

**enlist** [ɪnˈlɪst] vt recruter; *(support)* s'assurer ♦ vi s'engager

**enmity** [ˈenmɪtɪ] n inimitié f

**enormous** [ɪˈnɔːməs] adj énorme

**enough** [ɪˈnʌf] adj, pron: **~ time/books** assez *or* suffisamment de temps/livres ♦ adv: **big ~** assez *or* suffisamment grand; **have you got ~?** en avez-vous assez?; **he has not worked ~** il n'a pas assez *or* suffisamment travaillé; **to eat ~** assez à manger; **~!** assez!, ça suffit!; **that's ~, thanks** cela suffit *or* c'est assez, merci; **I've had ~ of him** j'en ai assez de lui; **... which, funnily** *or* **oddly ~** ... qui, chose curieuse

**enquire** [ɪnˈkwaɪəʳ] vt, vi = **inquire**

**enrage** [ɪnˈreɪdʒ] vt mettre en fureur *or* en rage, rendre furieux(-euse)

**enrol** [ɪnˈrəul] *(US* **enroll)** vt inscrire ♦ vi s'inscrire; **~ment** *(US* **enrollment)** n inscription f

**en suite** ['ɔnswiːt] adj: **with ~ bathroom** avec salle de bains en attenante

**ensure** [ɪn'ʃuɐr] vt assurer; garantir; **to ~ that** s'assurer que

**entail** [ɪn'teɪl] vt entraîner, occasionner

**entangled** [ɪn'tæŋɡld] adj: **to become ~ (in)** s'empêtrer (dans)

**enter** ['entɐr] vt (room) entrer dans, pénétrer dans; (club, army) entrer à; (competition) s'inscrire à pour; (sb for a competition) (faire) inscrire; (write down) inscrire, noter; (COMPUT) entrer, introduire ♦ vi entrer; **~ for** vt fus s'inscrire à, se présenter pour à; **~ into** vt fus (explanation) se lancer dans; (discussion, negotiations) entamer; (agreement) conclure

**enterprise** ['entɐpraɪz] n entreprise f; (initiative) (esprit m d')initiative f; **free ~** libre entreprise; **private ~** entreprise privée; **enterprising** adj entreprenant(e), dynamique; (scheme) audacieux(-euse)

**entertain** [entɐ'teɪn] vt amuser, distraire; (invite) recevoir (à dîner); (idea, plan) envisager; **~er** n artiste m/f de variétés; **~ing** adj amusant(e), distrayant(e); **~ment** n (amusement) divertissement m, amusement m; (show) spectacle m

**enthralled** [ɪn'θrɔːld] adj captivé(e)

**enthusiasm** [ɪn'θuːzɪæzəm] n enthousiasme m

**enthusiast** [ɪn'θuːzɪæst] n enthousiaste m/f; **~ic** [ɪnθuːzɪ'æstɪk] adj enthousiaste; **to be ~ic about** être enthousiasmé(e) par

**entire** [ɪn'taɪɐr] adj (tout) entier(-ère); **~ly** adv entièrement, complètement; **~ty** [ɪn'taɪɐrtɪ] n: **in its ~ty** dans sa totalité

**entitle** [ɪn'taɪtl] vt: **to ~ sb to sth** donner droit à qch à qn; **~d** [ɪn'taɪtld] adj (book) intitulé(e); **to be ~d to do** avoir le droit de ou être habilité à faire

**entrance** [n 'entrns, vb ɪn'trɑːns] n en-

trée f ♦ vt enchanter, ravir; **to gain ~ to** (university etc) être admis à; **~ examination** n examen m d'entrée; **~ fee** n (to museum etc) prix m d'entrée; (to join club etc) droit m d'inscription; **~ ramp** (US) n (AUT) bretelle f d'accès; **entrant** n participant(e); concurrent(e); (BRIT: in exam) candidat(e)

**entrenched** [en'trentʃt] adj retranché(e); (ideas) arrêté(e)

**entrepreneur** ['ɔntrəprə'nəːr] n entrepreneur m

**entrust** [ɪn'trʌst] vt: **to ~ sth to** confier qch à

**entry** ['entrɪ] n entrée f; (in register) inscription f; **no ~** défense d'entrer, entrée interdite; (AUT) sens interdit; **~ form** n feuille f d'inscription; **~ phone** (BRIT) n interphone m

**envelop** [ɪn'veləp] vt envelopper

**envelope** ['envələup] n enveloppe f

**envious** ['envɪəs] adj envieux(-euse)

**environment** [ɪn'vaɪərnmənt] n environnement m; (social, moral) milieu m; **~al** [ɪnvaɪərn'mentl] adj écologique; du milieu; **~friendly** adj écologique

**envisage** [ɪn'vɪzɪdʒ] vt (foresee) prévoir

**envoy** ['envɔɪ] n (diplomat) ministre m plénipotentiaire

**envy** ['envɪ] n envie f ♦ vt envier; **to ~ sb sth** envier qch à qn

**epic** ['epɪk] n épopée f ♦ adj épique

**epidemic** [epɪ'demɪk] n épidémie f

**epilepsy** ['epɪlepsɪ] n épilepsie f; **epileptic** [epɪ'leptɪk] adj épileptique m/f

**episode** ['epɪsəud] n épisode m

**epitome** [ɪ'pɪtəmɪ] n modèle m; **epitomize** vt incarner

**equal** ['iːkwl] adj égal(e) ♦ n égal(e) ♦ vt égaler; **~ to** (task) à la hauteur de; **~ity** [iː'kwɔlɪtɪ] n égalité f; **~ize** vi (SPORT) égaliser; **~ly** adv également; (just as) tout aussi

**equanimity** [ekwə'nɪmɪtɪ] n égalité f d'humeur

**equate** [ɪ'kweɪt] vt: **to ~ sth with** comparer qch à; assimiler qch à; **equa-**

**tion** n (MATH) équation f

**equator** [ɪ'kweɪtəʳ] n équateur m

**equilibrium** [i:kwɪ'lɪbrɪəm] n équilibre m

**equip** [ɪ'kwɪp] vt: **to ~ (with)** équiper (de); **to be well ~ped** être bien équipé(e); **~ment** n équipement m, (electrical etc) appareillage m, installation f

**equities** [ɪ'kwɪtɪz] (BRIT) npl (COMM) actions cotées en Bourse

**equivalent** [ɪ'kwɪvələnt] adj: **~ (to)** équivalent(e) (à) ♦ n équivalent m

**era** [ˈɪərə] n ère f, époque f

**eradicate** [ɪ'rædɪkeɪt] vt éliminer

**erase** [ɪ'reɪz] vt effacer; **~r** n gomme f

**erect** [ɪ'rekt] adj droit(e) ♦ vt construire; (monument) ériger, élever; (tent etc) dresser; **~ion** [ɪ'rekʃən] n (PHYSIOL) érection f; (of building) construction f; (of machinery) montage m

**ERM** n abbr (= Exchange Rate Mechanism) MTC m

**erode** [ɪ'rəud] vt éroder; (metal) ronger

**erotic** [ɪ'rɔtɪk] adj érotique

**errand** [ˈerənd] n course f, commission f

**erratic** [ɪ'rætɪk] adj irrégulier(-ère); inconstant(e)

**error** [ˈerəʳ] n erreur f

**erupt** [ɪ'rʌpt] vi entrer en éruption; (fig) éclater; **~ion** n éruption f

**escalate** [ˈeskəleɪt] vi s'intensifier

**escalator** [ˈeskəleɪtəʳ] n escalier roulant

**escapade** [eskə'peɪd] n (misdeed) fredaine f; (adventure) équipée f

**escape** [ɪs'keɪp] n fuite f; (from prison) évasion f ♦ vi s'échapper, fuir; (from jail) s'évader; (fig) s'en tirer; (leak) s'échapper ♦ vt échapper à; **to ~ from** (person) échapper à; (place) s'échapper de; (fig) fuir; **escapism** n (fig) évasion f

**escort** [n ˈeskɔːt, vb ɪs'kɔːt] n escorte f ♦ vt escorter

**Eskimo** [ˈeskɪməu] n Esquimau(de)

**especially** [ɪs'peʃlɪ] adv (particularly) particulièrement; (above all) surtout

**espionage** [ˈespɪənɑːʒ] n espionnage

**Esquire** [ɪs'kwaɪəʳ] n: **J Brown, ~** Monsieur J. Brown

**essay** [ˈeseɪ] n (SCOL) dissertation f; (LITERATURE) essai m

**essence** [ˈesns] n essence f

**essential** [ɪ'senʃl] adj essentiel(le); (basic) fondamental(e) ♦ n: **~s** éléments essentiels; **~ly** adv essentiellement

**establish** [ɪs'tæblɪʃ] vt établir; (business) fonder, créer; (one's power etc) asseoir, affirmer; **~ed** adj bien établi(e); **~ment** n établissement m; (founding) création f

**estate** [ɪs'teɪt] n (land) domaine m, propriété f; (LAW) biens mpl, succession f; (BRIT: also: housing ~) lotissement m, cité f; **~ agent** n agent immobilier; **~ car** (BRIT) n break m

**esteem** [ɪs'tiːm] n estime f

**esthetic** [ɪs'θetɪk] (US) adj = aesthetic

**estimate** [n ˈestɪmət, vb ˈestɪmeɪt] n estimation f; (COMM) devis m ♦ vt estimer; **estimation** [estɪ'meɪʃən] n opinion f; (calculation) estimation f

**estranged** [ɪs'treɪndʒd] adj séparé(e); dont on s'est séparé(e)

**etc.** abbr (= et cetera) etc

**eternal** [ɪ'təːnl] adj éternel(le)

**eternity** [ɪ'təːnɪtɪ] n éternité f

**ethical** [ˈeθɪkl] adj moral(e); **ethics** n éthique f ♦ npl moralité f

**Ethiopia** [iːθɪ'əupɪə] n Éthiopie f

**ethnic** [ˈeθnɪk] adj ethnique; (music etc) folklorique; **~ minority** minorité f ethnique

**ethos** [ˈiːθɔs] n génie m

**etiquette** [ˈetɪket] n convenances fpl, étiquette f

**EU** n abbr (= European Union) UE f

**euro** [ˈjuərəu] n (currency) euro m

**Euroland** [ˈjuərəulænd] n Euroland m

**Eurocheque** [ˈjuərəutʃek] n eurochèque m

**Europe** [ˈjuərəp] n Europe f; **~an** [juərə'piːən] adj européen(ne) ♦ n Européen(ne); **~an Community** Communauté f européenne

**evacuate** [ɪ'vækjueɪt] vt évacuer

**evade** [ɪ'veɪd] vt échapper à; (question etc) éluder; (duties) se dérober à; **to ~ tax** frauder le fisc

**evaporate** [ɪ'væpəreɪt] vi s'évaporer; **~d milk** n lait condensé non sucré

**evasion** [ɪ'veɪʒən] n dérobade f; **tax ~** fraude fiscale

**eve** [iːv] n: **on the ~ of** à la veille de

**even** ['iːvn] adj (level, smooth) régulier(-ère); (equal) égal(e); (number) pair(e) ♦ adv même; **if ~ me** site sit +indic; **~ though** alors même que +cond; **~ more** encore plus; **~ so** quand même; **not ~** pas même; **to get ~ with sb** prendre sa revanche sur qn

**evening** ['iːvnɪŋ] n soir m; (as duration, event) soirée f; **in the ~** le soir; **~ class** n cours m du soir; **~ dress** n tenue f de soirée

**event** [ɪ'vent] n événement m; (SPORT) épreuve f; **in the ~ of** en cas de; **~ful** adj mouvementé(e)

**eventual** [ɪ'ventʃuəl] adj final(e); **~ity** [ɪventʃu'ælɪtɪ] n possibilité f, éventualité f; **~ly** adv finalement

**ever** ['evə*] adv jamais; (at all times) toujours; **the best ~** le meilleur qu'on ait jamais vu; **have you ~ seen it?** l'as-tu déjà vu?, as-tu eu l'occasion or t'est-il arrivé de le voir?; **why ~ not?** mais enfin, pourquoi pas?; **~ since** adv depuis ♦ conj depuis que; **~green** n arbre m à feuilles persistantes; **~lasting** adj éternel(le)

**every** ['evrɪ] adj chaque; **~ day** tous les jours, chaque jour; **~ other/third day** tous les deux/trois jours; **~ other car** une voiture sur deux; **~ now and then** de temps en temps; **~body** pron tout le monde, tous pl; **~day** adj quotidien(ne), de tous les jours; **~one** pron = **everybody**; **~thing** pron tout; **~where** adv partout

**evict** [ɪ'vɪkt] vt expulser; **~ion** n expulsion f

**evidence** ['evɪdns] n (proof) preuve(s)

f(pl); (of witness) témoignage m; (sign): **to show ~ of** présenter des signes de; **to give ~** témoigner, déposer

**evident** ['evɪdnt] adj évident(e); **~ly** adv de toute évidence; (apparently) apparamment

**evil** ['iːvl] adj mauvais(e) ♦ n mal m

**evoke** [ɪ'vəʊk] vt évoquer

**evolution** [iːvə'luːʃən] n évolution f

**evolve** [ɪ'vɒlv] vt élaborer ♦ vi évoluer

**ewe** [juː] n brebis f

**ex-** [eks] prefix ex-

**exact** [ɪg'zækt] adj exact(e) ♦ vt: **to ~ sth (from)** extorquer qch (à); exiger qch (de); **~ing** adj exigeant(e); (work) astreignant(e); **~ly** adv exactement

**exaggerate** [ɪg'zædʒəreɪt] vt, vi exagérer; **exaggeration** [ɪgzædʒə'reɪʃən] n exagération f

**exalted** [ɪg'zɔːltɪd] adj (prominent) élevé(e); (: person) haut placé(e)

**exam** [ɪg'zæm] n abbr (SCOL) = **examination**

**examination** [ɪgzæmɪ'neɪʃən] n (SCOL, MED) examen m

**examine** [ɪg'zæmɪn] vt (gen) examiner; (SCOL: person) interroger; **~r** n examinateur(-trice)

**example** [ɪg'zɑːmpl] n exemple m; **for ~** par exemple

**exasperate** [ɪg'zɑːspəreɪt] vt exaspérer; **exasperation** [ɪgzɑːspə'reɪʃən] n exaspération f, irritation f

**excavate** ['ekskəveɪt] vt excaver; **excavation** [ekskə'veɪʃən] n fouilles fpl

**exceed** [ɪk'siːd] vt dépasser; (one's powers) outrepasser; **~ingly** adv extrêmement

**excellent** ['eksələnt] adj excellent(e)

**except** [ɪk'sept] prep (also: **~ for**, **~ing**) sauf, excepté ♦ vt excepter; **~ if/when** sauf si/quand; **~ that** sauf que, si ce n'est que; **~ion** n exception f; **to take ~ion to** s'offusquer de; **~ional** adj exceptionnel(le)

**excerpt** ['eksɜːpt] n extrait m

**excess** [ɪk'ses] n excès m; **~ baggage**

*n* excédent *m* de bagages; **~ fare** (BRIT) *n* supplément *m*; **~ive** *adj* excessif(-ive)

**exchange** [ɪks'tʃeɪndʒ] *n* échange *m*; (also: **telephone ~**) central *m* ♦ *vt*: **to ~ (for)** échanger (contre); **~ rate** *n* taux *m* de change

**Exchequer** [ɪks'tʃekəʳ] (BRIT) *n*: **the ~** l'Échiquier *m*, ≈ le ministère des Finances

**excise** [*n* 'eksaɪz, *vb* ek'saɪz] *n* taxe *f* ♦ *vt* exciser

**excite** [ɪk'saɪt] *vt* exciter; **to get ~d** s'exciter; **~ment** *n* excitation *f*; **exciting** *adj* passionnant(e)

**exclaim** [ɪks'kleɪm] *vi* s'exclamer; **exclamation** [ekskla'meɪʃən] *n* exclamation *f*; **exclamation mark** *n* point *m* d'exclamation

**exclude** [ɪks'klu:d] *vt* exclure; **exclusion zone** *n* zone interdite; **exclusive** *adj* exclusif(-ive); (club, district) sélect(e); (item of news) en exclusivité; **exclusive of VAT** TVA non comprise; **mutually exclusive** qui s'excluent l'un(e) l'autre

**excruciating** [ɪks'kru:ʃieɪtɪŋ] *adj* atroce

**excursion** [ɪks'kə:ʃən] *n* excursion *f*

**excuse** [*n* ɪks'kju:s, *vb* ɪks'kju:z] *n* excuse *f* ♦ *vt* excuser; **to ~ sb from** (activity) dispenser qn de; **~ me!** excusez-moi, pardon!; **now if you will ~ me**, ... maintenant, si je (vous) permettez ...

**ex-directory** ['eksdɪ'rektərɪ] (BRIT) *adj* sur la liste rouge

**execute** ['eksɪkju:t] *vt* exécuter; **execution** *n* exécution *f*

**executive** [ɪg'zekjutɪv] *n* (COMM) cadre *m*; (of organization, political party) bureau *m* ♦ *adj* exécutif(-ive)

**exemplify** [ɪg'zemplɪfaɪ] *vt* illustrer; (typify) incarner

**exempt** [ɪg'zempt] *adj*: **~ from** exempté(e) or dispensé(e) de ♦ *vt*: **to ~ sb from** exempter or dispenser qn de

**exercise** ['eksəsaɪz] *n* exercice *m* ♦ *vt* exercer; (patience etc) faire preuve de; (dog) promener ♦ *vi* prendre de l'exercice; **~ book** *n* cahier *m*

**exert** [ɪg'zə:t] *vt* exercer, employer; **to ~ o.s.** se dépenser; **~ion** *n* effort *m*

**exhale** [eks'heɪl] *vt* exhaler ♦ *vi* expirer

**exhaust** [ɪg'zɔ:st] *n* (also: **~ fumes**) gaz *mpl* d'échappement; (also: **~ pipe**) tuyau *m* d'échappement ♦ *vt* épuiser; **~ed** *adj* épuisé(e); **~ion** *n* épuisement *m*; **nervous ~ion** fatigue nerveuse; surmenage *m* mental; **~ive** *adj* très complet(-ète)

**exhibit** [ɪg'zɪbɪt] *n* (ART) pièce exposée, objet exposé; (LAW) pièce à conviction ♦ *vt* exposer; (courage, skill) faire preuve de; **~ion** [eksɪ'bɪʃən] *n* exposition *f*; (of ill-temper, talent etc) démonstration *f*

**exhilarating** [ɪg'zɪlɪreɪtɪŋ] *adj* grisant(e); stimulant(e)

**ex-husband** *n* ex-mari *m*

**exile** ['eksaɪl] *n* exil *m*; (person) exilé(e) ♦ *vt* exiler

**exist** [ɪg'zɪst] *vi* exister; **~ence** *n* existence *f*; **~ing** *adj* actuel(le)

**exit** ['eksɪt] *n* sortie *f* ♦ *vi* (COMPUT, THEATRE) sortir; **~ poll** *n* sondage *m* (fait à la sortie de l'isoloir); **~ ramp** *n* (AUT) bretelle *f* d'accès

**exodus** ['eksədəs] *n* exode *m*

**exonerate** [ɪg'zɔnəreɪt] *vt*: **to ~ from** disculper de

**exotic** [ɪg'zɔtɪk] *adj* exotique

**expand** [ɪks'pænd] *vt* agrandir; accroître ♦ *vi* (trade etc) se développer, s'accroître; (gas, metal) se dilater

**expanse** [ɪks'pæns] *n* étendue *f*

**expansion** [ɪks'pænʃən] *n* développement *m*, accroissement *m*

**expect** [ɪks'pekt] *vt* (anticipate) s'attendre à, s'attendre à ce que +sub; (count on) compter sur, escompter; (require) demander, exiger; (suppose) supposer; (await, also baby) attendre ♦ *vi*: **to be ~ing** être enceinte; **~ancy** *n* (anticipation) attente *f*; **life ~ancy** espérance *f* de vie; **~ant mother** *n* future maman; **~ation** [ekspek'teɪʃən] *n* attente *f*; espérance(s) *f(pl)*

**expedient** [ɪks'pi:dɪənt] *adj* indiqué(e),

opportun(e) ♦ n expédient m
expedition [ɛkspə'dɪʃən] n expédition f
expel [ɪks'pɛl] vt chasser, expulser; (SCOL) renvoyer
expend [ɪks'pɛnd] vt consacrer; (money) dépenser; ~iture [ɪks'pɛndɪtʃəʳ] n dépense f; dépenses fpl
expense [ɪks'pɛns] n dépense f, frais mpl; (high cost) coût m; ~s npl (COMM) frais mpl; at the ~ of aux dépens de; ~ account n (note f de) frais mpl; expensive adj cher (chère), coûteux (-euse); to be expensive coûter cher
experience [ɪks'pɪərɪəns] n expérience f ♦ vt connaître, faire l'expérience de; (feeling) éprouver; ~d adj expérimenté(e)
experiment [ɪks'pɛrɪmənt] n expérience f ♦ vi faire une expérience; to ~ with expérimenter
expert [ɛkspə:t] adj expert(e) ♦ n expert m; ~ise [ɛkspə:'ti:z] n (grande) compétence
expire [ɪks'paɪəʳ] vi expirer; expiry n expiration f
explain [ɪks'pleɪn] vt expliquer; explanation [ɛksplə'neɪʃən] n explication f; explanatory [ɪks'plænətrɪ] adj explicatif(-ive)
explicit [ɪks'plɪsɪt] adj explicite; (definite) formel(le)
explode [ɪks'pləʊd] vi exploser
exploit [n 'ɛksplɔɪt, vb ɪks'plɔɪt] n exploit m ♦ vt exploiter; ~ation [ɛksplɔ:'teɪʃən] n exploitation f
exploratory [ɪks'plɔrətrɪ] adj (expedition) d'exploration; (fig: talks) préliminaire
explore [ɪks'plɔ:ʳ] vt explorer; (possibilities) étudier, examiner; ~r n explorateur(-trice)
explosion [ɪks'pləʊʒən] n explosion f; explosive adj explosif(-ive) ♦ n explosif m
exponent [ɪks'pəʊnənt] n (of school of thought etc) interprète m, représentant m

export [vb ɛks'pɔ:t, n 'ɛkspɔ:t] vt exporter ♦ n exportation f ♦ cpd d'exportation; ~er n exportateur m
expose [ɪks'pəʊz] vt exposer; (unmask) démasquer, dévoiler; ~d adj (position, house) exposé(e); exposure n exposition f; (publicity) couverture f; (PHOT) (temps m de) pose f; (: shot) pose; to die from exposure (MED) mourir de froid; exposure meter n posemètre m
express [ɪks'prɛs] adj (definite) formel(le), exprès(-esse); (BRIT: letter etc) exprès inv ♦ n (train) rapide m; (bus) car m express ♦ vt exprimer; ~ion n expression f; ~ly adv expressément, formellement; ~way n (US) n (urban motorway) voie f express (à plusieurs files)
exquisite [ɛks'kwɪzɪt] adj exquis(e)
extend [ɪks'tɛnd] vt (visit, street) prolonger; (building) agrandir; (offer) présenter, offrir; (hand, arm) tendre ♦ vi s'étendre; extension n prolongation f; agrandissement m; (building) annexe f; (to wire, table) rallonge f; (telephone: in offices) poste m; (: in private house) téléphone m supplémentaire; extensive adj étendu(e), vaste; (damage, alterations) considérable; (inquiries) approfondi(e); extensively adv: he's travelled extensively il a beaucoup voyagé
extent [ɪks'tɛnt] n étendue f; to some ~ dans une certaine mesure; to what ~? dans quelle mesure?, jusqu'à quel point?; to the ~ of ... au point de ...; to such an ~ that ... à tel point que ...
extenuating [ɪks'tɛnjʊeɪtɪŋ] adj: ~ circumstances circonstances atténuantes
exterior [ɛks'tɪərɪəʳ] adj extérieur(e) ♦ n extérieur m; dehors m
external [ɛks'tə:nl] adj externe
extinct [ɪks'tɪŋkt] adj éteint(e)
extinguish [ɪks'tɪŋgwɪʃ] vt éteindre
extort [ɪks'tɔ:t] vt: ~ sth (from) extorquer qch (à); ~ionate [ɪks'tɔ:ʃnət] adj exorbitant(e)
extra ['ɛkstrə] adj supplémentaire, de plus ♦ adv (in addition) en plus ♦ n sup-

plément m; (perk) à-côté m; (THEATRE) figurant(e) ♦ ♦ prefix extra...

**extract** [vb iks'trækt, n 'ekstrækt] vt extraire; (tooth) arracher; (money, promise) soutirer ♦ n extrait m

**extracurricular** ['ekstrǝkǝ'rıkjulǝ*] adj parascolaire

**extradite** ['ekstrǝdaɪt] vt extrader

**extra...:** ~**marital** ['ekstrǝ'mærɪtl] adj extra-conjugal(e); ~**mural** ['ekstrǝ'mjuǝrl] adj hors faculté inv; (lecture) public(-que); ~**ordinary** [ɪks'trɔ:dnrɪ] adj extraordinaire

**extravagance** [ɪks'trævǝgǝns] n prodigalités fpl; (thing bought) folie f, dépense excessive; **extravagant** adj extravagant(e); (in spending: person) prodigue, dépensier(-ère); (: tastes) dispendieux(-euse)

**extreme** [ɪks'tri:m] adj extrême ♦ n extrême m; ~**ly** adv extrêmement; **extremist** adj, n extrémiste m/f

**extricate** ['ekstrɪkeɪt] vt: **to** ~ **sth (from)** dégager qch (de)

**extrovert** ['ekstrǝvɜ:t] n extraverti(e)

**ex-wife** n ex-femme f

**eye** [aɪ] n œil m (pl yeux); (of needle) trou m, chas m ♦ vt examiner; **to keep an** ~ **on** surveiller; ~**brow** n sourcil m; ~**drops** npl gouttes fpl pour les yeux; ~**lash** n cil m; ~**lid** n paupière f; ~**liner** n eye-liner m; ~**opener** n révélation f; ~**shadow** n ombre f à paupières; ~**sight** n vue f; ~**sore** n horreur f; ~**witness** n témoin m oculaire

# F, f

**F** [ef] n (MUS) fa m

**fable** ['feɪbl] n fable f

**fabric** ['fæbrɪk] n tissu m

**fabulous** ['fæbjulǝs] adj fabuleux(-euse); (inf: super) formidable

**face** [feɪs] n visage m, figure f; (expression) expression f; (of clock) cadran m; (of cliff) paroi f; (of mountain) face f; (of building) façade f ♦ vt faire face à; ~ **down** (person) à plat ventre; (card) face en dessous; **to lose/save** ~ perdre/sauver la face; **to make** or **pull a** ~ faire une grimace; **in the** ~ **of** (difficulties etc) face à, devant; **on the** ~ **of it** à première vue; ~ **to** ~ face à face; ~ **up to** vt fus faire face à, affronter; ~ **cloth** (BRIT) n gant m de toilette; ~ **cream** n crème f pour le visage; ~ **lift** n lifting m; (of building etc) ravalement m, retapage m; ~ **powder** n poudre f de riz; ~ **value** n (of coin) valeur nominale; **to take sth at** ~ **value** (fig) prendre qch pour argent comptant

**facilities** [fǝ'sɪlɪtɪz] npl installations fpl, équipement m; **credit** ~ facilités fpl de paiement

**facing** ['feɪsɪŋ] prep face à, en face de

**facsimile** [fæk'sɪmɪlɪ] n (exact replica) fac-similé m; (fax) télécopie f

**fact** [fækt] n fait m; **in** ~ en fait

**factor** ['fæktǝ*] n facteur m

**factory** ['fæktǝrɪ] n usine f, fabrique f

**factual** ['fæktjuǝl] adj basé(e) sur les faits

**faculty** ['fækǝltɪ] n faculté f; (US: teaching staff) corps enseignant

**fad** [fæd] n (craze) engouement m

**fade** [feɪd] vi se décolorer, passer; (light, sound) s'affaiblir; (flower) se faner

**fag** [fæg] (BRIT: inf) n (cigarette) sèche f

**fail** [feɪl] vt (exam) échouer à; (candidate) recaler; (subj: courage, memory) faire défaut à ♦ vi échouer; (brakes) lâcher; (eyesight, health, light) baisser, s'affaiblir; **to** ~ **to do sth** (neglect) négliger de faire qch; (be unable) ne pas arriver or parvenir à faire qch; **without** ~ à coup sûr; sans faute; ~**ing** n défaut m ♦ prep faute de; ~**ure** n échec m; (person) raté(e); (mechanical etc) défaillance f

**faint** [feɪnt] adj faible; (recollection) vague; (mark) à peine visible ♦ n évanouissement m ♦ vi s'évanouir; **to feel** ~ défaillir

**fair** [fɛəʳ] adj équitable, juste, impartial(e); (hair) blond(e); (skin, complexion) pâle, blanc, blanc (blanche); (weather) beau (belle); (good enough) assez bon(ne); (sizeable) considérable ♦ adv: **to play ~** jouer franc-jeu ♦ n foire f; (BRIT: funfair) fête (foraine); **~ly** adv équitablement; (quite) assez; **~ness** n justice f, équité f, impartialité f

**fairy** ['fɛərɪ] n fée f; **~ tale** n conte m de fées

**faith** [feɪθ] n foi f; (trust) confiance f; (specific religion) religion f; **~ful** adj fidèle; **~fully** adv see **yours**

**fake** [feɪk] n (painting etc) faux m; (person) imposteur m ♦ adj faux (fausse) ♦ vt simuler; (painting) faire un faux de

**falcon** ['fɔːlkən] n faucon m

**fall** [fɔːl] (pt **fell**, pp **fallen**) n chute f; (US: autumn) automne m ♦ vi tomber; (price, temperature, dollar) baisser; **~s** npl (waterfall) chute f d'eau, cascade f; **to ~ flat** vi (on one's face) tomber de tout son long, s'étaler; (joke) tomber à plat; (plan) échouer; **~ back** vi reculer, se retirer; **~ back on** vt fus se rabattre sur; **~ behind** vi prendre du retard; **~ down** vi (person) tomber; (building) s'effondrer, s'écrouler; **~ for** vt fus (trick, story etc) se laisser prendre à; (person) tomber amoureux de; **~ in** vi s'effondrer; (MIL) se mettre en rangs; **~ off** vi tomber; (diminish) baisser, diminuer; **~ out** vi (hair, teeth) tomber; (MIL) rompre les rangs; (friends etc) se brouiller; **~ through** vi (plan, project) tomber à l'eau

**fallacy** ['fæləsɪ] n erreur f, illusion f

**fallout** ['fɔːlaut] n retombées (radioactives)

**fallow** ['fæləu] adj en jachère; en friche

**false** [fɔːls] adj faux (fausse); **~ alarm** n fausse alerte; **~ pretences** npl: **under ~ pretences** sous un faux prétexte; **~ teeth** npl (BRIT) fausses dents

**falter** ['fɔːltəʳ] vi chanceler, vaciller

**fame** [feɪm] n renommée f, renom m

**familiar** [fə'mɪlɪəʳ] adj familier(-ère); **to be ~ with** (subject) connaître

**family** ['fæmɪlɪ] n famille f ♦ cpd (business, doctor etc) de famille; **has he any ~?** (children) a-t-il des enfants?

**famine** ['fæmɪn] n famine f

**famished** ['fæmɪʃt] (inf) adj affamé(e)

**famous** ['feɪməs] adj célèbre; **~ly** adv (get on) fameusement, à merveille

**fan** [fæn] n (folding) éventail m; (ELEC) ventilateur m; (of person) fan m, admirateur(-trice) m/f; (of team, sport etc) supporter m/f ♦ vt éventer; (fire, quarrel) attiser

**fanatic** [fə'nætɪk] n fanatique m/f

**fan belt** n courroie f de ventilateur

**fancy** ['fænsɪ] n fantaisie f, envie f; imagination f ♦ adj (de) fantaisie inv ♦ vt (feel like, want) avoir envie de; (imagine, think) imaginer; **to take a ~ to** se prendre d'affection pour; s'enticher de; **he fancies her** (inf) elle lui plaît; **~ dress** n déguisement m, travesti m; **~-dress ball** n bal masqué or costumé

**fang** [fæŋ] n croc m; (of snake) crochet m

**fantastic** [fæn'tæstɪk] adj fantastique

**fantasy** ['fæntəsɪ] n imagination f, fantaisie f; (dream) chimère f

**far** [fɑːʳ] adj lointain(e), éloigné(e) ♦ adv loin; **~ away** or **off** au loin, dans le lointain; **at the ~ side/end** à l'autre côté/bout; **~ better** beaucoup mieux; **~ from** loin de; **by ~** de loin, de beaucoup; **go as ~ as** the **~m** allez jusqu'à la ferme; **as I know** pour autant que je sache; **how ~ is it to ...?** combien y a-t-il ...?; **how ~ have you got?** où en êtes-vous?; **~away** ['fɑːrəweɪ] adj lointain(e); (look) distrait(e)

**farce** [fɑːs] n farce f

**fare** [fɛəʳ] n (on trains, buses) prix m du billet; (in taxi) prix de la course; (food) table f, chère f; **half ~** demi-tarif; **full ~** plein tarif

**Far East** n Extrême-Orient m

**farewell** [feə'wɛl] *excl* adieu ♦ *n* adieu *m*

**farm** [fɑ:m] *n* ferme *f* ♦ *vt* cultiver; **~er** *n* fermier(-ère); cultivateur(-trice); **~hand** *n* ouvrier(-ère) agricole; **~house** *n* (maison *f* de) ferme *f*; **~ing** *n* agriculture *f*; (*of animals*) élevage *m*; **~land** *n* terres cultivées; **~ worker** *n* = **farmhand**; **~yard** *n* cour *f* de ferme

**far-reaching** [fɑ:'ri:tʃɪŋ] *adj* d'une grande portée

**fart** [fɑ:t] (*inf!*) *vi* péter

**farther** [fɑ:ðə'] *adv* plus loin ♦ *adj* plus éloigné(e), plus lointain(e)

**farthest** [fɑ:ðɪst] *superl* of **far**

**fascinate** [fæsɪneɪt] *vt* fasciner; **fascinating** *adj* fascinant(e)

**fascism** [fæʃɪzəm] *n* fascisme *m*

**fashion** [fæʃən] *n* mode *f*; (*manner*) façon *f*, manière *f* ♦ *vt* façonner; **in ~** à la mode; **out of ~** démodé(e); **~able** *adj* à la mode; **~ show** *n* défilé *m* de mannequins or de mode

**fast** [fɑ:st] *adj* rapide; (*clock*): **to be ~** avancer; (*dye, colour*) grand or bon teint *inv* ♦ *adv* vite, rapidement; (*stuck, held*) solidement ♦ *n* jeûne *m* ♦ *vi* jeûner; **~ asleep** profondément endormi

**fasten** [fɑ:sn] *vt* attacher, fixer; (*coat*) attacher, fermer ♦ *vi* se fermer, s'attacher; **~er**, **~ing** *n* attache *f*

**fast food** *n* fast food *m*, restauration *f* rapide

**fastidious** [fæs'tɪdɪəs] *adj* exigeant(e), difficile

**fat** [fæt] *adj* gros(se) ♦ *n* graisse *f*; (*on meat*) gras *m*; (*for cooking*) matière grasse

**fatal** [feɪtl] *adj* (*injury etc*) mortel(le); (*mistake*) fatal(e); **~ity** [fə'tælɪtɪ] *n* (*road death etc*) victime *f*, décès *m*

**fate** [feɪt] *n* destin *m*; (*of person*) sort *m*; **~ful** *adj* fatidique

**father** [fɑ:ðə'] *n* père *m*; **~-in-law** *n* beau-père *m*; **~ly** *adj* paternel(le)

**fathom** [fæðəm] *n* brasse *f* (= 1828 mm) ♦ *vt* (*mystery*) sonder, pénétrer

**fatigue** [fə'ti:g] *n* fatigue *f*

**fatten** [fætn] *vt, vi* engraisser

**fatty** [fætɪ] *adj* (*food*) gras(se) ♦ *n* (*inf*) gros(se)

**fatuous** [fætjuəs] *adj* stupide

**faucet** [fɔ:sɪt] (*US*) *n* robinet *m*

**fault** [fɔ:lt] *n* faute *f*; (*defect*) défaut *m*; (*GEO*) faille *f* ♦ *vt* trouver des défauts à; **it's my ~** c'est de ma faute; (*to find ~ with* trouver à redire à or à critiquer à; **at ~** fautif(-ive), coupable; **~y** *adj* défectueux(-euse)

**fauna** [fɔ:nə] *n* faune *f*

**favour** [feɪvə'] (*US* **favor**) *n* faveur *f*; (*help*) service *m* ♦ *vt* (*proposition*) être en faveur de; (*pupil etc*) favoriser; (*team, horse*) donner gagnant; **to do sb a ~** rendre un service à qn; **to find ~ with** trouver grâce aux yeux de qn; **in ~ of** en faveur de; **~able** *adj* favorable; **~ite** [feɪvrɪt] *adj*, *n* favori(te)

**fawn** [fɔ:n] *n* faon *m* ♦ *adj* (*also: ~ colour*) fauve ♦ *vi*: **to ~ (up)on** flatter servilement

**fax** [fæks] *n* (*document*) télécopie *f*; (*machine*) télécopieur *m* ♦ *vt* envoyer par télécopie

**FBI** *n abbr* (*US*: Federal Bureau of Investigation*) F.B.I. *f*

**fear** [fɪə'] *n* crainte *f*, peur *f* ♦ *vt* craindre; **for ~ of** de peur que +*sub*, de peur de +*infin*; **~ful** *adj* craintif(-ive); (*sight, noise*) affreux(-euse), épouvantable; **~less** *adj* intrépide

**feasible** [fi:zəbl] *adj* faisable, réalisable

**feast** [fi:st] *n* festin *m*, banquet *m*; (*REL: also: ~ day*) fête *f* ♦ *vi* festoyer

**feat** [fi:t] *n* exploit *m*, prouesse *f*

**feather** [fɛðə'] *n* plume *f*

**feature** [fi:tʃə'] *n* caractéristique *f*; (*article*) chronique *f*, rubrique *f* ♦ *vt* (*subj: film*) avoir pour vedette(s) ♦ *vi*: **to ~ in** figurer (en bonne place) dans; (*in film*) jouer dans; **~s** *npl* (*of face*) traits *mpl*; **~ film** *n* long métrage *m*

**February** [fɛbruərɪ] *n* février *m*

**fed** [fɛd] *pt, pp* of **feed**

**federal** [fɛdərəl] *adj* fédéral(e)

**fed up** adj: **to be ~** en avoir marre, en avoir plein le dos

**fee** [fi:] n rémunération f; (of doctor, lawyer) honoraires mpl; (for examination) droits mpl; **school ~s** frais mpl de scolarité

**feeble** ['fi:bl] adj faible; (pathetic: attempt, excuse) pauvre; (: joke) piteux (-euse)

**feed** [fi:d] (pt, pp **fed**) n (of animal) fourrage m; pâture f; (on printer) mécanisme m d'alimentation ♦ vt (person) nourrir; (baby) allaiter; (with bottle) donner le biberon à; (horse etc) donner à manger à; (machine) alimenter; (data, information): **to ~ sth into** fournir qch à; **~ on** vt fus se nourrir de; **~back** n feed-back m inv

**feel** [fi:l] (pt, pp **felt**) n sensation f; (impression) impression f ♦ vt toucher; (explore) tâter, palper; (cold, pain) sentir; (grief, anger) ressentir, éprouver; (think, believe) trouver; **to ~ well** ne me sens pas bien; **it's ~ soft** c'est doux (douce) au toucher; **to ~ hungry/cold** avoir faim/froid; **to ~ lonely/better** se sentir seul/mieux; **I don't ~ well** je ne me sens pas bien; **to ~ like** (want) avoir envie de; **~ about** vi fouiller, tâtonner; **~er** n (of insect) antenne f; **~ing** n (physical) sensation f; (emotional) sentiment m

**feet** [fi:t] npl of **foot**

**feign** [fein] vt feindre, simuler

**fell** [fel] pt of **fall** ♦ vt (tree, person) abattre

**fellow** ['feləu] n type m; (comrade) compagnon m; (of learned society) membre m ♦ cpd: **their ~ prisoners/students** leurs camarades prisonniers/d'étude; **~ citizen** n concitoyen(ne) m/f; **~ countryman** (irreg) n compatriote m; **~ men** npl semblables mpl; **~ship** n (society) association f; (comradeship) amitié f, camaraderie f; (grant) sorte de bourse universitaire

**felony** ['feləni] n crime m, forfait m

**felt** [felt] pt, pp of **feel** ♦ n feutre m; **~-**

**tip pen** n stylo-feutre m

**female** ['fi:meil] n (ZOOL) femelle f; (pej: woman) bonne femme ♦ adj (BIO) femelle; (sex, character) féminin(e); (vote etc) des femmes

**feminine** ['feminin] adj féminin(e)

**feminist** ['feminist] n féministe m/f

**fence** [fens] n barrière f ♦ vt (also: ~ in) clôturer ♦ vi faire de l'escrime; **fencing** n escrime m

**fend** [fend] vi: **to ~ for o.s.** se débrouiller (tout seul); **~ off** vt (attack etc) parer

**fender** ['fendər] n garde-feu m inv; (on boat) défense f; (US: of car) aile f

**ferment** [vb fə'ment, n 'fɜ:ment] vi fermenter ♦ n (fig) agitation f, effervescence f

**fern** [fɜ:n] n fougère f

**ferocious** [fə'rəuʃəs] adj féroce

**ferret** ['ferit] n furet m

**ferry** ['feri] n (small) bac m; (large: also: **~boat**) ferry(-boat) m ♦ vt transporter

**fertile** ['fɜ:taɪl] adj fertile; (BIO) fécond(e); **fertilizer** ['fɜ:tɪlaɪzər] n engrais m

**fester** ['festər] vi suppurer

**festival** ['festɪvəl] n (REL) fête f; (ART, MUS) festival m

**festive** ['festɪv] adj de fête; **the ~ season** (BRIT: Christmas) la période des fêtes; **festivities** npl réjouissances fpl

**festoon** [fes'tu:n] vt: **to ~ with** orner de

**fetch** [fetʃ] vt aller chercher; (sell for) vendre

**fête** [feit] n fête f, kermesse f

**feud** [fju:d] n dispute f, dissension f

**fever** ['fi:vər] n fièvre f; **~ish** adj fiévreux(-euse), fébrile

**few** [fju:] adj (not many) peu de; **a ~** ♦ adj quelques ♦ pron quelques-uns (-unes), quelques; **~er** ['fju:ər] adj moins de; moins (nombreux); **~est** ['fju:ist] adj le moins (de)

**fiancé, e** [fɪ'ɑ:nseɪ] n fiancé(e) m/f

**fib** [fib] n bobard m

**fibre** ['faɪbər] (US **fiber**) n fibre f; **~glass**

['faɪbəglɑːs] (**Fiberglass** ® US) n fibre de verre

**fickle** ['fɪkl] adj inconstant(e), volage, capricieux(-euse)

**fiction** ['fɪkʃən] n romans mpl, littérature f romanesque; (invention) fiction f; **~al** adj fictif(-ive)

**fictitious** adj fictif(-ive), imaginaire

**fiddle** ['fɪdl] n (MUS) violon m; (cheating) combine f, escroquerie f ♦ vt (BRIT: accounts) falsifier, maquiller; **~ with** vt fus tripoter

**fidget** ['fɪdʒɪt] vi se trémousser, s'agiter

**field** [fiːld] n champ m; (fig) domaine m, champ; (SPORT: ground) terrain m; **~work** n travaux mpl pratiques (sur le terrain)

**fiend** [fiːnd] n démon m

**fierce** [fɪəs] adj (look, animal) féroce, sauvage; (wind, attack, person) violent(e); (fighting, enemy) acharné(e)

**fiery** ['faɪərɪ] adj ardent(e), brûlant(e); (temperament) fougueux(-euse)

**fifteen** [fɪf'tiːn] num quinze

**fifth** [fɪfθ] num cinquième

**fifty** ['fɪftɪ] num cinquante; **~-fifty** adj: a **~-fifty** chance une chance etc sur deux ♦ adv moitié-moitié

**fig** [fɪg] n figue f

**fight** [faɪt] (pt, pp fought) n (MIL) combat m; (between persons) bagarre f; (against cancer etc) lutte f ♦ vt se battre contre; (cancer, alcoholism, emotion) combattre, lutter contre; (election) se présenter à ♦ vi se battre; **~er** n (fig) lutteur m; (plane) chasseur m; **~ing** n combats mpl; (brawl) bagarres fpl

**figment** ['fɪgmənt] n: a **~ of the imagination** une invention

**figurative** ['fɪgjurətɪv] adj figuré(e)

**figure** ['fɪgə'] n figure f; (number, cipher) chiffre m; (body, outline) silhouette f; (shape) ligne f, formes fpl ♦ vt (think: esp US) supposer ♦ vi (appear) figurer; **~ out** vt (work out) calculer; **~head** n (NAUT) figure f de proue; (pej) prête-nom m; **~ of speech** n figure f de rhétorique

**file** [faɪl] n (dossier) dossier m; (folder) dossier, chemise f; (: with hinges) classeur m; (COMPUT) fichier m; (row) file f; (tool) lime f ♦ vt (nails, wood) limer; (papers) classer; (LAW: claim) faire enregistrer; déposer; ♦ vi: **to ~ in/out** entrer/sortir l'un derrière l'autre; **to ~ for divorce** faire une demande en divorce; **filing cabinet** n classeur m (meuble)

**fill** [fɪl] vt remplir; (need) répondre à ♦ n: **to eat one's ~** manger à sa faim; **to ~ with** remplir de; **~ in** vt (hole) boucher; (form) remplir; **~ up** vt remplir; **~ it up, please** (AUT) le plein, s'il vous plaît

**fillet** ['fɪlɪt] n filet m; **~ steak** n filet de bœuf, tournedos m

**filling** ['fɪlɪŋ] n (CULIN) garniture f, farce f; (for tooth) plombage m; **~ station** n station-service f

**film** [fɪlm] n film m; (PHOT) pellicule f, film; (of powder, liquid) couche f, pellicule ♦ vt (scene) filmer ♦ vi tourner; **~ star** n vedette f de cinéma

**filter** ['fɪltə'] n filtre m ♦ vt filtrer; **~ lane** n (AUT) voie f de sortie; **~-tipped** adj à bout filtre

**filth** [fɪlθ] n saleté f; **~y** adj sale, dégoûtant(e); (language) ordurier(-ère)

**fin** [fɪn] n (of fish) nageoire f

**final** ['faɪnl] adj final(e); (definitive) définitif(-ive) ♦ n (SPORT) finale f; **~s** npl (SCOL) examens mpl de dernière année; **~e** [fɪ'nɑːlɪ] n finale m; **~ist** n finaliste m/f; **~ize** vt mettre au point; **~ly** adv (eventually) enfin, finalement; (lastly) en dernier lieu

**finance** [faɪ'næns] n finance f ♦ vt financer; **~s** npl (financial position) finances fpl; **financial** [faɪ'nænʃəl] adj financier(-ère)

**find** [faɪnd] (pt, pp found) vt trouver; (lost object) retrouver ♦ n trouvaille f, découverte f; **to ~ sb guilty** (LAW) déclarer qn coupable; **~ out** vt (truth, se-

cret) découvrir; (person) démasquer ♦
vi: **to ~ out about** (make enquiries) se
renseigner; (by chance) apprendre; **~
ings** npl (LAW) conclusions fpl, verdict
m; (of report) conclusions
**fine** [faɪn] adj (excellent) excellent(e);
(thin, not coarse, subtle) fin(e); (weather) beau (belle) ♦ adv (well) très bien
♦ n (LAW) amende f; contravention f ♦
vt (LAW) condamner à une amende;
donner une contravention à; **to be ~**
(person) aller bien; (weather) être beau; **~
arts** npl beaux-arts mpl; **~ry** n parure
f
**finger** ['fɪŋgər] n doigt m ♦ vt palper,
toucher; **little ~** auriculaire m, petit
doigt; **~ index ~** index m; **~nail** n ongle
m (de la main); **~print** n empreinte digitale; **~tip** n bout m du doigt
**finish** ['fɪnɪʃ] n fin f; (SPORT) arrivée f;
(polish etc) finition f ♦ vt finir, terminer
♦ vi finir, se terminer; **to ~ doing sth**
finir de faire qch; **to ~ third** arriver or
terminer troisième; **~ off** vt finir, terminer; (kill) achever; **~ up** vi, vt finir; **~ing
line** n ligne f d'arrivée
**finite** ['faɪnaɪt] adj fini(e); (verb) conju-
gué(e)
**Finland** ['fɪnlənd] n Finlande f
**Finn** [fɪn] n Finlandais(e); **Finnish** adj finlan-
dais(e) ♦ n (LING) finnois m
**fir** [fɜːr] n sapin m

**fire** ['faɪər] n feu m; (accidental) incendie
m; (heater) radiateur m ♦ vt (fig) enflammer, animer; (inf: dismiss) mettre à
la porte, renvoyer; (discharge): **to ~ a
gun** tirer un coup de feu ♦ vi (shoot) tirer, faire feu; **on ~** en feu; **~ alarm** n
avertisseur m d'incendie; **~arm** n arme
f à feu; **~ brigade** n (sapeurs-)
pompiers mpl; **~ department** (US) n =
**fire brigade**; **~ engine** n (vehicle) voiture f de pompiers; **~ escape** n escalier m de secours; **~ extinguisher** n
extincteur m; **~man** n pompier m;
**~place** n cheminée f; **~side** n foyer m,
coin m du feu; **~ station** n caserne f

de pompiers; **~wood** n bois m de
chauffage; **~works** npl feux mpl d'artifice; (display) feu(x) d'artifice
**firing squad** ['faɪərɪŋ-] n peloton m
d'exécution
**firm** [fɜːm] adj ferme ♦ n compagnie f,
firme f
**first** [fɜːst] adj premier(-ère) ♦ adv (before all others) le premier, la première;
(before all other things) en premier,
d'abord; (when listing reasons etc) en
premier lieu, premièrement ♦ n (person:
in race) premier(-ère); (BRIT: SCOL) mention f très bien; (AUT) première f; **at ~**
au commencement, au début; **~ of all**
tout d'abord, pour commencer; **~ aid**
n premiers secours or soins; **~-aid kit**
n trousse f à pharmacie; **~-class** adj de
première classe; (excellent) excellent(e),
exceptionnel(le); **~-hand** adj de première main; **~ lady** (US) n femme f du
président; **~ly** adv premièrement, en
premier lieu; **~ name** n prénom m; **~-
rate** adj excellent(e)
**fish** [fɪʃ] n inv poisson m ♦ vt, vi pêcher;
**to go ~ing** aller à la pêche; **~erman** n
pêcheur m; **~ farm** n établissement m
piscicole; **~ fingers** (BRIT) npl bâtonnets
de poisson (congelés); **~ing boat** n
barque f or bateau m de pêche; **~ing
line** n ligne f (de pêche); **~ing rod** n
canne f à pêche; **~ing tackle** n attirail
m de pêche; **~monger's (shop)** n
poissonnerie f; **~ slice** n pelle f à poisson; **~ sticks** (US) npl = **fish fingers**;
**~y** adj (inf) suspect(e), louche

**fist** [fɪst] n poing m
**fit** [fɪt] adj (healthy) en (bonne) forme;
(proper) convenable; approprié(e) ♦ vt
(subj: clothes) aller à; (put in, attach)
installer, poser; adapter; (equip) équiper, garnir, munir; (suit) convenir à ♦ vi
(clothes) aller; (parts) s'adapter; (in
space, gap) entrer, s'adapter ♦ n (MED)
accès m, crise f (of anger) accès; (of
hysterics, jealousy) crise; **~ in** to en état
de; **~ for** digne de; apte à; **~ of**

**coughing** quinte *f* de toux; **a ~ of giggles** le fou rire; **this dress is a good ~** cette robe (me) va très bien; **by ~s and starts** par à-coups; **~ in** *vi* s'accorder; s'adapter; **~ful** *adj* (*sleep*) agité(e); **~ment** *n* meuble encastré, élément *m*; **~ness** *n* (*MED*) forme *f* physique; **~ted carpet** *n* (*BRIT*) moquette *f*; **~ted kitchen** (*BRIT*) cuisine équipée; **~ter** *n* monteur *m*; **~ting** *adj* approprié(e) ♦ *n* (*of dress*) essayage *m*; (*of piece of equipment*) pose *f*, installation *f*; **~tings** *npl* installations *fpl*; **~ting room** *n* cabine *f* d'essayage

**five** [faɪv] *num* cinq; **~r** (*inf*) *n* (*BRIT*) billet *m* de cinq livres; (*US*) billet *m* de cinq dollars

**fix** [fɪks] *vt* (*date, amount etc*) fixer; (*organize*) arranger; (*mend*) réparer; (*meal, drink*) préparer ♦ *n*: **to be in a ~** être dans le pétrin; **~ up** *vt* (*meeting*) arranger; **to ~ sb up with sth** faire avoir qch à qn; **~ation** [fɪkˈseɪʃən] *n* (*PSYCH*) fixation *f*; (*fig*) obsession *f*; **~ed** *adj* (*prices etc*) fixe; (*smile*) figé(e); **~ture** *n* installation *f* (fixe); (*SPORT*) rencontre *f* (au programme)

**fizzy** [ˈfɪzɪ] *adj* pétillant(e); gazeux(-euse)

**flabbergasted** [ˈflæbəgɑːstɪd] *adj* sidéré(e), ahuri(e)

**flabby** [ˈflæbɪ] *adj* mou (molle)

**flag** [flæɡ] *n* drapeau *m*; (*also:* **~stone**) dalle *f* ♦ *vi* faiblir; fléchir; **~ down** *vt* héler, faire signe (à un chauffeur etc) de s'arrêter à; **~pole** *n* mât *m*; **~ship** *n* vaisseau *m* amiral; (*fig*) produit *m* vedette

**flair** [flɛər] *n* flair *m*

**flak** [flæk] *n* (*MIL*) tir antiaérien; (*inf: criticism*) critiques *fpl*

**flake** [fleɪk] *n* (*of rust, paint*) écaille *f*; (*of snow, soap powder*) flocon *m* ♦ *vi* (*also:* **~ off**) s'écailler

**flamboyant** [flæmˈbɔɪənt] *adj* flamboyant(e), éclatant(e); (*person*) haut(e) en couleur

**flame** [fleɪm] *n* flamme *f*

**flamingo** [fləˈmɪŋɡəu] *n* flamant *m* (rose)

**flammable** [ˈflæməbl] *adj* inflammable

**flan** [flæn] (*BRIT*) *n* tarte *f*

**flank** [flæŋk] *n* flanc *m* ♦ *vt* flanquer

**flannel** [ˈflænl] *n* (*fabric*) flanelle *f*; (*BRIT: also:* **face ~**) gant *m* de toilette

**flap** [flæp] *n* (*of pocket, envelope*) rabat *m* ♦ *vt* (*wings*) battre (de) ♦ *vi* (*also: inf:* **be in a ~**) paniquer

**flare** [flɛər] *n* (*signal*) signal lumineux; (*in skirt etc*) évasement *m*; **~ up** *vi* s'embraser; (*fig: person*) se mettre en colère; (: *revolt etc*) éclater

**flash** [flæʃ] *n* éclair *m*; (*also:* **news ~**) flash *m* (d'information); (*PHOT*) flash *m* ♦ *vt* (*light*) projeter; (*send: message*) câbler; (*look*) jeter; (*smile*) lancer ♦ *vi* (*light*) clignoter; **a ~ of lightning** un éclair; **in a ~** en un clin d'œil; **to ~ one's headlights** faire un appel de phares; **to ~ by** *or* **past** (*person*) passer (devant) comme un éclair; **~bulb** *n* ampoule *f* de flash; **~cube** *n* cube-flash *m*; **~light** *n* lampe *f* de poche; **~y** (*pej*) *adj* tape-à-l'œil *inv*, tapageur(-euse)

**flask** [flɑːsk] *n* flacon *m*, bouteille *f*; (*also:* **vacuum ~**) thermos ® *m or f inv*

**flat** [flæt] *adj* plat(e); (*tyre*) dégonflé(e), à plat; (*beer*) éventé(e); (*denial*) catégorique; (*MUS*) bémol *inv*; (: *voice*) faux (fausse); (*fee, rate*) fixe ♦ *n* (*BRIT: apartment*) appartement *m*; (*AUT*) crevaison *f*; (*MUS*) bémol *m*; **to work ~ out** travailler d'arrache-pied; **~ly** *adv* catégoriquement; **~ten** *vt* (*also:* **~ten out**) aplatir; (*crop*) coucher; (*building(s)*) raser

**flatter** [ˈflætər] *vt* flatter; **~ing** *adj* flatteur(-euse); **~y** *n* flatterie *f*

**flaunt** [flɔːnt] *vt* faire étalage de

**flavour** [ˈfleɪvər] (*US* **flavor**) *n* goût *m*, saveur *f*; (*of ice cream etc*) parfum *m* ♦ *vt* parfumer; **vanilla-~ed** à l'arôme de vanille, à la vanille; **~ing** *n* arôme *m*

**flaw** [flɔː] *n* défaut *m*; **~less** *adj* sans défaut

**flax** [flæks] *n* lin *m*

# flea 403 fluent

**flea** [fliː] n puce f

**fleck** [flɛk] n tacheture f; moucheture f

**flee** [fliː] vt (pt, pp **fled**) vt fuir ♦ vi fuir, s'enfuir

**fleece** [fliːs] n toison f ♦ vt (inf) voler, filouter

**fleet** [fliːt] n flotte f; (of lorries etc) parc m, convoi m

**fleeting** [ˈfliːtɪŋ] adj fugace, fugitif (-ive); (visit) très bref (brève)

**Flemish** [ˈflɛmɪʃ] adj flamand(e)

**flesh** [flɛʃ] n chair f; ~ **wound** n blessure superficielle

**flew** [fluː] pt of **fly**

**flex** [flɛks] n fil m or câble m électrique ♦ vt (knee) fléchir; (muscles) tendre; **~ible** adj flexible

**flick** [flɪk] n petite tape; chiquenaude f; (of duster) petit coup ♦ vt donner un petit coup à; (switch) appuyer sur; **~ through** vt fus feuilleter

**flicker** [ˈflɪkəʳ] vi (light) vaciller; **his eyelids ~ed** il a cillé

**flier** [ˈflaɪəʳ] n aviateur m

**flight** [flaɪt] n vol m; (escape) fuite f; (also: ~ **of steps**) escalier m; **~ attendant** (US) n steward, hôtesse f de l'air; **~ deck** n (AVIAT) poste m de pilotage; (NAUT) pont m d'envol

**flimsy** [ˈflɪmzɪ] adj peu solide; (clothes) trop léger(-ère); (excuse) pauvre, mince

**flinch** [flɪntʃ] vi tressaillir; **to ~ from** se dérober à, reculer devant

**fling** [flɪŋ] (pt, pp **flung**) vt jeter, lancer

**flint** [flɪnt] n silex m; (in lighter) pierre f (à briquet)

**flip** [flɪp] vt (throw) lancer (d'une chiquenaude); **to ~ sth over** retourner qch

**flippant** [ˈflɪpənt] adj désinvolte, irrévérencieux(-euse)

**flipper** [ˈflɪpəʳ] n (of seal etc) nageoire f; (for swimming) palme f

**flirt** [fləːt] vi flirter ♦ n flirteur(-euse) m/f

**float** [fləut] n flotteur m; (in procession) char m; (money) réserve f ♦ vi flotter

**flock** [flɒk] n troupeau m; (of birds) vol

m; (REL) ouailles fpl ♦ vi: **to ~** se rendre en masse à

**flog** [flɒg] vt fouetter

**flood** [flʌd] n inondation f; (of letters, refugees etc) flot m ♦ vt inonder ♦ vi (people): **to ~ into** envahir; **~ing** n inondation f; **~light** n projecteur m

**floor** [flɔːʳ] n sol m; (storey) étage m; (of sea, valley) fond m ♦ vt (subj: question) déconcerter; (: blow) terrasser; **on the ~** par terre; **ground ~**, (US) **first ~** rez-de-chaussée m inv; **first ~**, (US) **second ~** premier étage; **~board** n planche f (du plancher); **~ show** n spectacle m de variétés

**flop** [flɒp] n fiasco ♦ vi être un fiasco; (fall: into chair) s'affaler, s'effondrer; **~py** adj lâche, flottant(e) ♦ n (COMPUT: also: **~py disk**) disquette f

**flora** [ˈflɔːrə] n flore f

**floral** [ˈflɔːrl] adj (dress) à fleurs

**florid** [ˈflɒrɪd] adj (complexion) coloré(e); (style) plein(e) de fioritures

**florist** [ˈflɒrɪst] n fleuriste m/f; **~'s (shop)** n magasin m ou boutique f de fleuriste

**flounder** [ˈflaundəʳ] vi patauger ♦ n (ZOOL) flet m

**flour** [ˈflauəʳ] n farine f

**flourish** [ˈflʌrɪʃ] vi prospérer ♦ n (gesture) moulinet m

**flout** [flaut] vt se moquer de, faire fi de

**flow** [fləu] n (ELEC, of river) courant m; (of blood in veins) circulation f; (of tide) flux m; (of orders, data) flot m ♦ vi couler; (traffic) s'écouler; (robes, hair) flotter; **the ~ of traffic** l'écoulement m de la circulation; **~ chart** n organigramme m

**flower** [ˈflauəʳ] n fleur f ♦ vi fleurir; **~ bed** n plate-bande f; **~pot** n pot m (de fleurs); **~y** adj fleuri(e)

**flown** [fləun] pp of **fly**

**flu** [fluː] n grippe f

**fluctuate** [ˈflʌktjueɪt] vi varier, fluctuer

**fluent** [ˈfluːənt] adj (speech) coulant(e), aisé(e); **he speaks ~ French, he's ~ in**

**French** il parle couramment le français

**fluff** [flʌf] n duvet m; (on jacket, carpet) peluche f; **~y** adj duveteux(-euse); (toy) en peluche

**fluid** ['flu:ɪd] adj fluide ♦ n fluide m

**fluke** [flu:k] (inf) n (luck) coup m de veine

**flung** [flʌŋ] pt, pp of **fling**

**fluoride** ['fluəraɪd] n fluorure f; ~ **toothpaste** dentifrice m au fluor

**flurry** ['flʌrɪ] n (of snow) rafale f, bourrasque f; **~ of activity/excitement** affairement m/excitation f soudain(e)

**flush** [flʌʃ] n (on face) rougeur f; (fig: of youth, beauty etc) éclat m ♦ vt nettoyer à grande eau ♦ vi rougir ♦ adj: **~ with** au ras de, de niveau avec; **to ~ the toilet** tirer la chasse (d'eau); **~ed** adj (tout)rouge

**flustered** ['flʌstəd] adj énervé(e)

**flute** [flu:t] n flûte f

**flutter** ['flʌtəʳ] n (of panic, excitement) agitation f; (of wings) battement m ♦ vi (bird) battre des ailes, voleter

**flux** [flʌks] n: **in a state of ~** fluctuant sans cesse

**fly** [flaɪ] (pt **flew**, pp **flown**) n (insect) mouche f; (on trousers: also: **flies**) braguette f ♦ vt piloter; (passengers, cargo) transporter par avion; (distances) parcourir ♦ vi voler; (passengers) aller en avion; (escape) s'enfuir, fuir; (flag) se déployer; **~ away** (bird, insect) s'envoler; **~ off** vi = **fly away**; **~-drive** n formule f avion plus voiture; **~ing** n (activity) aviation f; (action) vol m ♦ adj: **a ~ing visit** une visite éclair; **with ~ing colours** haut la main; **~ing saucer** n soucoupe volante; **~ing start** n: **to get off to a ~ing start** prendre un excellent départ; **~over** (BRIT) n (bridge) saut-de-mouton m; **~sheet** n (for tent) double toit m

**foal** [fəul] n poulain m

**foam** [fəum] n écume f; (on beer) mousse f; (also: **~ rubber**) caoutchouc mousse m ♦ vi (liquid) écumer; (soapy water) mousser

**fob** [fɔb] vt: **to ~ sb off** se débarrasser de qn

**focal point** ['fəukl-] n (fig) point central

**focus** ['fəukəs] (pl **~es**) n foyer m; (of interest) centre m ♦ vt (field glasses etc) mettre au point ♦ vi: **to ~ (on)** (with camera) régler la mise au point (sur); (person) fixer son regard (sur); **out of/ in ~** (picture) flou(e)/net(te); (camera) pas au point/au point

**fodder** ['fɔdəʳ] n fourrage m

**foe** [fəu] n ennemi m

**fog** [fɔg] n brouillard m; **~gy** adj: **it's ~gy** il y a du brouillard; **~ lamp** (US **~light**) n (AUT) phare m antibrouillard

**foil** [fɔɪl] vt déjouer, contrecarrer ♦ n feuille f de métal; (kitchen ~) papier m alu(minium); (complement) repoussoir m

**fold** [fəuld] n (bend, crease) pli m; (AGR) parc m à moutons; (fig) bercail m ♦ vt plier; (arms) croiser; **~ up** vi (map, table etc) se plier; (business) fermer boutique ♦ vt (map, clothes) plier; **~er** n (for papers) chemise f; (: with hinges) classeur m; (COMPUT) répertoire m; **~ing** adj (chair, bed) pliant(e)

**foliage** ['fəulɪdʒ] n feuillage m

**folk** [fəuk] npl gens mpl ♦ cpd folklorique; **~s** (inf) npl (parents) parents mpl; **~lore** ['fəuklɔ:ʳ] n folklore m; **~ song** n chanson f folklorique

**follow** ['fɔləu] vt suivre ♦ vi suivre; (result) s'ensuivre; **to ~ suit** (fig) faire de même; **~ up** vt (letter, offer) donner suite à; (case) suivre; **~er** n disciple m/f, partisan(e); **~ing** adj suivant(e) ♦ n partisans mpl, disciples mpl

**folly** ['fɔlɪ] n inconscience f; folie f

**fond** [fɔnd] adj (memory, look) tendre; (hopes, dreams) un peu fou (folle); **to be ~ of** aimer beaucoup

**fondle** ['fɔndl] vt caresser

**font** [fɔnt] n (in church: for baptism) fonts baptismaux; (TYP) fonte f

**food** [fu:d] n nourriture f; **~ mixer** n

mixer m; ~ **poisoning** n intoxication f alimentaire; ~ **processor** n robot m de cuisine; ~**stuffs** npl denrées fpl alimentaires

**fool** [fu:l] n idiot(e); (CULIN) mousse f de fruits ♦ vt berner, duper ♦ vi faire l'idiot or l'imbécile; ~**hardy** adj téméraire, imprudent(e); ~**ish** adj idiot(e), stupide; (rash) imprudent(e), insensé(e); ~**proof** adj (plan etc) infaillible

**foot** [fut] (pl **feet**) n (of person) pied m; (of animal) patte f; (measure) pied (= 30,48 cm; 12 inches) ♦ vt (bill) payer; **on** ~ à pied; ~**age** n (CINEMA: length) ≈ métrage m; (: material) séquences fpl; ~**ball** n ballon m (de football); (sport: BRIT) football m, foot m; (: US) football américain; ~**ball player** (BRIT) (also: ~**baller**) joueur m de football; ~**brake** n frein m à pédale; ~**bridge** n passerelle f; ~**hills** npl contreforts mpl; ~**hold** n prise f (de pied); ~**ing** n (fig) position f; **to lose one's** ~**ing** perdre pied; ~**lights** npl rampe f; ~**note** n note f (en bas de page); ~**path** n sentier m; (in street) trottoir m; ~**print** n trace f (de pas); ~**step** n pas m; ~**wear** n chaussure(s) f(pl)

---

football pools

*Les football pools - ou plus familièrement les "pools" - consistent à parier sur les résultats des matches de football qui se jouent tous les samedis. L'expression consacrée en anglais est "to do the pools". Les parieurs envoient à l'avance les fiches qu'ils ont complétées à l'organisme qui gère les paris et ils attendent 17 h le samedi que les résultats soient annoncés. Les sommes gagnées se comptent parfois en milliers (ou même en millions) de livres sterling.*

---

KEYWORD

**for** [fɔːʳ] prep 1 (indicating destination,

intention, purpose) pour; **the train for London** le train pour or à (destination de) Londres; **he went for the paper** il est allé chercher le journal; **it's time for lunch** c'est l'heure du déjeuner; **what's it for?** ça sert à quoi?; **what for?** (why) pourquoi?

2 (on behalf of, representing) pour; **the MP for Hove** le député de Hove; **to work for sb/sth** travailler pour qn/qch; **G for George** G comme Georges

3 (because of) pour; **for this reason** pour cette raison; **for fear of being criticized** de peur d'être critiqué

4 (with regard to) pour; **it's cold for July** il fait froid pour juillet; **a gift for languages** un don pour les langues

5 (in exchange for): **I sold it for £5** je l'ai vendu 5 livres; **to pay 50 pence for a ticket** payer un billet 50 pence

6 (in favour of) pour; **are you for or against us?** êtes-vous pour ou contre nous?

7 (referring to distance) pendant, sur; **there are roadworks for 5 km** il y a des travaux sur 5 km; **we walked for miles** nous avons marché pendant des kilomètres

8 (referring to time) pendant; depuis; pour; **he was away for 2 years** il a été absent pendant 2 ans; **she will be away for a month** elle sera absente (pendant) un mois; **I have known her for years** je la connais depuis des années; **can you do it for tomorrow?** est-ce que tu peux le faire pour demain?

9 (with infinitive clauses): **it is not for me to decide** ce n'est pas à moi de décider; **it would be best for you to leave** le mieux serait que vous partiez; **there is still time for you to do it** vous avez encore le temps de le faire; **for this to be possible ...** pour que cela soit possible ...

10 (in spite of): **for all his work/**

**efforts** malgré tout son travail/tous ses efforts; they're **very fond of her** il a beau se plaindre, il l'aime beaucoup ♦ *conj (since, as: rather formal)* car

**forage** ['fɔrɪdʒ] *vi* fourrager

**foray** ['fɔreɪ] *n* incursion *f*

**forbid** [fə'bɪd] (*pt* **forbad(e)**, *pp* **forbidden**) *vt* défendre, interdire; **to ~ sb to do** défendre *or* interdire à qn de faire; **~ding** *adj* sévère, sombre

**force** [fɔːs] *n* force *f* ♦ *vt* forcer; (*push*) pousser (de force); **the F~s** *npl* (MIL) l'armée *f*; **in ~** en vigueur; **~-feed** *vt* nourrir de force; **~ful** *adj* énergique, volontaire; **forcibly** *adv* par la force, de force; (*express*) énergiquement

**ford** [fɔːd] *n* gué *m*

**fore** [fɔːʳ] *n*: **to come to the ~** se faire remarquer; **~arm** *n* avant-bras *m inv*; **~boding** *n* pressentiment *m* (néfaste); **~cast** (*irreg: like* **cast**) *n* prévision *f* ♦ *vt* prévoir; **~court** *n* (*of garage*) devant *m*; **~finger** *n* index *m*; **~front** *n*: **in the ~front of** au premier rang *or* plan de

**foregone** ['fɔːgɒn] *adj*: **it's a ~ conclusion** c'est couru d'avance

**foreground** ['fɔːgraʊnd] *n* premier plan

**forehead** ['fɒrɪd] *n* front *m*

**foreign** ['fɒrɪn] *adj* étranger(-ère); (*trade*) extérieur(-e); **~er** *n* étranger (-ère); **~ exchange** *n* change *m*; **F~ Office** (BRIT) *n* ministère *m* des affaires étrangères; **F~ Secretary** (BRIT) *n* ministre *m* des affaires étrangères

**fore:** **~leg** *n* (*of cat, dog*) patte *f* de devant; (*of horse*) jambe antérieure; **~man** (*irreg*) *n* (*of factory, building site*) contremaître *m*, chef *m* d'équipe; **~most** *adj* le (la) plus en vue; premier(-ère) ♦ *adv*: **first and ~most** avant tout, tout d'abord

**forensic** [fə'rensɪk] *adj*: **~ medicine** médecine légale; **~ scientist** médecin

*m* légiste

**fore:** **~runner** *n* précurseur *m*; **~see** (*irreg: like* **see**) *vt* prévoir; **~seeable** *adj* prévisible; **~shadow** *vt* présager, annoncer, laisser prévoir; **~sight** *n* prévoyance *f*

**forest** ['fɒrɪst] *n* forêt *f*; **~ry** *n* sylviculture *f*

**foretaste** ['fɔːteɪst] *n* avant-goût *m*

**foretell** [fɔː'tel] (*irreg: like* **tell**) *vt* prédire

**forever** [fə'revəʳ] *adv* pour toujours; (*fig*) continuellement

**foreword** ['fɔːwəːd] *n* avant-propos *m inv*

**forfeit** ['fɔːfɪt] *vt* (*lose*) perdre

**forgave** [fə'geɪv] *pt of* **forgive**

**forge** [fɔːdʒ] *n* forge *f* ♦ *vt* (*signature*) contrefaire; (*wrought iron*) forger; **to ~ money** (BRIT) fabriquer de la fausse monnaie; **~ ahead** *vi* pousser de l'avant, prendre de l'avance; **~d** *adj* faux (fausse); **~r** *n* faussaire *m*; **~ry** *n* faux *m*, contrefaçon *f*

**forget** [fə'get] (*pt* **forgot**, *pp* **forgotten**) *vt*, *vi* oublier; **~ful** *adj* distrait(e), étourdi(e); **~-me-not** *n* myosotis *m*

**forgive** [fə'gɪv] (*pt* **forgave**, *pp* **forgiven**) *vt* pardonner; **to ~ sb for sth/for doing sth** pardonner qch à qn/à qn de faire qch; **~ness** *n* pardon *m*

**forgo** [fɔː'gəʊ] (*pt* **forwent**, *pp* **forgone**) *vt* renoncer à

**fork** [fɔːk] *n* (*for eating*) fourchette *f*; (*for gardening*) fourche *f*; (*of roads*) bifurcation *f*; (*of railways*) embranchement *m* ♦ *vi* (*road*) bifurquer; **~ out** (*inf*) *vt* allonger; **~-lift truck** *n* chariot élévateur

**forlorn** [fə'lɔːn] *adj* (*deserted*) abandonné(e); (*attempt, hope*) désespéré(e)

**form** [fɔːm] *n* forme *f*; (SCOL) classe *f*; (*questionnaire*) formulaire *m* ♦ *vt* former; (*habit*) contracter; **in top ~** en pleine forme

**formal** ['fɔːməl] *adj* (*offer, receipt*) en bonne et due forme; (*person*) cérémonieux(-euse); (*dinner*) officiel(le); (*clothes*) de soirée; (*garden*) à la française; (*education*) à proprement parler; **~ly** *adv* officiellement; cérémonieusement

**format** ['fɔːmæt] *n* format *m* ♦ *vt* (COMPUT) formater

**formation** [fɔː'meɪʃən] *n* formation *f*

**formative** ['fɔːmətɪv] *adj*: **~ years** années *fpl* d'apprentissage *or* de formation

**former** ['fɔːmə*] *adj* ancien(ne) (*before n*), précédent(e); **the ~ ... the latter** le premier ... le second, celui-là ... celui-ci; **~ly** *adv* autrefois

**formidable** ['fɔːmɪdəbl] *adj* redoutable

**formula** ['fɔːmjulə] (*pl* **~s** *or* **~e**) *n* formule *f*

**forsake** [fə'seɪk] (*pt* **forsook**, *pp* **forsaken**) *vt* abandonner

**fort** [fɔːt] *n* fort *m*

**forte** ['fɔːtɪ] *n* (*point*) fort *m*

**forth** [fɔːθ] *adv* en avant; **to go back and ~** aller et venir; **and so ~** et ainsi de suite; **~coming** *adj* (*event*) qui va avoir lieu prochainement; (*character*) ouvert(e), communicatif(-ive); (*available*) disponible; **~right** *adj* franc (franche), direct(e); **~with** *adv* sur-le-champ

**fortify** ['fɔːtɪfaɪ] *vt* fortifier

**fortitude** ['fɔːtɪtjuːd] *n* courage *m*

**fortnight** ['fɔːtnaɪt] (BRIT) *n* quinzaine *f*, quinze jours *mpl*; **~ly** (BRIT) *adj* bimensuel(le) ♦ *adv* tous les quinze jours

**fortunate** ['fɔːtʃənɪt] *adj* heureux(-euse); (*person*) chanceux(-euse); **it is ~ that** c'est une chance que; **~ly** *adv* heureusement

**fortune** ['fɔːtʃən] *n* chance *f*; (*wealth*) fortune *f*; **~-teller** *n* diseuse *f* de bonne aventure

**forty** ['fɔːtɪ] *num* quarante

**forward** ['fɔːwəd] *adj* (*ahead of schedule*) en avance; (*movement, position*) en avant, vers l'avant; (*not shy*) direct(e); effronté(e) ♦ *n* (SPORT) avant *m* ♦ *vt* (*letter*) faire suivre; (*parcel, goods*) expé-

dier; (*fig*) promouvoir, favoriser; **~(s)** *adv* en avant; **to move ~** avancer

**fossil** ['fɔsl] *n* fossile *m*

**foster** ['fɔstə*] *vt* encourager, favoriser; (*child*) élever (*sans obligation d'adopter*); **~ child** *n* enfant adopté(e)

**fought** [fɔːt] *pt, pp* of **fight**

**foul** [faul] *adj* (*weather, smell, food*) infect(e); (*language*) ordurier(-ère) ♦ *n* (SPORT) faute *f* ♦ *vt* (*dirty*) salir, encrasser; **he's got a ~ temper** il a un caractère de chien; **~ play** *n* (LAW) acte criminel

**found** [faund] *pt, pp* of **find** ♦ *vt* (*establish*) fonder; **~ation** [faun'deɪʃən] *n* (*act*) fondation *f*; (*base*) fondement *m*; (*also*: **~ation cream**) fond *m* de teint; **~ations** *npl* (*of building*) fondations *fpl*

**founder** ['faundə*] *n* fondateur *m* ♦ *vi* couler, sombrer

**foundry** ['faundrɪ] *n* fonderie *f*

**fountain** ['fauntɪn] *n* fontaine *f*; **~ pen** *n* stylo *m* (à encre)

**four** [fɔː*] *num* quatre; **on all ~s** à quatre pattes; **~-poster** *n* (*also*: **~-poster bed**) lit *m* à baldaquin; **~teen** *num* quatorze; **~th** *num* quatrième

**fowl** [faul] *n* volaille *f*

**fox** [fɔks] *n* renard *m* ♦ *vt* mystifier

**foyer** ['fɔɪeɪ] *n* (*hotel*) hall *m*; (THEATRE) foyer *m*

**fraction** ['frækʃən] *n* fraction *f*

**fracture** ['fræktʃə*] *n* fracture *f*

**fragile** ['frædʒaɪl] *adj* fragile

**fragment** ['frægmənt] *n* fragment *m*

**fragrant** ['freɪgrənt] *adj* parfumé(e), odorant(e)

**frail** [freɪl] *adj* fragile, délicat(e)

**frame** [freɪm] *n* charpente *f*; (*of picture, bicycle*) cadre *m*; (*of door, window*) encadrement *m*, chambranle *m*; (*of spectacles*: *also*: **~s**) monture *f* ♦ *vt* encadrer; **~ of mind** *n* disposition *f* d'esprit; **~work** *n* structure *f*

**France** [frɑːns] *n* France *f*

**franchise** ['fræntʃaɪz] *n* (POL) droit *m* de vote; (COMM) franchise *f*

**frank** [fræŋk] adj franc (franche) ♦ vt (letter) affranchir; **~ly** adv franchement

**frantic** ['fræntɪk] adj (hectic) frénétique; (distraught) hors de soi

**fraternity** [frə'tɜːnɪtɪ] n (spirit) fraternité f; (club) communauté f, confrérie f

**fraud** [frɔːd] n supercherie f, fraude f, tromperie f; (person) imposteur m

**fraught** [frɔːt] adj: **~ with** chargé(e) de, plein(e) de

**fray** [freɪ] vi s'effilocher

**freak** [friːk] n (also cpd) phénomène m, créature ou événement exceptionnel par sa rareté

**freckle** ['frekl] n tache f de rousseur

**free** [friː] adj libre; (gratis) gratuit(e) ♦ vt (prisoner etc) libérer; (jammed object or person) dégager; **~ (of charge), for ~** gratuitement; **~dom** n liberté f; **F~fone** ® n numéro vert; **~-for-all** n mêlée générale; **~ gift** n prime f; **~hold** n propriété foncière libre; **~ kick** n coup franc; **~lance** adj indépendant(e); **~ly** adv librement; (liberally) libéralement; **F~mason** n franc-maçon m; **F~post** ® n port payé; **~-range** adj (hen, eggs) de ferme; **~ trade** n libre-échange m; **~way** (US) n autoroute f; **~ will** n libre arbitre m; **of one's own ~ will** de son plein gré

**freeze** [friːz] (pt **froze**, pp **frozen**) vi geler ♦ vt geler; (food) congeler; (prices, salaries) bloquer, geler ♦ n gel m; (fig) blocage m; **~-dried** adj lyophilisé(e); **~r** n congélateur m; **freezing** adj: **freezing (cold)** adj (weather, water) glacial(e) ♦ n: **3 degrees below freezing** 3 degrés au-dessous de zéro; **freezing point** n point m de congélation

**freight** [freɪt] n (goods) fret m, cargaison f; (money charged) fret, prix m du transport; **~ train** n train m de marchandises

**French** [frentʃ] adj français(e) ♦ n (LING) français m; **the ~pl** (people) les Français; **~ bean** n haricot vert; **~ fried (potatoes)** (US ~ **fries**) npl (pommes

de terre fpl) frites fpl; **~ horn** n (MUS) cor m (d'harmonie); **~ loaf** n baguette f; **~man** (irreg) n Français m; **~ window** n porte-fenêtre f; **~woman** (irreg) n Française f

**frenzy** ['frenzɪ] n frénésie f

**frequency** ['friːkwənsɪ] n fréquence f

**frequent** [adj 'friːkwənt, vb frɪ'kwent] adj fréquent(e) ♦ vt fréquenter; **~ly** adv fréquemment

**fresh** [freʃ] adj frais (fraîche); (new) nouveau (nouvelle); (cheeky) familier(-ère), culotté(e); **~en** vi (wind, air) fraîchir; **~en up** vi faire un brin de toilette; **~er** (BRIT: inf) n (SCOL) bizuth m, étudiant(e) de 1ère année; **~ly** adv nouvellement, récemment; **~man** (US) (irreg) n = **fresher**; **~ness** n fraîcheur f; **~water** adj (fish) d'eau douce

**fret** [fret] vi s'agiter, se tracasser

**friar** ['fraɪə*] n moine m, frère m

**friction** ['frɪkʃən] n friction f

**Friday** ['fraɪdɪ] n vendredi m

**fridge** [frɪdʒ] (BRIT) n frigo m, frigidaire ® m

**fried** [fraɪd] adj frit(e); **~ egg** n œuf m sur le plat

**friend** [frend] n ami(e) m/f; **~ly** adj amical(e); gentil(le); (place) accueillant(e); **they were killed by ~ly fire** ils sont morts sous les tirs de leur propre camp; **~ship** n amitié f

**frieze** [friːz] n frise f

**fright** [fraɪt] n peur f, effroi m; **to take ~** prendre peur, s'effrayer; **~en** vt effrayer, faire peur à; **~ened** adj: **to be ~ened (of)** avoir peur de; **~ening** adj effrayant(e); **~ful** adj affreux(-euse)

**frigid** ['frɪdʒɪd] adj frigide

**frill** [frɪl] n (on dress) volant m; (on shirt) jabot m

**fringe** [frɪndʒ] n (BRIT: of hair) frange f; (edge: of forest etc) bordure f; **~ benefits** npl avantages sociaux or en nature

**Frisbee** ® ['frɪzbɪ] n Frisbee ® m

**frisk** [frɪsk] vt fouiller

**fritter** ['frɪtə'] n beignet m; ~ **away** vt gaspiller

**frivolous** ['frɪvələs] adj frivole

**frizzy** ['frɪzɪ] adj crépu(e)

**fro** [frəu] adv: **to go to and** ~ aller et venir

**frock** [frɔk] n robe f

**frog** [frɔg] n grenouille f; ~**man** n homme-grenouille m

**frolic** ['frɔlɪk] vi folâtrer, batifoler

━━━━━━━━━━━━━━
KEYWORD
━━━━━━━━━━━━━━

**from** [frɔm] prep **1** (indicating starting place, origin etc) de; **where do you come from?**, **where are you from?** d'où venez-vous?; **from London to Paris** de Londres à Paris; **a letter from my sister** une lettre de ma sœur; **to drink from the bottle** boire à (même) la bouteille

**2** (indicating time) (à partir) de; **from one o'clock to** or **until** or **till two** d'une heure à deux heures; **from January (on)** à partir de janvier

**3** (indicating distance) de; **the hotel is one kilometre from the beach** l'hôtel est à un kilomètre de la plage

**4** (indicating price, number etc) de; **the interest rate was increased from 9% to 10%** le taux d'intérêt est passé de 9 à 10%

**5** (indicating difference) de; **he can't tell red from green** il ne peut pas distinguer le rouge du vert

**6** (because of, on the basis of): **from what he says** d'après ce qu'il dit; **weak from hunger** affaibli par la faim

━━━━━━━━━━━━━━

**front** [frʌnt] n (of house, dress) devant m; (of coach, train) avant m; (promenade: also: **sea** ~) bord m de mer; (MIL, METEOROLOGY) front m; (fig: appearances) contenance f, façade f ♦ adj de devant; (seat) avant inv; **in** ~ (of) devant; ~ **age** n (of building) façade f; ~ **door** n porte f d'entrée; (of car) portière f avant; ~**ier**

['frʌntɪə'] n frontière f; ~ **page** n première page; ~ **room** n (BRIT) pièce f de devant, salon m; ~**wheel drive** n traction f avant

**frost** [frɔst] n gel m, gelée f; (also: **hoarfrost**) givre m; ~**bite** n engelures fpl; ~**ed** adj (glass) dépoli(e); ~**y** adj (weather, welcome) glacial(e)

**froth** [frɔθ] n mousse f; écume f

**frown** [fraun] vi froncer les sourcils

**froze** [frəuz] pt of freeze

**frozen** ['frəuzn] pp of freeze

**fruit** [fruːt] n inv fruit m; ~**erer** n fruitier m, marchand(e) de fruits; ~**ful** adj (fig) fructueux(-euse); ~**ion** [fruːˈɪʃən] n: **to come to** ~**ion** se réaliser; ~ **juice** n jus m de fruit; ~ **machine** (BRIT) n machine f à sous; ~ **salad** n salade f de fruits

**frustrate** [frʌsˈtreɪt] vt frustrer

**fry** [fraɪ] (pt, pp **fried**) vt (faire) frire; see **also small**; ~**ing pan** n poêle f (à frire)

**ft.** abbr = **feet**; **foot**

**fudge** [fʌdʒ] n (CULIN) caramel m

**fuel** ['fjuəl] n (for heating) combustible m; (for propelling) carburant m; ~ **oil** n mazout m; ~ **tank** n (in vehicle) réservoir m

**fugitive** ['fjuːdʒɪtɪv] n fugitif(-ive)

**fulfil** [fulˈfɪl] (US **fulfill**) vt (function, condition) remplir; (order) exécuter; (wish, desire) satisfaire, réaliser; ~**ment** (US **fulfillment**) n (of wishes etc) réalisation f; (feeling) contentement m

**full** [ful] adj plein(e); (details, information) complet(-ète); (skirt) ample, large ♦ adv: **to know** ~ **well** that savoir fort bien que; **I'm** ~ **(up)** j'ai bien mangé; **a** ~ **two hours** deux bonnes heures; **at** ~ **speed** à toute vitesse; **in** ~ (reproduce, quote) intégralement; (write) en toutes lettres; ~ **employment** plein emploi; **to pay in** ~ tout payer; ~**-length** adj (film) long métrage; (portrait, mirror) en pied; (coat) long(ue); ~ **moon** n pleine lune; ~**-scale** adj (attack, war) complet(-ète), total(e); (model) grandeur nature inv; ~ **stop** n point m; ~-

**time** adj, adv (work) à plein temps; **~y** adv entièrement, complètement; (at least) au moins; **~ licensed** (hotel, restaurant) autorisé(e) à vendre des boissons alcoolisées; **~y-fledged** adj (barrister etc) diplômé(e); (citizen, member) à part entière

**fumble** ['fʌmbl] vi: **~ with** tripoter

**fume** [fjuːm] vi rager; **~s** npl vapeurs fpl, émanations fpl, gaz mpl

**fun** [fʌn] n amusement m, divertissement m; **to have ~** s'amuser; **for ~** pour rire; **to make ~ of** se moquer de

**function** ['fʌŋkʃən] n fonction f; (social occasion) cérémonie f, soirée officielle ♦ vi fonctionner; **~al** adj fonctionnel(le)

**fund** [fʌnd] n caisse f, fonds m; (source, store) source f, mine f; **~s** npl (money) fonds mpl

**fundamental** [fʌndə'mɛntl] adj fondamental(e)

**funeral** ['fjuːnərəl] n enterrement m, obsèques fpl; **~ parlour** n entreprise f de pompes funèbres; **~ service** n service m funèbre

**funfair** ['fʌnfɛə*] (BRIT) n fête (foraine)

**fungi** ['fʌŋgaɪ] npl of **fungus**

**fungus** ['fʌŋgəs] (pl **fungi**) n champignon m; (mould) moisissure f

**funnel** ['fʌnl] n entonnoir m; (of ship) cheminée f

**funny** ['fʌnɪ] adj amusant(e), drôle; (strange) curieux(-euse), bizarre

**fur** [fəː*] n fourrure f; (BRIT: in kettle etc) (dépôt m de) tartre m

**furious** ['fjuərɪəs] adj furieux(-euse); (effort) acharné(e)

**furlong** ['fəːlɔŋ] n = 201,17 m

**furnace** ['fəːnɪs] n fourneau m

**furnish** ['fəːnɪʃ] vt meubler; (supply): **to ~ sb with sth** fournir qch à qn; **~ings** npl mobilier m, ameublement m

**furniture** ['fəːnɪtʃə*] n meubles mpl, mobilier m; **piece of ~** meuble m

**furrow** ['fʌrəu] n sillon m

**furry** ['fəːrɪ] adj (animal) à fourrure; (toy) en peluche

**further** ['fəːðə*] adj (additional) supplémentaire, autre; nouveau (nouvelle) ♦ adv plus loin; (more) davantage; (moreover) de plus ♦ vt faire avancer or progresser, promouvoir; **~ education** n enseignement m postscolaire; **~more** adv de plus, en outre

**furthest** ['fəːðɪst] superl of **far**

**fury** ['fjuərɪ] n fureur f

**fuse** [fjuːz] (US **fuze**) n fusible m; (for bomb etc) amorce f, détonateur m ♦ vt, vi (metal) fondre; **to ~ the lights** (BRIT) faire sauter les plombs; **~ box** n boîte à fusibles

**fuss** [fʌs] n (excitement) agitation f; (complaining) histoire(s) f(pl); **to make a ~** faire des histoires; **to make a ~ of sb** être aux petits soins pour qn; **~y** adj (person) tatillon(ne), difficile; (dress, style) tarabiscoté(e)

**future** ['fjuːtʃə*] adj futur(e) ♦ n avenir m; (LING) futur m; **in ~** à l'avenir

**fuze** [fjuːz] (US) n, vt, vi = **fuse**

**fuzzy** ['fʌzɪ] adj (PHOT) flou(e); (hair) crépu(e)

# G, g

**G** [dʒiː] n (MUS) sol m

**G7** n abbr (= Group of 7) le groupe des 7

**gabble** ['gæbl] vi bredouiller

**gable** ['geɪbl] n pignon m

**gadget** ['gædʒɪt] n gadget m

**Gaelic** ['geɪlɪk] adj gaélique ♦ n (LING) gaélique m

**gag** [gæg] n (on mouth) bâillon m; (joke) gag m ♦ vt bâillonner

**gaiety** ['geɪɪtɪ] n gaieté f

**gain** [geɪn] n (improvement) gain m; (profit) gain, profit m; (increase): **~ (in)** augmentation f (de) ♦ vt gagner ♦ vi (watch) avancer; **to ~ 3 lbs (in weight)** prendre 3 livres; **to ~ on sb** (catch up) rattraper qn; **to ~ from/by** gagner de/à

**gal.** abbr = **gallon**

**gale** [geɪl] n coup m de vent

**gallant** ['gælənt] adj vaillant(e), brave; (towards ladies) galant

**gall bladder** ['gɔ:l-] n vésicule f biliaire

**gallery** ['gælərɪ] n galerie f; (also: **art ~**) musée m; (: private) galerie

**gallon** ['gælən] n gallon m (BRIT: = 4,5 ℓ; US = 3,8 ℓ)

**gallop** ['gæləp] n galop m ♦ vi galoper

**gallows** ['gæləuz] n potence f

**gallstone** ['gɔ:lstəun] n calcul m biliaire

**galore** [gə'lɔ:ʳ] adv en abondance, à gogo

**Gambia** ['gæmbɪə] n: (**The**) **~** la Gambie

**gambit** ['gæmbɪt] n (fig): (**opening**) **~** ♦ vt asphyxier; **~ cooker** (BRIT) n cuisinière f à gaz; **~ cylinder** n bouteille de gaz; **~ fire** (BRIT) n radiateur m à gaz

**gamble** ['gæmbl] n pari m, risque calculé ♦ vt, vi jouer; **to ~ on** (fig) miser sur; **~r** n joueur m; **gambling** n jeu m

**game** [geɪm] n jeu m; (match) match m; (strategy, scheme) plan m; projet m; (HUNTING) gibier m ♦ adj (willing): **to be ~ (for)** être prêt(e) (à or pour); **big ~** gros gibier; **~keeper** n garde-chasse m

**gammon** ['gæmən] n (bacon) quartier m de lard fumé; (ham) jambon fumé

**gamut** ['gæmət] n gamme f

**gang** [gæŋ] n bande f; (of workmen) équipe f; **~ up** vi: **to ~ up on sb** se liguer contre qn; **~ster** n gangster m; **~way** ['gæŋweɪ] n passerelle f; (BRIT: of bus, plane) couloir central; (: in cinema) allée centrale

**gaol** [dʒeɪl] (BRIT) n = **jail**

**gap** [gæp] n trou m; (in time) intervalle m; (difference): **~ between** écart m entre

**gape** [geɪp] vi (person) être or rester bouche bée; (hole, shirt) être ouvert(e); **gaping** adj (hole) béant(e)

**garage** ['gæra:ʒ] n garage m

**garbage** ['ga:bɪdʒ] n (US: rubbish) ordures fpl, détritus mpl; (inf: nonsense) foutaises fpl; **~ can** (US) n poubelle f, boîte f à ordures

**garbled** ['ga:bld] adj (account, message) embrouillé(e)

**garden** ['ga:dn] n jardin m; **~s** npl jardin public; **~er** n jardinier m; **~ing** n jardinage m

**gargle** ['ga:gl] vi se gargariser

**garish** ['gɛərɪʃ] adj criard(e), voyant(e); (light) cru(e)

**garland** ['ga:lənd] n guirlande f; couronne f

**garlic** ['ga:lɪk] n ail m

**garment** ['ga:mənt] n vêtement m

**garrison** ['gærɪsn] n garnison f

**garter** ['ga:təʳ] n jarretière f; (US) jarretelle f

**gas** [gæs] n gaz m; (US: gasoline) essence f

**gash** [gæʃ] n entaille f; (on face) balafre f

**gasket** ['gæskɪt] n (AUT) joint m de culasse

**gas mask** n masque m à gaz

**gas meter** n compteur m à gaz

**gasoline** ['gæsəli:n] (US) n essence f

**gasp** [ga:sp] vi haleter

**gas: ~ ring** n brûleur m; **~ station** (US) n station-service f; **~ tap** n bouton m (de cuisinière à gaz); (on pipe) robinet m à gaz

**gastric** ['gæstrɪk] adj gastrique; **~ flu** grippe f intestinale

**gate** [geɪt] n (of garden) portail m; (of field) barrière f; (of building, at airport) porte f

**gateau** ['gætəu] n (pl **~x**) (gros) gâteau m à la crème

**gatecrash** vt s'introduire sans invitation dans

**gateway** n porte f

**gather** ['gæðəʳ] vt (flowers, fruit) cueillir; (pick up) ramasser; (assemble) rassembler, réunir; recueillir; (understand) comprendre; (SEWING) froncer ♦ vi (assemble) se rassembler; **to ~ speed** prendre de la vitesse; **~ing** n rassemblement m

**gaudy** ['gɔːdɪ] adj voyant(e)

**gauge** [geɪdʒ] n (instrument) jauge f ♦ vt jauger

**gaunt** [gɔːnt] adj (thin) décharné(e); (grim, desolate) désolé(e)

**gauntlet** ['gɔːntlɪt] n (glove) gant m

**gauze** [gɔːz] n gaze f

**gave** [geɪv] pt of **give**

**gay** [geɪ] adj (homosexual) homosexuel(le); (cheerful) réjoui(e); (colour etc) gai, vif (vive)

**gaze** [geɪz] n regard m fixe ♦ vi: **to ~ at** fixer du regard

**gazump** [gə'zʌmp] (BRIT) vi revenir sur une promesse de vente (pour accepter une offre plus intéressante)

**GB** abbr = **Great Britain**

**GCE** n abbr (BRIT) = **General Certificate of Education**

**GCSE** n abbr (BRIT) = **General Certificate of Secondary Education**

**gear** [gɪə*] n matériel m, équipement m; attirail m; (TECH) engrenage m; (AUT) vitesse f ♦ vt (fig: adapt): **to ~** sth to adapter qch à; **top** or (US) **high ~** quatrième (or cinquième) vitesse; **low ~** première vitesse; **in ~** en prise; **~ box** n boîte f de vitesses; **~ lever** (US **gear shift**) n levier m de vitesse

**geese** [giːs] npl of **goose**

**gel** [dʒel] n gel m

**gem** [dʒem] n pierre précieuse

**Gemini** ['dʒemɪnaɪ] n les Gémeaux mpl

**gender** ['dʒendə*] n genre m

**gene** [dʒiːn] n gène m

**general** ['dʒenərl] n général m ♦ adj général(e); **in ~** en général; **~ delivery** n poste restante; **~ election** n élection(s) législative(s); **~ knowledge** n connaissances générales; **~ly** adv généralement; **~ practitioner** n généraliste m/f

**generate** ['dʒenəreɪt] vt engendrer; (electricity etc) produire; **generation** n génération f; (of electricity etc) production f; **generator** n générateur m

**generosity** [dʒenə'rɔsɪtɪ] n générosité f

**generous** ['dʒenərəs] adj généreux (-euse); (copious) copieux(-euse)

**genetic** [dʒɪ'netɪk] adj: **~ engineering** ingénierie f génétique; **~ fingerprinting** système m d'empreinte génétique

**genetics** [dʒɪ'netɪks] n génétique f

**Geneva** [dʒɪ'niːvə] n Genève

**genial** ['dʒiːnɪəl] adj cordial(e), chaleureux(-euse)

**genitals** ['dʒenɪtlz] npl organes génitaux

**genius** ['dʒiːnɪəs] n génie m

**genteel** [dʒen'tiːl] adj de bon ton, distingué(e)

**gentle** ['dʒentl] adj doux (douce)

**gentleman** ['dʒentlmən] n monsieur m; (well-bred man) gentleman m

**gently** ['dʒentlɪ] adv doucement

**gentry** ['dʒentrɪ] n inv: **the ~** la petite noblesse

**gents** [dʒents] n W.-C. mpl (pour hommes)

**genuine** ['dʒenjuɪn] adj véritable, authentique; (person) sincère

**geographical** [dʒɪə'græfɪkl] adj géographique

**geography** [dʒɪ'ɔgrəfɪ] n géographie f

**geology** [dʒɪ'ɔlədʒɪ] n géologie f

**geometric(al)** [dʒɪə'metrɪk(l)] adj géométrique

**geometry** [dʒɪ'ɔmətrɪ] n géométrie f

**geranium** [dʒɪ'reɪnɪəm] n géranium m

**geriatric** [dʒerɪ'ætrɪk] adj gériatrique

**germ** [dʒəːm] n (MED) microbe m

**German** ['dʒəːmən] adj allemand(e) ♦ n Allemand(e); (LING) allemand m; **~ measles** (BRIT) n rubéole f

**Germany** ['dʒəːmənɪ] n Allemagne f

**gesture** ['dʒestjə*] n geste m

---

KEYWORD

**get** [get] (pt, pp **got**, pp **gotten** (US)) vi 1 (become, be) devenir; **to get old/tired** devenir vieux/fatigué, vieillir/se fatiguer; **to get drunk** s'enivrer; **to get killed** se faire tuer; **when do I get**

**paid?** quand est-ce que je serai payé?;
**it's getting late** il se fait tard

**2** (go): **to get to/from** aller à/de; **to
get home** rentrer chez soi; **how did
you get here?** comment es-tu arrivé
ici?

**3** (begin) commencer or se mettre à;
**I'm getting to like him** je commence
à l'apprécier; **let's get going** or
**started** allons-y

**4** (modal aux vb): **you've got to do it**
il faut que vous le fassiez; **I've got to
tell the police** je dois le dire à la police

♦ vt **1: to get sth done** (do) faire qch;
(have done) faire faire qch; **to get
one's hair cut** se faire couper les cheveux; **to get sb to do sth** faire faire
qch à qn; **to get sb drunk** enivrer qn
**2** (obtain: money, permission, results)
obtenir, avoir; (find: job, flat) trouver;
(fetch: person, doctor, object) aller chercher; **to get sth for sb** se procurer qch
à qn; **get me Mr Jones, please** (on
phone) passez-moi Mr Jones, s'il vous
plaît; **can I get you a drink?** est-ce
que je peux vous servir à boire?
**3** (receive: present, letter) recevoir,
avoir; (acquire: reputation) avoir; (:
prize) obtenir; **what did you get for
your birthday?** qu'est-ce que tu as eu
pour ton anniversaire?
**4** (catch) prendre, saisir, attraper; (hit:
target etc) atteindre; **to get sb by the
arm/throat** prendre or saisir qn par le
bras/à la gorge; **get him!** arrête-le!
**5** (take, move) faire parvenir; **do you
think we'll get it through the door?**
on arrivera à la faire passer par la porte?; **I'll get you there somehow** je
me débrouillerai pour t'y emmener
**6** (catch, take: plane, bus etc) prendre
**7** (understand) comprendre, saisir;
(hear) entendre; **I've got it!** j'ai
compris!, je saisis!; **I didn't get your
name** je n'ai pas entendu votre nom

**8** (have, possess): **to have got** avoir;
**how many have you got?** vous en
avez combien?

**get about** vi se déplacer; (news) se répandre

**get along** vi (agree) s'entendre; (depart) s'en aller; (manage) = **get by**

**get at** vt fus (attack) s'en prendre à;
(reach) attraper, atteindre

**get away** vi partir, s'en aller; (escape)
s'échapper

**get away with** vt fus en être quitte
pour; se faire passer or pardonner

**get back** vi (return) rentrer ♦ vt récupérer, recouver

**get by** vi (pass) passer; (manage) se
débrouiller

**get down** vi, vt fus descendre ♦ vt descendre; (depress) déprimer

**get down to** vt fus (work) se mettre à
(faire)

**get in** vi rentrer; (train) arriver

**get into** vt fus entrer dans; (car, train
etc) monter dans; (clothes) mettre, enfiler, endosser; **to get into bed/a rage**
se mettre au lit/en colère

**get off** vi (from train etc) descendre;
(depart: person, car) s'en aller; (escape)
s'en tirer ♦ vt (remove: clothes, stain)
enlever ♦ vt fus (train, bus) descendre
de

**get on** vi (at exam etc) se débrouiller;
(agree): **to get on (with)** s'entendre
(avec) ♦ vt fus monter dans; (horse)
monter sur

**get out** vi sortir; (of vehicle) descendre
♦ vt sortir

**get out of** vt fus sortir de; (duty etc)
échapper à, se soustraire à

**get over** vt fus (illness) se remettre de

**get round** vt fus contourner; (fig: person) entortiller

**get through** vi (TEL) avoir la communication; **to get through to sb** atteindre qn

**get together** vi se réunir ♦ vt assembler

**get up** vi (rise) se lever ♦ vt monter

**get up to** vt fus (reach) arriver à; (prank etc) faire

**getaway** ['getəweɪ] n: **to make one's ~** filer

**geyser** ['giːzə'] n (GEO) geyser m; (BRIT: water heater) chauffe-eau m inv

**Ghana** ['gɑːnə] n Ghana m

**ghastly** ['gɑːstlɪ] adj atroce, horrible; (pale) livide, blême

**gherkin** ['gəːkɪn] n cornichon m

**ghetto blaster** ['getəʊ'blɑːstə'] n stéréo f portable

**ghost** [gəʊst] n fantôme m, revenant m

**giant** ['dʒaɪənt] n géant(e) ♦ adj géant(e), énorme

**gibberish** ['dʒɪbərɪʃ] n charabia m

**giblets** ['dʒɪblɪts] npl abats mpl

**Gibraltar** [dʒɪ'brɔːltə'] n Gibraltar

**giddy** ['gɪdɪ] adj (dizzy): **to be** or **feel ~** avoir le vertige

**gift** [gɪft] n cadeau m; (donation, ability) don m; **~ed** adj doué(e); **~ shop** n boutique f de cadeaux; **~ token** n chèque-cadeau m

**gigantic** [dʒaɪ'gæntɪk] adj gigantesque

**giggle** ['gɪgl] vi pouffer (de rire), rire sottement

**gill** [dʒɪl] n (measure) = 0.25 pints (BRIT = 0.15 l, US = 0.12 l)

**gills** [gɪlz] npl (of fish) ouïes fpl, branchies fpl

**gilt** [gɪlt] adj doré(e) ♦ n dorure f; **~-edged** adj (COMM) de premier ordre

**gimmick** ['gɪmɪk] n truc m

**gin** [dʒɪn] n (liquor) gin m

**ginger** ['dʒɪndʒə'] n gingembre m; **~ ale, ~ beer** n boisson gazeuse au gingembre; **~bread** n pain m d'épices

**gingerly** ['dʒɪndʒəlɪ] adv avec précaution

**gipsy** ['dʒɪpsɪ] n = **gypsy**

**giraffe** [dʒɪ'rɑːf] n girafe f

**girder** ['gəːdə'] n poutrelle f

**girl** [gəːl] n fille f, fillette f; (young unmarried woman) jeune fille; (daughter) fille f; **an English ~** une jeune Anglaise; **~friend** n (of girl) amie f; (of boy) petite amie; **~ish** adj de petite or de jeune fille; (for a boy) efféminé(e)

**giro** ['dʒaɪrəʊ] n (bank ~) virement m bancaire; (post office ~) mandat m; (BRIT: welfare cheque) mandat d'allocation chômage

**gist** [dʒɪst] n essentiel m

**give** [gɪv] (pt **gave**, pp **given**) vt donner ♦ vi (break) céder; (stretch: fabric) se prêter; **to ~ sb sth, ~ sth to sb** donner qch à qn; **to ~ a cry/sigh** pousser un cri/un soupir; **~ away** vt donner; (free) faire cadeau de; (betray) trahir; (disclose) révéler; (bride) conduire à l'autel; **~ back** vt rendre; **~ in** vi céder ♦ vt donner; **~ off** vt dégager; **~ out** vt distribuer; annoncer; **~ up** vi renoncer ♦ vt renoncer à; **to ~ up smoking** arrêter de fumer; **to ~ o.s. up** se rendre; **~ way** (BRIT) vi céder; (AUT) céder la priorité

**glacier** ['glæsɪə'] n glacier m

**glad** [glæd] adj content(e); **~ly** adv volontiers

**glamorous** ['glæmərəs] adj (person) séduisant(e); (job) prestigieux(-euse)

**glamour** ['glæmə'] n éclat m, prestige m

**glance** [glɑːns] n coup m d'œil ♦ vi: **to ~ at** jeter un coup d'œil à; **glancing** adj (blow) oblique

**gland** [glænd] n glande f

**glare** [glɛə'] n (of anger) regard furieux; (of light) lumière éblouissante; (of publicity) feux mpl ♦ vi briller d'un éclat aveuglant; **to ~ at** lancer un regard furieux à; **glaring** adj (mistake) criant(e), qui saute aux yeux

**glass** [glɑːs] n verre m; **~es** npl (spectacles) lunettes fpl; **~house** (BRIT) n (for plants) serre f; **~ware** n verrerie f

**glaze** [gleɪz] vt (door, window) vitrer;

(pottery) vernir ♦ n (on pottery) vernis
m; ~d adj (pottery) verni(e); (eyes)
vitreux(-euse)

**glazier** ['gleɪzɪə'] n vitrier m

**gleam** [gli:m] n lueur f ♦ vi luire, briller

**glean** [gli:n] vt (information) glaner

**glee** [gli:] n joie f

**glib** [glɪb] adj (person) qui a du bagou;
(response) désinvolte, facile

**glide** [glaɪd] vi (aircraft, birds) planer; ~r n (AVIAT) planeur m; **gliding** n
(SPORT) vol m à voile

**glimmer** ['glɪmə'] n lueur f

**glimpse** [glɪmps] n vision passagère,
aperçu ♦ vt entrevoir, apercevoir

**glint** [glɪnt] vi étinceler

**glisten** ['glɪsn] vi briller, luire

**glitter** ['glɪtə'] vi scintiller, briller

**gloat** [gləʊt] vi: **to ~ (over)** jubiler (à
propos de)

**global** ['gləʊbl] adj mondial(e); **~
warming** réchauffement m de la planète

**globe** [gləʊb] n globe m

**gloom** [glu:m] n obscurité f; (sadness)
tristesse f, mélancolie f; **~y** adj sombre,
triste, lugubre

**glorious** ['glɔ:rɪəs] adj glorieux(-euse)·
splendide

**glory** ['glɔ:rɪ] n gloire f; splendeur f

**gloss** [glɒs] n (shine) brillant m, vernis
m; **~ over** vt fus glisser sur

**glossary** ['glɒsərɪ] n glossaire m

**glossy** ['glɒsɪ] adj brillant(e); **~ magazine** magazine m de luxe

**glove** [glʌv] n gant m; **~ compartment** n (AUT) boîte f à gants, vide-
poches m inv

**glow** [gləʊ] vi rougeoyer; (face) rayonner; (eyes) briller

**glower** ['glaʊə'] vi: **to ~ (at)** lancer des
regards mauvais (à)

**glucose** ['glu:kəʊs] n glucose m

**glue** [glu:] n colle f ♦ vt coller

**glum** [glʌm] adj sombre, morne

**glut** [glʌt] n surabondance f

**glutton** ['glʌtn] n glouton(ne); **a ~ for**

work un bourreau de travail; **a ~ for
punishment** un masochiste (fig)

**GM** abbr (= genetically modified) génétiquement modifié(e)

**gnat** [næt] n moucheron m

**gnaw** [nɔ:] vt ronger

**go** [gəʊ] (pt **went**, pp **gone**, pl **~es**) vi
aller; (depart) partir, s'en aller; (work)
marcher; (break etc) céder; (be sold):
**to ~ for £10** se vendre 10 livres; (fit, suit):
**to ~ with** aller avec; (become):
**to ~
pale/mouldy** pâlir/moisir ♦ n: **to have
a ~ (at)** essayer (de faire); **to be on
the ~** être en mouvement; **whose ~
is it?** à qui est-ce de jouer; **he's ~ing
to do it** il va le faire, il est sur le point de
faire; **to ~ for a walk** aller se promener; **to ~ dancing** aller danser; **how
did it ~?** comment est-ce que ça s'est
passé?; **to ~ round the back/by the
shop** passer par derrière/devant le magasin; **~ about** vi (rumour) se répandre
♦ vt fus: **how do I ~ about this?**
comment dois-je m'y prendre (pour faire ceci)?; **~ after** vt fus (pursue) poursuivre, courir après; (job, record etc) essayer d'obtenir; **~ ahead** vi (make progress) avancer; (get going) y aller; **~
along** vi aller, avancer ♦ vt fus longer,
parcourir; **to ~ along with** (agree with)
être d'accord avec; **~ away** vi partir, s'en aller;
**~ back** vi revenir; revenir; (~ again) retourner; **~ back on** vt fus (promise) revenir sur; **~ by** vi (years, time) passer,
s'écouler ♦ vt fus s'en tenir à; en croire;
**~ down** vi descendre; (ship) couler;
(sun) se coucher ♦ vt fus descendre; **~
for** vt fus (fetch) aller chercher; (like)
aimer; (attack) s'en prendre à, attaquer;
**~ in** vi entrer; **~ in for** vt fus (competition) se présenter à; (like) aimer; **~
into** vt fus (enter) entrer dans; (investigate)
étudier, examiner; (embark on) se lancer dans; **~ off** vi partir, s'en aller;
(food) se gâter; (explode) sauter; (event)
se dérouler ♦ vt fus ne plus aimer; **the
gun went off** le coup est parti; **~ on**
vi continuer; (happen) se passer; **to ~**

**on doing** continuer à faire; **~ out** vi sortir; (fire, light) s'éteindre; **~ over** (vi fus) (check) revoir, vérifier; **~ past** (vt: **to ~ past sth** passer devant qch; (vi): **to ~ past** passer devant qn); **~ round** vi (circulate: news, rumour) circuler; (revolve) tourner; (suffice) suffire (pour tout le monde); **to ~ round to sb's** (visit) passer chez qn; **to ~ round (by)** (make a detour) faire un détour (par); **~ through** vt fus (town etc) traverser; **~ up** vi monter; (price) augmenter ♦ vt fus gravir; **~ with** vt fus (suit) aller avec; **~ without** vt fus se passer de

**goad** [gəud] vt aiguillonner

**go-ahead** adj dynamique, entreprenant(e) ♦ n feu vert

**goal** [gəul] n but m; **~keeper** n gardien m de but; **~post** n poteau m de but

**goat** [gəut] n chèvre f

**gobble** ['gɔbl] vt (also: **~ down, ~ up**) engloutir

**go-between** ['gəubitwi:n] n intermédiaire m/f

**god** [gɔd] n dieu m; **G~** n Dieu m; **~child** n filleul(e); **~daughter** n filleule f; **~dess** n déesse f; **~father** n parrain m; **~forsaken** adj maudit(e); **~mother** n marraine f; **~send** n aubaine f; **~son** n filleul m

**goggles** ['gɔglz] npl (for skiing etc) lunettes protectrices

**going** ['gəuiŋ] n (conditions) état m du terrain ♦ adj: **the ~ rate** le tarif (en vigueur)

**gold** [gəuld] n or m ♦ adj en or; (reserves) d'or; **~en** adj (made of gold) en or; (gold in colour) doré(e); **~fish** n poisson m rouge; **~-plated** adj plaqué(e) or inv; **~smith** n orfèvre m

**golf** [gɔlf] n golf m; **~ ball** n balle f de golf; (on typewriter) boule m; **~ club** n club m de golf; (stick) club m, crosse f de golf; **~ course** n (terrain m de) golf m; **~er** n joueur/-euse) m/f de golf

**gone** [gɔn] pp of **go**

**gong** [gɔŋ] n gong m

**good** [gud] adj bon(ne); (kind) gentil(le); (child) sage ♦ n bien m; **~s** npl (COMM) marchandises fpl, articles mpl; **~!** bon!, très bien!; **to be ~ to** être bon envers; **to be ~ for** être bon pour; **would you be ~ enough to ...?** auriez-vous la bonté ou l'amabilité de ...?; **a ~ deal (of)** beaucoup (de); **a ~ many** beaucoup (de); **to make ~** vi (succeed) faire son chemin, réussir ♦ vt (deficit) combler; (losses) compenser; **it's no ~ complaining** cela ne sert à rien de se plaindre; **for ~** pour de bon, une fois pour toutes; **~ morning/afternoon!** bonjour!; **~ evening!** bonsoir!; **~ night!** bonsoir!; (on going to bed) bonne nuit; **~bye** excl au revoir!; **G~ Friday** n Vendredi saint; **~-looking** adj beau (belle), bien inv; **~-natured** adj (person) qui a un bon naturel; **~ness** n (of person) bonté f; **for ~ness sake!** je vous en prie!; **~ness gracious!** mon Dieu!; **~s train** n train m de marchandises; **~will** n bonne volonté

**goose** [gu:s] (pl **geese**) n oie f

**gooseberry** ['guzbəri] n groseille f à maquereau; **to play ~** (BRIT) tenir la chandelle

**gooseflesh** ['gu:sfleʃ] n, **goose pimples** npl chair f de poule

**gore** [gɔ:r] vt encorner ♦ n sang m

**gorge** [gɔ:dʒ] n gorge f ♦ vt: **to ~ o.s. (on)** se gorger (de)

**gorgeous** ['gɔ:dʒəs] adj splendide, superbe

**gorilla** [gə'rilə] n gorille m

**gorse** [gɔ:s] n ajoncs mpl

**gory** ['gɔ:ri] adj sanglant(e); (details) horrible

**go-slow** ['gəu'sləu] n (BRIT) grève perlée

**gospel** ['gɔspl] n évangile m

**gossip** ['gɔsip] n (chat) bavardages mpl; commérage m, cancans mpl; (person) commère f ♦ vi bavarder; (maliciously) cancaner, faire des commérages

**got** [gɔt] pt, pp of **get**; **~ten** (US) pp of

**get**

**gout** [gaut] n goutte f

**govern** ['gʌvən] vt gouverner; **~ess** n
gouvernante f; **~ment** n gouvernement m; (BRIT: ministers) ministère m;
**~or** n (of state, bank) gouverneur m; (of
school, hospital) ≃ membre m du
conseil d'établissement; (BRIT: of prison)
directeur(-trice)

**gown** [gaun] n robe f; (of teacher, BRIT:
of judge) toge f

**GP** n abbr = **general practitioner**

**grab** [græb] vt saisir, empoigner ♦ vi: to
~ **at** essayer de saisir

**grace** [greis] n grâce f ♦ vt honorer;
(adorn) orner; **5 days'** ~ cinq jours de
répit; **~ful** adj gracieux(-euse), élé-
gant(e); **gracious** ['greiʃəs] adj bien-
veillant(e)

**grade** [greid] n (COMM) qualité f; (in
hierarchy) catégorie f, grade m, échelon
m; (SCOL) note f; (US: school class) classe
f ♦ vt classer; **~ crossing** (US) n passage m à niveau; **~ school** (US) n école f
primaire

**gradient** ['greidiənt] n inclinaison f,
pente f

**gradual** ['grædjuəl] adj graduel(le),
progressif(-ive); **~ly** adv peu à peu, gra-
duellement

**graduate** [n 'grædjuit, vb 'grædjueit] n
diplômé(e), licencié(e); (US: of high
school) bachelier(-ère) ♦ vi obtenir un
diplôme; (US) obtenir son baccalauréat;
**graduation** [grædju'eiʃən] n (cérémonie f de) remise f des diplômes

**graffiti** [grə'fi:ti] npl graffiti mpl

**graft** [gra:ft] n (AGR, MED) greffe f; (bribery) corruption f ♦ vt greffer; **hard** ~
(BRIT: inf) boulot acharné

**grain** [grein] n grain m

**gram** [græm] n gramme m

**grammar** ['græmə*] n grammaire f; **~
school** (BRIT) n ≃ lycée m; **grammatical** [grə'mætikl] adj grammatical(e)

**gramme** [græm] n = **gram**

**grand** [grænd] adj magnifique, splendi-

de; (gesture etc) noble; **~children** npl
petits-enfants mpl; **~dad** (inf) n grand-
papa m; **~daughter** n petite-fille f;
**~father** n grand-père m; **~ma** (inf) n
grand-maman f; **~mother** n grand-
mère f; **~pa** (inf) n = **granddad**; **~-
parents** npl grands-parents mpl; **~
piano** n piano m à queue; **~son** n
petit-fils m; **~stand** n (SPORT) tribune f

**granite** ['grænit] n granit m

**granny** ['græni] (inf) n grand-maman f

**grant** [gra:nt] vt accorder; (a request)
accéder à; (admit) concéder ♦ n (SCOL)
bourse f; (ADMIN) subside m, subvention
f; **to take it for ~ed that** trouver tout
naturel que +sub; **to take sb for ~ed**
considérer qn comme faisant partie du
décor

**granulated sugar** ['grænjuleitid–] n
sucre m en poudre

**grape** [greip] n raisin m

**grapefruit** ['greipfru:t] n pamplemousse m

**graph** [gra:f] n graphique m; **~ic**
['græfik] adj graphique; (account, description) vivant(e); **~ics** n arts mpl graphiques; graphisme m ♦ npl représentations fpl graphiques

**grapple** ['græpl] vi: to ~ **with** être aux
prises avec

**grasp** [gra:sp] vt saisir ♦ n (grip) prise
f; (understanding) compréhension f,
connaissance f; **~ing** adj cupide

**grass** [gra:s] n herbe f; (lawn) gazon m;
**~hopper** n sauterelle f; **~roots** adj de
la base, du peuple

**grate** [greit] n grille f de cheminée ♦ vi
grincer ♦ vt (CULIN) râper

**grateful** ['greitful] adj reconnaissant(e)

**grater** ['greitə*] n râpe f

**gratifying** ['grætifaiiŋ] adj agréable

**grating** ['greitiŋ] n (iron bars) grille f
♦ adj (noise) grinçant(e)

**gratitude** ['grætitju:d] n gratitude f

**gratuity** [grə'tju:iti] n pourboire m

**grave** [greiv] n tombe f ♦ adj grave,
sérieux(-euse)

**gravel** ['grævl] n gravier m

**gravestone** ['greɪvstəun] n pierre tombale

**graveyard** ['greɪvjɑːd] n cimetière m

**gravity** ['grævɪtɪ] n (PHYSICS) gravité f, pesanteur f; (seriousness) gravité f

**gravy** ['greɪvɪ] n jus m (de viande); sauce f

**gray** [greɪ] (US) adj = **grey**

**graze** [greɪz] vi paître, brouter ♦ vt (touch lightly) frôler, effleurer; (scrape) écorcher ♦ n écorchure f

**grease** [griːs] n (fat) graisse f; (lubricant) lubrifiant m ♦ vt graisser; lubrifier; **~proof paper** (BRIT) n papier sulfurisé; **greasy** adj gras(se), graisseux(-euse)

**great** [greɪt] adj grand(e); (inf) formidable; **G~ Britain** n Grande-Bretagne f; **~grandfather** n arrière-grand-père m; **~grandmother** n arrière-grand-mère f; **~ly** adv très, grandement; (with verbs) beaucoup; **~ness** n grandeur f

**Greece** [griːs] n Grèce f

**greed** [griːd] n (also: **~iness**) avidité f; (for food) gourmandise f, gloutonnerie f; **~y** adj avide; gourmand(e), glouton(ne)

**Greek** [griːk] adj grec (grecque) ♦ n Grec (Grecque); (LING) grec m

**green** [griːn] adj vert(e); (inexperienced) (bien) jeune, naïf (naïve); (POL) vert(e), écologiste; (ecological) écologique ♦ n vert m; (stretch of grass) pelouse f; **~s** npl (vegetables) légumes verts; **the G~s** les Verts mpl; **the G~ Party** (BRIT: POL) le parti écologiste; **~ belt** n (round town) ceinture verte; **~ card** n (AUT) carte verte; (US) permis m de travail; **~ery** n verdure f; **~grocer's** (BRIT) n marchand m de fruits et légumes; **~house** n serre f; **~house effect** n effet m de serre; **~house gas** n gas m à effet de serre; **~ish** adj verdâtre

**Greenland** ['griːnlənd] n Groenland m

**greet** [griːt] vt accueillir; **~ing** n salutation f; **~ing(s) card** n carte f de vœux

sociable

**grenade** [grə'neɪd] n grenade f

**grew** [gruː] pt of **grow**

**grey** [greɪ] (US **gray**) adj gris(e); (dismal) sombre; **~-haired** adj grisonnant(e); **~hound** n lévrier m

**grid** [grɪd] n grille f; (ELEC) réseau m; **~lock** n (traffic jam) embouteillage m; **~locked** adj: **to be ~locked** (roads) être bloqué par un embouteillage; (talks etc) être suspendu

**grief** [griːf] n chagrin m, douleur f

**grievance** ['griːvəns] n doléance f, grief m

**grieve** [griːv] vi avoir du chagrin; se désoler ♦ vt faire de la peine à, affliger; **to ~ for sb** (dead person) pleurer qn

**grievous** ['griːvəs] adj (LAW): **grievous bodily harm** coups mpl et blessures fpl

**grill** [grɪl] n (on cooker) gril m; (food: also mixed ~) grillade(s) f(pl) ♦ vt (BRIT) griller; (inf: question) cuisiner

**grille** [grɪl] n grille f, grillage m; (AUT) calandre f

**grim** [grɪm] adj sinistre, lugubre; (serious, stern) sévère

**grimace** [grɪ'meɪs] n grimace f ♦ vi grimacer, faire une grimace

**grime** [graɪm] n crasse f, saleté f

**grin** [grɪn] n large sourire m ♦ vi sourire

**grind** [graɪnd] (pt, pp ground) vt écraser; (coffee, pepper etc) moudre; (US: meat) hacher; (make sharp) aiguiser ♦ n (work) corvée f

**grip** [grɪp] n (hold) prise f, étreinte f; (control) emprise f; (grasp) connaissance f; (handle) poignée f; (holdall) sac m de voyage ♦ vt saisir, empoigner; **to come to ~s with** en venir aux prises avec; **~ping** adj prenant(e), palpitant(e)

**grisly** ['grɪzlɪ] adj sinistre, macabre

**gristle** ['grɪsl] n cartilage m

**grit** [grɪt] n gravillon m; (courage) cran m ♦ vt (road) sabler; **to ~ one's teeth** serrer les dents

**groan** [grəun] n (of pain) gémissement

*m* ♦ *vi* gémir

**grocer** ['grəusə'] *n* épicier *m*; **~ies** *npl* provisions *fpl*; **~'s (shop)** *n* épicerie *f*

**groin** [grɔɪn] *n* aine *f*

**groom** [gruːm] *n* palefrenier *m*; (*also:* **bridegroom**) marié *m* ♦ *vt* (*horse*) panser; (*fig*): **to ~ sb for** former qn pour; **well-~ed** très soigné(e)

**groove** [gruːv] *n* rainure *f*

**grope** [grəup] *vi*: **to ~ for** chercher à tâtons

**gross** [grəus] *adj* grossier(-ère); (*COMM*) brut(e); **~ly** *adv* (*greatly*) très, grandement

**grotto** ['grɔtəu] *n* grotte *f*

**grotty** ['grɔtɪ] (*inf*) *adj* minable, affreux(-euse)

**ground** [graund] *pt, pp* of **grind** ♦ *n* sol *m*, terre *f*; (*land*) terrain *m*, terres *fpl*; (*SPORT*) terrain; (*US: also:* **~ wire**) terre *f*; (*reason: gen pl*) raison *f* ♦ *vt* (*plane*) empêcher de décoller, retenir au sol; (*US: ELEC*) équiper d'une prise de terre; **~s** *npl* (*of coffee etc*) marc *m*; (*gardens etc*) parc *m*, domaine *m*; **on the ~, to the ~** par terre; **to gain/lose ~** gagner/perdre du terrain; **~ cloth** (*US*) *n* = **groundsheet**; **~ing** *n* (*in education*) connaissances *fpl* de base; **~less** *adj* sans fondement; **~sheet** (*BRIT*) *n* tapis *m* de sol; **~ staff** *n* personnel *m* au sol; **~work** *n* préparation *f*

**group** [gruːp] *n* groupe *m* ♦ *vt* (*also:* **~ together**) grouper ♦ *vi* se grouper

**grouse** [graus] *n inv* (*bird*) grouse *f* ♦ *vi* (*complain*) rouspéter, râler

**grove** [grəuv] *n* bosquet *m*

**grovel** ['grɔvl] *vi* (*fig*) ramper

**grow** [grəu] (*pt* **grew**, *pp* **grown**) *vi* pousser, croître; (*person*) grandir; (*increase*) augmenter, se développer; (*become*): **to ~ rich/weak** s'enrichir/s'affaiblir; (*develop*): **he's ~n out of his jacket** sa veste est (devenue) trop petite pour lui ♦ *vt* cultiver, faire pousser; (*beard*) laisser pousser; **he'll ~ out of it!** ça lui passera!; **~ up** *vi* grandir; **~er** *n*

producteur *m*; **~ing** *adj* (*fear, amount*) croissant(e), grandissant(e)

**growl** [graul] *vi* grogner

**grown** [grəun] *pp* of **grow**; **~-up** *n* adulte *m/f*, grande personne

**growth** [grəuθ] *n* croissance *f*, développement *m*; (*what has grown*) pousse *f*, poussée *f*; (*MED*) grosseur *f*, tumeur *f*

**grub** [grʌb] *n* larve *f*; (*inf: food*) bouffe *f*

**grubby** ['grʌbɪ] *adj* crasseux(-euse)

**grudge** [grʌdʒ] *n* rancune *f* ♦ *vt*: **to ~ sb sth** (*in giving*) donner qch à qn à contre-cœur; (*resent*) reprocher qch à qn; **to bear sb a ~ (for)** garder rancune *or* en vouloir à qn

**gruelling** ['gruəlɪŋ] (*US* **grueling**) *adj* exténuant(e)

**gruesome** ['gruːsəm] *adj* horrible

**gruff** [grʌf] *adj* bourru(e)

**grumble** ['grʌmbl] *vi* rouspéter, ronchonner

**grumpy** ['grʌmpɪ] *adj* grincheux(-euse)

**grunt** [grʌnt] *vi* grogner

**G-string** ['dʒiːstrɪŋ] *n* (*garment*) cache-sexe *m inv*

**guarantee** [gærən'tiː] *n* garantie *f* ♦ *vt* garantir

**guard** [gɑːd] *n* garde *f*, surveillance *f*; (*one man*) garde *m*; (*BRIT: RAIL*) chef *m* de train; (*on machine*) dispositif *m* de sûreté; (*also:* **fireguard**) garde-feu *m* ♦ *vt* garder, surveiller; (*protect*): **to ~ (against** *or* **from**) protéger (contre); **~ against** *vt fus* (*prevent*) empêcher, se protéger de; **~ed** *adj* (*fig*) prudent(e); **~ian** *n* gardien(ne); (*of minor*) tuteur(-trice), tutrice); **~'s van** (*BRIT*) (*RAIL*) fourgon *m*

**guerrilla** [gə'rɪlə] *n* guérillero *m*

**guess** [ges] *vt* deviner; (*estimate*) évaluer; (*US*) croire, penser ♦ *vi* deviner ♦ *n* supposition *f*, hypothèse *f*; **to take** *or* **have a ~** essayer de deviner; **~work** *n* hypothèse *f*

**guest** [gest] *n* invité(e); (*in hotel*) client(e); **~house** *n* pension *f*; **~ room** *n* chambre *f* d'amis

**guffaw** [gʌ'fɔː] *vi* pouffer de rire

**guidance** ['gaɪdəns] n conseils mpl

**guide** [gaɪd] n (person, book etc) guide m; (BRIT: also: **girl** ~) guide f ♦ vt guider; **~book** n guide m; **~ dog** n chien m d'aveugle; **~lines** npl (fig) instructions (générales), conseils mpl

**guild** [gɪld] n corporation f; cercle m, association f

**guillotine** ['gɪlətiːn] n guillotine f

**guilt** [gɪlt] n culpabilité f; **~y** adj coupable

**guinea pig** ['gɪnɪ-] n cobaye m

**guise** [gaɪz] n aspect m, apparence f

**guitar** [gɪ'tɑːɪ] n guitare f

**gulf** [gʌlf] n golfe m; (abyss) gouffre m

**gull** [gʌl] n mouette f; (larger) goéland m

**gullible** ['gʌlɪbl] adj crédule

**gully** ['gʌlɪ] n ravin m; ravine f; couloir m

**gulp** [gʌlp] vi avaler sa salive ♦ vt (also: ~ **down**) avaler

**gum** [gʌm] n (ANAT) gencive f; (glue) colle f; (sweet: also ~**drop**) boule f de gomme; (also: **chewing~**) chewing-gum m ♦ vt coller; **~boots** (BRIT) npl bottes fpl en caoutchouc

**gun** [gʌn] n (small) revolver m, pistolet m; (rifle) fusil m; carabine f; (cannon) canon m; **~boat** n canonnière f; **~fire** n fusillade f; **~man** n bandit armé; **~point** n: **at ~point** sous la menace du pistolet (or fusil); **~powder** n poudre f à canon; **~shot** n coup m de feu

**gurgle** ['gɜːgl] vi gargouiller; (baby) gazouiller

**gush** [gʌʃ] vi jaillir; (fig) se répandre en effusions

**gust** [gʌst] n (of wind) rafale f; (of smoke) bouffée f

**gusto** ['gʌstəu] n enthousiasme m

**gut** [gʌt] n intestin m, boyau m; **~s** npl (inf: courage) cran m

**gutter** ['gʌtəɪ] n (in street) caniveau m; (of roof) gouttière f

**guy** [gaɪ] n (inf: man) type m; (also: **~rope**) corde f; (BRIT: figure) effigie de

Guy Fawkes (brûlée en plein air le 5 novembre)

**guzzle** ['gʌzl] vt avaler gloutonnement

**gym** [dʒɪm] n (also: **~nasium**) gymnase m; (also: **~nastics**) gym f; **~nast** n gymnaste m/f; **~nastics** [dʒɪm'næstɪks] n, npl gymnastique f; **~ shoes** npl chaussures fpl de gym; **~slip** (BRIT) n tunique f (d'écolière)

**gynaecologist** [gaɪnɪ'kɔlədʒɪst] (US **gynecologist**) n gynécologue m/f

**gypsy** ['dʒɪpsɪ] n gitan(e), bohémien(ne)

# H, h

**haberdashery** [hæbə'dæʃərɪ] (BRIT) n mercerie f

**habit** ['hæbɪt] n habitude f; (REL: costume) habit m; **~ual** adj habituel(le); (drinker, liar) invétéré(e)

**hack** [hæk] vt hacher, tailler ♦ n (pej: writer) nègre m; **~er** n (COMPUT) pirate m (informatique); (: enthusiast) passionné(e) m/f des ordinateurs

**hackneyed** ['hæknɪd] adj usé(e), rebattu(e)

**had** [hæd] *pt, pp* of **have**

**haddock** ['hædək] (*pl* ~ *or* ~**s**) *n* églefin *m*; **smoked** ~ haddock *m*

**hadn't** ['hædnt] = **had not**

**haemorrhage** ['hemərɪdʒ] (*US* **hemorrhage**) *n* hémorragie *f*

**haemorrhoids** ['hemərɔɪdz] (*US* **hemorrhoids**) *npl* hémorroïdes *fpl*

**haggle** ['hægl] *vi* marchander

**Hague** [heɪg] *n*: The ~ La Haye

**hail** [heɪl] *n* grêle *f* ♦ *vt* (*call*) héler; (*acclaim*) acclamer ♦ *vi* grêler; **~stone** *n* grêlon *m*

**hair** [hɛəʳ] *n* (of animal) pelage *m*, poils *mpl*; (of head) cheveux *mpl*; (single ~: on head) cheveu *m*; (: on body; of animal) poil *m*; **to do one's** ~ se coiffer; **~brush** *n* brosse *f* à cheveux; **~cut** *n* coupe *f* (de cheveux); **~do** *n* coiffure *f*; **~dresser** *n* coiffeur(-euse); **~dresser's** *n* salon *m* de coiffure, coiffeur *m*; **~ dryer** *n* sèche-cheveux *m*; **~ gel** *n* gel *m* pour cheveux; **~grip** *n* pince *f* à cheveux; **~net** *n* filet *m* à cheveux *f*; **~piece** *n* perruque *f*; **~pin** *n* épingle *f* à cheveux; **~pin bend** (*US* **hairpin curve**) *n* virage *m* en épingle *f* à cheveux; **~raising** *adj* à (vous) faire dresser les cheveux sur la tête; **~ removing cream** *n* crème *f* dépilatoire; **~ spray** *n* laque *f* (pour les cheveux); **~style** *n* coiffure *f*; **~y** *adj* poilu(e); (*inf: fig*) effrayant(e)

**hake** [heɪk] (*pl* ~ *or* ~**s**) *n* colin *m*, merlu *m*

**half** [hɑːf] (*pl* **halves**) *n* moitié *f*; (of beer: also ~ **pint**) ~ demi *m*; (*RAIL, bus: also* ~ **fare**) ~ demi-tarif *m* ♦ *adj* demi(e) ♦ *adv* à moitié, à demi; **a dozen** une demi-douzaine; **a pound** une demi-livre, ≃ 250 g; **two and a** ~ deux et demi; **to cut sth in** ~ couper qch en deux; **~-caste** ['hɑːfkɑːst] *n* métis(se); **~-hearted** *adj* tiède, sans enthousiasme; (*fig*) demi-heure *f*; **~-mast: at ~-mast** *adv* (*flag*) en berne; **~penny** (*BRIT*) *n* demi-penny *m*;

**~ price** *adj, adv*: (**at**) **~-price** à moitié prix; **~ term** (*BRIT*) *n* (*SCOL*) congé *m* de demi-trimestre; **~-time** *n* mi-temps *f*; **~-way** *adv* à mi-chemin

**hall** [hɔːl] *n* salle *f*; (*entrance way*) hall *m*, entrée *f*

**hallmark** ['hɔːlmɑːk] *n* poinçon *m*; (*fig*) marque *f*

**hallo** [hə'ləu] *excl* = **hello**

**hall of residence** (*BRIT*) (*pl* **halls of residence**) *n* résidence *f* universitaire

**Hallowe'en** ['hæləu'iːn] *n* veille *f* de la Toussaint

Selon la tradition, **Hallowe'en** est la nuit des fantômes et des sorcières. En Écosse et aux États-Unis surtout (beaucoup moins en Angleterre) les enfants, pour fêter Hallowe'en, se déguisent ce soir-là et ils vont ainsi de porte en porte en demandant de petits cadeaux (du chocolat, une pomme etc.).

**hallucination** [həluːsɪ'neɪʃən] *n* hallucination *f*

**hallway** ['hɔːlweɪ] *n* vestibule *m*

**halo** ['heɪləu] *n* (of saint etc) auréole *f*

**halt** [hɔːlt] *n* halt *f*, arrêt *m* ♦ *vt* (*progress*) interrompre ♦ *vi* faire halte, s'arrêter

**halve** [hɑːv] *vt* (*apple etc*) partager *or* diviser en deux; (*expense*) réduire de moitié; **~s** *npl* of **half**

**ham** [hæm] *n* jambon *m*

**hamburger** ['hæmbəːgəʳ] *n* hamburger *m*

**hamlet** ['hæmlɪt] *n* hameau *m*

**hammer** ['hæməʳ] *n* marteau *m* ♦ *vt* (*nail*) enfoncer; (*fig*) démolir ♦ *vi* (*on door*) frapper à coups redoublés; **to ~ an idea into sb** faire entrer de force une idée dans la tête de qn

**hammock** ['hæmək] *n* hamac *m*

**hamper** ['hæmpəʳ] *vt* gêner ♦ *n* panier *m* (d'osier)

**hamster** ['hæmstəʳ] *n* hamster *m*

**hand** [hænd] n main f; (of clock) aiguille f; (~writing) écriture f; (~worker) ouvrier(-ère); (at cards) jeu ♦ vt passer, donner; **to give** or **lend sb sth ~** donner un coup de main à qn; **at ~** à portée de la main; **in ~** (time) à disposition; (job, situation) en main; **to be on ~** (person) être disponible; (emergency services) se tenir prêt(e) (à intervenir); **to ~** (information etc) sous la main, à portée de la main; **on the one ~ ..., on the other ~** d'une part ..., d'autre part; **~ in** vt remettre; **~ out** vt distribuer; **~ over** vt transmettre; céder; **~bag** n sac m à main; **~book** n manuel m; **~brake** n frein m à main; **~cuffs** npl menottes fpl; **~ful** n poignée f

**handicap** ['hændɪkæp] n handicap m ♦ vt handicaper; **mentally/physically ~ped** handicapé(e) mentalement/physiquement

**handicraft** ['hændɪkrɑːft] n (travail m d')artisanat m, technique artisanale; (object) objet artisanal

**handiwork** ['hændɪwɜːk] n ouvrage m

**handkerchief** ['hæŋkətʃɪf] n mouchoir m

**handle** ['hændl] n (of door etc) poignée f; (of cup etc) anse f; (of knife etc) manche m; (of saucepan) queue f; (for winding) manivelle f ♦ vt toucher, manier; (deal with) s'occuper de; (treat: people) prendre; **"~ with care"** "fragile"; **to fly off the ~** s'énerver; **~bar(s)** n(pl) guidon m

**hand:** **~luggage** n bagages mpl à main; **~made** adj fait(e) à la main; **~out** n (from government, parents) aide f, don m; (leaflet) documentation f, prospectus m; (summary of lecture) polycopié m; **~rail** n rampe f, main courante; **~set** n (TEL) combiné m; **please replace the ~set** raccrochez s'il vous plaît; **~shake** n poignée f de main

**handsome** ['hænsəm] adj beau (belle); (profit, return) considérable

**handwriting** ['hændraɪtɪŋ] n écriture f

**handy** ['hændɪ] adj (person) adroit(e); (close at hand) sous la main; (convenient) pratique

**hang** [hæŋ] (pt, pp hung) vt accrocher; (criminal: pt, pp: ~ed) pendre ♦ vi pendre; (hair, drapery) tomber; **to get the ~ of (doing) sth** (inf) attraper le coup pour faire qch; **~ about** vi traîner; **~ around** vi = hang about; **~ on** vi (wait) attendre; **~ up** vi (TEL) raccrocher ♦ vt (coat, painting etc) accrocher, suspendre

**hangar** ['hæŋər] n hangar m

**hanger** ['hæŋər] n cintre m, portemanteau m; **~-on** n parasite m

**hang:** **~-gliding** n deltaplane m, vol m libre; **~over** n (after drinking) gueule f de bois; **~-up** n complexe m

**hanker** ['hæŋkər] vi: **to ~ after** avoir envie de

**hankie, hanky** ['hæŋkɪ] n abbr = **handkerchief**

**haphazard** [hæp'hæzəd] adj fait(e) au hasard, fait(e) au petit bonheur

**happen** ['hæpən] vi arriver; se passer, se produire; **it so ~s that** il se trouve que; **as it ~s** justement; **~ing** n événement m

**happily** ['hæpɪlɪ] adv heureusement; (cheerfully) joyeusement

**happiness** ['hæpɪnɪs] n bonheur m

**happy** ['hæpɪ] adj heureux(-euse); **~ with** (arrangements etc) satisfait(e) de; **to be ~ to do** faire volontiers; **~ birthday!** bon anniversaire!; **~-go-lucky** adj insouciant(e); **~ hour** n heure pendant laquelle les consommations sont à prix réduit

**harass** ['hærəs] vt accabler, tourmenter; **~ment** n tracasserie fpl

**harbour** ['hɑːbər] (US **harbor**) n port m ♦ vt héberger, abriter; (hope, fear etc) entretenir

**hard** [hɑːd] adj (question, problem) difficile, dure; (facts, evidence) concret(-ète) ♦ adv (work) dur; (think, *try)* sérieusement; **to look ~ at** regarder fixement; *(thing)* regarder de près; **no ~ feelings!** sans rancune!; **to be ~ of hearing** être dur(e) d'oreille; **to be ~ done by** être traité(e) injustement; **~back** *n* espèces *fpl*; **~ disk** *(COMPUT)* disque dur; **~** *vt* durcir; *(fig)* endurcir ♦ *vi* durcir; **~-headed** *adj* réaliste; décidé(e); **~ labour** *n* travaux forcés

**hardly** ['hɑ:dlɪ] *adv (scarcely, no count)* à peine; **~ anywhere/ever** presque nulle part/jamais

**hard: ~ship** *n* épreuves *fpl*; **~ shoulder** *(BRIT)* *n (AUT)* accotement stabilisé; **~ up** *(inf)* fauché(e); **~ware** *n* quincaillerie *f*; *(COMPUT, MIL)* matériel *m*; **~ware shop** *n* quincaillerie *f*; **~-wearing** *adj* solide; **~-working** *adj* travailleur(-euse)

**hardy** ['hɑ:dɪ] *adj* robuste; *(plant)* résistant(e) au gel

**hare** [heə*] *n* lièvre *m*; **~-brained** *adj* farfelu(e)

**harm** [hɑ:m] *n* mal *m*; *(wrong)* tort *m* ♦ *vt (person)* faire du mal ou du tort à; *(thing)* endommager; **out of ~'s way** à l'abri du danger, en lieu sûr; **~ful** *adj* nuisible; **~less** *adj* inoffensif(-ive); sans méchanceté

**harmony** ['hɑ:mənɪ] *n* harmonie *f*

**harness** ['hɑ:nɪs] *n* harnais *m*; *(safety ~)* harnais de sécurité ♦ *vt (horse)* harnacher; *(resources)* exploiter

**harp** [hɑ:p] *n* harpe *f* ♦ *vi*: **to ~ on about** rabâcher

**harrowing** ['hærəʊɪŋ] *adj* déchirant(e), très pénible

**harsh** [hɑ:ʃ] *adj (hard)* dur(e); *(severe)* sévère; *(unpleasant: sound)* discordant(e); *(: light)* cru(e)

**harvest** ['hɑ:vɪst] *n (of corn)* moisson *f*; *(of fruit)* récolte *f*; *(of grapes)* vendange *f* ♦ *vt* moissonner; récolter; vendanger

**has** [hæz] *vb see* **have**

**hash** [hæʃ] *n (CULIN)* hachis *m*; *(fig: mess)* gâchis *m*

**hasn't** ['hæznt] = **has not**

**hassle** ['hæsl] *n (inf: bother)* histoires *fpl*, tracas *mpl*

**haste** [heɪst] *n* hâte *f*; précipitation *f*; **~n** ['heɪsn] *vt* hâter, accélérer ♦ *vi* s'empresser; **hastily** *adv* à la hâte; précipitamment; **hasty** *adj* hâtif(-ive); précipité(e)

**hat** [hæt] *n* chapeau *m*

**hatch** [hætʃ] *n (NAUT: also: ~way)* écoutille *f*; *(also: service ~)* passe-plats *m inv* ♦ *vi* éclore; **~back** *n (AUT)* modèle *m* avec hayon arrière

**hatchet** ['hætʃɪt] *n* hachette *f*

**hate** [heɪt] *vt* haïr, détester ♦ *n* haine *f*; **~ful** *adj* odieux(-euse), détestable; **hatred** ['heɪtrɪd] *n* haine *f*

**haughty** ['hɔ:tɪ] *adj* hautain(e), arrogant(e)

**haul** [hɔ:l] *vt* traîner, tirer ♦ *n (of fish)* prise *f*; *(of stolen goods etc)* butin *m*; **~age** *n* transport routier; *(costs)* frais *mpl* de transport; **~ier** ['hɔ:lɪə*] *(US* **hauler)** *n (company)* transporteur (routier); *(driver)* camionneur *m*

**haunch** [hɔ:ntʃ] *n* hanche *f*; *(of meat)* cuissot *m*

**haunt** [hɔ:nt] *vt (subj: ghost, fear)* hanter; *(: person)* fréquenter ♦ *n* repaire *m*

KEYWORD

**have** [hæv] *(pt, pp* **had)** *aux vb* **1** *(gen)* avoir; être; **to have arrived/gone** être arrivé(e)/allé(e); **to have eaten/slept** avoir mangé/dormi; **he has been promoted** il a eu une promotion

**2** *(in tag questions)*: **you've done it, haven't you?** vous l'avez fait, n'est-ce pas?

**3** *(in short answers and questions)*: **no I haven't/yes we have!** mais non!/mais si!; **so I have!** ah oui!, oui c'est vrai!; **I've been there before, have you?** j'y suis déjà allé, et vous?

♦ *modal aux vb (be obliged)*: **to have (got) to do sth** devoir faire qch; être obligé(e) de faire qch; **she has (got)**

to do it elle doit le faire, il faut qu'elle le fasse; **you haven't to tell her** vous ne devez pas le lui dire

♦ vt **1** (*possess, obtain*) avoir; **he has (got) blue eyes/dark hair** il a les yeux bleus/les cheveux bruns; **may I have your address?** puis-je avoir votre adresse?

**2** (*+noun: take, hold etc*): **to have breakfast/a bath/a shower** prendre le petit déjeuner/un bain/une douche; **to have dinner/lunch** dîner/déjeuner; **to have a swim** nager; **to have a meeting** se réunir; **to have a party** organiser une fête

**3**: **to have sth done** faire faire qch; **to have one's hair cut** se faire couper les cheveux; **to have sb do sth** faire faire qch à qn

**4** (*experience, suffer*) avoir; **to have a cold/flu** avoir un rhume/la grippe; **to have an operation** se faire opérer

**5** (*inf: dupe*) avoir; **he's been had** il s'est fait avoir *or* rouler

**have out** vt: **to have it out with sb** (*settle a problem etc*) s'expliquer (franchement) avec qn

**haven** ['heɪvn] n port m; (*fig*) havre m

**haven't** ['hævnt] = **have not**

**havoc** ['hævək] n ravages mpl

**hawk** [hɔːk] n faucon m

**hay** [heɪ] n foin m; ~ **fever** n rhume m des foins; ~**stack** n meule f de foin

**haywire** (*inf*) adj: **to go** ~ (*machine*) se détraquer; (*plans*) mal tourner

**hazard** ['hæzəd] n (*danger*) danger m, risque m ♦ vt risquer, hasarder; ~ **(warning) lights** (AUT) feux mpl de détresse

**haze** [heɪz] n brume f

**hazelnut** ['heɪzlnʌt] n noisette f

**hazy** ['heɪzɪ] adj brumeux(-euse); (*idea*) vague

**he** [hiː] pron il; **it is** ~ **who** ... c'est lui qui ...

**head** [hɛd] n tête f; (*leader*) chef m; (*of*

*school*) directeur(-trice) ♦ vt (*list*) être en tête de; (*group*) être à la tête de; ~**s (or tails)** pile (ou face); ~ **first** tête la première; ~ **over heels in love** follement *or* éperdument amoureux(-euse); **to** ~ **a ball** faire une tête; ~ **for** vt fus se diriger vers; ~**ache** n mal m de tête; ~**dress** (BRIT) n (*of Red Indian etc*) coiffure f; ~**ing** n titre m; ~**lamp** (BRIT) n phare m; ~**light** n phare m; ~**land** n promontoire m, cap m; ~**line** n titre m; ~**long** adv (*fall*) la tête la première; (*rush*) tête baissée; ~**master** n directeur m; ~**mistress** n directrice f; ~ **office** n bureau central, siège m; ~-**on** adj (*collision*) de plein fouet; (*confrontation*) en face à face; ~**phones** npl casque m (à écouteurs); ~**quarters** npl bureau *or* siège central; (MIL) quartier général; ~**rest** n appui-tête m; ~**room** n (*in car*) hauteur f de plafond; (*under bridge*) hauteur limite; ~**scarf** n foulard m; ~**strong** adj têtu(e), entêté(e); ~ **teacher** n directeur(-trice); (*of secondary school*) proviseur m; ~ **waiter** n maître d'hôtel; ~**way** n: **to make** ~**way** avancer, faire des progrès; ~**wind** n vent m contraire; (NAUT) vent debout; ~**y** adj capiteux(-euse); enivrant(e); (*experience*) grisant(e)

**heal** [hiːl] vt, vi guérir

**health** [hɛlθ] n santé f; ~ **food** n aliment(s) naturel(s); ~ **food shop** n magasin m diététique; **H~ Service** n: **the H~ Service** ≈ la Sécurité sociale; ~**y** adj (*person*) en bonne santé; (*climate, food, attitude etc*) sain(e), bon(ne) pour la santé

**heap** [hiːp] n tas m ♦ vt: **to** ~ **(up)** entasser, amonceler; **she** ~**ed her plate with cakes** elle a chargé son assiette de gâteaux

**hear** [hɪəʳ] (*pt, pp* **heard**) vt entendre; (*news*) apprendre ♦ vi entendre; **to** ~ **about** entendre parler de; avoir des nouvelles de; **to** ~ **from sb** recevoir *or* avoir des nouvelles de qn; ~**ing** n (*sense*) ouïe *f*; (*of witnesses*) audition *f*; (*of a case*) audience *f*; **~ing aid** *n* appareil *m* acoustique; **~say:** by **~say** *adv* par ouï-dire *m*

**hearse** [hə:s] *n* corbillard *m*

**heart** [hɑ:t] *n* cœur *m*; **~s** *npl* (CARDS) cœur; **to lose/take ~** perdre/prendre courage; **at ~** au fond; **by ~** (*learn, know*) par cœur; **~ attack** *n* crise cardiaque; **~beat** *n* battement *m* du cœur; **~breaking** *adj* déchirant(e), qui fend le cœur; **~broken** *adj*: **to be ~broken** avoir beaucoup de chagrin ou le cœur brisé; **~burn** *n* brûlures *fpl* d'estomac; **~ failure** *n* arrêt *m* du cœur; **~felt** *adj* sincère

**hearth** [hɑ:θ] *n* foyer *m*, cheminée *f*

**heartily** ['hɑ:tɪlɪ] *adv* chaleureusement; (*laugh*) de bon cœur; (*eat*) de bon appétit; **to agree ~** être entièrement d'accord

**hearty** ['hɑ:tɪ] *adj* chaleureux(-euse); (*appetite*) robuste; (*dislike*) cordial(e)

**heat** [hi:t] *n* chaleur *f*; (*fig*) feu *m*, agitation *f*; (SPORT: *also:* **qualifying ~**) éliminatoire *f* ♦ *vt* chauffer; **~ up** *vi* (*water*) chauffer; (*room*) se réchauffer ♦ *vt* réchauffer; **~ed** *adj* chauffé(e); (*fig*) passionné(e), échauffé(e); **~er** *n* appareil *m* de chauffage; radiateur *m*; (*in car*) chauffage *m*; (*water heater*) chauffe-eau *m*

**heath** [hi:θ] (BRIT) *n* lande *f*

**heather** ['heðə'] *n* bruyère *f*

**heating** ['hi:tɪŋ] *n* chauffage *m*

**heatstroke** ['hi:tstrəuk] *n* (MED) coup *m* de chaleur

**heat wave** *n* vague *f* de chaleur

**heave** [hi:v] *vt* soulever (avec effort); (*drag*) traîner ♦ *vi* se soulever; (*retch*) avoir un haut-le-cœur; **to ~ a sigh** pousser un soupir

**heaven** ['hevn] *n* ciel *m*, paradis *m*; (*fig*) paradis; **~ly** *adj* céleste, divin(e)

**heavily** ['hevɪlɪ] *adv* lourdement; (*drink, smoke*) beaucoup; (*sleep, sigh*) profondément

**heavy** ['hevɪ] *adj* lourd(e); (*work, sea, rain, eater*) gros(se); (*snow*) beaucoup de; (*drinker, smoker*) grand(e); (*breathing*) bruyant(e); (*schedule, week*) chargé(e) ♦ (SPORT) poids lourd; **~ goods vehicle** *n* poids lourd; **~weight** *n* (SPORT) poids lourd

**Hebrew** ['hi:bru:] *adj* hébraïque ♦ *n* (LING) hébreu *m*

**Hebrides** ['hebrɪdi:z] *npl*: **the ~** les Hébrides *fpl*

**heckle** ['hekl] *vt* interpeller (*un orateur*)

**hectic** ['hektɪk] *adj* agité(e), trépidant(e)

**he'd** [hi:d] = **he would; he had**

**hedge** [hedʒ] *n* haie *f* ♦ *vi* se dérober; **to ~ one's bets** se couvrir

**hedgehog** ['hedʒhɔg] *n* hérisson *m*

**heed** [hi:d] *vt* (*also:* **take ~ of**) tenir compte de; **~less** *adj* insouciant(e)

**heel** [hi:l] *n* talon *m* ♦ *vt* retalonner

**hefty** ['heftɪ] *adj* (*person*) costaud(e); (*parcel*) lourd(e); (*profit*) gros(se)

**heifer** ['hefə'] *n* génisse *f*

**height** [haɪt] *n* (*of person*) taille *f*, grandeur *f*; (*of object*) hauteur *f*; (*of plane, mountain*) altitude *f*; (*high ground*) hauteur, éminence *f*; (*fig: of glory*) sommet *m*; (*: of luxury, stupidity*) comble *m*; **~en** *vt* (*fig*) augmenter

**heir** [εə'] *n* héritier *m*; **~ess** *n* héritière *f*; **~loom** *n* héritage *m*, meuble (*or* bijou *or* tableau *m*) de famille

**held** [held] *pt, pp of* **hold**

**helicopter** ['helɪkɔptə'] *n* hélicoptère *m*

**hell** [hel] *n* enfer *m*; **~!** (*inf*) merde!

**he'll** [hi:l] = **he will; he shall**

**hellish** ['helɪʃ] (*inf*) *adj* infernal(e)

**hello** [hə'ləu] *excl* bonjour!; (*to attract attention*) hé!; (*surprise*) tiens!

**helm** [helm] *n* (NAUT) barre *f*

**helmet** ['helmɪt] *n* casque *m*

**help** [help] *n* aide *f*; (*charwoman*) femme *f* de ménage ♦ *vt* aider; **~!** au secours!; **~ yourself** servez-vous; **he can't ~ it** il ne peut pas s'en empêcher; **~er** *n* aide *m/f*, assistant(e); **~ful** *adj* serviable, obligeant(e); (*useful*) utile;

**~ing** n portion f; **~less** adj impuissant(e); (defenceless) faible

**hem** [hem] n ourlet m ♦ vt ourler; **~ in** vt cerner

**hemorrhage** ['hemərɪdʒ] (US) n = **haemorrhage**

**hemorrhoids** ['hemərɔɪdz] (US) npl = **haemorrhoids**

**hen** [hen] n poule f

**hence** [hens] adv (therefore) d'où, de là; **2 years ~** d'ici 2 ans, dans 2 ans; **~forth** adv dorénavant

**her** [hɜːʳ] pron (direct) la, l'; (indirect) lui, (stressed, after prep) elle ♦ adj son (sa), ses pl; see also **me; my**

**herald** ['herəld] n héraut m ♦ vt annoncer; **~ry** n (study) héraldique f; (coat of arms) blason m

**herb** [hɜːb] n herbe f

**herd** [hɜːd] n troupeau m

**here** [hɪəʳ] adv (time) alors ♦ excl tiens!, tenez!; **~ is, ~ are** voici; **~ he/she is!** le/la voici!; **~after** adv après, plus tard; **~by** adv (formal: in letter) par la présente

**hereditary** [hɪ'redɪtrɪ] adj héréditaire

**heresy** ['herəsɪ] n hérésie f

**heritage** ['herɪtɪdʒ] n (of country) patrimoine m

**hermit** ['hɜːmɪt] n ermite m

**hernia** ['hɜːnɪə] n hernie f

**hero** ['hɪərəʊ] (pl **~es**) n héros m

**heroin** ['herəʊɪn] n héroïne f

**heroine** ['herəʊɪn] n héroïne f

**heron** ['herən] n héron m

**herring** ['herɪŋ] n hareng m

**hers** [hɜːz] pron le (la) sien(ne), les siens (siennes); see also **mine¹**

**herself** [hɜː'self] pron (reflexive) se; (emphatic) elle-même; (after prep) elle; see also **oneself**

**he's** [hiːz] = **he is; he has**

**hesitant** ['hezɪtənt] adj hésitant(e), indécis(e)

**hesitate** ['hezɪteɪt] vi hésiter; **hesitation** [hezɪ'teɪʃən] n hésitation f

**heterosexual** ['hetərəʊ'seksjʊəl] adj, n

hétérosexuel(le)

**heyday** ['heɪdeɪ] n: the **~ of** l'âge m d'or de, les beaux jours de

**HGV** n abbr = **heavy goods vehicle**

**hi** [haɪ] excl salut!; (to attract attention) hé!

**hiatus** [haɪ'eɪtəs] n (gap) lacune f; (interruption) pause f

**hibernate** ['haɪbəneɪt] vi hiberner

**hiccough, hiccup** ['hɪkʌp] vi hoqueter; **~s** npl hoquet m

**hide** [haɪd] (pt **hid**, pp **hidden**) n (skin) peau f ♦ vt cacher ♦ vi: to **~ (from sb)** se cacher (de qn); **~-and-seek** n cache-cache m

**hideous** ['hɪdɪəs] adj hideux(-euse)

**hiding** ['haɪdɪŋ] n (beating) correction f, volée f de coups; to **be in ~** (concealed) se tenir caché(e)

**hierarchy** ['haɪərɑːkɪ] n hiérarchie f

**hi-fi** ['haɪfaɪ] n hi-fi f inv ♦ adj hi-fi inv

**high** [haɪ] adj haut(e); (speed, respect, number) grand(e); (price) élevé(e); (wind) fort(e), violent(e); (voice) aigu (aiguë) ♦ adv haut; **20 m ~** haut(e de 20 m; **~brow** adj, n intellectuel(le); **~chair** n (child's) chaise haute; **~ education** n études supérieures; **~-handed** adj très autoritaire; très cavalier(-ère); **~-heeled** adj à hauts talons; **~ jump** n (SPORT) saut m en hauteur; **~lands** npl Highlands mpl; **~light** n (fig: of event) point culminant ♦ vt faire ressortir, souligner; **~lights** npl (in hair) reflets mpl; **~ly** adv très fort, hautement; to **speak/think ~ly of sb** dire/penser beaucoup de bien de qn; **~ly paid** adj très bien payé(e); **~ly strung** adj nerveux(-euse), toujours tendu(e); **~ness** n: Her (or His) H**~ness** Son Altesse f; **~-pitched** adj aigu (aiguë); **~-rise** adj: **~-rise block, ~-rise flats** tour f (d'habitation); **~ school** n lycée m; (US) établissement m d'enseignement supérieur; **~ season** (BRIT) n haute saison; **~ street** (BRIT) n grand-rue f; **~way** n route nationale;

**H~way Code** (BRIT) n code m de la route

**hijack** ['haɪdʒæk] vt (plane) détourner; **~er** n pirate m de l'air

**hike** [haɪk] vi aller or faire des excursions à pied ♦ n excursion f à pied, randonnée f; **~r** n promeneur(-euse), excursionniste m/f; **hiking** n excursions fpl à pied

**hilarious** [hɪ'lɛərɪəs] adj (account, event) désopilant(e)

**hill** [hɪl] n colline f; (fairly high) montagne f; (on road) côte f; **~side** n (flanc m de) coteau m; **~-walking** n randonnée f de basse montagne; **~y** adj vallonné(e); montagneux(-euse)

**hilt** [hɪlt] n (of sword) garde f; **to the ~** (fig: support) à fond

**him** [hɪm] pron (direct) le, l'; (stressed, indirect, after prep) lui; see also me; **~self** pron (reflexive) se; (emphatic) lui-même; (after prep) lui; see also oneself

**hinder** ['hɪndə*] vt gêner; (delay) retarder; **hindrance** n gêne f, obstacle m

**hindsight** ['haɪndsaɪt] n: **with ~** avec du recul, rétrospective

**Hindu** ['hɪndu:] adj hindou(e)

**hinge** [hɪndʒ] n charnière f ♦ vi (fig): **to ~ on** dépendre de

**hint** [hɪnt] n allusion f; (advice) conseil m ♦ vt: **to ~ that** insinuer que ♦ vi: **to ~ at** faire une allusion à

**hip** [hɪp] n hanche f

**hippie** ['hɪpɪ] n hippie m/f

**hippo** ['hɪpəu] (pl ~s), **hippopotamus** [hɪpə'pɔtəməs] (pl **~potamuses** or **~potami**) n hippopotame m

**hire** ['haɪə*] vt (BRIT: car, equipment) louer; (worker) embaucher, engager ♦ n location f; **for ~** à louer; (taxi) libre; **~(d) car** n voiture f de location; **~ purchase** (BRIT) n achat m (or vente f) à tempérament or crédit

**his** [hɪz] pron le (la) sien(ne), les siens (siennes) ♦ adj son (sa), ses pl; see also my; **mine¹**

**hiss** [hɪs] vi siffler

**historic** [hɪ'stɔrɪk] adj historique; **~al** adj historique

**history** ['hɪstərɪ] n histoire f

**hit** [hɪt] (pt, pp hit) vt frapper; (reach: target) atteindre, toucher; (collide with: car) entrer en collision avec, heurter; (fig: affect) toucher ♦ n coup m; (: success) succès m; (: song) tube m; **to ~ it off with sb** bien s'entendre avec qn; **~-and-run driver** n chauffard m (coupable du délit de fuite)

**hitch** [hɪtʃ] vt (fasten) accrocher, attacher; (also: **~ up**) remonter d'une saccade ♦ n (difficulty) anicroche f, contretemps m; **to ~ a lift** faire du stop; **~hike** vi faire de l'auto-stop; **~hiker** n auto-stoppeur(-euse)

**hi-tech** ['haɪ'tɛk] adj de pointe

**hitherto** [hɪðə'tu:] adv jusqu'ici

**hit man** n tueur m à gages

**HIV** n: **~-negative/-positive** adj séronégatif(-ive)/-positif(-ive)

**hive** [haɪv] n ruche f

**HMS** abbr = Her/His Majesty's Ship

**hoard** [hɔ:d] n (of food) provisions fpl, réserves fpl; (of money) trésor m ♦ vt amasser; **~ing** (BRIT) n (for posters) panneau m d'affichage or publicitaire

**hoarse** [hɔ:s] adj enroué(e)

**hoax** [həuks] n canular m

**hob** [hɔb] n plaque (chauffante)

**hobble** ['hɔbl] vi boitiller

**hobby** ['hɔbɪ] n passe-temps favori

**hobo** ['həubəu] (US) n vagabond m

**hockey** ['hɔkɪ] n hockey m

**hog** [hɔg] n porc (châtré) ♦ vt (fig) accaparer; **to go the whole ~** aller jusqu'au bout

**hoist** [hɔɪst] n (apparatus) palan m ♦ vt hisser

**hold** [həuld] (pt, pp held) vt tenir; (contain) contenir; (believe) considérer; (possess) avoir; (detain) détenir ♦ vt (withstand pressure) tenir (bon); (be valid) valoir ♦ n prise f; (fig) influence f; (NAUT) cale f; **~ the line!** (TEL) ne quittez pas!; **to ~ one's own** (fig) (bien) se défendre; **to catch** or **get (a) ~ of** saisir; **to get ~ of** (fig) trouver; **~ back** vt retenir; (secret) taire; **~ down** vt (person) maintenir à terre; (job) occuper; **~ off** vt tenir à distance; **~ on** vi tenir bon; (wait) attendre; **~ on!** (TEL) ne quittez pas!; **~ on to** vt fus se cramponner à; (keep) conserver, garder; **~ out** vt offrir ♦ vi (resist) tenir bon; **~ up** vt (raise) lever; (support) soutenir; (delay) retarder; (rob) braquer; **~all** (BRIT) n fourre-tout m inv; **~er** n (of ticket, record) détenteur(-trice); (of office, title etc) titulaire m/f; (container) support m; **~ing** n (share) intérêts mpl; (farm) ferme f; **~up** n (robbery) hold-up m; (delay) retard m; (BRIT: in traffic) bouchon m.

**hole** [həul] n trou m; **~-in-the-wall** n (cash dispenser) distributeur m de billets

**holiday** ['hɔlədeɪ] n vacances fpl; (day off) jour m de congé; (public) jour m férié; **on ~** en congé; **~ camp** n (also: **~ centre**) camp m de vacances; **~ maker** n (BRIT) vacancier(-ère); **~ resort** n centre m de villégiature or de vacances

**Holland** ['hɔlənd] n Hollande f

**hollow** ['hɔləu] adj creux(-euse) ♦ n creux m ♦ vt: **to ~ out** creuser, évider

**holly** ['hɔlɪ] n houx m

**holocaust** ['hɔləkɔːst] n holocauste m

**holster** ['həulstə*] n étui m de revolver

**holy** ['həulɪ] adj saint(e); (bread, water) bénit(e); (ground) sacré(e); **H~ Ghost** n Saint-Esprit m

**homage** ['hɔmɪdʒ] n hommage m; **to pay ~ to** rendre hommage à

**home** [həum] n foyer m, maison f; (country) pays natal, patrie f; (institution) maison ♦ adj de famille; (ECON, POL) national(e), intérieur(e); (SPORT: game) sur leur or notre terrain; (team) qui reçoit ♦ adv chez soi, à la maison; au pays natal; (right in: nail etc) à fond; **at ~** chez soi, à la maison; **make yourself at ~** faites comme chez vous; **~ address** n domicile permanent;

**~land** n patrie f; **~less** adj sans foyer; sans abri; **~ly** adj (plain) simple, sans prétention; **~-made** adj fait(e) à la maison; **~ match** n match m à domicile; **H~ Office** (BRIT) n ministère m de l'Intérieur; **~ page** n (COMPUT) page f d'accueil; **~ rule** n autonomie f; **H~ Secretary** (BRIT) n ministre m de l'Intérieur; **~sick** adj: **to be ~sick** avoir le mal du pays; s'ennuyer de sa famille; **~ town** n ville natale; **~ward** adj (journey) du retour; **~work** n devoirs mpl

**homoeopathic** [həumɪəu'pæθɪk] (US **homeopathic**) adj (medicine, methods) homéopathique; (doctor) homéopathe

**homogeneous** [hɔməu'dʒiːnɪəs] adj homogène

**homosexual** [hɔməu'seksjuəl] adj, n homosexuel(le)

**honest** ['ɔnɪst] adj honnête; (sincere) franc (franche); **~ly** adv honnêtement; franchement; **~y** n honnêteté f

**honey** ['hʌnɪ] n miel m; **~comb** n rayon m de miel; **~moon** n lune f de miel, voyage m de noces; **~suckle** (BOT) n chèvrefeuille m

**honk** [hɔŋk] vi (AUT) klaxonner

**honorary** ['ɔnərərɪ] adj honoraire; (duty, title) honorifique

**honour** ['ɔnə*] (US **honor**) vt honorer ♦ n honneur m; **hono(u)rable** adj honorable; **hono(u)rs degree** n (SCOL) licence avec mention

**hood** [hud] n capuchon m; (of cooker) hotte f; (AUT: BRIT) capote f; (: US) capot m

**hoof** [huːf] (pl **hooves**) n sabot m

**hook** [huk] n crochet m; (on dress) agrafe f; (for fishing) hameçon m ♦ vt accrocher; (fish) prendre

**hooligan** ['huːlɪgən] n voyou m

**hoop** [huːp] n cerceau m

**hooray** [huː'reɪ] excl hourra

**hoot** [huːt] vi (AUT) klaxonner; (siren) mugir; (owl) hululer; **~er** n (BRIT: AUT) klaxon m; (NAUT, factory) sirène f

**Hoover** ® ['huːvə*] (BRIT) n aspirateur

$m$ ♦ vt: **h~** passer l'aspirateur dans or sur

**hooves** [huːvz] npl of **hoof**

**hop** [hɔp] vi (on one foot) sauter à cloche-pied; (bird) sautiller

**hope** [həup] vt, vi espérer ♦ n espoir m; **I ~ so** je l'espère; **I ~ not** j'espère que non; **~ful** adj (person) plein(e) d'espoir; (situation) prometteur(-euse), encourageant(e); **~fully** adv (expectantly) avec espoir, avec optimisme; (one hopes) avec un peu de chance; **~less** adj désespéré(e); (useless) nul(le)

**hops** [hɔps] npl houblon m

**horizon** [həˈraɪzn] n horizon m; **~tal** [hɔrɪˈzɔntl] adj horizontal(e)

**horn** [hɔːn] n corne f; (MUS: also: **French ~**) cor m; (AUT) klaxon m

**hornet** [ˈhɔːnɪt] n frelon m

**horoscope** [ˈhɔrəskəup] n horoscope m

**horrendous** [həˈrendəs] adj horrible, affreux(-euse)

**horrible** [ˈhɔrɪbl] adj horrible, affreux (-euse)

**horrid** [ˈhɔrɪd] adj épouvantable

**horrify** [ˈhɔrɪfaɪ] vt horrifier

**horror** [ˈhɔrə*] n horreur f; **~ film** n film m d'épouvante

**hors d'œuvre** [ɔːˈdəːvrə] n (CULIN) hors-d'œuvre m inv

**horse** [hɔːs] n cheval m; **~back** n: on **~back** à cheval; **~ chestnut** n marron m (d'Inde); **~man** (irreg) n cavalier m; **~power** n puissance f (en chevaux); **~-racing** n courses fpl de chevaux; **~radish** n raifort m; **~shoe** n fer m à cheval

**hose** [həuz] n (also: **~pipe**) tuyau m; (also: **garden ~**) tuyau d'arrosage

**hospitable** [ˈhɔspɪtəbl] adj hospitalier(-ère)

**hospital** [ˈhɔspɪtl] n hôpital m; **in ~** à l'hôpital

**hospitality** [hɔspɪˈtælɪtɪ] n hospitalité f

**host** [həust] n hôte m; (TV, RADIO) animateur(-trice); (REL) hostie f; (large

number): **a ~ of** une foule de

**hostage** [ˈhɔstɪdʒ] n otage m

**hostel** [ˈhɔstl] n foyer m; (also: **youth ~**) auberge f de jeunesse

**hostess** [ˈhəustɪs] n hôtesse f; (TV, RADIO) animatrice f

**hostile** [ˈhɔstaɪl] adj hostile; **hostility** [hɔˈstɪlɪtɪ] n hostilité f

**hot** [hɔt] adj chaud(e); (as opposed to only warm) très chaud; (spicy) fort(e); (contest etc) acharné(e); (temper) passionné(e); **to be ~** (person) avoir chaud; (object) être très chaud; (weather) il fait chaud; **~bed** n (fig) foyer m, pépinière f; **~ dog** n hot-dog m

**hotel** [həuˈtel] n hôtel m

**hot: ~house** n serre (chaude); **~line** n (POL) téléphone m rouge, ligne directe; **~ly** adv passionnément, violemment; **~plate** n (on cooker) plaque chauffante; **~pot** (BRIT) n ragoût m, ≈ hachis; **~-water bottle** n bouillotte f

**hound** [haund] vt poursuivre avec acharnement ♦ n chien courant

**hour** [ˈauə*] n heure f; **~ly** adj, adv toutes les heures; (rate) horaire

**house** [n haus, vb hauz] n maison f; (POL) chambre f; (THEATRE) salle f, auditoire m ♦ vt (person) loger, héberger; (objects) abriter; on the **~** (fig) aux frais de la maison; **~ arrest** n assignation f à résidence; **~boat** n bateau m (aménagé en habitation); **~bound** adj confiné(e) chez soi; **~breaking** n cambriolage m (avec effraction); **~hold** n (persons) famille f, maisonnée f; (ADMIN etc) ménage m; **~keeper** n gouvernante f; **~keeping** n (work) ménage m; (also: **~keeping (money)**) argent m du ménage; **~-warming (party)** n pendaison f de crémaillère; **~wife** (irreg) n ménagère f; femme f au foyer; **~work** n (travaux mpl du) ménage m

**housing** [ˈhauzɪŋ] n logement m; **~ development**, **~ estate** n lotissement m

**hovel** ['hɔvl] n taudis m

**hover** ['hɔvəʳ] vi planer; **~craft** n aéroglisseur m

**how** [hau] adv comment; **~ are you?** comment allez-vous?; **~ do you do?** bonjour; enchanté(e); **~ far is it to?** combien y a-t-il jusqu'à ...?; **~ long have you been here?** depuis combien de temps êtes-vous là?; **~ lovely!** que or comme c'est joli!; **~ many/much?** combien?; **~ many people/much milk?** combien de gens/lait?; **~ old are you?** quel âge avez-vous?

**however** [hau'evəʳ] adv de quelque façon or manière que +subj; (+adj) quelque or si ... que +subj; (in questions) comment ♦ conj pourtant, cependant

**howl** [haul] vi hurler

**H.P.** abbr = **hire purchase**

**h.p.** abbr = **horsepower**

**HQ** abbr = **headquarters**

**hub** [hʌb] n (of wheel) moyeu m; (fig) centre m, foyer m; **~cap** n enjoliveur m

**huddle** ['hʌdl] vi: **to ~ together** se blottir les uns contre les autres

**hue** [hju:] n teinte f, nuance f

**huff** [hʌf] n: **in a ~** fâché(e)

**hug** [hʌg] vt serrer dans ses bras; (shore, kerb) serrer

**huge** [hju:dʒ] adj énorme, immense

**hulk** [hʌlk] n (ship) épave f; (car, building) carcasse f; (person) mastodonte m

**hull** [hʌl] n (of ship) coque f

**hullo** [hə'ləu] excl = **hello**

**hum** [hʌm] vt (tune) fredonner ♦ vi fredonner; (insect) bourdonner; (plane, tool) vrombir

**human** ['hju:mən] adj humain(e) ♦ n: **~ being** être humain; **~e** [hju:'meɪn] adj humain(e), humanitaire; **~itarian** [hju:mænɪ'tɛərɪən] adj humanitaire; **~ity** [hju:'mænɪtɪ] n humanité f

**humble** ['hʌmbl] adj humble, modeste ♦ vt humilier

**humdrum** ['hʌmdrʌm] adj monotone, banal(e)

**humid** ['hju:mɪd] adj humide

**humiliate** [hju:'mɪlɪeɪt] vt humilier

**humiliation** [hju:mɪlɪ'eɪʃən] n humiliation f

**humorous** ['hju:mərəs] adj humoristique; (person) plein(e) d'humour

**humour** ['hju:məʳ] (US **humor**) n humour m; (mood) humeur f ♦ vt (person) faire plaisir à; se prêter aux caprices de

**hump** [hʌmp] n bosse f

**hunch** [hʌntʃ] n (premonition) intuition f; **~back** n bossu(e); **~ed** adj voûté(e)

**hundred** ['hʌndrəd] num cent; **~s of** des centaines de; **~weight** n (BRIT) 50.8 kg, 112 lb; (US) 45.3 kg, 100 lb

**hung** [hʌŋ] pt, pp of **hang**

**Hungary** ['hʌŋgərɪ] n Hongrie f

**hunger** ['hʌŋgəʳ] n faim f ♦ vi: **to ~ for** avoir faim de, désirer ardemment

**hungry** ['hʌŋgrɪ] adj affamé(e); (keen): **~ for** avide de; **to be ~** avoir faim

**hunk** [hʌŋk] n (of bread etc) gros morceau

**hunt** [hʌnt] vt chasser; (criminal) pourchasser ♦ vi chasser; (search): **to ~ for** chercher (partout) ♦ n chasse f; **~er** n chasseur m; **~ing** n chasse f

**hurdle** ['hɜ:dl] n (SPORT) haie f; (fig) obstacle m

**hurl** [hɜ:l] vt lancer (avec violence); (abuse, insults) lancer

**hurrah** [hu'ra:] excl = **hooray**

**hurray** [hu'reɪ] excl = **hooray**

**hurricane** ['hʌrɪkən] n ouragan m

**hurried** ['hʌrɪd] adj pressé(e), précipité(e); (work) fait(e) à la hâte; **~ly** adv précipitamment, à la hâte

**hurry** ['hʌrɪ] (vb: also: **~ up**) n hâte f, précipitation f ♦ vi se presser, se dépêcher ♦ vt (person) faire presser, faire se dépêcher; (work) presser; **to be in a ~** être pressé(e); **to do sth in a ~** faire qch en vitesse; **to ~ in/out** entrer/sortir précipitamment

**hurt** [hɜ:t] (pt, pp **hurt**) vt (cause pain to) faire mal à; (injure, fig) blesser ♦ vi faire mal ♦ adj blessé(e); **~ful** adj (remark) blessant(e)

**hurtle** ['hɜːtl] *vi*: **to ~ past** passer en trombe; **to ~ down** dégringoler

**husband** ['hʌzbənd] *n* mari *m*

**hush** [hʌʃ] *n* calme *m*, silence *m* ♦ *vt* faire taire; **~!** chut!; **~ up** *vt* (*scandal*) étouffer

**husk** [hʌsk] *n* (*of wheat*) balle *f*; (*of rice, maize*) enveloppe *f*

**husky** ['hʌskɪ] *adj* rauque ♦ *n* chien *m* esquimau *or* de traîneau

**hustle** ['hʌsl] *vt* pousser, bousculer ♦ *n*: **~ and bustle** tourbillon *m* (d'activité)

**hut** [hʌt] *n* hutte *f*; (*shed*) cabane *f*

**hutch** [hʌtʃ] *n* clapier *m*

**hyacinth** ['haɪəsɪnθ] *n* jacinthe *f*

**hydrant** ['haɪdrənt] *n*, *also*: **fire ~**) bouche *f* d'incendie

**hydraulic** [haɪ'drɔːlɪk] *adj* hydraulique

**hydroelectric** ['haɪdrəʊ'lektrɪk] *adj* hydro-électrique

**hydrofoil** ['haɪdrəfɔɪl] *n* hydrofoil *m*

**hydrogen** ['haɪdrədʒən] *n* hydrogène *m*

**hyena** [haɪ'iːnə] *n* hyène *f*

**hygiene** ['haɪdʒiːn] *n* hygiène *f*; **hygienic** *adj* hygiénique

**hymn** [hɪm] *n* hymne *m*; cantique *m*

**hype** [haɪp] (*inf*) *n* battage *m* publicitaire

**hypermarket** ['haɪpəmɑːkɪt] (*BRIT*) *n* hypermarché *m*

**hypertext** ['haɪpətekst] *n* (*COMPUT*) hypertexte *m*

**hyphen** ['haɪfn] *n* trait *m* d'union

**hypnotize** ['hɪpnətaɪz] *vt* hypnotiser

**hypocrisy** [hɪ'pɒkrɪsɪ] *n* hypocrisie *f*; **hypocrite** ['hɪpəkrɪt] *n* hypocrite *m/f*; **hypocritical** *adj* hypocrite

**hypothesis** [haɪ'pɒθɪsɪs] (*pl* **hypotheses**) *n* hypothèse *f*

**hysterical** [hɪ'sterɪkl] *adj* hystérique; (*funny*) hilarant(e); **~ laughter** fou rire *m*

**hysterics** [hɪ'sterɪks] *npl*: **to be in/have ~** (*anger, panic*) avoir une crise de nerfs; (*laughter*) attraper un fou rire

## I, i

**I** [aɪ] *pron* je; (*before vowel*) j'; (*stressed*) moi

**ice** [aɪs] *n* glace *f*; (*on road*) verglas *m* ♦ *vt* (*cake*) glacer ♦ *vi* (*also*: **~ over, ~ up**) geler; (*window*) se givrer; **~berg** *n* iceberg *m*; **~box** *n* (*US*) réfrigérateur *m*; (*BRIT*) compartiment *m* à glace; (*insulated box*) glacière *f*; **~ cream** *n* glace *f*; **~ cube** *n* glaçon *m*; **~d** *adj* glacé(e); **~ hockey** *n* hockey *m* sur glace; **Iceland** *n* Islande *f*; **~ lolly** *n* (*BRIT*) esquimau *m* (glace); **~ rink** *n* patinoire *f*; **~-skating** *n* patinage *m* (sur glace)

**icicle** ['aɪsɪkl] *n* glaçon *m* (*naturel*)

**icing** ['aɪsɪŋ] *n* (*CULIN*) glace *f*; **~ sugar** *n* (*BRIT*) *n* sucre *m* glace

**icy** ['aɪsɪ] *adj* glacé(e); (*road*) verglacé(e); (*weather, temperature*) glacial(e)

**I'd** [aɪd] = I would; I had

**idea** [aɪ'dɪə] *n* idée *f*

**ideal** [aɪ'dɪəl] *n* idéal *m* ♦ *adj* idéal(e)

**identical** [aɪ'dentɪkl] *adj* identique

**identification** [aɪdentɪfɪ'keɪʃən] *n* identification *f*; **means of ~** pièce *f* d'identité

**identify** [aɪ'dentɪfaɪ] *vt* identifier

**Identikit picture** ® [aɪ'dentɪkɪt-] *n* portrait-robot *m*

**identity** [aɪ'dentɪtɪ] *n* identité *f*; **~ card** *n* carte *f* d'identité

**ideology** [aɪdɪ'ɒlədʒɪ] *n* idéologie *f*

**idiom** ['ɪdɪəm] *n* expression *f* idiomatique; (*style*) style *m*

**idiosyncrasy** [ɪdɪəʊ'sɪŋkrəsɪ] *n* (*of person*) particularité *f*, petite manie

**idiot** ['ɪdɪət] *n* idiot(e), imbécile *m/f*; **~ic** [ɪdɪ'ɒtɪk] *adj* idiot(e), bête, stupide

**idle** ['aɪdl] *adj* sans occupation, désœuvré(e); (*lazy*) oisif(-ive), paresseux (-euse); (*unemployed*) au chômage; (*question, pleasures*) vain(e), futile ♦ *vi* (*engine*) tourner au ralenti; **to lie ~** être arrêté(e), ne pas fonctionner

# idol

# impatience

**idol** ['aɪdl] *n* idole *f*; **~ize** *vt* idolâtrer, adorer

**i.e.** *adv abbr* (= *id est*) c'est-à-dire

**if** [ɪf] *conj* si; **~ so** si c'est le cas; **~ not** sinon; **~ only** si seulement

**ignite** [ɪg'naɪt] *vt* mettre le feu à, enflammer ♦ *vi* s'enflammer; **ignition** *n* (AUT) allumage *m*; **to switch on/off the ignition** mettre/couper le contact; **ignition key** *n* clé *f* de contact

**ignorant** ['ɪgnərənt] *adj* ignorant(e); **to be ~ of** (*subject*) ne rien connaître à; (*events*) ne pas être au courant de

**ignore** [ɪg'nɔː] *vt* ne tenir aucun compte de; (*person*) faire semblant de ne pas reconnaître; (*fact*) méconnaître

**ill** [ɪl] *adj* (*sick*) malade; (*bad*) mauvais(e) ♦ *n* mal *m* ♦ *adv*: **to speak/think ~ of** dire/penser du mal de; **~s** *npl* (*misfortunes*) maux *mpl*, malheurs *mpl*; **to be taken ~** tomber malade; **~-advised** *adj* (*decision*) peu judicieux(-euse); (*person*) malavisé(e); **~-at-ease** *adj* mal à l'aise

**I'll** [aɪl] = **I will**; **I shall**

**illegal** [ɪ'liːgl] *adj* illégal(e)

**illegible** [ɪ'ledʒɪbl] *adj* illisible

**illegitimate** [ɪlɪ'dʒɪtɪmət] *adj* illégitime

**ill-fated** [ɪl'feɪtɪd] *adj* malheureux(-euse); (*day*) néfaste

**ill feeling** *n* ressentiment *m*, rancune *f*

**illiterate** [ɪ'lɪtərət] *adj* illettré(e); (*letter*) plein(e) de fautes

**ill-mannered** [ɪl'mænəd] *adj* (*child*) mal élevé(e); **~ness** *n* maladie *f*; **~treat** *vt* maltraiter

**illuminate** [ɪ'luːmɪneɪt] *vt* (*room, street*) éclairer; (*for special effect*) illuminer; **illumination** [ɪluːmɪ'neɪʃən] *n* éclairage *m*; illumination *f*

**illusion** [ɪ'luːʒən] *n* illusion *f*

**illustrate** ['ɪləstreɪt] *vt* illustrer; **illustration** [ɪlə'streɪʃən] *n* illustration *f*

**ill will** *n* malveillance *f*

**I'm** [aɪm] = **I am**

**image** ['ɪmɪdʒ] *n* image *f*; (*public face*) image de marque; **~ry** *n* images *fpl*

**imaginary** [ɪ'mædʒɪnərɪ] *adj* imaginaire

**imagination** [ɪmædʒɪ'neɪʃən] *n* imagination *f*

**imaginative** [ɪ'mædʒɪnətɪv] *adj* imaginatif(-ive); (*person*) plein(e) d'imagination

**imagine** [ɪ'mædʒɪn] *vt* imaginer, s'imaginer; (*suppose*) imaginer, supposer

**imbalance** [ɪm'bæləns] *n* déséquilibre *m*

**imitate** ['ɪmɪteɪt] *vt* imiter; **imitation** [ɪmɪ'teɪʃən] *n* imitation *f*

**immaculate** [ɪ'mækjulət] *adj* impeccable; (*REL*) immaculé(e)

**immaterial** [ɪmə'tɪərɪəl] *adj* sans importance, insignifiant(e)

**immature** [ɪmə'tjuə] *adj* (*fruit*) (qui n'est) pas mûr(e); (*person*) qui manque de maturité

**immediate** [ɪ'miːdɪət] *adj* immédiat(e); **~ly** *adv* (*at once*) immédiatement; **~ly next to** juste à côté de

**immense** [ɪ'mens] *adj* immense; énorme

**immerse** [ɪ'mɜːs] *vt* immerger, plonger; **immersion heater** (*BRIT*) *n* chauffe-eau *m* électrique

**immigrant** ['ɪmɪgrənt] *n* immigrant(e); immigré(e); **immigration** [ɪmɪ'greɪʃən] *n* immigration *f*

**imminent** ['ɪmɪnənt] *adj* imminent(e)

**immoral** [ɪ'mɔrl] *adj* immoral(e)

**immortal** [ɪ'mɔːtl] *adj, n* immortel(le)

**immune** [ɪ'mjuːn] *adj*: **~ (to)** immunisé(e) (contre); (*fig*) à l'abri de; **immunity** *n* immunité *f*

**impact** ['ɪmpækt] *n* choc *m*, impact *m*; (*fig*) impact

**impair** [ɪm'pɛə] *vt* détériorer, diminuer

**impart** [ɪm'pɑːt] *vt* communiquer, transmettre; (*flavour*) donner

**impartial** [ɪm'pɑːʃl] *adj* impartial(e)

**impassable** [ɪm'pɑːsəbl] *adj* infranchissable; (*road*) impraticable

**impassive** [ɪm'pæsɪv] *adj* impassible

**impatience** [ɪm'peɪʃəns] *n* impatience *f*

**impatient** [ɪm'peɪʃənt] *adj* impatient(e); **to get** *or* **grow ~** s'impatienter; **~ly** *adv* avec impatience

**impeccable** [ɪm'pɛkəbl] *adj* impeccable, parfait(e)

**impede** [ɪm'piːd] *vt* gêner; **impediment** *n* obstacle *m*; (*also:* **speech impediment**) défaut *m* d'élocution

**impending** [ɪm'pɛndɪŋ] *adj* imminent(e)

**imperative** [ɪm'pɛrətɪv] *adj* (*need*) urgent(e), pressant(e); (*tone*) impérieux(-euse) ♦ *n* (LING) impératif *m*

**imperfect** [ɪm'pəːfɪkt] *adj* imparfait(e); (*goods etc*) défectueux(-euse)

**imperial** [ɪm'pɪərɪəl] *adj* impérial(e); (BRIT: *measure*) légal(e)

**impersonal** [ɪm'pəːsənl] *adj* impersonnel(le)

**impersonate** [ɪm'pəːsəneɪt] *vt* se faire passer pour; (THEATRE) imiter

**impertinent** [ɪm'pəːtɪnənt] *adj* impertinent(e), insolent(e)

**impervious** [ɪm'pəːvɪəs] *adj* (fig): **~ to** insensible à

**impetuous** [ɪm'pɛtjuəs] *adj* impétueux(-euse), fougueux(-euse)

**impetus** ['ɪmpətəs] *n* impulsion *f*; (*of runner*) élan *m*

**impinge** [ɪm'pɪndʒ]: **to ~ on** *fus* (*person*) affecter, toucher; (*rights*) empiéter sur

**implement** [*n* 'ɪmplɪmənt, *vb* 'ɪmplɪmɛnt] *n* outil *m*, instrument *m*; (*for cooking*) ustensile *m* ♦ *vt* exécuter

**implicit** [ɪm'plɪsɪt] *adj* implicite; (*complete*) absolu(e), sans réserve

**imply** [ɪm'plaɪ] *vt* suggérer, laisser entendre; indiquer, supposer

**impolite** [ɪmpə'laɪt] *adj* impoli(e)

**import** [*vb* ɪm'pɔːt, *n* 'ɪmpɔːt] *vt* importer ♦ *n* (COMM) importation *f*

**importance** [ɪm'pɔːtns] *n* importance *f*

**important** [ɪm'pɔːtənt] *adj* important(e)

**importer** [ɪm'pɔːtə*] *n* importateur (-trice)

**impose** [ɪm'pəuz] *vt* imposer ♦ *vi*: **to ~ on sb** abuser de la gentillesse de qn; **imposing** *adj* imposant(e), impressionnant(e); **imposition** [ɪmpə'zɪʃən] *n* (*of tax etc*) imposition *f*; **to be an imposition on** (*person*) abuser de la gentillesse *or* la bonté de

**impossible** [ɪm'pɔsɪbl] *adj* impossible

**impotent** ['ɪmpətnt] *adj* impuissant(e)

**impound** [ɪm'paund] *vt* confisquer, saisir

**impoverished** [ɪm'pɔvərɪʃt] *adj* appauvri(e), pauvre

**impractical** [ɪm'præktɪkl] *adj* pas pratique; (*person*) qui manque d'esprit pratique

**impregnable** [ɪm'prɛgnəbl] *adj* (*fortress*) imprenable

**impress** [ɪm'prɛs] *vt* impressionner, faire impression sur; (*mark*) imprimer, marquer; **to ~ sth on sb** faire bien comprendre qch à qn; **~ed** *adj* impressionné(e)

**impression** [ɪm'prɛʃən] *n* impression *f*; (*of stamp, seal*) empreinte *f*; (*imitation*) imitation *f*; **to be under the ~ that** avoir l'impression que; **~ist** *n* (ART) impressionniste *m/f*; (*entertainer*) imitateur(-trice) *m/f*

**impressive** [ɪm'prɛsɪv] *adj* impressionnant(e)

**imprint** ['ɪmprɪnt] *n* (*outline*) marque *f*, empreinte *f*

**imprison** [ɪm'prɪzn] *vt* emprisonner, mettre en prison

**improbable** [ɪm'prɔbəbl] *adj* improbable; (*excuse*) peu plausible

**improper** [ɪm'prɔpə*] *adj* (*unsuitable*) déplacé(e), de mauvais goût; (*indécent*(e); (*dishonest*) malhonnête

**improve** [ɪm'pruːv] *vt* améliorer ♦ *vi* s'améliorer; (*pupil etc*) faire des progrès; **~ment** *n* amélioration *f*; (*in sb*) progrès *m*

**improvise** ['ɪmprəvaɪz] *vt, vi* improviser

**impudent** ['ɪmpjudnt] *adj* impudent(e)

**impulse** ['ɪmpʌls] *n* impulsion *f*; **on ~**

impulsivement, sur un coup de tête; **impulsive** adj impulsif(-ive)

**in** [ɪn] prep 1 (indicating place, position) dans; **in the house/the fridge** dans la maison/le frigo; **in the garden** dans le ou au jardin; **in town** en ville; **in the country** à la campagne; **in school** à l'école; **in here/there** ici/là

2 (with place names: of town, region, country): **in London** à Londres; **in England** en Angleterre; **in Japan** au Japon; **in the United States** aux États-Unis

3 (indicating time: during): **in spring** au printemps; **in summer** en été; **in May/1992** en mai/1992; **in the afternoon** (dans) l'après-midi; **at 4 o'clock in the afternoon** à 4 heures de l'après-midi

4 (indicating time: in the space of) en; (: future) dans; **I did it in 3 hours/days** je l'ai fait en 3 heures/jours; **I'll see you in 2 weeks** or **in 2 weeks' time** je te verrai dans 2 semaines

5 (indicating manner etc) à; **in a loud/soft voice** à voix haute/basse; **in pencil** au crayon; **in French** en français; **the boy in the blue shirt** le garçon à or avec la chemise bleue

6 (indicating circumstances): **in the sun** au soleil; **in the shade** à l'ombre; **in the rain** sous la pluie

7 (indicating mood, state): **in tears** en larmes; **in anger** sous le coup de la colère; **in despair** au désespoir; **in good condition** en bon état; **to live in luxury** vivre dans le luxe

8 (with ratios, numbers): **1 in 10 (households), 1 (household) in 10** 1 (ménage) sur 10; **20 pence in the pound** 20 pence par livre sterling; **they lined up in twos** ils se mirent en rangs (deux) par deux; **in hundreds** par centaines

9 (referring to people, works) chez; **the disease is common in children** c'est

une maladie courante chez les enfants; **in (the works of) Dickens** chez Dickens, dans (l'œuvre de) Dickens

10 (indicating profession etc) dans; **to be in teaching** être dans l'enseignement

11 (after superlative) de; **the best pupil in the class** le meilleur élève de la classe

12 (with present participle): **in saying this** en disant ceci

♦ adv: **to be in** (person: at home, work) être là; (train, ship, plane) être arrivé(e); (in fashion) être à la mode; **to ask sb in** inviter qn à entrer; **to run/limp** etc **in** entrer en courant/boitant etc

♦ n: **the ins and outs (of)** (of proposal, situation etc) les tenants et aboutissants (de)

**in.** abbr = **inch**

**inability** [ɪnə'bɪlɪtɪ] n incapacité f

**inaccurate** [ɪn'ækjurət] adj inexact(e); (person) qui manque de précision

**inadequate** [ɪn'ædɪkwət] adj insuffisant(e), inadéquat(e)

**inadvertently** [ɪnəd'vɜːtntlɪ] adv par mégarde

**inadvisable** [ɪnəd'vaɪzəbl] adj (action) à déconseiller

**inane** [ɪ'neɪn] adj inepte, stupide

**inanimate** [ɪn'ænɪmət] adj inanimé(e)

**inappropriate** [ɪnə'prəuprɪət] adj inopportun(e), mal à propos; (word, expression) impropre

**inarticulate** [ɪnɑː'tɪkjulət] adj (person) qui s'exprime mal; (speech) indistinct(e)

**inasmuch as** [ɪnəz'mʌtʃ-] adv (insofar as) dans la mesure où; (seeing that) attendu que

**inauguration** [ɪnɔːgju'reɪʃən] n inauguration f; (of president) investiture f

**inborn** [ɪn'bɔːn] adj (quality) innée(e)

**inbred** [ɪn'bred] adj inné(e), naturel(le); (family) consanguin(e)

**Inc.** abbr = **incorporated**

**incapable** [ɪn'keɪpəbl] adj incapable

**incapacitate** [ɪnkəˈpæsɪteɪt] vt: **to ~ sb from doing** rendre qn incapable de faire

**incense** [n ˈɪnsens, vb ɪnˈsens] n encens m ♦ vt (anger) mettre en colère

**incentive** [ɪnˈsentɪv] n encouragement m, raison f de se donner de la peine

**incessant** [ɪnˈsesnt] adj incessant(e); **~ly** adv sans cesse, constamment

**inch** [ɪntʃ] n pouce m (= 25 mm; 12 in a foot); **within an ~ of** à deux doigts de; **he didn't give an ~** (fig) il n'a pas voulu céder d'un pouce

**incident** [ˈɪnsɪdnt] n incident m; **~al** [ɪnsɪˈdentl] adj (additional) accessoire; **~al to** qui accompagne; **~ally** adv (by the way) à propos

**inclination** [ɪnklɪˈneɪʃən] n (fig) inclination f

**incline** [n ˈɪnklaɪn, vb ɪnˈklaɪn] n pente f ♦ vt incliner ♦ vi (surface) s'incliner; **to be ~d to do** avoir tendance à faire

**include** [ɪnˈkluːd] vt inclure, comprendre; **including** prep y compris; **inclusive** adj inclus(e), compris(e); **inclusive of tax** etc taxes etc comprises

**income** [ˈɪnkʌm] n revenu m; **~ tax** n impôt m sur le revenu

**incoming** [ˈɪnkʌmɪŋ] adj qui arrive; (president) entrant(e); **~ mail** courrier m du jour; **~ tide** marée montante

**incompetent** [ɪnˈkɒmpɪtnt] adj incompétent(e), incapable

**incomplete** [ɪnkəmˈpliːt] adj incomplet(-ète)

**incongruous** [ɪnˈkɒŋɡruəs] adj incongru(e)

**inconsiderate** [ɪnkənˈsɪdərət] adj (person) qui manque d'égards; (action) inconsidéré(e)

**inconsistency** [ɪnkənˈsɪstənsɪ] n (of actions etc) inconséquence f; (of work) irrégularité f; (of statement etc) incohérence f

**inconsistent** [ɪnkənˈsɪstnt] adj inconséquent(e); irrégulier(-ère); peu cohérent(e); **~ with** incompatible avec

**inconspicuous** [ɪnkənˈspɪkjuəs] adj qui passe inaperçu(e); (colour, dress) discret(-ète)

**inconvenience** [ɪnkənˈviːnjəns] n inconvénient m; (trouble) dérangement m ♦ vt déranger

**inconvenient** [ɪnkənˈviːnjənt] adj (house) malcommode; (time, place) mal choisi(e), qui ne convient pas; (visitor) importun(e)

**incorporate** [ɪnˈkɔːpəreɪt] vt incorporer; (contain) contenir; **~d company** (US) n = société f anonyme

**incorrect** [ɪnkəˈrekt] adj incorrect(e)

**increase** [n ˈɪnkriːs, vb ɪnˈkriːs] n augmentation f ♦ vi, vt augmenter; **increasing** adj (number) croissant(e); **increasingly** adv de plus en plus

**incredible** [ɪnˈkredɪbl] adj incroyable

**incubator** [ˈɪnkjubeɪtə] n (for babies) couveuse f

**incumbent** [ɪnˈkʌmbənt] (president) président m en exercice; (REL) titulaire m/f ♦ adj: **it is ~ on him to ...** il lui incombe or appartient de ...

**incur** [ɪnˈkɜː] vt (expenses) encourir; (anger, risk) s'exposer à; (debt) contracter; (loss) subir

**indebted** [ɪnˈdetɪd] adj: **to be ~ to sb (for)** être redevable à qn (de)

**indecent** [ɪnˈdiːsnt] adj indécent(e), inconvenant(e); **~ assault** (BRIT) n attentat m à la pudeur; **~ exposure** n outrage m (public) à la pudeur

**indecisive** [ɪndɪˈsaɪsɪv] adj (person) indécis(e)

**indeed** [ɪnˈdiːd] adv vraiment; en effet; (furthermore) d'ailleurs; **yes ~!** certainement!

**indefinitely** [ɪnˈdefɪnɪtlɪ] adv (wait) indéfiniment

**indemnity** [ɪnˈdemnɪtɪ] n (safeguard) assurance f, garantie f; (compensation) indemnité f

**independence** [ɪndɪˈpendns] n indépendance f

**Independence Day**

L'**Independence Day** est la fête nationale aux États-Unis, le 4 juillet. Il commémore l'adoption de la déclaration d'Indépendance, en 1776, écrite par Thomas Jefferson et proclamant la séparation des 13 colonies américaines de la Grande-Bretagne.

**independent** [ɪndɪˈpɛndnt] *adj* indépendant(e); (*school*) privé(e); (*radio*) libre

**index** [ˈɪndɛks] *n* (*pl: ~es: in book*) index *m*; (*: in library etc*) catalogue *m*; (*pl: indices: ratio, sign*) indice *m*; ~ **finger** *n* index *m*; ~**-linked** *adj* indexé(e) (sur le coût de la vie *etc*)

**India** [ˈɪndɪə] *n* Inde *f*; ~**n** *adj* indien(ne) ♦ *n* Indien(ne); (**American**) ~**n** *n* Indien(ne) (d'Amérique); ~ **Ocean** *n* océan Indien

**indicate** [ˈɪndɪkeɪt] *vt* indiquer; **indication** [ɪndɪˈkeɪʃən] *n* indication *f*, signe *m*; **indicative** [ɪnˈdɪkətɪv] *adj*: **indicative of** symptomatique de ♦ *n* (LING) indicatif *m*; **indicator** *n* (*sign*) indicateur *m*; (AUT) clignotant *m*

**indices** [ˈɪndɪsiːz] *npl of* **index**

**indictment** [ɪnˈdaɪtmənt] *n* accusation *f*

**indifferent** [ɪnˈdɪfrənt] *adj* indifférent(e); (*poor*) médiocre, quelconque

**indigenous** [ɪnˈdɪdʒɪnəs] *adj* indigène

**indigestion** [ɪndɪˈdʒɛstʃən] *n* indigestion *f*, mauvaise digestion

**indignant** [ɪnˈdɪgnənt] *adj*: ~ **(at sth/ with sb)** indigné(e) (de qch/contre qn)

**indignity** [ɪnˈdɪgnɪtɪ] *n* indignité *f*, affront *m*

**indirect** [ɪndɪˈrɛkt] *adj* indirect(e)

**indiscreet** [ɪndɪsˈkriːt] *adj* indiscret (-ète); (*rash*) imprudent(e)

**indiscriminate** [ɪndɪsˈkrɪmɪnət] *adj* (*person*) qui manque de discernement; (*killings*) commis(e) au hasard

**indisputable** [ɪndɪsˈpjuːtəbl] *adj* in-

contestable, indiscutable

**individual** [ɪndɪˈvɪdjuəl] *n* individu *m* ♦ *adj* individuel(le); (*characteristic*) particulier(-ère), original(e)

**indoctrination** [ɪndɒktrɪˈneɪʃən] *n* endoctrinement *m*

**Indonesia** [ɪndəˈniːzɪə] *n* Indonésie *f*

**indoor** [ˈɪndɔːr] *adj* (*plant*) d'appartement; (*swimming pool*) couvert(e); (*sport, games*) pratiqué(e) en salle; ~**s** *adv* à l'intérieur

**induce** [ɪnˈdjuːs] *vt* (*persuade*) persuader; (*bring about*) provoquer; ~**ment** *n* (*incentive*) récompense *f*; (*pej: bribe*) pot-de-vin *m*

**indulge** [ɪnˈdʌldʒ] *vt* (*whim*) céder à, satisfaire; (*child*) gâter ♦ *vi*: **to ~ in sth** (*luxury*) se permettre qch; (*fantasies etc*) se livrer à qch; ~**nce** *n* fantaisie *f* (que l'on s'offre); (*leniency*) indulgence *f*; ~**nt** *adj* indulgent(e)

**industrial** [ɪnˈdʌstrɪəl] *adj* industriel(le); (*injury*) du travail; ~ **action** *n* action revendicative; ~ **estate** (BRIT) *n* zone industrielle; ~**ist** *n* industriel *m*; ~ **park** (US) *n* = **industrial estate**

**industrious** [ɪnˈdʌstrɪəs] *adj* travailleur(-euse)

**industry** [ˈɪndəstrɪ] *n* industrie *f*; (*diligence*) zèle *m*, application *f*

**inebriated** [ɪˈniːbrɪeɪtɪd] *adj* ivre

**inedible** [ɪnˈɛdɪbl] *adj* immangeable; (*plant etc*) non comestible

**ineffective** [ɪnɪˈfɛktɪv], **ineffectual** [ɪnɪˈfɛktʃuəl] *adj* inefficace

**inefficient** [ɪnɪˈfɪʃənt] *adj* inefficace

**inequality** [ɪnɪˈkwɒlɪtɪ] *n* inégalité *f*

**inescapable** [ɪnɪˈskeɪpəbl] *adj* inéluctable, inévitable

**inevitable** [ɪnˈɛvɪtəbl] *adj* inévitable; **inevitably** *adv* inévitablement

**inexpensive** [ɪnɪkˈspɛnsɪv] *adj* bon marché *inv*

**inexperienced** [ɪnɪkˈspɪərɪənst] *adj* inexpérimenté(e)

**infallible** [ɪnˈfælɪbl] *adj* infaillible

**infamous** [ˈɪnfəməs] *adj* infâme, abo-

**infancy** ['ɪnfənsɪ] n petite enfance, bas
âge

**infant** ['ɪnfənt] n (baby) nourrisson m;
(young child) petit(e) enfant; ~ **school**
(BRIT) n classes fpl préparatoires (entre 5
et 7 ans)

**infatuated** [ɪn'fætjʊeɪtɪd] adj: ~ **with**
entiché(e) de; **infatuation** [ɪnfæt-
ju'eɪʃən] n engouement m

**infect** [ɪn'fekt] vt infecter, contaminer;
~**ion** n infection f; (contagion) contagion f; ~**ious** adj infectieux(-euse);
(also fig) contagieux(-euse)

**infer** [ɪn'fɜ:ʳ] vt conclure, déduire

**inferior** [ɪn'fɪərɪəʳ] adj inférieur(e);
(goods) de qualité inférieure ♦ n infé-
rieur(e); (in rank) subalterne m/f; ~**ity**
[ɪnfɪərɪ'ɔrɪtɪ] n infériorité f

**infertile** [ɪn'fɜ:taɪl] adj stérile

**infighting** ['ɪnfaɪtɪŋ] n querelles fpl in-
ternes

**infinite** ['ɪnfɪnɪt] adj infini(e)

**infinitive** [ɪn'fɪnɪtɪv] n infinitif m

**infinity** [ɪn'fɪnɪtɪ] n infinité f; (also
MATH) infini m

**infirmary** [ɪn'fɜ:mərɪ] n (hospital)
hôpital m

**inflamed** [ɪn'fleɪmd] adj enflammé(e)

**inflammable** [ɪn'flæməbl] (BRIT) adj inflammable

**inflammation** [ɪnflə'meɪʃən] n inflammation f

**inflatable** [ɪn'fleɪtəbl] adj gonflable

**inflate** [ɪn'fleɪt] vt (tyre, balloon) gonfler; (price) faire monter; **inflation** f
(ECON) inflation f; **inflationary** adj in-
flationniste

**inflict** [ɪn'flɪkt] vt: to ~ **on** infliger à

**influence** ['ɪnfluəns] n influence f ♦ vt
influencer; **under the** ~ **of alcohol** en
état d'ébriété; **influential** [ɪnflu'enʃl]
adj influent(e)

**influenza** [ɪnflu'enzə] n grippe f

**influx** ['ɪnflʌks] n afflux m

**infomercial** [ɪn'fəuməːʃl] (US) n (for
product) publi-information f; (POL) émis-

sion où un candidat présente son programme
électoral

**inform** [ɪn'fɔ:m] vt: to ~ **sb** (of) informer or avertir qn (de) ♦ vi: to ~ **on sb**
dénoncer qn

**informal** [ɪn'fɔ:ml] adj (person, manner,
party) simple; (visit, discussion) dénué(e)
de formalités; (announcement, invitation) non officiel(le); (colloquial)
familier(-ère); ~**ity** [ɪnfɔ:'mælɪtɪ] n simplicité f, absence f de cérémonie; caractère non officiel

**informant** [ɪn'fɔ:mənt] n informa-
teur(-trice)

**information** [ɪnfə'meɪʃən] n information f; renseignements mpl; (knowledge)
connaissances fpl; **a piece of** ~ un renseignement; ~ **desk** n accueil m; ~
**office** n bureau m de renseignements

**informative** [ɪn'fɔ:mətɪv] adj
instructif(-ive)

**informer** [ɪn'fɔ:məʳ] n (also: **police** ~)
indicateur(-trice)

**infringe** [ɪn'frɪndʒ] vt enfreindre ♦ vi:
to ~ **on** empiéter sur; ~**ment** n:
~**ment** (of) infraction f (à)

**infuriating** [ɪn'fjuərɪeɪtɪŋ] adj exaspé-
rant(e)

**ingenious** [ɪn'dʒi:njəs] adj ingénieux
(-euse); **ingenuity** [ɪndʒɪ'nju:ɪtɪ] n in-
géniosité f

**ingenuous** [ɪn'dʒenjuəs] adj naïf
(naïve), ingénu(e)

**ingot** ['ɪŋgət] n lingot m

**ingrained** [ɪn'greɪnd] adj enraciné(e)

**ingratiate** [ɪn'greɪʃɪeɪt] vt: to ~ **o.s.**
**with** s'insinuer dans les bonnes grâces
de, se faire bien voir de

**ingredient** [ɪn'gri:dɪənt] n ingrédient
m; (fig) élément m

**inhabit** [ɪn'hæbɪt] vt habiter; ~**ant** n
habitant(e)

**inhale** [ɪn'heɪl] vt respirer; (smoke) avaler ♦ vi aspirer; (in smoking) avaler la fumée

**inherent** [ɪn'hɪərənt] adj: ~ (**in** or **to**)
inhérent(e) (à)

**inherit** [ɪn'hɛrɪt] vt hériter (de); **~ance** n héritage m

**inhibit** [ɪn'hɪbɪt] vt (PSYCH) inhiber; (growth) freiner; **~ion** [ɪnhɪ'bɪʃən] n inhibition f

**inhuman** [ɪn'hjuːmən] adj inhumain(e)

**initial** [ɪ'nɪʃl] adj initial(e) ♦ n initiale f ♦ vt parafer; **~s** npl (letters) initiales fpl; (as signature) parafe m; **~ly** adv initiale-ment, au début

**initiate** [ɪ'nɪʃɪeɪt] vt (start) entrepren-dre, amorcer; (enterprise) lancer; (per-son) initier; **to ~ proceedings against sb** intenter une action à qn; **initiative** n initiative f

**inject** [ɪn'dʒɛkt] vt injecter; (person): to **~ sb with sth** faire une piqûre de qch à qn; **~ion** n injection f, piqûre f

**injure** ['ɪndʒər] vt blesser; (reputation etc) compromettre; **~d** adj blessé(e); **injury** n blessure f; **~ time** n (SPORT) arrêts mpl de jeu

**injustice** [ɪn'dʒʌstɪs] n injustice f

**ink** [ɪŋk] n encre f

**inkling** ['ɪŋklɪŋ] n: **to have an/no ~ of** avoir une (vague) idée de/n'avoir au-cune idée de

**inlaid** ['ɪnleɪd] adj incrusté(e); (table etc) marqueté(e)

**inland** [adj 'ɪnlənd, adv ɪn'lænd] adj in-térieur(e) ♦ adv à l'intérieur, dans les terres; **Inland Revenue** n (BRIT) fisc m

**in-laws** ['ɪnlɔːz] npl beaux-parents mpl; belle famille

**inlet** ['ɪnlɛt] n (GEO) crique f

**inmate** ['ɪnmeɪt] n (in prison) déte-nu(e); (in asylum) interné(e)

**inn** [ɪn] n auberge f

**innate** [ɪ'neɪt] adj inné(e)

**inner** ['ɪnər] adj intérieur(e); **~ city** n centre m de zone urbaine; **~ tube** n (of tyre) chambre f à air

**innings** ['ɪnɪŋz] n (CRICKET) tour m de batte

**innocent** ['ɪnəsnt] adj innocent(e)

**innocuous** [ɪ'nɒkjuəs] adj inoffensif (-ive)

**innuendo** [ɪnju'ɛndəu] (pl **~es**) n insi-nuation f, allusion f (malveillante)

**innumerable** [ɪ'njuːmrəbl] adj innom-brable

**inpatient** ['ɪnpeɪʃənt] n malade hospi-talisé(e)

**input** ['ɪnput] n (resources) ressources fpl; (COMPUT) entrée f (de données); (: data) données fpl

**inquest** ['ɪnkwɛst] n enquête f; (coro-ner's) ~ enquête judiciaire

**inquire** [ɪn'kwaɪər] vi demander ♦ vt demander; **to ~ about** se renseigner sur; **~ into** vt fus faire une enquête sur; **inquiry** n demande f de renseigne-ments; (investigation) enquête f, investi-gation f; **inquiries** npl: **the inquiries** (RAIL etc) les renseignements; **inquiry** or **inquiries office** (BRIT) n bureau m des renseignements

**inquisitive** [ɪn'kwɪzɪtɪv] adj curieux (-euse)

**ins** abbr = **inches**

**insane** [ɪn'seɪn] adj fou (folle); (MED) aliéné(e); **insanity** [ɪn'sænɪtɪ] n folie f, (MED) aliénation (mentale)

**inscription** [ɪn'skrɪpʃən] n inscription f; (in book) dédicace f

**inscrutable** [ɪn'skruːtəbl] adj impéné-trable; (comment) obscur(e)

**insect** ['ɪnsɛkt] n insecte m; **~icide** [ɪn'sɛktɪsaɪd] n insecticide m; **~ repel-lent** n crème f anti-insecte

**insecure** [ɪnsɪ'kjuər] adj peu solide; peu sûr(e); (person) anxieux(-euse)

**insensitive** [ɪn'sɛnsɪtɪv] adj insensible

**insert** [ɪn'səːt] vt insérer; **~ion** n inser-tion f

**in-service** ['ɪn'səːvɪs] adj (training) continu(e), en cours d'emploi; (course) de perfectionnement

**inshore** ['ɪn'ʃɔːr] adj côtier(-ère) ♦ adv près de la côte; (move) vers la côte

**inside** ['ɪn'saɪd] n intérieur m ♦ adj in-térieur(e) ♦ adv à l'intérieur, dedans ♦ prep à l'intérieur de; (of time): **~5 minutes** en moins de 10 minutes; **~s**

npl (inf) intestins mpl; ~ **information** n renseignements obtenus à la source; ~ **lane** n (AUT: in Britain) voie f de gauche; (: in US, Europe etc) voie de droite; ~ **out** adv à l'envers; (know) à fond; ~r **dealing**, ~r **trading** n (St Ex) délit m d'initié

**insight** ['insait] n perspicacité f; (glimpse, idea) aperçu m

**insignificant** [insig'nifiknt] adj insignifiant(e)

**insincere** [insin'siər] adj hypocrite

**insinuate** [in'sinjueit] vt insinuer

**insist** [in'sist] vi insister; to ~ on doing insister pour faire; to ~ on sth exiger qch; to ~ that insister pour ... que; (claim) maintenir or soutenir que; ~ent adj insistant(e), pressant(e); (noise, action) ininterrompu(e)

**insole** ['insəul] n (removable) semelle intérieure

**insolent** ['insələnt] adj insolent(e)

**insolvent** [in'sɔlvənt] adj insolvable

**insomnia** [in'sɔmniə] n insomnie f

**inspect** [in'spekt] vt inspecter; contrôler; ~ion n inspection f; contrôle m; ~or n inspecteur-(trice); (BRIT: on buses, trains) contrôleur-(euse)

**inspire** [in'spaiər] vt inspirer

**install** [in'stɔ:l] vt installer; ~ation [instə'leiʃən] n installation f

**instalment** (US **installment**) n acompte m, versement partiel; (of TV serial etc) épisode m; in ~s (pay) à tempérament; (receive) en plusieurs fois

**instance** ['instəns] n exemple m; for ~ par exemple; in the first ~ tout d'abord, en premier lieu

**instant** ['instənt] n instant m ♦ adj immédiat(e); (coffee, food) instantané(e), en poudre; ~ly adv immédiatement, tout de suite

**instead** [in'sted] adv au lieu de cela; ~ of au lieu de; ~ of sb à la place de qn

**instep** ['instep] n cou-de-pied m; (of shoe) cambrure f

**instigate** ['instigeit] vt (rebellion) fo-

menter, provoquer; (talks etc) promouvoir

**instil** [in'stil] vt: to ~ (into) inculquer (à); (courage) insuffler (à)

**instinct** ['instiŋkt] n instinct m

**institute** ['institju:t] n institut m ♦ vt instituer, établir; (inquiry) ouvrir; (proceedings) entamer

**institution** [insti'tju:ʃən] n institution f; (educational) établissement m (scolaire); (mental home) établissement (psychiatrique)

**instruct** [in'strʌkt] vt: to ~ sb in sth enseigner qch à qn; to ~ sb to do charger qn or ordonner à qn de faire; ~ion n instruction f; ~ions npl (orders) directives fpl; ~ions (for use) mode m d'emploi; ~or n professeur m; (for skiing, driving) moniteur m

**instrument** ['instrumənt] n instrument m; ~al [instru'mentl] adj: to be ~al in contribuer à; ~ panel n tableau m de bord

**insufficient** [insə'fiʃənt] adj insuffisant(e)

**insular** ['insjulər] adj (outlook) borné(e); (person) aux vues étroites

**insulate** ['insjuleit] vt isoler; (against sound) insonoriser; **insulation** [insju'leiʃən] n isolation f; insonorisation f

**insulin** ['insjulin] n insuline f

**insult** [n 'insʌlt, vb in'sʌlt] n insulte f, affront m ♦ vt insulter, faire affront à

**insurance** [in'fuərəns] n assurance f; fire/life ~ assurance-incendie/-vie; ~ **policy** n police f d'assurance

**insure** [in'fuər] vt assurer; to ~ (o.s.) against (fig) parer à

**intact** [in'tækt] adj intact(e)

**intake** ['inteik] n (of food, oxygen) consommation f; (BRIT: SCOL): an ~ of 200 a year 200 admissions fpl par an

**integral** ['intigrəl] adj (part) intégrant(e)

**integrate** ['intigreit] vt intégrer ♦ vi s'intégrer

**intellect** ['ɪntəlekt] n intelligence f; **~ual** [ɪntə'lektjuəl] adj, n intellectuel(le)

**intelligence** [ɪn'telɪdʒəns] n intelligence f; (MIL etc) informations fpl, renseignements mpl; **~ service** n services secrets; **intelligent** adj intelligent(e)

**intend** [ɪn'tend] vt (gift etc): **to ~ sth for** destiner qch à; **to ~ to do** avoir l'intention de faire

**intense** [ɪn'tens] adj intense; (person) véhément(e); **~ly** adv intensément; profondément

**intensive** [ɪn'tensɪv] adj intensif(-ive); **~ care unit** n service m de réanimation

**intent** [ɪn'tent] n intention f ♦ adj attentif(-ive); **to all ~s and purposes** en fait, pratiquement; **to be ~ on doing sth** être (bien) décidé à faire qch; **~ion** n intention f; **~ional** adj intentionnel(le), délibéré(e); **~ly** adv attentivement

**interact** [ɪntər'ækt] vi avoir une action réciproque; (people) communiquer; **~ive** adj (COMPUT) interactif(-ive)

**interchange** [n 'ɪntətʃeɪndʒ, vb ɪntə'tʃeɪndʒ] n (exchange) échange m; (on motorway) échangeur m; **~able** adj interchangeable

**intercom** ['ɪntəkɔm] n interphone m

**intercourse** ['ɪntəkɔːs] n (sexual) rapports mpl

**interest** ['ɪntrɪst] n intérêt m; (pastime): **my main ~** ce qui m'intéresse le plus; (COMM) intérêts mpl ♦ vt intéresser; **to be ~ed in sth** s'intéresser à qch; **I am ~ed in going** ça m'intéresse d'y aller; **~ing** adj intéressant(e); **~ rate** n taux m d'intérêt

**interface** ['ɪntəfeɪs] n (COMPUT) interface f

**interfere** [ɪntə'fɪər] vi: **to ~ in** (quarrel) s'immiscer dans; (other people's business) se mêler de; **to ~ with** (object) toucher à; (plans) contrecarrer; (duty) être en conflit avec; **~nce** n (in affairs)

ingérance f; (RADIO, TV) parasites mpl

**interim** ['ɪntərɪm] adj provisoire ♦ n: **in the ~** dans l'intérim, entre-temps

**interior** [ɪn'tɪərɪər] n intérieur m ♦ adj intérieur(e); **~ (minister, department) de** l'Intérieur; **~ designer** n styliste m/f, designer m/f

**interjection** [ɪntə'dʒekʃən] n (interruption) interruption f; (LING) interjection f

**interlock** [ɪntə'lɔk] vi s'enclencher

**interlude** ['ɪntəluːd] n intervalle m; (THEATRE) intermède m

**intermediate** [ɪntə'miːdɪət] adj intermédiaire; (SCOL) moyen(ne)

**intermission** [ɪntə'mɪʃən] n pause f; (THEATRE, CINEMA) entracte m

**intern** [vb ɪn'tɜːn, n 'ɪntɜːn] vt interner ♦ n (US) interne m/f

**internal** [ɪn'tɜːnl] adj interne; (politics) intérieur(e); **~ly** adv: **"not to be taken ~ly"** "pour usage externe"; **I~ Revenue Service** (US) n fisc m

**international** [ɪntə'næʃənl] adj international(e)

**Internet** ['ɪntənet] n Internet m; **~ café** n cybercafé m; **~ service provider** n fournisseur m d'accès à Internet

**interplay** ['ɪntəpleɪ] n effet m réciproque, interaction f

**interpret** [ɪn'tɜːprɪt] vt interpréter ♦ vi servir d'interprète; **~er** n interprète m/f

**interrelated** [ɪntərɪ'leɪtɪd] adj en corrélation, en rapport étroit

**interrogate** [ɪn'terəgeɪt] vt interroger; (suspect etc) soumettre à un interrogatoire; **interrogation** [ɪnterəu'geɪʃən] n interrogation f, interrogatoire m

**interrupt** [ɪntə'rʌpt] vt, vi interrompre; **~ion** n interruption f

**intersect** [ɪntə'sekt] vi (roads) se croiser, se couper; **~ion** n (of roads) croisement m

**intersperse** [ɪntə'spɜːs] vt: **to ~ with** parsemer de

**intertwine** [ɪntə'twaɪn] vi s'entrelacer

**interval** ['ɪntəvl] n intervalle m; (THEATRE) entracte m; (: SPORT) mi-temps f; **at ~s** par intervalles

**intervene** [ɪntə'viːn] vi (person) intervenir; (event) survenir; (time) s'écouler (entre-temps); **intervention** n intervention f

**interview** ['ɪntəvjuː] n (RADIO, TV etc) interview f; (for job) entrevue f ♦ vt interviewer; avoir une entrevue avec; **~er** n (RADIO, TV) interviewer m

**intestine** [ɪn'testɪn] n intestin m

**intimacy** ['ɪntɪməsɪ] n intimité f

**intimate** [adj 'ɪntɪmət, vb 'ɪntɪmeɪt] adj intime; (friendship) profond(e); (knowledge) approfondi(e) ♦ vt (hint) suggérer, laisser entendre

**into** ['ɪntuː] prep dans; **~ pieces/French** en morceaux/français

**intolerant** [ɪn'tɒlərnt] adj: **~ (of)** intolérant(e) (de)

**intoxicated** [ɪn'tɒksɪkeɪtɪd] adj (drunk) ivre

**intractable** [ɪn'træktəbl] adj (child) indocile, insoumis(e); (problem) insoluble

**intranet** ['ɪntrənet] n intranet m

**intransitive** [ɪn'trænsɪtɪv] adj intransitif(-ive)

**intravenous** [ɪntrə'viːnəs] adj intraveineux(-euse)

**in-tray** ['ɪntreɪ] n courrier m "arrivée"

**intricate** ['ɪntrɪkət] adj complexe, compliqué(e)

**intrigue** [ɪn'triːɡ] n intrigue f ♦ vt intriguer; **intriguing** adj fascinant(e)

**intrinsic** [ɪn'trɪnsɪk] adj intrinsèque

**introduce** [ɪntrə'djuːs] vt introduire; (TV show, people to each other) présenter; **to ~ sb to** (pastime, technique) initier qn à; **introduction** n introduction f; (of person) présentation f; (to new experience) initiation f; **introductory** adj préliminaire, d'introduction; **introductory offer** n (COMM) offre f de lancement

**intrude** [ɪn'truːd] vi (person) être importun(e); **to ~ on** (conversation etc) s'immiscer dans; **~r** n intrus(e)

**intuition** [ɪntjuː'ɪʃən] n intuition f

**inundate** ['ɪnʌndeɪt] vt: **to ~ with**

inonder de

**invade** [ɪn'veɪd] vt envahir

**invalid** [n 'ɪnvəlɪd, adj ɪn'vælɪd] n malade m/f; (with disability) invalide m/f ♦ adj (not valid) non valide or valable

**invaluable** [ɪn'væljuəbl] adj inestimable, inappréciable

**invariably** [ɪn'veərɪəblɪ] adv invariablement; toujours

**invent** [ɪn'vent] vt inventer; **~ion** n invention f; **~ive** adj inventif(-ive); **~or** n inventeur(-trice)

**inventory** ['ɪnvəntrɪ] n inventaire m

**invert** [ɪn'vɜːt] vt intervertir; (cup, object) retourner; **~ed commas** (BRIT) npl guillemets mpl

**invest** [ɪn'vest] vt investir ♦ vi: **to ~ in** sth placer son argent dans qch; (fig) s'offrir qch

**investigate** [ɪn'vestɪɡeɪt] vt (crime etc) faire une enquête sur; **investigation** [ɪnvestɪ'ɡeɪʃən] n (of crime) enquête f

**investment** [ɪn'vestmənt] n investissement m, placement m

**investor** [ɪn'vestər] n investisseur m; actionnaire m/f

**invigilator** [ɪn'vɪdʒɪleɪtər] n surveillant(e)

**invigorating** [ɪn'vɪɡəreɪtɪŋ] adj vivifiant(e); (fig) stimulant(e)

**invisible** [ɪn'vɪzɪbl] adj invisible

**invitation** [ɪnvɪ'teɪʃən] n invitation f

**invite** [ɪn'vaɪt] vt inviter; (opinions etc) demander; **inviting** adj engageant(e), attrayant(e)

**invoice** ['ɪnvɔɪs] n facture f

**involuntary** [ɪn'vɒləntrɪ] adj involontaire

**involve** [ɪn'vɒlv] vt (entail) entraîner, nécessiter; (concern) concerner; (associate): **to ~ sb (in)** impliquer qn (dans), mêler qn (à); faire participer qn (à); **~d** adj (complicated) complexe; **to be ~d in** participer à; **~ment** n: **~ment (in)** participation f (à); rôle m (dans); (enthusiasm) enthousiasme m (pour)

**inward** ['ɪnwəd] adj (thought, feeling)

# iodine 442 itch

profond(e), intime; (*movement*) vers l'intérieur ♦ *adv* vers l'intérieur
**iodine** ['aɪədiːn] *n* iode *m*
**iota** [aɪ'əʊtə] *n* (*fig*) brin *m*, grain *m*
**IOU** *n abbr* (= *I owe you*) reconnaissance *f* de dette
**IQ** *n abbr* (= *intelligence quotient*) Q.I. *m*
**IRA** *n abbr* (= *Irish Republican Army*) IRA *f*
**Iran** [ɪ'rɑːn] *n* Iran *m*
**Iraq** [ɪ'rɑːk] *n* Irak *m*
**irate** [aɪ'reɪt] *adj* courroucé(e)
**Ireland** ['aɪələnd] *n* Irlande *f*
**iris** ['aɪrɪs] (*pl* ~**es**) *n* iris *m*
**Irish** ['aɪrɪʃ] *adj* irlandais(e) ♦ *npl*: **the** ~ les Irlandais; ~**man** (*irreg*) *n* Irlandais *m*; ~ **Sea** *n* mer *f* d'Irlande; ~**woman** (*irreg*) *n* Irlandaise *f*
**iron** ['aɪən] *n* fer *m*; (*for clothes*) fer à repasser ♦ *cpd* de or en fer; (*fig*) de fer ♦ *vt* (*clothes*) repasser; ~ **out** *vt* (*fig*) aplanir; faire disparaître
**ironic(al)** [aɪ'rɒnɪk(l)] *adj* ironique
**ironing** ['aɪənɪŋ] *n* repassage *m*; ~ **board** *n* planche *f* à repasser
**ironmonger's (shop)** ['aɪənmʌŋgəz-] *n* quincaillerie *f*
**irony** ['aɪrənɪ] *n* ironie *f*
**irrational** [ɪ'ræʃənl] *adj* irrationnel(le)
**irregular** [ɪ'regjʊlə] *adj* irrégulier(-ère); (*surface*) inégal(e)
**irrelevant** [ɪ'reləvənt] *adj* sans rapport, hors de propos
**irresistible** [ɪrɪ'zɪstɪbl] *adj* irrésistible
**irrespective** [ɪrɪ'spektɪv]: ~ **of** *prep* sans tenir compte de
**irresponsible** [ɪrɪ'spɒnsɪbl] *adj* (*act*) irréfléchi(e); (*person*) irresponsable
**irrigate** ['ɪrɪgeɪt] *vt* irriguer; **irrigation** [ɪrɪ'geɪʃən] *n* irrigation *f*
**irritate** ['ɪrɪteɪt] *vt* irriter
**irritating** *adj* irritant(e); **irritation** [ɪrɪ'teɪʃən] *n* irritation *f*
**IRS** *n abbr* = **Internal Revenue Service**
**is** [ɪz] *vb* see **be**
**Islam** ['ɪzlɑːm] *n* Islam *m*; ~**ic** *adj* islamique; ~**ic fundamentalists** intégris-

tes *mpl* musulmans
**island** ['aɪlənd] *n* île *f*; ~**er** *n* habitant(e) d'une île, insulaire *m/f*
**isle** [aɪl] *n* île *f*
**isn't** ['ɪznt] = **is not**
**isolate** ['aɪsəleɪt] *vt* isoler; ~**d** *adj* isolé(e); **isolation** *n* isolation *f*
**ISP** *n abbr* = **Internet service provider**
**Israel** ['ɪzreɪl] *n* Israël *m*; ~**i** [ɪz'reɪlɪ] *adj* israélien(ne) ♦ *n* Israélien(ne)
**issue** ['ɪʃjuː] *n* question *f*, problème *m*; (*of book*) publication *f*, parution *f*; (*of banknotes etc*) émission *f*; (*of newspaper etc*) numéro *m* ♦ *vt* (*rations, equipment*) distribuer; (*statement*) publier, faire; (*banknotes etc*) émettre, mettre en circulation; **at** ~ en jeu, en cause; **to take** ~ **with sb** (**over**) exprimer son désaccord avec qn (sur); **to make an** ~ **of sth** faire une montagne de qch

<hr>

KEYWORD

<hr>

**it** [ɪt] *pron* **1** (*specific: subject*) il (elle); (: *direct object*) le (la) (l'); (: *indirect object*) lui; **it's on the table** c'est or il (or elle) est sur la table; **about/from/of it** en; **I spoke to him about it** je lui en ai parlé; **what did you learn from it?** qu'est-ce que vous en avez retiré?; **I'm proud of it** j'en suis fier; **in/to it** y; **put the book in it** mettez-y le livre; **he agreed to it** il y a consenti; **did you go to it?** (*party, concert etc*) est-ce que vous y êtes allé(s)?
**2** (*impersonal*) il; **it's raining** il pleut; **it's Friday tomorrow** demain c'est vendredi or nous sommes vendredi; **it's 6 o'clock** il est 6 heures; **who is it? - it's me** qui est-ce? - c'est moi

**Italian** [ɪ'tæljən] *adj* italien(ne) ♦ *n* Italien(ne); (*LING*) italien *m*
**italics** [ɪ'tælɪks] *npl* italiques *fpl*
**Italy** ['ɪtəlɪ] *n* Italie *f*
**itch** [ɪtʃ] *n* démangeaison *f* ♦ *vi* (*person*) éprouver des démangeaisons; (*part of*

*body)* démanger; **I'm ~ing to do** l'envie me démange de faire; **~y** *adj* qui démange; **to be ~y** avoir des démangeaisons

**it'd** ['ɪtd] = **it would**; **it had**

**item** ['aɪtəm] *n* article *m*; *(on agenda)* question *f*, point *m*; *(also:* **news ~)** nouvelle *f*; **~ize** *vt* détailler, faire une liste de

**itinerary** [aɪ'tɪnərərɪ] *n* itinéraire *m*

**it'll** ['ɪtl] = **it will**; **it shall**

**its** [ɪts] *adj* son (sa), ses *pl*

**it's** [ɪts] = **it is**; **it has**

**itself** [ɪt'self] *pron (reflexive)* se; *(emphatic)* lui-même (elle-même)

**ITV** *n abbr (BRIT: Independent Television)* chaîne privée

**IUD** *n abbr (= intra-uterine device)* DIU *m*, stérilet *m*

**I've** [aɪv] = **I have**

**ivory** ['aɪvərɪ] *n* ivoire *m*

**ivy** ['aɪvɪ] *n* lierre *m*

# J, j

**jab** [dʒæb] *vt:* **to ~ sth into** enfoncer ou planter qch dans ♦ *n (inf: injection)* piqûre *f*

**jack** [dʒæk] *n (AUT)* cric *m*; *(CARDS)* valet *m*; **~ up** *vt* soulever (au cric)

**jackal** ['dʒækl] *n* chacal *m*

**jacket** ['dʒækɪt] *n* veste *f*, veston *m*; *(of book)* jaquette *f*, couverture *f*; **~ potato** *n* pomme *f* de terre en robe des champs

**jack-knife** *vi:* **the lorry ~knifed** la remorque (du camion) s'est mise en travers; **~ plug** *n (ELEC)* prise jack mâle *f*; **~pot** *n* gros lot

**jaded** ['dʒeɪdɪd] *adj* éreinté(e), fatigué(e)

**jagged** ['dʒægɪd] *adj* dentelé(e)

**jail** [dʒeɪl] *n* prison *f* ♦ *vt* emprisonner, mettre en prison

**jam** [dʒæm] *n* confiture *f*; *(also:* **traffic ~)** embouteillage *m* ♦ *vt (passage etc)*

encombrer, obstruer; *(mechanism, drawer etc)* bloquer, coincer; *(RADIO)* brouiller ♦ *vi* se coincer, se bloquer; *(gun)* s'enrayer; **to be in a ~** *(inf)* être dans le pétrin; **to ~ sth into** entasser qch dans; enfoncer qch dans

**Jamaica** [dʒə'meɪkə] *n* Jamaïque *f*

**jam:** **~ jar** *n* pot *m* à confiture; **~med** *adj (window etc)* coincé(e); **~-packed** *adj:* **~-packed (with)** bourré(e) (de)

**jangle** ['dʒæŋgl] *vi* cliqueter

**janitor** ['dʒænɪtər] *n* concierge *m*

**January** ['dʒænjuərɪ] *n* janvier *m*

**Japan** [dʒə'pæn] *n* Japon *m*; **~ese** [dʒæpə'niːz] *adj* japonais(e) ♦ *n inv* Japonais(e); *(LING)* japonais *m*

**jar** [dʒɑː] *n (stone, earthenware)* pot *m*; *(glass)* bocal *m* ♦ *vi (sound discordant)* produire un son grinçant ou discordant; *(colours etc)* jurer

**jargon** ['dʒɑːgən] *n* jargon *m*

**jaundice** ['dʒɔːndɪs] *n* jaunisse *f*

**javelin** ['dʒævlɪn] *n* javelot *m*

**jaw** [dʒɔː] *n* mâchoire *f*

**jay** [dʒeɪ] *n* geai *m*; **~walker** *n* piéton indiscipliné

**jazz** [dʒæz] *n* jazz *m*; **~ up** *vt* animer, égayer

**jealous** ['dʒeləs] *adj* jaloux(-ouse); **~y** *n* jalousie *f*

**jeans** [dʒiːnz] *npl* jean *m*

**jeer** [dʒɪər] *vi:* **to ~ (at)** se moquer cruellement (de), railler

**Jehovah's Witness** [dʒɪ'həʊvəz-] *n* témoin *m* de Jéhovah

**jelly** ['dʒelɪ] *n* gelée *f*; **~fish** ['dʒelɪfɪʃ] *n* méduse *f*

**jeopardy** ['dʒepədɪ] *n:* **to be in ~** être en danger ou péril

**jerk** [dʒɜːk] *n* secousse *f*; saccade *f*; sursaut *m*, spasme *m*; *(inf: idiot)* pauvre type *m* ♦ *vt (pull)* tirer brusquement ♦ *vi (vehicles)* cahoter

**jersey** ['dʒɜːzɪ] *n (pullover)* tricot *m*; *(fabric)* jersey *m*

**Jesus** ['dʒiːzəs] *n* Jésus *m*

**jet** [dʒet] *n (gas, liquid)* jet *m*; *(AVIAT)*

avion *m* à réaction, jet *m*; **~black** *adj* (d'un noir) de jais; **~ engine** *n* moteur *m* à réaction; **~ lag** *n* (fatigue due au) décalage *m* horaire

**jettison** ['dʒetɪsn] *vt* jeter par-dessus bord

**jetty** ['dʒetɪ] *n* jetée *f*, digue *f*

**Jew** [dʒu:] *n* Juif *m*

**jewel** ['dʒu:əl] *n* bijou *m*, joyau *m*; (in watch) rubis *m*; **~ler** (*US* **jeweler**) *n* bijoutier(-ère), joaillier *m*; **~ler's (shop)** *n* bijouterie *f*, joaillerie *f*; **~lery** (*US* **jewelry**) *n* bijoux *mpl*

**Jewess** ['dʒu:ɪs] *n* Juive *f*

**Jewish** ['dʒu:ɪʃ] *adj* juif (juive)

**jibe** [dʒaɪb] *n* sarcasme *m*

**jiffy** ['dʒɪfɪ] (*inf*) *n*: **in a ~** en un clin d'œil

**jigsaw** ['dʒɪgsɔ:] *n* (also: **~ puzzle**) puzzle *m*

**jilt** [dʒɪlt] *vt* laisser tomber, plaquer

**jingle** ['dʒɪŋgl] *n* (for advert) couplet *m* publicitaire ♦ *vi* cliqueter, tinter

**jinx** [dʒɪŋks] (*inf*) *n* (mauvais) sort

**jitters** ['dʒɪtəz] (*inf*) *npl*: **to get the ~** (*inf*) avoir la trouille ou la frousse

**job** [dʒɔb] *n* (chore, task) travail *m*, tâche *f*; (employment) emploi *m*, poste *m*, place *f*; **it's a good ~ that ...** c'est heureux ou c'est une chance que ...; **just the ~!** (c'est) juste ou exactement ce qu'il faut!; **~ centre** (*BRIT*) *n* agence *f* pour l'emploi; **~less** *adj* sans travail, au chômage

**jockey** ['dʒɔkɪ] *n* jockey *m* ♦ *vi*: **to ~ for position** manœuvrer pour être bien placé

**jog** [dʒɔg] *vt* secouer ♦ *vi* (*SPORT*) faire du jogging; **to ~ sb's memory** rafraîchir la mémoire de qn; **~ along** *vi* cheminer; trotter; **~ging** *n* jogging *m*

**join** [dʒɔɪn] *vt* (put together) unir, assembler; (become member of) s'inscrire à; (meet) rejoindre, retrouver; (queue) se joindre à ♦ *vi* (roads, rivers) se rejoindre, se rencontrer ♦ *n* raccord *m*; **~ in** *vi* se mettre de la partie, participer ♦

*vt fus* participer à, se mêler à; **~ up** *vi* (meet) se rejoindre; (*MIL*) s'engager

**joiner** ['dʒɔɪnə*] (*BRIT*) *n* menuisier *m*

**joint** [dʒɔɪnt] *n* (*TECH*) jointure *f*; joint *m*; (*ANAT*) articulation *f*, jointure *f*; (*CULIN*) rôti *m*; (*inf: place*) boîte *f*; (: of cannabis) joint *m* ♦ *adj* commun(e); **~ account** *n* (with bank etc) compte joint

**joke** [dʒəuk] *n* plaisanterie *f*; (also: **practical ~**) farce *f* ♦ *vi* plaisanter; **to play a ~ on** jouer un tour à, faire une farce à; **~r** *n* (*CARDS*) joker *m*

**jolly** ['dʒɔlɪ] *adj* gai(e), enjoué(e); (enjoyable) amusant(e), plaisant(e) ♦ *adv* (*BRIT: inf*) rudement, drôlement

**jolt** [dʒəult] *n* cahot *m*, secousse *f*; (shock) choc *m* ♦ *vt* cahoter, secouer

**Jordan** ['dʒɔ:dən] *n* (country) Jordanie *f*

**jostle** ['dʒɔsl] *vt* bousculer, pousser

**jot** [dʒɔt] *n*: **not one ~** pas un brin; **~ down** *vt* noter; **~ter** (*BRIT*) *n* cahier *m* (de brouillon); (pad) bloc-notes *m*

**journal** ['dʒɜ:nl] *n* journal *m*; **~ism** *n* journalisme *m*; **~ist** *n* journaliste *m/f*

**journey** ['dʒɜ:nɪ] *n* voyage *m*; (distance covered) trajet *m*

**joy** [dʒɔɪ] *n* joie *f*; **~ful** *adj* joyeux (-euse); **~rider** *n* personne qui fait une virée dans une voiture volée; **~stick** *n* (*AVIAT, COMPUT*) manche à balai

**JP** *n abbr* = **Justice of the Peace**

**Jr** *abbr* = **junior**

**jubilant** ['dʒu:bɪlnt] *adj* triomphant(e), réjoui(e)

**judge** [dʒʌdʒ] *n* juge *m* ♦ *vt* juger; **judg(e)ment** *n* jugement *m*

**judicial** [dʒu:'dɪʃl] *adj* judiciaire; **judiciary** *n* (pouvoir *m*) judiciaire

**judo** ['dʒu:dəu] *n* judo *m*

**jug** [dʒʌg] *n* pot *m*, cruche *f*

**juggernaut** ['dʒʌgənɔ:t] (*BRIT*) *n* (huge truck) énorme poids lourd

**juggle** ['dʒʌgl] *vi* jongler; **~r** *n* jongleur *m*

**juice** [dʒu:s] *n* jus *m*; **juicy** *adj* juteux (-euse)

**jukebox** ['dʒuːkbɒks] n juke-box m

**July** [dʒuː'laɪ] n juillet m

**jumble** ['dʒʌmbl] n fouillis m ♦ vt (also: ~ up) mélanger, brouiller; ~ **sale** (BRIT) n vente f de charité

---
**jumble sale**

Les jumble sales ont lieu dans les églises, salles de fêtes ou halls d'écoles, et l'on y vend des articles de toutes sortes, en général bon marché et surtout d'occasion, pour collecter des fonds pour une œuvre de charité, une école ou encore une église.

---

**jumbo (jet)** ['dʒʌmbəu-] n jumbo-jet m, gros porteur

**jump** [dʒʌmp] vi sauter, bondir; (start) sursauter; (increase) monter en flèche ♦ vt sauter, franchir ♦ n saut m, bond m; sursaut m; **to ~ the queue** (BRIT) passer avant son tour

**jumper** ['dʒʌmpər] n (BRIT: pullover) pull-over m; (US: dress) robe-chasuble f

**jumper cables** (US: BRIT **jump leads**) npl câbles mpl de démarrage

**jumpy** ['dʒʌmpɪ] adj nerveux(-euse), agité(e)

**Jun.** abbr = **junior**

**junction** ['dʒʌŋkʃən] (BRIT) n (of roads) carrefour m; (of rails) embranchement m

**juncture** ['dʒʌŋktʃər] n: **at this ~** à ce moment-là, sur ces entrefaites

**June** [dʒuːn] n juin m

**jungle** ['dʒʌŋgl] n jungle f

**junior** ['dʒuːnɪər] adj, n: **he's ~ to me (by 2 years)**, **he's my ~ (by 2 years)** il est mon cadet (de 2 ans), il est plus jeune que moi (de 2 ans); **he's ~ to me** (seniority) il est en dessous de moi (dans la hiérarchie), j'ai plus d'ancienneté que lui; ~ **school** (BRIT) n ≈ école f primaire

**junk** [dʒʌŋk] n (rubbish) camelote f; (cheap goods) bric-à-brac m inv; ~ **food** n aliments mpl sans grande valeur nutri-

tive; ~ **mail** n prospectus mpl (non sollicités); ~ **shop** n (boutique f de) brocanteur m

**Junr** abbr = **junior**

**juror** ['dʒuərər] n juré m

**jury** ['dʒuərɪ] n jury m

**just** [dʒʌst] adj juste ♦ adv: **he's ~ done it/left** il vient de le faire/partir; ~ **right/two o'clock** exactement ou juste ce qu'il faut/deux heures; **she's ~ as clever as you** elle est tout aussi intelligente que vous; **it's ~ as well (that)** ... heureusement que ...; ~ **as he was leaving** au moment or à l'instant précis où il partait; ~ **before/enough/here** juste avant/assez/ici; **it's ~ me/a mistake** ce n'est pas moi/(rien) qu'une erreur; ~ **missed/caught** manqué/attrapé de justesse; ~ **listen to this!** écoutez un peu ça!

**justice** ['dʒʌstɪs] n justice f; (US: judge) juge m de la Cour suprême; **J~ of the Peace** n juge m de paix

**justify** ['dʒʌstɪfaɪ] vt justifier

**jut** [dʒʌt] vi (also: ~ **out**) dépasser, faire saillie

**juvenile** ['dʒuːvənaɪl] adj juvénile; (court, books) pour enfants ♦ n adolescent(e)

# K, k

**K** abbr (= one thousand) K; (= kilobyte) Ko

**kangaroo** [kæŋgə'ruː] n kangourou m

**karate** [kə'rɑːtɪ] n karaté m

**kebab** [kə'bæb] n kébab m

**keel** [kiːl] n quille f; **on an even ~** (fig) à flot

**keen** [kiːn] adj (eager) plein(e) d'enthousiasme; (interest, desire, competition) vif (vive); (eye, intelligence) pénétrant(e); (edge) effilé(e); **to be ~ to do** or **on doing sth** désirer vivement faire qch, tenir beaucoup à faire qch; **to be ~ on sth/sb** aimer beaucoup qch/qn

**keep** [kiːp] (*pt, pp* **kept**) *vt* (*retain, preserve*) garder; (*detain*) retenir; (*shop, accounts, diary, promise*) tenir; (*house*) avoir; (*support*) entretenir; (*chickens, bees etc*) élever ♦ *vi* (*remain*) rester; (*food*) se conserver ♦ *n* (*of castle*) donjon *m*; (*food: inf*): **enough for his ~** assez pour (assurer) sa subsistance; (*inf*): **for ~s** pour de bon, pour toujours; **to ~ doing sth** ne pas arrêter de faire qch; **to ~ sb from doing sth** empêcher qn de faire or que qn ne fasse; **to ~ sb happy/a place tidy** faire que qn soit content/qu'un endroit reste propre; **to ~ sth to o.s.** garder qch pour soi, tenir qch secret; **to ~ sth (back) from sb** cacher qch à qn; **to ~ time** (*clock*) être à l'heure, ne pas retarder; **well kept** bien entretenu(e); **~ on** *vi*: **to ~ on doing** continuer à faire; **don't ~ on about it!** arrête (d'en parler)!; **~ out** *vt* empêcher d'entrer; **"~ out"** "défense d'entrer"; **~ up** *vt* continuer, maintenir ♦ *vi*: **to ~ up with sb** (*in race etc*) aller aussi vite que qn; (*in work etc*) se maintenir au niveau de qn; **~er** *n* gardien(ne); **~-fit** *n* gymnastique *f* d'entretien; **~ing** *n* (*care*) garde *f*; **in ~ing with** en accord avec; **~sake** *n* souvenir *m*

**kennel** ['kɛnl] *n* niche *f*; **~s** *npl* (*boarding ~s*) chenil *m*

**kerb** [kəːb] (*BRIT*) *n* bordure *f* du trottoir

**kernel** ['kəːnl] *n* (*of nut*) amande *f*; (*fig*) noyau *m*

**kettle** ['kɛtl] *n* bouilloire *f*; **~drum** *n* timbale *f*

**key** [kiː] *n* (*gen, MUS*) clé *f*; (*of piano, typewriter*) touche *f* ♦ *cpd* clé ♦ *vt* (*also*: **~ in**) introduire (au clavier), saisir; **~board** *n* clavier *m*; **~ed up** *adj* (*person*) surexcité(e); **~hole** *n* trou *m* de la serrure; **~hole surgery** *n* chirurgie *f* très minutieuse où l'incision est minimale; **~note** *n* (*of speech*) note *f* dominante; (*MUS*) tonique *f*; **~ ring** *n* porte-clés *m*

**khaki** ['kɑːkɪ] *n* kaki *m*

**kick** [kɪk] *vt* donner un coup de pied à ♦ *vi* (*horse*) ruer ♦ *n* coup *m* de pied; (*thrill*): **he does it for ~s** il le fait parce que ça l'excite, il le fait pour le plaisir; **to ~ the habit** (*inf*) arrêter; **~ off** *vi* (*SPORT*) donner le coup d'envoi

**kid** [kɪd] *n* (*inf: child*) gamin(e), gosse *m/f*; (*animal, leather*) chevreau *m* ♦ *vi* (*inf*) plaisanter, blaguer

**kidnap** ['kɪdnæp] *vt* enlever, kidnapper; **~per** *n* ravisseur(-euse); **~ping** *n* enlèvement *m*

**kidney** ['kɪdnɪ] *n* (*ANAT*) rein *m*; (*CULIN*) rognon *m*

**kill** [kɪl] *vt* tuer ♦ *n* mise *f* à mort; **~er** *n* tueur(-euse); meurtrier(-ère); **~ing** *n* meurtre *m*; (*of group of people*) tuerie *f*, massacre *m*; **to make a ~** (*inf*) réussir un beau coup (de filet); **~joy** *n* rabat-joie *m/f*

**kiln** [kɪln] *n* four *m*

**kilo** ['kiːləʊ] *n* kilo *m*; **~byte** *n* (*COMPUT*) kilo-octet *m*; **~gram(me)** *n* kilogramme *m*; **~metre** (*US* **kilometer**) *n* kilomètre *m*; **~watt** *n* kilowatt *m*

**kilt** [kɪlt] *n* kilt *m*

**kin** [kɪn] *n see* **next**

**kind** [kaɪnd] *adj* gentil(le), aimable ♦ *n* sorte *f*, espèce *f*, genre *m*; (*COMM*) nature *f*; **to be two of a ~** se ressembler; **in ~** (*COMM*) en nature

**kindergarten** ['kɪndəgɑːtn] *n* jardin *m* d'enfants

**kind-hearted** [kaɪnd'hɑːtɪd] *adj* bon (bonne)

**kindle** ['kɪndl] *vt* allumer, enflammer

**kindly** ['kaɪndlɪ] *adj* bienveillant(e), plein(e) de gentillesse ♦ *adv* avec bonté; **will you ...!** auriez-vous la bonté or l'obligeance de ...?

**kindness** ['kaɪndnɪs] *n* bonté *f*, gentillesse *f*

**king** [kɪŋ] *n* roi *m*; **~dom** *n* royaume *m*; **~fisher** *n* martin-pêcheur *m*; **~-size bed** *n* grand lit (de 1,95 *m* de large); **~-size(d)** *adj* format géant *inv*; (*cigarettes*) long (longue)

**kiosk** ['kiːɔsk] *n* kiosque *m*; (BRIT: TEL) cabine *f* (téléphonique)

**kipper** ['kɪpə'] *n* hareng fumé et salé

**kiss** [kɪs] *n* baiser *m* ♦ *vt* embrasser; **to ~ (each other)** s'embrasser; **~ of life** (BRIT) bouche à bouche *m*

**kit** [kɪt] *n* équipement *m*, matériel *m*; (set of tools etc) trousse *f*; (for assembly) kit *m*

**kitchen** ['kɪtʃɪn] *n* cuisine *f*; **~ sink** *n* évier *m*

**kite** [kaɪt] *n* (toy) cerf-volant *m*

**kitten** ['kɪtn] *n* chaton *m*, petit chat

**kitty** ['kɪtɪ] *n* (money) cagnotte *f*

**km** *abbr* = **kilometre**

**knack** [næk] *n*: **to have the ~ of doing** avoir le coup pour faire

**knapsack** ['næpsæk] *n* musette *f*

**knead** [niːd] *vt* pétrir

**knee** [niː] *n* genou *m*; **~cap** *n* rotule *f*

**kneel** [niːl] (*pt, pp* **knelt**) *vi* (also: **~ down**) s'agenouiller

**knew** [njuː] *pt of* **know**

**knickers** ['nɪkəz] (BRIT) *npl* culotte *f* (de femme)

**knife** [naɪf] (*pl* **knives**) *n* couteau *m* ♦ *vt* poignarder, frapper d'un coup de couteau

**knight** [naɪt] *n* chevalier *m*; (CHESS) cavalier *m*; **~hood** [-hud] *n* (title): **to get a ~hood** être fait chevalier

**knit** [nɪt] *vt* tricoter ♦ *vi* tricoter; (broken bones) se ressouder; **to ~ one's brows** froncer les sourcils; **~ting** *n* tricot *m*; **~ting needle** *n* aiguille *f* à tricoter; **~wear** *n* tricots *mpl*, lainages *mpl*

**knives** [naɪvz] *npl of* **knife**

**knob** [nɔb] *n* bouton *m*

**knock** [nɔk] *n* frapper; (bump into) heurter; (inf) dénigrer ♦ *vi* (at door etc): **to ~ at** *or* **on** frapper à ♦ *n* coup *m*; **~ down** *vt* renverser; **~ off** *vi* (inf: finish) s'arrêter (de travailler); ♦ *vt* (from price) faire un rabais de; (inf: steal) piquer; **~ out** *vt* assommer; (BOXING) mettre k.-o.; (defeat) éliminer; **~ over** *vt* renverser, faire tomber; **~** n (on door) heurtoir

*m*; **~out** *n* (BOXING) knock-out *m*, K.-O. *m*; **~out competition** compétition *f* avec épreuves éliminatoires

**knot** [nɔt] *n* (gen) nœud *m* ♦ *vt* nouer

**know** [nəu] (*pt* **knew**, *pp* **known**) *vt* savoir; (person, place) connaître; **to ~ how to do** savoir (comment) faire; **to ~ how to swim** savoir nager; **to ~ about** *or* **of sth** être au courant de qch; **to ~ about** *or* **of sb** avoir entendu parler de qn; **~-all** (pej) *n* je-sais-tout *m/f*; **~-how** *n* savoir-faire *m*; **~ing** *adj* (look etc) entendu(e); **~ingly** *adv* sciemment; (smile, look) d'un air entendu

**knowledge** ['nɔlɪdʒ] *n* connaissance *f*; (learning) connaissances, savoir *m*; **~able** *adj* bien informé(e)

**knuckle** ['nʌkl] *n* articulation *f* (des doigts), jointure *f*

**Koran** [kɔ'rɑːn] *n* Coran *m*

**Korea** [kə'rɪə] *n* Corée *f*

**kosher** ['kəuʃə'] *adj* kascher *inv*

**Kosovo** ['kɔsəvəu] *n* Kosovo *m*

# L, l

**L** *abbr* = (*lake*, *large*) L; (= *left*) g; (BRIT: AUT: *learner*) signale un conducteur débutant

**lab** [læb] *n abbr* (= *laboratory*) labo *m*

**label** ['leɪbl] *n* étiquette *f* ♦ *vt* étiqueter

**labor** *etc* ['leɪbə'] (US) = **labour** *etc*

**laboratory** [lə'bɔrətəri] *n* laboratoire *m*

**labour** ['leɪbə'] (US **labor**) *n* (work) travail *m*; (workforce) main-d'œuvre *f* ♦ *vi*: **to ~ (at)** travailler dur (à), peiner (sur) ♦ *vt*: **to ~ a point** insister sur un point; **in ~** (MED) en travail, en train d'accoucher; **L~, the L~ party** (BRIT) le parti travailliste, les travaillistes *mpl*; **~ed** ['leɪbəd] *adj* (breathing) pénible, difficile; **~er** *n* manœuvre *m*; **farm ~er** *n* ouvrier *m* agricole

**lace** [leɪs] *n* dentelle *f*; (of shoe etc) lacet *m* ♦ *vt* (shoe: also: **~ up**) lacer

**lack** [læk] *n* manque *m* ♦ *vt* manquer

de; (through or for) ~ faute de, par manque de; (to be ~ing) manquer, faire défaut; (to be ~ing in) manquer de

**lacquer** ['lækə*] n laque f

**lad** [læd] n garçon m, gars m

**ladder** ['lædə*] n échelle f; (BRIT: in tights) maille filée

**laden** ['leɪdn] adj: ~ (with) chargé(e) (de)

**ladle** ['leɪdl] n louche f

**lady** ['leɪdɪ] n dame f; (in address): **ladies and gentlemen** Mesdames (et) Messieurs; **young** ~ jeune fille f; (married) jeune femme f; **the ladies' (room)** les toilettes fpl (pour dames); ~**bird** (US **ladybug**) n coccinelle f; ~**like** adj distingué(e); ~**ship** n: **your** ~**ship** Madame la comtesse/la baronne etc

**lag** [læg] n retard m ♦ vi (also: ~ **behind**) rester en arrière, traîner; (fig) rester en traîne ♦ vt (pipes) calorifuger

**lager** ['lɑːɡə*] n bière blonde

**lagoon** [lə'ɡuːn] n lagune f

**laid** [leɪd] pt, pp of **lay**; ~**back** (inf) adj relaxe, décontracté(e); ~ **up** adj alité(e)

**lain** [leɪn] pp of **lie**

**lake** [leɪk] n lac m

**lamb** [læm] n agneau m; ~ **chop** n côtelette f d'agneau

**lame** [leɪm] adj boiteux(-euse)

**lament** [lə'ment] n lamentation f ♦ vt pleurer, se lamenter sur

**laminated** ['læmɪneɪtɪd] adj laminé(e); (windscreen) en verre feuilleté

**lamp** [læmp] n lampe f; ~**post** (BRIT) n réverbère m; ~**shade** n abat-jour m inv

**lance** [lɑːns] vt (MED) inciser

**land** [lænd] n (as opposed to sea) terre f (ferme); (soil) terre; terrain m; (estate) terre(s), domaine(s) m(pl); (country) pays m ♦ vi (AVIAT) atterrir; (fig) (re)tomber ♦ vt (passengers, goods) débarquer; **to ~ sb with sth** (inf) coller qch à qn; ~ **up** vi atterrir, (finir par) se retrouver; ~**fill site** n décharge f; ~**ing** n (AVIAT) atterrissage m; (of staircase)

palier m; (of troops) débarquement m; ~**ing strip** n piste f d'atterrissage; ~**lady** n propriétaire f, logeuse f; (of pub) patronne f; ~**locked** adj sans littoral; ~**lord** n propriétaire m, logeur m; (of pub etc) patron m; ~**mark** n (point de) repère m; **to be a ~mark** (fig) faire date or époque; ~**owner** n propriétaire foncier or terrien m; ~**scape** n paysage m; ~**scape gardener** n jardinier(-ère) paysagiste; ~**slide** n (GEO) glissement m (de terrain); (fig: POL) raz-de-marée (électoral)

**lane** [leɪn] n (in country) chemin m; (AUT) voie f; file f; (in race) couloir m; **"get in ~"** (AUT) "mettez-vous dans or sur la bonne file"

**language** ['læŋɡwɪdʒ] n langue f; (way one speaks) langage m; **bad** ~ grossièretés fpl, langage grossier; ~ **laboratory** n laboratoire m de langues

**lank** [læŋk] adj (hair) raide et terne

**lanky** ['læŋkɪ] adj grand(e) et maigre, efflanqué(e)

**lantern** ['læntən] n lanterne f

**lap** [læp] n (of track) tour m (de piste); (of body): **in** or **on one's** ~ sur les genoux ♦ vt (also: ~ **up**) laper ♦ vi (waves) clapoter; ~ **up** vt (fig) accepter béatement, gober

**lapel** [lə'pel] n revers m

**Lapland** ['læplænd] n Laponie f

**lapse** [læps] n défaillance f; (in behaviour) écart m de conduite ♦ vi (LAW) cesser d'être en vigueur; (contract) expirer; **to ~ into bad habits** prendre de mauvaises habitudes; ~ **of time** laps m de temps, intervalle m

**laptop (computer)** n ['læptɒp(-)] n portable m

**larceny** ['lɑːsənɪ] n vol m

**larch** [lɑːtʃ] n mélèze m

**lard** [lɑːd] n saindoux m

**larder** ['lɑːdə*] n garde-manger m inv

**large** [lɑːdʒ] adj grand(e); (person, animal) gros(se); **at** ~ (free) en liberté; (generally) en général; see also **by**; ~**ly**

**lark** [lɑːk] n (bird) alouette f; (joke) blague f, farce f

**laryngitis** [lærɪnˈdʒaɪtɪs] n laryngite f

**laser** [ˈleɪzəʳ] n laser m; ~ **printer** n imprimante f laser

**lash** [læʃ] n coup m de fouet; (also: **eyelash**) cil m ♦ vt fouetter; (tie) attacher; ~ **out** vi: **to ~ out at** or **against** attaquer violemment

**lass** [læs] (BRIT) n (jeune) fille f

**lasso** [læˈsuː] n lasso m

**last** [lɑːst] adj dernier(-ère) ♦ adv en dernier; (finally) finalement ♦ vi durer; ~ **week** la semaine dernière; ~ **night** (evening) hier soir; (night) la nuit dernière; **at** ~ enfin; **but one** avant-dernier(-ère); **~-ditch** adj (attempt) ultime, désespéré(e); **~ing** adj durable; **~ly** adv en dernier lieu, pour finir; **~-minute** adj de dernière minute

**latch** [lætʃ] n loquet m

**late** [leɪt] adj (not on time) en retard; (far on in day etc) tardif(-ive); (edition, delivery) dernier(-ère); (former) ancien(ne) ♦ adv tard; (behind time, schedule) en retard; **of** ~ dernièrement; **in** ~ **May** vers la fin (du mois) de mai, fin mai; **the** ~ **Mr X** feu M. X; **~comer** n retardataire m/f; **~ly** adv récemment; ~ (date etc) ultérieur(e); (version etc) plus récent(e) ♦ adv plus tard; **~r on** plus tard; **~st** adj tout(e) dernier(-ère); **at the ~st** au plus tard

**lathe** [leɪð] n tour m

**lather** [ˈlɑːðəʳ] n mousse f (de savon) ♦ vt savonner

**Latin** [ˈlætɪn] n latin m ♦ adj latin(e); ~ **America** n Amérique latine; ~ **American** adj latino-américain(e)

**latitude** [ˈlætɪtjuːd] n latitude f

**latter** [ˈlætəʳ] adj deuxième, dernier(-ère) ♦ n: **the** ~ ce dernier, celui-ci; **~ly** adv dernièrement, récemment

**laudable** [ˈlɔːdəbl] adj louable

**laugh** [lɑːf] n rire m ♦ vi rire; ~ **at** vt fus se moquer de; rire de; ~ **off** vt écarter par une plaisanterie or par une boutade; **~able** adj risible, ridicule; **~ing stock** n: **the ~ing stock of** la risée de; **~ter** n rire m; rires mpl

**launch** [lɔːntʃ] n lancement m; (motorboat) vedette f ♦ vt lancer; ~ **into** vt fus se lancer dans

**Launderette** ® [lɔːnˈdrɛt] (BRIT), **Laundromat** ® [ˈlɔːndrəmæt] (US) n laverie f (automatique)

**laundry** [ˈlɔːndrɪ] n (clothes) linge m; (business) blanchisserie f; (room) buanderie f

**laurel** [ˈlɔrl] n laurier m

**lava** [ˈlɑːvə] n lave f

**lavatory** [ˈlævətərɪ] n toilettes fpl

**lavender** [ˈlævəndəʳ] n lavande f

**lavish** [ˈlævɪʃ] adj (amount) copieux (-euse); (person): ~ **with** prodigue de ♦ vt: **to ~ sth on sb** prodiguer qch à qn; (money) dépenser sans compter pour qn/qch

**law** [lɔː] n loi f; (science) droit m; **~-abiding** adj respectueux(-euse) des lois; ~ **and order** n l'ordre public; ~ **court** n tribunal m, cour f de justice; **~ful** adj légal(e); **~less** adj (action) illégal(e)

**lawn** [lɔːn] n pelouse f; **~mower** n tondeuse f à gazon; ~ **tennis** n tennis m

**law school** (US) n faculté f de droit

**lawsuit** [ˈlɔːsuːt] n procès m

**lawyer** [ˈlɔːjəʳ] n (consultant, with company) juriste m; (for sales, wills etc) notaire m; (partner, in court) avocat m

**lax** [læks] adj relâché(e)

**laxative** [ˈlæksətɪv] n laxatif m

**lay** [leɪ] (pt, pp **laid**) pt of **lie** ♦ adj laïque; (not expert) profane ♦ vt poser, mettre; (eggs) pondre; **to ~ the table** mettre la table; ~ **aside** vt mettre de côté; ~ **by** vt = **lay aside**; ~ **down** vt poser; ~ **down the law** faire la loi; **to ~ down one's life** sacrifier sa vie; ~

**off** vt (workers) licencier; **~ on** vt (provide) fournir; **~ out** vt (display) disposer, étaler; **~about** (inf) n fainéant(e); **~by** (BRIT) n aire f de stationnement (sur le bas-côté)

**layer** ['leɪə*] n couche f

**layman** ['leɪmən] (irreg) n profane m

**layout** ['leɪaut] n disposition f, plan m, agencement m; (PRESS) mise f en page

**laze** [leɪz] vi (also: ~ about) paresser

**lazy** ['leɪzɪ] adj paresseux(-euse)

**lb** abbr = **pound** (weight)

**lead¹** [li:d] (pt, pp led) n (distance, time ahead) avance f; (clue) piste f; (THEATRE) rôle principal; (ELEC) fil m; (for dog) laisse f ♦ vt mener, conduire; (be ~er of) être à la tête de ♦ vi (street etc) mener, conduire; (SPORT) mener, être en tête; **in the ~** en tête; **to ~ the way** montrer le chemin; **~ away** vt emmener; **~ back** vt to ~ back to ramener à; **~ on** vt (tease) faire marcher; **~ on to** vt fus mener à; conduire à; **~ up to** vt fus conduire à

**lead²** [lɛd] n (metal) plomb m; (in pencil) mine f; **~ed petrol** n essence f au plomb; **~en** adj (sky, sea) de plomb

**leader** ['li:də*] n chef m; dirigeant(e), leader m; (SPORT: in league) leader; (: in race) coureur m de tête; **~ship** n direction f; (quality) qualités fpl de chef

**lead-free** ['lɛdfri:] adj (petrol) sans plomb

**leading** ['li:dɪŋ] adj principal(e); de premier plan; (in race) de tête; **~ lady** n (THEATRE) vedette (féminine); **~ light** n (person) vedette f, sommité f; **~ man** (irreg) n vedette (masculine)

**lead singer** [li:d-] n (in pop group) (chanteur m) vedette f

**leaf** [li:f] (pl **leaves**) n feuille f ♦ vi: **to ~ through** feuilleter; **to turn over a new ~** changer de conduite ou d'existence

**leaflet** ['li:flɪt] n prospectus m, brochure f; (POL, REL) tract m

**league** [li:g] n ligue f; (FOOTBALL) championnat m; **to be in ~ with** avoir partie liée avec, être de mèche avec

**leak** [li:k] n fuite f ♦ vi (pipe, liquid etc) fuir; (shoes) prendre l'eau; (ship) faire eau ♦ vt (information) divulguer

**lean** [li:n] (pt, pp **leaned** or **leant**) adj maigre ♦ vt: **to ~ sth on sth** appuyer qch sur qch ♦ vi (slope) pencher; (rest): **to ~ against** s'appuyer contre; être appuyé(e) contre; **to ~ on** s'appuyer sur; **to ~ back/forward** se pencher en arrière/avant; **~ out** vi se pencher au dehors; **~ over** vi se pencher; **~ing** n: **~ing (towards)** tendance f (à), penchant m (pour); **~t** [lɛnt] pt, pp of **lean**

**leap** [li:p] (pt, pp **leaped** or **leapt**) n bond m, saut m ♦ vi bondir, sauter; **~frog** n saute-mouton m; **~t** [lɛpt] pt, pp of **leap**; **~ year** n année f bissextile

**learn** [lə:n] (pt, pp **learned** or **learnt**) vt, vi apprendre; **to ~ to do sth** apprendre à faire qch; **to ~ about or of sth** (hear, read) apprendre qch; **~ed** ['lə:nɪd] adj érudit(e), savant(e); **~er** (BRIT) n (also: **~er driver**) (conducteur (-trice)) débutant(e); **~ing** n (knowledge) savoir m; **~t** pt, pp of **learn**

**lease** [li:s] n bail m ♦ vt louer à bail

**least** [li:st] n laisse f

**least** [li:st] adj: **the ~** (+noun) le (la) plus petit(e), le (la) moindre; (: smallest amount of) le moins de ♦ adv (+verb) le moins; (+adj): **the ~** le (la) moins; **at ~** au moins; (or rather) du moins; **not in the ~** pas le moins du monde

**leather** ['lɛðə*] n cuir m

**leave** [li:v] (pt, pp **left**) vt laisser; (go away from) quitter; (forget) oublier ♦ vi partir, s'en aller ♦ n (time off) congé m; (MIL also: consent) permission f; **to be left** rester; **there's some milk left** il reste du lait; **on ~** en permission; **~ behind** vt (person, object) laisser; (forget) oublier; **~ out** vt oublier, omettre; **~ of absence** n congé exceptionnel; (MIL) permission spéciale

**leaves** [li:vz] npl of **leaf**

**Lebanon** ['lebənən] n Liban m

**lecherous** ['letʃərəs] (pej) adj lubrique

**lecture** ['lektʃə$^r$] n conférence f; (SCOL) cours m ♦ vi donner des cours; enseigner ♦ vt (scold) sermonner, réprimander; **to give a ~ on** faire une conférence sur; donner un cours sur; **~r** (BRIT) n (at university) professeur m (d'université)

**led** [led] pt, pp of **lead**¹

**ledge** [ledʒ] n (of window, on wall) rebord m; (of mountain) saillie f, corniche f

**ledger** ['ledʒə$^r$] n (COMM) registre m, grand livre

**leech** [li:tʃ] n (also fig) sangsue f

**leek** [li:k] n poireau m

**leer** [lɪə$^r$] vi: **to ~ at sb** regarder qn d'un air mauvais ou concupiscent

**leeway** ['li:weɪ] n (fig): **to have some ~** avoir une certaine liberté d'action

**left** [left] pt, pp of **leave** ♦ adj (not right) gauche ♦ n gauche f ♦ adv à gauche; **on the ~, to the ~** à gauche; **the L~** (POL) la gauche; **~-handed** adj gaucher(-ère); **~-hand side** n gauche f; **~-luggage locker** n (casier m à) consigne f automatique; **~-luggage (office)** (BRIT) n consigne f; **~overs** npl restes mpl; **~-wing** adj (POL) de gauche

**leg** [leg] n jambe f; (of animal) patte f; (of furniture) pied m; (CULIN: of chicken, pork) cuisse f; (: of lamb) gigot m; (of journey) étape f; **1st/2nd ~** (SPORT) match m aller/retour

**legacy** ['legəsɪ] n héritage m, legs m

**legal** ['li:gl] adj légal(e); **~ holiday** (US) n jour férié; **~ tender** n monnaie légale

**legend** ['ledʒənd] n légende f

**leggings** ['legɪnz] npl caleçon n

**legible** ['ledʒəbl] adj lisible

**legislation** [ledʒɪs'leɪʃən] n législation f; **legislature** ['ledʒɪslətʃə$^r$] n (corps m) législatif m

**legitimate** [lɪ'dʒɪtɪmət] adj légitime

**leg-room** ['legru:m] n place f pour les jambes

**leisure** ['leʒə$^r$] n loisir m, temps m libre; loisirs mpl; **at ~** (tout) à loisir; à tête reposée; **~ centre** n centre m de loisirs; **~ly** adj tranquille; fait(e) sans se presser

**lemon** ['lemən] n citron m; **~ade** [lemə'neɪd] n limonade f; **~ tea** n thé m au citron

**lend** [lend] (pt, pp lent) vt: **to ~ sth (to sb)** prêter qch (à qn)

**length** [leŋθ] n longueur f; (section: of road, pipe etc) morceau m, bout m; (of time) durée f; **at ~** (at last) enfin, à la fin; (~ily) longuement, en long; **~en** vt allonger, prolonger ♦ vi s'allonger; **~ways** adv dans le sens de la longueur, en long; **~y** adj (très) long (longue)

**lenient** ['li:nɪənt] adj indulgent(e), clément(e)

**lens** [lenz] n lentille f; (of spectacles) verre m; (of camera) objectif m

**Lent** [lent] n carême m

**lent** [lent] pt, pp of **lend**

**lentil** ['lentl] n lentille f

**Leo** ['li:əu] n le Lion

**leotard** ['li:ata:d] n maillot m (de danseur etc), collant m

**leprosy** ['leprəsɪ] n lèpre f

**lesbian** ['lezbɪən] n lesbienne f

**less** [les] adj moins de ♦ pron, adv moins ♦ prep moins; **~ than that/you** moins que cela/vous; **~ than half** moins de la moitié; **~ than ever** moins que jamais; **~ and ~** de moins en moins; **the ~ he works ...** moins il travaille ...; **~en** vi diminuer, s'atténuer ♦ vt diminuer, réduire, atténuer; **~er** adj moindre; **to a ~er extent** à un degré moindre

**lesson** ['lesn] n leçon f; **to teach sb a ~** (fig) donner une bonne leçon à qn

**let** [let] (pt, pp let) vt laisser; (BRIT: lease) louer; **to ~ sb do sth** laisser qn faire qch; **to ~ sb know sth** faire savoir qch à qn, prévenir qn de qch; **~'s go** allons-y; **~ him come** qu'il vienne; **"to ~"** "à louer"; **~ down** vt (tyre) dégonfler; (person) décevoir, faire faux bond à; **~ go** vi lâcher prise ♦ vt lâcher; **~ in**

vt laisser entrer; (*visitor etc*) faire entrer; ~ **off** vt (*culprit*) ne pas punir; (*firework etc*) faire partir; ~ **on** (*inf*) vi dire; ~ **out** vt laisser sortir; (*scream*) laisser échapper; ~ **up** vi diminuer; (*cease*) s'arrêter

**lethal** ['li:θl] *adj* mortel(le), fatal(e)

**letter** ['lɛtəʳ] *n* lettre *f*; ~ **bomb** lettre piégée; ~**box** *n* boîte *f* aux lettres; ~**ing** *n* lettres *fpl*; caractères *mpl*

**lettuce** ['lɛtɪs] *n* laitue *f*, salade *f*

**let-up** ['lɛtʌp] *n* répit *m*, arrêt *m*

**leukaemia** [lu:'ki:mɪə] (*US* **leukemia**) *n* leucémie *f*

**level** ['lɛvl] *adj* plat(e), plan(e), uni(e); horizontal(e) ♦ *n* niveau *m* ♦ *vt* niveler, aplanir; **to be ~ with** être au même niveau que; **to draw ~ with** (*person, vehicle*) arriver à la hauteur de; **"A" ~s** (*BRIT*) baccalauréat *m*; **"O" ~s** (*BRIT*) ≃ B.E.P.C.; ~ *n* (*fig: honest*) régulier(-ère); ~ **off** vi (*prices etc*) se stabiliser; ~ **out** vi = level off; ~ **crossing** (*BRIT*) *n* passage à niveau; ~**-headed** *adj* équilibré(e)

**lever** ['li:vəʳ] *n* levier *m*; ~**age** *n*: ~**age** (**on** *or* **with**) prise *f* sur (*or* par)

**levy** ['lɛvɪ] *n* taxe *f*, impôt *m* ♦ *vt* prélever, imposer; percevoir

**lewd** [lu:d] *adj* obscène, lubrique

**liability** [laɪə'bɪlətɪ] *n* responsabilité *f*; (*handicap*) handicap *m*; **liabilities** *npl* (*on balance sheet*) passif *m*

**liable** ['laɪəbl] *adj* (*subject*): ~ **to** sujet(te) à; passible de; (*responsible*): ~ (**for**) responsable de; (*likely*): ~ **to do** susceptible de faire

**liaise** [li:'eɪz] *vi*: **to ~ (with)** assurer la liaison avec; **liaison** *n* liaison *f*

**liar** ['laɪəʳ] *n* menteur(-euse)

**libel** ['laɪbl] *n* diffamation *f*; (*document*) écrit *m* diffamatoire ♦ *vt* diffamer

**liberal** ['lɪbərl] *adj* libéral(e); (*generous*): ~ **with** prodigue de, généreux(-euse) avec; **the L~ Democrats** (*BRIT*) le parti libéral-démocrate

**liberation** [lɪbə'reɪʃən] *n* libération *f*

**liberty** ['lɪbətɪ] *n* liberté *f*; **to be at ~ to do** être libre de faire

**Libra** ['li:brə] *n* la Balance

**librarian** [laɪ'brɛərɪən] *n* bibliothécaire *m/f*

**library** ['laɪbrərɪ] *n* bibliothèque *f*

**libretto** [lɪ'brɛtəu] *n* livret *m*

**Libya** ['lɪbɪə] *n* Libye *f*

**lice** [laɪs] *npl of* **louse**

**licence** ['laɪsns] (*US* **license**) *n* autorisation *f*, permis *m*; (*RADIO, TV*) redevance *f*; **driving ~**, (*US*) **driver's license** permis *m* (de conduire); ~ **number** *n* numéro *m* d'immatriculation; ~ **plate** *n* plaque *f* minéralogique

**license** ['laɪsns] *n* (*US*) = licence ♦ *vt* donner une licence à; ~**d** *adj* (*car*) muni(e) de la vignette; (*to sell alcohol*) patenté(e) pour la vente des spiritueux, qui a une licence de débit de boissons

**lick** [lɪk] *vt* lécher; (*inf: defeat*) écraser; **to ~ one's lips** (*fig*) se frotter les mains

**licorice** ['lɪkərɪs] (*US*) *n* = **liquorice**

**lid** [lɪd] *n* couvercle *m*; (*eyelid*) paupière *f*

**lie** [laɪ] (*pt* **lay**, *pp* **lain**) *vi* (*rest*) être étendu(e) *or* allongé(e) *or* couché(e); (*in grave*) être enterré(e), reposer; (*be situated*) se trouver, être; (*be untruthful*: *pt, pp* ~**d**) mentir ♦ *n* mensonge *m*; **to ~ low** (*fig*) se cacher; ~ **about** *vi* traîner; ~ **around** *vi* = lie about; ~ **down** (*BRIT*) *vi*: **to have a ~-down** s'allonger, se reposer; ~-**in** (*BRIT*) *n*: **to have a ~-in** faire la grasse matinée

**lieutenant** [lɛf'tɛnənt, (*US*) lu:'tɛnənt] *n* lieutenant *m*

**life** [laɪf] (*pl* **lives**) *n* vie *f*; **to come to ~** (*fig*) s'animer; ~ **assurance** (*BRIT*) *n* = **life insurance**; ~**belt** (*BRIT*) *n* bouée *f* de sauvetage; ~**boat** *n* canot *m* *or* chaloupe *f* de sauvetage; ~**buoy** *n* bouée *f* de sauvetage; ~**guard** *n* surveillant *m* de baignade; ~ **insurance** *n* assurance-vie *f*; ~ **jacket** *n* gilet *m* *or* ceinture *f* de sauvetage; ~**less** *adj* sans vie, inanimé(e); (*dull*) qui manque de vie *or* de vigueur; **~like** *adj* qui semble vrai(e) *or* vivant(e); *(painting)* réaliste; **~long** *adj* de toute une vie, de toujours; **~ preserver** *(US)* *n* = **lifebelt**; **life jacket**; **~saving** *n* sauvetage *m*; **~ sentence** *n* condamnation *f* à perpétuité; **~-size(d)** *adj* grandeur nature *inv*; **~ span** *(durée f de)* vie *f*; **~style** *n* style *m or* mode *m* de vie; **~support system** *n (MED)* respirateur artificiel; **~time** *n* vie *f*; **in his ~time** de son vivant

**lift** [lɪft] *vt* soulever, lever; *(end)* supprimer, lever ♦ *vi (fog)* se lever ♦ *n (BRIT: elevator)* ascenseur *m*; **to give sb a ~** *(BRIT: AUT)* emmener *or* prendre qn en voiture; **~-off** *n* décollage *m*

**light** [laɪt] *(pt, pp lit)* *n* lumière *f*; *(lamp)* lampe *f*; *(AUT: rear)* feu *m*; *(: headlight)* phare *m*; *(for cigarette etc)*: **have you got a ~?** avez-vous du feu? ♦ *vt (candle, cigarette, fire)* allumer; *(room)* éclairer ♦ *adj (room, colour)* clair(e); *(not heavy)* léger(-ère); *(not strenuous)* peu fatigant(e); **~s** *npl (AUT: traffic ~s)* feux *mpl*; **to come to ~** être dévoilé(e) *or* découvert(e); **~ up** *vi (face)* s'éclairer ♦ *vt (illuminate)* éclairer, illuminer; **~ bulb** *n* ampoule *f*; **~en** *vt (make less heavy)* alléger; **~er** *n (also: cigarette ~er)* briquet *m*; **~-headed** *adj* étourdi(e); *(excited)* grisé(e); **~-hearted** *adj* gai(e), joyeux(-euse), enjoué(e); **~house** *n* phare *m*; **~ing** *n (on road)* éclairage *m*; *(in theatre)* éclairages; **~ly** *adv* légèrement; **to get off ~ly** s'en tirer à bon compte; **~ness** *n (in weight)* légèreté *f*

**lightning** [ˈlaɪtnɪŋ] *n* éclair *m*, foudre *f*; **~ conductor** *(US* **lightning rod)** *n* paratonnerre *m*

**light pen** *n* crayon *m* optique

**lightweight** [ˈlaɪtweɪt] *adj (suit)* léger(-ère) ♦ *n (BOXING)* poids léger

**like** [laɪk] *vt* aimer (bien) ♦ *prep* comme ♦ *adj* semblable, pareil(le) ♦ *n*: **and the ~** et d'autres du même genre; **his ~s**

**and dislikes** ses goûts *mpl or* préférences *fpl*; **I would ~, I'd ~** je voudrais, j'aimerais; **would you ~ a coffee?** voulez-vous du café?; **to be/look ~ sb/sth** ressembler à qn/qch; **what does it look ~?** de quoi est-ce que ça a l'air?; **what does it taste ~?** quel goût est-ce que ça a?; **that's just ~ him** c'est bien de lui, ça lui ressemble; **do it ~ this** fais-le comme ceci; **it's nothing ~ ...** ce n'est pas du tout comme ...; **~able** *adj* sympathique, agréable

**likelihood** [ˈlaɪklɪhʊd] *n* probabilité *f*

**likely** [ˈlaɪklɪ] *adj* probable; plausible; **he's ~ to leave** il va sûrement partir, il risque fort de partir; **not ~!** *(inf)* pas de danger!

**likeness** [ˈlaɪknɪs] *n* ressemblance *f*; **that's a good ~** c'est très ressemblant

**likewise** [ˈlaɪkwaɪz] *adv* de même, pareillement

**liking** [ˈlaɪkɪŋ] *n (for person)* affection *f*; *(for thing)* penchant *m*, goût *m*

**lilac** [ˈlaɪlək] *n* lilas *m*

**lily** [ˈlɪlɪ] *n* lis *m*; **~ of the valley** *n* muguet *m*

**limb** [lɪm] *n* membre *m*

**limber up** [ˈlɪmbə-] *vi* se dégourdir, faire des exercices d'assouplissement

**limbo** [ˈlɪmbəʊ] *n*: **to be in ~** *(fig)* être tombé(e) dans l'oubli

**lime** [laɪm] *n (tree)* tilleul *m*; *(fruit)* lime *f*, citron vert; *(GEO)* chaux *f*

**limelight** [ˈlaɪmlaɪt] *n*: **in the ~** *(fig)* en vedette, au premier plan

**limerick** [ˈlɪmərɪk] *n* poème *m* humoristique (de 5 vers)

**limestone** [ˈlaɪmstəʊn] *n* pierre *f* à chaux; *(GEO)* calcaire *m*

**limit** [ˈlɪmɪt] *n* limite *f* ♦ *vt* limiter; **~ed** *adj* limité(e), restreint(e); **to be ~ed to** se limiter à, ne concerner que; **~ed (liability) company** *(BRIT)* *n* ≈ société *f* anonyme

**limousine** [ˈlɪməziːn] *n* limousine *f*

**limp** [lɪmp] *n*: **to have a ~** boiter ♦ *vi*

boiter ♦ *adj* mou (molle)

**limpet** ['lɪmpɪt] *n* patelle *f*

**line** [laɪn] *n* ligne *f*; (*stroke*) trait *m*; (*wrinkle*) ride *f*; (*rope*) corde *f*; (*wire*) fil *m*; (*of poem*) vers *m*; (*row*, *series*) rangée *f*; (*of people*) file *f*, queue *f*; (*railway track*) voie *f*; (*COMM*: *series of goods*) article(s) *m*(*pl*); (*work*) métier *m*, type *m* d'activité; (*attitude*, *policy*) position *f* ♦ *vt* (*subj*: *trees*, *crowd*) border; **in a ~** aligné(e); **in his ~ of business** dans sa partie, dans son rayon; **in ~ with** en accord avec; **to ~** (**with**) (*clothes*) doubler (de); (*box*) garnir *or* tapisser (de); **~ up** *vi* s'aligner, se mettre en rang(s) ♦ *vt* aligner; (*event*) prévoir; préparer; **~d** *adj* (*face*) ridé(e), marqué(e); (*paper*) réglé(e)

**linen** ['lɪnɪn] *n* linge *m* (de maison); (*cloth*) lin *m*

**liner** ['laɪnə<sup>r</sup>] *n* paquebot *m* (de ligne); (*for bin*) sac *m* à poubelle

**linesman** ['laɪnzmən] (*irreg*) *n* juge *m* de touche; (*TENNIS*) juge *m* de ligne

**line-up** ['laɪnʌp] *n* (*US*: *queue*) file *f*; (*SPORT*) composition *f* de l'équipe *f*

**linger** ['lɪŋgə<sup>r</sup>] *vi* s'attarder; traîner; (*smell*, *tradition*) persister

**linguist** ['lɪŋgwɪst] *n*: **to be a good ~** être doué(e) par les langues; **~ics** [lɪŋ'gwɪstɪks] *n* linguistique *f*

**lining** ['laɪnɪŋ] *n* doublure *f*

**link** [lɪŋk] *n* lien *m*, rapport *m*; (*of a chain*) maillon *m* ♦ *vt* relier, lier, unir; **~s** *npl* (*GOLF*) (terrain *m* de) golf *m*; **~ up** *vt* relier ♦ *vi* se rejoindre; s'associer

**lino** ['laɪnəu] *n* = **linoleum**

**linoleum** [lɪ'nəuliəm] *n* linoléum *m*

**lion** ['laɪən] *n* lion *m*; **~ess** *n* lionne *f*

**lip** [lɪp] *n* lèvre *f*

**liposuction** ['lɪpəusʌkʃən] *n* liposuccion *f*

**lip:** **~-read** *vi* lire sur les lèvres; **~ salve** *n* pommade *f* rosat *or* pour les lèvres; **~ service** *n*: **to pay ~ service to sth** ne reconnaître le mérite de qch que pour la forme; **~stick** *n* rouge *m* à lèvres

**liqueur** [lɪ'kjuə<sup>r</sup>] *n* liqueur *f*

**liquid** ['lɪkwɪd] *adj* liquide ♦ *n* liquide *m*; **~ize** *vt* (*CULIN*) passer au mixer; **~izer** *n* mixer *m*

**liquor** ['lɪkə<sup>r</sup>] *n* spiritueux *m*, alcool *m*

**liquorice** ['lɪkərɪs] (*BRIT*) *n* réglisse *f*

**liquor store** (*US*) *n* magasin *m* de vins et spiritueux

**lisp** [lɪsp] *vi* zézayer

**list** [lɪst] *n* liste *f* ♦ *vt* (*write down*) faire une *or* la liste de; (*mention*) énumérer; **~ed building** (*BRIT*) *n* monument classé

**listen** ['lɪsn] *vi* écouter; **to ~ to** écouter; **~er** *n* auditeur(-trice)

**listless** ['lɪstlɪs] *adj* indolent(e), apathique

**lit** [lɪt] *pt*, *pp* **of light**

**liter** ['li:tə<sup>r</sup>] (*US*) *n* = **litre**

**literacy** ['lɪtərəsɪ] *n* degré *m* d'alphabétisation, fait *m* de savoir lire et écrire

**literal** ['lɪtərəl] *adj* littéral(e); **~ly** *adv* littéralement; (*really*) réellement

**literary** ['lɪtərərɪ] *adj* littéraire

**literate** ['lɪtərət] *adj* qui sait lire et écrire, instruit(e)

**literature** ['lɪtrɪtʃə<sup>r</sup>] *n* littérature *f*; (*brochures etc*) documentation *f*

**lithe** [laɪð] *adj* agile, souple

**litigation** [lɪtɪ'geɪʃən] *n* litige *m*; contentieux *m*

**litre** ['li:tə<sup>r</sup>] (*US* **liter**) *n* litre *m*

**litter** ['lɪtə<sup>r</sup>] *n* (*rubbish*) détritus *mpl*, ordures *fpl*; (*young animals*) portée *f*; **~ bin** (*BRIT*) *n* boîte *f* à ordures, poubelle *f*; **~ed** *adj*: **~ed with** jonché(e) de, couvert(e) de

**little** ['lɪtl] *adj* (*small*) petit(e) ♦ *adv* peu; **~ milk/time** peu de lait/temps; **a ~** un peu (de); **a ~ bit** un peu; **~ by ~** petit à petit, peu à peu

**live¹** [laɪv] *adj* (*animal*) vivant(e), en vie; (*wire*) sous tension; (*bullet*, *bomb*) non explosé(e); (*broadcast*) en direct; (*performance*) en public

**live²** [lɪv] *vi* vivre; (*reside*) vivre, habiter; **~ down** vt faire oublier (avec le temps); **~ on** vt fus (food, salary) vivre de; **~ together** vi vivre ensemble, cohabiter; **~ up to** vt fus se montrer à la hauteur de

**livelihood** ['laɪvlɪhud] n moyens mpl d'existence

**lively** ['laɪvlɪ] adj vif (vive), plein(e) d'entrain; (place, book) vivant(e)

**liven up** ['laɪvn-] vt animer ♦ vi s'animer

**liver** ['lɪvəʳ] n foie m

**lives** [laɪvz] npl of **life**

**livestock** ['laɪvstɔk] n bétail m, cheptel m

**livid** ['lɪvɪd] adj livide, blafard(e); (inf: furious) furieux(-euse), furibond(e)

**living** ['lɪvɪŋ] adj vivant(e), en vie ♦ n: **to earn** ou **make a ~** gagner sa vie; **~ conditions** npl conditions fpl de vie; **~ room** n salle f de séjour; **~ standards** npl niveau m de vie; **~ wage** n salaire m permettant de vivre (décemment)

**lizard** ['lɪzəd] n lézard m

**load** [ləud] n (weight) poids m; (thing carried) chargement m, charge f ♦ vt (also: **~ up**): **to ~ (with)** charger (de); (gun, camera) charger (avec); (COMPUT) charger; **a ~ of, ~s of** (fig) un ou des tas de, des masses de; **to talk a ~ of rubbish** dire des bêtises; **~ed** adj (question) insidieux(-euse); (inf: rich) bourré(e) de fric

**loaf** [ləuf] (pl **loaves**) n pain m, miche f ♦ vi (also: **~ about, ~ around**) fainéanter, traîner

**loan** [ləun] n prêt m ♦ vt prêter; **on ~** prêté(e), en prêt

**loath** [ləuθ] adj: **to be ~ to do** répugner à faire

**loathe** [ləuð] vt détester, avoir en horreur

**loaves** [ləuvz] npl of **loaf**

**lobby** ['lɔbɪ] n hall m, entrée f; (POL) groupe m de pression, lobby m ♦ vt faire pression sur

**lobster** ['lɔbstəʳ] n homard m

**local** ['ləukl] adj local(e) ♦ n (BRIT: pub) pub m ou café m du coin; **the ~s** npl (in-

habitants) les gens mpl du pays ou du coin; **~ anaesthetic** n anesthésie locale; **~ authority** n collectivité locale, municipalité f; **~ call** n communication urbaine; **~ government** n administration locale ou municipale; **~ity** [ləu'kælɪtɪ] n région f, environs mpl; (position) lieu m

**locate** [ləu'keɪt] vt (find) trouver, repérer; (situate): **to be ~d** être situé(e) à ou en; **location** n emplacement m; **on location** (CINEMA) en extérieur

**loch** [lɔx] n lac m, loch m

**lock** [lɔk] n (of door, box) serrure f; (of canal) écluse f; (of hair) mèche f, boucle f ♦ vt (with key) fermer à clé ♦ vi (door etc) fermer à clé; (wheels) se bloquer; **~ in** vt enfermer; **~ out** vt enfermer dehors; (deliberately) mettre à la porte; **~ up** vt (person) enfermer; (house) fermer à clé ♦ vi tout fermer (à clé)

**locker** ['lɔkəʳ] n casier m; (in station) consigne f automatique

**locket** ['lɔkɪt] n médaillon m

**locksmith** ['lɔksmɪθ] n serrurier m

**lockup** ['lɔkʌp] n (prison) prison f

**locum** ['ləukəm] n (MED) suppléant(e) (de médecin)

**lodge** [lɔdʒ] n pavillon m (de gardien); (hunting ~) pavillon de chasse ♦ vi (person): **to ~ (with)** être logé(e) (chez), être en pension (chez); (bullet) se loger ♦ vt: **to ~ a complaint** porter plainte; **~r** n locataire m/f; (with meals) pensionnaire m/f; **lodgings** npl chambre f, meublé m

**loft** [lɔft] n grenier m

**lofty** ['lɔftɪ] adj (noble) noble, élevé(e); (haughty) hautain(e)

**log** [lɔg] n (of wood) bûche f; (book) **logbook** n (record) noter; **~book** (NAUT) livre m ou journal m de bord; (AVIAT) carnet m de vol; (of car) ~ carte grise

**loggerheads** ['lɔgəhedz] npl: **at ~ (with)** à couteaux tirés (avec)

**logic** ['lɔdʒɪk] n logique f; **~al** adj logique

**loin** [lɔ̃ɛ̃] n (CULIN) filet m, longe f
**loiter** ['lɔɪtər] vi traîner
**loll** [lɔl] vi (also: ~ about) se prélasser, fainéanter
**lollipop** ['lɔlɪpɔp] n sucette f; ~ **man/lady** (BRIT: irreg) n contractuel qui fait traverser la rue aux enfants

---

**lollipop men/ladies**

Les lollipop men/ladies sont employés pour aider les enfants à traverser la rue à proximité des écoles à l'heure où ils entrent en classe et à la sortie. On les repère facilement à cause de leur long ciré blanc et du fait qu'ils portent une pancarte ronde pour faire signe aux automobilistes de s'arrêter. On les appelle ainsi car la forme circulaire de cette pancarte rappelle une sucette.

---

**lolly** ['lɔlɪ] (inf) n (lollipop) sucette f; (money) fric m
**London** ['lʌndən] n Londres m; ~er n Londonien(ne)
**lone** [ləun] adj solitaire
**loneliness** ['ləunlɪnɪs] n solitude f, isolement m
**lonely** ['ləunlɪ] adj seul(e); solitaire, isolé(e)
**long** [lɔŋ] adj long (longue) ♦ adv longtemps ♦ vi: **to ~ for sth** avoir très envie de qch; attendre qch avec impatience; **so** or **as ~ as** pourvu que; **don't be ~!** dépêchez-vous!; **how ~ is this river/course?** quelle est la longueur de ce fleuve/la durée de ce cours?; **6 metres ~** (long) de 6 mètres; **6 months ~** qui dure 6 mois, de 6 mois; **all night ~** toute la nuit; **he no ~er comes** il ne vient plus; **they're no ~er going out together** ils ne sortent plus ensemble; **I can't stand it any ~er** je ne peux plus le supporter; **~ before/after** longtemps avant/après; **before ~** (+future) avant

peu, dans peu de temps; (+past) peu (de temps) après; **at ~ last** enfin; **~-distance** adj (call) interurbain(e); **~er** ['lɔŋgər] adv see long; **~hand** n écriture normale or courante; **~ing** n désir m, envie f, nostalgie f
**longitude** ['lɔŋgɪtjuːd] n longitude f
**long:** ~ **jump** n saut m en longueur; **~-life** adj (batteries etc) longue durée inv; (milk) longue conservation; **~-lost** adj (person) perdu(e) de vue depuis longtemps; **~-range** adj à longue portée; **~-sighted** adj (MED) presbyte; **~-standing** adj de longue date; **~-suffering** adj empreint(e) d'une patience résignée; extrêmement patient(e); **~-term** adj à long terme; **~wave** n grandes ondes; **~-winded** adj intarissable, interminable
**loo** [luː] (BRIT: inf) n W.-C. mpl, petit coin
**look** [luk] vi regarder; (seem) sembler, paraître, avoir l'air; (building etc): **to ~ south/(out) onto the sea** donner au sud/sur la mer ♦ n regard m; (appearance) air m, allure f, aspect m; ~**s** npl (good ~s) physique m, beauté f; **to have a ~** regarder; **~! regardez!; ~ (here)!** (annoyance) écoutez!; **~ after** vt fus (care for, deal with) s'occuper de; **~ at** vt fus regarder; (problem etc) examiner; **~ back** vi: **to ~ back on** (event etc) évoquer, repenser à; **~ down on** vt fus (fig) regarder de haut, dédaigner; **~ for** vt fus chercher; **~ forward to** vt fus attendre avec impatience; **we ~ forward to hearing from you** (in letter) dans l'attente de vous lire; **~ into** vt fus examiner, étudier; **~ on** vi regarder (en spectateur); **~ out** vi (beware): **to ~ out (for)** prendre garde (à), faire attention (à); **~ out for** vt fus être à la recherche de; guetter; **~ round** vi faire demi-tour, se retourner; **~ to** vt fus (rely on) compter sur; **~ up** vi lever les yeux; (improve) s'améliorer ♦ vt (word, name) chercher; **~ up to** vt fus

avoir du respect pour ♦ n poste m de guet; (person) guetteur m; **to be on the ~ out (for)** guetter

**loom** [luːm] vi (also: **~ up**) surgir; (approach: event etc) être imminent(e); (threaten) menacer ♦ n (for weaving) métier m à tisser

**loony** ['luːnɪ] (inf) adj, n timbré(e), cinglé(e)

**loop** [luːp] n boucle f; **~hole** n (fig) porte f de sortie; échappatoire f

**loose** [luːs] adj (knot, screw) desserré(e); (clothes) ample, lâche; (hair) dénoué(e); (not firmly fixed) pas solide; (morals, discipline) relâché(e) ♦ n: **on the ~** en liberté; **~ change** n petite monnaie; **~ chippings** npl (on road) gravillons mpl; **~ end** n: **to be at a ~ end** or (US) **at ~ ends** ne pas trop savoir quoi faire; **~ly** adv sans serrer; (imprecisely) approximativement; **~n** vt desserrer

**loot** [luːt] n (inf: money) pognon m, fric m ♦ vt piller

**lopsided** ['lɒp'saɪdɪd] adj de travers, asymétrique

**lord** [lɔːd] n seigneur m; **L~ Smith** lord Smith; **the L~** le Seigneur; **good L~!** mon Dieu! **the (House of) L~s** (BRIT) la Chambre des lords; **my L~** = **your Lordship**; **L~ship** n: **your L~ship** Monsieur le comte/le baron/le juge; (to bishop) Monseigneur

**lore** [lɔː] n tradition(s) f(pl)

**lorry** ['lɒrɪ] (BRIT) n camion m; **~ driver** (BRIT) n camionneur m, routier m

**lose** [luːz] (pt, pp **lost**) vt, vi perdre; **to ~ (time)** (clock) retarder; **to get lost** vi se perdre; **~r** n perdant(e)

**loss** [lɒs] n perte f; **to be at a ~** être perplexe ou embarrassé(e)

**lost** [lɒst] pt, pp of **lose** ♦ adj perdu(e); **~ and found** (US), **~ property** n objets trouvés

**lot** [lɒt] n (set) lot m; **the ~** le tout; **a ~ (of)** beaucoup (de); **~s of** des tas de; **to draw ~s (for sth)** tirer (qch) au sort

**lotion** ['ləʊʃən] n lotion f

**lottery** ['lɒtərɪ] n loterie f

**loud** [laʊd] adj bruyant(e), sonore; (voice) fort(e); (support, condemnation) vigoureux(-euse); (gaudy) voyant(e), tapageur(-euse) ♦ adv (speak etc) fort; **out ~** tout haut; **~hailer** (BRIT) n porte-voix m inv; **~ly** adv fort, bruyamment; **~speaker** n haut-parleur m

**lounge** [laʊndʒ] n salon m; (at airport) salle f; (BRIT: also: **~ bar**) (salle de) café m or bar m ♦ vi (also: **~ about** or **around**) se prélasser, paresser; **~ suit** (BRIT) n complet m; (on invitation) "tenue de ville"

**louse** [laʊs] (pl lice) n pou m

**lousy** ['laʊzɪ] (inf) adj infect(e), moche; **I feel ~** je suis mal fichu(e)

**lout** [laʊt] n rustre m, butor m

**lovable** ['lʌvəbl] adj adorable; très sympathique

**love** [lʌv] n amour m ♦ vt aimer; (caringly, kindly) aimer beaucoup; **"~ (from) Anne"** "affectueusement, Anne"; **I ~ chocolate** j'adore le chocolat; **to be/fall in ~ with** être/tomber amoureux (-euse) de; **to make ~** faire l'amour; **"15 ~"** (TENNIS) "15 à rien or zéro"; **~ affair** n liaison (amoureuse); **~ life** n vie sentimentale

**lovely** ['lʌvlɪ] adj (très) joli(e), ravissant(e); (delightful: person) charmant(e); (holiday etc) (très) agréable

**lover** ['lʌvə] n amant m; (person in love) amoureux(-euse); (amateur): **a ~ of** un amateur de; un(e) amoureux (-euse) de

**loving** ['lʌvɪŋ] adj affectueux(-euse), tendre

**low** [laʊ] adj bas (basse); (quality) mauvais(e), inférieur(e); (person: depressed) déprimé(e) ♦ adv (fly) bas; (speak) bas, doucement ♦ n (METEOROLOGY) dépression f; **to be ~ on** être à court de; **to feel ~** se sentir déprimé(e); **to reach an all-time ~** être au plus bas; **~-alcohol** adj peu alcoolisé(e); **~-calorie** adj hypoca-

lorique; **~-cut** adj (dress) décolleté(e);
**~er** adj inférieur(e) ♦ vt abaisser, baisser; **~er sixth** (BRIT) n (SCOL) première
f; **~-fat** adj maigre; **~lands** npl (GEO)
plaines fpl; **~ly** adj humble, modeste
**loyal** ['lɔɪəl] adj loyal(e), fidèle; **~ty** n
loyauté f, fidélité f; **~ty card** n carte f
de fidélité
**lozenge** ['lɔzɪndʒ] n (MED) pastille f
**LP** n abbr = **long-playing record**
**L-plates** ['ɛlpleɪts] npl (BRIT) plaques fpl
d'apprenti conducteur

---

**L-plates**

Les L-plates sont des carrés blancs
portant un "L" rouge que l'on met à
l'avant et à l'arrière de sa voiture pour
montrer qu'on n'a pas encore son permis de conduire. Jusqu'à l'obtention
du permis, l'apprenti conducteur a un
permis provisoire et n'a le droit de
conduire que si un conducteur qualifié
est assis à côté de lui. Il est interdit
aux apprentis conducteurs de circuler
sur les autoroutes, même s'ils sont accompagnés.

---

**Ltd** abbr (= limited) ≈ S.A.
**lubricant** ['luːbrɪkənt] n lubrifiant m
**lubricate** ['luːbrɪkeɪt] vt lubrifier, graisser
**luck** [lʌk] n chance f; **bad ~** malchance
f, malheur m; **bad** or **hard** or **tough ~!**
pas de chance!; **good ~!** bonne chance!; **~ily** adv heureusement, par bonheur; **~y** adj (person) qui a de la chance; (coincidence, event) heureux(-euse); (object) porte-bonheur inv
**ludicrous** ['luːdɪkrəs] adj ridicule, absurde
**lug** [lʌg] (inf) vt traîner, tirer
**luggage** ['lʌgɪdʒ] n bagages mpl; **~**
**rack** n (in car) galerie f
**lukewarm** ['luːkwɔːm] adj tiède
**lull** [lʌl] n accalmie f; (in conversation)
pause f ♦ vt: **to ~ sb to sleep** bercer
qn pour qu'il s'endorme; **to be ~ed**

**into a false sense of security** s'endormir dans une fausse sécurité
**lullaby** ['lʌləbaɪ] n berceuse f
**lumbago** [lʌm'beɪgəu] n lumbago m
**lumber** ['lʌmbər] n (wood) bois m de
charpente; (junk) bric-à-brac m inv;
**~jack** n bûcheron m
**luminous** ['luːmɪnəs] adj lumineux(-euse)
**lump** [lʌmp] n morceau m; (swelling)
grosseur f ♦ vt: **to ~ together** réunir,
mettre en tas; **~ sum** n somme globale
or forfaitaire; **~y** adj (sauce) avec des
grumeaux; (bed) défoncé(e), peu
confortable
**lunar** ['luːnər] adj lunaire
**lunatic** ['luːnətɪk] adj fou (folle), cinglé(e) (inf)
**lunch** [lʌntʃ] n déjeuner m
**luncheon** ['lʌntʃən] n déjeuner m
(chic); **~ meat** n sorte de mortadelle; **~**
**voucher** (BRIT) n chèque-repas m
**lung** [lʌŋ] n poumon m
**lunge** [lʌndʒ] vi (also: **~ forward**) faire
un mouvement brusque en avant; **to ~**
**at** envoyer or assener un coup à
**lurch** [lɜːtʃ] vi vaciller, tituber ♦ n écart
m brusque; **to leave sb in the ~** laisser qn se débrouiller or se dépêtrer
tout(e) seul(e)
**lure** [luər] n (attraction) attrait m, charme m ♦ vt attirer or persuader par la
ruse
**lurid** ['luərɪd] adj affreux(-euse), atroce;
(pej: colour, dress) criard(e)
**lurk** [lɜːk] vi se tapir, se cacher
**luscious** ['lʌʃəs] adj succulent(e); appétissant(e)
**lush** [lʌʃ] adj luxuriant(e)
**lust** [lʌst] n (sexual) désir m; (fig): **~ for**
soif f de; **~y** adj vigoureux(-euse), robuste
**Luxembourg** ['lʌksəmbəːg] n Luxembourg m
**luxurious** [lʌg'zjuərɪəs] adj luxueux(-euse)
**luxury** ['lʌkʃərɪ] n luxe m ♦ cpd de luxe

**lying** ['laɪɪŋ] n mensonge(s) m(pl) ♦ vb see **lie**

**lyrical** ['lɪrɪkl] adj lyrique

**lyrics** ['lɪrɪks] npl (of song) paroles fpl

# M, m

**m.** abbr = metre; mile; million

**M.A.** abbr = Master of Arts

**mac** [mæk] (BRIT) n imper(méable) m

**macaroni** [mækə'rəʊnɪ] n macaroni mpl

**machine** [mə'ʃiːn] n machine f ♦ vt (TECH) façonner à la machine; (dress etc) coudre à la machine; **~ gun** n mitrailleuse f; **~ language** n (COMPUT) langage-machine m; **~ry** n machinerie f, machines fpl; (fig) mécanisme(s) m(pl)

**mackerel** ['mækrl] n inv maquereau m

**mackintosh** ['mækɪntɒʃ] (BRIT) n imperméable m

**mad** [mæd] adj fou (folle); (foolish) insensé(e); (angry) furieux(-euse); (keen): **to be ~ about** être fou (folle) de

**madam** ['mædəm] n madame f

**madden** ['mædn] vt exaspérer

**made** [meɪd] pt, pp of **make**

**Madeira** [mə'dɪərə] n (GEO) Madère f; (wine) madère m

**made-to-measure** ['meɪdtə'meʒə*] (BRIT) adj fait(e) sur mesure

**madly** ['mædlɪ] adv follement; **~ in love** éperdument amoureux(-euse)

**madman** ['mædmən] (irreg) n fou m

**madness** ['mædnɪs] n folie f

**magazine** [mægə'ziːn] n (PRESS) magazine m, revue f; (RADIO, TV: also: **~ programme**) magazine

**maggot** ['mægət] n ver m, asticot m

**magic** ['mædʒɪk] n magie f ♦ adj magique; **~al** adj magique; (experience, evening) merveilleux(-euse); **~ian** [mə'dʒɪ-ʃən] n magicien(ne); (conjurer) prestidigitateur m

**magistrate** ['mædʒɪstreɪt] n magistrat m; juge m

**magnet** ['mægnɪt] n aimant m; **~ic** [mæg'netɪk] adj magnétique

**magnificent** [mæg'nɪfɪsnt] adj superbe, magnifique; (splendid) magnifique; (robe, building) somptueux(-euse), magnifique

**magnify** ['mægnɪfaɪ] vt grossir; (sound) amplifier; **~ing glass** n loupe f

**magnitude** ['mægnɪtjuːd] n ampleur f

**magpie** ['mægpaɪ] n pie f

**mahogany** [mə'hɒgənɪ] n acajou m

**maid** [meɪd] n bonne f; **old ~** (pej) vieille fille

**maiden** ['meɪdn] n jeune fille f ♦ adj (aunt etc) non mariée; (speech, voyage) inaugural(e); **~ name** n nom m de jeune fille

**mail** [meɪl] n poste f; (letters) courrier m ♦ vt envoyer (par la poste); **~box** (US) n boîte f aux lettres; **~ing list** n liste f d'adresses; **~-order** n vente f or achat m par correspondance

**maim** [meɪm] vt mutiler

**main** [meɪn] adj principal(e) ♦ n: **the ~(s)** n(pl) (gas, water) conduite principale, canalisation f; (ELEC) secteur m; **the ~ thing** l'essentiel m; **in the ~** dans l'ensemble; **~frame** n (COMPUT) (gros) ordinateur, unité centrale; **~land** n continent m; **~ly** adv principalement, surtout; **~ road** n grand-route f; **~stay** n (fig) pilier m; **~stream** n courant principal

**maintain** [meɪn'teɪn] vt entretenir; (continue) maintenir; (affirm) soutenir; **maintenance** ['meɪntənəns] n entretien m; (alimony) pension f alimentaire

**maize** [meɪz] n maïs m

**majestic** [mə'dʒestɪk] adj majestueux (-euse)

**majesty** ['mædʒɪstɪ] n majesté f

**major** ['meɪdʒə*] n (MIL) commandant m ♦ adj (important) important(e); (most important) important(e); (MUS) majeur(e)

**Majorca** [mə'jɔːkə] n Majorque f

**majority** [mə'dʒɒrɪtɪ] n majorité f

**make** [meɪk] (pt, pp made) vt faire; (manufacture) faire, fabriquer; (earn) gagner; (cause to be): **to ~ sb sad** etc rendre qn triste etc; (force): **to ~ sb do sth** obliger qn à faire qch, faire faire font à qn; (equal): **2 and 2 ~ 4** 2 et 2 font 4 ♦ n fabrication f; (brand) marque f; **to ~ a fool of sb** (ridicule) ridiculiser qn; (trick) jouer un duper qn; **to ~ a profit** faire un ou des bénéfice(s); **to ~ a loss** essuyer une perte; **to ~ it** (arrive) arriver; (achieve sth) parvenir à qch, réussir; **what time do you ~ it?** quelle heure avez-vous?; **to ~ do with** se contenter de; **to ~ do with ou for** vt fus (place) se diriger vers; **~ out** vt (write out: cheque) faire; (decipher) déchiffrer; (understand) comprendre; (see) distinguer; **~ up** vt (constitute) constituer; (invent) imaginer, inventer; (parcel, bed) faire ♦ vi se réconcilier; (with cosmetics) se maquiller; **~ up for** vt fus compenser; **~-believe** n: **it's just ~-believe** (game) c'est pour faire semblant; (invention) c'est de l'invention pure; **~r** n fabricant m; **~shift** adj provisoire, improvisé(e); **~-up** n maquillage m

**making** ['meɪkɪŋ] n (fig): **in the ~** en formation ou gestation; **to have the ~s of** (actor, athlete etc) avoir l'étoffe de

**malaria** [mə'lɛərɪə] n malaria f

**Malaysia** [mə'leɪzɪə] n Malaisie f

**male** [meɪl] n (BIO) mâle m ♦ adj mâle; (sex, attitude) masculin(e); (child etc) du sexe masculin

**malevolent** [mə'levələnt] adj malveillant(e)

**malfunction** [mæl'fʌŋkʃən] n fonctionnement m défectueux

**malice** ['mælɪs] n méchanceté f, malveillance f; **malicious** [mə'lɪʃəs] adj méchant(e), malveillant(e)

**malignant** [mə'lɪgnənt] adj (MED) malin(-igne)

**mall** [mɔːl] n (also: **shopping ~**) centre commercial

**mallet** ['mælɪt] n maillet m

**malpractice** [mæl'præktɪs] n faute pro-

fessionnelle; négligence f

**malt** [mɔːlt] n malt m ♦ cpd (also: **~ whisky**) pur malt

**Malta** ['mɔːltə] n Malte f

**mammal** ['mæml] n mammifère m

**mammoth** ['mæməθ] n mammouth m ♦ adj géant(e), monstre

**man** [mæn] (pl **men**) n homme m ♦ vt (NAUT: ship) garnir d'hommes; (MIL: gun) servir; (: post) être de service à; (machine) assurer le fonctionnement de; **an old ~** un vieillard; **~ and wife** mari et femme

**manage** ['mænɪdʒ] vi se débrouiller ♦ vt (be in charge of) s'occuper de; (: business etc) gérer; (control: ship) manier, manœuvrer; (: person) savoir s'y prendre avec; **to ~ to do** réussir à faire; **~able** adj (task) faisable; (number) raisonnable; **~ment** n gestion f, administration f, direction f; **~r** n directeur m; administrateur m; (SPORT) manager m; (of artist) impresario m; **~ress** [mænɪdʒə'res] n directrice f; gérante f; **~rial** [mænɪ'dʒɪərəl] adj directorial(e); (skills) de cadre, de gestion; **managing director** n directeur général

**mandarin** ['mændərɪn] n (also: **~ orange**) mandarine f; (person) mandarin m

**mandatory** ['mændətərɪ] adj obligatoire

**mane** [meɪn] n crinière f

**maneuver** [mə'nuːvə] (US) vt, vi, n = **manoeuvre**

**manfully** ['mænfəlɪ] adv vaillamment

**mangle** ['mæŋgl] vt déchiqueter; mutiler

**mango** ['mæŋgəu] (pl **~es**) n mangue f

**mangy** ['meɪndʒɪ] adj galeux(-euse)

**man: ~handle** vt malmener; **~hole** n trou m d'homme; **~hood** n âge m d'homme; virilité f; **~-hour** n heure f de main-d'œuvre; **~hunt** n (POLICE) chasse f à l'homme

**mania** ['meɪnɪə] n manie f; **~c** ['meɪnɪæk] n maniaque m/f; (fig) fou (folie) m/f; **manic** ['mænɪk] adj maniaque

**manicure** ['mænɪkjʊəʳ] n manucure f

**manifest** ['mænɪfest] vt manifester ♦ adj manifeste, évident(e); **~ly** adj [mænɪ'festəʊ] n manifeste m

**manipulate** [mə'nɪpjʊleɪt] vt manipuler; (system, situation) exploiter

**man:** **~kind** [mæn'kaɪnd] n humanité f, genre humain; **~ly** adj viril(e); **~made** adj artificiel(le); (fibre) synthétique

**manner** ['mænəʳ] n manière f, façon f; (behaviour) attitude f, comportement m; (sort) **all** ~ of toutes sortes de; **~s** npl (behaviour) manières; **~ism** n particularité f de langage (or de comportement), tic m

**manoeuvre** [mə'nuːvəʳ] (US maneuver) vt (move) manœuvrer; (manipulate: person) manipuler; (: situation) exploiter ♦ vi manœuvrer ♦ n manœuvre f

**manor** ['mænəʳ] n (also: ~ house) manoir m

**manpower** ['mænpaʊəʳ] n maind'œuvre f

**mansion** ['mænʃən] n château m, manoir m

**manslaughter** ['mænslɔːtəʳ] n homicide m involontaire

**mantelpiece** ['mæntlpiːs] n cheminée f

**manual** ['mænjʊəl] adj manuel(le) ♦ n manuel m

**manufacture** [mænjʊ'fæktʃəʳ] vt fabriquer ♦ n fabrication f; **~r** n fabricant m

**manure** [mə'njʊəʳ] n fumier m

**manuscript** ['mænjʊskrɪpt] n manuscrit m

**many** ['menɪ] adj beaucoup de, de nombreux(-euses) ♦ pron beaucoup, un grand nombre; **a great** ~ un grand nombre (de); **a** ~ ... bien des ..., plus d'un(e) ...

**map** [mæp] n carte f; (of town) plan m; **~ out** vt tracer; (task) planifier

**maple** ['meɪpl] n érable m

**mar** [mɑːʳ] vt gâcher, gâter

**marathon** ['mærəθən] n marathon m

**marble** ['mɑːbl] n marbre m; (toy) bille f

**March** [mɑːtʃ] n mars m

**march** [mɑːtʃ] vi marcher au pas; (fig: protesters) défiler ♦ n marche f; (demonstration) manifestation f

**mare** [mɛəʳ] n jument f

**margarine** [mɑːdʒə'riːn] n margarine f

**margin** ['mɑːdʒɪn] n marge f; **~al (seat)** n (POL) siège disputé

**marigold** ['mærɪɡəʊld] n souci m

**marijuana** [mærɪ'wɑːnə] n marijuana f

**marina** [mə'riːnə] n (harbour) marina f

**marine** [mə'riːn] adj marin(e) ♦ n fusilier marin; (US) marine m

**marital** ['mærɪtl] adj matrimonial(e); **~ status** situation f de famille

**marjoram** ['mɑːdʒərəm] n marjolaine f

**mark** [mɑːk] n marque f; (of skid etc) trace f; (BRIT: SCOL) note f; (currency) mark m ♦ vt marquer; (stain) tacher; (BRIT: SCOL) noter; corriger; **to ~ time** marquer le pas; **~er** n (sign) jalon m; (bookmark) signet m

**market** ['mɑːkɪt] n marché m ♦ vt (COMM) commercialiser; **~ garden** (BRIT) n jardin maraîcher; **~ing** n marketing m; **~place** n place f du marché; (COMM) marché m; **~ research** n étude f de marché

**marksman** ['mɑːksmən] (irreg) n tireur m d'élite

**marmalade** ['mɑːməleɪd] n confiture f d'oranges

**maroon** [mə'ruːn] vt: **to be ~ed** être abandonné(e); (fig) être bloqué(e) ♦ adj bordeaux inv

**marquee** [mɑː'kiː] n chapiteau m

**marriage** ['mærɪdʒ] n mariage m; **~ certificate** n extrait m d'acte de mariage

**married** ['mærɪd] adj marié(e); (life, love) conjugal(e)

**marrow** ['mærəʊ] n moelle f; (vegetable) courge f

**marry** ['mærɪ] vt épouser, se marier

avec; (subj: father, priest etc) marier ♦ vi (also: **get married**) se marier

**Mars** [mɑːz] n (planet) Mars f

**marsh** [mɑːʃ] n marais m, marécage m

**marshal** [ˈmɑːʃl] n maréchal m; (US: fire, police) ≃ capitaine m; (SPORT) membre m du service d'ordre ♦ vt rassembler

**marshy** [ˈmɑːʃi] adj marécageux(-euse)

**martyr** [ˈmɑːtər] n martyr(e); **~dom** n martyre m

**marvel** [ˈmɑːvl] n merveille f ♦ vi: to **~ (at)** s'émerveiller (de); **~lous** (US **marvelous**) adj merveilleux(-euse)

**Marxist** [ˈmɑːksɪst] adj marxiste ♦ n marxiste m/f

**marzipan** [ˈmɑːzɪpæn] n pâte d'amandes

**mascara** [mæsˈkɑːrə] n mascara m

**masculine** [ˈmæskjulɪn] adj masculin(e)

**mash** [mæʃ] vt écraser, réduire en purée; **~ed potatoes** npl purée f de pommes de terre

**mask** [mɑːsk] n masque m ♦ vt masquer

**mason** [ˈmeɪsn] n (also: **stonemason**) maçon m; (also: **freemason**) franc-maçon m; **~ry** n maçonnerie f

**masquerade** [mæskəˈreɪd] vi: to **~ as** se faire passer pour

**mass** [mæs] n multitude f, masse f; (PHYSICS) masse f; (REL) messe f ♦ cpd (communication) de masse; (unemployment) massif(-ive) ♦ vi se masser; the **~es** les masses; **~es of** des tas de

**massacre** [ˈmæsəkər] n massacre m

**massage** [ˈmæsɑːʒ] n massage m ♦ vt masser

**massive** [ˈmæsɪv] adj énorme, massif (-ive)

**mass media** n inv mass-media mpl

**mass production** n fabrication f en série

**mast** [mɑːst] n mât m; (RADIO) pylône m

**master** [ˈmɑːstər] n maître m; (in secondary school) professeur m; (title for boys): **M~ X** Monsieur X ♦ vt maîtriser; (learn) apprendre à fond; **~ly** adj magistral(e); **~mind** n esprit supérieur ♦ vt diriger, être le cerveau de; **M~ of Arts/Science** n ≃ maîtrise f (en lettres/sciences); **~piece** n chef-d'œuvre m; **~plan** n stratégie f d'ensemble; **~y** n maîtrise f, connaissance parfaite

**mat** [mæt] n petit tapis; (also: **doormat**) paillasson m; (also: **tablemat**) napperon m ♦ adj = **matt**

**match** [mætʃ] n allumette f; (game) match m, partie f; (fig) égal(e) ♦ vt (also: **~ up**) assortir; (go well with) aller bien avec, s'assortir à; (equal) égaler, valoir ♦ vi être assorti(e); **to be a good ~** être bien assorti(e); **~box** n boîte d'allumettes; **~ing** adj assorti(e)

**mate** [meɪt] n (inf) copain (copine); (animal) partenaire m/f, mâle/femelle; (in merchant navy) second m ♦ vi s'accoupler

**material** [məˈtɪərɪəl] n (substance) matière f, matériau m; (cloth) tissu m, étoffe f; (information, data) données fpl ♦ adj matériel(le); (relevant: evidence) pertinent(e); **~s** npl (equipment) matériaux mpl

**maternal** [məˈtɜːnl] adj maternel(le)

**maternity** [məˈtɜːnɪti] n maternité f; **~ dress** n robe f de grossesse; **~ hospital** n maternité f

**mathematical** [mæθəˈmætɪkl] adj mathématique

**mathematics** [mæθəˈmætɪks] n mathématiques fpl

**maths** [mæθs] (US **math**) n math(s) fpl

**matinée** [ˈmætɪneɪ] n matinée f

**mating call** n appel m du mâle

**matrices** [ˈmeɪtrɪsiːz] npl of **matrix**

**matriculation** [mətrɪkjuˈleɪʃən] n inscription f

**matrimonial** [mætrɪˈməʊnɪəl] adj matrimonial(e), conjugal(e)

**matrimony** [ˈmætrɪmənɪ] n mariage m

**matrix** [ˈmeɪtrɪks] (pl **matrices**) n matrice f

**matron** ['meɪtrən] n (in hospital) infirmière-chef f; (in school) infirmière

**mat(t)** [mæt] adj mat(e)

**matted** ['mætɪd] adj emmêlé(e)

**matter** ['mætər] n question f; (PHYSICS) matière f; (content) contenu m, fond m; (MED: pus) pus m ♦ vi importer; **~s** npl (affairs, situation) la situation; **it doesn't ~** cela n'a pas d'importance; (I don't mind) cela ne fait rien; **what's the ~?** qu'est-ce qu'il y a?, qu'est-ce qui ne va pas?; **no ~ what** quoiqu'il arrive; **as a ~ of course** tout naturellement; **as a ~ of fact** en fait; **~-of-fact** adj terre à terre; (voice) neutre

**mattress** ['mætrɪs] n matelas m

**mature** [mə'tjʊər] adj mûr(e); (cheese) fait(e); (wine) arrivé(e) à maturité ♦ vi (person) mûrir; (wine, cheese) se faire

**maul** [mɔ:l] vt lacérer

**mauve** [məʊv] adj mauve

**maximum** ['mæksɪməm] (pl maxima) adj maximum ♦ n maximum m

**May** [meɪ] n mai m; **~ Day** n le Premier Mai; see also **mayday**

**may** [meɪ] (conditional **might**) vi (indicating possibility): **he ~ come** il se peut qu'il vienne; (be allowed to): **~ I smoke?** puis-je fumer?; (wishes): **~ God bless you!** (que) Dieu vous bénisse!; **you ~ as well go** à votre place, je partirais

**maybe** ['meɪbi:] adv peut-être; **~ he'll ...** peut-être qu'il ...

**mayday** ['meɪdeɪ] n SOS m

**mayhem** ['meɪhem] n grabuge m

**mayonnaise** [meɪə'neɪz] n mayonnaise f

**mayor** [mɛər] n maire m; **~ess** n épouse f du maire

**maze** [meɪz] n labyrinthe m, dédale m

**M.D.** n abbr = Doctor of Medicine) titre universitaire; = **managing director**

**me** [mi:] pron me, m' +vowel; (stressed, after prep) moi; **he heard ~** il m'a entendu(e); **give ~ a book** donnez-moi

un livre; **after ~** après moi

**meadow** ['medəʊ] n prairie f, pré m

**meagre** ['mi:gər] (US **meager**) adj maigre

**meal** [mi:l] n repas m; (flour) farine f; **~time** n l'heure f du repas

**mean** [mi:n] (pt, pp **meant**) adj (with money) avare, radin(e); (unkind) méchant(e); (shabby) misérable; (average) moyen(ne) ♦ vt signifier, vouloir dire; (refer to) faire allusion à, parler de; (intend): **to ~ to do** avoir l'intention de faire ♦ n moyenne f; **~s** npl (way, money) moyens mpl; **by ~s of** par l'intermédiaire de, au moyen de; **by all ~s!** je vous en prie!; **to be ~t for sb/sth** être destiné(e) à qn/qch; **do you ~ it?** vous êtes sérieux?; **what do you ~?** que voulez-vous dire?

**meander** [mɪ'ændər] vi faire des méandres

**meaning** ['mi:nɪŋ] n signification f; sens m; **~ful** adj significatif(-ive); (relationship, occasion) important(e); **~less** adj dénué(e) de sens

**meanness** ['mi:nnɪs] n (with money) avarice f; (unkindness) méchanceté f; (shabbiness) médiocrité f

**meant** [ment] pt, pp of **mean**

**meantime** ['mi:ntaɪm] adv (also: **in the ~**) pendant ce temps

**meanwhile** ['mi:nwaɪl] adv = **meantime**

**measles** ['mi:zlz] n rougeole f

**measure** ['meʒər] vt, vi mesurer ♦ n mesure f; (ruler) règle f (graduée); **~ments** npl mesures fpl; **chest/hip ~ment(s)** tour m de poitrine/hanches

**meat** [mi:t] n viande f; **~ball** n boulette f de viande

**Mecca** ['mekə] n La Mecque

**mechanic** [mɪ'kænɪk] n mécanicien m; **~al** adj mécanique; **~s** n (PHYSICS) mécanique f ♦ npl (of reading, government etc) mécanisme m

**mechanism** ['mekənɪzəm] n mécanisme m

**medal** ['medl] n médaille f; **~lion** [mɪ'dælɪən] n médaillon m; **~list** (US **medalist**) n (SPORT) médaillé(e)

**meddle** ['medl] vi: **to ~ in** se mêler de, s'occuper de; **to ~ with** toucher à

**media** ['miːdɪə] npl media mpl

**mediaeval** [medɪ'iːvl] adj = **medieval**

**median** ['miːdɪən] (US) n (also: **~ strip**) bande médiane

**mediate** ['miːdɪeɪt] vi servir d'intermédiaire

**Medicaid** ® ['medɪkeɪd] (US) n assistance médicale aux indigents

**medical** ['medɪkl] adj médical(e) ♦ n visite médicale

**Medicare** ® ['medɪkeəʳ] (US) n assistance médicale aux personnes âgées

**medication** [medɪ'keɪʃən] n (drugs) médicaments mpl

**medicine** ['medsɪn] n médecine f; (drug) médicament m

**medieval** [medɪ'iːvl] adj médiéval(e)

**mediocre** [miːdɪ'əʊkəʳ] adj médiocre

**meditate** ['medɪteɪt] vi méditer

**Mediterranean** [medɪtə'reɪnɪən] adj méditerranéen(ne); **the ~ (Sea)** la (mer) Méditerranée

**medium** ['miːdɪəm] (pl **media**) adj moyen(ne) ♦ n (means) moyen m; (pl **~s: person**) médium m; **the happy ~** le juste milieu; **~-sized** adj de taille moyenne; **~ wave** n ondes moyennes

**medley** ['medlɪ] n mélange m; (MUS) pot-pourri m

**meek** [miːk] adj doux (douce), humble

**meet** [miːt] (pt, pp **met**) vt rencontrer; (by arrangement) retrouver, rejoindre; (for the first time) faire la connaissance de; (go and fetch): **I'll ~ you at the station** j'irai te chercher à la gare; (opponent, danger) faire face à; (obligations) satisfaire à ♦ vi (friends) se rencontrer, se retrouver; (in session) se réunir; (join: lines, roads) se rejoindre; **~ with** vt fus rencontrer; **~ing** n rencontre f; (session: of club etc) réunion f; (POL) meeting m; **she's at a ~ing**

(COMM) elle est en conférence

**mega** ['megə] (inf) adv: **he's ~ rich** il est hyper-riche; **~byte** n (COMPUT) méga-octet m; **~phone** n porte-voix m inv

**melancholy** ['melənkəlɪ] n mélancolie f ♦ adj mélancolique

**mellow** ['meləʊ] adj velouté(e); doux (douce); (sound) mélodieux(-euse) ♦ vi (person) s'adoucir

**melody** ['melədɪ] n mélodie f

**melon** ['melən] n melon m

**melt** [melt] vi fondre ♦ vt faire fondre; (metal) fondre; **~ away** vi fondre complètement; **~ down** vt fondre; **~down** n fusion f (du cœur d'un réacteur nucléaire); **~ing pot** n (fig) creuset m

**member** ['membəʳ] n membre m; **M~ of Parliament** (BRIT) député m; **M~ of the European Parliament** Eurodéputé m; **~ship** n adhésion f; statut m de membre; (members) membres mpl, adhérents mpl; **~ship card** n carte f de membre

**memento** [mə'mentəʊ] n souvenir m

**memo** ['meməʊ] n note f (de service)

**memoirs** ['memwɑːz] npl mémoires mpl

**memorandum** [memə'rændəm] (pl **memoranda**) n note f (de service)

**memorial** [mɪ'mɔːrɪəl] n mémorial m ♦ adj commémoratif(-ive)

**memorize** ['meməraɪz] vt apprendre par cœur; retenir

**memory** ['memərɪ] n mémoire f; (recollection) souvenir m

**men** [men] npl of **man**

**menace** ['menɪs] n menace f; (nuisance) plaie f ♦ vt menacer; **menacing** adj menaçant(e)

**mend** [mend] vt réparer; (darn) raccommoder, repriser ♦ n: **on the ~** en voie de guérison; **to ~ one's ways** s'amender; **~ing** n réparation f; (clothes) raccommodage m

**menial** ['miːnɪəl] adj subalterne

**meningitis** [menɪnˈdʒaɪtɪs] n méningite f

**menopause** [ˈmɛnəupɔːz] n ménopause f

**menstruation** [mɛnstruˈeɪʃən] n menstruation f

**mental** [ˈmɛntl] adj mental(e); **~ity** [mɛnˈtælɪtɪ] n mentalité f

**mention** [ˈmɛnʃən] n mention f ♦ vt mentionner, faire mention de; **don't ~ it!** je vous en prie, il n'y a pas de quoi!

**menu** [ˈmɛnjuː] n (set ~, COMPUT) menu m; (list of dishes) carte f

**MEP** n abbr = **Member of the European Parliament**

**mercenary** [ˈmɜːsɪnərɪ] adj intéressé(e), mercenaire ♦ n mercenaire m

**merchandise** [ˈmɜːtʃəndaɪz] n marchandises fpl

**merchant** [ˈmɜːtʃənt] n négociant m, marchand m; **~ bank** (BRIT) n banque f d'affaires; **~ navy** (US **merchant marine**) n marine marchande

**merciful** [ˈmɜːsɪful] adj miséricordieux(-euse), clément(e); **a ~ release** une délivrance

**merciless** [ˈmɜːsɪlɪs] adj impitoyable, sans pitié

**mercury** [ˈmɜːkjurɪ] n mercure m

**mercy** [ˈmɜːsɪ] n pitié f, indulgence f; (REL) miséricorde f; **at the ~ of** à la merci de

**mere** [mɪəʳ] adj simple; (chance) pur(e); **a ~ two hours** seulement deux heures; **~ly** adv simplement, purement

**merge** [mɜːdʒ] vt unir ♦ vi (colours, shapes, sounds) se mêler; (roads) se joindre; (COMM) fusionner; **~r** n (COMM) fusion f

**meringue** [məˈræŋ] n meringue f

**merit** [ˈmɛrɪt] n mérite m, valeur f

**mermaid** [ˈmɜːmeɪd] n sirène f

**merry** [ˈmɛrɪ] adj gai(e); **M~ Christmas!** Joyeux Noël!; **~-go-round** n manège m

**mesh** [mɛʃ] n maille f

**mesmerize** [ˈmɛzməraɪz] vt hypnotiser; fasciner

**mess** [mɛs] n désordre m, fouillis m, pagaille f; (muddle: of situation) gâchis m; (dirt) saleté f; (MIL) mess m, cantine f; **~ about** (inf) vi perdre son temps; **~ about with** (inf) vt fus tripoter; **~ around** (inf) vi = **mess about**; **~ around with** vt fus = **mess about with**; **~ up** vt (dirty) salir; (spoil) gâcher

**message** [ˈmɛsɪdʒ] n message m

**messenger** [ˈmɛsɪndʒəʳ] n messager m

**Messrs** [ˈmɛsəz] abbr (on letters) MM

**messy** [ˈmɛsɪ] adj sale; en désordre

**met** [mɛt] pt, pp of **meet**

**metal** [ˈmɛtl] n métal m; **~lic** [mɪˈtælɪk] adj métallique

**meteorology** [miːtɪəˈrɒlədʒɪ] n météorologie f

**meter** [ˈmiːtəʳ] n (instrument) compteur m; (also: **parking ~**) parcomètre m; (US: unit) = **metre**

**method** [ˈmɛθəd] n méthode f; **~ical** [mɪˈθɒdɪkl] adj méthodique; **M~ist** n méthodiste m/f

**meths** [mɛθs] (BRIT), **methylated spirit** [ˈmɛθɪleɪtɪd-] (BRIT) n alcool m à brûler

**metre** [ˈmiːtəʳ] (US **meter**) n mètre m; **metric** [ˈmɛtrɪk] adj métrique

**metropolitan** [mɛtrəˈpɒlɪtn] adj métropolitain(e); **the M~ Police** (BRIT) la police londonienne

**mettle** [ˈmɛtl] n: **to be on one's ~** être d'attaque

**mew** [mjuː] vi (cat) miauler

**mews** [mjuːz] (BRIT) n: **~ cottage** cottage aménagé dans une ancienne écurie

**Mexico** [ˈmɛksɪkəu] n Mexique m

**mice** [maɪs] npl of **mouse**

**micro** [ˈmaɪkrəu] n (also: **~computer**) micro-ordinateur m; **~chip** n puce f; **~phone** n microphone m; **~scope** n microscope m; **~wave** n (also: **~wave oven**) four m à micro-ondes

**miaow** [miːˈau] vi miauler

**mid** [mɪd] adj: **in ~ May** à la mi-mai; **in ~ afternoon** le milieu de l'après-midi; **in**

~ **air** en plein ciel; **~day** n midi m

**middle** ['mɪdl] n milieu m; (waist) taille f ♦ adj du milieu; (average) moyen(ne); **in the ~ of the night** au milieu de la nuit; **~-aged** adj d'un certain âge; **M~ Ages** npl: **the M~ Ages** le moyen âge; **~-class** adj ≈ bourgeois(e); **~ class(es)** n(pl): **the ~ class(es)** ≈ les classes moyennes; **M~ East** n Proche-Orient m, Moyen-Orient m; **~man** (irreg) n intermédiaire m; **~ name** n deuxième nom m; **~-of-the-road** adj (politician) modéré(e); (music) neutre; **~weight** n (BOXING) poids moyen; **middling** adj moyen(ne)

**midge** [mɪdʒ] n moucheron m

**midget** ['mɪdʒɪt] n nain(e)

**Midlands** ['mɪdləndz] npl comtés du centre de l'Angleterre

**midnight** ['mɪdnaɪt] n minuit m

**midriff** ['mɪdrɪf] n estomac m, taille f

**midst** [mɪdst] n: **in the ~ of** au milieu de

**mid** [mɪd-]: **~summer** [mɪd'sʌmər] n milieu m de l'été; **~way** [mɪd'weɪ] adj, adv: **~way (between)** à mi-chemin (entre); **~way through ...** au milieu de ..., en plein(e) ...; **~week** [mɪd'wiːk] adj au milieu de la semaine

**midwife** ['mɪdwaɪf] (pl **midwives**) n sage-femme f

**might** [maɪt] vb see **may** ♦ n puissance f, force f; **~y** adj puissant(e)

**migraine** ['miːɡreɪn] n migraine f

**migrant** ['maɪɡrənt] adj (bird) migrateur(-trice); (worker) saisonnier(-ère)

**migrate** [maɪ'ɡreɪt] vi émigrer

**mike** [maɪk] n abbr (= microphone) micro m

**mild** [maɪld] adj doux (douce); (reproach, infection) léger(-ère); (illness) bénin(-igne); (interest) modéré(e); (taste) peu relevé(e); (in beer) bière légère; **~ly** adv doucement; légèrement; **to put it ~ly** c'est le moins qu'on puisse dire

**mile** [maɪl] n mi(l)le m (= 1609 m); **~age** n distance f en miles; ≈ kilométrage m; **~ometer** [maɪ'lɒmɪtər] n compteur m (kilométrique); **~stone** n borne f; (fig) jalon m

**militant** ['mɪlɪtnt] adj militant(e)

**military** ['mɪlɪtərɪ] adj militaire

**militia** [mɪ'lɪʃə] n milice(s) f(pl)

**milk** [mɪlk] n lait m ♦ vt (cow) traire; (fig: person) dépouiller, plumer; (: situation) exploiter à fond; **~ chocolate** n chocolat m au lait; **~man** (irreg) n laitier m; **~ shake** n milk-shake m; **~y** adj (drink) au lait; (colour) laiteux(-euse); **M~y Way** n voie lactée

**mill** [mɪl] n moulin m; (factory) ≈ aciérie f; (spinning) ≈ filature f; (flour~) ≈ minoterie f ♦ vt moudre, broyer ♦ vi (also: **~ about**) grouiller; **~er** n meunier m

**millennium bug** [mɪ'lenɪəm-] n bogue m or bug m de l'an 2000

**milligram(me)** ['mɪlɪɡræm] n milligramme m

**millimetre** ['mɪlɪmiːtər] (US **millimeter**) n millimètre m

**million** ['mɪljən] n million m; **~aire** n millionnaire m

**milometer** [maɪ'lɒmɪtər] n ≈ compteur m kilométrique

**mime** [maɪm] n mime m ♦ vt, vi mimer;

**mimic** ['mɪmɪk] n imitateur(-trice) ♦ vt imiter, contrefaire

**min.** abbr = **minute(s)**; **minimum**

**mince** [mɪns] vt hacher ♦ n (BRIT: CULIN) viande hachée, hachis m; **~meat** n (fruit) hachis de fruits secs utilisé en pâtisserie; (US: meat) viande hachée, hachis; **~ pie** n (sweet) sorte de tarte aux fruits secs; **~r** n hachoir m

**mind** [maɪnd] n esprit m ♦ vt (attend to, look after) s'occuper de; (be careful) faire attention à; (object to): **I don't ~ the noise** le bruit ne me dérange pas; **I don't ~** cela ne me dérange pas; **it is on my ~** cela me préoccupe; **to my ~** à mon avis or sens; **to be out of one's ~** ne plus avoir toute sa raison; **to**

keep *or* bear sth in ~ tenir compte de qch; **to make up one's ~** se décider; **~ you,** ... remarquez ...; **never** ~ ça ne fait rien; *(don't worry)* ne vous en faites pas; **"~ the step"** "attention à la marche"; **~er** n *(child-minder)* gardienne f; *(inf: bodyguard)* ange gardien *(fig)*; **~ful** adj: **~ful of** attentif(-ive) à, soucieux(-euse) de; **~less** adj irréfléchi(e); *(boring: job)* idiot(e)

**mine**[1] ['maɪn] pron le (la) mien(ne), les miens (miennes) ♦ adj: **this book is ~** ce livre est à moi

**mine**[2] ['maɪn] n mine f ♦ vt *(coal)* extraire; *(ship, beach)* miner; **~field** n champ m de mines; *(fig)* situation très délicate); **~r** n mineur m

**mineral** ['mɪnərəl] adj minéral(e) ♦ n minéral m; **~s** npl *(BRIT: soft drinks)* boissons gazeuses; **~ water** n eau minérale

**mingle** ['mɪŋgl] vi: **to ~ with** se mêler à

**miniature** ['mɪnətʃər] adj (en) miniature ♦ n miniature f

**minibus** ['mɪnɪbʌs] n minibus m

**minimal** ['mɪnɪml] adj minime

**minimize** ['mɪnɪmaɪz] vt *(reduce)* réduire au minimum; *(play down)* minimiser

**minimum** ['mɪnɪməm] (pl **minima**) adj, n minimum m

**mining** ['maɪnɪŋ] n exploitation minière

**miniskirt** ['mɪnɪskə:t] n mini-jupe f

**minister** ['mɪnɪstər] n *(BRIT: POL)* ministre m; *(REL)* pasteur m ♦ vi: **to ~ to sb's needs** pourvoir aux besoins de qn; **~ial** ['mɪnɪs'tɪərɪəl] *(BRIT)* adj *(POL)* ministériel(le); **ministry** n *(BRIT: POL)* ministère m; *(REL)*: **to go into the ministry** devenir pasteur

**mink** [mɪŋk] n vison m

**minor** ['maɪnər] adj petit(e), de peu d'importance; *(MUS, poet, problem)* mineur(e) ♦ n *(LAW)* mineur(e) f

**minority** [maɪ'nɒrɪtɪ] n minorité f

**mint** [mɪnt] n *(plant)* menthe f; *(sweet)* bonbon m à la menthe ♦ vt *(coins)* bat-

tre; **the (Royal) M~**, *(US)* **the (US) M~** ≈ l'Hôtel m de la Monnaie; **in ~ condition** à l'état de neuf

**minus** ['maɪnəs] n *(also:* **~ sign)** signe m moins ♦ prep moins

**minute**[1] [maɪ'nju:t] adj minuscule; *(detail, search)* minutieux(-euse)

**minute**[2] ['mɪnɪt] n minute f; **~s** npl *(official record)* procès-verbal, compte rendu

**miracle** ['mɪrəkl] n miracle m

**mirage** ['mɪrɑ:ʒ] n mirage m

**mirror** ['mɪrər] n miroir m, glace f; *(in car)* rétroviseur m

**mirth** [mə:θ] n gaieté f

**misadventure** [mɪsəd'ventʃər] n mésaventure f

**misapprehension** ['mɪsæprɪ'henʃən] n malentendu m, méprise f

**misappropriate** [mɪsə'prəuprɪeɪt] vt détourner

**misbehave** [mɪsbɪ'heɪv] vi mal se conduire

**miscalculate** [mɪs'kælkjuleɪt] vt mal calculer

**miscarriage** ['mɪskærɪdʒ] n *(MED)* fausse couche; **~ of justice** erreur f judiciaire

**miscellaneous** [mɪsɪ'leɪnɪəs] adj *(items)* divers(es); *(selection)* varié(es)

**mischief** ['mɪstʃɪf] n *(naughtiness)* sottises fpl; *(fun)* farce f; *(playfulness)* espièglerie f; *(maliciousness)* méchanceté f; **mischievous** ['mɪstʃɪvəs] adj *(playful, naughty)* coquin(e), espiègle

**misconception** ['mɪskən'sepʃən] n idée fausse

**misconduct** [mɪs'kɒndʌkt] n inconduite f; **professional ~** faute professionnelle

**misdemeanour** [mɪsdɪ'mi:nər] *(US* **misdemeanor)** n écart m de conduite; infraction f

**miser** ['maɪzər] n avare m/f

**miserable** ['mɪzərəbl] adj *(person, expression)* malheureux(-euse); *(conditions)* misérable; *(weather)* maussade;

*(offer, donation)* minable; *(failure)* pitoyable

**miserly** ['maɪzəlɪ] *adj* avare

**misery** ['mɪzərɪ] *n (unhappiness)* tristesse *f; (pain)* souffrances *fpl; (wretchedness)* misère *f*

**misfire** [mɪs'faɪə] *vi* rater

**misfit** ['mɪsfɪt] *n (person)* inadapté(e)

**misfortune** [mɪs'fɔːtʃən] *n* malchance *f*, malheur *m*

**misgiving** [mɪs'gɪvɪŋ] *n (apprehension)* craintes *fpl;* **to have ~s about** avoir des doutes quant à

**misguided** [mɪs'gaɪdɪd] *adj* malavisé(e)

**mishandle** [mɪs'hændl] *vt (mismanage)* mal s'y prendre pour faire ou résoudre *etc*

**mishap** ['mɪshæp] *n* mésaventure *f*

**misinform** [mɪsɪn'fɔːm] *vt* mal renseigner

**misinterpret** [mɪsɪn'tɜːprɪt] *vt* mal interpréter

**misjudge** [mɪs'dʒʌdʒ] *vt* méjuger

**mislay** [mɪs'leɪ] *(irreg: like* **lay**) *vt* égarer

**mislead** [mɪs'liːd] *(irreg: like* **lead**) *vt* induire en erreur; **~ing** *adj* trompeur(-euse)

**mismanage** [mɪs'mænɪdʒ] *vt* mal gérer

**misplace** [mɪs'pleɪs] *vt* égarer

**misprint** ['mɪsprɪnt] *n* faute *f* d'impression

**Miss** [mɪs] *n* Mademoiselle

**miss** [mɪs] *vt (fail to get, attend or see)* manquer, rater; *(regret the absence of):* **I ~ him/it** il/cela me manque ♦ *vi* manquer ♦ *n (shot)* coup manqué; **~ out** *(BRIT) vt* oublier

**misshapen** [mɪs'ʃeɪpən] *adj* difforme

**missile** ['mɪsaɪl] *n (MIL)* missile *m; (object thrown)* projectile *m*

**missing** ['mɪsɪŋ] *adj* manquant(e); *(after escape, disaster: person)* disparu(e); **to go ~** disparaître; **to be ~** avoir disparu

**mission** ['mɪʃən] *n* mission *f;* **~ary** ['mɪʃənrɪ] *n* missionnaire *m/f;* **~state-**

**-ment** *n* déclaration *f* d'intention

**mist** [mɪst] *n* brume *f* ♦ *vi (also:* **~ over:** *eyes)* s'embuer; *(: windows etc)* s'embuer; **~ over** *vi* = **mist over**

**mistake** [mɪs'teɪk] *(irreg: like* **take**) *n* erreur *f*, faute *f* ♦ *vt (meaning, remark)* mal comprendre; se méprendre sur; **to make a ~** se tromper, faire une erreur; **by ~** par erreur, par inadvertance; **to ~ for** prendre pour; **~n** *pp of* **mistake** ♦ *adj (idea etc)* erroné(e); **to be ~n** faire erreur, se tromper

**mister** ['mɪstə*] (inf)* Monsieur *m;* see *also* **Mr**

**mistletoe** ['mɪsltəu] *n* gui *m*

**mistook** [mɪs'tuk] *pt of* **mistake**

**mistress** ['mɪstrɪs] *n* maîtresse *f; (BRIT: in primary school)* institutrice *f; (: in secondary school)* professeur *m*

**mistrust** [mɪs'trʌst] *vt* se méfier de

**misty** ['mɪstɪ] *adj* brumeux(-euse); *(glasses, window)* embué(e)

**misunderstand** [mɪsʌndə'stænd] *(irreg)* *vt, vi* mal comprendre; **~ing** *n* méprise *f*, malentendu *m*

**misuse** [*n* mɪs'juːs, *vb* mɪs'juːz] *n* mauvais emploi; *(of power)* abus *m* ♦ *vt* mal employer; abuser de; **~ of funds** détournement *m* de fonds

**mitigate** ['mɪtɪgeɪt] *vt* atténuer

**mitt(en)** ['mɪt(n)] *n* mitaine *f;* moufle *f*

**mix** [mɪks] *vt* mélanger; *(sauce, drink etc)* préparer ♦ *vi* se mélanger; *(socialize):* **he doesn't ~ well** il est peu sociable ♦ *n* mélange *m;* **to ~ with** *(people)* fréquenter; **~ up** *vt* mélanger; *(confuse)* confondre; **~ed** *adj (feelings, reactions)* contradictoire; *(salad)* mélangé(e); *(school, marriage)* mixte; **~ed grill** *n* assortiment de grillades; **~ed-up** *adj (confused)* désorienté(e), embrouillé(e); **~er** *n (for food)* batteur *m*, mixer *m; (person):* **he is a good ~er** il est très liant; **~ture** *n* assortiment *m*, mélange *m; (MED)* préparation *f;* **~up** *n* confusion *f*

**moan** [məʊn] n gémissement m ♦ vi gémir; (inf: complain): **to ~ (about)** se plaindre (de)

**moat** [məʊt] n fossé m, douves fpl

**mob** [mɒb] n foule f; (disorderly) cohue f ♦ vt assaillir

**mobile** ['məʊbaɪl] adj mobile ♦ n mobile m; ~ **home** n (grande) caravane; ~ **phone** n téléphone portatif

**mock** [mɒk] vt ridiculiser; (laugh at) se moquer de ♦ adj faux (fausse); ~ **exam** n examen blanc; **~ery** n moquerie f, raillerie f; **to make a ~ery of** tourner en dérision; **~-up** n maquette f

**mod** [mɒd] adj see **convenience**

**mode** [məʊd] n mode m

**model** ['mɒdl] n modèle m; (person: for fashion) mannequin m; (: for artist) modèle ♦ vt (with clay etc) modeler ♦ vi travailler comme mannequin ♦ adj (railway: toy) modèle réduit inv; (child, factory) modèle; **to ~ clothes** présenter des vêtements; **to o.s.** imiter

**modem** ['məʊdem] n (COMPUT) modem m

**moderate** [adj 'mɒdərət, vb 'mɒdəreɪt] adj modéré(e) ♦ (amount, change) peu important(e) ♦ vi se calmer ♦ vt modérer

**modern** ['mɒdən] adj moderne; **~ize** vt moderniser

**modest** ['mɒdɪst] adj modeste; **~y** n modestie f

**modify** ['mɒdɪfaɪ] vt modifier

**mogul** ['məʊgl] n (fig) nabab m

**mohair** ['məʊhɛə] n mohair m

**moist** [mɔɪst] adj humide, moite; **~en** vt humecter, mouille(e) légèrement; **~ure** n humidité f; **~urizer** n produit hydratant

**molar** ['məʊlə] n molaire f

**molasses** [mə'læsɪz] n mélasse f

**mold** [məʊld] (US) n, vt = **mould**

**mole** [məʊl] n (animal, fig: spy) taupe f; (spot) grain m de beauté

**molest** [mə'lest] vt (harass) molester; (LAW: sexually) attenter à la pudeur de

**mollycoddle** ['mɒlɪkɒdl] vt chouchouter, couver

**molt** [məʊlt] (US) vi = **moult**

**molten** ['məʊltən] adj fondu(e); (rock) en fusion

**mom** [mɒm] (US) n = **mum**

**moment** ['məʊmənt] n moment m, instant m; **at the ~** en ce moment; **at that ~** à ce moment-là; **~ary** momentané(e), passager(-ère); **~ous** [məʊ'mentəs] adj important(e), capital(e)

**momentum** [məʊ'mentəm] n élan m, vitesse acquise; (fig) dynamique f; **to gather ~** prendre de la vitesse

**mommy** ['mɒmɪ] (US) n maman f

**Monaco** ['mɒnəkəʊ] n Monaco m

**monarch** ['mɒnək] n monarque m; **~y** n monarchie f

**monastery** ['mɒnəstərɪ] n monastère m

**Monday** ['mʌndɪ] n lundi m

**monetary** ['mʌnɪtərɪ] adj monétaire

**money** ['mʌnɪ] n argent m; **to make ~** gagner de l'argent; **~ belt** n ceinture-portefeuille f; **~ order** n mandat m; **~-spinner** (inf) n mine f d'or (fig)

**mongrel** ['mʌŋgrəl] n (dog) bâtard m

**monitor** ['mɒnɪtə] n (TV, COMPUT) moniteur m ♦ vt contrôler; (broadcast) être à l'écoute de; (progress) suivre (de près)

**monk** [mʌŋk] n moine m

**monkey** ['mʌŋkɪ] n singe m; ~ **nut** (BRIT) n cacahuète f

**monopoly** [mə'nɒpəlɪ] n monopole m

**monotone** ['mɒnətəʊn] n ton m (or voix f) monocorde; **monotonous** [mə'nɒtənəs] adj monotone

**monsoon** [mɒn'suːn] n mousson f

**monster** ['mɒnstə] n monstre m; **monstrous** ['mɒnstrəs] adj monstrueux(-euse); (huge) gigantesque

**month** [mʌnθ] n mois m; **~ly** adj mensuel(le) ♦ adv mensuellement

**monument** ['mɒnjumənt] n monument m

**moo** [muː] vi meugler, beugler

**mood** [muːd] n humeur f, disposition f;
**to be in a good/bad** ~ être de
bonne/mauvaise humeur; ~ adj (variable) d'humeur changeante, lunatique;
(sullen) morose, maussade

**moon** [muːn] n lune f; ~light n clair m
de lune; ~lighting n travail m au noir;
~lit adj: a ~lit night une nuit de lune

**moor** [muə<sup>r</sup>] n lande f ♦ vt (ship) amarrer ♦ vi mouiller; ~land n lande f

**moose** [muːs] n inv élan m

**mop** [mɔp] n balai m à laver; (for dishes)
lavette f (à vaisselle) ♦ vt essuyer; ~ of
hair tignasse f; ~ up vt éponger

**mope** [məup] vi avoir le cafard, se morfondre

**moped** ['məuped] n cyclomoteur m

**moral** ['mɔrl] adj moral(e) ♦ n morale f;
~s npl (attitude, behaviour) moralité f

**morale** [mɔ'rɑːl] n moral m

**morality** [mə'rælɪtɪ] n moralité f

**morass** [mə'ræs] n marais m, marécage
m

---

**more** [mɔː<sup>r</sup>] adj 1 (greater in number
etc) plus (de), davantage; **more
people/work (than)** plus de gens/de
travail (que)

2 (additional) encore (de); **do you
want (some) more tea?** voulez-vous
encore un peu de thé?; **I have no** or **I don't
have any more money** je n'ai plus
d'argent; **it'll take a few more weeks**
ça prendra encore quelques semaines
♦ pron plus, davantage; **more than 10**
plus de 10; **it cost more than we expected** cela a coûté plus que prévu; **I
want more** je n'en veux plus or davantage; **is there any more?** est-ce qu'il en
reste?; **there's no more** il n'y en a
plus; **a little more** un peu plus;
**many/much more** beaucoup plus,
bien davantage

♦ adv: **more dangerous/easily (than)**
plus dangereux/facilement (que); **more
and more expensive** de plus en plus

cher; **more or less** plus ou moins;
**more than ever** plus que jamais

---

**moreover** [mɔː'rəuvə<sup>r</sup>] adv de plus

**morning** ['mɔːnɪŋ] n matin m; matinée
f ♦ cpd matinal(e); (paper) du matin; **in
the** ~ le matin; **7 o'clock in the** ~ 7
heures du matin; ~ **sickness** n nau-
sées matinales

**Morocco** [mə'rɔkəu] n Maroc m

**moron** ['mɔːrɔn] (inf) n idiot(e)

**Morse** [mɔːs] n: ~ **code** code morse m

**morsel** ['mɔːsl] n bouchée f

**mortar** ['mɔːtə<sup>r</sup>] n mortier m

**mortgage** ['mɔːgɪdʒ] n hypothèque f;
(loan) prêt m (or crédit m) hypothécaire
♦ vt hypothéquer; ~ **company** (US) n
société f de crédit immobilier

**mortuary** ['mɔːtjuəri] n morgue f

**mosaic** [mə'zeɪɪk] n mosaïque f

**Moscow** ['mɔskəu] n Moscou

**Moslem** ['mɔzləm] adj, n = **Muslim**

**mosque** [mɔsk] n mosquée f

**mosquito** [mɔs'kiːtəu] (pl ~es) n
moustique m

**moss** [mɔs] n mousse f

**most** [məust] adj la plupart de; le plus
de ♦ pron la plupart ♦ adv le plus; (very)
très, extrêmement; **the** ~ (also: + adjective) le plus; ~ **of** la plus grande
partie de; ~ **of them** la plupart d'entre
eux; **I saw the** ~ j'en ai vu la plupart; c'est moi qui en ai vu le plus; **at
the (very)** ~ au plus; **to make the** ~
**of** profiter au maximum de; ~**ly** adv
(chiefly) surtout; (usually) généralement

**MOT** n abbr (BRIT: Ministry of Transport):
**the MOT (test)** la visite technique (annuelle) obligatoire des véhicules à moteur

**motel** [məu'tel] n motel m

**moth** [mɔθ] n papillon m de nuit; (in
clothes) mite f

**mother** ['mʌðə<sup>r</sup>] n mère f ♦ vt (act as ~
to) servir de mère à; (pamper, protect)
materner; ~ **country** mère patrie;
~**hood** n maternité f; ~**-in-law** n
belle-mère f; ~**ly** adj maternel(le); ~-

**motion** -of-pearl *n* nacre *f*; **M~'s Day** *n* fête *f* des Mères; **~-to-be** *n* future maman; **~ tongue** *n* langue maternelle

**motion** ['məʊʃən] *n* mouvement *m*; (gesture) geste *m*; (at meeting) motion *f* ♦ *vt, vi*: **to ~ (to) sb to do** faire signe à qn de faire; **~less** *adj* immobile, sans mouvement; **~ picture** *n* film *m*

**motivated** ['məʊtɪveɪtɪd] *adj* motivé(e); **motivation** [məʊtɪ'veɪʃən] *n* motivation *f*

**motive** ['məʊtɪv] *n* motif *m*, mobile *m*

**motley** ['mɒtlɪ] *adj* hétéroclite

**motor** ['məʊtə<sup>r</sup>] *n* moteur *m*; (BRIT: inf: vehicle) auto *f* ♦ *cpd* (industry, vehicle) automobile; **~bike** *n* moto *f*; **~boat** *n* bateau *m* à moteur; **~car** (BRIT) *n* automobile *f*; **~cycle** *n* vélomoteur *m*; **~cycle racing** *n* course *f* de motos; **~cyclist** *n* motocycliste *m/f*; **~ing** (BRIT) *n* tourisme *m* automobile; **~ist** *n* automobiliste *m/f*; **~ mechanic** *n* mécanicien *m* garagiste; **~ racing** (BRIT) *n* course *f* automobile; **~way** (BRIT) *n* autoroute *f*

**mottled** ['mɒtld] *adj* tacheté(e), marbré(e)

**motto** ['mɒtəʊ] (*pl* **~es**) *n* devise *f*

**mould** [məʊld] (US **mold**) *n* moule *m*; (mildew) moisissure *f* ♦ *vt* mouler, modeler; (fig) façonner; **mo(u)ldy** *adj* moisi(e); (smell) de moisi

**moult** [məʊlt] (US **molt**) *vi* muer

**mound** [maʊnd] *n* monticule *m*, tertre *m*; (heap) monceau *m*, tas *m*

**mount** [maʊnt] *n* mont *m*, montagne *f* ♦ *vt* monter ♦ *vi* (inflation, tension) augmenter; (also: **~ up**: problems etc) s'accumuler; **~ up** *vi* (bills, costs, savings) s'accumuler

**mountain** ['maʊntɪn] *n* montagne *f* ♦ *cpd* de montagne; **~ bike** *n* VTT *m*, vélo tout-terrain; **~eer** [maʊntɪ'nɪə<sup>r</sup>] *n* alpiniste *m/f*; **~eering** *n* alpinisme *m*; **~ous** *adj* montagneux(-euse); **~ rescue team** *n* équipe *f* de secours en montagne; **~side** *n* flanc *m* or versant

*m* de la montagne

**mourn** [mɔːn] *vt* pleurer ♦ *vi*: **to ~ (for)** (person) pleurer (la mort de); **~er** *n* parent(e) *f* du défunt; personne *f* en deuil; **~ing** *n* deuil *m*; **in ~ing** en deuil

**mouse** [maʊs] (*pl* **mice**) *n* (also COMPUT) souris *f*; **~ mat** *n* (COMPUT) tapis *m* de souris; **~trap** *n* souricière *f*

**moustache** [məs'tɑːʃ] (US **mustache**) *n* moustache *f(pl)*

**mousy** ['maʊsɪ] *adj* (hair) d'un châtain terne

**mouth** [maʊθ] (*pl* **~s**) *n* bouche *f*; (of dog, cat) gueule *f*; (of river) embouchure *f*; (of hole, cave) ouverture *f*; **~ful** *n* bouchée *f*; **~ organ** *n* harmonica *m*; **~piece** *n* (of musical instrument) embouchure *f*; (spokesman) porte-parole *m inv*; **~wash** *n* eau *f* dentifrice; **~watering** *adj* qui met l'eau à la bouche

**movable** ['muːvəbl] *adj* mobile

**move** [muːv] (**~ment**) *n* mouvement *m*; (in game) coup *m*; (: turn to play) tour *m*; (change of house) déménagement *m*; (: of job) changement *m* d'emploi ♦ *vt* déplacer, bouger; (emotionally) émouvoir; (POL: resolution etc) proposer; (in game) jouer ♦ *vi* (gen) bouger, remuer; (traffic) circuler; (also: ~ **house**) déménager; (situation) progresser; **that was a good ~** bien joué!; **to get a ~ on** se dépêcher, se remuer; **to ~ sb to do sth** pousser or inciter qn à faire qch; **~ about** *vi* (fidget) remuer; (travel) voyager, se déplacer; (change residence, job) ne pas rester au même endroit; **~ along** *vi* se pousser; **~ around** *vi* = **move about**; **~ away** *vi* s'en aller; **~ back** *vi* revenir, retourner; **~ forward** *vi* avancer; **~ in** *vi* (to a house) emménager; (police, soldiers) intervenir; **~ on** *vi* se remettre en route; **~ out** *vi* (of house) déménager; **~ over** *vi* se pousser, se déplacer; **~ up** *vi* (pupil) passer dans la classe supérieur; (*employee*) avoir de l'avancement; **~able** adj = **movable**

**movement** ['mu:vmənt] n mouvement m

**movie** ['mu:vɪ] n film m; **the ~s** le cinéma

**moving** ['mu:vɪŋ] adj en mouvement; (*emotional*) émouvant(e)

**mow** [məu] (*pt* mowed, *pp* mowed *or* mown) vt faucher; (*lawn*) tondre; **~ down** vt faucher; **~er** n (*also:* **lawnmower**) tondeuse f à gazon

**MP** n abbr = **Member of Parliament**

**mph** n abbr = **miles per hour**

**Mr** ['mɪstəʳ] n: **~ Smith** Monsieur Smith, M. Smith

**Mrs** ['mɪsɪz] n: **~ Smith** Madame Smith, Mme Smith

**Ms** [mɪz] n (= Miss or Mrs): **~ Smith** Madame Smith, Mme Smith

**MSc** abbr = **Master of Science**

**MSP** [emes'pi:] n abbr = **Member of the Scottish Parliament**

**much** [mʌtʃ] adj beaucoup de ♦ adv, n, pron beaucoup; **how ~ is it?** combien est-ce que ça coûte?; **too ~** trop (de); **as ~ as** autant de

**muck** [mʌk] n (*dirt*) saleté f; (*mud*) boue f; **~ about** *or* **around** (*inf*) vi faire l'imbécile; **~ up** (*inf*) vt (*exam, interview*) se planter à (*fam*); **~y** adj (*very*) sale

**mud** [mʌd] n boue f

**muddle** ['mʌdl] n (*mess*) pagaille f, désordre m; (*mix-up*) confusion f ♦ vt (*also:* **~ up**) embrouiller; **~ through** vi se débrouiller

**muddy** ['mʌdɪ] adj boueux(-euse)

**mudguard** ['mʌdgɑ:d] n garde-boue m inv

**muesli** ['mju:zlɪ] n muesli m

**muffin** ['mʌfɪn] n muffin m

**muffle** ['mʌfl] vt (*sound*) assourdir, étouffer; (*against cold*) emmitoufler; **~d** adj (*sound*) étouffé(e); **~r** n (*US*) (*AUT*) silencieux m

**mug** [mʌg] n (*cup*) grande tasse (*sans*

soucoupe); (: *for beer*) chope f; (*inf: face*) bouille f; (: *fool*) poire f ♦ vt (*assault*) agresser; **~ger** n agresseur m; **~ging** n agression f

**muggy** ['mʌgɪ] adj lourd(e), moite

**mule** [mju:l] n mule f

**multi-level** ['mʌltɪlevl] (*US*) adj = **multistorey**

**multiple** ['mʌltɪpl] adj multiple ♦ n multiple m; **~ sclerosis** [-sklɪ'rəusɪs] n sclérose f en plaques

**multiplex cinema** ['mʌltɪpleks-] n cinéma m multisalles

**multiplication** [mʌltɪplɪ'keɪʃən] n multiplication f; **multiply** ['mʌltɪplaɪ] vt multiplier ♦ vi se multiplier

**multistorey** ['mʌltɪ'stɔ:rɪ] (*BRIT*) adj (*building*) à étages, (*car park*) à étages *or* niveaux multiples ♦ n (*car park*) parking m à plusieurs étages

**mum** [mʌm] (*BRIT: inf*) n maman f ♦ adj: **to keep ~** ne pas souffler mot

**mumble** ['mʌmbl] vt, vi marmotter, marmonner

**mummy** ['mʌmɪ] n (*BRIT: mother*) maman f; (*embalmed*) momie f

**mumps** [mʌmps] n oreillons mpl

**munch** [mʌntʃ] vt, vi mâcher

**mundane** [mʌn'deɪn] adj banal(e), terre à terre inv

**municipal** [mju:'nɪsɪpl] adj municipal(e)

**murder** ['mɜ:dəʳ] n meurtre m, assassinat m ♦ vt assassiner; **~er** n meurtrier m, assassin m; **~ous** ['mɜ:dərəs] adj meurtrier(-ère)

**murky** ['mɜ:kɪ] adj sombre, ténébreux(-euse); (*water*) trouble

**murmur** ['mɜ:məʳ] n murmure m ♦ vt, vi murmurer

**muscle** ['mʌsl] n muscle m; (*fig*) force f; **~ in** (*on territory*) envahir; (*on profits*) exploiter; **muscular** ['mʌskjuləʳ] adj musculaire; (*person, arm*) musclé(e)

**muse** [mju:z] vi méditer, songer

**museum** [mju:'zɪəm] n musée m

**mushroom** ['mʌʃrum] n champignon m ♦ vi pousser comme un champignon

**music** ['mjuːzɪk] n musique f; **~al** adj musical(e); (person) musicien(ne) ♦ n (show) comédie musicale; **~al instrument** n instrument m de musique; **~ centre** n chaîne compacte; **~ian** [mjuːˈzɪʃən] n musicien(ne)

**Muslim** ['mazlɪm] adj, n musulman(e)

**muslin** ['mazlɪn] n mousseline f

**mussel** ['masl] n moule f

**must** [mast] aux vb (obligation): **I ~ do it** je dois le faire, il faut que je le fasse; (probability): **he ~ be there by now** il doit y être maintenant, il y est probablement maintenant; (suggestion, invitation): **you ~ come and see me** il faut que vous veniez me voir; (indicating sth unwelcome): **why ~ he behave so badly?** qu'est-ce qu'il le pousse à se conduire si mal? ♦ n nécessité f, impératif m; **it's a ~** c'est indispensable

**mustache** ['mastæʃ] (US) n = moustache

**mustard** ['mastəd] n moutarde f

**muster** ['mastə'] vt rassembler

**mustn't** ['masnt] = must not

**mute** [mjuːt] adj muet(te); **~d** adj (colour) sourd(e); (sound) voilé(e)

**mutiny** ['mjuːtɪnɪ] n mutinerie f ♦ vi se mutiner

**mutter** ['matə'] vt, vi marmonner, marmotter

**mutton** ['matn] n mouton m

**mutual** ['mjuːtʃuəl] adj mutuel(le), réciproque; (benefit, interest) commun(e); **~ly** adv mutuellement

**muzzle** ['mazl] n museau m; (protective device) muselière f; (of gun) gueule f ♦ vt museler

**my** [maɪ] adj mon (ma), mes pl; **~ house/car/gloves** ma maison/mon auto/mes gants; **I've washed ~ hair/cut ~ finger** je me suis lavé les cheveux/coupé le doigt; **~self** [maɪˈself] pron (reflexive) me; (emphatic) moi-même; (after prep) moi; see also **oneself**

**mysterious** [mɪsˈtɪərɪəs] adj mysté-

rieux(-euse)

**mystery** ['mɪstərɪ] n mystère m

**mystify** ['mɪstɪfaɪ] vt mystifier; (puzzle) ébahir

**myth** [mɪθ] n mythe m; **~ology** [mɪˈθɒlədʒɪ] n mythologie f

# N, n

**n/a** abbr = **not applicable**

**naff** [næf] (BRIT: inf) adj nul(le)

**nag** [næg] vt (scold) être toujours après, reprendre sans arrêt; **~ging** (doubt, pain) persistant(e)

**nail** [neɪl] n (human) ongle m; (metal) clou m ♦ vt clouer; **to ~ sb down to a date/price** contraindre qn à accepter ou donner une date/un prix; **~brush** n brosse f à ongles; **~file** n lime f à ongles; **~ polish** n vernis m à ongles; **~ polish remover** n dissolvant m; **~ scissors** npl ciseaux mpl à ongles; **~ varnish** (BRIT) n = **nail polish**

**naive** [naɪˈiːv] adj naïf(-ïve)

**naked** ['neɪkɪd] adj nu(e)

**name** [neɪm] n nom m; (reputation) réputation f ♦ vt nommer; (identify: accomplice etc) citer; (price, date) fixer, donner; **by ~** par son nom; **in the ~ of** au nom de; **what's your ~?** comment vous appelez-vous?; **~less** adj sans nom; (witness, contributor) anonyme; **~ly** adv à savoir; **~sake** n homonyme m

**nanny** ['nænɪ] n bonne f d'enfants

**nap** [næp] n (sleep) (petit) somme ♦ vi: **to be caught ~ping** être pris à l'improviste ou en défaut

**nape** [neɪp] n: **~ of the neck** nuque f

**napkin** ['næpkɪn] n serviette f (de table)

**nappy** ['næpɪ] (BRIT) n couche f (gen pl); **~ rash** n: **to have ~ rash** avoir les fesses rouges

**narcissus** [nɑːˈsɪsəs] (pl **narcissi**) n narcisse m

**narcotic** ['nɑː'kɔtɪk] n (drug) stupéfiant m; (MED) narcotique m

**narrative** ['nærətɪv] n récit m

**narrow** ['nærəʊ] adj étroit(e); (fig) restreint(e), limité(e) ♦ vi (road) devenir plus étroit, se rétrécir; (gap, difference) se réduire; **to have a ~ escape** l'échapper belle; **to ~ sth down to** réduire qch à; **~ly** adv: **he ~ly missed injury/the tree** il a failli se blesser/rentrer dans l'arbre; **~-minded** adj à l'esprit étroit, borné(e); (attitude) borné

**nasty** ['nɑːstɪ] adj (person: malicious) méchant(e); (: rude) très désagréable; (smell) dégoûtant(e); (wound, situation, disease) mauvais(e)

**nation** ['neɪʃən] n nation f

**national** ['næʃənl] adj national(e) ♦ n (abroad) ressortissant(e); (when home) national(e); **~ anthem** n hymne national; **~ dress** n costume national; **N~ Health Service** (BRIT) n service national de santé, ≈ Sécurité Sociale; **N~ Insurance** (BRIT) n ≈ Sécurité Sociale; **~ism** n nationalisme m; **~ist** adj, n nationaliste m/f; **~ity** [næʃə'nælɪtɪ] n nationalité f; **~ize** vt nationaliser; **~ly** adv (as a nation) du point de vue national; (as a country) dans le pays entier; **~ park** n parc national

---

**National Trust**

Le **National Trust** est un organisme indépendant, à but non lucratif, dont la mission est de protéger et de mettre en valeur les monuments et les sites britanniques en raison de leur intérêt historique ou de leur beauté naturelle.

---

**nationwide** ['neɪʃənwaɪd] adj s'étendant à l'ensemble du pays; (problem) à l'échelle du pays entier ♦ adv à travers or dans tout le pays

**native** ['neɪtɪv] n autochtone m/f, habitant(e) du pays ♦ adj du pays, indigène; (country) natal(e); (ability) inné(e); **a ~**

**of Russia** une personne originaire de Russie; **a ~ speaker of French** une personne de langue maternelle française; **N~ American** n Indien(ne) d'Amérique; **~ language** n langue maternelle

**NATO** ['neɪtəʊ] n abbr (= North Atlantic Treaty Organization) OTAN f

**natural** ['nætʃrəl] adj naturel(le); **~ gas** n gaz naturel; **~ist** n naturaliste m/f; **~ly** adv naturellement

**nature** ['neɪtʃəʳ] n nature f; **by ~** par tempérament, de nature

**naught** [nɔːt] n = nought

**naughty** ['nɔːtɪ] adj (child) vilain(e), pas sage

**nausea** ['nɔːsɪə] n nausée f

**naval** ['neɪvl] adj naval(e); **~ officer** n officier m de marine

**nave** [neɪv] n nef f

**navel** ['neɪvl] n nombril m

**navigate** ['nævɪgeɪt] vt (steer) diriger; (plot course) naviguer ♦ vi naviguer; **navigation** [nævɪ'geɪʃən] n navigation f

**navvy** ['nævɪ] (BRIT) n terrassier m

**navy** ['neɪvɪ] n marine f; **~(-blue)** adj bleu marine inv

**Nazi** ['nɑːtsɪ] n Nazi(e)

**NB** abbr (= nota bene) NB

**near** [nɪəʳ] adj proche ♦ adv près ♦ prep (also: **~ to**) près de ♦ vt approcher de; **~by** [nɪə'baɪ] adj proche ♦ adv tout près, à proximité; **~ly** adv presque; **I ~ly fell** j'ai failli tomber; **~ miss** n (AVIAT) quasi-collision f; **that was a ~ miss** (gen) il s'en est fallu de peu; (of shot) c'est passé très près; **~side** n (AUT: in Britain) côté m gauche; (: in US, Europe etc) côté droit; **~-sighted** adj myope

**neat** [niːt] adj (person, work) soigné(e); (room etc) bien tenu(e) or rangé(e); (skilful) habile; (spirits) pur(e); **~ly** adv avec soin or ordre; habilement

**necessarily** ['nesɪsrɪlɪ] adv nécessairement

**necessary** ['nesɪsrɪ] adj nécessaire; ne-

**cessity** [nɪˈsɛsɪtɪ] n nécessité f; (thing needed) chose nécessaire or essentielle; **necessities** npl nécessaire m

**neck** [nɛk] n cou m; (of animal, garment) encolure f; (of bottle) goulot m ♦ vi (inf) se peloter; ~ **and** ~ à égalité; ~**lace** n collier m; ~**line** n encolure f; ~**tie** n cravate f.

**need** [niːd] n besoin m; to ~ to devoir faire; avoir besoin de faire; (state of ~) abandon m; ~**ed** adj négligé(e); à l'abandon

**needle** [ˈniːdl] n aiguille f ♦ vt asticoter, tourmenter

**needless** [ˈniːdlɪs] adj inutile

**needlework** [ˈniːdlwɜːk] n (activity) travaux mpl d'aiguille; (object(s)) ouvrage m

**needn't** [ˈniːdnt] = need not

**needy** [ˈniːdɪ] adj nécessiteux(-euse)

**negative** [ˈnɛgətɪv] n (PHOT, ELEC) négatif m; (LING) terme m de négation ♦ adj négatif(-ive); ~ **equity** situation dans laquelle la valeur d'une maison est inférieure à celle de l'emprunt-logement contracté pour la payer

**neglect** [nɪˈglɛkt] vt négliger ♦ n le fait de négliger; (state of ~) abandon m; ~**ed** adj négligé(e); à l'abandon

**negligee** [ˈnɛglɪʒeɪ] n déshabillé m

**negotiate** [nɪˈgəʊʃɪeɪt] vi, vt négocier; **negotiation** [nɪgəʊʃɪˈeɪʃən] n négociation f, pourparlers mpl

**neigh** [neɪ] vi hennir

**neighbour** [ˈneɪbər] (US **neighbor**) n voisin(e); ~**hood** n (place) quartier m; (people) voisinage m; ~**ing** adj voisin(e), avoisinant(e); ~**ly** adj obligeant(e); (action) amical(e)

**neither** [ˈnaɪðər] adj, pron aucun(e) (des deux), ni l'un(e) ni l'autre ♦ conj: I **didn't move and ~ did Claude** je n'ai pas bougé, (et) Claude non plus ♦ adv: ~ **good nor bad** ni bon ni mauvais; ..., ~ **did I refuse** ..., (et or mais) je n'ai pas non plus refusé ...

**neon** [ˈniːɔn] n néon m; ~ **light** n lampe f au néon

**nephew** [ˈnɛvjuː] n neveu m

**nerve** [nɜːv] n nerf m; (fig: courage) sang-froid m, courage m; (: impudence) aplomb m, toupet m; to **have a fit of** ~**s** avoir le trac; ~**racking** adj angoissant(e)

**nervous** [ˈnɜːvəs] adj nerveux(-euse); (anxious) inquiet(-ète), plein(e) d'appréhension; (timid) intimidé(e); ~ **breakdown** n dépression nerveuse

**nest** [nɛst] n nid m ♦ vi (se) nicher, faire son nid; ~ **egg** n (fig) bas m de laine, magot m

**nestle** [ˈnɛsl] vi se blottir

**net** [nɛt] n filet m; **the N~** (Internet) le Net m; adj net(te) ♦ vt (fish etc) prendre au filet; (profit) rapporter; ~**ball** n netball m

**Netherlands** [ˈnɛðələndz] npl: **the** ~ les Pays-Bas mpl

**nett** [nɛt] adj = **net**

**netting** [ˈnɛtɪŋ] n (for fence etc) treillis m, grillage m

**nettle** [ˈnɛtl] n ortie f

**network** [ˈnɛtwɜːk] n réseau m

**neurotic** [njuˈrɔtɪk] adj névrosé(e)

**neuter** [ˈnjuːtər] adj neutre ♦ vt (cat etc) châtrer, couper

**neutral** [ˈnjuːtrəl] adj neutre ♦ n (AUT) point mort; ~**ize** vt neutraliser

**never** [ˈnɛvər] adv (ne ...) jamais; ~ **again** plus jamais; ~ **in my life** jamais de ma vie; see also **mind**; ~**ending** adj interminable; ~**theless** adv néanmoins, malgré tout

**new** [njuː] adj nouveau (nouvelle), (brand) ~ neuf (neuve); **N~ Age** n New Age m; ~**born** adj nouveau/nouvelle-né(e); ~**comer** n nouveau venu/nouvelle venue; ~**fangled** [ˈnjuːˈfæŋgld] (pej) adj ultramoderne (et farfelu(e)); ~**found** (friend) nouveau (nouvelle); (enthusiasm) de fraîche date; ~**ly** adv nouvellement, récemment; ~**ly-weds** npl jeunes mariés mpl

**news** [nju:z] n nouvelle(s) f(pl); (RADIO, TV) informations fpl, actualités fpl; **a piece of ~** une nouvelle; **~ agency** n agence f de presse; **~agent** (BRIT) n marchand m de journaux; **~caster** n présentateur(-trice); **~ flash** n flash m d'information; **~letter** n bulletin m, ~**paper** n journal m; **~print** n papier m (de) journal; **~reader** n = newscaster; **~reel** n actualités (filmées); **~ stand** n kiosque m à journaux

**newt** [nju:t] n triton m

**New Year** n Nouvel An, le jour de l'An; **~'s Day** n le jour de l'An; **~'s Eve** n la Saint-Sylvestre

**New Zealand** [-'zi:lənd] n la Nouvelle-Zélande; **~er** n Néo-zélandais(e)

**next** [nekst] adj (seat, room) voisin(e), d'à côté; (meeting, bus stop) suivant(e); (in time) prochain(e) ♦ adv (place) à côté; (time) la fois suivante, la prochaine fois; (afterwards) ensuite; **~ day** le lendemain, le jour suivant or d'après; **~ year** l'année prochaine; **~ time** la prochaine fois; **~ to** à côté de; **~ to nothing** presque rien; **~, please!** (at doctor's etc) au suivant!; **~ door** adv à côté ♦ adj d'à côté; **~-of-kin** n parent m le plus proche

**NHS** n abbr = **National Health Service**

**nib** [nib] n (bec m de) plume f

**nibble** [nibl] vt grignoter

**nice** [nais] adj (pleasant, likeable) agréable; (pretty) joli(e); (kind) gentil(le); **~ly** adv agréablement; joliment; gentiment

**niceties** ['naisitiz] npl subtilités fpl

**nick** [nik] n (indentation) encoche f; (wound) entaille f ♦ vt (BRIT: inf) faucher, piquer; **in the ~ of time** juste à temps

**nickel** ['nikl] n nickel m; (US) pièce f de 5 cents

**nickname** ['nikneim] n surnom m ♦ vt surnommer

**nicotine patch** ['nikəti:n-] n timbre m anti-tabac, patch m

**niece** [ni:s] n nièce f

**Nigeria** [nai'dʒiəriə] n Nigéria m or f

**niggling** ['niglin] adj (person) tatillon(ne); (detail) insignifiant(e); (doubts, injury) persistant(e)

**night** [nait] n nuit f; (evening) soir m; **at ~** la nuit; **by ~** de nuit; **the ~ before last** avant-hier soir; **~cap** n boisson prise avant le coucher; **~ club** n boîte f de nuit; **~dress** n chemise f de nuit; **~fall** n tombée f de la nuit; **~gown** n chemise f de nuit; **~ie** ['naiti] n chemise f de nuit; **~ingale** ['naitiŋgeil] n rossignol m; **~life** n vie f nocturne; **~ly** adj de chaque nuit or soir; (by night) nocturne ♦ adv chaque nuit or soir; **~mare** n cauchemar m; **~ porter** n gardien de nuit, concierge f de la nuit; **~ school** n cours mpl du soir; **~ shift** n équipe f de nuit; **~time** n nuit f; **~ watchman** n veilleur m or gardien m de nuit

**nil** [nil] n rien m; (BRIT: SPORT) zéro m

**Nile** [nail] n: **the ~** le Nil

**nimble** ['nimbl] adj agile

**nine** [nain] num neuf; **~teen** ['nain'ti:n] num dix-neuf; **~ty** ['nainti] num quatre-vingt-dix; **ninth** [nainθ] num neuvième

**nip** [nip] vt pincer

**nipple** ['nipl] n (ANAT) mamelon m, bout m du sein

**nitrogen** ['naitrədʒən] n azote m

---

**no** [nəu] (pl noes) adv (opposite of "yes") non; **are you coming? - no (I'm not)** est-ce que vous venez? - non; **would you like some more? - no thank you** vous en voulez encore? - non merci

♦ adj (not any) pas de, aucun(e) (used with "ne"); **I have no money/books** je n'ai pas d'argent or de livres; **no student would have done it** aucun étudiant ne l'aurait fait; **"no smoking"** "défense de fumer"; **"no dogs"** "les

chiens ne sont pas admis"
♦ n non m

**nobility** [nəu'bılıtı] n noblesse f

**noble** ['nəubl] adj noble

**nobody** ['nəubədı] pron personne

**nod** [nɔd] vi faire un signe de tête (affirmatif ou amical); (sleep) somnoler ♦ vt: **to ~ one's head** faire un signe de (la) tête; (in agreement) faire signe que oui ♦ n signe m de (la) tête; **~ off** vi s'assoupir

**noise** [nɔız] n bruit m; **noisy** adj bruyant(e)

**nominal** ['nɔmınl] adj symbolique

**nominate** ['nɔmıneıt] vt (propose) proposer; (appoint) nommer; **nominee** [nɔmı'ni:] n candidat agréé; personne nommée

**non...** [nɔn] prefix non-; **~alcoholic** adj non-alcoolisé(e); **~committal** adj évasif(-ive); **~descript** adj quelconque, indéfinissable

**none** [nʌn] pron aucun(e); **~ of you** aucun d'entre vous, personne parmi vous; **I've ~ left** je n'en ai plus; **he's ~ the worse for it** il ne s'en porte pas plus mal

**nonentity** [nɔ'nentıtı] n personne insignifiante

**nonetheless** ['nʌnðə'les] adv néanmoins

**non-existent** [nɔnıg'zıstənt] adj inexistant(e)

**non-fiction** [nɔn'fıkʃən] n littérature f non-romanesque

**nonplussed** [nɔn'plʌst] adj perplexe

**nonsense** ['nɔnsəns] n absurdités fpl, idioties fpl; **~!** ne dites pas d'idioties!

**non:** **~smoker** n non-fumeur m; **~smoking** adj non-fumeur; **~stick** adj qui n'attache pas; **~stop** adj direct(e), sans arrêt (or arrêté); **~stop** adv sans arrêt

**noodles** ['nu:dlz] npl nouilles fpl

**nook** [nuk] n: **~s and crannies** recoins mpl

**noon** [nu:n] n midi m

**no one** ['nəuwʌn] pron = **nobody**

**noose** [nu:s] n nœud coulant; (hangman's) corde f

**nor** [nɔ:r] conj = **neither** ♦ adv see **neither**

**norm** [nɔ:m] n norme f

**normal** adj normal(e); **~ly** ['nɔ:məlɪ] adv normalement

**Normandy** ['nɔ:məndɪ] n Normandie f

**north** [nɔ:θ] n nord m ♦ adj du nord, nord inv ♦ adv au or vers le nord; **N~ America** n Amérique f du Nord; **~east** n nord-est m; **~erly** ['nɔ:ðəlɪ] adj du nord; **~ern** ['nɔ:ðən] adj du nord, septentrional(e); **N~ern Ireland** n Irlande f du Nord; **N~ Pole** n pôle m Nord; **N~ Sea** n mer f du Nord; **~ward(s)** adv vers le nord; **~west** n nord-ouest m

**Norway** ['nɔ:weı] n Norvège f; **Norwegian** [nɔ:'wi:dʒən] adj norvégien(ne) ♦ n Norvégien(ne); (LING) norvégien m

**nose** [nəuz] n nez m; **~ about, ~ around** vi fouiner ou fureter (partout); **~bleed** n saignement m du nez; **~dive** n (descente f en) piqué m; **~y** (inf) adj = **nosy**

**nostalgia** [nɔs'tældʒɪə] n nostalgie f

**nostril** ['nɔstrıl] n narine f; (of horse) naseau m

**nosy** ['nəuzı] (inf) adj curieux(-euse)

**not** [nɔt] adv (ne ...) pas; **he is ~ or isn't here** il n'est pas ici; **you must ~ or you mustn't do that** tu ne dois pas faire ça; **it's too late, isn't it or is it ~?** c'est trop tard, n'est-ce pas?; **~ yet/now** pas encore/maintenant; **~ at all** pas du tout; see also **all; only**

**notably** ['nəutəblɪ] adv (particularly) en particulier; (markedly) spécialement

**notary** ['nəutərı] n notaire m

**notch** [nɔtʃ] n encoche f

**note** [nəut] n note f; (letter) mot m; (banknote) billet m ♦ vt (also: **~ down**) noter; (observe) constater; **~book** n carnet m; **~d** adj réputé(e); **~pad** n bloc-notes *m*; **~paper** *n* papier *m* à lettres

**nothing** ['nʌθɪŋ] *n* rien *m*; **he does ~** il ne fait rien; **~ new** rien de nouveau; **for ~** pour rien

**notice** ['nəʊtɪs] *n* (announcement, warning) avis *m*; (period of time) délai *m*; (resignation) démission *f*; (dismissal) congé *m* ♦ *vt* remarquer, s'apercevoir de; **to take ~ of** prêter attention à; **to bring sth to sb's~** porter qch à la connaissance de qn; **at short ~** dans un délai très court; **until further ~** jusqu'à nouvel ordre; **to hand in one's ~** donner sa démission, démissionner; **~able** *adj* visible; **~ board** (BRIT) *n* panneau *m* d'affichage

**notify** ['nəʊtɪfaɪ] *vt*: **to ~ sth to sb** notifier qch à qn; **to ~ sb (of sth)** avertir qn (de qch)

**notion** ['nəʊʃən] *n* idée *f*; (concept) notion *f*

**notorious** [nəʊ'tɔːrɪəs] *adj* notoire (souvent en mal)

**nought** [nɔːt] *n* zéro *m*

**noun** [naʊn] *n* nom *m*

**nourish** ['nʌrɪʃ] *vt* nourrir; **~ing** *adj* nourrissant(e); **~ment** *n* nourriture *f*

**novel** ['nɔvl] *n* roman *m* ♦ *adj* nouveau (nouvelle), original(e); **~ist** *n* romancier *m*; **~ty** *n* nouveauté *f*

**November** [nəʊ'vembər] *n* novembre *m*

**now** [naʊ] *adv* maintenant ♦ *conj*: **~ (that)** maintenant que; **right ~** tout de suite; **by ~** à l'heure qu'il est; **just ~**: **that's the fashion just ~** c'est la mode en ce moment; **~ and then, ~ and again** de temps en temps; **from ~ on** dorénavant; **~adays** *adv* de nos jours

**nowhere** ['nəʊwɛər] *adv* nulle part

**nozzle** ['nɔzl] *n* (of hose etc) ajutage *m*; (of vacuum cleaner) suceur *m*

**nuclear** ['njuːklɪər] *adj* nucléaire

**nucleus** ['njuːklɪəs] *n* (pl **nuclei**) noyau *m*

**nude** [njuːd] *adj* nu(e) ♦ *n* nu *m*; **in the ~** (tout(e)) nu(e)

**nudge** [nʌdʒ] *vt* donner un (petit) coup de coude à

**nudist** ['njuːdɪst] *n* nudiste *m/f*

**nuisance** ['njuːsns] *n*: **it's a ~** c'est (très) embêtant; **he's a ~** il est assommant *or* casse-pieds; **what a ~!** quelle barbe!

**null** [nʌl] *adj*: **~ and void** nul(le) et non avenu(e)

**numb** [nʌm] *adj* engourdi(e); (with fear) paralysé(e)

**number** ['nʌmbər] *n* nombre *m*; (numeral) chiffre *m*; (of house, bank account etc) numéro *m* ♦ *vt* numéroter; (amount to) compter; **a ~ of** un certain nombre de; **they were seven in ~** ils étaient (au nombre de) sept; **to be ~ed among** compter parmi; **~ plate** (AUT) *n* plaque *f* minéralogique *or* d'immatriculation

**numeral** ['njuːmərəl] *n* chiffre *m*

**numerate** ['njuːmərɪt] *adj*: **to be ~** avoir des notions d'arithmétique

**numerical** [njuː'merɪkl] *adj* numérique

**numerous** ['njuːmərəs] *adj* nombreux(-euse)

**nun** [nʌn] *n* religieuse *f*, sœur *f*

**nurse** [nɜːs] *n* infirmière *f* ♦ *vt* (patient, cold) soigner

**nursery** ['nɜːsərɪ] *n* (room) nursery *f*; (institution) crèche *f*; (for plants) pépinière *f*; **~ rhyme** *n* comptine *f*, chansonnette *f* pour enfants; **~ school** *n* école maternelle; **~ slope** (SKI) *n* piste *f* pour débutants

**nursing** ['nɜːsɪŋ] *n* (profession) profession *f* d'infirmière; (care) soins *mpl*; **~ home** *n* clinique *f*; maison *f* de convalescence

**nut** [nʌt] *n* (of metal) écrou *m*; (fruit) noix *f*, noisette *f*; cacahuète *f*; **~crackers** *npl* casse-noix *m inv*, casse-noisette(s) *m*

**nutmeg** ['nʌtmeg] *n* (noix *f*) muscade *f*

**nutritious** [njuː'trɪʃəs] *adj* nutritif(-ive),

nourrissant(e)

**nuts** [nʌts] (inf) adj dingue

**nutshell** ['nʌtʃel] n: **in a ~** en un mot

**nutter** ['nʌtər] (BRIT: inf) n: **he's a complete ~** il est complètement cinglé

**nylon** ['naɪlɔn] n nylon m ♦ adj de or en nylon

# O, o

**oak** [əuk] n chêne m ♦ adj de or en (bois de) chêne

**OAP** (BRIT) n abbr = **old-age pensioner**

**oar** [ɔːr] n aviron m, rame f

**oasis** [əu'eɪsɪs] (pl **oases**) n oasis f

**oath** [əuθ] n serment m; (swear word) juron m; **under ~**, (BRIT) **on ~** sous serment

**oatmeal** ['əutmiːl] n flocons mpl d'avoine

**oats** [əuts] n avoine f

**obedience** [ə'biːdɪəns] n obéissance f; **obedient** adj obéissant(e)

**obey** [ə'beɪ] vt obéir à; (instructions) se conformer à

**obituary** [ə'bɪtjuərɪ] n nécrologie f

**object** [n 'ɔbdʒɪkt, vb əb'dʒɛkt] n objet m; (purpose) but m, objet; (LING) complément m d'objet ♦ vi: **to ~ to** (attitude) désapprouver; (proposal) protester contre; **expense is no ~** l'argent n'est pas un problème; **he ~ed** that ... il a fait valoir or a objecté que ...; **I ~!** je proteste!; **~ion** [əb'dʒɛkʃən] n objection f; **~ionable** adj très désagréable; (language) choquant(e); **~ive** n objectif m ♦ adj objectif(-ive)

**obligation** [ɔblɪ'geɪʃən] n obligation f, devoir m; **without ~** sans engagement; **obligatory** [ə'blɪɡətərɪ] adj obligatoire

**oblige** [ə'blaɪdʒ] vt (force): **to ~ sb to do** obliger or forcer qn à faire; (do a favour) rendre service à, obliger; **to be ~d to sb for sth** être obligé(e) à qn de qch; **obliging** adj obligeant(e), serviable

**oblique** [ə'bliːk] adj oblique; (allusion) indirect(e)

**obliterate** [ə'blɪtəreɪt] vt effacer

**oblivion** [ə'blɪvɪən] n oubli m; **oblivious** adj: **oblivious of** oublieux (-euse) de

**oblong** ['ɔblɔŋ] adj oblong (oblongue) ♦ n rectangle m

**obnoxious** [əb'nɔkʃəs] adj odieux (-euse); (smell) nauséabond(e)

**oboe** ['əubəu] n hautbois m

**obscene** [əb'siːn] adj obscène

**obscure** [əb'skjuər] adj obscur(e) ♦ vt obscurcir; (hide: sun) cacher

**observant** [əb'zɜːvnt] adj observateur(-trice)

**observation** [ɔbzə'veɪʃən] n (remark) observation f; (watching) surveillance f

**observatory** [əb'zɜːvətrɪ] n observatoire m

**observe** [əb'zɜːv] vt observer; (remark) faire observer or remarquer; **~r** n observateur(-trice)

**obsess** [əb'sɛs] vt obséder; **~ive** adj obsédant(e)

**obsolete** ['ɔbsəliːt] adj dépassé(e); démodé(e)

**obstacle** ['ɔbstəkl] n obstacle m; **~ race** n course f d'obstacles

**obstinate** ['ɔbstɪnɪt] adj obstiné(e)

**obstruct** [əb'strʌkt] vt (block) boucher, obstruer; (hinder) entraver

**obtain** [əb'teɪn] vt obtenir

**obvious** ['ɔbvɪəs] adj évident(e), manifeste; **~ly** adv manifestement; **~ly not!** bien sûr que non!

**occasion** [ə'keɪʒən] n occasion f; (event) événement m; **~al** adj pris(e) or fait(e) etc de temps en temps, occasionnel(le); **~ally** adv de temps en temps, quelquefois

**occupation** [ɔkju'peɪʃən] n occupation f; (job) métier m, profession f; **~al hazard** n risque m du métier

**occupier** ['ɔkjupaɪər] n occupant(e)

**occupy** ['ɔkjupaɪ] vt occuper; **to ~ o.s.**

in *or* with doing s'occuper à faire
**occur** [əˈkəːʳ] vi (event) se produire; (phenomenon, error) se rencontrer; **to ~ to sb** venir à l'esprit de qn; **~rence** n (existence) présence f, existence f; (event) cas m, fait m f

**ocean** [ˈəuʃən] n océan m
**o'clock** [əˈklɔk] adv: **it is 5 ~** il est 5 heures
**OCR** n abbr = **optical character reader; optical character recognition**
**October** [ɔkˈtəubəʳ] n octobre m
**octopus** [ˈɔktəpəs] n pieuvre f
**odd** [ɔd] adj (strange) bizarre, curieux (-euse); (number) impair(e); (not of a set) dépareillé(e); **60-~** 60 et quelques; **at ~ times** de temps en temps; **the ~ one out** l'exception f; **~ity** n (person) excentrique m/f; (thing) curiosité f; **job man** n homme à tout faire; **~ jobs** npl petits travaux divers; **~ly** adv bizarrement, curieusement; **~ments** npl (COMM) fins fpl de série; **~s** npl (in betting) cote f; **it makes no ~s** cela n'a pas d'importance; **at ~s** en désaccord; **~s and ends** de petites choses
**odour** [ˈəudəʳ] (US **odor**) n odeur f

**of** [ɔv, əv] prep 1 (gen) de; **a friend of ours** un de nos amis; **a boy of 10** un garçon de 10 ans; **that was kind of you** c'était gentil de votre part
2 (expressing quantity, amount, dates etc) de; **a kilo of flour** un kilo de farine; **how much of this do you need?** combien vous en faut-il?; **there were 3 of them** (people) ils étaient 3; (objects) il y en avait 3; **3 of us went** 3 d'entre nous y sont allé(e)s; **the 5th of July** le 5 juillet
3 (from, out of) en, de; **a statue of marble** une statue de *or* en marbre; **made of wood** (fait) en bois

**off** [ɔf] adj, adv (engine) coupé(e); (tap) fermé(e); (BRIT: food: bad) mauvais(e); (:

milk: bad) tourné(e); (CULIN) absent(e); (absent) absent(e); (cancelled) annulé(e) ♦ prep de; sur; **to be ~** (to leave) partir, s'en aller; **to be ~ sick** être absent pour cause de maladie; **a day ~** un jour de congé; **to have an ~ day** n'être pas en forme; **he had his coat ~** il avait enlevé son manteau; **10% ~** (COMM) 10% de rabais; **~ the coast** au large de la côte; **I'm ~ meat** je ne mange plus de viande, je n'aime plus la viande; **on the ~ chance** à tout hasard

**offal** [ˈɔfl] n (CULIN) abats mpl
**off-colour** [ˈɔfˈkʌləʳ] (BRIT) adj (ill) malade, mal fichu(e)
**offence** [əˈfɛns] (US **offense**) n (crime) délit m, infraction f; **to take ~ at** se vexer de, s'offenser de
**offend** [əˈfɛnd] vt (person) offenser, blesser; **~er** n délinquant(e)
**offense** [əˈfɛns] (US) n = **offence**
**offensive** [əˈfɛnsɪv] adj offensant(e), choquant(e); (smell etc) très déplaisant(e); (weapon) offensif(-ive) ♦ n (MIL) offensive f
**offer** [ˈɔfəʳ] n offre f, proposition f ♦ vt offrir, proposer; **"on ~"** (COMM) "en promotion"; **~ing** n offrande f
**offhand** [ˈɔfˈhænd] adj désinvolte ♦ adv spontanément
**office** [ˈɔfɪs] n (place, room) bureau m; (position) charge f, fonction f; **doctor's ~** (US) cabinet (médical); **to take ~** entrer en fonctions; **~ automation** n bureautique f; **~ block** (US **office building**) n immeuble m de bureaux; **~ hours** npl heures fpl de bureau; (US: MED) heures de consultation
**officer** [ˈɔfɪsəʳ] n (MIL etc) officier m; (also: **police ~**) agent m (de police); (of organization) membre m du bureau directeur
**office worker** n employé m de bureau
**official** [əˈfɪʃl] adj officiel(le) ♦ n officiel m; (civil servant) fonctionnaire m/f; employé(e)
**officiate** [əˈfɪʃɪeɪt] vi (REL) officier; **to ~**

**at a marriage** célébrer un mariage

**officious** [ə'fɪʃəs] *adj* trop empressé(e)

**offing** ['ɒfɪŋ] *n*: **in the ~** (*fig*) en perspective

**off**: **~-licence** (*BRIT*) *n* (*shop*) débit *m* de vins et de spiritueux; **~-line** *adj*, *adv* (*COMPUT*) (en mode) autonome; (: *switched off*) non connecté(e); **~-peak** *adj* aux heures creuses; (*electricity*, *ticket*) au tarif heures creuses; **~-putting** (*BRIT*) *adj* (*remark*) rébarbatif (-ive); (*person*) rebutant(e), peu engageant(e); **~-road vehicle** *n* véhicule *m* tout-terrain; **~-season** *adj*, *adv* hors-saison *inv*; **~set** (*irreg*) *vt* (*counteract*) contrebalancer, compenser; **~shoot** *n* (*fig*) ramification *f*, antenne *f*; **~shore** *adj* (*breeze*) de terre; (*fishing*) côtier (-ère); **~side** *adj* (*SPORT*) hors jeu; (*AUT*: *in Britain*) droit(e); (: *in US, Europe*) de gauche; **~spring** *n* progéniture *f*, **~stage** *adv* dans les coulisses; **~-the-peg** (*US* **off-the-rack**) *adv* en prêt-à-porter; **~-white** *adj* blanc cassé *inv*

---

*Un off-licence est un magasin où l'on vend de l'alcool (à emporter) aux heures où les pubs sont fermés. On peut également y acheter des boissons non alcoolisées, des cigarettes, des chips, des bonbons, des chocolats etc.*

---

**Oftel** ['ɒftel] *n* organisme qui supervise les télécommunications

**often** ['ɒfn] *adv* souvent; **how ~ do you go?** vous y allez tous les combien?; **how ~ have you gone there?** vous y êtes allé combien de fois?

**Ofwat** ['ɒfwɒt] *n* organisme qui surveille les activités des compagnies des eaux

**oh** [əʊ] *excl* ô!, oh!, ah!

**oil** [ɔɪl] *n* huile *f*; (*petroleum*) pétrole *m*; (*for central heating*) mazout *m* ♦ *vt* (*machine*) graisser; **~can** *n* burette *f* de graissage; (*for storing*) bidon *m* à huile;

**~field** *n* gisement *m* de pétrole; **~ filter** *n* (*AUT*) filtre *m* à huile; **~ painting** *n* peinture *f* à l'huile; **~ refinery** *n* raffinerie *f*; **~ rig** *n* derrick *m*; (*at sea*) plate-forme pétrolière; **~ slick** *n* nappe *f* de mazout; **~ tanker** *n* (*ship*) pétrolier *m*; (*truck*) camion-citerne *m*; **~ well** *n* puits *m* de pétrole; **~y** *adj* huileux (-euse); (*food*) gras(se)

**ointment** ['ɔɪntmənt] *n* onguent *m*

**O.K., okay** ['əʊ'keɪ] *excl* d'accord! ♦ *adj* (*average*) pas mal ♦ *vt* approuver, donner son accord à; **is it ~?, are you ~?** ça va?

**old** [əʊld] *adj* vieux (vieille); (*person*) vieux, âgé(e); (*former*) ancien(ne), vieux, vieux; **how ~ are you?** quel âge avez-vous?; **he's 10 years ~** il a 10 ans, il est âgé de 10 ans; **~er brother/sister** frère/sœur aîné(e); **~ age** *n* vieillesse *f*; **~ age pensioner** (*BRIT*) *n* retraité(e); **~-fashioned** *adj* démodé(e); (*person*) vieux jeu *inv*

**olive** ['ɒlɪv] *n* (*fruit*) olive *f*; (*tree*) olivier *m* ♦ *adj* (*also*: **~-green**) (vert) olive *inv*; **~ oil** *n* huile *f* d'olive

**Olympic** [əʊ'lɪmpɪk] *adj* olympique; **the ~ Games, the ~s** les Jeux *mpl* olympiques

**omelet(te)** ['ɒmlɪt] *n* omelette *f*

**omen** ['əʊmən] *n* présage *m*

**ominous** ['ɒmɪnəs] *adj* menaçant(e), inquiétant(e); (*event*) de mauvais augure

**omit** [əʊ'mɪt] *vt* omettre; **to ~ to do** omettre de faire

---

KEYWORD

**on** [ɒn] *prep* **1** (*indicating position*) sur; **on the table** sur la table; **on the wall** sur le *ou* au mur; **on the left** à gauche **2** (*indicating means, method, condition etc*): **on foot** à pied; **on the train/plane** (*be*) dans le train/l'avion; (*go*) en train/avion; **on the telephone/radio/television** au téléphone/à la radio/à la télévision; **to be on drugs** se droguer;

on holiday en vacances

3 (*referring to time*): **on Friday** vendredi; **on Fridays** le vendredi; **on June 20th** le 20 juin; **a week on Friday** vendredi en huit; **on arrival** à l'arrivée; **on seeing this** en voyant cela

4 (*about, concerning*) sur, de; **a book on Balzac/physics** un livre sur Balzac/la physique

♦ *adv* 1 (*referring to dress, covering*): **to have one's coat on** avoir (mis) son manteau; **to put one's coat on** mettre son manteau; **what's she got on?** qu'est-ce qu'elle porte?; **screw the lid on tightly** vissez bien le couvercle

2 (*further, continuously*): **to walk** *etc* **on** continuer à marcher *etc*; **on and off** de temps à autre

♦ *adj* 1 (*in operation: machine*) en marche; (: *radio, TV, light*) allumé(e); (: *tap, gas*) ouvert(e); (: *brakes*) mis(e); **is the meeting still on?** (*not cancelled*) est-ce que la réunion a bien lieu?; (*in progress*) la réunion dure-t-elle encore?; **when is this film on?** quand passe ce film?

2 (*inf*): **that's not on!** (*not acceptable*) cela ne se fait pas!; (*not possible*) pas question!

**once** [wʌns] *adv* une fois; (*formerly*) autrefois ♦ *conj* une fois que; **he had left/it was done** une fois qu'il fut parti/que ce fut terminé; **at ~** tout de suite, immédiatement; (*simultaneously*) à la fois; **~ a week** une fois par semaine; **~ more** encore une fois; **~ and for all** une fois pour toutes; **~ upon a time** il y avait une fois, il était une fois

**oncoming** [ˈɔnkʌmɪŋ] *adj* (*traffic*) venant en sens inverse

**one** [wʌn] *num* un(e); **one hundred and fifty** cent cinquante; **one day** un jour

♦ *adj* 1 (*sole*) seul(e), unique; **the one**

**book which** l'unique *or* le seul livre qui; **the one man who** le seul (homme) qui

2 (*same*) même; **they came in the one car** ils sont venus dans la même voiture

♦ *pron* 1: **this one** celui-ci (celle-ci); **that one** celui-là (celle-là); **I've already got one/a red one** j'en ai déjà un(e)/un(e) rouge; **one by one** un(e) à *or* par un(e)

2: **one another** l'un(e) l'autre; **to look at one another** se regarder

3 (*impersonal*) on; **one never knows** on ne sait jamais; **to cut one's finger** se couper le doigt

**one:** **~-day excursion** (*US*) *n* billet *m* d'aller-retour (valable pour la journée); **~-man** *adj* (*business*) dirigé(e) *etc* par un seul homme; **~-man band** *n* homme-orchestre *m*; **~-off** (*BRIT: inf*) *n* exemplaire *m* unique

**oneself** [wʌnˈself] *pron* (*reflexive*) se; (*after prep*) soi(-même); (*emphatic*) soimême; **to hurt ~** se faire mal; **to keep sth for ~** garder qch pour soi; **to talk to ~** se parler à soi-même

**one:** **~-sided** *adj* (*argument*) unilatéral; **~-to-~** *adj* (*relationship*) univoque; **~-way** *adj* (*street, traffic*) à sens unique

**ongoing** [ˈɔngəʊɪŋ] *adj* en cours; (*relationship*) suivi(e)

**onion** [ˈʌnjən] *n* oignon *m*

**on-line** [ˈɔnlaɪn] *adj, adv* (*COMPUT*) en ligne; (: *switched on*) connecté(e)

**onlooker** [ˈɔnlukəʳ] *n* spectateur(-trice) *m/f*

**only** [ˈəʊnlɪ] *adv* seulement ♦ *adj* seul(e), unique ♦ *conj* seulement, mais; **an ~ child** un enfant unique; **not ~ ... but also** non seulement ... mais aussi

**onset** [ˈɔnset] *n* début *m*; (*of winter, old age*) approche *f*

**onshore** [ˈɔnʃɔːʳ] *adj* (*wind*) du large

**onslaught** [ˈɔnslɔːt] *n* attaque *f*, assaut *m*

**onto** [ˈɔntu] *prep* = **on to**

**onward(s)** [ˈɔnwəd(z)] *adv* (move) en avant; **from that time ~** à partir de ce moment

**ooze** [uːz] *vi* suinter

**opaque** [əuˈpeik] *adj* opaque

**OPEC** [ˈaupek] *n abbr* (= Organization of Petroleum-Exporting Countries) O.P.E.P. *f*

**open** [ˈəupn] *adj* ouvert(e); (car) découvert(e); (road, view) dégagé(e); (meeting) public(-ique); (admiration) manifeste ♦ *vt* ouvrir ♦ *vi* (flower, eyes, door, debate) s'ouvrir; (shop, bank, museum) ouvrir; (book etc. commence) commencer, débuter; **in the ~ (air)** en plein air; **~ on to** *vt fus* (subj: room, door) donner sur; **~ up** ouvrir ♦ *vi* s'ouvrir; **~ing** *n* ouverture *f*; (opportunity) occasion *f* ♦ *adj* (remarks) préliminaire; **~ing hours** *npl* heures *fpl* d'ouverture; **~ly** *adv* ouvertement; **~-minded** *adj* à l'esprit ouvert; **~-necked** *adj* à col ouvert; **~-plan** *adj* sans cloisons

---

**Open University**

L'**Open University** a été fondée en 1969. Ce type d'enseignement comprend des cours (certaines plages horaires sont réservées à cet effet à la télévision et à la radio), des devoirs qui sont envoyés par l'étudiant à son directeur ou sa directrice d'études, et un séjour obligatoire en université d'été. Il faut couvrir un certain nombre d'unités de valeur pendant une période de temps déterminée et obtenir la moyenne à un certain nombre d'entre elles pour recevoir le diplôme visé.

---

**opera** [ˈɔpərə] *n* opéra *m*; **~ singer** *n* chanteur(-euse) d'opéra

**operate** [ˈɔpəreit] *vt* (machine) faire marcher, faire fonctionner ♦ *vi* fonctionner; (MED): **to ~ (on sb)** opérer (qn)

**operatic** [ɔpəˈrætik] *adj* d'opéra

**operating table** *n* table *f* d'opération

**operating theatre** *n* salle *f* d'opération

**operation** [ɔpəˈreiʃən] *n* opération *f*; (of machine) fonctionnement *m*; **to be in ~** (system, law) être en vigueur; **to have an ~** (MED) se faire opérer

**operative** [ˈɔpərətiv] *adj* (measure) en vigueur

**operator** [ˈɔpəreitə] *n* (of machine) opérateur(-trice); (TEL) téléphoniste *m/f*

**opinion** [əˈpinjən] *n* opinion *f*, avis *m*; **in my ~** à mon avis; **~ated** *adj* aux idées bien arrêtées; **~ poll** *n* sondage *m* (d'opinion)

**opponent** [əˈpəunənt] *n* adversaire *m/f*

**opportunity** [ɔpəˈtjuːnitɪ] *n* occasion *f*; **to take the ~ of doing** profiter de l'occasion pour faire; en profiter pour faire

**oppose** [əˈpəuz] *vt* s'opposer à; **~d to** à opposé(e) à; **as ~d to** par opposition à; **opposing** *adj* (side) opposé(e)

**opposite** [ˈɔpəzit] *adj* opposé(e); (house etc) d'en face ♦ *adv* en face ♦ *prep* en face de ♦ *n* opposé *m*, contraire *m*; **the ~ sex** l'autre sexe, le sexe opposé; **opposition** [ɔpəˈziʃən] *n* opposition *f*

**oppressive** [əˈpresiv] *adj* (political regime) oppressif(-ive); (weather) lourd(e); (heat) accablant(e)

**opt** [ɔpt] *vi*: **to ~ for** opter pour; **to ~ to do** choisir de faire; **to ~ out of** choisir de ne pas participer à or de ne pas faire

**optical** [ˈɔptikl] *adj* optique; (instrument) d'optique; **~ character recognition/reader** *n* lecture *f*/ lecteur *m* optique

**optician** [ɔpˈtiʃən] *n* opticien(ne)

**optimist** [ˈɔptimist] *n* optimiste *m/f*; **~ic** [ɔptiˈmistik] *adj* optimiste

**option** [ˈɔpʃən] *n* choix *m*, option *f*; (SCOL) matière *f* à option; (COMM) option; **~al** *adj* facultatif(-ive); (COMM) en option

**or** [ɔː] *conj* ou; (with negative): **he hasn't seen ~ heard anything** il n'a rien vu ni entendu; **~ else** sinon; ou bien

**oral** ['ɔːrəl] *adj* oral(e) ♦ *n* oral *m*

**orange** ['ɔrɪndʒ] *n* (*fruit*) orange *f* ♦ *adj* orange *inv*

**orbit** ['ɔːbɪt] *n* orbite *f* ♦ *vt* graviter autour de; **~al (motorway)** *n* périphérique *m*

**orchard** ['ɔːtʃəd] *n* verger *m*

**orchestra** ['ɔːkɪstrə] *n* orchestre *m*; (*US: seating*) (fauteuils *mpl* d')orchestre

**orchid** ['ɔːkɪd] *n* orchidée *f*

**ordain** [ɔː'deɪn] *vt* (*REL*) ordonner

**ordeal** [ɔː'diːl] *n* épreuve *f*

**order** ['ɔːdəʳ] *n* ordre *m*; (*COMM*) commande *f* ♦ *vt* ordonner; (*COMM*) commander; **in ~** en ordre; (*document*) en règle; **in (working) ~** en état de marche; **out of ~** (*not in correct ~*) en désordre; (*not working*) en dérangement; **in ~ to do/that** pour faire/que +*sub*; **on ~** (*COMM*) en commande; **to ~ sb to do** ordonner à qn de faire; **~ form** *n* bon *m* de commande; **~ly** *n* (*MIL*) ordonnance *f*; (*MED*) garçon *m* de salle ♦ *adj* (*room*) en ordre; (*person*) qui a de l'ordre

**ordinary** ['ɔːdnrɪ] *adj* ordinaire, normal(e); (*pej*) ordinaire, quelconque; **out of the ~** exceptionnel(le)

**Ordnance Survey map** ['ɔːdnəns-] *n* ≈ carte *f* d'État-Major

**ore** [ɔːʳ] *n* minerai *m*

**organ** ['ɔːgən] *n* organe *m*; (*MUS*) orgue *m*, orgues *fpl*; **~ic** [ɔː'gænɪk] *adj* organique; (*food*) biologique

**organization** [ɔːgənaɪ'zeɪʃən] *n* organisation *f*

**organize** ['ɔːgənaɪz] *vt* organiser; **~r** *n* organisateur(-trice)

**orgasm** ['ɔːgæzəm] *n* orgasme *m*

**Orient** ['ɔːrɪənt] *n*: **the ~** l'Orient *m*; **o~al** [ɔːrɪ'ɛntl] *adj* oriental(e)

**origin** ['ɔrɪdʒɪn] *n* origine *f*

**original** [ə'rɪdʒɪnl] *adj* original(e); (*earliest*) originel(le) ♦ *n* original *m*; **~ly** *adv* (*at first*) à l'origine

**originate** [ə'rɪdʒɪneɪt] *vi*: **to ~ from** (*person*) être originaire de; (*suggestion*) provenir de; **to ~ in** prendre naissance dans; avoir son origine dans

**Orkney** ['ɔːknɪ] *n* (*also*: **the ~ Islands**) les Orcades *fpl*

**ornament** ['ɔːnəmənt] *n* ornement *m*; (*trinket*) bibelot *m*; **~al** [ɔːnə'mɛntl] *adj* décoratif(-ive); (*garden*) d'agrément

**ornate** [ɔː'neɪt] *adj* très orné(e)

**orphan** ['ɔːfn] *n* orphelin(e)

**orthopaedic** [ɔːθə'piːdɪk] (*US* **orthopedic**) *adj* orthopédique

**ostensibly** [ɔs'tɛnsɪblɪ] *adv* en apparence

**ostentatious** [ɔstɛn'teɪʃəs] *adj* prétentieux(-euse)

**ostracize** ['ɔstrəsaɪz] *vt* frapper d'ostracisme

**ostrich** ['ɔstrɪtʃ] *n* autruche *f*

**other** ['ʌðəʳ] *adj* autre ♦ *pron*: **the ~ (one)** l'autre; **~s** (*~ people*) d'autres; **~ than** autrement que; à part; **~wise** *adv*, *conj* autrement

**otter** ['ɔtəʳ] *n* loutre *f*

**ouch** [autʃ] *excl* aïe!

**ought** [ɔːt] (*pt* **ought**) *aux vb*: **I ~ to do it** je devrais le faire, il faudrait que je le fasse; **this ~ to have been corrected** cela aurait dû être corrigé; **he ~ to win** il devrait gagner

**ounce** [auns] *n* once *f* (= 28.35g; 16 in a pound)

**our** ['auəʳ] *adj* notre, nos *pl*; *see also* **my**; **~s** *pron* le (la) nôtre, les nôtres; *see also* **mine¹**; **~selves** [auə'sɛlvz] *pron pl* (*reflexive, after preposition*) nous; (*emphatic*) nous-mêmes; *see also* **oneself**

**oust** [aust] *vt* évincer

**out** [aut] *adv* dehors; (*published, not at home etc*) sorti(e); (*light, fire*) éteint(e); **~ here** ici; **~ there** là-bas; **he's ~** (*absent*) il est sorti; (*unconscious*) il s'est sans connaissance; **to be ~ in one's calculations** s'être trompé dans ses calculations; **to run/back etc ~** sortir en courant/en reculant *etc*; **~ loud** à haute voix; **~ of**

(~side) en dehors de; (because of: anger etc) par; (from among): ~ of 10 sur 10; (without): ~ of petrol sans essence, à court d'essence; ~ of order (machine) en panne; (TEL: line) en dérangement; ~-and--- adj (liar, thief etc) véritable; ~back n (in Australia): the ~back l'intérieur m; ~board n (also: ~board motor) (moteur m) hors-bord m; ~break n (of war, disease) début m; (of violence) éruption f; ~burst n explosion f, accès m; ~cast n exilé(e); (socially) paria m; ~come n issue f, résultat m; ~crop n (of rock) affleurement m; ~cry n tollé (général); ~dated adj démodé(e); ~do (irreg) vt surpasser; ~door adj de or en plein air; ~doors adv dehors; au grand air

outer ['autə*] adj extérieur(e); ~ space n espace m cosmique

outfit n (clothes) tenue f

out: ~going adj (character) ouvert(e), extraverti(e); (departing) sortant(e); ~goings (BRIT) npl (expenses) dépenses fpl; ~grow (irreg) vt (clothes) devenir trop grand(e) pour; ~house n appentis m, remise f

outing ['autɪŋ] n sortie f; excursion f

out: ~law n hors-la-loi m inv ♦ vt mettre hors-la-loi; ~lay n dépenses fpl; (investment) mise f de fonds; ~let n (for liquid etc) issue f, sortie f; (US: ELEC) prise f de courant; (also: retail ~let) point m de vente; ~line n (shape) contour m; (summary) esquisse f, grandes lignes ♦ vt (fig: theory, plan) exposer à grands traits; ~live vt survivre à; ~look n perspective f; ~lying adj écarté(e); ~moded adj démodé(e); ~number vt surpasser en nombre; ~of-date adj (passport) périmé(e); (theory etc) dépassé(e); (clothes) démodé(e); ~of-the-way adj loin de tout; ~patient n malade m/f en consultation externe; ~post n avant-poste m; ~put n rendement m, production f; (COMPUT) sortie f

outrage ['autreɪdʒ] n (anger) indignation f; (violent act) atrocité f; (scandal) scandale m ♦ vt outrager; ~ous [aut'reɪdʒəs] adj atroce; scandaleux (-euse)

outright [adv aut'raɪt, adj 'autraɪt] adv complètement; (deny, refuse) catégoriquement; (ask) carrément; (kill) sur le coup ♦ adj complet(-ète); catégorique

outset ['autset] n début m

outside [aut'saɪd] n extérieur m ♦ adj extérieur(e) ♦ adv (au) dehors, à l'extérieur ♦ prep hors de, à l'extérieur de; at the ~ (fig) au plus or maximum; ~ lane n (AUT: in Britain) voie f de droite; (: in US, Europe) voie f de gauche; ~ line n (TEL) ligne extérieure; ~r n (stranger) étranger(-ère)

out: ~size ['autsaɪz] adj énorme; (clothes) grande taille inv; ~skirts npl faubourgs mpl; ~spoken adj très franc (franche); ~standing adj remarquable, exceptionnel(le); (unfinished) en suspens; (debt) impayé(e); (problem) non réglé(e); ~stay vt: to ~stay one's welcome abuser de l'hospitalité de son hôte; ~stretched [aut'stretʃt] adj (hand) tendu(e); ~strip [aut'strɪp] vt (competitors, demand) dépasser; ~ tray n courrier m "départ"

outward ['autwəd] adj (sign, appearance) extérieur(e); (journey) d'aller

outweigh [aut'weɪ] vt l'emporter sur

outwit [aut'wɪt] vt se montrer plus malin que

oval ['əuvl] adj ovale ♦ n ovale m

Oval Office

L'Oval Office est le bureau personnel du président des États-Unis à la Maison-Blanche, ainsi appelé du fait de sa forme ovale. Par extension, ce terme désigne la présidence elle-même.

ovary ['əuvəri] n ovaire m

oven ['ʌvn] n four m; ~proof adj allant au four

**over** ['əuvəʳ] adv (par-)dessus ♦ adj (finished) terminé(e); (too much) en plus ♦ prep sur; par-dessus; (above) au-dessus de; (on the other side of) de l'autre côté de; (more than) plus de; (during) pendant; ~ **here** ici; ~ **there** là-bas; **all** ~ (everywhere) partout, fini(e); ~ **and** ~ (again) à plusieurs reprises; ~ **and above** en plus de lo; **to ask sb** ~ inviter qn (à passer)

**overall** [adj, n 'əuvərɔ:l, adv əuvər'ɔ:l] adj (length, cost etc) total(e); (study) d'ensemble ♦ n (BRIT) blouse f ♦ adv dans l'ensemble, en général; ~**s** npl bleus mpl (de travail)

**over:** ~**awe** vt impressionner; ~**balance** vi basculer; ~**board** adv (NAUT) par-dessus bord; **to go** ~**board** faire du surbooking; ~**cast** adj couvert(e)

**overcharge** [əuvə'tʃɑ:dʒ] vt: **to** ~ **sb for sth** faire payer qch trop cher à qn

**overcoat** ['əuvəkəut] n pardessus m

**overcome** [əuvə'kʌm] vt (defeat) triompher de; (difficulty) surmonter

**over:** ~**crowded** adj bondé(e); ~**do** (irreg) vt exagérer; (overcook) trop cuire; **to** ~ **it do** (work etc) se surmener; ~**dose** n dose excessive; ~**draft** n découvert m; ~**drawn** adj (account) à découvert; (person) dont le compte est à découvert; ~**due** adj en retard; (change, reform) qui tarde; ~**estimate** vt surestimer

**overflow** [vb əuvə'fləu] vi déborder ♦ n (also: ~ **pipe**) tuyau m d'écoulement, trop-plein m

**overgrown** [əuvə'grəun] adj (garden) envahi(e) par la végétation

**overhaul** [vb əuvə'hɔ:l, n 'əuvəhɔ:l] vt réviser ♦ n révision f

**overhead** [adv əuvə'hed, adj, n 'əuvəhed] adv au-dessus ♦ adj aérien(ne); (lighting) vertical(e) n (US) = **overheads:** ~**s** npl (expenses) frais généraux; ~ **projector** n rétroprojecteur m

**over:** ~**hear** (irreg) vt entendre (par

hasard); ~**heat** vi (engine) chauffer; ~**joyed** adj: ~**joyed (at)** ravi(e) (de), enchanté(e) (de)

**overland** ['əuvəlænd] adj, adv par voie de terre

**overlap** [əuvə'læp] vi se chevaucher

**over:** ~**leaf** adv au verso; ~**load** vt surcharger; ~**look** vt (have view of) donner sur; (miss: by mistake) oublier; (forgive) fermer les yeux sur

**overnight** [adv əuvə'naɪt, adj 'əuvənaɪt] adv (happen) durant la nuit; (fig) soudain adj d'une (or de) nuit; **he stayed there** ~ il y a passé la nuit

**overpass** ['əuvəpɑ:s] n pont autoroutier

**overpower** [əuvə'pauəʳ] vt vaincre; (fig) accabler; ~**ing** adj (heat, stench) suffocant(e)

**over:** ~**rate** vt surestimer; ~**ride** (irreg: like **ride**) vt (order, objection) passer outre à; ~**riding** adj prépondérant(e); ~**rule** vt (decision) annuler; (claim) rejeter; (person) rejeter l'avis de; ~**run** (irreg: like **run**) vt (country) occuper; (time limit) dépasser

**overseas** [əuvə'si:z] adv outre-mer; (abroad) à l'étranger ♦ adj (trade) extérieur(e); (visitor) étranger(-ère)

**overshadow** [əuvə'ʃædəu] vt (fig) éclipser

**oversight** ['əuvəsaɪt] n omission f, oubli m

**oversleep** [əuvə'sli:p] (irreg) vi se réveiller (trop) tard

**overstep** [əuvə'step] vt: **to** ~ **the mark** dépasser la mesure

**overt** [əu'vɜ:t] adj non dissimulé(e)

**overtake** [əuvə'teɪk] (irreg) vt (AUT) dépasser, doubler

**over:** ~**throw** (irreg) vt (government) renverser; ~**time** n heures fpl supplémentaires; ~**tone** n (also: ~**tones**) note f, sous-entendus mpl

**overture** ['əuvətʃuəʳ] n (MUS, fig) ouverture f

**over:** ~**turn** vt renverser ♦ vi se retourner; **~weight** *adj* (*person*) trop gros(se); **~whelm** *vt* (*subj: emotion*) accabler; (*enemy, opponent*) écraser; **~whelming** *adj* (*victory, defeat*) écrasant(e); (*desire*) irrésistible

**overwrought** [əuvə'rɔːt] *adj* excédé(e).

**owe** [au] *vt*: **to ~ sb sth, to ~ sth to sb** devoir qch à qn; **owing to** *prep* à cause de, en raison de

**owl** [aul] *n* hibou *m*

**own** [aun] *vt* posséder ♦ *adj* propre; **a room of my ~** une chambre à moi, ma propre chambre; **to get one's ~ back** prendre sa revanche; **on one's ~** tout(e) seul(e); **~ up** *vi* avouer; **~er** *n* propriétaire *m/f*; **~ership** *n* possession *f*

**ox** [ɔks] (*pl* **~en**) *n* bœuf *m*; **~tail** *n*: **~tail soup** soupe *f* à la queue de bœuf

**oxygen** ['ɔksidʒən] *n* oxygène *m*

**oyster** ['ɔistə*] *n* huître *f*

**oz.** *abbr* = **ounce(s)**

**ozone** ['əuzəun]: **~-friendly** *adj* qui n'attaque pas *or* qui préserve la couche d'ozone; **~ hole** *n* trou *m* d'ozone; **~ layer** *n* couche *f* d'ozone

# P, p

**p** *abbr* = **penny; pence**

**PA** *n abbr* = **personal assistant; public address system**

**pa** [paː] (*inf*) *n* papa *m*

**p.a.** *abbr* = **per annum**

**pace** [peis] *n* pas *m*; (*speed*) allure *f*; vitesse *f* ♦ *vi*: **to ~ up and down** faire les cent pas; **to keep ~ with** aller à la même vitesse que; **~maker** *n* (*MED*) stimulateur *m* cardiaque; (*SPORT: also:* **~setter**) meneur(-euse) de train

**Pacific** [pə'sifik] *n*: **the ~ (Ocean)** le Pacifique, l'océan *m* Pacifique

**pack** [pæk] *n* (*~et, US of cigarettes*) paquet *m*; (*of hounds*) meute *f*; (*of thieves etc*) bande *f*; (*back ~*) sac *m* à dos; (*of cards*) jeu *m* ♦ *vt* (*goods*) empaqueter, emballer; (*box*) remplir; (*cram*) entasser;

**to ~ one's suitcase** faire sa valise; **to ~ (one's bags)** faire ses bagages; **to ~ sb off** expédier qn à; **~ it in!** laisse tomber!, écrase!

**package** ['pækidʒ] *n* paquet *m*; (*also:* **~ deal**) forfait *m*; **~ tour** (*BRIT*) *n* voyage organisé

**packed** *adj* (*crowded*) bondé(e); **~ lunch** (*BRIT*) *n* repas froid

**packet** ['pækit] *n* paquet *m*

**packing** ['pækiŋ] *n* emballage *m*; **~ case** *n* caisse *f* (d'emballage)

**pact** [pækt] *n* pacte *m*, traité *m*

**pad** [pæd] *n* bloc(-notes) *m*; (*to prevent friction*) tampon *m*; (*inf: home*) piaule *f* ♦ *vt* rembourrer; **~ding** *n* rembourrage *m*

**paddle** ['pædl] *n* (*oar*) pagaie *f*; (*US: for table tennis*) raquette *f* de ping-pong ♦ *vt*: **to ~ a canoe** *etc* pagayer ♦ *vi* barboter, faire trempette; **paddling pool** (*BRIT*) *n* petit bassin

**paddock** ['pædək] *n* enclos *m*; (*RACING*) paddock *m*

**padlock** ['pædlɔk] *n* cadenas *m*

**paediatrics** [piːdi'ætriks] (*US* **pediatrics**) *n* pédiatrie *f*

**pagan** ['peigən] *adj, n* païen(ne)

**page** [peidʒ] *n* (*of book*) page *f*; (*also:* **~ boy**) groom, chasseur *m*; (*at wedding*) garçon *m* d'honneur ♦ *vt* (*in hotel etc*) (faire) appeler

**pageant** ['pædʒənt] *n* spectacle *m* historique; **~ry** *n* apparat *m*, pompe *f*

**pager** ['peidʒə*] *n*, **paging device** *n* (*TEL*) récepteur d'appels

**paid** [peid] *pt, pp of* **pay** ♦ *adj* (*work, official*) rémunéré(e); (*holiday*) payé(e); **to put ~ to** (*BRIT*) mettre fin à, régler

**pail** [peil] *n* seau *m*

**pain** [pein] *n* douleur *f*; **to be in ~** souffrir, avoir mal; **to take ~s to do** se donner du mal pour faire; **~ed** *adj* peiné(e), chagrin(e); **~ful** *adj* douloureux(-euse); (*fig*) difficile, pénible; **~fully** *adv* (*fig: very*) terriblement; **~killer** *n* analgésique *m*; **~less** *adj* indolore; **~staking** ['peɪnteɪkɪŋ] adj (person) soigneux(-euse); (work) soigné(e)

**paint** [peɪnt] n peinture f ♦ vt peindre; **to ~ the door blue** peindre la porte en bleu; **~brush** n pinceau m; **~er** n peintre m; **~ing** n peinture f; (picture) tableau m; **~work** n peinture f

**pair** [pɛəʳ] n (of shoes, gloves etc) paire f; (of people) couple m; **~ of scissors** (paire de) ciseaux mpl; **~ of trousers** pantalon m

**pajamas** [pə'dʒɑ:məz] (US) npl pyjama(s) m(pl)

**Pakistan** [pɑ:kɪ'stɑ:n] n Pakistan m; **~i** adj pakistanais(e) ♦ n Pakistanais(e)

**pal** [pæl] (inf) n copain (copine)

**palace** ['pæləs] n palais m

**palatable** ['pælɪtəbl] adj bon (bonne), agréable au goût

**palate** ['pælɪt] n palais m (ANAT)

**pale** [peɪl] adj pâle ♦ n: **beyond the ~** (behaviour) inacceptable; **to grow ~** pâlir

**Palestine** ['pælɪstaɪn] n Palestine f; **Palestinian** [pælɪs'tɪnɪən] adj palestinien(ne) ♦ n Palestinien(ne)

**palette** ['pælɪt] n palette f

**pall** [pɔ:l] n (of smoke) voile m ♦ vi venir lassant(e)

**pallet** ['pælɪt] n (for goods) palette f

**pallid** ['pælɪd] adj blême

**palm** [pɑ:m] n (of hand) paume f; (also: **~ tree**) palmier m ♦ vt: **to ~ sth off on sb** (inf) refiler qch à qn; **P~ Sunday** n le dimanche des Rameaux

**paltry** ['pɔ:ltrɪ] adj dérisoire

**pamper** ['pæmpəʳ] vt gâter, dorloter

**pamphlet** ['pæmflət] n brochure f

**pan** [pæn] n (also: **saucepan**) casserole f; (also: **frying ~**) poêle f; **~cake** n crêpe f

**panda** ['pændə] n panda m

**pandemonium** [pændɪ'məʊnɪəm] n tohu-bohu m

**pander** ['pændəʳ] vi: **to ~ to** flatter bassement; obéir servilement à

**pane** [peɪn] n carreau m, vitre f

**panel** ['pænl] n (of wood, cloth etc) panneau m; (RADIO, TV) experts mpl; (for interview, exams) jury m; **~ling** (US **paneling**) n boiseries fpl

**pang** [pæŋ] n: **~s of remorse/jealousy** affres mpl du remords/de la jalousie; **~s of hunger/conscience** tiraillements mpl d'estomac/de la conscience

**panic** ['pænɪk] n panique f, affolement m ♦ vi s'affoler, paniquer; **~ky** adj (person) qui panique ou s'affole facilement; **~-stricken** adj affolé(e)

**pansy** ['pænzɪ] n (BOT) pensée f; (inf: pej) tapette f, pédé m

**pant** [pænt] vi haleter

**panther** ['pænθəʳ] n panthère f

**panties** ['pæntɪz] npl slip m

**pantomime** ['pæntəmaɪm] (BRIT) n spectacle m de Noël

---

**pantomime**

Une **pantomime**, que l'on appelle également de façon familière "panto", est un genre de farce ou le personnage principal est souvent un jeune garçon et où il y a toujours une **dame**, c'est-à-dire une vieille femme jouée par un homme, et un méchant. La plupart du temps, l'histoire est basée sur un conte de fées comme Cendrillon ou Le Chat botté, et le public est encouragé à participer en prévenant le héros d'un danger imminent. Ce genre de spectacle, qui s'adresse surtout aux enfants, vise également un public d'adultes au travers de nombreuses plaisanteries faisant allusion à des faits d'actualité.

---

**pantry** ['pæntrɪ] n garde-manger m inv

**pants** [pænts] npl (BRIT: woman's) slip m; (: man's) slip, caleçon m; (US: trousers) pantalon m

**pantyhose** ['pæntɪhəʊz] (US) npl collant m

**paper** ['peɪpəʳ] n papier m; (also: **wallpaper**) papier peint; (also: **newspaper**) journal *m*; (*academic essay*) article *m*; (*exam*) épreuve écrite ♦ *adj* en cuir or papier ♦ *vt* tapisser (*de papier peint*); **~s** *npl* (*also*: **identity ~s**) papiers (d'identité); **~back** *n* livre de poche; livre broché or non relié; **~ bag** *n* sac en papier; **~ clip** *n* trombone *m*; **~ hankie** *n* mouchoir *m* en papier; **~weight** *n* presse-papiers *m inv*; **~work** *n* papiers *mpl*, (*pej*) paperasserie *f*

**par** [paːʳ] *n* pair *m*; (*GOLF*) normale *f* du parcours; **on a ~ with** à égalité avec, au même niveau que

**parachute** [ˈpærəʃuːt] *n* parachute *m*

**parade** [pəˈreɪd] *n* défilé *m* ♦ *vt* (*fig*) faire étalage de ♦ *vi* défiler

**paradise** [ˈpærədaɪs] *n* paradis *m*

**paradox** [ˈpærədɒks] *n* paradoxe *m*; **~ically** [pærəˈdɒksɪklɪ] *adv* paradoxalement

**paraffin** [ˈpærəfɪn] *n* (*BRIT*) (*also*: **~ oil**) pétrole (lampant)

**paragon** [ˈpærəgən] *n* modèle *m*

**paragraph** [ˈpærəgrɑːf] *n* paragraphe *m*

**parallel** [ˈpærəlɛl] *adj* parallèle; (*fig*) semblable *n* (*line*) parallèle *f*; (*fig*, *GEO*) parallèle *m*

**paralyse** [ˈpærəlaɪz] (*BRIT*) *vt* paralyser; **paralysis** [pəˈrælɪsɪs] *n* paralysie *f*; **paralyze** (*US*) *vt* = **paralyse**

**paramount** [ˈpærəmaunt] *adj*: **of ~ importance** de la plus haute or grande importance

**paranoid** [ˈpærənɔɪd] *adj* (*PSYCH*) paranoïaque

**paraphernalia** [pærəfəˈneɪlɪə] *n* attirail *m*

**parasol** [ˈpærəsɔl] *n* ombrelle *f*; (*over table*) parasol *m*

**paratrooper** [ˈpærətruːpəʳ] *n* parachutiste *m* (*soldat*)

**parcel** [ˈpɑːsl] *n* paquet *m*, colis *m* ♦ *vt* (*also*: **~ up**) empaqueter

**parchment** [ˈpɑːtʃmənt] *n* parchemin *m*

**pardon** [ˈpɑːdn] *n* pardon *m*; grâce *f*

♦ *vt* pardonner à; **~ me!, I beg your ~! pardon!, je suis désolé!; (I beg your) ~?, (US) ~ me? pardon?**

**parent** [ˈpɛərənt] *n* père *m* or mère *f*; **~s** *npl* parents *mpl*

**Paris** [ˈpærɪs] *n* Paris

**parish** [ˈpærɪʃ] *n* paroisse *f*; (*BRIT*: *civil*) ≃ commune *f*

**Parisian** [pəˈrɪzɪən] *adj* parisien(ne) ♦ *n* Parisien(ne)

**park** [pɑːk] *n* parc *m*, jardin public ♦ *vt* garer *vi* se garer

**parking** [ˈpɑːkɪŋ] *n* stationnement *m*; **"no ~"** "stationnement interdit"; **~ lot** (*US*) *n* parking *m*, parc *m* de stationnement; **~ meter** *n* parcomètre *m*; **~ ticket** *n* P.V.

**parliament** [ˈpɑːləmənt] *n* parlement *m*; **~ary** [pɑːləˈmɛntərɪ] *adj* parlementaire

**parlour** [ˈpɑːləʳ] (*US* **parlor**) *n* salon *m*

**parochial** [pəˈrəukɪəl] (*pej*) *adj* à l'esprit de clocher

**parole** [pəˈrəul] *n*: **on ~** en liberté conditionnelle

**parrot** [ˈpærət] *n* perroquet *m*

**parry** [ˈpærɪ] *vt* (*blow*) esquiver

**parsley** [ˈpɑːslɪ] *n* persil *m*

**parsnip** [ˈpɑːsnɪp] *n* panais *m*

**parson** [ˈpɑːsn] *n* ecclésiastique *m*; (*Church of England*) pasteur *m*

**part** [pɑːt] *n* partie *f*; (*of machine*) pièce *f*; (*THEATRE etc*) rôle *m*; (*of serial*) épisode *m*; (*US*: *in hair*) raie *f* ♦ *adv* = **partly** ♦ *vt* séparer ♦ *vi* (*people*) se séparer; (*crowd*) s'ouvrir; **to take ~ in** participer à, prendre part à; **to take sth in good ~** prendre qch du bon côté; **to take sb's ~** prendre le parti de qn, prendre parti pour qn; **for my ~** en ce qui me concerne; **for the most ~** dans la plupart des cas; **~ with** *vt fus* se séparer de; **~ exchange** (*BRIT*) *n*: **in ~ exchange** en reprise

**partial** [ˈpɑːʃl] *adj* (*not complete*) partiel(le); **to be ~ to** avoir un faible pour

**participate** [pɑːˈtɪsɪpeɪt] *vi*: **to ~ (in**

participer (à), prendre part (à); **partici-pation** [pɑːtɪsɪˈpeɪʃən] n participation f
**participle** [ˈpɑːtɪsɪpl] n participe m
**particle** [ˈpɑːtɪkl] n particule f
**particular** [pəˈtɪkjulər] adj particulier (-ère); (special) spécial(e); (fussy) difficile; méticuleux(-euse); **~s** npl (details) détails mpl; (personal) nom, adresse etc; **in ~** en particulier; **~ly** adv particulièrement
**parting** [ˈpɑːtɪŋ] n séparation f; (BRIT: in hair) raie f ♦ adj d'adieu
**partisan** [pɑːtɪˈzæn] n partisan(e) ♦ adj partisan(e); de parti
**partition** [pɑːˈtɪʃən] n (wall) cloison f; (POL) partition f, division f
**partly** [ˈpɑːtlɪ] adv en partie, partiellement
**partner** [ˈpɑːtnər] n partenaire m/f; (in marriage) conjoint(e); (boyfriend, girl-friend) ami(e); (COMM) associé(e); (at dance) cavalier(-ère); **~ship** n association f
**partridge** [ˈpɑːtrɪdʒ] n perdrix f
**part-time** [ˈpɑːtˈtaɪm] adj, adv à mi-temps, à temps partiel
**party** [ˈpɑːtɪ] n (POL) parti m; (group) groupe m; (LAW) partie f; (celebration) réception f, soirée f, fête f ♦ cpd (POL) de or du parti; **~ dress** n robe habillée
**pass** [pɑːs] vt passer; (place) passer devant; (friend) croiser; (overtake) dépasser; (exam) être reçu(e) à, réussir; (ap-prove) approuver, accepter ♦ vi passer; (SCOL) être reçu(e) or admis(e), réussir ♦ n (permit) laissez-passer m inv; carte f d'accès or d'abonnement; (in moun-tains) col m; (SPORT) passe f; (SCOL: also: **~ mark**): **to get a ~** être reçu(e) (sans mention); **to make a ~ at sb** (inf) faire des avances à qn; **~ away** vi mourir; **~ by** vi passer ♦ vt négliger; **~ on** vt (news, object) transmettre; (illness) passer; **~ out** vi s'évanouir; **~ up** vt (op-portunity) laisser passer; **~able** adj (road) praticable; (work) acceptable
**passage** [ˈpæsɪdʒ] n (also: **~way**) cou-loir m; (gen, in book) passage m; (by boat) traversée f
**passbook** [ˈpɑːsbuk] n livret m
**passenger** [ˈpæsɪndʒər] n passager (-ère)
**passer-by** [pɑːsəˈbaɪ] n (pl **~s-~**) pas-sant(e)
**passing** [ˈpɑːsɪŋ] adj (fig) passager (-ère); **in ~** en passant; **~ place** n (AUT) aire f de croisement
**passion** [ˈpæʃən] n passion f; **~ate** adj passionné(e)
**passive** [ˈpæsɪv] adj (also LING) passif (-ive); **~ smoking** n tabagisme m passif
**Passover** [ˈpɑːsəuvər] n Pâque f (juive)
**passport** [ˈpɑːspɔːt] n passeport m; **~ control** n contrôle m des passeports; **~ office** n bureau m de délivrance des passeports
**password** [ˈpɑːswɜːd] n mot m de pas-se
**past** [pɑːst] prep (in front of) devant; (further than) au delà de, plus loin que; après; (later than) après ♦ adj passé(e); (president etc) ancien(ne) ♦ n passé m; **he's ~ forty** il a plus de or passé quarante ans; **for the ~ few/3 days** depuis quelques/3 jours; ces derniers/3 der-niers jours; **ten/quarter ~ eight** huit heures dix/un or et quart
**pasta** [ˈpæstə] n pâtes fpl
**paste** [peɪst] n (meat ~) pâté m (à tartiner); (tomato ~) purée f, concen-tré m; (glue) colle f (de pâte) ♦ vt coller
**pasteurized** [ˈpæstʃəraɪzd] adj pasteuri-sé(e)
**pastille** [ˈpæstɪl] n pastille f
**pastime** [ˈpɑːstaɪm] n passe-temps m inv
**pastry** [ˈpeɪstrɪ] n pâte f; (cake) pâtisserie f
**pasture** [ˈpɑːstʃər] n pâturage m
**pasty** [n ˈpæstɪ, adj ˈpeɪstɪ] n petit pâté (en croûte) ♦ adj (complexion) terreux (-euse)
**pat** [pæt] vt tapoter; (dog) caresser
**patch** [pætʃ] n (of material) pièce f; (eye

~) cache m; (spot) tache f; (on tyre) rustine f ♦ vt (clothes) rapiécer; (to go through) a bad ~ (passer par) une période difficile; (to ~ up réparer (grossièrement); to ~ up a quarrel se raccommoder; ~y adj inégal(e); (incomplete) fragmentaire

**pâté** ['pɑteɪ] n pâté m, terrine f

**patent** ['peɪtnt] n brevet m (d'invention) ♦ vt faire breveter ♦ adj patent(e), manifeste; ~ **leather** n cuir verni

**paternal** [pə'tɜːnl] adj paternel(le)

**path** [pɑːθ] n chemin m, sentier m; (in garden) allée f; (trajectory) trajectoire f

**pathetic** [pə'θetɪk] adj (pitiful) pitoyable; (very bad) lamentable, minable

**pathological** [pæθə'lɒdʒɪkl] adj pathologique

**pathway** ['pɑːθweɪ] n sentier m, passage m

**patience** ['peɪʃns] n patience f; (BRIT: CARDS) réussite f

**patient** ['peɪʃnt] n malade m/f; (of dentist etc) patient(e) ♦ adj patient(e)

**patio** ['pætɪəʊ] n patio m

**patriotic** [pætrɪ'ɒtɪk] adj patriotique; (person) patriote

**patrol** [pə'trəʊl] n patrouille f ♦ vt patrouiller dans; ~ **car** n voiture f de police; ~**man** (irreg) (US) n agent m de police

**patron** ['peɪtrən] n (in shop) client(e); (of charity) patron(ne); ~ **of the arts** mécène m; ~**ize** ['pætrənaɪz] vt (pej) traiter avec condescendance; (shop, club) être (un) client ou un habitué de

**patter** ['pætəʳ] n crépitement m, tapotement m; (sales talk) boniment m ♦

**pattern** ['pætən] n (design) motif m; (SEWING) patron m

**pauper** ['pɔːpəʳ] n indigent(e)

**pause** [pɔːz] n pause f, arrêt m ♦ vi faire une pause, s'arrêter

**pave** [peɪv] vt paver, daller; **to ~ the way for** ouvrir la voie à

**pavement** ['peɪvmənt] n (BRIT) trottoir m

**pavilion** [pə'vɪlɪən] n pavillon m; tente f

**paving** ['peɪvɪŋ] n (material) pavé m, dalle f; ~ **stone** n pavé m

**paw** [pɔː] n patte f

**pawn** [pɔːn] n (CHESS, also fig) pion m ♦ vt mettre en gage; ~**broker** n prêteur m sur gages; ~**shop** n mont-de-piété m

**pay** [peɪ] (pt, pp **paid**) n salaire m; paie f ♦ vt payer ♦ vi payer; (be profitable) être rentable; **to ~ attention (to)** prêter attention (à); **to ~ sb a visit** rendre visite à qn; **to ~ one's respects to sb** présenter ses respects à qn; ~ **back** vt rembourser; ~ **for** vt fus payer; ~ **in** vt verser; ~ **off** vt régler, acquitter; (person) rembourser ♦ vi (scheme, decision) se révéler payant(e); ~ **up** vt (money) payer; ~**able** adj; ~**able to sb** (cheque) à l'ordre de qn; ~**ee** [peɪ'iː] n = **pay packet**; ~**envelope** (US) n = **pay packet**; ~**ment** n paiement m; règlement m; **monthly** ~**ment** mensualité f; ~ **packet** (BRIT) n paie f; ~ **phone** n cabine f téléphonique, téléphone public; ~**roll** n registre m du personnel; ~ **slip** (BRIT) n bulletin m de paie; ~ **television** n chaînes fpl payantes

**PC** n abbr = **personal computer**

**p.c.** abbr = **per cent**

**pea** [piː] n (petit) pois

**peace** [piːs] n paix f; (calm) calme m, tranquillité f; ~**ful** adj paisible, calme

**peach** [piːtʃ] n pêche f

**peacock** ['piːkɒk] n paon m

**peak** [piːk] n (mountain) pic m, cime f; (of cap) visière f; (fig: highest level) maximum m; (: of career, fame) apogée m; ~ **hours** npl heures fpl de pointe

**peal** [piːl] n (of bells) carillon m; ~ **of laughter** éclat m de rire

**peanut** ['piːnʌt] n arachide f, cacahuète f; ~ **butter** n beurre m de cacahuète

**pear** [pɛəʳ] n poire f

**pearl** [pɜːl] n perle f

**peasant** ['peznt] n paysan(ne)

**peat** [pi:t] n tourbe f

**pebble** ['pebl] n caillou m, galet m

**peck** [pek] vt (also: ~ at) donner un coup de bec à ♦ n coup m de bec; (kiss) bise f; ~ing order m ordre m des préséances; ~ish (BRIT: inf) adj: I feel ~ish je mangerais bien quelque chose

**peculiar** [pɪ'kju:lɪə] adj étrange, bizarre, curieux(-euse); ~ to particulier(-ère) à

**pedal** ['pedl] n pédale f ♦ vi pédaler

**pedantic** [pɪ'dæntɪk] adj pédant(e)

**peddler** ['pedlə'] n (of drugs) revendeur(-euse)

**pedestal** ['pedəstl] n piédestal m

**pedestrian** [pɪ'destrɪən] n piéton m; ~ **crossing** (BRIT) n passage clouté; ~**ized** adj: a ~ized street une rue piétonne

**pediatrics** [pi:dɪ'ætrɪks] (US) n = **paediatrics**

**pedigree** ['pedɪgri:] n ascendance f; (of animal) pedigree m ♦ cpd (animal) de race

**pee** [pi:] (inf) vi faire pipi, pisser

**peek** [pi:k] vi jeter un coup d'œil (furtif)

**peel** [pi:l] n pelure f, épluchure f; (of orange, lemon) écorce f ♦ vt peler, éplucher ♦ vi (paint etc) s'écailler; (wallpaper) se décoller; (skin) peler

**peep** [pi:p] n (BRIT: look) coup d'œil furtif; (sound) pépiement m ♦ vi (BRIT) jeter un coup d'œil (furtif); ~ **out** (BRIT) vi se montrer (furtivement); ~**hole** n judas m

**peer** [pɪə'] vi: **to ~ at** regarder attentivement, scruter ♦ n (noble) pair m; (equal) pair, égal(e); ~**age** ['pɪərɪdʒ] n pairie f

**peeved** [pi:vd] adj irrité(e), fâché(e)

**peg** [peg] n (for coat etc) patère f; (BRIT: also: clothes ~) pince f à linge

**Pekin(g)ese** [pi:kɪ'ni:z] n (dog) pékinois m

**pelican** ['pelɪkən] n pélican m; ~ **crossing** (BRIT) n (AUT) feu à commande manuelle

**pellet** ['pelɪt] n boulette f; (of lead) plomb m

**pelt** [pelt] vt: **to ~ sb (with)** bombarder qn (de) ♦ vi (rain) tomber à seaux; (inf: run) courir à toutes jambes ♦ n peau f

**pelvis** ['pelvɪs] n bassin m

**pen** [pen] n (for writing) stylo m; (for sheep) parc m

**penal** ['pi:nl] adj pénal(e); (system, colony) pénitentiaire; ~**ize** ['pi:nəlaɪz] vt pénaliser

**penalty** ['penltɪ] n pénalité f; sanction f; (fine) amende f; (SPORT) pénalisation f; (FOOTBALL) penalty m; (RUGBY) pénalité f

**penance** ['penəns] n pénitence f

**pence** [pens] (BRIT) npl of **penny**

**pencil** ['pensl] n crayon m; ~ **case** n trousse f (d'écolier); ~ **sharpener** n taille-crayon(s) m inv

**pendant** ['pendnt] n pendentif m

**pending** ['pendɪŋ] prep en attendant ♦ adj en suspens

**pendulum** ['pendjuləm] n (of clock) balancier m

**penetrate** ['penɪtreɪt] vt pénétrer dans; pénétrer

**penfriend** ['penfrend] (BRIT) n correspondant(e)

**penguin** ['peŋgwɪn] n pingouin m

**penicillin** [penɪ'sɪlɪn] n pénicilline f

**peninsula** [pə'nɪnsjulə] n péninsule f

**penis** ['pi:nɪs] n pénis m, verge f

**penitentiary** [penɪ'tenʃərɪ] n prison f

**penknife** ['pennaɪf] n canif m

**pen name** n nom m de plume, pseudonyme m

**penniless** ['penɪlɪs] adj sans le sou

**penny** ['penɪ] (pl **pennies** or (BRIT) **pence**) n penny m

**penpal** ['penpæl] n correspondant(e)

**pension** ['penʃən] n pension f; (from company) retraite f; ~**er** (BRIT) n retraité(e); ~ **fund** n caisse f de pension; ~ **plan** n plan m de retraite

**Pentagon**

*Le Pentagon est le nom donné aux bureaux du ministère de la Défense américain, situés à Arlington en Virginie, à cause de la forme pentagonale du bâtiment dans lequel ils se trouvent. Par extension, ce terme est également utilisé en parlant du ministère lui-même.*

**pentathlon** [pɛn'tæθlən] n pentathlon m

**Pentecost** ['pɛntikɔst] n Pentecôte f

**penthouse** ['pɛnthaus] n appartement m (de luxe) (en attique)

**pent-up** ['pɛntʌp] adj (feelings) refoulé(e)

**penultimate** [pe'nʌltimət] adj avant-dernier(-ère)

**people** ['pi:pl] npl gens mpl; personnes fpl; (inhabitants) population f; (POL) peuple m ♦ n (nation, race) peuple m; **several ~ came** plusieurs personnes sont venues; **~ say that ...** on dit que ...

**pep up** [pɛp-] (inf) vt remonter

**pepper** ['pepə'] n poivre m; (vegetable) poivron m ♦ vt (fig): **to ~ with** bombarder de; **~ mill** n moulin m à poivre; **~mint** n (sweet) pastille f de menthe

**peptalk** ['pɛptɔ:k] (inf) n (petit) discours d'encouragement

**per** [pə:'] prep par; **~ hour** (miles etc) à l'heure; (fee) de l'heure; **~ kilo** etc le kilo etc; **~ annum** par an; **~ capita** par personne, par habitant

**perceive** [pə'si:v] vt percevoir; (notice) remarquer, s'apercevoir de

**per cent** adv pour cent; **percentage** [pə'sɛntidʒ] n pourcentage m

**perception** [pə'sɛpʃən] n perception f; (insight) perspicacité f

**perceptive** [pə'sɛptiv] adj pénétrant(e); (person) perspicace

**perch** [pə:tʃ] n (fish) perche f; (for bird) perchoir m ♦ vi: **to ~ on** se percher sur

**percolator** ['pə:kəleitə'] n cafetière f (électrique)

**percussion** [pə'kʌʃən] n percussion f

**perennial** [pə'rɛniəl] adj perpétuel(le); (BOT) vivace

**perfect** [adj, n 'pə:fikt, vb pə'fɛkt] adj parfait(e) ♦ n (also: ~ **tense**) parfait m ♦ vt parfaire; mettre au point; **~ly** adv parfaitement

**perforate** ['pə:fəreit] vt perforer, percer; **perforation** [pə:fə'reiʃən] n perforation f

**perform** [pə'fɔ:m] vt (carry out) exécuter; (concert etc) jouer, donner ♦ vi jouer; **~ance** n représentation f, spectacle m; (of an artist) interprétation f; (SPORT) performance f; (of car, engine) fonctionnement m; (of company, economy) résultats mpl; (of person) interprétation f; **~er** n artiste m/f, interprète m/f

**perfume** ['pə:fju:m] n parfum m

**perhaps** [pə'hæps] adv peut-être

**peril** ['pɛril] n péril m

**perimeter** [pə'rimitə'] n périmètre m

**period** ['piəriəd] n période f; (of history) époque f; (SCOL) cours m; (full stop) point m; (MED) règles fpl ♦ adj (costume, furniture) d'époque; **~ic(al)** [piəri'ɔd-ik(l)] adj périodique; **~ical** [piəri'ɔdikl] n périodique m

**peripheral** [pə'rifərəl] adj périphérique ♦ n (COMPUT) périphérique m

**perish** ['pɛriʃ] vi périr; (decay) se détériorer; **~able** adj périssable

**perjury** ['pə:dʒəri] n parjure m, faux serment

**perk** [pə:k] n avantage m accessoire, à-côté m; **~ up** vi (cheer up) se ragaillardir; **~y** adj (cheerful) guilleret(te)

**perm** [pə:m] n (for hair) permanente f

**permanent** ['pə:mənənt] adj permanent(e)

**permeate** ['pə:mieit] vi s'infiltrer ♦ vt s'infiltrer dans; pénétrer

**permissible** [pə'misibl] adj permis(e), acceptable

**permission** [pə'miʃən] n permission f,

autorisation f

**permissive** [pə'mɪsɪv] adj tolérant(e), permissif(-ive)

**permit** [n 'pɜːmɪt, vb pə'mɪt] n permis m ♦ vt permettre

**perpendicular** [pɜːpən'dɪkjuləʳ] adj perpendiculaire

**perplex** [pə'plɛks] vt (person) rendre perplexe

**persecute** ['pɜːsɪkjuːt] vt persécuter

**persevere** [pɜːsɪ'vɪəʳ] vi persévérer

**Persian** ['pɜːʃən] adj persan(e) ♦ n (LING) persan m; **the ~ Gulf** le golfe Persique

**persist** [pə'sɪst] vi: **to ~ (in doing)** persister ou s'obstiner (à faire); **~ent** [pə'sɪstənt] adj persistant(e), tenace; **~ent vegetative state** état m végétatif persistant

**person** ['pɜːsn] n personne f; **in ~** en personne; **~al** adj personnel(le); **~al assistant** n secrétaire privé(e); **~al column** n annonces personnelles; **~al computer** n ordinateur personnel; **~ality** [pɜːsə'nælɪtɪ] n personnalité f; **~ally** adv personnellement; **to take sth ~ally** se sentir visé(e) (par qch); **~al organizer** n filofax ® m; **~al stereo** n Walkman ® m, baladeur m

**personnel** [pɜːsə'nɛl] n personnel m

**perspective** [pə'spɛktɪv] n perspective f; **to get things into ~** faire la part des choses

**Perspex** ['pɜːspɛks] ® n plexiglas ® m

**perspiration** [pɜːspɪ'reɪʃən] n transpiration f

**persuade** [pə'sweɪd] vt: **to ~ sb to do sth** persuader qn de faire qch; **persuasion** [pə'sweɪʒən] n persuasion f; (creed) religion f

**perverse** [pə'vɜːs] adj pervers(e); (contrary) contrariant(e); **pervert** [n 'pɜːvɜːt, vb pə'vɜːt] n perverti(e) ♦ vt pervertir; (words) déformer

**pessimist** ['pɛsɪmɪst] n pessimiste m/f; **~ic** [pɛsɪ'mɪstɪk] adj pessimiste

**pest** [pɛst] n animal m (or insecte m) nuisible; (fig) fléau m

**pester** ['pɛstəʳ] vt importuner, harceler

**pet** [pɛt] n animal m familier ♦ cpd (favourite) favori(te) ♦ vt (stroke) caresser, câliner; **teacher's ~** chouchou du professeur; ♦ **hate** bête noire

**petal** ['pɛtl] n pétale m

**peter out** ['piːtə-] vi (stream, conversation) tarir; (meeting) tourner court; (road) se perdre

**petite** [pə'tiːt] adj menu(e)

**petition** [pə'tɪʃən] n pétition f

**petrified** ['pɛtrɪfaɪd] adj (fig) mort(e) de peur

**petrol** ['pɛtrəl] (BRIT) n essence f; **fourstar ~** super m; **~ can** n bidon m à essence

**petroleum** [pə'trəʊlɪəm] n pétrole m

**petrol: ~ pump** (BRIT) n pompe f à essence; **~ station** (BRIT) n station-service f; **~ tank** (BRIT) n réservoir m d'essence

**petticoat** ['pɛtɪkəʊt] n combinaison f

**petty** ['pɛtɪ] adj (mean) mesquin(e); (unimportant) insignifiant(e), sans importance; **~ cash** n caisse f des dépenses courantes; **~ officer** n second-maître m

**petulant** ['pɛtjulənt] adj boudeur (-euse), irritable

**pew** [pjuː] n banc m (d'église)

**pewter** ['pjuːtəʳ] n étain m

**phantom** ['fæntəm] n fantôme m

**pharmacy** ['fɑːməsɪ] n pharmacie f

**phase** [feɪz] n phase f ♦ vt: **to ~ sth in/out** introduire/supprimer qch progressivement

**PhD** abbr = **Doctor of Philosophy** ♦ n abbr (title) ≈ docteur m (en droit ou lettres etc), ≈ doctorat m; (person) titulaire m/f d'un doctorat

**pheasant** ['fɛznt] n faisan m

**phenomenon** [fə'nɔmɪnən] (pl **phenomena**) n phénomène m

**philosophical** [fɪlə'sɔfɪkl] adj philosophique

**philosophy** [fɪ'lɔsəfɪ] n philosophie f

**phobia** ['fəʊbjə] n phobie f

**phone** [fəʊn] n téléphone m ♦ vt téléphoner; **to be on the ~** avoir le téléphone; (be calling) être au téléphone; **~ back** vt, vi rappeler; **~ up** vt téléphoner à ♦ vi téléphoner; **~bill** n facture f de téléphone; **~ book** n annuaire m de téléphone; **~ booth**, **~ box** (BRIT) n cabine f téléphonique; **~ call** n coup m de fil or de téléphone; **~card** n carte f de téléphone; **~-in** [BRIT] n (RADIO, TV) programme m à ligne ouverte; **~ number** n numéro m de téléphone

**phonetics** [fə'nɛtɪks] n phonétique f

**phoney** ['fəʊnɪ] adj faux (fausse), factice; (person) pas franc (franche), poseur(-euse)

**photo** ['fəʊtəʊ] n photo f; **~copier** n photocopieuse f; **~copy** n photocopie f ♦ vt photocopier; **~graph** n photographie f ♦ vt photographier; **~grapher** [fə'tɒgrəfə[sup]r[/sup]] n photographe m/f; **~graphy** [fə'tɒgrəfɪ] n photographie f

**phrase** [freɪz] n expression f (LING) locution f ♦ vt exprimer; **~ book** n recueil m d'expressions (pour touristes)

**physical** ['fɪzɪkl] adj physique; **~ education** n éducation f physique; **~ly** adv physiquement

**physician** [fɪ'zɪʃən] n médecin m

**physicist** ['fɪzɪsɪst] n physicien(ne)

**physics** ['fɪzɪks] n physique f

**physiotherapist** [fɪzɪəʊ'θɛrəpɪst] n kinésithérapeute m/f

**physiotherapy** [fɪzɪəʊ'θɛrəpɪ] n kinésithérapie f

**physique** [fɪ'ziːk] n physique m; constitution f

**pianist** ['piːənɪst] n pianiste m/f

**piano** [pɪ'ænəʊ] n piano m

**pick** [pɪk] n (tool: also: **~axe**) pic m, pioche f ♦ vt choisir; (fruit etc) cueillir; (remove) prendre; (lock) forcer; **take your ~** faites votre choix; **the ~ of** le (la) meilleur(e) de; **to ~ one's nose** se mettre les doigts dans le nez; **to ~ one's teeth** se curer les dents; **to ~ a**

**quarrel with sb** chercher noise à qn; **~ at** vt fus: **to ~ at one's food** manger du bout des dents, chipoter; **~ on** vt fus (person) harceler; **~ out** vt choisir; (distinguish) distinguer; **~ up** vi (improve) s'améliorer ♦ vt ramasser; (collect) passer prendre; (AUT: give lift to) prendre, emmener; (learn) apprendre; (RADIO) capter; **to ~ up speed** prendre de la vitesse; **to ~ o.s. up** se relever

**picket** ['pɪkɪt] n (in strike) piquet m de grève ♦ vt mettre un piquet de grève devant

**pickle** ['pɪkl] n (also: **~s**: as condiment) pickles mpl; petits légumes macérés dans du vinaigre ♦ vt conserver dans du vinaigre or dans de la saumure; **to be in a ~** (mess) être dans le pétrin

**pickpocket** ['pɪkpɔkɪt] n pickpocket m

**pick-up** ['pɪkʌp] n (small truck) pick-up m inv

**picnic** ['pɪknɪk] n pique-nique m

**picture** ['pɪktʃə[sup]r[/sup]] n image f; (painting) peinture f, tableau m; (etching) gravure f; (photograph) photo(graphie) f; (drawing) dessin m; (film) film m; (fig) description f; tableau m ♦ vt se représenter; **the ~s** (BRIT: inf) le cinéma; **~ book** n livre m d'images

**picturesque** [pɪktʃə'rɛsk] adj pittoresque

**pie** [paɪ] n tourte f; (of fruit) tarte f; (of meat) pâté m en croûte

**piece** [piːs] n morceau m; (item): **a ~ of furniture/advice** un meuble/conseil m; **~ together** vt rassembler; **to take to ~s** démonter; **~meal** adv (irregularly) au coup par coup; (bit by bit) par bouts; **~work** n travail m aux pièces

**pie chart** n graphique m circulaire, camembert m

**pier** [pɪə[sup]r[/sup]] n jetée f

**pierce** [pɪəs] vt percer, transpercer; **~d** adj (ears etc) percé(e)

**pig** [pɪg] n cochon m, porc m

**pigeon** ['pɪdʒən] n pigeon m; **~hole** n casier m

**piggy bank** ['pɪgɪ-] n tirelire f

**pig:** ~**headed** adj entêté(e), têtu(e); ~**let** n porcelet m, petit cochon; ~**skin** n peau m de porc; ~**sty** n porcherie f; ~**tail** n natte f, tresse f

**pike** [paɪk] n (fish) brochet m

**pilchard** ['pɪltʃəd] n pilchard m (sorte de sardine)

**pile** [paɪl] n (pillar, of books) pile f; (heap) tas m; (of carpet) poils m pl ♦ vt (also: ~ **up**) empiler, entasser ♦ vi (also: ~ **up**) s'entasser, s'accumuler; **to ~ into** (car) s'entasser dans; ~**s** npl hémorroïdes fpl; ~**-up** n (AUT) télescopage m, collision f en série

**pilfering** ['pɪlfərɪŋ] n chapardage m

**pilgrim** ['pɪlgrɪm] n pèlerin m

**pill** [pɪl] n pilule f

**pillage** ['pɪlɪdʒ] vt piller

**pillar** ['pɪlə'] n pilier m; ~ **box** (BRIT) n boîte f aux lettres (publique)

**pillion** ['pɪljən] n: **to ride** ~ (on motorcycle) monter derrière

**pillow** ['pɪləu] n oreiller m; ~**case** n taie f d'oreiller

**pilot** ['paɪlət] n pilote m ♦ cpd (scheme etc) pilote, expérimental(e) ♦ vt piloter; ~ **light** n veilleuse f

**pimp** [pɪmp] n souteneur m, maquereau m

**pimple** ['pɪmpl] n bouton m

**pin** [pɪn] n épingle f; (TECH) cheville f ♦ vt épingler; ~**s and needles** fourmis fpl; **to ~ sb down** (fig) obliger qn à répondre; **to ~ sth on sb** (fig) mettre qch sur le dos de qn

**PIN** [pɪn] n abbr (= personal identification number) numéro m d'identification personnel

**pinafore** ['pɪnəfɔː'] n tablier m

**pinball** ['pɪnbɔːl] n flipper m

**pincers** ['pɪnsəz] npl tenailles fpl; (of crab etc) pinces fpl

**pinch** [pɪntʃ] n (of salt etc) pincée f ♦ vt pincer; (inf: steal) piquer, chiper; **at a ~** à la rigueur

**pincushion** ['pɪnkuʃən] n pelote f à

épingles

**pine** [paɪn] n (also: ~ **tree**) pin m ♦ vi: **to ~ for** s'ennuyer de, désirer ardemment; ~ **away** vi dépérir

**pineapple** ['paɪnæpl] n ananas m

**ping** [pɪŋ] n (noise) tintement m; ~**pong** ® n ping-pong ® m

**pink** [pɪŋk] adj rose ♦ n (colour) rose m; (BOT) œillet m, mignardise f

**PIN (number)** ['pɪn(-)] n code m confidentiel

**pinpoint** ['pɪnpɔɪnt] vt indiquer or localiser (avec précision); (problem) mettre le doigt sur

**pint** [paɪnt] n pinte f (BRIT = 0.57l; US = 0.47l); (BRIT: inf) ≈ demi m

**pioneer** [paɪə'nɪə'] n pionnier m

**pious** ['paɪəs] adj pieux(-euse)

**pip** [pɪp] n (seed) pépin m; **the ~s** npl (BRIT: time signal on radio) le(s) top(s) sonore(s)

**pipe** [paɪp] n tuyau m, conduite f; (for smoking) pipe f ♦ vt amener par tuyau; ~**s** npl (also: **bagpipes**) cornemuse f; ~ **cleaner** n cure-pipe m; ~ **dream** n chimère f, château m en Espagne; ~**line** n pipe-line m; ~**r** n joueur(-euse) de cornemuse

**piping** ['paɪpɪŋ] adv: ~ **hot** très chaud(e)

**pique** ['piːk] n dépit m

**pirate** ['paɪərət] n pirate m; ~**d** adj pirate

**Pisces** ['paɪsiːz] n les Poissons mpl

**piss** [pɪs] (inf!) vi pisser; ~**ed** (inf!) adj (drunk) bourré(e)

**pistol** ['pɪstl] n pistolet m

**piston** ['pɪstən] n piston m

**pit** [pɪt] n trou m, fosse f; (also: **coal** ~) puits m de mine; (quarry) carrière f ♦ vt: **to ~ one's wits against sb** se mesurer à qn; ~**s** npl (AUT) aire f de service

**pitch** [pɪtʃ] n (MUS) ton m; (SPORT) terrain m; (tar) poix f; (fig) degré m; point m ♦ vt (throw) lancer ♦ vi (fall) tomber; **to ~ a tent** dresser une tente; ~**black** adj noir(e) (comme du cirage);

**~ed battle** n bataille rangée

**pitfall** ['pɪtfɔ:l] n piège m

**pith** [pɪθ] n (of orange etc) intérieur m de l'écorce; (fig) essence f

**pithy** ['pɪθɪ] adj piquant(e)

**pitiful** ['pɪtɪful] adj (touching) pitoyable

**pitiless** ['pɪtɪlɪs] adj impitoyable

**pittance** ['pɪtns] n salaire m de misère

**pity** ['pɪtɪ] n pitié f ♦ vt plaindre; **what a ~!** quel dommage!

**pizza** ['pi:tsə] n pizza f

**placard** ['plækɑ:d] n affiche f; (in march) pancarte f

**placate** [plə'keɪt] vt apaiser, calmer

**place** [pleɪs] n endroit m, lieu m; (proper position, job, rank, seat) place f; (home): **at/to his ~** chez lui ♦ vt (object) placer, mettre; (identify) situer, reconnaître; **to take ~** avoir lieu; **out of ~** (not suitable) déplacé(e), inopportun(e); **to change ~s with sb** changer de place avec qn; **in the first ~** d'abord, en premier

**plague** [pleɪg] n fléau m; (MED) peste f ♦ vt tourmenter

**plaice** [pleɪs] n inv carrelet m

**plaid** [plæd] n tissu écossais

**plain** [pleɪn] n (one colour) uni(e); (simple) simple; (clear) clair(e), évident(e); (not handsome) quelconque, ordinaire ♦ adv franchement, carrément ♦ n plaine f; **~ chocolat** n chocolat à croquer; **~ clothes** adj (police officer) en civil; **~ly** adv clairement; (frankly) carrément, sans détours

**plaintiff** ['pleɪntɪf] n plaignant(e)

**plait** [plæt] n tresse f, natte f

**plan** [plæn] n plan m; (scheme) projet m ♦ vt (think in advance) projeter; (prepare) organiser; (house) dresser les plans de, concevoir ♦ vi faire des projets; **to ~ to do** prévoir de faire

**plane** [pleɪn] n (AVIAT) avion m; (ART, MATH etc) plan m; (fig) niveau m, plan; (tool) rabot m; (also: **~ tree**) platane m ♦ vt raboter

**planet** ['plænɪt] n planète f

**plank** [plæŋk] n planche f

**planner** ['plænə<sup>r</sup>] n planificateur(-trice); (town) urbaniste m/f

**planning** ['plænɪŋ] n planification f; **family ~** planning familial; **~ permission** n permis m de construire

**plant** [plɑ:nt] n plante f; (machinery) matériel m; (factory) usine f ♦ vt planter; (bomb) poser; (microphone, incriminating evidence) cacher

**plaster** ['plɑ:stə<sup>r</sup>] n plâtre m; (also: **~ of Paris**) plâtre à mouler; (BRIT: also: **sticking ~**) pansement adhésif ♦ vt plâtrer; (cover): **to ~ with** couvrir de; **~ed** (inf) soûl(e)

**plastic** ['plæstɪk] n plastique m ♦ adj (made of ~) en plastique; **~ bag** n sac m en plastique

**Plasticine** ® ['plæstɪsi:n] n pâte f à modeler

**plastic surgery** n chirurgie f esthétique

**plate** [pleɪt] n (dish) assiette f; (in book) gravure f, planche f; (dental ~) dentier m

**plateau** ['plætəu] (pl **~s** or **~x**) n plateau m

**plate glass** n verre m (de vitrine)

**platform** ['plætfɔ:m] n plate-forme f; (at meeting) tribune f; (stage) estrade f; (RAIL) quai m

**platinum** ['plætɪnəm] n platine m

**platter** ['plætə<sup>r</sup>] n plat m

**plausible** ['plɔ:zɪbl] adj plausible; (person) convaincant(e)

**play** [pleɪ] n (THEATRE) pièce f (de théâtre) ♦ vt (game) jouer à; (team, opponent) jouer contre; (instrument) jouer de; (part, piece of music, note) jouer; (record etc) passer ♦ vi jouer; **to ~ safe** ne prendre aucun risque; **~ down** vt minimiser; **~ up** vi (cause trouble) faire des siennes; **~boy** n playboy m; **~er** n joueur(-euse); (THEATRE) acteur(-trice); (MUS) musicien(ne); **~ful** adj enjoué(e); **~ground** n cour f de récréation; (in park) aire f de jeux; **~group** n garderie f; **~ing card** n carte f à jouer; **~ing**

**field** *n* terrain *m* de sport; **~mate** *n* camarade *m/f*, copain (copine) *f* ♦; **~off** *n* (SPORT) belle *f*; **~pen** *n* parc *m* (pour bébé); **~thing** *n* jouet *m*; **~** *n* récréation *f*; **~wright** *n* dramaturge *m*

**plc** *abbr* (= *public limited company*) SARL *f*

**plea** [pli:] *n* (*request*) appel *m*; (LAW) défense *f*

**plead** [pli:d] *vt* plaider; (*give as excuse*) invoquer ♦ *vi* plaider; (*beg*): **to ~ with sb** implorer qn

**pleasant** ['plɛznt] *adj* agréable; **~ries** *npl* (*polite remarks*) civilités *fpl*

**please** [pli:z] *excl* s'il te (*or* vous) plaît ♦ *vt* plaire à ♦ *vi* plaire; (*think fit*): **do as you ~** faites comme il vous plaira; **~ yourself!** à ta (*or* votre) guise!; **~d** *adj*: **~d (with)** content(e) (de); **~d to meet you** enchanté (de faire votre connaissance); **pleasing** *adj* plaisant(e), qui fait plaisir

**pleasure** ['plɛʒər] *n* plaisir *m*; "**it's a ~**" "je vous en prie"

**pleat** [pli:t] *n* pli *m*

**pledge** [plɛdʒ] *n* (*promise*) promesse *f* ♦ *vt* engager; promettre

**plentiful** ['plɛntɪful] *adj* abondant(e), copieux(-euse)

**plenty** ['plɛntɪ] *n*: **~ of** beaucoup de; (*bien*) assez de

**pliable** ['plaɪəbl] *adj* flexible; (*person*) malléable

**pliers** ['plaɪəz] *npl* pinces *fpl*

**plight** [plaɪt] *n* situation *f* critique

**plimsolls** ['plɪmsəlz] (BRIT) *npl* chaussures *fpl* de tennis, tennis *mpl*

**plinth** [plɪnθ] *n* (*of statue*) socle *m*

**P.L.O.** *n abbr* (= *Palestine Liberation Organization*) OLP *f*

**plod** [plɔd] *vi* avancer péniblement; (*fig*) peiner

**plonk** [plɔŋk] (*inf*) *n* (BRIT: *wine*) pinard *m*, piquette *f* ♦ *vt*: **to ~ sth down** poser brusquement qch

**plot** [plɔt] *n* complot *m*, conspiration *f*; (*of story, play*) intrigue *f*; (*of land*) lot *m*

de terrain, lopin *m* ♦ *vt* (*sb's downfall*) comploter; (*mark out*) pointer; relever, déterminer ♦ *vi* comploter

**plough** [plau] (*US* **plow**) *n* charrue *f* ♦ *vt* (*earth*) labourer; **to ~ money into** investir dans; **~ through** *vt fus* (*snow etc*) avancer péniblement dans; **~man's lunch** (BRIT) *n* assiette froide avec du pain, du fromage et des pickles

**ploy** [plɔɪ] *n* stratagème *m*

**pluck** [plʌk] *n* (*fruit*) cueillir; (*musical instrument*) pincer; (*bird*) plumer; (*eyebrow*) épiler ♦ *n* courage *m*, cran *m*; **to ~ up courage** prendre son courage à deux mains

**plug** [plʌg] *n* (ELEC) prise *f* de courant; (*stopper*) bouchon *m*, bonde *f*; (AUT: *also*: **spark(ing) ~**) bougie *f* ♦ *vt* (*hole*) boucher; (*inf: advertise*) faire de la battage pour; **~ in** *vt* (ELEC) brancher

**plum** [plʌm] *n* (*fruit*) prune *f* ♦ *cpd*: **~ job** (*inf*) travail *m* en or

**plumb** [plʌm] *vt*: **to ~ the depths** (*fig*) toucher le fond (du désespoir)

**plumber** ['plʌmər] *n* plombier *m*

**plumbing** ['plʌmɪŋ] *n* (*trade*) plomberie *f*; (*piping*) tuyauterie *f*

**plummet** ['plʌmɪt] *vi*: **to ~ (down)** plonger, dégringoler

**plump** [plʌmp] *adj* rondelet(te), dodu(e), bien en chair *f* ♦ *vi*: **to ~ for** (*inf: choose*) se décider pour

**plunder** ['plʌndər] *n* pillage *m*; (*loot*) butin *m* ♦ *vt* piller

**plunge** [plʌndʒ] *n* plongeon *m*; (*fig*) chute *f* ♦ *vt* plonger ♦ *vi* plonger; (*fall*) tomber, dégringoler; **to take the ~** se jeter à l'eau; **plunging** ['plʌndʒɪŋ] *adj*: **plunging neckline** décolleté plongeant

**pluperfect** [plu:'pə:fɪkt] *n* plus-que-parfait *m*

**plural** ['pluərl] *adj* pluriel(le) ♦ *n* pluriel *m*

**plus** [plʌs] *n* (*also*: **~ sign**) signe *m* plus ♦ *prep* plus; **ten/twenty ~** plus de dix/vingt

**plush** [plʌʃ] adj somptueux(-euse)

**ply** [plaɪ] vt (a trade) exercer ♦ vi (ship) faire la navette ♦ n (of wool, rope) fil m, brin m; **to ~ sb with drink** donner continuellement à boire à qn; **to ~ sb with questions** presser qn de questions; **~wood** n contre-plaqué m

**PM** abbr = **Prime Minister**

**p.m.** adv abbr (= post meridiem) de l'après-midi

**pneumatic drill** [njuːˈmætɪk-] n marteau-piqueur m

**pneumonia** [njuːˈməʊnɪə] n pneumonie f

**poach** [pəʊtʃ] vt (cook) pocher, (steal) pêcher (or chasser) sans permis ♦ vi braconner; **~ed egg** n œuf poché m; **~er** n braconnier m

**P.O. box** n abbr = **post office box**

**pocket** [ˈpɒkɪt] n poche f, vt empocher; **to be out of ~** (BRIT) en être de sa poche; **~book** n (US) (wallet) portefeuille m; **~ calculator** n calculette f; **~ knife** n canif m; **~ money** n argent m de poche

**pod** [pɒd] n cosse f

**podgy** [ˈpɒdʒɪ] adj rondelet(te)

**podiatrist** [pɒˈdiːətrɪst] n (US) n pédicure m/f, podologue m/f

**poem** [ˈpəʊɪm] n poème m

**poet** [ˈpəʊɪt] n poète m; **~ic** [pəʊˈetɪk] adj poétique; **~ry** [ˈpəʊɪtrɪ] n poésie f

**poignant** [ˈpɔɪnjənt] adj poignant(e); (sharp) vif (vive)

**point** [pɔɪnt] n point m; (tip) pointe f; (in time) moment m; (in space) endroit m; (subject, idea) point, sujet m; (purpose) sens m; (ELEC) prise f; (also: **decimal ~**): **2 ~ 3 (2.3)** 2 virgule 3 (2,3) ♦ vt (show) indiquer; (gun etc): **to ~ sth at** braquer or diriger qch sur ♦ vi: **to ~ at** montrer du doigt; **~s** npl (AUT) vis platinées f; (RAIL) aiguillage m; **to be on the ~ of doing sth** être sur le point de faire qch; **to make a ~ of doing** ne pas manquer de faire; **to get the ~** comprendre, saisir; **to miss the ~** ne

pas comprendre; **to come to the ~** en venir au fait; **there's no ~ (in doing)** cela ne sert à rien (de faire); **~ out** vt faire remarquer, souligner; **~ to** vt fus (fig) indiquer; **~-blank** adv (fig) catégoriquement; (also: **at ~-blank range**) à bout portant; **~ed** adj (shape) pointu(e); (remark) plein(e) de sous-entendus; **~er** n (needle) aiguille f; (piece of advice) conseil m; (clue) indice m; **~less** adj inutile, vain(e); **~ of view** n point m de vue

**poise** [pɔɪz] n (composure) calme m

**poison** [ˈpɔɪzn] n poison m ♦ vt empoisonner; **~ous** adj (snake) venimeux (-euse); (plant) vénéneux(-euse); (fumes etc) toxique

**poke** [pəʊk] vt (fire) tisonner; (jab with finger, stick etc) piquer; (put): **to ~ sth in(to)** fourrer or enfoncer qch dans; **~ about** vi fureter; **~r** n tisonnier m; (CARDS) poker m

**poky** [ˈpəʊkɪ] adj exigu(ë)

**Poland** [ˈpəʊlənd] n Pologne f

**polar** [ˈpəʊlə*] adj polaire; **~ bear** n ours blanc

**Pole** [pəʊl] n Polonais(e)

**pole** [pəʊl] n poteau m; (of wood) mât m, perche f; (GEO) pôle m; **~ bean** n (US) haricot m (à rames); **~ vault** n saut m à la perche

**police** [pəˈliːs] npl police f ♦ vt maintenir l'ordre dans; **~ car** n voiture f de police; **~man** (irreg) n agent m de police, policier m; **~ station** n commissariat m de police; **~woman** (irreg) n femme-agent f

**policy** [ˈpɒlɪsɪ] n politique f; (also: **insurance ~**) police f (d'assurance)

**polio** [ˈpəʊlɪəʊ] n polio f

**Polish** [ˈpəʊlɪʃ] adj polonais(e) ♦ n (LING) polonais m

**polish** [ˈpɒlɪʃ] n (for shoes) cirage m; (for floor) cire f, encaustique f; (shine) éclat m, poli m; (fig: refinement) raffinement m ♦ vt (put ~ on shoes, wood) cirer; (make shiny) astiquer, faire briller;

**off** (inf) vt (food) liquider; **~ed** adj (fig) raffiné(e)

**polite** [pə'laɪt] adj poli(e); **in ~ society** dans la bonne société; **~ly** adv poliment; **~ness** n politesse f

**political** [pə'lɪtɪkl] adj politique; **~ly correct** politiquement correct(e)

**politician** [pɔlɪ'tɪʃən] n homme m/femme f politique

**politics** ['pɔlɪtɪks] npl politique f

**poll** [pəul] n scrutin m, vote m; (also: **opinion ~**) sondage m (d'opinion) ♦ vt obtenir

**pollen** ['pɔlən] n pollen m

**polling day** ['pəulɪŋ-] (BRIT) n jour m des élections

**polling station** (BRIT) n bureau m de vote

**pollute** [pə'lu:t] vt polluer; **pollution** n pollution f

**polo** ['pəuləu] n polo m; **~-necked** adj à col roulé; **~ shirt** n polo m

**polyester** [pɔlɪ'estə'] n polyester m

**polystyrene** [pɔlɪ'staɪri:n] n polystyrène m

**polythene** ['pɔlɪθi:n] n polyéthylène m; **~ bag** n sac m en plastique

**pomegranate** ['pɔmɪɡrænɪt] n grenade f

**pomp** [pɔmp] n pompe f, faste m, apparat m; **~ous** adj pompeux(-euse)

**pond** [pɔnd] n étang m, mare f

**ponder** ['pɔndə'] vt considérer, peser; **~ous** adj pesant(e), lourd(e)

**pong** [pɔŋ] (BRIT: inf) n puanteur f

**pony** ['pəunɪ] n poney m; **~tail** n queue f de cheval; **~ trekking** (BRIT) n randonnée f à cheval

**poodle** ['pu:dl] n caniche m

**pool** [pu:l] n (of rain) flaque f; (pond) mare f; (also: **swimming ~**) piscine f; (billiards) poule f ♦ vt mettre en commun; **~s** npl (football ~s) ≃ loto sportif

**poor** [puə'] adj pauvre; (mediocre) médiocre, faible, mauvais(e) ♦ npl: **the ~** les pauvres mpl; **~ly** adj souffrant(e),

malade ♦ adv mal; médiocrement

**pop** [pɔp] n (MUS) musique f pop; (drink) boisson gazeuse; (US: inf: father) papa m; (noise) bruit sec ♦ vt (put) mettre (rapidement) ♦ vi éclater; (cork) sauter; **~ in** vi entrer en passant; **~ out** vi sortir (brièvement); **~ up** vi apparaître, surgir; **~corn** n pop-corn m

**pope** [pəup] n pape m

**poplar** ['pɔplə'] n peuplier m

**popper** ['pɔpə'] (BRIT: inf) n bouton-pression m

**poppy** ['pɔpɪ] n coquelicot m; pavot m

**Popsicle** ® ['pɔpsɪkl] (US) n esquimau m (glace)

**popular** ['pɔpjulə'] adj populaire; (fashionable) à la mode

**population** [pɔpju'leɪʃən] n population f

**porcelain** ['pɔ:slɪn] n porcelaine f

**porch** [pɔ:tʃ] n porche m; (US) véranda f

**porcupine** ['pɔ:kjupaɪn] n porc-épic m

**pore** [pɔ:'] n pore m ♦ vi: **to ~ over** s'absorber dans, être plongé(e) dans

**pork** [pɔ:k] n porc m

**porn** [pɔ:n] (inf) adj, n porno m

**pornographic** [pɔ:nə'ɡræfɪk] adj pornographique

**pornography** [pɔ:'nɔɡrəfɪ] n pornographie f

**porpoise** ['pɔ:pəs] n marsouin m

**porridge** ['pɔrɪdʒ] n porridge m

**port** [pɔ:t] n (harbour) port m; (NAUT: left side) bâbord m; (wine) porto m; **~ of call** escale f

**portable** ['pɔ:tǝbl] adj portatif(-ive)

**porter** ['pɔ:tə'] n (for luggage) porteur m; (doorkeeper) gardien(ne); portier m

**portfolio** [pɔ:t'fəuliəu] n portefeuille m; (of artist) portfolio m

**porthole** ['pɔ:thəul] n hublot m

**portion** ['pɔ:ʃən] n portion f, part f

**portrait** ['pɔ:treɪt] n portrait m

**portray** [pɔ:'treɪ] vt faire le portrait de; (in writing) dépeindre, représenter; (subj: actor) jouer

**Portugal** ['pɔ:tjuɡl] n Portugal m; Por-

**tuguese** [pɔːtjuːgiːz] adj portugais(e)
♦ n inv Portugais(e); (LING) portugais m

**pose** [pəuz] n pose f ♦ vi (pretend): **to ~
as** se poser en ♦ vt poser; (problem)
créer

**posh** [pɔʃ] (inf) adj chic inv

**position** [pəˈzɪʃən] n position f; (job) situation f ♦ vt placer

**positive** [ˈpɔzɪtɪv] adj positif(-ive); (certain) sûr(e), certain(e); (definite) for-
mel(le), catégorique

**possess** [pəˈzɛs] vt posséder; **~ion** n
possession f

**possibility** [pɔsɪˈbɪlɪtɪ] n possibilité f;
éventualité f

**possible** [ˈpɔsɪbl] adj possible; **as big
as ~** aussi gros que possible; **possibly**
adv (perhaps) peut-être; **if you possibly
can** si cela vous est possible; **I
cannot possibly come** il m'est impossible de venir

**post** [pəust] n poste f; (BRIT: letters,
delivery) courrier m; (job, situation, MIL)
poste m; (pole) poteau m ♦ vt (send
by ~) poster; (: appoint): **to ~ to** affecter à; **~age** n tarifs mpl d'affranchissement; **~al order** n mandat(-poste) m;
**~box** (BRIT) n boîte f aux lettres; **~card**
n carte postale; **~code** (BRIT) n code
postal

**poster** [ˈpəustə'] n affiche f

**poste restante** [pəustˈrɛstɑ̃ːt] (BRIT)
n poste restante

**postgraduate** [ˈpəustˈɡrædjuət] n ≈
étudiant(e) de troisième cycle

**posthumous** [ˈpɔstjuməs] adj posthume

**postman** [ˈpəustmən] (irreg) n facteur
m

**postmark** [ˈpəustmɑːk] n cachet m (de
la poste)

**postmortem** [pəustˈmɔːtəm] n autopsie f

**post office** n (building) poste f; (organization): **the P~ O~** les Postes; **~ ~
box** n boîte postale

**postpone** [pəusˈpəun] vt remettre (à

plus tard)

**posture** [ˈpɔstʃə'] n posture f; (fig) attitude f

**postwar** [pəustˈwɔː'] adj d'après-guerre

**postwoman** n factrice f

**posy** [ˈpəuzɪ] n petit bouquet

**pot** [pɔt] n pot m; (for cooking) marmite
f, casserole f; (teapot) théière f; (coffee-
pot) cafetière f; (inf: marijuana) herbe f
♦ vt (plant) mettre en pot; **to go to ~**
(inf: work, performance) aller à vau-l'eau

**potato** [pəˈteɪtəu] (pl ~es) n pomme f
de terre; **~ peeler** n épluche-légumes
m inv

**potent** [ˈpəutnt] adj puissant(e); (drink)
fort(e), très alcoolisé(e); (man) viril

**potential** [pəˈtɛnʃl] adj potentiel(le) ♦ n
potentiel m

**pothole** [ˈpɔthəul] n (in road) nid m de
poule; (BRIT: underground) gouffre m,
caverne f; **potholing** (BRIT) n: **to go
potholing** faire de la spéléologie

**potluck** [pɔtˈlʌk] n: **to take ~** tenter
sa chance

**pot plant** n plante f d'appartement

**potted** [ˈpɔtɪd] adj (food) en conserve;
(plant) en pot; (abbreviated) abrégé(e)

**potter** [ˈpɔtə'] n potier m ♦ vi: **to ~
around**, **~ about** (BRIT) bricoler; **~y** n
poterie f

**potty** [ˈpɔtɪ] adj (inf: mad) dingue ♦ n
(child's) pot m

**pouch** [pautʃ] n (ZOOL) poche f; (for tobacco) blague f; (for money) bourse f

**poultry** [ˈpəultrɪ] n volaille f

**pounce** [pauns] vi: **to ~ (on)** bondir
(sur), sauter (sur)

**pound** [paund] n (unit of money) livre f;
(unit of weight) livre ♦ vt (beat) bourrer
de coups, marteler; (crush) piler, pulvériser ♦ vi (heart) battre violemment, taper

**pour** [pɔː'] vt verser ♦ vi couler à flots;
**to ~ (with rain)** pleuvoir à verse; **to ~
sb a drink** verser or servir à boire à qn;
**~ away** vt vider; **~ in** vi (people) affluer, se précipiter; (news, letters etc) ar-

river en masse; **~ off** vt = **pour away**;
**~ out** vi (people) sortir en masse ♦ vt
vider; (fig) déverser; (serve: a drink) verser; **~ing** ['pɔːrɪŋ] adj: **~ing rain** pluie
torrentielle

**pout** [paut] vi faire la moue

**poverty** ['pɔvətɪ] n pauvreté f, misère f;
**~-stricken** adj pauvre, déshérité(e)

**powder** ['paudəʳ] n poudre f ♦ vt: **to ~
one's face** se poudrer; **~ compact** n
poudrier m; **~ed milk** n lait m en poudre; **~ room** n toilettes fpl (pour dames)

**power** ['pauəʳ] n (strength) puissance f,
force f; (ability, authority) pouvoir m; (of
speech, thought) faculté f; (ELEC) courant
m; **to be in ~** (POL etc) être au pouvoir;
**~ cut** (BRIT) n coupure f de courant;
**~ed** adj: **~ed by** actionné(e) par, fonctionnant à; **~ failure** n panne f de courant; **~ful** adj puissant(e); **~less** adj impuissant(e); **~ point** (BRIT) n prise f de
courant; **~ station** n centrale f électrique; **~ struggle** n lutte f pour le pouvoir

**p.p.** abbr (= per procurationem): **p.p. J.
Smith** pour M. J. Smith

**PR** n abbr = **public relations**

**practical** ['præktɪkl] adj pratique; **~ity**
[præktɪˈkælɪtɪ] (no pl) n (of person) sens
m pratique; **~ities** npl (of situation) aspect m pratique; **~ joke** n farce f; **~ly**
adv (almost) pratiquement

**practice** ['præktɪs] n pratique f; (of profession) exercice m; (at football etc) entraînement m; (business) cabinet m ♦ vt,
vi (US) = **practise**; **in ~** (in reality) en
pratique; **out of ~** rouillé(e)

**practise** ['præktɪs] (US **practice**) vt (musical instrument) travailler; (train for:
sport) s'entraîner à; (a sport, religion)
pratiquer; (profession) exercer ♦ vi
s'exercer, travailler; (train) s'entraîner;
(lawyer, doctor) exercer; **practising** adj
(Christian etc) pratiquant(e); (lawyer) en
exercice

**practitioner** [prækˈtɪʃənəʳ] n prati-

cien(ne)

**prairie** ['prɛərɪ] n steppe f, prairie f

**praise** [preɪz] n éloge(s) m(pl), louange(s) f(pl) ♦ vt louer, faire l'éloge de;
**~worthy** adj digne d'éloges

**pram** [præm] (BRIT) n landau m, voiture
f d'enfant

**prance** [prɑːns] vi (also: ~ about: person) se pavaner

**prank** [præŋk] n farce f

**prawn** [prɔːn] n crevette f (rose); **~
cocktail** n cocktail m de crevettes

**pray** [preɪ] vi prier; **~er** [prɛəʳ] n prière f

**preach** [priːtʃ] vt, vi prêcher

**precaution** [prɪˈkɔːʃən] n précaution f

**precede** [prɪˈsiːd] vt précéder

**precedent** ['presɪdənt] n précédent m

**preceding** adj qui précède/précédait etc

**precinct** ['priːsɪŋkt] n (US: district) circonscription f, arrondissement m; **~s** npl (neighbourhood) alentours mpl, environs mpl;
**pedestrian ~** (BRIT) zone piétonnière
or piétonne; **shopping ~** (BRIT) centre
commercial

**precious** ['preʃəs] adj précieux(-euse)

**precipitate** [prɪˈsɪpɪteɪt] vt précipiter

**precise** [prɪˈsaɪs] adj précis(e); **~ly** adv
précisément

**precocious** [prɪˈkəʊʃəs] adj précoce

**precondition** [priːkənˈdɪʃən] n condition f nécessaire

**predecessor** ['priːdɪsesəʳ] n prédécesseur m

**predicament** [prɪˈdɪkəmənt] n situation f difficile

**predict** [prɪˈdɪkt] vt prédire; **~able** adj
prévisible

**predominantly** [prɪˈdɒmɪnəntlɪ] adv
en majeure partie; surtout

**pre-empt** [priːˈemt] vt anticiper, devancer

**preen** [priːn] vt: **to ~ itself** (bird) se lisser les plumes; **to ~ o.s.** s'admirer

**prefab** ['priːfæb] n bâtiment m préfabriqué

**preface** ['prefəs] n préface f

**prefect** ['pri:fekt] (BRIT) n (in school) élève chargé(e) de certaines fonctions de discipline

**prefer** [pri'fə:ʳ] vt préférer; **~ably** ['prefrəbli] adv de préférence; **~ence** ['prefrəns] n préférence f; **~ential** [prefə'renʃəl] adj: **~ential treatment** traitement m de faveur ou préférentiel

**prefix** ['pri:fɪks] n préfixe m

**pregnancy** ['pregnənsi] n grossesse f

**pregnant** ['pregnənt] adj enceinte; (animal) pleine

**prehistoric** ['pri:hɪs'tɔrɪk] adj préhistorique

**prejudice** ['predʒudɪs] n préjugé m; ~d adj (person) plein(e) de préjugés; (in a matter) partial(e)

**premarital** ['pri:'mærɪtl] adj avant le mariage

**premature** ['prematjuəʳ] adj prématuré(e)

**premenstrual syndrome** [pri:'menstrual-] n syndrome prémenstruel

**premier** ['premɪəʳ] adj premier(-ère), principal(e) ♦ n (POL) Premier ministre

**première** ['premɪɛəʳ] n première f

**Premier League** n première division

**premise** ['premɪs] n prémisse f; ~s npl (building) locaux mpl; **on the ~s** sur les lieux; sur place

**premium** ['pri:mɪəm] n prime f; **to be at a ~** faire prime; **~ bond** (BRIT) n bon m à lot, obligation f à prime

**premonition** [premə'nɪʃən] n prémonition f

**preoccupied** [pri:'ɔkjupaɪd] adj préoccupé(e)

**prep** [prep] n (SCOL) étude f

**prepaid** [pri:'peɪd] adj payé(e) d'avance

**preparation** [prepə'reɪʃən] n préparation f; ~s npl (for trip, war) préparatifs mpl

**preparatory** [pri'pærətəri] adj préliminaire; **~ school** (BRIT) n école primaire privée

**prepare** [pri'peəʳ] vt préparer ♦ vi: **to ~ for** se préparer à; **~d to** prêt(e) à

**preposition** [prepə'zɪʃən] n préposition f

**preposterous** [pri'pɔstərəs] adj absurde

**prep school** n = preparatory school

**prerequisite** [pri:'rekwɪzɪt] n condition f préalable

**Presbyterian** [prezbɪ'tɪərɪən] adj, n presbytérien(ne) m/f

**prescribe** [pri'skraɪb] vt prescrire; **prescription** [pri'skrɪpʃən] n (MED) ordonnance f; (: medicine) médicament (obtenu sur ordonnance)

**presence** ['prezns] n présence f; **~ of mind** présence d'esprit

**present** [adj, n 'preznt, vb pri'zent] adj présent(e) ♦ n (gift) cadeau m; (actuality) présent m ♦ vt présenter; (prize, medal) remettre; (give): **to ~ sb with sth** ou **sth to sb** offrir qch à qn; **to give sb a ~** offrir un cadeau à qn; **at ~** en ce moment; **~ation** [prezn'teɪʃən] n présentation f; (ceremony) remise f du cadeau (or de la médaille etc); **~-day** adj contemporain(e), actuel(le); **~er** n (RADIO, TV) présentateur(-trice); **~ly** adv (with verb in past) peu après; (soon) tout à l'heure, bientôt; (at present) en ce moment

**preservative** [pri'zə:vətɪv] n agent m de conservation

**preserve** [pri'zə:v] vt (keep safe) préserver, protéger; (maintain) conserver, garder; (food) mettre en conserve ♦ n (often pl: jam) confiture f

**president** ['prezɪdənt] n président(e); **~ial** [prezɪ'denʃl] adj présidentiel(le)

**press** [pres] n presse f; (for wine) pressoir m ♦ vt (squeeze) presser, serrer; (push) appuyer sur; (clothes: iron) repasser; (put ~ure on) faire pression sur; (insist): **to ~ sth on sb** presser qn d'accepter qch ♦ vi appuyer, peser; **to ~ for sth** faire pression pour obtenir qch; **we are ~ed for time/money** sous temps/l'argent nous manque; **~ on** vi continuer; **~ conference** n conférence f de presse; **~ing** adj urgent(e), pressant(e); **~ stud** (BRIT) n bouton-pression m; **~-up** (BRIT) n traction f

**pressure** ['prɛʃər] n pression f; (stress) tension f; **to put ~ on sb (to do)** faire pression sur qn (pour qu'il/elle fasse); **~ cooker** n cocotte-minute f; **~ gauge** n manomètre m; **~ group** n groupe m de pression

**prestige** [prɛs'tiːʒ] n prestige m; **prestigious** [prɛs'tɪdʒəs] adj prestigieux(-euse)

**presumably** [prɪ'zjuːməblɪ] adv vraisemblablement

**presume** [prɪ'zjuːm] vt présumer, supposer

**pretence** [prɪ'tɛns] (US **pretense**) n (claim) prétention f; (pretext) prétexte m; **under false ~s** sous de faux prétextes; sous des prétextes fallacieux

**pretend** [prɪ'tɛnd] vt (feign) feindre, simuler ♦ vi faire semblant

**pretext** ['priːtɛkst] n prétexte m

**pretty** ['prɪtɪ] adj joli(e) ♦ adv assez

**prevail** [prɪ'veɪl] vi (be usual) avoir cours; (win) l'emporter, prévaloir; **~ing** adj dominant(e); **prevalent** ['prɛvələnt] adj répandu(e), courant(e)

**prevent** [prɪ'vɛnt] vt: **to ~ (from doing)** empêcher (de faire); **~ative** [prɪ'vɛntətɪv], **~ive** [prɪ'vɛntɪv] adj préventif(-ive)

**preview** ['priːvjuː] n (of film etc) avant-première f

**previous** ['priːvɪəs] adj précédent(e); antérieur(e); **~ly** adv précédemment, auparavant

**prewar** [priː'wɔːr] adj d'avant-guerre

**prey** [preɪ] n proie f ♦ vi: **to ~ on** s'attaquer à; **it was ~ing on his mind** cela le travaillait

**price** [praɪs] n prix m ♦ vt (goods) fixer le prix de; **~less** adj sans prix, inestimable; **~ list** n liste f des prix, tarif m

**prick** [prɪk] n piqûre f ♦ vt piquer; **to ~ up one's ears** dresser or tendre l'oreille

**prickle** ['prɪkl] n (of plant) épine f; (sensation) picotement m; **prickly** adj piquant(e), épineux(-euse); **prickly heat** n fièvre f miliaire

**pride** [praɪd] n orgueil m; fierté f ♦ vt: **to ~ o.s.** on se flatter de; s'enorgueillir de

**priest** [priːst] n prêtre m; **~hood** n prêtrise f, sacerdoce m

**prim** [prɪm] adj collet monté inv, guindé(e)

**primarily** ['praɪmərɪlɪ] adv principalement, essentiellement

**primary** ['praɪmərɪ] adj (first in importance) premier(-ère), primordial(e), principal(e) ♦ n (US: election) (élection f) primaire f; **~ school** (BRIT) n école f primaire f

**prime** [praɪm] adj primordial(e), fondamental(e); (excellent) excellent(e) ♦ n: **in the ~ of life** dans la fleur de l'âge ♦ vt (wood) apprêter; (fig) mettre au courant; **P~ Minister** n Premier ministre m

**primeval** adj primitif(-ive); **~ forest** forêt f vierge

**primitive** ['prɪmɪtɪv] adj primitif(-ive)

**primrose** ['prɪmrəuz] n primevère f

**primus (stove)** ® ['praɪməs-] (BRIT) n réchaud m de camping

**prince** [prɪns] n prince m

**princess** [prɪn'sɛs] n princesse f

**principal** ['prɪnsɪpl] adj principal(e) ♦ n (headmaster) directeur(-trice), principal m

**principle** ['prɪnsɪpl] n principe m; **in/ on ~** en/par principe

**print** [prɪnt] n (mark) empreinte f; (letters) caractères mpl; (ART) gravure f, estampe f; (photograph) photo f ♦ vt imprimer; (publish) publier; (write in block letters) écrire en caractères d'imprimerie; **out of ~** épuisé(e); **~ed matter** n imprimé(s) m(pl); **~er** n imprimeur m; (machine) imprimante f; **~ing** n impression f; **~-out** n copie f papier

**prior** ['praɪər] adj antérieur(e), précé-

dent(e); (more important) prioritaire ♦
adv: **~ to doing** avant de faire; **~ity**
[praɪˈɒrɪtɪ] n priorité f

**prise** [praɪz] vt: **to ~ open** forcer

**prison** [ˈprɪzn] n prison f ♦ cpd pénitentiaire; **~er** n prisonnier(-ère)

**pristine** [ˈprɪstiːn] adj parfait(e)

**privacy** [ˈprɪvəsɪ] n intimité f, solitude f

**private** [ˈpraɪvɪt] adj privé(e); (personal)
personnel(le); (house, lesson)
particulier(-ère); (quiet: place) tranquille;
(reserved: person) secret(-ète) ♦ n soldat
m de deuxième classe; **"~"** (on envelope) "personnelle"; **in ~** en privé; **~**
**detective** n détective privé; **~ enterprise** n l'entreprise privée; **~ property**
n propriété privée; **privatize** vt privati-
ser

**privet** [ˈprɪvɪt] n troène m

**privilege** [ˈprɪvɪlɪdʒ] n privilège m

**privy** [ˈprɪvɪ] adj: **to be ~ to** être au
courant de

**prize** [praɪz] n prix m ♦ adj (example,
idiot) parfait(e); (bull, novel) primé(e) ♦
vt priser, faire grand cas de; **~-giving** n
distribution f des prix; **~-winner** n ga-
gnant(e)

**pro** [prəu] n (SPORT) professionnel(le);
**the ~s and cons** le pour et le contre

**probability** [prɒbəˈbɪlɪtɪ] n probabilité f

**probable** [ˈprɒbəbl] adj probable;
**probably** adv probablement

**probation** [prəˈbeɪʃən] n: **on ~** (LAW)
en liberté surveillée, en sursis; (employee) à l'essai

**probe** [prəub] n (MED, SPACE) sonde f;
(enquiry) enquête f, investigation f ♦ vt
sonder, explorer

**problem** [ˈprɒbləm] n problème m

**procedure** [prəˈsiːdʒə] n (ADMIN, LAW)
procédure f; (method) marche f à suivre, façon f de procéder

**proceed** [prəˈsiːd] vi continuer; (go forward) avancer; **to ~ (with)** continuer,
poursuivre; **to ~ to do** se mettre à faire; **~ings** npl (LAW) poursuites fpl;
(meeting) réunion f, séance f; **~s**

[ˈprəusiːdz] npl produit m, recette f

**process** [ˈprəuses] n processus m;
(method) procédé m ♦ vt traiter; **~ing** n
(PHOT) développement m; **~ion**
[prəˈsɛʃən] n défilé m, cortège m; (REL)
procession f; **funeral ~ion** (on foot)
cortège m funèbre; (in cars) convoi m
mortuaire

**proclaim** [prəˈkleɪm] vt déclarer, proclamer

**procrastinate** [prəuˈkræstɪneɪt] vi faire
traîner les choses, vouloir tout remettre
au lendemain

**procure** [prəˈkjuə] vt obtenir

**prod** [prɒd] vt pousser

**prodigal** [ˈprɒdɪgl] adj prodigue

**prodigy** [ˈprɒdɪdʒɪ] n prodige m

**produce** [n ˈprɒdjuːs, vb prəˈdjuːs] n
(AGR) produits mpl ♦ vt produire; (to
show) présenter; (cause) provoquer,
causer; (THEATRE) monter, mettre en
scène; **~r** n producteur m; (THEATRE)
metteur m en scène

**product** [ˈprɒdʌkt] n produit m

**production** [prəˈdʌkʃən] n production
f; (THEATRE) mise f en scène; **~ line**
chaîne f (de fabrication)

**productivity** [prɒdʌkˈtɪvɪtɪ] n productivité f

**profession** [prəˈfɛʃən] n profession f;
**~al** n professionnel(le) ♦ adj profession-
nel(le); (work) de professionnel; **~ally**
adv professionnellement; (SPORT): **play**
**~ally** jouer en professionnel; **she sings**
**~ally** elle chante professionnellement; **I only**
**know him ~ally** je n'ai avec lui que
des relations de travail

**professor** [prəˈfɛsə] n professeur m (titulaire d'une chaire)

**proficiency** [prəˈfɪʃənsɪ] n compétence f,
aptitude f

**profile** [ˈprəufaɪl] n profil m

**profit** [ˈprɒfɪt] n bénéfice m; profit m
♦ vi: **to ~ (by** or **from)** profiter (de);
**~able** adj lucratif(-ive), rentable

**profound** [prəˈfaund] adj profond(e)

**profusely** [prəˈfjuːslɪ] adv abondamment; avec effusion

**prognosis** [prɒgˈnəusɪs] (pl **prognoses**) n pronostic m

**programme** [ˈprəugræm] (US **program**) n programme m; (RADIO, TV) émission f ♦ vt programmer; **~r** (US **programer**) n programmeur(-euse);
**programming** (US **programing**) n programmation f

**progress** [n ˈprəugres, vb prəˈgres] n progrès m(pl) ♦ vi progresser, avancer; **in ~** en cours; **~ive** [prəˈgresɪv] adj progressif(-ive); (person) progressiste

**prohibit** [prəˈhɪbɪt] vt interdire, défendre

**project** [n ˈprɒdʒekt, vb prəˈdʒekt] n (plan) projet m, plan m; (venture) opération f, entreprise f; (research) étude f, dossier m ♦ vt projeter ♦ vi faire saillie, s'avancer; **~ion** n projection f; (overhang) saillie f; **~or** n projecteur m

**prolong** [prəˈlɒŋ] vt prolonger

**prom** [prɒm] n abbr = **promenade**; (US: ball) bal m d'étudiants

**promenade** [prɒməˈnɑːd] n (by sea) esplanade f, promenade f; **~ concert** (BRIT) n concert m populaire (de musique classique)

promenade concert

En Grande-Bretagne, un *promenade concert* (ou *prom*) est un concert de musique classique, ainsi appelé car, à l'origine, le public restait debout et se promenait au lieu de rester assis. De nos jours, une partie du public reste debout, mais il y a également des places assises (plus chères). Les *Proms* les plus connus sont les *Proms* londoniens. La dernière séance (the *Last Night of the Proms*) est un grand événement médiatique où se jouent des airs traditionnels et patriotiques. Aux États-Unis et au Canada, le *prom* ou *promenade* est un bal organisé par le lycée.

**prominent** [ˈprɒmɪnənt] adj (standing out) proéminent(e); (important) important(e)

**promiscuous** [prəˈmɪskjuəs] adj (sexually) de mœurs légères

**promise** [ˈprɒmɪs] n promesse f ♦ vt, vi promettre; **promising** adj prometteur(-euse)

**promote** [prəˈməut] vt promouvoir; (new product) faire la promotion de; **~r** n (of event) organisateur(-trice); (of cause, idea) promoteur(-trice); **promotion** n promotion f

**prompt** [prɒmpt] adj rapide ♦ adv (punctually) à l'heure ♦ n (COMPUT) message m (de guidage) ♦ vt provoquer; (person) inciter, pousser; (THEATRE) souffler (son rôle or ses répliques) à; **~ly** adv rapidement, sans délai; ponctuellement

**prone** [prəun] adj (lying) couché(e) (face contre terre); **~ to** enclin(e) à

**prong** [prɒŋ] n (of fork) dent f

**pronoun** [ˈprəunaun] n pronom m

**pronounce** [prəˈnauns] vt prononcer; **pronunciation** [prənʌnsɪˈeɪʃən] n prononciation f

**proof** [pruːf] n preuve f; (TYP) épreuve f ♦ adj: **~ against** à l'épreuve de

**prop** [prɒp] n support m, étai m; (fig) soutien m ♦ vt (also: **~ up**) étayer, soutenir; (lean): **to ~ sth against** appuyer qch contre or à

**propaganda** [prɒpəˈgændə] n propagande f

**propel** [prəˈpel] vt propulser, faire avancer; **~ler** n hélice f

**propensity** [prəˈpensɪtɪ] n: a **~ for** or **to/to do** une propension à/à faire

**proper** [ˈprɒpə*] adj (suited, right) approprié(e), bon (bonne); (seemly) correct(e), convenable; (authentic) vrai(e), véritable; (referring to place): **the village ~** le village proprement dit; **~ly** adv correctement, convenablement; **~ noun** n nom m propre

**property** [ˈprɒpətɪ] n propriété f;

# prophecy    507    psychic

(things owned) biens mpl; propriété(s)
f(pl); (land) terres fpl

**prophecy** ['prɒfɪsɪ] n prophétie f

**prophesy** ['prɒfɪsaɪ] vt prédire

**prophet** ['prɒfɪt] n prophète m

**proportion** [prə'pɔːʃən] n proportion f;
(share) part f, partie f; ~al, ~ate adj
proportionnel(le)

**proposal** [prə'pəuzl] n proposition f,
offre f; (plan) projet m; (of marriage)
demande f en mariage

**propose** [prə'pəuz] vt proposer, suggérer ♦ vi faire sa demande en mariage;
to ~ to do avoir l'intention de faire;
**proposition** [prɒpə'zɪʃən] n proposition f

**proprietor** [prə'praɪətər] n propriétaire
m/f

**propriety** [prə'praɪətɪ] n (seemliness)
bienséance f, convenance f

**prose** [prəuz] n (not poetry) prose f

**prosecute** ['prɒsɪkjuːt] vt poursuivre;
**prosecution** [prɒsɪ'kjuːʃən] n poursuites fpl judiciaires; (accusing side) partie
plaignante; **prosecutor** n (us: plaintiff)
plaignant(e); (also: **public prosecutor**)
procureur m, ministère public

**prospect** [n 'prɒspekt, vb prə'spekt] n
perspective f ♦ vt, vi prospecter; ~s npl
(for work etc) possibilités fpl d'avenir,
débouchés mpl; ~ing n (for gold, oil etc)
prospection f; ~ive adj (possible) éven-
tuel(le); (future) futur(e)

**prospectus** [prə'spektəs] n prospectus
m

**prosperity** [prɒ'sperɪtɪ] n prospérité f

**prostitute** ['prɒstɪtjuːt] n prostituée f

**protect** [prə'tekt] vt protéger; ~ion n
protection f; ~ive adj protecteur(-trice);
(clothing) de protection

**protein** ['prəutiːn] n protéine f

**protest** [n 'prəutest, vb prə'test] n protestation f ♦ vi, vt: to ~ (that) protester
(que)

**Protestant** ['prɒtɪstənt] adj, n protes-
tant(e)

**protester** [prə'testər] n manifestant(e)

**protracted** [prə'træktɪd] adj prolon-
gé(e)

**protrude** [prə'truːd] vi avancer, dépasser

**proud** [praud] adj fier(-ère); (pej)
orgueilleux(-euse)

**prove** [pruːv] vt prouver, démontrer ♦
vi: to ~ (to be) correct etc s'avérer juste etc; to ~ o.s. montrer ce dont on est
capable

**proverb** ['prɒvɜːb] n proverbe m

**provide** [prə'vaɪd] vt fournir; to ~ sb
with sth fournir qch à qn; ~ for vt fus
(person) subvenir aux besoins de; (future event) prévoir; ~d (that) conj à
condition que +sub; **providing** conj:
**providing (that)** à condition que +sub

**province** ['prɒvɪns] n province f; (fig)
domaine m; **provincial** [prə'vɪnʃəl] adj
provincial(e)

**provision** [prə'vɪʒən] n (supplying)
fourniture f; approvisionnement m;
(stipulation) disposition f; ~s npl (food)
provisions fpl; ~al adj provisoire

**proviso** [prə'vaɪzəu] n condition f

**provocative** [prə'vɒkətɪv] adj
provocateur(-trice), provocant(e)

**provoke** [prə'vəuk] vt provoquer

**prowess** ['prauɪs] n prouesse f

**prowl** [praul] vi (also: ~ about, ~
around) rôder ♦ n: on the ~ à l'affût;
~er n rôdeur(-euse)

**proxy** ['prɒksɪ] n procuration f

**prudent** ['pruːdnt] adj prudent(e)

**prune** [pruːn] n pruneau m ♦ vt élaguer

**pry** [praɪ] vi: to ~ into fourrer son nez
dans

**PS** n abbr (= postscript) p.s.

**psalm** [sɑːm] n psaume m

**pseudonym** ['sjuːdənɪm] n pseudonyme m

**psyche** ['saɪkɪ] n psychisme m

**psychiatrist** [saɪ'kaɪətrɪst] n psychiatre
m/f

**psychic** ['saɪkɪk] adj (also: ~al) (méta)psychique; (person) doué(e) d'un
sixième sens

**psychoanalyst** [saɪkəʊ'ænəlɪst] *n* psychanalyste *m/f*

**psychological** [saɪkə'lɒdʒɪkl] *adj* psychologique

**psychologist** [saɪ'kɒlədʒɪst] *n* psychologue *m/f*

**psychology** [saɪ'kɒlədʒɪ] *n* psychologie *f*

**PTO** *abbr* (= *please turn over*) T.S.V.P.

**pub** [pʌb] *n* (*public house*) pub *m*

---

**pub**

Un pub comprend en général deux salles: l'une ("the lounge") est plutôt confortable, avec des fauteuils et des bancs capitonnés, tandis que l'autre ("the public bar") est simplement un bar où les consommations sont en général moins chères. Cette dernière est souvent aussi une salle de jeux, les jeux les plus courants étant les fléchettes, les dominos et le billard. Il y a parfois aussi une petite arrière-salle douillette appelée "the snug". Beaucoup de pubs servent maintenant des repas, surtout à l'heure du déjeuner, et c'est alors le seul moment où les enfants sont acceptés, à condition d'être accompagnés. Ils sont en général ouverts de 11 h à 23 h, mais cela peut varier selon leur licence; certains pubs ferment l'après-midi.

---

**public** ['pʌblɪk] *adj* public(-ique) ♦ *n* public *m*; **in ~** en public; **to make ~** rendre public; **to ~ address system** *n* (système *m* de) sonorisation *f*; hauts-parleurs *mpl*

**publican** ['pʌblɪkən] *n* patron *m* de pub

**public:** **~ company** *n* société *f* anonyme (*cotée en Bourse*); **~ convenience** (*BRIT*) *n* toilettes *fpl*; **~ holiday** (*BRIT*) *n* jour férié; **~ house** (*BRIT*) *n* pub *m*

**publicity** [pʌb'lɪsɪtɪ] *n* publicité *f*

**publicize** ['pʌblɪsaɪz] *vt* faire connaître, rendre public(-ique)

**public:** **~ opinion** *n* opinion publique; **~ relations** *n* relations publiques; **~ school** *n* (*BRIT*) école (secondaire) privée; (*US*) école publique; **~-spirited** *adj* qui fait preuve de civisme; **~ transport** *n* transports *mpl* en commun

**publish** ['pʌblɪʃ] *vt* publier; **~er** *n* éditeur *m*; **~ing** *n* édition *f*

**pub lunch** *n* repas *m* de bistrot

**pucker** ['pʌkər] *vt* plisser

**pudding** ['pʊdɪŋ] *n* pudding *m*; (*BRIT*: *sweet*) dessert *m*, entremets *m*; **black ~**, (*US*) **blood ~** boudin (noir)

**puddle** ['pʌdl] *n* flaque *f* (d'eau)

**puff** [pʌf] *n* bouffée *f* ♦ *vt*: **to ~ one's pipe** tirer sur sa pipe ♦ *vi* (*pant*) haleter; **~ out of** (*with air*) gonfler; **~ pastry** (*US* **puff paste**) *n* pâte feuilletée; **~y** *adj* bouffi(e), boursouflé(e)

**pull** [pʊl] *n* (*tug*): **to give sth a ~** tirer sur qch ♦ *vt* tirer; (*trigger*) presser ♦ *vi* tirer; **to ~ to pieces** mettre en morceaux; **to ~ one's punches** ménager son adversaire; **to ~ one's weight** faire sa part (du travail); **to ~ o.s. together** se ressaisir; **to ~ sb's leg** (*fig*) faire marcher qn; **~ apart** *vt* (*break*) mettre en pièces, démantibuler; **~ down** *vt* (*house*) démolir; **~ in** *vi* (*AUT*) rentrer; (*RAIL*) entrer en gare; **~ off** *vt* enlever, ôter; (*deal etc*) mener à bien, conclure; **~ out** *vi* démarrer, partir ♦ *vt* sortir; arracher; **~ over** *vi* (*AUT*) se ranger; **~ through** *vi* s'en sortir; **~ up** *vi* (*stop*) s'arrêter ♦ *vt* remonter; (*uproot*) déraciner, arracher

**pulley** ['pʊlɪ] *n* poulie *f*

**pullover** ['pʊləʊvər] *n* pull(-over) *m*, tricot *m*

**pulp** [pʌlp] *n* (*of fruit*) pulpe *f*

**pulpit** ['pʊlpɪt] *n* chaire *f*

**pulsate** [pʌl'seɪt] *vi* battre, palpiter; (*music*) vibrer

**pulse** [pʌls] *n* (*of blood*) pouls *m*; (*of heart*) battement *m*; (*of music, engine*) vibrations *fpl*; (*BOT, CULIN*) légume sec

**pump** [pʌmp] *n* pompe *f*; (*shoe*) escarpin ♦ vt pomper; **~ up** vt gonfler

**pumpkin** ['pʌmpkɪn] n potiron m, citrouille f

**pun** [pʌn] n jeu de mots, calembour m

**punch** [pʌntʃ] n (blow) coup m de poing; (tool) poinçon m; (drink) punch m ♦ vt (hit): **to ~ sb/sth** donner un coup de poing à qn/sur qch; **~line** n (of joke) conclusion f; **~-up** (BRIT: inf) n bagarre f

**punctual** ['pʌŋktjuəl] adj ponctuel(le)

**punctuation** [pʌŋktju'eɪʃən] n ponctuation f

**puncture** ['pʌŋktʃə'] n crevaison f

**pundit** ['pʌndɪt] n individu m qui pontifie, pontife m

**pungent** ['pʌndʒənt] adj piquant(e), âcre

**punish** ['pʌnɪʃ] vt punir; **~ment** n punition f, châtiment m

**punk** [pʌŋk] n (also: ~ **rocker**) punk m/f; (also: ~ **rock**) le punk rock; (US: inf: hoodlum) voyou m

**punt** [pʌnt] n (boat) bachot m

**punter** ['pʌntə'] n (gambler) parieur(-euse); (inf): **the ~s** le public

**puny** ['pju:nɪ] adj chétif(-ive); (effort) piteux(-euse)

**pup** [pʌp] n chiot m

**pupil** ['pju:pl] n (SCOL) élève m/f; (of eye) pupille f

**puppet** ['pʌpɪt] n marionnette f, pantin m

**puppy** ['pʌpɪ] n chiot m, jeune chien(ne)

**purchase** ['pə:tʃɪs] n achat m ♦ vt acheter; **~r** n acheteur(-euse)

**pure** [pjuə'] adj pur(e); **~ly** adv purement

**purge** [pə:dʒ] n purge f ♦ vt purger

**purple** ['pə:pl] adj violet(te); (face) cramoisi(e)

**purpose** ['pə:pəs] n intention f, but m; **on ~** exprès; **~ful** adj déterminé(e), résolu(e)

**purr** [pə:'] vi ronronner

**purse** [pə:s] n (BRIT: for money) portemonnaie m inv; (US: handbag) sac m à main ♦ vt serrer, pincer

**purser** n (NAUT) commissaire m du bord

**pursue** [pə'sju:] vt poursuivre; **pursuit** [pə'sju:t] n poursuite f; (occupation) occupation f, activité f

**push** [puʃ] n poussée f ♦ vt pousser; (button) appuyer sur; (product) faire de la publicité pour; (thrust): **to ~ sth (into)** enfoncer qch (dans) ♦ vi pousser; (demand): **to ~ for** exiger, demander avec insistance; **~ aside** vt écarter; **~ off** (inf) vi filer, ficher le camp; **~ on** vi (continue) continuer; **~ through** vi se frayer un chemin ♦ vt (measure) faire accepter; **~ up** vt (total, prices) faire monter; **~chair** (BRIT) n poussette f; **~er** n (drug pusher) revendeur(-euse) (de drogue), ravitailleur(-euse) (en drogue); **~over** (inf) n: **it's a ~over** c'est un jeu d'enfant; **~-up** (US) n traction f; **~y** (pej) adj arriviste

**puss** [pus], **pussy (cat)** ['pusɪ(kæt)] (inf) n minet m

**put** [put] (pt, pp **put**) vt mettre, poser, placer; (say) dire, exprimer; (a question) poser; (case, view) exposer, présenter; (estimate) estimer; **~ about** vt (rumour) faire courir; **~ across** vt (ideas etc) communiquer; **~ away** vt (store) ranger; **~ back** vt (replace) remettre, replacer; (postpone) remettre; (delay) retarder; **~ by** vt (money) mettre de côté, économiser; **~ down** vt (parcel etc) poser, déposer; (in writing) mettre par écrit, inscrire; (suppress: revolt etc) réprimer, faire cesser; (animal) abattre; (dog, cat) faire piquer; (attribute) attribuer; **~ forward** vt (ideas) avancer; **~ in** vt (gas, electricity) installer; (application, complaint) soumettre; (time, effort) consacrer; **~ off** vt (light etc) éteindre; (postpone) remettre à plus tard, ajourner; (discourage) dissuader; **~ on** vt (clothes, lipstick, record) mettre; (light etc) allumer; (play etc) monter; (food:

cook) mettre à cuire or à chauffer; (gain): **to ~ on weight** prendre du poids, grossir; **to ~ the brakes on** freiner; **to ~ the kettle on** mettre l'eau à chauffer; **~ out** vt (take out) mettre dehors; (one's hand) tendre; (light etc) éteindre; (person: inconvenience) déranger, gêner; **~ through** vt (TEL: call) passer; (: person) mettre en communication; (: plan) faire accepter; **~ up** vt (raise) lever, relever, remonter; (pin up) afficher; (hang) accrocher; (build) construire, ériger; (tent) monter; (umbrella) ouvrir; (increase) augmenter; (accommodate) loger; **~ up with** vt fus supporter

**putt** [pʌt] n coup roulé; **~ing green** n green m

**putty** ['pʌtɪ] n mastic m

**put-up** ['pʊtʌp] (BRIT) adj: **~~ job** coup monté

**puzzle** ['pʌzl] n énigme f, mystère m; (jigsaw) puzzle m ♦ vt intriguer, rendre perplexe ♦ vi se creuser la tête; **~d** adj perplexe; **puzzling** adj déconcertant(e)

**pyjamas** [pə'dʒɑːməz] (BRIT) npl pyjama(s) m(pl)

**pylon** ['paɪlən] n pylône m

**pyramid** ['pɪrəmɪd] n pyramide f

**Pyrenees** [pɪrə'niːz] npl: **the ~** les Pyrénées fpl

# Q, q

**quack** [kwæk] n (of duck) coin-coin m inv; (pej: doctor) charlatan m

**quad** [kwɒd] n abbr = **quadrangle**; **quadruplet**

**quadrangle** ['kwɒdræŋgl] n (courtyard) cour f

**quadruple** [kwɒ'druːpl] vt, vi quadrupler; **~ts** npl quadruplés

**quail** [kweɪl] n (ZOOL) caille f ♦ vi: **to ~** at or **before** reculer devant

**quaint** [kweɪnt] adj bizarre; (house, village) au charme vieillot, pittoresque

**quake** [kweɪk] vi trembler

**qualification** [kwɒlɪfɪ'keɪʃən] n (often pl: degree etc) diplôme m; (training) qualification(s) f(pl); (experience) expérience f; (ability) compétence(s) f(pl); (limitation) réserve f, restriction f

**qualified** ['kwɒlɪfaɪd] adj (trained) qualifié(e); (professionally) diplômé(e); (fit, competent) compétent(e), qualifié(e); (limited) conditionnel(le)

**qualify** ['kwɒlɪfaɪ] vt qualifier; (modify) atténuer, nuancer ♦ vi: **to ~ (as)** obtenir son diplôme (de); **to ~ (for)** remplir les conditions requises (pour); (SPORT) se qualifier (pour)

**quality** ['kwɒlɪtɪ] n qualité f; **~ time** moments privilégiés

---

### The quality (news)papers

Les **quality (news)papers** (ou la **quality press**) englobent les journaux sérieux, quotidiens ou hebdomadaires, par opposition aux journaux populaires (**tabloid press**). Ces journaux visent un public qui souhaite des informations détaillées sur un éventail très vaste de sujets et qui est prêt à consacrer beaucoup de temps à leur lecture. Les **quality newspapers** sont en général de grand format.

---

**qualm** [kwɑːm] n doute m; scrupule m

**quandary** ['kwɒndrɪ] n: **in a ~** devant un dilemme, dans l'embarras

**quantity** ['kwɒntɪtɪ] n quantité f; **~ surveyor** n métreur m vérificateur

**quarantine** ['kwɒrəntiːn] n quarantaine f

**quarrel** ['kwɒrl] n querelle f, dispute f ♦ vi se disputer, se quereller

**quarry** ['kwɒrɪ] n (for stone) carrière f; (animal) proie f, gibier m

**quart** [kwɔːt] n ≈ litre m

**quarter** ['kwɔːtər] n quart m; (US: coin: 25 cents) quart de dollar; (of year) trimestre m; (district) quartier m ♦ vt (divide) partager en quartiers or en quatre;

**~s** npl (living ~) logement m; (MIL) quartiers mpl, cantonnement m ♦ **~ of an hour** un quart d'heure; **~ final** n quart m de finale; **~ly** adj trimestriel(le) ♦ adv tous les trois mois

**quartet(te)** [kwɔː'tet] n quatuor m; (jazz players) quartette m

**quartz** [kwɔːts] n quartz m

**quash** [kwɔʃ] vt (verdict) annuler

**quaver** ['kweɪvəʳ] vi trembler

**quay** [kiː] n (also: **~side**) quai m

**queasy** ['kwiːzɪ] adj: **to feel ~** avoir mal au cœur

**queen** [kwiːn] n reine f; (CARDS etc) dame f; **~ mother** n reine mère f

**queer** [kwɪəʳ] adj étrange, curieux (-euse); (suspicious) louche ♦ n (inf!) homosexuel m

**quell** [kwel] vt réprimer, étouffer

**quench** [kwentʃ] vt: **to ~ one's thirst** se désaltérer

**query** ['kwɪərɪ] n question f ♦ vt remettre en question, mettre en doute

**quest** [kwest] n recherche f, quête f

**question** ['kwestʃən] n question f ♦ vt (person) interroger; (plan, idea) remettre en question, mettre en doute; **beyond ~** sans aucun doute; **out of the ~** hors de question; **~able** adj discutable; **~ mark** n point m d'interrogation; **~naire** [kwestʃə'nɛəʳ] n questionnaire m

**queue** [kjuː] (BRIT) n queue f, file f ♦ vi (also: **~ up**) faire la queue

**quibble** ['kwɪbl] vi: **~ (about)** or (**over**) or (**with sth**) ergoter (sur qch)

**quick** [kwɪk] adj rapide; (agile) agile, vif (vive) ♦ n (fig) touché(e) au vif; **be ~!** dépêche-toi!; **~en** vt accélérer, presser ♦ vi s'accélérer, devenir plus rapide; **~ly** adv vite, rapidement; **~sand** n sables mouvants; **~-witted** adj à l'esprit vif

**quid** [kwɪd] (BRIT: inf) n, pl inv livre f

**quiet** ['kwaɪət] adj tranquille, calme; (voice) bas(se); (ceremony, colour) discret(-ète) ♦ n tranquillité f, calme m;

(silence) silence m ♦ vt, vi (US) = **quieten; keep ~!** tais-toi; **~en** vi (also: **~en down**) se calmer, s'apaiser ♦ vt calmer, apaiser; **~ly** adv tranquillement, calmement; (silently) silencieusement; **~ness** n tranquillité f, calme m; (silence) silence m

**quilt** [kwɪlt] n édredon m; (continental ~) couette f

**quin** [kwɪn] n abbr = **quintuplet**

**quintuplets** [kwɪn'tjuːplɪts] npl quintuplé(e)s

**quip** [kwɪp] n remarque piquante or spirituelle, pointe f

**quirk** [kwɜːk] n bizarrerie f

**quit** [kwɪt] (pt, pp quit or quitted) vt quitter; (smoking, grumbling) arrêter de ♦ vi (give up) abandonner, renoncer; (resign) démissionner

**quite** [kwaɪt] adv (rather) assez, plutôt; (entirely) complètement, tout à fait; (following a negative = almost): **that's not ~ big enough** ce n'est pas tout à fait assez grand; **I ~ understand** je comprends très bien; **~ a few of them** un assez grand nombre d'entre eux; **~ (so)!** exactement!

**quits** [kwɪts] adj: **~ (with)** quitte (envers); **let's call it ~** restons-en là

**quiver** ['kwɪvəʳ] vi trembler, frémir

**quiz** [kwɪz] n (game) jeu-concours m ♦ vt interroger; **~zical** adj narquois(e)

**quota** ['kwəʊtə] n quota m

**quotation** [kwəʊ'teɪʃən] n citation f; (estimate) devis m; **~ marks** npl guillemets mpl

**quote** [kwəʊt] n citation f; (estimate) devis m ♦ vt citer; (price) indiquer; **~s** npl guillemets mpl

# R, r

**rabbi** ['ræbaɪ] n rabbin m

**rabbit** ['ræbɪt] n lapin m; ~ **hutch** n clapier m

**rabble** ['ræbl] (pej) n populace f

**rabies** ['reɪbiːz] n rage f

**RAC** n abbr (BRIT) = **Royal Automobile Club**

**rac(c)oon** [rə'kuːn] n raton laveur

**race** [reɪs] n (species) race f; (competition, rush) course f ♦ vt (horse) faire courir ♦ vi (compete) faire la course, courir; (hurry) aller à toute vitesse, courir; (engine) s'emballer; (pulse) augmenter; ~ **car** (US) n = **racing car**; ~ **car driver** n (US) = **racing driver**; ~**course** n champ m de courses; ~**horse** n cheval m de course; ~**r** n (bike) vélo m de course; ~**track** n piste f

**racial** ['reɪʃl] adj racial(e)

**racing** ['reɪsɪŋ] n course f; ~ **car** (BRIT) n voiture f de course; ~ **driver** (BRIT) n pilote m de course

**racism** ['reɪsɪzəm] n racisme m; **racist** adj raciste ♦ n raciste m/f

**rack** [ræk] n (for guns, tools) râtelier m; (also: luggage ~) porte-bagages m inv, filet m à bagages; (also: roof ~) galerie f; (dish ~) égouttoir m ♦ vt tourmenter; **to ~ one's brains** se creuser la cervelle

**racket** ['rækɪt] n (for tennis) raquette f; (noise) tapage m, vacarme m; (swindle) escroquerie f

**racquet** ['rækɪt] n raquette f

**racy** ['reɪsɪ] adj plein(e) de verve; (slightly indecent) osé(e)

**radar** ['reɪdɑː] n radar m

**radial** ['reɪdɪəl] adj (also: ~-ply) à carcasse radiale

**radiant** ['reɪdɪənt] adj rayonnant(e)

**radiate** ['reɪdɪeɪt] vt (heat) émettre, dégager; (emotion) rayonner de ♦ vi (lines) rayonner; **radiation** [reɪdɪ'eɪʃən] n rayonnement m; (radioactive) radia-

tion f; **radiator** ['reɪdɪeɪtə'] n radiateur m

**radical** ['rædɪkl] adj radical(e)

**radii** ['reɪdɪaɪ] npl of **radius**

**radio** ['reɪdɪəu] n radio f ♦ vt appeler par radio; **on the ~** à la radio; ~**active** ['reɪdɪəʊ'æktɪv] adj radioactif(-ive); ~ **cassette** n radiocassette m; ~-**controlled** adj téléguidé(e); ~ **station** n station f de radio

**radish** ['rædɪʃ] n radis m

**radius** ['reɪdɪəs] (pl **radii**) n rayon m

**RAF** n abbr = **Royal Air Force**

**raffle** ['ræfl] n tombola f

**raft** [rɑːft] n (craft; also: life ~) radeau m

**rafter** ['rɑːftə'] n chevron m

**rag** [ræg] n chiffon m; (pej: newspaper) feuille f de chou, torchon m; (student ~) attractions organisées au profit d'œuvres de charité; ~**s** npl (torn clothes etc) haillons mpl; ~ **doll** n poupée f de chiffon

**rage** [reɪdʒ] n (fury) rage f, fureur f ♦ vi (person) être fou (folle) de rage; (storm) faire rage, être déchaîné(e); **it's all the ~** cela fait fureur

**ragged** ['rægɪd] adj (edge) inégal(e); (clothes) en loques; (appearance) déguenillé(e)

**raid** [reɪd] n (attack, also: MIL) raid m; (criminal) hold-up m inv; (by police) descente f, rafle f ♦ vt faire un raid sur ou un hold-up ou une descente dans

**rail** [reɪl] n (on stairs) rampe f; (on bridge, balcony) balustrade f; (of ship) bastingage m; (for train) rail m; ~**s** npl (track) rails mpl, voie ferrée; **by** ~ par chemin de fer, en train; ~**ing(s)** n(pl) grille f; ~**road** (US), ~**way** (BRIT) n (track) voie ferrée; (company) chemin m de fer; ~**way line** (BRIT) n ligne f de chemin de fer; ~**wayman** (BRIT) (irreg) n cheminot m; ~**way station** (BRIT) n gare f

**rain** [reɪn] n pluie f ♦ vi pleuvoir; **in the** ~ sous la pluie; **it's ~ing** il pleut; ~**bow** n arc-en-ciel m; ~**coat** n imperméable m; ~**drop** n goutte f de pluie; ~**fall** n chute f de pluie; (measurement) hauteur f des précipitations; **~forest** n forêt f tropicale humide; **~y** adj pluvieux(-euse)

**raise** [reɪz] n augmentation f ♦ vt (lift) lever; hausser; (increase) augmenter; (morale) remonter; (standards) améliorer; (question, doubt) provoquer, soulever; (cattle, family) élever; (crop) faire pousser; (funds) rassembler; (loan) obtenir; (army) lever; **to ~ one's voice** élever la voix

**raisin** ['reɪzn] n raisin sec

**rake** [reɪk] n (tool) râteau m ♦ vt (garden, leaves) ratisser

**rally** ['rælɪ] n (POL etc) meeting m, rassemblement m; (AUT) rallye m; (TENNIS) échange m ♦ vt (support) gagner ♦ vi (sick person) aller mieux; (Stock Exchange) reprendre; **~ round** vt fus venir en aide à

**RAM** [ræm] n abbr (= random access memory) mémoire vive

**ram** [ræm] n bélier m ♦ vt enfoncer; (crash into) emboutir, percuter

**ramble** ['ræmbl] n randonnée f ♦ vi (walk) se promener, faire une randonnée; (talk: also: **~ on**) discourir, pérorer; **~r** n promeneur(-euse), randonneur (-euse); (BOT) rosier grimpant; **rambling** adj (speech) décousu(e); (house) plein(e) de coins et de recoins; (BOT) grimpant(e)

**ramp** [ræmp] n (incline) rampe f; dénivellation f; **on ~, off ~** (US: AUT) bretelle f d'accès

**rampage** [ræm'peɪdʒ] n: **to be on the ~** se déchaîner

**rampant** ['ræmpənt] adj (disease etc) qui sévit

**ram raiding** [-reɪdɪŋ] n pillage d'un magasin en enfonçant la vitrine avec une voiture

**ramshackle** ['ræmʃækl] adj (house) délabré(e); (car etc) déglingué(e)

**ran** [ræn] pt of **run**

**ranch** [rɑːntʃ] n ranch m; **~er** n propriétaire m de ranch

**rancid** ['rænsɪd] adj rance

**rancour** ['ræŋkəʳ] (US **rancor**) n rancune f

**random** ['rændəm] adj fait(e) or établi(e) au hasard; (MATH) aléatoire ♦ n: **at ~** au hasard; **~ access** n (COMPUT) accès sélectif

**randy** ['rændɪ] (BRIT: inf) adj excité(e); lubrique

**rang** [ræŋ] pt of **ring**

**range** [reɪndʒ] n (of mountains) chaîne f; (of missile, voice) portée f; (of products) choix m, gamme f; (MIL: also: **shooting ~**) champ m de tir; (indoor) stand m de tir; (also: **kitchen ~**) fourneau m (de cuisine) ♦ vt (place in a line) mettre en rang, ranger ♦ vi: **to ~ over** (extend) couvrir; **to ~ from ... to** aller de ... à; **a ~ of** (series: of proposals etc) divers(e)

**ranger** ['reɪndʒəʳ] n garde forestier

**rank** [ræŋk] n (row) rangée f; (MIL) grade m; (BRIT: also: **taxi ~**) station f de taxis ♦ vi: **to ~ among** compter or se classer parmi ♦ adj (stinking) fétide, puant(e); **the ~ and file** (fig) la masse, la base

**ransack** ['rænsæk] vt fouiller (à fond); (plunder) piller

**ransom** ['rænsəm] n rançon f; **to hold to ~** (fig) exercer un chantage sur

**rant** [rænt] vi fulminer

**rap** [ræp] vt frapper sur or à; taper sur ♦ n: **~ music** rap m

**rape** [reɪp] n viol m; (BOT) colza m ♦ vt violer; **~(seed) oil** n huile f de colza

**rapid** ['ræpɪd] adj rapide; **~s** npl (GEO) rapides mpl

**rapist** ['reɪpɪst] n violeur m

**rapport** [ræ'pɔːʳ] n entente f

**rapturous** ['ræptʃərəs] adj enthousiaste, frénétique

**rare** [rɛəʳ] adj rare; (CULIN: steak) saignant(e)

**raring** ['rɛərɪŋ] adj: **~ to go** (inf) très impatient(e) de commencer

**rascal** ['rɑːskl] n vaurien m

**rash** [ræʃ] adj imprudent(e), irréfléchi(e)

**rasher** ['ræʃəʳ] *n* fine tranche (de lard)

**raspberry** ['rɑ:zbərɪ] *n* framboise *f*; ~ **bush** *n* framboisier *m*

**rasping** ['rɑ:spɪŋ] *adj*: ~ **noise** grincement *m*

**rat** [ræt] *n* rat *m*

**rate** [reɪt] *n* taux *m*; (speed) vitesse *f*, rythme *m*; (price) tarif *m* ♦ *vt* classer; évaluer; ~**s** *npl* (BRIT: tax) impôts locaux; (fees) tarifs *mpl*; **to** ~ **sb/sth as** considérer qn/qch comme; ~**able value** (BRIT) *n* valeur locative imposable; ~**payer** ['reɪtpeɪəʳ] (BRIT) *n* contribuable *m/f* (payant les impôts locaux)

**rather** ['rɑ:ðəʳ] *adv* plutôt; it's ~ **expensive** c'est assez cher; (too much) c'est un peu cher; **there's** ~ **a lot** il y en a beaucoup; **I would** ~ **go** j'aimerais mieux or je préférerais partir

**rating** ['reɪtɪŋ] *n* (assessment) évaluation *f*; (score) classement *m*; ~**s** *npl* (RADIO, TV) indice *m* d'écoute

**ratio** ['reɪʃɪəʊ] *n* proportion *f*

**ration** ['ræʃən] *n* (gen pl) ration(s) f(pl)

**rational** ['ræʃənl] *adj* raisonnable, sensé(e); (solution, reasoning) logique; ~**e** [ræʃəˈnɑ:l] *n* raisonnement *m*; ~**ize** *vt* rationaliser; (conduct) essayer d'expliquer or de motiver

**rat race** *n* foire *f* d'empoigne

**rattle** ['rætl] *n* (of door, window) battement *m*; (of coins, chain) cliquetis *m*; (of train, engine) bruit *m* de ferraille; (object: for baby) hochet *m*; (: of car, bus): **to** ~ **along** rouler dans un bruit de ferraille ♦ *vi* cliqueter; (car, bus) rouler dans un bruit de ferraille ♦ *vt* agiter (bruyamment); (unnerve) déconcerter; ~**snake** *n* serpent *m* à sonnettes

**raucous** ['rɔ:kəs] *adj* rauque; (noisy) bruyant(e), tapageur(-euse)

**rave** [reɪv] *vi* (in anger) s'emporter; (with enthusiasm) s'extasier; (MED) délirer ♦ *n* (BRIT: inf: party) rave *f*, soirée *f* techno

**raven** ['reɪvən] *n* corbeau *m*

**ravenous** ['rævənəs] *adj* affamé(e)

**ravine** [rəˈvi:n] *n* ravin *m*

**raving** ['reɪvɪŋ] *adj*: ~ **lunatic** ♦ *n* fou (folle) furieux(-euse)

**ravishing** ['rævɪʃɪŋ] *adj* enchanteur(-eresse)

**raw** [rɔ:] *adj* (uncooked) cru(e); (not processed) brut(e); (sore) à vif, irrité(e); (inexperienced) inexpérimenté(e); (weather, day) froid(e) et humide; ~ **deal** (inf) *n* sale coup *m*; ~ **material** *n* matière première

**ray** [reɪ] *n* rayon *m*; ~ **of hope** lueur *f* d'espoir

**raze** [reɪz] *vt* (also: ~ **to the ground**) raser, détruire

**razor** ['reɪzəʳ] *n* rasoir *m*; ~ **blade** *n* lame *f* de rasoir

**Rd** *abbr* = **road**

**RE** *n abbr* = **religious education**

**re** [ri:] *prep* concernant

**reach** [ri:tʃ] *n* portée *f*, atteinte *f*; (of river etc) étendue *f* ♦ *vt* atteindre; (conclusion, decision) parvenir à ♦ *vi* s'étendre, étendre le bras; **out of/within** ~ hors de/à portée; **within** ~ **of the shops** pas trop loin des or à proximité des magasins; ~ **out** *vt* tendre ♦ *vi*: **to** ~ **out (for)** allonger le bras (pour prendre)

**react** [ri:ˈækt] *vi* réagir; ~**ion** *n* réaction *f*

**reactor** [ri:ˈæktəʳ] *n* réacteur *m*.

**read** [ri:d, *pt, pp* red] (*pt, pp* **read**) *vi* lire ♦ *vt* lire; (understand) comprendre, interpréter; (study) étudier; (meter) relever; ~ **out** *vt* lire à haute voix; ~**able** *adj* facile or agréable à lire; (writing) lisible; ~**er** *n* lecteur(-trice); (BRIT: at university) chargé(e) d'enseignement; ~**ship** *n* (of paper etc) (nombre *m* de) lecteurs *mpl*

**readily** ['redɪlɪ] *adv* volontiers, avec empressement; (easily) facilement

**readiness** ['redɪnɪs] *n* empressement *m*; **in** ~ (prepared) prêt(e)

**reading** ['ri:dɪŋ] *n* lecture *f*; (under-

**ready** ['rɛdɪ] adj prêt(e); (willing) prêt, disposé(e); (available) disponible ♦ n: at the ~ (MIL) prêt à faire feu; to get ~ vi se préparer ♦ vt préparer; ~-made adj tout(e) fait(e); ~-to-wear adj prêt(e) à porter

**real** [rɪəl] adj véritable; réel(le); in ~ terms dans la réalité; ~ estate n biens fonciers or immobiliers; ~istic [rɪə'lɪstɪk] adj réaliste; ~ity [riː'ælɪtɪ] n réalité f

**realization** [rɪəlaɪ'zeɪʃən] n (awareness) prise f de conscience; (fulfilment; also: of asset) réalisation f

**realize** ['rɪəlaɪz] vt (understand) se rendre compte de; (a project, COMM: asset) réaliser

**really** ['rɪəlɪ] adv vraiment; ~? vraiment?, c'est vrai?

**realm** [rɛlm] n royaume m; (fig) domaine m

**realtor** ® ['rɪəltɔː] (US) n agent immobilier

**reap** [riːp] vt moissonner; (fig) récolter

**reappear** [riːə'pɪə] vi réapparaître, reparaître

**rear** [rɪə] adj de derrière, arrière inv (AUT: wheel etc) arrière ♦ n arrière m ♦ vt (cattle, family) élever ♦ vi (also: ~ up: animal) se cabrer; ~guard n (MIL) arrière-garde f; ~-view mirror n (AUT) rétroviseur m

**reason** ['riːzn] n raison f ♦ vi: to ~ with sb raisonner qn, faire entendre raison à qn; to have ~ to think avoir lieu de penser; it stands to ~ that il va sans dire que; ~able adj raisonnable; (not bad) acceptable; ~ably adv raisonnablement; ~ing n raisonnement m

**reassurance** [riːə'ʃuərəns] n réconfort m; (factual) assurance f, garantie f

**reassure** [riːə'ʃuə] vt rassurer

**rebate** ['riːbeɪt] n (on tax etc) dégrèvement m

**rebel** [n 'rɛbl, vb rɪ'bɛl] n rebelle m/f ♦ vi se rebeller, se révolter; ~lious [rɪ'bɛljəs] adj rebelle

**rebound** [vb rɪ'baund, n 'riːbaund] vi (ball) rebondir ♦ n rebond m; to marry on the ~ se marier immédiatement après une déception amoureuse

**rebuff** [rɪ'bʌf] n rebuffade f

**rebuke** [rɪ'bjuːk] vt réprimander

**rebut** [rɪ'bʌt] vt réfuter

**recall** [vb rɪ'kɔːl, n 'riːkɔl] vt rappeler; (remember) se rappeler, se souvenir de ♦ n rappel m; (ability to remember) mémoire f

**recant** [rɪ'kænt] vi se rétracter; (REL) abjurer

**recap** ['riːkæp], **recapitulate** [riːkə'pɪtjuleɪt] vt, vi récapituler

**rec'd** abbr = received

**recede** [rɪ'siːd] vi (tide) descendre; (disappear) disparaître peu à peu; (memory, hope) s'estomper; **receding** adj (chin) fuyant(e); **receding hairline** front dégarni

**receipt** [rɪ'siːt] n (document) reçu m; (for parcel etc) accusé m de réception; (act of receiving) réception f; ~s npl (COMM) recettes fpl

**receive** [rɪ'siːv] vt recevoir; ~r n (TEL) récepteur m, combiné m; (RADIO) récepteur m; (of stolen goods) receleur m; (LAW) administrateur m judiciaire

**recent** ['riːsnt] adj récent(e); ~ly adv récemment

**receptacle** [rɪ'sɛptɪkl] n récipient m

**reception** [rɪ'sɛpʃən] n réception f; (welcome) accueil m, réception; ~ desk n réception f; ~ist n réceptionniste m/f

**recess** [rɪ'sɛs] n (in room) renfoncement m, alcôve f; (secret place) recoin m; (POL etc: holiday) vacances fpl

**recession** [rɪ'sɛʃən] n récession f

**recipe** ['rɛsɪpɪ] n recette f

**recipient** [rɪ'sɪpɪənt] n (of payment) bénéficiaire m/f; (of letter) destinataire m/f

**recital** [rɪ'saɪtl] n récital m

**recite** [rɪ'saɪt] vt (poem) réciter

**reckless** ['rɛkləs] adj (driver etc) imprudent(e)

**reckon** ['rɛkən] vt (count) calculer, compter; (think): **I ~ that ...** je pense que ...; **~ on** fus compter sur, s'attendre à; **~ing** n compte m, calcul m; estimation f

**reclaim** [rɪ'kleɪm] vt (demand back) réclamer (le remboursement ou la restitution de); (land: from sea) assécher; (waste materials) récupérer

**recline** [rɪ'klaɪn] vi être allongé(e) or étendu(e); **reclining** adj (seat) à dossier réglable

**recluse** [rɪ'kluːs] n reclus(e), ermite m

**recognition** [rɛkəg'nɪʃən] n reconnaissance f; **to gain ~** être reconnu(e); **transformed beyond ~** méconnaissable

**recognizable** ['rɛkəgnaɪzəbl] adj: **~ (by)** reconnaissable (à)

**recognize** ['rɛkəgnaɪz] vt: **to ~ (by/as)** reconnaître (à/comme étant)

**recoil** [vb rɪ'kɔɪl, n 'riːkɔɪl] vi (person): **to ~ (from sth/doing sth)** reculer (devant qch/l'idée de faire qch) ♦ n (of gun) recul m

**recollect** [rɛkə'lɛkt] vt se rappeler, se souvenir de; **~ion** n souvenir m

**recommend** [rɛkə'mɛnd] vt recommander

**reconcile** ['rɛkənsaɪl] vt (two people) réconcilier; (two facts) concilier, accorder; **to ~ o.s.** se résigner à

**recondition** [riːkən'dɪʃən] vt remettre à neuf; réviser entièrement

**reconnoitre** [rɛkə'nɔɪtə*] (US **reconnoiter**) vt (MIL) reconnaître

**reconsider** [riːkən'sɪdə*] vt reconsidérer

**reconstruct** [riːkən'strʌkt] vt (building) reconstruire; (crime, policy, system) reconstituer

**record** [n 'rɛkɔːd, vb rɪ'kɔːd] n rapport m, récit m; (of meeting etc) procès-verbal m; (register) registre m; (file) dossier m; (also: **criminal ~**) casier m judiciaire; (MUS: disc) disque m; (SPORT) record m; (COMPUT) article m ♦ vt (set down) noter; (MUS: song etc) enregistrer; **in ~ time** en un temps record inv; **~ off the ~** adj officieux(-euse) ♦ adv officieusement; **~ card** n (in file) fiche f; **~ed delivery** n (BRIT: POST): **~ed delivery letter** etc lettre etc recommandée; **~er** n (MUS) flûte f à bec; **~ holder** n (SPORT) détenteur(-trice) du record; **~ing** n (MUS) enregistrement m; **~ player** n tourne-disque m

**recount** [rɪ'kaʊnt] vt raconter

**re-count** ['riːkaʊnt] n (POL: of votes) deuxième compte m

**recoup** [rɪ'kuːp] vt: **to ~ one's losses** récupérer ce qu'on a perdu, se refaire

**recourse** [rɪ'kɔːs] n: **to have ~ to** avoir recours à

**recover** [rɪ'kʌvə*] vt récupérer ♦ vi (from (illness) se rétablir (de); (from shock) se remettre (de); **~y** n récupération f; rétablissement m; (ECON) redressement m

**recreation** [rɛkrɪ'eɪʃən] n récréation f, détente f; **~al** adj pour la détente, récréatif(-ive)

**recruit** [rɪ'kruːt] n recrue f ♦ vt recruter

**rectangle** ['rɛktæŋgl] n rectangle m

**rectangular** [rɛk'tæŋgjʊlə*] adj rectangulaire

**rectify** ['rɛktɪfaɪ] vt (error) rectifier, corriger

**rector** ['rɛktə*] n (REL) pasteur m

**recuperate** [rɪ'kjuːpəreɪt] vi récupérer; (from illness) se rétablir

**recur** [rɪ'kəː*] vi se reproduire; (symptoms) réapparaître; **~rence** n répétition f; réapparition f; **~rent** adj périodique, fréquent(e)

**recycle** [riː'saɪkl] vt recycler; **recycling** n recyclage m

**red** [rɛd] n rouge m; (POL: pej) rouge m/f ♦ adj rouge; (hair) roux (rousse); **in the ~** (account) à découvert; (business) en déficit; **~ carpet treatment** n réception f en grande pompe; **R~ Cross**

Croix-Rouge f; **~currant** n groseille f
(rouge); **~den** vt, vi rougir
**redecorate** [riː'dekəreɪt] vt (with wallpaper) retapisser; (with paint) refaire les peintures
**redeem** [rɪ'diːm] vt (debt) rembourser; (sth in pawn) dégager; (fig, also REL) racheter; **~ing** adj (feature) qui sauve, qui rachète (le reste)
**redeploy** [riːdɪ'plɔɪ] vt (resources) réorganiser
**red:** **~haired** adj roux (rousse); **~handed** adj: **to be caught ~handed** être pris(e) en flagrant délit ou la main dans le sac; **~head** n roux (rousse); **~ herring** n (fig) diversion f, fausse piste; **~hot** adj chauffé(e) au rouge, brûlant(e)
**redirect** [riːdaɪ'rekt] vt (mail) faire suivre
**red light** n: **to go through a ~** (AUT) brûler un feu rouge; **red-light district** n quartier m des prostituées
**redo** [riː'duː] (irreg) vt refaire
**redress** [rɪ'dres] n réparation f ♦ vt réparer
**red:** **R~ Sea** n mer Rouge f; **~skin** n Peau-Rouge m/f; **~ tape** n (fig) paperasserie (administrative)
**reduce** [rɪ'djuːs] vt réduire; (lower) abaisser; **"~ speed now"** (AUT) "ralentir"; **reduction** [rɪ'dʌkʃən] n réduction f; (discount) rabais m
**redundancy** [rɪ'dʌndənsɪ] (BRIT) n licenciement m, mise f au chômage
**redundant** [rɪ'dʌndnt] adj (BRIT: worker) mis(e) au chômage, licencié(e); (detail, object) superflu(e); **to be made ~** être licencié(e), être mis(e) au chômage
**reed** [riːd] n (BOT) roseau m; (MUS: of clarinet etc) hanche f
**reef** [riːf] n (at sea) récif m, écueil m
**reek** [riːk] vi: **to ~ (of)** puer, empester
**reel** [riːl] n bobine f; (FISHING) moulinet m; (CINEMA) bande f; (dance) quadrille écossais ♦ vi (sway) chanceler; **~ in** vt

(fish, line) ramener
**ref** [ref] (inf) n abbr (= referee) arbitre m
**refectory** [rɪ'fektərɪ] n réfectoire m
**refer** [rɪ'fɜːʳ] vt: **to ~ sb to** (inquirer: for information, patient: to specialist) adresser qn à; (reader: to text) renvoyer qn à; (dispute, decision): **to ~ sth to** soumettre qch à ♦ vi: **to ~** (allude to) parler de, faire allusion à; (consult) se reporter à
**referee** [refə'riː] n arbitre m; (BRIT: for job application) répondant(e)
**reference** [refrəns] n référence f, renvoi m; (mention) allusion f, mention f; (for job application: letter) références, lettre f de recommandation; **with ~ to** (COMM: in letter) me référant à, suite à; **~ book** n ouvrage m de référence
**refill** vt [riː'fɪl], n ['riːfɪl] vt remplir à nouveau; (pen, lighter etc) recharger ♦ n (for pen etc) recharge f
**refine** [rɪ'faɪn] vt (sugar, oil) raffiner; (taste) affiner; (theory, idea) fignoler (inf); **~d** adj (person, taste) raffiné(e); **~ry** n raffinerie f
**reflect** [rɪ'flekt] vt (light, image) réfléchir, refléter; (fig) refléter ♦ vi (think) réfléchir, méditer; **it ~s badly on him** cela le discrédite; **it ~s well on him** c'est tout à son honneur; **~ion** n réflexion f; (image) reflet m; (criticism): **~ion on** critique f de; atteinte f à; **on ~ion** réflexion faite
**reflex** ['riːfleks] adj réflexe ♦ n réflexe m; **~ive** [rɪ'fleksɪv] adj (LING) réfléchi(e)
**reform** [rɪ'fɔːm] n réforme f ♦ vt réformer; **~atory** [rɪ'fɔːmətən] (US) n ≃ centre m d'éducation surveillée
**refrain** [rɪ'freɪn] vi: **to ~ from doing** s'abstenir de faire ♦ n refrain m
**refresh** [rɪ'freʃ] vt rafraîchir; (subj: sleep) reposer; **~er course** (BRIT) n cours m de recyclage; **~ing** adj (drink) rafraîchissant(e); (sleep) réparateur(-trice); **~ments** npl rafraîchissements mpl
**refrigerator** [rɪ'frɪdʒəreɪtəʳ] n réfrigérateur m, frigidaire m ® m

**refuel** ['ri:fjuəl] vi se ravitailler en carburant

**refuge** ['refju:dʒ] n refuge m; **to take ~ in** se réfugier dans; **~e** [refju'dʒi:] n réfugié(e)

**refund** [n 'ri:fʌnd, vb ri'fʌnd] n remboursement m ♦ vt rembourser

**refurbish** [ri:'fɜ:bɪʃ] vt remettre à neuf

**refusal** [ri'fju:zəl] n refus m; **to have first ~ on** avoir droit de préemption sur

**refuse¹** [ri'fju:z] vt, vi refuser

**refuse²** ['refju:s] n ordures fpl, détritus mpl; **~ collection** n ramassage m d'ordures

**regain** [ri'geɪn] vt regagner; retrouver

**regal** ['ri:gl] adj royal(e)

**regard** [ri'gɑ:d] n respect m, estime f, considération f ♦ vt considérer; **to give one's ~s to** faire ses amitiés à; **"with kindest ~s"** "bien amicalement"; **as ~s, with ~ to** = **regarding**; **~ing** prep en ce qui concerne; **~less** adv quand même; **~less of** sans se soucier de

**régime** [rei'ʒi:m] n régime m

**regiment** ['redʒimənt] n régiment m; **~al** [redʒi'mentl] adj d'un ou du régiment

**region** ['ri:dʒən] n région f; **in the ~ of** (fig) aux alentours de; **~al** adj régional(e)

**register** ['redʒistə'] n registre m; (also: **electoral ~**) liste électorale ♦ vt enregistrer; (birth, death) déclarer; (vehicle) immatriculer; (POST: letter) envoyer en recommandé; (subj: instrument) marquer ♦ vi s'inscrire; (at hotel) signer le registre; (make impression) être (bien) compris(e); **~ed** adj (letter, parcel) recommandé(e); **~ed trademark** n marque déposée; **registrar** ['redʒistrɑ:'] n officier m de l'état civil; **registration** [redʒis'treɪʃən] n enregistrement m; (BRIT: AUT: also: **registration number**) numéro m d'immatriculation

**registry** ['redʒistri] n bureau m de l'enregistrement; **~ office** (BRIT) n bureau

m de l'état civil; **to get married in a ~ office** ≈ se marier à la mairie

**regret** [ri'gret] n regret m ♦ vt regretter; **~fully** adv à ou avec regret

**regular** ['regjulə'] adj régulier(-ère); (usual) habituel(le); (soldier) de métier ♦ n (client etc) habitué(e); **~ly** adv régulièrement

**regulate** ['regjuleit] vt régler; **regulation** [regju'leiʃən] n (rule) règlement m; (adjustment) réglage m

**rehabilitation** ['ri:əbili'teiʃən] n (of offender) réinsertion f; (of addict) réadaptation f

**rehearsal** [ri'hɜ:səl] n répétition f

**rehearse** [ri'hɜ:s] vt répéter

**reign** [rein] n règne m ♦ vi régner

**reimburse** [ri:im'bɜ:s] vt rembourser

**rein** [rein] n (for horse) rêne f

**reindeer** ['reindiə'], n pl inv renne m

**reinforce** [ri:in'fɔ:s] vt renforcer; **~d concrete** n béton armé; **~ments** npl (MIL) renfort(s) m(pl)

**reinstate** [ri:in'steit] vt rétablir, réintégrer

**reject** [n 'ri:dʒekt, vb ri'dʒekt] n (COMM) article m de rebut ♦ vt refuser; (idea) rejeter; **~ion** n rejet m, refus m

**rejoice** [ri'dʒɔis] vi: **to ~ (at or over)** se réjouir (de)

**rejuvenate** [ri'dʒu:vəneit] vt rajeunir

**relapse** [ri'læps] n (MED) rechute f

**relate** [ri'leit] vt (tell) raconter; (connect) établir un rapport entre ♦ vi: **this ~s to** ceci se rapporte à; **to ~ to sb** entretenir des rapports avec qn; **~d** adj apparenté(e); **relating to** prep concernant

**relation** [ri'leiʃən] n (person) parent(e); (link) rapport m, lien m; **~ship** n rapport m, lien m; (personal ties) relations fpl, rapports; (also: **family ~ship**) lien de parenté

**relative** ['relətiv] n parent(e) ♦ adj relatif(-ive); **all her ~s** toute sa famille; **~ly** adv relativement

**relax** [ri'læks] vi (muscle) se relâcher;

*(person: unwind)* se détendre ♦ vt re-lâcher; *(mind, person)* détendre; **~ation** [riːlækˈseɪʃən] n relâchement m; *(of mind)* relaxation f; *(recreation)* détente f, délassement m; **~ed** adj détendu(e); **~ing** adj délassant(e)

**relay** [n 'riːleɪ, vb riːˈleɪ] n *(SPORT)* course f de relais f; *(message)* retransmettre, relayer

**release** [rɪˈliːs] n *(from prison, obligation)* libération f; *(of gas etc)* émission f; *(of film etc)* sortie f; *(new recording)* disque m ♦ vt *(prisoner)* libérer; *(gas etc)* émettre, dégager; *(free: from wreckage etc)* dégager; *(TECH: catch, spring etc)* faire jouer; *(book, film)* sortir; *(report, news)* rendre public, publier

**relegate** ['relɪɡeɪt] vt reléguer; *(BRIT: SPORT)*: **to be ~d** descendre dans une division inférieure

**relent** [rɪˈlent] vi se laisser fléchir; **~less** adj implacable; *(unceasing)* continuel(le)

**relevant** ['reləvənt] adj *(question)* pertinent(e); *(fact)* significatif(-ive); *(information)* utile; **~ to** ayant rapport à, approprié à

**reliable** [rɪˈlaɪəbl] adj *(person, firm)* sérieux(-euse), fiable; *(method, machine)* fiable; *(news, information)* sûr(e); **reliably** adv: **to be reliably informed** savoir de source sûre

**reliance** [rɪˈlaɪəns] n: **~ (on)** *(person)* confiance f en); *(drugs, promises)* besoin m (de), dépendance f (de)

**relic** ['relɪk] n *(REL)* relique f; *(of the past)* vestige m

**relief** [rɪˈliːf] n *(from pain, anxiety etc)* soulagement m; *(help, supplies)* secours m(pl); *(ART, GEO)* relief m

**relieve** [rɪˈliːv] vt *(pain, patient)* soulager; *(fear, worry)* dissiper; *(bring help)* secourir; *(take over from: gen)* relayer; *(: guard)* relever; **to ~ sb of sth** débarrasser qn de qch; **to ~ o.s.** se soulager

**religion** [rɪˈlɪdʒən] n religion f; **religious** adj religieux(-euse); *(book)* de piété

**relinquish** [rɪˈlɪŋkwɪʃ] vt abandonner; *(plan, habit)* renoncer à

**relish** ['relɪʃ] n *(CULIN)* condiment m; *(enjoyment)* délectation f; *(of food etc)* savourer; **to ~ doing** se délecter à faire

**relocate** [riːləuˈkeɪt] vt installer ailleurs ♦ vi déménager, s'installer ailleurs

**reluctance** [rɪˈlʌktəns] n répugnance f

**reluctant** [rɪˈlʌktənt] adj peu disposé(e), qui hésite; **~ly** adv à contrecœur

**rely on** [rɪˈlaɪ-] vt fus *(be dependent)* dépendre de; *(trust)* compter sur

**remain** [rɪˈmeɪn] vi rester; **~der** n reste m; **~ing** adj qui reste; **~s** npl restes mpl

**remake** ['riːmeɪk] n *(CINEMA)* remake m

**remand** [rɪˈmɑːnd] n: **on ~** en détention préventive ♦ vt: **to be ~ed in custody** être placé(e) en détention préventive

**remark** [rɪˈmɑːk] n remarque f, observation f ♦ vt *(faire)* remarquer, dire; **~able** adj remarquable; **~ably** adv remarquablement

**remarry** [riːˈmærɪ] vi se remarier

**remedial** [rɪˈmiːdɪəl] adj *(tuition, classes)* de rattrapage; **~ exercises** gymnastique corrective

**remedy** ['remədɪ] n: **~ (for)** remède m (contre à) ♦ vt remédier à

**remember** [rɪˈmembə*] vt se rappeler, se souvenir de; *(send greetings)*: **~ me to him** saluez-le de ma part; **remembrance** n souvenir m; mémoire f; **Remembrance Day** n le jour de l'Armistice

---

**Remembrance Sunday**

Remembrance Sunday ou Remembrance Day est le dimanche le plus proche du 11 novembre, jour où la Première Guerre mondiale a officiellement pris fin, et rend hommage aux victimes des deux guerres mondiales. À cette occasion, un silence de deux minutes est observé à 11 h, heure de la signature de l'armistice avec l'Alle-

magne en 1918; certains membres de
la famille royale et du gouvernement
déposent des gerbes de coquelicots au
cénotaphe de Whitehall, et des cou-
ronnes sont placées sur les monuments aux morts dans toute la
Grande-Bretagne; par ailleurs, les gens
portent des coquelicots artificiels fabri-
qués et vendus par des membres de la
légion britannique blessés au combat,
au profit des blessés de guerre et de
leur famille.

**remind** [rɪ'maɪnd] vt: **to ~ sb of** rappeler à qn; **to ~ sb to do** faire penser
à qn à faire, rappeler à qn qu'il doit faire; **~er** n (souvenir) souvenir m; (letter)
rappel m

**reminisce** [remɪ'nɪs] vi: **to ~ (about)**
évoquer ses souvenirs (de); **~nt** adj: **to
be ~nt of** rappeler, faire penser à

**remiss** [rɪ'mɪs] adj négligent(e); **~ion** n
(of illness, sins) rémission f; (of debt,
prison sentence) remise f

**remit** [rɪ'mɪt] vt (send: money) envoyer;
**~tance** n paiement m

**remnant** ['remnənt] n reste m, restant
m; (of cloth) coupon m; **~s** npl (COMM)
fins fpl de série

**remorse** [rɪ'mɔːs] n remords m; **~ful**
adj (plein(e) de remords; **~less** adj (fig)
impitoyable

**remote** [rɪ'məʊt] adj éloigné(e), loin-
tain(e); (person) distant(e); (possibility)
vague; **~ control** n télécommande f;
**~ly** adv au loin; (slightly) très vaguement

**remould** ['riːməʊld] n (BRIT) (tyre) pneu
rechapé

**removable** [rɪ'muːvəbl] adj (detachable) amovible

**removal** [rɪ'muːvəl] n (taking away)
enlèvement m; suppression f; (BRIT: from
house) déménagement m; (from office:
dismissal) renvoi m; (of stain) nettoyage
m; (MED) ablation f; **~ van** n camion m de déménagement

**remove** [rɪ'muːv] vt enlever, retirer;
(employee) renvoyer; (stain) faire partir;
(abuse) supprimer; (doubt) chasser

**render** ['rendə'] vt rendre; **~ing** n (MUS
etc) interprétation f

**rendezvous** ['rɒndɪvuː] n rendez-vous
m inv

**renew** [rɪ'njuː] vt renouveler; (negotiations) reprendre; (acquaintance) renouer; **~able** adj (energy) renouvelable;
**~al** n renouvellement m; reprise f

**renounce** [rɪ'naʊns] vt renoncer à

**renovate** ['renəveɪt] vt rénover; (art
work) restaurer

**renown** [rɪ'naʊn] n renommée f; **~ed**
adj renommé(e)

**rent** [rent] n loyer m ♦ vt louer; **~al** n
(for television, car) (prix m de) location f

**reorganize** [riː'ɔːɡənaɪz] vt réorganiser

**rep** [rep] n abbr = **representative**; **repertory**

**repair** [rɪ'peə'] n réparation f ♦ vt réparer; **in good/bad ~** en bon/mauvais
état; **~ kit** n trousse f de réparation

**repatriate** [riː'pætrɪeɪt] vt rapatrier

**repay** [riː'peɪ] (irreg) vt (money, creditor)
rembourser; (sb's efforts) récompenser;
**~ment** n remboursement m

**repeal** [rɪ'piːl] n (of law) abrogation f
♦ vt (law) abroger

**repeat** [rɪ'piːt] n (RADIO, TV) reprise f ♦ vt
répéter; (COMM: order) renouveler;
(SCOL: a class) redoubler ♦ vi répéter;
**~edly** adv souvent, à plusieurs reprises

**repel** [rɪ'pel] vt repousser; **~lent** adj
repoussant(e) ♦ n: **insect ~lent** insectifu-
ge m

**repent** [rɪ'pent] vi: **to ~ (of)** se repentir
(de); **~ance** n repentir m

**repertory** ['repətəri] n (also: ~ theatre)
théâtre m de répertoire

**repetition** [repɪ'tɪʃən] n répétition f

**repetitive** [rɪ'petɪtɪv] adj (movement,
work) répétitif(-ive); (speech) plein(e) de
redites

**replace** [rɪ'pleɪs] vt (put back) remettre,
replacer; (take the place of) remplacer;

~**ment** n (substitution) remplacement m; (person) remplaçant(e)
**replay** ['ri:pleɪ] n (of match) match rejoué, (of tape, film) répétition f
**replenish** [rɪ'plenɪʃ] vt (glass) remplir (de nouveau); (stock etc) réapprovisionner
**replica** ['replɪkə] n réplique f, copie exacte
**reply** [rɪ'plaɪ] n réponse f ♦ vi répondre
**report** [rɪ'pɔːt] n (account) rapport m, (PRESS etc) reportage m; (BRIT: also: **school** ~) bulletin m (scolaire); (of gun) détonation f ♦ vt rapporter, faire un compte rendu de; (PRESS etc) faire un reportage sur; (bring to notice: occurrence) signaler ♦ vi (make a ~) faire un rapport (or un reportage); (present o.s.): **to** ~ **(to sb)** se présenter (chez qn); (be responsible to): **to** ~ **to sb** être sous les ordres de qn; ~ **card** (US, SCOTTISH) n bulletin m scolaire; ~**edly** adv: **she is** ~**edly living in** ... elle habiterait ...; **he** ~**edly told them to** ... il leur aurait ordonné de ...; ~**er** n reporter m
**repose** [rɪ'pəʊz] n: **in** ~ en or au repos
**represent** [reprɪ'zent] vt représenter; (view, belief) présenter, expliquer; (describe): **to** ~ **sth as** présenter or décrire qch comme; ~**ation** [reprɪzen'teɪʃən] n représentation f, ~**ations** npl (protest) démarche f, ~**ative** [reprɪ'zentətɪv] n représentant(e); (US: POL) député m ♦ adj représentatif(-ive), caractéristique
**repress** [rɪ'pres] vt réprimer; ~**ion** n répression f
**reprieve** [rɪ'priːv] n (LAW) grâce f; (fig) sursis m, délai m
**reprisal** [rɪ'praɪzl] n: ~**s** npl représailles fpl
**reproach** [rɪ'prəʊtʃ] vt: **to** ~ **sb with sth** reprocher qch à qn; ~**ful** adj de reproche
**reproduce** [riːprə'djuːs] vt reproduire ♦ vi se reproduire; **reproduction** [riːprə'dʌkʃən] n reproduction f
**reproof** [rɪ'pruːf] n reproche m

**reptile** ['reptaɪl] n reptile m
**republic** [rɪ'pʌblɪk] n république f; ~**an** adj républicain(e)
**repudiate** [rɪ'pjuːdɪeɪt] vt répudier, rejeter
**repulsive** [rɪ'pʌlsɪv] adj repoussant(e), répulsif(-ive)
**reputable** ['repjʊtəbl] adj de bonne réputation; (occupation) honorable
**reputation** [repjʊ'teɪʃən] n réputation f
**reputed** [rɪ'pjuːtɪd] adj (supposed) supposé(e); ~**ly** adv d'après ce qu'on dit
**request** [rɪ'kwest] n demande f; (formal) requête f ♦ vt: **to** ~ **(of or from sb)** demander (à qn); ~ **stop** (BRIT) n (for bus) arrêt facultatif
**require** [rɪ'kwaɪə*] vt (need: subj: person) avoir besoin de; (: thing, situation) demander; (want) exiger; (order): **to** ~ **sb to do sth/of sb** exiger que qn fasse qch/qch de qn; ~**ment** n exigence f; besoin m; condition requise
**requisition** [rekwɪ'zɪʃən] n: ~ **(for)** demande f (de) ♦ vt (MIL) réquisitionner
**rescue** ['reskjuː] n (from accident) sauvetage m; (help) secours mpl ♦ vt sauver; ~ **party** n équipe f de sauvetage; ~**r** n sauveteur m
**research** [rɪ'sɜːtʃ] n recherche(s) f(pl) ♦ vt faire des recherches sur
**resemblance** [rɪ'zembləns] n ressemblance f
**resemble** [rɪ'zembl] vt ressembler à
**resent** [rɪ'zent] vt être contrarié(e) par; ~**ful** adj irrité(e), plein(e) de ressentiment; ~**ment** n ressentiment m
**reservation** [rezə'veɪʃən] n (booking) réservation f; (doubt) réserve f; (for tribe) réserve f; **to make a** ~ **(in a hotel/a restaurant/on a plane)** réserver or retenir une chambre/une table/une place
**reserve** [rɪ'zɜːv] n réserve f; (SPORT) remplaçant(e); (seats etc) réserve, retenir; ~**s** npl (MIL) réservistes mpl; **in** ~ en réserve; ~**d** adj réservé(e)

**reshuffle** [riːˈʃʌfl] n: **Cabinet ~** (POL) remaniement ministériel

**residence** [ˈrezɪdəns] n résidence f; **~ permit** (BRIT) n permis m de séjour

**resident** [ˈrezɪdənt] n résident(e) ♦ adj résidant(e); [rezɪˈdenʃəl] adj résidentiel(le); (course) avec hébergement sur place; **~ial school** n internat m

**residue** [ˈrezɪdjuː] n reste m, (CHEM, PHYSICS) résidu m

**resign** [rɪˈzaɪn] vt (one's post) démissionner de ♦ vi démissionner; **to ~ o.s. to** se résigner à; **~ation** [rezɪgˈneɪʃən] n (of post) démission f; (state of mind) résignation f; **~ed** adj résigné(e)

**resilient** [rɪˈzɪlɪənt] adj (material) élastique; (person) qui réagit, qui a du ressort

**resist** [rɪˈzɪst] vt résister à; **~ance** n résistance f

**resit** [riːˈsɪt] vt (exam) repasser à deuxième session f (d'un examen)

**resolution** [rezəˈluːʃən] n résolution f

**resolve** [rɪˈzɔlv] n résolution f ♦ vt (problem) résoudre ♦ vi: **to ~ to do** résoudre or décider de faire

**resort** [rɪˈzɔːt] n (seaside town) station f balnéaire; (ski ~) station de ski; (recourse) recours m ♦ vi: **to ~ to** avoir recours à; **in the last ~** en dernier ressort

**resounding** [rɪˈzaʊndɪŋ] adj retentissant(e)

**resource** [rɪˈsɔːs] n ressource f; **~s** npl (supplies, wealth etc) ressources fpl; **~ful** adj ingénieux(-euse), débrouillard(e)

**respect** [rɪsˈpekt] n respect m ♦ vt respecter; **~s** npl (compliments) respects, hommages mpl; **with ~ to** en ce qui concerne; **in this ~** à cet égard; **~able** adj respectable; **~ful** adj respectueux(-euse); **~ively** adv respectivement

**respite** [ˈrespaɪt] n répit m

**respond** [rɪsˈpɔnd] vi répondre; (react) réagir; **response** n réponse f, réaction f

**responsibility** [rɪspɔnsɪˈbɪlɪtɪ] n responsabilité f

**responsible** [rɪsˈpɔnsɪbl] adj (liable): **~ (for)** responsable (de); (person) digne de confiance; (job) qui comporte des responsabilités

**responsive** [rɪsˈpɔnsɪv] adj qui réagit; (person) qui n'est pas réservé(e) or indifférent(e)

**rest** [rest] n repos m; (stop) arrêt m, pause f; (MUS) silence m; (support) support m, appui m; (remainder) reste m, restant m ♦ vi se reposer; (be supported): **to ~ on** appuyer or reposer sur; (remain) rester ♦ vt (lean): **to ~ sth on/against** appuyer qch sur/contre; **the ~ of them** les autres; **it ~s with him to ...** c'est à lui de ...

**restaurant** [ˈrestərɔŋ] n restaurant m; **~ car** (BRIT) n wagon-restaurant m

**restful** [ˈrestful] adj reposant(e)

**restive** [ˈrestɪv] adj agité(e), impatient(e); (horse) rétif(-ive)

**restless** [ˈrestləs] adj agité(e)

**restoration** [restəˈreɪʃən] n restauration f; restitution f; rétablissement m

**restore** [rɪsˈtɔː] vt (building) restaurer; (sth stolen) restituer; (peace, health) rétablir; **to ~ to** (former state) ramener à

**restrain** [rɪsˈtreɪn] vt contenir; (person): **to ~ (from doing)** retenir (de faire); **~ed** adj (style) sobre; (manner) mesuré(e); **~t** n (restriction) contrainte f; (moderation) retenue f

**restrict** [rɪsˈtrɪkt] vt restreindre, limiter; **~ion** n restriction f, limitation f

**rest room** (US) n toilettes fpl

**result** [rɪˈzʌlt] n résultat m ♦ vi: **to ~ in** aboutir à, se terminer par; **as a ~ of** à la suite de

**resume** [rɪˈzjuːm] vt, vi (work, journey) reprendre

**résumé** [ˈreɪzjuːmeɪ] n résumé m; (US) curriculum vitae m

**resumption** [rɪˈzʌmpʃən] n reprise f

**resurgence** [rɪˈsɜːdʒəns] n (of energy, activity) regain m

**resurrection** [rezəˈrekʃən] n résurrection f

**resuscitate** [rɪˈsʌsɪteɪt] vt (MED) réanimer

**retail** [ˈriːteɪl] adj de or au détail ♦ adv au détail; **~er** n détaillant(e); **~ price** n prix m de détail

**retain** [rɪˈteɪn] vt (keep) garder, conserver; **~er** n (fee) acompte m, provision f

**retaliate** [rɪˈtælɪeɪt] vi: **to ~ (against)** se venger (de); **retaliation** [rɪtælɪˈeɪʃən] n représailles fpl, vengeance f

**retarded** [rɪˈtɑːdɪd] adj retardé(e)

**retch** [retʃ] vi avoir des haut-le-cœur

**retentive** [rɪˈtentɪv] adj: **~ memory** excellente mémoire

**retina** [ˈretɪnə] n rétine f

**retire** [rɪˈtaɪə*] vi (give up work) prendre sa retraite; (withdraw) se retirer, partir; (go to bed) (aller) se coucher; **~d** adj (person) retraité(e); **~ment** n retraite f; **retiring** adj (shy) réservé(e); (leaving) sortant(e)

**retort** [rɪˈtɔːt] vi riposter

**retrace** [riːˈtreɪs] vt: **to ~ one's steps** revenir sur ses pas

**retract** [rɪˈtrækt] vt (statement, claws) rétracter; (undercarriage, aerial) rentrer, escamoter

**retrain** [riːˈtreɪn] vt (worker) recycler

**retread** [ˈriːtred] n (tyre) pneu rechapé

**retreat** [rɪˈtriːt] n retraite f ♦ vi battre en retraite

**retribution** [retrɪˈbjuːʃən] n châtiment m

**retrieval** [rɪˈtriːvəl] n (see vb) récupération f; réparation f

**retrieve** [rɪˈtriːv] vt (sth lost) récupérer; (situation, honour) sauver; (error, loss) réparer; **~r** n chien m d'arrêt

**retrospect** [ˈretrəspekt] n: **in ~** rétrospectivement, après coup; **~ive** [retrəˈspektɪv] adj rétrospectif(-ive); (law) rétroactif(-ive)

**return** [rɪˈtɜːn] n (going or coming back) retour m; (of sth stolen) restitution f; (FINANCE: from land, shares) rendement m, rapport m ♦ cpd (journey) de retour; (BRIT: ticket) aller et retour; (match) retour ♦ vi (come back) revenir; (go back) retourner ♦ vt rendre; (bring back) rapporter; (send back; also: mail) renvoyer; (put back) remettre; (POL: candidate) élire; **~s** npl (COMM) recettes fpl; (FINANCE) bénéfices mpl; **in ~ (for)** en échange (de); **by ~ (of post)** par retour (du courrier); **many happy ~s (of the day)!** bon anniversaire!

**reunion** [riːˈjuːnɪən] n réunion f

**reunite** [riːjuːˈnaɪt] vt réunir

**reuse** [riːˈjuːz] vt réutiliser

**rev** [rev] n abbr (AUT: = revolution) tour m ♦ vt (also: rev up) emballer

**revamp** [riːˈvæmp] vt (firm, system etc) réorganiser

**reveal** [rɪˈviːl] vt (make known) révéler; (display) laisser voir; **~ing** adj révélateur(-trice); (dress) au décolleté généreux or suggestif

**revel** [ˈrevl] vi: **to ~ in sth/in doing** se délecter de qch/à faire

**revenge** [rɪˈvendʒ] n vengeance f; **to take ~ on** (enemy) se venger sur

**revenue** [ˈrevənjuː] n revenu m

**reverberate** [rɪˈvɜːbəreɪt] vi (sound) retentir, se répercuter; (fig: shock etc) se propager

**reverence** [ˈrevərəns] n vénération f, révérence f

**Reverend** [ˈrevərənd] adj (in titles): **the ~ John Smith** (Anglican) le révérend John Smith; (Catholic) l'abbé (John) Smith; (Protestant) le pasteur (John) Smith

**reversal** [rɪˈvɜːsl] n (of opinion) revirement m; (of order) renversement m; (of direction) changement m

**reverse** [rɪˈvɜːs] n contraire m, opposé m; (back) dos m, envers m; (of paper) verso m; (of coin) revers m; (setback) revers m; (AUT: also: **~ gear**) marche f arrière ♦ adj (order, direction) opposé(e), inverse ♦ vt (order, position) changer, inverser; (direction, policy) changer complètement de; (decision) annuler; (roles) renverser; (car) faire marche arrière avec ♦ vi (BRIT: AUT) faire marche arrière; **he ~d (the car) into a wall** il a embouti un mur en marche arrière; **~d charge call** (BRIT) (TEL) communication f en PCV; **reversing lights** (BRIT) npl (AUT) feux mpl de marche arrière ou de recul

**revert** [rɪ'vəːt] vi: **to ~ to** revenir à, retourner à

**review** [rɪ'vjuː] n revue f; (of book, film) critique f, compte rendu; (of situation, policy) examen m, bilan m ♦ vt passer en revue; faire la critique de; examiner; **~er** n critique m

**revise** [rɪ'vaɪz] vt réviser, modifier; (manuscript) revoir, corriger ♦ vi (study) réviser; **revision** [rɪ'vɪʒən] n révision f

**revival** [rɪ'vaɪvəl] n reprise f; (recovery) rétablissement m; (of faith) renouveau m

**revive** [rɪ'vaɪv] vt (person) ranimer; (custom) rétablir; (economy) relancer; (hope, courage) raviver, faire renaître; (play) reprendre ♦ vi (person) reprendre connaissance; (: from ill health) se rétablir; (hope etc) renaître; (activity) reprendre

**revoke** [rɪ'vəuk] vt révoquer; (law) abroger

**revolt** [rɪ'vəult] n révolte f ♦ vi se révolter, se rebeller ♦ vt révolter, dégoûter; **~ing** adj dégoûtant(e)

**revolution** [revə'luːʃən] n révolution f; (of wheel etc) tour m, révolution; **~ary** adj révolutionnaire ♦ n révolutionnaire m/f

**revolve** [rɪ'vɔlv] vi tourner

**revolver** [rɪ'vɔlvəʳ] n revolver m

**revolving** [rɪ'vɔlvɪŋ] adj tournant(e); (chair) pivotant(e); **~ door** n (porte f à) tambour m

**revulsion** [rɪ'vʌlʃən] n dégoût m, répugnance f

**reward** [rɪ'wɔːd] n récompense f ♦ vt: **to ~ (for)** récompenser (de); **~ing** adj (fig) qui (en) vaut la peine, gratifiant(e)

**rewind** [riː'waɪnd] (irreg) vt (tape) rembobiner

**rewire** [riː'waɪəʳ] vt (house) refaire l'installation électrique de

**rheumatism** [ˈruːmətɪzm] n rhumatisme m

**Rhine** [raɪn] n Rhin m

**rhinoceros** [raɪ'nɔsərəs] n rhinocéros m

**Rhone** [rəun] n Rhône m

**rhubarb** [ˈruːbɑːb] n rhubarbe f

**rhyme** [raɪm] n rime f; (verse) vers mpl

**rhythm** [ˈrɪðm] n rythme m

**rib** [rɪb] n (ANAT) côte f

**ribbon** [ˈrɪbən] n ruban m; **in ~s** (torn) en lambeaux

**rice** [raɪs] n riz m; **~ pudding** n riz au lait

**rich** [rɪtʃ] adj riche; (gift, clothes) somptueux(-euse) ♦ npl: **the ~** les riches mpl; **~es** npl richesses fpl; **~ly** adv richement; (deserved, earned) largement

**rickets** [ˈrɪkɪts] n rachitisme m

**rid** [rɪd] (pt, pp rid) vt: **to ~ sb of** débarrasser qn de; **to get ~ of** se débarrasser de

**riddle** [ˈrɪdl] n (puzzle) énigme f ♦ vt: **to be ~d with** être criblé(e) de; (fig: guilt, corruption, doubts) être en proie à

**ride** [raɪd] (pt rode, pp ridden) n promenade f, tour m; (distance covered) trajet m ♦ vi (as sport) monter (à cheval), faire du cheval; (go somewhere: on horse, bicycle) aller (à cheval ou bicyclette etc); (journey: on bicycle, motorcycle, bus) rouler ♦ vt (a certain horse) monter; (distance) parcourir, faire; **to take sb for a ~** (fig) faire marcher qn; **to ~ a horse/bicycle** monter à cheval/à bicyclette; **~r** n cavalier(-ère); (in race) jockey m; (on bicycle) cycliste m/f; (on motorcycle) motocycliste m/f

**ridge** [rɪdʒ] n (of roof, mountain) arête f; (of hill) faîte m; (on object) strie f

**ridicule** [ˈrɪdɪkjuːl] n ridicule m; dérision f

**ridiculous** [rɪ'dɪkjuləs] adj ridicule

**riding** [ˈraɪdɪŋ] n équitation f;

**school** n manège m, école f d'équitation

**rife** [raɪf] adj répandu(e); ~ **with** abondant(e) en, plein(e) de

**riffraff** ['rɪfræf] n racaille f

**rifle** [raɪfl] n fusil m (à canon rayé) ♦ vt vider, dévaliser; ~ **through** vt (belongings) fouiller; (papers) feuilleter; ~ **range** n champ m de tir; (at fair) stand m de tir

**rift** [rɪft] n fente f, fissure f; (fig: disagreement) désaccord m

**rig** [rɪg] n (also: **oil** ~: at sea) plateforme pétrolière f ♦ vt (election etc) truquer; ~ **out** (BRIT) vt: **to** ~ **out as/in** habiller en/de; ~ **up** vt arranger, faire avec des moyens de fortune; ~**ging** n (NAUT) gréement m

**right** [raɪt] adj (correctly chosen: answer, road etc) bon (bonne); (true) juste, exact(e); (suitable) approprié(e), convenable; (just) juste, équitable; (morally good) bien inv; (not left) droit(e) ♦ n (what is morally ~) bien m; (title, claim) droit m; (not left) droite f ♦ adv (answer) correctement, juste; (treat) bien, comme il le faut; (not on the left) à droite ♦ vt redresser ♦ excl bon!; **to be** ~ (person) avoir raison; (answer) être juste ou correct(e); (clock) être à l'heure (juste); **by** ~**s** en toute justice; **on the** ~ à droite; **to be in the** ~ avoir raison; ~ **now** en ce moment même; tout de suite; ~ **away** immédiatement; ~ **angle** n (MATH) angle droit; ~**eous** ['raɪtʃəs] adj droit(e), vertueux(-euse); (anger) justifié(e); ~**ful** adj légitime; ~**-handed** adj (person) droitier(-ère); ~**-hand man** n bras droit (fig); ~**-hand side** n la droite; ~**ly** adv (with reason) à juste titre; ~ **of way** n droit m de passage; (AUT) priorité f; ~**-wing** adj (POL) de droite

**rigid** ['rɪdʒɪd] adj rigide; (principle, control) strict(e)

**rigmarole** ['rɪgmərəʊl] n comédie f

**rigorous** ['rɪgərəs] adj rigoureux(-euse)

**rile** [raɪl] vt agacer

**rim** [rɪm] n bord m; (of spectacles) monture f; (of wheel) jante f

**rind** [raɪnd] n (of bacon) couenne f; (of lemon etc) écorce f, zeste m; (of cheese) croûte f

**ring** [rɪŋ] (pt **rang**, pp **rung**) n anneau m; (on finger) bague f; (also: **wedding** ~) alliance f; (of people, objects) cercle m; (of spies) réseau m; (of smoke etc) rond m; (arena) piste f, arène f; (for boxing) ring m; (sound of bell) sonnerie f ♦ vi (telephone, bell) sonner; (person: by telephone) téléphoner; (also: ~ **out**: voice, words) retentir; (ears) bourdonner ♦ vt (BRIT: TEL: also: ~ **up**) téléphoner à, appeler; (bell) faire sonner; **to** ~ **the bell** sonner; **to give sb a** ~ (BRIT: TEL) appeler qn; ~ **back** (BRIT) vt, vi (TEL) rappeler; ~ **off** (BRIT) vi (TEL) raccrocher; ~ **up** (BRIT) vt (TEL) appeler; ~ **binder** n classeur m à anneaux; ~**ing** ['rɪŋɪŋ] n (of telephone) sonnerie f; (of bell) tintement m; (in ears) bourdonnement m; ~**ing tone** n (TEL) sonnerie f; ~**leader** n (of gang) chef m, meneur m; ~**lets** npl anglaises fpl; ~ **road** (BRIT) n route f de ceinture; (motorway) périphérique m

**rink** [rɪŋk] n (also: **ice** ~) patinoire f

**rinse** [rɪns] vt rincer

**riot** ['raɪət] n émeute f; (of flowers, colour) profusion f ♦ vi faire une émeute, manifester avec violence; **to run** ~ se déchaîner; ~**ous** adj (mob, assembly) séditieux(-euse), déchaîné(e); (living, behaviour) débauché(e); (party) très animé(e); (welcome) délirant(e)

**rip** [rɪp] n déchirure f ♦ vt déchirer ♦ vi se déchirer; ~**cord** n poignée f d'ouverture

**ripe** [raɪp] adj (fruit) mûr(e); (cheese) fait(e); ~**n** vt mûrir ♦ vi mûrir

**rip-off** (inf) n: **it's a** ~~! c'est de l'arnaque!

**ripple** ['rɪpl] n ondulation f; (of applause, laughter) cascade f ♦ vi onduler

**rise** [raɪz] (*pt* **rose**, *pp* **risen**) *n* (*slope*) côte *f*, pente *f*; (*hill*) hauteur *f*; (*increase: in wages: BRIT*) augmentation *f*; (*: in prices, temperature*) hausse *f*, augmentation; (*fig: to power etc*) ascension *f* ♦ *vi* s'élever; monter; (*prices, numbers*) augmenter; (*waters*) monter; (*sun; person: from chair, bed*) se lever; (*also: ~ up: tower, building*) s'élever; (*: rebel*) se révolter; se rebeller; (*in rank*) s'élever; **to give ~ to** donner lieu à; **to ~ to the occasion** se montrer à la hauteur; **~r** *n*: **to be an early ~r** être matinal(le); **rising** *adj* (*number, prices*) en hausse; (*tide*) montant(e); (*sun, moon*) levant(e)

**risk** [rɪsk] *n* risque *m* ♦ *vt* risquer; **at ~** en danger; **at one's own ~** à ses risques et périls; **~y** *adj* risqué(e)

**rissole** ['rɪsəʊl] *n* croquette *f*

**rite** [raɪt] *n* rite *m*; **last ~s** derniers sacrements

**ritual** ['rɪtjuəl] *adj* rituel(le) ♦ *n* rituel *m*

**rival** ['raɪvl] *adj*, *n* rival(e); (*in business*) concurrent(e) ♦ *vt* (*match*) égaler; **~ry** ['raɪvlrɪ] *n* rivalité *f*, concurrence *f*

**river** ['rɪvə*] *n* rivière *f*, (*also fig*) fleuve *m* ♦ *cpd* (*port, traffic*) fluvial(e); **up/down ~** en amont/aval; **~bank** *n* rive *f*, berge *f*; **~bed** *n* lit *m* (de rivière *or* de fleuve)

**rivet** ['rɪvɪt] *n* rivet *m* ♦ *vt* (*fig*) river, fixer

**Riviera** [rɪvɪ'eərə] *n*: **the (French) ~** la Côte d'Azur; **the Italian ~** la Riviera (italienne)

**road** [rəʊd] *n* route *f*, (*in town*) rue *f*; (*fig*) chemin, voie *f*; **major/minor ~** route principale *or* à priorité/voie secondaire; **~ accident** *n* accident *m* de la circulation; **~block** *n* barrage routier; **~hog** *n* chauffard *m*; **~ map** *n* carte routière; **~ rage** *n* comportement très agressif de certains usagers de la route; **~ safety** *n* sécurité routière; **~side** *n* bord *m* de la route, bas-côté *m*; **~ sign** *n* panneau *m* de signalisation; **~way** *n* chaussée *f*; **~ works** *npl* travaux *mpl*

(de réfection des routes); **~worthy** *adj* en bon état de marche

**roam** [rəʊm] *vi* errer, vagabonder

**roar** [rɔː*] *n* rugissement *m*; (*of crowd*) hurlements *mpl*; (*of vehicle, thunder, storm*) grondement *m* ♦ *vi* rugir; hurler; gronder; **to ~ with laughter** éclater de rire; **to do a ~ing trade** faire des affaires d'or

**roast** [rəʊst] *n* rôti *m* ♦ *vt* (faire) rôtir; (*coffee*) griller, torréfier; **~ beef** *n* rôti *m* de bœuf, rosbif *m*

**rob** [rɒb] *vt* (*person*) voler; (*bank*) dévaliser; **to ~ sb of sth** voler *or* dérober qch à qn; (*fig: deprive*) priver qn de qch; **~ber** *n* bandit *m*, voleur *m*; **~bery** *n* vol *m*

**robe** [rəʊb] *n* (*for ceremony etc*) robe *f*; (*also*: **bathrobe**) peignoir *m*; (*US*) couverture *f*

**robin** ['rɒbɪn] *n* rouge-gorge *m*

**robot** ['rəʊbɒt] *n* robot *m*

**robust** [rəʊ'bʌst] *adj* robuste; (*material, appetite*) solide

**rock** [rɒk] *n* (*substance*) roche *f*, roc *m*; (*boulder*) rocher *m*; (*US: small stone*) caillou *m*; (*BRIT: sweet*) = sucre *m* d'orge ♦ *vt* (*swing gently: cradle*) balancer; (*: child*) bercer; (*shake*) ébranler, secouer ♦ *vi* (se) balancer; être ébranlé(e) *or* secoué(e); **on the ~s** (*drink*) avec des glaçons; (*marriage etc*) en train de craquer; **~ and roll** *n* rock (and roll) *m*, rock'n'roll *m*; **~-bottom** *adj* (*fig: prices*) sacrifié(e); **~ery** *n* (jardin *m* de) rocaille *f*

**rocket** ['rɒkɪt] *n* fusée *f*; (*MIL*) fusée, roquette *f*

**rocking chair** *n* fauteuil *m* à bascule

**rocking horse** *n* cheval *m* à bascule

**rocky** ['rɒkɪ] *adj* (*hill*) rocheux(-euse); (*path*) rocailleux(-euse)

**rod** [rɒd] *n* (*wooden*) baguette *f*; (*metallic*) tringle *f*; (*TECH*) tige *f*; (*also*: **fishing ~**) canne *f* à pêche

**rode** [rəʊd] *pt of* **ride**

**rodent** ['rəʊdnt] *n* rongeur *m*

# rodeo 527 rot

**rodeo** ['rəudɪəu] (*US*) rodéo *m*

**roe** [rəu] *n* (*species: also*: ~ **deer**) chevreuil *m*; (*of fish: also*: **hard** ~) œufs *mpl* de poisson; **soft** ~ laitance *f*

**rogue** [rəug] *n* coquin(e)

**role** [rəul] *n* rôle *m*; ~ **play** *n* jeu *m* de rôle

**roll** [rəul] *n* rouleau *m*; (*of banknotes*) liasse *f*; (*also*: **bread** ~) petit pain; (*register*) liste *f*; (*sound: of drums etc*) roulement *m* ♦ *vt* rouler; (*also*: ~ **up**: *string*) enrouler; (: *sleeves*) retrousser; (*also*: ~ **out**: *pastry*) étendre au rouleau, abaisser ♦ *vi* rouler; ~ **about** *vi* rouler ça et là; (*person*) se rouler par terre; ~ **around** *vi* = **roll about**; ~ **by** *vi* (*time*) s'écouler, passer; ~ **over** *vi* se retourner; ~ **up** *vi* (*inf: arrive*) arriver, s'amener ♦ *vt* rouler; ~ **call** *n* appel *m*; ~**er** *n* rouleau *m*; (*wheel*) roulette *f*; (*for road*) rouleau compresseur; ~**er blade** *n* patin *m* en ligne; ~**er coaster** *n* montagnes *fpl* russes; ~**er skates** *npl* patins *mpl* à roulettes; ~**er skating** *n* patin *m* à roulettes; ~**ing** *adj* (*landscape*) onduleux(-euse); ~**ing pin** *n* rouleau *m* à pâtisserie; ~**ing stock** *n* (*RAIL*) matériel roulant

**ROM** [rɔm] *n abbr* (= *read only memory*) mémoire morte

**Roman** ['rəumən] *adj* romain(e); ~ **Catholic** *adj*, *n* catholique *m/f*

**romance** [rə'mæns] *n* (*love affair*) idylle *f*; (*charm*) poésie *f*; (*novel*) roman *m* à l'eau de rose

**Romania** [rəu'meɪnɪə] *n* Roumanie *f*; ~**n** *adj* roumain(e) ♦ *n* Roumain(e); (*LING*) roumain *m*

**Roman numeral** *n* chiffre romain

**romantic** [rə'mæntɪk] *adj* romantique; sentimental(e)

**Rome** [rəum] *n* Rome

**romp** [rɔmp] *n* jeux bruyants ♦ *vi* (*also*: ~ **about**) s'ébattre, jouer bruyamment; ~**ers** *npl* barboteuse *f*

**roof** [ruːf] (*pl* ~**s**) *n* toit *m* ♦ *vt* couvrir (d'un toit); **the** ~ **of the mouth** la voûte du palais; ~**ing** *n* toiture *f*; ~ **rack** *n* (*AUT*) galerie *f*

**rook** [ruk] *n* (*bird*) freux *m*; (*CHESS*) tour *f*

**room** [ruːm] *n* (*in house*) pièce *f*; (*also*: **bedroom**) chambre *f* (à coucher); (*in school etc*) salle *f*; (*space*) place *f*; ~**s** *npl* (*lodging*) meublé *m*; "~**s to let**" (*BRIT*) or "~**s for rent**" (*US*) "chambres à louer"; **single/double** ~ chambre pour une personne/deux personnes; **there is** ~ **for improvement** cela laisse à désirer; ~**ing house** (*US*) *n* maison *f* or immeuble *m* de rapport; ~**mate** *n* camarade *m/f* de chambre; ~ **service** *n* service *m* des chambres (*dans un hôtel*); ~**y** *adj* spacieux(-euse); (*garment*) ample

**roost** [ruːst] *vi* se jucher

**rooster** ['ruːstə<sup>r</sup>] *n* (*esp US*) coq *m*

**root** [ruːt] *n* (*BOT, MATH*) racine *f*; (*fig: of problem*) origine *f*, fond *m* ♦ *vi* (*plant*) s'enraciner; ~ **about** *vi* (*fig*) fouiller; ~ **for** *vt fus* encourager, applaudir; ~ **out** *vt* (*find*) dénicher

**rope** [rəup] *n* corde *f*; (*NAUT*) cordage *m* ♦ *vt* (*tie up or together*) attacher; (*climbers: also*: ~ **together**) encorder; (*area*: ~ *off*) interdire l'accès de; (: *divide off*) séparer; **to know the** ~**s** (*fig*) être au courant, connaître les ficelles; ~ **in** *vt* (*fig: person*) embringuer

**rosary** ['rəuzərɪ] *n* chapelet *m*

**rose** [rəuz] *pt of* **rise** ♦ *n* rose *f*; (*also*: ~**bush**) rosier *m*; (*on watering can*) pomme *f*

**rosé** ['rəuzeɪ] *n* rosé *m*

**rosebud** ['rəuzbʌd] *n* bouton *m* de rose

**rosemary** ['rəuzmərɪ] *n* romarin *m*

**roster** ['rɔstə<sup>r</sup>] *n*: **duty** ~ tableau *m* de service

**rostrum** ['rɔstrəm] *n* tribune *f* (*pour un orateur etc*)

**rosy** ['rəuzɪ] *adj* rose; **a** ~ **future** un bel avenir

**rot** [rɔt] *n* (*decay*) pourriture *f*; (*fig: pej*)

**rota** 528 **rpm**

**rota** fpl ♦ vt, vi pourrir

idioties fpl

**rota** ['rəutə] n liste f, tableau m de service; **on a ~ basis** par roulement

**rotary** ['rəutəri] adj rotatif(-ive)

**rotate** [rəu'teit] vt (revolve) faire tourner; (change round: jobs) faire à tour de rôle ♦ vi (revolve) tourner; **rotating** adj (movement) tournant(e)

**rotten** ['rɔtn] adj (decayed) pourri(e); (dishonest) corrompu(e); (inf: bad) mauvais(e), moche; **to feel ~** (ill) être mal fichu(e)

**rotund** [rəu'tʌnd] adj (person) rondelet(te)

**rough** [rʌf] adj (cloth, skin) rêche, rugueux(-euse); (terrain) accidenté(e); (path) rocailleux(-euse); (voice) rauque, rude; (person, manner: coarse) rude, fruste; (: violent) brutal(e); (district, weather) mauvais(e); (sea) houleux(-euse); (plan etc) ébauché(e); (guess) approximatif(-ive) ♦ n (GOLF) rough m ♦ vt: **to ~** (it) vivre à la dure; **to sleep ~** (BRIT) coucher à la dure; **~age** n fibres fpl alimentaires; **~-and-ready** adj rudimentaire; **~ copy, ~ draft** n brouillon m; **~ly** adv (handle) rudement, brutalement; (speak) avec brusquerie; (make) grossièrement; (approximately) à peu près, en gros

**roulette** [ru:'let] n roulette f

**Roumania** [ru:'meiniə] n = Romania

**round** [raund] adj rond(e) ♦ n (BRIT: of toast) tranche f; (duty: of policeman, milkman etc) tournée f; (: of doctor) visites fpl; (game: of cards, in competition) partie f; (BOXING) round m; (of talks) série f ♦ vt (corner) tourner ♦ prep autour de ♦ adv: **all ~** tout autour; **the long way ~** (par) le chemin le plus long; **all the year ~** toute l'année; **it's just ~ the corner** (fig) c'est tout près; **~ the clock** 24 heures sur 24; **to go ~ to sb's (house)** aller chez qn; **go ~ the back** passez par derrière; **enough to go ~** assez pour tout le monde; **~ of ammunition** cartouche f; **~ of ap-**

plause ban m, applaudissements mpl; **~ of drinks** tournée f; **~ of sandwiches** sandwich m; **~ off** vt (speech etc) terminer; **~ up** vt rassembler; (criminals) effectuer une rafle de; (price, figure) arrondir (au chiffre supérieur); **~about** n (BRIT: AUT) rond-point m (à sens giratoire); (: at fair) manège m (de chevaux de bois) ♦ adj (route, means) détourné(e); **~ers** n (game) sorte de baseball; **~ly** adv (fig) tout net, carrément; **~ trip** n (voyage m) aller et retour m; **~up** n rassemblement m; (of criminals) rafle f

**rouse** [rauz] vt (wake up) réveiller; (stir up) susciter; provoquer; éveiller; **rousing** adj (welcome) enthousiaste

**route** [ru:t] n itinéraire m; (of bus) parcours m; (of trade, shipping) route f

**routine** [ru:'ti:n] adj (work) ordinaire, courant(e); (procedure) d'usage ♦ n (habits) habitudes fpl; (pej) train-train m; (THEATRE) numéro m

**rove** [rəuv] vt (area, streets) errer dans

**row¹** [rəu] n (line) rangée f; (of people, seats, KNITTING) rang m; (behind one another: of cars, people) file f ♦ vi (in boat) ramer; (as sport) faire de l'aviron ♦ vt (boat) faire aller à la rame ♦ a l'aviron; **in a ~** (fig) d'affilée

**row²** [rau] n (noise) vacarme m, (dispute) dispute f, querelle f; (scolding) réprimande f, savon m ♦ vi se disputer, se quereller

**rowboat** ['rəubəut] (US) n canot m (à rames)

**rowdy** ['raudi] adj chahuteur(-euse); (occasion) tapageur(-euse)

**rowing** ['rəuiŋ] n canotage m; (as sport) aviron m; **~ boat** (BRIT) n canot m (à rames)

**royal** ['rɔiəl] adj royal(e); **R~ Air Force** (BRIT) n armée de l'air britannique; **~ty** n (royal persons) (membres mpl de la) famille royale; (payment: to author) droits mpl d'auteur; (: to inventor) royalties fpl

**rpm** abbr (AUT) (= revolutions per minute)

tr/mn

**RSVP** *abbr* (= répondez s'il vous plaît) R.S.V.P.

**Rt Hon.** *abbr* (BRIT: *Right Honourable*) titre donné aux députés de la Chambre des communes

**rub** [rʌb] *vt* frotter; frictionner; (*hands*) se frotter ♦ *n* (*with cloth*) coup *m*; **to give sth a ~** donner un coup de chiffon *or* de torchon à; **to ~ sb up** (BRIT) *or* **to ~ sb** (US) **the wrong way** prendre qn à rebrousse-poil; **~ off** *vi* partir; **~ off on** *vt fus* déteindre sur; **~ out** *vt* effacer

**rubber** ['rʌbə*r*] *n* caoutchouc *m*; (BRIT: *eraser*) gomme *f* (à effacer); **~ band** *n* élastique *m*; **~ plant** *n* caoutchouc *m* (*plante verte*)

**rubbish** ['rʌbɪʃ] *n* (*from household*) ordures *fpl*; (*fig*: *pej*) camelote *f*; (: *nonsense*) bêtises *fpl*, idioties *fpl*; **~ bin** *n* (BRIT) poubelle *f*; **~ dump** *n* décharge publique, dépotoir *m*

**rubble** ['rʌbl] *n* décombres *mpl*; (*smaller*) gravats *mpl*; (CONSTR) blocage *m*

**ruby** ['ru:bɪ] *n* rubis *m*

**rucksack** ['rʌksæk] *n* sac à dos

**rudder** ['rʌdə*r*] *n* gouvernail *m*

**ruddy** ['rʌdɪ] *adj* (*face*) coloré(e); (*inf*: *damned*) sacré(e), fichu(e)

**rude** [ru:d] *adj* (*impolite*) impoli(e); (*coarse*) grossier(-ère); (*shocking*) indécent(e), inconvenant(e)

**ruffle** ['rʌfl] *vt* (*hair*) ébouriffer; (*clothes*) chiffonner; (*fig*: *person*): **to get ~d** s'énerver

**rug** [rʌg] *n* petit tapis; (BRIT: *blanket*) couverture *f*

**rugby** ['rʌgbɪ] *n* (*also*: **~ football**) rugby *m*

**rugged** ['rʌgɪd] *adj* (*landscape*) accidenté(e); (*features*, *character*) rude

**ruin** ['ru:ɪn] *n* ruine *f* ♦ *vt* ruiner; (*spoil*: *clothes*) abîmer; (*event*) gâcher; **~s** *npl* (*of building*) ruine(s)

**rule** [ru:l] *n* règle *f*; (*regulation*) règlement *m*; (*government*) autorité *f*,

gouvernement *m* ♦ *vt* (*country*) gouverner; (*person*) dominer ♦ *vi* commander; (LAW) statuer; **as a ~** normalement, en règle générale; **~ out** *vt* exclure; **~d** *adj* (*paper*) réglé(e); **~r** *n* (*sovereign*) souverain(e); (*for measuring*) règle *f*; **ruling** *adj* (*party*) au pouvoir; (*class*) dirigeant(e) ♦ *n* (LAW) décision *f*

**rum** [rʌm] *n* rhum *m*

**Rumania** [ruːˈmeɪnɪə] *n* = Romania

**rumble** ['rʌmbl] *vi* gronder; (*stomach*, *pipe*) gargouiller

**rummage** ['rʌmɪdʒ] *vi* fouiller

**rumour** ['ruːmə*r*] (US **rumor**) *n* rumeur *f*, bruit *m* (qui court) ♦ *vt*: **it is ~ed that** le bruit court que

**rump** [rʌmp] *n* (*of animal*) croupe *f*; (*inf*: *of person*) postérieur *m*; **~ steak** *n* romsteck *m*

**rumpus** ['rʌmpəs] (*inf*) *n* tapage *m*, chahut *m*

**run** [rʌn] (*pt* **ran**, *pp* **run**) *n* (*fast pace*) (pas *m* de) course *f*; (*outing*) tour *m* *or* promenade *f* (en voiture); (*distance travelled*) parcours *m*, trajet *m*; (*series*) suite *f*, série *f*; (THEATRE) série de représentations; (SKI) piste *f*; (CRICKET, BASEBALL) point *m*; (*in tights*, *stockings*) maille filée, échelle *f* ♦ *vt* (*operate*: *business*) diriger; (: *competition*, *course*) organiser; (: *hotel*, *house*) tenir; (*race*) participer à; (COMPUT) exécuter; (*to pass*: *hand*, *finger*) passer; (*water*, *bath*) faire couler; (PRESS: *feature*) publier ♦ *vi* courir; (*flee*) s'enfuir; (*work*: *machine*, *factory*) marcher; (*bus*, *train*) circuler; (*continue*: *play*) se jouer; (: *contract*) être valide; (*flow*: *river*, *bath*; *nose*) couler; (*colours*, *washing*) déteindre; (*in election*) être candidat, se présenter; **to go for a ~** faire un peu de course à pied; **there was a ~ on** ... (*meat*, *tickets*) les gens se sont rués sur ...; **in the long ~** à longue échéance; à la longue; **on the ~** en fuite; **I'll ~ you to the station** je vais vous emmener *or* conduire à la gare; **to ~ a risk** courir un risque; **~ about** vi (children) courir çà et là; **~ across** vt fus (find) trouver par hasard; **~ around** vi = run about; **~ away** vi s'enfuir; **~ down** vt (production) réduire progressivement; (factory) réduire progressivement la production de; (AUT) renverser; (criticize) critiquer, dénigrer; **to be ~ down** (person: tired) être fatigué(e) or à plat; **~ in** (BRIT) vt (car) roder; **~ into** vt fus (meet: person) rencontrer par hasard; (trouble) se heurter à; (collide with) heurter; **~ off** vi s'enfuir ♦ vt (water) laisser s'écouler; (copies) tirer; **~ out** vi (person) sortir en courant; (liquid) couler; (lease) expirer; (money) être épuisé(e); **~ out of** vt fus se trouver à court de; **~ over** vt (AUT) écraser ♦ vt fus (revise) revoir, reprendre; **~ through** vt fus (recapitulate) reprendre; (play) répéter; **~ up** vt: **to ~ up against** (difficulties) se heurter à; **to ~ up a debt** s'endetter; **~away** adj (horse) emballé(e); (truck) fou (folle); (person) fugitif(-ive); (teenager) fugueur(-euse)

**rung** [rʌŋ] pp of **ring** ♦ n (of ladder) barreau m

**runner** ['rʌnə*] n (in race: person) coureur(-euse); (: horse) partant m; (on sledge) patin m; (for drawer etc) coulisseau m; **~ bean** (BRIT) n haricot m (à rames); **~up** n second(e)

**running** ['rʌnɪŋ] n course f, (of business, organization) gestion f, direction f ♦ adj (water) courant(e); **to be in/out of the ~ for sth** être/ne pas être sur les rangs pour qch; **6 days ~** 6 jours de suite; **~ commentary** n commentaire détaillé; **~ costs** npl frais mpl d'exploitation

**runny** ['rʌnɪ] adj qui coule

**run-of-the-mill** ['rʌnəvðə'mɪl] adj ordinaire, banal(e)

**runt** [rʌnt] n avorton m

**run-up** ['rʌnʌp] n: **~~ to sth** (election etc) période f précédant qch

**runway** ['rʌnweɪ] n (AVIAT) piste f

**rupture** ['rʌptʃə*] n (MED) hernie f

**rural** ['ruərl] adj rural(e)

**rush** [rʌʃ] n (hurry) hâte f, précipitation f; (of crowd, COMM: sudden demand) ruée f; (current) flot m; (of emotion) vague f; (BOT) jonc m ♦ vt (hurry) transporter or envoyer d'urgence ♦ vi se précipiter; **~ hour** n heures fpl de pointe

**rusk** [rʌsk] n biscotte f

**Russia** ['rʌʃə] n Russie f; **~n** adj russe ♦ n Russe m/f; (LING) russe m

**rust** [rʌst] n rouille f ♦ vi rouiller

**rustic** ['rʌstɪk] adj rustique

**rustle** ['rʌsl] vi bruire, produire un bruissement ♦ vt froisser

**rustproof** ['rʌstpruːf] adj inoxydable

**rusty** ['rʌstɪ] adj rouillé(e)

**rut** [rʌt] n ornière f; (ZOOL) rut m; **to be in a ~** suivre l'ornière, s'encroûter

**ruthless** ['ruːθlɪs] adj sans pitié, impitoyable

**rye** [raɪ] n seigle m

# S, s

**Sabbath** ['sæbəθ] n (Jewish) sabbat m; (Christian) dimanche m

**sabotage** ['sæbətɑːʒ] n sabotage m ♦ vt saboter

**saccharin(e)** ['sækərɪn] n saccharine f

**sachet** ['sæʃeɪ] n sachet m

**sack** [sæk] n (bag) sac m ♦ vt (dismiss) renvoyer, mettre à la porte; (plunder) piller, mettre à sac; **to get the ~** être renvoyé(e), être mis(e) à la porte; **~ing** n (material) toile f à sac; (dismissal) renvoi m

**sacrament** ['sækrəmənt] n sacrement m

**sacred** ['seɪkrɪd] adj sacré(e)

**sacrifice** ['sækrɪfaɪs] n sacrifice m ♦ vt sacrifier

**sad** [sæd] adj triste; (deplorable) triste, fâcheux(-euse)

**saddle** ['sædl] n selle f ♦ vt (horse) seller; **to be ~d with sth** (inf) avoir qch sur les bras; **~bag** n sacoche f

**sadistic** [sə'dɪstɪk] adj sadique

**sadly** ['sædlɪ] adv tristement; (unfortunately) malheureusement; (seriously) fort

**sadness** ['sædnɪs] n tristesse f

**s.a.e.** n abbr = **stamped addressed envelope**

**safe** [seɪf] adj (out of danger) hors de danger, en sécurité; (not dangerous) sans danger; (cautious) prudent(e); (sure: bet etc) assuré(e) ♦ n coffre-fort m; **~ from** à l'abri de; **~ and sound** sain(e) et sauf (sauve); (just) to be on the **~ side** pour plus de sûreté, par précaution; **~ journey!** bon voyage!; **~-conduct** m; sauf-conduit m; **~-deposit** n (vault) dépôt m de coffres-forts; (box) coffre-fort m; **~guard** n sauvegarde f, protection f ♦ vt sauvegarder, protéger; **~keeping** n bonne garde; **~ly** adv (assume, say) sans risque d'erreur; (drive, arrive) sans accident; **~ sex** n rapports mpl sexuels sans risque

**safety** ['seɪftɪ] n sécurité f; **~ belt** n ceinture f de sécurité; **~ pin** n épingle f de sûreté ou de nourrice; **~ valve** n soupape f de sûreté

**sag** [sæg] vi s'affaisser; (hem, breasts) pendre

**sage** [seɪdʒ] n (herb) sauge f; (person) sage m

**Sagittarius** [sædʒɪ'tɛərɪəs] n le Sagittaire

**Sahara** [sə'hɑːrə] n: the **~ (Desert)** le (désert du) Sahara

**said** [sɛd] pt, pp of **say**

**sail** [seɪl] n (on boat) voile f; (trip): to go for a **~** faire un tour en bateau ♦ vt (boat) manœuvrer, piloter ♦ vi (travel: ship) avancer, naviguer; (set off) partir, prendre la mer; (SPORT) faire de la voile; **they ~ed into Le Havre** ils sont entrés dans le port du Havre; **~ through** vi, vt fus (fig) réussir haut la main; **~boat** (US) n bateau m à voiles, voilier m; **~ing** n (SPORT) voile f; **to go ~ing** faire de la

voile; **~ing boat** n bateau m à voiles, voilier m; **~ing ship** n grand voilier; **~or** n marin m, matelot m

**saint** [seɪnt] n saint(e)

**sake** [seɪk] n: **for the ~ of** pour (l'amour de), dans l'intérêt de; par égard pour

**salad** ['sæləd] n salade f; **~ bowl** n saladier m; **~ cream** (BRIT) n (sorte f de) mayonnaise f; **~ dressing** n vinaigrette f

**salami** [sə'lɑːmɪ] n salami m

**salary** ['sælərɪ] n salaire m

**sale** [seɪl] n vente f; (at reduced prices) soldes mpl; **"for ~"** "à vendre"; **on ~** en vente; **on ~ or return** vendu(e) avec faculté de retour; **~room** n salle f des ventes; **~s assistant** (US **sales clerk**) n vendeur(-euse); **~sman** (irreg) n vendeur m; (representative) représentant m; **~s rep** (COMM) représentant(e) m/f; **~swoman** (irreg) n vendeuse f; (representative) représentante f

**salmon** ['sæmən] n inv saumon m

**salon** ['sælɔn] n salon m

**saloon** [sə'luːn] n (US) bar m; (BRIT: AUT) berline f; (ship's lounge) salon m

**salt** [sɔːlt] n sel m ♦ vt saler; **~ cellar** n salière f; **~water** adj de mer; **~y** adj salé(e)

**salute** [sə'luːt] n salut m ♦ vt saluer

**salvage** ['sælvɪdʒ] n (saving) sauvetage m; (things saved) biens sauvés ou récupérés ♦ vt sauver, récupérer

**salvation** [sæl'veɪʃən] n salut m; **S~ Army** n armée f du Salut

**same** [seɪm] adj même ♦ pron: **the ~** (la) même, les mêmes; **the ~ book as** le même livre que; **at the ~ time** en même temps; **all** ou **just the ~** tout de même, quand même; **to do the ~** faire de même, en faire autant; **to do the ~ as sb** faire comme qn; **the ~ to you!** à vous de même!; (after insult) toi-même!

**sample** ['sɑːmpl] n échantillon m; (blood) prélèvement m ♦ vt (food, wine) goûter

**sanction** ['sæŋkʃən] n approbation f, sanction f

**sanctity** ['sæŋktɪtɪ] n sainteté f, caractère sacré

**sanctuary** ['sæŋktjuərɪ] n (holy place) sanctuaire m; (refuge) asile m; (for wild life) réserve f

**sand** [sænd] n sable m ♦ vt (furniture: also: ~ **down**) poncer

**sandal** ['sændl] n sandale f

**sand:** ~**box** (US) n tas m de sable; ~**castle** n château m de sable; ~**paper** n papier m de verre; ~**pit** (BRIT) n (for children) tas m de sable; ~**stone** n grès m

**sandwich** ['sændwɪtʃ] n sandwich m; **cheese/ham** ~ sandwich au fromage/jambon; ~ **course** (BRIT) n cours m de formation professionnelle

**sandy** ['sændɪ] adj sablonneux(-euse); (colour) sable inv, blond roux inv

**sane** [seɪn] adj (person) sain(e) d'esprit; (outlook) sensé(e), sain(e)

**sang** [sæŋ] pt of **sing**

**sanitary** ['sænɪtərɪ] adj (system, arrangements) sanitaire; (clean) hygiénique; ~ **towel** (US **sanitary napkin**) n serviette f hygiénique

**sanitation** [sænɪ'teɪʃən] n (in house) installations fpl sanitaires; (in town) système m sanitaire; ~ **department** (US) n service m de voirie

**sanity** ['sænɪtɪ] n santé mentale; (common sense) bon sens

**sank** [sæŋk] pt of **sink**

**Santa Claus** [sæntə'klɔːz] n le père Noël

**sap** [sæp] n (of plants) sève f ♦ vt (strength) miner, saper

**sapling** ['sæplɪŋ] n jeune arbre m

**sapphire** ['sæfaɪə*] n saphir m

**sarcasm** ['sɑːkæzm] n sarcasme m, raillerie f; **sarcastic** [sɑː'kæstɪk] adj sarcastique

**sardine** [sɑː'diːn] n sardine f

**Sardinia** [sɑː'dɪnɪə] n Sardaigne f

**sash** [sæʃ] n écharpe f

**sat** [sæt] pt, pp of **sit**

**satchel** ['sætʃl] n cartable m

**satellite** ['sætəlaɪt] n satellite m; ~ **dish** n antenne f parabolique; ~ **television** n télévision f par câble

**satin** ['sætɪn] n satin m ♦ adj en or de satin, satiné(e)

**satire** ['sætaɪə*] n satire f

**satisfaction** [sætɪs'fækʃən] n satisfaction f

**satisfactory** [sætɪs'fæktərɪ] adj satisfaisant(e)

**satisfied** ['sætɪsfaɪd] adj satisfait(e)

**satisfy** ['sætɪsfaɪ] vt satisfaire, contenter; (convince) convaincre, persuader; ~**ing** adj satisfaisant(e)

**Saturday** ['sætədɪ] n samedi m

**sauce** [sɔːs] n sauce f; ~**pan** n casserole f

**saucer** ['sɔːsə*] n soucoupe f

**Saudi** ['saudɪ]: ~ **Arabia** n Arabie Saoudite; ~ **(Arabian)** adj saoudien(ne)

**sauna** ['sɔːnə] n sauna m

**saunter** ['sɔːntə*] vi: **to** ~ **along/in/out** etc marcher/entrer/sortir etc d'un pas nonchalant

**sausage** ['sɔsɪdʒ] n saucisse f; (cold meat) saucisson m; ~ **roll** n ~ friand m

**savage** ['sævɪdʒ] adj (cruel, fierce) brutal(e), féroce; (primitive) primitif(-ive), sauvage ♦ n sauvage m/f

**save** [seɪv] vt (person, belongings) sauver; (money) mettre de côté, économiser; (time) (faire) gagner; (keep) garder; (COMPUT) sauvegarder; (SPORT: stop) arrêter; (avoid: trouble) éviter ♦ vi (also: ~ **up**) mettre de l'argent de côté ♦ n (SPORT) arrêt m (du ballon) ♦ prep sauf, à l'exception de

**saving** ['seɪvɪŋ] n économie f ♦ adj: **the** ~ **grace of sth** ce qui rachète qch; ~**s** npl (money saved) économies fpl; ~**s account** n compte m d'épargne; ~**s bank** n caisse f d'épargne

**saviour** ['seɪvjə*] (US **savior**) n sauveur m

**savour** ['seɪvər] (US **savor**) vt savourer; **~y** (US **savory**) adj (dish: not sweet) salé(e)

**saw** [sɔ:] (pt **sawed**, pp **sawed** or **sawn**) vt scier ♦ n (tool) scie f ♦ pt of **see**; **~dust** n sciure f; **~mill** n scierie f; **~n-off** adj: **~n-off shotgun** carabine f à canon scié

**sax** [sæks] (inf) n saxo m

**saxophone** ['sæksəfəʊn] n saxophone m

**say** [seɪ] (pt, pp **said**) n: **to have one's ~** dire ce qu'on a à dire ♦ vt dire; **to have a** or **some ~ in sth** avoir voix au chapitre; **could you ~ that again?** pourriez-vous répéter ce que vous venez de dire?; **that goes without ~ing** cela va sans dire, cela va de soi; **~ing** n dicton m, proverbe m

**scab** [skæb] n croûte f; (pej) jaune m

**scaffold** ['skæfəld] n échafaud m; **~ing** n échafaudage m

**scald** [skɔːld] n brûlure f ♦ vt ébouillanter

**scale** [skeɪl] n (of fish) écaille f; (MUS) gamme f; (of ruler, thermometer etc) graduation f, échelle (graduée) f; (of salaries, fees etc) barème m; (of map, also: size, extent) échelle ♦ vt (mountain) escalader; **~s** npl (for weighing) balance f; (also: **bathroom ~s**) pèse-personne m; **on a large ~** sur une grande échelle, en grand; **~ of charges** tableau m des tarifs; **~ down** vt réduire

**scallop** ['skɒləp] n coquille f Saint-Jacques; (SEWING) feston m

**scalp** [skælp] n cuir chevelu ♦ vt scalper

**scampi** ['skæmpɪ] npl langoustines (frites), scampi mpl

**scan** [skæn] vt scruter, examiner; (glance at quickly) parcourir; (TV, RADAR) balayer ♦ n (MED) scanographie f

**scandal** ['skændl] n scandale m; (gossip) ragots mpl

**Scandinavia** [skændɪ'neɪvɪə] n Scandinavie f; **~n** adj scandinave

**scant** [skænt] adj insuffisant(e); **~y** ['skæntɪ] adj peu abondant(e), insuffisant(e); (underwear) minuscule

**scapegoat** ['skeɪpgəʊt] n bouc m émissaire

**scar** [skɑ:] n cicatrice f ♦ vt marquer (d'une cicatrice)

**scarce** [skɛəs] adj rare, peu abondant(e); **to make o.s. ~** (inf) se sauver; **~ly** adv à peine; **scarcity** n manque m, pénurie f

**scare** [skɛər] n peur f, panique f; (to threaten) frayeur, faire peur à; **to ~ sb stiff** faire une peur bleue à qn; **bomb ~** alerte f à la bombe; **~ away** vt faire fuir; **~ off** vt = **scare away**; **~crow** n épouvantail m; **~d** adj: **to be ~d** avoir peur

**scarf** [skɑ:f] (pl **~s** or **scarves**) n (long) écharpe f; (square) foulard m

**scarlet** ['skɑ:lɪt] adj écarlate; **~ fever** n scarlatine f

**scary** ['skɛərɪ] (inf) adj effrayant(e)

**scathing** ['skeɪðɪŋ] adj cinglant(e), acerbe

**scatter** ['skætər] vt éparpiller, répandre; (crowd) disperser ♦ vi se disperser; **~brained** adj écervelé(e), étourdi(e)

**scavenger** ['skævəndʒər] n (person: in bins etc) pilleur m de poubelles

**scene** [si:n] n scène f; (of crime, accident) lieu(x) m(pl); (sight, view) spectacle m, vue f; **~ry** ['si:nərɪ] n (THEATRE) décor(s) m(pl); (landscape) paysage m; **scenic** adj (picturesque) offrant de beaux paysages or panoramas

**scent** [sent] n parfum m, odeur f; (track) piste f

**sceptical** ['skeptɪkl] (US **skeptical**) adj sceptique

**schedule** ['ʃedjuːl, (US) 'skedjuːl] n programme m, plan m; (of trains) horaire m; (of prices etc) barème m, tarif m ♦ vt prévoir; **on ~** à l'heure (prévue); **to be ahead of/behind ~** avoir de l'avance/du retard; **~d flight** n vol régulier

**scheme** [skiːm] n plan m, projet m,

(dishonest plan, plot) complot m, combine m, (arrangement) arrangement m, classification f; (pension - etc) régime m ♦ vi comploter, manigancer; **scheming** adj rusé(e), intrigant(e) ♦ n manigances fpl, intrigues fpl

**scholar** ['skɔlər] n érudit(e); (pupil) boursier(-ère); **~ship** n (knowledge) érudition f; (grant) bourse f (d'études)

**school** [sku:l] n école f; (secondary ~) collège m, lycée m; (us: university) université f; (in university) faculté f ♦ cpd scolaire; **~book** n livre m scolaire or de classe; **~boy** n écolier m; collégien m; lycéen m; **~children** npl écoliers mpl; collégiens mpl; lycéens mpl; **~girl** n écolière f; collégienne f, lycéenne f; **~ing** n instruction f, études fpl; **~master** n professeur m, (primary) instituteur m; **~mistress** n professeur m, (primary) institutrice f; **~teacher** n instituteur(-trice); professeur m

**science** ['saɪəns] n science f; **~ fiction** n science-fiction f; **scientific** [saɪən'tɪfɪk] adj scientifique; **scientist** n scientifique m/f; (eminent) savant m

**scissors** ['sɪzəz] npl ciseaux mpl

**scoff** [skɔf] vt (BRIT: inf: eat) avaler, bouffer ♦ vi: to ~ (at) (mock) se moquer (de)

**scold** [skəuld] vt gronder

**scone** [skɔn] n sorte de petit pain rond au lait

**scoop** [sku:p] n (for ice cream) boule f à glace; (PRESS) scoop m; ~ **out** vt évider, creuser; ~ **up** vt ramasser

**scooter** ['sku:tər] n (also: **motor ~**) scooter m; (toy) trottinette f

**scope** [skəup] n (capacity: of plan, undertaking) portée f, envergure f; (: of person) compétence f, capacités fpl; (opportunity) possibilités fpl; **within the ~** of dans les limites de

**scorch** [skɔ:tʃ] vt (clothes) brûler (légèrement), roussir; (earth, grass) dessécher, brûler

**score** [skɔ:r] n score m, décompte m

des points; (MUS) partition f; (twenty) vingt ♦ vt (goal, point) marquer; (success) remporter ♦ vi marquer des points; (FOOTBALL) marquer un but; (keep ~) compter les points; ~**s of** (very many) beaucoup de, un tas de (fam); **on that ~** sur ce chapitre, à cet égard; **to ~ 6 out of 10** obtenir 6 sur 10; ~ **out** vt rayer, barrer, biffer; ~**board** n tableau m

**scorn** [skɔ:n] n mépris m, dédain m

**Scorpio** ['skɔ:pɪəu] n le Scorpion

**Scot** [skɔt] n Écossais(e)

**Scotch** [skɔtʃ] n whisky m, scotch m

**scot-free** ['skɔt'fri:] adv: **to get off ~~** s'en tirer sans être puni(e)

**Scotland** ['skɔtlənd] n Écosse f; **Scots** adj écossais(e); **Scotsman** (irreg) n Écossais; **Scotswoman** (irreg) n Écossaise f; **Scottish** adj écossais(e); **Scottish Parliament** n Parlement m écossais

**scoundrel** ['skaundrl] n vaurien m

**scour** ['skauər] vt (search) battre, parcourir

**scout** [skaut] n (MIL) éclaireur m; (also: **boy ~**) scout m; girl ~ (us) guide f; ~ **around** vi explorer, chercher

**scowl** [skaul] vi avoir l'air maussade; **to ~ at** regarder de travers

**scrabble** ['skræbl] vi (also: ~ **around**: search) chercher à tâtons; (claw): **to ~ (at)** gratter ♦ n: S~ ® Scrabble ®

**scram** [skræm] (inf) vi ficher le camp

**scramble** ['skræmbl] n (rush) bousculade f, ruée f ♦ vi: **to ~ up/down** grimper/descendre tant bien que mal; **to ~ out** sortir or descendre à toute vitesse; **to ~ through** se frayer un passage (à travers); **to ~ for** se bousculer or se disputer pour (avoir); ~**d eggs** npl œufs brouillés

**scrap** [skræp] n bout m, morceau m; (fight) bagarre f; (also: ~ **iron**) ferraille f ♦ vt jeter, mettre au rebut; (fig) abandonner, laisser tomber ♦ vi (fight) se bagarrer; ~**s** npl (waste) déchets mpl;

**~book** n album m; **~ dealer** n marchand m de ferraille

**scrape** [skreɪp] vt à gratter, racler ♦ n: **to get into a ~** s'attirer des ennuis; **to ~ through** réussir de justesse; **~ together** vt (money) racler ses fonds de tiroir pour réunir

**scrap:** **~ heap** n: **on the ~ heap** (fig) au rancart or rebut; **~ merchant** (BRIT) n marchand m de ferraille; **~ paper** n papier m brouillon

**scratch** [skrætʃ] n égratignure f, rayure f; éraflure f; (from claw) coup m de griffe ♦ cpd: **~ team** équipe de fortune or improvisée ♦ vt (rub) (se) gratter; (record) rayer; (paint etc) érafler; (with claw, nail) griffer ♦ vi (se) gratter; **to start from ~** partir de zéro; **to be up to ~** être à la hauteur

**scrawl** [skrɔːl] vi gribouiller

**scrawny** ['skrɔːnɪ] adj décharné(e)

**scream** [skriːm] n cri perçant, hurlement m ♦ vi crier, hurler

**screech** [skriːtʃ] vi hurler; (tyres) crisser; (brakes) grincer

**screen** [skriːn] n écran m; (in room) paravent m; (fig) écran, rideau m ♦ vt (conceal) masquer, cacher; (from the wind etc) abriter, protéger; (film) projeter; (candidates etc) filtrer; **~ing** n (MED) test m (or tests) de dépistage; **~play** n scénario m

**screw** [skruː] n vis f ♦ vt (also: **~ in**) visser; **~ up** vt (paper) froisser; **to ~ up one's eyes** plisser les yeux; **~driver** n tournevis m

**scribble** ['skrɪbl] vt, vi gribouiller, griffonner

**script** [skrɪpt] n (CINEMA etc) scénario m, texte m; (system of writing) écriture (f) script m

**Scripture(s)** ['skrɪptʃə(-əz)] n(pl) (Christian) Écriture sainte; (other religions) écritures saintes

**scroll** [skrəʊl] n rouleau m

**scrounge** [skraʊndʒ] (inf) vt: **to ~ sth off** or **from sb** taper qn de qch; **~r**

(inf) n parasite m

**scrub** [skrʌb] n (land) broussailles fpl ♦ vt (floor) nettoyer à la brosse; (pan) récurer; (washing) frotter; (inf: cancel) annuler

**scruff** [skrʌf] n: **by the ~ of the neck** par la peau du cou

**scruffy** ['skrʌfɪ] adj débraillé(e)

**scrum(mage)** ['skrʌm(ɪdʒ)] n (RUGBY) mêlée f

**scruple** ['skruːpl] n scrupule m

**scrutiny** ['skruːtɪnɪ] n examen minutieux

**scuff** [skʌf] vt érafler

**scuffle** ['skʌfl] n échauffourée f, rixe f

**sculptor** ['skʌlptə'] n sculpteur m

**sculpture** ['skʌlptʃə'] n sculpture f

**scum** [skʌm] n écume f, mousse f; (pej: people) rebut m, lie f

**scurry** ['skʌrɪ] vi filer à toute allure; **to ~ off** détaler, se sauver

**scuttle** ['skʌtl] n (also: **coal ~**) seau m (à charbon) ♦ vt (ship) saborder ♦ vi (scamper): **to ~ away** or **off** détaler

**scythe** [saɪð] n faux f

**SDP** n abbr (= Social Democratic Party)

**sea** [siː] n mer f ♦ cpd marin(e), (de la) mer; **by ~** (travel) par mer, en bateau; **on the ~** (boat) en mer; (town) au bord de la mer; **to be all at ~** (fig) nager complètement; **out to ~** au large; (out) **~** en mer; **~board** n côte f; **~food** n fruits mpl de mer; **~front** n bord m de mer; **~going** adj (ship) de mer; **~gull** n mouette f

**seal** [siːl] n (animal) phoque m; (stamp) sceau m, cachet m ♦ vt sceller; (envelope) coller; (: with ~) cacheter; **~ off** vt (forbid entry to) interdire l'accès de

**sea level** n niveau m de la mer

**sea lion** n otarie f

**seam** [siːm] n couture f; (of coal) veine f, filon m

**seaman** ['siːmən] (irreg) n marin m

**seance** ['seɪɔns] n séance f de spiritisme

**seaplane** ['si:pleɪn] n hydravion m

**search** [sɜ:tʃ] n (for person, thing, COMPUT) recherche(s) f(pl); (LAW: at sb's home) perquisition f ♦ vt fouiller; (examine) examiner minutieusement; scruter ♦ vi: **to ~ for** chercher; **in ~ of** à la recherche de; **to ~ through** vt fus fouiller; **~ing** adj pénétrant(e); **~light** n projecteur m; **~ party** n expédition f de secours; **~ warrant** n mandat m de perquisition

**sea:** **~shore** n rivage m, plage f, bord m de (la) mer; **~sick** adj: **to be ~sick** avoir le mal de mer; **~side** n bord de la mer; **~side resort** n station f balnéaire

**season** ['si:zn] n saison f ♦ vt assaisonner, relever; **to be in/out of ~** être/ne pas être en saison; **~al** adj (work) saisonnier(-ère); **~ed** adj (fig) expérimenté(e); **~ ticket** n carte f d'abonnement

**seat** [si:t] n siège m; (in bus, train: place) place f; (buttocks) postérieur m; (of trousers) fond m ♦ vt faire asseoir, placer; (have room for) avoir des places assises pour, pouvoir accueillir; **~ belt** n ceinture f de sécurité

**sea:** **~water** n eau f de mer; **~weed** n algues fpl; **~worthy** adj en état de naviguer

**sec.** abbr = **second(s)**

**secluded** [sɪ'klu:dɪd] adj retiré(e), à l'écart

**seclusion** [sɪ'klu:ʒən] n solitude f

**second¹** [sɪ'kɒnd] (BRIT) vt (employee) affecter provisoirement

**second²** ['sekənd] adj deuxième, second(e) ♦ adv (in race etc) en seconde position ♦ n (unit of time) seconde f; (AUT: ~ gear) seconde; (COMM: imperfect) article m de second choix; (BRIT: UNIV) licence f avec mention ♦ vt (motion) appuyer; **~ary** adj secondaire; **~ary school** n collège m, lycée m; **~class** adj de deuxième classe; (RAIL) de seconde (classe); (POST) au tarif réduit;

(pej) de qualité inférieure ♦ adv (RAIL) en seconde; (POST) au tarif réduit; **~hand** adj d'occasion, de seconde main; **~ hand** n (on clock) trotteuse f de la deuxième; **~ment** [sɪ'kɒndmənt] (BRIT) n détachement m; **~rate** adj de deuxième ordre, de qualité inférieure; **~ thoughts** npl doutes mpl; **on ~ thoughts** or (US) **thought** à la réflexion

**secrecy** ['si:krəsɪ] n secret m

**secret** ['si:krɪt] adj secret(-ète) ♦ n secret m; **in ~** en secret, secrètement, en cachette

**secretary** ['sekrətərɪ] n secrétaire m/f; (COMM) secrétaire général; **S~ of State (for)** (BRIT: POL) ministre m (de)

**secretive** ['si:krətɪv] adj dissimulé(e)

**secretly** ['si:krɪtlɪ] adv en secret, secrètement

**sectarian** [sek'teərɪən] adj sectaire

**section** ['sekʃən] n section f; (of document) section, article m, paragraphe m; (cut) coupe f

**sector** ['sektə'] n secteur m

**secular** ['sekjulə'] adj profane, laïque; séculier(-ère)

**secure** [sɪ'kjuə'] adj (free from anxiety) sans inquiétude, sécurisé(e); (firmly fixed) solide, bien attaché(e) or fermé(e) etc); (in safe place) en lieu sûr, en sûreté ♦ vt (fix) fixer, attacher; (get) obtenir, se procurer

**security** [sɪ'kjuərɪtɪ] n sécurité f, mesures fpl de sécurité; (for loan) caution f, garantie f; **~ guard** n garde chargé de la sécurité; (when transporting money) convoyeur m de fonds

**sedate** [sɪ'deɪt] adj calme; posé(e) ♦ vt (MED) donner des sédatifs à

**sedative** ['sedɪtɪv] n calmant m, sédatif m

**seduce** [sɪ'dju:s] vt séduire; **seduction** [sɪ'dʌkʃən] n séduction f; **seductive** [sɪ'dʌktɪv] adj séduisant(e); (smile) séducteur (-trice); (offer) alléchant(e)

**see** [si:] (pt **saw**, pp **seen**) vt voir; (accompany): **to ~ sb to the door** reconduire or raccompagner qn jusqu'à la porte ♦ vi voir ♦ n évêché m; **to ~ that** (ensure) veiller à ce que +sub, faire en sorte que +sub, s'assurer que; **~ you soon!** à bientôt!; **~ about** vt fus s'occuper de; **~ off** vt accompagner (à la gare ou à l'aéroport etc); **~ through** vt mener à bonne fin ♦ vt fus voir clair dans; **~ to** vt fus s'occuper de, se charger de

**seed** [si:d] n graine f; (sperm) semence f; (fig) germe m; (TENNIS etc) tête f de série; **to go to ~** monter en graine; (fig) se laisser aller, **~ling** n jeune plant m, semis m; **~y** adj (shabby) minable, miteux(-euse)

**seeing** [si:ŋ] conj: **~ (that)** vu que, étant donné que

**seek** [si:k] (pt, pp sought) vt chercher, rechercher

**seem** [si:m] vi sembler, paraître; **there ~s to be ...** il semble qu'il y a ...; **on dirait qu'il y a ...; **~ingly** adv apparemment

**seen** [si:n] pp of **see**

**seep** [si:p] vi suinter, filtrer

**seesaw** [si:sɔ:] n (jeu m de) bascule f

**seethe** [si:ð] vi être en effervescence; **to ~ with anger** bouillir de colère

**see-through** [si:θru:] adj transparent(e)

**segment** [segmənt] n segment m; (of orange) quartier m

**segregate** [segrɪgeɪt] vt séparer, isoler

**seize** [si:z] vt saisir, attraper; (take possession of) s'emparer de; (opportunity) saisir; **~ up** vi (TECH) se gripper; **~ (up)on** vt fus saisir, sauter sur

**seizure** [si:ʒəʳ] n (MED) crise f, attaque f; (of power) prise f

**seldom** [seldəm] adv rarement

**select** [sɪ'lekt] adj choisi(e), d'élite ♦ vt sélectionner, choisir; **~ion** n sélection f, choix m

**self** [self] (pl selves) n: **the ~** le moi inv ♦ prefix auto-; **~assured** adj sûr(e) de soi; **~catering** (BRIT) adj avec cuisi-ne, où l'on peut faire sa cuisine; **~centred** (US self-centered) adj égocentrique; **~confidence** n confiance f en soi; **~conscious** adj timide, qui manque d'assurance; **~contained** (BRIT) adj (flat) avec entrée particulière, indépendant(e); **~control** n maîtrise f de soi; **~defence** (US self-defense) n (LAW) légitime défense f; **~discipline** n discipline personnelle; **~employed** adj qui travaille à son compte; **~evident** adj: **to be ~evident** être évident(e), aller de soi; **~governing** adj autonome; **~indulgent** adj qui ne se refuse rien; **~interest** n intérêt personnel; **~ish** adj égoïste; **~ishness** n égoïsme m; **~less** adj désintéressé(e); **~pity** n apitoiement m sur soi-même; **~possessed** adj assuré(e); **~preservation** n instinct m de conservation; **~respect** n respect m de soi, amour-propre m; **~righteous** adj suffisant(e); **~sacrifice** n abnégation f; **~satisfied** adj content(e) de soi, suffisant(e); **~service** adj libre-service, self-service; **~sufficient** adj autosuffisant(e); (person: independent) indépendant(e); **~taught** adj (artist, pianist) qui a appris par lui-même

**sell** [sel] (pt, pp sold) vt vendre ♦ vi se vendre; **to ~ at or for 10 F** se vendre 10 F; **~ off** vt liquider; **~ out** vi: **to ~ out (of sth)** (use up stock) vendre tout son stock (de qch); **the tickets are all sold out** il ne reste plus de billets; **~ by date** n date f limite de vente; **~er** n vendeur(-euse), marchand(e); **~ing price** n prix m de vente

**Sellotape** ® [seləʊteɪp] (BRIT) n papier m collant, scotch ® m

**selves** [selvz] npl of **self**

**semblance** [sembləns] n semblant m

**semen** [si:mən] n sperme m

**semester** [sɪ'mestəʳ] (esp US) n semestre m

**semi** [semɪ] prefix semi-, demi-; à demi,

à moitié; **~circle** n demi-cercle m; **~colon** n point-virgule m; **~detached (house)** (BRIT) n maison jumelée or jumelle; **~final** n demi-finale f

**seminar** ['semɪnɑːʳ] n séminaire m; **~y** n (REL: for priests) séminaire m

**semiskilled** ['semɪ'skɪld] adj: **~ worker** ouvrier(-ère) spécialisé(e)

**semi-skimmed milk** [semɪ'skɪmd-] n lait m demi-écrémé

**senate** ['senɪt] n sénat m; **senator** n sénateur m

**send** [send] (pt, pp **sent**) vt envoyer; **~ away** vt (letter, goods) envoyer, expédier; (unwelcome visitor) renvoyer; **~ away for** vt fus commander par correspondance, se faire envoyer; **~ back** vt renvoyer; **~ for** vt fus envoyer chercher; faire venir; **~ off** vt (goods) envoyer, expédier; (BRIT SPORT: player) expulser ou renvoyer du terrain; **~ out** vt (invitation) envoyer (par la poste); (light, heat, signal) émettre; **~ up** vt faire monter; (BRIT: parody) mettre en boîte, parodier; **~er** n expéditeur (-trice); **~-off** n: **a good ~-off** des adieux chaleureux

**senior** ['siːnɪəʳ] adj (high-ranking) de haut niveau; (of higher rank): **to be ~ to sb** être le supérieur de qn (hiérarchiquement); (older): **she is 15 years his ~** elle est son aînée de 15 ans, elle est plus âgée que lui de 15 ans; **~ citizen** n personne âgée; **~ity** [siːnɪ'ɔrɪtɪ] n (in service) ancienneté f

**sensation** [sen'seɪʃən] n sensation f; **~al** adj qui fait sensation; (marvellous) sensationnel(le)

**sense** [sens] n sens m; (feeling) sentiment m; (meaning) sens m; (wisdom) bon sens ♦ vt sentir, pressentir; **it makes ~** c'est logique, ça se tient; **~less** adj insensé(e), stupide; (unconscious) sans connaissance

**sensible** ['sensɪbl] adj sensé(e), raisonnable; sage

**sensitive** ['sensɪtɪv] adj sensible

**sensual** ['sensjuəl] adj sensuel(le)

**sensuous** ['sensjuəs] adj voluptueux (-euse), sensuel(le)

**sent** [sent] pt, pp of **send**

**sentence** ['sentns] n (LING) phrase f; (LAW: judgment) condamnation f, sentence f; (: punishment) peine ♦ vt: **to ~ sb to death/to 5 years in prison** condamner qn à mort/à 5 ans de prison

**sentiment** ['sentɪmənt] n sentiment m; (opinion) opinion f, avis m; **~al** [sentɪ'mentl] adj sentimental(e)

**sentry** ['sentrɪ] n sentinelle f

**separate** [adj 'seprɪt, vb 'sepəreɪt] adj séparé(e), indépendant(e), différent(e) ♦ vt séparer; (make a distinction between) distinguer ♦ vi se séparer; **~ly** adv séparément; **~s** npl (clothes) coordonnés mpl; **separation** [sepə'reɪʃən] n séparation f

**September** [sep'tembəʳ] n septembre m

**septic** ['septɪk] adj (wound) infecté(e); **~ tank** n fosse f septique

**sequel** ['siːkwl] n conséquence f, séquelles fpl; (of story) suite f

**sequence** ['siːkwəns] n ordre m, suite f; (film ~) séquence f; (dance ~) numéro m

**sequin** ['siːkwɪn] n paillette f

**Serbia** ['sɜːbɪə] n Serbie f

**serene** [sɪ'riːn] adj serein(e), calme, paisible

**sergeant** ['sɑːdʒənt] n sergent m; (POLICE) brigadier m

**serial** ['sɪərɪəl] n feuilleton m; **~ killer** n meurtrier m tuant en série; **~ number** n numéro m de série

**series** ['sɪərɪz] n inv série f; (PUBLISHING) collection f

**serious** ['sɪərɪəs] adj sérieux(-euse); (ill-ness) grave; **~ly** adv sérieusement; (hurt) gravement

**sermon** ['sɜːmən] n sermon m

**serrated** [sɪ'reɪtɪd] adj en dents de scie

**servant** ['sɜːvənt] n domestique m/f;

(fig) serviteur/servante

**serve** [sɜːv] vt (employer etc) servir, être au service de; (purpose) servir à; (customer, food, meal) servir; (subj: train) desservir; (apprenticeship) faire, accomplir; (prison term) purger ♦ vt servir; (be useful): **to ~ as/for/to do** servir de/à/à faire ♦ n (TENNIS) service m; **it ~s him right** c'est bien fait pour lui; **~ out, ~ up** vt (food) servir

**service** ['sɜːvɪs] n service m; (AUT: maintenance) révision f ♦ vt (car, washing machine) réviser; **the S~s** les forces armées; **to be of ~ to** rendre service à qn; **15% ~ included** service 15% compris; **~ not included** service non compris; **~able** adj pratique, commode; **~ area** n (on motorway) aire f de services; **~ charge** (BRIT) n service m; **~man** (irreg) n militaire m; **~ station** n station-service f

**serviette** [sɜːvɪ'et] (BRIT) n serviette f (de table)

**session** ['seʃən] n séance f

**set** [set] (pt, pp set) n série f, assortiment m; (of tools etc) jeu m; (RADIO, TV) poste m; (TENNIS) set m; (group of people) cercle m, milieu m; (THEATRE: stage) scène f; (: scenery) décor m; (MATH) ensemble m; (HAIRDRESSING) mise f en plis ♦ adj (fixed) fixe, déterminé(e); (ready) prêt(e) ♦ vt (place) placer; (fix, establish) fixer; (: record) établir; (adjust) régler; (decide: rules etc) fixer, choisir; (task) donner; (exam) composer ♦ vi (sun) se coucher; (jam, jelly, concrete) prendre; (bone) se ressouder; **to be ~ on doing** être résolu à faire; **to ~ the table** mettre la table; **to ~ (to music)** mettre en musique; **to ~ on fire** mettre le feu à; **to ~ free** libérer; **to ~ sth going** déclencher qch; **to ~ sail** prendre la mer; **~ about** vt fus (task) entreprendre, se mettre à; **~ aside** vt mettre de côté; (time) garder; **~ back** vt (in time): **to ~ back (by)** retarder (de); (cost): **to ~ sb back £5** coûter 5 livres

à qn; **~ off** vi se mettre en route, partir ♦ vt (bomb) faire exploser; (cause to start) déclencher; (show up well) mettre en valeur, faire valoir; **~ out** vi se mettre en route, partir ♦ vt (arrange) disposer; (arguments) présenter, exposer; **to ~ out to do** entreprendre de faire, avoir pour but or intention de faire; **~ up** vt (organization) fonder, créer; **~back** n (hitch) revers m, contretemps m; **~ menu** n menu m

**settee** [se'tiː] n canapé m

**setting** ['setɪŋ] n cadre m; (of jewel) monture f; (position: of controls) réglage m

**settle** ['setl] vt (argument, matter, account) régler; (problem) résoudre; (MED: calm) calmer ♦ vi (bird, dust etc) se poser; (also: **~ down**) s'installer, se fixer; (calm down) se calmer; **to ~ for sth** accepter qch, se contenter de qch; **to ~ on sth** opter or se décider pour qch; **to ~ in** vi s'installer; **~ up** vi: **to ~ up with sb** régler (ce que l'on doit à) qn; **~ment** n (payment) règlement m; (agreement) accord m; (village etc) établissement m; hameau m; **~r** n colon m

**setup** ['setʌp] n (arrangement) manière f dont les choses sont organisées; (situation) situation f

**seven** ['sevn] num sept; **~teen** num dix-sept; **~th** num septième; **~ty** num soixante-dix

**sever** ['sevə¹] vt couper, trancher; (relations) rompre

**several** ['sevrəl] adj, pron plusieurs m/ fpl; **~ of us** plusieurs d'entre nous

**severance** ['sevərəns] n (of relations) rupture f; **~ pay** n indemnité f de licenciement

**severe** [sɪ'vɪə¹] adj (stern) sévère, strict(e); (serious) grave, sérieux(-euse); (plain) sévère, austère; **severity** [sɪ'verɪtɪ] n sévérité f; gravité f; rigueur f

**sew** [səʊ] (pt sewed, pp sewn) vt, vi coudre; **~ up** vt (re)coudre

**sewage** ['su:ɪdʒ] n vidange(s) f(pl)

**sewer** ['su:ə*] n égout m

**sewing** ['səʊɪŋ] n couture f; (item(s)) ouvrage m; **~ machine** n machine f à coudre

**sewn** [səʊn] pp of **sew**

**sex** [seks] n sexe m; **to have ~ with** avoir des rapports (sexuels) avec; **~ism** n sexisme m; **~ist** n sexiste; **~ual** ['seksjuəl] adj sexuel(le); **~uality** [seksjuˈælɪtɪ] n sexualité f; **~y** adj inv

**shabby** ['ʃæbɪ] adj miteux(-euse); (behaviour) mesquin(e), méprisable

**shack** [ʃæk] n cabane f, hutte f

**shackles** ['ʃæklz] npl chaînes fpl, entraves fpl

**shade** [ʃeɪd] n ombre f; (for lamp) abat-jour m inv; (of colour) nuance f, ton m ♦ vt abriter du soleil, ombrager; **in the ~** à l'ombre; **a ~ too large/more** un tout petit peu trop grand(e)/plus

**shadow** ['ʃædəʊ] n ombre f ♦ vt (follow) filer; **~ cabinet** (BRIT) n (POL) cabinet parallèle formé par l'Opposition; **~y** adj ombragé(e); (dim) vague, indistinct(e)

**shady** ['ʃeɪdɪ] adj ombragé(e); (fig: dishonest) louche, véreux(-euse)

**shaft** [ʃɑːft] n (of arrow, spear) hampe f; (AUT, TECH) arbre m; (of mine) puits m; (of lift) cage f; (of light) rayon m, trait m

**shaggy** ['ʃægɪ] adj hirsute; en broussaille

**shake** [ʃeɪk] (pt **shook**, pp **shaken**) vt secouer; (bottle, cocktail) agiter; (house, confidence) ébranler ♦ vi trembler; **to ~ one's head** (in refusal) dire or faire non de la tête; (in dismay) secouer la tête; **to ~ hands with sb** serrer la main à qn; **~ off** vt secouer; (pursuer) se débarrasser de; **~ up** vt secouer; **~n** pp of **shake**; **shaky** adj (hand, voice) tremblant(e); (building) branlant(e), peu solide

**shall** [ʃæl] aux vb: **I ~ go** j'irai; **~ I open the door?** j'ouvre la porte?; **I'll get**

the coffee, **~ I?** je vais chercher le café, d'accord?

**shallow** ['ʃæləʊ] adj peu profond(e); (fig) superficiel(le)

**sham** [ʃæm] n frime f ♦ vt simuler

**shambles** ['ʃæmblz] n (muddle) confusion f, pagaïe f, fouillis m

**shame** [ʃeɪm] n honte f ♦ vt faire honte à; **it is a ~ (that/to do)** c'est une honte ou dommage (que +sub/de faire); **what a ~!** quel dommage!; **~ful** adj honteux(-euse), scandaleux(-euse); **~less** adj éhonté(e), effronté(e)

**shampoo** [ʃæmˈpuː] n shampooing m ♦ vt faire un shampooing à; **~ and set** n shampooing m (et) mise f en plis

**shamrock** ['ʃæmrɒk] n trèfle m (emblème de l'Irlande)

**shandy** ['ʃændɪ] n bière panachée

**shan't** [ʃɑːnt] = **shall not**

**shanty town** ['ʃæntɪ-] n bidonville m

**shape** [ʃeɪp] n forme f ♦ vt façonner, modeler; (sb's ideas) former; (sb's life) déterminer ♦ vi (also: **~ up**: events) prendre tournure; (: person) faire des progrès, s'en sortir; **to take ~** prendre forme or tournure; **~d suffix: heart~d** en forme de cœur; **~less** adj informe, sans forme; **~ly** adj bien proportionné(e), beau (belle)

**share** [ʃɛə*] n part f; (COMM) action f ♦ vt partager; (have in common) avoir en commun; **~ out** vi partager; **~holder** n actionnaire m

**shark** [ʃɑːk] n requin m

**sharp** [ʃɑːp] adj (razor, knife) tranchant(e), bien aiguisé(e); (point, voice) aigu(-guë); (nose, chin) pointu(e); (outline, increase) net(te); (cold, pain) vif (vive); (taste) piquant(e), âcre; (MUS) dièse; (person: quick-witted) vif (vive), éveillé(e); (: unscrupulous) malhonnête ♦ adv (precisely): **at 2 o'clock ~** à 2 heures pile or précises; **~en** vt aiguiser; (pencil) tailler; **~ener** n (also: **pencil ~ener**) taille-crayon(s) m inv; **~-eyed** adj à qui rien n'échappe;

**~ly** *adv* (*turn, stop*) brusquement; (*stand out*) nettement; (*criticize, retort*) sèchement, vertement

**shatter** ['ʃætə'] *vt* briser; (*fig: upset*) bouleverser; (: *ruin*) briser, ruiner ♦ *vi* voler en éclats, se briser

**shave** [ʃeɪv] *vt* raser ♦ *vi* se raser ♦ **to have a ~** se raser; **~r** *n* (*also:* **electric ~r**) rasoir *m* électrique

**shaving** ['ʃeɪvɪŋ] (*action*) rasage *m*; **~s** *npl* (*of wood etc*) copeaux *mpl*; **~ brush** *n* blaireau *m*; **~ cream** *n* crème *f* à raser; **~ foam** *n* mousse *f* à raser

**shawl** [ʃɔːl] *n* châle *m*

**she** [ʃiː] *pron* elle ♦ *prefix*: **~cat** chatte *f*; **~-elephant** éléphant *m* femelle

**sheaf** [ʃiːf] (*pl* **sheaves**) *n* gerbe *f*; (*of papers*) liasse *f*

**shear** [ʃɪə'] (*pt* **sheared**, *pp* **shorn**) *vt* (*sheep*) tondre; **~s** *npl* (*for hedge*) cisaille(s) *f(pl)*

**sheath** [ʃiːθ] *n* gaine *f*, fourreau *m*, étui *m*; (*contraceptive*) préservatif *m*

**shed** [ʃed] (*pt, pp* **shed**) *n* remise *f*, resserre *f* ♦ *vt* perdre; (*tears*) verser, répandre; (*workers*) congédier

**she'd** [ʃiːd] = **she had; she would**

**sheen** [ʃiːn] *n* lustre *m*

**sheep** [ʃiːp] *n inv* mouton *m*; **~dog** *n* chien *m* de berger; **~skin** *n* peau *f* de mouton

**sheer** [ʃɪə'] *adj* (*utter*) pur(e), pur et simple; (*steep*) à pic, abrupt(e); (*almost transparent*) extrêmement fin(e) ♦ *adv* à pic, abruptement

**sheet** [ʃiːt] *n* (*on bed*) drap *m*; (*of paper*) feuille *f*; (*of glass, metal etc*) feuille, plaque *f*

**sheik(h)** [ʃeɪk] *n* cheik *m*

**shelf** [ʃelf] (*pl* **shelves**) *n* étagère *f*, rayon *m*

**shell** [ʃel] *n* (*on beach*) coquillage *m*; (*of egg, nut etc*) coquille *f*; (*explosive*) obus *m*; (*of building*) carcasse *f* ♦ *vt* (*peas*) écosser; (MIL) bombarder (d'obus)

**she'll** [ʃiːl] = **she will; she shall**

**shellfish** ['ʃelfɪʃ] *n inv* (*crab etc*) crusta-

cé *m*; (*scallop etc*) coquillage *m* ♦ *npl* (*as food*) fruits *mpl* de mer

**shell suit** *n* survêtement *m* (*en synthétique froissé*)

**shelter** ['ʃeltə'] *n* abri *m*, refuge *m* ♦ *vt* abriter, protéger; (*give lodging to*) donner asile à ♦ *vi* s'abriter, se mettre à l'abri; **~ed housing** *n* foyers *mpl* (*pour personnes âgées ou handicapées*)

**shelve** [ʃelv] *vt* (*fig*) mettre en suspens ou en sommeil; **~s** *npl of* **shelf**

**shepherd** ['ʃepəd] *n* berger *m* ♦ *vt* (*guide*) guider, escorter; **~'s pie** (BRIT) *n* ≈ hachis *m* Parmentier

**sheriff** ['ʃerɪf] (US) *n* shérif *m*

**sherry** ['ʃerɪ] *n* xérès *m*, sherry *m*

**she's** [ʃiːz] = **she is; she has**

**Shetland** ['ʃetlənd] *n* (*also:* **the ~ Islands**) les îles *fpl* Shetland

**shield** [ʃiːld] *n* bouclier *m*; (*protection*) écran *m* de protection ♦ *vt*: **to ~ (from)** protéger (de ou contre)

**shift** [ʃift] *n* (*change*) changement *m*; (*work period*) période *f* de travail; (*of workers*) équipe *f*, poste *m* ♦ *vt* déplacer, changer de place; (*remove*) enlever ♦ *vi* changer de place, bouger; **~ work** *n* travail en équipe ou par relais ou par roulement; **~y** *adj* sournois(e); (*eyes*) fuyant(e)

**shimmer** ['ʃimə'] *vi* miroiter, chatoyer

**shin** [ʃin] *n* tibia *m*

**shine** [ʃain] (*pt, pp* **shone**) *n* éclat *m*, brillant *m* ♦ *vi* briller ♦ *vt* (*torch etc*): **to ~ on** braquer sur; (*polish: pt, pp* **~d**) faire briller ou reluire

**shingle** ['ʃiŋgl] *n* (*on beach*) galets *mpl*; **~s** *n* (MED) zona *m*

**shiny** ['ʃaini] *adj* brillant(e)

**ship** [ʃip] *n* bateau *m*; (*large*) navire *m* ♦ *vt* transporter (par mer); (*send*) expédier (par mer); **~building** *n* construction navale; **~ment** *n* cargaison *f*, **~ping** *n* (*ships*) navires *mpl*; (*the industry*) industrie navale; (*transport*) transport *m*; **~wreck** *n* (*ship*) épave *f*; (*event*) naufrage *m* ♦ *vt*: **to be**

~wrecked faire naufrage; ~yard n chantier naval

shire [ˈʃaɪə] n (BRIT) n comté m

shirt [ʃəːt] n (man's) chemise f; (woman's) chemisier m; in (one's) ~ sleeves en bras de chemise

shit [ʃɪt] (infl) n, excl merde f (!)

shiver [ˈʃɪvə] n frisson m ♦ vi frissonner

shoal [ʃəʊl] n (of fish) banc m (fig: also: ~s) masse f, foule f

shock [ʃɔk] n choc m; (ELEC) secousse f, (MED) commotion f, choc ♦ vt (offend) choquer, scandaliser; (upset) bouleverser; ~ absorber n amortisseur m; ~ing adj (scandalizing) choquant(e), scandaleux(-euse); (appalling) épouvantable

shoddy [ˈʃɔdɪ] adj de mauvaise qualité, mal fait(e)

shoe [ʃuː] (pt, pp shod) n chaussure f, soulier m; (also: horseshoe) fer m à cheval; (of horse) ferrer; ~lace n lacet m (de soulier); ~ polish n cirage m; ~ shop n magasin m de chaussures; ~string n (fig): on a ~string avec un budget dérisoire

shone [ʃɔn] pt, pp of shine

shook [ʃuk] pt of shake

shoot [ʃuːt] (pt, pp shot) n (on branch, seedling) pousse f ♦ vt (game) chasser; tirer; abattre; (person) blesser or tuer) d'un coup de fusil (or de revolver); (execute) fusiller; (arrow) tirer; (gun) tirer un coup de; (film) tourner ♦ vi (with gun, bow): to ~ (at) tirer (sur); (FOOTBALL) shooter, tirer; ~ down vt (plane) abattre; ~ in vi entrer comme une flèche; ~ out vi sortir comme une flèche; ~ up vi (fig) monter en flèche; ~ing n (shots) coups mpl de feu, fusillade f; (HUNTING) chasse f; ~ing star n étoile filante

shop [ʃɔp] n magasin m; (workshop) atelier m ♦ vi (also: go ~ping) faire ses courses or ses achats; ~ assistant (BRIT) n vendeur(-euse); ~ floor (BRIT) n (INDUSTRY: fig) ouvriers mpl; ~keeper n

commerçant(e); ~lifting n vol m à l'étalage; ~per n personne f qui fait ses courses, acheteur(-euse); ~ping n (goods) achats mpl, provisions fpl; ~ping bag n sac m (à provisions); ~ping centre (US shopping center) n centre commercial; ~-soiled adj défraîchi(e), qui a fait la vitrine; ~ steward (BRIT) n (INDUSTRY) délégué(e) syndical(e); ~ window n vitrine f

shore [ʃɔː] n (of sea, lake) rivage m, rive f ♦ vt: to ~ (up) étayer; on ~ à terre

shorn [ʃɔːn] pp of shear

short [ʃɔːt] adj (not long) court(e); (soon finished) court, bref (brève); (person, step) petit(e); (curt) brusque, sec (sèche); (insufficient) insuffisant(e); to be/run ~ of sth être à court de or manquer de qch; in ~ bref; en bref; ~ of doing ... à moins de faire ...; everything ~ of tout sauf; it is ~ for c'est l'abréviation or le diminutif de; to cut ~ (speech, visit) abréger, écourter; to fall ~ of ne pas être à la hauteur de; to run ~ of arriver à court de, venir à manquer de; to stop ~ s'arrêter net; to stop ~ of ne pas aller jusqu'à; ~age n manque m, pénurie f; ~bread n = sablé m; ~change vt ne pas rendre assez à; ~circuit n court-circuit m; ~coming n défaut m; ~(crust) pastry (BRIT) n pâte brisée; ~cut n raccourci m; ~en vt raccourcir; (text, visit) abréger; ~fall n déficit m; ~hand (BRIT) n sténo(graphie) f; ~hand typist (BRIT) n sténodactylo m/f; ~list (BRIT) n (for job) liste f des candidats sélectionnés; ~ly adv bientôt, sous peu; ~ notice n: at ~ notice au dernier moment; ~s npl: (a pair of) ~s un short; ~sighted (BRIT) adj myope; (fig) qui manque de clairvoyance; ~staffed adj à court de personnel; ~stay adj (car park) de courte durée; ~story n nouvelle f; ~tempered adj qui s'emporte facilement; ~term adj (effect) à court terme; ~wave n (RADIO) ondes courtes

**shot** [ʃɔt] *pt, pp of* **shoot ♦** *n* coup *m* (de feu); (*try*) coup, essai *m*; (*injection*) piqûre *f*; (PHOT) photo *f*; **he's a good/ poor ~** il tire bien/mal; **like a ~** comme une flèche; (*very readily*) sans hésiter; **~gun** *n* fusil *m* de chasse

**should** [ʃud] *aux vb*: **I ~ go now** je devrais partir maintenant; **he ~ be there now** il devrait être arrivé maintenant; **I ~ go if I were you** si j'étais vous, j'irais; **I ~ like to** j'aimerais bien, volontiers

**shoulder** ['ʃəuldər] *n* épaule *f* ♦ *vt* (*fig*) endosser, se charger de; **~ bag** *n* sac *m* à bandoulière; **~blade** *n* omoplate *f*

**shouldn't** ['ʃudnt] = **should not**

**shout** [ʃaut] *n* cri *m* ♦ *vt* crier ♦ *vi* (*also*: **~ out**) crier, pousser des cris; **~ down** *vt* huer; **~ing** *n* cris *mpl*

**shove** [ʃʌv] *vt* pousser; (*inf*: *put*): **to ~ sth in** fourrer ou ficher qch dans; **~ off** (*inf*) *vi* ficher le camp

**shovel** ['ʃʌvl] *n* pelle *f*

**show** [ʃəu] (*pt* **showed**, *pp* **shown**) *n* (*of emotion*) manifestation *f*, démonstration *f*; (*semblance*) semblant *m*, apparence *f*; (*exhibition*) exposition *f*, salon *m*; (THEATRE, TV) spectacle *m* ♦ *vt* montrer; (*film*) donner; (*courage etc*) faire preuve de, manifester; (*exhibit*) exposer ♦ *vi* se voir, être visible; **for ~** pour l'effet; **on ~** (*exhibits etc*) exposé(e); **~ in** *vt* (*person*) faire entrer; **~ off** (*pej*) *vi* crâner ♦ *vt* (*display*) faire valoir; **~ out** *vt* (*person*) reconduire (jusqu'à la porte); **~ up** *vi* (*stand out*) ressortir; (*inf*: *turn up*) se montrer ♦ *vt* (*flaw*) faire ressortir; **~ business** *n* le monde du spectacle; **~down** *n* épreuve *f* de force

**shower** ['ʃauər] *n* (*rain*) averse *f*; (*of stones etc*) pluie *f*, grêle *f*; (*~bath*) douche *f* ♦ *vi* prendre une douche, se doucher ♦ *vt*: **to ~ sb** (*with gifts etc*) combler qn de; **to have** *ou* **take a ~** prendre une douche; **~proof** *adj* imperméabilisé(e)

**showing** ['ʃəuiŋ] *n* (*of film*) projection *f*

**show jumping** *n* concours *m* hippique

**shown** [ʃəun] *pp of* **show**

**show: ~-off** *n* (*person*) crâneur (-euse), m'as-tu-vu(e); **~piece** *n* (*of exhibition*) trésor *m*; **~room** *n* magasin *m* d'exposition

**shrank** [ʃræŋk] *pt of* **shrink**

**shrapnel** ['ʃræpnl] *n* éclats *mpl* d'obus

**shred** [ʃred] *n*. (*gen pl*) lambeau *m*, petit morceau *f* ♦ *vt* mettre en lambeaux, déchirer; (CULIN: *grate*) râper; (: *lettuce etc*) couper en lanières; **~der** *n* (*for vegetables*) râpeur *m*; (*for documents*) déchiqueteuse *f*

**shrewd** [ʃru:d] *adj* astucieux(-euse), perspicace; (*businessman*) habile

**shriek** [ʃri:k] *n* cri perçant, hurlement, cri ♦ *vi* hurler, crier

**shrill** [ʃril] *adj* perçant(e), .aigu(-guë), strident(e)

**shrimp** [ʃrimp] *n* crevette *f*

**shrine** [ʃrain] *n* (*place*) lieu *m* de pèlerinage

**shrink** [ʃriŋk] (*pt* **shrank**, *pp* **shrunk**) *vi* rétrécir; (*fig*) se réduire, diminuer; (*move: also*: **~ away**) reculer ♦ *vt* (*wool*) faire rétrécir ♦ *n* (*inf*: *neg*) psychiatre *m/f*, psy *m/f*; **to ~ from** (*doing*) **sth** reculer devant (la pensée de faire) qch; **~wrap** *vt* emballer sous film plastique

**shrivel** ['ʃrivl] *vt* (*also*: **~ up**) ratatiner, flétrir ♦ *vi* se ratatiner, se flétrir

**shroud** [ʃraud] *n* linceul *m* ♦ *vt*: **~ed in mystery** enveloppé(e) de mystère

**Shrove Tuesday** ['ʃrəuv-] *n* (le) Mardi gras

**shrub** [ʃrʌb] *n* arbuste *m*; **~bery** *n* massif *m* d'arbustes

**shrug** [ʃrʌg] *vt, vi*: **to ~** (*one's shoulders*) hausser les épaules; **~ off** *vt* faire fi de

**shrunk** [ʃrʌŋk] *pp of* **shrink**

**shudder** ['ʃʌdər] *n* frissonnement, frémir

**shuffle** ['ʃʌfl] *vt* (*cards*) battre; **to ~** (*one's feet*) traîner les pieds

**shun** [ʃʌn] *vt* éviter, fuir

**shunt** [ʃʌnt] *vt* (RAIL) aiguiller

**shut** [ʃʌt] (*pt, pp* **shut**) *vt* fermer ♦ *vi*

(se) fermer; ~ **down** vt, vi fermer définitivement; ~ **off** vt couper, arrêter; ~ **up** vi (inf: keep quiet) se taire ♦ vt (close) fermer; (silence) faire taire; ~**ter** n volet m; (PHOT) obturateur m

**shuttle** ['ʃʌtl] n navette f; (also: ~ **service**) (service m de) navette f; ~**cock** volant m (de badminton); ~ **diplomacy** n navettes fpl diplomatiques

**shy** [ʃaɪ] adj timide

**Siberia** [saɪ'bɪərɪə] n Sibérie f

**Sicily** ['sɪsɪlɪ] n Sicile f

**sick** [sɪk] adj (ill) malade; (vomiting): **to be** ~ vomir; (humour) noir(e), macabre; **to feel** ~ avoir envie de vomir, avoir mal au cœur; **to be** ~ **of** (fig) en avoir assez de; ~ **bay** n infirmerie f; ~**en** vt écœurer; ~**ening** adj (fig) écœurant(e), dégoûtant(e)

**sickle** ['sɪkl] n faucille f

**sick**: ~ **leave** n congé m de maladie; ~**ly** adj maladif(-ive), souffreteux(-euse); (causing nausea) écœurant(e); ~**ness** n maladie f; (vomiting) vomissement(s) m(pl); ~ **note** n (from parents) mot d'absence; (from doctor) certificat médical; ~ **pay** n indemnité f de maladie

**side** [saɪd] n côté m; (of lake, road) bord m; (team camp m, équipe f of adj (door, entrance) latéral(e) ♦ vi: **to** ~ **with sb** prendre le parti de qn, se ranger du côté de qn; **by the** ~ **of** au bord de; **by** ~ côte à côte; **from** ~ **to** ~ d'un côté à l'autre; **to take** ~**s** (**with**) prendre parti (pour); ~**board** n buffet m; ~**boards** (BRIT), ~**burns** npl (whiskers) pattes fpl; ~ **drum** n tambour m; ~ **effect** n effet m secondaire; ~**light** n (AUT) veilleuse f; ~**line** n (SPORT) (ligne f de) touche f; (fig) travail m secondaire; ~**long** adj oblique; ~**show** n attraction f; ~**step** vt (fig) éviter; ~ **street** n (petite) rue transversale; ~**track** vt (fig) faire dévier de son sujet; ~**walk** n (US) trottoir m; ~**ways** adv de côté

**siding** ['saɪdɪŋ] n (RAIL) voie f de garage

---

**siege** [siːdʒ] n siège m

**sieve** [sɪv] n tamis m, passoire f

**sift** [sɪft] vt (fig: also: ~ **through**) passer en revue; (lit: flour etc) passer au tamis

**sigh** [saɪ] n soupir m ♦ vi soupirer, pousser un soupir

**sight** [saɪt] n (faculty) vue f; (spectacle) spectacle m; (on gun) mire f ♦ vt apercevoir; **in** ~ visible; **out of** ~ hors de vue; ~**seeing** n tourisme m; **to go** ~**seeing** faire du tourisme

**sign** [saɪn] n signe m; (with hand etc) signe, geste m; (notice) panneau m, écriteau m ♦ vt signer; ~ **on** vi (as unemployed) s'inscrire au chômage; (for course) s'inscrire ♦ vt (employee) embaucher; ~ **over** vt: **to** ~ **sth over to sb** céder qch par écrit à qn; ~ **up** vt engager ♦ vi (MIL) s'engager; (for course) s'inscrire

**signal** ['sɪgnl] n signal m ♦ vi (AUT) mettre son clignotant ♦ vt (person) faire signe à; (message) communiquer par signaux; ~**man** (irreg) n (RAIL) aiguilleur m

**signature** ['sɪgnətʃə] n signature f; ~ **tune** n indicatif musical

**signet ring** ['sɪgnət-] n chevalière f

**significance** [sɪg'nɪfɪkəns] n signification f; importance f

**significant** [sɪg'nɪfɪkənt] adj significatif(-ive); (important) important(e), considérable

**sign language** n langage m par signes

**signpost** n poteau indicateur

**silence** ['saɪləns] n silence m ♦ vt faire taire, réduire au silence; ~**r** n (on gun, BRIT: AUT) silencieux m

**silent** ['saɪlənt] adj silencieux(-euse); (film) muet(te); **to remain** ~ garder le silence, ne rien dire; ~ **partner** n (COMM) bailleur m de fonds, commanditaire m

**silhouette** [sɪluː'et] n silhouette f

**silicon chip** ['sɪlɪkən-] n puce f électronique

**silk** [sɪlk] n soie f ♦ cpd de or en soie; ~**y**

**silly** 545 **sit-in**

*adj* soyeux(-euse)

**silly** ['sɪlɪ] *adj* stupide, sot(te), bête

**silt** [sɪlt] *n* vase *f*, limon *m*

**silver** ['sɪlvəʳ] *n* argent *m*; *(money)* monnaie *f* (en pièces d'argent); *(also:* **~ware**) argenterie *f* ♦ *adj* d'argent, en argent; **~smith** *n* orfèvre *m/f*; **~** **paper** *(BRIT)* *n* papier *m* d'argent or d'étain; **~-plated** *adj* plaqué(e) argent inv; **~smith** *n* orfèvre *m/f*; *adj* argenté(e)

**similar** ['sɪmɪləʳ] *adj*: **~ (to)** semblable (à); **~ly** *adv* de la même façon, de même

**simmer** ['sɪməʳ] *vi* cuire à feu doux, mijoter

**simple** ['sɪmpl] *adj* simple; **simplicity** [sɪm'plɪsɪtɪ] *n* simplicité *f*; **simply** *adv* (without fuss) avec simplicité

**simultaneous** [sɪməl'teɪnɪəs] *adj* simultané(e)

**sin** [sɪn] *n* péché *m* ♦ *vi* pécher

**since** [sɪns] *adv*, *prep* depuis ♦ *conj (time)* depuis que; *(because)* puisque, étant donné que, comme; **~ then, ever ~** depuis ce moment-là

**sincere** [sɪn'sɪəʳ] *adj* sincère; **~ly** *adv* see **yours**; **sincerity** [sɪn'sɛrɪtɪ] *n* sincérité *f*

**sinew** ['sɪnjuː] *n* tendon *m*

**sing** [sɪŋ] *(pt* **sang**, *pp* **sung**) *vt*, *vi* chanter

**Singapore** [sɪŋə'pɔː] *n* Singapour *m*

**singe** [sɪndʒ] *vt* brûler légèrement; *(clothes)* roussir

**singer** ['sɪŋəʳ] *n* chanteur(-euse)

**singing** ['sɪŋɪŋ] *n* chant *m*

**single** ['sɪŋgl] *adj* seul(e), unique; *(unmarried)* célibataire; *(not double)* simple ♦ *n (BRIT: also:* **~ ticket**) aller *m* simple; *(record)* 45 tours *m*; **~ out** *vt* choisir; *(distinguish)* distinguer; **~ bed** *n* lit *m* d'une personne; **~-breasted** *adj* droit(e); **~ file** *n*: **in ~ file** en file indienne; **~-handed** *adv* tout(e) seul(e), sans (aucune) aide; **~-minded** *adj* résolu(e), tenace; **~ parent** *n* parent *m* unique; **~ room** *n* chambre *f* à un lit or

pour une personne; **~s** *n (TENNIS)* simple *m*; **~-track road** *n* route *f* à voie unique; **singly** *adv* séparément

**singular** ['sɪŋgjuləʳ] *adj* singulier(-ère), étrange; *(outstanding)* remarquable; *(LING)* (au) singulier, du singulier ♦ *n* singulier *m*

**sinister** ['sɪnɪstəʳ] *adj* sinistre

**sink** [sɪŋk] *(pt* **sank**, *pp* **sunk**) *n* évier *m* ♦ *vt (ship)* (faire) couler, faire sombrer; *(foundations)* creuser ♦ *vi* couler, sombrer; *(ground etc)* s'affaisser; *(also:* **~ back, ~ down**) s'affaisser, se laisser retomber; **to ~ sth into** enfoncer qch dans; **my heart sank** j'ai complètement perdu courage; **~ in** *vi (fig)* pénétrer, être compris(e)

**sinner** ['sɪnəʳ] *n* pécheur(-eresse)

**sinus** ['saɪnəs] *n* sinus *m* inv

**sip** [sɪp] *n* gorgée *f* ♦ *vt* boire à petites gorgées

**siphon** ['saɪfən] *n* siphon *m*; **~ off** *vt* siphonner; *(money: illegally)* détourner

**sir** [sɜːʳ] *n* monsieur *m*; **S~ John Smith** sir John Smith; **yes ~** oui, Monsieur

**siren** ['saɪərn] *n* sirène *f*

**sirloin** ['sɜːlɔɪn] *n (also:* **~ steak**) aloyau *m*

**sissy** ['sɪsɪ] *n (inf) (coward)* poule mouillée

**sister** ['sɪstəʳ] *n* sœur *f*; *(nun)* religieuse *f*, sœur; *(BRIT: nurse)* infirmière *f* en chef; **~-in-law** *n* belle-sœur *f*

**sit** [sɪt] *(pt, pp* **sat**) *vi* s'asseoir; *(be ~ting)* être assis(e); *(assembly)* être en séance, siéger; *(for painter)* poser ♦ *vt (exam)* passer, se présenter à; **~ down** *vi* s'asseoir; **~ in on** *vt fus* assister à; **~ up** *vi* s'asseoir; *(straight)* se redresser; *(not go to bed)* rester debout, ne pas se coucher

**sitcom** ['sɪtkɒm] *n abbr (= situation comedy)* comédie *f* de situation

**site** [saɪt] *n* emplacement *m*, site *m*; *(also:* **building ~**) chantier *m* ♦ *vt* placer

**sit-in** ['sɪtɪn] *n (demonstration)* sit-in *m* inv, occupation *f* (de locaux)

**sitting** ['sɪtɪŋ] n (of assembly etc) séance f; (in canteen) service m; ~ **room** n salon m

**situated** ['sɪtjueɪtɪd] adj situé(e)

**situation** [sɪtju'eɪʃən] n situation f; "~s **vacant**" (BRIT) "offres d'emploi"

**six** [sɪks] num six; ~**teen** num seize; ~**th** num sixième; ~**ty** num soixante

**size** [saɪz] n taille f; dimensions fpl; (of clothing) taille; (of shoes) pointure f; (fig) ampleur f; (of glue) colle f; ~ **up** vt juger, jauger; ~**able** adj assez grand(e); assez important(e)

**sizzle** ['sɪzl] vi grésiller

**skate** [skeɪt] n patin m; (fish: pl inv) raie f ♦ vi patiner; ~**board** n skateboard m, planche f à roulettes; ~**boarding** n skateboard m; ~**r** n patineur(-euse); **skating** n patinage m; **skating rink** n patinoire f

**skeleton** ['skelɪtn] n squelette m; (outline) schéma m; ~ **staff** n effectifs réduits

**skeptical** ['skeptɪkl] (US) adj = **sceptical**

**sketch** [sketʃ] n (drawing) croquis m, esquisse f; (THEATRE) sketch m, saynète f ♦ vt esquisser, faire un croquis or une esquisse de; ~ **book** n carnet m à dessin; ~**y** adj incomplet(-ète), fragmentaire

**skewer** ['skju:ə'] n brochette f

**ski** [ski:] n ski m ♦ vi skier, faire du ski; ~ **boot** n chaussure f de ski

**skid** [skɪd] n dérapage m ♦ vi déraper

**ski: ~er** n skieur(-euse); ~**ing** n ski m; ~ **jump** n saut m à skis

**skilful** ['skɪlful] (US **skillful**) adj habile, adroit(e)

**ski lift** n remonte-pente m inv

**skill** [skɪl] n habileté f, adresse f, talent m; (requiring training: gen pl) compétences fpl; ~**ed** adj habile, adroit(e); (worker) qualifié(e)

**skim** [skɪm] vt (milk) écrémer; (glide over) raser, effleurer ♦ vi: **to ~ through** (fig) parcourir; ~**med milk** n lait écré-

mé

**skimp** [skɪmp] vt (also: ~ **on**: work) bâcler, faire à la va-vite; (: cloth etc) lésiner sur; ~**y** adj (skirt) étriqué(e)

**skin** [skɪn] n peau f ♦ vt (fruit etc) éplucher; (animal) écorcher; **~ cancer** n cancer m de la peau; ~**-deep** adj superficiel(le); ~**-diving** n plongée sousmarine; ~**head** n skinhead m/f; ~**ny** adj maigre, maigrichon(ne); ~**tight** adj (jeans etc) moulant(e), ajusté(e)

**skip** [skɪp] n petit bond or saut; (BRIT: container) benne f ♦ vi gambader, sautiller; (with rope) sauter à la corde ♦ vt sauter

**ski pass** n forfait-skieur(s) m

**ski pole** n bâton m de ski

**skipper** ['skɪpə'] n capitaine m; (in race) skipper m

**skipping rope** ['skɪpɪŋ-] (BRIT) n corde f à sauter

**skirmish** ['skɜ:mɪʃ] n escarmouche f, accrochage m

**skirt** [skɜ:t] n jupe f ♦ vt longer, contourner; ~**ing board** (BRIT) n plinthe f

**ski: ~ slope** n piste f de ski; ~ **suit** n combinaison f (de ski); ~ **tow** n remonte-pente m inv

**skittle** ['skɪtl] n quille f; ~**s** n (game) (jeu m de) quilles fpl

**skive** [skaɪv] (BRIT: inf) vi tirer au flanc

**skull** [skʌl] n crâne m

**skunk** [skʌŋk] n mouffette f

**sky** [skaɪ] n ciel m; ~**light** n lucarne f; ~**scraper** n gratte-ciel m inv

**slab** [slæb] n (of stone) dalle f; (of food) grosse tranche

**slack** [slæk] adj (loose) lâche, desserré(e); (slow) stagnant(e); (careless) négligent(e), peu sérieux(-euse) or consciencieux(-euse); ~**s** npl (trousers) pantalon m; ~**en** vi ralentir, diminuer ♦ vt (speed) réduire; (grip) relâcher; (clothing) desserrer

**slag heap** [slæg-] n crassier m

**slag off** (BRIT: inf) vt dire du mal de

547

**slam** [slæm] vt (door) (faire) claquer; (throw) jeter violemment, flanquer (fam); (criticize) démolir ♦ vi claquer

**slander** ['slɑ:ndə*] n calomnie f; diffamation f

**slang** [slæŋ] n argot m

**slant** [slɑ:nt] n inclinaison f, (fig) angle m, point de vue; **~ing** adj en pente, incliné(e); **~ing eyes** yeux bridés

**slap** [slæp] n claque f, gifle f, tape f ♦ vt donner une claque or une gifle or une tape à; (paint) appliquer rapidement ♦ adv (directly) tout droit, en plein; **~dash** adj fait(e) sans soin or à la va-vite; (person) insouciant(e), négligent(e); **~stick** n (comedy) grosse farce, style m tarte à la crème; **~up** adj: **a ~up meal** un repas extra or fameux

**slash** [slæʃ] vt entailler, taillader, (fig: criticize) casser; (fig: prices) casser

**slat** [slæt] n latte f, lame f

**slate** [sleɪt] n ardoise f ♦ vt (fig: criticize) éreinter, démolir

**slaughter** ['slɔ:tə*] n carnage m, massacre m ♦ vt (animal) abattre; (people) massacrer; **~house** n abattoir m

**slave** [sleɪv] n esclave m/f ♦ vi (also: **~ away**) trimer, travailler comme un forçat; **~ry** n esclavage m

**slay** [sleɪ] (pt slew, pp slain) vt tuer

**sleazy** ['sli:zɪ] adj miteux(-euse), minable

**sledge** [sledʒ] n luge f ♦ vi: **to go sledging** faire de la luge

**sledgehammer** n marteau m de forgeron

**sleek** [sli:k] adj (hair, fur etc) brillant(e), lisse; (car, boat etc) aux lignes pures et élégantes

**sleep** [sli:p] (pt, pp slept) n sommeil m ♦ vi dormir; (spend night) dormir, coucher; **to go to ~** s'endormir; **~ around** vi coucher à droite et à gauche; **~ in** vi (oversleep) se réveiller trop tard; **~er** (BRIT) n (RAIL: train) train-

couchettes m; (: berth) couchette f; **~ing bag** n sac m de couchage; **~ing car** n (RAIL) wagon-lit m, voiture-lit f; **~ing partner** (BRIT) n = silent partner; **~ing pill** n somnifère m; **~less** adj: **a ~less night** une nuit sans sommeil; **~walker** n somnambule m/f; **~y** adj qui a sommeil; (fig) endormi(e)

**sleet** [sli:t] n neige fondue

**sleeve** [sli:v] n manche f; (of record) pochette f

**sleigh** [sleɪ] n traîneau m

**sleight** [slaɪt] n: **~ of hand** tour m de passe-passe

**slender** ['slendə*] adj svelte, mince; (fig) faible, ténu(e)

**slept** [slept] pt, pp of sleep

**slew** [slu:] vi (also: **~ around**) virer, pivoter ♦ pt of slay

**slice** [slaɪs] n tranche f; (round) rondelle f; (utensil) spatule f, truelle f ♦ vt couper en tranches (or en rondelles)

**slick** [slɪk] adj (skilful) brillant(e) (en apparence); (salesman) qui a du bagout ♦ n (also: **oil ~**) nappe f de pétrole, marée noire

**slide** [slaɪd] (pt, pp slid) n (in playground) toboggan m; (PHOT) diapositive f; (BRIT: also: **hair ~**) barrette f (in prices) chute f, baisse f ♦ vt (faire) glisser ♦ vi glisser; **sliding** adj coulissant(e); **sliding scale** n échelle f mobile

**slight** [slaɪt] adj (slim) mince, menu(e); (frail) frêle; (trivial) faible, insignifiant(e); (small) petit(e), léger(-ère) (before n) ♦ n offense f, affront m; **not in the ~est** pas le moins du monde, pas du tout; **~ly** adv légèrement, un peu

**slim** [slɪm] adj mince ♦ vi maigrir; (diet) suivre un régime amaigrissant

**slime** [slaɪm] n (mud) vase f; (other substance) substance visqueuse

**slimming** ['slɪmɪŋ] adj (diet, pills) amaigrissant(e); (foodstuff) qui ne fait pas grossir

**sling** [slɪŋ] (pt, pp slung) n (MED) écharpe f; (for baby) porte-bébé m; (weapon) fronde f, lance-pierre m ♦ vt lancer, jeter

**slip** [slɪp] n faux pas; (mistake) erreur f, étourderie f; (underskirt) combinaison f; (of paper) petite feuille, fiche f ♦ vt (slide) glisser ♦ vi glisser; (decline) baisser; (move smoothly): **to ~ into/out of** se glisser or se faufiler dans/hors de; **to ~ sth on/off** enfiler/enlever qch; **to give sb the ~** fausser compagnie à qn; **~ away** vi s'esquiver; **~ in** vt glisser ♦ vi (errors) s'y glisser; **~ out** vi sortir; **~ up** vi faire une erreur, gaffer; **~ped disc** n déplacement m de vertèbre

**slipper** ['slɪpə*] n pantoufle f

**slippery** ['slɪpərɪ] adj glissant(e)

**slip:** **~ road** n (to motorway) bretelle f d'accès; **~-up** n bévue f; **~way** n cale f (de construction or de lancement)

**slit** [slɪt] (pt, pp **slit**) n fente f; (cut) incision f ♦ vt fendre; couper; inciser

**slither** ['slɪðə*] vi (person, snake) onduler

**sliver** ['slɪvə*] n (of glass, wood) éclat m; (of cheese etc) petit morceau, fine tranche

**slob** [slɒb] (inf) n rustaud(e)

**slog** [slɒg] (BRIT) vi travailler très dur ♦ n gros effort; tâche fastidieuse

**slogan** ['sləugən] n slogan m

**slope** [sləup] n pente f, côte f; (side of mountain) versant m; (slant) inclinaison f ♦ vi: **to ~ down** être or descendre en pente; **to ~ up** monter; **sloping** adj en pente; (writing) penché(e)

**sloppy** ['slɒpɪ] adj (work) peu soigné(e), bâclé(e); (appearance) négligé(e), débraillé(e)

**slot** [slɒt] n fente f ♦ vt: **to ~ sth into** encastrer or insérer qch dans

**sloth** [sləuθ] n (laziness) paresse f

**slouch** [slautʃ] vi avoir le dos rond, être voûté(e)

**slovenly** ['slʌvənlɪ] adj sale, débrail-

lé(e); (work) négligé(e)

**slow** [sləu] adj lent(e); (watch): **to be ~** retarder ♦ adv lentement ♦ vt, vi (also: **~ down, ~ up**) ralentir; **"~"** (road sign) "ralentir"; **~ly** adv lentement; **~ motion** n: **in ~ motion** au ralenti

**sludge** [slʌdʒ] n boue f

**slug** [slʌg] n limace f; (bullet) balle f

**sluggish** ['slʌgɪʃ] adj (person) mou (molle), lent(e); (stream, engine, trading) lent

**sluice** [slu:s] n (also: **~ gate**) vanne f

**slum** [slʌm] n (house) taudis m

**slump** [slʌmp] n baisse soudaine, effondrement m; (ECON) crise f ♦ vi s'effondrer, s'affaisser

**slung** [slʌŋ] pt, pp of **sling**

**slur** [slɜː*] n (fig: smear): **~ (on)** atteinte f (à); insinuation f (contre) ♦ vt mal articuler

**slush** [slʌʃ] n neige fondue

**slut** [slʌt] (pej) n salope f

**sly** [slaɪ] adj (person) rusé(e); (smile, expression, remark) sournois(e)

**smack** [smæk] n (slap) tape f; (on face) gifle f ♦ vt donner une tape à; (on face) gifler; (on bottom) donner la fessée à ♦ vi: **to ~ of** avoir des relents de, sentir

**small** [smɔːl] adj petit(e); **~ ads** npl petites annonces; **~ change** n petite or menue monnaie; **~holder** n (BRIT) petit cultivateur; **~ hours** npl: **in the ~ hours** au petit matin; **~pox** n variole f; **~ talk** n menus propos

**smart** [smɑːt] adj (neat, fashionable) élégant(e), chic inv; (clever) intelligent(e), astucieux(-euse), futé(e); (quick) rapide, vif (vive), prompt(e) ♦ vi faire mal, brûler; (fig) être piqué(e) au vif; **~ card** n carte f à puce; **~en up** vi devenir plus élégant(e), se faire beau (belle) ♦ vt rendre plus élégant(e)

**smash** [smæʃ] n (also: **~-up**) collision f, accident m; (also: **~ hit**) succès foudroyant ♦ vt casser, briser, fracasser; (opponent) écraser; (SPORT: record) pulvériser ♦ vi se briser, se fracasser; s'écraser; **~ing** (inf) adj formidable

**smattering** ['smætərɪŋ] n: a ~ of quelques notions de

**smear** [smɪə] n tache f, salissure f; trace f; (MED) frottis m ♦ vt enduire; (make dirty) salir; **~ campaign** n campagne f de diffamation

**smell** [smel] (pt, pp **smelt** or **smelled**) n odeur f; (sense) odorat m ♦ vt sentir ♦ vi (food etc): **to ~ (of)** sentir de; (pej) sentir mauvais; **~y** adj qui sent mauvais, malodorant(e)

**smile** [smaɪl] n sourire m ♦ vi sourire

**smirk** [smɜːk] n petit sourire suffisant or affecté

**smock** [smɒk] n blouse f

**smog** [smɒg] n brouillard mêlé de fumée, smog m

**smoke** [sməuk] n fumée f ♦ vt, vi fumer; **~d** adj (bacon, glass) fumé(e); **~r** n (person) fumeur(-euse); (RAIL) wagon m fumeurs; **~ screen** n rideau m or écran m de fumée; (fig) paravent m; **smoking** n tabagisme m; **"no smoking"** (sign) "défense de fumer"; **to give up smoking** arrêter de fumer; **smoking compartment** (US **smoking car**) n wagon m fumeurs; **smoky** adj enfumé(e); (taste) fumé(e)

**smolder** ['sməuldə] (US) vi = **smoulder**

**smooth** [smu:ð] adj lisse; (sauce) onctueux(-euse); (flavour, whisky) moelleux(-euse); (movement) régulier (-ère), sans à-coups or heurts; (pej: person) doucereux(-euse), mielleux(-euse) ♦ vt (also: ~ out): skirt, paper) lisser, défroisser; (: creases, difficulties) faire disparaître

**smother** ['smʌðə] vt étouffer

**smoulder** ['sməuldə] (US **smolder**) vi couver

**smudge** [smʌdʒ] n tache f, bavure f ♦ vt salir, maculer

**smug** [smʌg] adj suffisant(e)

**smuggle** ['smʌgl] vt passer en contrebande or en fraude; **~r** n

contrebandier(-ère); **smuggling** n contrebande f

**smutty** ['smʌtɪ] adj (fig) grossier(-ère), obscène

**snack** [snæk] n casse-croûte m inv; **~ bar** n snack(-bar) m

**snag** [snæg] n inconvénient m, difficulté f

**snail** [sneɪl] n escargot m

**snake** [sneɪk] n serpent m

**snap** [snæp] n (sound) claquement m, bruit sec; (photograph) photo f, instantané m ♦ adj subit(e); fait(e) sans réfléchir ♦ vt (break) casser net; (fingers) faire claquer ♦ vi se casser net or avec un bruit sec; (speak sharply) parler d'un ton brusque; **to ~ shut** se refermer brusquement; **~ at** vt fus (subj: dog) essayer de mordre; **~ off** vi (break) casser net; **~ up** vt sauter sur, saisir; **~py** (inf) adj prompt(e); (slogan) qui a du punch; **make it ~py!** (inf) grouille-toi, magne-toi!; **~shot** n photo f, instantané m

**snare** [snɛə] n piège m

**snarl** [snɑːl] vi gronder

**snatch** [snætʃ] n (small amount): **~es of** des fragments mpl or bribes fpl de ♦ vt saisir (d'un geste vif); (steal) voler

**sneak** [sni:k] vi: **to ~ in/out** entrer/ sortir furtivement or à la dérobée ♦ n (inf: pej: informer) faux jeton; **to ~ up on sb** s'approcher de qn sans faire de bruit; **~ers** npl tennis mpl, baskets mpl

**sneer** [snɪə] vi ricaner; **to ~** traiter avec mépris

**sneeze** [sni:z] vi éternuer

**sniff** [snɪf] vi renifler ♦ vt renifler, flairer; (glue, drugs) sniffer, respirer

**snigger** ['snɪgə] vi ricaner; pouffer de rire

**snip** [snɪp] n (cut) petit coup m; (BRIT: inf: bargain) (bonne) occasion or affaire f ♦ vt couper

**sniper** ['snaɪpə] n tireur embusqué

**snippet** ['snɪpɪt] n bribe(s) f(pl)

**snob** [snɒb] n snob m/f; **~bish** adj snob inv

**snooker** ['snu:kə*r*] *n* sorte de jeu de billard

**snoop** [snu:p] *vi:* **to ~ about** fureter

**snooze** [snu:z] *n* petit somme ♦ *vi* faire un petit somme

**snore** [snɔ:*r*] *vi* ronfler

**snorkel** ['snɔ:kl] *n* (*of swimmer*) tuba *m*

**snort** [snɔ:t] *vi* grogner; (*horse*) renâcler

**snout** [snaut] *n* museau *m*

**snow** [snəu] *n* neige *f* ♦ *vi* neiger; **~ball** *n* boule *f* de neige; **~bound** *adj* enneigé(e), bloqué(e) par la neige; **~drift** *n* congère *f*; **~drop** *n* perce-neige *m or f*; **~fall** *n* chute *f* de neige; **~flake** *n* flocon *m* de neige; **~man** (*irreg*) *n* bonhomme *m* de neige; **~plough** (*US* **~plow**) *n* chasse-neige *m inv*; **~shoe** *n* raquette *f* (*pour la neige*); **~storm** *n* tempête *f* de neige

**snub** [snʌb] *vt* repousser, snober ♦ *n* rebuffade *f*; **~-nosed** *adj* au nez retroussé

**snuff** [snʌf] *n* tabac *m* à priser

**snug** [snʌg] *adj* douillet(te), confortable; (*person*) bien au chaud

**snuggle** ['snʌgl] *vi:* **to ~ up to sb** se serrer *or* se blottir contre qn

---

KEYWORD

**so** [səu] *adv* **1** (*thus, likewise*) ainsi; **if so** si oui; **so do** *or* **have I** moi aussi; **it's 5 o'clock – so it is!** il est 5 heures – en effet! *or* c'est vrai!; **I hope/think so** je l'espère/le crois; **so far** jusqu'ici, jusqu'à maintenant; (*in past*) jusque-là

**2** (*in comparisons etc: to such a degree*) si, tellement; **so big (that)** si *or* tellement grand (que); **she's not so clever as her brother** elle n'est pas aussi intelligente que son frère

**3: so much**

♦ *adj* autant de (tde); **I've got so much work** j'ai tant de travail; **I love you so much** je vous aime tant; **so many** tant (de)

**4** (*phrases*): **10 or so** à peu près *or* environ 10; **so long!** (*inf: goodbye*) au re-

voir!, à un de ces jours!

♦ *conj* **1** (*expressing purpose*): **so as to do** pour faire, afin de faire; **so (that)** pour que *or* afin que +*sub*

**2** (*expressing result*) donc, par conséquent; **so that** si bien que, de (telle) sorte que

---

**soak** [səuk] *vt* faire tremper; (*drench*) tremper ♦ *vi* tremper; **~ in** être absorbé(e); **~ up** *vt* absorber; **~ing** *adj* trempé(e)

**soap** [səup] *n* savon *m*; **~flakes** *npl* paillettes *fpl* de savon; **~ opera** *n* feuilleton télévisé; **~ powder** *n* lessive *f*; **~y** *adj* savonneux(-euse)

**soar** [sɔ:*r*] *vi* monter (en flèche), s'élancer; (*building*) s'élancer

**sob** [sɔb] *n* sanglot *m* ♦ *vi* sangloter

**sober** ['səubə*r*] *adj* qui n'est pas (*or* plus) ivre; (*serious*) sérieux(-euse), sensé(e); (*colour, style*) sobre, discret(-ète); **~ up** *vt* dessoûler (*inf*) ♦ *vi* dessoûler (*inf*)

**so-called** ['səu'kɔ:ld] *adj* soi-disant *inv*

**soccer** ['sɔkə*r*] *n* football *m*

**social** ['səuʃl] *adj* social(e); (*sociable*) sociable ♦ *n* (petite) fête; **~ club** *n* amicale *f*, foyer *m*; **~ism** *n* socialisme *m*; **~ist** *adj* socialiste ♦ *n* socialiste *m/f*; **~ize** *vi:* **to ~ize (with)** lier connaissance (avec); parler (avec); **~ security** (*BRIT*) *n* aide sociale; **~ work** *n* assistance sociale, travail social; **~ worker** *n* assistant(e) social(e)

**society** [sə'saɪətɪ] *n* société *f*; (*club*) société, association *f*; (*also:* **high ~**) (haute) société, grand monde

**sociology** [səusɪ'ɔlədʒɪ] *n* sociologie *f*

**sock** [sɔk] *n* chaussette *f*

**socket** ['sɔkɪt] *n* cavité *f*; (*BRIT: ELEC: also:* **wall ~**) prise *f* de courant

**sod** [sɔd] *n* (*of earth*) motte *f*; (*BRIT: inf!*) con *m* (!); salaud *m* (!)

**soda** ['səudə] *n* (*CHEM*) soude *f*; (*also:* **~ water**) eau *f* de Seltz; (*US: also:* **~ pop**) soda *m*

**sofa** ['səʊfə] n sofa m, canapé m

**soft** [sɒft] adj (not rough) doux (douce); (not hard) doux; mou (molle); (not loud) doux, léger(-ère); (kind) doux, gentil(le); ~ **drink** n boisson non alcoolisée; ~**en** vt (r)amollir; (fig) adoucir; atténuer ♦ vi se ramollir; s'adoucir; s'atténuer; ~**ly** adv doucement; gentiment; ~**ness** n douceur f; ~**ware** n (COMPUT) logiciel m, software m

**soggy** ['sɒgɪ] adj trempé(e); détrempé(e)

**soil** [sɔɪl] n (earth) sol m, terre f ♦ vt salir; (fig) souiller

**solar** ['səʊlə*] adj solaire; ~ **panel** n panneau m solaire; ~ **power** n énergie solaire

**sold** [səʊld] pt, pp of **sell**

**solder** ['səʊldə*] vt souder (au fil à souder) ♦ n soudure f

**soldier** ['səʊldʒə*] n soldat m, militaire m

**sole** [səʊl] n (of foot) plante f; (of shoe) semelle f; (fish: pl inv) sole f ♦ adj seul(e), unique

**solemn** ['sɒləm] adj solennel(le); (person) sérieux(-euse), grave

**sole trader** n (COMM) chef m d'entreprise individuelle

**solicit** [sə'lɪsɪt] vt (request) solliciter ♦ vi (prostitute) racoler

**solicitor** [sə'lɪsɪtə*] n (for wills etc) ≈ notaire m; (in court) ≈ avocat m

**solid** ['sɒlɪd] adj solide; (not hollow) plein(e), compact(e), massif(-ive); (entire): **3** ~ **hours** 3 heures entières ♦ n solide m

**solidarity** [sɒlɪ'dærɪtɪ] n solidarité f

**solitary** ['sɒlɪtərɪ] adj solitaire; ~ **confinement** n (LAW) isolement m

**solo** ['səʊləʊ] n solo m ♦ adv (fly) en solitaire; ~**ist** n soliste m/f

**soluble** ['sɒljʊbl] adj soluble

**solution** [sə'lu:ʃən] n solution f

**solve** [sɒlv] vt résoudre

**solvent** ['sɒlvənt] adj (COMM) solvable ♦ n (CHEM) (dis)solvant m

**some** [sʌm] adj **1** (a certain amount or number of): **some tea/water/ice cream** du thé/de l'eau/de la glace; **some children/apples** des enfants/pommes

**2** (certain: in contrasts): **some people say that ...** il y a des gens qui disent que ...; **some films were excellent, but most ...** certains films étaient excellents, mais la plupart ...

**3** (unspecified): **some woman was asking for you** il y avait une dame qui vous demandait; **he was asking for some book (or other)** il demandait un livre quelconque; **some day** un de ces jours; **some day next week** un jour la semaine prochaine

♦ pron **1** (a certain number) quelques-un(e)s, certain(e)s; **I've got some** (books etc) j'en ai (quelques-uns); **some (of them) have been sold** certains ont été vendus

**2** (a certain amount) un peu; **I've got some** (money, milk) j'en ai (un peu)

♦ adv: **some 10 people** quelque 10 personnes, 10 personnes environ

**some: ~body** ['sʌmbədɪ] pron = **someone; ~how** adv d'une façon ou d'une autre; (for some reason) pour une raison ou une autre; ~**one** pron quelqu'un; ~**place** (US) adv = **somewhere**

**somersault** ['sʌməsɔ:lt] n culbute f, saut périlleux ♦ vi faire la culbute or un saut périlleux; (car) faire un tonneau

**some: ~thing** pron quelque chose; ~**thing interesting** quelque chose d'intéressant; ~**time** adv (in future) un de ces jours, un jour ou l'autre; (in past): ~**time last month** au cours du mois dernier; ~**times** adv quelquefois, parfois; ~**what** adv quelque peu, un peu; ~**where** adv quelque part

**son** [sʌn] n fils m

**song** [sɒŋ] n chanson f; (of bird) chant

*m*

**son-in-law** *n* gendre *m*, beau-fils *m*

**soon** [su:n] *adv* bientôt; (*early*) tôt; **~ afterwards** peu après; *see also* **as**; **~er** *adv* (*time*) plus tôt; (*preference*): **I would ~er do** j'aimerais autant or je préférerais faire; **~er or later** tôt ou tard

**soot** [sut] *n* suie *f*

**soothe** [su:ð] *vt* calmer, apaiser

**sophisticated** [sə'fɪstɪkeɪtɪd] *adj* raffiné(e); sophistiqué(e); (*machinery*) hautement perfectionné(e), très complexe

**sophomore** ['sɔfəmɔː'] (*US*) *n* étudiant(e) de seconde année

**sopping** ['sɔpɪŋ] *adj* (*also:* **~ wet**) complètement trempé(e)

**soppy** ['sɔpɪ] (*pej*) *adj* sentimental(e)

**soprano** [sə'prɑːnəu] *n* (*singer*) soprano *m/f*

**sorcerer** ['sɔːsərə'] *n* sorcier *m*

**sore** [sɔː'] *adj* (*painful*) douloureux (-euse), sensible ♦ *n* plaie *f*; **~ly** ['sɔːlɪ] *adv* (*tempted*) fortement

**sorrow** ['sɔrəu] *n* peine *f*, chagrin *m*

**sorry** ['sɔrɪ] *adj* désolé(e); (*condition, excuse*) triste, déplorable; **~!** pardon!, excusez-moi!; **~?** pardon?; **to feel ~ for sb** plaindre qn

**sort** [sɔːt] *n* genre *m*, espèce *f*, sorte *f* ♦ *vt* (*also:* **~ out**) trier; classer; ranger; (: *problems*) résoudre, régler; **~ing office** ['sɔːtɪŋ-] *n* bureau *m* de tri

**SOS** *n* S.O.S. *m*

**so-so** ['səusəu] *adv* comme ci comme ça

**sought** [sɔːt] *pt, pp of* **seek**

**soul** [səul] *n* âme *f*; **~ful** ['səulful] *adj* sentimental(e); (*eyes*) expressif(-ive)

**sound** [saund] *adj* (*healthy*) en bonne santé, sain(e); (*safe, not damaged*) solide, en bon état; (*reliable, not superficial*) sérieux(-euse), solide; (*sensible*) sensé(e) ♦ *adv*: **~ asleep** profondément endormi(e) ♦ *n* (*noise*) bruit *m*; (*GEO*) détroit *m*, bras *m* de mer ♦ *vt* (*alarm*) sonner ♦ *vi* sonner, retentir; (*fig: seem*) sembler

(être); **to ~ like** ressembler à; **~ out** *vt* sonder; **~ barrier** *n* mur *m* du son; **~ bite** *n* phrase *f* toute faite (*pour être citée dans les médias*); **~ effects** *npl* bruitage *m*; **~ly** *adv* (*sleep*) profondément; (*beat*) complètement, à plate couture; **~proof** *adj* insonorisé(e); **~track** *n* (*of film*) bande *f* sonore

**soup** [su:p] *n* soupe *f*, potage *m*; **~ plate** *n* assiette creuse or à soupe; **~spoon** *n* cuiller *f* à soupe

**sour** ['sauə'] *adj* aigre; **it's ~ grapes** (*fig*) c'est du dépit

**source** [sɔːs] *n* source *f*

**south** [sauθ] *n* sud *m* ♦ *adj* sud *inv*, du sud ♦ *adv* au sud, vers le sud; **S~ Africa** *n* Afrique *f* du Sud; **S~ African** *adj* sud-africain(e) ♦ *n* Sud-Africain(e); **S~ America** *n* Amérique *f* du Sud; **S~ American** *adj* sud-américain(e) ♦ *n* Sud-Américain(e); **~east** *n* sud-est *m*; **~erly** ['sʌðəlɪ] *adj* du sud; au sud; **~ern** ['sʌðən] *adj* (du) sud; méridional(e); **S~ Pole** *n* Pôle *m* Sud; **S~ Wales** *n* le Pays de Galles; **~ward(s)** *adv* vers le sud; **~west** *n* sud-ouest *m*

**souvenir** [su:və'nɪə'] *n* (*objet*) souvenir *m*

**sovereign** ['sɔvrɪn] *n* souverain(e)

**soviet** ['səuvɪət] *adj* soviétique; **the S~ Union** l'Union *f* soviétique

**sow**[1] [sau] *n* truie *f*

**sow**[2] [səu] (*pt* **sowed**, *pp* **sown**) *vt* semer

**sown** [səun] *pp of* **sow**[2]

**soya** ['sɔɪə] (*US* **soy**) *n*: **~ bean** graine *f* de soja; **soy(a) sauce** sauce *f* au soja

**spa** [spɑː] *n* (*town*) station thermale; (*US: also:* **health ~**) établissement *m* de cure de rajeunissement *etc*

**space** [speɪs] *n* espace *m*; (*room*) place *f*; espace; (*length of time*) laps *m* de temps ♦ *cpd* spatial(e) ♦ *vt* (*also:* **~ out**) espacer; **~craft** *n* engin spatial; **~man** (*irreg*) *n* astronaute *m*, cosmonaute *m*; **~ship** *n* = **spacecraft**; **spacing** *n* espacement m; **spacious** ['speiʃəs] adj spacieux(-euse), grand(e)

**spade** [speid] n (tool) bêche f, pelle f; (child's) pelle; ~s npl (CARDS) pique m

**Spain** [spein] n Espagne f

**span** [spæn] n (of bird, plane) envergure f; (of arch) portée f; (in time) espace m de temps, durée f ♦ vt enjamber, franchir; (fig) couvrir, embrasser

**Spaniard** ['spænjəd] n Espagnol(e)

**spaniel** ['spænjəl] n épagneul m

**Spanish** ['spæniʃ] adj espagnol(e) ♦ n (LING) espagnol m; **the ~** npl les Espagnols mpl

**spank** [spæŋk] vt donner une fessée à

**spanner** ['spænə'] (BRIT) n clé f (de mécanicien)

**spare** [speə'] adj de réserve, de rechange; (surplus) de or en trop, de reste ♦ n (part) pièce f de rechange, pièce détachée ♦ vt (do without): to ~ se passer de; (afford to give) donner, accorder; (refrain from hurting) épargner; **to ~** (surplus) en surplus, de trop; **~ part** n pièce f de rechange, pièce détachée; **~ time** n moments mpl de loisir, temps m libre; **~ wheel** n (AUT) roue f de secours; **sparingly** adv avec modération

**spark** [spɑːk] n étincelle f; **~(ing) plug** n bougie f

**sparkle** ['spɑːkl] n scintillement m, éclat m ♦ vi étinceler, scintiller; **sparkling** adj (wine) mousseux(-euse), pétillant(e); (water) pétillant(e); (fig: conversation, performance) étincelant(e), pétillant(e)

**sparrow** ['spærəu] n moineau m

**sparse** [spɑːs] adj clairsemé(e)

**spartan** ['spɑːtən] adj (fig) spartiate

**spasm** ['spæzəm] n (MED) spasme m; **~odic** [spæz'mɔdik] adj (fig) intermittent(e)

**spastic** ['spæstik] n handicapé(e) moteur

**spat** [spæt] pt, pp of **spit**

**spate** [speit] n (fig): **a ~ of** une avalanche or un torrent de

**spawn** [spɔːn] vi frayer ♦ n frai m

**speak** [spiːk] (pt **spoke**, pp **spoken**) vt parler; (truth) dire ♦ vi parler; (make a speech) prendre la parole; **to ~ to sb/ of** or **about sth** parler à qn/de qch; **~ up!** parle plus fort!; **~er** n (in public) orateur m; (also: **loudspeaker**) haut-parleur m; **the S~er** (BRIT: POL) le président de la chambre des Communes; (US: POL) le président de la chambre des Représentants

**spear** [spiə'] n lance f ♦ vt transpercer; **~head** vt (attack etc) mener

**spec** [spek] (inf) n: **on ~** à tout hasard

**special** ['speʃl] adj spécial(e); **~ist** n spécialiste m/f; **~ity** [speʃi'æliti] n spécialité f; **~ize** vi: **to ~ize (in)** se spécialiser (dans); **~ly** adv spécialement, particulièrement; **~ty** (esp US) n = **speciality**

**species** ['spiːʃiːz] n inv espèce f

**specific** [spə'sifik] adj précis(e), particulier(-ère); (BOT, CHEM etc) spécifique; **~ally** adv expressément, explicitement; **~ation** [spesifi'keiʃən] n (TECH) spécification f; (requirement) stipulation f

**specimen** ['spesimən] n spécimen m, échantillon m; (of blood) prélèvement m

**speck** [spek] n petite tache, petit point; (particle) grain m

**speckled** ['spekld] adj tacheté(e), moucheté(e)

**specs** [speks] (inf) npl lunettes fpl

**spectacle** ['spektəkl] n spectacle m; **~s** npl (glasses) lunettes fpl; **spectacular** [spek'tækjulə'] adj spectaculaire

**spectator** [spek'teitə'] n spectateur (-trice)

**spectrum** ['spektrəm] (pl **spectra**) n spectre m

**speculation** [spekju'leiʃən] n spéculation f

**speech** [spiːtʃ] n (faculty) parole f; (talk) discours m, allocution f; (manner of speaking) façon f de parler, langage m; (enunciation) élocution f; **~less** adj muet(te)

**speed** [spiːd] n vitesse f; (promptness) rapidité f ♦ vi: **to ~ along/past** etc aller/passer etc à toute vitesse or allure; **at full** or **top ~** à toute vitesse or allure; **~ up** vi aller plus vite, accélérer ♦ vt accélérer; **~boat** n vedette f, hors-bord m inv; **~ily** adv rapidement, promptement; **~ing** n (AUT) excès m de vitesse; **~ limit** n limitation f de vitesse, vitesse maximale permise; **~ometer** [spɪˈdɒmɪtəʳ] n compteur m (de vitesse); **~way** n (SPORT: also: **~way racing**) courses f(pl) de vitesse de motos; **~y** adj rapide, prompt(e)

**spell** [spel] (pt, pp **spelt** or **spelled**) n (also: **magic ~**) sortilège m, charme m; (period of time) (courte) période ♦ vt (in writing) écrire, orthographier; (aloud) épeler; (fig) signifier; **to cast a ~ on sb** jeter un sort à qn; **he can't ~** il fait des fautes d'orthographe; **~bound** adj envoûté(e), subjugué(e); **~ing** n orthographe f

**spend** [spend] (pt, pp **spent**) vt (money) dépenser; (time, life) passer; consacrer; **~thrift** n dépensier(-ère)

**sperm** [spəːm] n sperme m

**sphere** [sfɪəʳ] n sphère f

**spice** [spaɪs] n épice f; **spicy** adj épicé(e), relevé(e); (fig) piquant(e)

**spider** [ˈspaɪdəʳ] n araignée f

**spike** [spaɪk] n pointe f; (BOT) épi m

**spill** [spɪl] (pt, pp **spilt** or **spilled**) vt renverser; répandre ♦ vi se répandre; **~ over** vi déborder

**spin** [spɪn] (pt **spun** or **span**, pp **spun**) n (revolution of wheel) tour m; (AVIAT) (chute f en) vrille f; (trip in car) petit tour, balade f ♦ vt (wool etc) filer; (wheel) faire tourner ♦ vi filer; (turn) tourner, tournoyer

**spinach** [ˈspɪnɪtʃ] n épinard m; (as food) épinards

**spinal** [ˈspaɪnl] adj vertébral(e), spinal(e); **~ cord** n moelle épinière

**spin doctor** n personne employée pour pré-

senter un parti politique sous un jour favorable

**spin-dryer** [spɪnˈdraɪəʳ] (BRIT) n essoreuse f

**spine** [spaɪn] n colonne vertébrale; (thorn) épine f; **~less** adj (fig) mou (molle)

**spinning** [ˈspɪnɪŋ] n (of thread) filature f; **~ top** n toupie f

**spin-off** [ˈspɪnɔf] n avantage inattendu; sous-produit m

**spinster** [ˈspɪnstəʳ] n célibataire f; vieille fille (péj)

**spiral** [ˈspaɪərl] n spirale f ♦ vi (fig) monter en flèche; **~ staircase** n escalier m en colimaçon

**spire** [ˈspaɪəʳ] n flèche f, aiguille f

**spirit** [ˈspɪrɪt] n esprit m; (mood) état d'esprit; (courage) courage m, énergie f; **~s** npl (drink) spiritueux mpl, alcool m; **in good ~s** de bonne humeur; **~ed** adj vif (vive), fougueux(-euse), plein(e) d'allant; **~ual** adj spirituel(le) (religious) religieux(-euse)

**spit** [spɪt] (pt, pp **spat**) n (for roasting) broche f; (saliva) salive f ♦ vi cracher; (sound) crépiter

**spite** [spaɪt] n rancune f, dépit m ♦ vt contrarier, vexer; **in ~ of** en dépit de, malgré; **~ful** adj méchant(e), malveillant(e)

**spittle** [ˈspɪtl] n salive f; (of animal) bave f; (spat out) crachat m

**splash** [splæʃ] n (sound) plouf m; (of colour) tache f ♦ vt éclabousser ♦ vi (also: **~ about**) barboter, patauger

**spleen** [spliːn] n (ANAT) rate f

**splendid** [ˈsplendɪd] adj splendide, superbe, magnifique

**splint** [splɪnt] n attelle f, éclisse f

**splinter** [ˈsplɪntəʳ] n (wood) écharde f; (glass) éclat m ♦ vi se briser, se fendre

**split** [splɪt] (pt, pp **split**) n fente f, déchirure f; (fig: POL) scission f ♦ vt diviser; (work, profits) partager, répartir ♦ vi (divide) se diviser; **~ up** vi (couple) se séparer, rompre; (meeting) se disperser

# spoil 555 sprinkle

**spoil** [spɔɪl] (*pt, pp* **spoilt** *or* **spoiled**) *vt* (*damage*) abîmer; (*mar*) gâcher; (*child*) gâter; **~s** *npl* butin *m*; (*fig: profits*) bénéfices *npl*, profits *npl*; **~sport** *n* trouble-fête *m*, rabat-joie *m*

**spoke** [spəʊk] *pt of* **speak** ♦ *n* (*of wheel*) rayon *m*

**spoken** ['spəʊkn] *pp of* **speak**

**spokesman** ['spəʊksmən], **spokes-woman** ['spəʊkswʊmən] (*irreg*) *n* porte-parole *m inv*

**sponge** [spʌndʒ] *n* éponge *f*; (*also: ~ cake*) = biscuit *m* de Savoie ♦ *vt* éponger ♦ *vi*: **to ~ off** *or* **on** vivre aux crochets de; **~ bag** (*BRIT*) *n* trousse *f* de toilette

**sponsor** ['spɒnsə*] *n* (*RADIO, TV, SPORT*) sponsor *m*; (*for application*) parrain *m*, marraine *f*; (*BRIT: for fund-raising event*) donateur(-trice) *m/f* ♦ *vt* sponsoriser; parrainer; faire un don à; **~ship** *n* sponsoring *m*; parrainage *m*; dons *mpl*

**spontaneous** [spɒn'teɪnɪəs] *adj* spontané(e)

**spooky** ['spuːkɪ] (*inf*) *adj* qui donne la chair de poule

**spool** [spuːl] *n* bobine *f*

**spoon** [spuːn] *n* cuiller *f*; **~feed** *vt* nourrir à la cuiller; (*fig*) mâcher le travail à; **~ful** *n* cuillerée *f*

**sport** [spɔːt] *n* sport *m*; (*person*) chic type (*fille*) ♦ *vt* arborer; **~ing** *adj* sportif(-ive); **to give sb a ~ing chance** donner sa chance à qn; **~ jacket** (*US*) *n* = **sports jacket**; **~s car** *n* voiture *f* de sport; **~s jacket** (*BRIT*) *n* veste *f* de sport; **~sman** (*irreg*) *n* sportif *m*; **~smanship** *n* esprit sportif, sportivité *f*; **~swear** *n* vêtements *mpl* de sport; **~swoman** (*irreg*) *n* sportive *f*; **~y** *adj* sportif(-ive)

**spot** [spɒt] *n* tache *f*; (*dot: on pattern*) pois *m*; (*pimple*) bouton *m*; (*place*) endroit *m*, coin *m*; (*RADIO, TV: in programme*) numéro *m*; (*: for person*) rubrique *f*; (*small amount*): **a ~ of** un peu de ♦ *vt* (*notice*) apercevoir,

repérer; **on the ~** sur place, sur les lieux; (*immediately*) sur-le-champ; (*in difficulty*) dans l'embarras; **~ check** *n* sondage *m*, vérification ponctuelle; **~less** *adj* immaculé(e); **~light** *n* projecteur *m*; **~ted** *adj* (*fabric*) à pois; **~ty** *adj* (*face, person*) boutonneux(-euse)

**spouse** [spaʊs] *n* époux (épouse)

**spout** [spaʊt] *n* (*of jug*) bec *m*; (*of pipe*) orifice *m* ♦ *vi* jaillir

**sprain** [spreɪn] *n* entorse *f*, foulure *f* ♦ *vt*: **to ~ one's ankle** *etc* se fouler *or* se tordre la cheville *etc*

**sprang** [spræŋ] *pt of* **spring**

**sprawl** [sprɔːl] *vi* s'étaler

**spray** [spreɪ] *n* jet *m* (en fines gouttelettes); (*from sea*) embruns *mpl*, vaporisateur *m*; (*for garden*) pulvérisateur *m*; (*aerosol*) bombe *f*; (*of flowers*) petit bouquet ♦ *vt* vaporiser, pulvériser; (*crops*) traiter

**spread** [spred] (*pt, pp* **spread**) *n* (*distribution*) répartition *f*; (*CULIN*) pâte *f* à tartiner; (*inf: meal*) festin *m* ♦ *vt* étendre, étaler; répandre; (*wealth, workload*) distribuer ♦ *vi* (*disease, news*) se propager; (*also: ~ out: stain*) s'étaler; **~ out** *vi* (*people*) se disperser; **~-eagled** *adj* bras et jambes écartés; **~sheet** *n* (*COMPUT*) tableur *m*

**spree** [spriː] *n*: **to go on a ~** faire la fête

**sprightly** ['spraɪtlɪ] *adj* alerte

**spring** [sprɪŋ] (*pt* **sprang**, *pp* **sprung**) *n* (*leap*) bond *m*, saut *m*; (*coiled metal*) ressort *m*; (*season*) printemps *m*; (*of water*) source *f* ♦ *vi* (*leap*) bondir, sauter; **in ~** au printemps; **to ~ from** provenir de; **~ up** *vi* (*problem*) se présenter, surgir; (*plant, buildings*) surgir de terre; **~board** *n* tremplin *m*; **~-clean(ing)** *n* grand nettoyage de printemps; **~time** *n* printemps *m*

**sprinkle** ['sprɪŋkl] *vt*: **to ~ water on, ~ with water** *etc* asperger d'eau *etc*; **to ~ sugar** *etc* **on, ~ with sugar** *etc* saupoudrer de sucre *etc*; **~r** *n* (*for* *lawn*) arroseur m; *(to put out fire)* diffuseur m d'extincteur automatique d'incendie

**sprint** [sprɪnt] n sprint m ♦ vi courir à toute vitesse; *(SPORT)* sprinter; **~er** n sprinteur(-euse)

**sprout** [spraʊt] vi germer, pousser; **~s** npl *(also:* **Brussels ~s)** choux mpl de Bruxelles

**spruce** [spruːs] n inv épicéa m ♦ adj net(te), pimpant(e)

**sprung** [sprʌŋ] pp of **spring**

**spun** [spʌn] pt, pp of **spin**

**spur** [spəːʳ] n éperon m; *(fig)* aiguillon m ♦ vt *(also:* **~ on)** éperonner; aiguillonner; **on the ~ of the moment** sous l'impulsion du moment

**spurious** ['spjʊərɪəs] adj faux (fausse)

**spurn** [spəːn] vt repousser avec mépris

**spurt** [spəːt] n *(of blood)* jaillissement m; *(of energy)* regain m, sursaut m ♦ vi jaillir, gicler

**spy** [spaɪ] n espion(ne) m ♦ vi: **to ~ on** espionner, épier; *(see)* apercevoir; **~ing** n espionnage m

**sq.** abbr = **square**

**squabble** ['skwɔbl] vi se chamailler

**squad** [skwɔd] n *(MIL, POLICE)* escouade f, groupe m; *(FOOTBALL)* contingent m

**squadron** ['skwɔdrən] n *(MIL)* escadron m; *(AVIAT, NAUT)* escadrille f

**squalid** ['skwɔlɪd] adj sordide

**squall** [skwɔːl] n rafale f, bourrasque f

**squalor** ['skwɔləʳ] n conditions fpl sordides

**squander** ['skwɔndəʳ] vt gaspiller, dilapider

**square** [skwɛəʳ] n carré m; *(in town)* place f ♦ adj carré(e); *(inf: ideas, tastes)* vieux jeu inv ♦ vt *(arrange)* régler; arranger; *(MATH)* élever au carré ♦ vi *(reconcile)* concilier; **all ~** quitte; à égalité; **a ~ meal** un repas convenable; **2 metres ~** de 2 mètres sur 2; **2 metres 2** mètres carrés; **~ly** adv carrément

**squash** [skwɔʃ] n *(BRIT: drink):* **lemon/**

orange **~** citronnade f/orangeade f; *(US: marrow)* courge f; *(SPORT)* squash m ♦ vt écraser

**squat** [skwɔt] adj petit(e) et épais(se), ramassé(e) ♦ vi *(also:* **~ down)** s'accroupir; **~ter** n squatter m

**squeak** [skwiːk] vi grincer, crier; *(mouse)* pousser un petit cri

**squeal** [skwiːl] vi pousser un or des cri(s) aigu(s) or perçant(s); *(brakes)* grincer

**squeamish** ['skwiːmɪʃ] adj facilement dégoûté(e)

**squeeze** [skwiːz] n pression f; *(ECON)* restrictions fpl de crédit ♦ vt presser; *(hand, arm)* serrer; **~ out** vt exprimer

**squelch** [skwɛltʃ] vi faire un bruit de succion

**squid** [skwɪd] n calmar m

**squiggle** ['skwɪgl] n gribouillis m

**squint** [skwɪnt] vi loucher ♦ n: **he has a ~** il louche, il souffre de strabisme

**squirm** [skwəːm] vi se tortiller

**squirrel** ['skwɪrəl] n écureuil m

**squirt** [skwəːt] vi jaillir, gicler

**Sr** abbr = **senior**

**St** abbr = **saint; street**

**stab** [stæb] n *(with knife etc)* coup m *(de couteau etc)*; *(of pain)* lancée f; *(inf: try):* **to have a ~ at (doing) sth** s'essayer à (faire) qch ♦ vt poignarder

**stable** ['steɪbl] n écurie f ♦ adj stable

**stack** [stæk] n tas m, pile f ♦ vt *(also:* **~ up)** empiler, entasser

**stadium** ['steɪdɪəm] n *(pl* **stadia** or **~s)** n stade m

**staff** [stɑːf] n *(workforce)* personnel m; *(BRIT: SCOL)* professeurs mpl ♦ vt pourvoir en personnel

**stag** [stæg] n cerf m

**stage** [steɪdʒ] n scène f; *(platform)* estrade f ♦ n *(point)* étape f, stade m; *(profession):* **the ~** le théâtre ♦ vt *(play)* monter, mettre en scène; *(demonstration)* organiser; **in ~s** par étapes, par degrés; **~coach** n diligence f; **~ manager** n régisseur m

**stagger** ['stægə<sup>r</sup>] vi chanceler, tituber ♦ vt (person) amaze) stupéfier; (hours, holidays) étaler, échelonner; **~ing** adj (amazing) stupéfiant(e), renversant(e).

**stagnate** [stæg'neɪt] vi stagner, croupir

**stag party** n enterrement m de vie de garçon

**staid** [steɪd] adj posé(e), rassis(e)

**stain** [steɪn] n tache f; (colouring) colorant m ♦ vt tacher; (wood) teindre; **~ed glass window** n vitrail m; **~less** adj (steel) inoxydable; **~less steel** n acier m inoxydable, inox m; **~ remover** n détachant m

**stair** [stɛə<sup>r</sup>] n (step) marche f; **~s** npl (flight of steps) escalier m; **~case**, **~way** n escalier m

**stake** [steɪk] n pieu m, poteau m; (BETTING) enjeu m; (COMM: interest) intérêts mpl ♦ vt risquer, jouer; (also ~ out: area) marquer, délimiter; **to be at ~** être en jeu; **to ~ one's claim (to)** revendiquer

**stale** [steɪl] adj (bread) rassis(e); (food) pas frais (fraîche); (beer) éventé(e); (smell) de renfermé; (air) confiné(e)

**stalemate** ['steɪlmeɪt] n (CHESS) pat m; (fig) impasse f

**stalk** [stɔːk] n tige f ♦ vt traquer ♦ vi: to ~ out/off sortir/partir d'un air digne

**stall** [stɔːl] n (in street, market etc) éventaire m, étal m; (in stable) stalle f ♦ vt (AUT) caler; (delay) retarder ♦ vi (AUT) caler; (fig) essayer de gagner du temps; **~s** npl (BRIT: in cinema, theatre) orchestre m

**stallion** ['stæljən] n étalon m (cheval)

**stamina** ['stæmɪnə] n résistance f, endurance f

**stammer** ['stæmə<sup>r</sup>] n bégaiement m ♦ vi bégayer

**stamp** [stæmp] n timbre m; (rubber ~) tampon m; (mark, also fig) empreinte f ♦ vi (also: ~ one's foot) taper du pied ♦ vt (letter) timbrer; (with rubber ~) tamponner; **~ album** n album m de timbres(-poste); **~ collecting** n philatélie f

**stampede** [stæm'piːd] n ruée f

**stance** [stæns] n position f

**stand** [stænd] (pt, pp stood) n (position) position f; (for taxis) station f (de taxis); (music) pupitre m à musique; (COMM) étalage m, stand m; (SPORT: also: ~s) tribune f ♦ vi (be upright) se tenir (debout); (rise) se lever, se mettre debout; (be placed) se trouver; (remain: offer etc) rester valable; (BRIT: in election) être candidat(e) ♦ vt (place) mettre, poser; (tolerate, withstand) supporter; (treat, invite to) offrir, payer; **to make** or **take a ~** prendre position; **to ~ at** (score, value etc) être de; **to ~ for parliament** (BRIT) se présenter aux élections législatives; **~ by** vi (be ready) se tenir prêt(e) ♦ vt fus (opinion) s'en tenir à; (person) ne pas abandonner, soutenir; **~ down** vi (withdraw) se retirer; **~ for** vt fus (signify) représenter, signifier; (tolerate) supporter, tolérer; **~ in for** vt fus remplacer; **~ out** vi (be prominent) ressortir; **~ up** vi (rise) se lever, se mettre debout; **~ up for** vt fus défendre; **~ up to** vt fus tenir tête à, résister à

**standard** ['stændəd] n (level) niveau m (voulu); (norm) norme f, étalon m; (criterion) critère m; (flag) étendard m ♦ adj (size etc) ordinaire, normal(e); courant(e); (text) de base; **~s** npl (morals) morale f, principes mpl; **~ lamp** n lampadaire m; **~ of living** n niveau m de vie

**stand-by** ['stændbaɪ] n remplaçant(e); **to be on ~~** se tenir prêt(e) à intervenir; être de garde; **~~ ticket** n (AVIAT) billet m stand-by

**stand-in** ['stændɪn] n remplaçant(e)

**standing** ['stændɪŋ] adj debout inv; (permanent) permanent(e) ♦ n réputation f, rang m, standing m; **of many years'** ~ qui dure or existe depuis longtemps; **~ joke** n vieux sujet de plaisanterie; **~ order** (BRIT) n (at bank) virement m automatique, prélèvement m bancaire; **~ room** n places fpl debout

**standpoint** ['stændpɔɪnt] n point m de vue

**standstill** ['stændstɪl] n: **at a ~** paralysé(e); **to come to a ~** s'immobiliser, s'arrêter

**stank** [stæŋk] pt of **stink**

**staple** ['steɪpl] n (for papers) agrafe f ♦ adj (food etc) de base ♦ vt agrafer; **~r** n agrafeuse f

**star** [stɑːʳ] n étoile f; (celebrity) vedette f ♦ vi: **to ~ (in)** être la vedette (de) ♦ vt (CINEMA etc) avoir pour vedette; **the ~s** npl l'horoscope m

**starboard** ['stɑːbəd] n tribord m

**starch** [stɑːtʃ] n amidon m; (in food) fécule f

**stardom** ['stɑːdəm] n célébrité f

**stare** [stɛəʳ] n regard m fixe ♦ vi: **to ~ at** regarder fixement

**starfish** ['stɑːfɪʃ] n étoile f de mer

**stark** [stɑːk] adj (bleak) désolé(e), morne ♦ adv: **~ naked** complètement nu(e)

**starling** ['stɑːlɪŋ] n étourneau m

**starry** ['stɑːrɪ] adj étoilé(e); **~-eyed** adj (innocent) ingénu(e)

**start** [stɑːt] n commencement m, début m; (of race) départ m; (sudden movement) sursaut m; (advantage) avance f, avantage m ♦ vt commencer; (found) créer; (engine) mettre en marche ♦ vi partir, se mettre en route; (jump) sursauter; **to ~ doing** or **to do sth** se mettre à faire qch; **~ off** vi commencer; (leave) partir; **~ up** vi commencer; (car) démarrer ♦ vt (business) créer; (car) mettre en marche; **~er** n (AUT) démarreur m; (SPORT: official) starter m; (BRIT: CULIN) entrée f; **~ing point** n point m de départ

**startle** ['stɑːtl] vt faire sursauter; donner un choc à; **startling** adj (news) surprenant(e)

**starvation** [stɑːˈveɪʃən] n faim, famine f

**starve** [stɑːv] vi mourir de faim; être affamé(e) ♦ vt affamer

**state** [steɪt] n état m; (POL) État m ♦ vt dé-

clarer, affirmer; **the S~s** npl (America) les États-Unis mpl; **to be in a ~** être dans tous ses états; **~ly** adj majestueux(-euse), imposant(e); **~ly home** n château m; **~ment** n déclaration f; **~sman** (irreg) n homme m d'État

**static** ['stætɪk] n (RADIO, TV) parasites mpl ♦ adj statique

**station** ['steɪʃən] n gare f; (police ~) poste m de police ♦ vt placer, poster

**stationary** ['steɪʃnərɪ] adj à l'arrêt, immobile

**stationer** ['steɪʃənəʳ] n papetier(-ère); **~'s (shop)** n papeterie f; **~y** n papier m à lettres, petit matériel de bureau

**stationmaster** ['steɪʃənmɑːstəʳ] n (RAIL) chef m de gare

**station wagon** (US) n break m

**statistic** [stəˈtɪstɪk] n statistique f; **~s** [stəˈtɪstɪks] n (science) statistique f

**statue** ['stætjuː] n statue f

**status** ['steɪtəs] n position f, situation f; (official) statut m; (prestige) prestige m; **~ symbol** n signe extérieur de richesse

**statute** ['stætjuːt] n loi f, statut m; **statutory** adj statutaire, prévu(e) par un article de loi

**staunch** [stɔːntʃ] adj sûr(e), loyal(e)

**stay** [steɪ] n (period of time) séjour m ♦ vi rester; (reside) loger; (spend some time) séjourner; **to ~ put** ne pas bouger; **to ~ with friends** loger chez des amis; **to ~ the night** passer la nuit; **~ behind** vi rester en arrière; **~ in** vi (at home) rester à la maison; **~ on** vi rester; **~ out** vi (of house) ne pas rentrer; **~ up** vi (at night) ne pas se coucher; **~ing power** n endurance f

**stead** [stɛd] n: **in sb's ~** à la place de qn; **to stand sb in good ~** être très utile à qn

**steadfast** ['stɛdfɑːst] adj ferme, résolu(e)

**steadily** ['stɛdɪlɪ] adv (regularly) progressivement; (firmly) fermement; (: walk) d'un pas ferme; (fixedly: look) sans détourner les yeux

**steady** ['stɛdɪ] adj stable, solide, ferme; (regular) constant(e), régulier(-ère); (person) calme, pondéré(e) ♦ vt stabiliser; (nerves) calmer; **a ~ boyfriend** un petit ami

**steak** [steɪk] n (beef) bifteck m, steak m; (fish, pork) tranche f

**steal** [stiːl] (pt **stole**, pp **stolen**) vt voler ♦ vi voler; (move secretly) se faufiler, se déplacer furtivement

**stealth** [stɛlθ] n: **by ~** furtivement

**steam** [stiːm] n vapeur f ♦ vt (CULIN) cuire à la vapeur ♦ vi fumer; **~ engine** n locomotive f à vapeur; **~er** n (bateau m à) vapeur m; **~ship** n = steamer; **~y** adj embué(e), humide

**steel** [stiːl] n acier m ♦ adj d'acier; **~works** n aciérie f

**steep** [stiːp] adj raide, escarpé(e); (price) excessif(-ive)

**steeple** ['stiːpl] n clocher m

**steer** [stɪəʳ] vt diriger; (boat) gouverner; (person) guider, conduire ♦ vi tenir le gouvernail; **~ing** n (AUT) conduite f; **~ing wheel** n volant m

**stem** [stem] n (of plant) tige f; (of glass) pied m ♦ vt contenir, arrêter, juguler; **~ from** vt fus provenir de, découler de

**stench** [stɛntʃ] n puanteur f

**stencil** ['stɛnsl] n stencil m; (pattern used) pochoir m ♦ vt polycopier

**stenographer** [stɛ'nɔgrəfəʳ] (US) n sténographe m/f

**step** [step] n pas m; (stair) marche f; (action) mesure f, disposition f ♦ vi: **to ~ forward/back** faire un pas en avant/arrière, avancer/reculer; **~s** npl (BRIT) = stepladder; **to be in/out of ~ (with)** (fig) aller dans le sens de/être déphasé(e) (par rapport à); **~ down** vi (fig) se retirer, se désister; **~ up** vt augmenter; intensifier; **~brother** n demi-frère m; **~daughter** n belle-fille f; **~father** n beau-père m; **~ladder** (BRIT) n escabeau m, échelle f; **~mother** n belle-mère f; **~ping stone** n pierre f de gué; (fig) tremplin m; **~sister** n demi-sœur f;

**~son** n beau-fils m

**stereo** ['stɛrɪəu] n (sound) stéréo f; (hi-fi) chaîne f stéréo inv ♦ adj (also: **~phonic**) stéréo(phonique)

**sterile** ['stɛraɪl] adj stérile; **sterilize** ['stɛrɪlaɪz] vt stériliser

**sterling** ['stəːlɪŋ] adj (silver) de bon aloi, fin(e) ♦ n (ECON) livres fpl sterling inv; **a pound ~** une livre sterling

**stern** [stəːn] adj sévère ♦ n (NAUT) arrière m, poupe f

**stew** [stjuː] n ragoût m ♦ vt, vi cuire (à la casserole)

**steward** ['stjuːəd] n (on ship, plane, train) steward m; **~ess** n hôtesse f (de l'air)

**stick** [stɪk] (pt, pp **stuck**) n bâton m; (walking ~) canne f ♦ vt (glue) coller; (inf: put) mettre, fourrer; (: tolerate) supporter; (thrust): **to ~ sth into** planter or enfoncer qch dans ♦ vi (become attached) rester collé(e) or fixé(e); (be unmoveable: wheels etc) se bloquer; (remain) rester; **~ out** vi dépasser, sortir; **~ up** vi = stick out; **~ up for** vt fus défendre; **~er** n auto-collant m; **~ing plaster** n sparadrap m, pansement adhésif

**stick-up** ['stɪkʌp] (inf) n braquage m, hold-up m inv

**sticky** ['stɪkɪ] adj poisseux(-euse); (label) adhésif(-ive); (situation) délicat(e)

**stiff** [stɪf] adj raide; rigide; dur(e); (difficult) difficile, ardu(e); (cold) froid(e), distant(e); (strong, high) fort(e), élevé(e) ♦ adv: **to be bored/scared/frozen** s'ennuyer à mort/être mort(e) de peur/froid; **~en** vi se raidir; **~ neck** n torticolis m

**stifle** ['staɪfl] vt étouffer, réprimer

**stigma** ['stɪgmə] n stigmate m

**stile** [staɪl] n échalier m

**stiletto** [stɪ'lɛtəu] (BRIT) n (also: **~ heel**) talon m aiguille

**still** [stɪl] adj immobile ♦ adv (up to this time) encore, toujours; (even) encore; (nonetheless) quand même, tout de

**stilt**; **~born** adj mort-né(e); **~ life** n nature morte

**stilt** [stɪlt] n (for walking on) échasse f; (pile) pilotis m

**stilted** ['stɪltɪd] adj guindé(e), emprunté(e)

**stimulate** ['stɪmjuleɪt] vt stimuler

**stimuli** ['stɪmjulaɪ] npl of **stimulus**

**stimulus** ['stɪmjuləs] (pl **stimuli**) n stimulant m; (BIOL, PSYCH) stimulus m

**sting** [stɪŋ] (pt, pp **stung**) n piqûre f; (organ) dard m ♦ vt, vi piquer

**stingy** ['stɪndʒɪ] adj avare, pingre

**stink** [stɪŋk] (pt **stank**, pp **stunk**) n puanteur f ♦ vi puer, empester; **~ing** (inf) adj (fig) infect(e), vache; **a ~ing ...** un(e) foutu(e) ...

**stint** [stɪnt] n part f de travail ♦ vi: **to ~ on** lésiner sur, être chiche de

**stir** [stəːr] n agitation f, sensation f ♦ vt remuer ♦ vi remuer, bouger; **~ up** (trouble) fomenter, provoquer

**stirrup** ['stɪrəp] n étrier m.

**stitch** [stɪtʃ] n (SEWING) point m; (KNITTING) maille f; (MED) point de suture; (pain) point de côté ♦ vt coudre, piquer; (MED) suturer

**stoat** [stəut] n hermine f (avec son pelage d'été)

**stock** [stɔk] n réserve f, provision f; (COMM) stock m; (AGR) cheptel m, bétail m; (CULIN) bouillon m; (descent, origin) souche f; (FINANCE) valeurs fpl, titres mpl ♦ adj (fig: reply etc) classique ♦ vt (have in ~) avoir, vendre; **~s and shares** valeurs (mobilières); titres; **in/out of ~** en stock ou en magasin/épuisé(e); **to take ~ of** (fig) faire le point de; **~ up** vi: **to ~ up (with)** s'approvisionner (en); **~broker** n agent m de change; **~ cube** n bouillon-cube m; **~ exchange** n Bourse f

**stocking** ['stɔkɪŋ] n bas m

**stock-**: **~ market** n Bourse f, marché financier; **~pile** n stock m, réserve f ♦ vt stocker, accumuler; **~taking** (BRIT) n (COMM) inventaire m

**stocky** ['stɔkɪ] adj trapu(e), râblé(e)

**stodgy** ['stɔdʒɪ] adj bourratif(-ive), lourd(e)

**stoke** [stəuk] vt (fire) garnir, entretenir; (boiler) chauffer

**stole** [stəul] pt of **steal** ♦ n étole f.

**stolen** ['stəuln] pp of **steal**

**stomach** ['stʌmək] n estomac m; (abdomen) ventre m ♦ vt digérer, supporter; **~ache** n mal m à l'estomac ou au ventre

**stone** [stəun] n pierre f; (pebble) caillou m, galet m; (in fruit) noyau m; (MED) calcul m; (BRIT: weight) 6,348 kg ♦ adj de ou en pierre ♦ vt (person) lancer des pierres sur, lapider; **~-cold** adj complètement froid(e); **~-deaf** adj sourd(e) comme un pot; **~work** n maçonnerie f

**stood** [stud] pt, pp of **stand**

**stool** [stuːl] n tabouret m

**stoop** [stuːp] vi (also: **have a ~**) être voûté(e); (also: **~ down**: bend) se baisser

**stop** [stɔp] n arrêt m; halte f; (in punctuation: also: **full ~**) point m ♦ vt arrêter, bloquer; (break off) interrompre; (also: **put a ~ to**) mettre fin à ♦ vi s'arrêter; (rain, noise etc) cesser, s'arrêter; **to ~ doing sth** cesser ou arrêter de faire qch; **~ dead** vi s'arrêter net; **~ off** vi faire une courte halte; **~ up** vt (hole) boucher; **~gap** n (person) bouche-trou m; (measure) mesure f intérimaire; **~over** n halte f; (AVIAT) escale f; **~page** n (strike) arrêt de travail; (blockage) obstruction f; **~per** n bouchon m; **~ press** n nouvelles fpl de dernière heure; **~watch** n chronomètre m

**storage** ['stɔːrɪdʒ] n entreposage m; **~ heater** n radiateur m électrique par accumulation

**store** [stɔːr] n (stock) provision f, réserve f; (depot) entrepôt m; (BRIT: large shop) grand magasin; (US) magasin m ♦ vt emmagasiner; (information) enregistrer; **~s** npl (food) provisions fpl; **in ~** en réserve; **~ up** vt mettre en réserve; accumuler; **~room** n réserve f, magasin m

**storey** ['stɔːrɪ] (US **story**) n étage m

**stork** [stɔːk] n cigogne f

**storm** [stɔːm] n tempête f; (thunderstorm) orage m ♦ vi (fig) fulminer ♦ vt prendre d'assaut; **~y** adj orageux(-euse)

**story** ['stɔːrɪ] n histoire f, récit m; (US) = **storey**; **~book** n livre m d'histoires or de contes

**stout** [staut] adj solide; (fat) gros(se), corpulent(e) ♦ n bière brune

**stove** [stəuv] n (for cooking) fourneau m; (: small) réchaud m; (for heating) poêle m

**stow** [stəu] vt (also: ~ away) ranger; **~away** n passager(-ère) clandestin(e)

**straddle** ['strædl] vt enjamber, être à cheval sur

**straggle** ['strægl] vi être (or marcher) en désordre

**straight** [streɪt] adj droit(e); (hair) raide; (frank) honnête, franc (franche); (simple) simple ♦ adv (tout) droit; (drink) sec, sans eau; **to put** or **get** ~ (fig) mettre au clair; ~ **away**, ~ **off** (at once) tout de suite; **~en** vt ajuster; (bed) arranger; **~en out** vt (fig) débrouiller; **~faced** adj impassible; **~forward** adj simple; (honest) honnête, direct(e)

**strain** [streɪn] n tension f; pression f; (physical) effort m; (mental) tension (nerveuse); (breed) race f ♦ vt (stretch: resources etc) mettre à rude épreuve, grever; (hurt: back etc) se faire mal à; (vegetables) égoutter; **~s** npl (MUS) accords mpl, accents mpl; **back** ~ tour de rein; **~ed** adj (muscle) froissé(e); (laugh etc) forcé(e), contraint(e); (relations) tendu(e); **~er** n passoire f

**strait** [streɪt] n (GEO) détroit m; **~s** npl: **to be in dire** ~ avoir de sérieux ennuis (d'argent); **~jacket** n camisole f de force; **~-laced** adj collet monté inv

**strand** [strænd] n (of thread) fil m, brin m; (of rope) toron m; (of hair) mèche f;

**~ed** adj en rade, en plan

**strange** [streɪndʒ] adj (not known) inconnu(e); (odd) étrange, bizarre; **~ly** adv étrangement, bizarrement; see also **enough**; **~r** n inconnu(e); (from another area) étranger(-ère)

**strangle** ['stræŋgl] vt étrangler; **~hold** n (fig) emprise totale, mainmise f

**strap** [stræp] n lanière f, courroie f, sangle f; (of slip, dress) bretelle f; **~py** adj (dress) à bretelles; (sandals) à lanières

**strategy** ['strætɪdʒɪ] n stratégie f

**straw** [strɔː] n paille f; **that's the last** ~! ça, c'est le comble!

**strawberry** ['strɔːbərɪ] n fraise f

**stray** [streɪ] adj (animal) perdu(e), errant(e); (scattered) isolé(e) ♦ vi s'égarer; ~ **bullet** n balle perdue

**streak** [striːk] n bande f, filet m; (in hair) raie f ♦ vt zébrer, strier ♦ vi: **to** ~ **past** passer à toute allure

**stream** [striːm] n (brook) ruisseau m; (current) courant m, flot m; (of people) défilé ininterrompu, flot ♦ vt (SCOL) répartir par niveau ♦ vi ruisseler; **to** ~ **in/out** entrer/sortir à flots

**streamer** ['striːmər] n serpentin m; (banner) banderole f

**streamlined** ['striːmlaɪnd] adj aérodynamique; (fig) rationalisé(e)

**street** [striːt] n rue f; **~car** (US) n tramway m; **~ lamp** n réverbère m; **~ plan** n plan m (des rues); **~wise** (inf) adj futé(e), réaliste

**strength** [streŋθ] n force f; (of girder, knot etc) solidité f; **~en** vt (muscle etc) fortifier; (nation, case etc) renforcer; (building, ECON) consolider

**strenuous** ['strenjuəs] adj vigoureux (-euse), énergique

**stress** [stres] n (force, pressure) pression f; (mental strain) tension (nerveuse), stress m; (accent) accent m ♦ vt insister sur, souligner

**stretch** [stretʃ] n (of sand etc) étendue f ♦ vi s'étirer; (extend): **to** ~ **to** or **as far**

**as** s'étendre jusqu'à ♦ *vt* tendre, étirer; *(fig)* pousser (au maximum); **~ out** *vi* s'étendre ♦ *vt* *(arm etc)* allonger, tendre; *(spread)* étendre

**stretcher** ['strɛtʃə*r*] *n* brancard *m*, civière *f*

**stretchy** ['strɛtʃɪ] *adj* élastique

**strewn** [struːn] *adj*: **~ with** jonché(e) de

**stricken** ['strɪkən] *adj* *(person)* très éprouvé(e); *(city, industry etc)* dévasté(e); **~ with** *(disease etc)* frappé(e) ou atteint(e) de

**strict** [strɪkt] *adj* strict(e)

**stride** [straɪd] *(pt* **strode,** *pp* **stridden)** *n* grand pas, enjambée *fretar* ♦ *vi* marcher à grands pas

**strife** [straɪf] *n* conflit *m*, dissensions *fpl*

**strike** [straɪk] *(pt, pp* **struck)** *n* grève *f*; *(of oil etc)* découverte *f*; *(attack)* raid *m* ♦ *vt* frapper; *(oil etc)* trouver, découvrir; *(deal)* conclure ♦ *vi* faire grève; *(attack)* attaquer; *(clock)* sonner; **on ~** *(workers)* en grève; **to ~ a match** frotter une allumette; **~ down** *vt* terrasser; **~ up** *(MUS)* se mettre à jouer; **to ~ up a friendship** se lier d'amitié avec; **to ~ up a conversation (with)** engager une conversation (avec); **~r** *n* gréviste *m/f*; *(SPORT)* buteur *m*; **striking** *adj* frappant(e), saisissant(e); *(attractive)* éblouissant(e)

**string** [strɪŋ] *(pt, pp* **strung)** *n* ficelle *f*; *(row: of beads)* rang *m*; *(: of onions)* chapelet *m*; *(MUS)* corde *f* ♦ *vt*: **to ~ out** échelonner; **the ~s** *npl* *(MUS)* les instruments *mpl* à cordes; **to ~ together** enchaîner; **to pull ~s** *(fig)* faire jouer le piston; **~(ed) instrument** *n* *(MUS)* instrument *m* à cordes

**stringent** ['strɪndʒənt] *adj* rigoureux (-euse)

**strip** [strɪp] *n* bande *f* ♦ *vt* *(undress)* déshabiller; *(paint)* décaper; *(also: ~ down: machine)* démonter ♦ *vi* se déshabiller; **~ cartoon** *n* bande dessinée

**stripe** [straɪp] *n* raie *f*, rayure *f*; *(MIL)* ga-

lon *m*; **~d** *adj* rayé(e), à rayures

**strip: ~ lighting** *(BRIT)* *n* éclairage *m* au néon ou fluorescent; **~per** *n* stripteaseur(-euse) *f*; **~ search** *n* fouille corporelle *(en faisant se déshabiller la personne)* ♦ *vt*: **he was ~ searched** on l'a fait se déshabiller et soumis à une fouille corporelle

**stripy** ['straɪpɪ] *adj* rayé(e)

**strive** [straɪv] *(pt* **strove,** *pp* **striven)** *vi*: **to ~ to do/for sth** s'efforcer de faire/ d'obtenir qch

**strode** [strəʊd] *pt of* **stride**

**stroke** [strəʊk] *n* coup *m*; *(SWIMMING)* nage *f*; *(MED)* attaque *f* ♦ *vt* caresser; **at a ~** d'un (seul) coup

**stroll** [strəʊl] *n* petite promenade ♦ *vi* flâner, se promener nonchalamment; **~er** *(US)* *n* *(pushchair)* poussette *f*

**strong** [strɒŋ] *adj* fort(e); vigoureux (-euse); *(heart, nerves)* solide; **they are 50 ~** ils sont au nombre de 50; **~hold** *n* bastion *m*; **~ly** *adv* fortement, avec force; vigoureusement; solidement; **~room** *n* chambre forte

**strove** [strəʊv] *pt, pp of* **strive**

**struck** [strʌk] *pt, pp of* **strike**

**structural** ['strʌktʃ*r*əl] *adj* structural(e); *(CONSTR)* de construction; *(damage)* affectant les parties portantes

**structure** ['strʌktʃə*r*] *n* structure *f*; *(building)* construction *f*

**struggle** ['strʌɡl] *n* lutte *f* ♦ *vi* lutter, se battre

**strum** [strʌm] *vt* *(guitar)* jouer (en sourdine) de

**strung** [strʌŋ] *pt, pp of* **string**

**strut** [strʌt] *n* étai *m*, support *m* ♦ *vi* se pavaner

**stub** [stʌb] *n* *(of cigarette)* bout *m*, mégot *m*; *(of cheque etc)* talon *m* ♦ *vt*: **to ~ one's toe** se cogner le doigt de pied; **~ out** *vt* écraser

**stubble** ['stʌbl] *n* chaume *m*; *(on chin)* barbe *f* de plusieurs jours

**stubborn** ['stʌbən] *adj* têtu(e), obstiné(e), opiniâtre

**stuck** [stʌk] *pt, pp of* **stick** ♦ *adj* (*jammed*) bloqué(e), coincé(e); **~-up** (*inf*) *adj* prétentieux(-euse)

**stud** [stʌd] *n* (*on boots etc*) clou *m*; (*on collar*) bouton *m* de col; (*earring*) petite boucle d'oreille; (*of horses: also:* **~ farm**) écurie *f*, haras *m*; (*also:* **~ horse**) étalon *m* ♦ *vt* (*fig*): **~ded with** parsemé(e) or criblé(e) de

**student** ['stju:dənt] *n* étudiant(e) ♦ *adj* estudiantin(e); d'étudiant; **~ driver** (*US*) *n* (*conducteur*-*trice*) débutant(e)

**studio** ['stju:dɪəʊ] *n* studio *m*, atelier *m*; (*TV etc*) studio

**studious** ['stju:dɪəs] *adj* studieux(-euse), appliqué(e); (*attention*) soutenu(e); **~ly** *adv* (*carefully*) soigneusement

**study** ['stʌdɪ] *n* étude *f*; (*room*) bureau *m* ♦ *vt* étudier; (*examine*) examiner ♦ *vi* étudier, faire ses études

**stuff** [stʌf] *n* chose(s) *f(pl)*; affaires *fpl*, trucs *mpl*; (*substance*) substance *f* ♦ *vt* rembourrer; (*CULIN*) farcir; (*inf: push*) fourrer; **~ing** *n* bourre *f*, rembourrage *m*; (*CULIN*) farce *f*; **~y** *adj* (*room*) mal ventilé(e) *or* aéré(e); (*ideas*) vieux jeu *inv*

**stumble** ['stʌmbl] *vi* trébucher; **to ~ across** *or* **on** (*fig*) tomber sur; **stumbling block** *n* pierre *f* d'achoppement

**stump** [stʌmp] *n* souche *f*; (*of limb*) moignon *m* ♦ *vt*: **to be ~ed** sécher, ne pas savoir que répondre

**stun** [stʌn] *vt* étourdir; (*fig*) abasourdir

**stung** [stʌŋ] *pt, pp of* **sting**

**stunk** [stʌŋk] *pp of* **stink**

**stunned** [stʌnd] *adj* sidéré(e)

**stunning** ['stʌnɪŋ] *adj* (*news etc*) stupéfiant(e); (*girl etc*) éblouissant(e)

**stunt** [stʌnt] *n* (*in film*) cascade *f*, acrobatie *f*; (*publicity* ~) truc *m* publicitaire ♦ *vt* retarder, arrêter; **~man** ['stʌntmæn] (*irreg*) *n* cascadeur *m*

**stupendous** [stju:'pɛndəs] *adj* prodigieux(-euse), fantastique

**stupid** ['stju:pɪd] *adj* stupide, bête; **~ity** [stju:'pɪdɪtɪ] *n* stupidité *f*, bêtise *f*

**sturdy** ['stə:dɪ] *adj* robuste; solide

**stutter** ['stʌtə*] *vi* bégayer

**sty** [staɪ] *n* (*for pigs*) porcherie *f*

**stye** [staɪ] *n* (*MED*) orgelet *m*

**style** [staɪl] *n* style *m*; (*distinction*) allure *f*, cachet *m*, style; **stylish** *adj* élégant(e), chic *inv*

**stylus** ['staɪləs] (*pl* **styli** *or* **~es**) *n* (*of record player*) pointe *f* de lecture

**suave** [swɑ:v] *adj* doucereux(-euse), onctueux(-euse)

**sub...** [sʌb] *prefix* sub..., sous-; **~conscious** *adj* subconscient(e); **~contract** *vt* sous-traiter

**subdue** [səb'dju:] *vt* subjuguer, soumettre; **~d** *adj* (*light*) tamisé(e); (*person*) qui a perdu de son entrain

**subject** [*n* 'sʌbdʒɪkt, *vb* səb'dʒɛkt] *n* sujet *m*; (*SCOL*) matière *f* ♦ *vt*: **to ~ to** soumettre à; exposer à; **to be ~ to** (*law*) être soumis(e) à; (*disease*) être sujet(te) à; **~ive** [səb'dʒɛktɪv] *adj* subjectif(-ive); **~ matter** *n* (*content*) contenu *m*

**sublet** [sʌb'lɛt] *vt* sous-louer

**submarine** [sʌbmə'ri:n] *n* sous-marin *m*

**submerge** [səb'mə:dʒ] *vt* submerger ♦ *vi* plonger

**submission** [səb'mɪʃən] *n* soumission *f*; **submissive** *adj* soumis(e)

**submit** [səb'mɪt] *vt* soumettre ♦ *vi* se soumettre

**subnormal** [sʌb'nɔ:məl] *adj* au-dessous de la normale

**subordinate** [sə'bɔ:dɪnət] *adj* subalterne ♦ *n* subordonné(e)

**subpoena** [səb'pi:nə] *n* (*LAW*) citation *f*, assignation *f*

**subscribe** [səb'skraɪb] *vi* cotiser; **to ~ to** (*opinion, fund*) souscrire à; (*newspaper*) s'abonner à; être abonné(e) à; **~r** *n* (*to periodical, telephone*) abonné(e); **subscription** [səb'skrɪpʃən] *n* (*to magazine etc*) abonnement *m*

**subsequent** ['sʌbsɪkwənt] *adj* ultérieur(e), suivant(e); consécutif(-ive); **~ly**

*adv* par la suite

**subside** [səb'saɪd] *vi* (*flood*) baisser; (*wind*, *feelings*) tomber; **~nce** [səb'saɪdns] *n* affaissement *m*

**subsidiary** [səb'sɪdɪərɪ] *adj* subsidiaire, accessoire ♦ *n* filiale *f*

**subsidize** ['sʌbsɪdaɪz] *vt* subventionner; **subsidy** ['sʌbsɪdɪ] *n* subvention *f*

**substance** ['sʌbstəns] *n* substance *f*

**substantial** [səb'stænʃl] *adj* substantiel(le); (*fig*) important(e); **~ly** *adv* considérablement; (*in essence*) en grande partie

**substantiate** [səb'stænʃɪeɪt] *vt* étayer, fournir des preuves à l'appui de

**substitute** ['sʌbstɪtjuːt] *n* (*person*) remplaçant(e); (*thing*) succédané *m* ♦ *vt*: to ~ sth/sb for substituer qch/qn à, remplacer qch/qn

**subterranean** [sʌbtə'reɪnɪən] *adj* souterrain(e)

**subtitle** ['sʌbtaɪtl] *n* (CINEMA, TV) sous-titre *m*; **~d** *adj* sous-titré(e)

**subtle** ['sʌtl] *adj* subtil(e)

**subtotal** [sʌb'təʊtl] *n* total partiel

**subtract** [səb'trækt] *vt* soustraire, retrancher; **~ion** *n* soustraction *f*

**suburb** ['sʌbəːb] *n* faubourg *m*; **the ~s** *npl* la banlieue; **~an** [sə'bəːbən] *adj* de banlieue, suburbain(e); **~ia** [sə'bəːbɪə] *n* la banlieue

**subway** ['sʌbweɪ] *n* (US: railway) métro *m*; (BRIT: underpass) passage souterrain

**succeed** [sək'siːd] *vi* réussir ♦ *vt* succéder à; to ~ in doing réussir à faire; **~ing** *adj* (following) suivant(e)

**success** [sək'ses] *n* succès *m*; réussite *f*; **~ful** *adj* (venture) couronné(e) de succès; to be **~ful (in doing)** réussir (à faire); **~fully** *adv* avec succès

**succession** [sək'seʃən] *n* succession *f*; **3 days in ~** 3 jours de suite

**successive** [sək'sesɪv] *adj* successif (-ive); consécutif(-ive)

**such** [sʌtʃ] *adj* tel (telle); (of that kind): ~ **a book** un livre de ce genre, un livre pareil, un tel livre; (so much): ~ **cour-**

**age** un tel courage ♦ *adv* si; ~ **books** des livres de ce genre, des livres pareils, de tels livres; ~ **a long trip** un si long voyage; ~ **a lot of** tellement de; ~ **as** (like) tel que, comme; **as** ~ en tant que tel, à proprement parler; **~-and-~** *adj* tel ou tel

**suck** [sʌk] *vt* sucer; (breast, bottle) téter; **~er** *n* ventouse *f*; (inf) poire *f*

**suction** ['sʌkʃən] *n* succion *f*

**sudden** ['sʌdn] *adj* soudain(e), subit(e); **all of a** ~ soudain, tout à coup; **~ly** *adv* brusquement, tout à coup, soudain

**suds** [sʌdz] *npl* eau savonneuse

**sue** [suː] *vt* poursuivre en justice, intenter un procès à

**suede** [sweɪd] *n* daim *m*

**suet** ['sʊɪt] *n* graisse *f* de rognon

**suffer** ['sʌfəʳ] *vi* souffrir, subir; (bear) tolérer, supporter ♦ *vi* souffrir; **~er** *n* (MED) malade *m/f*; **~ing** *n* souffrance(s) *f(pl)*

**sufficient** [sə'fɪʃnt] *adj* suffisant(e); ~ **money** suffisamment d'argent; **~ly** *adv* suffisamment, assez

**suffocate** ['sʌfəkeɪt] *vi* suffoquer; étouffer

**sugar** ['ʃʊɡəʳ] *n* sucre *m* ♦ *vt* sucrer; ~ **beet** *n* betterave sucrière; ~ **cane** *n* canne *f* à sucre

**suggest** [sə'dʒest] *vt* suggérer, proposer; (indicate) dénoter; **~ion** *n* suggestion *f*

**suicide** ['sʊɪsaɪd] *n* suicide *m*; see also **commit**

**suit** [suːt] *n* (man's) costume *m*, complet *m*; (woman's) tailleur *m*, ensemble *m*; (LAW) poursuite(s) *f(pl)*, procès *m*; (CARDS) couleur *f* ♦ *vt* aller à; convenir à; (adapt): to ~ **sth to** adapter ou approprier qch à; **well ~ed** (well matched) faits l'un pour l'autre, très bien assortis; **~able** *adj* qui convient; approprié(e); **~ably** *adv* comme il se doit (or se devait etc), convenablement

**suitcase** ['suːtkeɪs] *n* valise *f*

**suite** [swiːt] *n* (of rooms, also MUS) suite

f; *(furniture)*: **bedroom/dining room ~** (ensemble m de) chambre f à coucher/salle f à manger

**suitor** ['su:tər] n soupirant m, prétendant m

**sulfur** ['sʌlfər] *(US)* n = **sulphur**

**sulk** [sʌlk] vi bouder; **~y** adj boudeur (-euse), maussade

**sullen** ['sʌlən] adj renfrogné(e), maussade

**sulphur** ['sʌlfər] *(US **sulfur**)* n soufre m

**sultana** [sʌl'tɑːnə] n *(CULIN)* raisin (sec) de Smyrne

**sultry** ['sʌltrɪ] adj étouffant(e)

**sum** [sʌm] n somme f; *(SCOL etc)* calcul m; **~ up** vt, vi résumer

**summarize** ['sʌməraɪz] vt résumer

**summary** ['sʌmərɪ] n résumé m

**summer** ['sʌmər] n été m ♦ adj d'été, estival(e); **~house** n *(in garden)* pavillon m; **~time** n été m; **~ time** n *(by clock)* heure f d'été

**summit** ['sʌmɪt] n sommet m

**summon** ['sʌmən] vt appeler, convoquer; **~ up** vt rassembler, faire appel à; **~s** n citation f, assignation f

**sun** [sʌn] n soleil m; **in the ~** au soleil; **~bathe** vi prendre un bain de soleil; **~block** n écran m total; **~burn** n coup m de soleil; **~burned**, **~burnt** *(tanned)* bronzé(e)

**Sunday** ['sʌndɪ] n dimanche m; **~ school** n ≈ catéchisme m

**sundial** ['sʌndaɪəl] n cadran m solaire

**sundown** ['sʌndaʊn] n coucher m du *(or de)* soleil

**sundries** ['sʌndrɪz] npl articles divers

**sundry** ['sʌndrɪ] adj divers(e), différent(e) ♦ n: **all and ~** tout le monde, n'importe qui

**sunflower** ['sʌnflaʊər] n tournesol m

**sung** [sʌŋ] pp of **sing**

**sunglasses** ['sʌnglɑːsɪz] npl lunettes fpl de soleil

**sunk** [sʌŋk] pp of **sink**

**sun: ~light** n *(lumière f du)* soleil m; **~lit** adj ensoleillé(e); **~ny** adj ensoleil-

lé(e); **~rise** n lever m du *(or de)* soleil; **~ roof** n *(AUT)* toit ouvrant; **~screen** n crème f solaire; **~set** n coucher m du *(or de)* soleil; **~shade** n *(over table)* parasol m; **~shine** n *(lumière f du)* soleil m; **~stroke** n insolation f; **~tan** n bronzage m; **~tan lotion** n lotion f or lait m solaire; **~tan oil** n huile f solaire

**super** ['su:pər] *(inf)* adj formidable

**superannuation** [su:pərænju'eɪʃən] n *(contribution)* cotisations fpl pour la pension

**superb** [su:'pə:b] adj superbe, magnifique

**supercilious** [su:pə'sɪliəs] adj hautain(e), dédaigneux(-euse)

**superficial** [su:pə'fɪʃəl] adj superficiel(le)

**superimpose** ['su:pərɪm'pəʊz] vt superposer

**superintendent** [su:pərɪn'tendənt] n directeur(-trice); *(POLICE)* ≈ commissaire m

**superior** [su'pɪərɪər] adj, n supérieur(e); **~ity** [supɪərɪ'ɔrɪtɪ] n supériorité f

**superlative** [su'pə:lətɪv] adj *(LING)* superlatif m

**superman** ['su:pəmæn] *(irreg)* n surhomme m

**supermarket** ['su:pəmɑːkɪt] n supermarché m

**supernatural** [su:pə'nætʃərəl] adj surnaturel(le)

**superpower** ['su:pəpaʊər] n *(POL)* superpuissance f

**supersede** [su:pə'si:d] vt remplacer, supplanter

**superstitious** [su:pə'stɪʃəs] adj superstitieux(-euse)

**supervise** ['su:pəvaɪz] vt surveiller; diriger; **supervision** [su:pə'vɪʒən] n surveillance f; contrôle m; **supervisor** n surveillant(e); *(in shop)* chef m de rayon

**supper** ['sʌpər] n dîner m; *(late)* souper m

**supple** ['sʌpl] adj souple

**supplement** [n 'sʌplɪmənt, vb

sʌplɪ'mənt] n supplément m ♦ vt
compléter; **~ary** [sʌplɪ'mentərɪ] adj
supplémentaire; **~ary benefit** (BRIT)
n allocation f (supplémentaire) d'aide sociale

**supplier** [sə'plaɪə*] n fournisseur m

**supply** [sə'plaɪ] vt (provide) fournir;
(equip): **to ~ (with)** approvisionner or
ravitailler (en); fournir (en) ♦ n provision f, réserve f; (~ing) approvisionnement m; **supplies** npl (food) vivres mpl;
(MIL) subsistances fpl; **~ teacher** (BRIT)
n (suppléant(e)

**support** [sə'pɔːt] n (moral, financial etc)
soutien m, appui m; (TECH) support m,
soutien ♦ vt soutenir; (financi-
ally) subvenir aux besoins de; (uphold)
être pour, être partisan de, appuyer;
**~er** (POL etc) partisan(e) m/f; (SPORT)
supporter m

**suppose** [sə'pəuz] vt supposer; imaginer; **to be ~d to do** être censé(e) faire;
**~dly** [sə'pəuzɪdlɪ] adv soi-disant; **supposing** conj si, à supposer que +sub

**suppress** [sə'pres] vt (revolt) réprimer;
(information) supprimer; (yawn) étouffer; (feelings) réprimer

**supreme** [su'priːm] adj suprême

**surcharge** ['sɜːtʃɑːdʒ] n surcharge f

**sure** [ʃuə*] adj sûr(e); (definite, con-
vinced) sûr, certain(e); **~! (of course)** bien
sûr!; **~ enough** effectivement; **to make
~ of sth** s'assurer de or vérifier qch;
**to make ~ that** s'assurer or vérifier
que; **~ly** adv sûrement; certainement

**surf** [sɜːf] n (waves) ressac m

**surface** ['sɜːfɪs] n surface f ♦ vt (road)
poser un revêtement sur ♦ vi remonter
à la surface; faire surface; **~ mail** n
courrier m par voie de terre (or maritime)

**surfboard** ['sɜːfbɔːd] n planche f de
surf

**surfeit** ['sɜːfɪt] n: **a ~ of** un excès de;
une indigestion de

**surfing** ['sɜːfɪŋ] n surf m

**surge** [sɜːdʒ] n vague f, montée f ♦ vi

déferler

**surgeon** ['sɜːdʒən] n chirurgien m

**surgery** ['sɜːdʒərɪ] n chirurgie f; (BRIT:
room) cabinet m (de consultation);
(: also: **~ hours**) heures fpl de consultation

**surgical** ['sɜːdʒɪkl] adj chirurgical(e); **~
spirit** (BRIT) n alcool m à 90°

**surname** ['sɜːneɪm] n nom m de famille

**surplus** ['sɜːpləs] n surplus m, excédent
m ♦ adj en surplus, de trop; (COMM) ex-
cédentaire

**surprise** [sə'praɪz] n surprise f; (astonishment) étonnement m ♦ vt surprendre; (astonish) étonner; **surprising** adj
surprenant(e), étonnant(e); **surpris-
ingly** adv (easy, helpful) étonnamment

**surrender** [sə'rendə*] n reddition f, capi-
tulation f ♦ vi se rendre, capituler

**surreptitious** [sʌrəp'tɪʃəs] adj subrepti-
ce, furtif(-ive)

**surrogate** ['sʌrəgɪt] n substitut m; **~
mother** n mère porteuse or de substitution

**surround** [sə'raund] vt entourer; (MIL
etc) encercler; **~ing** adj environnant(e);
**~ings** npl environs mpl, alentours mpl

**surveillance** [sɜː'veɪləns] n surveillance
f

**survey** [n 'sɜːveɪ, vb sɜː'veɪ] n enquête
f, étude f; (in housebuying etc) inspection f, (rapport m d')expertise f; (of
land) levé m ♦ vt enquêter sur; inspecter; (look at) embrasser du regard; **~or**
n (of house) expert m; (of land) (arpenteur m) géomètre m

**survival** [sə'vaɪvl] n survie f; (relic) vestige m

**survive** [sə'vaɪv] vi survivre; (custom
etc) subsister ♦ vt survivre à; **survivor**
n survivant(e); (fig) battant(e)

**susceptible** [sə'septəbl] adj: **~ (to)**
sensible (à); (disease) prédisposé(e) (à)

**suspect** [adj, n 'sʌspekt, vb sə'spekt]
adj, n suspect(e) ♦ vt soupçonner, suspecter

**suspend** [səs'pɛnd] vt suspendre; **~ed sentence** n condamnation f avec sursis; **~er belt** n porte-jarretelles m inv; **~ers** npl (BRIT) jarretelles fpl; (US) bretelles fpl

**suspense** [səs'pɛns] n attente f, incertitude f; (in film etc) suspense m

**suspension** [səs'pɛnʃən] n suspension f; (of driving licence) retrait m provisoire; **~ bridge** n pont suspendu

**suspicion** [səs'pɪʃən] n soupçon(s) m(pl); **suspicious** adj (suspecting) soupçonneux(-euse), méfiant(e); (causing suspicion) suspect(e)

**sustain** [səs'teɪn] vt soutenir; (suffer) subir; recevoir; **~able** adj (development, growth etc) viable; **~ed** adj (effort) soutenu(e), prolongé(e); **sustenance** ['sʌstɪnəns] n nourriture f; (money) moyens mpl de subsistance

**swab** [swɔb] n (MED) tampon m

**swagger** ['swægə*] vi plastronner

**swallow** ['swɔləu] n (bird) hirondelle f ♦ vt avaler; **~ up** vt engloutir

**swam** [swæm] pt of **swim**

**swamp** [swɔmp] n marais m, marécage m ♦ vt submerger

**swan** [swɔn] n cygne m

**swap** [swɔp] vt: **to ~ (for)** échanger (contre), troquer (contre)

**swarm** [swɔːm] n essaim m ♦ vi fourmiller, grouiller

**swastika** ['swɔstɪkə] n croix gammée

**swat** [swɔt] vt écraser

**sway** [sweɪ] vi se balancer, osciller ♦ vt (influence) influencer

**swear** [swɛə*] (pt **swore**, pp **sworn**) vt, vi jurer; **~word** n juron m, gros mot

**sweat** [swɛt] n sueur f, transpiration f ♦ vi suer

**sweater** ['swɛtə*] n tricot m, pull m

**sweaty** ['swɛtɪ] adj en sueur, moite ou mouillé(e) de sueur

**Swede** [swiːd] n Suédois(e)

**swede** [swiːd] (BRIT) n rutabaga m

**Sweden** ['swiːdn] n Suède f; **Swedish**

adj suédois(e) ♦ n (LING) suédois m

**sweep** [swiːp] (pt, pp **swept**) n (also: **chimney ~**) ramoneur m ♦ vt balayer; (subj: current) emporter; **~ away** vt balayer; entraîner; emporter; **~ past** vi passer majestueusement ou rapidement; **~ up** vt, vi balayer; **~ing** adj (gesture) large; circulaire; a **~ing statement** une généralisation hâtive

**sweet** [swiːt] n (candy) bonbon m; (BRIT: pudding) dessert m ♦ adj doux (douce); (not savoury) sucré(e); (fig: kind) gentil(le); (baby) mignon(ne); **~corn** ['swiːtkɔːn] n maïs m; **~en** vt adoucir; (with sugar) sucrer; **~heart** n amoureux(-euse); **~ness** n goût sucré; douceur f; **~ pea** n pois m de senteur

**swell** [swɛl] n (of sea) houle f ♦ adj (US: inf) chouette ♦ vi grossir, augmenter; (sound) s'enfler; (MED) enfler; **~ing** n (MED) enflure f; (lump) grosseur f

**sweltering** ['swɛltərɪŋ] adj étouffant(e), oppressant(e)

**swept** [swɛpt] pt, pp of **sweep**

**swerve** [swəːv] vi faire une embardée ou un écart; dévier

**swift** [swɪft] n (bird) martinet m ♦ adj rapide, prompt(e)

**swig** [swɪg] (inf) n (drink) lampée f

**swill** [swɪl] n (also: **~ out, ~ down**) laver à grande eau

**swim** [swɪm] (pt **swam**, pp **swum**) n: **to go for a ~** aller nager ou se baigner ♦ vi nager; (SPORT) faire de la natation; (head, room) tourner ♦ vt traverser (à la nage); (a length) faire (à la nage); **~mer** n nageur(-euse); **~ming** n natation f; **~ming cap** n bonnet m de bain; **~ming costume** (BRIT) n maillot m (de bain); **~ming pool** n piscine f; **~ming trunks** npl caleçon ou slip m de bain; **~suit** n maillot m (de bain)

**swindle** ['swɪndl] n escroquerie f

**swine** [swaɪn] (inf!) n inv salaud m (!)

**swing** [swɪŋ] (pt, pp **swung**) n balançoire f; (movement) balancement m, oscillations fpl; (change: in opinion etc) revirement m ♦ vt balancer, faire osciller; (also: ~ round) tourner, faire virer ♦ vi se balancer, osciller; (also: ~ round) virer, tourner; **to be in full ~** battre son plein; **~ bridge** n pont tournant; **~ door** (US **swinging door**) n porte battante

**swingeing** ['swɪndʒɪŋ] (BRIT) adj écrasant(e); (cuts etc) considérable

**swipe** [swaɪp] (inf) vt (steal) piquer °

**swirl** [swɜːl] vi tourbillonner, tournoyer

**Swiss** [swɪs] adj suisse ♦ n inv Suisse m/f

**switch** [swɪtʃ] n (for light, radio etc) bouton m; (change) changement m, revirement m ♦ vt changer; **~ off** vt éteindre; (engine) arrêter; **~ on** vt allumer; (engine, machine) mettre en marche; **~board** n (TEL) standard m

**Switzerland** ['swɪtsələnd] n Suisse f

**swivel** ['swɪvl] vi (also: ~ round) pivoter, tourner

**swollen** ['swəʊlən] pp of **swell**

**swoon** [swuːn] vi se pâmer

**swoop** [swuːp] n (by police) descente f ♦ vi (also: ~ down) descendre en piqué, piquer

**swop** [swɒp] vt = **swap**

**sword** [sɔːd] n épée f; **~fish** n espadon m

**swore** [swɔːʳ] pt of **swear**

**sworn** [swɔːn] pp of **swear** ♦ adj (statement, evidence) donné sous serment

**swot** [swɒt] vi bûcher, potasser

**swum** [swʌm] pp of **swim**

**swung** [swʌŋ] pt, pp of **swing**

**syllable** ['sɪləbl] n syllabe f

**syllabus** ['sɪləbəs] n programme m

**symbol** ['sɪmbl] n symbole m

**symmetry** ['sɪmɪtrɪ] n symétrie f

**sympathetic** [sɪmpə'θetɪk] adj compatissant(e); bienveillant(e), compréhensif(-ive); (likeable) sympathique; **~ towards** bien disposé(e) envers

**sympathize** ['sɪmpəθaɪz] vi: **to ~ with sb** plaindre qn; (in grief) s'associer à la

douleur de qn; **to ~ with sth** comprendre qch; **~r** n (POL) sympathisant(e)

**sympathy** ['sɪmpəθɪ] n (pity) compassion f, sympathies npl (support) soutien m; **left-wing etc sympathies** penchants mpl à gauche etc; **in ~ with** (strike) en or par solidarité avec; **with our deepest ~** en vous priant d'accepter nos sincères condoléances

**symphony** ['sɪmfənɪ] n symphonie f

**symptom** ['sɪmptəm] n symptôme m, indice m

**syndicate** ['sɪndɪkɪt] n syndicat m, coopérative f

**synopsis** [sɪ'nɒpsɪs] (pl **synopses**) n résumé m

**synthetic** [sɪn'θetɪk] adj synthétique

**syphon** ['saɪfən] n, vb = **siphon**

**Syria** ['sɪrɪə] n Syrie f

**syringe** [sɪ'rɪndʒ] n seringue f

**syrup** ['sɪrəp] n sirop m; (also: **golden ~**) mélasse raffinée

**system** ['sɪstəm] n système m; (ANAT) organisme m; **~atic** [sɪstə'mætɪk] adj systématique; méthodique; **~ disk** n (COMPUT) disque m système; **~s analyst** n analyste fonctionnel(le)

# T, t

**ta** [tɑː] (BRIT: inf) excl merci!

**tab** [tæb] n (label) étiquette f; (on drinks can etc) languette f; **to keep ~s on** (fig) surveiller

**tabby** ['tæbɪ] n (also: ~ **cat**) chat(te) tigré(e)

**table** ['teɪbl] n table f ♦ vt (BRIT: motion etc) présenter; **to lay** or **set the ~** mettre le couvert or la table; **~cloth** n nappe f; **~ d'hôte** [tɑːbl'dəʊt] adj (meal) à prix fixe; **~ lamp** n lampe f de table; **~mat** n (for plate) napperon m, set m; (for hot dish) dessous-de-plat m inv; **~ of contents** n table f des matières; **~spoon** n cuiller f de service;

# tablet                       569                       talent

*(also:* ~**spoonful**) *as measurement)* cuillerée *f* à soupe

**tablet** ['tæblɪt] *n* (MED) comprimé *m*

**table tennis** *n* ping-pong ® *m*, tennis *m* de table

**table wine** *n* vin *m* de table

**tabloid** ['tæblɔɪd] *n* quotidien *m* populaire

### tabloid press

*Le terme* tabloid press *désigne les journaux populaires de demi-format où l'on trouve beaucoup de photos et qui adoptent un style très concis. Ce type de journaux vise des lecteurs s'intéressant aux faits divers ayant un parfum de scandale; voir* quality (news)papers.

**tack** [tæk] *n (nail)* petit clou ♦ *vt* clouer; *(fig)* direction *f; (BRIT: stitch)* faufiler ♦ *vi* tirer un *or* des bord(s)

**tackle** ['tækl] *n* matériel *m,* équipement *m; (for lifting)* appareil *m* de levage; *(RUGBY)* plaquage *m* ♦ *vt (difficulty, animal, burglar etc)* s'attaquer à; *(person: challenge)* s'expliquer avec; *(RUGBY)* plaquer

**tacky** ['tækɪ] *adj* collant(e); *(pej: of poor quality)* miteux(-euse)

**tact** [tækt] *n* tact *m;* ~**ful** *adj* plein(e) de tact

**tactical** ['tæktɪkl] *adj* tactique

**tactics** ['tæktɪks] *npl* tactique *f*

**tactless** ['tæktlɪs] *adj* qui manque de tact

**tadpole** ['tædpəʊl] *n* têtard *m*

**tag** [tæg] *n* étiquette *f;* ~ **along** *vi* suivre

**tail** [teɪl] *n* queue *f; (of shirt)* pan *m* ♦ *vt (follow)* suivre, filer; ~**s** *npl* habit *m;* ~ **away,** ~ **off** *vi (in size, quality etc)* baisser peu à peu; ~**back** (BRIT) *n* (AUT) bouchon *m;* ~ **end** *n* bout *m,* fin *f;* ~**gate** *n* (AUT) hayon *m* arrière

**tailor** ['teɪlə*] *n* tailleur *m;* ~**ing** *n (cut)* coupe *f;* ~-**made** *adj* fait(e) sur mesure;

*(fig)* conçu(e) spécialement

**tailwind** ['teɪlwɪnd] *n* vent *m* arrière *inv*

**tainted** ['teɪntɪd] *adj (food)* gâté(e); *(water, air)* infecté(e); *(fig)* souillé(e)

**take** [teɪk] *(pt* **took***, pp* **taken***) vt* prendre; *(gain: prize)* remporter; *(require: effort, courage)* demander; *(tolerate)* accepter, supporter; *(hold: passengers etc)* contenir; *(accompany)* emmener, accompagner; *(bring, carry)* apporter, emporter; *(exam)* passer, se présenter à; ~ **to** ~ **sth from** *(drawer etc)* prendre qch dans; *(person)* prendre qch à; **I** ~ **it that ...** je suppose que ...; ~ **after** *vt fus* ressembler à; ~ **apart** *vt* démonter; ~ **away** *vt* enlever; *(carry off)* emporter; ~ **back** *vt (return)* rendre, rapporter; *(one's words)* retirer; ~ **down** *vt (building)* démolir; *(letter etc)* prendre, écrire; ~ **in** *vt (deceive)* tromper, rouler; *(understand)* comprendre, saisir; *(include)* comprendre, inclure; *(lodger)* prendre; ~ **off** *vi (AVIAT)* décoller ♦ *vt (remove)* enlever; ~ **on** *vt (work)* accepter, se charger de; *(employee)* prendre, embaucher; *(opponent)* accepter de se battre contre; ~ **out** *vt (invite)* emmener, sortir; *(remove)* enlever; ~ **sth out of sth** *(drawer, pocket etc)* prendre qch dans qch; ~ **over** *vt (business)* reprendre ♦ *vi:* **to** ~ **over from sb** prendre la relève de qn; ~ **to** *vt fus (person)* se prendre d'amitié pour; *(thing)* prendre goût à; ~ **up** *vt (activity)* se mettre à; *(dress)* raccourcir; *(occupy: time, space)* prendre, occuper; **to** ~ **sb up on an offer** accepter la proposition de qn; ~**away** (BRIT) *adj (food)* à emporter ♦ *n (shop, restaurant)* café *m* qui vend de plats à emporter; ~-**off** *n (AVIAT)* décollage *m;* ~**over** *n (COMM)* rachat *m;* **takings** *npl (COMM)* recette *f*

**talc** [tælk] *n (also:* ~**um powder**) talc *m*

**tale** [teɪl] *n (story)* conte *m,* histoire *f; (account)* récit *m;* **to tell** ~**s** *(fig)* rapporter

**talent** ['tælnt] *n* talent *m,* don *m;* ~**ed**

*adj* doué(e), plein(e) de talent

**talk** [tɔːk] *n* (*a speech*) causerie *f*, exposé *m*; (*conversation*) discussion *f*, entretien *m*; (*gossip*) racontars *mpl* ♦ *vi* parler; **~s** *npl* (POL *etc*) entretiens *mpl*; **to ~ about** parler de; **to ~ sb into/out of doing** persuader qn de faire/ne pas faire; **to ~ shop** parler métier or affaires; **~ over** *vt* discuter (de); **~ative** *adj* bavard(e); **~ show** *n* causerie (télévisée or radiodiffusée)

**tall** [tɔːl] *adj* (*person*) grand(e); (*building, tree*) haut(e); **to be 6 feet ~** ≃ mesurer 1 mètre 80; **~ story** *n* histoire *f* invraisemblable

**tally** [ˈtælɪ] *n* compte *m* ♦ *vi*: **to ~ (with)** correspondre (à)

**talon** [ˈtælən] *n* griffe *f*; (*of eagle*) serre *f*

**tame** [teɪm] *adj* apprivoisé(e); (*fig: story, style*) insipide

**tamper** [ˈtæmpər] *vi*: **to ~ with** toucher à

**tampon** [ˈtæmpən] *n* tampon *m* (hygiénique or périodique)

**tan** [tæn] *n* (*also*: **suntan**) bronzage *m* ♦ *vi, vt* bronzer ♦ *adj* (*colour*) brun roux *inv*

**tang** [tæŋ] *n* odeur (*or* saveur) piquante

**tangent** [ˈtændʒənt] *n* (MATH) tangente *f*; **to go off at a ~** (*fig*) changer de sujet

**tangerine** [tændʒəˈriːn] *n* mandarine *f*

**tangle** [ˈtæŋgl] *n* enchevêtrement *m*; **to get in(to) a ~** s'embrouiller

**tank** [tæŋk] *n* (*water* ~) réservoir *m*; (*for fish*) aquarium *m*; (MIL) char *m* d'assaut, tank *m*

**tanker** [ˈtæŋkər] *n* (*ship*) pétrolier *m*, tanker *m*; (*truck*) camion-citerne *m*

**tantalizing** [ˈtæntəlaɪzɪŋ] *adj* (*smell*) extrêmement appétissant(e); (*offer*) terriblement tentant(e)

**tantamount** [ˈtæntəmaunt] *adj*: **~ to** qui équivaut à

**tantrum** [ˈtæntrəm] *n* accès *m* de colère

**tap** [tæp] *n* (*on sink etc*) robinet *m*; (*gentle blow*) petite tape *f* ♦ *vt* frapper or taper légèrement; (*resources*) exploiter, utiliser; (*telephone*) mettre sur écoute; **on ~** (*fig: resources*) disponible; **~-dancing** *n* claquettes *fpl*

**tape** [teɪp] *n* ruban *m*; (*also*: **magnetic ~**) bande *f* (magnétique); (*cassette*) cassette *f*; (*sticky*) scotch *m* ® (R) (*record*) enregistrer; (*stick with* ~) coller avec du scotch; **~ deck** *n* platine *f* d'enregistrement; **~ measure** *n* mètre *m* à ruban

**taper** [ˈteɪpər] *vi* s'effiler

**tape recorder** *n* magnétophone *m*

**tapestry** [ˈtæpɪstrɪ] *n* tapisserie *f*

**tar** [tɑː] *n* goudron *m*

**target** [ˈtɑːgɪt] *n* cible *f*; (*fig*) objectif *m*

**tariff** [ˈtærɪf] *n* (COMM) tarif *m*; (*taxes*) tarif douanier

**tarmac** [ˈtɑːmæk] *n* (BRIT: *on road*) macadam *m*; (AVIAT) piste *f*

**tarnish** [ˈtɑːnɪʃ] *vt* ternir

**tarpaulin** [tɑːˈpɔːlɪn] *n* bâche (goudronnée)

**tarragon** [ˈtærəgən] *n* estragon *m*

**tart** [tɑːt] *n* (CULIN) tarte *f*; (BRIT: *inf: prostitute*) putain *f* ♦ *adj* (*flavour*) âpre, aigrelet(te); **~ up** (BRIT: *inf*) *vt* (*object*) retaper; **to ~ o.s. up** se faire beau (belle), s'attifer (*pej*)

**tartan** [ˈtɑːtn] *n* tartan *m* ♦ *adj* écossais(e)

**tartar** [ˈtɑːtər] *n* (*on teeth*) tartre *m*; **~(e) sauce** *n* sauce *f* tartare

**task** [tɑːsk] *n* tâche *f*; **to take sb to ~** prendre qn à partie; **~ force** *n* (MIL, POLICE) détachement spécial

**tassel** [ˈtæsl] *n* gland *m*; pompon *m*

**taste** [teɪst] *n* goût *m*; (*fig: glimpse, idea*) idée *f*, aperçu *m* ♦ *vt* goûter ♦ *vi*: **to ~ of** (*fish etc*) avoir le or un goût de; **you can ~ the garlic (in it)** on sent bien l'ail; **can I have a ~ of this wine?** puis-je goûter un peu de ce vin?; **in good/bad ~** de bon/mauvais goût; **~ful** *adj* de bon goût; **~less** *adj* (*food*) fade; (*remark*) de mauvais goût;

**tasty** *adj* savoureux(-euse), délicieux(-euse)

**:atters** ['tætəz] *npl*: **in ~** en lambeaux

**tattoo** [tə'tu:] *n* (BRIT: *inf*) *adj* (*spectacle*) parade *f* militaire ♦ *vt* tatouer

**:atty** ['tætɪ] *adj* (*clothes*) fripé(e); (*shop, area*) délabré(e)

**taught** [tɔːt] *pt, pp of* **teach**

**taunt** [tɔːnt] *n* raillerie *f* ♦ *vt* railler

**Taurus** ['tɔːrəs] *n* le Taureau

**taut** [tɔːt] *adj* tendu(e)

**tax** [tæks] *n* (*on goods etc*) taxe *f*; (*on income*) impôts *mpl*, contributions *fpl* ♦ *vt* taxer; imposer; (*fig: patience etc*) mettre à l'épreuve; **~able** *adj* (*income*) imposable; **~ation** [tæk'seɪʃən] *n* taxation *f*; impôts *mpl*, contributions *fpl*; **~ avoidance** *n* dégrèvement fiscal; **~ disc** (BRIT) *n* (AUT) vignette *f* (automobile); **~ evasion** *n* fraude fiscale; **~-free** *adj* exempt(e) d'impôts

**taxi** ['tæksɪ] *n* taxi *m* ♦ *vi* (AVIAT) rouler (lentement) au sol; **~ driver** *n* chauffeur *m* de taxi; **~ rank** (BRIT) *n* station *f* de taxis; **~ stand** *n* = taxi rank

**tax**: **~ payer** *n* contribuable *m/f*; **~ relief** *n* dégrèvement fiscal; **~ return** *n* déclaration *f* d'impôts or de revenus

**TB** *n abbr* = **tuberculosis**

**tea** [tiː] *n* thé *m*; (BRIT: *snack: for children*) goûter *m*; **high ~** collation combinant goûter et dîner, **~ bag** *n* sachet *m* de thé; **~ break** (BRIT) *n* pause-thé *f*

**teach** [tiːtʃ] (*pt, pp* **taught**) *vt*: **to ~ sb sth, ~ sth to sb** apprendre qch à qn; (*in school etc*) enseigner qch à qn ♦ *vi* enseigner; **~er** *n* (*in secondary school*) professeur *m*; (*in primary school*) instituteur(-trice); **~ing** *n* enseignement *m*

**tea**: **~ cloth** *n* torchon *m*; **~ cosy** *n* cloche *f* à thé; **~cup** *n* tasse *f* à thé

**teak** [tiːk] *n* teck *m*

**team** [tiːm] *n* équipe *f*; (*of animals*) attelage *m*; **~work** *n* travail *m* d'équipe

**teapot** ['tiːpɔt] *n* théière *f*

**tear¹** [tɛəʳ] (*pt* **tore**, *pp* **torn**) *n* déchirure *f* ♦ *vt* déchirer ♦ *vi* se déchirer; **~ along** *vi* (*rush*) aller à toute vitesse; **~ up** *vt* (*sheet of paper etc*) déchirer, mettre en morceaux or pièces

**tear²** [tɪəʳ] *n* larme *f*; **in ~s** en larmes; **~ful** *adj* larmoyant(e); **~ gas** *n* gaz *m* lacrymogène

**tearoom** ['tiːrum] *n* salon *m* de thé

**tease** [tiːz] *vt* taquiner; (*unkindly*) tourmenter

**tea set** *n* service *m* à thé

**teaspoon** ['tiːspuːn] *n* petite cuiller; (*also:* **~ful**: *as measurement*) ≈ cuillerée *f* à café

**teat** [tiːt] *n* tétine *f*

**teatime** ['tiːtaɪm] *n* l'heure *f* du thé

**tea towel** (BRIT) *n* torchon *m* (à vaisselle)

**technical** ['tɛknɪkl] *adj* technique; **~ity** [tɛknɪ'kælɪtɪ] *n* (*detail*) détail *m* technique; (*point of law*) vice *m* de forme; **~ly** *adv* techniquement; (*strictly speaking*) en théorie

**technician** [tɛk'nɪʃən] *n* technicien(ne)

**technique** [tɛk'niːk] *n* technique *f*

**techno** ['tɛknəʊ] *n* (*music*) techno *f*

**technological** [tɛknə'lɔdʒɪkəl] *adj* technologique

**technology** [tɛk'nɔlədʒɪ] *n* technologie *f*

**teddy (bear)** ['tɛdɪ(-)] *n* ours *m* en peluche

**tedious** ['tiːdɪəs] *adj* fastidieux(-euse)

**tee** [tiː] *n* (GOLF) tee *m*

**teem** [tiːm] *vi*: **to ~ (with)** grouiller (de); **it is ~ing (with rain)** il pleut à torrents

**teenage** ['tiːneɪdʒ] *adj* (*fashions etc*) pour jeunes, pour adolescents; (*children*) adolescent(e); **~r** *n* adolescent(e)

**teens** [tiːnz] *npl*: **to be in one's ~** être adolescent(e)

**tee-shirt** ['tiːʃəːt] *n* = **T-shirt**

**teeter** ['tiːtəʳ] *vi* chanceler, vaciller

**teeth** [tiːθ] *npl of* **tooth**

**teethe** [tiːð] *vi* percer ses dents

**teething troubles** npl (fig) difficultés initiales

**teetotal** ['tiː'təʊtl] adj (person) qui ne boit jamais d'alcool

**tele:** ~**communications** npl télécommunications fpl; ~**conferencing** n téléconférence(s) f(pl); ~**gram** n télégramme m; ~**graph** n télégraphe m; ~**graph pole** n poteau m télégraphique

**telephone** ['telɪfəʊn] n téléphone m ♦ vt (person) téléphoner à; (message) téléphoner; **on the** ~ au téléphone; **to be on the** ~ (BRIT: have a ~) avoir le téléphone; ~ **booth,** ~ **box** (BRIT) n cabine f téléphonique; ~ **call** n coup m de téléphone, appel m téléphonique; ~ **directory** n annuaire m (du téléphone); ~ **number** n numéro m de téléphone; **telephonist** [tə'lefənɪst] (BRIT) n téléphoniste m/f

**telesales** ['telɪseɪlz] n télévente f

**telescope** ['telɪskəʊp] n télescope m

**television** ['telɪvɪʒən] n télévision f; **on** ~ à la télévision; ~ **set** n (poste f de) télévision m

**telex** ['teleks] n télex m

**tell** [tel] (pt, pp told) vt dire; (relate: story) raconter; (distinguish): **to** ~ **sth from** distinguer qch de ♦ vi (talk): **to** ~ (**of**) parler de; (have effect) se faire sentir, se voir; **to** ~ **sb to do** dire à qn de faire; ~ **off** vt réprimander, gronder; ~**er** n (in bank) caissier(-ère); ~**ing** adj (remark, detail) révélateur(-trice); ~**tale** adj (sign) éloquent(e), révélateur(-trice)

**telly** ['telɪ] (BRIT: inf) n abbr (= television) télé f

**temp** [temp] n abbr (= temporary) (secrétaire f) intérimaire f

**temper** ['tempər] n (nature) caractère m; (mood) humeur f; (fit of anger) colère f ♦ vt (moderate) tempérer, adoucir; **to be in a** ~ être en colère; **to lose one's** ~ se mettre en colère

**temperament** ['temprəmənt] n (nature) tempérament m; ~**al** [temprə'mentl] adj capricieux(-euse)

**temperate** ['tempərət] adj (climate, country) tempéré(e)

**temperature** ['temprətʃər] n température f; **to have** o **run a** ~ avoir de la fièvre

**temple** ['templ] n (building) temple m; (ANAT) tempe f

**temporary** ['tempərərɪ] adj temporaire, provisoire; (job, worker) temporaire

**tempt** [tempt] vt tenter; **to** ~ **sb into doing** persuader qn de faire; ~**ation** [temp'teɪʃən] n tentation f; ~**ing** adj tentant(e)

**ten** [ten] num dix

**tenacity** [tə'næsɪtɪ] n ténacité f

**tenancy** ['tenənsɪ] n location f; état m de locataire

**tenant** ['tenənt] n locataire m/f

**tend** [tend] vt s'occuper de ♦ vi: **to** ~ **to do** avoir tendance à faire; ~**ency** ['tendənsɪ] n tendance f

**tender** ['tendər] adj tendre; (delicate) délicat(e); (sore) sensible ♦ n (COMM: offer) soumission f ♦ vt offrir

**tenement** ['tenəmənt] n immeuble m

**tennis** ['tenɪs] n tennis m; ~ **ball** n balle f de tennis; ~ **court** n (court m de) tennis; ~ **player** n joueur(-euse) de tennis; ~ **racket** n raquette f de tennis; ~ **shoes** npl (chaussures fpl de) tennis mpl

**tenor** ['tenər] n (MUS) ténor m

**tenpin bowling** ['tenpɪn-] (BRIT) n bowling m (à dix quilles)

**tense** [tens] adj tendu(e) ♦ n (LING) temps m

**tension** ['tenʃən] n tension f

**tent** [tent] n tente f

**tentative** ['tentətɪv] adj timide, hésitant(e); (conclusion) provisoire

**tenterhooks** ['tentəhʊks] npl: **on** ~ sur des charbons ardents

**tenth** [tenθ] num dixième

**tent peg** n piquet m de tente

**tent pole** n montant m de tente

**tenuous** ['tenjʊəs] adj ténu(e)

**tenure** ['tenjʊər] n (of property) bail

**tepid** (of job) période f de jouissance

**tepid** ['tepid] adj tiède

**term** [tɜ:m] n terme m; (SCOL) trimestre m ♦ vt appeler; ~s npl (conditions) conditions fpl; (COMM) tarif m; **in the short/long** ~ à court/long terme; **to come to ~s with** (problem) faire face à

**terminal** ['tɜ:mɪnl] adj (disease) dans sa phase terminale; (patient) incurable ♦ n (ELEC) borne f; (for oil, ore etc, COMPUT) terminal m; (also: **air** ~) aérogare f; (BRIT: also: **coach** ~) gare routière; **~ly** adv: **to be ~ly ill** être condamné(e)

**terminate** ['tɜ:mɪneɪt] vt mettre fin à; (pregnancy) interrompre

**termini** ['tɜ:mɪnaɪ] npl of **terminus**

**terminus** ['tɜ:mɪnəs] (pl **termini**) n terminus m inv

**terrace** ['terəs] n terrasse f; (BRIT: row of houses) rangée f de maisons (attenantes); **the ~s** npl (BRIT: SPORT) les gradins mpl; **~d** adj (garden) en terrasses

**terracotta** ['terə'kɒtə] n terre cuite

**terrain** [te'reɪn] n terrain m (sol)

**terrible** ['terɪbl] adj terrible, atroce; (weather, conditions) affreux(-euse), épouvantable; **terribly** adv terriblement; (very badly) affreusement mal

**terrier** ['terɪər] n terrier m (chien)

**terrific** [tə'rɪfɪk] adj fantastique, incroyable, terrible; (wonderful) formidable, sensationnel(le)

**terrify** ['terɪfaɪ] vt terrifier

**territory** ['terɪtərɪ] n territoire m

**terror** ['terər] n terreur f; **~ism** n terrorisme m; **~ist** n terroriste m/f

**test** [test] n (trial, check) essai m; (of courage etc) épreuve f; (MED) examen m; (CHEM) analyse f; (SCOL) interrogation f; (also: **driving** ~) (examen du) permis m de conduire ♦ vt essayer; mettre à l'épreuve; examiner; analyser; faire subir une interrogation à

**testament** ['testəmənt] n testament m; **the Old/New T~** l'Ancien/le Nouveau Testament

**testicle** ['testɪkl] n testicule m

**testify** ['testɪfaɪ] vi (LAW) témoigner, déposer; **to ~ to sth** attester qch

**testimony** ['testɪmənɪ] n témoignage m; (clear proof): **to be (a)** ~ **to** être la preuve de

**test match** n (CRICKET, RUGBY) match international

**test tube** n éprouvette f

**tetanus** ['tetənəs] n tétanos m

**tether** ['teðər] vt attacher ♦ n: **at the end of one's** ~ à bout (de patience)

**text** [tekst] n texte m; **~book** n manuel m

**textile** ['tekstaɪl] n textile m

**texture** ['tekstʃər] n texture f; (of skin, paper etc) grain m

**Thailand** ['taɪlænd] n Thaïlande f

**Thames** [temz] n: **the** ~ la Tamise

**than** [ðæn, ðən] conj que; (with numerals): **more** ~ **10**/once plus de 10/d'une fois; **I have more/less** ~ **you** j'en ai plus/moins que toi; **she has more apples** ~ **pears** elle a plus de pommes que de poires

**thank** [θæŋk] vt remercier, dire merci à; ~s npl (gratitude) remerciements mpl ♦ excl merci!; ~ **you (very much)** merci (beaucoup); ~s **to** grâce à; ~ **God!** Dieu merci!; ~**ful:** ~**ful (for)** reconnaissant(e) (de); ~**less** adj ingrat(e); **T~sgiving (Day)** n jour m d'action de grâce (fête américaine)

---

**Thanksgiving Day**

Thanksgiving Day est un jour de congé aux États-Unis, le quatrième jeudi du mois de novembre, commémorant la bonne récolte que les Pèlerins venus de Grande-Bretagne ont eue en 1621; traditionnellement, c'est un jour où l'on remerciait Dieu et où l'on organisait un grand festin. Une fête semblable a lieu au Canada le deuxième lundi d'octobre.

KEYWORD

**that** [ðæt] adj (demonstrative: pl those) ce, cet +vowel or h mute, cette f; **that man/woman/book** cet homme/cette femme/ce livre; (not "this") cet homme-là/cette femme-là/ce livre-là; **that one** celui-là (celle-là)

♦ pron 1 (demonstrative: pl those) ce; (not "this one") cela, ça; **who's that?** qui est-ce?; **what's that?** qu'est-ce que c'est?; **is that you?** c'est toi?; **I prefer this to that** je préfère ceci à cela or ça; **that's what he said** c'est or voilà ce qu'il a dit; **that is (to say)** c'est-à-dire, à savoir

2 (relative: subject) qui; (: object) que; (: indirect) lequel (laquelle), lesquels (lesquelles) pl; **the book that I read** le livre que j'ai lu; **the books that are in the library** les livres qui sont dans la bibliothèque; **all that I have** tout ce que j'ai; **the box that I put it in** la boîte dans laquelle je l'ai mis; **the people that I spoke to** les gens auxquels or à qui j'ai parlé

3 (relative: of time) où; **the day that he came** le jour où il est venu

♦ conj que; **he thought that I was ill** il pensait que j'étais malade

♦ adv (demonstrative): **I can't work that much** je ne peux pas travailler autant que cela; **I didn't know it was that bad** je ne savais pas que c'était si or aussi mauvais; **it's about that high** c'est à peu près de cette hauteur

**thatched** [θætʃt] adj (roof) de chaume; **~ cottage** chaumière f

**thaw** [θɔ:] n dégel m ♦ vi (ice) fondre; (food) dégeler ♦ vt (food: also: **~ out**) (faire) dégeler

KEYWORD

**the** [ði:, ðə] def art 1 (gen) le, la f, l' +vowel or h mute, les pl; **the boy/girl/ink** le garçon/la fille/l'encre; **the child-**

ren les enfants; **the history of the world** l'histoire du monde; **give it to the postman** donne-le au facteur; **to play the piano/flute** jouer du piano/de la flûte; **the rich and the poor** les riches et les pauvres

2 (in titles): **Elizabeth the First** Elisabeth première; **Peter the Great** Pierre le Grand

3 (in comparisons): **the more he works, the more he earns** plus il travaille, plus il gagne de l'argent

**theatre** [ˈθɪətəˈ] n théâtre m; (also: **lecture ~**) amphi(théâtre) m; (MED: also: **operating ~**) salle f d'opération; **~goer** n habitué(e) du théâtre; **theatrical** [θɪˈætrɪkl] adj théâtral(e)

**theft** [θeft] n vol m (larcin)

**their** [ðɛəˈ] adj leur; (pl) leurs; see also **my; ~s** pron le (la) leur; (pl) les leurs; see also **mine**

**them** [ðɛm, ðəm] pron (direct) les; (indirect) leur; (stressed, after prep) eux (elles); see also **me**

**theme** [θi:m] n thème m; **~ park** n parc m (d'attraction) à thème; **~ song** n chanson principale

**themselves** [ðəmˈselvz] pl pron (reflexive) se; (emphatic, after prep) eux-mêmes (elles-mêmes); see also **oneself**

**then** [ðen] adv (at that time) alors, à ce moment-là; (next) puis, ensuite; (and also) et puis ♦ conj (therefore) alors, dans ce cas ♦ adj: **the ~ president** le président d'alors or de l'époque; **by ~** (past) à ce moment-là; (future) d'ici là; **from ~ on** dès lors

**theology** [θɪˈɒlədʒɪ] n théologie f

**theoretical** [θɪəˈretɪkl] adj théorique

**theory** [ˈθɪərɪ] n théorie f

**therapy** [ˈθerəpɪ] n thérapie f

KEYWORD

**there** [ðɛəˈ] adv 1: **there is, there are** il y a; **there are 3 of them** (people, things) il y en a 3; **there has been an**

**accident** il y a eu un accident
**2** (referring to place) là, là-bas; **it's there** c'est là(-bas); **in/on/up/down there** là-dedans/là-dessus/là-haut/en bas; **he went there on Friday** il y est allé vendredi; **I want that book there** je veux ce livre-là; **there he is!** le voilà!
**3: there, there** (esp to child) allons, allons!

**there: ~abouts** adv (place) par là, près de là; (amount) environ, à peu près; **~after** adv par la suite; **~by** adv ainsi; **~fore** adv donc, par conséquent; **~'s = there is; there is**
**thermal** ['θəːml] adj (springs) thermal(e); (underwear) en thermolactyl ®; (COMPUT: paper) thermosensible; (: printer) thermique
**thermometer** [θə'mɔmɪtəʳ] n thermomètre m
**Thermos** ® ['θəːməs] n (also: **~ flask**) thermos m or f inv
**thermostat** ['θəːməustæt] n thermostat m
**thesaurus** [θɪ'sɔːrəs] n dictionnaire m des synonymes
**these** [ðiːz] pl adj ces; (not "those"): **~ books** ces livres-ci ♦ pl pron ceux-ci (celles-ci)
**thesis** ['θiːsɪs] (pl **theses**) n thèse f
**they** [ðeɪ] pl pron ils (elles); (stressed) eux (elles); **~ say that ...** (it is said that) on dit que ...; **~'d =** they had; they would; **~'ll =** they shall; they will; **~'re =** they are; **~'ve =** they have
**thick** [θɪk] adj épais(se); (stupid) bête, borné(e) ♦ n: **in the ~ of** au beau milieu de, en plein cœur de; **it's 20 cm ~** il/elle a 20 cm d'épaisseur; **~en** vi s'épaissir ♦ vt (sauce etc) épaissir; **~ness** n épaisseur f; **~set** adj trapu(e), costaud(e)
**thief** [θiːf] (pl **thieves**) n voleur(-euse)
**thigh** [θaɪ] n cuisse f
**thimble** ['θɪmbl] n dé m (à coudre)
**thin** [θɪn] adj mince; (skinny) maigre;

(soup, sauce) peu épais(se), clair(e); (hair, crowd) clairsemé(e) ♦ vt: **to ~ (down)** (sauce, paint) délayer
**thing** [θɪŋ] n (object) objet m; (contraption) truc m; (mania): **to have a ~ about** être obsédé(e) par; **~s** npl (belongings) affaires fpl; **poor ~!** le (la) pauvre!; **the best ~ would be to** le mieux serait de; **how are ~s?** comment ça va?
**think** [θɪŋk] (pt, pp **thought**) vi penser, réfléchir; (believe) penser ♦ vt (imagine) imaginer; **what did you ~ of them?** qu'avez-vous pensé d'eux?; **to ~ about sth/sb** penser à qch/qn; **I'll ~ about it** je vais y réfléchir; **to ~ of doing** avoir l'idée de faire; **I ~ so/not** je crois que oui/non; **to ~ well of** avoir une haute opinion de; **~ over** vt bien réfléchir à; **~ up** vt inventer, trouver; **~ tank** n groupe m de réflexion
**thinly** ['θɪnlɪ] adv (cut) en fines tranches; (spread) en une couche mince
**third** [θəːd] num troisième ♦ n (fraction) tiers m; (AUT) troisième (vitesse) f; (BRIT: SCOL: degree) ≈ licence f sans mention; **~ly** adv troisièmement; **~ party insurance** (BRIT) n assurance f au tiers; **~ rate** adj de qualité médiocre; **the T~ World** n le tiers monde
**thirst** [θəːst] n soif f; **~y** adj (person) qui a soif, assoiffé(e); (work) qui donne soif; **to be ~y** avoir soif
**thirteen** [θəː'tiːn] num treize
**thirty** ['θəːtɪ] num trente

---

**KEYWORD**

**this** [ðɪs] adj (demonstrative: pl **these**) ce, cet +vowel or h mute, cette f; **this man/woman/book** cet homme/cette femme/ce livre; (not "that") cet homme-ci/cette femme-ci/ce livre-ci; **this one** celui-ci (celle-ci)
♦ pron (demonstrative: pl **these**) ce; (not "that one") celui-ci (celle-ci), ceci; **who's this?** qui est-ce?; **what's this?** qu'est-ce que c'est?; **I prefer this to**

that je préfère ceci à cela; **this is what he said** voici ce qu'il a dit; **this is Mr Brown**; (in introductions) je vous présente Mr Brown; (in photo) c'est Mr Brown; (on telephone) ici Mr Brown
♦ adv (demonstrative): **it was about this big** c'était à peu près de cette grandeur or grand comme ça; **I didn't know it was this bad** je ne savais pas que c'était si or aussi mauvais

**thistle** ['θɪsl] n chardon m

**thorn** [θɔːn] n épine f

**thorough** ['θʌrə] adj (search) minutieux(-euse); (knowledge, research) approfondi(e); (work, person) consciencieux(-euse); (cleaning) à fond; **~bred** n (horse) pur-sang m inv; **~fare** n route f; **"no ~fare"** "passage interdit"; **~ly** adv minutieusement; en profondeur; à fond; (very) tout à fait

**those** [ðəʊz] pl adj ces; (not "these") **~ books** ces livres-là ♦ pl pron ceux-là (celles-là)

**though** [ðəʊ] conj bien que +sub, quoique +sub ♦ adv pourtant

**thought** [θɔːt] pt, pp of **think** ♦ n pensée f; (idea) idée f; (opinion) avis m; **~ful** adj (deep in thought) pensif(-ive); (serious) réfléchi(e); (considerate) prévenant(e); **~less** adj étourdi(e); qui manque de considération

**thousand** ['θaʊzənd] num mille; **two ~** deux mille; **~s of** des milliers de; **~th** num millième

**thrash** [θræʃ] vt rouer de coups; donner une correction à; (defeat) battre à plate couture; **~ about**, **~ around** vi se débattre; **~ out** vt débattre de

**thread** [θrɛd] n fil m; (TECH) pas m, filetage m ♦ vt (needle) enfiler; **~bare** adj râpé(e), élimé(e)

**threat** [θrɛt] n menace f; **~en** vi menacer ♦ vt: **to ~en sb with sth/to do** menacer qn de qch/de faire

**three** [θriː] num trois; **~-dimensional** adj à trois dimensions; **~-piece suit** n

complet m (avec gilet); **~-piece suite** n salon m comprenant un canapé et deux fauteuils assortis; **~-ply** adj (wool) trois fils inv

**threshold** ['θrɛʃhəʊld] n seuil m

**threw** [θruː] pt of **throw**

**thrifty** ['θrɪftɪ] adj économe

**thrill** [θrɪl] n (excitement) émotion f, sensation forte; (shudder) frisson m ♦ vt (audience) électriser; **to be ~ed** (with gift etc) être ravi(e); **~er** n film m or roman m or pièce f) à suspense; **~ing** adj saisissant(e), palpitant(e)

**thrive** [θraɪv] (pt, pp **thrived**) vi pousser, se développer; (business) prospérer; **he ~s on it** cela lui réussit; **thriving** adj (business, community) prospère

**throat** [θrəʊt] n gorge f; **to have a sore ~** avoir mal à la gorge

**throb** [θrɒb] vi (heart) palpiter; (engine) vibrer; **my head is ~bing** j'ai des élancements dans la tête

**throes** [θrəʊz] npl: **in the ~ of** au beau milieu de

**throne** [θrəʊn] n trône m

**throng** ['θrɒŋ] n foule f ♦ vt se presser dans

**throttle** ['θrɒtl] n (AUT) accélérateur m ♦ vt étrangler

**through** [θruː] prep à travers; (time) pendant, durant; (by means of) par, par l'intermédiaire de; (owing to) à cause de ♦ adj (ticket, train, passage) direct(e) ♦ adv à travers; **to put sb ~ to** (BRIT: TEL) passer qn à qn; **to be ~** (BRIT: TEL) avoir la communication; (esp US: have finished) avoir fini; **to be ~ with sb** (relationship) avoir rompu avec qn; **"no road"** (BRIT) "impasse"; **~out** prep (place) partout dans; (time) durant tout(e) la ♦ adv partout

**throw** [θrəʊ] (pt **threw**, pp **thrown**) n jet m; (SPORT) lancer m ♦ vt lancer, jeter; (SPORT) lancer; (rider) désarçonner; (fig) décontenancer; **to ~ a party** donner une réception; **~ away** vt jeter; **~ off** vt se débarrasser de; **~ out** vt jeter; (reject) rejeter; (*person*) mettre à la porte; **~ up** *vi* vomir; **~away** *adj* à jeter; (*remark*) fait(e) en passant; **~-in** *n* (SPORT) remise *f* en jeu

**thru** [θruː] (*US*) = **through**

**thrush** [θrʌʃ] *n* (*bird*) grive *f*

**thrust** [θrʌst] (*pt, pp* **thrust**) *n* (TECH) poussée *f* ♦ *vt* pousser brusquement; (*push in*) enfoncer

**thud** [θʌd] *n* bruit sourd

**thug** [θʌg] *n* voyou *m*

**thumb** [θʌm] *n* (ANAT) pouce *m* ♦ *vt*: to **~ a lift** faire de l'auto-stop, arrêter une voiture; **~ through** (*book*) feuilleter; **~tack** (*US*) *n* punaise *f* (*clou*)

**thump** [θʌmp] *n* grand coup; (*sound*) bruit sourd ♦ *vt* cogner sur ♦ *vi* cogner, battre fort

**thunder** ['θʌndə<sup>r</sup>] *n* tonnerre *m* ♦ *vi* tonner; (*train etc*): to **~ past** passer dans un grondement *or* un bruit de tonnerre; **~bolt** *n* foudre *f*; **~clap** *n* coup *m* de tonnerre; **~storm** *n* orage *m*; **~y** *adj* orageux(-euse)

**Thursday** ['θɜːzdɪ] *n* jeudi *m*

**thus** [ðʌs] *adv* ainsi

**thwart** [θwɔːt] *vt* contrecarrer

**thyme** [taɪm] *n* thym *m*

**tiara** [tɪ'ɑːrə] *n* diadème *m*

**tick** [tɪk] *n* (*sound: of clock*) tic-tac *m*; (*mark*) coche *f*; (ZOOL) tique *f*; (BRIT: *inf*): **in a ~** dans une seconde ♦ *vi* faire tic-tac ♦ *vt* (*item on list*) cocher; **~ off** *vt* (*item on list*) cocher; (*person*) réprimander, attraper; **~ over** *vi* (*engine*) tourner au ralenti; (*fig*) aller *or* marcher doucettement

**ticket** ['tɪkɪt] *n* billet *m*; (*for bus, tube*) ticket *m*; (*in shop: on goods*) étiquette *f*; (*for library*) carte *f*; (*parking ~*) papillon *m*, p.-v. *m*; **~ collector, ~ inspector** *n* contrôleur(-euse); **~ office** *n* guichet *m*, bureau *m* de vente des billets

**tickle** ['tɪkl] *vt, vi* chatouiller; **ticklish** *adj* (*person*) chatouilleux(-euse); (*problem*) épineux(-euse)

**tidal** ['taɪdl] *adj* (*force*) de la marée; (*estuary*) à marée; **~ wave** *n* raz-de-marée *m inv*

**tidbit** ['tɪdbɪt] (*US*) *n* = **titbit**

**tiddlywinks** ['tɪdlɪwɪŋks] *n* jeu *m* de puce

**tide** [taɪd] *n* marée *f*; (*fig: of events*) cours *m* ♦ *vt*: to **~ sb over** dépanner qn; **high/low ~** marée haute/basse

**tidy** ['taɪdɪ] *adj* (*room*) bien rangé(e); (*dress, work*) net(te), soigné(e); (*person*) ordonné(e), qui a de l'ordre ♦ *vt* (*also: ~ up*) ranger

**tie** [taɪ] *n* (*string etc*) cordon *m*; (BRIT: *also: necktie*) cravate *f*; (*fig: links*) lien *m*; (SPORT: *draw*) égalité *f* de points; match nul ♦ *vt* (*parcel*) attacher; (*ribbon, shoelaces*) nouer ♦ *vi* (SPORT) faire match nul; finir à égalité de points; to **~ sth in a bow** faire un nœud à *or* avec qch; to **~ a knot in sth** faire un nœud à qch; **~ down** *vt* (*fig*): to **~ sb down** (*to*) contraindre qn (à accepter); to **be ~d down** (*by relationship*) se fixer; **~ up** *vt* (*parcel*) ficeler; (*dog, boat*) attacher; (*prisoner*) ligoter; (*arrangements*) conclure; to **be ~d up** (*busy*) être pris(e) *or* occupé(e)

**tier** [tɪə<sup>r</sup>] *n* gradin *m*; (*of cake*) étage *m*

**tiger** ['taɪgə<sup>r</sup>] *n* tigre *m*

**tight** [taɪt] *adj* (*rope*) tendu(e), raide; (*clothes*) étroit(e), très juste; (*budget, programme, bend*) serré(e); (*control*) strict(e), sévère; (*inf: drunk*) ivre, rond(e) ♦ *adv* (*squeeze*) très fort; (*shut*) hermétiquement, bien; **~en** *vt* (*rope*) tendre; (*screw*) resserrer; (*control*) renforcer ♦ *vi* se tendre, se resserrer; **~fisted** *adj* avare; **~ly** *adv* (*grasp*) bien, très fort; **~rope** *n* corde *f* raide; **~s** *npl* collant *m*

**tile** [taɪl] *n* (*on roof*) tuile *f*; (*on wall or floor*) carreau *m*; **~d** *adj* en tuiles; carrelé(e)

**till** [tɪl] *n* caisse (enregistreuse) ♦ *vt* (*land*) cultiver ♦ *prep, conj* = **until**

**tiller** ['tɪlə<sup>r</sup>] *n* (NAUT) barre *f* (du gouvernail)

**tilt** [tɪlt] vt pencher, incliner ♦ vi pencher, être incliné(e)

**timber** ['tɪmbə*] n (material) bois m (de construction); (trees) arbres mpl

**time** [taɪm] n temps m; (epoch: often pl) époque f, temps; (by clock) heure f; (moment) moment m; (occasion, also MATH) fois f ♦ vt (race) chronométrer; (programme) minuter; (visit) fixer; (remark etc) choisir le moment de; **a long ~** un long moment, longtemps; **for the ~ being** pour le moment; **4 at a ~** 4 à la fois; **from ~ to ~** de temps en temps; **at ~s** parfois; **in ~** (soon enough) à temps; (after some ~) avec le temps, à la longue; (MUS) en mesure; **in a week's ~** dans une semaine; **in no ~** en un rien de temps; **any ~** n'importe quand; **on ~** à l'heure; **5 ~s 5** 5 fois 5; **what ~ is it?** quelle heure est-il?; **to have a good ~** bien s'amuser; **~ bomb** bombe f à retardement; **~ lag** (BRIT) n décalage m; (in travel) décalage horaire; **~less** adj éternel(le); **~ly** adj opportun(e); **~ off** n temps m libre; **~r** n (TECH) minuteur m; (in kitchen) compte-minutes m inv; **~scale** n délais mpl; **~share** n maison f/appartement m en multipropriété; **~switch** (BRIT) n minuterie f; (for lighting) minuterie f; **~table** n (RAIL) (indicateur m) horaire m; (SCOL) emploi m du temps; **~ zone** n fuseau m horaire

**timid** ['tɪmɪd] adj timide; (easily scared) peureux(-euse)

**timing** ['taɪmɪŋ] n minutage m; chronométrage m; **the ~ of his resignation** le moment choisi pour sa démission

**timpani** ['tɪmpənɪ] npl timbales fpl

**tin** [tɪn] n étain m; (also: ~ **plate**) ferblanc m; (BRIT: can) boîte f (de conserve); (for storage) boîte f; **~foil** n papier m d'étain ou aluminium

**tinge** [tɪndʒ] n nuance f ♦ vt: **~d with** teinté(e) de

**tingle** ['tɪŋgl] vi picoter; (person) avoir des picotements

**tinker** ['tɪŋkə*] n (gipsy) romanichel m; **~ with** vt fus bricoler, rafistoler

**tinkle** ['tɪŋkl] vi tinter

**tinned** [tɪnd] (BRIT) adj (food) en boîte, en conserve

**tin opener** (BRIT) n ouvre-boîte(s) m

**tinsel** ['tɪnsl] n guirlandes fpl de Noël (argentées)

**tint** [tɪnt] n teinte f; (for hair) shampooing colorant; **~ed** adj (hair) teint(e); (spectacles, glass) teinté(e)

**tiny** ['taɪnɪ] adj minuscule

**tip** [tɪp] n (end) bout m; (gratuity) pourboire m; (BRIT: for rubbish) décharge f; (advice) tuyau m ♦ vt (waiter) donner un pourboire à; (tilt) incliner; (overturn: also: ~ **over**) renverser; (empty: also: ~ **out**) déverser; **~-off** n (hint) tuyau m, renseignement m; **~ped** (BRIT) adj (cigarette) (à bout) filtre inv

**tipsy** ['tɪpsɪ] (inf) adj un peu ivre, éméché(e)

**tiptoe** ['tɪptəu] n: **on ~** sur la pointe des pieds

**tiptop** ['tɪp'tɔp] adj: **in ~ condition** en excellent état

**tire** ['taɪə*] n (US) = **tyre** ♦ vt fatiguer ♦ vi se fatiguer; **~d** adj fatigué(e); **to be ~d of** en avoir assez de, être las (lasse) de; **~less** adj (person) infatigable; (efforts) inlassable; **~some** adj ennuyeux(-euse); **tiring** adj fatigant(e)

**tissue** ['tɪʃuː] n tissu m; (paper handkerchief) mouchoir m en papier, kleenex ® m; **~ paper** n papier m de soie

**tit** [tɪt] n (bird) mésange f; **to give ~ for ~** rendre la pareille

**titbit** ['tɪtbɪt] n (food) friandise f; (news) potin m

**title** ['taɪtl] n titre m; **~ deed** n (LAW) titre (constitutif) de propriété; **~ role** n rôle principal

**TM** abbr = **trademark**

---

KEYWORD

---

**to** [tuː, tə] prep **1** (direction) à; **to go to**

**France/Portugal/London/school** aller en France/au Portugal/à Londres/à l'école; **to go to Claude's/the doctor's** aller chez Claude/le docteur; **the road to Edinburgh** la route d'Édimbourg

**2** (as far as) (jusqu')à; **to count to 10** compter jusqu'à 10; **from 40 to 50 people** de 40 à 50 personnes

**3** (with expressions of time); **a quarter to 5** 5 heures moins le quart; **it's twenty to 3** il est 3 heures moins vingt

**4** (for, of) de; **the key to the front door** la clé de la porte d'entrée; **a letter to his wife** une lettre (adressée) à sa femme

**5** (expressing indirect object) à; **to give sth to sb** donner qch à qn; **to talk to sb** parler à qn

**6** (in relation to) à; **3 goals to 2** 3 (buts) à 2; **30 miles to the gallon** 9,4 litres aux cent (km)

**7** (purpose, result): **to come to sb's aid** venir au secours de qn, porter secours à qn; **to sentence sb to death** condamner qn à mort; **to my surprise** à ma grande surprise

♦ with vb **1** (simple infinitive): **to go/eat** aller/manger

**2** (following another vb): **to want/try/start to do** vouloir/essayer de/commencer à faire

**3** (with vb omitted): **I don't want to** je ne veux pas

**4** (purpose, result) pour; **I did it to help you** je l'ai fait pour vous aider

**5** (equivalent to relative clause): **I have things to do** j'ai des choses à faire; **the main thing is to try** l'important est d'essayer

**6** (after adjective etc): **ready to go** prêt(e) à partir; **too old/young to ...** trop vieux/jeune pour ...

♦ adv: **push/pull the door to** tirez/poussez la porte

**toad** [təud] n crapaud m

**toadstool** ['təudstu:l] n champignon (vénéneux)

**toast** [təust] n (CULIN) pain grillé, toast m; (drink, speech) toast m ♦ vt (CULIN) faire griller; (drink) to porter un toast à; **~er** n grille-pain m inv

**tobacco** [tə'bækəu] n tabac m; **~nist** n marchand(e) de tabac; **~nist's (shop)** n (bureau m de) tabac m

**toboggan** [tə'bɔgən] n toboggan m; (child's) luge f ♦ vi: **to go ~ing** faire de la luge

**today** [tə'deɪ] adv (also fig) aujourd'hui ♦ n aujourd'hui m

**toddler** ['tɔdlər] n enfant m/f qui commence à marcher, bambin m

**toe** [təu] n doigt m de pied, orteil m; (of shoe) bout m ♦ vt: **to ~ the line** (fig) obéir, se conformer; **~nail** n ongle m du pied

**toffee** ['tɔfi] n caramel m; **~ apple** (BRIT) n pomme caramélisée

**together** [tə'gɛðər] adv ensemble; (at same time) en même temps; **~ with** avec

**toil** [tɔil] n dur travail, labeur m ♦ vi peiner

**toilet** ['tɔilət] n (BRIT: lavatory) toilettes fpl ♦ cpd (accessories etc) de toilette; **~ bag** n nécessaire m de toilette; **~ paper** n papier m hygiénique; **~ries** npl articles mpl de toilette; **~ roll** n rouleau m de papier hygiénique

**token** ['təukən] n (sign) marque f, témoignage m; (metal disc) jeton m ♦ adj (strike, payment etc) symbolique; **book/record ~** (BRIT) chèque-livre/-disque m; **gift ~** n bon-cadeau m

**told** [təuld] pt, pp of **tell**

**tolerable** ['tɔlərəbl] adj (bearable) tolérable; (fairly good) passable

**tolerant** ['tɔlərnt] adj: **~ (of)** tolérant(e) (à l'égard de)

**tolerate** ['tɔləreɪt] vt supporter, tolérer

**toll** [təul] n (tax, charge) péage m ♦ vi (bell) sonner; **the accident ~ on the**

**roads** le nombre des victimes de la route

**tomato** [tə'mɑːtəʊ] (pl ~es) n tomate f

**tomb** [tuːm] n tombe f

**tomboy** ['tɒmbɔɪ] n garçon manqué

**tombstone** ['tuːmstəʊn] n pierre tombale

**tomcat** ['tɒmkæt] n matou m

**tomorrow** [tə'mɒrəʊ] adv (also fig) demain ♦ n demain m; **the day after ~** après-demain; **~ morning** demain matin

**ton** [tʌn] n tonne f (BRIT = 1016kg; US = 907kg); (metric) tonne (= 1000 kg); **~s of** (inf) des tas de

**tone** [təʊn] n ton m ♦ vi (also: ~ **in**) s'harmoniser; **~ down** vt (colour, criticism) adoucir; (sound) baisser; **~ up** vt (muscles) tonifier; **~-deaf** adj qui n'a pas d'oreille

**tongs** [tɒŋz] npl (for coal) pincettes fpl; (for hair) fer m à friser

**tongue** [tʌŋ] n langue f; **~ in cheek** ironiquement; **~-tied** adj (fig) muet(te); **~ twister** n phrase f très difficile à prononcer

**tonic** ['tɒnɪk] n (MED) tonique m; (also: **~ water**) tonic m, Schweppes ® m

**tonight** [tə'naɪt] adv, n cette nuit; (this evening) ce soir

**tonsil** ['tɒnsl] n amygdale f; **~litis** [tɒnsɪ'laɪtɪs] n angine f

**too** [tuː] adv (excessively) trop; (also) aussi; **~ much** adv trop ♦ adj trop de; **~ many** trop de; **~ bad!** tant pis!

**took** [tʊk] pt of **take**

**tool** [tuːl] n outil m; **~ box** boîte f à outils

**toot** [tuːt] n (of car horn) coup m de klaxon; (of whistle) coup de sifflet ♦ vi (with car horn) klaxonner

**tooth** [tuːθ] (pl **teeth**) n (ANAT, TECH) dent f; **~ache** n mal m de dents; **~brush** n brosse f à dents; **~paste** n (pâte f) dentifrice m; **~pick** n cure-dent m

**top** [tɒp] n (of mountain, head) sommet

m; (of page, ladder, garment) haut m; (of box, cupboard, table) dessus m; (lid: of box, jar) couvercle m; (: of bottle) bouchon m; (toy) toupie f ♦ adj (of the haut; (in rank) premier(-ère); (best) meilleur(e) ♦ vt (exceed) dépasser; (be first in) être en tête de; **on ~ of** sur; (in addition to) en plus de; **from ~ to bottom** de fond en comble; **~ up** (US = **~ off**) vt (bottle) remplir; (salary) compléter; **~ floor** n dernier étage; **~ hat** n haut-de-forme m; **~-heavy** adj (object) trop lourd(e) du haut

**topic** ['tɒpɪk] n sujet m, thème m; **~al** adj d'actualité

**top:** **~less** adj (bather etc) aux seins nus; **~-level** adj (talks) au plus haut niveau; **~most** adj le (la) plus haut(e)

**topple** ['tɒpl] vt renverser, faire tomber ♦ vi basculer, tomber

**top-secret** ['tɒp'siːkrɪt] adj top secret (-ète)

**topsy-turvy** ['tɒpsɪ'tɜːvɪ] adj, adv sens dessus dessous

**torch** [tɔːtʃ] n torche f; (BRIT: electric) lampe f de poche

**tore** [tɔː*] pt of **tear[1]**

**torment** [n 'tɔːment, vb tɔː'ment] n tourment m ♦ vt tourmenter; (fig: annoy) harceler

**torn** [tɔːn] pp of **tear[1]**

**tornado** [tɔː'neɪdəʊ] (pl ~es) n tornade f

**torpedo** [tɔː'piːdəʊ] (pl ~es) n torpille f

**torrent** ['tɔrənt] n torrent m; **~ial** [tɔ'renʃl] adj torrentiel(le)

**tortoise** ['tɔːtəs] n tortue f; **~shell** adj en écaille

**torture** ['tɔːtʃə*] n torture f ♦ vt torturer

**Tory** ['tɔːrɪ] (BRIT: POL) adj, n tory (m/f), conservateur(-trice)

**toss** [tɒs] vt lancer, jeter; (pancake) faire sauter; (head) rejeter en arrière; **to ~ a coin** jouer à pile ou face; **to ~ up for sth** jouer qch à pile ou face; **to ~ and turn** (in bed) se tourner et se retourner

**tot** [tɒt] n (BRIT: drink) petit verre; (child)

bambin m

**total** ['təʊtl] adj total(e) ♦ n total m ♦ vt *(add up)* faire le total de, additionner; *(amount to)* s'élever à; **~ly** adv totalement

**totter** ['tɒtə*] vi chanceler

**touch** [tʌtʃ] n contact m, toucher m; *(sense, also skill: of pianist etc)* toucher ♦ vt toucher; *(tamper with)* toucher à; **a ~ of** *(fig)* un petit peu de; une touche de; **to get in ~ with** prendre contact avec; **to lose ~** *(friends)* se perdre de vue; **~ on** vt fus *(topic)* effleurer, aborder; **~ up** vt *(paint)* retoucher; **~-and-go** adj incertain(e); **~down** n atterrissage m; *(on sea)* amerrissage m; *(US: FOOTBALL)* touché-en-but m; **~ed** adj *(moved)* touché(e); **~ing** adj touchant(e), attendrissant(e); **~line** n *(SPORT)* ligne f de touche f; **~y** adj *(person)* susceptible

**tough** [tʌf] adj dur(e); *(resistant)* résistant(e), solide; *(meat)* dur, coriace; *(firm)* inflexible; *(task)* dur, pénible; **~en** vt *(character)* endurcir; *(glass etc)* renforcer

**toupee** ['tu:peɪ] n postiche m

**tour** ['tʊə*] n voyage m; *(also: **package ~**)* voyage organisé; *(of town, museum)* tour m, visite f; *(by artist)* tournée f ♦ vt visiter; **~ guide** n *(person)* guide m/f

**tourism** ['tʊərɪzm] n tourisme m

**tourist** ['tʊərɪst] n touriste m/f ♦ cpd touristique; **~ office** n syndicat m d'initiative

**tournament** ['tʊənəmənt] n tournoi m

**tousled** ['taʊzld] adj *(hair)* ébouriffé(e)

**tout** [taʊt] vi: **to ~ for** essayer de racrocher, racoler ♦ n *(also: **ticket ~**)* revendeur m de billets

**tow** [təʊ] vt remorquer; *(caravan, trailer)* tracter; **"on ~"** *(BRIT)* or **"in ~"** *(US)* *(AUT)* "véhicule en remorque"

**toward(s)** [tə'wɔ:d(z)] prep vers; *(of attitude)* envers, à l'égard de; *(of purpose)* pour

**towel** ['taʊəl] n serviette f *(de toilette)*;

**~ling** n *(fabric)* tissu éponge m; **~ rail** *(US **towel rack**)* n porte-serviettes m inv

**tower** ['taʊə*] n tour f; **~ block** *(BRIT)* n tour f *(d'habitation)*; **~ing** adj très haut(e), imposant(e)

**town** [taʊn] n ville f; **to go to ~** aller en ville; *(fig)* et mettre le paquet; **~ centre** n centre m de la ville, centreville m; **~ council** n conseil municipal; **~ hall** n ≈ mairie f; **~ plan** n plan m de la ville; **~ planning** n urbanisme m

**towrope** ['təʊrəʊp] n *(câble m de)* remorque f

**tow truck** *(US)* n dépanneuse f

**toy** [tɔɪ] n jouet m; **~ with** vt fus jouer avec; *(idea)* caresser

**trace** [treɪs] n trace f ♦ vt *(draw)* tracer, dessiner; *(follow)* suivre la trace de; *(locate)* retrouver; **tracing paper** n papier-calque m

**track** [træk] n *(mark)* trace f; *(path: gen)* chemin m, piste f; *(: of bullet etc)* trajectoire f; *(: of suspect, animal)* piste f; *(RAIL)* voie ferrée, rails mpl; *(on tape, SPORT)* piste f; *(on record)* plage f; ♦ vt suivre la trace or la piste de; **to keep ~ of** suivre; **~ down** vt *(prey)* trouver et capturer; *(sth lost)* finir par retrouver; **~suit** n survêtement m

**tract** [trækt] n *(of land)* étendue f

**traction** ['trækʃən] n traction f; *(MED)*: **in ~** en extension

**tractor** ['træktə*] n tracteur m

**trade** [treɪd] n commerce m; *(skill, job)* métier m ♦ vi faire du commerce ♦ vt *(exchange)*: **to ~ sth (for sth)** échanger qch *(contre qch)*; **~ in** vt *(old car etc)* faire reprendre; **~ fair** n foireexposition f; **~-in price** n prix m à la reprise; **~mark** n marque f de fabrique; **~ name** n nom m de marque; **~r** n commerçant(e), négociant(e); **~sman** *(irreg)* n *(shopkeeper)* commerçant m; **~ union** n syndicat m; **~ unionist** n syndicaliste m/f

**tradition** [trə'dɪʃən] n tradition f; **~al** adj traditionnel(le)

**traffic** ['træfɪk] n trafic m; (cars) circulation ♦ vi: **to ~ in** (pej: liquor, drugs) faire le trafic de; **~ calming** n ralentissement m de la circulation; **~ circle** (US) n rond-point m; **~ jam** n embouteillage m; **~ lights** npl feux mpl (de signalisation); **~ warden** n contractuel(le)

**tragedy** ['trædʒədɪ] n tragédie f

**tragic** ['trædʒɪk] adj tragique

**trail** [treɪl] n (tracks) trace f, piste f; (path) chemin m, piste; (of smoke etc) traînée f ♦ vt traîner, tirer; (follow) suivre ♦ vi traîner; (in game, contest) être en retard; **~ behind** vi traîner, être à la traîne; **~er** n (AUT) remorque f; (US) caravane f; (CINEMA) bande-annonce f; **~er truck** (US) n (camion m à) semi-remorque m

**train** [treɪn] n train m; (in underground) rame f; (of dress) traîne f ♦ vt (apprentice, doctor etc) former; (sportsman) entraîner; (dog) dresser; (memory) exercer; (point: gun etc): **to ~ sth on** braquer qch sur ♦ vi suivre une formation; (SPORT) s'entraîner; **one's ~ of thought** le fil de sa pensée; **~ed** adj qualifié(e), qui a reçu une formation; (animal) dressé(e); **~ee** [treɪ'niː] n stagiaire m/f; (in trade) apprenti(e); **~er** n (SPORT: coach) entraîneur(-euse); (: shoe) chaussure f de sport; (of dogs etc) dresseur(-euse); **~ing** n formation f; entraînement m; **in ~ing** (SPORT) à l'entraînement; (fit) en forme; **~ing college** n école professionnelle; (for teachers) ≃ école normale; **~ing shoes** npl chaussures fpl de sport

**trait** [treɪt] n trait m (de caractère)

**traitor** ['treɪtəʳ] n traître m

**tram** [træm] (BRIT) n (also: **~car**) tram(way) m

**tramp** [træmp] n (person) vagabond(e), clochard(e); (inf: pej: woman): **to be a ~** être coureuse ♦ vi marcher d'un pas lourd

**trample** ['træmpl] vt: **to ~ (underfoot)** piétiner

**trampoline** ['træmpəliːn] n trampoline m

**tranquil** ['træŋkwɪl] adj tranquille; **~lizer** (US **tranquilizer**) n (MED) tranquillisant m

**transact** [træn'zækt] vt (business) traiter; **~ion** n transaction f

**transatlantic** ['trænzət'læntɪk] adj transatlantique

**transfer** [n 'trænsfəʳ, vb træns'fəːʳ] n (gen, also SPORT) transfert m; (POL: of power) passation f; (picture, design) décalcomanie f; (: stick-on) autocollant m ♦ vt transférer; passer; **to ~ the charges** (BRIT: TEL) téléphoner en P.C.V.; **~ desk** n (AVIAT) guichet m de transit

**transform** [træns'fɔːm] vt transformer

**transfusion** [træns'fjuːʒən] n transfusion f

**transient** ['trænzɪənt] adj transitoire, éphémère

**transistor** [træn'zɪstəʳ] n (~ radio) transistor m

**transit** ['trænzɪt] n: **in ~** en transit

**transitive** ['trænzɪtɪv] adj (LING) transitif(-ive)

**transit lounge** n salle f de transit

**translate** [trænz'leɪt] vt traduire; **translation** n traduction f; **translator** n traducteur(-trice)

**transmission** [trænz'mɪʃən] n transmission f

**transmit** [trænz'mɪt] vt transmettre; (RADIO, TV) émettre

**transparency** [træns'pɛərnsɪ] n (of glass etc) transparence f; (BRIT: PHOT) diapositive f

**transparent** [træns'pærnt] adj transparent(e)

**transpire** [træns'paɪəʳ] vi (turn out): **it ~d that ...** on a appris que ...; (happen) arriver

**transplant** [vb træns'plɑːnt, n 'trænsplɑːnt] vt transplanter; (seedlings) repiquer ♦ n (MED) transplantation f

**transport** [n 'trænspɔːt, vb træns'pɔːt]

**trap**

n transport m; (car) moyen m de transport, voiture f ♦ vt transporter; **~ation** ['trænspɔː'teɪʃən] n transport m; (means of transportation) moyen m de transport; **~ café** (BRIT) n ≈ restaurant m de routiers

**trap** [træp] n (snare, trick) piège m; (carriage) cabriolet m ♦ vt prendre au piège; (confine) coincer; **~ door** n trappe f

**trapeze** [trə'piːz] n trapèze m

**trappings** ['træpɪŋz] npl ornements mpl; attributs mpl

**trash** [træʃ] (pej) n (goods) camelote f; (nonsense) sottises fpl; **~ can** (US) n poubelle f; **~y** (inf) adj de camelote; (novel) de quatre sous

**trauma** ['trɔːmə] n traumatisme m; **~tic** [trɔː'mætɪk] adj traumatisant(e)

**travel** ['trævl] n voyage(s) m(pl) ♦ vi voyager; (news, sound) circuler, se propager ♦ vt (distance) parcourir; **~ agency** n agence f de voyages; **~ agent** n agent m de voyages; **~ler** (US **traveler**) n voyageur(-euse); **~ler's cheque** (US **traveler's check**) n chèque m de voyage; **~ling** (US **traveling**) n voyage(s) m(pl); **~ sickness** n mal m de la route (ou de mer ou de l'air)

**trawler** ['trɔːlə'] n chalutier m

**tray** [treɪ] n (for carrying) plateau m; (on desk) corbeille f

**treacherous** ['tretʃərəs] adj (person, look) traître(-esse); (ground, tide) dont il faut se méfier

**treacle** ['triːkl] n mélasse f

**tread** [tred] (pt **trod**, pp **trodden**) n pas m; (sound) bruit m de pas; (of tyre) chape f, bande f de roulement ♦ vi marcher; **~ on** vt fus marcher sur

**treason** ['triːzn] n trahison f

**treasure** ['treʒə'] n trésor m ♦ vt (value) tenir beaucoup à; **~r** n trésorier(-ère);

**treasury** n: **the Treasury**, (US) **the Treasury Department** le ministère des Finances

**treat** [triːt] n petit cadeau, petite surpri-

se ♦ vt traiter; **to ~ sb to sth** offrir qch à qn

**treatment** n traitement m

**treaty** ['triːtɪ] n traité m

**treble** ['trebl] adj triple ♦ vt, vi tripler; **~ clef** n (MUS) clé f de sol

**tree** [triː] n arbre m

**trek** [trek] n (journey) voyage m; (on foot) (longue) marche, tirée f

**tremble** ['trembl] vi trembler

**tremendous** [trɪ'mendəs] adj (enormous) énorme, fantastique; (excellent) formidable

**tremor** ['tremə'] n tremblement m; (also: **earth ~**) secousse f sismique

**trench** [trentʃ] n tranchée f

**trend** [trend] n (tendency) tendance f; (of events) cours m; (fashion) mode f; **~y** adj (idea, person) dans le vent; (clothes) dernier cri inv

**trespass** ['trespəs] vi: **to ~ on** s'introduire sans permission dans; **"no ~ing"** "propriété privée", "défense d'entrer"

**trestle** ['tresl] n tréteau m

**trial** ['traɪəl] n (LAW) procès m, jugement m; (test of machine etc) essai m; **~s** npl (unpleasant experiences) épreuves fpl; **to be on ~** (LAW) passer en jugement; **by ~ and error** par tâtonnements; **~ period** n période f d'essai

**triangle** ['traɪæŋgl] n (MATH, MUS) triangle m; **triangular** [traɪ'æŋgjulə'] adj triangulaire

**tribe** [traɪb] n tribu f; **~sman** (irreg) n membre m d'une tribu

**tribunal** [traɪ'bjuːnl] n tribunal m

**tributary** ['trɪbjutərɪ] n (river) affluent m

**tribute** ['trɪbjuːt] n tribut m, hommage m; **to pay ~ to** rendre hommage à

**trick** [trɪk] n (magic ~) tour m; (joke, prank) tour, farce f; (skill, knack) astuce f, truc m; (CARDS) levée f ♦ vt attraper, rouler; **to play a ~ on sb** jouer un tour à qn; **that should do the ~** ça devrait faire l'affaire; **~ery** n ruse f

**trickle** ['trɪkl] n (of water etc) filet m

♦ vi couler en un filet or goutte à goutte

**tricky** ['trɪkɪ] adj difficile, délicat(e)

**tricycle** ['traɪsɪkl] n tricycle m

**trifle** ['traɪfl] n bagatelle f; (CULIN) ≃ diplomate m ♦ adv: **a ~ long** un peu long; **trifling** adj insignifiant(e)

**trigger** ['trɪgə*] n (of gun) gâchette f; **~ off** vt déclencher

**trim** [trɪm] adj (house, garden) bien tenu(e); (figure) svelte ♦ n (haircut etc) légère coupe; (on car) garnitures fpl ♦ vt (cut) couper légèrement; (NAUT: a sail) gréer; (decorate): **to ~ (with)** décorer (de); **~mings** npl (CULIN) garniture f

**trinket** ['trɪŋkɪt] n bibelot m; (piece of jewellery) colifichet m

**trip** [trɪp] n voyage m; (excursion) excursion f; (stumble) faux pas ♦ vi faire un faux pas, trébucher; **on a ~** en voyage; **~ up** vi trébucher ♦ vt faire un croc-en-jambe à

**tripe** [traɪp] n (CULIN) tripes fpl; (pej: rubbish) idioties fpl

**triple** ['trɪpl] adj triple; **~ts** npl triplés (-ées); **triplicate** ['trɪplɪkət] n: **in triplicate** en trois exemplaires

**tripod** ['traɪpɔd] n trépied m

**trite** [traɪt] adj (pej) banal(e)

**triumph** ['traɪʌmf] n triomphe m ♦ vi: **to ~ (over)** triompher (de)

**trivia** ['trɪvɪə] (pej) futilités fpl; **~l** adj insignifiant(e); (commonplace) banal(e)

**trod** [trɔd] pt of **tread**; **~den** pp of **tread**

**trolley** ['trɔlɪ] n chariot m

**trombone** [trɔm'bəun] n trombone m

**troop** [truːp] n bande, groupe m ♦ vi: **~ in/out** entrer/sortir en groupe; **~s** npl (MIL) troupes fpl; (: men) hommes mpl, soldats mpl; **~ing the colour** (BRIT) n (ceremony) le salut au drapeau

**trophy** ['trəufɪ] n trophée m

**tropic** ['trɔpɪk] n tropique m; **~al** adj tropical(e)

**trot** [trɔt] n trot m ♦ vi trotter; **on the ~** (BRIT: fig) d'affilée

**trouble** ['trʌbl] n difficulté(s) f(pl), problème(s) m(pl); (worry) ennuis mpl, soucis mpl; (bother, effort) peine f; (POL) troubles mpl; (MED): **stomach etc ~** troubles gastriques etc ♦ vt (disturb) déranger, gêner; (worry) inquiéter ♦ vi: **to ~ to do** prendre la peine de faire; **~s** npl (POL etc) troubles mpl; (personal) ennuis, soucis; **to be in ~** avoir des ennuis; (ship, climber etc) être en difficulté; **what's the ~?** qu'est-ce qui ne va pas?; **~d** adj (person) inquiet(-ète); (epoch, life) agité(e); **~maker** n élément perturbateur, fauteur de troubles; **~shooter** n (in conflict) médiateur m; **~some** adj (child) fatigant(e), difficile; (cough etc) gênant(e)

**trough** [trɔf] n (also: **drinking ~**) abreuvoir m; (also: **feeding ~**) auge f; (depression) creux m

**trousers** ['trauzəz] npl pantalon m; **short ~** culottes courtes

**trout** [traut] n inv truite f

**trowel** ['trauəl] n truelle f; (garden tool) déplantoir m

**truant** ['truːənt] (BRIT) n: **to play ~** faire l'école buissonnière

**truce** [truːs] n trêve f

**truck** [trʌk] n camion m; (RAIL) wagon m à plate-forme; **~ driver** n camionneur m; **~ farm** (US) n jardin maraîcher

**true** [truː] adj vrai(e); (accurate) exact(e); (genuine) vrai, véritable; (faithful) fidèle; **to come ~** se réaliser

**truffle** ['trʌfl] n truffe f

**truly** ['truːlɪ] adv vraiment, réellement; (truthfully) sans mentir; see also **yours**

**trump** [trʌmp] n (also: **~ card**) atout m

**trumpet** ['trʌmpɪt] n trompette f

**truncheon** ['trʌntʃən] n (BRIT) n bâton m (d'agent de police); matraque f

**trundle** ['trʌndl] vt, vi: **to ~ along** rouler lentement et bruyamment

**trunk** [trʌŋk] n (of tree, person) tronc m; (of elephant) trompe f; (case) malle f; (US: AUT) coffre m; **~s** npl (also: **swimming ~s**) maillot m or slip m de bain

**truss** [trʌs] vt: **to ~ (up)** ligoter

**trust** [trʌst] n confiance f (responsibility) charge f; (LAW) fidéicommis m ♦ vt (rely on) avoir confiance en; (hope) espérer; (entrust): **to ~ sth to sb** confier qch à qn; **to take sb on ~** accepter qch les yeux fermés; **~ed** adj en qui l'on a confiance; **~ee** [trʌs'tiː] n (LAW) fidéicommissaire m/f; (of school etc) administrateur(-trice); **~ful, ~ing** adj confiant(e); **~worthy** adj digne de confiance

**truth** [truːθ] n vérité f; **~ful** adj (person) qui dit la vérité; (answer) sincère

**try** [traɪ] n essai m, tentative f; (RUGBY) essai ♦ vt (attempt) essayer, tenter; (test: sth new: also: ~ out) essayer, tester; (LAW: person) juger; (strain) éprouver ♦ vi essayer; **to have a ~** essayer; **to ~ to do** essayer de faire; (seek) chercher à faire; **~ on** vt (clothes) essayer; **~ing** adj pénible

**T-shirt** ['tiːʃəːt] n tee-shirt m

**T-square** ['tiːskwɛəʳ] n équerre f en T, té m

**tub** [tʌb] n cuve f; (for washing clothes) baquet m; (bath) baignoire f

**tubby** ['tʌbɪ] adj rondelet(te)

**tube** [tjuːb] n tube m; (BRIT: underground) métro m; (for tyre) chambre f à air

**tuberculosis** [tjubəːkjuˈləʊsɪs] n tuberculose f

**TUC** n abbr (BRIT: Trades Union Congress) confédération des syndicats britanniques

**tuck** [tʌk] vt (put) mettre; **~ away** vt cacher, ranger; vi rentrer; (child) border ♦ vt (eat) manger (de bon appétit); **~ up** vt (child) border; **~ shop** (BRIT) n boutique f à provisions (dans une école)

**Tuesday** ['tjuːzdɪ] n mardi m

**tuft** [tʌft] n touffe f

**tug** [tʌg] n (ship) remorqueur m ♦ vt tirer (sur); **~-of-war** n lutte f à la corde; (fig) lutte acharnée

**tuition** [tjuˈɪʃən] n (BRIT) leçons fpl; (: private ~) cours particuliers; (US: school fees) frais mpl de scolarité

**tulip** ['tjuːlɪp] n tulipe f

**tumble** ['tʌmbl] n (fall) chute f, culbute f ♦ vi tomber, dégringoler; **to ~ to sth** (inf) réaliser qch; **~down** adj délabré(e); **~ dryer** (BRIT) n séchoir m à air chaud

**tumbler** ['tʌmbləʳ] n (glass) verre (droit), gobelet m

**tummy** ['tʌmɪ] (inf) n ventre m; **~ upset** n maux mpl de ventre

**tumour** ['tjuːməʳ] (US **tumor**) n tumeur f

**tuna** ['tjuːnə] n inv (also: ~ **fish**) thon m

**tune** [tjuːn] n (melody) air m ♦ vt (MUS) accorder; (RADIO, TV, AUT) régler; **to be in/out of ~** (instrument) être accordé/désaccordé; (singer) chanter juste/faux; **to be in/out of ~ with** (fig) être en accord/désaccord avec; **~ in** vi (RADIO, TV): **to ~ in (to)** se mettre à l'écoute (de); **~ up** vi (musician) accorder son instrument; **~ful** adj mélodieux(-euse); **~r** n: **piano ~r** accordeur m (de pianos)

**Tunisia** [tjuˈnɪzɪə] n Tunisie f

**tunic** ['tjuːnɪk] n tunique f

**Tunisia** [tjuˈnɪzɪə] n Tunisie f

**tunnel** ['tʌnl] n tunnel m; (in mine) galerie f ♦ vi percer un tunnel

**turbulence** ['təːbjuləns] n (AVIAT) turbulence f

**tureen** [təˈriːn] n (for soup) soupière f; (for vegetables) légumier m

**turf** [təːf] n gazon m; (clod) motte f (de gazon) ♦ vt gazonner; **~ out** (inf) vt (person) jeter dehors

**Turk** [təːk] n Turc (Turque)

**Turkey** ['təːkɪ] n Turquie f

**turkey** ['təːkɪ] n dindon m, dinde f

**Turkish** ['təːkɪʃ] adj turc (turque) ♦ n (LING) turc m

**turmoil** ['təːmɔɪl] n trouble m, bouleversement m; **in ~** en émoi, en effervescence

**turn** [təːn] n tour m; (in road) tournant m; (of mind, events) tournure f; (performance) numéro m; (MED) crise f, attaque *f* ♦ *vt* tourner; (*collar, steak*) retourner; (*change*): **to ~ sth into** changer qch en ♦ *vi* (*object, wind, milk*) tourner; (*person: look back*) se (re)tourner; (*reverse direction*) faire demi-tour; (*become*) devenir; (*age*) atteindre; **to ~ into** se changer en; **a good ~** un service; **it gave me quite a ~** ça m'a fait un coup; **"no left ~"** (*AUT*) "défense de tourner à gauche"; **it's your ~** c'est (à) votre tour; **in ~** à son tour; **to take ~s (at)** se relayer (pour *or* à); **~ away** *vi* (*applicants*) refuser; **~ back** *vi* revenir, faire demi-tour ♦ *vt* (*person, vehicle*) faire faire demi-tour à; (*clock*) reculer; **~ down** *vt* (*refuse*) rejeter, refuser; (*reduce*) baisser; (*fold*) rabattre; **~ in** (*inf: go to bed*) aller se coucher ♦ *vt* (*fold*) rentrer; **~ off** *vi* (*from road*) tourner ♦ *vt* (*light, radio etc*) éteindre; (*tap*) fermer; (*engine*) arrêter; **~ on** *vt* (*light, radio etc*) allumer; (*tap*) ouvrir; (*engine*) mettre en marche; **~ out** *vt* (*light, gas*) éteindre; (*produce*) produire ♦ *vi* (*voters, troops etc*) se présenter; **to ~ out to be ...** s'avérer ..., se révéler ...; **~ over** *vi* (*person*) se retourner ♦ *vt* (*object*) retourner; (*page*) tourner; **~ round** *vi* faire demi-tour; (*rotate*) tourner; **~ up** *vi* (*person*) arriver, se pointer (*inf*); (*lost object*) être retrouvé(e) ♦ *vt* (*collar*) remonter; (*radio, heater*) mettre plus fort; **~ing** *n* (*in road*) tournant *m*; **~ing point** *n* (*fig*) tournant *m*, moment décisif

**turnip** ['tə:nɪp] *n* navet *m*

**turn: ~out** *n* (*of voters*) taux *m* de participation; **~over** *n* (*COMM: amount of money*) chiffre *m* d'affaires; (*: of goods*) roulement *m*; (*: of staff*) renouvellement *m*, changement *m*; **~pike** (*US*) *n* autoroute *f* à péage; **~stile** *n* tourniquet *m* (*d'entrée*); **~table** *n* (*on record player*) platine *f*; **~up** (*BRIT*) *n* (*on trousers*) revers *m*

**turpentine** ['tə:pəntaɪn] *n* (*also:* **turps**)

(*essence f de*) térébenthine *f*

**turquoise** ['tə:kwɔɪz] *n* (*stone*) turquoise *f* ♦ *adj* turquoise *inv*

**turret** ['tʌrɪt] *n* tourelle *f*

**turtle** ['tə:tl] *n* tortue marine *or* d'eau douce; **~neck (sweater)** *n* (*BRIT*) pullover *m* à col montant; (*US*) pullover à col roulé

**tusk** [tʌsk] *n* défense *f*

**tutor** ['tju:tə*ʳ*] *n* (*in college*) directeur (-trice) d'études; (*private teacher*) précepteur(-trice); **~ial** [tju:'tɔ:rɪəl] *n* (*SCOL*) (séance *f* de) travaux *mpl* pratiques

**tuxedo** [tʌk'si:dəu] (*US*) *n* smoking *m*

**TV** *n abbr* (*= television*) télé *f*

**twang** [twæŋ] *n* (*of instrument*) son vibrant; (*of voice*) ton nasillard

**tweed** [twi:d] *n* tweed *m*

**tweezers** ['twi:zəz] *npl* pince *f* à épiler

**twelfth** [twelfθ] *num* douzième

**twelve** [twelv] *num* douze; **at ~** (**o'clock**) à midi; (*midnight*) à minuit

**twentieth** ['twentɪθ] *num* vingtième

**twenty** ['twentɪ] *num* vingt

**twice** [twaɪs] *adv* deux fois; **~ as much** deux fois plus

**twiddle** ['twɪdl] *vt, vi*: **to ~ (with)** sth tripoter qch; **to ~ one's thumbs** (*fig*) se tourner les pouces

**twig** [twɪg] *n* brindille *f* ♦ *vi* (*inf*) piger

**twilight** ['twaɪlaɪt] *n* crépuscule *m*

**twin** [twɪn] *adj, n* jumeau(-elle) ♦ *vt* jumeler; **~(-bedded) room** *n* chambre *f* à deux lits; **~ beds** *npl* lits jumeaux

**twine** [twaɪn] *n* ficelle *f* ♦ *vi* (*plant*) s'enrouler

**twinge** [twɪndʒ] *n* (*of pain*) élancement *m*; **a ~ of conscience** un certain remords; **a ~ of regret** un pincement au cœur

**twinkle** ['twɪŋkl] *vi* scintiller; (*eyes*) pétiller

**twirl** [twə:l] *vt* faire tournoyer ♦ *vi* tournoyer

**twist** [twɪst] *n* torsion *f*, tour *m*; (*in road*) virage *m*; (*in wire, flex*) tortillon *m; (in story)* coup *m* de théâtre ♦ *vt* tordre; *(weave)* entortiller ▶ *vi (roll around)* enrouler; *(fig)* déformer ▶ *vi (road, river)* serpenter

**twit** [twɪt] *(inf)* n crétin/e

**twitch** [twɪtʃ] n *(pull)* coup *m* sec, saccade *f; (nervous)* tic *m* ♦ *vi* se convulser; avoir un tic

**two** [tu:] *num* deux; **to put ~ and ~ together** *(fig)* faire le rapprochement; **~-door** *adj (AUT)* à deux portes; **~-faced** *(pej) adj (person)* faux (fausse); **~-fold** *adv:* **~fold** *(woman's)* **to increase ~fold** doubler; **~-piece (suit)** n *(man's)* costume *m* (deux-pièces); *(woman's)* tailleur *m* deux-pièces *m inv*; **~-piece (swimsuit)** n *(maillot m* de bain) deux-pièces *m inv*; **~some** n *(people)* couple *m*; **~-way** *adj (traffic)* dans les deux sens

**tycoon** [taɪˈku:n] n: *(business)* **~** gros homme *m* d'affaires

**type** [taɪp] n *(category)* type *m*, genre *m*, espèce *f; (model, example)* type *m*, modèle *m; (TYP)* type, caractère *m; (letter etc)* taper (à la machine); **~cast** *adj (actor)* condamné(e) à toujours jouer le même rôle; **~face** n *(TYP)* œil *m* de caractère; **~script** n texte dactylographié; **~writer** n machine *f* à écrire; **~written** *adj* dactylographié(e)

**typhoid** [ˈtaɪfɔɪd] n typhoïde *f*

**typical** [ˈtɪpɪkl] *adj* typique, caractéristique

**typing** [ˈtaɪpɪŋ] n dactylo(graphie) *f*

**typist** [ˈtaɪpɪst] n dactylo *m/f*

**tyrant** [ˈtaɪərənt] n tyran *m*

**tyre** [ˈtaɪər] *(us tire)* n pneu *m; ~* **pressure** n pression *f* (de gonflage)

# U, u

**U-bend** [ˈju:bɛnd] n *(in pipe)* coude *m*

**ubiquitous** [ju:ˈbɪkwɪtəs] *adj* omniprésent(e)

**udder** [ˈʌdər] n pis *m*, mamelle *f*

**UFO** [ˈju:fəu] n *abbr (= unidentified flying object)* OVNI *m*

**Uganda** [ju:ˈgændə] n Ouganda *m*

**ugh** [ə:h] *excl* pouah!

**ugly** [ˈʌglɪ] *adj* laid(e), vilain(e); *(situation)* inquiétant(e)

**UHT** *adj abbr (= ultra heat treated)*: **UHT milk** lait *m* UHT *or* longue conservation

**UK** n *abbr* = **United Kingdom**

**ulcer** [ˈʌlsər] n ulcère *m; (also:* **mouth ~)** aphte *m*

**Ulster** [ˈʌlstər] n Ulster *m; (inf: Northern Ireland)* Irlande *f* du Nord

**ulterior** [ʌlˈtɪərɪər] *adj:* **~ motive** arrière-pensée *f*

**ultimate** [ˈʌltɪmət] *adj* ultime, final(e); *(authority)* suprême; **~ly** *adv (at last)* en fin de compte; *(fundamentally)* finalement

**ultrasound** [ˈʌltrəsaund] n ultrason *m*

**umbilical cord** [ʌmˈbɪlɪkl-] n cordon ombilical

**umbrella** [ʌmˈbrɛlə] n parapluie *m; (for sun)* parasol *m*

**umpire** [ˈʌmpaɪər] n arbitre *m*

**umpteen** [ʌmpˈti:n] *adj* je ne sais combien de; **~th** *adj:* **for the ~th time** pour la nième fois

**UN** n *abbr* = **United Nations**

**unable** [ʌnˈeɪbl] *adj:* **to be ~ to** ne pas pouvoir, être dans l'impossibilité de; *(incapable)* être incapable de

**unacceptable** [ʌnəkˈsɛptəbl] *adj (behaviour)* inadmissible; *(price, proposal)* inacceptable

**unaccompanied** [ʌnəˈkʌmpənid] *adj (child, baby)* non accompagné(e); *(song)* sans accompagnement

**unaccustomed** [ʌnəˈkʌstəmd] *adj:* **to be ~** ne pas avoir l'habitude de qch

**unanimous** [ju:ˈnænɪməs] *adj* unanime; **~ly** *adv* à l'unanimité

**unarmed** [ʌnˈɑ:md] *adj (without a weapon)* non armé(e); *(combat)* sans armes

**unattached** [ʌnəˈtætʃt] *adj* libre, sans attaches; *(part)* non attaché(e), indépendant(e)

**unattended** [ʌnəˈtɛndɪd] adj (car, child, luggage) sans surveillance

**unattractive** [ʌnəˈtræktɪv] adj peu attrayant(e); (character) peu sympathique

**unauthorized** [ʌnˈɔːθəraɪzd] adj non autorisé(e), sans autorisation

**unavoidable** [ʌnəˈvɔɪdəbl] adj inévitable

**unaware** [ʌnəˈwɛəʳ] adj: to be ~ of ignorer, être inconscient(e) de; ~s adv à l'improviste, au dépourvu

**unbalanced** [ʌnˈbælənst] adj déséquilibré(e); (report) peu objectif(-ive)

**unbearable** [ʌnˈbɛərəbl] adj insupportable

**unbeatable** [ʌnˈbiːtəbl] adj imbattable

**unbeknown(st)** [ʌnbɪˈnəʊn(st)] adv: ~ to me/Peter à mon insu/l'insu de Peter

**unbelievable** [ʌnbɪˈliːvəbl] adj incroyable

**unbend** [ʌnˈbɛnd] (irreg) vi se détendre ♦ vt (wire) redresser, détordre

**unbiased** [ʌnˈbaɪəst] adj impartial(e)

**unborn** [ʌnˈbɔːn] adj à naître, qui n'est pas encore né(e)

**unbreakable** [ʌnˈbreɪkəbl] adj incassable

**unbroken** [ʌnˈbrəʊkən] adj intact(e), (fig) continu(e), ininterrompu(e)

**unbutton** [ʌnˈbʌtn] vt déboutonner

**uncalled-for** [ʌnˈkɔːldfɔːʳ] adj déplacé(e), injustifié(e)

**uncanny** [ʌnˈkænɪ] adj étrange, troublant(e)

**unceremonious** [ʌnsɛrɪˈməʊnɪəs] adj (abrupt, rude) brusque

**uncertain** [ʌnˈsɜːtn] adj incertain(e); (hesitant) hésitant(e); in no ~ terms sans équivoque possible; ~ty n incertitude f, doute(s) m(pl)

**uncivilized** [ʌnˈsɪvɪlaɪzd] adj (gen) non civilisé(e); (fig: behaviour etc) barbare; (hour) indu(e)

**uncle** [ˈʌŋkl] n oncle m

**uncomfortable** [ʌnˈkʌmfətəbl] adj in-comfortable, peu confortable; (uneasy) mal à l'aise, gêné(e); (situation) désagréable

**uncommon** [ʌnˈkɔmən] adj rare, singulier(-ère), peu commun(e)

**uncompromising** [ʌnˈkɔmprəmaɪzɪŋ] adj intransigeant(e), inflexible

**unconcerned** [ʌnkənˈsɜːnd] adj: to be ~ (about) ne pas s'inquiéter de

**unconditional** [ʌnkənˈdɪʃənl] adj sans conditions

**unconscious** [ʌnˈkɔnʃəs] adj sans connaissance, évanoui(e); (unaware): ~ of inconscient(e) de ♦ n: the ~ l'inconscient m; ~ly adv inconsciemment

**uncontrollable** [ʌnkənˈtrəʊləbl] adj indiscipliné(e); (temper, laughter) irrépressible

**unconventional** [ʌnkənˈvɛnʃənl] adj peu conventionnel(le)

**uncouth** [ʌnˈkuːθ] adj grossier(-ère), fruste

**uncover** [ʌnˈkʌvəʳ] vt découvrir

**undecided** [ʌndɪˈsaɪdɪd] adj indécis(e), irrésolu(e)

**under** [ˈʌndəʳ] prep sous; (less than) (de) moins de; au-dessous de; (according to) selon, en vertu de ♦ adv au-dessous; en dessous; ~ there là-dessous; ~ repair (en cours de) réparation; ~age adj (person) qui n'a pas l'âge réglementaire; ~carriage n (AVIAT) train m d'atterrissage; ~charge vt ne pas faire payer assez à; ~coat n (paint) couche f de fond; ~cover adj secret(-ète), clandestin(e); ~current n courant m ou sentiment sous-jacent; ~cut (irreg) vt vendre moins cher que; ~dog n opprimé m; ~done adj (CULIN) saignant(e); (pej) pas assez cuit(e); ~estimate vt sous-estimer; ~fed adj sous-alimenté(e); ~foot adv sous les pieds; ~go (irreg) vt subir; (treatment) suivre; ~graduate n étudiant(e) (qui prépare la licence); ~ground n (BRIT: railway) métro m; (POL) clandestinité f ♦ adj souterrain(e); (fig) clandestin(e) ♦ adv dans la clandestinité, clandestinement; **~growth** n broussailles fpl, sous-bois m; **~hand(ed)** adj (fig: behaviour, method etc) en dessous; **~lie** (irreg) vt être à la base de; **~line** vt souligner; **~mine** vt saper, miner; **~neath** adv (en) dessous ♦ prep sous, au-dessous de; **~paid** adj sous-payé(e); **~pants** (BRIT) npl caleçon m, slip m; **~pass** (BRIT) n passage souterrain; (on motorway) passage inférieur; **~privileged** adj défavorisé(e), économiquement faible; **~rate** vt sous-estimer; **~shirt** (US) n tricot de corps; **~shorts** (US) npl caleçon m, slip m; **~side** n dessous m; **~skirt** (BRIT) n jupon m

**understand** [ʌndə'stænd] (irreg: like stand), vt, vi comprendre; **I ~ that ...** je me suis laissé dire que ...; je crois comprendre que ...; **~able** adj compréhensible; **~ing** adj compréhensif(-ive) ♦ n compréhension f; (agreement) accord m

**understatement** [ʌndə'steɪtmənt] n: **that's an ~** c'est (bien) peu dire, le terme est faible

**understood** [ʌndə'stud] pt, pp of **understand** ♦ adj entendu(e); (implied) sous-entendu(e)

**understudy** ['ʌndəstʌdɪ] n doublure f

**undertake** [ʌndə'teɪk] (irreg) vt entreprendre; se charger de; **to ~ to do sth** s'engager à faire qch

**undertaker** [ʌndə'teɪkər] n entrepreneur m des pompes funèbres, croquemort m

**undertaking** [ʌndə'teɪkɪŋ] n entreprise f; (promise) promesse f

**under: ~tone** n: **in an ~tone** à mivoix; **~water** adv sous l'eau ♦ adj sous-marin(e); **~wear** n sousvêtements mpl; (women's only) dessous mpl; **~world** n (of crime) milieu m, pègre f; **~write** n (INSURANCE) assureur m

**undies** ['ʌndɪz] (inf) npl dessous mpl, lingerie f

**undiplomatic** [ʌndɪplə'mætɪk] adj peu diplomatique

**undo** [ʌn'du:] (irreg) vt défaire; **~ing** n ruine f, perte f

**undoubted** [ʌn'dautɪd] adj indubitable, certain(e); **~ly** adv sans aucun doute

**undress** [ʌn'dres] vi se déshabiller

**undue** [ʌn'dju:] adj indu(e), excessif (-ive)

**undulating** ['ʌndjuleɪtɪŋ] adj ondoyant(e), onduleux(-euse)

**unduly** [ʌn'dju:lɪ] adv trop, excessivement

**unearth** [ʌn'ə:θ] vt déterrer; (fig) dénicher

**unearthly** [ʌn'ə:θlɪ] adj (hour) indu(e), impossible

**uneasy** [ʌn'i:zɪ] adj mal à l'aise, gêné(e); (worried) inquiet(-ète); (feeling) désagréable; (peace, truce) fragile

**uneconomic(al)** [ʌni:kə'nɔmɪk(l)] adj peu économique

**uneducated** [ʌn'edjukeɪtɪd] adj (person) sans instruction

**unemployed** [ʌnɪm'plɔɪd] adj sans travail, en or au chômage ♦ n: **the ~** les chômeurs mpl; **unemployment** n chômage m

**unending** [ʌn'endɪŋ] adj interminable, sans fin

**unerring** [ʌn'ə:rɪŋ] adj infaillible, sûr(e)

**uneven** [ʌn'i:vn] adj inégal(e); (quality, work) irrégulier(-ère)

**unexpected** [ʌnɪks'pektɪd] adj inattendu(e), imprévu(e); **~ly** [ʌnɪks'pektɪdlɪ] adv (arrive) à l'improviste; (succeed) contre toute attente

**unfailing** [ʌn'feɪlɪŋ] adj inépuisable; (remedy) infaillible

**unfair** [ʌn'feər] adj: **~ (to)** injuste (envers)

**unfaithful** [ʌn'feɪθful] adj infidèle

**unfamiliar** [ʌnfə'mɪlɪər] adj étrange, inconnu(e); **to be ~ with** mal connaître

**unfashionable** [ʌn'fæʃnəbl]

*(clothes)* démodé(e); *(place)* peu chic *inv*

**unfasten** [ʌnˈfɑːsn] *vt* défaire; détacher; *(open)* ouvrir

**unfavourable** [ʌnˈfeɪvrəbl] *(US* **unfavorable)** *adj* défavorable

**unfeeling** [ʌnˈfiːlɪŋ] *adj* insensible, dur(e)

**unfinished** [ʌnˈfɪnɪʃt] *adj* inachevé(e)

**unfit** [ʌnˈfɪt] *adj* en mauvaise santé; pas en forme; *(incompetent)*: **~ (for)** impropre (à); *(work, service)* inapte (à)

**unfold** [ʌnˈfəʊld] *vt* déplier ♦ *vi* se dérouler

**unforeseen** [ʌnfɔːˈsiːn] *adj* imprévu(e)

**unforgettable** [ʌnfəˈɡetəbl] *adj* inoubliable

**unfortunate** [ʌnˈfɔːtʃənət] *adj* malheureux(-euse); *(event, remark)* malencontreux(-euse); **~ly** *adv* malheureusement

**unfounded** [ʌnˈfaʊndɪd] *adj* sans fondement

**unfriendly** [ʌnˈfrendlɪ] *adj* inimical(e), peu aimable

**ungainly** [ʌnˈɡeɪnlɪ] *adj* gauche, dégingandé(e)

**ungodly** [ʌnˈɡɒdlɪ] *adj (hour)* indu(e)

**ungrateful** [ʌnˈɡreɪtful] *adj* ingrat(e)

**unhappiness** [ʌnˈhæpɪnɪs] *n* tristesse *f*, peine *f*

**unhappy** [ʌnˈhæpɪ] *adj* triste, malheureux(-euse); **~ about** *or* **with** *(arrangements etc)* mécontent(e) de, peu satisfait(e) de

**unharmed** [ʌnˈhɑːmd] *adj* indemne, sain(e) et sauf (sauve)

**UNHCR** *n abbr (= United Nations High Commission for refugees)* HCR *m*

**unhealthy** [ʌnˈhelθɪ] *adj* malsain(e); *(person)* maladif(-ive)

**unheard-of** [ʌnˈhɜːdɒv] *adj* inouï(e), sans précédent

**unhurt** [ʌnˈhɜːt] *adj* indemne

**unidentified** [ʌnaɪˈdentɪfaɪd] *adj* non identifié(e); *see also* **UFO**

**uniform** [ˈjuːnɪfɔːm] *n* uniforme *m* ♦ *adj* uniforme

**uninhabited** [ʌnɪnˈhæbɪtɪd] *adj* inhabité(e)

**unintentional** [ʌnɪnˈtenʃənəl] *adj* involontaire

**union** [ˈjuːnjən] *n* union *f*; *(also:* **trade ~)** syndicat *m* ♦ *cpd* du syndicat, syndical(e); **U~ Jack** *n* drapeau du Royaume-Uni

**unique** [juːˈniːk] *adj* unique

**UNISON** [ˈjuːnɪsn] *n* grand syndicat des services publics en Grande-Bretagne

**unison** [ˈjuːnɪsn] *n*: **in ~** *(sing)* à l'unisson; *(say)* en chœur

**unit** [ˈjuːnɪt] *n* unité *f*; *(section: of furniture etc)* élément *m*, bloc *m*; **kitchen ~** élément de cuisine

**unite** [juːˈnaɪt] *vt* unir ♦ *vi* s'unir; **~d** *adj* uni(e); unifié(e); *(effort)* conjugué(e); **U~d Kingdom** *n* Royaume-Uni *m*; **U~d Nations (Organization)** *n* (Organisation *f* des) Nations unies; **U~d States (of America)** *n* États-Unis *mpl*

**unit trust** *(BRIT)* *n* fonds commun de placement

**unity** [ˈjuːnɪtɪ] *n* unité *f*

**universal** [juːnɪˈvɜːsl] *adj* universel(le)

**universe** [ˈjuːnɪvɜːs] *n* univers *m*

**university** [juːnɪˈvɜːsɪtɪ] *n* université *f*

**unjust** [ʌnˈdʒʌst] *adj* injuste

**unkempt** [ʌnˈkempt] *adj* négligé(e), débraillé(e); *(hair)* mal peigné(e)

**unkind** [ʌnˈkaɪnd] *adj* peu gentil(le), méchant(e)

**unknown** [ʌnˈnəʊn] *adj* inconnu(e)

**unlawful** [ʌnˈlɔːful] *adj* illégal(e)

**unleaded** [ʌnˈledɪd] *adj (petrol, fuel)* sans plomb

**unleash** [ʌnˈliːʃ] *vt (fig)* déchaîner, déclencher

**unless** [ʌnˈles] *conj*: **~ he leaves** à moins qu'il ne parte

**unlike** [ʌnˈlaɪk] *adj* dissemblable, différent(e) ♦ *prep* contrairement à

**unlikely** [ʌnˈlaɪklɪ] *adj (happening)* improbable; *(explanation)* invraisemblable

**unlimited** [ʌnˈlɪmɪtɪd] *adj* illimité(e)

**unlisted** [ˈʌnˈlɪstɪd] *(US)* *adj (TEL)* sur la

liste rouge

**unload** [ʌn'ləud] *vt* décharger

**unlock** [ʌn'lɒk] *vt* ouvrir

**unlucky** [ʌn'lʌki] *adj* (*person*) malchanceux(-euse); (*object, number*) qui porte malheur; **to be ~** (*person*) ne pas avoir de chance

**unmarried** [ʌn'mærid] *adj* célibataire

**unmistak(e)able** [ʌnmis'teikəbl] *adj* indubitable; qu'on ne peut pas ne pas reconnaître

**unmitigated** [ʌn'mitigeitid] *adj* non mitigé(e), absolu(e), pur(e)

**unnatural** [ʌn'nætʃrəl] *adj* non naturel(le); (*habit*) contre nature

**unnecessary** [ʌn'nesəsəri] *adj* inutile, superflu(e)

**unnoticed** [ʌn'nəutist] *adj*: (**to go** *or* **pass**) **~** (passer) inaperçu(e)

**UNO** *n abbr* = **United Nations Organization**

**unobtainable** [ʌnəb'teinəbl] *adj* impossible à obtenir

**unobtrusive** [ʌnəb'tru:siv] *adj* discret(-ète)

**unofficial** [ʌnə'fiʃl] *adj* (*news*) officieux(-euse); (*strike*) sauvage

**unorthodox** [ʌn'ɔ:θədɒks] *adj* peu orthodoxe; (*REL*) hétérodoxe

**unpack** [ʌn'pæk] *vi* défaire sa valise ♦ *vt* (*suitcase*) défaire; (*belongings*) déballer

**unpalatable** [ʌn'pælətəbl] *adj* (*meal*) mauvais(e); (*truth*) désagréable (à entendre)

**unparalleled** [ʌn'pærəleld] *adj* incomparable, sans égal

**unpleasant** [ʌn'pleznt] *adj* déplaisant(e), désagréable

**unplug** [ʌn'plʌg] *vt* débrancher

**unpopular** [ʌn'pɒpjulə*] *adj* impopulaire

**unprecedented** [ʌn'presidentid] *adj* sans précédent

**unpredictable** [ʌnpri'diktəbl] *adj* imprévisible

**unprofessional** [ʌnprə'feʃənl] *adj*: **~**

**conduct** manquement *m* aux devoirs de la profession

**UNPROFOR** *n abbr* (= United Nations Protection Force) FORPRONU *f*

**unqualified** [ʌn'kwɔlifaid] *adj* (*teacher*) non diplômé(e), sans titres; (*success, disaster*) sans réserve, total(e)

**unquestionably** [ʌn'kwestʃənəbli] *adv* incontestablement

**unravel** [ʌn'rævl] *vt* démêler

**unreal** [ʌn'riəl] *adj* irréel(le); (*extraordinary*) incroyable

**unrealistic** ['ʌnriə'listik] *adj* irréaliste; peu réaliste

**unreasonable** [ʌn'ri:znəbl] *adj* qui n'est pas raisonnable

**unrelated** [ʌnri'leitid] *adj* sans rapport; sans lien de parenté

**unreliable** [ʌnri'laiəbl] *adj* sur qui (*or* quoi) on ne peut pas compter, peu fiable

**unremitting** [ʌnri'mitiŋ] *adj* inlassable, infatigable, acharné(e)

**unreservedly** [ʌnri'zə:vidli] *adv* sans réserve

**unrest** [ʌn'rest] *n* agitation *f*, troubles *mpl*

**unroll** [ʌn'rəul] *vt* dérouler

**unruly** [ʌn'ru:li] *adj* indiscipliné(e)

**unsafe** [ʌn'seif] *adj* (*in danger*) en danger; (*journey, car*) dangereux(-euse)

**unsaid** [ʌn'sed] *adj*: **to leave sth ~** passer qch sous silence

**unsatisfactory** ['ʌnsætis'fæktəri] *adj* peu satisfaisant(e)

**unsavoury** [ʌn'seivəri] (*US* **unsavory**) *adj* (*fig*) peu recommandable

**unscathed** [ʌn'skeiðd] *adj* indemne

**unscrew** [ʌn'skru:] *vt* dévisser

**unscrupulous** [ʌn'skru:pjuləs] *adj* sans scrupules

**unsettled** [ʌn'setld] *adj* perturbé(e); instable

**unshaven** [ʌn'ʃeivn] *adj* non *or* mal rasé(e)

**unsightly** [ʌn'saitli] *adj* disgracieux (-euse), laid(e)

**unskilled** [ʌnˈskɪld] adj: ~ **worker** manœuvre m

**unspeakable** [ʌnˈspiːkəbl] adj indicible; (awful) innommable

**unstable** [ʌnˈsteɪbl] adj instable

**unsteady** [ʌnˈstedɪ] adj mal assuré(e),
chancelant(e), instable

**unstuck** [ʌnˈstʌk] adj: **to come** ~ se
décoller; (plan) tomber à l'eau

**unsuccessful** [ʌnsəkˈsesful] adj (attempt) infructueux(-euse), vain(e); (writer, proposal) qui n'a pas de succès; **to
be** ~ (in attempting sth) ne pas réussir;
ne pas avoir de succès; (application) ne
pas être retenu(e)

**unsuitable** [ʌnˈsuːtəbl] adj qui ne
convient pas, peu approprié(e); inop-
portun(e)

**unsure** [ʌnˈʃuəʳ] adj pas sûr(e); **to be** ~
**of o.s.** manquer de confiance en soi

**unsuspecting** [ʌnsəsˈpɛktɪŋ] adj qui
ne se doute de rien

**unsympathetic** [ˈʌnsɪmpəˈθɛtɪk] adj
(person) antipathique; (attitude) peu
compatissant(e)

**untapped** [ʌnˈtæpt] adj (resources)
inexploité(e)

**unthinkable** [ʌnˈθɪŋkəbl] adj impensable, inconcevable

**untidy** [ʌnˈtaɪdɪ] adj (room) en désordre; (appearance, person) débraillé(e);
(person: in character) sans ordre, désordonné

**untie** [ʌnˈtaɪ] vt (knot, parcel) défaire;
(prisoner, dog) détacher

**until** [ʌnˈtɪl] prep jusqu'à; (after negative) avant ♦ conj jusqu'à ce que +sub;
(in past, after negative) avant que +sub;
~ **he comes** jusqu'à ce qu'il vienne,
jusqu'à son arrivée; ~ **now** jusqu'à présent, jusqu'ici; ~ **then** jusque-là

**untimely** [ʌnˈtaɪmlɪ] adj inopportun(e);
(death) prématuré(e)

**untold** [ʌnˈtəuld] adj (story) jamais ra-
conté(e); (wealth) incalculable; (joy, suffering) indescriptible

**untoward** [ʌntəˈwɔːd] adj fâcheux

(-euse), malencontreux(-euse)

**unused¹** [ʌnˈjuːzd] adj (clothes) neuf
(neuve)

**unused²** [ʌnˈjuːst] adj: **to be** ~ **to
sth/to doing sth** ne pas avoir l'habitude de qch/de faire qch

**unusual** [ʌnˈjuːʒuəl] adj insolite, ex-
ceptionnel(le), rare

**unveil** [ʌnˈveɪl] vt dévoiler

**unwanted** [ʌnˈwɒntɪd] adj (child, pregnancy) non désiré(e); (clothes etc) à
donner

**unwelcome** [ʌnˈwɛlkəm] adj impor-
tun(e); (news) fâcheux(-euse)

**unwell** [ʌnˈwɛl] adj souffrant(e); **to feel**
~ ne pas se sentir bien

**unwieldy** [ʌnˈwiːldɪ] adj (object) difficile à manier; (system) lourd(e)

**unwilling** [ʌnˈwɪlɪŋ] adj: **to be** ~ **to
do** ne pas vouloir faire; ~**ly** adv à
contrecœur, contre son gré

**unwind** [ʌnˈwaɪnd] (irreg) vt dérouler
♦ vi (relax) se détendre

**unwise** [ʌnˈwaɪz] adj irréfléchi(e), im-
prudent(e)

**unwitting** [ʌnˈwɪtɪŋ] adj involontaire

**unworkable** [ʌnˈwəːkəbl] adj (plan)
impraticable

**unworthy** [ʌnˈwəːðɪ] adj indigne

**unwrap** [ʌnˈræp] vt défaire; ouvrir

**unwritten** [ʌnˈrɪtn] adj (agreement) ta-
cite

---
KEYWORD
---

**up** [ʌp] prep: **he went up the stairs/
the hill** il a monté l'escalier/la colline;
**the cat was up a tree** le chat était
dans un arbre; **they live further up
the street** ils habitent plus haut dans
la rue

♦ adv 1 (upwards, higher): **up in the
sky/the mountains** (là-haut) dans le
ciel/les montagnes; **put it a bit higher
up** mettez-le un peu plus haut; **up
there** là-haut; ~ **above** au-dessus

**2: to be up** (out of bed) être levé(e);
(prices) avoir augmenté or monté

**up-and-coming** [ˌʌpənˈkʌmɪŋ] *adj* plein(e) d'avenir or de promesses

**upbringing** [ˈʌpbrɪŋɪŋ] *n* éducation *f*

**update** [ʌpˈdeɪt] *vt* mettre à jour

**upgrade** [ʌpˈgreɪd] *vt* (*house*) moderniser; (*job*) revaloriser; (*employee*) promouvoir

**upheaval** [ʌpˈhiːvl] *n* bouleversement *m*; branle-bas *m*

**uphill** [ˈʌpˈhɪl] *adj* qui monte; (fig: *task*) difficile, pénible ♦ *adv* (*face, look*) en amont; **to go** ~ monter

**uphold** [ʌpˈhəʊld] (*irreg*) *vt* (*law, decision*) maintenir

**upholstery** [ʌpˈhəʊlstərɪ] *n* rembourrage *m*; (*cover*) tissu *m* d'ameublement; (*of car*) garniture *f*

**upkeep** [ˈʌpkiːp] *n* entretien *m*

**upon** [əˈpɒn] *prep* sur

**upper** [ˈʌpər] *adj* supérieur(e); du dessus ♦ *n* (*of shoe*) empeigne *f*; **~-class** *adj* de la haute société, aristocratique; **~ hand** *n*: **to have the ~ hand** avoir le dessus; **~most** *adj* le (la) plus haut(e); **what was ~most in my mind** ce à quoi je pensais surtout; **~ sixth** *n* terminale *f*

**upright** [ˈʌpraɪt] *adj* droit(e); vertical(e); (fig) droit, honnête

**uprising** [ˈʌpraɪzɪŋ] *n* soulèvement *m*, insurrection *f*

**uproar** [ˈʌprɔːr] *n* tumulte *m*; (*protests*) tempête *f* de protestations

**uproot** [ʌpˈruːt] *vt* déraciner

**upset** [*n* ˈʌpset, *vb, adj* ʌpˈset] (*irreg: like* set) *n* bouleversement *m*; (*stomach* ~) indigestion *f* ♦ *vt* (*glass etc*) renverser; (*plan*) déranger; (*person: offend*) contrarier; (: *grieve*) faire de la peine à; bouleverser ♦ *adj* contrarié(e); peiné(e); (*stomach*) dérangé(e)

**upshot** [ˈʌpʃɒt] *n* résultat *m*

**upside-down** [ˈʌpsaɪdˈdaʊn] *adv* à l'envers; **to turn ~ ~** mettre sens dessus dessous

**upstairs** [ˈʌpˈsteəz] *adv* en haut ♦ *adj* (*room*) du dessus, d'en haut ♦ *n*: **the ~** l'étage *m*

**upstart** [ˈʌpstɑːt] (*pej*) *n* parvenu(e)

**upstream** [ˈʌpˈstriːm] *adv* en amont

**uptake** [ˈʌpteɪk] *n*: **to be quick/slow on the ~** comprendre vite/être lent à comprendre

**uptight** [ʌpˈtaɪt] (*inf*) *adj* très tendu(e), crispé(e)

**up-to-date** [ˈʌptəˈdeɪt] *adj* moderne; (*information*) très récent(e)

**upturn** [ˈʌptəːn] *n* (*in luck*) retournement *m*; (*COMM: in market*) hausse *f*

**upward** [ˈʌpwəd] *adj* ascendant(e); vers le haut; **~(s)** *adv* vers le haut; **~(s) of 200** 200 et plus

**urban** [ˈəːbən] *adj* urbain(e); **~ clearway** *n* rue *f* à stationnement interdit

**urbane** [əːˈbeɪn] *adj* urbain(e), courtois(e)

**urchin** [ˈəːtʃɪn] *n* polisson *m*

**urge** [əːdʒ] *n* besoin *m*; envie *f*; forte envie, désir *m* ♦ *vt*: **to ~ sb to do** exhorter qn à faire, pousser qn à faire; recommander vivement à qn de faire

**urgency** [ˈəːdʒənsɪ] *n* urgence *f*; (*of tone*) insistance *f*

**urgent** [ˈəːdʒənt] *adj* urgent(e); (*tone*) insistant(e), pressant(e)

**urinal** [ˈjuərɪnl] *n* urinoir *m*

**urine** [ˈjuərɪn] *n* urine *f*

**urn** [əːn] *n* urne *f*; (*also: tea* ~) fontaine *f* à thé

**US** *n abbr* = **United States**

**us** [ʌs] *pron* nous; *see also* **me**

**USA** *n abbr* = **United States of America**

**use** [*n* juːs, *vb* juːz] *n* emploi *m*, utilisa-

tion f; usage m; (~fulness) utilité f ♦ vt
se servir de, utiliser, employer; **in ~** en
usage; **out of ~** hors d'usage; **to be
of ~** servir, être utile; **it's no ~** ça ne
sert à rien; **she ~d to do it** elle le faisait (autrefois), elle avait coutume de le
faire; **~d to: to be ~d to** avoir l'habitude de, être habitué(e) à; **~ up** vt finir,
épuiser; consommer; **~d** [ju:zd] adj
(car) d'occasion; **~ful** ['ju:sful] adj utile;
**~fulness** n utilité f; **~less** ['ju:slɪs]
adj inutile; (person: hopeless) nul(le); **~r**
['ju:zər] n utilisateur(-trice), usager m;
**~r-friendly** adj (computer) convivial(e),
facile d'emploi

**usher** ['ʌʃər] n (at wedding ceremony)
placeur m; **~ette** [ʌʃə'rɛt] n (in cinema)
ouvreuse f

**usual** ['ju:ʒuəl] adj habituel(le); **as ~**
comme d'habitude; **~ly** ['ju:ʒuəlɪ] adv
d'habitude, d'ordinaire

**utensil** [ju:'tɛnsl] n ustensile m

**uterus** ['ju:tərəs] n utérus m

**utility** [ju:'tɪlɪtɪ] n utilité f; (also: public
~) service public; **~ room** n buanderie
f

**utmost** ['ʌtməust] adj extrême, le (la)
plus grand(e) ♦ n: **to do one's ~** faire
tout son possible

**utter** ['ʌtər] adj total(e), complet(-ète)
♦ vt (words) prononcer, émettre;
(sounds) émettre; **~ance** n paroles fpl;
**~ly** adv complètement, totalement

**U-turn** ['ju:'tɜ:n] n demi-tour m

# V, v

**v.** abbr = **verse; versus; volt;** (= vide)
voir

**vacancy** ['veɪkənsɪ] n (BRIT: job) poste
vacant; (room) chambre f disponible;
**"no vacancies"** "complet"

**vacant** ['veɪkənt] adj (seat etc) libre,
disponible; (expression) distrait(e)

**vacate** [və'keɪt] vt quitter

**vacation** [və'keɪʃən] n vacances fpl

**vaccinate** ['væksɪneɪt] vt vacciner

**vacuum** ['vækjum] n vide m; **~ cleaner** n aspirateur m; **~-packed** adj em-
ballé(e) sous vide

**vagina** [və'dʒaɪnə] n vagin m

**vagrant** ['veɪgrənt] n vagabond/e

**vague** [veɪg] adj vague, imprécis(e);
(blurred: photo, outline) flou(e); **~ly** adv
vaguement

**vain** [veɪn] adj (useless) vain(e); (conceited) vaniteux(-euse); **in ~** en vain

**valentine** ['væləntaɪn] n (also: ~ card)
carte f de la Saint-Valentin; (person)
bien-aimé(e) (le jour de la Saint-
Valentin); **V~'s day** n Saint-Valentin f

**valiant** ['vælɪənt] adj vaillant(e)

**valid** ['vælɪd] adj valable; (document)
valable, valide

**valley** ['vælɪ] n vallée f

**valour** ['vælər] (US **valor**) n courage m

**valuable** ['væljuəbl] adj (jewel) de valeur; (time, help) précieux(-euse); **~s** npl
objets mpl de valeur

**valuation** [vælju'eɪʃən] n (price) estimation f; (quality) appréciation f

**value** ['vælju:] n valeur f ♦ vt (fix price)
évaluer, expertiser; (appreciate) apprécier; **~ added tax** (BRIT) n taxe f à la
valeur ajoutée; **~d** adj (person) esti-
mé(e); (advice) précieux(-euse)

**valve** [vælv] n (in machine) soupape f,
valve f; (MED) valve, valvule f

**van** [væn] n (AUT) camionnette f

**vandal** ['vændl] n vandale m/f; **~ism** n
vandalisme m; **~ize** vt saccager

**vanguard** ['vænga:d] n (fig): **in the ~
of** à l'avant-garde de

**vanilla** [və'nɪlə] n vanille f

**vanish** ['vænɪʃ] vi disparaître

**vanity** ['vænɪtɪ] n vanité f

**vantage point** ['vɑ:ntɪdʒ-] n bonne
position

**vapour** ['veɪpər] (US **vapor**) n vapeur f;
(on window) buée f

**variable** ['vɛərɪəbl] adj variable; (mood)
changeant(e)

**variance** ['vɛərɪəns] n: **to be at ~**

**varicose** ['værɪkəʊs] adj: ~ **veins** varices fpl

**varied** ['veərɪd] adj varié(e), divers(e)

**variety** [və'raɪətɪ] n variété f; (quantity) nombre m, quantité f; ~ **show** n (spectacle m de) variétés fpl

**various** ['veərɪəs] adj divers(e), différent(e); (several) divers, plusieurs

**varnish** ['vɑːnɪʃ] n vernis m ♦ vt vernir

**vary** ['veərɪ] vt, vi varier, changer

**vase** [vɑːz] n vase m

**Vaseline** ® ['væsɪliːn] n vaseline f

**vast** [vɑːst] adj vaste, immense; (amount, success) énorme

**VAT** [væt] n abbr (= value added tax) TVA f

**vat** [væt] n cuve f

**vault** [vɔːlt] n (of roof) voûte f; (tomb) caveau m; (in bank) salle f des coffres; chambre forte ♦ vt (also: ~ over) sauter (d'un bond)

**vaunted** ['vɔːntɪd] adj: **much-~** tant vanté(e)

**VCR** n abbr = **video cassette recorder**

**VD** n abbr = **venereal disease**

**VDU** n abbr = **visual display unit**

**veal** [viːl] n veau m

**veer** [vɪər] vi tourner; virer

**vegan** ['viːgən] n végétalien(ne)

**vegeburger** ['vedʒɪbɜːgər] n burger végétarien

**vegetable** ['vedʒtəbl] n légume m ♦ adj végétal(e)

**vegetarian** [vedʒɪ'teərɪən] adj, n végétarien(ne)

**vehement** ['viːɪmənt] adj violent(e), impétueux(-euse); (impassioned) ardent(e)

**vehicle** ['viːɪkl] n véhicule m

**veil** [veɪl] n voile m

**vein** [veɪn] n veine f; (on leaf) nervure f

**velocity** [vɪ'lɒsɪtɪ] n vitesse f

**velvet** ['velvɪt] n velours m

**vending machine** ['vendɪŋ-] n distributeur m automatique

**veneer** [və'nɪər] n (on furniture) placage m; (fig) vernis m

**venereal** [vɪ'nɪərɪəl] adj: ~ **disease** maladie vénérienne

**Venetian blind** [vɪ'niːʃən-] n store vénitien

**vengeance** ['vendʒəns] n vengeance f; **with a ~** (fig) vraiment, pour de bon

**venison** ['venɪsn] n venaison f

**venom** ['venəm] n venin m

**vent** [vent] n conduit m d'aération; (in dress, jacket) fente f ♦ vt (fig: one's feelings) donner libre cours à

**ventilator** ['ventɪleɪtər] n ventilateur m

**ventriloquist** [ven'trɪləkwɪst] n ventriloque m/f

**venture** ['ventʃər] n entreprise f ♦ vt risquer, hasarder ♦ vi s'aventurer, se risquer

**venue** ['venjuː] n lieu m

**verb** [vɜːb] n verbe m; ~**al** adj verbal(e); (translation) littéral(e)

**verbatim** [vɜː'beɪtɪm] adj, adv mot pour mot

**verdict** ['vɜːdɪkt] n verdict m

**verge** [vɜːdʒ] n (BRIT) bord m, bas-côté m; "**soft ~s**" (BRIT: AUT) "accotement non stabilisé"; **on the ~ of doing** sur le point de faire; ~ **on** vt fus approcher de

**verify** ['verɪfaɪ] vt vérifier; (confirm) confirmer

**vermin** ['vɜːmɪn] npl animaux mpl nuisibles; (insects) vermine f

**vermouth** ['vɜːməθ] n vermouth m

**versatile** ['vɜːsətaɪl] adj polyvalent(e)

**verse** [vɜːs] n (poetry) vers mpl; (stanza) strophe f; (in Bible) verset m

**version** ['vɜːʃən] n version f

**versus** ['vɜːsəs] prep contre

**vertical** ['vɜːtɪkl] adj vertical(e) ♦ n verticale f

**vertigo** ['vɜːtɪgəʊ] n vertige m

**verve** [vɜːv] n brio m, enthousiasme m

**very** ['verɪ] adv très ♦ adj: **the ~ book which** le livre même que; **the ~ last** tout dernier; **at the ~ least** tout au moins; **~ much** beaucoup

**vessel** ['vesl] n (ANAT, NAUT) vaisseau m; (container) récipient m

**vest** [vest] n (BRIT) tricot m de corps; (US: waistcoat) gilet m

**vested interest** n (COMM) droits acquis

**vet** [vet] n abbr (BRIT: veterinary surgeon) vétérinaire m/f ♦ vt examiner soigneusement

**veteran** ['vetərn] n vétéran m; (also: war ~) ancien combattant

**veterinary surgeon** ['vetrinəri-] (BRIT), **veterinarian** [vetri'neəriən] (US) n vétérinaire m/f

**veto** ['viːtəu] (pl **~es**) n veto m ♦ vt opposer son veto à

**vex** [veks] vt fâcher, contrarier; **~ed** adj (question) controversé(e)

**via** ['vaiə] prep par, via

**viable** ['vaiəbl] adj viable

**vibrate** [vai'breit] vi vibrer

**vicar** ['vikə'] n pasteur m (de l'Église anglicane); **~age** n presbytère m

**vicarious** [vi'keəriəs] adj indirect(e)

**vice** [vais] n (evil) vice m; (TECH) étau m

**vice-** [vais] prefix vice-

**vice squad** n ≈ brigade mondaine

**vice versa** ['vaisi'vəːsə] adv vice versa

**vicinity** [vi'siniti] n environs mpl, alentours mpl

**vicious** ['viʃəs] adj (remark) cruel(le), méchant(e); (blow) brutal(e); (dog) méchant(e), dangereux(-euse); (horse) vicieux(-euse); **~ circle** n cercle vicieux

**victim** ['viktim] n victime f

**victor** ['viktə'] n vainqueur m

**Victorian** [vik'tɔːriən] adj victorien(ne)

**victory** ['viktəri] n victoire f

**video** ['vidiəu] cpd vidéo inv ♦ n (~ film) vidéo f; (also: ~ **cassette**) vidéocassette f; (also: ~ **cassette recorder**) magnétoscope m; **~ tape** n bande f vidéo inv; (cassette) vidéocassette f; **~ wall** n mur m d'images vidéo

**vie** [vai] vi: **to ~ with** rivaliser avec

**Vienna** [vi'enə] n Vienne

**Vietnam** ['vjet'næm] n Viêt-Nam m,

Vietnam m; **~ese** [vjetnæ'miːz] adj vietnamien(ne) ♦ n inv Vietnamien(ne); (LING) vietnamien m

**view** [vjuː] n vue f; (opinion) avis m, vue f ♦ vt voir, regarder; (situation) considérer; (house) visiter; **in full ~ of** sous les yeux de; **in ~ of the weather/the fact that** étant donné le temps/que; **in my ~** à mon avis; **~er** n (TV) téléspectateur(-trice); **~finder** n viseur m; **~point** n point m de vue

**vigorous** ['vigərəs] adj vigoureux (-euse)

**vile** [vail] adj (action) vil(e); (smell, food) abominable; (temper) massacrant(e)

**villa** ['vilə] n villa f

**village** ['vilidʒ] n village m; **~r** n villageois(e)

**villain** ['vilən] n (scoundrel) scélérat m; (BRIT: criminal) bandit m; (in novel etc) traître m

**vindicate** ['vindikeit] vt (person) innocenter; (action) justifier

**vindictive** [vin'diktiv] adj vindicatif (-ive), rancunier(-ère)

**vine** [vain] n vigne f; (climbing plant) plante grimpante

**vinegar** ['vinigə'] n vinaigre m

**vineyard** ['vinjɑːd] n vignoble m

**vintage** ['vintidʒ] n (year) année f, millésime m; **~ car** n voiture f d'époque; **~ wine** n vin de grand cru

**viola** [vi'əulə] n (MUS) alto m

**violate** ['vaiəleit] vt violer

**violence** ['vaiələns] n violence f

**violent** ['vaiələnt] adj violent(e)

**violet** ['vaiələt] adj violet(te) ♦ n (colour) violet m; (plant) violette f

**violin** [vaiə'lin] n violon m; **~ist** [vaiə'linist] n violoniste m/f

**VIP** n abbr (= very important person) V.I.P. m

**virgin** ['vəːdʒin] n vierge f ♦ adj vierge

**Virgo** ['vəːgəu] n la Vierge

**virile** ['virail] adj viril(e)

**virtually** ['vəːtjuəli] adv (almost) pratiquement

**virtual reality** ['vəːtjuəl-] n (COMPUT) réalité virtuelle

**virtue** ['vəːtjuː] n vertu f; (advantage) mérite m, avantage m; **by ~ of** en raison de; **virtuous** adj vertueux(-euse)

**virus** ['vaɪərəs] n (COMPUT) virus m

**visa** ['viːzə] n visa m

**visibility** [vɪzɪ'bɪlɪtɪ] n visibilité f

**visible** ['vɪzəbl] adj visible

**vision** ['vɪʒən] n (sight) vue f, vision f; (foresight, in dream) vision

**visit** ['vɪzɪt] n visite f; (stay) séjour m ♦ vt (person) rendre visite à; (place) visiter; **~ing hours** npl (in hospital etc) heures fpl de visite; **~or** n visiteur(-euse); (to one's house) visite f, invité(e); **~or centre** n hall m or centre m d'accueil

**visor** ['vaɪzər] n visière f

**vista** ['vɪstə] n vue f

**visual** ['vɪzjuəl] adj visuel(le); **~ aid** n support visuel; **~ display unit** n console f de visualisation, visuel m; **~ize** vt se représenter, s'imaginer; **~ly-impaired** adj malvoyant(e)

**vital** ['vaɪtl] adj vital(e); (person) plein d'entrain; **~ly** adv (important) absolument; **~ statistics** npl (fig) mensurations fpl

**vitamin** ['vɪtəmɪn] n vitamine f

**vivacious** [vɪ'veɪʃəs] adj animé(e), qui a de la vivacité

**vivid** ['vɪvɪd] adj (account) vivant(e); (light, imagination) vif (vive); **~ly** adv (describe) d'une manière vivante; (remember) de façon précise

**V-neck** ['viːnɛk] n décolleté m en V

**vocabulary** [vəu'kæbjulərɪ] n vocabulaire m

**vocal** ['vəukl] adj vocal(e); (articulate) qui sait s'exprimer; **~ cords** npl cordes vocales

**vocation** [vəu'keɪʃən] n vocation f; **~al** adj professionnel(le)

**vociferous** [və'sɪfərəs] adj bruyant(e)

**vodka** ['vɔdkə] n vodka f

**vogue** [vəug] n: **in ~** en vogue f

**voice** [vɔɪs] n voix f ♦ vt (opinion) exprimer, formuler; **~ mail** n (system) messagerie f vocale; (device) boîte f vocale

**void** [vɔɪd] n vide m ♦ adj nul(le); **~ of** vide de, dépourvu(e) de

**volatile** ['vɔlətaɪl] adj volatil(e); (person) versatile; (situation) explosif(-ive)

**volcano** [vɔl'keɪnəu] (pl **~es**) n volcan m

**volition** [və'lɪʃən] n: **of one's own ~** de son propre gré

**volley** ['vɔlɪ] n (of gunfire) salve f; (of stones etc) grêle f, volée f; (of questions) multitude f, série f; (TENNIS etc) volée f; **~ball** n volley(-ball) m

**volt** [vəult] n volt m; **~age** n tension f, voltage m

**volume** ['vɔljuːm] n volume m

**voluntarily** ['vɔləntrɪlɪ] adv volontairement

**voluntary** ['vɔləntərɪ] adj volontaire; (unpaid) bénévole

**volunteer** [vɔlən'tɪər] n volontaire m/f ♦ vi (MIL) s'engager comme volontaire; **to ~ to do** se proposer pour faire

**vomit** ['vɔmɪt] vt, vi vomir

**vote** [vəut] n vote m, suffrage m; (cast) voix f, vote; (franchise) droit m de vote ♦ vt (elect): **to be ~d chairman** etc être élu président etc; (propose): **to ~ that** proposer que ♦ vi voter; **~ of thanks** discours m de remerciement; **~r** n électeur(-trice); **voting** n scrutin m, vote m

**voucher** ['vautʃər] n (for meal, petrol, gift) bon m

**vouch for** ['vautʃ-] vt fus se porter garant de

**vow** [vau] n vœu m, serment m ♦ vi jurer

**vowel** ['vauəl] n voyelle f

**voyage** ['vɔɪdʒ] n voyage m par mer, traversée f; (by spacecraft) voyage

**vulgar** ['vʌlgər] adj vulgaire

**vulnerable** ['vʌlnərəbl] adj vulnérable

**vulture** ['vʌltʃər] n vautour m

# W, w

**wad** [wɒd] n (of cotton wool, paper) tampon m; (of banknotes etc) liasse f

**waddle** ['wɒdl] vi se dandiner

**wade** [weɪd] vi: to ~ **through** marcher dans, patauger dans; (fig: book) s'évertuer à lire

**wafer** ['weɪfə'] n (CULIN) gaufrette f

**waffle** ['wɒfl] n (CULIN) gaufre f; (inf) verbiage m, remplissage m ♦ vi parler pour ne rien dire, faire du remplissage

**waft** [wɒft] vt porter ♦ vi flotter

**wag** [wæg] vt agiter, remuer ♦ vi remuer

**wage** [weɪdʒ] n (also: ~s) salaire m, paye f ♦ vt: to ~ **war** faire la guerre; **~ earner** n salarié(e); **~ packet** n (enveloppe f de) paye f

**wager** ['weɪdʒə'] n pari m

**wag(g)on** ['wægən] n (horse-drawn) chariot m; (BRIT: RAIL) wagon m (de marchandises)

**wail** [weɪl] vi gémir; (siren) hurler

**waist** [weɪst] n taille f; **~coat** n (BRIT) gilet m; **~line** n (tour m de) taille f

**wait** [weɪt] n attente f ♦ vi attendre; **to keep sb ~ing** faire attendre qn; **to ~ for** attendre; **I can't ~ to ...** je meurs d'envie de ...; **~ behind** vi rester (à attendre); **~ on** vt fus servir; **~er** n garçon m (de café), serveur m; **~ing** n: **"no ~ing"** (BRIT: AUT) "stationnement interdit"; **~ing list** n liste f d'attente; **~ing room** n salle f d'attente; **~ress** n serveuse f

**waive** [weɪv] vt renoncer à, abandonner

**wake** [weɪk] (pt **woke**, **waked**, pp **woken**, **waked**) vt (also: ~ **up**) réveiller ♦ vi (also: ~ **up**) se réveiller ♦ n (for dead person) veillée f mortuaire; (NAUT) sillage m

**Wales** [weɪlz] n pays m de Galles; **the Prince of ~** le prince de Galles

**walk** [wɔːk] n promenade f; (short) petit tour; (gait) démarche f; (path) chemin m; (in park etc) allée f ♦ vi marcher; (for pleasure, exercise) se promener ♦ vt (distance) faire à pied; (dog) promener; **10 minutes' ~ from** à 10 minutes à pied de; **from all ~s of life** de toutes conditions sociales; **~ out** vi (audience) sortir, quitter la salle; (workers) se mettre en grève; **~ out on** (inf) vt fus quitter, plaquer; **~er** n (person) marcheur (-euse); **~ie-talkie** n talkie-walkie m; **~ing** n marche f à pied; **~ing shoes** npl chaussures fpl de marche; **~ing stick** n canne f; **W~man** ® n Walkman ® m; **~out** n (of workers) grève-surprise f; **~over** (inf) n victoire f or examen m etc facile; **~way** n promenade f

**wall** [wɔːl] n mur m; (of tunnel, cave etc) paroi f; **~ed** adj (city) fortifié(e); (garden) entouré(e) d'un mur, clos(e)

**wallet** ['wɒlɪt] n portefeuille m

**wallflower** ['wɔːlflaʊə'] n giroflée f; **to be a ~** (fig) faire tapisserie

**wallow** ['wɒləʊ] vi se vautrer

**wallpaper** ['wɔːlpeɪpə'] n papier peint ♦ vt tapisser

**walnut** ['wɔːlnʌt] n noix f; (tree, wood) noyer m

**walrus** ['wɔːlrəs] (pl ~ or ~es) n morse m

**waltz** [wɔːlts] n valse f ♦ vi valser

**wand** [wɒnd] n (also: **magic ~**) baguette f (magique)

**wander** ['wɒndə'] vi (person) errer; (thoughts) vagabonder, errer ♦ vt errer dans

**wane** [weɪn] vi (moon) décroître; (reputation) décliner

**wangle** ['wæŋgl] (BRIT: inf) vt se débrouiller pour avoir; carotter

**want** [wɒnt] vt (wish for) vouloir; (need) avoir besoin de ♦ n: **for ~ of** par manque de, faute de; **~s** npl (needs) besoins mpl; **to ~ to do** vouloir faire; **to ~ sb to do** vouloir que qn fasse; **~ed** adj (criminal) recherché(e) par la police; "**cook** ~**ed**" "on recherche un cuisinier"; ~**ing** adj:

**to be found** ~**ing** ne pas être à la hauteur

**war** [wɔːʀ] n guerre f; **to make** ~ (**on**) faire la guerre (à)

**ward** [wɔːd] n (in hospital) salle f; (POL) canton m; (LAW: child) pupille m/f; ~ **off** vt (attack, enemy) repousser, éviter

**warden** ['wɔːdn] n (in institution) directeur(-trice); (: also: **traffic** ~) contractuel(le); (of youth hostel) père m ou mère f aubergiste

**warder** ['wɔːdəʀ] n (BRIT) gardien m de prison

**wardrobe** ['wɔːdrəub] n (cupboard) armoire f; (clothes) garde-robe f; (THEATRE) costumes mpl

**warehouse** ['wɛəhaus] n entrepôt m

**wares** [wɛəz] npl marchandises fpl

**warfare** ['wɔːfɛəʀ] n guerre f

**warhead** ['wɔːhɛd] n (MIL) ogive f

**warily** ['wɛərɪlɪ] adv avec prudence

**warm** [wɔːm] adj chaud(e); (thanks, welcome, applause, person) chaleureux(-euse); **it's** ~ il fait chaud; **I'm** ~ j'ai chaud; ~ **up** vi (person, room) se réchauffer; (water) chauffer; (athlete) s'échauffer ♦ vt (food) (faire) réchauffer; (faire) chauffer; (engine) (faire) chauffer; ~**-hearted** adj affectueux(-euse); ~**ly** adv chaudement; chaleureusement; ~**th** n chaleur f

**warn** [wɔːn] vt avertir, prévenir; **to** ~ **sb** (**not**) **to do** conseiller à qn de (ne pas) faire; ~**ing** n avertissement m; (notice) avis m; (signal) avertisseur m; ~**ing light** n avertisseur lumineux; ~**ing triangle** n (AUT) triangle m de présignalisation

**warp** [wɔːp] vi (wood) travailler, se déformer ♦ vt (fig: character) pervertir

**warrant** ['wɔrnt] n (guarantee) garantie f; (LAW: to arrest) mandat m d'arrêt; (: to search) mandat de perquisition; ~**y** n garantie f

**warren** ['wɔrən] n (of rabbits) terrier m;

(fig: of streets etc) dédale m

**warrior** ['wɔrɪəʀ] n guerrier(-ère)

**Warsaw** ['wɔːsɔː] n Varsovie

**warship** ['wɔːʃɪp] n navire m de guerre

**wart** [wɔːt] n verrue f

**wartime** ['wɔːtaɪm] n: **in** ~ en temps de guerre

**wary** ['wɛərɪ] adj prudent(e)

**was** [wɔz] pt of **be**

**wash** [wɔʃ] vt laver ♦ vi se laver; (sea): **to** ~ **over/against sth** inonder/ baigner qch ♦ n (clothes) lessive f; (~ing programme) lavage m; (of ship) sillage m; **to have a** ~ se laver, faire sa toilette; **to give sth a** ~ laver qch; ~ **away** vt (stain) enlever au lavage; (subj: river etc) emporter; ~ **off** vi partir au lavage; ~ **up** vi (BRIT) faire la vaisselle; (US) se débarbouiller; ~**able** adj lavable; ~**basin** (US **washbowl**) n lavabo m; ~**cloth** (US) n gant m de toilette; ~**er** n (TECH) rondelle f, joint m; ~**ing** n (dirty) linge m; (clean) lessive f; ~**ing machine** n machine f à laver; ~**ing powder** (BRIT) n lessive f (en poudre); ~**ing-up** n vaisselle f; ~**ing-up liquid** n produit m pour la vaisselle; ~**-out** (inf) n désastre m; ~**room** (US) n toilettes fpl

**wasn't** ['wɔznt] = **was not**

**wasp** [wɔsp] n guêpe f

**wastage** ['weɪstɪdʒ] n gaspillage m; (in manufacturing, transport etc) pertes fpl, déchets mpl; **natural** ~ départs naturels

**waste** [weɪst] n gaspillage m; (of time) perte f; (rubbish) déchets mpl; (also: **household** ~) ordures fpl ♦ adj (land, ground: in city) à l'abandon; (leftover): ~ **material** déchets mpl ♦ vt gaspiller; (time, opportunity) perdre; ~**s** npl (area) étendue f désertique; ~ **away** vi dépérir; ~ **disposal unit** (BRIT) n broyeur m d'ordures; ~**ful** adj gaspilleur(-euse); (process) peu économique; ~ **ground** (BRIT) n terrain m vague; ~**paper basket** n corbeille f à papier

**watch** [wɔtʃ] n montre f; (act of ~ing)

surveillance f; guet m; (MIL: guards) garde f; (NAUT: guards, spell of duty) quart m ♦ vt (look at) observer; (: match, programme, TV) regarder; (spy on, guard) surveiller; (: be careful of) faire attention à ♦ vi regarder; (keep guard) monter la garde; ~ **out** vi faire attention; ~**dog** n chien m de garde; (fig) gardien(ne); ~**ful** adj attentif(-ive), vigilant(e); ~**maker** n horloger(-ère); ~**man** (irreg) n see **night**; ~**strap** n bracelet m de montre

**water** ['wɔːtə*] n eau f ♦ vt (plant, garden) arroser ♦ vi (eyes) larmoyer; (mouth): **it makes my mouth ~** j'en ai l'eau à la bouche; **in British ~s** dans les eaux territoriales britanniques; ~ **down** vt (milk) couper d'eau; (fig: story) édulcorer; ~**colour** (US **watercolor**) n aquarelle f; ~**cress** n cresson m (de fontaine); ~**fall** n chute f d'eau; ~ **heater** n chauffe-eau m; ~**ing can** n arrosoir m; ~ **lily** n nénuphar m; ~ **line** n (NAUT) ligne f de flottaison; ~**logged** adj (ground) détrempé(e); ~ **main** n canalisation f d'eau; ~**melon** n pastèque f; ~**proof** adj imperméable; ~**shed** n (GEO) ligne f de partage des eaux; (fig) moment m critique, point décisif; ~**skiing** n ski m nautique; ~**tight** adj étanche; ~**works** n (building) station f hydraulique; ~**y** adj (coffee, soup) trop faible; (eyes) humide, larmoyant(e)

**watt** [wɔt] n watt m

**wave** [weɪv] n vague f; (of hand) geste m, signe m; (RADIO) onde f; (in hair) ondulation f ♦ vi (flag) flotter au vent; (grass) ondoyer ♦ vt (handkerchief) agiter; (stick) brandir; ~**length** n longueur f d'ondes

**waver** ['weɪvə*] vi vaciller; (voice) trembler; (person) hésiter

**wavy** ['weɪvɪ] adj (hair, surface) ondulé(e); (line) onduleux(-euse)

**wax** [wæks] n cire f; (for skis) fart m ♦ vt cirer; (car) lustrer; (skis) farter ♦ vi (moon) croître; ~**works** npl personnages mpl de cire ♦ n musée m de cire

**way** [weɪ] n chemin m, voie f; (distance) distance f; (direction) sens m, direction f; (manner) façon f, manière f; (habit) habitude f, façon f; **which ~? - this ~** par où? - par ici; **on the ~** (en route) en route; **to be on one's ~** être en route; **to go out of one's ~ to do** (fig) se donner du mal pour faire; **to be in the ~** bloquer le passage; (fig) gêner; **to lose one's ~** perdre son chemin; **under ~** en cours; **in a ~** dans un sens; **in some ~s** à certains égards; **no ~!** (inf) pas question!; **by the ~ ...** à propos ...; **"~ in"** (BRIT) "entrée"; **"~ out"** (BRIT) "sortie"; **the ~ back** le chemin du retour; **"give ~"** (BRIT AUT) "cédez le passage"; ~**lay** (irreg) vt attaquer

**wayward** ['weɪwəd] adj capricieux(-euse), entêté(e)

**W.C.** n abbr w.c. mpl, waters mpl

**we** [wiː] pl pron nous

**weak** [wiːk] adj faible; (health) fragile; (beam etc) peu solide; ~**en** vi faiblir, décliner ♦ vt affaiblir; ~**ling** n (physically) gringalet m; (morally etc) faible m/f; ~**ness** n faiblesse f; (fault) point m faible; **to have a ~ness for** avoir un faible pour

**wealth** [welθ] n (money, resources) richesse(s) f(pl); (of details) profusion f; ~**y** adj riche

**wean** [wiːn] vt sevrer

**weapon** ['wepən] n arme f

**wear** [wɛə*] (pt wore, pp worn) n (use) usage m; (deterioration through use) usure f; (clothing): **sports/babywear** vêtements mpl de sport/pour bébés ♦ vt (clothes) porter; (put on) mettre; (damage: through use) user ♦ vi (last) faire de l'usage; (rub etc through) s'user; **town/evening ~** tenue f de ville/soirée; ~ **away** vt user, ronger ♦ vi (inscription) s'effacer; ~ **down** vt (strength, person) épuiser; ~ **off** vi disparaître; ~ **out** vt user; (person, strength) épuiser; ~ **and tear** n usure f

# weary

**601**

# Welsh

**weary** ['wɪərɪ] *adj* (tired) épuisé(e); (dispirited) las (lasse), abattu(e) ♦ *vi*: **to ~ of** se lasser de

**weasel** ['wiːzl] *n* (ZOOL) belette *f*

**weather** ['weðəʳ] *n* temps *m* ♦ *vt* (tempest, crisis) essuyer, réchapper à, survivre à; **under the ~** (*fig*: ill) mal fichu(e); **~-beaten** *adj* (person) hâlé(e); (building) dégradé(e) par les intempéries; **~cock** *n* girouette *f*; **~ forecast** *n* prévisions *fpl* météorologiques, météo *f*; **~ man** (*irreg*) (*inf*) météorologue *m*; **~ vane** *n* **= weathercock**

**weave** [wiːv] (*pt* **wove**, *pp* **woven**) *vt* (cloth) tisser; (basket) tresser; **~r** *n* tisserand(e)

**web** [wɛb] *n* (of spider) toile *f*; (on foot) palmure *f*; (fabric, also fig) tissu *m*; **the (World Wide) W~** le Web

**website** ['wɛbsaɪt] *n* (COMPUT) site *m* Web

**wed** [wɛd] (*pt*, *pp* **wedded**) *vt* épouser ♦ *vi* se marier

**we'd** [wiːd] = **we had**; **we would**

**wedding** [wɛdɪŋ] *n* mariage *m*; **silver/golden ~** (anniversary) noces *fpl* d'argent/d'or; **~ day** *n* jour *m* du mariage; **~ dress** *n* robe *f* de mariée; **~ ring** *n* alliance *f*

**wedge** [wɛdʒ] *n* (of wood etc) coin *m*, cale *f*; (of cake) part *f* ♦ *vt* (fix) caler; (pack tightly) enfoncer

**Wednesday** ['wɛnzdɪ] *n* mercredi *m*

**wee** [wiː] (SCOTTISH) *adj* (tout(e)) petit(e)

**weed** [wiːd] *n* mauvaise herbe *f* ♦ *vt* désherber; **~killer** *n* désherbant *m*; **~y** *adj* (man) gringalet

**week** [wiːk] *n* semaine *f*; **a ~ today/on Friday** aujourd'hui/vendredi en huit; **~day** *n* jour *m* de semaine; (COMM) jour ouvrable; **~end** *n* week-end *m*; **~ly** *adv* une fois par semaine, chaque semaine ♦ *adj* hebdomadaire

**weep** [wiːp] (*pt*, *pp* **wept**) *vi* (person) pleurer; **~ing willow** *n* saule pleureur

**weigh** [weɪ] *vt*, *vi* peser; **to ~ anchor** lever l'ancre; **~ down** *vt* (person, ani-

mal) écraser; (fig: with worry) accabler; **~ up** *vt* examiner

**weight** [weɪt] *n* poids *m*; **to lose/put on ~** maigrir/grossir; **~ing** *n* (allowance) indemnité *f*, allocation *f*; **~lifter** *n* haltérophile *m*; **~lifting** *n* haltérophilie *f*; **~y** *adj* lourd(e); (important) de poids, important(e)

**weir** [wɪəʳ] *n* barrage *m*

**weird** [wɪəd] *adj* bizarre

**welcome** ['wɛlkəm] *adj* bienvenu(e) ♦ *n* accueil *m* ♦ *vt* accueillir; (also: **bid ~**) souhaiter la bienvenue à; (be glad of) se réjouir de; **thank you - you're ~!** merci - de rien or il n'y a pas de quoi!

**welder** [wɛldəʳ] *n* soudeur(-euse)

**welfare** ['wɛlfɛəʳ] *n* (wellbeing) bien-être *m*; (social work) assistance sociale; **~ state** *n* État-providence *m*

**well** [wɛl] *n* puits *m* ♦ *adv* bien ♦ *adj*: **to be ~** aller bien ♦ *excl* eh bien!; (relief also) bon!; (resignation) enfin!; **as ~** aussi, également; **as ~ as** en plus de; **~ done!** bravo!; **get ~ soon** remets-toi vite!; **to do ~** bien réussir; (business) prospérer; **~ up** *vi* monter

**we'll** [wiːl] = **we will**; **we shall**

**well: ~-behaved** *adj* sage, obéissant(e); **~-being** *n* bien-être *m*; **~-built** *adj* (person) bien bâti(e); **~-deserved** *adj* (bien) mérité(e); **~-dressed** *adj* bien habillé(e); **~-heeled** (*inf*) *adj* (wealthy) nanti(e)

**wellingtons** ['wɛlɪŋtənz] *npl* (also: **wellington boots**) bottes *fpl* de caoutchouc

**well: ~-known** *adj* (person) bien connu(e); **~-mannered** *adj* bien élevé(e); **~-meaning** *adj* bien intentionné(e); **~-off** *adj* aisé(e); **~-read** *adj* cultivé(e); **~-to-do** *adj* aisé(e); **~-wishers** *npl* amis *mpl* et admirateurs *mpl*; (friends) amis *mpl*

**Welsh** [wɛlʃ] *adj* gallois(e) ♦ *n* (LING) gallois *m*; **the ~** *npl* (people) les Gallois *mpl*; **~ Assembly** *n* Parlement *m* gallois; **~man** (*irreg*) *n* Gallois *m*;

**~woman** (irreg) n Galloise f

**went** [wɛnt] pt of **go**

**wept** [wɛpt] pt, pp of **weep**

**were** [wəːʳ] pt of **be**

**we're** [wɪəʳ] = we are

**weren't** [wəːnt] = were not

**west** [wɛst] n ouest m ♦ adj ouest inv, de or à l'ouest ♦ adv à or vers l'ouest; **the W~** l'Occident m, l'Ouest; **the W~ Country** (BRIT) ♦ n le sud-ouest de l'Angleterre; **~erly** adj (wind) d'ouest; (point) à l'ouest; **~ern** adj occidental(e), de or à l'ouest ♦ n (CINEMA) western m; **W~ Indian** adj antillais(e) ♦ n Antillais(e); **W~ Indies** npl Antilles fpl; **~ward(s)** adv vers l'ouest

**wet** [wɛt] adj mouillé(e); (damp) humide; (soaked) trempé(e); (rainy) pluvieux(-euse) ♦ n (BRIT: POL) modéré m du parti conservateur; **to get ~** se mouiller; **"~ paint"** "attention peinture fraîche"; **~ suit** n combinaison f de plongée

**we've** [wiːv] = we have

**whack** [wæk] vt donner un grand coup à

**whale** [weɪl] n (ZOOL) baleine f

**wharf** [wɔːf] (pl **wharves**) n quai m

KEYWORD

**what** [wɔt] adj quel(le); **what size is he?** quelle taille fait-il?; **what colour is it?** de quelle couleur est-ce?; **what books do you need?** quels livres vous faut-il?; **what a mess!** quel désordre!
♦ pron **1** (interrogative) que, prep +quoi; **what are you doing?** que faites-vous?, qu'est-ce que vous faites?; **what is happening?** qu'est-ce qui se passe?, que se passe-t-il?; **what are you talking about?** de quoi parlez-vous?; **what is it called?** comment est-ce que ça s'appelle?; **what about me?** et moi?; **what about doing ...?** et si on faisait ...?
**2** (relative: subject) ce qui; (: direct object) ce que; (: indirect object) ce +prep

+quoi, ce dont; **I saw what you did/was on the table** j'ai vu ce que vous avez fait/ce qui était sur la table; **tell me what you remember** dites-moi ce dont vous vous souvenez
♦ excl (disbelieving) quoi!, comment!

**whatever** [wɔtˈɛvəʳ] adj: **~ book** quel que soit le livre que (or qui) +sub; n'importe quel livre ♦ pron: **do ~ is necessary** faites tout (ce qui est nécessaire); **~ happens** quoi qu'il arrive; **no reason ~** pas la moindre raison; **nothing ~** rien du tout

**whatsoever** [wɔtsəuˈɛvəʳ] adj = whatever

**wheat** [wiːt] n blé m, froment m

**wheedle** [ˈwiːdl] vt: **~ sb into doing sth** cajoler ou enjôler qn pour qu'il fasse qch; **~ sth out of sb** obtenir qch de qn par des cajoleries

**wheel** [wiːl] n roue f; (also: **steering ~**) volant m; (NAUT) gouvernail m ♦ vt (pram etc) pousser ♦ vi (birds) tournoyer; (also: **~ round**: person) virevolter; **~barrow** n brouette f; **~chair** n fauteuil roulant; **~ clamp** n (AUT) sabot m (de Denver)

**wheeze** [wiːz] vi respirer bruyamment

KEYWORD

**when** [wɛn] adv quand; **when did he go?** quand est-ce qu'il est parti?
♦ conj **1** (at, during, after the time that) quand, lorsque; **she was reading when I came in** elle lisait quand or lorsque je suis entré
**2** (on, at which): **on the day when I met him** le jour où je l'ai rencontré
**3** (whereas) alors que; **I thought I was wrong when in fact I was right** je cru que j'avais tort alors qu'en fait j'avais raison

**whenever** [wɛnˈɛvəʳ] adv quand donc
♦ conj quand; (every time that) chaque fois que

**where** [wɛəʳ] adv, conj où; **this is ~** c'est là que; **~abouts** ['wɛərəbauts] adv où donc ♦ n: nobody knows his **~abouts** personne ne sait où il se trouve; **~as** [wɛərˈæz] conj alors que; **~by** adv par lequel (or laquelle etc); **~ever** [wɛərˈevəʳ] adv où donc ♦ conj où que +sub; **~withal** ['wɛəwɪðɔːl] n moyens mpl

**whether** ['wɛðəʳ] conj si; **I don't know ~ to accept** or not je ne sais pas si je dois accepter ou non; **it's doubtful ~** il est peu probable que +sub; **~ you go or not** que vous y alliez ou non

**which** [wɪtʃ] adj (interrogative: direct, indirect) quel(le); **which picture do you want?** quel tableau voulez-vous?; **which one?** lequel (laquelle)?; **in which case** auquel cas

♦ pron 1 (interrogative) lequel (laquelle, lesquels (lesquelles) pl; **I don't mind which** peu importe lequel; **which (of these) are yours?** lesquels sont à vous?; **tell me which you want** dites-moi lesquels or ceux que vous voulez

2 (relative: subject) qui; (: object) que, prep +lequel (laquelle) etc; **the apple which you ate/which is on the table** la pomme que vous avez mangée/qui est sur la table; **the chair on which you are sitting** la chaise sur laquelle vous êtes assis; **the book of which you spoke** le livre dont vous avez parlé; **he knew, which is true/I feared** il le savait, ce qui est vrai/ce que je craignais; **after which** après quoi

**whichever** [wɪtʃˈevəʳ] adj: **take ~ book you prefer** prenez le livre que vous préférez, n'importe lequel; **~ book you take** quel que soit le livre que vous preniez

**while** [waɪl] n moment m ♦ conj pendant que; (as long as) tant que;

(whereas) alors que; bien que +sub; **for a ~** pendant quelque temps; **~ away** vt (time) (faire) passer

**whim** [wɪm] n caprice m

**whimper** ['wɪmpəʳ] vi geindre

**whimsical** ['wɪmzɪkəl] adj (person) capricieux(-euse); (look, story) étrange

**whine** [waɪn] vi gémir, geindre

**whip** [wɪp] n fouet m; (for riding) cravache f; (POL: person) chef de file assurant la discipline dans son groupe parlementaire ♦ vt fouetter; (eggs) battre; (move quickly) enlever/sortir brusquement; **~ped cream** n crème fouettée; **~round** (BRIT) n collecte f

**whirl** [wəːl] vi tourbillonner; (dancers) tournoyer ♦ vt faire tourbillonner; faire tournoyer; **~pool** n tourbillon m; **~wind** n tornade f

**whirr** [wəːʳ] vi (motor etc) ronronner; (: louder) vrombir

**whisk** [wɪsk] n (CULIN) fouet m ♦ vt fouetter; (eggs) battre; **to ~ sb away** or off emmener qn rapidement

**whiskers** ['wɪskəz] npl (of animal) moustaches fpl; (of man) favoris mpl

**whisky** ['wɪski] (IRELAND, US **whiskey**) n whisky m

**whisper** ['wɪspəʳ] vt, vi chuchoter

**whistle** ['wɪsl] n (sound) sifflement m; (object) sifflet m ♦ vi siffler

**white** [waɪt] adj blanc (blanche); (with fear) blême ♦ n blanc m; (person) blanc (blanche); **~ coffee** (BRIT) n café au lait; (café) crème m; **~-collar worker** n employé/e de bureau; **~ elephant** n (fig) objet dispendieux et superflu; **~ lie** n pieux mensonge; **~ paper** n (POL) livre blanc; **~wash** vt blanchir à la chaux; (fig) blanchir ♦ n (paint) blanc m de chaux

**whiting** ['waɪtɪŋ] n inv (fish) merlan m

**Whitsun** ['wɪtsn] n la Pentecôte

**whizz** [wɪz] vi: **to ~ past** or **by** passer à toute vitesse; **~ kid** (inf) n petit prodige

**who** [huː] pron qui; **~dunit** [huːˈdʌnɪt] (inf) n roman policier

**whoever** ['huː'evə'] pron: ~ finds it celui (celle) qui le trouve, qui que ce soit), quiconque le trouve; **ask ~ you like** demandez à qui vous voulez; **he marries** quelle que soit la personne qu'il épouse; **~ told you that?** qui a bien pu vous dire ça?

**whole** [həʊl] adj (complete) entier(-ère), tout(e); (not broken) intact(e), complet(-ète) ♦ n (all): **the ~ of** la totalité de, tout(e) le (la); (entire unit) tout m; **the ~ of the town** la ville tout entière; **on the ~, as a ~** dans l'ensemble; **~food(s)** n(pl) aliments complets; **~hearted** adj sans réserve(s); **~meal** (BRIT) adj (bread, flour) complet(-ète); **~sale** (vente f en) gros m ♦ adj (price) de gros; (destruction) systématique ♦ adv en gros; **~saler** n grossiste m/f ♦ **~some** adj sain(e); **~wheat** adj = **wholemeal; wholly** ['həʊlɪ] adv entièrement, tout à fait

**whom** [huːm] pron **1** (interrogative) qui; **whom did you see?** qui avez-vous vu?; **to whom did you give it?** à qui l'avez-vous donné?

**2** (relative) que, prep +qui: **the man whom I saw/to whom I spoke** l'homme que j'ai vu/à qui j'ai parlé

**whooping cough** ['huːpɪŋ-] n coqueluche f

**whore** [hɔː'] n (inf: pej) n putain f

**whose** [huːz] adj **1** (possessive: interrogative): **whose book is this?** à qui est ce livre?; **whose pencil have you taken?** à qui est le crayon que vous avez pris?, c'est le crayon de qui que vous avez pris?; **whose daughter are you?** de qui êtes-vous la fille?

**2** (possessive: relative): **the man whose son you rescued** l'homme dont or de qui vous avez sauvé le fils; **the girl**

**whose sister you were speaking to** la fille à la sœur de qui or de laquelle vous parliez; **the woman whose car was stolen** la femme dont la voiture a été volée

♦ pron à qui; **whose is this?** à qui est ceci?; **I know whose it is** je sais à qui c'est

**why** [waɪ] adv pourquoi ♦ excl eh bien!, tiens!; **the reason ~** la raison pour laquelle; **tell me ~** dites-moi pourquoi; **~ not?** pourquoi pas?

**wicked** ['wɪkɪd] adj mauvais(e), méchant(e); (crime) pervers(e); (mischievous) malicieux(-euse)

**wicket** ['wɪkɪt] n (CRICKET) guichet m; terrain m (entre les deux guichets)

**wide** [waɪd] adj large; (area, knowledge) vaste, très étendu(e); (choice) grand(e) ♦ adv: **to open ~** ouvrir tout grand; **to shoot ~** tirer à côté; **~-awake** adj bien éveillé(e); **~ly** adv (differing) radicalement; (spaced) sur une grande étendue; (believed) généralement; (travel) beaucoup; **~n** vt élargir ♦ vi s'élargir; **~ open** adj grand(e) ouvert(e); **~spread** adj (belief etc) très répandu(e)

**widow** ['wɪdəʊ] n veuve f; **~ed** adj veuf (veuve); **~er** n veuf m

**width** [wɪdθ] n largeur f

**wield** [wiːld] vt (power) exercer

**wife** [waɪf] (pl **wives**) n femme f, épouse f

**wig** [wɪg] n perruque f

**wiggle** ['wɪgl] vt agiter, remuer

**wild** [waɪld] adj sauvage; (sea) déchaîné(e); (idea, life) fou (folle); (behaviour) extravagant(e), déchaîné(e); **to make a ~ guess** émettre une hypothèse tout hasard; **~card** n (COMPUT) (caractère m) joker m; **~erness** ['wɪldənɪs] n désert m, région f sauvage; **~life** n (animals) faune f; **~ly** adv (behave) de manière déchaînée; (applaud) frénétiquement; (hit, guess) au hasard; (happy) follement; **~s** n(pl (re-

*mote area)* régions *fpl* sauvages

**wilful** ['wilful] *(US* **willful)** *adj (person)* obstiné(e); *(action)* délibéré(e)

---

**KEYWORD**

**will** [wil] *(vt: pt, pp* **willed** ) *aux vb* **1** *(forming future tense)*: **I will finish it tomorrow** je le finirai demain; **I will have finished it by tomorrow** je l'aurai fini d'ici demain; **will you do it? - yes I will/no I won't** le ferez-vous? - oui/non

**2** *(in conjectures, predictions)*: **he will or he'll be there by now** il doit être arrivé à l'heure qu'il est; **that will be the postman** ça doit être le facteur

**3** *(in commands, requests, offers)*: **will you be quiet!** voulez-vous bien vous taire!; **will you help me?** est-ce que vous pouvez m'aider?; **will you have a cup of tea?** voulez-vous une tasse de thé?; **I won't put up with it!** je ne le tolérerai pas!

♦ *vt*: **to will sb to do** souhaiter ardemment que qn fasse; **he willed himself to go on** par un suprême effort de volonté, il continua

♦ *n* volonté *f*; testament *m*

---

**willing** ['wiliŋ] *adj* de bonne volonté, serviable; **he's ~ to do it** il est disposé à le faire, il veut bien le faire; **~ly** *adv* volontiers; **~ness** *n* bonne volonté

**willow** ['wiləu] *n* saule *m*

**willpower** ['wil'pauə'] *n* volonté *f*

**willy-nilly** ['wili'nili] *adv* bon gré mal gré

**wilt** [wilt] *vi* dépérir; *(flower)* se faner

**win** [win] *(pt, pp* **won)** *n (in sports etc)* victoire *f* ♦ *vt* gagner; *(prize)* remporter; *(popularity)* acquérir ♦ *vi* gagner; **~ over** *vt* convaincre; **~ round** *(BRIT)* *vt* = **win over**

**wince** [wins] *vi* tressaillir

**winch** [wintʃ] *n* treuil *m*

**wind¹** [wind] *n (also MED)* vent *m*; *(breath)* souffle *m* ♦ *vt (take breath)*
couper le souffle à

**wind²** [waind] *(pt, pp* **wound)** *vt* enrouler; *(wrap)* envelopper; *(clock, toy)* remonter ♦ *vi (road, river)* serpenter; **~ up** *vt (clock)* remonter; *(debate)* terminer, clôturer

**windfall** ['windfɔ:l] *n* coup *m* de chance

**winding** ['waindiŋ] *adj (road)* sinueux(-euse); *(staircase)* tournant(e)

**wind instrument** [wind-] *n (MUS)* instrument *m* à vent

**windmill** ['windmil] *n* moulin *m* à vent

**window** ['windəu] *n* fenêtre *f*; *(in car, train, also:* ~ *pane)* vitre *f*; *(in shop etc)* vitrine *f*; **~ box** *n* jardinière *f*; **~ cleaner** *n (person)* laveur(-euse) de vitres; **~ ledge** *n* rebord de la fenêtre; **~ pane** *n* vitre *f*, carreau *m*; **~-shopping** *n*: **to go ~-shopping** faire du lèche-vitrines; **~sill** ['windəusil] *n (inside)* appui *m* de la fenêtre; *(outside)* rebord *m* de la fenêtre

**windpipe** ['windpaip] *n* trachée *f*

**wind power** [wind-] *n* énergie éolienne

**windscreen** ['windskri:n] *n* pare-brise *m inv*; **~ washer** *n* lave-glace *m inv*; **~ wiper** *n* essuie-glace *m inv*

**windshield** ['windʃi:ld] *(US)* *n* = **windscreen**

**windswept** ['windswept] *adj* balayé(e) par le vent; *(person)* ébouriffé(e)

**windy** ['windi] *adj* venteux(-euse); **it's ~** il y a du vent

**wine** [wain] *n* vin *m*; **~ bar** *n* bar *m* à vin; **~ cellar** *n* cave *f* à vin; **~ glass** *n* verre *m* à vin; **~ list** *n* carte *f* des vins; **~ waiter** *n* sommelier *m*

**wing** [wiŋ] *n* aile *f*; **~s** *npl (THEATRE)* coulisses *fpl*; **~er** *n (SPORT)* ailier *m*

**wink** [wiŋk] *n* clin *m* d'œil ♦ *vi* faire un clin d'œil; *(blink)* cligner des yeux

**winner** ['winə'] *n* gagnant(e)

**winning** ['winiŋ] *adj (team)* gagnant(e); *(goal)* décisif(-ive); **~s** *npl* gains *mpl*

**winter** ['wɪntər] n hiver m; **in ~** en hiver; **~ sports** npl sports mpl d'hiver; **wintry** adj hivernal(e)

**wipe** [waɪp] n: **to give sth a ~** donner un coup de torchon/de chiffon/d'éponge à qch ♦ vt essuyer; (erase: tape) effacer; **~ off** vt enlever; **~ out** vt (debt) éteindre, amortir; (memory) effacer; (destroy) anéantir; **~ up** vt essuyer

**wire** ['waɪər] n fil m (de fer); (ELEC) fil électrique; (TEL) télégramme m ♦ vt (house) faire l'installation électrique de; (also: **~ up**) brancher; (person: send telegram to) télégraphier à; **~less** (BRIT) n poste m de radio; **wiring** n installation f électrique; **wiry** adj noueux(-euse), nerveux(-euse); (hair) dru(e)

**wisdom** ['wɪzdəm] n sagesse f; (of action) prudence f; **~ tooth** n dent f de sagesse

**wise** [waɪz] adj sage, prudent(e); (remark) judicieux(-euse) ♦ suffix: **...wise**: **timewise** etc en ce qui concerne le temps etc

**wish** [wɪʃ] n (desire) désir m; (specific desire) souhait m, vœu m ♦ vt souhaiter, désirer, vouloir; **best ~es** (on birthday etc) meilleurs vœux; **with best ~es** (in letter) bien amicalement; **to ~ sb goodbye** dire au revoir à qn; **he ~ed me well** il m'a souhaité bonne chance; **to ~ to do/sb to do** désirer or vouloir faire/que qn fasse; **to ~ for** souhaiter; **~ful** adj: **it's ~ful thinking** c'est prendre ses désirs pour des réalités

**wistful** ['wɪstful] adj mélancolique

**wit** [wɪt] n (gen pl) intelligence f, esprit m; (presence of mind) présence f d'esprit; (wittiness) esprit; (person) homme/femme d'esprit

**witch** [wɪtʃ] n sorcière f; **~craft** n sorcellerie f

KEYWORD

**with** [wɪð, wɪθ] prep 1 (in the company of) avec; (at the home of) chez; **we stayed with friends** nous avons logé chez des amis; **I'll be with you in a minute** je suis à vous dans un instant

2 (descriptive): **a room with a view** une chambre avec vue; **the man with the grey hat/blue eyes** l'homme au chapeau gris/aux yeux bleus

3 (indicating manner, means, cause): **with tears in her eyes** les larmes aux yeux; **to walk with a stick** marcher avec une canne; **red with anger** rouge de colère; **to shake with fear** trembler de peur; **to fill sth with water** remplir qch d'eau

4: **I'm with you** (I understand) je vous suis; **to be with it** (inf: up-to-date) être dans le vent

**withdraw** [wɪθ'drɔː] (irreg) vt retirer ♦ vi se retirer; **~al** n retrait m; **~al symptoms** npl (MED): **to have ~al symptoms** être en état de manque; **~n** adj (person) renfermé(e)

**wither** ['wɪðər] vi (plant) se faner

**withhold** [wɪθ'həuld] (irreg) vt (money) retenir; **to ~ (from)** (information) cacher (à); (permission) refuser (à)

**within** [wɪð'ɪn] prep à l'intérieur de ♦ adv à l'intérieur; **~ his reach** à sa portée; **~ sight of** en vue de; **~ a kilometre of** à moins d'un kilomètre de; **~ the week** avant la fin de la semaine

**without** [wɪð'aut] prep sans; **~ a coat** sans manteau; **~ speaking** sans parler; **to go ~ sth** se passer de qch

**withstand** [wɪθ'stænd] (irreg) vt résister à

**witness** ['wɪtnɪs] n (person) témoin m ♦ vt (event) être témoin de; (document) attester l'authenticité de; **to bear ~ (to)** (fig) attester; **~ box** (US **witness stand**) n barre f des témoins

**witty** ['wɪtɪ] adj spirituel(le), plein(e) d'esprit

**wives** [waɪvz] npl of **wife**

**wizard** ['wɪzəd] n magicien m

**wk** abbr = **week**

**wobble** ['wɔbl] vi trembler; (chair)

branler

**woe** [wəu] n malheur m

**woke** [wəuk] pt of **wake**; **~n** pp of **wake**

**wolf** [wulf] (pl **wolves**) n loup m

**woman** ['wumən] (pl **women**) n femme f; **~ doctor** n femme f médecin; **~ly** adj féminin(e)

**womb** [wu:m] n (ANAT) utérus m

**women** ['wimin] npl of **woman**; **~'s lib** (inf) n MLF m; **W~'s (Liberation) Movement** n mouvement m de libération de la femme

**won** [wʌn] pt, pp of **win**

**wonder** [wʌndə*] n merveille f, miracle m; (feeling) émerveillement m ♦ vi: **to ~ whether/why** se demander si/pourquoi; **to ~ at** (marvel) s'émerveiller de; **to ~ about** songer à; **it's no ~ (that)** il n'est pas étonnant (que +sub); **~ful** adj merveilleux(-euse)

**won't** [wəunt] = **will not**

**wood** [wud] n (timber, forest) bois m; **~ carving** n sculpture f en or sur bois; **~ed** adj boisé(e); **~en** adj en bois; (fig) raide; inexpressif(-ive); **~pecker** n pic m (oiseau); **~wind** n (MUS): **the ~wind** les bois mpl; **~work** n menuiserie f; **~worm** n ver m du bois

**wool** [wul] n laine f; **to pull the ~ over sb's eyes** (fig) en faire accroire à qn; **~len** (US **woolen**) adj de or en laine; (industry) lainier(-ère); **~lens** npl (clothes) lainages mpl; **~ly** (US **wooly**) adj laineux(-euse); (fig: ideas) confus(e)

**word** [wə:d] n mot m; (promise) parole f; (news) nouvelles fpl ♦ vt rédiger, formuler; **in other ~s** en d'autres termes; **to break/keep one's ~** manquer à sa parole/tenir parole; **~ing** n termes mpl; libellé m; **~ processing** n traitement m de texte; **~ processor** n machine f de traitement de texte

**wore** [wɔ:*] pt of **wear**

**work** [wə:k] n travail m; (ART, LITERATURE) œuvre f ♦ vi travailler; (mechanism) marcher, fonctionner; (plan etc) mar-

cher; (medicine) agir ♦ vt (clay, wood etc) travailler; (mine etc) exploiter; (machine) faire marcher or fonctionner; (miracles, wonders etc) faire; **to be out of ~** être sans emploi; **~ loose** se défaire, se desserrer; **~ on** vt fus travailler à; (influence) (essayer d')influencer; **~ out** vi (plans etc) marcher ♦ vt (problem) résoudre; (plan) élaborer; **it ~s out at £100** ça fait 100 livres; **~ up** vt: **to get ~ed up** se mettre dans tous ses états; **~able** adj (solution) réalisable; **~aholic** [wə:kə'hɔlik] n bourreau m de travail; **~er** n travailleur(-euse), ouvrier(-ère); **~ experience** n stage m; **~force** n main-d'œuvre f; **~ing class** n classe ouvrière; **~ing-class** adj ouvrier(-ère); **~ing order** n: **in ~ing order** en état de marche; **~man** (irreg) n ouvrier m; **~manship** (skill) n métier m, habileté f; **~s** n (BRIT: factory) usine f ♦ npl (of clock, machine) mécanisme m; **~ sheet** n (COMPUT) feuille f de programmation; **~shop** n atelier m; **~ station** n poste m de travail; **~-to-rule** (BRIT) n grève f du zèle

**world** [wə:ld] n monde m ♦ cpd (champion) du monde; (power, war) mondial(e); **to think the ~ of sb** (fig) ne jurer que par qn; **~ly** adj de ce monde; (knowledgeable) qui a l'expérience du monde; **~-wide** adj universel(le); **W~-Wide Web** n Web m

**worm** [wə:m] n ver m

**worn** [wɔ:n] pp of **wear** ♦ adj usé(e); **~-out** adj (object) complètement usé(e); (person) épuisé(e)

**worried** ['wʌrid] adj inquiet(-ète)

**worry** ['wʌri] n souci m ♦ vt inquiéter ♦ vi s'inquiéter, se faire du souci

**worse** [wə:s] adj pire, plus mauvais(e) ♦ adv plus mal ♦ n pire m; **a change for the ~** une détérioration; **~n** vt, vi empirer; **~ off** adj moins à l'aise financièrement; (fig): **you'll be ~ off this way** ça ira moins bien de cette façon

**worship** ['wə:ʃip] n culte m ♦ vt (God)

rendre un culte à; (person) adorer; **Your W~** (BRIT: to mayor) Monsieur le maire; (: to judge) Monsieur le juge

**worst** [wɜːst] adj le (la) plus mauvais(e) ♦ adv le plus mal ♦ n pire m; **at ~** au pis aller

**worth** [wɜːθ] n valeur f ♦ adj: **to be ~** valoir; **it's ~ it** cela en vaut la peine, ça vaut la peine; **it is ~ one's while (to do)** on gagne (à faire); **~less** adj qui ne vaut rien; **~while** adj (activity, cause) utile, louable

**worthy** [wɜːðɪ] adj (person) digne; (motive) louable; **~ of** digne de

**would** [wʊd] aux vb **1** (conditional tense): **if you asked him he would do it** si vous le lui demandiez, il le ferait; **if you had asked him he would have done it** si vous le lui aviez demandé, il l'aurait fait

**2** (in offers, invitations, requests): **would you like a biscuit?** voulez-vous un biscuit?; **would you close the door please?** voulez-vous fermer la porte, s'il vous plaît?

**3** (in indirect speech): **I said I would do it** j'ai dit que je le ferais

**4** (emphatic): **it WOULD have to snow today!** naturellement il neige aujourd'hui! or il fallait qu'il neige aujourd'hui!

**5** (insistence): **she wouldn't do it** elle n'a pas voulu or elle a refusé de le faire

**6** (conjecture): **it would go there on Mondays** il y allait le lundi

**7** (indicating habit): **he would go there on Mondays** il y allait le lundi

**would-be** ['wʊdbiː] adj (pej) soi-disant

**wouldn't** ['wʊdnt] = **would not**

**wound¹** [wuːnd] n blessure f ♦ vt blesser

**wound²** [waʊnd] pt, pp of **wind²**

**wove** [wəʊv] pt of **weave**; **~n** pp of **weave**

---

rendre un culte à; (person) adorer; **Your W~** (BRIT: to mayor) Monsieur le maire; (: to judge) Monsieur le juge

**wrap** [ræp] vt (also: ~ **up**) envelopper, emballer; (wind) enrouler; **~per** n (of book) couverture f; (on chocolate) emballage m, papier m; **~ping paper** n papier m d'emballage; (for gift) papier cadeau

**wreak** [riːk] vt: **to ~ havoc (on)** avoir un effet désastreux (sur)

**wreath** [riːθ] (pl **~s**) n couronne f

**wreck** [rek] n (ship) épave f; (vehicle) véhicule accidenté; (pej: person) loque humaine ♦ vt démolir; (fig) briser, ruiner; **~age** n débris mpl; (of building) décombres mpl; (of ship) épave f

**wren** [ren] n (ZOOL) roitelet m

**wrench** [rentʃ] n (TECH) clé f (à écrous); (tug) violent mouvement de torsion; (fig) déchirement m ♦ vt tirer violemment sur, tordre; **to ~ sth from** arracher qch à or de

**wrestle** ['resl] vi: **to ~ (with sb)** lutter (avec qn); **~r** n lutteur(-euse); **wrestling** n lutte f; (also: **all-in wrestling**) catch m, lutte f libre

**wretched** ['retʃɪd] adj misérable; (inf) maudit(e)

**wriggle** ['rɪgl] vi (also: ~ **about**) se tortiller

**wring** [rɪŋ] (pt, pp **wrung**) vt tordre; (wet clothes) essorer; (fig): **to ~ sth out of sb** arracher qch à qn

**wrinkle** ['rɪŋkl] n (on skin) ride f; (on paper etc) pli m ♦ vt plisser ♦ vi se plisser; **~d** adj (skin, face) ridé(e)

**wrist** [rɪst] n poignet m; **~watch** n montre-bracelet f

**writ** [rɪt] n acte m judiciaire

**write** [raɪt] (pt **wrote**, pp **written**) vt, vi écrire; (prescription) rédiger; **~ down** vt noter; (put in writing) mettre par écrit; **~ off** vt (debt) passer aux profits et pertes; (project) mettre une croix sur; **~ out** vt écrire; **~ up** vt rédiger; **~-off** n perte totale; **~r** n auteur m, écrivain m

**writhe** [raɪð] vi se tordre

**writing** ['raɪtɪŋ] n écriture f; (of author) œuvres fpl; **in ~** par écrit; **~ paper** n papier m à lettres

**wrong** [rɒŋ] *adj (incorrect)* faux (fausse); *(morally)* mauvais(e); *(wicked)* mal; *(unfair)* injuste ♦ *adv* mal ♦ *n* tort m; faire du tort à, léser; **you are ~ to do** it tu as tort de le faire; **you are ~ about that, you've got it ~** tu te trompes; **what's ~?** qu'est-ce qui ne va pas?; **you've got the ~ number** vous vous êtes trompé de numéro; **to go ~** *(person)* se tromper; *(plan)* mal tourner; *(machine)* tomber en panne; **to be in the ~** avoir tort; **~ful** *adj* injustifié(e); **~ly** *adv* mal, incorrectement; **~ side** *n (of material)* envers m

**wrote** [rəʊt] *pt of* **write**

**wrought iron** [rɔːt-] *n* fer forgé

**wrung** [rʌŋ] *pt, pp of* **wring**

**wt.** *abbr* = **weight**

**WWW** *n abbr* (= World Wide Web): **the ~** le Web

# X, x

**Xmas** ['eksməs] *n abbr* = **Christmas**

**X-ray** ['eksreɪ] *n (ray)* rayon m X; *(photo)* radio(graphie) f

**xylophone** ['zaɪləfəʊn] *n* xylophone m

# Y, y

**Y2K** *abbr* (= year 2000) l'an m 2000

**yacht** [jɒt] *n* yacht m; voilier m; **~ing** *n* yachting m, navigation f de plaisance; **~sman** *(irreg)* n plaisancier m

**Yank** [jæŋk], **Yankee** ['jæŋkɪ] *(pej) n* Amerloque m/f

**yap** [jæp] *vi (dog)* japper

**yard** [jɑːd] *n (of house etc)* cour f; *(measure)* yard m (= 91,4 cm); **~stick** *n (fig)* mesure f, critère mpl

**yarn** [jɑːn] *n* fil m; *(tale)* longue histoire

**yawn** [jɔːn] *n* bâillement m ♦ *vi* bâiller; **~ing** *adj (gap)* béant(e)

**yd.** *abbr* = **yard(s)**

**yeah** [jeə] *(inf) adv* ouais

**year** [jɪər] *n an m*, année f; **to be 8 ~s old** avoir 8 ans; **an eight-~-old child** un enfant de huit ans; **~ly** *adj* annuel(le) ♦ *adv* annuellement

**yearn** [jɜːn] *vi:* **to ~ for sth** aspirer à qch, languir après qch

**yeast** [jiːst] *n* levure f

**yell** [jel] *vi* hurler

**yellow** ['jeləʊ] *adj* jaune

**yelp** [jelp] *vi* japper; glapir

**yes** [jes] *adv* oui; *(answering negative question)* si ♦ *n* oui m; **to say/answer ~** dire/répondre oui

**yesterday** ['jestədɪ] *adv* hier ♦ *n* hier m; **~ morning/evening** hier matin/soir; **all day ~** toute la journée d'hier

**yet** [jet] *adv* encore; déjà ♦ *conj* pourtant, néanmoins; **it is not finished ~** ce n'est pas encore fini *or* toujours pas fini; **the best ~** le meilleur jusqu'ici *or* jusque-là; **as ~** jusqu'ici, encore

**yew** [juː] *n* if m

**yield** [jiːld] *n* production f, rendement m; rapport m ♦ *vt* produire, rendre, rapporter; *(surrender)* céder ♦ *vi* céder; *(US: AUT)* céder la priorité

**YMCA** *n abbr* (= Young Men's Christian Association) YMCA m

**yob** [jɒb] *(BRIT: inf) n* loubard(e) m

**yoghourt** ['jəʊgət] *n* yaourt m

**yog(h)urt** ['jəʊgət] *n* = **yoghourt**

**yoke** [jəʊk] *n* joug m

**yolk** [jəʊk] *n* jaune m (d'œuf)

| KEYWORD |

**you** [juː] *pron* **1** *(subject)* tu; *(polite form)* vous; *(plural)* vous; **you French enjoy your food** vous autres Français, vous aimez bien manger; **you and I will go** toi et moi *or* vous et moi, nous irons

**2** *(object: direct, indirect)* te, t' +*vowel*, vous; **I know you** je te *or* vous connais; **I gave it to you** je vous l'ai donné, je te l'ai donné

**3** *(stressed)* toi; vous; **I told YOU to do it** c'est à toi *or* vous que j'ai dit de le faire

**4** (after prep, in comparisons) toi; vous; **it's for you** c'est pour toi or vous; **she's younger than you** elle est plus jeune que toi or vous

**5** (impersonal: one) on; **fresh air does you good** l'air frais fait du bien; **you never know** on ne sait jamais

---

**you'd** [ju:d] = **you had**; **you would**

**you'll** [ju:l] = **you will**; **you shall**

**young** [jʌŋ] adj jeune ♦ npl (of animal) petits mpl; (people): **the ~** les jeunes, la jeunesse; **~er** [jʌŋgəʳ] adj (brother etc) cadet(te); **~ster** n jeune m (garçon m); (child) enfant m/f

**your** [jɔːʳ] adj ton (ta), tes pl; (polite form, pl) votre, vos pl; see also **my**

**you're** [juəʳ] = **you are**

**yours** [jɔːz] pron (le) (la) tien(ne), les tiens (tiennes); (polite form, pl) le (la) vôtre, les vôtres; **~ sincerely/faithfully/truly** veuillez agréer l'expression de mes sentiments les meilleurs; see also **mine**[1]

**yourself** [jɔːˈself] pron (reflexive) te; (: polite form) vous; (after prep) toi; vous; (emphatic) toi-même; vous-même; see also **oneself**; **yourselves** pl pron vous; (emphatic) vous-mêmes

**youth** [ju:θ] n jeunesse f; (young man: pl **~s**) jeune homme m; **~ club** n centre m de jeunes; **~ful** adj jeune; (enthusiasm) de jeunesse, juvénile; **~ hostel** n auberge f de jeunesse

**you've** [ju:v] = **you have**

**YTS** n abbr (BRIT: Youth Training Scheme) ≃ TUC m

**Yugoslav** [ˈjuːgəuslɑːv] adj yougoslave ♦ n Yougoslave m/f

**Yugoslavia** [ˈjuːgəuˈslɑːvɪə] n Yougoslavie f

**yuppie** [ˈjʌpɪ] (inf) n yuppie m/f

**YWCA** n abbr (= Young Women's Christian Association) YWCA m

---

# Z, z

**zany** [ˈzeɪnɪ] adj farfelu(e), loufoque

**zap** [zæp] vt (COMPUT) effacer

**zeal** [ziːl] n zèle m, ferveur f; empressement m

**zebra** [ˈziːbrə] n zèbre m; **~ crossing** (BRIT) n passage clouté or pour piétons

**zero** [ˈzɪərəu] n zéro m

**zest** [zest] n entrain m, élan m; (of orange) zeste m

**zigzag** [ˈzɪgzæg] n zigzag m

**Zimbabwe** [zɪmˈbɑːbwɪ] n Zimbabwe m

**Zimmer frame** [ˈzɪmə-] n déambulateur m

**zinc** [zɪŋk] n zinc m

**zip** [zɪp] n fermeture f éclair ® ♦ vt (also: **~ up**) fermer avec une fermeture éclair ®; **~ code** (US) n code postal; **~per** (US) n = **zip**

**zit** [zɪt] (inf) n bouton m

**zodiac** [ˈzəudɪæk] n zodiaque m

**zone** [zəun] n zone f

**zoo** [zuː] n zoo m

**zoom** [zuːm] vi: **to ~ past** passer en trombe; **~ lens** n zoom m

**zucchini** [zuːˈkiːnɪ] (US) n(pl) courgette(s) f(pl)

# VERB TABLES

*1* Participe présent *2* Participe passé *3* Présent *4* Imparfait *5* Futur *6* Conditionnel *7* Subjonctif présent

**acquérir** *1* acquérant *2* acquis *3* acquiers, acquérons, acquièrent *4* acquérais *5* acquerrai *7* acquière

**ALLER** *1* allant *2* allé *3* vais, vas, va, allons, allez, vont *4* allais *5* irai *6* irais *7* aille

**asseoir** *1* asseyant *2* assis *3* assieds, asseyons, asseyez, asseyent *4* asseyais *5* assiérai *7* asseye

**atteindre** *1* atteignant *2* atteint *3* atteins, atteignons, atteignent *4* atteignais *7* atteigne

**AVOIR** *1* ayant *2* eu *3* ai, as, a, avons, avez, ont *4* avais *5* aurai *6* aurais *7* aie, aies, ait, ayons, ayez, aient

**battre** *1* battant *2* battu *3* bats, bat, battons *4* battais *7* batte

**boire** *1* buvant *2* bu *3* bois, buvons, boivent *4* buvais *7* boive

**bouillir** *1* bouillant *2* bouilli *3* bous, bouillons *4* bouillais *7* bouille

**conclure** *1* concluant *2* conclu *3* conclus, concluons *4* concluais *7* conclue

**conduire** *1* conduisant *2* conduit *3* conduis, conduisons *4* conduisais *7* conduise

**connaître** *1* connaissant *2* connu *3* connais, connaît, connaissons *4* connaissais *7* connaisse

**coudre** *1* cousant *2* cousu *3* couds, cousons, cousez, cousent *4* cousais *7* couse

**courir** *1* courant *2* couru *3* cours, courons *4* courais *5* courrai *7* coure

**couvrir** *1* couvrant *2* couvert *3* couvre, couvrons *4* couvrais *7* couvre

**craindre** *1* craignant *2* craint *3* crains, craignons *4* craignais *7* craigne

**croire** *1* croyant *2* cru *3* crois, croyons, croient *4* croyais *7* croie

**croître** *1* croissant *2* crû, crue, crus, crues *3* croîs, croissons *4* croissais *7* croisse

**cueillir** *1* cueillant *2* cueilli *3* cueille, cueillons *4* cueillais *5* cueillerai *7* cueille

**devoir** *1* devant *2* dû, due, dus, dues *3* dois, devons, doivent *4* devais *5* devrai *7* doive

**dire** *1* disant *2* dit *3* dis, disons, dites, disent *4* disais *7* dise

**dormir** *1* dormant *2* dormi *3* dors, dormons *4* dormais *7* dorme

**écrire** *1* écrivant *2* écrit *3* écris, écrivons *4* écrivais *7* écrive

**ÊTRE** *1* étant *2* été *3* suis, es, est, sommes, êtes, sont *4* étais *5* serai *6* serais *7* sois, sois, soit, soyons, soyez, soient

**FAIRE** *1* faisant *2* fait *3* fais, fais, fait, faisons, faites, font *4* faisais *5* ferai *6* ferais *7* fasse

**falloir** *2* fallu *3* faut *4* fallait *5* faudra *6* faudrait *7* faille

**FINIR** *1* finissant *2* fini *3* finis, finis, finit, finissons, finissez, finissent *4* finissais *5* finirai *6* finirais *7* finisse

**fuir** *1* fuyant *2* fui *3* fuis, fuyons, fuient *4* fuyais *7* fuie

**joindre** *1* joignant *2* joint *3* joins, joignons *4* joignais *7* joigne

**lire** *1* lisant *2* lu *3* lis, lisons *4* lisais *7* lise

**luire** *1* luisant *2* lui *3* luis, luisons *4* luisais *7* luise

**maudire** *1* maudissant *2* maudit *3*

maudis, maudissons *4* maudissait *7* maudisse

mentir *1* mentant *2* menti *3* mens, mentons *4* mentais *7* mente

mettre *1* mettant *2* mis *3* mets, mettons *4* mettais *7* mette

mourir *1* mourant *2* mort *3* meurs, mourons, meurent *4* mourais *5* mourrai *7* meure

naître *1* naissant *2* né *3* nais, naît, naissons *4* naissais *7* naisse

offrir *1* offrant *2* offert *3* offre, offrons *4* offrais *7* offre

PARLER *1* parlant *2* parlé *3* parle, parles, parle, parlons, parlez, parlent *4* parlais, parlais, parlait, parlions, parliez, parlaient *5* parlerai, parleras, parlera, parlerons, parlerez, parleront *6* parlerais, parlerais, parlerait, parlerions, parleriez, parleraient *7* parle, parles, parle, parlons, parliez, parlent *impératif* parle! parlez!

partir *1* partant *2* parti *3* pars, partons *4* partais *7* parte

plaire *1* plaisant *2* plu *3* plais, plaît, plaisons *4* plaisais *7* plaise

pleuvoir *1* pleuvant *2* plu *3* pleut, pleuvent *4* pleuvait *5* pleuvra *7* pleuve

pourvoir *1* pourvoyant *2* pourvu *3* pourvois, pourvoyons, pourvoient *4* pourvoyais *7* pourvoie

pouvoir *1* pouvant *2* pu *3* peux, peut, pouvons, peuvent *4* pouvais *5* pourrai *7* puisse

prendre *1* prenant *2* pris *3* prends, prenons, prennent *4* prenais *7* prenne

prévoir *like* voir *5* prévoirai

RECEVOIR *1* recevant *2* reçu *3* reçois, reçois, reçoit, recevons, recevez, reçoivent *4* recevais *5* recevrai *6* recevrais *7* reçoive

RENDRE *1* rendant *2* rendu *3* rends, rends, rend, rendons, rendez, rendent *4* rendais *5* rendrai *6* rendrais *7* rende

résoudre *1* résolvant *2* résolu *3* résous, résolvons *4* résolvais *7* résolve

rire *1* riant *2* ri *3* ris, rions *4* riais *7* rie

savoir *1* sachant *2* su *3* sais, savons, savent *4* savais *5* saurai *7* sache *impératif* sache, sachons, sachez

servir *1* servant *2* servi *3* sers, servons *4* servais *7* serve

sortir *1* sortant *2* sorti *3* sors, sortons *4* sortais *7* sorte

souffrir *1* souffrant *2* souffert *3* souffre, souffrons *4* souffrais *7* souffre

suffire *1* suffisant *2* suffi *3* suffis, suffisons *4* suffisais *7* suffise

suivre *1* suivant *2* suivi *3* suis, suivons *4* suivais *7* suive

taire *1* taisant *2* tu *3* tais, taisons *4* taisais *7* taise

tenir *1* tenant *2* tenu *3* tiens, tenons, tiennent *4* tenais *5* tiendrai *7* tienne

vaincre *1* vainquant *2* vaincu *3* vaincs, vainc, vainquons *4* vainquais *7* vainque

valoir *1* valant *2* valu *3* vaux, vaut, valons *4* valais *5* vaudrai *7* vaille

venir *1* venant *2* venu *3* viens, venons, viennent *4* venais *5* viendrai *7* vienne

vivre *1* vivant *2* vécu *3* vis, vivons *4* vivais *7* vive

voir *1* voyant *2* vu *3* vois, voyons, voient *4* voyais *5* verrai *7* voie

vouloir *1* voulant *2* voulu *3* veux, veut, voulons, veulent *4* voulais *5* voudrai *7* veuille *impératif* veuillez

# VERBES IRRÉGULIERS

| present | pt | pp | present | pt | pp |
|---|---|---|---|---|---|
| arise | arose | arisen | draw | drew | drawn |
| awake | awoke | awaked | dream | dreamed, | dreamed, |
| be (am, is, | was, were | been | | dreamt | dreamt |
| are; being) | | | drink | drank | drunk |
| bear | bore | born(e) | drive | drove | driven |
| beat | beat | beaten | dwell | dwelt | dwelt |
| become | became | become | eat | ate | eaten |
| begin | began | begun | fall | fell | fallen |
| behold | beheld | beheld | feed | fed | fed |
| bend | bent | bent | feel | felt | felt |
| beset | beset | beset | fight | fought | fought |
| bet | bet, | bet, | find | found | found |
| | betted | betted | flee | fled | fled |
| bid | bid, bade | bid, | fling | flung | flung |
| | | bidden | fly (flies) | flew | flown |
| bind | bound | bound | forbid | forbade | for- |
| bite | bit | bitten | | | bidden |
| bleed | bled | bled | forecast | forecast | forecast |
| blow | blew | blown | forget | forgot | forgotten |
| break | broke | broken | forgive | forgave | forgiven |
| breed | bred | bred | forsake | forsook | forsaken |
| bring | brought | brought | freeze | froze | frozen |
| build | built | built | get | got | got, (US) |
| burn | burnt, | burnt, | | | gotten |
| | burned | burned | give | gave | given |
| burst | burst | burst | go (goes) | went | gone |
| buy | bought | bought | grind | ground | ground |
| can | could | (been | grow | grew | grown |
| | | able) | hang | hung, | hung, |
| cast | cast | cast | | hanged | hanged |
| catch | caught | caught | have (has; | had | had |
| choose | chose | chosen | having) | | |
| cling | clung | clung | hear | heard | heard |
| come | came | come | hide | hid | hidden |
| cost | cost | cost | hit | hit | hit |
| creep | crept | crept | hold | held | held |
| cut | cut | cut | hurt | hurt | hurt |
| deal | dealt | dealt | keep | kept | kept |
| dig | dug | dug | kneel | knelt, | knelt, |
| do (3rd | did | done | | kneeled | kneeled |
| person; | | | know | knew | known |
| he/she/it/ | | | lay | laid | laid |
| does) | | | lead | led | led |

| present | pt | pp | present | pt | pp |
|---------|-----|-----|---------|-----|-----|
| lean | leant, leaned | leant, leaned | shine | shone | shone |
| leap | leapt, leaped | leapt, leaped | shoot | shot | shot |
| | | | show | showed | shown |
| learn | learnt, learned | learnt, learned | shrink | shrank | shrunk |
| | | | shut | shut | shut |
| leave | left | left | sing | sang | sung |
| lend | lent | lent | sink | sank | sunk |
| let | let | let | sit | sat | sat |
| lie (lying) | lay | lain | slay | slew | slain |
| light | lit, lighted | lit, lighted | sleep | slept | slept |
| | | | slide | slid | slid |
| | | | sling | slung | slung |
| lose | lost | lost | slit | slit | slit |
| make | made | made | smell | smelt, smelled | smelt, smelled |
| may | might | — | | | |
| mean | meant | meant | sow | sowed | sown, sowed |
| meet | met | met | | | |
| mistake | mistook | mistaken | speak | spoke | spoken |
| mow | mowed | mown, mowed | speed | sped, speeded | sped, speeded |
| must | (had to) | (had to) | spell | spelt, spelled | spelt, spelled |
| pay | paid | paid | | | |
| put | put | put | spend | spent | spent |
| quit | quit, quitted | quit, quitted | spill | spilt, spilled | spilt, spilled |
| | | | spin | spun | spun |
| read | read | read | spit | spat | spat |
| rid | rid | rid | split | split | split |
| ride | rode | ridden | spoil | spoiled, spoilt | spoiled, spoilt |
| ring | rang | rung | | | |
| rise | rose | risen | spread | spread | spread |
| run | ran | run | spring | sprang | sprung |
| saw | sawed | sawn | stand | stood | stood |
| say | said | said | steal | stole | stolen |
| see | saw | seen | stick | stuck | stuck |
| seek | sought | sought | sting | stung | stung |
| sell | sold | sold | stink | stank | stunk |
| send | sent | sent | stride | strode | stridden |
| set | set | set | strike | struck | struck, stricken |
| shake | shook | shaken | | | |
| shall | should | — | | | |
| shear | sheared | shorn, sheared | strive | strove | striven |
| | | | swear | swore | sworn |
| shed | shed | shed | sweep | swept | swept |

615

| present | pt | pp | present | pt | pp |
|---------|-----|-----|---------|-----|-----|
| swell | swelled | swollen, swelled | wake | woke, waked | woken, waked |
| swim | swam | swum | wear | wore | worn |
| swing | swung | swung | weave | wove, weaved | woven, weaved |
| take | took | taken | | | |
| teach | taught | taught | wed | wedded, wed | wedded, wed |
| tear | tore | torn | | | |
| tell | told | told | weep | wept | wept |
| think | thought | thought | win | won | won |
| throw | threw | thrown | wind | wound | wound |
| thrust | thrust | thrust | wring | wrung | wrung |
| tread | trod | trodden | write | wrote | written |

# LES NOMBRES

# NUMBERS

| | | |
|---|---|---|
| un(une) | 1 | one |
| deux | 2 | two |
| trois | 3 | three |
| quatre | 4 | four |
| cinq | 5 | five |
| six | 6 | six |
| sept | 7 | seven |
| huit | 8 | eight |
| neuf | 9 | nine |
| dix | 10 | ten |
| onze | 11 | eleven |
| douze | 12 | twelve |
| treize | 13 | thirteen |
| quatorze | 14 | fourteen |
| quinze | 15 | fifteen |
| seize | 16 | sixteen |
| dix-sept | 17 | seventeen |
| dix-huit | 18 | eighteen |
| dix-neuf | 19 | nineteen |
| vingt | 20 | twenty |
| vingt et un(une) | 21 | twenty-one |
| vingt-deux | 22 | twenty-two |
| trente | 30 | thirty |
| quarante | 40 | forty |
| cinquante | 50 | fifty |
| soixante | 60 | sixty |
| soixante-dix | 70 | seventy |
| soixante et onze | 71 | seventy-one |
| soixante-douze | 72 | seventy-two |
| quatre-vingts | 80 | eighty |
| quatre-vingt-un(-une) | 81 | eighty-one |
| quatre-vingt-dix | 90 | ninety |
| quatre-vingt-onze | 91 | ninety-one |
| cent | 100 | a hundred |
| cent un(une) | 101 | a hundred and one |
| trois cents | 300 | three hundred |
| trois cent un(une) | 301 | three hundred and one |
| mille | 1 000 | a thousand |
| un million | 1 000 000 | a million |

| | |
|---|---|
| premier(première), 1er | first, 1st |
| deuxième, 2e or 2ème | second, 2nd |
| troisième, 3e or 3ème | third, 3rd |
| quatrième | fourth, 4th |
| cinquième | fifth, 5th |
| sixième | sixth, 6th |

# LES NOMBRES

septième
huitième
neuvième
dixième
onzième
douzième
treizième
quatorzième
quinzième
seizième
dix-septième
dix-huitième
dix-neuvième
vingtième
vingt-et-unième
vingt-deuxième
trentième
centième
cent-unième
millième

## Les Fractions etc

un demi
un tiers
deux tiers
un quart
un cinquième
zéro virgule cinq, 0,5
trois virgule quatre, 3,4
dix pour cent
cent pour cent

## Exemples

il habite au dix
c'est au chapitre sept
à la page sept
il habite au septième (étage)
il est arrivé (le) septième
une part d'un septième
échelle au vingt-cinq millième

# NUMBERS

seventh
eighth
ninth
tenth
eleventh
twelfth
thirteenth
fourteenth
fifteenth
sixteenth
seventeenth
eighteenth
nineteenth
twentieth
twenty-first
twenty-second
thirtieth
hundredth
hundred-and-first
thousandth

## Fractions etc

a half
a third
two thirds
a quarter
a fifth
(nought) point five, 0.5
three point four, 3.4
ten per cent
a hundred per cent

## Examples

he lives at number 10
it's in chapter 7
on page 7
he lives on the 7th floor
he came in 7th
a share of one seventh
scale one to twenty-five thousand

# L'HEURE

*quelle heure est-il?*

il est ...

minuit
une heure (du matin)

une heure cinq
une heure dix
une heure et quart
une heure vingt-cinq

une heure et demie, une heure
trente
une heure trente-cinq, deux heures moins vingt-cinq
deux heures moins vingt, une
heure quarante
deux heures moins le quart, une
heure quarante-cinq
deux heures moins dix, une heure cinquante
midi
deux heures (de l'après-midi)

sept heures (du soir)

*à quelle heure?*

à minuit
à sept heures

dans vingt minutes
il y a quinze minutes

# THE TIME

*what time is it?*

it's ...

midnight, twelve p.m.
one o'clock (in the morning),
one (a.m.)
five past one
ten past one
a quarter past one, one fifteen
twenty-five past one, one
twenty-five
half past one, one thirty

twenty-five to two, one thirty-
five
twenty to two, one forty

a quarter to two, one forty-five

ten to two, one fifty

twelve o'clock, midday, noon
two o'clock (in the afternoon),
two (p.m.)
seven o'clock (in the evening),
seven (p.m.)

*at what time?*

at midnight
at seven o'clock

in twenty minutes
fifteen minutes ago